"I know where to go to learn what I don't know."

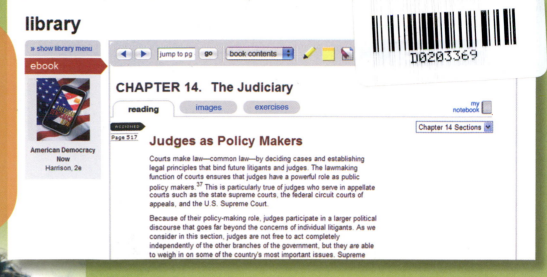

library

» show library menu

ebook

American Democracy Now
Harrison, 2e

jump to pg | go | book contents

CHAPTER 14. The Judiciary

reading | images | exercises

my notebook

ASSIGNED
Page 517

Chapter 14 Sections

Judges as Policy Makers

Courts make law—common law—by deciding cases and establishing legal principles that bind future litigants and judges. The lawmaking function of courts ensures that judges have a powerful role as public policy makers.[37] This is particularly true of judges who serve in appellate courts such as the state supreme courts, the federal circuit courts of appeals, and the U.S. Supreme Court.

Because of their policy-making role, judges participate in a larger political discourse that goes far beyond the concerns of individual litigants. As we consider in this section, judges are not free to act completely independently of the other branches of the government, but they *are* able to weigh in on some of the country's most important issues. Supreme

The integrated eBook takes students to the place in the text where the material they don't know is explained.

"I get an individual learning plan."

The rich reporting tools give students and instructors detailed views of how well a student is performing during the semester.

LearnSmart generates an individualized learning plan so students study most what they understand least.

Published by McGraw-Hill, an imprint of The McGraw-Hill Companies, Inc., 1221 Avenue of the Americas, New York, NY 10020. Copyright © 2011 and 2009 by The McGraw-Hill Companies. All rights reserved. No part of this publication may be reproduced or distributed in any form or by any means, or stored in a database or retrieval system, without the prior written consent of The McGraw-Hill Companies, Inc., including, but not limited to, in any network or other electronic storage or transmission, or broadcast for distance learning. This book is printed on acid-free paper.

1 2 3 4 5 6 7 8 9 0 DOW/DOW 9 8 7 6 5 4 3 2 1 0

ISBN: 978-0-07-734214-2
MHID: 0-07-734214-3

Vice President, Editorial: *Michael Ryan*
Director, Editorial: *Beth Mejia*
Sponsoring Editor: *Mark Georgiev*
Marketing Manager: *Patrick Brown*
Director of Development: *Dawn Groundwater*
Developmental Editors: *Judith Kromm and Naomi Friedman*
Editorial Coordinator: *Amy Flauaus*
Text Permissions Editor: *Marcy Lunetta*
Production Editor: *Leslie Racanelli*
Manuscript Editor: *Carole Crouse*
Illustrator: *Ayelet Arbel*
Designers: *Cassandra Chu & Linda Beaupré*
Photo Research Coordinator: *Alexandra Ambrose*
Photo Researcher: *David Tietz*
Buyer: *Louis Swaim*
Media Project Managers: *Thomas Brierly & Jami Woy*
Composition: *10/12 ITC Legacy Serif Book by Thompson Type*
Printing: *45# Liberty Dull by R.R. Donnelley & Sons*
Cover: Flag © Stockbyte/Getty Images; iPhone © Kacper Kida/Alamy

Credits: The credits section for this book begins on page 848 and is considered an extension of the copyright page.

Library of Congress Cataloging-in-Publication Data

American Democracy Now / Brigid Callahan Harrison ... [et al.].
     p. cm.
   Includes bibliographical references and index.
   ISBN-13: 978-0-07-734214-2
   MHID: 0-07-734214-3
   1. United States—Politics and government—Textbooks.   2. Political participation—
United States—Textbooks.   I. Harrison, Brigid, C.

2010940520

The Internet addresses listed in the text were accurate at the time of publication. The inclusion of a Web site does not indicate an endorsement by the authors or McGraw-Hill, and McGraw-Hill does not guarantee the accuracy of the information presented at these sites.

www.mhhe.com

AMERICAN DEMOCRACY NOW

TEXAS EDITION

BRIGID CALLAHAN HARRISON
Montclair State University

JEAN WAHL HARRIS
University of Scranton

GARY M. HALTER
Texas A & M University

WITH

MICHELLE D. DEARDORFF
Jackson State University

SECOND EDITION

Boston   Burr Ridge, IL   Dubuque, IA   Madison, WI   New York   San Francisco   St. Louis
Bangkok   Bogotá   Caracas   Kuala Lumpur   Lisbon   London   Madrid   Mexico City
Milan   Montreal   New Delhi   Santiago   Seoul   Singapore   Sydney   Taipei   Toronto

BRIEF CONTENTS

APPENDIXES

CONTENTS

Part I: Foundations of American Democracy

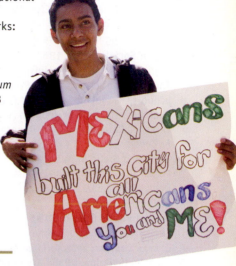

Part II: Fundamental Principles

Part III: Linkages Between the People and Government

Part IV: Institutions of Government

Part V: Public Policy

15 ECONOMIC POLICY 462

Part VI: State and Local Government

PERFORMANCE

means students actively and critically engage in discussing their government—a course in which students' opinions are well formed and evidence based.

Introducing Performance-Based Learning for *American Democracy Now*

Imagine that YOU . . .

- could recreate the one-on-one experience of working through difficult concepts in office hours with every one of your students
- could see at a glance how well each of your students or sections was performing in each segment of your course
- could spend more time in class teaching what you want to teach

Imagine *American Democracy Now!*

American Democracy Now does what no other learning program does. It directly complements the way instructors teach by directly reinforcing core learning objectives for the course. *American Democracy Now* benefits instructors by allowing them easily to see all student activity and progress, identifying challenging learning objectives, and evaluating each student's degree of mastery. Equipped with this information, instructors can tailor lectures, assignments, and exams for each class and each student.

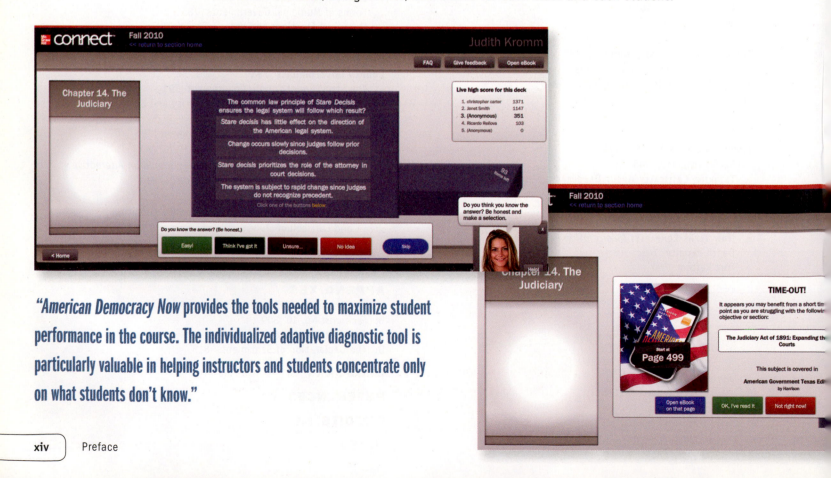

"American Democracy Now provides the tools needed to maximize student performance in the course. The individualized adaptive diagnostic tool is particularly valuable in helping instructors and students concentrate only on what students don't know."

Imagine that YOUR STUDENTS . . .

- are actively and critically engaged in discussing their government
- have opinions that are well formed and evidence based
- come to class prepared and perform better on quizzes and exams

Imagine *American Democracy Now!*

American Democracy Now is a first: a truly integrated learning program for American government that provides individualized instruction through an adaptive diagnostic coupled with pedagogical tools that are anchored in research on critical thinking. By showing students what they know, *American Democracy Now* focuses students on specific learning objectives they need to master in order to achieve better performance in the course. Better performance leads to greater student engagement and ultimately to a classroom in which true critical thinking can be achieved and applied. *American Democracy Now*'s individualized, adaptive learning program guides students away from merely expressing opinion to forming a point of view based in critical thinking, analysis, and evidence.

"I know that I know"

Individualized adaptive learning and outcomes based activities

"I am confident"

Engage in the content and participate in the course

Think critically about the issues in American government

"I know how to ask questions. I analyze issues. I apply what I learn."

Judith Kromm

AQ Give feedback Open eBook

Live high score for this deck

1. christopher carter   1371
2. Janet Smith   1147
3. (Anonymous)   351
4. Ricardo Reilova   103
5. (Anonymous)   0

In this way, *American Democracy Now*'s individualized, adaptive learning program is both a studying environment and a teaching environment—researched and designed to help students interact more with material, perform better during the course, and become more active, engaged citizens in the world.

Thinking Critically About American Government

At the heart of *American Democracy Now* is a rich set of instructional tools that move students along the path to critical thinking.

12 CHAPTER

The Presidency

THEN
Presidential power grew over the centuries to "imperial" proportions and then ebbed in the late twentieth century in the wake of scandals.

NOW
The power of modern presidents varies, and is affected by congressional actions and public opinion.

NEXT
Will future presidents continue down the path of an imperial presidency?

What checks will constrain future presidents' exercise of power?

[How] will the relationship between [... the] people change

367

A *Then, Now, Next* framework encourages students to understand historical contexts and precedents, so they can weigh them against current political events and actions, begin to formulate an informed judgment about politics, and consider how the past and present might shape the future.

THEN NOW NEXT

How the Media Have Shaped Entertainment and the Information Highways

THEN (1960s)	NOW (2011)
Television programming matured and revolutionized how the media entertained and provided information.	The Internet matures and revolutionizes how we are entertained and how we get information.
Television accentuated a new set of candidate qualities—including being telegenic—that had not mattered much in earlier political campaigns.	The Internet accentuates a new set of candidate qualities—including being tech savvy and Net organized—that were unheard of a generation ago.
Communication between the media and voters was one-way: people got information but could not "talk back."	Information flow is two-way, thanks to talk radio and the Internet—including blogs, YouTube, and social-networking sites.

WHAT'S NEXT?

> What new media technologies will shape campaigns and political participation in the future?

> For individuals seeking information about policy issues and political campaigns, what might be the negative consequences of the abundance of information flowing through the electronic media?

> How will technology change political participation in the future?

ANALYZING THE SOURCES

CONFIDENCE IN THE MEDIA

The Gallup Organization has asked the following question in surveys since 1972: "In general, how much trust and confidence do you have in the mass media—such as newspapers, T.V., and radio—when it comes to reporting the news fully, accurately, and fairly: a great deal, a fair amount, not very much, or none at all?"

Evaluating the Evidence

① Describe trends during the 1970s in people's confidence in the media, citing specific data from the graph.

② Describe trends since 2001 in people's confidence in the media, citing specific data.

③ What do the latest surveys indicate about respondents' opinions on the issue of confidence in the media?

④ What do the data say about the overall trends with regard to people's confidence in the media? [...] factors could have contributed [...] people's assess- [...]

Great deal/fair amount

68 69 72   53 55 51 54 55 50   56 55
                                    49   49   43 45
        30 29 26   46 44 49 46 44

Not very much/none at all

Percentage: 100, 80, 60, 40, 20, 0

Year: 1972 1976 1997 2000 2003 2006 2009

SOURCE: The Gallup Poll, Media Use and Evaluation, www.galluppoll.com/poll/1663/Media-Use-Evaluation.aspx

The line graph illustrates survey respondents' views on that question, showing data at various times between May 1972 and September 2009. You can see tha[...] able changes have occurred in people's assessment of news organizations in t[...]

THINKING CRITICALLY ABOUT DEMOCRACY

SHOULD CONGRESS REGULATE THE INTERNET INFRASTRUCTURE?

The Issue: The technological revolution has brought ongoing, exponential growth in Internet traffic. As rising numbers of people turn to the Internet for more and more uses—from viewing videos online to sending pictures to Grandma, and from buying gifts and personal items to calling friends and relatives—the volume of information that the broadband infrastructure of the Internet must transmit is becoming overwhelming. The owners of that infrastructure—corporate giants such as AT&T, Verizon, and Comcast—seek legislation that would allow them to charge companies that produce high volumes of traffic. In effect, this legislation would set up a two-tiered system of broadband access in which one tier is an "express lane" with tolls, and the other an older, slower lane with free access. One problem is that many of today's services require the faster access to make them effective.

Yes: Congress should regulate the Internet infrastructure. We need a two-tiered system of broadband access. The telecommunications titans in command of the Internet infrastructure argue that to keep up with the increasing demand for broadband space, they will have to expand and improve the system continually. Corporate advocates of a two-tiered system of broadband access are also interested in providing premium-quality broadband service to their own clientele. Thus, for example, Verizon wants to ensure that its Internet subscribers (rather than the subscribers of its competitors) have high-quality access to the broadband infrastructure technology that Verizon owns so that its subscribers do not get caught in an Internet traffic jam.

with soaring demand. In addition, the security of the system is crucial to continued business activity and corporate financial growth, as well as to national economic health. Broadband availability is a national security issue because if law enforcers, airports, hospitals, nuclear power plants, and first responders do not have adequate or immediate access to the information they need to perform their jobs, human lives are at risk. Because of these critical financial and security implications, a tax or user fee could be instituted that would pay for Internet infrastructure improvements.

What do you think?

① Do you believe that Congress should reject proposals to create a for-fee fast lane for Internet traffic? If so, why? Or do you think the marketplace should determine which services get faster access to broadband lines? If so, why would the latter be preferable?

② What impact would the creation of a two-tiered Internet structure have on Internet business development? On national security?

③ Should the federal government help to defray the costs of improvements to the Internet infrastructure? Why, or why not?

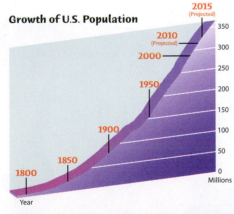

Growth of U.S. Population

2015 (Projected)
2010 (Projected)
2000
1950
1900
1850
1800

Year

350, 300, 250, 200, 150, 100, 50, 0

Millions

POLITICAL INQUIRY

FIGURE 1.2 ■ From 1790 to 1900, the population of the United States increased gradually, and it did not reach 100 million until the second decade of the twentieth century. What factors caused the steep rise during the twentieth century? How will these forces continue to affect the size of the U.S. population during this century?

SOURCE: U.S. Census, www.census.gov/population/www/documentation/twps0056.html, and www.census.gov/compendia/statab/cats/population/estimates_and_projections _by_age_sex_raceethnicity.html.

Teaching and Studying *American Democracy Now*

American Democracy Now is supported by a set of integrated supplements for instructors teaching and students studying American Government. Together with the core materials, these supplements are readily available on the instructor side of the Online Learning Center for *American Democracy Now*.

ONLINE LEARNING CENTER

The password-protected instructor side of the Online Learning Center (**www.mhhe.com/harrisonadn2e**) contains the Instructor's Manual that goes beyond lecture topics and outlines by tying all text features to individual and group projects in and out of class and a full test item file tied to Bloom's taxonomy, as well as PowerPoint slides, Classroom Performance System (CPS) Questions, and an Image Gallery. See more information about specific assets below. Ask your local McGraw-Hill representative for password information.

- The **Instructor's Manual** includes chapter summaries, chapter outlines, lecture outlines with integrated PowerPoints, and abundant class activities.

- The **Test Bank** includes more than 1000 multiple-choice and short-answer questions to accompany the chapters in *American Democracy Now,* along with questions to be used in class (with PowerPoints) and student self check questions.

CREATE Craft your teaching resources to match the way you teach! With McGraw-Hill Create, **www.mcgrawhillcreate.com,** you can easily rearrange chapters, combine material from other content sources, and quickly upload content you have written like your course syllabus or teaching notes. Find the content you need in Create by searching through thousands of leading McGraw-Hill textbooks. Arrange your book to fit your teaching style. Create even allows you to personalize your book's appearance by selecting the cover and adding your name, school, and course information. Order a Create book and you'll receive a complimentary print review copy in 3–5 business days or a complimentary electronic review copy (eComp) via email in about one hour. Go to www.mcgrawhillcreate.com today and register. Experience how McGraw-Hill Create empowers you to teach your students *your* way.

COURSESMART E-TEXTBOOK This text is available as an e-Textbook at **www .CourseSmart.com.** At CourseSmart your students can take advantage of significant savings off the cost of a print textbook, reduce their impact on the environment, and gain access to powerful web tools for learning. CourseSmart e-Textbooks can be viewed online or downloaded to a computer. The e-Textbooks allow students to do full text searches, add highlighting and notes, and share notes with classmates. CourseSmart has the largest selection of e-Textbooks available anywhere. Visit www.CourseSmart.com to learn more and to try a sample chapter.

Do More

BLACKBOARD McGraw-Hill Higher Education and Blackboard have teamed up. What does this mean for you?

1. **Your life, simplified.** Now you and your students can access McGraw-Hill's Connect™ and Create™ right from within your Blackboard course—all with one single sign-on. Say goodbye to the days of logging in to multiple applications.

2. **Deep integration of content and tools.** Not only do you get single sign-on with Connect™ and Create™, you also get deep integration of McGraw-Hill content and content engines right in Blackboard. Whether you're choosing a book for your course or building Connect™ assignments, all the tools you need are right where you want them—inside of Blackboard.

3. **Seamless gradebooks.** Are you tired of keeping multiple gradebooks and manually synchronizing grades into Blackboard? We thought so. When a student completes an integrated Connect™ assignment, the grade for that assignment automatically (and instantly) feeds your Blackboard grade center.

4. **A solution for everyone.** Whether your institution is already using Blackboard or you just want to try Blackboard on your own, we have a solution for you. McGraw-Hill and Blackboard can now offer you easy access to industry leading technology and content, whether your campus hosts it, or we do. Be sure to ask your local McGraw-Hill representative for details.

Staying Current

CHAPTER BY CHAPTER CHANGES IN AMERICAN DEMOCRACY NOW, SECOND EDITION

CHAPTER 1 PEOPLE, POLITICS, AND PARTICIPATION

- Updated coverage of the changing demographics and ideological shifts in American politics
- Revised coverage of the role of technology in politics

CHAPTER 2 THE CONSTITUTION

- Reorganized for better flow and to increase understanding of how the Constitution addressed the concerns of the framers, state rights advocates, and citizens
- Revised, more comprehansive coverage of the first state constitutions and their influence on the U.S. Constitution's separation of powers and Bill of Rights
- Additional coverage of the deficiencies of the Articles of Confederation and the call for a Constitutional convention
- Added a critical presentation of the innovative constitutional ratification process

CHAPTER 3 FEDERALISM

- Updated data in tables and figures throughout the chapter
- Added tables and figures on the number of local governments in each state and the number of recognized Indian tribes in each state
- Added information on the Race to the Top grant program
- Added information on the 2009 American Recovery and Reinvestment Act (ARRA)
- Added coverage on the minimum drinking age debate
- Revised section on Today's Federalism captures the difference between the federal system of government presented by Madison in *Federalist* No. 45 and the reality of today's federalism–intergovernmental relations

CHAPTER 4 CIVIL LIBERTIES

- Emphasis on the theoretical framework of the tension between liberty and societal order integrated throughout
- Added coverage of new Supreme Court civil liberties decisions
- Updated coverage of the Obama Administration's approach to ethnic profiling and the infringement of personal liberties in the War on Terror
- Integration of new sources that reflect current events
- New emphasis on social networking media
- New charts addressing changes in the death penalty and marriage rights by the states

CHAPTER 5 CIVIL RIGHTS

- Tests used by the courts to determine legal and illegal discrimination moved to the beginning of the chapter, establishing a framework for the civil rights evolution
- Updated information on voter registration and minority representation in elected offices

- Added information on the Indian Gaming Regulatory Act
- Added discussion of the 2008 ADA amendments

CHAPTER 6 POLITICAL SOCIALIZATION AND PUBLIC OPINION

- Updated with the most recent data available concerning U.S. public opinion, including confidence in institution trends and policy priorities

CHAPTER 7 INTEREST GROUPS

- New coverage of the regulatory environment that structures interest group behavior

CHAPTER 8 POLITICAL PARTIES

- New discussion of the Tea Party movement, the struggle in the national Republican party, and an Obama-led Democratic party
- New discussion of the post-2010 party environment, including the use of technology by the political parties

CHAPTER 9 ELECTIONS, CAMPAIGNS, AND VOTING

- New discussion of California's Proposition 8
- New discussion of how technology has revolutionized the art of political campaigning
- Added discussion of the *Citizen United* decision, including its impact on the PACs
- Increased discussion of voter turnout within states

CHAPTER 10 THE MEDIA

- Increased discussion of media consumers' responsibility
- Increased discussion of verifiability, particularly concerning the role of citizen journalists in politics
- Expanded coverage of the changing face of the media

CHAPTER 11 CONGRESS

- Preliminary discussion of the impact of the 2010 census on reapportionment and redistricting
- Added coverage of the 2010 congressional election
- Increased discussion of congressional policymaking, including earmarks and health care legislation

CHAPTER 12 THE PRESIDENCY

- Increased comparisons of Bush and Obama administration policies—including stimulus spending
- Included the latest presidential communication research
- Added coverage of the Obama administration personnel
- New discussion of Obama presidential approval ratings

CHAPTER 13 THE BUREAUCRACY

- Updated data on demographics of bureaucrats and added data on the type of work bureaucrats do
- Updated data on the number of federal bureaucrats in each department and each department's budget

Chapter 14 The Judiciary
- New coverage of the Roberts court, including the appointments of Sotomayor and Kagan
- Added coverage of new policy decisions

Chapter 15 Economic Policy
- Integrated discussion of the Bush and Obama administrations' use of fiscal policy to bolster faltering financial institutions and address the Great Recession
- New Analyzing the Sources box critiquing the GDP and the unemployment rate as measures of economic health
- Increased coverage of the Federal Reserve System
- Added coverage of the debate over new financial and banking regulations
- Updated coverage of the status of U.S. economy, the global economy, and the American dream

Chapter 16 Domestic Policy
- Coverage of the April 2010 Masey mine disaster in West Virginia and the BP oil rig disaster in the discussion of threats posed by energy production
- Discussion of the Obama administration's work on climate change legislation, the House of Representatives American Clean Energy and Security Act, and the Senate Energy and Natural Resources Committee's Clean Energy and Leadership Act
- New discussion of the sustainability of OASI
- New discussion of the March 2010 federal health care law, the Patient Protection and Affordable Care Act, and the debate over requiring people to purchase health care
- Revised section on homeland security policy to focus on dilemmas legislators confront in policy deliberations
- New coverage of the controversial Arizona immigration law

Chapter 17 Foreign Policy and National Security
- New coverage of the Obama doctrine in foreign policy
- Increased coverage of the war in Afghanistan
- Re-evaluation of the motivations driving U.S. foreign policy

Chapter 18 State and Local Government
- Information on recent ballot measures and recall efforts
- New discussion of the battle for Washington, D.C. statehood
- Enhanced discussion of the federal government's role as fiscal equalizer, with a focus on the impact of the American Recovery and Reinvestment Act (ARRA) on state budgets
- Updated data on minority representation and female representation in state legislatures

Chapter 19 Introduction to Texas Government
- Updated statistics on population growth, emphasizing how demographic changes have influenced politics
- Added coverage of the impact of the 2008 global financial crisis on the Texas economy
- Updated statistics on illegal immigration
- New feature analyzes Texas's top five exports

Chapter 20 The State Constitution
- Updated tables and figures throughout the chapter
- New examples illustrate the process of amending the Texas Constitution and the importance of ballot wording
- New discussion of how the amendment process might indicate changes in Texas's political culture

Chapter 21 Participation and Interest Groups in Texas Politics
- Updated figures demonstrate how political participation in Texas compares to political participation in other states
- New coverage of fundamentalist groups in Texas

Chapter 22 Political Parties and Elections in Texas
- Updated through the 2008–2010 election cycles
- Reorganized and revised coverage of straight ticket voting
- Additional information about how Texas candidates are using the Internet to raise support for their campaigns

Chapter 23 The Texas Legislature
- Updated to reflect the results of the 2010 election
- Revised section on the re-redistricting debate in 2003
- New emphasis on how redistricting in Texas sparked nationwide policy changes
- Updated tables and figures, including a new figure about bill survival rate in the Texas legislature
- Revised exploration of competitive races in recent elections
- Reorganized section on the role of the speaker of the House includes additional information about Representative Joe Straus

Chapter 24 The Office of Governor and State Agencies in Texas
- New map illustrates which states have current or past women governors, including the 2010 election results
- Updated tables and figures
- Additional information about the unsuccessful proposal to limit Texas governors to serving two terms
- Coverage of Governor Rick Perry's policies

Chapter 25 The Court System in Texas
- Revised chart on the structure of the court system in Texas
- Updated tables and figures
- Up-to-date look at the rising caseload in Texas
- The section on "Issues in the Justice System" now emphasizes racial disparities and includes a new pie chart that shows percentages of Texas inmates by race
- Additional coverage of the continuing death penalty debate in Texas includes updates from 2010

Chapter 26 Public Policy in Texas
- Updated tables and figures
- New discussion of an abstinence-only curriculum and teen pregnancy rates in Texas
- Additional information about the potential effects of global warming on Texas

Chapter 27
- New line graph demonstrates school completion rates

ACKNOWLEDGMENTS

We owe a debt of thanks to all of the people who contributed their thoughts and suggestions to the development of *American Democracy Now*.

Manuscript Reviewers

Stephen Anthony, *Georgia State University*
Stephen Baker, *Jacksonville University*
Michael Baranowski, *Northern Kentucky University*
Kyle Barbieri, *Georgia Perimeter College*
Wendell Broadwell, *Georgia Perimeter College*
Vida Davoudi, *Lone Star College–Kingwood*
Jacqueline DeMerritt, *University of North Texas*
Kevin Dockerty, *Kalamazoo Valley Community College*
Cecil Dorsey, *San Jacinto College*
Matthew Eshabaugh-Soha, *University of North Texas*
Glen Findley, *Odessa College*
John Forshee, *San Jacinto College*
Myrtle Freeman, *Tarrant County College–South*
Dana Glencross, *Oklahoma City Community College*
James Michael Greig, *University of North Texas*
Alexander Hogan, *Lone Star College–CyFair*
Richard Kiefer, *Waubonsee Community College*
Melinda Kovacs, *Sam Houston State University*
Nancy Kral, *Lone Star College–Tomball*
Fred Lokken, *Truckee Meadows*
Vinette Meikle-Harris, *Houston Community College–Central*
Fran Moran, *New Jersey City University*
Joseph Moskowitz, *New Jersey City University*
Yamini Munipalli, *Florida State College*
Kathleen Murnan, *Ozarks Technical Community College*
Martha Musgrove, *Tarrant County College–South*
Glynn Newman, *Eastfield College*
Cecil Larry Pool, *El Centro College*
Sean Reed, *Wharton County Junior College*
Shauna Reilly, *Northern Kentucky University*
Elizabeth Rexford, *Wharton County Junior College*
Shyam Sriram, *Georgia Perimeter College*
Adam Stone, *Georgia Perimeter College*
Steve Tran, *Houston Community College*
Dennis Toombs, *San Jacinto College–North*
David Uranga, *Pasadena City College*
Ron Vardy, *University of Houston*
Sarah Velasquez, *Fresno Community College*

American Government Symposia

Since 2006, McGraw-Hill has conducted several symposia in American Government for instructors from across the country. These events offered a forum for instructors to exchange ideas and experiences with colleagues they might not have met otherwise. They also provided an opportunity for editors from McGraw-Hill to gather information about the needs and challenges of instructors of American Government. The feedback we have received has been invaluable and has contributed—directly and indirectly—to the development of *American Democracy Now*. We would like to thank the participants for their insights.

Melvin Aaron, *Los Angeles City College*
Yan Bai, *Grand Rapids Community College*
Robert Ballinger, *South Texas College*
Nancy Bednar, *Antelope Valley College*
Jeffrey Birdsong, *Northeastern Oklahoma A&M College*
Amy Brandon, *San Jacinto College-North*
Jane Bryant, *John A. Logan College*
Dan R. Brown, *Southwestern Oklahoma State University*
Monique Bruner, *Rose State College*
Anita Chadha, *University of Houston–Downtown*
John Clark, *Western Michigan University–Kalamazoo*
Kathleen Collihan, *American River College*
Steven Collins, *Oklahoma State University–Oklahoma City*
John Davis, *Howard University*
Kevin Davis, *North Cedntral Texas College*
Paul Davis, *Truckee Meadows Community College*
Vida Davoudi, *Lone Star College – Kingwood*
Robert De Luna, *Saint Philips College*
Jeff DeWitt, *Kennesaw State University*
Kevin Dockerty, *Kalamazoo Valley Community College*
Cecil Dorsey, *San Jacinto College – South*
Hien Do, *San Jose State University*
Jay Dow, *University of Missouri–Columbia*
Manar Elkhaldi, *University of Central Florida*
Karry Evans, *Austin Community College*
Pearl Ford, *University of Arkansas–Fayetteville*
John Forshee, *San Jacinto College–Central*
Ben Riesner Fraser, *San Jacinto College*
Daniel Fuerstman, *Dutchess Community College*
Jarvis T. Gamble, *Owens Community College*
Marilyn Gaar, *Johnson County Community College*

Michael Gattis, *Gulf Coast Community College*
William Gillespie, *Kennesaw State University*
Dana K. Glencross, *Oklahoma City Community College*
Larry Gonzalez, *Houston Community College–Southwest*
Nirmal Goswami, *Texas A&M University–Kingsville*
Daniel Gutierrez, *El Paso Community College*
Richard Gutierrez, *University of Texas, El Paso*
Michelle Kukoleca Hammes, *St. Cloud State University*
Cathy Hanks, *University of Nevada, Las Vegas*
Wanda Hill, *Tarrant County Community College*
Joseph Hinchliffe, *University of Illinois at Urbana–Champaign*
John Hitt, *North Lake College*
Mark Jendrysik, *University of North Dakota*
Brenda Jones, *Houston Community College–Central*
Franklin Jones, *Texas Southern University*
Lynn Jones, *Collin County Community College*
James Joseph, *Fresno City College*
Jason Kassel, *Valdosta State University*
Manoucher Khosrowshahi, *Tyler Junior College*
Rich Kiefer, *Waubonsee Community College*
Robert J. King, *Georgia Perimeter College*
Melinda Kovacs, *Sam Houston State University*
Chien-Pin Li, *Kennesaw State University*
Fred Lokken, *Truckee Meadows Community College*
John Mercurio, *San Diego State University*
Janna Merrick, *University of South Florida*
Joe Meyer, *Los Angeles City College*
Eric Miller, *Blinn College*
Kent Miller, *Weatherford College*
Charles Moore, *Georgia State University*
Eduardo Munoz, *El Camino College*
Kay Murnan, *Ozarks Technical Community College*
Carolyn Myers, *Southwestern Illinois College*
Blaine Nelson, *El Paso Community College*
Theresa Nevarez, *El Paso Community College*
James A. Norris, *Texas A & M International University*
Kent Park, *U.S. Military Academy at West Point*
Eric Rader, *Henry Ford Community College*
Elizabeth Rexford, *Wharton County Junior College*
Tara Ross, *Keiser University*
Carlos Rovelo, *Tarrant Community College–South*
Ryan Rynbrandt, *Collin County Community College*
Ray Sandoval, *Richland College*
Craig Scarpelli, *California State University–Chico*
Louis Schubert, *City College of San Francisco*
Edward Senu-Oke, *Joliet Junior College*
Mark Shomaker, *Blinn College*
Thomas Simpson, *Missouri Southern University*
Henry Sirgo, *McNeese State University*
Amy Smith, *North Lake College*
Daniel Smith, *Northwest Missouri State University*
John Speer, *Houston Community College–Southwest*
Jim Startin, *University of Texas at San Antonio*
Sharon Sykora, *Slippery Rock University*
Tressa Tabares, *American River College*
Beatrice Talpos, *Wayne County Community College*
Alec Thomson, *Schoolcraft College*
Judy Tobler, *Northwest Arkansas Community College*

Steve Tran, *Houston Community College*
Beth Traxler, *Greenville Technical College*
William Turk, *University of Texas–Pan American*
Ron Vardy, *University of Houston*
Sarah Velasquez, *Fresno City College*
Ron VonBehren, *Valencia Community College–Osceola*
Albert C. Waite, *Central Texas College*
Van Allen Wigginton, *San Jacinto College–Central*
Charlotte Williams, *Pasadena City College*
Ike Wilson, *U.S. Military Academy*
Paul Wilson, *San Antonio College*
John Wood, *Rose State College*
Robert Wood, *University of North Dakota*
Larry Wright, *Florida A & M University*
Ann Wyman, *Missouri Southern State University*
Kathryn Yates, *Richland College*

Personal Acknowledgments

We must thank our team at McGraw-Hill: Steve Debow, president of the Humanities, Social Science, and Languages group; James Headley, national sales manager; Mike Ryan, vice president and editor in-chief; and Lisa Pinto, executive director of development have supported this project with amazing talent and resources. Beth Mejia, editorial director for political science, has been a strong advocate for this project, and a dear friend. With kind and thoughtful leadership and sharp intellect, Mark Georgiev, sponsoring editor, took us by the hand and gently led us to where we needed to be. We benefited from steady guidance and wisdom from Dawn Groundwater, director of development. Senior developmental editor Judith Kromm has been a pleasure to work with. Naomi Friedman and Marjorie Anderson provided valuable development support. Marketing manager Patrick Brown's energy and enthusiasm have meant a great deal to us. Leslie Racanelli, our production editor, and her team showed patience, innovation, and flexibility. We would particularly like to thank Cassandra Chu and Linda Beaupré, our designers; Ayelet Arbel, our illustrator; and David Tietz, our photo researcher. Amy Flauaus provided invaluable support with good humor in her role as editorial coordinator. We are extraordinarily grateful to all of you.

We would also like to thank the contributors to our first edition: Susan Tolchin at George Mason University, Suzanne U. Samuels at Ramapo College, Elizabeth Bennion at Indiana University, Carol Whitney, and Naomi Friedman.

For their patience, understanding, and support, the authors also wish to thank: Caroline, Alexandra, and John Harrison, Paul Meilak, Rosemary Fitzgerald, Patricia Jillard, Kathleen Cain, John Callahan, Teresa Biebel, Thomas Callahan, Michael Harris, Jim and Audrey Wahl and the Wahl "girls"—Eileen Choynowski, Laura McAlpine, Audrey Messina, and Jaimee Conner.

John and Rosemary Callahan and Jim and Audrey Wahl first began the conversation of democracy with us and we thank them and all of the students and colleagues, friends and family members, who continue that conversation now.

BRIGID CALLAHAN HARRISON

JEAN WAHL HARRIS

A letter from the AUTHORS

Welcome to the second edition of *American Democracy Now!* In creating the first edition of this text, we sought to merge our years of experience as classroom instructors and our desire to captivate students with the compelling story of their democracy into a student-centered text. In this second edition, we are delighted to refine those goals with an integrated learning program for American government that will maximize student performance.

One of the most exciting facets of the second edition is the ability to create individualized study plans. Using an adaptive diagnostic tool combined with research-based teaching tools, students are guided in their critical thinking about American government. These tools value student performance by showing what they know, and then creating individualized learning objectives that will facilitate their success in completing the course. The result is higher student achievement, greater interest, more critical thinking, and a classroom environment that sizzles with the excitement of success, learning, mastery, and engagement.

The key to student success is the ability to think critically about American government and politics. *American Democracy Now,* 2e, teaches students the essential elements, institutions, and dynamics of American government. As they gain an understanding of the fundamental character of our political process, they also learn to ask the questions that make their understanding of American government meaningful to them. They learn how the fundamental principles of American democracy inform their understanding of the politics and policies of today, so that they can think about the policies they would like to see take shape tomorrow. In short, they learn to inquire: how does then and now shape what's going to happen next? This then, now, next approach to critical thinking serves as the basis for student participation.

American Democracy Now, 2e, takes a broader view of participation than the textbooks we have used in the past. To us, participation encompasses a variety of activities from the modest, creative, local or even personal actions students can take to the larger career choices they can make. And today, technology plays an enormous role in shaping political participation – particularly the participation of young people. By recognizing the legitimacy of new forms of political participation, we are giving students the tools to define what participation means to them and make active choices about where, when, and how to participate. And choosing how to participate makes American government matter.

As the students in our American Government classroom become ever more diverse, the challenge is not to appeal directly to their personal backgrounds; the challenge is to hone their critical thinking skills, foster and harness their energy, and create tools that facilitate their success in the American government course. We know we have succeeded when students apply their knowledge and sharpened skills to consider the outcomes they—as students, citizens, and participants—would like to see.

Facilitating their success means joining students where they are. The second edition of *American Democracy Now* further integrates technology into our students' study of politics, so that their engagement with content is seamless. Facebook, YouTube, and Twitter are not only powerful social networking tools, but also powerful political and educational tools. New technologies help politicians to communicate with citizens, citizens to communicate with each other, and you to communicate with your students. We invite you to, and we wish you and your students success.

BRIGID CALLAHAN HARRISON

JEAN WAHL HARRIS

ABOUT THE AUTHORS

Brigid Callahan Harrison

Brigid Harrison specializes in the civic engagement and political participation of Americans, especially the Millennial Generation, the U.S. Congress, and the Presidency. Brigid has taught American government for over fifteen years. She takes particular pride in creating in the classroom a learning experience that shapes students' lifelong understanding of American politics, sharpens their critical thinking about American government, and encourages their participation in civic life. She enjoys supervising student internships in political campaigns and government and is a frequent commentator in print and electronic media on national and New Jersey politics. She currently serves as president of the National Women's Caucus for Political Science. She received her B.A. from The Richard Stockton College, her M.A. from Rutgers, The State University of New Jersey, and her Ph.D. from Temple University. Harrison lives in Galloway, NJ and has three children: Caroline (16), Alexandra (10), and John (7). Born and raised in New Jersey, Harrison is a fan of Bruce Springsteen and professor of political science and law at Montclair State University.

Jean Wahl Harris

Jean Harris's research interests include political socialization and engagement, federalism, and the evolution and institutionalization of the first ladyship and the vice presidency. She regularly teaches introductory courses in local, state, and national government and upper level courses in public administration and public policy. In the classroom, Jean seeks to cultivate students' participation in the political conversation so vital to American civic life and to convey the profound opportunities that the American political system affords an active, critical, and informed citizenry. She earned her B.A., M.A., and Ph.D. from the State University of New York at Binghamton. In 1994 the University of Scranton named her its CASE (Council for Advancement and Support of Education) professor of the year. She was an American Council on Education (ACE) Fellow during the 2007–2008 academic year. She currently serves as chairperson for the Political Science Department at the University of Scranton. Jean lives in Nicholson, Pennsylvania with her husband Michael. She enjoys reading on her deck overlooking the Endless Mountains of Northeast Pennsylvania.

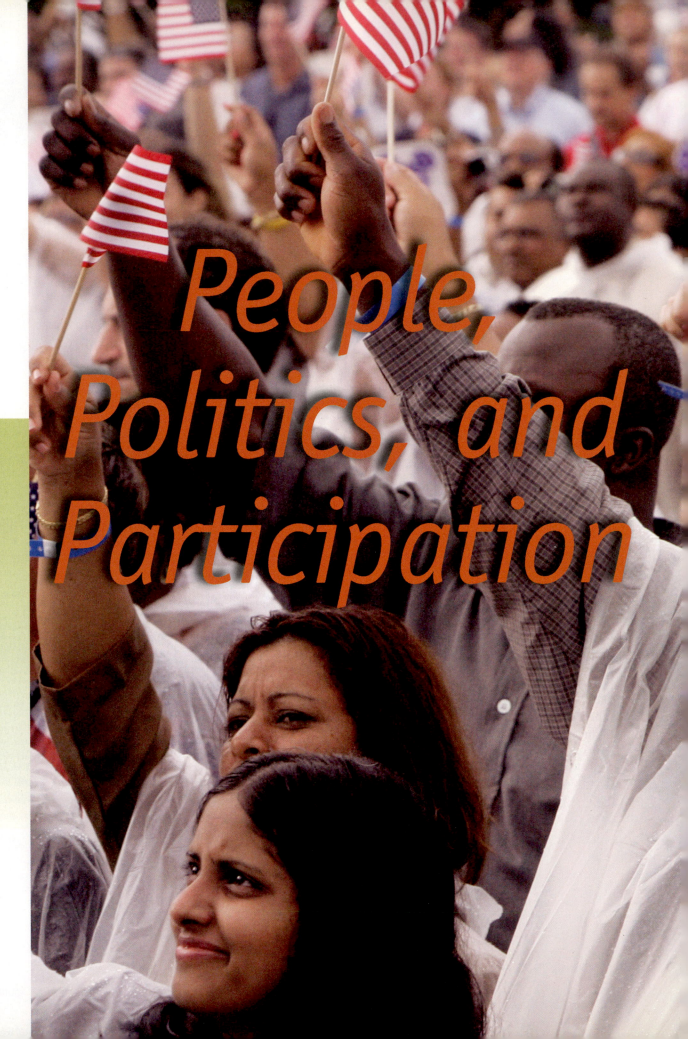

CHAPTER

1

People, Politics, and Participation

THEN

Cynicism, distrust, and apathy characterized Americans' relationship with their government for the past generation.

NOW

New information technologies, new political leadership, generational politics, and a diversifying population give cause for optimism as the nation responds to the challenges of a new millennium.

NEXT

Will the present generation break the cycle of cynicism that has pervaded the politics of the recent past?

Will new information technologies facilitate and energize political participation?

Will the face of American politics change as the nation's population grows and shifts?

3

This chapter provides a framework for your study of American government in this textbook.

FIRST, we delve into the basic question, *why should you study American democracy now?*

SECOND, we explore *what government does.*

THIRD, we explain how political scientists categorize the various *types of government.*

FOURTH, we consider the *origins of American democracy,* including the ideas of natural law, a social contract, and representative democracy.

FIFTH, we examine *political culture and American values,* which centrally include liberty; equality; consent of the governed; capitalism; and the importance of the individual, the family, and the community.

SIXTH, we focus on *the changing face of American democracy* as the population grows and diversifies.

SEVENTH, we look at *ideology as a prism* through which American politics can be viewed.

The United States was founded

by individuals who believed in the power of democracy to respond to the will of citizens. Historically, citizen activists have come from all walks of life, but they have shared one common attribute: the belief that, in the ongoing conversation of democracy, their government listens to *people like them.* This idea is vital if individuals are to have an impact on their government; people who don't believe they can have any influence rarely try. From the Pilgrims' flight from religious persecution, to the War for Independence, to the Civil War, to the Great Depression, to World War II, and to the great movements for social justice—civil rights, women's liberation, and more—the story of the United States is the story of people who are involved with their government, who know what they want their government to do, and who have confidence in their ability to influence its policies.[1] *American Democracy Now* tells the story of how today's citizen activists are participating in the conversation of democracy—in the politics, governance, and civic life of their communities and their nation during a time of technological revolution and unprecedented global change. This story is the next chapter in America's larger story.

The history of democracy in the United States is rife with examples of ordinary people who have made and are making a difference.[2] Throughout this book, we describe the impact that individuals and groups have had, and continue to have, in creating and changing the country's institutions of government. We also explore how individuals have influenced the ways in which our governments—national, state, and local—create policy.[3] These stories are important not only in and of themselves but also as motivators for all of us who want to live in a democracy that responds to all its citizens.

A fundamental principle underlying this book is that your beliefs and your voice—and ultimately how you use those beliefs and that voice—matter. Whatever your beliefs, it is important that you come to them thoughtfully, by employing introspection and critical thinking. Similarly, however you choose to participate, it is crucial that you take part in the civic life of your community. This book seeks both to inform and to inspire your participation. A sentiment voiced by American anthropologist Margaret Mead expresses a powerful truth: "Never doubt that a small group of thoughtful, committed citizens can change the world. Indeed, it's the only thing that ever has."

y shd u stdy am dem now? Or, Why Should You Study American Democracy Now?

politics
the process of deciding who benefits in society and who does not

Politics as practiced today is not your parents' brand of politics. **Politics**—the process of deciding who benefits in society and who does not—is a much different process today than it was even a decade ago. Advances in technology have altered the political landscape in many ways, including how voters and candidates communicate with each other, how governments provide information to individuals, how people get their news about events, and how governments administer laws. The political landscape has also changed because of world events. In particular, the terrorist attacks of September 11, 2001, and the wars in Afghanistan and Iraq have markedly changed many aspects of American life. Americans have become immune to the latest reports of suicide bombings in Iraq, Afghanistan, and elsewhere, and they have become all too familiar with reports of local soldiers killed in war. These shifts in how Americans interact with government and in what issues concern them represent distinct changes that make the study of politics today interesting, exciting, and important.

How Technology Has Changed Politics

It would be difficult to overstate the impact of the technological revolution on politics as it is practiced today. In electoral politics, faster computers and the Internet have revolutionized a process that, until the advent of the personal computer and the Internet, was not very different in 1990 from the way it was carried out in 1890. Today, many voters get much of their information from Internet-based news sites and Weblogs. Campaigns rely on e-mail; instant and text messaging; Web sites; and social-networking pages on MySpace, Facebook, BlackPlanet, Cyloop, and similar sites to communicate with and organize supporters. State governments rely on computers to conduct elections.

But the impact of technology is not limited to elections. Would you like to help your grandfather apply for his Social Security benefits? You no longer need to go to the local Social Security office or even mail an application; instead, you can help him apply online, and his check can be deposited into his bank account electronically. Do you want to communicate your views to your representatives in Congress? You do not need to call or send a letter by snail mail—their e-mail addresses are available online. Do you want to find out which government agencies are hiring recent college graduates? Go to usajobs.gov. Do you need to ship a package using the U.S. Postal Service? The postal service Web site provides guidelines.

Because of these unprecedented shifts in the ways politics happens and government is administered, Americans today face both new opportunities and new challenges. How might we use technology to ensure that elections are conducted fairly? How might the abundance and reach of media technology be directed toward informing and enriching us rather than overwhelming us or perpetuating the citizen cynicism of recent years? What privacy rights can we be sure of in the present digital age? Whatever your age, as a student, you are a member of one of the most tech-savvy groups in the country, and your input, expertise, and participation are vital to sorting out the opportunities and obstacles of this next stage of American democracy.

The Political Context Now

September 11, 2001, and the subsequent wars in Afghanistan and Iraq have had a marked effect on the U.S. political environment. These events have been a catalyst for changes in the attitudes of many Americans, including young Americans, about their government and their role in it.

Since the early 1970s—a decade blemished by the intense unpopularity of the Vietnam War and by scandals that ushered in the resignation of President Richard Nixon in 1974—Americans' attitudes about government have been dismal.[4] Numerous surveys, including an ongoing Gallup poll that has tracked Americans' opinions, have demonstrated low levels of trust in government and of confidence in government's ability to solve problems.[5] Young people's views have mirrored those of the nation as a whole. In 2000, one study of undergraduate college students, for example, showed that nearly two-thirds (64 percent) did not trust the federal government to do the right thing most of the time, an attitude that reflected the views of the larger population.[6] Distrust; lack of **efficacy,** which is a person's belief that he or she has the ability to achieve something desirable and that the government genuinely listens to individuals; and apathy among young people were reflected in the voter turnout for the 2000 presidential election, when only 36 percent of eligible college-age voters went to the polls.

The events of September 11, 2001, jolted American politics and the nation, and the altered political context provoked changes in popular views—notably, young people's opinions. "The attacks of 9/11 . . . changed the way the Millennial Generation thinks about

efficacy
citizens' belief that they have the ability to achieve something desirable and that the government listens to people like them

Technology and Political Participation

THEN (1970s)	NOW (2011)
47 percent of 18- to 20-year-olds voted in the 1976 presidential election.	About 53 percent of 18- to 20-year-olds voted in the 2008 presidential election, though that figure dropped in the 2010 congressional midterm elections.
People got their national news from one half-hour-long nightly news broadcast.	People get their news from an array of sources, including twenty-four-hour news networks and Internet news services available on demand via computers and cell phones.
Many people participated in civic life primarily through demonstrations, protests, and voting.	People still participate through demonstrations and protests but Tea Party activists rely on electronic communications to spread the word about demonstrations and protests. Other forms of political participation, including volunteerism, social networking, and targeted purchasing, characterize civic participation now.

WHAT'S NEXT?

> How might advancing media technologies further transform the ways that people "consume" their news?

> Will the upswing of voter participation by 18- to 20-year-olds continue?

> What new forms of civic participation will emerge?

> Will the highly competitive 2008 presidential race motivate a new wave of voters to remain active participants in the electoral process?

politics. Overnight, their attitudes were more like [those of] the Greatest Generation [the generation of Americans who lived through the Great Depression and World War II]," observed John Della Volpe, a pollster who helped Harvard University students construct a national poll of young people's views.[7]

As patriotic spirits soared, suddenly 60 percent of college students trusted government to do the right thing. Ninety-two percent considered themselves patriotic. Some 77 percent thought that politics was relevant to their lives.[8] In the immediate aftermath of the September 11, 2001 attacks, then-President George W. Bush and Congress enjoyed record-high approval ratings. Roughly 80 percent of young people and nearly that same percentage of all Americans supported U.S. military actions in Afghanistan. Beyond opinions, actions changed as well:

- More than 70 percent of college students gave blood, donated money, or volunteered in relief efforts.
- Nearly 70 percent volunteered in their communities (up from 60 percent in 2000).
- Eighty-six percent believed their generation was ready to lead the United States into the future.[9]

Then the political context changed again, over months and then years, as wars in Afghanistan and Iraq wore on, as casualties mounted, and as military spending skyrocketed. Trust in government, particularly of the president, plummeted. The changes after September 11, 2001 continued to affect how Americans, particularly young Americans, participate in politics.

An important trend is visible in one of the most easily measured contexts: voter turnout. Figure 1.1 shows the jump in participation by young voters in the 2004 presidential election. (In contrast, for voters aged 66–74, participation actually *de*creased in 2004.) Among voters aged 18–21, the largest increases in turnout occurred among 19-year-olds, whose turnout rivaled that of voters in their 30s. Americans are debating the importance of this upswing in turnout over the long haul. (See "Thinking Critically About Democracy" on page 8.) In 2008, that trend continued, with estimates indicating that voters aged 18–20 increased by 2.2 million, surpassing the young voter turnout since 18-year-olds voted for the first time in 1972.

As these statistics demonstrate, lingering media characterizations of a cynical young electorate are off the mark. Evidence indicates that many young people are enthusiastic participants in civic and political life.[10] Witness the strong political support that Barack Obama's presidential campaign garnered from young people, some of whom packed their bags and traveled with the Obama team during the primary season that led to the Democratic convention in August 2008 (see "Analyzing the Sources") on page 9. Others are taking part in ways that have not traditionally been thought of, and measured as, participation. These include, for example, Internet activism and using one's power as a consumer to send political messages. For many students, that foundation of political participation, volunteerism, or community action has already provided them with a rationale for increasing their knowledge of, and participation in, their communities.

Individuals who engage in politics and civic life experience many benefits. Engaged citizens are knowledgeable about public issues; actively communicate with policy makers and others; press government officials to carry out the people's will; advocate for their own self-interest and the interests of others; and hold public officials accountable for their decisions and actions. You will find that advocating for your own interests or working with others in similar situations will sometimes (perhaps to your surprise) lead to desired outcomes. This is efficacy in action. And you will discover that with experience you will become more effective at advocacy—the more you do, the better you get. Furthermore, you will derive social and psychological benefits from being civically engaged.

In addition, and importantly, local communities, states, and the nation benefit from an engaged populace. Governments are more effective when people voice their views. As we explore throughout this book, American democracy provides citizens and others more opportunities to influence governmental action than at any other time in history. If you have the knowledge and tools, you should be able to make the most of these opportunities.

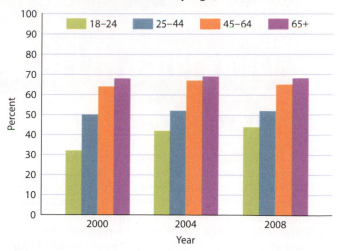

Voter Turnout by Age, 2000–2008

FIGURE 1.1 ■ **VOTER TURNOUT IN PRESIDENTIAL ELECTIONS (2000–2008) BY VOTER AGE** How has the turnout rate changed over time for voters aged 18–24? For other age groups?

SOURCE: www.census.gov/hhes/www/socdemo/voting/publications/historical/index.html.

POLITICAL INQUIRY

Civic Engagement: Acting on Your Views

One vitally important goal of this book is to encourage you to engage in a respectful, continuing conversation about your views and to make the connection between having ideas and opinions and acting on them. Political scientist Michael Delli Carpini has defined **civic engagement** as

> individual and collective actions designed to identify and address issues of public concern. Civic engagement can take many forms, from individual voluntarism to organizational involvement to electoral participation. It can include efforts to directly address an issue, work with others in a community to solve a problem or interact with the institutions of representative democracy.[11]

The possibilities for citizen involvement are so broad and numerous that the idea of civic engagement encompasses a range of activities. Civic engagement might include everything from tutoring an underprivileged child to volunteering at a conservative think tank. In this book, we focus in particular on civic engagement that takes the form of **political engagement**—that is, citizen actions that are intended to solve public problems through political means. As you will find as you read the book, a wide variety of political actions are possible, from boycotting and *buycotting* (buying goods produced by companies whose policies you agree with) to running for office.

We hope that this book not only empowers you by teaching you about the institutions, policies, and processes of the government but also inspires you to become civically and politically engaged. You can take part in your democracy by organizing a fund-raising event, joining a volunteer group,

civic engagement
individual and collective actions designed to identify and address issues of public concern

political engagement
citizen actions that are intended to solve public problems through political means

> One way in which individuals articulate their political views is through the products they choose to purchase. By purchasing "fair trade" coffee, consumers use their purchasing power to express their political viewpoints. Have you ever boycotted or buycotted a manufacturer based on your political view?

DOES THE YOUTH VOTE MATTER?

The Issue: During the 2008 presidential election, much emphasis was placed on the importance of the youth vote. Many pollsters and pundits, noting the strong support among younger voters for candidate Barack Obama, asserted that the youth vote had the potential to determine the outcome of that year's presidential race.

To that end, we saw a plethora of individuals from politicians to rappers to clothing designers urging young people to come out and vote. The national political parties took notice too: because Americans aged 18–29, drawn exclusively from the vast millennial generation, constitute a larger cohort than similar age brackets, the parties sought to tap the potential of this potential sleeping giant in the 2008 election.

Yes: The youth vote did matter in 2008, and it will continue to play an important role in future elections. The 2008 presidential election saw near-historic participation by young Americans: about 44 percent of those aged 18–24 voted. And although that is not a turnout rate comparable to that of older segments of the population (whose turnout rate ranged from 52 to 68 percent, depending upon age), it was the highest turnout for younger Americans in nearly forty years, when turnout was bolstered in the first presidential election in which 18–20 year-olds could vote. But the significance of the higher turnout rate was magnified by the large proportion of young Americans who voted for Barack Obama. Fully 66 percent of those aged 18–29 voted for Obama. This breakdown was the first sign of a new era of generational politics, and those who came of age politically in the era of Obama will be loyal to the Democratic party for years to come.

No: The turnout of young Americans, though increasing historically, will not be the determining factor in federal elections. The low participation rate by young Americans in 2010 indicates that the Obama phenomenon was a flash-in-the-pan occurrence, and that Democrats cannot count young Americans among their loyal party supporters. As a candidate, Barack Obama relied upon a message and an electronic medium that was attractive to young Americans, but those tactics are difficult to replicate in the complicated process of governing, and the 2010 turnout among young people is indicative of a disenchantment with both President Obama in particular and politics in general by those young voters.

Other approaches: Younger voters were attracted to Obama's brand of politics, and they will remain loyal to him in 2012. But as the 2010 turnout indicated, that support does not translate into support for other Democratic candidates. Nonetheless, today's younger voters—millennial voters—will become the determining constituency in federal elections in years to come, both because of the size of their generation and because of the unique set of political viewpoints they bring to the political table as a result of being socialized in a post–September 11 world.

What do you think?

① How did the impact of the youth vote in 2010 compare with that of 2008?

② What issues motivate young voters to vote? What kinds of candidates motivate younger voters?

③ Do the positions of millennial voters differ from those of older voters?

---

volunteering for a campaign, calling or writing to an elected official, or even participating in a protest march, to name just a few of the many options available to you. Consider which potential volunteer activities pique your interest. Think about what might best suit your schedule, lifestyle, and personal and professional goals. By taking part, you will ensure that your voice is heard, and you will derive the satisfaction of knowing that your community and the nation benefit from your actions as well.

government
the institution that creates and implements policies and laws that guide the conduct of the nation and its citizens

citizens
members of the polity who, through birth or naturalization, enjoy the rights, privileges, and responsibilities attached to membership in a given nation

What Government Does

In this section, we look at the nature of government and the functions a government performs. **Government** is an institution that creates and implements the policy and laws that guide the conduct of a nation and its citizens. **Citizens** are those members of a political community—town, city, state, or country—who, through birth or naturalization, enjoy the rights, privileges, and responsibilities attached to membership in a given nation. **Natural-**

ANALYZING THE SOURCES

The figure below shows the results of a Gallup poll that measures party identification by age. Notice that there are significant differences between people of various ages when it comes to their party identification.

Democrats currently enjoy a party identification advantage over Republicans among Americans at every age between 18 and 85. The Democrats' greatest advantages come from those in their 20s and from baby boomers in their late 40s and 50s. Republicans, on the other hand, come closest to parity with Democrats among Generation Xers in their late 30s and early 40s and among seniors in their late 60s.

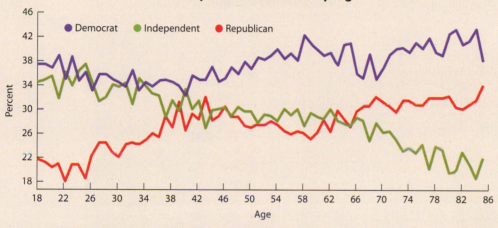

Party Identification by Age

SOURCE: www.gallup.com/poll/118285/Democrats-Best-Among-Generation-Baby-Boomers.aspx.

Evaluating the Evidence

① Describe the party breakdown of the millennial generation. Which party are members of that generation most likely to identify with? The least likely to identify with? Why do you think this is the case?

② Among which generation are there likely to be nearly equal proportions of Democrats and Republicans?

③ Which voters are least likely to be Independents? Why do you think this might be the case?

---

ization is the process of becoming a citizen by means other than birth, as in the case of immigrants. Although governments vary widely in how well they perform, most national governments share some common functions.

To get a clear sense of the business of government, consider the following key functions performed by government in the United States and many other national governments:

■ **To protect their sovereign territory and their citizenry and to provide national defense.** Governments protect their *sovereign territory* (that is, the territory over which they have the ultimate governing authority) and their citizens at home and abroad. Usually they carry out this responsibility by maintaining one or more types of armed services, but governments also provide for the national defense through counter-terrorism efforts.

In the United States, the armed services include the Army, Navy, Marines, Air Force, and Coast Guard. In 2008, the U.S. Department of Defense budget was approximately $480 billion. This excludes about $235 billion in emergency appropriations for military operations in Afghanistan and Iraq, plus about $38 billion in funding for the Department of Homeland Security.

Governments also preserve order domestically. In the United States, domestic order is preserved through the National Guard and federal, state, and local law enforcement agencies.

naturalization

the process of becoming a citizen by means other than birth, as in the case of immigrants

What Government Does   9

CHALLENGES FOR THE GOVERNMENT OF AFGHANISTAN

When Barack Obama was elected president of the United States in November 2008, many Americans applauded, others were disappointed, but acceptance of the election results as a free and fair expression of the will of the American people was near universal. Contrast that with the Afghani elections held in August 2009. In the aftermath of those elections, both international and domestic critics charged that the elections were corrupt, thereby tainting the reelection of Afghan president Hamid Karzai, and calling into question the legitimacy of the Afghani government. In fact, when the Gallup polling organization surveyed 1,000 Afghanis in June 2009, it found that eight in ten Afghans had asserted that corruption was widespread.

Because of the pervasive perception of corruption, the government's ability to perform other functions, including preserving order and stability and establishing a legitimate legal system, also suffers. Nonetheless, many Afghanis view the current situation as an improvement over earlier times.

SOURCE: Gallup World Poll, http://74.125.155.132/search?sourceid=navclient &ie=UTF-8&rlz=1T4DKUS_enUS304US304&q=cache:http%3A%2F%2F www.gallup.com%2Fpoll%2Fworld.aspx.

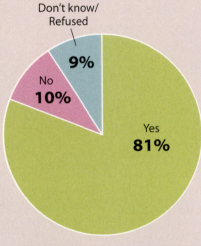

Is Corruption Widespread Throughout the Government of Afghanistan, or Not?

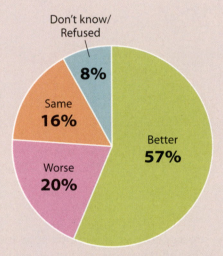

Afghans' View on Life Since the Fall of the Taliban

■ **To preserve order and stability.** Governments also preserve order by providing emergency services and security in the wake of disasters. For example, after Hurricane Katrina struck the Gulf Coast and the city of New Orleans in August 2005, the National Guard was sent in to provide security in the midst of an increasingly dangerous situation (though in the eyes of many critics, including local and state elected officials, the action came too late to preserve order). Governments also maintain stability by providing a political structure that has **legitimacy:** a quality conferred on government by citizens who believe that its exercise of power is right and proper.[12] (See "Global Context.")

legitimacy
a quality conferred on government by citizens who believe that its exercise of power is right and proper

■ **To establish and maintain a legal system.** Governments create legal structures by enacting and enforcing laws that restrict or ban certain behaviors. In the United States, the foundation of this legal structure is the federal Constitution.[13] Governments also provide the means to implement laws through the actions of local police and other state and national law enforcement agencies. By means of the court system, governments administer justice and impose penalties.

■ **To provide services.** Governments distribute a wide variety of services to their citizens. In the United States, government agencies provide services ranging from inspecting the meat we consume to ensuring the safety of our workplaces. Federal, state, and local governments provide roads, bridges, transportation, education, and health services. They facilitate communication, commerce, air travel, and entertainment.

Many of the services governments provide are called **public goods** because their benefits, by their nature, cannot be limited to specific groups or individuals. For example, everyone enjoys national defense, equal access to clean air and clean water, airport security, highways, and other similar services. Because the value and the benefits of these goods are extended to everyone, government makes them available through revenue collected by taxes. Not all goods that government provides are public goods, however; some goods, such as access to government-provided health care, are available only to the poor or to older Americans.

■ **To raise and spend money.** All the services that governments provide, from national protection and defense to health care, cost money.[14] Governments at all levels spend money collected through taxes. Depending on personal income, between 25 and 35 cents of every dollar earned by those working in the United States and earning above a certain level goes toward federal, state, and local income taxes. Governments also tax *commodities* (commercially exchanged goods and services) in various ways—through sales taxes, property taxes, sin taxes, and luxury taxes.

■ **To socialize new generations.** Governments play a role in *socialization,* the process by which individuals develop their political values and opinions. Governments perform this function, for example, by providing funding for schools, by introducing young people to the various "faces" of government (perhaps through a police officer's visiting a school or a mayor's bestowing an honor on a student), and by facilitating participation in civic life through institutions such as libraries, museums, and public parks. In these ways, governments transmit cultural norms and values such as patriotism and build commitment to fundamental values such as those we explore later in this chapter. For a detailed discussion of political socialization, see Chapter 6.

> Children are socialized to the dominant political culture from a very early age. When children emulate firefighters, for example, they begin the process of learning about the functions governments perform.

Types of Government

When social scientists categorize the different systems of government operating in the world today, two factors influence their classifications. The first factor is *who participates in governing or in selecting those who govern.* These participants vary as follows, depending on whether the government is a monarchy, an oligarchy, or a democracy:

monarchy
government in which a member of a royal family, usually a king or a queen, has absolute authority over a territory and its government

- In a **monarchy,** a member of a royal family, usually a king or a queen, has absolute authority over a territory and its government. Monarchies typically are inherited—they pass down from generation to generation. Most modern monarchies, such as those in Great Britain and Spain, are *constitutional monarchies,* in which the monarch plays a ceremonial role but has little actual say in governance, which is carried out by elected leaders. In contrast, in traditional monarchies, such as the Kingdom of Saudi Arabia, the monarch is both the ceremonial and the governmental head of state.

oligarchy
government in which an elite few hold power

- In an **oligarchy,** an elite few hold power. Some oligarchies are *dictatorships,* in which a small group, such as a political party or a military junta, supports a dictator. North Korea and Myanmar (formerly Burma) are present-day examples of oligarchies.

democracy
government in which supreme power of governance lies in the hands of its citizens

- In a **democracy,** the supreme power of governance lies in the hands of citizens. The United States and most other modern democracies are *republics,* sometimes called *representative democracies,* in which citizens elect leaders to represent their views. We discuss the republican form of government in Chapter 2.

Social scientists also consider *how governments function* and *how they are structured* when classifying governments:

totalitarianism
system of government in which the government essentially controls every aspect of people's lives

- Governments that rule according to the principles of **totalitarianism** essentially control every aspect of their citizens' lives. In these tyrannical governments, citizens enjoy neither rights nor freedoms, and the state is the tool of the dictator. Totalitarian regimes tend to center on a particular ideology, religion, or personality. North Korea is a contemporary example of a totalitarian regime, as was Afghanistan under the Islamic fundamentalist regime of the Taliban.

authoritarianism
system of government in which the government holds strong powers but is checked by some forces

- When a government rules by the principles of **authoritarianism,** it holds strong powers, but they are checked by other forces within the society. China and Cuba are examples of authoritarian states because their leaders are restrained in their exercise of power by political parties, constitutions, and the military. Individuals living under an authoritarian regime may enjoy some rights, but often those rights are not protected by the government.

constitutionalism
government that is structured by law, and in which the power of government is limited

limited government
government that is restricted in what it can do so that the rights of the people are protected

- **Constitutionalism,** a form of government structured by law, provides for **limited government**—a government that is restricted in what it can do so that the rights of the people are protected. Constitutional governments can be democracies or monarchies. In the United States, the federal Constitution created the governmental structure, and this system of government reflects both the historical experiences and the norms and values of the founders.

The Constitution's framers (authors) structured American government as a *constitutional democracy.* In this type of government, a constitution creates a representative democracy in which the rights of the people are protected. We can trace the roots of this modern constitutional democracy back to ancient times.

The Origins of American Democracy

The ancient Greeks first developed the concept of a democracy. The Greeks used the term *demokratia* (literally, "people power") to describe some of the 1,500 *poleis* ("city-states"; also the root of *politics*) on the Black and Mediterranean seas. These city-states were not democracies in the modern sense of the term, but the way they were governed provided the philosophical origins of American democracy. For example, citizens decided public issues using majority rule in many of the city-states. However, in contrast to modern democracies, the Greek city-states did not count women as citizens. The Greeks also did not count slaves as citizens. American democracy also traces some of its roots to the Judeo-Christian tradition and the English common law, particularly the ideas that thrived during the Protestant Reformation.[15]

Democracy's Origins in Popular Protest: The Influence of the Reformation and the Enlightenment

We can trace the seeds of the idea of modern democracy almost as far back as the concept of monarchy—back to several centuries ago, when the kings and emperors who ruled in Europe claimed that they reigned by divine sanction, or God's will. The monarchs' claims reflected the political theory of the **divine right of kings,** articulated by Jacques-Benigne Bossuet (1627–1704), who argued that monarchies, as a manifestation of God's will, could rule absolutely without regard to the will or well-being of their subjects. Challenging the right of a monarch to govern or questioning one of his or her decisions thus represented a challenge to the will of God.

At odds with the theory of the divine right of kings was the idea that people could challenge the crown and the church—institutions that seemed all-powerful. This idea took hold during the Protestant Reformation, a movement to reform the Catholic Church. In October 1517, Martin Luther, a German monk who would later found the Lutheran Church, posted his *95 Theses,* criticizing the harmful practices of the Catholic Church, to the door of the church at Wittenberg Castle. The Reformation continued throughout the sixteenth century, during which time reform-minded Protestants (whose name is derived from *protest*) challenged basic tenets of Catholicism and sought to *purify* the church.

In England, some extreme Protestants, known as Puritans, thought that the Reformation had not gone far enough in reforming the church. Puritans asserted their right to communicate directly with God through prayer rather than through an intermediary such as a priest. This idea that an individual could speak directly with God lent support to the notion that the people could govern themselves. Faced with persecution in England, congregations of Puritans, known to us today as the Pilgrims, fled to America, where they established self-governing colonies, a radical notion at the time. Before the Pilgrims reached shore in 1620, they drew up the Mayflower Compact, an example of a **social contract**—an agreement between people and their leaders, whereby the people give up some liberties so that their other liberties will be protected. In the Mayflower Compact, the Pilgrims agreed to be governed by the structure of government they formed, thereby establishing consent of the governed.

In the late seventeenth century came the early beginnings of the Enlightenment, a philosophical movement that stressed the importance of individuality, reason, and scientific endeavor. Enlightenment scientists such as Sir Isaac Newton (1642–1727) drastically changed how people thought about the universe and the world around them, including government. Newton's work in physics, astronomy, math, and mechanics demonstrated the power of science and repudiated prevalent ideas based on magic and superstition. Newton's ideas about **natural law,** the assertion that the laws that govern human behavior are derived from the nature of humans themselves and can be universally applied, laid the foundation for the ideas of the political philosophers of the Enlightenment.

divine right of kings
the assertion that monarchies, as a manifestation of God's will, could rule absolutely without regard to the will or well-being of their subjects

social contract
an agreement between people and their leaders in which the people agree to give up some liberties so that their other liberties are protected

natural law
the assertion that standards that govern human behavior are derived from the nature of humans themselves and can be universally applied

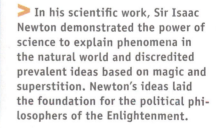

> In his scientific work, Sir Isaac Newton demonstrated the power of science to explain phenomena in the natural world and discredited prevalent ideas based on magic and superstition. Newton's ideas laid the foundation for the political philosophers of the Enlightenment.

The Modern Political Philosophy of Hobbes and Locke

The difficulty of individual survival under the rule of an absolute monarch is portrayed in British philosopher Thomas Hobbes' book *Leviathan* (1651). Hobbes (1588–1679), who

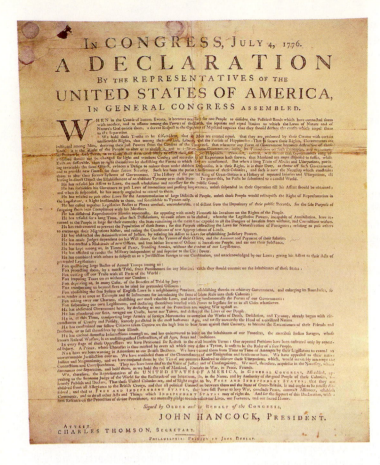

believed in the righteousness of absolute monarchies, argued that the strong naturally prey upon the weak and that through a social contract, individuals who relinquish their rights can enjoy the protection offered by a sovereign. Without such a social contract and without an absolute monarch, Hobbes asserted, anarchy prevails, describing this state as one lived in "continuall feare, and danger of violent death; And the life of man, solitary, poore, nasty, brutish, and short."[16]

John Locke (1632–1704) took Hobbes's reasoning concerning a social contract one step further. In the first of his *Two Treatises on Civil Government* (1689), Locke systematically rejected the notion that the rationale for the divine right of kings is based on scripture. By providing a theoretical basis for discarding the idea of a monarch's divine right to rule, Locke paved the way for more radical notions about the rights of individuals and the role of government. In the second *Treatise,* Locke argued that individuals possess certain unalienable (or natural) rights, which he identified as the rights to life, liberty, and property, ideas that would prove pivotal in shaping Thomas Jefferson's articulation of the role of government and the rights of individuals found in the Declaration of Independence. Locke, and later Jefferson, stressed that these rights are inherent in people as individuals; that is, government can neither bestow them nor take them away. When people enter into a social contract, Locke said, they do so with the understanding that the government will protect their natural rights. At the same time, according to Locke, they agree to accept the government's authority; but if the government fails to protect the inherent rights of individuals, the people have the right to rebel.

The French philosopher Jean-Jacques Rousseau (1712–1778) took Locke's notion further, stating that governments formed by social contract rely on **popular sovereignty,** the theory that government is created by the people and depends on the people for the authority to rule. **Social contract theory,** which assumes that individuals possess free will and that every individual possesses the God-given right of self-determination and the ability to consent to be governed, would eventually form the theoretical framework of the Declaration of Independence.

The Creation of the United States as an Experiment in Representative Democracy

The American colonists who eventually rebelled against Great Britain and who became the citizens of the first thirteen states were shaped by their experiences of living under European monarchies. Many rejected the ideas of absolute rule and the divine right of kings, which had been central to rationalizing the monarchs' authority. The logic behind the rejection of the divine right of kings—the idea that monarchs were not chosen by God—was that people could govern themselves.

In New England, where many colonists settled after fleeing England to escape religious persecution, a form of **direct democracy,** a structure of government in which citizens discuss and decide policy through majority rule, emerged in *town meetings* (which still take place today). In every colony, the colonists themselves decided who was eligible to participate in government, and so in some localities, women and people of color who owned property participated in government well before they were granted formal voting rights under amendments to the federal Constitution.

Beyond the forms of direct democracy prevalent in the New England colonies, nearly all the American colonies had councils structured according to the principle of representative democracy, sometimes called **indirect democracy,** in which citizens elect representatives

popular sovereignty
the theory that government is created by the people and depends on the people for the authority to rule

social contract theory
the idea that individuals possess free will, and every individual is equally endowed with the God-given right of self-determination and the ability to consent to be governed

direct democracy
a structure of government in which citizens discuss and decide policy through majority rule

indirect democracy
sometimes called a *representative democracy,* a system in which citizens elect representatives who decide policies on behalf of their constituents

who decide policies on their behalf. These representative democracies foreshadow important political values that founders such as Thomas Jefferson and James Madison would incorporate into key founding documents, including the Declaration of Independence and the Constitution.

Political Culture and American Values

On September 11, 2002, the first anniversary of the terrorist attacks on the United States, the *New York Times* ran an editorial, "America Enduring," that described how the United States and its residents had weathered the difficult year after 9/11. "America isn't bound together by emotion. It's bound together by things that transcend emotion, by principles and laws, by ideals of freedom and justice that need constant articulation."[17] These ideals are part of American **political culture**—the people's collective beliefs and attitudes about government and the political process. These ideals include liberty, equality, capitalism, consent of the governed, and the importance of the individual (as well as family and community).

Liberty

The most essential quality of American democracy, **liberty** is both freedom from government interference in our lives and freedom to pursue happiness. Many of the colonies that eventually became the United States were founded by people who were interested in one notion of liberty: religious freedom. Those who fought in the War for Independence were intent on obtaining economic and political freedom. The framers of the Constitution added

political culture
the people's collective beliefs and attitudes about government and political processes

liberty
the most essential quality of American democracy; it is both the freedom from governmental interference in citizens' lives and the freedom to pursue happiness

> **Thomas Jefferson's ideas about the role of government shaped the United States for generations to come. In 1999, descendants of Thomas Jefferson, including those he fathered with his slave, Sally Hemings, posed for a group photo at his plantation, Monticello, in Charlottesville, Virginia.**

to the structure of the U.S. government many other liberties,[18] including freedom of speech, freedom of the press, and freedom of association.[19]

There is evidence all around us of ongoing tensions between people attempting to assert their individual liberty on the one hand and the government's efforts to exert control on the other. For example, issues of religious freedom are in play in school districts where some parents object to the teaching of the theory of evolution because the theory contradicts their religious beliefs. The struggle for privacy rights—and how those rights are defined—continues unabated as the government's counterterrorism efforts result in officials' seeking greater access to our communications.

Throughout history and to the present day, liberties have often conflicted with efforts by the government to ensure a secure and stable society by exerting restraints on liberties. When government officials infringe on personal liberties, they often do so in the name of security, arguing that such measures are necessary to protect the rights of other individuals, institutions (including the government itself), or society as a whole. As we consider in Chapter 4, these efforts include, for example, infringing on the right to free speech by regulating or outlawing hate speech or speech that compels others to violence. Governments may also impinge on privacy rights; think of the various security measures that you are subject to before boarding an airplane.

> Many Americans began to change their views about their country on September 11, 2001, when terror attacks killed more than 2,700 people with the destruction of the World Trade Center, the crash at the Pentagon, and United Airlines Flight 93 in Shanksville, Pennsylvania. Here, a woman and child look over the flowers in the reflecting pool at Ground Zero during a memorial ceremony on September 11, 2009 in New York City. Nearly a decade later these views are still evolving.

The meaning of liberty—how we define our freedoms—is constantly evolving. In light of September 11 and the digital revolution, difficult questions have arisen about how much liberty Americans should have and how far the government should go in curtailing liberties to provide security. Should law enforcement officers be allowed to listen in on an individual's phone conversations if that person is suspected of a crime? Or should they be required to get a warrant first? What if that person is suspected of plotting a terrorist attack—should the officer be required to obtain a warrant first in that situation? What if one of the suspected plotters is not a U.S. citizen?

Equality

The Declaration of Independence states that "all men are created equal . . ." But the founders' notions of equality were vastly different from those that prevail today. Their ideas of equality evolved from the emphasis the ancient Greeks placed on equality of opportunity. The Greeks envisioned a merit-based system in which educated freemen could participate in democratic government rather than inheriting their positions as a birthright. The Judeo-Christian religions also emphasize the idea of equality. All three major world religions—Christianity, Judaism, and Islam—stress that all people are equal in the eyes of God. These notions of equality informed both Jefferson's assertion about equality in the Declaration of Independence and, later, the framers' structuring of the U.S. government in the Constitution.[20]

The idea of equality evolved during the nineteenth and twentieth centuries. In the early American republic, all women, as well as all men of color, were denied fundamental rights, including the right to vote. Through long, painful struggles—including the abolition movement to free the slaves; the suffrage movement to gain women the right to vote; various immigrants' rights movements; and later the civil rights, Native American rights, and women's rights movements of the 1960s and 1970s (see Chapter 5)—members of these disenfranchised groups won the rights previously denied to them.

Several groups are still engaged in the struggle for legal equality today, notably gay and lesbian rights organizations and groups that advocate for fathers', children's, and immigrants' rights. And historic questions about the nature of equality have very modern implications: Are certain forms of inequality, such as preventing gay couples from enjoying the rights of married heterosexual couples, acceptable in American society? Are the advantages of U.S. democracy reserved only for citizens, or should immigrants living legally in the United States also enjoy these advantages?

Beyond these questions of legal equality, today many arguments over equality focus on issues of economic equality, a concept about which there is substantial disagreement. Some in the United States believe that the government should do more to eliminate disparities in wealth—by taxing wealthy people more heavily than others, for example, or by providing more subsidies and services to the poor. Others disagree, however, and argue that although people should have equal opportunities for economic achievement, their attainment of that success should depend on factors such as education and hard work, and that success should be determined in the marketplace rather than through government intervention.

Capitalism

Although the founders valued the notion of equality, capitalism was equally important to them. **Capitalism** is an economic system in which the means of producing wealth are privately owned and operated to produce profits. In a pure capitalist economy, the marketplace determines the regulation of production, the distribution of goods and services, wages, and prices. In this type of economy, for example, businesses pay employees the wage that they are willing to work for, without the government's setting a minimum wage by law. Although capitalism is an important value in American democracy, the U.S. government imposes certain regulations on the economy: it mandates a minimum wage, regulates and inspects goods and services, and imposes tariffs on imports and taxes on domestically produced goods that have an impact on pricing.

One key component of capitalism is **property**—anything that can be owned. There are various kinds of property: businesses, homes, farms, the material items we use every day, and even ideas are considered property. Property holds such a prominent position in American culture that it is considered a natural right, and the Constitution protects some aspects of property ownership.

capitalism
an economic system in which the means of producing wealth are privately owned and operated to produce profits

property
anything that can be owned

Consent of the Governed

The idea that, in a democracy, the government's power derives from the consent of the people is called the **consent of the governed.** As we have seen, this concept, a focal point of the rebellious American colonists and eloquently expressed in Jefferson's Declaration of Independence, is based on John Locke's idea of a social contract. Implicit in Locke's social contract is the principle that the people agree to the government's authority, and if the government no longer has the consent of the governed, the people have the right to revolt.

The concept of consent of the governed also implies **majority rule**—the principle that, in a democracy, only policies with 50 percent plus one vote are enacted, and only candidates who attain 50 percent plus one vote are elected. In the United States and other democracies, often the candidate with a plurality (the most votes, but not necessarily a majority) wins. Governments based on majority rule include the idea that the majority has the right of self-governance and typically also protect the rights of people in the minority. A particular question about this ideal of governing by the consent of the governed has important implications for the United States in the early twenty-first century: Can a democracy remain stable and legitimate if less than a majority of its citizens participate in elections?

consent of the governed
the idea that, in a democracy, the government's power derives from the consent of the people

majority rule
the idea that, in a democracy, only policies with 50 percent plus one vote are enacted, and only candidates that win 50 percent plus one vote are elected

Individual, Family, and Community

Emphasis on the individual is a preeminent feature of American democratic thought. In the Constitution, rights are bestowed on, and exercised by, the individual. The importance of the individual—an independent, hearty entity exercising self-determination—has powerfully shaped the development of the United States, both geographically and politically.

Family and community have also played central roles in the U.S. political culture, both historically and in the present day. A child first learns political behavior from his or her family, and in this way the family serves to perpetuate the political culture. And from the earliest colonial settlements to today's blogosphere, communities have channeled individuals' political participation. Indeed, the intimate relationship between individualism and community life is reflected in the First Amendment of the Constitution, which ensures individuals' freedom of assembly—one component of which is their right to form or join any type of organization, political party, or club without penalty.

The Changing Face of American Democracy

Figure 1.2 shows how the U.S. population has grown since the first census in 1790. At that point, there were fewer than 4 million Americans. By 2000, the U.S. population had reached 281 million, and it will soar well over 300 million by the next census, in 2010.

Immigrants have always been part of the country's population growth, and over the centuries they have made innumerable contributions to American life and culture.[21] Immigrants from lands all around the world have faced the kinds of struggles that today's undocumented immigrants encounter. Chinese Americans, for example, were instrumental in pioneering the West and completing the construction of the transcontinental railroad in the mid-nineteenth century, but the Chinese Exclusion Act of 1881 prevented them from becoming U.S. citizens. Faced with the kinds of persecution that today would be considered hate crimes, Chinese Americans used civil disobedience to fight against the so-called Dog Tag Laws that required them to carry registration cards. In one incident, in 1885, they fought back against unruly mobs that drove them out of the town of Eureka, California, by suing the city for reparations and compensation.[22]

A Population That Is Growing— and on the Move

Between 1960 and 2000, the population of the United States increased by more than 50 percent. As the population increases, measures of who the American people are and what percentage of each demographic group makes up the population have significant implications for the policies, priorities, values, and preferred forms of civic and political participation of the people. All the factors contributing to U.S. population growth—including immigration, the birth rate, falling infant mortality rates, and longer life spans—influence both politics and policy as the ongoing debate about immigration reform shows. Generational differences in preferred methods of participation are yet another, as is the national conversation about the future of Social Security.

Accompanying the increase in population over the years has been a shift in the places where people live. For example, between 1990 and 2000, 684 of the nation's 3,142 counties, most of them in the Midwest and Plains states, reported a loss in population. But 80 counties, primarily in the West and the South, had population growth of more than 50 percent. In five counties, two in Georgia and three in Colorado, the population jumped by more than 100 percent.

An Aging Population

As the U.S. population increases and favors new places of residence, it is also aging. Figure 1.3 shows the distribution of the population by age and by sex as a series of three pyramids for three different years. The 2000 pyramid shows the "muffin top" of the baby boom-

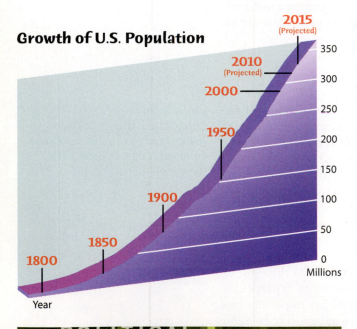

Growth of U.S. Population

2015 (Projected)
2010 (Projected)
2000
1950
1900
1850
1800

350
300
250
200
150
100
50
0
Millions

Year

POLITICAL INQUIRY

FIGURE 1.2 ■ From 1790 to 1900, the population of the United States increased gradually, and it did not reach 100 million until the second decade of the twentieth century. What factors caused the steep rise during the twentieth century? How will these forces continue to affect the size of the U.S. population during this century?

SOURCE: U.S. Census, www.census.gov/population/www/documentation/twps0056.html, and www.census.gov/compendia/stabab/cats/population/estimates_and_projections _by_age_sex_raceethnicity.html.

ers, who were 36 to 55 years old in that year. A quarter-century later, the echo boom of the millennials, who will be between the ages of 30 and 55 in 2025, is clearly visible. The pyramid evens out and thickens by 2050, showing the effects of increased population growth and the impact of extended longevity, with a large number of people (women in particular) expected to live to the age of 85 and older.

Some areas of the United States are well-known meccas for older Americans. For example, the reputation of Florida and the Southwest as the premier retirement destinations in the United States is highlighted in Figure 1.4 on page 20, which shows that older Americans are concentrated in those areas, as well as in a broad north–south band that runs down the United States' midsection. Older people are concentrated in the Midwest and Plains states because of the high levels of emigration from these areas by younger Americans, who are leaving their parents behind to look for opportunity elsewhere.

A Changing Complexion: Race and Ethnicity in the United States Today

The population of the United States is becoming not only older but also more racially and ethnically diverse. Figure 1.5 on page 20 shows the racial and ethnic composition of the U.S. population in 2010. Notice that Hispanics* now make up a greater proportion of the U.S. population than do blacks. As Figure 1.5 also shows, this trend has been continuous over the past several decades. Figure 1.5 also indicates that the percentage of Asian Americans has more than doubled in recent decades, from just over 2 percent of the U.S. population in 1980 to over 4 percent today. The Native American population has increased marginally but still constitutes less than 1 percent of the whole population. Figure 1.5 also shows the proportion of people reporting that they belonged to two or more racial groups, a category that was not an option on the census questionnaire until 2000.

As Figures 1.6 (on page 21) and 1.7 (on page 22) show, minority populations tend to be concentrated in different areas of the United States. Figure 1.6 shows the concentration of non-Hispanic African Americans. At 12 percent of the population, African Americans are the largest racial minority in the United States. (Hispanics are an ethnic minority.) As the map illustrates, the African American population tends to be centered in urban areas and in the South, where, in some counties, African Americans constitute a majority of the population.

Hispanics, on the other hand, tend to cluster in Texas and California along the border between the United States and Mexico and in the urban centers of New Mexico, as shown in Figure 1.7 (on page 22). Concentrations of Hispanic populations are also found in Florida and the Northeast. Hispanics are the fastest-growing ethnic group in the United States, with a projected 16 percent of the U.S. population identifying themselves as Hispanic in 2010, an increase of nearly 10 percent since 1980. Among people of Hispanic ethnicity, Mexicans make up the largest number (about 7 percent of the total U.S. population), followed by Puerto Ricans (1 percent in 2000) and Cubans (0.4 percent).

* A note about terminology: When discussing data for various races and ethnicities for the purpose of making comparisons, we use the terms *black* and *Hispanic,* because these labels are typically used in measuring demographics by the Bureau of the Census and other organizations that collect this type of data. In more descriptive writing that is not comparative, we use the terms *African American* and *Latino* and *Latina,* which are the preferred terms at this time. Although the terms *Latino* and *Latina* exclude Americans who came from Spain (or whose ancestors did), these people compose a very small proportion of this population in the United States.

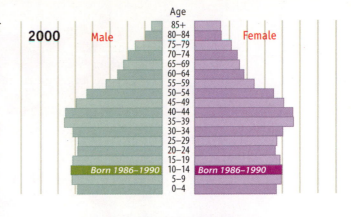
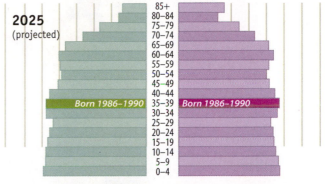
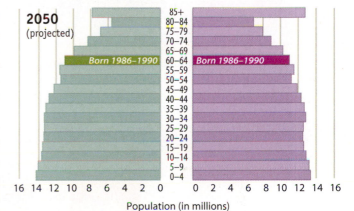

FIGURE 1.3

The Aging U.S. Population, 2000–2050

SOURCE: U.S. Census Bureau, National Population Projections, www.census.gov/population/www/projections/natchart.html.

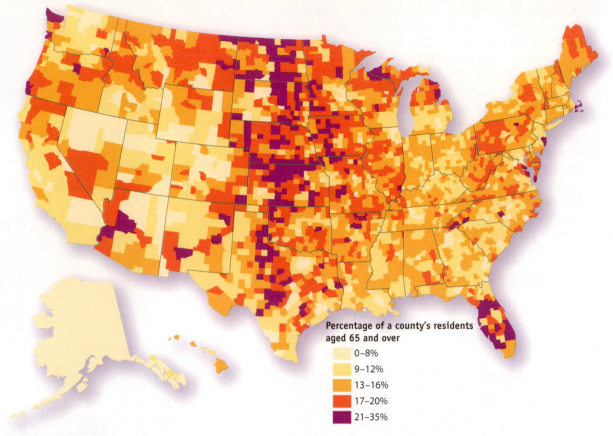

Percentage of a county's residents
aged 65 and over

- 0–8%
- 9–12%
- 13–16%
- 17–20%
- 21–35%

FIGURE 1.4

Where the Older Americans Are

SOURCE: www.CensusScope.org, Social Science Data Analysis Network, University of Michigan, www.ssdan.net.

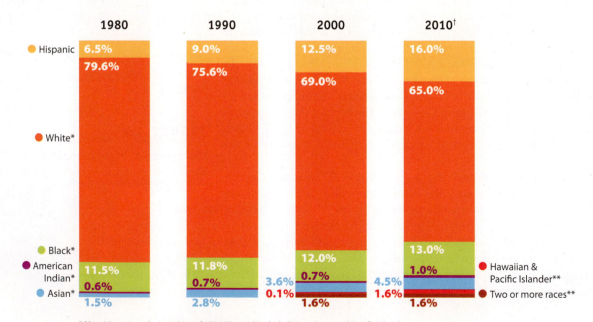

	1980	1990	2000	2010†
● Hispanic	6.5%	9.0%	12.5%	16.0%
● White*	79.6%	75.6%	69.0%	65.0%
● Black*	11.5%	11.8%	12.0%	13.0%
● American Indian*	0.6%	0.7%	0.7%	1.0%
● Asian*	1.5%	2.8%	3.6%	4.5%
● Hawaiian & Pacific Islander**			0.1%	1.6%
● Two or more races**			1.6%	1.6%

Non-Hispanic only; in 1980 and 1990 "Asians" included Hawaiians and Pacific Islanders
**Option available for the first time in 2000 census*
†*Projected*

FIGURE 1.5

Population by Race Since 1980

SOURCE: www.CensusScope.org, Social Science Data Analysis Network, University of Michigan, www.ssdan.net, and www.census.gov/compendia/statab/cats/population/estimates_and_projections_by_age_sex_raceethnicity.html.

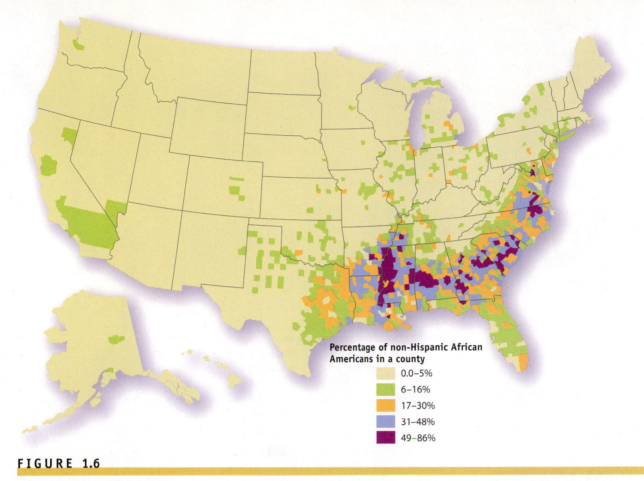

Percentage of non-Hispanic African
Americans in a county

- 0.0–5%
- 6–16%
- 17–30%
- 31–48%
- 49–86%

FIGURE 1.6

Where African Americans Live

SOURCE: www.CensusScope.org, Social Science Data Analysis Network, University of Michigan, www.ssdan.net.

Changing Households: American Families Today

The types of families that are counted by the U.S. census are also becoming more diverse. The *nuclear family,* consisting of a stay-at-home mother, a breadwinning father, and their children, was at one time the stereotypical "ideal family" in the United States. Many—though hardly all—American families were able to achieve that cultural ideal during the prosperous 1950s and early 1960s. But since the women's liberation movement of the 1970s, in which women sought equal rights with men, the American family has changed drastically. As Figure 1.8 on page 23 shows, these changes continued between 1990 and 2000, with the percentage of married couples declining from 55 percent to 52 percent. Explanations for this decline include the trend for people to marry at an older age and the fact that as the population ages, rising numbers of individuals are left widowed. The percentage of female householders without spouses (both with and without children) remained constant between 1990 and 2000 after experiencing a significant increase from 1970 through 1990. The proportion of male householders without spouses increased slightly, and men without a spouse are more likely to be raising children than they were in 1980. Finally, the proportion of the population living in nonfamily households, both those living alone and those living with others, rose slightly.

Why the Changing Population Matters
for Politics and Government

Each of the changes to the U.S. population described here has implications for American democracy. As the nature of the electorate shifts, a majority of the nation's people may have different priorities, and various policies may become more and less important. For example,

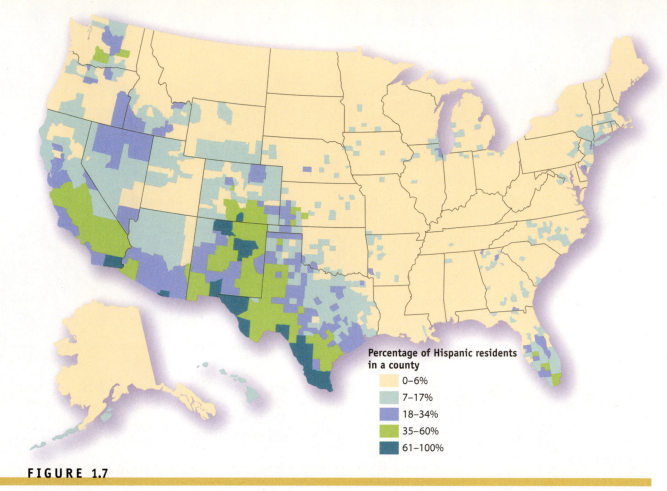

FIGURE 1.7

Where Hispanics Live

SOURCE: www.CensusScope.org, Social Science Data Analysis Network, University of Michigan, www.ssdan.net.

swift population growth means that demand for the services government provides—from schools, to highways, to health care—will continue to increase. The aging population will inevitably increase the burden on the nation's Social Security and government-supported health care system, which will be forced to support the needs of that rising population.

Changes in the population's racial and ethnic composition also matter, as does the concentration of racial minorities in specific geographic areas. The racial and ethnic makeup of the population (along with other influences) can significantly affect the nation's political culture and people's political attitudes. It has implications, too, for who will govern, as more and more representatives of the country's various racial and ethnic groups become candidates for political office and as *all* political candidates must reach out to increasingly diverse groups of voters—or possibly pay the price at the ballot box for failing to do so.

Ideology: A Prism for Viewing American Democracy

political ideology

integrated system of ideas or beliefs about political values in general and the role of government in particular

Besides focusing on the demographic characteristics of the U.S. population, another way of analyzing political events and trends is by looking at them through the prism of ideology. **Political ideology** is an integrated system of ideas or beliefs about political values in general and the role of government in particular. Political ideology provides a framework for thinking about politics, about policy issues, and about the role of government in people's everyday lives. In the United States, one key component of various ideologies is the extent to which adherents believe that the government should have a role in people's everyday

U.S. Household Trends

	1990 *Total households 92 million*	**2000** *Total households 105 million*	**2008** *Total households 117 million*
Married couple	55%	52%	50%
With children	26%	24%	28%
Without children	30%	28%	21%
Female householder, no spouse	12%	12%	12%
Male householder, no spouse	3%	4%	4%
Non-family households	30%	32%	32%
Living alone	25%	26%	27%
Two or more persons	5%	6%	5%

POLITICAL INQUIRY

FIGURE 1.8 ■ **What factors might explain the increase in male householders without spouses between 1990 and 2000? What factors might explain the increase in nonfamily households? What impact, if any, might these trends have on policy in the future?**

SOURCE: www.CensusScope.org/us/chart_house.html, Social Science Data Analysis Network, University of Michigan, www.ssdan.net, and www.census.gov/population/www/socdemo/hh-fam/cps2008.html.

lives, in particular, the extent to which the government should promote economic equality in society.

For all of the twentieth century, the ideologies of liberalism and conservatism dominated U.S. politics. Although liberalism and conservatism have remained powerful ideologies in the early years of the twenty-first century, neoconservatism has also become increasingly important. Table 1.1 on page 24 summarizes the key ideologies we consider in this section.

Liberalism

Modern **liberalism** in the United States is associated with the ideas of liberty and political equality; its advocates favor change in the social, political, and economic realms to better protect the well-being of individuals and to produce equality within society. They emphasize the importance of civil liberties, including freedom of speech, assembly, and the press, as outlined in the Bill of Rights. Modern liberals also advocate the separation of church and state, often opposing measures that bring religion into the public realm, such as prayer in the public schools. In addition, they support political equality, advocating contemporary movements that promote the political rights of gay and lesbian couples and voting rights for the disenfranchised.

The historical roots of modern liberalism reach back to the ideals of classical liberalism: freedom of thought and the free exchange of ideas, limited governmental authority, the consent of the governed, the rule of law in society, the importance of an unfettered market economy, individual initiative as a determinant of success, and access to free public education. These also were the founding ideals that shaped American democracy as articulated in the Declaration of Independence and the Constitution.

liberalism

an ideology that advocates change in the social, political, and economic realms to better protect the well-being of individuals and to produce equality within society

The Traditional Ideological Spectrum

TABLE 1.1

	Socialism	Liberalism	Middle of Road (Moderate)	Conservatism	Libertarianism
Goal of government	Equality	Equality of opportunity, protection of fundamental liberties	Nondiscrimination in opportunity, protection of some economic freedoms, security, stability	Traditional values, order, stability, economic freedom	Absolute economic and social freedom
Role of government	Strong government control of economy	Government action to promote opportunity	Government action to balance the wants of workers and businesses; government fosters stability	Government action to protect and bolster capitalist system, few limitations on fundamental rights	No governmental regulation of economy, no limitations on fundamental rights

Modern liberalism, which emerged in the early twentieth century, diverged from its classical roots in a number of ways. Most important, modern liberals expect the government to play a more active role in ensuring political equality and economic opportunity. Whereas classical liberals emphasized the virtues of a free market economy, modern liberals, particularly after the Great Depression that began in 1929, advocated government involvement in economic affairs. Today, we see this expectation in action when liberals call for affirmative action; increases in social welfare programs such as Social Security, Medicare, and Medicaid; and government regulation of business and workplace conditions.

Conservatism

conservatism
an ideology that emphasizes preserving tradition and relying on community and family as mechanisms of continuity in society

Advocates of **conservatism** recognize the importance of preserving tradition—of maintaining the status quo, or keeping things the way they are. Conservatives emphasize community and family as mechanisms of continuity in society. Ironically, some conservative ideals are consistent with the views of classical liberalism. In particular, the emphasis on individual initiative, the rule of law, limited governmental authority, and an unfettered market economy are key components of both classical liberalism and contemporary conservatism.

Traditionally, one of the key differences between modern liberals and conservatives has been their view of the role of government. In fact, one of the best ways of determining your own ideology is to ask yourself the question, To what extent should the government be involved in people's everyday lives? Modern liberals believe that the government should play a role in ensuring the public's well-being, whether through the regulation of industry or the economy, through antidiscrimination laws, or by providing an economic "safety net" for the neediest members of society. By contrast, conservatives believe that government should play a more limited role in people's everyday lives. They think that government should have a smaller role in regulating business and industry and that market forces, rather than the government, should largely determine economic policy. Conservatives believe that families, faith-based groups, and private charities should be more responsible for protecting the neediest and the government less so. When governments must act, conservatives prefer decentralized action by state governments rather than a nationwide federal policy. Conservatives also believe in the importance of individual initiative as a key determinant of success. Conservative ideas are the fundamental basis of policies such as the Welfare Reform Act of 1996, which placed the development and administration of welfare (Temporary Aid to Needy Families, or TANF) in the hands of the states rather than the federal government.

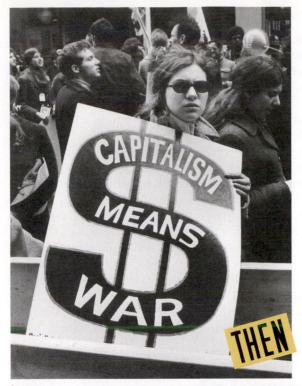

> Protests and demonstrations are tactics that have been used by people across the ideological spectrum. Often, those who rely on protests are outside the mainstream power structure. What groups do you think will be most likely to use protest as a key method in the next several years?

Other Ideologies on a Traditional Spectrum: Socialism and Libertarianism

Although liberals and conservatives dominate the U.S. political landscape, other ideologies reflect the views of some Americans. In general, those ideologies tend to be more extreme than liberalism or conservatism. Advocates of certain of these ideologies call for *more* governmental intervention than modern liberalism does, and supporters of other views favor even *less* governmental interference than conservatism does.

For example, **socialism**—an ideology that stresses economic equality, theoretically achieved by having the government or workers own the means of production (businesses and industry)—lies to the left of liberalism on the political spectrum.[23] Although socialists play a very limited role in modern American politics, this was not always the case.[24] In the early part of the twentieth century, socialists had a good deal of electoral success. Two members of Congress (Representative Meyer London of New York and Representative Victor Berger of Wisconsin), more than seventy mayors of cities of various sizes, and numerous state legislators (including five in the New York General Assembly and many municipal council members throughout the country) were socialists. In 1912, Socialist Party presidential candidate Eugene Debs garnered 6 percent of the presidential vote—six times what Green Party candidate Ralph Nader netted in 2004.

According to **libertarianism,** on the other hand, government should take a "hands-off" approach in most matters. This ideology can be found to the right of conservatism on a traditional ideological spectrum. Libertarians believe that the less government intervention, the better. They chafe at attempts by the government to foster economic equality or to promote a social agenda, whether that agenda is the equality espoused by liberals or the traditional values espoused by conservatives. Libertarians strongly support the rights of property owners and a *laissez-faire* (French for "let it be") capitalist economy.

socialism
an ideology that advocates economic equality, theoretically achieved by having the government or workers own the means of production (businesses and industry)

libertarianism
an ideology whose advocates believe that government should take a "hands-off" approach in most matters

Neoconservatism

The term *neoconservatism,* which emerged in the early 1970s, describes the "new conservatives," or "neo-cons"; the prefix *neo* indicates that many of the prominent thinkers who developed this ideology were new to conservatism. Many people who espouse neoconservative ideology were previously socialists or liberal Democrats who then turned to a more traditional perspective.

Neoconservatives differ from traditional conservatives in several ways. Whereas traditional conservatives tend to advocate an isolationist foreign policy and reliance on traditional foreign policy tactics such as diplomacy, neoconservatives are often characterized as "hawks" because they tend to advocate military over diplomatic solutions. Often, too, neoconservatives press for unilateral (one-sided) military action rather than the collective effort of a multinational military coalition. And unlike traditional conservatives, who emphasize a limited role for government, particularly in social policy, neoconservatives are less concerned with restraining government activity than they are with taking an aggressive foreign policy stand. During the Cold War, neoconservatives were defined by their militaristic opposition to communism. Today they are defined by their fierce advocacy of U.S. superiority and their stance against predominantly Arab states that are alleged to support or harbor terrorists or pose a threat to the state of Israel.

The ideology of neoconservatism was a powerful force during the George W. Bush administration (2000–2008). Indeed, the U.S. war in Iraq is often cited as an example of the power of neoconservatives in that era

neoconservatism
an ideology that advocates military over diplomatic solutions in foreign policy and is less concerned with restraining government activity in domestic politics than traditional conservatives

A Three-Dimensional Political Compass

The rise of neoconservatism demonstrates the limitations of a one-dimensional ideological continuum. For example, although an individual may believe that government should play a strong role in regulating the economy, he or she may also believe that the government should allow citizens a high degree of personal freedom of speech or religion. Even the traditional ideologies do not always fit easily into a single continuum that measures the extent to which the government should play a role in citizens' lives. Liberals supposedly advocate a larger role for the government. But while this may be the case in matters related to economic equality, liberals generally take a more laissez-faire approach when it comes to personal liberties, advocating strongly for privacy and free speech. And although conservatives support less governmental intervention in the economy, they sometimes advocate government action to promote traditional values, such as constitutional amendments to ban flag burning and abortion and laws that mandate prayer in public schools.

Scholars have developed various *multidimensional scales* that attempt to represent peoples' ideologies more accurately.[25] Many of these scales measure people's opinions on the proper role of government in the economy on one axis and their beliefs about personal freedom on a second axis. As shown in Figure 1.9, these scales demonstrate that traditional liberals (upper left quadrant) and traditional conservatives (lower right quadrant) believe in social liberty and economic equality, and economic liberty and social order, respectively. But the scale also acknowledges that some people prioritize economic equality and social order, whereas others embrace economic liberty and social order. One Web site, *The Political Compass* (www.politicalcompass.org), allows visitors to plot their ideology on the site's multidimensional scale.

Multi-Dimensional Ideological Scale

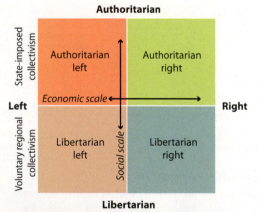

POLITICAL INQUIRY

FIGURE 1.9 ■ Where would you place yourself on this scale? How has your socialization formed your ideology? Can you imagine future circumstances that might cause your views to change?

SOURCE: http://politicalcompass.org/analysis2.

Now is an exciting time to study American democracy. And the fast-paced changes in American society today make participation in government and civic life more vitally important than ever. The effects of participating in the continuing conversation of American democracy through both words and actions are unequivocally positive—for you, for others, and for the government—and can have large ripple effects.

Will the present generation break the cycle of cynicism that has pervaded the politics of the recent past? Today, it is clear that generational changes, particularly the distinctive political opinions of the millennial generation, underscore why it is essential for members of that generation to voice their views. Millennials are participating in the civic life of their communities and the nation through unprecedented—and efficacious—new forms of political participation and community activism. Technology will continue to play a significant role in how they and the population at large communicate and participate in politics and how government creates and administers policy. Exciting changes have come to pass in the political realm, and there is no end to them in sight.

Demographic changes in American society—particularly the aging and growing diversity of the U.S. population—are giving rise to new public policy demands and creating new challenges. Challenges mean opportunities for those who are ready for them, and citizens who respond to those challenges will have an impact on the future of the nation.

Summary

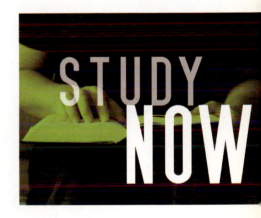

1. y shd u stdy am dem now? Or, Why Should You Study American Democracy Now?

American democracy is at a crossroads with respect to the impact of technology, war, and the continuing terrorist threat on politics. The young Americans of today differ from earlier generations in notable ways, and their fresh opinions and means of organizing and communicating with one another make them a significant political force.

2. What Government Does

Governments perform a variety of essential functions. They provide for the national defense, preserve order and stability, establish and maintain a legal system, distribute services, raise and spend money, and socialize new generations of citizens.

3. Types of Government

In categorizing governmental systems, political scientists evaluate two factors. One factor is who participates in governing or in selecting those who govern. In a monarchy, a king or a queen has absolute authority over a territory and its government (though most of today's monarchies are constitutional), whereas in an oligarchy, an elite few hold power. In a democracy, the people hold and exercise supreme power. Scholars also categorize governmental systems according to how governments function and are structured. Totalitarian governments effectively control every aspect of their citizens' lives. Authoritarian governments have strong powers but are checked by other forces within the society. In democracies, the people have a say in their governance either by voting directly or, as in the United States, by electing representatives to carry out their will.

4. The Origins of American Democracy

American democracy was shaped by individuals who believed in the right of citizens to have a voice in their government. Through principles developed by Enlightenment philosophers such as Thomas Hobbes, John Locke, and Jean-Jacques Rousseau, the key tenets of American democracy emerged, including the idea of a social contract creating a representative democracy.

5. Political Culture and American Values

Political culture refers to the people's collective beliefs and attitudes about the government and the political process. Though aspects of political culture change over time, certain fundamental values have remained constant in American democracy. These include liberty, which is both freedom *from* government interference in daily life and freedom *to* pursue happiness; and equality, the meaning of which has fluctuated significantly over the course of U.S. history. Capitalism—an economic system in which the means of producing wealth are privately owned and operated to produce profits—is also a core value of American political culture, as is consent of the governed, with its key components of popular sovereignty and majority rule. Finally, the American political system values the importance of the individual, the family, and the community.

6. The Changing Face of American Democracy

The population of the United States is growing, aging, and becoming increasingly diverse. Hispanics now make up the country's largest ethnic minority. U.S. families have undergone fundamental structural alterations, as the number of nonfamily households and of households headed by single people has increased in recent times. These changes have already had an impact on communities, and their effect on government policies will intensify. The demographic shifts may create demand for changes in current policies, or they may indicate that the nature of the electorate has shifted and that different priorities are favored by a majority of the people.

7. Ideology: A Prism for Viewing American Democracy

Liberals emphasize civil liberties, separation of church and state, and political equality. Conservatives prefer small government, individual initiative, and an unfettered market economy. Socialists advocate government intervention in the economy to promote economic equality, whereas libertarians argue that government should take a "hands-off" approach to most matters. Neoconservatism, with its emphasis on military rather than diplomatic solutions in foreign policy, and with its comparatively small concern for restraining government activity, has become a growing force in politics and government. Some social scientists prefer to use a three-dimensional framework rather than a two-dimensional continuum for understanding and analyzing political ideology. Regardless of their ideology, citizens can and should act upon their views through civic and political engagement.

Key Terms

authoritarianism 12	indirect democracy 14	political culture 15
capitalism 17	legitimacy 10	political engagement 7
citizens 8	liberalism 23	political ideology 22
civic engagement 7	libertarianism 25	politics 4
consent of the governed 17	liberty 15	popular sovereignty 14
conservatism 24	limited government 12	property 17
constitutionalism 12	majority rule 17	public goods 11
democracy 12	monarchy 12	social contract 13
direct democracy 14	natural law 13	social contract theory 14
divine right of kings 13	naturalization 9	socialism 25
efficacy 5	neoconservatism 26	totalitarianism 12
government 8	oligarchy 12	

For Review

1. In what ways has technology changed how politics happens and how government works? What impact did September 11, 2001 and the subsequent war on terror have on how Americans thought—and think—about their government?

2. Explain the functions that governments perform.

3. Describe how social scientists categorize governments.

4. How did the ideas of the Enlightenment shape people's views on the proper role of government?

5. Explain the fundamental values of American democracy.

6. Describe the general trends with regard to population change in the United States.

7. Contrast liberals' and conservatives' views on government. How do the views of neo-conservatives differ from these other perspectives?

For Critical Thinking and Discussion

1. In what ways do you use technology in your daily life? Do you use technology to get information about politics or to access government services? How? If not, what information and services may be obtained using technological tools?

2. Do you believe there are differences between your political views and those held by members of other generations? Explain. Have the wars in Afghanistan and Iraq changed how you view government? Describe.

3. Why do governments perform the functions they do? Can you think of any private entities that provide public goods?

4. Think of the advantages and disadvantages of direct versus indirect democracies. Do you participate in any form of direct decision making? If so, how well, or poorly, does it work?

5. Examine the demographic maps of the United States in this chapter, and describe what they reveal about the population in your home state.

PRACTICE QUIZ

MULTIPLE CHOICE: Choose the lettered item that answers the question correctly.

1. The institution that creates and implements policies and laws that guide the conduct of the nation and its citizens is called
   a. a democracy.
   b. efficacy.
   c. government.
   d. citizenry.

2. Public goods include
   a. clean air.
   b. clean water.
   c. highways.
   d. all of the above.

3. The economic system in which the means of producing wealth are privately owned and operated to produce profits is
   a. capitalism.
   b. monetarism.
   c. socialism.
   d. communism.

4. Emphasizing the importance of conserving tradition and of relying on community and family as mechanisms of continuity in society is known as
   a. communism.
   b. conservatism.
   c. liberalism.
   d. libertarianism.

5. Citizens' belief that they have the ability to achieve something desirable and that the government listens to them is called
   a. popular sovereignty.
   b. democracy.
   c. civic engagement.
   d. efficacy.

6. A system in which citizens elect representatives who decide policies on behalf of their constituents is referred to as
   a. an indirect democracy.
   b. a representative democracy.
   c. consent of the governed.
   d. both (a) and (b).

7. A belief by the people that a government's exercise of power is right and proper is
   a. authoritarianism.
   b. democracy.
   c. popular sovereignty.
   d. legitimacy.

8. The principle that the standards that govern human behavior are derived from the nature of humans themselves and can be universally applied is called
   a. the social contract.
   b. neoconservatism.
   c. natural law.
   d. representative democracy.

9. An agreement between the people and their leaders in which the people agree to give up some liberties so that other liberties are protected is called
   a. a Mayflower compact.
   b. a social contract.
   c. republicanism.
   d. natural law.

10. A form of government that essentially controls every aspect of people's lives is
    a. socialism.
    b. neoconservatism.
    c. liberalism.
    d. totalitarianism.

FILL IN THE BLANKS.

11. _____ is individual and collective actions designed to identify and address issues of public concern.

12. _____ is the institution that creates and implements policy and laws that guide the conduct of the nation and its citizens.

13. _____ is the idea that in a democracy, only policies with 50 percent plus one vote are enacted.

14. _____ are services governments provide that are available to everyone, such as clean air, clean water, airport security, and highways.

15. A form of government that is structured by law, and in which the power of government is limited, is called _____ .

Answers: 1. c; 2. d; 3. a; 4. b; 5. d; 6. d; 7. d; 8. c; 9. b; 10. d; 11. Civic engagement; 12. Government; 13. Majority rule; 14. Public goods; 15. constitutionalism.

Internet Resources

American Democracy Now

Web site www.mhhe.com/harrison2e Consult the book's Web site for study guides, interactive activities, simulations, and current hotlinks for additional information on American politics and political and civic engagement in the United States.

Circle: the Center for Information & Research on Civic Learning & Engagement

www.civicyouth.org Circle is the premier clearinghouse for research and analysis on civic engagement.

American Association of Colleges and Universities

www.aacu.org/resources/civicengagement/index.cfm The AACU's Web site offers a clearinghouse of Internet resources on civic engagement.

American Political Science Association

www.apsanet.org/section_245.cfm The professional association for political scientists offers many resources on research about civic engagement, education, and participation.

The Statistical Abstract of the United States

www.census.gov/compendia/statab This is "the authoritative and comprehensive summary of statistics on the social, political, and economic organization of the United States." It provides a plethora of data about the population of the United States.

The 2010 Census

http://2010.census.gov/2010census/ The U.S. Census Bureau's 2010 census Web site is a clearinghouse for information about the census, including information on why the census is important, data, and how you can get involved in the census.

Internet Activism

The Census Bureau

http://2010.census.gov/2010census/index.php The U.S. Census is one of the most important sources of demographic information. Go to the Web site and use the interactive tools to learn how census data affects funding levels for institutions such as hospitals and schools, and how the data collected even shape congressional representation.

Recommended Readings

Levine, Peter. *The Future of Democracy: Developing the Next Generation of American Citizens.* Medford, MA: Tufts University Press (UPNE), 2007. An examination of how today's youth are participating in politics differently from previous generations and of how they lack the skills necessary to facilitate some forms of civic participation. The author proposes educational, political, and institutional changes to correct this problem.

Putnam, Robert D. *Bowling Alone: The Collapse and Revival of American Community.* New York: Touchstone, 2000. A classic volume demonstrating the decline in traditional forms of civic participation.

Verba, Sidney, Kay Lehman Schlozman, and Henry E. Brady. *Voice and Equality: Civic Voluntarism in American Politics.* Cambridge, MA: Harvard University Press, 1995. An analysis of how people come to be activists in their communities, what issues they raise when they participate, and how activists from various demographic groups differ.

Winograd, Morley, and Michael D. Hais. *Millennial Makeover: MySpace, YouTube, and the Future of American Politics.* New Brunswick, NJ: Rutgers University Press, 2008. A study of the impact of millennials' use of changing technology on political life.

Zukin, Cliff, Scott Keeter, Molly Andolina, Krista Jenkins, and Michael X. Delli Carpini. *A New Engagement? Political Participation, Civic Life and the Changing American Citizen.* Oxford: Oxford University Press, 2006. A study of participation and political viewpoints across generations.

Movies of Interest

The Messenger (2009)

This film, starring Ben Foster and Woody Harrelson, depicts one side of the ravages of war through the experiences of Army's Casualty Notification service officers. Through their experiences, viewers explore the values of the families of fallen soldiers, as well as those of society at large.

V for Vendetta (2005)

Actor Natalie Portman becomes a revolutionary in this thriller, which depicts an uprising against an authoritarian government.

Blind Shaft (2003)

This Chinese thriller explores the interaction between free market incentives and aspects of political culture, including traditional communal values and human decency, in the context of an increasingly globalized economy.

Blue Collar (1978)

This classic film tracing the experience of three autoworkers in the late 1970s explores racial and economic strife in the United States.

The Constitution

Erie/Michigan

THEN

The Constitution's framers distributed government power between the federal and the state governments, and divided power and created checks and balances among the three branches of the national government to ensure a representative democracy that protected individual liberties.

NOW

The courts continue to probe and interpret the Constitution's meaning, and members of Congress introduce proposed constitutional amendments annually.

NEXT

How will the courts resolve the continuing tensions between individual liberties and majority rule?

Will Congress call for a second constitutional convention?

Will the Constitution's third century witness a greater volume of ratified constitutional amendments as the people's efforts to ensure "a more perfect union" intensify?

We trace various constitutional conflicts throughout this textbook. So that you can understand these conflicts, this chapter concentrates on the roots of the U.S. Constitution and the basic governing principles, structures, and procedures it establishes.

FIRST, we probe the question, *what is a constitution?* by considering the three main components of constitutional documents: descriptions of mission, foundational structures, and essential operating procedures.

SECOND, we explore the political, economic, and social factors that were the catalysts for *the creation of the United States of America.*

THIRD, we survey the *crafting of the Constitution* and the processes of *compromise, ratification, and quick amendment.*

FOURTH, we focus on *the Constitution as a living, evolving document*—a vitality that derives from the alteration (formal amendment) of its written words and from the Supreme Court's (re)interpretation of its existing language to create new meaning.

People in the United States of

America have lived under two constitutions since the American colonies declared their independence from Great Britain in 1776. The Articles of Confederation (1781–1789)—the first U.S. constitution—and the Constitution of the United States (1789–present)—the second and current constitution—established very different government bodies and operating procedures to achieve the same vision of government. The framers of both constitutions were striving to achieve the vision presented in the Declaration of Independence.

The Declaration of Independence (Appendix A) claims that the "laws of nature and of nature's God" give people the rights of life, liberty, and the pursuit of happiness. In addition, the Declaration argues that people have a natural right to create governments in order to protect their life, liberty, and pursuit of happiness. Moreover, when a government infringes on its citizens' natural rights, the Declaration maintains that the people have not only a right but also an obligation to separate from the offending government and establish a new government.

In their efforts to create a new government that would protect their natural rights better than did the government of Great Britain, the newly independent colonists sought a democratic system of government. By ratifying the Articles of Confederation, the founding generation of Americans established a friendly alliance (a confederation) among the existing state governments that composed the United States of America. Within a few years, citizens were criticizing this system of government for its inability to protect life, liberty, and the pursuit of happiness. Less than a decade after the Articles went into effect, the "people of the United States, in order to form a more perfect union," replaced it with the Constitution of the United States. The Constitution established an innovative system of government, which, its framers argued, would better protect the people's natural rights and would create and maintain a healthy economy and a strong nation.

This chapter explores the colonists' experiences under British rule and their subsequent efforts to create the structures and operating procedures of a democratic government that protects the people's life, liberty, and pursuit of happiness. In the process of replacing the problematic confederation with a more perfect union, the architects of the Constitution resolved major conflicts over principles and structures of government through compromise and agreement on frequently ambiguous language. Today, the debates over the vision of the Declaration and the meaning of constitutional language that began even before the states ratified the Constitution continue (see "Thinking Critically About Democracy").

What Is a Constitution?

constitution
the fundamental principles of a government and the basic structures and procedures by which the government operates to fulfill those principles; may be written or unwritten

A **constitution** presents the fundamental principles of a government and establishes the basic structures and procedures by which the government operates to fulfill those principles. Constitutions may be written or unwritten. An *unwritten constitution,* such as the constitution of Great Britain, is a collection of written laws approved by a legislative body and unwritten common laws established by judges, based on custom, culture, habit, and previ-

SHOULD CONGRESS CALL FOR A SECOND CONSTITUTIONAL CONVENTION?

The Issue: Today, many citizens believe that parts of the Constitution are not working. Major national economic problems, including huge deficits and debt, excessive influence of special interest groups, a presidential election decided by the U.S. Supreme Court, and questions about the balance between civil rights and liberties and national security have led citizens and several political scientists to call for a second constitutional convention. Should Congress call for a second constitutional convention?

Yes: The framers expected that the conversation of democracy would be ongoing, as would be attempts to perfect the union. To accommodate those expectations, they authorized two distinct factions (or interests) to propose constitutional amendments. Congress can propose constitutional amendments. Recognizing that the interests of the states may differ from those of Congress, the framers also gave the states authority to propose amendments by means of a constitutional convention. Unfortunately, the states must apply to Congress for a constitutional convention. Although applications for a constitutional convention have been submitted to Congress by all fifty state legislatures, Congress has never called for a constitutional convention. Article V of the Constitution states that Congress "shall call a convention for proposing amendments" to the Constitution "on the application of the legislatures of two thirds of the several states." Congress must call a convention, or else it is violating the Constitution.

No: Article V does not specify how Congress determines when two-thirds of the states have applied for a constitutional convention, nor does it detail how the convention would operate. In 1788, Virginia, New York, and North Carolina submitted applications for a constitutional convention. Should Congress count those applications as three of the thirty-four required today (two-thirds of the fifty states) to call a convention? No! Congress and the states already addressed concerns of 1788 with the states' ratification of the Bill of Rights in 1791. Moreover, the lack of specificity in the Constitution means that a convention could be free to consider and propose any amendments, including a whole new constitution, which is what happened at the last constitutional convention. Given the overwhelming success of the current Constitution, no one wants that.

Other approaches: Before calling a convention, Congress could propose legislation to fill in the gaps left by Article V's lack of details. That could ease fears that a runaway convention would propose a new constitution. Those fears could also be allayed by reminding the public that any proposal produced by a convention would need the approval of three-quarters of the states. Such a supermajority vote would prevent ratification of radical changes for which there is not a national consensus.

What do you think?

① Who should decide if the 750 applications for a convention submitted previously by the fifty states are valid? Explain your answer.

② Should the states review their previous applications and then report to Congress whether or not they are valid? How do you think Congress would react to that?

③ Do you think the states have grounds to sue Congress for violation of Article V? Explain.

④ Should citizens with specific proposals to amend the Constitution work through their members of Congress to get them proposed? How successful do you think they would be? Justify your answer.

ous judicial decisions. A *written constitution,* such as the Constitution of the United States, is one specific document supplemented by judicial interpretations that clarify its meaning.

If you read a government's written constitution, or even your school's student government constitution, you will find a statement of the government's mission, descriptions of its foundational structures, which are the core government bodies that will do what is necessary to accomplish the mission, and details of its essential operating procedures. Typically, constitutions begin with a description of the mission, the long-term goals of the government as envisioned by its founders. For example, the first sentence in the Constitution of the United States, known as the Preamble, states:

> We the People of the United States, in Order to form a more perfect Union, establish Justice, insure domestic Tranquility, provide for the common defence, promote the general Welfare, and secure the Blessings of Liberty to ourselves and our Posterity, do ordain and establish this Constitution for the United States of America.

The U.S. Constitution describes three foundational government bodies—the legislative, executive, and judicial branches—and articulates the responsibilities of each body as well as the relationships among those bodies. The Constitution also details essential operating procedures, including those used to select national government officials, to make laws, and to amend the Constitution, as well as the process by which the Constitution was to be ratified.

In addition to finding the mission statement, descriptions of foundational structures, and details of essential operating procedures in a constitution, you will typically find some vague and ambiguous language. For example, reread the Constitution's Preamble. What do you think "promote the general welfare" means? Does it mean that the government is responsible for ensuring that all people living in the nation have decent health care so that people do not pass their illnesses to others? Does it mean that the government needs to ensure that all people have sufficient and nutritious food and safe housing? Do you know what liberties the government must secure for you and your children and grandchildren? Does it include the freedom to marry whomever you want? Does it include the freedom to decide whether to buy health insurance?

Debates over the meaning of constitutional language were taking place in living rooms, in bars, in legislative chambers, in executive offices, in courtrooms, and on the streets even before the states ratified the Constitution. Ultimately, the United States Supreme Court has the final word on the meaning of constitutional language. You will learn as you read the chapters in this book that members of the Supreme Court do not always agree on what constitutional language means. Moreover, throughout U.S. history, as the members of the Supreme Court changed and the nation's economy, technology, and culture evolved, societal understanding of constitutional language changed, as has citizen and judicial interpretation.

To comprehend today's debates about constitutional language, we need to first develop an understanding of what the framers of the Constitution and the citizens who debated it were hoping to achieve. What was their vision of a more perfect union?

The Creation of the United States of America

Unlike British subjects living in England in the period before the War for Independence (1775–1783), the colonists, who also regarded themselves as British subjects, were largely shut out of participating in the political processes. As the eighteenth century unfolded, that exclusion increasingly rankled the American colonists, especially as parliamentary legislation put more and more restrictions on their freedoms and their pursuit of economic well-being. Eventually, the colonists' private and public conversations about the British government's damaging treatment of them coalesced around the principles of government by the people (popular sovereignty) and for the people (government established to protect the people's liberties).

Colonization and Governance of America

In the 1600s, waves of Europeans made the dangerous sea voyage to America to start new lives. Some people with connections to the king of England were rewarded with large grants of land and the authority to govern. Many more voyagers came as *indentured servants,* who would work for a number of years for a master who paid for their passage. Others came to create communities with people of the same religion so that they could practice their faith without government interference. Countless others—Africans who were brought to the colonies as slaves—came against their will. In short, a diversity of people and a mix of economic classes migrated to the colonies, joining the Native American peoples who already inhabited North America.

By the early eighteenth century, a two-tier system of governing the American colonies had evolved, with governance split between the colonies and Britain. The colonists elected local officials to assemblies that had the authority to rule on day-to-day matters (including criminal law and civil law) and to set and collect taxes. Back in England, Parliament, with no representatives from the colonies, enacted laws with which the colonists had to comply.

Governors appointed by the king oversaw the enforcement of British law in the colonies. Initially, those laws focused on international trade—the regulation of colonial imports and exports. But that focus soon shifted.

British Policy Incites a Rebellion

Between 1756 and 1763, Britain and France were engaged in the Seven Years' War, a military conflict that involved all the major European powers of the era. At the same time they were fighting on European soil, British and French forces (and France's Native American allies) were battling in North America, in a conflict known as the French and Indian War. To help pay the towering costs of waging the Seven Years' War and the French and Indian War, and postwar costs of maintaining peace in America as westward-moving colonists encroached on Indian lands, the British Parliament turned to the colonies for increased revenues. The first new tariff imposed after the end of the war was the Sugar Act (1764). In addition to increasing the taxes on such imported goods as molasses, coffee, and textiles, the Sugar Act directed that all the taxes thus collected be sent directly to Britain instead of to the colonial assemblies, as had been the practice until then.[1] Almost immediately, the colonists condemned the law, saying that because they had no representatives in Parliament, they had no obligation to pay taxes imposed by that body. Their anger intensified in 1765 when Parliament passed the Stamp Act, which taxed the paper used for all legal documents, bills of sale, deeds, advertisements, newspapers, and even playing cards.[2] The Stamp Act introduced a new level of British involvement (some thought interference) in the day-to-day matters of the colonies.

The colonists responded to the Sugar and Stamp acts by boycotting imported goods from Great Britain. Women, including groups of upper-class women known as Daughters of Liberty, substituted homegrown or homespun goods for the banned items. Although the boycotts were largely peaceful, other acts of resistance were not. The Sons of Liberty, founded by Boston brewer Samuel Adams in 1765, opposed the Stamp Act by intimidating British stamp commissioners and sometimes engaging in acts of violence.

Parliament followed the Sugar and Stamp acts with passage of the Quartering Act in 1765. The Quartering Act directed each colonial assembly to provide supplies to meet the basic needs of the British soldiers stationed within its colony. Parliament expanded this law in 1766 to require the assemblies to ensure housing for the soldiers.[3] Throughout the colonies, violent reactions to the quartering law erupted.[4]

Although Parliament repealed the hated Stamp Act in 1766, it paired that repeal with passage of the Declaratory Act. This new law gave Parliament the blanket power to assert control over colonies "in any way whatsoever."[5] This development was a clear indication that the two-tier system of colonial government, in which the colonies exerted some local governing authority, was dissolving. The next year, the colonists understood how momentous this law was, when Parliament used the Declaratory Act as the basis for a new series of laws that would culminate in war. Significant among these laws was the Townshend Duties Act of 1767, which not only expanded the list of imported goods that would be taxed but also stated that Parliament had unilateral power to impose taxes as a way of raising revenue and that the colonists had no right to object.[6] With this new law, the colonists dramatically stepped up their civic resistance.

Specifically, activist Samuel Adams circulated a letter arguing against British taxation of the colonists without their representation in Parliament, and calling for repeal of the Townshend Act. In 1768, the Massachusetts colonial legislature petitioned King George III to repeal the Act. In 1770, Parliament repealed the Townshend duties, except for the duty on tea. At the same time, Parliament reaffirmed its right to tax the colonists.

A "MASSACRE" AND A TEA PARTY   By 1770, more than 4,000 British soldiers were quartered in the homes of the 16,000 civilians living in Boston. To make matters worse, the British soldiers quartered in the city sought additional work as rope makers and in other crafts, competing with the colonists for those jobs.[7] On March 5, 1770, an angry mob of nearly 1,800 struggling colonists clashed with the British soldiers, who shot into the crowd, leaving five dead and six wounded.

Almost immediately, Samuel Adams—an expert at "spinning" a news story—condemned the event as "the Boston Massacre." Partnering with Adams to shape public opinion were silversmith Paul Revere and wealthy shipping merchant John Hancock. The communications of the two men stressed that the colonists respected the rule of law but emphasized that the British king, George III, cared more about preserving his own power than about his subjects' well-being. Therefore, Revere and Hancock asserted, there could be no assurance that he would respect the colonists' rights and liberties. This problem, they argued, could be rectified only by ending the American colonists' relationship with Britain.

In 1772, Adams created the Massachusetts Committee of Correspondence, a group dedicated to encouraging and maintaining the free flow of information and the spread of calls for rebellion among the Massachusetts colonists. Radicals in other colonies followed his lead.[8] Revere published pamphlets aimed at keeping the colonists together in their battle with the Crown, talking boldly about "our rights," "our liberties," and "our union."[9] These communication networks served as a kind of colonial-era Internet, facilitating the sharing of news among the colonists. But in this case, the swift transmission of information occurred by way of riders on horseback and printers at their presses rather than by the keystrokes of citizens typing on computers and cell phones—today's vital communication network for rallying people behind a cause and mobilizing political activism.

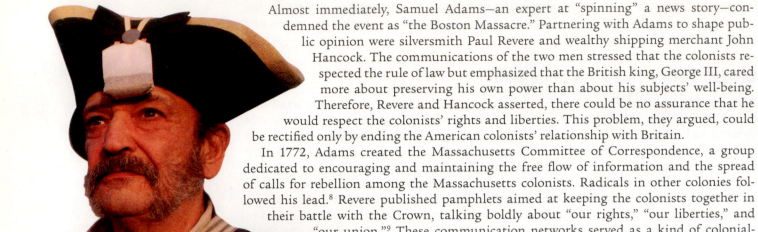

> The Tea Party movement emerged in 2009 evoking images and themes of the pre-Revolutionary era, specifically the Boston Tea Party's (1773) anti-tax and government-by-the-people messages. Tea Party protesters demand fewer and lower taxes and cuts in government spending, greater protection of individual liberties, and less government regulation of the economy.

Adding fuel to the fire, in 1773 Parliament passed the Tea Act, which gave the East India Tea Company a monopoly on tea imported into the colonies. By questioning the Act's legitimacy, the Sons of Liberty successfully swayed public opinion and became the catalyst for an event that would become known as the Boston Tea Party. In November 1773, the first post–Tea Act shipment of tea arrived in Boston Harbor on three East India ships. Under cover of darkness on the night of December 16, 1773, fifty colonists, dressed as Mohawk Indians, boarded the three ships, broke open hundreds of crates, and dumped thousands of pounds of tea into the harbor.[10] The Boston Tea Party had a cataclysmic effect, not only on the relationship between Britain and the colonies, but also on relationships among the colonists themselves.

Parliament responded with the Coercive Acts (Intolerable Acts), which closed the port of Boston and kept it closed until the colonists paid for the lost tea. In addition, the new laws imposed martial law, shut down the colonial assembly, and banned virtually all town meetings, thus curtailing legal opportunities for political engagement.[11] At the same time, the Crown stepped up enforcement of the Quartering Act.

THE CONTINENTAL CONGRESS'S DEMANDS FOR POLITICAL RIGHTS

Sympathy for Massachusetts's plight, along with rising concerns about how the Crown was generally abusing its powers, reinforced the colonists' growing sense of community and their shared consciousness of the need for collective action. The Massachusetts and Virginia colonial assemblies requested a meeting of delegates from all the colonies to develop a joint statement of concern that would be sent to the king. In September 1774, every colony but Georgia sent delegates to what became known as the First Continental Congress.

The Congress (the assembled delegates) adopted and sent to the king the Declaration of Rights and Grievances. This declaration listed numerous rights to which the delegates argued the colonists were entitled. Some of the rights included in the list were life, liberty, and property; participation in colonial legislatures; participation in Parliament's policy-making processes when the policies affected them; peaceable assembly; consideration of their grievances and petitions to the king; and protection from the king's standing armies.[12] The Congress also adopted the Articles of Association, which put forth a plan of association for the colonies, detailed the colonies' agreement to boycott (no longer import or consume) goods from Great Britain, and the creation of county, city, and town committees to monitor this boycott.[13] Finally, the Congress scheduled a second meeting—the Second Continental Congress—to discuss the king's response to their declaration of rights and list of grievances.

When the king refused to respond to the Congress's declaration, private and public discussions about pursuing independence from Great Britain increased. On April 19, 1775, before the Second Continental Congress met, shots rang out at Lexington and Concord, Massachusetts, as British troops moved inland to seize the colonists' store of guns and ammunition. On May 10, 1775, the Second Continental Congress convened. The assembled delegates empowered the Congress to function as an independent government and to prepare for war with Britain, appointing George Washington to command the to-be-created Continental Army.

The Common Sense of Declaring Independence

In July 1775, the Second Continental Congress made one last effort to avert a full-blown war. The Congress petitioned King George III to end hostile actions against the colonists. The king refused and sent even more troops to the colonies to put down the rebellion. Yet even as the Congress prepared for war, many colonists remained unsure about cutting their ties with Britain. A pamphlet written by Thomas Paine, a recently arrived radical from Britain, and published in January 1776 transformed many such wavering colonists into patriots. Paine's *Common Sense* argued that war with Great Britain was not only necessary but also unavoidable. Without war, the colonies and their people would continue to suffer "injuries" and disadvantages. Only through independence would Americans attain civil and religious liberty.[14]

In May 1776, Richard Henry Lee, Virginia delegate to the Congress, asserted "that these united Colonies are, and of right ought to be free and independent States, [and] that they are absolved from all allegiance to the British crown."[15] This "declaration of independence," which congressional delegates from other colonies subsequently echoed, led the Congress to approve a resolution empowering a committee of five to write down, in formal language, a collective declaration of independence. The committee selected Virginia delegate Thomas Jefferson, a wealthy plantation owner, to draft the declaration.

Unanimously endorsed by the Second Continental Congress on July 4, 1776, Jefferson's Declaration of Independence drew upon the work of John Locke and Jean-Jacques Rousseau, as Table 2.1 on page 40 highlights. Recall from Chapter 1 that Thomas Hobbes (1588–1679) argued that people enter into social contracts that create governments, giving up some of their liberties to protect their life and property. Locke built on this social contract theory, arguing that people, all of whom are born free and equal, agree to create government to protect their **natural rights** (also called **unalienable rights**), which are rights possessed by all humans as a gift from nature, or God, including the rights to life, liberty, and the pursuit of happiness. Rousseau took Locke's theory further, stating that people create governments, and therefore governments get their authority from the people.

Jefferson's Declaration was a radical statement. Its two central principles—that all men are equal and have rights that are unalienable (that is, fundamental and existing before governments are established) and that all government must be based on the consent of the governed—may seem obvious from the vantage point of the twenty-first century. But in 1776, the idea that the people had a right not only to choose their government but also to abolish it made the Declaration of Independence unlike anything before it.

After establishing those two central principles, the Declaration spelled out a list of grievances against King George in an attempt to convince the colonists and the European powers that the break with England was necessary

natural rights
(also called *unalienable rights*), the rights possessed by all humans as a gift from nature, or God, including the rights to life, liberty, and the pursuit of happiness

> Jefferson's Declaration of Independence, drawing on the work of philosophers John Locke and Jean-Jacques Rousseau, delivered the radical message that people have a right not only to choose their government but also to abolish it when it no longer serves them.

TABLE 2.1

The Theories of Locke and Rousseau as Applied by Jefferson

John Locke's Theories:
Two Treatises of Government (1690)

All people are born free and equal.

All people are born into a "state of nature" and choose to enter into government for protection against being harmed.

Every person has the right to "life, liberty and property," and government may not interfere with this right.

Jean-Jacques Rousseau's Theories:
The Social Contract (1762)

All power ultimately resides in the people.

People enter into a "social contract" with the government to ensure protection of their lives, liberties, and property.

If government abuses its powers and interferes with the people's exercise of their civil liberties, then the people have both the right and the duty to create a new government.

Thomas Jefferson's Application of Locke and Rousseau: Declaration of Independence (1776)

All men are created equal.

All men are endowed with certain unalienable rights, among which are life, liberty, and the pursuit of happiness.

To secure these rights, men create governments, which derive their powers from the consent of the governed.

King George III failed to respect the unalienable rights of the American colonists and instead created an "absolute tyranny" over them.

If government is destructive of people's rights, the people can alter or abolish it and create a new government.

POLITICAL INQUIRY

What ideas did Jefferson take from Locke and Rousseau with respect to human rights and liberties? How would you summarize the views of the three men on the purposes of government and the source of government power?

and justified. The Declaration won the hearts and minds of people in the colonies and abroad. Until this point, the patriots were united in their hatred toward Britain but lacked a rallying point. The Declaration provided that rallying point by promising a new government that would be based on the consent of the people, with liberty and equality as its central goals.

In 1777, as a brutal war over colonial independence raged between England and the colonies, the Second Continental Congress turned to the pressing task of establishing a new, *national* government by drafting a constitution, the Articles of Confederation. By that year, too, each colony had adopted a constitution, establishing new *state* governments. In these ways, the colonies had become thirteen states with independent, functioning governments. It was to those governments that the Second Continental Congress sent the Articles of Confederation for ratification in 1777.

The State Constitutions

In May 1776, the Continental Congress encouraged the legislative assembly of each colony to write a state constitution establishing its independence from Great Britain. By the end of 1776, eight states had enacted state constitutions. New York, Georgia, and Vermont followed suit in 1777. After four years of intense deliberation, Massachusetts adopted a state constitution in 1780. Connecticut and Rhode Island continued to operate under their royal charters until they enacted new constitutions in 1818 and 1843, respectively.[16] In Massachusetts, citizen voters ratified the state constitution; in all other states, elected representatives ratified the state constitutions. The new state constitutions were revolutionary for two primary reasons. First, they were each a single, written document that specified the principles, structures, and operating procedures of the government established by the consent of the people. Second, they were adopted at a specific moment in time, unlike constitutions before them, which were accumulations of disparate laws written over time or created by judges through the years, based on customs and traditions.[17]

The framers of the first state constitutions attempted to implement the principles of popular sovereignty and natural rights presented in the Declaration of Independence. Each state constitution established a **republic,** better known today as representative democracy. Moreover, most state constitutions explicitly asserted that the people held the power—government was by consent of the people. Whereas the Articles of Confederation would create one national governing body, state governments included three governing bodies—the legislative, executive, and judicial branches. **Bicameral legislatures,** which are legislatures comprising two parts, called *chambers,* were the norm in the states. State legislators, who were directly elected by voters in most states, were delegated more governing powers than members of the other two branches, who were not typically elected by voters. The prevailing view of people of the time was that the legislature offered the best prospects for representative government.

The mission of all the state governments was to ensure natural rights. Two weeks before adopting its state constitution, Virginia representatives approved a Declaration of Rights. In addition to affirming that all government's power derives from the people, this declaration endorsed rights such as trial by jury and religious freedom. Other state constitutions included protections for liberties including free speech and press, protection from excessive fines and bail, the right of the accused to be informed of the charges against them, and protection from unreasonable search and seizure. Authors of the first state constitutions wrote into them limits to prevent state governments from infringing on individuals' life, liberties, and pursuit of happiness, infringements the colonists experienced under British rule. Hence, the inclusion of a written list of citizens' liberties, a **bill of rights,** limited government by ensuring that both the people and the government knew what freedoms the government could not violate.

The states of the new American republic used their new constitutions to guide them in handling their day-to-day domestic matters. Meanwhile, members of the Second Continental Congress turned their attention to creating a national government that would allow the states to engage collectively in international affairs.

republic
a government that derives its authority from the people and in which citizens elect government officials to represent them in the processes by which laws are made; a representative democracy

bicameral legislature
legislature comprising two parts, called chambers

bill of rights
a written list of citizens' liberties within a constitution that establishes a limited government by ensuring that both the people and the government know what freedoms the government cannot violate

confederation
a union of independent states in which each state retains its sovereignty, rights, and power, which is not by their agreement expressly delegated to a central governing body

unicameral legislature
a legislative body with a single chamber

The Articles of Confederation (1781–1789)

Because of the colonists' bitter experience under the British Crown, the people and their delegates to the Second Continental Congress distrusted a strong, distant central government; they preferred limited local government, which they established in their state constitutions. The delegates nevertheless recognized the need for a unified authority to engage in international trade, foreign affairs, and defense. For a model of government, they needed to look no further than a league formed by several Indian tribes of the northeastern United States and eastern Canada.

The Iroquois League was an alliance of five tribes. Under the league, the tribes pursued their own self-interest independently of one another, and the only condition was that they maintain peace with one another. A Grand Council presided over the league, and its fifty representatives, who were chosen by the tribes, had very limited authority. This council served as a unified front and was charged simply with keeping intertribal peace—and later, with negotiating with the Europeans.[18]

The Iroquois League's influence is evident in the first four articles in the Articles of Confederation, which was submitted to the states for ratification in 1777 and which the required number of states (thirteen) ratified by 1781. The Articles of Confederation established a **confederation:** a union of independent states in which each state retains its sovereignty, rights, and power, which is not by their agreement expressly delegated to a central governing body. Through the Articles of Confederation, the states created an alliance for mutual well-being in the international realm yet continued to pursue their own self-interest independently.

STRUCTURE AND AUTHORITY OF THE CONFEDERATION Structurally, the Articles created only one governing body, a Congress. The Congress was a **unicameral legislature,** meaning that it had only one chamber. Every state had from two to seven delegates in Congress, but only one vote. Each state determined how its delegates would be

> This flag represents the original five nations of the Iroquois Confederacy: Seneca, Cayuga, Onondaga, Mohawk, and Oneida. The needles of the white pine, in the middle, grow in clusters of five. The influence of the Iroquois Confederacy is evident in the first four articles of the first constitution of the United States, the Articles of Confederation.

selected. However, the Articles specified one-year terms and a term limit of no more than three out of every six years. Approving policies and ratifying treaties required nine affirmative votes. The Articles did not create a judicial branch, an executive branch, or a chief executive officer. Congressional delegates would select one of their members to serve as president, to preside over the meetings of Congress. State courts would resolve legal conflicts, unless the dispute was between states, in which case Congress would resolve it. State governments would implement and pay for congressionally approved policies. Finally, and important to remember, amending the Articles of Confederation required unanimous agreement among all thirteen states.

The Congress had very limited authority. Although it could approve policies relevant to foreign affairs, defense, and the coining of money, it was not authorized to raise revenue through taxation. Only state governments could levy and collect taxes. Therefore, to pay the national government's bills, Congress had to request money from each state.

WEAKNESSES OF THE CONFEDERATION The Articles of Confederation emphasized the sovereignty of individual, independent states at the expense of a powerful national government and national identity. Citizens' allegiance was to their states; there was no mass national conscience. Under the Articles of Confederation, the states retained ultimate authority in matters of commerce. As a result, other nations were not willing to negotiate trade policies with national officials. In addition, each state taxed all goods coming into the state from foreign nations and from other states. Moreover, the states issued their own money and required the use of that currency for all business within the state. The cumulative effect of these state policies hampered interstate and international commerce, putting the nation's economic health in jeopardy.[19] Many politicians and the elite viewed the uprisings that resulted from these economic problems as examples of the dangers of democracy.

In Massachusetts, economic pressures reached a head in 1786 when small farmers, many of whom had fought in the War for Independence, could not pay their legal debts and faced bankruptcy and the loss of their land. Farmer and war veteran Daniel Shays led an uprising, today known as Shays's Rebellion, of those debt-burdened farmers. The rebels first broke into county courthouses and burned all records of their debts, then proceeded to the federal arsenal. Massachusetts asked Congress for assistance in putting down the rebellion. Congress appealed to each state for money to fulfill that request, but only Virginia complied. Eventually, through private donations, Massachusetts raised enough money to hire a militia to end the rebellion, but the weaknesses of the national confederacy and the need for a stronger central government were becoming apparent.

Five states sent delegates to Annapolis, Maryland, in 1786, to "remedy defects of the Federal Government," as the government created by the Articles of Confederation was known at that time. The states charged their delegates with considering the trade and commerce problems of the United States. However, in the report of their proceedings, the delegates noted that the "embarrassments which characterize the present State of our national affairs, foreign and domestic" suggested that trade and commerce were not the only problems of the federal government. Therefore, the delegates called for a future convention, to be attended by representatives from all thirteen states, to devise amendments to the Articles of Confederation that would fix its weaknesses and to submit its proposals to "the United States in Congress assembled."[20]

Crafting the Constitution: Compromise, Ratification, and Quick Amendment

The convention called to address the defects of the Articles of Confederation was held in Philadelphia from May 25 through September 17, 1787. All states except Rhode Island sent delegates. The delegates to this Constitutional Convention were among the most elite Americans. Some 80 percent had served as members of the Continental Congress, and most were lawyers, businessmen, or plantation owners. Many were engaged in highly lucrative international trade, and all were wealthy. These elites contrasted sharply with the masses, who included the country's hard-pressed farmers, struggling local merchants, and those engaged in trade. In fact, historian Charles Beard contended in 1913 that the Constitution's framers succeeded in forging a government that protected their elite status.[21]

Early in the convention, the delegates agreed on the need for a stronger national government than the Articles had created, but there was conflict over how best to structure a representative democracy that would protect liberties, with property rights a priority for the delegates. There was also conflict over the issue of slavery. In working through those conflicts to create compromises they could support, the delegates were pragmatic. They had to balance their preference for a strong central government with the citizens' distrust of a strong central government. Ultimately, the delegates framed a new constitution, establishing new foundational government structures and operating procedures to achieve the principles laid out in the Declaration of Independence. Thereafter, proponents of the Constitution would win its ratification only after acknowledging the need to amend it quickly by adding a bill of rights to limit the power of the national government it created.

Consensus

The framers had to send their final proposal to Congress for action. Remember that the Congress, as structured by the Articles of Confederation—the constitution in effect at the time of the convention—was made up of representatives of the state governments. The framers recognized that these representatives were not likely to ratify a document that created a strong central government at the expense of the existing state governments. Therefore, the framers had to balance a strong central government, national sovereignty, and existing state sovereignty. That balance would hinge on delegating governing powers to the national government in the policy areas that were problematic under the Articles—interstate and international trade, foreign affairs, and defense—and leaving the remaining domestic matters with the states.

DUAL SOVEREIGNTY   The framers created an innovative system of government with **dual sovereignty**—a system of government in which ultimate governing authority is divided between two levels of government—a central government and regional governments—with each level having ultimate authority over different policy matters. Today, we call this a *federal system* of government. Article I of the Constitution lists the matters over which the national legislature (Congress) has lawmaking authority, such as regulating interstate and foreign commerce, coining money, raising and funding an army, and declaring war. Article I also prohibits state governments from engaging in several specific activities, such as negotiating treaties. (Chapter 3 focuses on dual sovereignty and the constitutional distribution of power between the national and the state governments.)

dual sovereignty
a system of government in which ultimate governing authority is divided between two levels of government, a central government and regional governments, with each level having ultimate authority over different policy matters

NATIONAL SUPREMACY   Being pragmatic, the framers anticipated that this system of dual sovereignty would cause tension between the national government and the state governments. Therefore, they included in Article VI of the Constitution a **supremacy clause,** which states that the Constitution and the treaties and laws created by the national government in compliance with the Constitution are the supreme law of the land.

The framers did not include a list or even a vague outline of the matters over which the states had sovereignty. Citizens apprehensive of a strong central government would argue that this vacuum of information on state sovereignty was a major fault in the Constitution, because it would allow the national government to infringe on state sovereignty. The lack of a list of individual liberties to limit the power of the national government was also a major concern for citizens afraid of a strong central government.

supremacy clause
a clause in Article VI of the Constitution that states that the Constitution and the treaties and laws created by the national government in compliance with the Constitution are the supreme law of the land

SEPARATION OF POWERS WITH INTEGRATED CHECKS AND BALANCES
Another area where there was convergence of opinion among the framers was that of the foundational structures of the new government they were creating. Borrowing from the states and from *The Spirit of the Laws* (1748), by French political thinker Baron de Montesquieu

separation of powers

the Constitution's delegation of authority for the primary governing functions among three branches of government so that no one group of government officials controls all the governing functions

checks and balances

a system in which each branch of government can monitor and limit the functions of the other branches

Virginia Plan

the new governmental structure proposed by the Virginia delegation to the Constitutional Convention, which consisted of a bicameral legislature (Congress), an executive elected by the legislature, and a separate national judiciary; state representation in Congress would be proportional, based on state population; the people would elect members to the lower house, and members of the lower house would elect the members of the upper house

New Jersey Plan

the proposal presented in response to the Virginia Plan by the less populous states at the Constitutional Convention, which called for a unicameral national legislature in which all states would have an equal voice (equal representation), an executive office composed of several people elected by Congress, and a Supreme Court whose members would be appointed by the executive office

Connecticut Compromise

(also known as the *Great Compromise*), the compromise between the Virginia Plan and the New Jersey Plan that created a bicameral legislature with one chamber's representation based on population and the other chamber having two members for each state

(1689–1755), the framers separated the primary governing functions among three branches of government—referred to as the **separation of powers**—so that no one group of government officials controlled all the governing functions. Under the terms of the separation of powers, each branch of the government has specific powers and responsibilities that allow it to operate independently of the other branches: the legislative branch has authority to formulate policy; the executive branch has authority to implement policy; the judicial branch has authority to resolve conflicts over the law.

As suggested by Montesquieu's work, once the framers separated the primary functions, they established various mechanisms by which each branch can monitor and limit the functions of the other branches to ensure that no branch acts to the detriment of citizens' natural rights. These mechanisms collectively form a system of **checks and balances.** If one branch tries to move beyond its own sphere or to behave tyrannically, this arrangement ensures that the other branches can take action to stop it. Figure 2.1 shows how specific checks and balances contribute to the separation of powers.

The delegates spent most of the first two months of debate arguing about the national legislature and focused primarily on the question of state representation in Congress. They devoted less than a month to the other issues before them, including the structure of the executive and judicial branches; the relationship between the federal and the state governments; the process for amending the new plan of government, should the need arise to do so; the procedures for the Constitution's ratification; and a series of compromises over the slave trade.[22]

Conflict and Compromise over Representative Democracy

Among the delegates' top points of contention was representation in the national government. There was disagreement about two elements of representation. First, how should the government officials in each of the three branches of this newly formed republican national government be selected? Second, how would the states be represented in the national government?

THE CONNECTICUT COMPROMISE Virginian James Madison arrived at the convention with a plan in hand for restructuring the national government. The **Virginia Plan,** drafted by Madison and proposed by the Virginia delegation, called for a radically revamped government, consisting of three branches: a bicameral legislature (Congress), an executive elected by the legislature, and a separate national judiciary. State representation in Congress would be proportional, based on state population. The people would elect members to the lower house, and members of the lower house would elect the members of the upper house.

The states with smaller populations quickly and aggressively responded to Madison's Virginia Plan with a proposal of their own. Their concerns about the Virginia Plan were obvious. Because the Virginia Plan called for proportional representation in Congress based on state population, the small states stood to lose significant power. (Remember that under the Articles of Confederation, each state, no matter what its population and no matter how many representatives it had in the Congress, had one vote.) On behalf of the less populous states, William Paterson of New Jersey presented a series of resolutions known as the **New Jersey Plan.** Unlike the Virginia Plan, this was not a radical proposal—it essentially reworked the Articles of Confederation. Under the New Jersey Plan, a unicameral national legislature would remain the centerpiece of the government, and all states would have an equal voice (equal representation) in this government. The New Jersey Plan also called for Congress to elect several people to form an executive office, and the executive office had the authority to appoint members to a Supreme Court.

The disagreement and negotiation over the Virginia and New Jersey plans resulted in several compromises, most notably the **Connecticut Compromise** (also known as the *Great Compromise*). This compromise created today's bicameral Congress, with state representation in the House of Representatives based on state population and equal state representation in the Senate (two senators per state).

THE CONSTITUTION'S CHECKS ON REPRESENTATIVE DEMOCRACY At the heart of representative democracy is the participation of citizens in electing their government officials. Yet the framers built a number of checks into the Constitution that

Separation of Powers with Checks and Balances

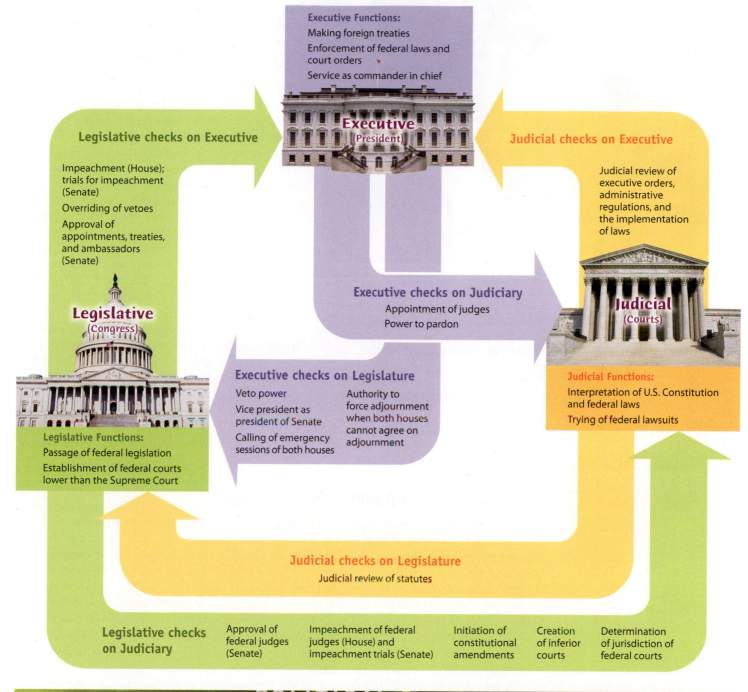

Executive Functions:

Making foreign treaties

Enforcement of federal laws and court orders

Service as commander in chief

Executive (President)

Legislative checks on Executive

Impeachment (House); trials for impeachment (Senate)

Overriding of vetoes

Approval of appointments, treaties, and ambassadors (Senate)

Judicial checks on Executive

Judicial review of executive orders, administrative regulations, and the implementation of laws

Legislative (Congress)

Executive checks on Judiciary

Appointment of judges

Power to pardon

Judicial (Courts)

Executive checks on Legislature

Veto power

Vice president as president of Senate

Calling of emergency sessions of both houses

Authority to force adjournment when both houses cannot agree on adjournment

Legislative Functions:

Passage of federal legislation

Establishment of federal courts lower than the Supreme Court

Judicial Functions:

Interpretation of U.S. Constitution and federal laws

Trying of federal lawsuits

Judicial checks on Legislature

Judicial review of statutes

| **Legislative checks on Judiciary** | Approval of federal judges (Senate) | Impeachment of federal judges (House) and impeachment trials (Senate) | Initiation of constitutional amendments | Creation of inferior courts | Determination of jurisdiction of federal courts |

POLITICAL INQUIRY

FIGURE 2.1 ■ Why did the Constitution's framers separate powers among the three branches of the national government? What specific powers does each branch have? What is the purpose of the Constitution's checks and balances? For each branch of the government—legislative, executive, judicial—name a specific check that it can exert on each of the other two.

significantly *limited* representative democracy, and in doing so they effectively took most of the governing institutions out of the hands of the people. Although the Constitution allowed citizens to elect members of the House directly, it specified the election of senators by the state legislatures. This protocol remained in effect until 1913, when the ratification of the Seventeenth Amendment to the Constitution gave voters the power to elect the members of the Senate.

The process that the framers devised for the election of the president and the vice president prevented citizens from directly selecting the nation's chief executive and the second-in-command. The Constitution delegates to states the authority to appoint individuals (*electors*), using a process determined by the state legislature, to elect the president and the vice president. Before ratification of the Twelfth Amendment (1804), these electors would cast two votes for president. The candidate receiving the largest majority of electors' votes would become president and the candidate receiving the second largest number of votes would become vice president. Since ratification of the Twelfth Amendment, each elector casts one vote for president and one vote for vice president. Today, in nearly every state, your presidential vote, combined with the votes of other citizens from your state, determines which political party's slate of representatives (*electors*) will participate on behalf of your state in the **Electoral College,** the name given to the body of electors that actually selects the president and the vice president.

In addition to limiting the number of officials directly elected by citizens, the framers effectively limited voting rights to a minority of citizens. Existing state constitutions had established that only property-owning white men could vote. The one exception was New Jersey, where property-owning white women could also vote until 1807, when the state constitution was amended to deny women the right to the vote. The framers left to the states the authority to determine eligibility to vote. Hence, women and many men, including Native Americans and slaves, were denied the right to vote under the new Constitution.

> Charnisha Thomas signs in to vote in New Orleans during Louisiana's 2008 presidential primary. Before the Constitution was formally amended, it did not guarantee any citizen the right to vote. Rather, state governments determined voting rights. Today the Constitution guarantees the right to vote to citizens who are at least 18 years old (Twenty-Sixth Amendment), regardless of their race (Fifteenth Amendment) or sex (Nineteenth Amendment).

Electoral College

the name given to the body of representatives elected by voters in each state to elect the president and the vice president

Conflict and Compromise Over Slavery

Delegates to the Constitutional Convention also disagreed on the "peculiar institution" (as Thomas Jefferson called it) of slavery. In 1790, slaves made up almost 20 percent of the U.S. population, and most slaves resided in the southern states.[23] Delegates from the southern states feared that a strong central government would abolish slavery. During the constitutional debates, they therefore refused to budge on the slavery issue. Meanwhile, northern delegates, who were widely concerned that a weak national government would limit the United States' ability to engage in commerce and international trade, believed that the nation needed a more powerful central government than had existed under the Articles of Confederation. Ultimately, to get the southern states to agree to a stronger central government, the northern states compromised on the slavery issue.

A provision in Article I, Section 9, of the Constitution postponed debate on the legality of slavery—and consequently kept it legal—by prohibiting Congress from addressing the importation of new slaves into the United States until January 1, 1808. Moreover, Article IV, which deals with interstate relations, established the states' obligation to deliver all fugitive slaves back to their owners. This measure aimed to ensure that people in non-slaveholding states would continue to respect the property rights of slaveholders—including the right to own slaves, who were legally property, not people with natural rights.

Although the slaves were legally property, Article I, Section 2, established a formula for "counting" slaves for purposes of representation in the House of Representatives, apportionment of electors for the Electoral College, and the allocation of tax burdens among the states. This **Three-Fifths Compromise** counted each slave as three-fifths of a free man. The southern states benefited by this compromise: they gained greater representa-

Three-Fifths Compromise

the negotiated agreement by the delegates to the Constitutional Convention to count each slave as three-fifths of a free man for the purpose of representation and taxes

tion in the House and in the Electoral College than they would have if only nonslaves were counted. The benefit to the northern states was that if the national government imposed a direct tax on the states based on their populations, southern states would pay more than they would if only nonslaves were counted (The national government has never imposed such a direct tax on the states.)

James Madison, while deploring slavery, argued that the delegates' "compromise" over slavery was "in the spirit of accommodation which governed the Convention." He insisted that without the compromise, the Constitution would never have been signed.

So in the delegates' debates and deliberations, they resolved some disagreements, such as the large state–small state conflict over congressional representation. They put on hold other differences, such as their divisions over slavery. In the end, the document that the framers sent to the states for ratification described a government structure that aimed to fulfill the principles of the Declaration of Independence, for a select group of people. Foremost among those principles was the idea that it is up to the people to found a government that protects their natural rights to life, liberty, and the pursuit of happiness. To ensure those rights, which were initially meant only for white, property-owning men, the framers devised two key arrangements: the separation of powers with an integrated system of checks and balances, and a federal system in which the national and state governments had distinct, ultimate authorities.

The Changing Face of Popular Representation

	CONSTITUTIONAL CONVENTION (1787)	111TH CONGRESS (2009–2010)	CURRENT U.S. POPULATION*
Women	0%	17%**	51%
African Americans	0%	8%†	12%
Asian Americans	0%	2%	4%
Hispanics	0%	6%	15%
Native Americans	0%	0%	1%

*U.S. Census Bureau, 2006 American Community Survey.
**www.cawp.rutgers.edu/Facts2.html.
†www.ethnicmajority.com/congress.htm.

WHAT'S NEXT?

> What is different about the composition of the delegates to the Constitutional Convention and the composition of the 111th Congress? What explains the differences?

> Why do you think the demographic representation among lawmakers in the 111th Congress does not mirror the composition of the U.S. population at large more closely?

> Do you think future Congresses will be more "representative" of the nation's population? Explain.

Congress Sends the Constitution to the States for Ratification

On September 17, 1787, thirty-nine convention delegates signed the Constitution. Following the Articles of Confederation, the delegates delivered their proposed constitution to the standing Congress. However, fearful that the document would not garner the approval of all thirteen state legislatures as mandated by the Articles' amendment process, the framers suggested an innovative ratification process.

The framers requested that Congress send the proposed constitution to the states and that the state legislatures each establish a special, popularly elected convention to review and ratify the Constitution. One argument made to support this suggested ratification process, which violated the Articles of Confederation, was that ratification by popularly elected conventions would validate the Constitution as the supreme law of the land, legitimized by the consent of the people. Congress acquiesced to the framers' request, and sent the proposed constitution to the states for ratification votes in special conventions.

The proposed constitution sent to the states was a product of conflict, deliberation, discernment, compromise, and pragmatism. In seven articles, the framers established a new national government with structures modeled after the state governments—distributing the basic governing functions among three branches and giving each branch a means to check the others—and a radical new system of government, a federal system, with dual sovereignty. Before exploring the states' debate and ratification of the Constitution, we review the blueprint of government embodied in the constitution sent to the states. To explore the entire Constitution, as amended since 1791, turn to the annotated Constitution that follows this chapter on pages 61–79.

ARTICLE I: THE LEGISLATIVE BRANCH

Article I of the Constitution delegates lawmaking authority to Congress, describes the structure of the legislative branch, and outlines the legislative process. Article I specifies that the legislature is bicameral, comprising the House of Representatives and the Senate. Each state is represented in the House based on its population. In contrast, state representation in the Senate is equal, with each state having two senators.

According to Article I, a proposed piece of legislation—a *bill*—requires simple majority votes (50 percent plus one vote) in both the House and the Senate to become a law. This requirement means that the House and the Senate can check each other in the legislative process, because even if one chamber garners a majority vote, the other chamber can kill the bill if its majority does not support it. Because all pieces of legislation supported by the majority of the House and the majority of the Senate go to the president for approval or rejection, the president has a check on the legislative authority of Congress.

ARTICLE II: THE EXECUTIVE BRANCH

Article II of the Constitution describes the authority of the president. This article gives the president authority to ensure that the laws are faithfully executed, to appoint people to assist in administering the laws, to negotiate treaties, and to command the military. In addition to those executive functions, Article II allows the president several checks on the power of the other two branches of government.

As already noted, the president checks the legislative authority of Congress. All pieces of legislation approved by the House and the Senate are forwarded to the president's desk. The president has ten days to act on a bill, or it will automatically become law. Within those ten days, the president can either sign the bill into law or send it back to Congress—**veto** it—with his objections noted. Because Congress has primary responsibility for legislative functions, it can set aside the president's veto—that is, override the veto—with two-thirds of House members and two-thirds of the senators voting to approve the vetoed bill.

With respect to the legislature's checks on the executive, the Constitution gives the Senate a check on presidential authority to negotiate treaties by specifying that the Senate can approve or reject any negotiated treaties. The Senate also checks the executive power through its constitutional authority of **advice and consent,** which is the power to approve or reject the president's appointments. The Senate's advice and consent authority extends to the president's judicial nominees as well. Although the president nominates the individuals who will serve as judges in the federal judicial branch—ultimately, the people who will interpret the Constitution—the Senate must approve those candidates.

ARTICLE III: THE JUDICIAL BRANCH

Article III describes the judicial branch. More specifically, Article III establishes the U.S. Supreme Court, and it delegates to Congress the authority to establish other, inferior (lower) courts. The Supreme Court and the other federal courts established by Congress have the authority to resolve lawsuits arising under the Constitution, federal laws, and international treaties. In 1803, in the case of *Marbury v. Madison,* the Supreme Court interpreted Article III to mean that the Court has the authority to determine whether an action taken by any government official or governing body violates the Constitution; this is the power of **judicial review.**

ARTICLE IV: STATE-TO-STATE RELATIONS

The Constitution does not include a list of state powers, rights, or responsibilities as it does for the national government. However, in Article IV, the Constitution does describe how the states must respect the rights and

veto
the president's rejection of a bill, which is sent back to Congress with the president's objections noted

advice and consent
the Senate's authority to approve or reject the president's appointments

Marbury v. Madison
the 1803 Supreme Court case that established the power of judicial review, which allows courts to determine that an action taken by any government official or governing body violates the Constitution

judicial review
court authority to determine that an action taken by any government official or governing body violates the Constitution; established by the Supreme Court in the 1803 *Marbury v. Madison* case

liberties of the citizens of all states as well as the legal proceedings and decisions of the other states. Article IV also establishes the means by which Congress can add new states to the union at the same time it prohibits Congress from changing state borders without consent of the affected states. This amendment also obligates the national government to ensure that all states are representative democracies and to protect the states from domestic violence.

ARTICLE V: THE AMENDMENT PROCESS The framers recognized that the Constitution was a compromise born of their attempts to resolve existing problems, and therefore future generations would want to, and need to, revise the document in light of their own experiences and circumstances. Therefore, the framers provided processes to amend the Constitution.

The Constitution's framers wanted to ensure that widespread deliberation among the American people would precede any and all changes in the written Constitution. Thus, they made it no easy matter to amend the U.S. Constitution—that is, to change its written language. Amendment is a two-step process, entailing, first, the proposal of the amendment and, second, the ratification of the proposed amendment. Article V describes two different procedures for *proposing* an amendment (see Figure 2.2). The first method requires a two-thirds majority vote in both the House and the Senate, after which the congressionally approved proposal is sent to the states for ratification. The second method (which has never been used) requires a special constitutional convention. If two-thirds of the state legislatures petition Congress to consider an amendment, such a convention, where state delegates vote on the possible amendment, takes place; an approved proposal then goes to the states for ratification.

Article V also outlines two avenues by which the second step, ratifying a proposed amendment, may occur. An amendment is ratified by a vote of approval in either three-quarters of the state legislatures or three-quarters of the special state conventions. Citizens have no vote in the process by which the U.S. Constitution is amended, nor did they have a vote in the original Constitution's ratification. In contrast, forty-nine of the fifty states in the United States do mandate that their citizens approve amendments to their state constitutions as well as new state constitutions. Many countries also mandate citizen approval of constitutional amendments.

ARTICLE VI: SUPREMACY OF THE CONSTITUTION Article VI proclaims that the new national government will be legally responsible for all debts incurred by the Congress of the United States established by the Articles of Confederation. In addition, the article states that the Constitution, and laws and treaties made in compliance with it by the national government, are the supreme law of the land. Moreover, all national and state government officials must uphold the Constitution of the United States.

ARTICLE VII: THE CONSTITUTIONAL RATIFICATION PROCESS According to Article VII of the Constitution, ratification of the Constitution required the affirmative vote of special conventions in nine of the thirteen original states. After the delegates signed the Constitution, the standing Congress forwarded it to the states, directing them to hold ratification conventions. See "Global Context" on page 50 for a description of the recent constitutional development and ratification process in Iraq.

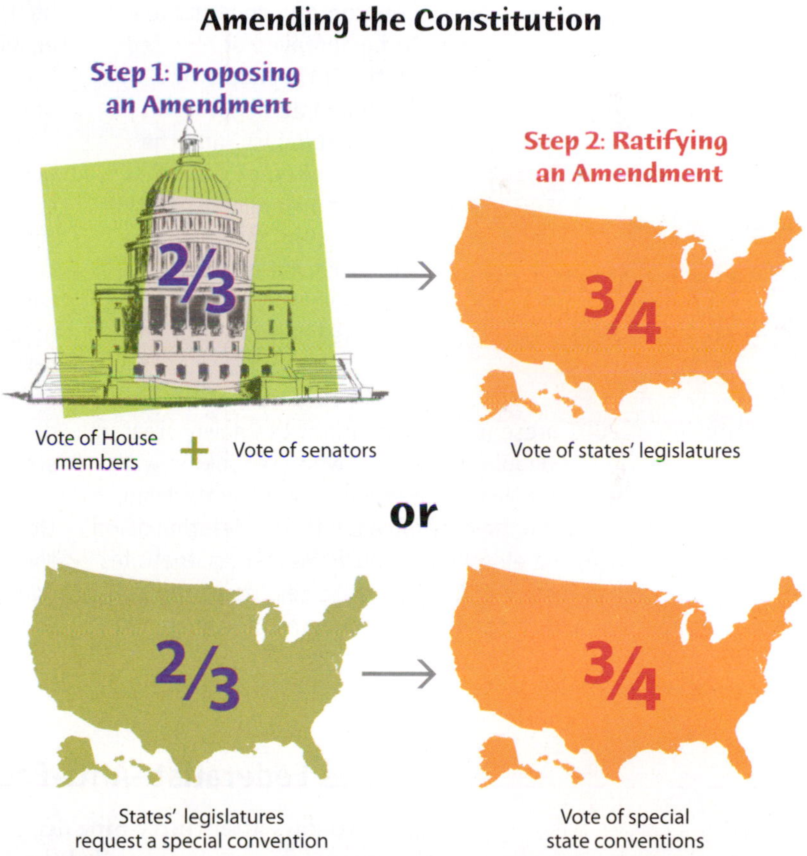

Amending the Constitution

Step 1: Proposing an Amendment

2/3

Vote of House members + Vote of senators

Step 2: Ratifying an Amendment

3/4

Vote of states' legislatures

or

2/3

States' legislatures request a special convention

3/4

Vote of special state conventions

POLITICAL INQUIRY

FIGURE 2.2 ■ What steps are involved in proposing a constitutional amendment? In what two ways can an amendment be ratified? Who has the authority to ratify amendments to the Constitution? Why is the designation of this authority important to the balance of power between the national and state governments? Explain.

THE IRAQI CONSTITUTION OF 2005

On March 20, 2003, multinational forces led by the United States and the United Kingdom invaded Iraq to search for nuclear weapons allegedly created and maintained in violation of United Nations (UN) resolutions prohibiting them. Within one month of the invasion, the United States established the Coalition Provisional Authority (CPA), which the UN and the international community recognized as the legitimate government in Iraq as it transitioned from rule under Saddam Hussein to a democratic government.

Will the Iraqi Constitution of 2005 stay in force for as long as the U.S. Constitution has been in force?

The CPA appointed an Iraqi Governing Council, which drafted a temporary constitution mandating the creation of a constitution to be approved or rejected by the Iraqi people. After considerable negotiation and compromise, and the promise of quick consideration of amendments to the constitution once ratification occurred, the Iraqi people voted to approve the proposed constitution on October 15, 2005.

The Preamble of the Iraqi Constitution of 2005 presents the mission of the newly created government. "We the people of Iraq . . . who are looking with confidence to the future through a republican, federal, democratic, pluralistic system, have resolved with the determination of our men, women, the elderly and youth, to respect the rules of law, to establish justice and equality, to cast aside the politics of aggression, and to tend to the concerns of women and their rights, and to the elderly and their concerns, and to children and their affairs, and to spread a culture of diversity and defusing terrorism."

The document goes on to describe fundamental principles of the Republic of Iraq, among them the concept of popular sovereignty, with government by consent of the people. It further enumerates civil and political rights and liberties of Iraqis, including equality before the law for all Iraqis, the right to personal privacy, and prohibitions against inhumane treatment.

> An Iraqi woman takes advantage of her constitutional right to vote in a parliamentary election in March 2010.

The foundational government bodies established by the Iraqi Constitution include a central (federal) government with the executive, legislative, and judicial powers distributed among three branches. Iraqis elect the members of one of the two chambers of the legislative branch, and these elected members will then elect the president of the republic. The fourth section of the Iraqi Constitution enumerates the powers of the federal government, and the fifth section enumerates the powers of the regional governments. The regional governments are delegated the authority to adopt constitutions that define the structure of regional government bodies. The final section of the Iraqi Constitution presents provisions for the transition to this new system of government, including the requirement that the constitution will go into force after the approval of the majority of the people voting in a general referendum.

The Federalist–Anti-Federalist Debate

Two days after thirty-nine delegates signed the Constitution, it was published in a special issue of a newspaper called the *Pennsylvania Packet*. Almost immediately, opponents of the proposed Constitution began to write letters, issue pamphlets, and make stirring speeches urging the state legislatures to reject the document. The debate developed as one between the Federalists and the Anti-Federalists. The **Federalists** supported the Constitution as presented by the convention delegates. The **Anti-Federalists** opposed the Constitution on the grounds that it gave the national government too much power—power that would erode states' authority and endanger individual freedoms.

The weak national government created by the Articles of Confederation was a federal government, as Americans understood the term before the ratification battle. Indeed, the critics of the Articles who called for the constitutional convention called for remedying the "defects of the *federal government*." However, those supporting ratification of the Constitution called themselves federalists in an effort to persuade citizens that the states retained considerable powers under the Constitution.

It was in the Pennsylvania debate between the Federalists and the Anti-Federalists that the call first clearly emerged for the inclusion of a bill of rights that would limit the powers of the federal government. Geared toward addressing the main Anti-Federalist complaints about the Constitution, the proposal for a bill of rights became the dominant point of contention in the ratification campaign. In the end, the success or failure of the ratification process would hinge on it.

THE FEDERALIST PAPERS: IN SUPPORT OF A STRONG NATIONAL GOVERNMENT

The Federalists made their most famous arguments in a series of essays known as *The Federalist Papers,* which appeared in newspapers across the new nation. The authors, James Madison, Alexander Hamilton, and John Jay, knew that achieving ratification depended on convincing the public and state legislators that the Constitution would empower the new nation to succeed. They also understood that many of the Anti-Federalists' concerns centered on how much power the national government would have under the Constitution and how that authority would affect the states and individual freedoms. Consequently, they approached the ratification debate strategically, penning eloquently reasoned essays (in the form of letters) to consider those specific issues.

Addressing fears of lost state power, Hamilton argues in *Federalist* No. 9 that "a FIRM Union will be of the utmost moment to the peace and liberty of the States, as a barrier against domestic faction and insurrection."[24] Similarly, in *Federalist* No. 51, Madison explains how the Constitution's provision of both a separation of powers and a system of checks and balances would prevent the national government from usurping the powers of the states and also ensure that no one branch of the federal government would dominate the other two.[25]

With regard to protecting individual rights, in *Federalist* No. 10, Madison reassuringly details how the republican government created by the Constitution would ensure that

Federalists
individuals who supported the new Constitution as presented by the Constitutional Convention in 1787

Anti-Federalists
individuals who opposed ratification of the Constitution because they were deeply suspicious of the powers it gave to the national government and of the impact those powers would have on states' authority and individual freedoms

The Federalist Papers
a series of essays, written by James Madison, Alexander Hamilton, and John Jay, that argued for the ratification of the Constitution

> James Madison, Alexander Hamilton, and John Jay wrote *The Federalist Papers,* a series of newspaper articles that justified and argued for the governing structures and procedures established in the U.S. Constitution. Because Madison and Hamilton had attended the Constitutional Convention, they had an insider's view of the arguments for and against the Constitution.

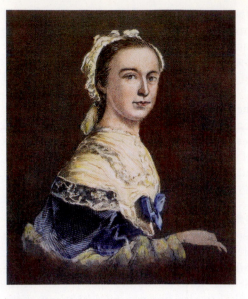

> Mercy Otis Warren was one of the rare, respected, politically engaged women of the eighteenth century. Her significant influence extended to the citizenry and to the authors of the Constitution and the Bill of Rights, with many of whom she discussed and debated governance and politics. Her political writings include the *Anti-Federalist Papers* and her extraordinary *History of the Rise, Progress, and Termination of the American Revolution* (1805).

many views would be heard and that a majority of the population would not be permitted to trample the rights of the numerical minority.[26] And writing in *Federalist* No. 84, Hamilton argues that because "the people surrender nothing, and as they retain every thing" by way of the Constitution, there was no danger that the new government would usurp individual rights and liberties.[27]

THE ANTI-FEDERALIST RESPONSE: IN OPPOSITION TO A STRONG NATIONAL GOVERNMENT On the other side of the debate, Anti-Federalists penned countless letters, speeches, and essays warning of the dangers of the new government and urging Americans to reject it. Anti-Federalists agonized that the Constitution ceded much too much power to the national government, at the expense of both the states and the people. Without a bill of rights, they reasoned, there was no way of truly limiting the actions the new government might take to achieve its goals.

Articulating Anti-Federalist views, Thomas Jefferson insisted that the inclusion of a bill of rights in the Constitution was essential. Federalist Alexander Hamilton countered that listing those rights might endanger the very kind of individual freedoms and rights they sought to safeguard. It was possible, Hamilton reasoned, that the list would be incomplete and that at some future time people might legitimately argue that because a given right was not specifically enumerated, it did not exist. (Was Hamilton correct? Consider the debate today about abortion.) Jefferson's response was that "half a loaf is better than no bread" and that "if we cannot secure all our rights, let us secure what we can."[28]

Along with Jefferson, Mercy Otis Warren was among the most influential Anti-Federalists. Through her political writings and personal relationships with many of the leading politicians of her time, Warren affected the public debate over declaring independence from Great Britain and ratifying the Articles of Confederation and the Constitution. Under the pen name "A Columbian Patriot," Warren wrote a pamphlet that presented a comprehensive argument against the proposed Constitution. The circulation of her pamphlet was larger than that of Hamilton, Madison, and Jay's *Federalist Papers*. Political scientist James McGregor Burns cited the "Columbian Patriot"—that is, Warren—as the spokesperson for the Anti-Federalist position.[29]

In the end, Jefferson's and Warren's views and the larger civic discourse about states' rights and individuals' liberties placed significant pressure on the Federalists to reconsider their opposition to a bill of rights. With the proviso that a bill of rights would be the first order of business for the new Congress, Massachusetts, Maryland, South Carolina, and New Hampshire—the last four states of the nine needed for ratification—ratified the Constitution in 1788. Ultimately, all original thirteen states ratified the Constitution.

The Bill of Rights (1791): Establishing Civil Liberties

In the opening days of the first session of the newly constituted Congress in March 1789, Virginia congressman James Madison introduced a bill of rights. Comprising twelve amendments, this proposed addition to the Constitution powerfully reflected the public concerns voiced during the ratification debates by enumerating limits on the government's right to infringe on the natural rights of life, liberty, and the pursuit of happiness, and by preserving the states' authority. Congress passed all twelve amendments and sent them to the states for approval. By 1791, the required number of states had quickly ratified ten of the twelve amendments, which we refer to today as the **Bill of Rights.**

The first eight amendments in the Bill of Rights establish the government's legal obligation to protect several specific liberties to which the Declaration of Independence re-

Bill of Rights
the first ten amendments to the Constitution, which were ratified in 1791, constituting an enumeration of the individual liberties with which the government is forbidden to interfere

ferred when it stated that men were "endowed by their creator with certain unalienable rights." These natural rights became government-protected liberties, *civil liberties,* through the ratification process. The Ninth Amendment indicates that the list of liberties in the first eight amendments is not exhaustive and therefore "shall not be construed to deny or disparage others retained by the people." (Chapter 4 discusses in depth the civil liberties established in the Bill of Rights.) The tenth and last amendment in the Bill of Rights, preserves the states' rights. The Tenth Amendment states that the powers not delegated to the national government by the Constitution "nor prohibited by it to the states, are reserved to the states respectively, or to the people."

The Constitution as a Living, Evolving Document

The authors of the Constitution were pragmatic men who were willing to compromise to resolve the problems confronting the new nation and to get a new constitution ratified.[30] To garner the votes needed to move the document from first draft through ratification, the framers had to negotiate and compromise over constitutional language. As a result of this give-and-take, the Constitution is replete with vague and ambiguous phrases, which the framers expected judges to interpret later. Alexander Hamilton wrote, "A constitution is in fact, and must be, regarded by judges as a fundamental law. It therefore belongs to them to ascertain its meaning as well as the meaning of any particular act proceeding from the legislative body. . . . The courts must declare the sense of the law. . . ."[31] As Supreme Court justice Charles Evans Hughes (1862–1948) more recently observed, "The Constitution is what the Judges say it is."[32]

Judges—and principally the justices sitting on the U.S. Supreme Court, which has the final authority to rule on what the Constitution means—have reinterpreted constitutional clauses many times. The Constitution has been formally amended, meaning the states have approved changes to the words in the document, only twenty-seven times, however. The reason for the relatively low number of constitutional amendments is that the framers established a difficult amendment process, requiring supermajority votes in Congress and among the states. They did so to ensure that nationwide public discourse would take place before the Constitution, the supreme law of the land, could be formally changed.

The alteration of this document—through both the formal passage of amendments and the less formal, but no less important, judicial reinterpretation of key clauses—derives from a continuing conversation among citizens about the core beliefs and principles of the framers and the generations that have followed them, including Americans today. In this concluding section, we consider the amendments that have been approved to date as the American people have undertaken efforts to perfect the union established by the Constitution, and we look at the process by which these amendments became a reality.

Formal Amendment of the Constitution

Every term, members of Congress introduce between one hundred and two hundred proposals for new constitutional amendments. That amounts to more than ten thousand proposals since 1789! Members of Congress who oppose a ruling by the U.S. Supreme Court or a law that engenders a great deal of public debate may propose an amendment to supersede the Court ruling or the law. Often, members of Congress introduce amendments knowing that they will never be ratified but wanting to appease their core constituencies by at least instigating public discourse about how our government should function and what rights and freedoms individuals possess.

Only a tiny fraction of the thousands of proposed amendments have cleared Congress—in fact, only thirty-three have achieved the two-thirds vote necessary in Congress—and, as noted, the states have ratified only twenty-seven. The amendments that the states have ratified fit into one of three categories: they have (1) extended civil liberties and civil rights (equal protection of laws for citizens), (2) altered the selection or operation of the branches of the national government, or (3) dealt with important policy issues. Table 2.2 (on page 54) summarizes the eleventh through the twenty-seventh constitutional amendments and organizes them by category.

TABLE 2.2

The Eleventh Through Twenty-Seventh Amendments to the Federal Constitution

Amendments That Protect Civil Liberties and Civil Rights

Thirteenth	1865	Banned slavery
Fourteenth	1868	Established that all people have the right to equal protection and due process before the law, and that all citizens are guaranteed the same privileges and immunities
Fifteenth	1870	Guaranteed that the right to vote could not be abridged on the basis of race or color
Nineteenth	1920	Guaranteed that the right to vote could not be abridged on the basis of sex
Twenty-third	1961	Defined how the District of Columbia would be represented in the Electoral College
Twenty-fourth	1964	Outlawed the use of a poll tax, which prevented poor people from exercising their right to vote
Twenty-sixth	1971	Lowered the voting age to 18 years

Amendments That Relate to the Selection of Government Officials or the Operation of the Branches of Government

Eleventh	1795	Limited federal court jurisdiction by barring citizens of one state from suing another state in federal court
Twelfth	1804	Required the electors in the Electoral College to vote twice: once for president and once for vice president
Seventeenth	1913	Mandated the direct election of senators by citizens
Twentieth	1933	Set a date for the convening of Congress and the inauguration of the president
Twenty-second	1951	Limited to two the number of terms the president can serve
Twenty-fifth	1967	Established the procedure for presidential succession in the event of the disability or death of the president; established the procedure for vice-presidential replacement when the position becomes vacant before the end of the term
Twenty-seventh	1992	Required that there be an intervening election between the time when Congress votes itself a raise and when that raise can be implemented

Amendments That Address Specific Public Policies

Sixteenth	1913	Empowered Congress to establish an income tax
Eighteenth	1919	Banned the manufacture, sale, and transportation of liquor
Twenty-first	1933	Repealed the ban on the manufacture, sale, and transportation of liquor

Interpretation by the U.S. Supreme Court

Beyond the addition of formal amendments, the Constitution has changed over time through reinterpretation by the courts. This reinterpretation began with the U.S. Supreme Court's landmark *Marbury v. Madison* decision in 1803, in which the Court established the important power of judicial review—the authority of the courts to rule on whether acts of government officials and governing bodies violate the Constitution. Although the U.S. Su-

ANALYZING THE SOURCES

CONSTITUTIONAL PRINCIPLES IN RECENT SECOND AMENDMENT CASES

Consider the following chronology related to the Second Amendment and its legal protections. Has the court made the meaning of the Second Amendment clear and unambiguous?

1791 **Second Amendment** states that "a well regulated Militia, being necessary to the security of a free State, the right of the people to keep and bear Arms, shall not be infringed."

1976 **Washington, D.C., law** is passed banning all handguns in homes unless they were registered before 1976. The law's intent is to decrease gun violence.

2007 **Majority opinion of the U.S. Court of Appeals for D.C. Circuit, *Parker v. District of Columbia,*** finds the 1976 Washington, D.C., ban unconstitutional and explains, "We . . . take it as an expression of the drafters' view that the people possessed a natural right to keep and bear arms, and that the preservation of the militia was the right's most salient political benefit—and thus the most appropriate to express in a political document."*

2008 **Majority opinion of the U.S. Supreme Court in *District of Columbia and Adrian M. Felty v. Dick Anthony Heller*** declares, "There seems to us no doubt, on the basis of both text and history, that the Second Amendment conferred an individual right to keep and bear arms." The decision goes on to say, "Like most rights, the Second Amendment right is not unlimited. It is not a right to keep and carry any weapon whatsoever in any manner whatsoever and for whatever purpose."**

**Parker v. District of Columbia, 478 F. 3d 370 (D.C. Circuit 2007).*
***District of Columbia and Adrian M. Fenty v. Dick Anthony Heller, 544 U.S.*

Evaluating the Evidence

① What do you think was the intent of the authors of the Second Amendment? Did they intend to protect a natural, individual right to bear arms? Did they mean to ensure that resources (that is, people with the right to bear arms) for protecting domestic tranquility and national defense would be readily available? Did they seek to ensure both?

② What do you imagine the majority of Americans think the Second Amendment means? Why? Where might you get data to support your prediction?

③ Do you agree with the majority opinion in the *Parker* case or the majority opinion in the *D.C. v. Heller* case? Explain.

④ What impact on public safety will the divergent interpretations of the Second Amendment have?

preme Court's interpretation is final, if the Supreme Court does not review constitutional interpretations made by lower federal courts, then the interpretations of those lower courts are the final word.

How do judges decide what the Constitution means? To interpret its words, they may look at how courts have ruled in past cases on the phrasing in question or what the custom or usage of the words has generally been. They may try to ascertain what the authors of the Constitution meant. Alternatively, the judges may consider the policy implications of differing interpretations, gauging them against the mission presented in the Constitution's Preamble. In any given case, the deciding court must determine which of those points of reference it will use and how it will apply them to interpret the constitutional principles under consideration. For a taste of how the courts determine the meaning of the Constitution, see "Analyzing the Sources."

The power of judicial review has allowed the courts to continue to breathe life into the Constitution to keep up with societal norms and technological change. For example, in 1896 the Supreme Court decreed that the Fourteenth Amendment allowed laws requiring the segregation of white and black citizens.[33] Then in 1954, in the case of *Brown v. The Board of Education of Topeka, Kansas,*[34] the Supreme Court declared such segregation to be an unconstitutional violation of the Fourteenth Amendment.

> In 2004, the U.S. Supreme Court ruled that U.S. federal courts had jurisdiction to decide lawsuits filed by foreigners detained at the U.S. naval base in Guantanamo Bay, Cuba (Gitmo). President George W. Bush and Congress responded to that ruling by enacting a law removing those lawsuits from federal court jurisdiction. In 2006, the Supreme Court found that law unconstitutional because of procedural errors in its enactment. Then Congress passed another law, following correct procedures, to remove the detainees' lawsuits from federal court jurisdiction. In 2008, the Supreme Court ruled that the Gitmo detainees had a constitutionally guaranteed right to have their lawsuits resolved in the federal courts. Today, federal courts hear lawsuits filed by Gitmo detainees.

Technology also drives constitutional reinterpretation. The framers naturally never conceived of the existence of computers and telecommunications. Yet by reviewing and freshly interpreting the Fourth Amendment, which prohibits unreasonable searches and seizures by government officials, the courts have uncovered the principles behind this amendment that apply to our technologically advanced society. Consequently, this provision, whose original intent was to limit governments' physical searches of one's property and person, can be used today to determine, for example, whether governmental surveillance of computer databases is permissible.

Sometimes, the Supreme Court's opinions ignite a debate or intensify a debate already under way. Court decisions that are viewed as a "win" for one side and a "loss" for the other often generate fierce responses in the other branches or levels of the government. For example, the executive branch might decide not to implement a Court decision. Or the legislative branch might write a new law that challenges a Court decision. Unless a lawsuit allows the Court to rule the new law unconstitutional, the new law takes effect.

Although controversial Court decisions often capture significant media attention, in most cases, the Court's rulings are in step with public opinion. Analysts note that the Court does not often lead public opinion—in fact, it more often follows it.[35] And even if the justices wanted to take some very controversial and unpopular action, the system of checks and balances forces them to consider how the other branches would react. Recall that the Court has the power to interpret the law; it does not have the power to implement or to enforce the law and must be concerned about how the other branches might retaliate against it for highly unpopular decisions. Therefore, for the most part, changes to the Constitution, both formal and informal, are incremental and further the will of the people because they are the product of widespread public discourse—an ongoing conversation of democracy.

The governing principles proclaimed in the Declaration of Independence successfully unified American colonists to fight the War for Independence. Government created by the consent of the people with the mission of protecting the people's natural rights of life, liberty, and the pursuit of happiness has proven difficult. The tensions between individual liberties and popular sovereignty first witnessed under the Articles of Confederation have continued under the Constitution of the United States. These tensions loom large, especially during times when national security is threatened and economic health is poor. Under such circumstances, the courts often play a role in interpreting the language of the Constitution. How will the courts resolve the continuing tensions between individual liberties and popular sovereignty?

Today, many Americans believe that parts of the Constitution are not working. Some argue that the government is not serving the people well; that the government is infringing on individual liberties and the pursuit of happiness. Others focus on the foundational structures and operating procedures established by the Constitution, claiming that the government is not properly implementing them. Many argue that the more perfect union envisioned by the founders is not being fulfilled. To address these contemporary governing defects, some have proposed constitutional amendments. Others are calling for a constitutional convention.

As Americans continue to work for a more perfect union, will Congress respond to state applications for a constitutional convention by calling for a second constitutional convention? Will the Constitution's third century witness a greater volume of ratified constitutional amendments as the people's efforts to ensure a more perfect union intensify?

Summary

1. What Is a Constitution?

A constitution presents the fundamental principles of a government and establishes the basic structures and procedures by which the government operates to fulfill those principles. Constitutions may be written or unwritten.

2. The Creation of the United States of America

By the mid-eighteenth century, the American colonists were protesting the effect of British rule on their lives and livelihoods. Pamphlets, newspaper articles, public discourse, and eloquent revolutionaries persuaded the colonists that it was common sense, as well as their obligation, to declare their independence from Britain and to create a new government. Yet the weak national government established by the country's first constitution, the Articles of Confederation, did not serve the people well.

3. Crafting the Constitution: Compromise, Ratification, and Quick Amendment

In response to severe economic problems and tensions among the states, and to growing desires for a more perfect union of the states, representatives from the states met in Philadelphia in 1787 to amend the Articles of Confederation. Debate and deliberation led to compromise and a new constitution, supported by the Federalists and opposed by the Anti-Federalists. The addition of the Bill of Rights two years after the states ratified the Constitution addressed the primary concerns about individual liberties and states' authority that the Anti-Federalists had raised during the debates over ratification of the Constitution of the United States.

4. The Constitution as a Living, Evolving Document

The Constitution of the United States has been formally amended a mere twenty-seven times over its 220-plus years of life. This rare occurrence of formal change to the Constitution's written words belies the reality of its perpetual revision through the process of judicial review and interpretation. The U.S. Supreme Court ultimately decides what the written words in the Constitution mean, and through that authority, the Court clarifies and modifies (hence, revises) the Constitution yearly.

Key Terms

advice and consent 48	constitution 34	New Jersey Plan 44
Anti-Federalists 51	dual sovereignty 43	republic 41
bicameral legislature 41	Electoral College 46	separation of powers 44
bill of rights 41	*The Federalist Papers* 51	supremacy clause 43
Bill of Rights 52	Federalists 51	Three-Fifths Compromise 46
checks and balances 44	judicial review 48	unicameral legislature 41
confederation 41	*Marbury v. Madison* 48	veto 48
Connecticut Compromise (Great Compromise) 44	natural rights (unalienable rights) 39	Virginia Plan 44

For Review

1. Describe the three main components of a written constitution.
2. How did the events leading up to the War for Independence shape the core principles of the U.S. Constitution?
3. How did conflict and compromise influence the drafting and ratification of the Constitution? What specific issues caused conflict and required compromise for their resolution? On what matters was there early consensus among the framers?
4. What are the formal and informal mechanisms for changing the Constitution?

For Critical Thinking and Discussion

1. What was the relationship between the state constitutions, many of which were created immediately after the signing of the Declaration of Independence, and the U.S. Constitution, which was written more than a decade later?
2. Think about important debates in American society today. Describe one that you think is linked in some way to the compromises upon which the Constitution is based.
3. Imagine that you are living during the Revolutionary era and writing an article for a newspaper in England. You are trying to explain why the colonists have destroyed thousands of pounds of British tea at the Boston Tea Party. How might you, as an English citizen living in England, characterize the colonists' motives? How might you, as an English citizen living in the colonies, characterize the colonists' motives?
4. What do you think would have happened had the Anti-Federalists, rather than the Federalists, prevailed in the ratification process of the Constitution? What kind of government would they have shaped? How would that government have dealt with the difficult issues facing the new republic—slavery, concerns about mob rule, and continuing hostility in the international community?

PRACTICE QUIZ

MULTIPLE CHOICE: Choose the lettered item that answers the question correctly.

1. According to the Declaration of Independence, the natural, unalienable rights include all the following except
   a. liberty.
   b. life.
   c. property.
   d. the pursuit of happiness.

2. The existence of three branches of government, each responsible for a different primary governing function, is the implementation of the foundational organizational structure called
   a. judicial review.
   b. the federal system.
   c. representative democracy.
   d. separation of powers.

3. *Marbury v. Madison* (1803) is a landmark case because it
   a. clarified the Electoral College system.
   b. clarified congressional legislative authority.
   c. clarified the courts' judicial review authority.
   d. clarified presidential appointment authority.

4. Ratification of an amendment to the U.S. Constitution requires
   a. approval of the majority of citizens voting in a referendum.
   b. approval of three-quarters of the members of Congress.
   c. approval of three-quarters of either the House or the Senate.
   d. approval of three-quarters of the state legislatures or special conventions.

5. All of the following were authors of *The Federalist Papers* except
   a. John Jay.
   b. Thomas Jefferson.
   c. Alexander Hamilton.
   d. James Madison.

6. The document (or set of documents), grounded in social contract theory and stating that citizens have an obligation to replace their government if it is not serving them and protecting their unalienable rights, is
   a. the Articles of Confederation.
   b. the Constitution of the United States of America.
   c. the Declaration of Independence.
   d. *The Federalist Papers*.

7. At the Constitutional Convention, the delegates devoted the bulk of their time to resolving the issue of
   a. procedures for electing the president and the vice president.
   b. representation in the national legislature.
   c. the necessity for a bill of rights.
   d. slavery.

8. The ultimate authority to interpret the meaning of constitutional language, and hence to decide what is the supreme law of the land, comes from
   a. the majority of members of Congress.
   b. the majority of members of state legislatures.
   c. the majority of justices on the U.S. Supreme Court.
   d. the president of the United States.

9. The required nine states ratified the Constitution of the United States in
   a. 1776.
   b. 1781.
   c. 1788.
   d. 1791.

10. One check that the Senate has on both the executive branch and the judicial branch is its power of
    a. advice and consent.
    b. impeachment.
    c. ratification of treaties.
    d. veto override.

FILL IN THE BLANKS.

11. Currently there are _____ amendments to the U.S. Constitution, and the last amendment was added in the year _____ .

12. The United States' first constitution was the _____ .

13. _____ wrote a pamphlet that summarized the Anti-Federalist position in the debate leading to ratification of the Constitution.

14. The Virginia delegate to the Second Continental Congress who wrote the Declaration of Independence was _____ .

15. Many of the Anti-Federalist criticisms of the Constitution were addressed in 1791 with the ratification of the _____ .

Answers: 1. c; 2. d; 3. c; 4. d; 5. b; 6. c; 7. b; 8. c; 9. c; 10. a; 11. 27 and 1992; 12. Articles of Confederation; 13. Mercy Otis Warren (the Columbian Patriot); 14. Thomas Jefferson; 15. Bill of Rights

RESOURCES FOR RESEARCH AND ACTION

Internet Resources

FindLaw
www.findlaw.com This site offers links to news regarding current cases before the U.S. Supreme Court as well as access to decisions of all federal and state appellate courts.

Library of Congress Memory Project
www.loc.gov/rr/program/bib/ourdocs/PrimDocsHome.htm
This comprehensive Web site, created by the Library of Congress as part of its Memory Project, includes a wealth of information about the early American republic, including primary documents such as *The Federalist Papers*.

The U.S. Constitution Online
www.USConstitution.net This interesting site helps to place the U.S. Constitution in a contemporary context. Its current events section discusses how the pending issues are affected by constitutional principles.

Internet Activism

YouTube
www.youtube.com/watch?v=TtGOyznDDEM&feature=related
Take a short test, developed by the Friends of the Article V Convention, to assess how much you know about the U.S. Constitution.

Twitter
http://twitter.com/aclu The American Civil Liberties Union (ACLU) is a nonprofit, nonpartisan, public interest organization devoted to protecting the basic civil liberties of everyone in America.

Facebook
www.facebook.com/pages/Philadelphia-PA/National -Constitution-Center/59543893235?ref=nfl The National Constitution Center is an interactive museum about the history of the Constitution.

Blog
http://blogs.archives.gov/aotus/ David Ferriero, the archivist for the National Archives, offers his take on transparency, collaboration, and participation at the National Archives. The National Archives preserves and makes accessible more than 9 billion valuable records of the Federal government, including the Declaration of Independence and the U.S. Constitution.

Recommended Readings

Breyer, Stephen. *Active Liberty: Interpreting Our Democratic Constitution.* New York: Random House, 2005. A short, readable book in which Supreme Court justice Stephen Breyer argues that constitutional interpretation must be guided by the foundational principle of government by the people and that the courts must ensure that they protect and facilitate citizens' participation in government.

Hamilton, Alexander, James Madison, and John Jay. *The Federalist Papers.* Cutchogue, NY: Buccaneer Books, 1992. A compilation of the eighty-five newspaper articles written by the authors to persuade the voters of New York to ratify the proposed Constitution of the United States, featuring a comprehensive introduction that puts the articles in context and outlines their principal themes—and hence, the underlying principles of the Constitution.

Roberts, Cokie. *Founding Mothers: The Women Who Raised Our Nation.* New York: Perennial Press, 2004. An examination of the Revolution and its aftermath, focusing on how women contributed to the war effort and to wider discussions about how the new government should be structured and what goals it should advance.

Sabato, Larry. *A More Perfect Constitution: 23 Proposals to Revitalize Our Constitution and Make America a Fairer Country.* New York: Walker Publishing, 2007. An exploration by political scientist Larry Sabato into why a constitutional convention is needed. The book includes proposals for twenty-three amendments—many of which citizens support, according to a poll commissioned by the author—that Sabato argues will perfect the Constitution. His real goal in writing the book was to kindle a national conversation on what he perceives as the deficiencies in U.S. representative democracy.

Movies of Interest

National Treasure (2004)
Starring Nicholas Cage, this adventure-packed film traces a hunt for treasure that a family's oral history says the nation's founding fathers buried. Clues are found hidden in the country's early currency and even on the back of the Declaration of Independence. The hunt exposes the viewer to the workings of the National Archives and its Preservation Room and features images of the founding fathers not typically reproduced in textbooks.

Return to the Land of Wonder (2004)
This documentary follows Adnan Pachachi's return to Iraq in 2003, after thirty-seven years in exile, to head a committee charged with drafting a new constitution and bill of rights. The movie focuses on the torturous process of trying to resolve conflicts created by the demands of the United States and the expectations of Iraqis, as well as the realities of everyday life in Iraq in 2003.

An Empire of Reason (1998)
A thought-provoking answer to an intriguing "what if?" question: What if the ratification debates were held using the media tools of the twenty-first century, specifically television?

Amistad (1997)
This film depicts the mutiny and subsequent trial of Africans aboard the ship *Amistad* in 1839–1840. Viewers get a glimpse of the intense civic discourse over slavery in the period leading up to the Civil War.

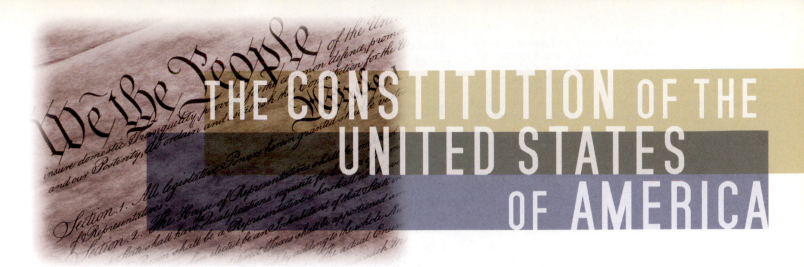

Preamble

We the People of the United States, in Order to form a more perfect Union, establish Justice, insure domestic Tranquility, provide for the common defence, promote the general Welfare, and secure the Blessings of Liberty to ourselves and our Posterity, do ordain and establish this Constitution for the United States of America.

ARTICLE I. (Legislative Branch)

Section 1. (Bicameral Legislative Branch)

All legislative Powers herein granted shall be vested in a Congress of the United States, which shall consist of a Senate and House of Representatives.

Section 2. (The House of Representatives)

Clause 1: The House of Representatives shall be composed of Members chosen every second Year by the People of the several States, and the Electors in each State shall have the Qualifications requisite for Electors of the most numerous Branch of the State Legislature.

Clause 2: No Person shall be a Representative who shall not have attained to the age of twenty five Years, and been seven Years a Citizen of the United States, and who shall not, when elected, be an Inhabitant of that State in which he shall be chosen.

Clause 3: Representatives and direct Taxes shall be apportioned among the several States which may be included within this Union, according to their respective Numbers, which shall be determined by adding to the whole Number of free Persons, including those bound to Service for a Term of Years, and excluding Indians not taxed, three fifths of all other Persons. The actual Enumeration shall be made within three Years after the first Meeting of the Congress of the United States, and within every subsequent Term of ten Years, in such Manner as they shall by Law direct. The Number of Representatives shall not exceed one for every thirty Thousand, but each State shall have at Least one Representative; and until such enumeration shall be made, the State of New Hampshire shall be entitled to chuse three, Massachusetts eight, Rhode-Island and Providence Plantations one, Connecticut five, New-York six, New Jersey four, Pennsylvania eight, Delaware one, Maryland six, Virginia ten, North Carolina five, South Carolina five, and Georgia three.

Clause 4: When vacancies happen in the Representation from any State, the Executive Authority thereof shall issue Writs of Election to fill such Vacancies.

> The Preamble states that "the People" are creating a new government, which is described in the Constitution. The Preamble also decrees that it is the mission of this new government to serve the people better than did the government established by the Articles of Confederation, which had been in effect since before the end of the War for Independence.

> Article I presents the organization, procedures, and authority of the lawmaking branch, the Congress, a bicameral (two-chamber) legislature comprising the House of Representatives and the Senate.

> House members are elected to serve a two-year term.

> The Constitution specifies only three qualifications to be elected to the House: you must be at least 25 years old; you must be a U.S. citizen for at least seven years (so a foreign-born, naturalized citizen can be a House member); and you must be a resident of the state you will represent. By tradition, House members live in the district that they represent.

> The number of seats in the House increased as the population of each state grew until 1911, when Congress set the number of House seats at 435. Congress distributes these seats among the fifty states according to each state's share of the total population, as determined by a census (official count of the country's inhabitants) conducted every ten years. Every state must have at least one seat in the House. The "three-fifths" clause decreed that when conducting the census the government would not count Native Americans and would count each slave as three-fifths of a person while counting every other inhabitant as one person. The Thirteenth Amendment (1865) abolished slavery, and the Fourteenth Amendment (1868) repealed the three-fifths clause. Today every inhabitant of the United States is counted as one person in the census, and House seats are redistributed every ten years based on the census to ensure that each House member is elected by (and therefore represents) approximately the same number of people.

> Governors have the authority to call for a special election to fill any of their states' House seats that become vacant.

> House members select their presiding officer, the Speaker of the House. The Speaker is in line to succeed the president if both the president and the vice president are unable to serve. The Constitution gives the House a check on officials of the executive and judicial branches through its power of impeachment: the power to accuse such officials formally of offenses such as treason, bribery, and abuse of power. If the officials are subsequently found guilty in a trial held by the Senate, they are removed from office.

> Initially, senators were selected by the members of their state's legislature, not by their state's voters. The Seventeenth Amendment (1913) changed this election process; today, senators are elected by the voters in their state. This amendment also authorized each state's governor to call for elections to fill vacancies as well as authorizing the state's legislature to determine how its state's vacant Senate seats would be temporarily filled until the election of a new senator.

> Every even-numbered year, congressional elections are held in which one-third of the Senate's 100 seats and all 435 House seats are up for election. Every state elects two senators, who serve six-year terms.

> Senators must be at least 30 years old, either natural-born citizens or immigrants who have been citizens for at least nine years, and—like members of the House—residents of the state they are elected to represent.

> The vice president serves as the president of the Senate, with the authority to preside over meetings of the Senate and to vote when there is a tie.

> Although the first few vice presidents did preside over daily meetings of the Senate, the vice president rarely does so today.

> The Senate exercises a check on officials of the executive and judicial branches of the federal government by trying them once they have been impeached by the House of Representatives.

> If the Senate convicts an impeached official, he or she is removed from office and may be subject to prosecution in the criminal courts.

Clause 5: The House of Representatives shall chuse their Speaker and other Officers; and shall have the sole Power of Impeachment.

POLITICAL INQUIRY: *Because members of the House of Representatives run for reelection every two years, they are perpetually raising money for, and worrying about, their next election campaign. Recently an amendment was introduced that would increase their term from two to four years. What would be the consequences of such a change? How would this change make members of the House more, or less, responsive to their constituents' concerns?*

Section 3. (The Senate)

Clause 1: The Senate of the United States shall be composed of two Senators from each State, chosen by the Legislature thereof, for six Years; and each Senator shall have one Vote.

Clause 2: Immediately after they shall be assembled in Consequence of the first Election, they shall be divided as equally as may be into three Classes. The Seats of the Senators of the first Class shall be vacated at the Expiration of the second Year, of the second Class at the Expiration of the fourth Year, and of the third Class at the Expiration of the sixth Year, so that one third may be chosen every second Year; and if Vacancies happen by Resignation, or otherwise, during the Recess of the Legislature of any State, the Executive thereof may make temporary Appointments until the next Meeting of the Legislature, which shall then fill such Vacancies.

Clause 3: No Person shall be a Senator who shall not have attained to the Age of thirty Years, and been nine Years a Citizen of the United States, and who shall not, when elected, be an Inhabitant of that State for which he shall be chosen.

Clause 4: The Vice President of the United States shall be President of the Senate but shall have no Vote, unless they be equally divided.

Clause 5: The Senate shall chuse their other Officers, and also a President pro tempore, in the Absence of the Vice President, or when he shall exercise the Office of President of the United States.

Clause 6: The Senate shall have the sole Power to try all Impeachments. When sitting for that Purpose, they shall be on Oath or Affirmation. When the President of the United States is tried the Chief Justice shall preside: And no Person shall be convicted without the Concurrence of two thirds of the Members present.

Clause 7: Judgment in Cases of Impeachment shall not extend further than to removal from Office, and disqualification to hold and enjoy any Office of honor, Trust or Profit under the United States: but the Party convicted shall nevertheless be liable and subject to Indictment, Trial, Judgment and Punishment, according to Law.

POLITICAL INQUIRY: *The framers of the Constitution, who did not expect members of Congress to serve more than one or two terms, would be shocked to learn that Senator Robert C. Byrd (D-West Virginia) was in his fifty-first year of service to the Senate when he died in 2010 at the age of 92. Concerned about such longevity in office, some have proposed a constitutional amendment that would limit the number of times a House member or a senator could win reelection to the same seat. How would term limits benefit citizens? What problems might term limits cause?*

Section 4. (Congressional Elections)

Clause 1: The Times, Places and Manner of holding Elections for Senators and Representatives, shall be prescribed in each State by the Legislature thereof; but the Congress may at any time by Law make or alter such Regulations, except as to the Places of chusing Senators.

> Though states have the authority to organize and conduct elections, today they rely heavily on local governments to assist them. Congress has passed numerous laws to ensure constitutionally guaranteed voting rights. The first such law was passed shortly after ratification of the Fifteenth Amendment to criminalize attempts to deny black men their newly won right to vote. Congress has also enacted laws to make voter registration easier. For example, a 1996 federal law requires states to allow citizens to register to vote through the mail.

POLITICAL INQUIRY: *Voter turnout (the percentage of eligible voters that vote on election day) has increased in Oregon since that state changed its laws to allow voters to vote by mail. What are some additional arguments that could be made in support of a national law allowing citizens to vote by mail? What are some arguments that could be made against such a national law?*

Clause 2: The Congress shall assemble at least once in every Year, and such Meeting shall be on the first Monday in December, unless they shall by Law appoint a different Day.

> Congress must meet at least once each year. Since ratification of the Twentieth Amendment (1933), the regular annual session of Congress begins on January 3 of each year; however, the Twentieth Amendment gives Congress the authority to change the date on which its session begins.

Section 5. (Powers and Responsibilities of the House)

Clause 1: Each House shall be the Judge of the Elections, Returns and Qualifications of its own Members, and a Majority of each shall constitute a Quorum to do Business; but a smaller Number may adjourn from day to day, and may be authorized to compel the Attendance of absent Members, in such Manner, and under such Penalties as each House may provide.

> Each chamber decides whether the election of each of its members is legitimate. A majority of the members of each chamber must be present to conduct business: at least 218 members for the House and 51 senators for the Senate.

Clause 2: Each House may determine the Rules of its Proceedings, punish its Members for disorderly Behaviour, and, with the Concurrence of two thirds, expel a Member.

> After each congressional election, both the House and the Senate determine how they will conduct their business, and each chamber selects from among its members a presiding officer. Moreover, the members of each chamber establish codes of behavior, which they use to judge and—if necessary—punish members' misconduct.

Clause 3: Each House shall keep a Journal of its Proceedings, and from time to time publish the same, excepting such Parts as may in their Judgment require Secrecy; and the Yeas and Nays of the Members of either House on any question shall, at the Desire of one fifth of those Present, be entered on the Journal.

> The House and the Senate must keep and publish records of their proceedings, including a record of all votes for and against proposals, except those that they decide require secrecy. However, if one-fifth of the members of a chamber demand that a vote be recorded, it must be recorded. Congress publishes a record of its debates called the *Congressional Record*.

Clause 4: Neither House, during the Session of Congress, shall, without the Consent of the other, adjourn for more than three days, nor to any other Place than that in which the two Houses shall be sitting.

> To close down business for more than three days during a session, or to conduct business at another location, each chamber needs to get approval from the other one. This ensures that one chamber cannot stop the legislative process by refusing to meet.

Section 6. (Rights of Congressional Members)

Clause 1: The Senators and Representatives shall receive a Compensation for their Services, to be ascertained by Law, and paid out of the Treasury of the United States. They shall in all Cases, except Treason, Felony and Breach of the Peace, be privileged from Arrest during their Attendance at the Session of their respective Houses, and in going to and returning from the same; and for any Speech or Debate in either House, they shall not be questioned in any other Place.

> Today, each member of Congress earns at least $174,000 per year, paid by taxes collected by the national government. Members of Congress are protected from civil lawsuits and criminal prosecution for the work they do as legislators. They are also protected from arrest while Congress is in session except for a charge of treason, of committing a felony, or of committing a breach of the peace.

Clause 2: No Senator or Representative shall, during the Time for which he was elected, be appointed to any civil Office under the Authority of the United States, which shall have been created, or the Emoluments whereof shall have been increased during such time; and no Person holding any Office under the United States, shall be a Member of either House during his Continuance in Office.

> To ensure the separation of basic governing functions, no member of Congress can hold another federal position while serving in the House or Senate. Moreover, members of Congress cannot be appointed to a position in the executive or judicial branch that was created during their term of office.

Section 7. (The Legislative Process)

Clause 1: All Bills for raising Revenue shall originate in the House of Representatives; but the Senate may propose or concur with amendments as on other Bills.

> This section details the legislative process.

> Although all revenue-raising bills, such as tax bills, must originate in the House, the Senate reviews them and has the authority to make modifications; ultimately the House and the Senate must approve the identical bill for it to become law.

> After the House and the Senate approve, by a simple majority vote in each chamber, the identical bill, it is sent to the president for approval or rejection. The president has ten days in which to act, or the bill will automatically become law (unless Congress has adjourned, in which case the bill dies—a pocket veto). If the president signs the bill within ten days, it becomes law. If the president rejects—vetoes—the bill, he or she sends it back to the chamber of its origin with objections. Congress can then rewrite the vetoed bill and send the revised bill through the legislative process. Or Congress can attempt to override the veto by garnering a supermajority vote of approval (two-thirds majority) in each chamber.

> The president must approve or veto everything that Congress approves except its vote to adjourn or any resolutions that do not have the force of law.

> This section specifies the constitutionally established congressional powers. These powers are limited to those listed and any other powers that Congress believes are "necessary and proper" for Congress to fulfill its listed powers. Congress has used the "necessary and proper" clause (Clause 18) to justify laws that expand its listed powers. Laws that appear to go beyond the listed powers can be challenged in the courts, with the Supreme Court ultimately deciding their constitutionality.

> The power to raise money and to authorize spending it for common defense and the general welfare is one of the most essential powers of Congress. The Sixteenth Amendment (1913) authorizes a national income tax, which was not previously possible given the "uniformity" requirement in Clause 1.

> Today, after years of borrowing money to pay current bills, the national government has a debt of over $13 trillion.

Clause 2: Every Bill which shall have passed the House of Representatives and the Senate, shall, before it become a law, be presented to the President of the United States: If he approve he shall sign it, but if not he shall return it, with his Objections to that House in which it shall have originated, who shall enter the Objections at large on their Journal, and proceed to reconsider it. If after such Reconsideration two thirds of that House shall agree to pass the Bill, it shall be sent, together with the Objections, to the other House, by which it shall likewise be reconsidered, and if approved by two thirds of that House, it shall become a Law. But in all such Cases the Votes of both Houses shall be determined by Yeas and Nays, and the Names of the Persons voting for and against the Bill shall be entered on the Journal of each House respectively. If any Bill shall not be returned by the President within ten Days (Sundays excepted) after it shall have been presented to him, the Same shall be a Law, in like Manner as if he had signed it, unless the Congress by their Adjournment prevent its Return, in which Case it shall not be a Law.

Clause 3: Every Order, Resolution, or Vote to which the Concurrence of the Senate and House of Representatives may be necessary (except on a question of Adjournment) shall be presented to the President of the United States; and before the Same shall take Effect, shall be approved by him, or being disapproved by him, shall be repassed by two thirds of the Senate and House of Representatives, according to the Rules and Limitations prescribed in the Case of a Bill.

POLITICAL INQUIRY: *The presidential veto power is limited to an all-or-nothing decision. Presidents must either approve or veto entire bills; they cannot approve part of a bill and veto other parts of it. Many who worry about the national debt have called for a new type of presidential veto: a line-item veto. This type of veto would authorize the president to overrule parts of a bill that provide spending authority while approving other parts of the same bill. Would giving the president authority to exercise a line-item veto make it easier for the national government to enact a balanced annual budget (a budget in which the money spent in the budget year is equal to or less than the money raised in that year)? Why or why not? What arguments might members of Congress make against giving the president a line-item veto, hence giving up their final say on spending bills?*

Section 8. (The Lawmaking Authority of Congress)

Clause 1: The Congress shall have Power To lay and collect Taxes, Duties, Imposts and Excises, to pay the Debts and provide for the common Defence and general Welfare of the United States; but all Duties, Imposts and Excises shall be uniform throughout the United States;

Clause 2: To borrow Money on the credit of the United States;

POLITICAL INQUIRY: *Some economists, politicians, and citizens fear that the national debt harms the United States by limiting the amount of money available to invest in growing the economy. Moreover, citizens worry that their children and grandchildren, saddled with the obligation of paying back this debt, may face limited government services. Therefore, there have been repeated calls for a balanced budget amendment, which would force Congress to spend no more than the money it raises in each budget year. What arguments might the members of Congress, elected officials who want to be reelected, put forth against ratification of a balanced budget amendment? What national situations might require spending more money than is raised in a budget year?*

Clause 3: To regulate Commerce with foreign Nations, and among the several States, and with the Indian Tribes;

Clause 4: To establish an uniform Rule of Naturalization, and uniform Laws on the subject of Bankruptcies throughout the United States;

Clause 5: To coin Money, regulate the Value thereof, and of foreign Coin, and fix the Standard of Weights and Measures;

Clause 6: To provide for the Punishment of counterfeiting the Securities and current Coin of the United States;

Clause 7: To establish Post Offices and post Roads;

Clause 8: To promote the Progress of Science and useful Arts, by securing for limited Times to Authors and Inventors the exclusive Right to their respective Writings and Discoveries;

Clause 9: To constitute Tribunals inferior to the supreme Court;

Clause 10: To define and punish Piracies and Felonies committed on the high Seas, and Offences against the Law of Nations;

Clause 11: To declare War, grant Letters of Marque and Reprisal, and make Rules concerning Captures on Land and Water;

Clause 12: To raise and support Armies, but no Appropriation of Money to that Use shall be for a longer Term than two Years;

Clause 13: To provide and maintain a Navy;

Clause 14: To make Rules for the Government and Regulation of the land and naval Forces;

Clause 15: To provide for calling forth the Militia to execute the Laws of the Union, suppress Insurrections and repel Invasions;

Clause 16: To provide for organizing, arming, and disciplining, the Militia, and for governing such Part of them as may be employed in the Service of the United States, reserving to the States respectively, the Appointment of the Officers, and the Authority of training the Militia according to the discipline prescribed by Congress;

> With the Supreme Court's support, Congress has interpreted Clause 3 in a way that has allowed it to expand its involvement in the economy and the daily lives of U.S. citizens, using this clause to regulate business as well as to outlaw racial segregation. However, state governments have frequently challenged Congress's expansion of power by way of the commerce clause when they believe that Congress is infringing on their constitutional authority.

> Congress has the authority to establish the process by which foreigners become citizens (Clause 4). Recently, national legislation has made it more difficult for individuals to file for bankruptcy.

> The authority to make and regulate money as well as to standardize weights and measures is essential to the regulation of commerce (Clause 5).

> Congress exercised its authority under Clause 9 to create the federal court system other than the Supreme Court, which was established under Article III of the Constitution.

> Every nation in the world possesses the authority to establish its own laws regarding crimes outside its borders and violations of international law (Clause 10).

> Clauses 11 through 15 collectively delegate to Congress the authority to raise and support military troops, to enact rules to regulate the troops, to call the troops to action, and to declare war. However, the president as commander in chief (Article II) has the authority to wage war. Presidents have committed armed troops without a declaration of war, leading to disputes over congressional and presidential war powers. Clause 11 also provides Congress with the authority to hire an individual for the purpose of retaliating against another nation for some harm it has caused the United States—that is, to provide a *letter of Marque,* an outdated practice.

> Clauses 15 and 16 guarantee the states the right to maintain and train a militia (today's National Guard), but state control of the militia is subordinate to national control when the national government needs the support of these militias to ensure that laws are executed, to suppress domestic uprisings, and to repel invasion.

POLITICAL INQUIRY: *Several state governments, specifically states that have needed their National Guard troops to help with crises such as massive forest fires, have raised questions about the right of the national government to send National Guard troops to foreign lands such as Afghanistan. Imagine you are arguing in front of the Supreme Court on behalf of the states. What argument would you make to support the states' claim that the national government does not have the right to send National Guard troops to Afghanistan? Now imagine that you are arguing in front of the Court on behalf of the national government. What argument would you make to support the right of the national government to send National Guard troops anywhere in the world?*

Clause 17: To exercise exclusive Legislation in all Cases whatsoever, over such District (not exceeding ten Miles square) as may, by Cession of Particular States, and the Acceptance of Congress, become the Seat of the Government of the United States, and to exercise like Authority over all Places purchased by the Consent of the Legislature of the State in which the Same shall be, for the Erection of Forts, Magazines, Arsenals, dock-Yards and other needful Buildings;—And

> Congress has the authority to govern Washington D.C., which is the seat of the national government. Today, citizens living in Washington D.C. elect local government officials to govern the city with congressional oversight. The national government also governs federal lands throughout the states that are used for federal purposes, such as military installations.

POLITICAL INQUIRY: *Article IV of the Constitution delegates to Congress the authority to admit new states to the union. The citizens of Washington D.C. have petitioned Congress to become a state. What would be the benefits* of making Washington D.C. a state? What problems might arise if Washington D.C. were to become a state?

> Clause 18 grants Congress authority to make all laws it deems necessary and proper to fulfill its responsibilities under the Constitution, including those listed in Section 8. This clause also authorizes Congress to pass laws it deems necessary to ensure that the other two branches are able to fulfill their responsibilities. Congress has also used this clause to expand its powers.

> Article I, Section 9 limits Congress's lawmaking authority and mandates that Congress be accountable to the people in how it spends the public's money.

> Clause 1 barred Congress from passing laws to prohibit the slave trade until 1808 at the earliest. The Thirteenth Amendment (1865) made slavery illegal.

> Clauses 2 and 3 guarantee protections to those accused of crimes. Clause 2 establishes the right of imprisoned persons to challenge their imprisonment in court (through a *writ of habeas corpus*). It notes that Congress can deny the right to a writ of habeas corpus during times of a rebellion or invasion if public safety is at risk.

> Congress cannot pass laws that declare a person or a group of people guilty of an offense (Bills of Attainder). Only courts have the authority to determine guilt. Congress is also prohibited from passing a law that punishes a person tomorrow for an action he or she took that was legal today (ex post facto law).

> Clause 4 prohibits Congress from directly taxing individual people, such as imposing an income tax. The Sixteenth Amendment (1913) authorized congressional enactment of a direct income tax on individual people.

> Congress is prohibited from taxing goods that are exported from any state, either those sent to foreign lands or to other states (Clause 5).

> Congress cannot favor any state over another in its regulation of trade (Clause 6).

> The national government can spend money only as authorized by Congress through enacted laws (no more than authorized and only for the purpose authorized) and must present a public accounting of revenues and expenditures.

> Congress cannot grant individuals special rights, privileges, or a position in government based on their heredity (birth into a family designated as nobility), which is how kings, queens, and other officials were granted their positions in the British monarchy. In addition, federal officials cannot accept gifts from foreign nations except those Congress allows (which today are gifts of minimal value).

> Clause 1 specifically prohibits states from engaging in several activities that the Constitution delegates to the national government, including engaging in foreign affairs and creating currency. In addition, it extends several of the prohibitions on Congress to the states.

> Clause 2 prevents states from interfering in foreign trade without congressional approval.

> States cannot, without congressional approval, levy import taxes, sign agreements or treaties with foreign nations, or enter into compacts (agreements) with other states.

Clause 18: To make all Laws which shall be necessary and proper for carrying into Execution the foregoing Powers and all other Powers vested by this Constitution in the Government of the United States, or in any Department or Officer thereof.

Section 9. (Prohibitions on Congress)

Clause 1: The Migration or Importation of such Persons as any of the States now existing shall think proper to admit, shall not be prohibited by the Congress prior to the Year one thousand eight hundred and eight, but a Tax or duty may be imposed on such Importation, not exceeding ten dollars for each Person.

Clause 2: The Privilege of the Writ of Habeas Corpus shall not be suspended, unless when in Cases of Rebellion or Invasion the public Safety may require it.

Clause 3: No Bill of Attainder or ex post facto Law shall be passed.

Clause 4: No Capitation, or other direct, Tax shall be laid, unless in Proportion to the Census of Enumeration herein before directed to be taken.

Clause 5: No Tax or Duty shall be laid on Articles exported from any State.

Clause 6: No Preference shall be given by any Regulation of Commerce or Revenue to the Ports of one State over those of another: nor shall Vessels bound to, or from, one State, be obliged to enter, clear or pay Duties in another.

Clause 7: No Money shall be drawn from the Treasury, but in Consequence of Appropriations made by Law; and a regular Statement and Account of the Receipts and Expenditures of all public Money shall be published from time to time.

Clause 8: No Title of Nobility shall be granted by the United States: And no Person holding any Office of Profit or Trust under them, shall, without the Consent of the Congress, accept of any present, Emolument, Office, or Title, of any kind whatever, from any King, Prince or foreign State.

Section 10. (Prohibitions on the States)

Clause 1: No State shall enter into any Treaty, Alliance, or Confederation; grant Letters of Marque and Reprisal; coin Money; emit Bills of Credit; make any Thing but gold and silver Coin a Tender in Payment of Debts; pass any Bill of Attainder, ex post facto Law, or Law impairing the Obligation of Contracts, or grant any Title of Nobility.

Clause 2: No State shall, without the Consent of the Congress, lay any Imposts or Duties on Imports or Exports, except what may be absolutely necessary for executing its inspection Laws: and the net Produce of all Duties and Imposts, laid by any State on Imports or Exports, shall be for the Use of the Treasury of the United States; and all such Laws shall be subject to the Revision and Controul of the Congress.

Clause 3: No State shall, without the Consent of Congress, lay any Duty of Tonnage, keep Troops, or Ships of War in time of Peace, enter into any Agreement or Compact with another State, or with a foreign Power, or engage in War, unless actually invaded, or in such imminent Danger as will not admit of delay.

ARTICLE II. (Executive Branch)

Section 1. (Executive Powers of the President)

Clause 1: The executive Power shall be vested in a President of the United States of America. He shall hold his Office during the Term of four Years, and, together with the Vice President, chosen for the same Term, be elected, as follows:

Clause 2: Each State shall appoint, in such Manner as the Legislature thereof may direct, a Number of Electors, equal to the whole Number of Senators and Representatives to which the State may be entitled in the Congress: but no Senator or Representative, or Person holding an Office of Trust or Profit under the United States, shall be appointed an Elector.

Clause 3: The Electors shall meet in their respective States, and vote by Ballot for two Persons, of whom one at least shall not be an Inhabitant of the same State with themselves. And they shall make a List of all the Persons voted for, and of the Number of Votes for each; which List they shall sign and certify, and transmit sealed to the Seat of the Government of the United States, directed to the President of the Senate. The President of the Senate shall, in the Presence of the Senate and House of Representatives, open all the Certificates, and the Votes shall then be counted. The Person having the greatest Number of Votes shall be the President, if such Number be a Majority of the whole Number of Electors appointed; and if there be more than one who have such Majority, and have an equal Number of Votes, then the House of Representatives shall immediately chuse by Ballot one of them for President; and if no Person have a Majority, then from the five highest on the List the said House shall in like Manner chuse the President. But in chusing the President, the Votes shall be taken by States, the Representatives from each State having one Vote; a quorum for this Purpose shall consist of a Member or Members from two thirds of the States, and a Majority of all the States shall be necessary to a Choice. In every Case, after the Choice of the President, the Person having the greatest Number of Votes of the Electors shall be the Vice President. But if there should remain two or more who have equal Votes, the Senate shall chuse from them by Ballot the Vice President.

POLITICAL INQUIRY: *The Electoral College system is criticized for many reasons. Some argue that deciding the presidential election by any vote other than that of the citizens is undemocratic. Others complain that in 2000 the system allowed George W. Bush to become president, even though he had not won the popular vote. Many argue that the Electoral College system should be eliminated and replaced by direct popular election of the president and the vice president. What is (are) the benefit(s) of eliminating the Electoral College? What might be the potential harm to the nation of eliminating the Electoral College?*

Clause 4: The Congress may determine the Time of chusing the Electors, and the Day on which they shall give their Votes; which Day shall be the same throughout the United States.

Clause 5: No Person except a natural born Citizen, or a Citizen of the United States, at the time of the Adoption of this Constitution, shall be eligible to the Office of President; neither shall any person be eligible to that Office who shall not have attained to the Age of thirty five Years, and been fourteen Years a Resident within the United States.

> Article II outlines the authority of the president and the vice president and the process of their selection.

> The Constitution delegates to the president the authority to administer the executive branch of the national government. The term of office for the president and his vice president is four years. No term limit was specified; until President Franklin D. Roosevelt, there was a tradition of a two-term limit. President Roosevelt served four terms.

> The Electoral College system was established as a compromise between those who wanted citizens to elect the president directly and others who wanted Congress to elect the president. Each state government has the authority to determine how their state's electors will be selected.

> Electors, who are selected through processes established by the legislatures of each state, have the authority to select the president and the vice president. Citizens' votes determine who their state's electors will be. Electors are individuals selected by officials of the state's political parties to participate in the Electoral College if the party wins the presidential vote in the state. Before passage of the Twelfth Amendment (1804), each elector had two votes. The candidate receiving the majority of votes won the presidency, and the candidate with the second highest number of votes won the vice presidency. Today, when the electors meet as the Electoral College, each elector casts one vote for the presidency and one vote for the vice presidency. If no presidential candidate wins a majority of the electoral votes, the House selects the president. If no vice-presidential candidate wins a majority of the electoral votes, the Senate selects the vice president.

> Today, by law, national elections are held on the Tuesday following the first Monday in November, in even-numbered years. During presidential election years, the electors gather in their state capitals on the Monday after the second Wednesday in December to vote for the president and the vice president. When Congress convenes in January after the presidential election, its members count the electoral ballots and formally announce the newly elected president and vice president.

> The president (and the vice president) must be at least 35 years old and must have lived within the United States for at least fourteen years. Unlike the citizenship qualification for members of the House and Senate, the president and vice president must be natural-born citizens; they cannot be immigrants who have become citizens after arriving in the United States. Therefore, prominent public figures such as California governor Arnold Schwarzenegger, who was born in Austria, Madeleine Albright, secretary of state under President Clinton, who was born in what is now the Czech Republic, and Senator Mel Martinez (R-Florida), who was born in Cuba, could never be elected president.

> Clause 6 states that the powers and duties of the presidency are transferred to the vice president when the president is no longer able to fulfill them. It also states that Congress can pass legislation to indicate who shall act as president if both the president and the vice president are unable to fulfill the president's powers and duties. The "acting" president would serve until the disability is removed or a new president is elected. The Twenty-Fifth Amendment (1967) clarifies when the vice president acts as president temporarily—such as when the president undergoes surgery—and when the vice president actually becomes president.

> Currently the president's salary is $400,000 per year plus numerous benefits including a nontaxable expense account.

> Under the Constitution, the authority to ensure that laws are carried out is delegated to the president. The president and the vice president are elected to serve concurrent four-year terms. The call for a term limit followed President Franklin Roosevelt's election to a fourth term. The Twenty-Second Amendment (1951) established a two-term limit for presidents.

> The president is the commander of the military and of the National Guard (militia of the several states) when it is called to service by the president. When they are not called to service by the president, the state divisions of the National Guard are commanded by their governors. The president is authorized to establish the cabinet, the presidential advisory body comprising the top officials (secretaries) of each department of the executive branch. As the chief executive officer, the president can exercise a check on the judicial branch by decreasing or eliminating sentences and even pardoning (eliminating guilty verdicts of) federal prisoners.

> The Constitution provides a check on the president's authority to negotiate treaties and appoint foreign ambassadors, top officials in the executive branch, and Supreme Court justices by requiring that treaties be ratified or appointments confirmed by the Senate. Congress can create additional executive branch positions and federal courts and can decree how these legislatively created positions will be filled.

Clause 6: In Case of the Removal of the President from Office, or of his Death, Resignation, or Inability to discharge the Powers and Duties of the said Office, the Same shall devolve on the Vice President, and the Congress may by Law provide for the Case of Removal, Death, Resignation or Inability, both of the President and Vice President, declaring what Officer shall then act as President, and such Officer shall act accordingly, until the Disability be removed, or a President shall be elected.

Clause 7: The President shall, at stated Times, receive for his Services, a Compensation, which shall neither be encreased nor diminished during the Period for which he shall have been elected, and he shall not receive within that Period any other Emolument from the United States, or any of them.

Clause 8: Before he enter on the Execution of his Office, he shall take the following Oath or Affirmation:—"I do solemnly swear (or affirm) that I will faithfully execute the Office of President of the United States, and will to the best of my Ability, preserve, protect and defend the Constitution of the United States."

Section 2. (Powers of the President)

Clause 1: The President shall be Commander in Chief of the Army and Navy of the United States, and of the Militia of the several States, when called into the actual Service of the United States; he may require the Opinion, in writing, of the principal Officer in each of the executive Departments, upon any Subject relating to the Duties of their respective Offices, and he shall have Power to Grant Reprieves and Pardons for Offences against the United States, except in Cases of Impeachment.

Clause 2: He shall have Power, by and with the Advice and Consent of the Senate, to make Treaties, provided two thirds of the Senators present concur; and he shall nominate, and by and with the Advice and Consent of the Senate, shall appoint Ambassadors, other public Ministers and Consuls, Judges of the supreme Court, and all other Officers of the United States, whose Appointments are not herein otherwise provided for, and which shall be established by Law: but the Congress may by Law vest the Appointment of such inferior Officers, as they think proper, in the President alone, in the Courts of Law, or in the Heads of Departments.

Clause 3: The President shall have Power to fill up all Vacancies that may happen during the Recess of the Senate, by granting Commissions which shall expire at the End of their next Session.

> If vacancies occur when the Senate is not in session and is therefore not available to confirm presidential appointees, the president can fill the vacancies. The appointees serve through the end of the congressional session.

POLITICAL INQUIRY: *In recent years, Presidents Bush and Obama have both taken advantage of the constitutional loophole that allows presidents to appoint people without Senate confirmation to make controversial appointments. Should the Constitution be amended to limit further the time an appointee who has not been confirmed can serve by requiring the Senate to consider the appointment when it next reconvenes? Why or why not?*

Section 3. (Responsibilities of the President)

He shall from time to time give to the Congress Information on the State of the Union, and recommend to their Consideration such Measures as he shall judge necessary and expedient; he may, on extraordinary Occasions, convene both Houses, or either of them, and in Case of Disagreement between them, with Respect to the Time of Adjournment, he may adjourn them to such Time as he shall think proper; he shall receive Ambassadors and other public Ministers; he shall take Care that the Laws be faithfully executed, and shall Commission all the Officers of the United States.

> As chief executive officer of the nation, the president is required to ensure that laws are properly implemented by overseeing the executive-branch agencies to be sure they are doing the work of government as established in law. The president is also required from time to time to give an assessment of the status of the nation to Congress and to make recommendations for the good of the country. This has evolved into the annual televised State of the Union Address, which is followed within days by the presentation of the president's budget proposal to Congress. The president can also call special sessions of Congress.

Section 4. (Impeachment)

The President, Vice President and all Civil Officers of the United States, shall be removed from Office on Impeachment for and Conviction of, Treason, Bribery, or other high Crimes and Misdemeanors.

> Presidents, vice presidents, and other federal officials can be removed from office if the members of the House of Representatives formally accuse them of treason (giving assistance to the nation's enemies), bribery, or other vaguely defined abuses of power ("high Crimes and Misdemeanors") and two-thirds of the Senate find them guilty of these charges.

ARTICLE III. (Judicial Branch)

Section 1. (Federal Courts and Rights of Judges)

The judicial Power of the United States, shall be vested in one supreme Court, and in such inferior Courts as the Congress may from time to time ordain and establish. The Judges, both of the supreme and inferior Courts, shall hold their Offices during good Behaviour, and shall, at stated Times, receive for their Services, a Compensation, which shall not be diminished during their Continuance in Office.

> Article III presents the organization and authority of the U.S. Supreme Court and delegates to Congress the authority to create other courts as its members deem necessary.

> To ensure that judges make neutral and objective decisions, and are protected from political influences, federal judges serve until they retire, die, or are impeached by the House and convicted by the Senate. In addition, Congress cannot decrease a judge's pay.

POLITICAL INQUIRY: *Although age discrimination is illegal, the government has allowed a retirement age to be established for some positions. For example, there is a retirement age for airline pilots, and most states have established retirement ages for state judges. What would be the arguments for or against amending the Constitution to establish a retirement age for federal judges?*

Section 2. (Jurisdiction of Federal Courts)

Clause 1: The judicial Power shall extend to all Cases, in Law and Equity, arising under this Constitution, the Laws of the United States, and Treaties made, or which shall be made, under their Authority;—to all Cases affecting Ambassadors, other public ministers and Consuls;—to all Cases of admiralty and maritime Jurisdiction;—to Controversies to which the United States shall be a Party;—to Controversies between two or more States;—between a State and Citizens of another State;—between Citizens of different States;—between Citizens of the same

> Federal courts have the authority to hear all lawsuits pertaining to national laws, the Constitution of the United States, and treaties. They also have jurisdiction over cases involving citizens of different states and citizens of foreign nations. Note that the power of judicial review, that is, the power to declare acts of government officials or bodies unconstitutional, is not enumerated in the Constitution.

State claiming Lands under Grants of different States, and between a State, or the Citizens thereof, and foreign States, Citizens or Subjects.

POLITICAL INQUIRY: *Today there are nine Supreme Court justices, yet the Constitution does not set a specific number for Supreme Court justices. With the increasing number of cases appealed to the Supreme Court, what would be the arguments for or against increasing the number of Supreme Court justices?*

> The Supreme Court hears cases involving foreign diplomats and cases in which states are a party. Today, such cases are rare. For the most part, the Supreme Court hears cases on appeal from lower federal courts.

Clause 2: In all Cases affecting Ambassadors, other public Ministers and Consuls, and those in which a State shall be Party, the supreme Court shall have original Jurisdiction. In all the other Cases before mentioned, the supreme Court shall have appellate Jurisdiction, both as to Law and Fact, with such Exceptions, and under such Regulations as the Congress shall make.

> Defendants accused of federal crimes have the right to a jury trial in a federal court located in the state in which the crime was committed.

Clause 3: The Trial of all Crimes, except in Cases of Impeachment, shall be by Jury; and such Trial shall be held in the State where the said Crimes shall have been committed; but when not committed within any State, the Trial shall be at such Place or Places as the Congress may by Law have directed.

Section 3. (Treason)

> This clause defines treason as making war against the United States or helping its enemies. At least two witnesses to the crime are required for a conviction.

Clause 1: Treason against the United States, shall consist only in levying War against them, or in adhering to their Enemies, giving them Aid and Comfort. No Person shall be convicted of Treason unless on the Testimony of two Witnesses to the same overt Act, or on Confession in open Court.

> This clause prevents Congress from redefining treason. Those found guilty of treason can be punished, but their family members cannot be (no "Corruption of Blood").

Clause 2: The Congress shall have Power to declare the Punishment of Treason, but no Attainder of Treason shall work Corruption of Blood, or Forfeiture except during the Life of the Person attainted.

ARTICLE IV. (State-to-State Relations)

> Article IV establishes the obligations states have to each other and to the citizens of other states.

Section 1. (Full Faith and Credit of legal proceedings and decisions)

> States must respect one another's legal judgments and records, and a contract agreed to in one state is binding in the other states.

Full Faith and Credit shall be given in each State to the public Acts, Records, and judicial Proceedings of every other State. And the Congress may by general Laws prescribe the Manner in which such Acts, Records and Proceedings shall be proved, and the Effect thereof.

POLITICAL INQUIRY: *States have had the authority to legally define marriage since before the Constitution was ratified. Today, one of the many issues being debated is whether states with laws defining marriage as a contract between one man and one woman need to give full faith and credit to a same-sex marriage contract from a state where such marriages are legal, such as Massachusetts. Which level of government do you think has the right to define marriage? Explain your choice. Does the full faith and credit clause require states that deny marriage contracts to same-sex couples to recognize legal same-sex marriage contracts from other states? Can you identify a compelling public interest that you believe can only be achieved by the government denying marriage contracts to same-sex couples?*

Section 2. (Privileges and Immunities of Citizens)

> No matter what state they find themselves in, all U.S. citizens are entitled to the same privileges and rights as the citizens of that state.

Clause 1: The Citizens of each State shall be entitled to all Privileges and Immunities of Citizens in the several States.

> If requested by a governor of another state, a state is obligated to return an accused felon to the state from which he or she fled.

Clause 2: A Person charged in any State with Treason, Felony, or other Crime, who shall flee from Justice, and be found in another State, shall on Demand of the executive Authority of the State from which he fled, be delivered up, to be removed to the State having Jurisdiction of the Crime.

Clause 3: No Person held to Service or Labour in one State, under the Laws thereof, escaping into another, shall, in Consequence of any Law or Regulation therein, be discharged from such Service or Labour, but shall be delivered up on Claim of the Party to whom such Service or Labour may be due.

Section 3. (Admission of New States)

Clause 1: New States may be admitted by the Congress into this Union; but no new State shall be formed or erected within the Jurisdiction of any other State; nor any State be formed by the Junction of two or more States, or Parts of States, without the Consent of the Legislatures of the States concerned as well as of the Congress.

Clause 2: The Congress shall have Power to dispose of and make all needful Rules and Regulations respecting the Territory or other Property belonging to the United States; and nothing in this Constitution shall be so construed as to Prejudice any Claims of the United States, or of any particular State.

Section 4. (National Government Obligations to the States)

The United States shall guarantee to every State in this Union a Republican Form of Government, and shall protect each of them against Invasion; and on Application of the Legislature, or of the Executive (when the Legislature cannot be convened) against domestic Violence.

ARTICLE V. (Formal Constitutional Amendment Process)

The Congress, whenever two thirds of both Houses shall deem it necessary, shall propose Amendments to this Constitution, or, on the Application of the Legislatures of two thirds of the several States, shall call a Convention for proposing Amendments, which, in either Case, shall be valid to all Intents and Purposes, as Part of this Constitution, when ratified by the Legislatures of three fourths of the several States, or by Conventions in three fourths thereof, as the one or the other Mode of Ratification may be proposed by the Congress; Provided that no Amendment which may be made prior to the Year One thousand eight hundred and eight shall in any Manner affect the first and fourth Clauses in the Ninth Section of the first Article; and that no State, without its Consent, shall be deprived of its equal Suffrage in the Senate.

ARTICLE VI. (Supremacy of the Constitution)

Clause 1: All Debts contracted and Engagements entered into, before the Adoption of this Constitution, shall be as valid against the United States under this Constitution, as under the Confederation.

Clause 2: This Constitution, and the Laws of the United States which shall be made in Pursuance thereof; and all Treaties made, or which shall be made, under the Authority of the United States, shall be the supreme Law of the Land; and the Judges in every State shall be bound thereby, any Thing in the Constitution or Laws of any state to the Contrary notwithstanding.

Clause 3: The Senators and Representatives before mentioned, and the Members of the several State Legislatures, and all executive and judicial Officers, both of the United States and of the several States, shall be bound by Oath or Affirmation, to support this Constitution; but no religious Test shall ever be required as a Qualification to any Office or public Trust under the United States.

> The Thirteenth Amendment (1865) eliminated a state's obligation to return slaves fleeing from their enslavement in another state.

> Congress can admit new states to the union, but it cannot alter established state borders without the approval of the states that would be affected by the change.

> The federal government has authority to administer all federal lands, wherever they are located, including national parks and historic sites as well as military installations.

> The national government must ensure that every state has a representative democracy, protect each state from foreign invasion, and assist states in addressing mass breaches of domestic tranquility. Under this section, Congress has authorized the president to send in federal troops to protect public safety. During the civil rights movement, for example, federal troops ensured the safety of black students attending newly desegregated high schools and colleges.

> Article V details the process by which the Constitution can be amended.

> Amendments can be proposed either by Congress or by a special convention called at the request of the states. States have the authority to ratify amendments to the Constitution; three-fourths of the state legislatures must ratify an amendment for it to become part of the Constitution. Every year dozens of constitutional amendments are proposed in Congress, yet only twenty-seven have been ratified since 1789.

> Article VI decrees that the Constitution is the supreme law of the land.

> This provision states that the new federal government created by the Constitution was responsible for the financial obligations of the national government created by the Articles of Confederation.

> The Constitution, and all laws made to fulfill its mission that are in compliance with it, is the supreme law of the land; no one is above the supreme law of the land.

> All national and state officials must take an oath promising to uphold the Constitution. This article also prohibits the government from requiring officeholders to submit to a religious test or swear a religious oath, hence supporting a separation of government and religion.

> Article VII outlines the process by which the Constitution will be ratified.

> When the Constitutional Convention presented the proposed second constitution, the Constitution of the United States, to the states for ratification, the Articles of Confederation (the first constitution) were still in effect. The Articles required agreement from all thirteen states to amend it, which some argued meant that all thirteen states had to agree to replace the Articles of Confederation with the Constitution. Yet the proposed second constitution decreed that it would replace the Articles when nine states had ratified it. The first Congress met under the Constitution of the United States in 1789.

ARTICLE VII. (Constitutional Ratification Process)

Clause 1: The Ratification of the Conventions of nine States, shall be sufficient for the Establishment of this Constitution between the States so ratifying the same.

Clause 2: Done in Convention by the Unanimous Consent of the States present the Seventeenth Day of September in the Year of our Lord one thousand seven hundred and Eighty seven and of the Independence of the United States of America the Twelfth. In witness whereof We have hereunto subscribed our Names,

G. Washington—Presid't.
and deputy from Virginia

Delaware	George Read
	Gunning Bedford, Jr.
	John Dickinson
	Richard Bassett
	Jacob Broom
Maryland	James McHenry
	Daniel of St. Thomas Jenifer
	Daniel Carroll
Virginia	John Blair
	James Madison, Jr.
North Carolina	William Blount
	Richard Dobbs Spaight
	Hugh Williamson
South Carolina	John Rutledge
	Charles Cotesworth Pinckney
	Charles Pinckney
	Pierce Butler
Georgia	William Few
	Abraham Baldwin

New Hampshire	John Langdon
	Nicholas Gilman
Massachusetts	Nathaniel Gorham
	Rufus King
Connecticut	William Samuel Johnson
	Roger Sherman
New York	Alexander Hamilton
New Jersey	William Livingston
	David Brearley
	William Patterson
	Jonathan Dayton
Pennsylvania	Benjamin Franklin
	Thomas Mifflin
	Robert Morris
	George Clymer
	Thomas FitzSimons
	Jared Ingersoll
	James Wilson
	Gouverneur Morris

Amendments to the Constitution of the United States of America

THE BILL OF RIGHTS: AMENDMENTS I–X
(ratified in 1791)

Amendment I (1791)

Congress shall make no law respecting an establishment of religion, or prohibiting the free exercise thereof; or abridging the freedom of speech, or of the press; or the right of the people peaceably to assemble, and to petition the Government for a redress of grievances.

> Government cannot make laws that limit freedom of expression, which includes freedom of religion, speech, and the press, as well as the freedom to assemble and to petition the government to address grievances. None of these individual freedoms is absolute, however; courts balance the protection of individual freedoms (as provided for in this Constitution) with the protection of public safety, including national security.

POLITICAL INQUIRY: *Currently, freedom of speech protects symbolic speech such as the burning of the U.S. flag to make a statement of protest. What reasons are there to amend the Constitution to make burning the flag unconstitutional and hence a form of speech that is not protected by the Constitution? What reasons are there not to do so?*

Amendment II (1791)

A well regulated Militia, being necessary to the security of a free State, the right of the people to keep and bear Arms, shall not be infringed.

> Today, states and the federal government balance the right of the people to own guns with the need to protect the public.

POLITICAL INQUIRY: *Does the phrase "a well regulated Militia" limit the right to bear arms to those engaged in protecting public peace and safety? Why or why not?*

Amendment III (1791)

No Soldier shall, in time of peace be quartered in any house, without the consent of the Owner, nor in time of war, but in a manner to be prescribed by law.

> Military troops cannot take control of private homes during peacetime.

Amendment IV (1791)

The right of the people to be secure in their persons, houses, papers, and effects, against unreasonable searches and seizures, shall not be violated, and no Warrants shall issue, but upon probable cause, supported by Oath or affirmation, and particularly describing the place to be searched, and the persons or things to be seized.

> Government officials must obtain approval before they search or seize a person's property. The approval must come either from the person whose private property they are searching or seizing or from a judge who determines that the government is justified in taking this action to protect public safety and therefore signs a search warrant.

POLITICAL INQUIRY: *Since the terrorist attacks on September 11, 2001, the national government has tried to balance the right of people to be secure in their person and property with public safety and national security. What reasons have the president and members of Congress offered in defense of allowing intelligence agencies to bypass the requirement to get judicial permission to conduct searches or seizures of phone records of suspected terrorists? How valid are those reasons? In your opinion, can they be reconciled with constitutional protections?*

Amendment V (1791)

No person shall be held to answer for a capital, or otherwise infamous crime, unless on a presentment or indictment of a Grand Jury, except in cases arising in the land or naval forces, or in the Militia, when in actual service in time of War or public danger; nor shall any person be

> The Fifth Amendment provides much more than the familiar protection against self-incrimination that we hear people who are testifying before Congress and the courts claim by "taking the Fifth." For example, before the government can punish a person for a crime (take away a person's life, liberty, or pursuit of happiness), it must follow certain procedures specified in law; it must follow *due process of the law*. The federal government guarantees those accused of federal crimes a grand jury hearing in which the government presents its evidence to a selected group of citizens who determine whether there is sufficient evidence to go to trial. If a defendant is found not guilty of a specific criminal offense, he or she cannot be brought to trial again by the same government for the same offense. If the government determines it needs private property for a public use, the owner is compelled to sell the land, and the government must pay a fair price based on the market value of the property.

> The Sixth Amendment outlines additional procedures that the government must follow before taking away a person's life, liberty, or pursuit of happiness. People accused of crimes have the right to know what they are accused of doing, to hear from witnesses against them, and to defend themselves in a trial that is open to the public within a reasonable amount of time after the accusations are made. An indigent (very poor) person is guaranteed a government-provided lawyer in serious criminal cases. It is assumed all others can afford to hire a lawyer.

> Either party (the complainant or the person accused of causing harm or violating a contract) in a federal civil lawsuit involving more than $20 can demand a jury trial.

> The Eighth Amendment protects those accused of crimes as well as those found guilty from overly punitive decisions. Bail, a payment to the government that can be required to avoid incarceration before and during trial, cannot be set at an excessively high amount, unless the judge determines that freedom for the accused would jeopardize public safety or that he or she might flee. The punishment imposed on those convicted of crimes is expected to "fit" the crime: it is to be reasonable given the severity of the crime. Punishment cannot be excessive or cruel.

> The Ninth Amendment acknowledges that there are additional rights, not listed in the preceding eight amendments, that the government cannot deny to citizens. The Supreme Court has interpreted the First Amendment, Fifth Amendment, and the Ninth Amendment to collectively provide individuals with a right to privacy.

> The Tenth Amendment acknowledges that state governments retain all authority they had before ratification of the Constitution that has not been delegated to the national government by the Constitution. This amendment was demanded by the Anti-Federalists, who opposed ratification of this Constitution. The Anti-Federalists feared that the national government would infringe on people's freedoms and on the authority of the state governments. The vagueness of the rights retained by the states continues to cause tensions and disputes between the state governments and the national government.

> The courts have interpreted this amendment to mean that federal courts do not have the authority to hear lawsuits brought by citizens against their own state or against another state, or brought by foreigners against a state.

subject for the same offence to be twice put in jeopardy of life or limb; nor shall be compelled in any criminal case to be a witness against himself, nor be deprived of life, liberty, or property, without due process of law; nor shall private property be taken for public use, without just compensation.

Amendment VI (1791)

In all criminal prosecutions, the accused shall enjoy the right to a speedy and public trial, by an impartial jury of the State and district wherein the crime shall have been committed, which district shall have been previously ascertained by law, and to be informed of the nature and cause of the accusation; to be confronted with the witnesses against him; to have compulsory process for obtaining witnesses in his favor, and to have the Assistance of Counsel for his defence.

POLITICAL INQUIRY: *The resources needed to provide an adequate defense in a criminal case can be quite steep. For example, to ensure a fair trial, a lawyer may use government money to pay for expert witnesses. Argue for or against the need to limit such expenditures for indigent defendants accused of serious crimes.*

Amendment VII (1791)

In Suits at common law, where the value in controversy shall exceed twenty dollars, the right of trial by jury shall be preserved, and no fact tried by a jury, shall be otherwise re-examined in any Court of the United States, than according to the rules of the common law.

Amendment VIII (1791)

Excessive bail shall not be required, nor excessive fines imposed, nor cruel and unusual punishments inflicted.

POLITICAL INQUIRY: *When the Constitution was written, imprisonment was viewed as cruel and unusual punishment of the convicted. Today, there is debate over whether the death penalty (capital punishment) is cruel and unusual. Whatever your opinion is of the death penalty itself, consider some of the techniques used by the government to put people to death. Are they cruel and unusual? Make a case for or against the use of lethal injection, for example.*

Amendment IX (1791)

The enumeration in the Constitution, of certain rights, shall not be construed to deny or disparage others retained by the people.

Amendment X (1791)

The powers not delegated to the United States by the Constitution, nor prohibited by it to the States, are reserved to the States respectively, or to the people.

Amendment XI (1795)

The Judicial power of the United States shall not be construed to extend to any suit in law or equity, commenced or prosecuted against one of the United States by Citizens of another State, or by Citizens or Subjects of any Foreign State.

Amendment XII (1804)

The Electors shall meet in their respective states and vote by ballot for President and Vice-President, one of whom, at least, shall not be an inhabitant of the same state with themselves; they shall name in their ballots the person voted for as President, and in distinct ballots the person voted for as Vice-President, and they shall make distinct lists of all persons voted for as President, and of all persons voted for as Vice-President, and of the number of votes for each, which lists they shall sign and certify, and transmit sealed to the seat of the government of the United States, directed to the President of the Senate;—The President of the Senate shall, in the presence of the Senate and House of Representatives, open all the certificates and the votes shall then be counted;—The person having the greatest Number of votes for President, shall be the President, if such number be a majority of the whole number of Electors appointed; and if no person have such majority, then from the persons having the highest numbers not exceeding three on the list of those voted for as President, the House of Representatives shall choose immediately, by ballot, the President. But in choosing the President, the votes shall be taken by states, the representation from each state having one vote; a quorum for this purpose shall consist of a member or members from two-thirds of the states, and a majority of all the states shall be necessary to a choice. And if the House of Representatives shall not choose a President whenever the right of choice shall devolve upon them, before the fourth day of March next following, then the Vice-President shall act as President, as in the case of the death or other constitutional disability of the President— The person having the greatest number of votes as Vice-President, shall be the Vice-President, if such number be a majority of the whole number of Electors appointed, and if no person have a majority, then from the two highest numbers on the list, the Senate shall choose the Vice-President; a quorum for the purpose shall consist of two-thirds of the whole number of Senators, and a majority of the whole number shall be necessary to a choice. But no person constitutionally ineligible to the office of President shall be eligible to that of Vice-President of the United States.

> The presidential election in 1800 ended with a tie in Electoral College votes between Thomas Jefferson and Aaron Burr. Because the candidate with the most votes was to become president and the candidate with the second highest number of votes was to become vice president, the tie meant that the job of selecting the president was turned over to the House of Representatives. The House selected Jefferson. Calls to change the procedure were answered by the enactment of this amendment. Today, each elector has two votes; one for a presidential candidate and one for a vice-presidential candidate. The presidential candidate who wins the majority of electoral votes wins the presidency, and the same is true for the vice-presidential candidate. If no presidential candidate wins a majority of the votes, the House selects the president. If no vice-presidential candidate wins a majority of the votes, the Senate selects the vice president.

Amendment XIII (1865)

Section 1. Neither slavery nor involuntary servitude, except as a punishment for crime whereof the party shall have been duly convicted, shall exist within the United States, or any place subject to their jurisdiction.

Section 2. Congress shall have power to enforce this article by appropriate legislation.

> This amendment abolished slavery.

Amendment XIV (1868)

Section 1. All persons born or naturalized in the United States and subject to the jurisdiction thereof, are citizens of the United States and of the State wherein they reside. No State shall make or enforce any law which shall abridge the privileges or immunities of citizens of the United States; nor shall any State deprive any person of life, liberty, or property, without due process of law; nor deny to any person within its jurisdiction the equal protection of the laws.

> This amendment extends the rights of citizenship to all those born in the United States and those who have become citizens through naturalization. States are prohibited from denying U.S. citizens their rights and privileges and must provide all people with due process before taking away their life, liberty, or pursuit of happiness. States must also treat all people equally and fairly. The courts have also used this section of the Fourteenth Amendment to require that states ensure citizens their protections under the Bill of Rights.

POLITICAL INQUIRY: *Recently some citizens and politicians have claimed that illegal immigrants and their children, who are citizens if they were born in the United States, cost the nation's taxpayers a great deal of money in public services guaranteed to all citizens, including public education. Argue for or against amending the Constitution to deny citizenship to those born in the United States to parents who are in the country illegally.*

Section 2. Representatives shall be apportioned among the several States according to their respective numbers, counting the whole number of

> This section of the Fourteenth Amendment is the first use of the term "male" in the Constitution. This section requires that if a state denies men over the age of 21 the right to vote, its representation in the House will be diminished accordingly. The Fifteenth Amendment makes this section unnecessary.

> The intent of this section was to prevent government officials who supported the Confederacy during the Civil War from serving in government. In 1898 Congress voted to eliminate this prohibition.

> All male citizens meeting their state's minimum age requirement are guaranteed the right to vote.

> This amendment authorizes the national government to establish taxes on personal and corporate income.

> Since the ratification of the Seventeenth Amendment in 1913, senators are elected by the citizens in each state rather than by state legislatures. The amendment also allows each state legislature to establish the process by which vacancies in the Senate will be filled, either through special election or by gubernatorial appointment.

persons in each State, excluding Indians not taxed. But when the right to vote at any election for the choice of electors for President and Vice President of the United States, Representatives in Congress, the Executive and Judicial officers of a State, or the members of the Legislature thereof, is denied to any of the male inhabitants of such State, being twenty-one years of age, and citizens of the United States, or in any way abridged, except for participation in rebellion, or other crime, the basis of representation therein shall be reduced in the proportion which the number of such male citizens shall bear to the whole number of male citizens twenty-one years of age in such State.

Section 3. No person shall be a Senator or Representative in Congress, or elector of President and Vice President, or hold any office, civil or military, under the United States, or under any State, who, having previously taken an oath, as a member of Congress, or as an officer of the United States, or as a member of any State legislature, or as an executive or judicial officer of any State, to support the Constitution of the United States, shall have engaged in insurrection or rebellion against the same, or given aid or comfort to the enemies thereof. But Congress may by a vote of two-thirds of each House, remove such disability.

Section 4. The validity of the public debt of the United States, authorized by law, including debts incurred for payment of pensions and bounties for services in suppressing insurrection or rebellion, shall not be questioned. But neither the United States nor any State shall assume or pay any debt or obligation incurred in aid of insurrection or rebellion against the United States, or any claim for the loss or emancipation of any slave; but all such debts, obligations and claims shall be held illegal and void.

Section 5. The Congress shall have power to enforce, by appropriate legislation, the provisions of this article.

POLITICAL INQUIRY: *According to the courts' interpretation, the Fourteenth Amendment prohibits discrimination under the law based on a person's race, religion, color, and national origin unless such discrimination is necessary for the government to accomplish a compelling public interest. However, the courts have allowed discrimination based on sex when a government successfully argues that the discrimination is substantially related to the achievement of an important public interest. Argue for or against amending the Constitution so that sex-based discrimination is treated the same as other forms of discrimination.*

Amendment XV (1870)

Section 1. The right of citizens of the United States to vote shall not be denied or abridged by the United States or by any State on account of race, color, or previous condition of servitude.

Section 2. The Congress shall have power to enforce this article by appropriate legislation.

Amendment XVI (1913)

The Congress shall have power to lay and collect taxes on incomes, from whatever source derived, without apportionment among the several States, and without regard to any census or enumeration.

Amendment XVII (1913)

The Senate of the United States shall be composed of two Senators from each State, elected by the people thereof, for six years; and each Senator shall have one vote. The electors in each State shall have the qualifications requisite for electors of the most numerous branch of the State legislatures.

When vacancies happen in the representation of any State in the Senate, the executive authority of such State shall issue writs of election to fill such vacancies: Provided, That the legislature of any State may empower the executive thereof to make temporary appointments until the people fill the vacancies by election as the legislature may direct.

This amendment shall not be so construed as to affect the election or term of any Senator chosen before it becomes valid as part of the Constitution.

Amendment XVIII (1919)

Section 1. After one year from the ratification of this article the manufacture, sale, or transportation of intoxicating liquors within, the importation thereof into, or the exportation thereof from the United States and all territory subject to the jurisdiction thereof for beverage purposes is hereby prohibited.

> The "Prohibition" amendment—making it illegal to manufacture, sell, or transport alcoholic beverages in the United States—was widely disobeyed during the years it was in effect. The Twenty-First amendment repealed this amendment.

Section 2. The Congress and the several States shall have concurrent power to enforce this article by appropriate legislation.

Section 3. This article shall be inoperative unless it shall have been ratified as an amendment to the Constitution by the legislatures of the several States, as provided in the Constitution, within seven years from the date of the submission hereof to the States by the Congress.

Amendment XIX (1920)

The right of citizens of the United States to vote shall not be denied or abridged by the United States or by any State on account of sex. Congress shall have power to enforce this article by appropriate legislation.

> All female citizens meeting their state's minimum age requirement are guaranteed the right to vote.

Amendment XX (1933)

Section 1. The terms of the President and Vice President shall end at noon on the 20th day of January, and the terms of Senators and Representatives at noon on the 3d day of January, of the years in which such terms would have ended if this article had not been ratified; and the terms of their successors shall then begin.

Section 2. The Congress shall assemble at least once in every year, and such meeting shall begin at noon on the 3d day of January, unless they shall by law appoint a different day.

> The first two sections of the Twentieth Amendment establish new starting dates for the president's and vice president's terms of office (January 20) as well as for members of Congress (January 3). Section 2 also decrees that the annual meeting of Congress will begin on January 3 unless Congress specifies a different date.

Section 3. If, at the time fixed for the beginning of the term of the President, the President elect shall have died, the Vice President elect shall become President. If a President shall not have been chosen before the time fixed for the beginning of his term, or if the President elect shall have failed to qualify, then the Vice President elect shall act as President until a President shall have qualified; and the Congress may by law provide for the case wherein neither a President elect nor a Vice President elect shall have qualified, declaring who shall then act as President, or the manner in which one who is to act shall be selected, and such person shall act accordingly until a President or Vice President shall have qualified.

> Sections 3 and 4 of this amendment establish that if the president elect dies before his or her term of office begins, the vice president elect becomes president. If the president elect has not been selected or is unable to begin the term, the vice president elect serves as acting president until the president is selected or is able to serve.

Section 4. The Congress may by law provide for the case of the death of any of the persons from whom the House of Representatives may choose a President whenever the right of choice shall have devolved upon them, and for the case of the death of any of the persons from whom the Senate may choose a Vice President whenever the right of choice shall have devolved upon them.

Section 5. Sections 1 and 2 shall take effect on the 15th day of October following the ratification of this article.

Section 6. This article shall be inoperative unless it shall have been ratified as an amendment to the Constitution by the legislatures of three-fourths of the several States within seven years from the date of its submission.

> With this amendment, the Eighteenth Amendment's prohibition of the manufacture, sale, and transportation of alcoholic beverages was repealed.

> This amendment established a two-term limit for the presidency, or in the case of a vice president succeeding to the presidency and then running for reelection, a maximum limit of ten years in office.

> Citizens living in Washington D.C. are given the right to elect three voting members to the Electoral College. Before this amendment, these citizens were not represented in the Electoral College.

> Governments are prohibited from requiring a person to pay a tax in order to vote.

Amendment XXI (1933)

Section 1. The eighteenth article of amendment to the Constitution of the United States is hereby repealed.

Section 2. The transportation or importation into any State, Territory, or possession of the United States for delivery or use therein of intoxicating liquors, in violation of the laws thereof, is hereby prohibited.

Section 3. This article shall be inoperative unless it shall have been ratified as an amendment to the Constitution by conventions in the several States, as provided in the Constitution, within seven years from the date of the submission hereof to the States by the Congress.

Amendment XXII (1951)

Section 1. No person shall be elected to the office of the President more than twice, and no person who has held the office of President, or acted as President, for more than two years of a term to which some other person was elected President shall be elected to the office of the President more than once. But this Article shall not apply to any person holding the office of President, when this Article was proposed by the Congress, and shall not prevent any person who may be holding the office of President, or acting as President, during the term within which this Article becomes operative from holding the office of President or acting as President during the remainder of such term.

Section 2. This article shall be inoperative unless it shall have been ratified as an amendment to the Constitution by the legislatures of three-fourths of the several States within seven years from the date of its submission to the States by the Congress.

POLITICAL INQUIRY: *Critics of term limits in general argue that they are undemocratic because they may force out of office an official whom the voters want to keep in office as their representative. Other critics of term limits for the president argue that forcing out a popular, successful president during a time of war may be harmful to the nation. Argue for or against eliminating the two-term limit for the presidency.*

Amendment XXIII (1961)

Section 1. The District constituting the seat of Government of the United States shall appoint in such manner as the Congress may direct: A number of electors of President and Vice President equal to the whole number of Senators and Representatives in Congress to which the District would be entitled if it were a State, but in no event more than the least populous State; they shall be in addition to those appointed by the States, but they shall be considered, for the purposes of the election of President and Vice President, to be electors appointed by a State; and they shall meet in the District and perform such duties as provided by the twelfth article of amendment.

Section 2. The Congress shall have power to enforce this article by appropriate legislation.

Amendment XXIV (1964)

Section 1. The right of citizens of the United States to vote in any primary or other election for President or Vice President, for electors for President or Vice President, or for Senator or Representative in Congress, shall not be denied or abridged by the United States or any State by reason of failure to pay any poll tax or other tax.

Section 2. The Congress shall have power to enforce this article by appropriate legislation.

Amendment XXV (1967)

Section 1. In case of the removal of the President from office or of his death or resignation, the Vice President shall become President.

Section 2. Whenever there is a vacancy in the office of the Vice President, the President shall nominate a Vice President who shall take office upon confirmation by a majority vote of both Houses of Congress.

Section 3. Whenever the President transmits to the President pro tempore of the Senate and the Speaker of the House of Representatives his written declaration that he is unable to discharge the powers and duties of his office, and until he transmits to them a written declaration to the contrary, such powers and duties shall be discharged by the Vice President as Acting President.

Section 4. Whenever the Vice President and a majority of either the principal officers of the executive departments or of such other body as Congress may by law provide, transmit to the President pro tempore of the Senate and the Speaker of the House of Representatives their written declaration that the President is unable to discharge the powers and duties of his office, the Vice President shall immediately assume the powers and duties of the office as Acting President.

Thereafter, when the President transmits to the President pro tempore of the Senate and the Speaker of the House of Representatives his written declaration that no inability exists, he shall resume the powers and duties of his office unless the Vice President and a majority of either the principal officers of the executive department or of such other body as Congress may by law provide, transmit within four days to the President pro tempore of the Senate and the Speaker of the House of Representatives their written declaration that the President is unable to discharge the powers and duties of his office. Thereupon Congress shall decide the issue, assembling within forty-eight hours for that purpose if not in session. If the Congress, within twenty-one days after receipt of the latter written declaration, or, if Congress is not in session, within twenty-one days after Congress is required to assemble, determines by two-thirds vote of both Houses that the President is unable to discharge the powers and duties of his office, the Vice President shall continue to discharge the same as Acting President; otherwise, the President shall resume the powers and duties of his office.

Amendment XXVI (1971)

Section 1. The right of citizens of the United States, who are eighteen years of age or older, to vote shall not be denied or abridged by the United States or by any State on account of age.

Section 2. The Congress shall have power to enforce this article by appropriate legislation.

Amendment XXVII (1992)

No law varying the compensation for the services of the Senators and Representatives shall take effect, until an election of Representatives shall have intervened.

> The vice president becomes president if the president resigns or dies.

> The president can nominate a person to fill a vice-presidential vacancy. Congress must approve the nominee. President Richard Nixon appointed and Congress confirmed Gerald Ford to the vice presidency when Vice President Spiro Agnew resigned. When President Nixon resigned, Vice President Ford, who had not been elected, became president. He subsequently appointed and Congress confirmed Nelson Rockefeller to be vice president.

> If the president indicates in writing to Congress that he or she cannot carry out the duties of office, the vice president becomes acting president until the president informs Congress that he or she is again fit to resume the responsibilities of the presidency.

> If the vice president in concert with a majority of cabinet officials (or some other body designated by Congress) declares to Congress in writing that the president is unable to fulfill the duties of office, the vice president becomes acting president until the president claims he or she is again fit for duty. However, if the vice president and a majority of cabinet officials challenge the president's claim, then Congress must decide within three weeks if the president can resume office.

> The Twenty-Sixth Amendment guarantees citizens 18 years of age and older the right to vote.

> Proposed in 1789, this amendment prevents members of Congress from raising their own salaries. Approved salary increases cannot take effect until after the next congressional election.

Federalism

THEN

The newly created national government and the preexisting state governments acted independently as they implemented the innovative federal system of government established in 1789.

NOW

National, state, and local governments challenge one another regularly over the proper interpretation of the Constitution's distribution of power in the federal system.

NEXT

Will Supreme Court justices continue to issue conflicting interpretations of federalism?

Will state and local governments continue their efforts to be laboratories for the creation of effective domestic policies?

Will intergovernmental relations evolve so that government can provide more efficient, effective public service?

This chapter examines the nature and evolution of the constitutional distribution of authority between the national and state governments in the U.S. federal system of government.

FIRST, we take an *overview of the U.S. federal system* and its distinct dual sovereignty.

SECOND, we explore the details of dual sovereignty by considering the *constitutional distribution of authority* between the national and state governments.

THIRD, we focus on the *evolution of the federal system* and see how national and state governments' power relationships have changed over time.

FOURTH, we survey the complex intergovernmental relations that dominate *today's federalism: intergovernmental relations.*

The framers of the Constitution

of the United States balanced their preference for a strong central government with their critics' calls for retaining state government authority over day-to-day matters by creating a system of government with dual sovereignty. That is, the Constitution established a new central government that would coexist with the existing state governments and distributed governing authority to these two levels of government—the national and the state—with each level having ultimate authority over different policy matters and different geographic areas. The framers called this new system of government a *federal system*. Because the federal system was a product of negotiation and compromise, as Chapter 2 explored, the constitutional language that distributes authority between the national and the state governments is not always clear.

Since the 1789 creation of the federal system, the number of governments in the United States has grown, as new states have joined the union and state governments have created local governments to help them serve their states' citizens better. Today, with more than 89,000 distinct governments in the United States—one national, 50 state, and over 89,476 local governments—and given vague constitutional language regarding the proper authority of national and state governments, the courts frequently must interpret the framers' intent with respect to the distribution of authority. Among the conflicts over jurisdiction that have reached the courts are disagreements over which level of government has the authority to set the legal drinking age, to establish gun-free school zones, to legalize the medical use of marijuana, and to determine which votes count in a presidential election.

Wherever you live in the United States, at least four or five governments collect taxes from you, provide services to you, and establish your rights and responsibilities. With so many governments in action, citizens who are interested in influencing public policies have many access points. Yet which government has the authority to address your concerns may not be clear to you. It may not even be clear to government officials. Ultimately, the Constitution, as interpreted by the U.S. Supreme Court justices, determines which government is responsible for which matters.

Even as the wrangling continues over the proper interpretation of the constitutional distribution of authority between governments, the U.S. national, state, and local governments engage every day in collaborative efforts to fulfill the complex, costly needs of the people whom they serve. Such intergovernmental efforts are essential in today's world. But they complicate attempts to clarify which level of government is ultimately responsible for which services and policies.

An Overview of the U.S. Federal System

federal system
a governmental structure with two levels of government in which each level has sovereignty over different policy matters and geographic areas

The U.S. Constitution established an unprecedented government structure characterized by a federal system of governance. A **federal system** has two constitutionally recognized levels of government, each with sovereignty—that is, ultimate governing authority, with no legal superior—over different policy matters and geographic areas. According to the Constitution, the national government has ultimate authority over some matters, and the state governments hold ultimate authority over different matters. In addition, the national government's jurisdiction covers the entire geographic area of the nation, and each state government's jurisdiction covers the geographic area within the state's borders. The existence of two governments, each with ultimate authority over different matters and geographic areas—an arrangement called dual sovereignty—is what distinguishes the federal system of government from the two other most common systems of government, known as unitary and confederal. The American colonists' experience with a unitary system, and subsequently the early U.S. citizens' life under a confederal system (1781–1788), led to the creation of the innovative federal system.

Unitary System

Colonial Americans lived under Great Britain's unitary system of government. Today, the majority of the world's nations, including Great Britain, have unitary governments. In a **unitary system,** the central government is sovereign. It can create other governments (regional governments) and delegate powers and responsibilities to them. The central government in a unitary system can also unilaterally take away any responsibilities it has delegated to the regional governments it creates and can even eliminate the regional governments.

Indeed, under Britain's unitary system of government during the American colonial period, the British Crown (the sovereign government) created colonial governments and gave them authority to handle day-to-day matters such as regulating marriages, resolving business conflicts, providing for public safety, and maintaining roads. As the central government in Britain approved tax and trade policies that harmed the colonists' quality of life, growing public discourse and dissension spurred the colonists to protest. It was the colonists' failed attempts to influence the central government's policies—by lobbying the king's selected colonial governors, sending petitions to the king, and boycotting certain goods—that eventually sparked more radical acts such as the Boston Tea Party and the colonists' declaration of independence from Great Britain.

unitary system
a governmental structure in which one central government has sovereignty, although it may create regional governments to which it delegates responsibilities

Confederal System

When the colonies declared their independence from Great Britain in 1776, each became an independent sovereign state and adopted its own constitution. As a result, no state had a legal superior. In 1777, delegates from every state except Rhode Island met in a convention and agreed to a proposed alliance of the thirteen sovereign state governments. In 1781, the thirteen independent state governments ratified the Articles of Confederation, the first U.S. constitution, which created a confederal system of government.

In a **confederal system,** several independent sovereign governments (such as the thirteen state governments in the American case) agree to cooperate on specified matters while each retains ultimate authority over all other governmental matters within its borders. The cooperating sovereign governments delegate some responsibilities to a central governing body. Each sovereign government selects its own representatives to the central governing body. The sovereign governments retain ultimate authority in a confederal system for the simple reason that they can recall their delegates from the central government at any time and can either carry out or ignore the central government's policies.

As detailed in Chapter 2, the effectiveness of the confederation created by the Articles of Confederation increasingly came into question. In February 1787, the national Congress passed a resolution calling for a constitutional convention "for the sole and express purpose of revising the Articles of Confederation" in order to preserve the Union. Clear-eyed about the failures of the unitary and confederal systems, the colonists decided to experiment with a unique government system—a federal system. The federal system created by the Constitution of the United States has succeeded in preserving the union for over 220 years.

confederal system
a structure of government in which several independent sovereign governments agree to cooperate on specified governmental matters while retaining sovereignty over all other governmental matters within their jurisdictions

Federal System

The state delegates who met in Philadelphia in 1787 drafted a new constitution that created an innovative federal system of government with dual sovereignty. The Constitution's framers established dual sovereignty by detailing a new, sovereign national government for

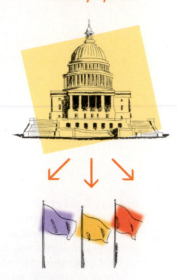

Unitary System

The central government is sovereign, with no legal superior. It may create state governments and delegate legal authority to them. It can also eliminate such governments.

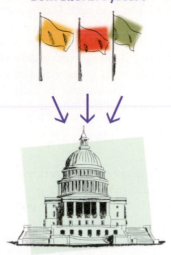

Confederal System

An alliance exists among independent sovereign governments, which delegate limited authority to a central government of their making. The independent sovereign governments retain sovereignty, with no legal superior, over all matters they do not delegate to the central government.

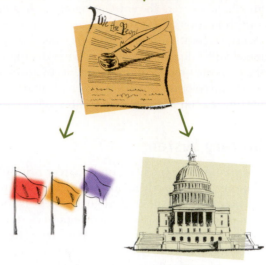

Federal System

State governments are sovereign in specified matters, and a central (national) government is sovereign in other specified matters. The matters over which each government is sovereign are set forth in a constitution, which is the supreme law of the land. Dual sovereignty is the distinguishing characteristic of a federal system.

POLITICAL INQUIRY

FIGURE 3.1 ■ **Who is sovereign in a unitary system of government? In a confederal system of government? In a federal system of government? Which of the systems of government does the United States have, and why?**

the United States and modifying the sovereignty of the existing state governments. The national government thus created has no legal superior on matters over which the Constitution gives it authority, and the state governments have no legal superior on the matters over which they are granted authority by the Constitution.

Such dual sovereignty does not exist in unitary and confederal systems, where sovereignty is held by one level of government (the central government in a unitary system and the regional governments in a confederal system). Figure 3.1 compares the three types of governing systems. The European Union (EU), or United States of Europe, represents the most recent innovation in governmental systems. See "Global Context" for a look at this new governing system.

The federal system, as it works in the United States today, can be confusing—not only to citizens but also to elected officials and even Supreme Court justices. The confusion occurs because in addition to the one national and fifty distinct state governments that are operating in the country today, more than 89,000 local governments are functioning, even though the Constitution does not mention local governments.

It is state constitutions that authorize states to create local governments. State governments delegate some of their responsibilities to these local governments through legislation and/or the approval of a *charter*, which is a local government's version of a constitution. At the same time, state governments have the authority to take back delegated responsibilities and even to eliminate local governments. Because the state government retains ultimate authority over all the matters it delegates to its local governments and can eliminate its local governments, the relationship between a state government and its local governments is *unitary* (following a unitary system of governmental structure).

INTERGOVERNMENTAL RELATIONS (IGR)   To govern, a government must have the authority to formulate and approve a plan of action, to raise and spend money to finance the plan, and to hire workers to put the plan into action. In the U.S. federal system

GLOBAL CONTEXT

THE UNITED STATES OF EUROPE

Clearly not a unitary system, the European Union (EU) claims to be "more than just a confederation of countries, but . . . not a federal State." The principles, institutions, and power relationships of the EU have developed over the last fifty years through a series of treaties among European nations. The current twenty-seven EU member states have delegated some of their national sovereignty to several shared institutions (each with legislative, executive, and/or judicial functions) through a series of treaties, not in one single document such as the Constitution of the United States.

What are some potential future impacts of EU membership—good and bad—for EU member nations?

Each European country that joins the EU has its own constitution and maintains its national sovereignty— with all inherent powers of sovereignty—in order to further its national interests. (Each state in the United States has its own constitution; however, the Constitution of the United States is the supreme law of the land and distributes sovereignty between the national government and the state governments.) Yet when a country joins the EU, it agrees to follow the decisions of the EU institutions, which focus on the collective interests of European nations.

The roots of the EU reach back to 1951. That year, six countries—Belgium, the Federal Republic of Germany, France, Italy, Luxembourg, and the Netherlands—signed a treaty establishing among themselves a common market for their coal and steel. By the 1960s, these six countries had signed additional treaties in which they expanded their common market to a wide range of goods and services, eliminated import taxes on one another's goods, and established common trade and agricultural policies. The success of those policies soon led to agreement on common social and environmental policies as well. Moreover, additional European countries joined what the world knew as the European Economic Community (EEC).

By 1990, twelve European countries belonged to the EEC, and they turned their attention to negotiating a new treaty to clarify the principles and the institutions of their government system. In 1992, the presidents and prime ministers of the EEC countries signed the Treaty on European Union, better known as the Treaty of Maastricht, for the Dutch city in which it was signed. The Treaty of Maastricht, which took effect in 1993, defines the foundations for the current EU institutions and the relationships among these bodies.

Originally, the collaborative efforts of European countries focused on a common European market for the sale of goods and services, as noted above. Today, however, EU policies range well beyond economic considerations. Indeed, the EU targets a wide range of policy areas, including environmental protection, public health, consumer rights, transportation, education, economic development, and fundamental human rights.

> Traditionally, the number twelve is a symbol of perfection, completeness, and unity. The circle of twelve gold stars on the European Union flag represents solidarity, harmony, and unity among the peoples and nations of Europe.

SOURCE: "Europe in 12 Lessons," *Europa*, http://europa.eu/abc/12lessons/index_en.htm.

---

today, the responsibility for these three elements of any given public policy—the policy *statement,* the policy *financing,* and the policy *implementation*—may rest entirely with one level of government (national, state, or local), or it may be shared in a collaborative effort by two or more of these levels. Political scientists label the collaborative efforts of two or more levels of government working to serve the public **intergovernmental relations (IGR).** The provision of elementary and secondary public education is an example of IGR.

Education is a policy matter that the U.S. Constitution reserves for the states. In all but four states, the state governments have created school districts—which are local-level governments—to provide elementary and secondary education. In providing education, the school districts implement national and state policy, as well as their own policy statements.

intergovernmental relations (IGR)
collaborative efforts of two or more levels of government working to serve the public

For example, Titles VI and IX of the national Civil Rights Act require equal educational opportunities for all children no matter their race, religion, ethnicity, color, or sex. The national Individuals with Disabilities Education Act mandates equal educational opportunity for all children no matter their disabilities. Among other policies, state laws determine what requirements an individual must meet to earn state certification to teach in public schools. State compulsory education laws determine for how many years, or until what grade, children must attend school. School districts determine policies for the day-to-day operations of elementary and secondary schools, including school dress codes, the hours of the school day, and discipline procedures.

All three levels of government provide some funding for elementary and secondary education. School districts collect property taxes from those who own property within the geographic area covered by the district. State governments grant money to each school district to supplement its property tax revenue. On average, state grants to school districts cover about 50 percent of the total cost of elementary and secondary education. Historically, the federal government provided grants to pay for less than 10 percent of elementary and secondary education costs. However, in 2009 the national government designated $4 billion for school reform efforts. Known as the Race to the Top Fund, these federal dollars were given to states to encourage and reward their creation of the conditions for education innovation and reform; their achievement of significant improvement in student outcomes; and their implementation of plans to improve student assessment, teacher effectiveness, and data collection.[1] State and federal grant money comes with rules and regulations that direct the policies and the actions of grant recipients.

School districts hire the personnel—teachers, custodians, coaches, librarians, cafeteria workers, principals, superintendents, and others—who implement national, state, and school district policies. The United States thus delivers the public service of elementary and secondary education through a complex network of intergovernmental relations wherein the three levels of government share policy making and financing, and the school districts dominate policy implementation.

We can measure the scope of IGR today by looking at the distribution of the workers whom national, state, and local governments hire to deliver specific public services. The graphs in Figure 3.2 show some policies that are purely national and several that are truly intergovernmental. Another gauge of the extent of IGR is the percentage of national grant money that state and local governments spend on the delivery of specific services. In 2007, federal grants to state and local governments made up 28 percent of all state and local expenditures.[2]

WHAT A FEDERAL SYSTEM MEANS FOR CITIZENS

For citizens, living in a federal system of government means that their legal rights and liberties and their civic responsibilities vary depending on where they live. The majority of U.S. citizens live under the jurisdiction of at least five governments: national, state, county (called *borough* in Alaska and *parish* in Louisiana), municipal or township, and school district. Each of these governments can impose responsibilities on the people living in its jurisdiction. The most obvious responsibility is to pay taxes. These taxes can include the national personal income tax; state sales and personal income taxes; and county, municipal, township, and school district property taxes. Each government can also guarantee personal liberties and rights. The Constitution lists individual liberties in the Bill of Rights. In addition, every state constitution has its own bill of rights, and some local governments offer further protections to their citizens. For example, some cities and counties prohibit discrimination based on an individual's sexual orientation, yet most states do not, nor does the national government.

Thus, the federal system can be confusing for citizens. It can also be confusing for the many governments created to serve the people. Which government is responsible for what services and policies? Because the Constitution of the United States is the supreme law of the land, it is to the Constitution that we must turn to answer that question. Yet constitutional language is not always clear. As we saw in Chapter 2, the framers hammered out the Constitution through intensive bargaining and compromise that produced a text that is often vague and ambiguous.

Also as discussed in Chapter 2, the U.S. Supreme Court has the authority to determine what the Constitution means and hence what is constitutional. This authority came from the Court's decision in the *Marbury v. Madison* case (1803), in which the justices established the principle of judicial review: the Court's authority to determine whether an action of any government operating within the United States violates the Constitution.[3]

Although the Supreme Court is the final interpreter of the Constitution, the Court's *constructions* (interpretations) have changed over time. For example, it is true that dual sovereignty—and therefore a federal system—still exists in the United States today, but the courts have interpreted the Constitution in such a way that the authority of the national government has expanded significantly over the last 220-plus years. In addition, the determination of which government has ultimate authority over specific matters has become even less clear because of the evolution of a complex arrangement of various levels of government working together to meet the various responsibilities that the Constitution delegates, implies, or reserves to them.

Later in this chapter, we consider this evolution of the U.S. federal system. Before we do, it is useful to examine the constitutional distribution of authority to the national and state governments.

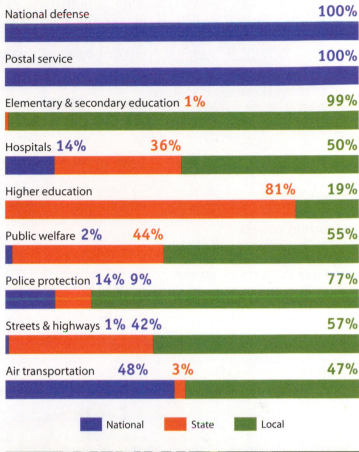

Who Employs the Public Servants?

	National	State	Local
National defense	100%		
Postal service	100%		
Elementary & secondary education	1%		99%
Hospitals	14%	36%	50%
Higher education		81%	19%
Public welfare	2%	44%	55%
Police protection	14%	9%	77%
Streets & highways	1%	42%	57%
Air transportation	48%	3%	47%

National **State** **Local**

POLITICAL INQUIRY

FIGURE 3.2 ■ What proportion of employees working in the postal service is national? What proportion of employees working in elementary and secondary education is national? What explains the difference in these two cases?

SOURCE: U.S. Census Bureau, "All Governments—Employment and Payroll by Function: 2006," www.census.gov/compendia/statab/tables/09s0444.pdf.

Constitutional Distribution of Authority

By distributing some authority to the national government and different authority to the state governments, the Constitution creates the dual sovereignty that defines the U.S. federal system. The Constitution specifically lists the several matters over which the national government has ultimate authority, and it implies additional national authority. The Constitution spells out just a few matters over which the state governments have authority. Part of the reason there is a lack of constitutional detail on state authority is that at the time of the Constitution's drafting, the states expected to retain their authority, except for matters that, by way of the Constitution, they agreed to turn over to the newly created national government.

To fulfill their responsibilities to their citizens, both the national and the state governments have the authority to engage in the functions inherent to all sovereign governments. This authority extends to the concurrent powers, the first topic in this section.

Concurrent Sovereign Authority

concurrent powers
basic governing functions of all sovereign governments, in the United States they are held by the national, state, and local governments and include the authority to tax, to make policy, and to implement policy

To function, sovereign governments need the authority to make policy, raise money, establish courts to interpret policy when a conflict arises about its meaning, and implement policy. These authorities are recognized as *inherent* to all governments—they are defining characteristics of governments. In the U.S. federal system, we designate these inherent governing functions as the **concurrent powers** because the national and the state governments hold these powers jointly and each can use them at the same time. For example, national and state governments make their own public policies, raise their own revenues, and spend those revenues to implement their policies. State governments delegate these authorities, in limited ways, to the local governments they create so that they can function as governments. (Figure 3.3 presents the number of local governments in each state.)

Number of Local Governments in Each State

WA 1,845
OR 1,546
ID 1,240
MT 1,273
ND 2,699
MN 3,526
WI 3,120
MI 2,893
NH 545
VT 733
ME 850
NY 3,403
MA 861
RI 134
CT 649
NJ 1,383
DE 338
MD 256
NV 198
UT 599
WY 726
SD 1,983
NE 2,659
IA 1,954
IL 6,994
IN 3,231
OH 3,702
PA 4,871
WV 663
VA 511
CA 4,344
CO 2,416
KS 3,931
MO 3,723
KY 1,346
AZ 645
NM 863
OK 1,880
AR 1,548
TN 928
NC 963
SC 698
AL 1,185
GA 1,439
MS 1,000
LA 526
TX 4,835
FL 1,623
AK 177
HI 19

POLITICAL INQUIRY

FIGURE 3.3 ■ What might explain the range in the number of local governments that exist in the fifty states? Do the states with the largest geographic area have the largest number of local governments? Are there regional patterns? Do states with smaller populations have fewer local governments?

SOURCE: www.census.gov/govs/cog/GovOrgTab03ss.html.

In addition to the inherent governing powers that the national and state governments hold concurrently, in the federal system of dual sovereignty, the national government and the state governments have sovereignty over different matters. We now consider these distinct sovereign powers.

National Sovereignty

The Constitution distributes powers that are (1) enumerated, or specifically listed, and (2) implied for the national government's three branches—legislative, executive, and judicial. For example, Article I of the Constitution enumerates (lists) the matters over which Congress holds the authority to make laws, including interstate and foreign commerce, the system of money, general welfare, and national defense. These matters are **enumerated powers** of the national government. The Constitution also gives Congress **implied powers**—that is, powers that are not explicitly described but may be interpreted to be necessary to fulfill the enumerated powers. Congress specifically receives implied powers through the Constitution's **necessary and proper clause,** sometimes called the **elastic clause** because the national government uses this passage to stretch its enumerated authority. The necessary and proper clause states that Congress has the power to "make all laws which shall be necessary and proper" for carrying out its enumerated powers.

Articles II and III of the Constitution also enumerate powers of the national government. Article II delegates to the president the authority to ensure the proper implementation of national laws and, with the advice and consent of the U.S. Senate, the authority to make treaties with foreign nations and to appoint foreign ambassadors. With respect to the U.S. Supreme Court and the lower federal courts, Article III enumerates jurisdiction over legal cases involving constitutional issues, national legislation, and treaties. The jurisdiction of the Supreme Court also extends to disagreements between two or more state governments, as well as to conflicts between citizens from different states. Figure 3.4 lists the national powers enumerated in Articles I, II, and III of the Constitution.

THE SUPREMACY CLAUSE The country's founders obviously anticipated disagreements over the interpretation of constitutional language and prepared for them by creating the Supreme Court. The Court has mostly supported the national government when states, citizens, or interest groups have challenged Congress's use of the necessary and proper clause to take on new responsibilities beyond its enumerated powers. Unless the Supreme Court finds a national law to be outside of the enumerated or implied powers, that law is constitutional and hence the **supreme law of the land,** as defined by the supremacy clause in Article VI of the Constitution: "This Constitution, and the laws of the United States which shall be made in pursuance thereof; and all treaties made, or which shall be made, under the authority of the United States, shall be the supreme law of the land." State and local governments are thereby obligated to comply with national laws that implement national enumerated and implied powers, as well as with treaties—including treaties with Native American nations.

NATIONAL TREATIES WITH INDIAN NATIONS

Throughout U.S. history, the national government has signed treaties with Native American nations, which are legally viewed as sovereign foreign nations. As with all treaties, treaties with Native American nations are

enumerated powers
the powers of the national government that are listed in the Constitution

implied powers
powers of the national government that are not enumerated in the Constitution but that Congress claims are necessary and proper for the national government to fulfill its enumerated powers in accordance with the necessary and proper clause of the Constitution

necessary and proper clause (elastic clause)
a clause in Article I, Section 8, of the Constitution that gives Congress the power to do whatever it deems necessary and constitutional to meet its enumerated obligations; the basis for the implied powers

supreme law of the land
the Constitution's description of its own authority, meaning that all laws made by governments within the United States must be in compliance with the Constitution

NATIONAL POWERS

- Punish offenses against the laws of the nation
- Lay and collect taxes for the common defense and the general welfare
- Coin and regulate money
- Establish courts inferior to the U.S. Supreme Court
- Raise and support armies
- Administer the Capitol district and military bases
- Declare war
- Organize, arm, and discipline state militias when called to suppress insurrections and invasions
- Provide for copyrights for authors and inventors
- Regulate interstate and foreign commerce
- Regulate the armed forces
- Provide and maintain a navy
- Establish standard weights and measures
- Create naturalization laws
- Punish the counterfeiting of money
- Punish piracies and felonies on the seas
- Develop roads and postal service
- Define bankruptcy

FIGURE 3.4

Enumerated Powers of National Government

supreme law with which the national government and state and local governments must comply. The core issue in the majority of these treaties is the provision of land (reservations) on which the native peoples could resettle after non-Indians took their lands during the eighteenth and nineteenth centuries. Today, the federal government recognizes more than 550 Indian tribes. Although most Native Americans no longer live on reservations—most native peoples have moved to cities—approximately three hundred reservations remain, in thirty-four states.[4] Figure 3.5 indicates the number of federally recognized tribes in each state.

Even though Indian reservations lie within state borders, national treaties and national laws, not state or local laws, apply to the reservation populations and lands. State and local laws, including laws having to do with taxes, crime, and the environment, are unenforceable on reservations. Moreover, Native American treaty rights to hunt, fish, and gather on reservations and on public lands supersede national, state, and local environmental regulations.[5]

With the exception of Native American reservations, state governments are sovereign within their state borders over matters the Constitution distributes to them. What are the matters that fall within state sovereignty?

State Sovereignty

The Constitution specifies only a few state powers. It provides the states with a role in national politics and gives them the final say on formally amending the Constitution. One reason for the lack of constitutional specificity regarding state authority is that the state governments were already functioning when the states ratified the Constitution. Other than those responsibilities that the states agreed to delegate to the newly created federal government through their ratification of the Constitution, the states expected to retain

Federally Recognized Indian Tribes and Groups

FIGURE 3.5

Federally Recognized Indian Tribes and Groups

SOURCE: www.ncsl.org/?tabid=13278.

their sovereignty over all the day-to-day matters internal to their borders that they were already handling. Yet the original Constitution did not speak of this sovereignty explicitly.

POWERS DELEGATED TO THE STATES The state powers enumerated in the Constitution give the states a distinct voice in the composition and priorities of the national government. Members of Congress are elected by voters in their home state (in the case of senators) or their home district (in the case of representatives in the House). Voters also participate in the election of their state's Electoral College electors, who vote for the president and the vice president on behalf of their state, as we saw in Chapter 2. Overall, state voters expect that the officials whom they elect to the national government will carefully consider their concerns when creating national policy. This is representative government in action.

In addition to establishing the various electoral procedures that give voice to state interests in the national policy-making process, the Constitution creates a formal means by which the states can ensure that their constitutional authority is not changed or eliminated without their approval. Specifically, the Constitution stipulates that three-fourths of the states (through votes in either their legislatures or special conventions, as discussed in Chapter 2) must ratify amendments to the Constitution. By having the final say in whether the supreme law of the land will be changed through the passage of amendments, the states can protect their constitutional powers. Indeed, they did just that when they ratified the Tenth Amendment (1791).

POWERS RESERVED TO THE STATES The Constitution's extremely limited attention to state authority caused concern among citizens of the early American republic. Many people feared that the new national government would meddle in matters for which states had been responsible, in that way compromising state sovereignty. Citizens were also deeply concerned about their freedoms, corresponding to the protections listed in each state constitution's bill of rights. As described in Chapter 2, the states ratified the Bill of Rights, the first ten amendments to the Constitution, in response to those concerns.

The Tenth Amendment asserts that the "powers not delegated to the United States by the Constitution, nor prohibited by it to the states, are *reserved to the states* [emphasis added] respectively, or to the people." This **reserved powers** clause of the Tenth Amendment acknowledged the domestic matters over which the states had exercised authority since the ratification of their own constitutions. These matters included the ordinary, daily affairs of the people—birth, death, marriage, intrastate business, commerce, crime, health, morals, and safety. The states' reserved powers to protect the health, safety, lives, and property of their citizens are referred to as their **police powers.** It was over these domestic matters, internal to each state, that the states retained sovereignty according to the Tenth Amendment. In addition, state courts retained sovereignty over legal cases that involve their state's constitution and legislation (and that do not also raise issues involving the U.S. Constitution). Figure 3.6 summarizes the constitutionally reserved and enumerated powers of the states at the time of the Tenth Amendment's ratification.

The Tenth Amendment's affirmation of state sovereignty is brief and vague, and the Supreme Court continues to this day to resolve conflicts over its interpretation. New cases, leading to fresh interpretations, come before the Court when state governments challenge national laws that the states deem to infringe on their reserved powers but that the national government claims to fulfill its enumerated or implied powers. New interpretations by the Court also arise when the national government or citizens challenge the constitutionality of a state or local government action. Citizens, local

reserved powers
the matters referred to in the Tenth Amendment over which states retain sovereignty

police powers
the states' reserved powers to protect the health, safety, lives, and properties of residents in a state

STATE POWERS

- Conduct local, state, and national elections
- Establish republican forms of government
- Build and maintain infrastructure (roads, bridges, canals, ports)
- Administer family laws (e.g., marriage and divorce)
- Establish criminal laws (except on the high seas)
- Provide education
- Tax estates and inheritance
- Protect public health and safety
- Regulate occupations and professions
- Regulate intrastate commerce
- Protect property rights
- Regulate banks and credit
- Establish insurance laws
- Regulate charities
- Conduct public works
- Regulate land use

FIGURE 3.6

Constitutionally Delegated and Reserved State Powers

governments, state governments, and the national government persistently ask the courts to resolve constitutional conflicts in order to protect their liberties, their rights, and, in the case of governments, their sovereignty.

The Supreme Court's Interpretation of National versus State Sovereignty

McCulloch v. Maryland
established that the necessary and proper clause justifies broad understandings of enumerated powers

The landmark case of ***McCulloch v. Maryland*** (1819) exemplifies a Supreme Court ruling that established the use of the implied powers to expand the national government's enumerated authority.[6] The case stemmed from Congress's establishment of a national bank, and in particular a branch of that bank located in the state of Maryland, which the Maryland state authorities tried to tax. Attorneys for the state of Maryland argued that if the federal government had the authority to establish a national bank and to locate a branch in Maryland, then Maryland had the power to tax the bank. On a more basic level, Maryland's legal counsel asserted that Congress did not have the constitutional authority to establish a national bank, noting that doing so was not an enumerated power. Lawyers for the national government in turn argued that federal authority to establish a national bank was implied and that Maryland's levying a tax on the bank was unconstitutional, for it impinged on the national government's ability to fulfill its constitutional responsibilities by taking some of its financial resources.

The Supreme Court decided in favor of the national government. The justices based their ruling on their interpretation of the Constitution's necessary and proper clause and the enumerated powers of Congress to "lay and collect taxes, to borrow money . . . and to regulate commerce among the several states." The Court said that combined, these powers implied that the national government had the authority to charter a bank and to locate a branch in Maryland. In addition, the Court found that Maryland did not have the right to tax that bank, because taxation by the state would interfere with the exercise of federal authority. In addition to establishing that the necessary and proper clause justifies broad understandings of the enumerated powers, the Court affirmed once and for all that in the event of a conflict between national legislation (the law chartering the national bank) and state legislation (Maryland's tax law), the national law is supreme *as long as* it is in compliance with the Constitution's enumerated and implied powers.

THE POWER TO REGULATE COMMERCE A few years later, in the case of *Gibbons v. Ogden* (1824), the Supreme Court again justified a particular national action on the basis of the implications of an enumerated power.[7] The *Gibbons* case was the first suit brought to the Supreme Court seeking clarification on the constitutional meaning of *commerce* in the Constitution's clause on the regulation of interstate commerce. The Court established a broad definition of commerce: "all commercial intercourse—meaning all business dealings." The conflict in this case concerned which government, New York State or the national government, had authority to regulate the operation of boats on the waterways between New York and New Jersey. The Court ruled that regulation of commerce implied regulation of navigation and that therefore the national government had authority to regulate it, not New York State.

Following the *Gibbons* decision, the national government frequently justified many of its actions by arguing that they were necessary to fulfill its enumerated powers to regulate interstate commerce, and the Court typically agreed. The case of *United States v. Lopez* (1995) is an example, however, of the Court's recent trend of being more critical of Congress's at-

> In 1995, the U.S. Supreme Court ruled the national Gun-Free School Zones legislation unconstitutional and affirmed that the Constitution reserves to the *states* the power to establish gun-free school zones. Notice the bilingual gun-free and drug-free school zone signs at this Phoenix, Arizona, school.

tempts to use the commerce clause to justify a national law.[8] The context for the case is the national Gun-Free School Zones Act of 1990, which mandated gun-free zones within a specified area surrounding schools. The lawyers for Alfonso Lopez, a twelfth-grader charged with violating this national law by bringing a .38-caliber handgun to school, successfully argued that the law was unconstitutional. The Court rejected the national government attorney's argument that the 1990 law was a necessary and proper means to regulate interstate commerce. Instead, the Court found that the law was a criminal statute, for which the state governments, not the national government, have authority.[9]

THE POWER TO PROVIDE FOR THE GENERAL WELFARE Another enumerated power that has expanded through Court interpretation of what the Constitution implies is the power of the national government to provide for the general welfare. The national government's landmark Social Security Act of 1935 was a response to the Great Depression's devastating impact on the financial security of countless Americans. The congressional vote to establish Social Security was overwhelmingly favorable. Yet the constitutionality of this very expansive program, which has become the most expensive national program, was tested in the courts shortly after its passage. In 1937, the Supreme Court had to decide: Was Social Security indeed a matter of general welfare for which Congress is delegated the authority to raise and spend money? Or was Social Security a matter for the state governments to address?[10] The Court found the national policy to be constitutional—a reasonable congressional interpretation, the justices wrote, of the enumerated and implied powers of the national government.

The Supreme Court's decisions in the *McCulloch, Gibbons,* and Social Security cases set precedents for the expansion of national power in domestic policy matters by combining the necessary and proper clause with such enumerated powers as the regulation of commerce and providing for the general welfare. The Court continues today to support Congress's use of the elasticity provided by the implied powers clause to expand its delegated powers. The Court also continues to protect national enumerated powers. Yet Congress does not always get its way, as the justices' decision in the *Lopez* case indicates.

In addition to establishing dual sovereignty and creating two independently operating levels of government, the Constitution enumerates some obligations that the national government has to the states—the topic to which we now turn.

National Obligations to the States

On August 27, 2005, the day before Katrina (a powerful category 3 hurricane) hit the Gulf Coast states, National Hurricane Center director Max Mayfield personally called the governors of Mississippi and Louisiana and the mayor of New Orleans. Mayfield wanted to be sure that these state and local officials understood the severity of the approaching storm.[11] That same day, President George W. Bush declared a national state of emergency for the area, and Mississippi governor Haley Barbour did the same for his state. Louisiana governor Kathleen Blanco had declared a state of emergency for her state the day before. New Orleans mayor Ray Nagin ordered a mandatory evacuation of the city's 485,000 residents.[12] Federal Emergency Management Administration (FEMA) director Michael Brown told state and local officials in the Gulf states that FEMA was ready with all available assistance and was "going to move quick . . . and going to do whatever it takes to help disaster victims."[13]

Even with this apparent readiness at all levels of government, the impact of Katrina's subsequent flooding in New Orleans because of a levee break was devastating: over 1,200 people dead, more than 1 million evacuees, and an estimated $200 billion-plus of damage.[14] The devastation prompted questions about the national government's obligations to local and state governments and to citizens in times of disaster. The Constitution describes several obligations that the national government has to the states, including assistance during times of domestic upheaval (see Table 3.1).

Department of Homeland Security (DHS) secretary Michael Chertoff explained four days after Katrina hit that the national government steps in "to assist local and state authorities. Under the Constitution, state and local authorities have the principal first line of response

> President George W. Bush, New Orleans Mayor Ray Nagin (to the left of the president), and Louisiana Governor Kathleen Blanco (far left, behind the mayor) visit with homeowner Ethel Williams, whose home was devastated by Hurricane Katrina. Federal, state, and local governments, as well as non-profit organizations receiving government funds and charitable donations, worked together to address Katrina's devastation.

TABLE 3.1

National Obligations to the States

The federal government:

- must treat states equally in matters of the regulation of commerce and the imposition of taxes
- cannot approve the creation of a new state from the property of an existing state without the consent of the legislatures of the states concerned
- cannot change state boundaries without the consent of the states concerned
- must guarantee a republican form of government
- must protect states from foreign invasion
- at their request, must protect states against domestic violence

obligation. DHS has the coordinating role, or the managing role. The president has, of course, the ultimate responsibility for all the federal effort here. I want to emphasize the federal government does not supersede the state and local government."[15]

There is no denying the national government's constitutional obligation to assist state and local governments in times of domestic upheaval. Yet does the national government have to wait for state or local officials to ask for help before it takes action? The Constitution is not clear about that question, and to date the courts have not rendered an interpretation on the matter.

State-to-State Obligations: Horizontal Federalism

Just as the Constitution establishes national obligations to the states, it also defines state-to-state obligations. In Article IV, the Constitution sets forth obligations that the states have to one another. Collectively, these state-to-state obligations and the relationships they mandate are forms of **horizontal federalism.** For example, state governments have the right to forge agreements with other states, known as **interstate compacts.** Congress must review and approve interstate compacts to ensure that they do not harm the states that are not party to them and the nation as a whole. States enter into cooperative agreements to provide services and benefits for one another, such as monitoring paroled inmates from other states; sharing and conserving natural resources that spill over state borders, such as water; and decreasing pollution that crosses state borders.

States also cooperate through a procedure called **extradition,** the legal process of sending individuals back to a state that accuses them of having committed a crime, and from which they have fled. The Constitution establishes a state governor's right to request the extradition of an accused criminal. Yet the courts have also supported governors' refusals to extradite individuals.

The Constitution asserts, too, that each state must guarantee the same **privileges and immunities** to all U.S. citizens—that is, citizens from other states who visit or move into the state—that it provides its own citizens. This guarantee does not prohibit states from imposing reasonable requirements before extending rights to visiting or new state residents. For example, states can and do charge higher tuition costs to out-of-state college students. In addition, in many states, new state residents must wait thirty days before they can register to vote. Yet no state can deny new state residents who are U.S. citizens the right to register to vote once they meet a reasonable state residency requirement.

Today, one very controversial state-to-state obligation stems from the full faith and credit clause of Article IV, Section 1, of the Constitution. The **full faith and credit clause** asserts that each state must recognize as legally binding (that is, valid and enforceable) the public acts, records, and judicial proceedings of every other state. For example, states must recognize the validity of out-of-state driver's licenses. Currently, public debate is ongoing about the impact of the full faith and credit clause on same-sex marriage contracts, and hence the constitutionality of the national Defense of Marriage Act (DOMA) of 1996, which allows states to determine whether they will recognize same-sex marriage contracts or same-sex civil union contracts legalized in other states. President Obama's Justice Department is also reviewing the constitutionality of DOMA.

The debates over same-sex marriage and civil unions raise several challenging constitutional questions. Because the Constitution is supreme, answers to those questions will eventually come from the Supreme Court's interpretation of the Constitution. Recently, the Supreme Court ruled that although the Constitution *is* the supreme law, state and local governments can guarantee their citizens more liberties and rights than are found in the Constitution, which guarantees only the required minimum.

> The Justice Department, under the direction of U.S. Attorney General Eric Holder, is tackling a variety of federalism questions as it considers the constitutionality of numerous pieces of state and national legistlation including the Defense of Marriage Act (1996), which allows states discretion in providing "full faith and credit" to same-sex marriage and civil union contracts made in other states.

The New Judicial Federalism

Political scientists use the phrase **new judicial federalism** to describe the practice whereby state judges base decisions regarding citizens' legal rights and liberties on their state constitutions when those laws guarantee more than the minimum rights or liberties enumerated in the U.S. Constitution. In fact, many state and local governments grant more liberties and rights than the Constitution guarantees, and can do so, according to the Supreme Court.

In *Pruneyard Shopping Center and Fred Sahadi v. Michael Robins et al.* (1980), the Court considered the case of a group of politically active high school students who had set up tables in a mall to hand out informational pamphlets and obtain signatures on a petition.[16] The pamphlets and petition dealt with opposition to the United Nations' stand on Zionism—that is, the existence of the Jewish state of Israel. After the owner of the shopping center asked the students to leave his private property, the students sued him on the basis of their belief that the California state constitution specifically protected their freedom of speech and expression, even in a privately owned shopping center. The Supreme Court agreed with the students that California's constitution gave its citizens more freedom of expression than the U.S. Constitution guaranteed, and judged that greater freedom to be constitutional.

New judicial federalism expands the authority of state governments in an era when the Supreme Court is ever more frequently being asked to clarify the constitutional distribution of authority. As we have seen, the delineation among national powers (enumerated and implied) and the states' reserved powers has never been clear. To complicate matters, over the course of U.S. history, national, state, and local governments' interactions have evolved into collaborative efforts whereby the creation, financing, and implementation of a given public policy are shared by two or more levels of government through intergovernmental relations. We now explore the evolution of intergovernmental relations in the U.S. federal system.

Evolution of the Federal System

Evolution is a slow and continuous change, often from the simple to the complex. The federal system established by the Constitution has evolved from a simple system of *dual federalism* to a complex system of intergovernmental relations characterized by *conflicted federalism*.

Evolution has occurred in the power relationship between the national government and the states, the state governments and their local governments, and the national government

horizontal federalism
the state-to-state relationships created by the U.S. Constitution

interstate compacts
agreements between states that Congress has the authority to review and reject

extradition
the return of individuals accused of a crime to the state in which the crime was committed upon the request of that state's governor

privileges and immunities clause
the Constitution's requirement that a state extend to other states' citizens the privileges and immunities it provides for its own citizens

full faith and credit clause
the constitutional clause that requires states to comply with and uphold the public acts, records, and judicial decisions of other states

new judicial federalism
the practice whereby state judges base decisions regarding civil rights and liberties on their state's constitution, rather than the U.S. Constitution, when their state's constitution guarantees more than minimum rights

and local governments. However, our focus here is on the evolution of the dual sovereignty established by the U.S. federal system of government. We first survey four types of federalism, characterized by four different power relationships between the national and the state governments, all of which continue to this day. We then explore various means by which the national government has altered the power relationship between it and the state governments.

Dual Federalism

dual federalism
the relationship between the national and state governments, dominant between 1789 and 1932, whereby the two levels of government functioned independently of each other to address their distinct constitutional responsibilities

Initially, the dual sovereignty of the U.S. federal system was implemented in such a way that the national and state governments acted independently of each other, as in political scientist Deil Wright's coordinate model of intergovernmental relations. (See "Analyzing the Sources.") Political scientists give the name **dual federalism** to this pattern of implementation of the federal system, whereby the national government takes care of its enumerated powers and the states independently take care of their reserved powers. From 1789 through 1932, dual federalism was the dominant pattern of national-state relations. Congresses and presidents did enact some laws that states argued infringed on their powers, and the Courts typically found in favor of the states in those cases. Yet as the 1819 *McCulloch* case shows, sometimes the Court ruled in favor of the national government.

Cooperative Federalism

grant-in-aid (intergovernmental transfer)
transfer of money from one government to another government that does not need to be paid back

A crippling economic depression that reached global proportions, known as the Great Depression, began in 1929. To help state governments deal with the domestic problems spawned by the economic collapse, Congress and President Franklin D. Roosevelt (1933–1945) approved numerous policies, collectively called the New Deal. Through those policies, the independent actions of national and state governments to fulfill their respective responsibilities evolved into cooperative efforts. **Grants-in-aid**—transfers of money from one level of government to another (also known as **intergovernmental transfers**)—became a main mechanism of President Roosevelt's New Deal programs.

The national grants of money offered to the state governments, and eventually also to local governments, during the Great Depression had few specific terms and conditions and did not need to be paid back. State and local governments welcomed the national grants, which assisted them in addressing the domestic matters that fell within their sovereignty while allowing them to make most of the specific program decisions to implement the policy. The era of federalism that began during the Depression, with its growing number of collaborative, intergovernmental efforts to address domestic matters reserved to the states, is the period of **cooperative federalism** (1932–1963), described by Wright's overlapping model. (See "Analyzing the Sources.")

cooperative federalism
the relationship between the national and state governments whereby the two levels of government work together to address domestic matters reserved to the states, driven by the policy priorities of the states

Centralized Federalism

centralized federalism
the relationship between the national and state governments whereby the national government imposes its policy preferences on state governments

By the time of Lyndon Johnson's presidency (1963–1969), a new kind of federalism was replacing cooperative federalism. In this new form of federalism, the national government imposed its own policy preferences on state and local governments. Specifically, in **centralized federalism,** directives in national legislation, including grant-in-aid programs with ever-increasing conditions or strings attached to the money, force state and local governments to implement a particular national policy. Wright's inclusive model comes closest to diagramming centralized federalism. (See "Analyzing the Sources.")

devolution
the process whereby the national government returns policy responsibilities to state and/or local governments

Presidents since Richard Nixon (1969–1974) have fought against this centralizing tendency by proposing to return policy responsibilities (policy making, policy financing, and policy implementation) to state and local governments. Presidents Nixon and Ronald Reagan (1981–1989) gave the name *new federalism* to their efforts to revert such obligations to state and local governments, and today we use the term **devolution** to refer to the return of policy responsibilities to state and local governments.

ANALYZING THE SOURCES

DEIL WRIGHT'S MODELS OF INTERGOVERNMENTAL RELATIONS IN A FEDERAL SYSTEM

The diagram below presents Deil Wright's models of intergovernmental relations in the United States.* The *coordinate model,* indicates that the relationship between the national government and state governments is one of independence. Each government has autonomy over its functions. The *overlapping model* shows the interdependent relationships among all three levels of government in the United States. Wright argues that the authority pattern in the overlapping model is based on bargaining between the national and the state governments. Finally, the *inclusive model* shows dependent relationships with a hierarchical pattern of authority.

*Deil Wright, *Understanding Intergovernmental Relations,* 3rd ed. © 1988 Wadsworth, a part of Cengage Learning, Inc.

Evaluating the Evidence

① Which of Wright's models do you think the Constitution's framers—the creators of the U.S. federal system—had in mind? Justify your selection.

② Which of Wright's models do you think best presents the relationships among the national, state, and local governments today? Explain.

③ Which model displays the relationships and pattern of authority that you believe will best serve you and your family? Justify your selection.

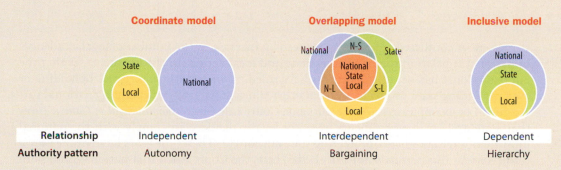

	Coordinate model	Overlapping model	Inclusive model
Relationship	Independent	Interdependent	Dependent
Authority pattern	Autonomy	Bargaining	Hierarchy

Republicans and Democrats (including presidents, members of Congress, and state and local lawmakers) broadly support devolution, but they debate *which elements of the policy-making process* should be devolved: policy creation, financing, and/or implementation. They also butt heads over *which policies* to devolve. The legislation and court decisions that result from these debates make for a complicated coexistence of dual federalism, cooperative federalism, and centralized federalism.

Conflicted Federalism

David B. Walker, a preeminent scholar of federalism and intergovernmental relations, uses the term **conflicted federalism** to describe today's national-state governmental relations, which involve the conflicting elements of dual, cooperative, and centralized federalisms.[17] Efforts to centralize policy making at the national level are evident, as are efforts to decentralize the implementation of national policies to the state and local levels. For some policy matters, the national and state governments operate independently of each other, and hence dual federalism is at work. For most policies, however, intergovernmental efforts are the norm. These efforts may be voluntary and a means to advance state policy priorities (cooperative federalism), or they may be compelled by national legislation (centralized federalism).

conflicted federalism
the current status of national-state relations that involve the conflicting elements of dual, cooperative, and centralized federalisms

> Benjamin Franklin's 1754 cartoon, displaying a rattlesnake cut in eight pieces and the phrase "Join, or Die," emphasized the need for the colonies to work together against threats by Native Americans. During the War for Independence, the cartoon became popular as a symbol of the need for colonies to unite. In 1775, the newly established U.S. Navy first flew the Gadsden Flag, which portrays a coiled rattlesnake with 13 rattles and the phrase "Don't Tread on Me," symbolizing the power and persistence of the united colonies. Today's Tea Party movement members, angered by a national government they perceive to be too involved in their lives and the economy—in violation of the founders' notion of federalism—have adopted the Gadsden Flag as a symbol of their patriotic anger.

The era of conflicted federalism, has seen an increase in the number of legal challenges to national legislation that mandates state and local action. In the various cases that the Supreme Court has heard, the justices have ruled inconsistently, sometimes upholding or even expanding state sovereignty and at other times protecting or expanding national sovereignty. For example, in 1976 the Supreme Court ruled in *National League of Cities v. Usery* that state and local governments were not legally required to comply with the national minimum wage law—hence protecting state authority.[18] Then nine years later, in the *Garcia v. San Antonio Transportation Authority* (1985) case, the Court ruled that national minimum wage laws did apply to state and local government employees—thus expanding national authority.[19]

Another policy matter that has been subject to conflicting Court decisions is the medical use of marijuana. California has fought an up-and-down battle with the national government over medical uses of marijuana. In 1996, California voters approved the Compassionate Use Act, allowing people to grow, obtain, or smoke marijuana for medical needs, with a doctor's recommendation. Then in 2001, the U.S. Supreme Court ruled that the national government could charge people who distributed marijuana for medical use with a crime, even in California, where the state law allowed such activity.[20] The Court interpreted the national supremacy clause to mean that national narcotics laws took precedence over California's law, which California had argued was grounded in the reserved powers of the states. But in 2003, the Court refused to review a case challenging a California law allowing doctors to recommend marijuana use to their patients.[21] As a consequence of the Court's refusal to take on the case, the decision from the lower court prevailed. The lower court's ruling had been that doctors could *not* be charged with a crime for recommending marijuana to patients. To add to the confused legal status of medicinal marijuana in California, the U.S. Supreme Court in 2005 upheld the right of the national government to prosecute people who smoke the drug at the recommendation of their doctors, as well as those who grow it for medical purposes.[22]

The confusion caused by conflicting Court decisions regarding medical marijuana has become even more problematic since October 2009, when President Obama's attorney general announced that the federal government will not prosecute individuals who are dispensing marijuana or who are using it in compliance with state law in one of the states that

has legalized such activities. How did the U.S. federal system evolve from dual federalism to today's conflicted federalism?

Landmarks in the Evolution of Federalism: Key Constitutional Amendments

Understanding the U.S. federal system's evolution from dual federalism to conflicted federalism requires a brief review of the tools the national government uses to expand its authority to direct state and local governments' domestic policies. Although the formal language of the Constitution with regard to the distribution of national and state sovereignty remains essentially as it was in 1791 (when the Tenth Amendment was ratified), three amendments—the Fourteenth, Sixteenth, and Seventeenth—have had a tremendous impact on the power relationship between national and state government. The Civil War, which was a catalyst for the ratification of the Fourteenth Amendment, also influenced the national-state power relationship.

THE CIVIL WAR AND THE POSTWAR AMENDMENTS

The military success of the northern states in the Civil War (1861–1865) meant the preservation of the union—the United States of America. The ratification of the Thirteenth Amendment (1865) brought the legal end of slavery in every state. In addition, the Fourteenth Amendment (1868), which extended the rights of citizenship to individuals who were previously enslaved, also placed certain limits and obligations on state governments.

The Fourteenth Amendment authorizes the national government to ensure that the state governments follow fair procedures (due process) before taking away a person's life, liberties, or pursuit of happiness and that the states guarantee all people the same rights (equal protection of the laws) to life, liberties, and the pursuit of happiness, without discrimination. In addition, the amendment guarantees the privileges and immunities of U.S. citizenship to all citizens in all states. Accordingly, since the Fourteenth Amendment's ratification, Congresses and presidents have approved national laws that direct the states to ensure due process and equal protection. This legislation includes, for example, laws mandating that all government buildings, including state and local edifices, provide access to all persons, including individuals with physical disabilities. In addition, the Supreme Court has used the Fourteenth Amendment to justify extending the Bill of Rights' limits on national government to state and local governments (under incorporation theory, which

Chapter 4 considers). And in *Bush v. Gore* (2000), the Supreme Court used the amendment's equal protection clause to end a controversial Florida ballot recount in the 2000 presidential election.[23]

Conducting elections is a power reserved for the states. Therefore, state laws detail how citizens will cast their votes and how the state will count them to determine the winners. In the 2000 presidential election, Democratic candidate Al Gore successfully challenged, through Florida's court system, the vote count in that state. The Florida State Supreme Court interpreted Florida election law to require the state to count ballots that it initially did not count. In response, Republican candidate George W. Bush challenged the Florida Supreme Court's finding by appealing to the U.S. Supreme Court. Lawyers for candidate Bush argued that Florida's election law violated the Fourteenth Amendment's equal protection clause by not ensuring that the state would treat each person's vote equally. The U.S. Supreme Court found in favor of candidate Bush, putting an end to the vote recount called for by the Florida Supreme Court. Candidate Bush became President Bush. (For more on the 2000 election, see Chapter 9.)

> A Broward County, Florida, election official attempts to determine whether there is a countable vote on this ballot during the 2000 presidential election. The Florida Supreme Court called for a recount of ballots in several counties, but the U.S. Supreme Court stopped the Florida recount, finding that the subjectivity of election officials determining which votes were countable violated the Constitution's equal protection clause.

THE SIXTEENTH AMENDMENT Passage of the Sixteenth Amendment (1913) powerfully enhanced the ability of the national government to raise money. It granted Congress the authority to collect income taxes from workers and corporations without apportioning those taxes among the states on the basis of population (which had been mandated by the Constitution before this amendment). The national government uses these resources to meet its constitutional responsibilities and to assist state governments in meeting their constitutional responsibilities. Moreover, the national government also uses these resources as leverage over state and local governments, encouraging or coercing them to pursue and implement policies that the national government thinks best. Specifically, by offering state and local governments grants-in-aid, national officials have gained the power to determine many of the policies these governments approve, finance, and implement. For example, by offering grants to the states for highways, the federal government encouraged each state to establish a legal drinking age of 21 years (which we explore later in the chapter).

THE SEVENTEENTH AMENDMENT Before ratification of the Seventeenth Amendment in 1913, the Constitution called for state legislatures to select U.S. senators. By that arrangement, the framers strove to ensure that Congress and the president would take the concerns of state governments into account in national policy making. Essentially, the original arrangement provided the state legislatures with lobbyists in the national policy-making process who would be accountable to the states. Once ratified, the Seventeenth Amendment shifted the election of U.S. senators to a system of popular vote by the citizens in a state.

With that change, senators were no longer directly accountable to the state legislatures' because the latter no longer selected the senators. Consequently, state governments lost their direct access to national policy makers. Some scholars of federalism and intergovernmental relations argue that this loss has decreased the influence of state governments in national policy making.[24]

Further Evolutionary Landmarks: Grants-in-Aid

In 1837, the national government shared its revenue surplus with the states in the form of a monetary grant. But the government did not make a habit of such financial grants-in-aid until the Great Depression of the 1930s. Today, there is growing controversy over the strings attached to the various kinds of grants issued by the federal government.

CATEGORICAL GRANTS Historically, the most common type of grant-in-aid has been the **categorical formula grant**—a grant of money from the federal government to state and local governments for a narrow purpose, as defined by the federal government. The legis-

categorical formula grant
money granted by the national government to state and local governments for a specified program area and in an amount based on a legislated formula

lation that creates such a grant includes a formula determining how much money is available to each grant recipient. The formula is typically based on factors related to the purpose of the grant, such as the number of people in the state in need of the program's benefits. The Census Bureau collects much of the data used in grant formulas through the decennial (occurring every ten years) census, which is mandated by the U.S. Constitution. (More than 400 billion grant dollars will be distributed based on the data collected in the 2010 Census.) Categorical grants come with strings—that is, rules and regulations with which the recipient government must comply.

One typical condition is a matching funds requirement, which obligates the government receiving the grant to spend some of its own money to match a specified percentage of the grant money provided. Matching funds requirements allow the national government to influence the budget decisions of state and local governments by forcing them to spend some of their own money on a national priority, which may or may not also be a state priority, in order to receive national funding.

Since the 1960s, the national government has also offered categorical project grants. Like the categorical formula grant, a **categorical project grant** covers a narrow purpose (program area), but unlike the formula grant, a project grant does not include a formula specifying how much money a recipient will receive. Instead, state and local governments interested in receiving such a grant must compete for it by writing proposals detailing what programs they wish to implement and what level of funding they need. A categorical project grant has strings attached to it and typically offers much less funding than a categorical formula grant.

The National Decennial Census

THEN (1990)	NOW (2010)
State and local governments played a limited role in updating the Census Bureau address lists for the 1990 Census.	State and local governments are very involved in updating the Census Bureau address lists for the 2010 Census.
State and local governments played a limited role in educating people about, and encouraging people to complete, the Census.	State and local governments, as well as community organizations, are very involved in educating people about, and encouraging people to complete, the Census, with a focus on illegal immigrants.
One in six households received the long Census questionnaire, with 100 questions.	All households receive the same Census questionnaire, with 10 questions.
Respondents were instructed to select one of the listed races to define themselves.	Respondents are instructed to select all relevant races from the list to define themselves.

WHAT'S NEXT?

> Do you think the response rate for the 2010 Census will surpass the response rate of the 2000 Census? Explain your answer.

> Will state and local governments become even more involved in the Census in the future? Explain your answer.

BLOCK GRANTS Another type of formula-based intergovernmental transfer of money, the **block grant,** differs from categorical formula and categorical project grants in that the use of the grant money is less narrowly defined by the national government. Whereas a categorical grant might specify that the money is to be used for a child care program, a block grant gives the recipient government more discretion to determine what program it will be used for within a broad policy area such as assistance to economically needy families with children. When first introduced by the Nixon administration in the 1970s, the block grant also had fewer strings attached to it than the categorical grants. Today, however, the number and the specificity of conditions included in block grants are increasing.

AMERICAN RECOVERY AND REINVESTMENT ACT OF 2009 In February 2009, President Obama and the 111th Congress enacted the American Recovery and Reinvestment Act (ARRA). The goal of the ARRA was to stimulate the nation's economy, which was in the depths of what some have called the Great Recession. The ARRA included

categorical project grant
money granted by the national government to state and local governments for a specified program area; state and local governments compete for these grants by proposing specific projects they want to implement

block grant
money granted by the national government to states or localities for broadly defined policy areas, with fewer strings than categorical grants, and in amounts based on complicated formulas

$499 billion in spending, $280 billion of which went to state and local governments through grants. Most of the money that was quickly distributed to state and local governments was in the form of categorical formula grants for specific government programs related to health, nutrition, and income security, such as unemployment. Where states had more discretion over the use of grant money, they used it to keep people employed or to create new jobs. For example, state and local governments used the grants to keep teachers and police officers on the job. Moreover, they created jobs in the construction industry by hiring private construction firms to do government construction projects. The federal government stimulus money in the form of competitive categorical project grants was distributed more slowly because state and local governments had to prepare proposals that made a case for the federal government to fund their projects. Categorical project grants provided funds for energy efficiency programs, broadband access, high-speed rail transportation projects, and educational reforms.[25]

State and local governments have grown dependent on national financial assistance, and so grants are an essential tool of national power to direct state and local government activity. Although the states welcome federal grant money, they do not welcome the strings attached to the funds.

STATE ATTEMPTS TO INFLUENCE GRANT-IN-AID CONDITIONS
State government opposition to the conditions attached to national grants came to a head in 1923 in the case of *Massachusetts v. Mellon*.[26] In this case, the Supreme Court found the conditions of national grants-in-aid to be constitutional, arguing that grants-in-aid are voluntary cooperative arrangements. By voluntarily accepting the national grant, the justices ruled, the state government agrees to the grant conditions. This 1923 Court decision was essential to the proliferation of national grants in subsequent years and to the evolution of federalism and intergovernmental relations as well. But the Court's decision did not end states' challenges to grant conditions.

In 1987, South Dakota challenged a 1984 national transportation law that penalized states whose legal drinking age was lower than 21 years. The intent of the national law was to decrease "drinking while intoxicated" (DWI) car accidents. States with legal drinking ages lower than 21 years would lose 10 percent of their national grant money for transportation. South Dakota argued that Congress was using grant conditions to put a law into effect that Congress could not achieve through national legislation because the law dealt with a power reserved to the states—determining the legal age for drinking alcoholic beverages.

In its decision in *South Dakota v. Dole,* the Court found that the national government could not impose a national drinking age because setting a drinking age is indeed a reserved power of the states.[27] Yet, the Court ruled, the national government could *encourage* states to set a drinking age of 21 years by threatening to decrease their grants-in-aid for highway construction. In other words, conditions attached to voluntarily accepted grants-in-aid are constitutional. Ultimately, the national policy goal of a 21-year-old drinking age was indeed accomplished by 1988—not through a national law but through a condition attached to national highway funds offered to state governments, funds on which the states are dependent. The national "encouragement" for states to establish 21 years as the legal drinking age is still controversial, as this chapter's "Thinking Critically About Democracy" section highlights.

Over time, the number and specificity of the grant conditions have grown. State and local governments have increasingly lobbied national lawmakers during the policy-making processes that create and reauthorize grants. One goal of this **intergovernmental lobbying** is to limit the grant conditions—or at least to influence them to the states' advantage. In other words, lobbyists for an individual state work to ensure that the conditions, including the grants' formulas, benefit that state. Beyond the efforts of lobbyists hired by individual states, coordinated lobbying on behalf of *multiple* states, municipal governments, and county governments is common.

If a state does not want to comply with a grant condition, then it need not accept the grant. The problem for state and local governments is that they have come to rely on national grant funds. In 2009 and 2010, almost half of state and local revenue came from national grants. However, after the ARRA grant money is distributed, the

> The Constitution reserves to the states the authority to establish the legal drinking age. However, the national government's grant-in-aid for highways requires states to set 21 years as the age when people can legally purchase alcohol, or the states risk losing a percentage of their highway grant dollars.

SHOULD STATE GOVERNMENTS LOWER THE MINIMUM LEGAL DRINKING AGE TO 18?

The Issue: The 1984 National Minimum Drinking Age Act mandated that any state that did not raise its minimum purchase and public possession of alcohol age to 21 years would lose 10 percent of its federal highway grants-in-aid. By 1988, all states had established 21 years as their minimum age for purchasing and public possession of alcohol. (Note that although it is illegal to sell alcohol to a person under the age of 21 in all states, most states allow parents to provide their children with alcohol in the privacy of their own homes.)[28] In 2009, John McCardell Jr., president emeritus of Middlebury College, and 135 college and university presidents issued the Amethyst Initiative. This initiative called on elected officials to support a public debate over the effects of the 21-year-old drinking age. The question, Should state governments lower the drinking age?, fuels the debate.

Yes: The traditional argument for lowering the minimum legal drinking age (MLDA) is that it is not moral or logical for governments to say that at the age of 18 citizens are responsible enough to vote, decide guilt or innocence as a juror in a trial, and take up arms for the nation, but they are not responsible enough to drink a beer. Other supporters of a lower MLDA argue that it will decrease the rate of binge drinking among college students, which has increased among college students, especially women, since the 1980s.

No: According to the National Institutes of Health, "since the early 1980s, alcohol-related traffic fatalities have been cut in half, with the greatest proportional declines among persons 16–20 years old." Moreover, the U.S. Department of Transportation estimates that increasing the drinking age to 21 years prevents 1,000 traffic deaths each year.[29]

Other approaches: McCardell and his supporters are calling on the federal government to provide a waiver of the 10 percent reduction in highway grants-in-aid penalty to states that participate in a pilot alcohol-education program coupled with an MLDA of 18 years. A certified educator, trained to cover alcohol-related legal, ethical, health, and safety issues, would teach the education program. Community involvement, such as attending DWI court hearings and establishing safe-ride programs, would complement in-class instruction. Students who successfully complete the program and pass a required final exam would receive a license entitling them to the same drinking privileges and responsibilities currently guaranteed to those 21 years of age and older.

What do you think?

① What role, if any, do you think increased car safety (air bags, for example) had in the decrease of alcohol-related traffic fatalities since the early 1980s? Do you think seat-belt laws can explain some of the decrease? What factors, other than the change in MLDA, might help account for the decrease in alcohol-related traffic fatalities?

② Other than an increase in binge drinking, what negative effects might you attribute to the states lowering MLDA to 18 years?

③ Does the fact that so many people under the age of 21 years drink threaten the legitimacy of the law or the authority of the government? Explain.

---

percentage of state and local revenue coming from the national government will probably decrease to what it was before the Great Recession, about 30 percent.[30] Because the national government has no constitutional obligation to offer grants-in-aid to state or local governments, intergovernmental lobbies persistently lobby Congress to ensure not only favorable grant formulas but also the survival of grants-in-aid on which state and local governments depend. They also lobby to prevent the passage of national laws mandating specific state and local actions.

Federalism's Continuing Evolution: Mandates

In our earlier analysis of the constitutional distribution of sovereignty, we considered specific examples of the Court's expansion of national authority through its decisions in cases involving conflicts over constitutional interpretation. The constitutional clauses most often questioned are

intergovernmental lobbying efforts by groups representing state and local governments to influence national public policy

- the necessary and proper clause (Article I, Section 9)
- the national supremacy clause (Article VI)
- the general welfare clause (Article I, Section 8)
- the regulation of interstate commerce clause (Article I, Section 8)

With those Court decisions in hand, the national government is able to *mandate* certain state and local government actions. In addition, through a process known as *preemption,* the federal government can take away states' and localities' policy authority and impose its policy choices on state and local governments.

National **mandates** are clauses in national laws, including grants-in-aid, that direct state and local governments to do something specified by the national government. Many mandates relate to ensuring citizens' civil rights and civil liberties, as in the case of the mandate in the Rehabilitation Act of 1973 requiring that all government buildings, including those of state and local authorities, be accessible to persons with disabilities. When the national government assumes the entire cost of a mandate, it is a *funded mandate.* When the state or local government must cover all or some of the cost, it is an *unfunded mandate.*

Also common is the federal government's use of preemption. **Preemption** means that a national policy supersedes a state or local policy because it deals with an enumerated or implied national power. Therefore, people must obey, and states must enforce, the national law even if the state or local government has its own law on the matter.

The Supreme Court typically has supported the federal government's arguments that the national supremacy clause and the necessary and proper clause—coupled with the powers delegated to the national government to provide for the general welfare and to regulate interstate commerce—give the federal government the authority to force state and local governments to implement its mandates. The Court has also supported the national government's argument that it can attach conditions to the grants-in-aid it offers state and local governments, hence forcing those that voluntarily accept national grants to implement policies established by national lawmakers.

Today's Federalism: Intergovernmental Relations

In *Federalist* No. 45, James Madison argued that under the proposed Constitution, the states will retain "a very extensive portion of active sovereignty." More specifically, he notes that

> the powers delegated by the proposed Constitution to the federal government are few and defined. Those which are to remain in the State governments are numerous and indefinite. The former will be exercised principally on external objects, as war, peace, negotiation, and foreign commerce; with which last the power of taxation will, for the most part, be connected. The powers reserved to the several States will extend to all the objects which, in the ordinary course of affairs, concern the lives, liberties, and properties of people, and the internal order, improvement, and prosperity of the State.

How well does today's federalism match Madison's description of the federal system the Constitution would create?

There are signs of the dual federalism that Madison forecasted—the national and state governments acting independently to create, finance, and implement policies to fulfill their distinct constitutional responsibilities. The national government is undeniably the principal actor in the "external objects" of war, diplomacy, and international commerce. The national government creates, finances, and implements policies in these external matters. However, when we consider the internal objects reserved to the states, Madison's dual federalism is harder to find.

Several realities account for today's intergovernmental relations—the complex networks of national, state, and local governments' collaborative efforts—in domestic policy matters. Foremost is the reality that since passage of the Sixteenth Amendment and without a constitutional requirement to balance its budget, the national government is able to acquire the money needed to pay its expenses and a share of the expenses incurred by state and local governments. State constitutions mandate balanced state and local government bud-

---

mandates
clauses in legislation that direct state and local governments to comply with national legislation and national standards

preemption
constitutionally based principle that allows a national law to supersede state or local laws

gets, which limit the ability of state and local governments to engage in the level of long-term borrowing that the national government can incur. Voters in numerous states have used direct democracy procedures, which provide them the legal right to vote on public policies, to place limits on their state and local governments' abilities to increase taxes as well as increase expenditures. The combination of the national government's greater pool of resources and state governments' taxing and spending constraints help to explain **fiscal federalism**—the large number and size (in dollar value) of national grants-in-aid to state and local governments.

Federal grants may support innovative state and local programs targeting societal problems that face citizens throughout the nation, such as unemployment, poverty, hunger, and housing insecurity during times of severe economic downturns and air, land, and water pollution (cooperative federalism). Federal grants may also encourage state or local governments to change their laws and policies in support of national government priorities or preferences, such as changing their legal drinking age (centralized federalism).

In addition to using its financial resources to support or direct state and local policies, the national government has successfully used its enumerated and implied powers to create and expand its role in domestic policy matters. Supported by the U.S. Supreme Court in its interpretation of constitutionally enumerated and implied powers, and the national supremacy clause, the national government's policies extend to all the objects which, in the ordinary course of affairs, concern lives, liberties, and properties of people, and the internal order, improvement, and prosperity of the states and the local governments that the states create. Through preemption and mandates (funded and unfunded), state and local governments must work with the national government to help finance and implement national policy. Hence, when it comes to domestic matters, intergovernmental relations characterize today's federal system.

Knowing that they can benefit from federal grants, state and local governments perpetually lobby national policy makers in hopes of influencing the policies they will have to implement. At the same time, debates continue over the proper interpretation of the constitutional distribution of powers between the national and the state governments. State and local governments challenge national policies in the courts. The national government challenges state and local policies in the courts. Hence, the conversation about the proper interpretation of the federal system of government created by the U.S. Constitution continues today.

fiscal federalism
the relationship between the national government and state and local governments whereby the national government provides grant money to state and local governments

CONCLUSION

THINKING CRITICALLY ABOUT WHAT'S NEXT FOR FEDERALISM

Until recent decades, the pattern of Supreme Court interpretation of the distribution of constitutional power between the national and the state governments favored an expansion of the national government's enumerated and implied powers in domestic policy matters. However, the last few decades have witnessed inconsistency in the Court's interpretations. The Court protects and even expands national powers in some cases while protecting states' powers in other cases. Will U.S. Supreme Court Justices continue to issue conflicting interpretations of federalism?

Traditionally, state and local governments have been laboratories for domestic policies. Addressing long-term problems, such as poverty, and confronting new problems, such as global warming, while working within fiscal constraints, state and local governments have regularly experimented with innovative policies and programs. Federal grants-in-aid have supported, and sometimes even encouraged, state and local governments to work out solutions to domestic problems. Will state and local governments maintain their efforts to be laboratories for the creation of effective domestic policies?

The reality of federalism, as evidenced by the inadequate response to Hurricane Katrina, can be ineffective and inefficient. Governments can disagree on which government, if any, is responsible for addressing a problem. They may also disagree on what action needs to occur. Moreover, two or more levels of government may decide to act independently of each other, causing overlap in efforts and waste of resources. Will IGR evolve so that government can provide more efficient, effective public service?

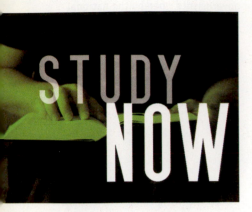

Summary

1. An Overview of the U.S. Federal System
Dual sovereignty is the defining characteristic of the United States' federal system of government. Under a federal system, the national government is sovereign over specific matters, and state governments are sovereign over different matters. Today, it is often difficult to differentiate between national sovereignty and state sovereignty.

2. Constitutional Distribution of Authority
The vagueness of the U.S. Constitution's language providing for enumerated and implied national powers, reserved state powers, concurrent powers, and national supremacy has provoked ongoing conflict between the federal government and the states over the proper distribution of sovereignty. The U.S. Supreme Court has the final word on the interpretation of the Constitution—and hence the final say on national and state sovereignty.

3. Evolution of the Federal System
The Supreme Court's interpretations of the Constitution's distribution of authority have reinforced the ability of national officials to compel state and local governments to implement national policy preferences. Mandates and preemption, as well as conditions placed on voluntarily accepted national grants-in-aid, require states to assist in financing and implementing national policies. As a result, relations between the national government and the states have evolved from a simple arrangement of dual federalism to a complex system of intergovernmental relations (IGR).

4. Today's Federalism: Intergovernmental Relations
Federalism's dual sovereignty is clearly seen in the external matters delegated to the national government, such as war, diplomacy, and foreign commerce, but very difficult to identify in the domestic matters reserved to the state governments, which are dominated by intergovernmental relations.

Key Terms

block grant 101
categorical formula grant 100
categorical project grant 101
centralized federalism 96
concurrent powers 88
confederal system 83
conflicted federalism 97
cooperative federalism 96
devolution 96
dual federalism 96
enumerated powers 89
extradition 95
federal system 82

fiscal federalism 105
full faith and credit clause 95
grants-in-aid
   (intergovernmental
   transfers) 96
horizontal federalism 95
implied powers 89
intergovernmental
   lobbying 103
intergovernmental relations
   (IGR) 85
interstate compacts 95
mandates 104

McCulloch v. Maryland 92
necessary and proper clause
   (elastic clause) 89
new judicial federalism 95
preemption 104
police powers 91
privileges and immunities
   clause 95
reserved powers 91
supreme law of the land 89
unitary system 83

For Review

1. In terms of which government is sovereign, differentiate among a unitary system, a confederal system, and a federal system of government.

2. To which level of government does the Constitution distribute the enumerated powers? Implied powers? Concurrent authorities? Reserved powers? Provide several examples of each power and authority.

3. What matters fall within the scope of state sovereignty?

4. Differentiate among dual federalism, cooperative federalism, centralized federalism, and conflicted federalism.

5. How does the national government use grants-in-aid, mandates, and preemption to direct the policy of state and local governments?

6. What do we mean by intergovernmental relations (IGR)? Why is the term a good description of U.S. federalism today?

For Critical Thinking and Discussion

1. Is the federal system of government that provides citizens with the opportunity to elect a large number of officials each year a benefit or a burden for citizens? Explain your answer.

2. Would the amount of money citizens pay for their governments through taxes and fees decrease if there were fewer levels of governments serving them? Defend your answer.

3. Would the quality or quantity of government services decrease if there were fewer levels of government in the United States? Why or why not?

4. Note at least three societal problems you believe the national government can address best (more effectively and efficiently than state or local governments). Discuss why you believe the national government is best suited to address these problems. Do these problems fit in the category of enumerated national powers? Explain your answer.

5. Note at least three societal problems you believe state or local governments can address best (more effectively and efficiently than the national government). Discuss why you believe state or local governments are best suited to address these problems. Do these problems fit in the category of powers reserved to the states? Explain your answer.

MULTIPLE CHOICE: Choose the lettered item that answers the question correctly.

1. The characteristic that distinguishes a federal system of government from both a unitary and a confederal system is
   a. dual sovereignty.
   b. the existence of three levels of government.
   c. sovereignty held by only the central government.
   d. sovereignty held by only the regional governments.

2. The authorities to make policy, raise money, establish courts, and implement policy that are inherent to all governments are examples of
   a. concurrent powers.   c. implied powers.
   b. enumerated powers.   d. reserved powers.

3. The necessary and proper clause of the Constitution establishes the
   a. enumerated powers of the national government.
   b. implied powers of the national government.
   c. implied powers of the state governments.
   d. reserved powers of the state governments.

4. The authority to coin and regulate money, to regulate interstate and foreign commerce, and to make treaties with foreign nations (including Native American nations) are examples of
   a. concurrent powers.   c. implied powers.
   b. enumerated powers.   d. reserved powers.

5. The Supreme Court used implied powers to confirm the national government's authority to establish a national bank, and applied the national supremacy clause to deny state authority to tax branches of the national bank, in the case of
   a. *Gibbons v. Ogden.*   c. *Marbury v. Madison.*
   b. *United States v. Lopez.*   d. *McCulloch v. Maryland.*

6. The state-to-state obligations detailed in the Constitution create state-to-state relationships known as
   a. centralized federalism.   c. dual federalism.
   b. cooperative federalism.   d. horizontal federalism.

7. The current debate over states' recognizing same-sex marriage contracts from other states may eventually force the Supreme Court to interpret the Article IV clause that concerns
   a. extradition.   c. interstate compacts.
   b. full faith and credit.   d. privileges and immunities.

8. The powers that the Tenth Amendment to the Constitution establishes are the
   a. enumerated powers.   c. implied powers.
   b. concurrent powers.   d. reserved powers.

9. Political scientists label today's federalism
   a. centralized federalism.
   b. conflicted federalism.
   c. dual federalism.
   d. horizontal federalism.

10. _____ provide(s) state governments with the most discretion over their policy actions (including policy formulation, policy financing, and policy implementation).
   a. National block grants
   b. National categorical grants
   c. National mandates
   d. National preemption

FILL IN THE BLANKS.

11. _____ is the name political scientists give to the collaborative efforts of two or more levels of government working to serve the public.

12. All national, state, and local laws must comply with the Constitution of the United States, for the Constitution is the _____ .

13. The practice whereby state judges base decisions regarding civil rights and liberties on their state constitutions, rather than on the U.S. Constitution, when their state constitution guarantees more than the minimum rights, is labeled _____ .

14. The national government has used the _____ clause of the Constitution, also known as the elastic clause, to stretch its enumerated powers.

15. Beginning in the 1970s, state governments and presidents began to respond to centralized federalism by calling for _____ , which is the return of policy creation, financing, and/or implementation to the state governments.

Answers: 1. a; 2. a; 3. b; 4. b; 5. d; 6. d; 7. b; 8. d; 9. b; 10. a; 11. Intergovernmental relations; 12. supreme law of the land; 13. new judicial federalism; 14. necessary and proper; 15. devolution.

RESOURCES FOR RESEARCH AND ACTION

Internet Resources

Bureau of the Census
www.census.gov Access the *Statistical Abstract of the United States* as well as other sources of data about national and state governments at this site.

Council of State Governments
www.csg.org This site is a place where state officials can share information on common problems and possible solutions.

National Conference of State Legislatures
www.ncsl.org/statefed/statefed.htm This site is dedicated to state-federal issues and relationships.

National Governors Association (NGA)
www.nga.org The NGA lobbies the national government on behalf of governors and also provides the governors with opportunities to share information on policies.

Internet Activism

Facebook
www.facebook.com/uscensusbureau Census Bureau Facebook, Blogs, Twitter, YouTube, and other social media channels allow visitors to interact with the agency and others, and encourage visitors to freely comment and give welcomed feedback.

Blog
http://ncsl.typepad.com/the_thicket/federalism/ This National Council of State Legislatures (NCSL) blog focuses on issues of federalism and their impacts on state governments.

Twitter
http://twitter.com/tenthamendment The Tenth Amendment Center works to preserve and protect states' rights and federalism through education about the Tenth Amendment to the U.S. Constitution.

YouTube
www.youtube.com/watch?v=dBdQP-8izDc The national president of Mothers Against Drunk Drivers (MADD) and the founder of Amethyst present two sides of the debate on lowering the minimum drinking age.

Recommended Readings

O'Toole, Laurence J. *American Intergovernmental Relations: Foundations, Perspectives, and Issues,* 3rd ed. Washington, DC: CQ Press, 2000. A collection of readings giving a comprehensive overview of U.S. federalism and intergovernmental relations, covering historical, theoretical, and political perspectives as well as fiscal and administrative views.

Rehnquist, William H. *The Supreme Court: Revised and Updated.* New York: Vintage Books, 2001. A history of the Supreme Court by the deceased chief justice, probing the inner workings of the Court, key Court decisions in the evolution of federalism, and insights into the debates among the justices.

Walker, David B. *The Rebirth of Federalism: Slouching Toward Washington,* 2nd ed. Washington, DC: CQ Press, 2000. Both a history of U.S. federalism and an assessment of the status of U.S. federalism today.

Movies of Interest

When the Levees Broke: A Requiem in Four Acts (2006)
This Spike Lee documentary critically examines the responses of federal, state, and local governments to Hurricane Katrina. Through images of the disaster, interviews with Katrina's victims, and clips of government officials' media interviews, Lee focuses on racial issues and intergovernmental ineptitude—from the poor construction of the levees to the delayed and inadequate federal, state, and local response.

Hoxie: The First Stand (2003)
This documentary presents one of the first integration battles in the South post–*Brown v. Board of Education of Topeka, Kansas.* The opponents are the Hoxie Board of Education, which in the summer of 1955 decided to integrate its schools, and grassroots citizens' organizations that resisted integration through petitions, harassment, and threats of violence against the school board members, their families, and the school superintendent.

Dances with Wolves (1990)
Sent to command the U.S. Army's westernmost outpost in the 1860s, Lieutenant John Dunbar witnesses, as an observer and a participant, the conflicts created in the Dakota Territory as white settlers encroach on territory of the Sioux Indians. Movie critics and historians praised Kevin Costner (the movie's director and lead actor) for correcting the erroneous image of Native Americans presented in classic Hollywood Westerns.

Civil Liberties

THEN

The Bill of Rights was designed to protect citizens' rights to speak and act without undue monitoring by or interference from the national government; however, Congress soon legislated exceptions to those protections.

NOW

As part of a global war on terrorism, the national government increasingly monitors the words and actions of citizens and others, while people continue to protest and challenge governmental policies.

Will the Supreme Court uphold post-9/11 laws allowing the president to place terrorist suspects under surveillance without a court order?

Will airports and national security agencies further develop and deploy security systems based on methods such as thumbprint and eye-scan technology?

Will the Court uphold post-9/11 laws that require Internet providers to secretly share personal information about their clients with the FBI?

NEXT

civil liberties
constitutionally established guarantees that protect citizens, opinions, and property against arbitrary government interference

A strong belief in civil liberties

is deeply embedded in our understanding of what it means to be an American. Civil liberties protect people from government intrusion and allow them to follow their own belief systems. Civil liberties also empower people to speak out against the government, as long as they do not harm others.

Since the nation's founding, political discourse among the people has often focused on the ideals of liberty and freedom. The colonists took up arms against Britain because the king and Parliament refused to recognize their liberties as English citizens—freedoms their counterparts in Great Britain took for granted: freedom of speech and assembly and the right to be free from unrestrained governmental power, especially in the investigation and prosecution of crimes. As scholar Stephen L. Carter noted, by declaring their independence, the colonists engaged in the ultimate act of dissent.[1] Withdrawing their consent to be governed by the king, they created a new government that would tolerate political discourse and disagreement and that could not legally disregard the collective or individual will of citizens.

Ideologies of liberty and freedom inspired the War for Independence and the founding of the new nation.[2] Those rights, though guaranteed, were never absolute. In fact, one of the early acts passed by Congress after the Bill of Rights was the Alien and Sedition Acts (1789), which not only limited immigration but also prohibited certain criticisms of the government. From its origins, the Constitution guaranteed basic liberties, but those protections were tempered by other goals and values, perhaps most importantly by the goal of order and the need to protect people and their property. Following the terrorist attacks of September 11, 2001, the national government enacted laws aimed at protecting American citizens and property from further attack. But those laws have had a dramatic impact on individual freedoms and rights, in some cases overturning decades of legal precedent in the area of civil liberties. Our civil liberties—though protected—have always been threatened, challenged, contested, and defended—especially during a time of war, when they are often most important.

Civil Liberties in the American Legal System

Civil liberties are individual liberties established in the Constitution and safeguarded by state and federal courts. We also refer to civil liberties as *personal freedoms* and often use the concepts of "liberty" and "freedom" interchangeably.

Civil liberties differ from civil rights. **Civil liberties** are constitutionally established guarantees that protect citizens, opinions, and property *against* arbitrary government interference. In contrast, civil rights (the focus of Chapter 5) reflect positive acts of government (in the form of constitutional provisions or statutes) *for* the purpose of protecting individuals against arbitrary or discriminatory actions. For example, the freedom of speech, a liberty established in the First Amendment to the U.S. Constitution, protects citizens against the government's censorship of their words, in particular when those words are politically charged. In contrast, the constitutionally protected right to vote requires the government to step in to ensure that all citizens be allowed to vote, without restriction by individuals, groups, or governmental officials.

The Freedoms Protected in the American System

The U.S. Constitution, through the Bill of Rights, and state constitutions explicitly recognize and protect civil liberties. As Table 4.1 summarizes, the first ten amendments to the Constitution explicitly limited the power of the legislative, executive, and judicial branches of the national government.

The Bill of Rights established the freedoms that are essential to individuals' and groups' free and effective participation in the larger community. Consider how the absence of freedom to speak one's mind or the absence of protection against the arbitrary exercise of police powers might affect the nature and the extent of people's engagement in political and community debates and discussions. Without these protections, citizens could not freely express their opinions through rallies, speeches, protests, letters, pamphlets, public meetings, blogs, e-mail, and other forms of civic engagement. The Constitution's framers, who had been denied these liberties under British rule, saw them as indispensable to forming a new democratic republic.

The meanings of these precious freedoms have shifted over the course of U.S. history, as presidents, legislators, judges, and ordinary citizens have changed their minds about how much freedom the people should have. When Americans have not perceived themselves as being under some external threat, they generally have adopted an expansive interpretation of civil liberties. At those times, citizens tend to believe that the government should interfere as little as necessary in individuals' lives. Accordingly, they strongly support people's right to gather with others and to speak their minds, even when the content of that speech is controversial. When the nation has been under some perceived threat, citizens have often allowed the government to limit protected freedoms.[3] (See "Analyzing the Sources" on page 114.) Limits have also extended to many **due process** protections—legal safeguards that

due process
legal safeguards that prevent the government from arbitrarily depriving citizens of life, liberty, or property; guaranteed by the Fifth and Fourteenth amendments

TABLE 4.1

The Bill of Rights: Limiting Government Power

Amendment I: Limits on Congress	Congress cannot make any law establishing a religion or abridging the freedom of religious exercise, speech, assembly, or petition.
Amendments II, III, IV: Limits on the Executive	The executive branch cannot infringe on the right of the people to bear arms (II), cannot house soldiers in citizens' houses (III), and cannot search for or seize evidence without a legal warrant from a court of law (IV).
Amendments V, VI, VII, VIII: Limits on the Judiciary	The courts cannot hold trials for serious offenses without providing for a grand jury (V), a trial jury (VII), a fair trial (VI), and legal counsel (VI). The accused also have the right to hear the charges against them (VI), to confront hostile witnesses (VI), and to refrain from giving testimony against themselves (V); and they cannot be tried more than once for the same crime (V). In addition, neither bail nor punishment can be excessive (VIII), and no property can be taken from private citizens without "just compensation" (V).
Amendments IX, X: Limits	Any rights not listed specifically in the Constitution for the National Government are reserved to the states or to the people (X), and the enumeration of certain rights in the Constitution should not be interpreted to mean that those are the only rights the people have (IX).

ANALYZING THE SOURCES

BALANCING THE CONSTITUTIONAL TENSION

Two of the leading intellectuals of the Founding Era, Benjamin Franklin and Thomas Jefferson, have interpreted this tension between personal freedom and national security in different ways.

"Those who would give up essential liberty to purchase a little temporary safety deserve neither liberty or safety."

—Benjamin Franklin

"A strict observance of the written laws is doubtless one of the highest duties of a good citizen, but it is not the highest. The laws of necessity, of self-preservation, of serving our country when in danger, are of higher obligation." **—Thomas Jefferson**

Evaluating the Evidence

① Why is Jefferson easier to believe in times of war and Franklin in times of peace?

② How does the Constitution and its interpretation ensure that both views are kept at the forefront of the American consciousness?

prevent the government from arbitrarily depriving people of life, liberty, or property without adhering to strict legal procedures. In this chapter, we consider not only the historical context of our civil liberties but also recent changes in how Congress, the president, and the courts interpret these liberties.

The Historical Basis for American Civil Liberties: The Bill of Rights

The framers vividly remembered the censorship and suppression of speech that they had suffered under British rule. Colonists had been harshly punished, often by imprisonment and confiscation of their property and even death, if they criticized the British government, through both speech and the publication of pamphlets. The framers understandably viewed liberty as a central principle guiding the creation of a new democratic republic. Federalists such as Alexander Hamilton saw the Constitution itself as a bill of rights because it delegated specific powers to the national government and contained specific provisions designed to protect citizens against an abusive government (see Table 4.2).

The protections listed in Table 4.2 were designed to protect people from being punished, imprisoned, or executed for expressing political beliefs or opposition. However, the Anti-Federalists still stressed the need for a written bill of rights. As we saw in Chapter 2, the ratification of the Constitution stalled because citizens feared that the government might use its expanded powers to limit individual freedoms, particularly those associated with political speech and engagement. The First Amendment, which ensures freedom of religion, the press, assembly, and speech, was essential to political speech and to discourse in the larger society.

The freedoms embodied in the Bill of Rights are broad principles rather than specific prohibitions against governmental action. From the nation's beginnings, the vagueness of the Bill of Rights led to serious disagreement about how to interpret its amendments. For example, the First Amendment's establishment clause states simply that "Congress shall make no law respecting an establishment of religion." Some commentators, most notably Thomas Jefferson, argued that the clause mandated a "wall of separation between church and state" and barred any federal support of religion. Others more narrowly interpreted the clause as barring only the establishment of a national religion or the requirement that all public officials swear an oath to some particular religion. This disagreement about the breadth of the establishment clause is ongoing today, as courts and lawyers continue to try to determine what the proper relationship should be between church and state.

Other freedoms, too, have been subject to differing interpretations, including the First Amendment guarantees of freedom of speech, assembly, and the press. These conflicting interpretations often arise in response to public crises or security concerns. Security concerns also affect the protections offered to those accused of threatening the safety of the nation. For example, the USA PATRIOT Act, passed by Congress almost immediately after the September 11 attacks and amended in 2002, allows law enforcement a good deal of legal leeway. It permits agents to sidestep well-established rules that govern how searches and seizures may be conducted and to restrict criminal due process protections severely, particularly for persons suspected of involvement in organizations thought to have ties to

TABLE 4.2

Citizens' Protections in the Original Constitution

Clause	Protection
Article I, Sec. 9	Guarantee of *habeas corpus*—a court order requiring that an individual in custody be brought into court and told the cause for detention
Article I, Sec. 9	Prohibition of *bills of attainder*—laws that declare a person guilty of a crime without a trial
Article I, Sec. 9	Prohibition of *ex post facto laws*—retroactive laws that punish people for committing an act that was legal when the act was committed
Article III	Guarantee of a trial by jury in the state where the crime was committed

> According to the Supreme Court, public schools cannot sponsor religious activities, including teacher-led school prayer, without violating the First Amendment's establishment clause. Here, students at an Illinois high school bow their heads in student-initiated prayer. Does the ban on prayer in public schools violate the free exercise clause in your view?

> Since September 11, 2001, the struggle to balance national security with civil liberties has become more dynamic. Here, demonstrators rally to demand the closure of Guantanamo Bay prison camp and end indefinite detention without charges or trial.

suspected terrorists. Civil liberties advocates worry that fear is causing Americans to give up their most precious freedoms.

Incorporation of the Bill of Rights to Apply to the States

The framers intended the Bill of Rights to restrict the powers of only the *national government*. They did not see the Bill of Rights as applicable to the state governments. In general, there was little public worry that the states would curtail civil liberties, because most state constitutions included a bill of rights that protected the individual against abuses of state power. Further, it was generally believed that because the state governments were geographically closer to the people than the national government, they would be less likely to encroach upon individual rights and liberties.

Through most of early U.S. history, the Bill of Rights applied to the national government, but not to the states. That assumption is illustrated by the case of *Barron v. Baltimore* (1833), in which a wharf owner named Barron sued the city of Baltimore. Barron claimed that the city had violated the "takings clause" of the Fifth Amendment, which bars the taking of private property for public use without just compensation. *Barron* argued that by paving its streets, the city of Baltimore had changed the natural course of certain streams; the resulting buildup of silt and gravel in the harbor made his wharf unusable. The case centered on the idea that the Fifth Amendment protects individuals from actions taken by both the national and the state or local governments. The Supreme Court disagreed, ruling that the Fifth Amendment was restricted to suits brought against the federal government.[4]

In 1868, three years after the Civil War ended, the Fourteenth Amendment was added to the U.S. Constitution. The Fourteenth Amendment reads as if it were meant to extend the protections of the Bill of Rights to citizens' interactions with *state governments*:

> No State shall make or enforce any law which shall abridge the privileges or immunities of citizens of the United States; nor shall any State deprive any person of life, liberty, or property, without due process of law; nor deny to any person within its jurisdiction the equal protection of the laws.

total incorporation
the theory that the Fourteenth Amendment's due process clause requires the states to uphold all freedoms in the Bill of Rights; rejected by the Supreme Court in favor of selective incorporation

selective incorporation
the process by which, over time, the Supreme Court applied those freedoms that served some fundamental principle of liberty or justice to the states, thus rejecting total incorporation

Although this language sounds like an effort to protect citizens' rights and liberties from arbitrary interference by state governments, the Supreme Court rejected the doctrine of **total incorporation:** that is, the application of *all* the protections contained in the Bill of Rights to the states. Instead, beginning with a series of cases decided by the Court in the 1880s, the justices formulated a narrower approach, known as **selective incorporation.**[5] This approach considered each protection individually, one case at a time, for possible incorporation into the Fourteenth Amendment and application to the states. In each case, the justices rejected the plaintiff's specific claims of protection against the state. But the Court held that due process mandates the incorporation of those rights that serve the fundamental principles of liberty and justice, those that were at the core of the "very idea of free government" and that were unalienable rights of citizenship.

Despite those early cases, the Supreme Court continued to embrace the idea that although citizenship meant being a citizen of a state and of the nation as a whole, the Bill of Rights protected citizens only against the national government. As Table 4.3 shows, not until 1925 did the Court gradually begin the process of incorporation, starting with the First Amendment protections most central to democratic government and civic engagement. That year, in the case of *Gitlow v. New York*, the Court held that freedom of speech is "among the fundamental personal rights and 'liberties' protected by the due process clause of the Fourteenth Amendment from impairment by the states."[6] In 1931, in its decision in

Selective Incorporation of the Bill of Rights

TABLE 4.3

Amendment	Liberty	Date	Key Case
I	Freedom of speech	1925	*Gitlow v. New York*
	Freedom of the press	1931	*Near v. Minnesota*
	Freedom of assembly and petition	1937	*DeJonge v. Oregon*
	Freedom to practice religion	1940	*Cantwell v. Connecticut*
	Freedom from government-established religion	1947	*Everson v. Board of Education*
II	Right to bear arms	2010	*McDonald v. City of Chicago*
III	No quartering of soldiers		Not incorporated
IV	No unreasonable searches and seizures	1949	*Wolf v. Colorado*
	Exclusionary rule	1961	*Mapp v. Ohio*
V	Right to just compensation (for property taken by government)	1897	*Chicago, B&Q RR Co. v. Chicago*
	No compulsory self-incrimination	1964	*Malloy v. Hogan*
	No double jeopardy	1969	*Benton v. Maryland*
	Right to grand jury indictment		Not incorporated
VI	Right to a public trial	1948	*In re Oliver*
	Right to counsel in criminal cases	1963	*Gideon v. Wainwright*
	Right to confront witnesses	1965	*Pointer v. Texas*
	Right to an impartial jury	1966	*Parker v. Gladden*
	Right to a speedy trial	1967	*Klopfer v. North Carolina*
	Right to a jury in criminal trials	1968	*Duncan v. Louisiana*
VII	Right to a jury in civil trials		Not incorporated
VIII	No cruel and unusual punishments	1962	*Robinson v. California*
	No excessive fines or bail		Not incorporated

Near v. Minnesota, the Court added freedom of the press, and in 1937 it added freedom of assembly to the list of incorporated protections.[7]

Incorporation progressed further with the landmark case of *Palko v. Connecticut* (1937), in which the Court laid out a formula for defining fundamental rights that later courts have used time and time again in incorporation cases, as well as in due process cases more generally. The justices found that fundamental rights were rooted in the traditions and conscience of the American people. Moreover, if those rights were eliminated, the justices argued, neither liberty nor justice could exist.[8] Judges in subsequent cases have used this formula to determine which Bill of Rights protections should be applied to the states. In case after case, the justices have considered whether such a right is fundamental—that is, rooted in the American tradition and conscience and essential for liberty and justice—and they have been guided by the principle that citizen participation in government and society is necessary for democracy in gauging the importance of each constitutionally protected right.

Over time, the Supreme Court has incorporated most Bill of Rights protections, as Table 4.3 summarizes. Among the few notable exceptions to the trend of incorporation are the Third Amendment's prohibition against the quartering of soldiers in citizens' homes, which has not been an issue since colonial times. The Fifth Amendment's provision for a grand jury indictment, whereby a panel of citizens determines whether or not there is enough evidence for prosecutors to bring a criminal case, runs counter to a trend in state criminal cases away from a reliance on grand juries; a grand jury is not required to guarantee that states adhere to Fifth and Sixth amendment protections during the arrest, interrogation, and trial of criminal defendants. Similarly, the Seventh Amendment's provision of a jury in a civil trial is widely viewed as less important than the Sixth Amendment's guarantee of a jury trial in criminal cases in which life and liberty may be at stake.

Freedoms of Speech, Assembly, and the Press: First Amendment Freedoms Supporting Civic Discourse

Civic discourse and free participation in the political process have certain requirements. As we consider in this section, an individual must be able to express his or her political views through speech, assembly, and petition. The person must also live in a society with a press that is independent of government censorship. Freedom of speech, assembly, petition, and the press is essential to an open society and to democratic rule. These freedoms ensure that individuals can discuss the important issues facing the nation and try to agree about how to address these matters. Scholars have referred to this sharing of contrasting opinions as the **marketplace of ideas.** It is through the competition of ideas—some of them radical, some even loathsome—that solutions emerge. Freedom of the press allows for the dissemination and discussion of these varying ideas and encourages consensus building.

The marketplace of ideas enables people to voice their concerns and views freely and allows individuals to reconsider their ideas on important national and local issues. The centrality of the freedom of political expression to the First Amendment reflects the founders' belief that democracy would flourish only through robust discussion and candid debate.

The First Amendment and Political Instability

Over time, the Supreme Court has distinguished between political expression that the First Amendment protects and expression that the government may limit or even prohibit. The government has tried to limit speech, assembly, and the press during times of national emergency, when it has viewed that expression as more threatening than it would be in normal times.

THE TENSION BETWEEN FREEDOM AND ORDER
A fundamental tension exists between the Bill of Rights, with its goal of protecting individual freedoms, and the government's central goal of ensuring order. Not even a decade had gone by after the Constitution's ratification when Congress passed the Alien and Sedition Acts (1798). These laws placed the competing goals of freedom and order directly in conflict. The Sedition Act criminalized all speech and writings judged to be critical of the government, Congress, or the president. This was just the first of many times in U.S. history that lawmakers sacrificed free speech and freedom of the press in an effort to ensure national security and order. For example, President Abraham Lincoln attempted to silence political dissidents during the Civil War by mandating that they be tried in military courts, without the due process protections afforded in a civilian court. Lincoln also suspended the writ of **habeas corpus** (Latin, meaning "you have the body"), an ancient right and constitutional guarantee that protects an individual in custody from being held without the right to be heard in a court of law.[9] Again, political dissidents were targeted for indefinite detention without trial. Whenever the nation has perceived itself under attack or threat, pressure has been placed on the government by some citizens to limit individual freedom to ensure societal order, and other citizens have pressured the government to maintain freedom while securing order.

The struggle for a balance between freedom and order continues today as the United States fights a global war on terrorism. Part of the 1789 Alien and Sedition Acts, known as the Alien Enemies Act, empowered the president to deport aliens suspected of threatening the nation's security or to imprison them indefinitely.[10] After the September 11 terrorist attacks on U.S. soil, President George W. Bush invoked those same powers for enemy combatants, insurgents, and suspected terrorists captured in the United States or abroad. Like President Lincoln, President Bush also argued that military combatants and suspected ter-

---

marketplace of ideas
a concept at the core of the freedoms of expression and press, based on the belief that true and free political discourse depends on a free and unrestrained discussion of ideas

habeas corpus
an ancient right that protects an individual in custody from being held without the right to be heard in a court of law

THE ELECTION PROTESTS IN IRAN

Neda Agha-Soltan, a 27-year-old musician, became politically engaged for the first time after the 2009 presidential elections in Iran. Four hours after the polls closed on June 12, the Iranian government had announced the reelection of President Mahmoud Ahmadinejad, claiming he had received more than 60 percent of the 40 million paper ballots cast in the election. The leading opposition candidate, Mir-Hossein Mousavi, had been ahead in the polls before the election. During his campaign, he promised to reverse the country's hard-line policies and limits on civil liberties. Under President Ahmadinejad, authorities had curbed Internet access, shut down almost all liberal newspapers, jailed Iranian-American scholars, and kept activists under close surveillance and frequently summoned them for questioning.

How will technology affect the exercise of political liberties in Iran and around the world?

In addition to Mousavi, there had been several other candidates who boasted of substantial followings in the weeks leading to the election. As the outcome of the election was announced, protests erupted across Tehran and spread across the country. Mousavi challenged the outcome and declared himself the winner, suggesting that election irregularities were widespread. Almost immediately young people, women, moderate religious officials, and intellectuals took to the streets to demonstrate their opposition to Ahmadinejad. The police closed the universities in Tehran—detaining over 200 students—and arresting over 170 people in a crackdown on protests. The Supreme Leader Ayatollah Khamenei soon announced support for President Ahmadinejad, despite popular pressure to support a fair election. The Basij, a paramilitary force that supports Khamenei, joined the police and military in attacking and subduing the protesters; they have been accused of invading college dorms at night and destroying property, and they were filmed shooting into crowds.

As part of the crackdown against political protest, the government blocked citizens' cell-phone transmissions and access to such Web sites as Facebook, and they shut down text-messaging services. Despite those measures, messages reached the rest of the world, as protesters posted on international blogs, sent tweets, and downloaded video on YouTube and other sites as evidence of violence against the protesters. Opposition leaders claim that protesters were tortured and raped while in prison. Protesters in their turn attacked police, burned vehicles, and destroyed property.

On June 20th, on her way to a protest, Neda Agha-Soltan was killed as she stood beside her car. She was shot through the heart and died in the street; citizens nearby filmed her death and quickly posted the video on the Internet. Her death became a symbol of the abuses in Iran and inspired a call for continued protest. Because the Ahmadinejad administration had blamed outside forces for instigating rebellion, international journalists were banned from leaving their offices or from reporting stories on the protests. Despite that, over one hundred video clips of a July 20 protest were posted on the Internet. Regardless of governmental crackdown, arrests, and torture, protesting bloggers found ways to post and tweet continuously to the outside world what they were experiencing.

In the months following the election, the Iranian government has reported thirty-six deaths from the protests, but opposition leaders claim that twice as many deaths have resulted from government repression of protest. World humanitarian agencies have repeatedly called for investigation of the civil and human rights abuses resulting from this election. President Ahmadinejad was sworn into office in August 2009.

rorists should be tried in military tribunals and denied the protections of civilian courts, including the right to a speedy and public trial.[11] While the Obama Adminstration has moved to try some detainees in civilian criminal courts,[12] it has also been publicly struggling with the decision to retain Guantánamo detainees indefinitely without trials.[13]

THE HISTORICAL CONTEXT FOR FREE SPEECH LAWS The Supreme Court's willingness to suppress or punish political speech has changed over time in response to perceived internal and external threats to the nation. During World War I, the Court upheld the conviction of socialist and war protester Charles Schenck for distributing a pamphlet to recently drafted men urging them to resist the draft.[14] For the first time, the Court created through its ruling a test to evaluate such government actions, called the **clear and present danger test.** Under this standard, the government may silence speech or expression only when there is a clear and present danger that such speech will bring about some harm that the government has the power to prevent. In the *Schenck* case, the Court noted that the circumstances of war permit greater restrictions on the freedom of speech than would be allowable during peacetime. The justices ruled that Schenck's actions could endanger the nation's ability to carry out the draft and prosecute the war.

Soon after the *Schenck* case, a majority of the justices adopted a far more restrictive test that made it easier to punish citizens for the content of their speech. This test, known as the **bad tendency test,** was extended in the case of Benjamin Gitlow, who was convicted of violating a New York State criminal anarchy law by publishing pamphlets calling for a revolutionary mass action to create a socialist government.[15] The political context of Gitlow's conviction is revealing: a so-called red scare—fears that the socialist revolution in the Soviet Union would spread to other nations with large populations of workers—was sweeping the nation. Gitlow's lawyer contended that there was no proof that Gitlow's pamphlet created a clear and present danger of a violent uprising. The Court disagreed, however, ruling that any speech that had the tendency to incite crime or disturb the public peace could be silenced.

This highly restrictive test required only that the government demonstrate that some speech may at some time help to bring about harm. The threat did not need to be immediate or even direct. The test sacrificed the freedoms of speech and the press to concerns about public safety and protection of the existing order. The bad tendency test lasted only a short while; by the late 1930s, the Court had reverted to the clear and present danger test, which the justices interpreted more broadly to protect speech and participation. The relative peace and stability of the period between the two world wars is apparent in the Court's handling of speech and press cases, as the justices required government officials to demonstrate that the speech clearly posed a danger to public safety.

Even after the Court reverted to the clear and present danger test, however, it still allowed concerns about national security to control its handling of First Amendment cases. In the wake of World War II, a war of conflicting ideologies emerged between the United States and the Soviet Union. Termed the *Cold War* because it did not culminate in a direct military confrontation between the countries, this development nevertheless created a climate of fear and insecurity in both nations. Concerns about the spread of communism in the United States led to prosecutions of individuals deemed to be sympathetic to communism and socialism under the Smith Act of 1940. This federal law barred individuals from advocating or teaching about "the duty, necessity, desirability, or propriety of overthrowing or destroying any government in the United States by force or violence."

In the most important case of this period, the Supreme Court upheld the conviction of several individuals who were using the writings of German philosophers Karl Marx and Friedrich Engels, along with those of Soviet leaders Vladimir Lenin and Josef Stalin, to teach about socialism and communism.[16] In upholding the convictions, the justices found that although the use of these writings did not pose a risk of imminent danger to the government, it created the *probability* that such harm would result. Because there was a probability that these readings would lead to the destruction of the government, the Court reasoned, the speech could be barred. The seriousness of the evil was key to the test that came out of this ruling, known as the **clear and probable danger test.** Because the government was suppressing speech to avoid the gravest danger, an armed takeover of the United States, the Supreme Court majority ruled that it was justified in its actions—even if the risk or probability of this result was relatively remote.

As the Cold War subsided and concerns diminished about a potential communist takeover of the United States, the Court shifted to a broader interpretation of the First Amendment speech and press protections. Beginning with *Brandenburg v. Ohio* (1969), the Court signaled that it would give more weight to First Amendment claims and less to government concerns about security and order. In this case, the Court considered the convictions of the leaders of an Ohio Ku Klux Klan group who were arrested after they made a speech at a

---

clear and present danger test
a standard established in the 1919 Supreme Court case *Schenck v. U.S.* whereby the government may silence speech or expression when there is a clear and present danger that such speech will bring about some harm that the government has the power to prevent

bad tendency test
a standard extended in the 1925 case *Gitlow v. New York* whereby any speech that has the tendency to incite crime or disturb the public peace can be silenced

clear and probable danger test
a standard established in the 1951 case *Dennis v. U.S.* whereby the government could suppress speech to avoid grave danger, even if the probability of the dangerous result was relatively remote; replaced by the imminent lawless action (incitement) test in 1969

televised rally, during which they uttered racist and anti-Semitic comments and showed guns and rifles. Local officials charged them with violating a state law that banned speech that disturbed the public peace and threatened armed overthrow. In overturning the convictions, the Court reverted to a strict reading of the clear and present danger test. The justices held that government officials had to demonstrate that the speech they sought to silence went beyond mere advocacy, or words, and that it created the risk of imminent disorder or lawlessness.[17]

THE STANDARD TODAY: THE IMMINENT LAWLESS ACTION TEST

The *Brandenburg* test, known as both the **imminent lawless action test** and the **incitement test,** altered the clear and present danger test by making it even more stringent. Specifically, after the *Brandenburg* decision, any government in the United States—national, state, or local—trying to silence speech would need to show that the risk of harm from the speech was highly likely and that the harm was imminent or immediate. The imminent lawless action test is the standard the courts use today to determine whether speech is protected from government interference.

Even though the *Brandenburg* test is well established, the issue of whether speech is protected continues to be debated. For example, since the September 11 attacks, public attention has increasingly focused on Web sites operated by terrorists and terrorist sympathizers, especially members of militant Islamic groups. Some of these sites carry radical messages; for example, one site urges viewers to eliminate all "enemies of Allah" by any necessary means and gives instructions on loading weapons. Do First Amendment guarantees protect such sites? What about Web sites that encouraged property damage against offices of the Democratic Party after the health care reform bill passed? Courts examining this question must determine not only whether the speech intends to bring about a bad result—most would agree that intent exists—but also whether the speech incites lawless action that is imminent.

Freedom of Speech

The freedom to speak publicly, even critically, about government and politics is central to the democratic process. Citizens cannot participate fully in a political system if they are unable to share information, opinions, advice, and calls to action. Citizens cannot hold government accountable if they cannot criticize government actions or demand change.

PURE SPEECH VERSUS SYMBOLIC SPEECH

The Supreme Court has made a distinction between pure speech that is "just words" and advocacy that couples words with actions. With respect to civic discourse, both are important. When speech moves beyond words into the realm of action, it is considered to be **symbolic speech,** nonverbal "speech" in the form of an action such as picketing or wearing an armband to signify a protest.

Unless words threaten imminent lawless action, the First Amendment will likely protect the speaker. But in civic discourse, words are often combined with action. For example, in the 1960s, antiwar protesters were arrested for burning their draft cards to demonstrate their refusal to serve in Vietnam, and public high school students were suspended from school for wearing black armbands to protest the war. When the two groups brought their cases to the Supreme Court, the justices had to determine whether their conduct rose to the level of political expression and merited First Amendment protection. Together, these cases help to define the parameters for symbolic speech.

In the first of these cases, *U.S. v. O'Brien,* the justices considered whether the government could punish several Vietnam War protesters for burning their draft cards in violation of

> Demonstrators gather outside the Capitol Building to protest the passage of President Barack Obama's health care reform bill. With the Democratic Party in control after the 2008 election, conservatives became more outspoken in exercising their right to protest.

imminent lawless action test (incitement test)
a standard established in the 1969 *Brandenburg v. Ohio* case whereby speech is restricted only if it goes beyond mere advocacy, or words, to create a high likelihood of imminent disorder or lawlessness

symbolic speech
nonverbal "speech" in the form of an action such as picketing, flag burning, or wearing an armband to signify a protest

commercial speech
advertising statements that describe products

the Selective Service Act, which made it a crime to "destroy or mutilate" those cards. The Court balanced the free expression guarantee against the government's need to prevent the destruction of the cards. Because the cards were critical to the nation's ability to raise an army, the Court ruled that the government had a compelling interest in preventing their destruction. Moreover, because the government had passed the Selective Service Act to facilitate the draft and not to suppress speech, the impact of the law on speech was incidental. When the justices balanced the government's interest in making it easy to raise an army against the incidental impact that this law had on speech, they found that the government's interest overrode that of the political protesters.[18]

In contrast, when the Court considered the other symbolic speech case of this era, *Tinker v. Des Moines,* they found that the First Amendment did protect the speech in question. In this case, the justices ruled that the political expression in the form of the students' wearing black armbands to school to protest the Vietnam War was protected.[19] On what basis did the justices distinguish the armbands in the *Tinker* case from the draft cards in the *O'Brien* case? They cited legitimate reasons for the government to ban the burning of draft cards: in a time of war, the cards were especially important to aid in the military draft. But there were no comparable reasons to ban the wearing of armbands, apart from the school district's desire to curb or suppress political expression on school grounds. School officials could not show that the armbands had disrupted normal school activities.[20] For that reason, the Court argued, the symbolic speech in *Tinker* warranted more protection than that in *O'Brien.*

The highly controversial case of *Texas v. Johnson* (1989) tested the Court's commitment to protecting symbolic speech of a highly unpopular nature. At issue was a man's conviction under state law for burning the American flag during the Republican National Convention in 1984 to emphasize his disagreement with the policies of the administration of President Ronald Reagan (1981–1989). The Supreme Court overturned the man's conviction, finding that the flag burning was political speech worthy of protection under the First Amendment.[21] After the *Johnson* decision, Congress quickly passed the Flag Protection Act in an attempt to reverse the Court's ruling. Subsequently, however, in the case of *U.S. v. Eichman* (1990), the Court struck down the new law by the same 5–4 majority as in the *Johnson* ruling.[22]

The decisions in these flag-burning cases were very controversial and have prompted Congress to pursue the only remaining legal avenue to enact flag protection statutes—a constitutional amendment. Indeed, each Congress since the *Johnson* decision has considered creating a flag-desecration amendment. Every other year from 1995 to 2006, the proposed amendment has received the two-thirds majority necessary for approval in the U.S. House of Representatives, but it has consistently failed to achieve the same constitutionally required supermajority vote in the U.S. Senate. Senate opponents of the ban argue that ratification of the amendment would undermine the principles bolstering the meaning of the flag. Although the amendment is still regularly proposed in both houses, in recent years it has not moved from committee consideration to a vote on the floor.

NOT ALL SPEECH IS CREATED EQUAL: UNPROTECTED SPEECH The Supreme Court long ago rejected the extreme view that all speech should be free in the United States. Whereas *political speech* tends to be protected against government suppression, other forms of speech can be limited or prohibited.

The courts afford **commercial speech,** that is, advertising statements, limited protection under the First Amendment. According to the Supreme Court, commercial speech may be restricted as long as the restriction "seeks to implement a substantial government interest, directly advances that interest, and goes no further than necessary to accomplish its objective." Restrictions on tobacco advertising, for example, limit free

> Here, anti-war demonstrators exercise their right to free speech and assembly, protesting the war in Iraq. Protected speech can be verbal or symbolic, as in the alteration to the American flag below.

speech in the interest of protecting the health of society. In 2010, the Supreme Court, in the controversial *Citizens United v. Federal Elections Commission* decision, revised its previous rulings and determined that the First Amendment also protected corporate spending during elections as a form of free speech. Legislation that limits such spending was an unconstitutional banning of political speech.[23]

Other forms of speech, including libel and slander, receive no protection under the First Amendment. **Libel** (written statements) and **slander** (verbal statements) are false statements that harm the reputation of another person. To qualify as libel or slander, the defamatory statement must be made publicly and with fault, meaning that reporters, for example, must undertake reasonable efforts to verify allegations. The statement must extend beyond mere name-calling or insults that cannot be proven true or false. Those who take a legal action on the grounds that they are victims of libel or slander, such as government officials, celebrities, and people involved with specific public controversies, are required to prove that the defendant acted with malice—with knowledge that the statement was false or recklessly disregarded the truth or falsity of the statement.

Obscenity, indecent or offensive speech or expression, is another form of speech that is not protected under the First Amendment. After many unsuccessful attempts to define obscenity, in 1973 the Supreme Court developed a three-part test in *Miller v. California*.[24] The Court ruled that a book, a film, or another form of expression is legally obscene if

- the average person applying contemporary standards finds that the work taken as a whole appeals to the prurient interest—that is, tends to excite unwholesome sexual desire
- the work depicts or describes, in a patently offensive way, a form of sexual conduct specifically prohibited by an antiobscenity law
- the work taken as a whole lacks serious literary, artistic, political, or scientific value

Of course, these standards do not guarantee that people will agree upon what materials are obscene. What is obscene to some may be acceptable to others. For that reason, the Court has been reluctant to limit free speech, even in the most controversial cases.

The Court may also ban speech known as **fighting words**—speech that inflicts injury or results in public disorder. The Court first articulated the fighting-words doctrine in *Chaplinsky v. New Hampshire* (1942). Walter Chaplinsky was convicted of violating a New Hampshire statute that prohibited the use of offensive, insulting language toward persons in public places after he made several inflammatory comments to a city official. The Court, in upholding the statute as constitutional, explained the limits of free speech: "These include the lewd and obscene, the profane, the libelous, and the insulting or fighting words—those which by their very utterance inflict injury or tend to incite an immediate breach of the peace."[25] Thus the Court ruled that, like slander, libel, and obscenity, "fighting words" do not advance the democratic goals of free speech. Cross burning, for example, has been a form of symbolic speech that in the United States has come to represent racial violence and intimidation against African Americans and other vulnerable groups. In 2005, the Supreme Court in *Virginia v. Black* found that a state could ban cross burning when it was used to threaten or attempt to silence other individuals, but that the state law could not assume all cross burnings attempt to communicate that message.

Even the types of "unprotected speech" we have considered enjoy broad protection under the law. Although cigarette ads are banned from television, many products are sold through every media outlet imaginable. Though a tabloid such as the *National Inquirer* sometimes faces lawsuits for the false stories it prints, most celebrities do not pursue legal action because of the high burden of proving that the paper knew the story was false, intended to damage the subject's reputation, and in fact caused real harm. Even though network television is censored for broadcasting objectionable material, the Supreme Court has ruled that the government cannot ban (adult) pornography on the Internet or on paid cable television channels.[26] The Court even struck down a ban on the transmission of "virtual" child pornography, arguing that no real children were harmed in the creation of these photographic or computer-generated images.[27] And, despite continued reaffirmation of the fighting-words doctrine, the Supreme Court has declined to uphold any convictions for fighting words since *Chaplinsky*. In short, the Court is reluctant to do anything that might

libel
false written statements about others that harm their reputation

slander
false verbal statements about others that harm their reputation

obscenity
indecent or offensive speech or expression

fighting words
speech that is likely to bring about public disorder or chaos; the Supreme Court has held that such speech may be banned in public places to ensure the preservation of public order

limit the content of adults' free speech and expression, even when that speech is unpopular or offensive.

Freedom of Assembly and Redress of Grievances

The First Amendment says that people have the freedom to assemble peaceably and to seek redress of (compensation for) grievances against the government; yet, there are limits placed on assembly. As the Supreme Court has considered free assembly cases, it has been most concerned about ensuring that individuals and groups can get together to discuss their concerns and that they can take action in the public arena that advances their political goals.

The Court's stance in free speech cases provides insight into its leanings in cases concerning freedom of assembly. The Court is keenly aware of the need for order in public forums and will clamp down on speech that is intended and likely to incite public unrest and anger. That is one reason the Court has reaffirmed the fighting-words doctrine. Although officials cannot censor speech before it occurs, they can take action to limit speech once it becomes apparent that public disorder is going to erupt. In its rulings, the Court has also allowed content-neutral **time, place, and manner restrictions**—regulations regarding when, where, or how expression may occur. Such restrictions do not target speech based on content, and to stand up in court, they must be applied in a content-neutral manner. For example, people have the right to march in protest, but not while chanting into bullhorns at four o'clock in the morning in a residential neighborhood.

The Court's rulings in these various cases illustrate how the government is balancing the freedom of public assembly against other concerns, notably public safety and the right of an individual to be left alone. The Court is carefully weighing the freedoms of one group of individuals against another and attempting to ensure the protection of free public expression.

Freedom of the Press

Throughout American history, the press has played a crucial role in the larger debate about political expression. Before the War for Independence, when the British monarchy sought to clamp down on political dissent in the colonies, the king and Parliament quickly recognized the urgency of silencing the press. A free press is essential to democratic ideals, and democracy cannot survive when a government controls the press. The First Amendment's guarantees of a free press ensure not only that American government remains accountable to its constituents but also that the people hear competing ideas about how to deal with matters of public concern. Increasingly, the Internet has become the place where ordinary citizens share their views on important political issues.

Ensuring a free press can complicate the work of government. Consider the challenge presented to the George W. Bush administration when the *New York Times* broke a story in late 2005 that the National Security Agency (NSA) had been using futuristic spy technology against thousands of individuals inside the United States.[28],[29] The NSA is responsible for monitoring the communications of foreigners outside U.S. borders and does not have authority to engage in surveillance of Americans in the United States. Moreover, the Fourth Amendment protects American citizens against searches without either a warrant or a court order. Despite claims to the contrary during his campaign, President Obama has not changed that policy and has sided with the Bush Administration in legislation challenging it.[30]

Certain well-established principles govern freedom of the press in the United States. First and foremost, the courts almost never allow the government to engage in prior restraint. **Prior restraint** means censorship—the attempt to block the publication of material that is considered to be harmful. The Supreme Court established this rule against censorship in 1931 in the landmark case of *Near v. Minnesota*. After editor

time, place, and manner restrictions
regulations regarding when, where, or how expression may occur; must be content neutral

prior restraint
a form of censorship by the government whereby it blocks the publication of news stories viewed as libelous or harmful

Jay Near wrote a story in the *Saturday Press* alleging that Jews were responsible for corruption, bribery, and prostitution in Minneapolis, a state judge barred all future sales of the newspaper. The Court overturned the state judge's ruling, finding that the sole purpose of the order was to suppress speech. Because freedom of the press has strong historical foundations, the Court concluded, censorship is clearly prohibited.

In the *Near* ruling, the Court recognized, however, that there might be times when governmental officials could limit the publication of certain stories. Specifically, such censorship might be justified under extraordinary circumstances related to ensuring public safety or national security or in cases involving obscenity. In reality, though, the Court has disallowed prior restraint in the vast majority of cases. For example, in the most important case examining the national security exception, *New York Times v. U.S.* (1971), the Court rejected the government's attempt to prevent publication of documents that detailed the history of the United States' involvement in Vietnam. In this case, also known as the *Pentagon Papers* case, the government argued that censorship was necessary to prevent "irreparable injury" to national security. But the Court dismissed that argument, asserting that full disclosure was in the interest of all Americans and that publication of the documents could contribute to the ongoing debate about the U.S. role in the Vietnam War.[31] In their ruling, the justices recognized that some materials are clearly necessary for full and fair discussion of issues facing the nation, whereas others are far less important to political discourse. (The Court, for example, has allowed the government to censor publications that are far less central to public debate, such as obscene materials.)

The Court is far more willing to allow the government to impose constraints on broadcast media than on print media. Why should a distinction be made between print and broadcast media? Probably the most important justification is that only a limited number of channels can be broadcast, and the government is responsible for parceling out those channels. Because the public owns the airwaves, the people may also impose reasonable regulations on those who are awarded licenses to operate broadcast channels.

The Court views the Internet to be more like print media than like broadcast media. Thus far, the Court has signaled its interpretation that the Internet is an enormous resource for democratic forums, one that allows users access to virtually unlimited sites at very low cost (*Reno v. ACLU*, 1997). The Court's fine distinctions are between media that allow more and media that allow less access to individuals and groups to engage in political discourse. The Court's assumption is that print media and the Internet provide relatively cheap and virtually unlimited access and enable people to tap easily into discussions about issues facing the nation. In contrast, broadcast media, with much scarcer channels, represent a much more limited arena for dialogue and thus can reasonably be regulated.

Freedoms of Religion, Privacy, and Criminal Due Process: Encouraging Community and Civic Engagement

The Constitution's framers understood that the government they were creating could use its powers to single out certain groups for either favorable or unfavorable treatment and in that way could interfere with the creation of community—and with citizens' engagement within that community. The founders' commitment to community building and citizens' engagement lies at the heart of several constitutional amendments in the Bill of Rights. Specifically these are the amendments establishing the freedom of religion, the right to privacy, and the right to due process for individuals in the criminal justice system.

The First Amendment and the Freedom of Religion

The religion clauses of the First Amendment—the establishment clause and the free exercise clause—essentially do two things. First, they bar the government from establishing or supporting any one religious sect over another, and second, they ensure that individuals are not hindered in the exercise of their religion. Whereas the establishment clause requires that the government be neutral toward religious institutions, favoring neither one specific religion over others nor all religious groups over nonreligious groups, the free exercise clause prohibits the government from taking action that is hostile toward individuals' practice of their religion. As we now consider, there is tension between these two clauses.

THE ESTABLISHMENT CLAUSE Stating only that "Congress shall make no law respecting an establishment of religion," the **establishment clause** does little to clarify what the relationship between church and state should be. The Constitution's authors wanted to ensure that Congress could not create a national religion, as a number of European powers (notably France and Spain) had done; the framers sought to avoid that level of government entanglement in religious matters. Further, many colonists had immigrated to America to escape religious persecution in Europe, and although many were deeply religious, uncertainty prevailed about the role that government should play in the practice of religion. That uncertainty, too, is reflected in the brevity of the establishment clause. The question arises, does the clause prohibit the government from simply preferring one sect over another, or is it broader, encompassing any kind of support of religion?

This is a crucial question because religious institutions have always been important forums for community building and engagement in the United States. Americans continue to be a very religious people. In 2009, over 81 percent of Americans surveyed said religion was fairly or very important in their lives.[32] But even given their strong religious affiliations, most Americans believe in some degree of separation between religious organizations and the government. The actual debate has been about how much separation the establishment clause requires.

Over time, scholars and lawyers have considered three possible interpretations of the establishment clause. One interpretation, called separationism, is that the establishment clause requires a *strict separation of church and state* and bars most or all government support for religious sects. Supporters of the strict separationist view invoke the writings of Thomas Jefferson, James Madison, and others that call for a "wall of separation" between church and state.[33] They also point to societies outside the United States in which religious leaders dictate how citizens may dress, act, and pray as examples of what can happen without strict separation.

A second, and more flexible, interpretation allows the government to offer support to religious sects as long as that support is neutral and not biased toward one sect. This interpretation, known as *neutrality* or the *preferential treatment standard*, would permit government support provided that this support extended to all religious groups. The third interpretation is the most flexible and reads the establishment clause as barring only establishment of a state religion. This interpretation, known as *accommodationism,* allows the government to offer support to any or all religious groups provided that this support does not rise to the level of recognizing an official religion.[34]

Which of these three vastly different interpretations of the establishment clause is correct? Over time, the Supreme Court has shifted back and forth in its opinions, usually depending on the kind of government support in question. Overall, the courts have rejected the strictest interpretation of the establishment clause, which would ban virtually any form of aid to religion. Instead, they have allowed government support for religious schools, programs, and institutions if the support advances a secular (nonreligious) goal and does not specifically endorse a particular religious belief.

For example, in 1974, the Court upheld a New Jersey program that provided funds to the parents of parochial school students to pay for bus transportation to and from school.[35] The Court reasoned that the program was necessary to help students to get to school safely and concluded that if the state withdrew funding for any of these programs for parochial school students, it would be impossible to operate these schools. The impact would be the hindrance of the free exercise of religion for students and their parents.

In another landmark case, *Lemon v. Kurtzman* (1971), however, the Court struck down a state program that used cigarette taxes to reimburse parochial schools for the costs of teachers' salaries and textbooks. The Court found that subsidizing parochial schools furthered a process of religious teaching and that the "continuing state surveillance" that would be necessary to enforce the specific provisions of the laws would inevitably entangle the state in religious affairs.[36]

establishment clause
First Amendment clause that bars the government from passing any law "respecting an establishment of religion"; often interpreted as a separation of church and state but increasingly questioned

In the *Lemon* case ruling, the Court refined the establishment clause standard to include three considerations.

- Does the state program have a secular, as opposed to a religious, purpose?
- Does it have as its principal effect the advancement of religion?
- Does the program create an excessive entanglement between church and state?

This three-part test is known as the **Lemon test.** The programs most likely to withstand scrutiny under the establishment clause are those that have a secular purpose, have only an incidental effect on the advancement of religion, and do not excessively entangle church and state.

More recently, the Court upheld an Ohio program that gave vouchers to parents to offset the cost of parochial schooling.[37] The justices ruled that the purpose of the program was secular, not religious, because it was intended to provide parents with an alternative to the Cleveland public schools. Any aid to religious institutions—in this case, mostly Catholic schools—was indirect, because the primary beneficiaries were the students themselves. Finally, there was little entanglement between the church and state, because the parents received the vouchers based on financial need and then were free to use these vouchers as they pleased. There was no direct relationship between the religious schools and the state.

So where the government program offers financial support, the Court has tended to evaluate this program by using either the preferential treatment standard or the accommodationist standard. Where the program or policy involves prayer in the school or issues related to the curriculum, however, the Court has adopted a standard that looks more like strict separationism. Table 4.4 summarizes the Court's decisions in a variety of school-related free exercise and establishment clause cases.

As Table 4.4 illustrates, a series of cases beginning with *Engel v. Vitale* (1962) has barred formalized prayer in the school, finding that such prayer has a purely religious purpose and that prayer is intended to advance religious, as opposed to secular, ideals.[38] For that reason, the Court has barred school-organized prayer in public elementary and secondary schools on the grounds that it constitutes a state endorsement of religion. Student-organized prayer is constitutional because the state is not engaging in any coercion by mandating or encouraging student participation.

Recently, courts have begun to grapple with the decision of some school boards to mandate the inclusion of intelligent design in the curriculum.[39] **Intelligent design** is the assertion that the apparent design in the universe and in living things is the product of an intelligent cause rather than of an undirected process such as natural selection. Though

Lemon test

a three-part test established by the Supreme Court in the 1971 case *Lemon v. Kurtzman* to determine whether government aid to parochial schools is constitutional; the test is also applied to other cases involving the establishment clause

intelligent design

theory that the apparent design in the universe and in living things is the product of an intelligent cause rather than of an undirected process such as natural selection; its primary proponents believe that the designer is God and seek to redefine science to accept supernatural explanations

TABLE 4.4

Religion and Schools: Permissible and Impermissible Activities

Public Funding Not Permitted	Supreme Court Case	Year
Parochial school salaries	*Lemon v. Kurtzman*	1971
Parochial school textbooks	*Lemon v. Kurtzman*	1971
Public Funding Permitted	**Supreme Court Case**	**Year**
Parochial school busing	*Everson v. Board of Education*	1947
Parochial/private school computers	*Mitchell v. Helms*	2000
Public/private school vouchers	*Zelman v. Simmons-Harris*	2002
Public School Activities Not Permitted	**Supreme Court Case**	**Year**
Teacher-led nondenominational prayer	*Engel v. Vitale*	1962
Banning the teaching of evolution	*Epperson v. Arkansas*	1968
Requiring teaching of creationism	*Edward v. Aguillard*	1987
Requiring Ten Commandments posting	*Stone v. Graham*	1980
Official graduation ceremony prayers	*Lee v. Weisman*	1992
Moment of silence for voluntary prayer	*Wallace v. Jaffree*	1985
Student-led prayers using PA system	*Santa Fe School District v. Doe*	2000
Requiring all students to say the Pledge	*W. Virginia Board of Ed. v. Barnette*	1943
Public School Activities Permitted	**Supreme Court Case**	**Year**
Off-campus release-time religion classes	*Zorach v. Clauson*	1952
After-school student-led religion club	*Board of Education of Westside Community Schools v. Mergens*	1990
Use of public school building by religious groups (after hours)	*Lamb's Chapel v. Center Moriches School District*	1993
Public school teachers teaching in parochial schools	*Agostini v. Felton*	1997
Voluntary after-school Bible study	*Good News Club v. Milford Central School*	2001

creationism

theory of the creation of the earth and humankind based on a literal interpretation of the biblical story of Genesis

free exercise clause

First Amendment clause prohibiting the government from enacting laws prohibiting an individual's practice of his or her religion; often in contention with the establishment clause

not stated by its primary proponents, many supporters believe that the designer is God, and they seek to redefine science to accept supernatural explanations.

Advocates of intelligent design claim that unlike **creationism,** which defends a literal interpretation of the biblical story of Genesis, intelligent design is a scientific theory. For that reason, they say, school boards should be permitted to include it in the curriculum, alongside evolution. Opponents claim that intelligent design is just another form of creationism, because it is based upon a belief in a divine being, does not generate any predictions, and cannot be tested by experiment. Mandating that schools teach intelligent design, critics argue, constitutes an endorsement of religion by the state.

THE FREE EXERCISE CLAUSE   The tension between the establishment and free exercise clauses arises because the establishment clause bars the state from helping religious institutions, whereas the **free exercise clause** makes it illegal for the government to enact laws prohibiting the free practice of religion by individuals. Establishment clause cases often raise free exercise claims, and so courts must frequently consider whether by banning state aid, they are interfering with the free exercise of religion.

Although free exercise and establishment cases raise many of the same concerns, they are different kinds of cases, whose resolution depends on distinct legal tests. Establishment clause cases typically involve well-established and well-known religious institutions. Because establishment clause cases often center on state aid to religious schools, many involve the Roman Catholic Church, which administers the largest number of private elementary and secondary schools in the country. In contrast, free exercise clause cases tend to involve less mainstream religious groups, among them Mormons, Jehovah's Witnesses, Christian Scientists, and Amish. These groups' practices tend to be less well known—or more controversial. For example, free exercise clause cases have involved the right to practice polygamy, to use hallucinogens, to refuse conventional medical care for a child, and to refuse to salute the flag.

The Supreme Court has refused to accept that the government is barred from *ever* interfering with religious exercise. Free exercise claims are difficult to settle because they require that courts balance the individual's right to free practice of religion against the government's need to adopt some policy or program. First and foremost, the Court has always distinguished between religious beliefs, which government may not interfere with, and religious actions, which government is permitted to regulate. For example, although adults may refuse lifesaving medical care on the basis of their own religious beliefs, they may not refuse medical procedures required to save the lives of their children.[40]

In assessing those laws that interfere with religiously motivated action, the Court has distinguished between laws that are neutral and generally applicable to all religious sects and laws that single out one sect for unfavorable treatment. In *Employment Division, Department of Human Resources v. Smith* (1990), the Court allowed the state of Oregon to deny unemployment benefits to two substance-abuse counselors who were fired from their jobs after using peyote as part of their religious practice. Oregon refused to provide benefits because the two men had been fired for engaging in an illegal activity. The Court concluded that there was no free exercise challenge, because Oregon had good reason for denying benefits to lawbreakers who had been fired from their jobs. The justices concluded that the state was simply applying a neutral and generally applicable law to the men as opposed to singling them out for bad treatment.[41] One consequence of this case was that several states, including Oregon, passed laws excluding members of the Native American Church, who smoke peyote as part of traditional religious rites, from being covered by their controlled-substance laws.

In summary, people are free to hold and profess their own beliefs, to build and actively participate in religious communities, and to allow their religious beliefs to inform their participation in politics and civil society. However, individual *actions* based on religious beliefs may be limited if those actions conflict with existing laws that are neutrally applied in a nondiscriminatory fashion.

The Right to Privacy

So far in this section, we have explored the relationship between civil liberties and some key themes of this book: civic participation, inclusiveness, community building, and community engagement. We now shift our focus somewhat to consider the **right to privacy,** the right of an individual to be left alone and to make decisions freely, without the interference of others. Privacy is a core principle for most Americans, and the right to make decisions, especially about intimate or personal matters, is at the heart of this right. Yet the right to privacy is also necessary for genuine inclusiveness and community engagement, because it ensures that each individual is able to act autonomously and to make decisions about how he or she will interact with others.

The right to privacy is highly controversial and the subject of much public debate. In large part, the reason is that this right is tied to some of the most divisive issues of our day, including abortion, aid in dying, and sexual orientation. The right to privacy is also controversial because, unlike the freedoms of speech, the press, assembly, and religion, it is not explicitly mentioned anywhere in the Constitution. A further reason for the debate surrounding the right to privacy is that the Supreme Court has only recently recognized it.

THE EMERGENT RIGHT TO PRIVACY   For more than one hundred years, Supreme Court justices and lower-court judges have concluded that the right to privacy is implied in all the other liberties spelled out in the Bill of Rights. Not until the landmark Supreme Court case *Griswold v. Connecticut* (1965) did the courts firmly establish the right to privacy. The issue in this case may seem strange to us today: whether the state of Connecticut had the power to prohibit married couples from using birth control. In their decision, the justices concluded that the state law violated the privacy right of married couples by preventing them from seeking to access birth control, and the Court struck down the Connecticut prohibition. The Court argued that the right to privacy was inherent in many of the other constitutional guarantees, most importantly the First Amendment freedom of association, the Third Amendment right to be free from the quartering of soldiers, the Fourth Amendment right to be free from unreasonable searches and seizures, the Fifth Amendment protection against self-incrimination, and the Ninth Amendment assurance of rights not explicitly listed in the Bill of Rights. Justice William O. Douglas and his colleagues effectively argued that a zone of privacy surrounded every person in the United States and that government could not pass laws that encroached upon this zone.[42]

In its ruling, the Court asserted that the right to privacy existed quite apart from the law. It was implicit in the Bill of Rights and fundamental to the American system of law and justice. The right to privacy hinged in large part on the right of individuals to associate with one another, and specifically the right of marital partners to engage in intimate association.

In a 1984 case, the Supreme Court ruled that the Constitution protects two kinds of freedom of association: (1) intimate associations and (2) expressive associations.[43] The protection of intimate associations allows Americans to maintain intimate human relationships as part of their personal liberty. The protection of expressive associations allows people to form associations with others and to practice their First Amendment freedoms of speech, assembly, petition, and religion.

> Thirteen-year-old Savanna Redding was suspected of possessing prescription strength ibuprofen and over-the-counter naproxen pills in her public school. Female school officials questioned her, asked her to strip down to her underwear, and then show she had nothing hidden in her underwear. In *Safford v. Redding* (2009), the Court found this "strip-search" to be unreasonable.

THE RIGHT TO PRIVACY APPLIED TO OTHER ACTIVITIES   The challenge for the Court since *Griswold* has been to determine which activities fall within the scope of the privacy right, and that question has placed the justices at the center of some of the most controversial issues of the day. For example, the first attempt to extend the privacy right, which raised the question of whether the right protected abortion, remains at least as controversial today as it was in 1973 when the Court decided the first abortion rights case, *Roe v. Wade*.[44] In *Roe* and the many abortion cases the Court has heard since, the justices have tried to establish whether a woman's right to abortion takes precedence over any interests the state may have in either the woman's health or the fetus's life. Over time, the Court has adopted a compromise position by rejecting the view that the right to abortion is absolute and by attempting to determine when states can regulate, or even prohibit, access to abortion. In 1992, the Court established the "undue burden" test, which asks whether a state abortion law places a "substantial obstacle in the path of a woman seeking an abortion before the fetus attains viability."[45] Although the Court used this standard to strike down spousal notification requirements, it has upheld other requirements imposed by some states, including waiting periods, mandatory counseling, and parental consent.

The Court has also stepped gingerly around other privacy rights, such as the right to choose one's sexual partners and the right to terminate medical treatment or engage in physician-assisted suicide. Both of these rights have been presented to the Court as hinging on the much broader right to privacy. With respect to the right to terminate medical treatment, the Court has been fairly clear. Various Court decisions have confirmed that as long as an individual is competent to terminate treatment, the state may not stop him or her from taking this action, even if stopping treatment will lead to the person's death.[46]

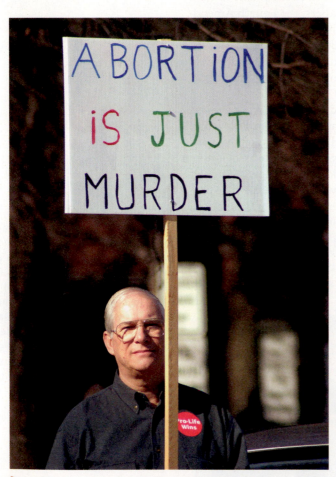 

> Public debate over abortion was not settled by the Supreme Court's 1973 decision in *Roe v. Wade.* In this photo taken more than three decades later, pro-life and pro-choice activists in Washington, D.C., hold signs supporting their differing viewpoints. Abortion rights advocates frame the issue in terms of a woman's right to privacy and to control her own body. Abortion rights opponents view abortion as murder and frame the issue in terms of the rights of an unborn child.

The Court has been less clear in its rulings when an incompetent person's right is advanced by another individual, such as a spouse, a parent, or a child. In these circumstances, the Court has accepted the state's argument that before treatment may be terminated, the state may require that the person seeking to end life show that his or her loved one would have wanted that course of action.[47] When a person's wishes are not clear, loved ones may wage legal battles over whether to discontinue life support (see Chapter 14).

In cases involving the right to engage in consensual sexual activities with a partner of one's choosing, the Supreme Court has also employed a less than absolute approach. For many years, the Court allowed states to criminalize homosexual activity, finding that the right to engage in consensual sexual activity did not extend to same-sex partners.[48] In a 2003 case, *Lawrence v. Texas,* the Court changed course by ruling that the right to engage in intimate sexual activity was protected as a liberty right, especially when the activity occurred inside one's home, and that states could not criminalize this activity.[49] Since that decision, rights activists have worked through the courts and state and federal legislatures to secure for same-sex partners the same rights that heterosexual couples enjoy, including benefits provided by group health insurance and marriage. Marriage is regulated by the states, and as Figure 4.1 shows, there is a wide range of state laws pertaining to marriage; many of these laws have only been recently passed. The *Lawrence* decision aside, states are still free

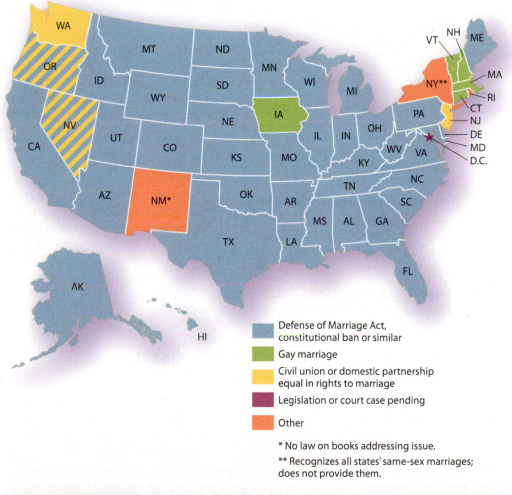

Defense of Marriage Act, constitutional ban or similar

Gay marriage

Civil union or domestic partnership equal in rights to marriage

Legislation or court case pending

Other

* No law on books addressing issue.

** Recognizes all states' same-sex marriages; does not provide them.

POLITICAL INQUIRY

FIGURE 4.1 ■ STATE MARRIAGE LAWS What regional variations do you see regarding these laws? How would you explain the existence of both a ban on gay marriage and a law protecting civil unions and domestic partnerships in Nevada and Oregon? How does your home state currently address same-sex marriages or civil unions?

Sharing Personal Information on the Internet

WEB SITE	THEN (2003)	NOW (2010)
Facebook	0 active users >	117 million unique users per month
MySpace	0 active users >	42 million unique users per month
Twitter	0 active users >	20 million unique users a month
LinkedIn	0 active users >	13.8 million unique users a month

WHAT'S NEXT?

> Will social-networking Web sites be required to share personal information about their clients, and their clients' Internet behavior, with federal investigators?

> How will our conceptions of privacy (and privacy rights) change as people post increasing amounts of information about themselves on the Web?

> Will the courts continue to protect virtually unlimited speech on the Web?

SOURCE: http://blog.nielson.com/nielsonwire/global/facebook-and-twitter-post-large-year-over-year-gains-in-unique-users. May 4, 2010.

to prohibit a range of sexual activities, including prostitution, child sexual abuse, and sex in public places.[50] In the Court's view, these activities can be prohibited primarily because they are not consensual or do not take place in the home, a place that accords special protection by the privacy right.

The right to privacy remains very controversial. Cases brought under the right to privacy tend to link this right with some other civil liberty, such as the protection against unreasonable search and seizure, the right to free speech, or the protection against self-incrimination. In other words, the privacy right, which the justices themselves created, seems to need buttressing by other rights that the Bill of Rights *explicitly* establishes. The explanation for this development may be the contentiousness of Americans' civic discourse about abortion, aid in dying, and other privacy issues. In short, continuing civic disagreement may have forced the Court to fall back on rights that are well established and more widely accepted.

Public discourse about privacy is constantly evolving as people voluntarily share more and more information about themselves through online networking sites such as Facebook, MySpace, Twitter, and LinkedIn. (See "Then, Now, Next.") Users of such sites and bloggers share stories, photos, and videos of themselves—as well as of others, who may be unaware that they are the subject of a posting, a blog, or a video. Civil libertarians worry about the misuse and theft of personal information in a high-tech society where people's financial, employment, consumer, legal, and personal histories are so easily accessible. Government and law enforcement agencies are still deciding how they may use such materials in criminal investigations. Legal implications remain unclear.

The Fourth, Fifth, Sixth, and Eighth Amendments: Ensuring Criminal Due Process

The last category of civil liberties that bear directly on civic engagement consists of the criminal due process protections established in the Fourth, Fifth, Sixth, and Eighth amendments. Does it surprise you that so many of the Bill of Rights amendments focus on the rights of individuals accused of crimes? The context for this emphasis is the founders' concern with how the British monarchy had abused its power and used criminal law to impose its will on the American colonists. The British government had used repeated trials, charges of treason, and imprisonment without bail to stifle political dissent. The founders therefore wanted to ensure that there were effective checks on the power of the federal government, especially in the creation and enforcement of criminal law. As we have seen, the Bill of Rights amendments were incorporated to apply to the states and to their criminal codes through the process of selective incorporation. Thus, criminal due process protections are the constitutional limits imposed on law enforcement personnel.

These four amendments together are known as the **criminal due process rights** because they establish the guidelines that the government must follow in investigating, bringing to trial, and punishing individuals who violate criminal law. Each amendment guides the government in administering some facet of law enforcement, and all are intended to ensure justice and fairness in the administration of the law. Criminal due process is essential to guarantee that individuals can participate in the larger society and that no one person is singled out for better or worse treatment under the law. Like the First Amendment, due process protects political speech and freedom. Without these liberties, government officials could selectively target those who disagree with the laws and policies they advocate.

Moreover, without these rights, there would be little to stop the government from using criminal law to punish those who want to take action that is protected by the other amendments we have examined in this chapter. For example, what good would it do to talk about the freedom of speech if the government could isolate or punish someone who spoke out critically against it without having to prove in a public venue that the speech threatened public safety or national security? The criminal due process protections are essential to ensuring meaningful participation and engagement in the larger community and to safeguarding justice and fairness.

THE FOURTH AMENDMENT AND THE PROTECTION AGAINST UNREASONABLE SEARCHES AND SEIZURES

The Fourth Amendment requires police to get a warrant before engaging in a search and guides law enforcement personnel in conducting criminal investigations and in searching an individual's body or property. It has its roots in colonial history—specifically, in the British government's abuse of its law enforcement powers to prosecute and punish American colonists suspected of being disloyal.

The Fourth Amendment imposes significant limits on law enforcement. In barring police from conducting any unreasonable searches and seizures, it requires that they show probable cause that a crime has been committed before they can obtain a search warrant. The warrant ensures that police officers can gather evidence only when they have probable cause. Further, a judicially created ruling known as the **exclusionary rule** compels law enforcers to carry out searches properly. Established for federal prosecutions in 1914, the exclusionary rule forbids the courts to admit illegally seized evidence during trial.[51] This rule was extended to state court proceedings in the Supreme Court decision *Mapp v. Ohio* (1961).[52] In this case, the Court overturned an Ohio court's conviction of Dollree Mapp for the possession of obscene materials. Police had found pornographic books in Mapp's apartment after searching it without a search warrant and despite the defendant's refusal to let them in. Critics of the exclusionary rule note that securing a warrant is not always necessary or feasible and that guilty people sometimes go free because of procedural technicalities. They argue that reasonable searches should not be defined solely by the presence of a court-ordered search warrant.[53]

What are "reasonable" and "unreasonable" searches under the Fourth Amendment? Over time, the U.S. Supreme Court has established criteria to guide both police officers and judges hearing cases. In the strictest definition of reasonableness, there is a warrant: where there is no warrant, the search is considered to be unreasonable. However, the Supreme Court has ruled that even without a warrant, some searches would still be reasonable. In 1984, for example, the Court held that illegally obtained evidence could be admitted at trial if law enforcers could prove that they would have obtained the evidence legally anyway.[54]

In another case the same year, the Court created a "good faith" exception to the exclusionary rule by upholding the use of evidence obtained with a technically incorrect warrant, because the police officer had acted in good faith.[55]

More broadly, a warrantless search is valid if the person subjected to it has no reasonable expectation of privacy in the place or thing being searched. From colonial times to the present, the assumption has been that individuals have a reasonable expectation of privacy in their homes. Where there is no reasonable expectation of privacy, however, there can be no unreasonable search, and so the police are not required to get a warrant before conducting the search or surveillance. Since the 1990s, the Court has expanded the situations in which there is no reasonable expectation of privacy and hence no need for a warrant. For example, there is no reasonable expectation of privacy in one's car, at least in those areas that are in plain view, such as the front and back seats. There is also no expectation of privacy in public

criminal due process rights
safeguards for those accused of crime; these rights constrain government conduct in investigating crimes, trying cases, and punishing offenders

exclusionary rule
criminal procedural rule stating that evidence obtained illegally cannot be used in a trial

places such as parks and stores, because it is reasonable to assume that a person knowingly exposes his or her activities to public view in those places. The same is true of one's trash: because there is no reasonable expectation of privacy in the things that one discards, police may search this material without a warrant.[56]

In instances where there is a reasonable expectation of privacy, individuals or their property may be searched if law enforcement personnel acquire a warrant from a judge. To obtain a warrant, the police must provide the judge with evidence that establishes probable cause that a crime has been committed. Further, the warrant must be specific about the place to be searched and the materials that the agents are seeking. These requirements limit the ability of police simply to go on a "fishing expedition" to find some bit of incriminating evidence.

As society changes, expectations of privacy change as well. For example, technological innovation has given us e-mail and the Internet, and Fourth Amendment law has had to adapt to these inventions. Is there a reasonable expectation of privacy in our communications on the Internet? This is an important question, especially in light of citizens' heightened concerns about terrorism and white-collar crime.

THE FIFTH AND SIXTH AMENDMENTS: THE RIGHT TO A FAIR TRIAL AND THE RIGHT TO COUNSEL The Fifth and Sixth amendments establish the rules for conducting a trial. These two amendments ensure that criminal defendants are protected at the formal stages of legal proceedings. Although less than 10 percent of all charges result in trials, these protections have significant symbolic and practical importance, because they hold the state to a high standard whenever it attempts to use its significant power to prosecute a case against an individual.

The Fifth Amendment bars **double jeopardy** and compelled self-incrimination. These safeguards mean, respectively, that a person may not be tried twice for the same crime or forced to testify against himself or herself when accused of a crime. These safeguards are meant to protect people from persecution, harassment, and forced confessions. A single criminal action, however, can lead to multiple trials if each trial is based on a separate offense.

The Sixth Amendment establishes the rights to a speedy and public trial, to a trial by a jury of one's peers, to information about the charges against oneself, to the confrontation of witnesses testifying against oneself, and to legal counsel. The protection of these Fifth and Sixth Amendment liberties is promoted by the *Miranda* **rights,** based on the Supreme Court decision in *Miranda v. Arizona* (1966).[57] In the *Miranda* case, the Court outlined the requirement that "prior to questioning, the person must be warned that he has a right to remain silent, that any statement he does make may be used against him, and that he has a right to the presence of an attorney, either retained or appointed." Later cases have created some exceptions to *Miranda* (see Table 4.5).

Together, the Fourth, Fifth, and Sixth amendments ensure the protection of individuals against abuses of power by the state, and in so doing they promote a view of justice that the community widely embraces. Because these rights extend to individuals charged with violating the community's standards of right and wrong, they promote a broad sense of inclusiveness—a respect even for persons who allegedly have committed serious offenses, and a desire to ensure that the justice system treats all people fairly.

The Court has considered the community's views in reaching its decisions in cases brought before it. For example, through a series of Supreme Court cases culminating with *Gideon v. Wainwright* (1963), the justices interpreted the right to counsel to mean that the government must provide lawyers to individuals who are too poor to hire their own.[58] The justices adopted this standard because they came to believe that the community's views of fundamental fairness dic-

double jeopardy
the trying of a person again for the same crime that he or she has been cleared of in court; barred by the Fifth Amendment

***Miranda* rights**
criminal procedural rule, established in the 1966 case *Miranda v. Arizona*, requiring police to inform criminal suspects, on their arrest, of their legal rights, such as the right to remain silent and the right to counsel; these warnings must be read to suspects before interrogation

TABLE 4.5

Cases Weakening Protection Against Self-Incrimination

Year	Case	Ruling
1986	*Moran v. Burbine*	Confession is not inadmissible because police failed to inform suspect of attorney's attempted contacts.
1991	*Arizona v. Fulminante*	Conviction is not automatically overturned in cases of coerced confession if other evidence is strong enough to justify conviction.
1994	*Davis v. U.S.*	Suspect must unequivocally and assertively state his right to counsel to stop police questioning.

tated this result. Before this decision, states had to provide attorneys only in cases that could result in capital punishment.

THE EIGHTH AMENDMENT: PROTECTION AGAINST CRUEL AND UN-USUAL PUNISHMENT   The meaning of *cruel* and *unusual* has changed radically since the Eighth Amendment was ratified, especially with regard to the imposition of capital punishment—the death penalty. Moreover, Americans have always disagreed among themselves about the death penalty itself. Throughout the country's history, citizens and lawmakers have debated the morality of capital punishment as well as the circumstances under which the death penalty should be used. Central to the public debate have been the questions of which crimes should be punished by death and how capital punishment should be carried out.

Generally, the Court has supported the constitutionality of the death penalty. An exception was the landmark case *Furman v. Georgia* (1972), in which, in a 5–4 decision, the Court suspended the use of the death penalty.[59] Justices Brennan and Marshall believed the death penalty to be "incompatible with evolving standards of decency in contemporary society." The dissenting justices argued in turn that capital punishment had always been regarded as appropriate under the Anglo-American legal tradition for serious crimes and that the Constitution implicitly authorized death penalty laws because of the Fourteenth Amendment's reference to the taking of "life." The majority decision came about as a result of concurring opinions by justices Stewart, White, and Douglas, who focused on the arbitrary nature with which death sentences had been imposed. The Court's decision forced the states and the national legislature to rethink their statutes for capital offenses to ensure that the death penalty would not be administered in a capricious or discriminatory manner.[60] Over time, the courts have also interpreted the Eighth Amendment as requiring that executions be carried out in the most humane and least painful manner. Public discourse and debate have strongly influenced thinking about which methods of execution are appropriate.

Recent studies, however, suggest that states' administration of the sedative sodium pentothal has left individuals conscious and in agony but paralyzed and thus unable to cry out while they are dying. But in 2008, the Supreme Court ruled in a 7–2 decision that lethal injection does not constitute cruel and unusual punishment,[61] paving the way for ten states, which had halted lethal injections pending the case's outcome, to resume executions. The 2008 decision of *Baze v. Rees* marked the first time the Supreme Court reviewed the constitutionality of a method of execution since 1878, when the Court upheld Utah's use of a firing squad.[62]

In that early ruling, the Court said the Constitution prohibits executions that involve torture, such as burning alive or drawing and quartering an individual, as well as other infliction of "unnecessary cruelty" that the justices did not define. As Figure 4.2 on page 136 demonstrates, states have greatly differed in their interpretation of a constitutionally legitimate means of execution. In the recent case, lawyers for the Kentucky inmates argued that the state is violating that standard by using drugs that pose a risk of extreme pain if something goes wrong and by failing to provide adequate safeguards. But in its decision in 2008, the Court ruled that there is no Eighth Amendment requirement that a government-sanctioned execution be pain free, only that it does not involve a "substantial" or "objectively intolerable" risk of serious harm—a risk greater than possible alternatives.

Freedoms in Practice: Controversy Over the Second Amendment and the Right to Bear Arms

The fierce debate today over gun control illustrates much about the nature of political discourse and citizen action in the United States. Americans disagree about how to interpret the Second Amendment of the Constitution, but they do agree to have their disputes settled through laws and court rulings rather than armed conflict. Private citizens and political interest groups use their First Amendment freedoms of speech and assembly to voice their opinions about the place of guns in society. They also work behind the scenes to influence elected officials through campaign contributions and lobbying (see Chapter 7). At the heart of this debate is the question of the role of guns in creating a safe and free society.

States with and without the Death Penalty

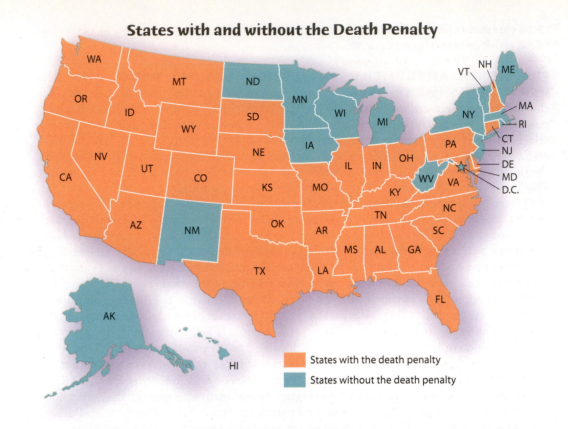

■ States with the death penalty
■ States without the death penalty

Nationwide Murder Rates, 2008
per 100,000 People

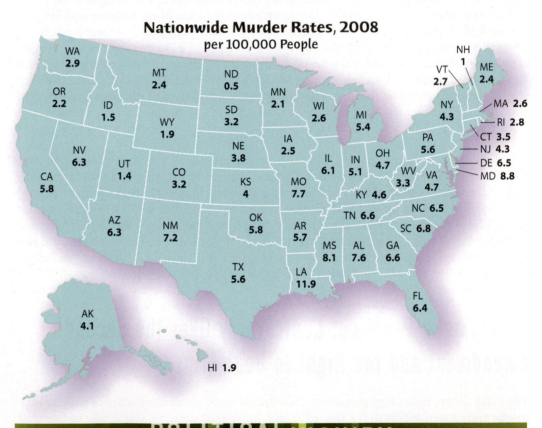

FIGURE 4.2 ■ **STATE LAWS REGARDING CAPITAL PUNISHMENT** What relationship do you see between the two maps? Are states with death penalties likely to have higher or lower murder rates than states without death penalties? What might this mean for public policy decisions?

Competing Interpretations of the Second Amendment

Americans disagree about the purpose and the contemporary significance of the Second Amendment, which reads

> A well regulated Militia, being necessary to the security of a free State, the right of the people to keep and bear Arms, shall not be infringed.

Some people argue that the amendment gives individual citizens the right to bear arms, free from government control.[63] On the opposing side, others stress that the Second Amendment's original purpose was to ensure that state militias could back the government in maintaining public order.[64] These people suggest that the right to bear arms is thus a group right subject to regulation by Congress and the states.[65] The unorganized militia has not been activated since before the Civil War, and the government now has adequate weapons to defend the nation, these critics say.

States differ widely in the degree to which citizens have access to guns. Some states allow residents to carry concealed weapons for personal protection, but others do not. In 1976, Washington, D.C., passed the nation's toughest gun control laws, including a ban on handguns, rifles, and automatic weapons, except for individuals with a special permit—mostly police and security guards. In a 2008 ruling, the Supreme Court ruled in a 5–2 decision that "the right of the people to keep and bear arms" is not limited to state militias but, rather, is a part of "the inherent right of self-defense," striking down the district's handgun ban.[66] In 2010, the Court ruled that the Fourteenth Amendment incorporates the Second Amendment to the states, requiring them to respect these rights in state law. [67]

Citizens Engaged: Fighting for a Safer Nation

This disagreement over the Second Amendment's meaning is reflected in the actions of ordinary citizens and organized interest groups. For example, the Million Moms and the Second Amendment Sisters are two interest groups with clashing views on the issue of gun control. The Million Moms see stronger gun control laws as a way to prevent the alarmingly high number of U.S. deaths of young people from gun violence, an estimated ten deaths per day.[68] The Second Amendment Sisters believe that guns are a woman's best tool for self-defense and give her the ability to protect herself and her family.[69] Both groups have joined vocally in the public debate, exercising their freedom of speech and assembly to influence opinions about guns in the United States. They disagree over how best to protect themselves and their families in a dangerous world. Each group struggles to interpret the Second Amendment to fit its members' own understandings of social needs and problems today.

> The Second Amendment Sisters and the Million Mom March represent women on different sides of the gun control debate. What are your views on gun control?

Civil Liberties in Post-9/11 America

Public discussion about the proper balance between individual freedom and public safety is not limited to gun control policies. Debate has intensified as the nation struggles with the aftermath of the September 11, 2001 terrorist attacks and the continuing global war on terror. Citizens and government leaders are rethinking their beliefs about the proper scope of government power. Over the course of U.S. history, liberty and security have coexisted in a state of tension.

In the wake of September 11, this tension has become more acute, as the federal, state, and local governments have taken certain actions that directly intrude upon individual freedoms. The government argues these actions are necessary to protect life and property. But civil libertarians shudder at what they see as unprecedented violations of individual freedoms and rights.

Perceived Intrusions on Free Speech and Assembly

Although the tension between liberty and order has been clear since the origins of our republic, this conflict has become more intense in recent years. For instance, the Foreign Intelligence Surveillance Act (FISA) of 1978, which empowers the government to conduct secret searches where necessary to protect national security, significantly broadened the powers of law enforcement agencies to engage in investigation. Agencies must go before a designated court, the Foreign Intelligence Surveillance Act Court, to justify a secret search. Civil libertarians are concerned about the FISA court's concealed location and sealed records, as well as its judicial proceedings, in which the suspect is never told about the investigation and probable cause is not required to approve surveillance or searches of any person suspected of having some link to terrorism.

Following September 11, 2001, a number of government agencies engaged in the surveillance of political groups in the United States. In late 2005, the media exposed a program by the Bush administration and the National Security Administration (NSA) to target U.S. civilians for electronic surveillance without judicial oversight. Members of the Bush administration claimed that they had monitored only communications where one party was suspected of links to terrorism and was currently overseas. Beginning in 2005, however, the American Civil Liberties Union (ACLU) issued a series of reports demonstrating that the Federal Bureau of Investigation (FBI) spied not only on people suspected of taking part in terrorist plots but also on individuals involved in peaceful political activities.[70] In one instance, the FBI monitored the organizers of an antiwar protest who had gathered at a Denver bookstore, and agents compiled a list with the descriptions and license plates of cars in the store's vicinity. In 2009, the ACLU filed a lawsuit challenging the constitutionality of the 2008 FISA Amendment Act, which increased the ability of the federal government to engage in the warrantless surveillance of American citizens.[71] The ACLU has released similar reports describing the Pentagon's database of peaceful war protesters.[72]

The ACLU and other critics of the domestic surveillance program have argued that the federal government is targeting political protest, not

POLITICAL INQUIRY

A CHOICE BETWEEN FREEDOM AND SECURITY What message is the cartoonist trying to convey? Do you think citizens must choose between freedom and security? Explain. Do you support the central provisions of the USA PATRIOT Act and the NSA wiretapping program? Why or why not? Do such programs increase security or threaten liberty? Explain.

SOURCE: By Clay Bennett. Reproduced with permission from the October 29, 2001 issue of The Christian Science Monitor (www.CSMonitor.com). © 2001 The Christian Science Monitor.

domestic terrorism plots. Opponents of the policy warn that the FBI and other agencies are infringing upon free speech, assembly, and expression. But employees of the NSA and the Department of Justice have defended the government's expanded investigation and enforcement activities, claiming that the threats to national security are grave and that the government must be given the power it needs to protect against these dangers.[73]

Perceived Intrusions on Criminal Due Process

Even though several years have passed since September 11, 2001, concern lingers about another terrorist attack on U.S. soil, and many Americans are willing to accept some infringement on their freedoms if it makes them safer. These citizens assume that criminal activity may be afoot and that the surveillance is not being used to target groups that are politically unpopular or critical of the administration. Much of the debate about the surveillance activities of the FBI and other groups centers on the distinction between criminally active groups and politically unpopular groups. How do we know which groups the federal government is using its powers to investigate?

To what extent must administration officials provide evidence of criminal intent before placing a suspect under surveillance? Since September 11, 2001, the laws that govern domestic spying have been modified in such a way that the government has much more leeway in conducting searches and investigations, even where there is no proof of criminal activity.

The terrorism of September 11 led to important shifts in U.S. policy. One example is the USA PATRIOT Act, which Congress passed six weeks after the attacks with little debate in either the House or the Senate.[74] This law, reauthorized in 2005, allows the FBI and other intelligence agencies to access personal information and records without getting permission from, or even informing, targeted individuals. Much of the data come from private sources, which are often ordered to hand over their records. For example, the USA PATRIOT Act authorized the FBI to order Internet service providers to give information about their clients to the FBI. The USA PATRIOT Act also empowered intelligence agencies to order public libraries to hand over records of materials that the targeted individuals borrowed or viewed.

On July 28, 2007, President Bush called on Congress to pass legislation to reform the FISA in order to ease restrictions on the surveillance of terrorist suspects in cases where one party or both parties to the communication are located overseas. The Protect America Act of 2007, signed into law on August 5, 2007, essentially legalized ongoing NSA practices.[75] Under the act, the U.S. government may wiretap without FISA court supervision any communications that begin or end in a foreign country. The act removes from the definition of "electronic surveillance" in FISA any surveillance directed at a person reasonably believed to be located outside the United States. This means that the government may listen to conversations without a court order as long as the U.S. attorney general approves the surveillance. Supporters stress that flexibility is needed to monitor the communications of suspected terrorists and their networks. Critics, however, worry that the law is too vague and provides the government with the ability to monitor any group or individual it opposes, regardless of whether it has links to terrorism. In 2009, the Inspectors General of the Department of Defense, the Department of Justice, the CIA, the NSA, and the Office of the Director of National Intelligence revealed that the surveillance program had a much larger scope than previously believed. The report also demonstrated conflict within the Obama and Bush administrations as to how helpful the information obtained through these measures was in combating terrorism.[76]

Although many Americans are concerned about domestic surveillance, especially in situations where it targets political speech and expression, these laws remain on the books, and this surveillance likely will continue. For the time being, the line between suspected criminal activity and purely political expression remains blurred. Civic discourse about how to balance liberty and national security continues to evolve as Americans consider how much freedom they should sacrifice to protect public safety.

In addition to conversations about search and surveillance procedures, the nation is struggling with larger questions about the rights of detainees accused of conducting or supporting terrorist activities. Some political commentators argue that the torture of these individuals is appropriate in specific situations.[77] They point to a "ticking time bomb" scenario, in which the torture of a single suspect known to have information about the location of a nuclear bomb would be justified in order to save thousands or millions of innocent lives. Critics of this logic note that information obtained through torture is unreliable and not worth the price of violating our moral codes. Further, they argue that if the United States legalizes torture, Americans will lose their standing as a moral society and alienate potential allies in the war against terror.[78]

In response to the criticism of torture, Congress and the president passed the Detainee Treatment Act of 2005, which bans cruel, inhuman, or degrading treatment of detainees in U.S. custody, but provides significant exceptions to the definition of torture, such as waterboarding (the practice of pouring water over the nose and mouth while the victim is strapped to an inclined board to induce the sensation of drowning.)[79] Despite this legislation, questions remain. For example, in 2006 various media outlets reported the practice of **rendition,** which involves the transfer of custody of suspected terrorists to other nations for imprisonment and interrogation. Critics saw the practice as an attempt to circumvent U.S. law, which requires due process and prohibits torture. Former secretary of state Condoleezza Rice denied that U.S. officials transfer suspects to places where they know these individuals will be tortured.[80] But according to a February 2007 European Parliament report, the CIA conducted 1,245 flights over European territory between 2001 and April 2006, many of them to destinations where suspects could face torture.[81] The Obama Adminstration continued the policy of rendition but pledged to closely monitor the treatment of the incarcerated to ensure that they were not tortured.[82] Unquestionably, the global war on terror has caused U.S. citizens and public officials to reconsider the boundaries of acceptable behavior as they balance the need to protect the civil liberties of the accused with the desire to prevent terrorist attacks. Events such as the attempted 2009 Christmas airplane attack increase the tension between liberty and order.

rendition
transfer of suspected terrorists to other nations for imprisonment and interrogation; this practice circumvents U.S. law, which requires due process and prohibits torture

Discrimination Against Muslim Americans

Immediately after September 11, members of the Bush administration said repeatedly that the war on terror was not a war on immigrants or a war on Islam. Despite assurances, civil libertarians and leaders in the Muslim American community criticized administration policies targeting Muslims. Among these were policies allowing racial profiling of Arab and Muslim men; the use of secret evidence in national security cases; widespread FBI interviews of Muslims; raids of Muslim homes, schools, and mosques; the special registration and fingerprinting of Muslims from specific Arab nations; and the detention and deportation of many Arab and Muslim nationals without the right to legal representation.[83]

President Obama's administration has faced similar criticism for its policies. In response to critics, in March 2010 President Obama appointed the legal director of the American-Arab Anti-Discrimination Committee, Nawar Shora, to the Transportation Security Administration as a senior adviser to the office reviewing civil rights and liberties.[84] Members of these presidential administrations have explained aggressive policing in Muslim communities as a way to catch would-be terrorists and to cause them to delay or abandon their plans. Critics have argued that the policies deny Muslims due process and violate their civil liberties, as well as cause officials to ignore non-Muslim terrorist potentials. As American-born Muslims continue to participate in "home-grown" terrorism, this tension between liberty and security will only intensify.

Critics contend that administration policies have violated Muslims' freedoms of speech, religion, and association as law enforcers monitor their words, religious ceremonies, and organizational ties and as Muslims have become targets of government interrogation and even detention. In a government profiling program designed to catch would-be terrorists, race, age, and national origin, too, can lead to interrogation. Many in the executive branch argue that they are required to do whatever they can to protect U.S. citizens from another terrorist strike. Critics worry that racial and religious profiling will alienate the 7 million Muslim citizens and will, in fact, jeopardize officials' ability to gather valuable intelligence. (See "Thinking Critically About Democracy.") The nation's struggles to balance the demands of freedom and order are clearly illustrated in the ongoing conversation about how to protect personal liberty while ensuring national security.

THINKING CRITICALLY ABOUT DEMOCRACY

SHOULD U.S. AUTHORITIES USE ETHNIC PROFILING IN THE INTEREST OF NATIONAL SECURITY?

The Issue: In light of the ongoing terrorist threat, should airport security and law enforcement officials practice ethnic and religious profiling to prevent a hijacking or a terrorist attack?

Yes: The most serious threat we face as a nation is the threat posed by militant Islamic fundamentalists. Militant Islam, or fundamentalism, is a radical ideology that teaches its adherents to apply the laws of Islam, the Shari'a, to all people by creating Islamic states.

Given the nature of the threat, it makes sense for police seeking suspects after a terrorist attack to search mosques rather than churches or synagogues and to question pedestrians who appear to be Middle Eastern or wear head scarves. To avoid an attack, it also makes sense to focus on the people most likely to threaten our safety. Heightened scrutiny for young Middle Eastern men fitting the profile of al-Qaeda recruits is reasonable. Should we require an 85-year-old grandmother from Wisconsin to remove her shoes at the airline gate simply because we just asked a 25-year-old single man from Saudi Arabia to do the same? Common sense tells us that we can more efficiently use resources by concentrating our attention on those who are most likely to pose a risk.

Although profiling may inconvenience law-abiding Muslims, they must be willing to endure mild inconvenience for the larger goal of saving lives. Indeed, integrationist Muslims who seek to live successfully within the U.S. constitutional framework react with fear and loathing when Islamist extremists commit acts of terror in the name of Islam.*

No: Racial, ethnic, and religious profiling is inefficient, counterproductive, and morally wrong. Race and ethnic appearance are poor predictors of behavior. First, it is difficult to determine a person's religion by appearance alone. People from the Middle East have a wide range of skin tones and facial features. They include Christians and Jews as well as Muslims. Cases of mistaken identity are widespread. Many of those who found themselves the victims of anti-Muslim hate crimes after September 11 included numerous non-Muslims such as Chaldeans, Hindus, and Sikhs. More important, focusing on race and ethnicity keeps security officials' attention on a set of surface details that tell us little about a person and that draw officers' attention away from what is much more important and concrete: behavior.

Focusing on ethnic appearance can cause us to miss genuine threats. John Walker Lindh, a 20-year-old white Californian, fought with the Taliban in Afghanistan. Does an 85-year-old Middle Eastern grandmother deserve closer scrutiny than a 25-year-old white American man who has just bought a one-way ticket and looks nervous and sweaty?

Subjecting all Muslims or Middle Easterners to intrusive questioning, stops, or searches will harm our enforcement and detection efforts. First, profiling will drain enforcement efforts away from the close observation of suspicious behavior. Second, profiling will alienate law-abiding Muslims whose cooperation is critical for effective information gathering and counterterrorist intelligence. Alienating law-abiding Muslims by treating them like terrorist suspects will ultimately harm our ability to gather information about real terrorist threats.

We must find effective ways to secure the nation without giving up what is best about our country. Enacting discriminatory policies that take away individual liberty destroys the values for which we are fighting.**

Other approaches: The issue of ethnic profiling is more complicated than proponents and opponents often indicate in their arguments. In some cases, law enforcement use ethnic profiling based on specific threats. But law enforcement officials need to recognize that ethnic profiling limits their ability to detect terror suspects who may not fit the mold of the stereotypical terrorist—including women.

What do you think?

① Should airport security officers pay greater attention to passengers who appear to be Middle Eastern or Muslim? Why or why not?

② Should the FBI use ethnic or religious profiling to select people to interview as part of its counterterrorism efforts?

③ Will profiling strengthen or weaken our intelligence-gathering efforts? Explain.

④ Is racial, ethnic, or religious profiling ever justified? If so, in what cases? If not, why not?

*For a fuller exposition of this argument, see Daniel Pipes, "Fighting Militant Islam, Without Bias," *City Journal,* November 2001.
**For a fuller exposition of this argument, see David A. Harris, "Flying While Arab, Immigration Issues, and Lessons from the Racial Profiling Controversy." Testimony before the U.S. Commission on Civil Rights (October 12, 2001).

At the core of the U.S. political and legal system lies a strong belief in individual liberties and rights. This belief is reflected in the Bill of Rights, the first ten amendments to the Constitution. The freedoms therein are at the heart of civic engagement and ensure that individuals can freely participate in the political and social life of their communities. But these freedoms are also malleable, and at times the government has starkly limited them, as when officials perceive a threat to national security.

The inevitable tension between freedom and order is heightened in a post-9/11 world. Americans and their government struggle to protect essential liberties while guarding the nation against future terrorist attacks. This tension between national security and personal freedom is reflected in contemporary debates over free speech, political protest, and due process.

Do antiwar protests threaten the nation's success in Iraq? Will airports and national security agencies further develop and deploy security systems based on methods such as thumbprint and eye-scan technology? Should the government be able to track citizens' phone calls and e-mail messages? Should security officials profile Muslims and Arabs? Is torture ever justifiable? Will the Court uphold new laws that require Internet providers to secretly share personal information about their clients with the FBI? Those are the questions we confront in a post-9/11 world as we struggle to maintain the commitment to liberty that defines our nation while preserving the nation itself.

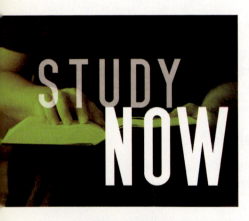

Summary

1. Civil Liberties in the American Legal System
The U.S. Constitution—and more specifically, the Bill of Rights, the first ten amendments—protects individuals against the unrestrained exercise of power by the federal government. The framers intended the Bill of Rights to ensure that individuals could engage freely in political speech and civic discourse in the larger society. Although the Bill of Rights was initially interpreted as imposing limits only on the national government, over time the Supreme Court has interpreted most of its protections as applying to the state governments as well.

2. Freedoms of Speech, Assembly, and the Press: First Amendment Freedoms Supporting Civic Discourse
Civic engagement is possible only in a society that fully protects civil liberties. Some of the civil liberties guaranteed in the Bill of Rights relate specifically to political participation and discourse. Most importantly, the freedoms of speech, assembly, petition, and the press empower individuals to engage actively and freely in politics and public life. These freedoms have always existed in a state of tension with the goal of national security; in times of crisis or instability, the judicial system has interpreted them narrowly.

3. Freedoms of Religion, Privacy, and Criminal Due Process: Encouraging Community and Civic Engagement
Other Bill of Rights freedoms encourage inclusiveness and community building, ensuring that individuals can be fully engaged in the social life of the nation. The freedom of religion, right to privacy, and criminal due process protections ensure that no one individual or group may be singled out for either favorable or unfavorable treatment.

4. Freedoms in Practice: Controversy Over the Second Amendment and the Right to Bear Arms
Historical context is crucial to our understanding of the freedoms protected by the Bill of Rights. Americans actively disagree about the proper interpretation of the Second Amendment and about the role of guns in maintaining a free and safe society.

5. Civil Liberties in Post-9/11 America

The tension between liberty and security, always present in U.S. political culture, has become more acute since the terrorist attacks of September 11, 2001. In the wake of those attacks, federal and state law enforcement officials have limited the speech, assembly, and petition rights of some American citizens and nationals and have curtailed the due process protections of those suspected of engaging in or supporting domestic and international terrorism.

Key Terms

bad tendency test 120

civil liberties 112

clear and present danger test 120

clear and probable danger test 120

commercial speech 122

creationism 128

criminal due process rights 133

double jeopardy 134

due process 113

establishment clause 126

exclusionary rule 133

fighting words 123

free exercise clause 128

habeas corpus 118

imminent lawless action test (incitement test) 121

intelligent design 127

Lemon test 127

libel 123

marketplace of ideas 118

Miranda rights 134

obscenity 123

prior restraint 124

rendition 140

right to privacy 129

selective incorporation 116

slander 123

symbolic speech 121

time, place, and manner restrictions 124

total incorporation 116

For Review

1. What are civil liberties? How do civil liberties differ from civil rights? Why do we protect civil liberties?

2. How does the First Amendment support civic discourse?

3. What protections does the Bill of Rights provide to those accused of committing a crime?

4. What are the two sides of the issue of Second Amendment rights? How has the Supreme Court interpreted this right?

5. How have the terrorist attacks of September 11, 2001, affected civil liberties in the United States?

For Critical Thinking and Discussion

1. Under what circumstances should the government be allowed to regulate or punish speech?

2. Should Congress pass a constitutional amendment banning flag burning? Why or why not?

3. Under what circumstances should government be able to punish people for practicing their religious beliefs?

4. Should the government be allowed to search people and property without a warrant based on probable cause that a crime was committed? Explain.

5. Do you believe that the USA PATRIOT Act and the NSA domestic surveillance program make the nation safer? Why or why not?

6. Will giving up liberty to enhance security protect the nation against terrorists, or will it destroy the fundamental values upon which the nation was founded? Defend your position.

PRACTICE QUIZ

MULTIPLE CHOICE: Choose the lettered item that answers the question correctly.

1. Civil liberties
   a. are protected only in Article III of the U.S. Constitution.
   b. entitle all citizens to equal protection of the laws.
   c. protect individuals against an abuse of government power.
   d. did not exist until the twenty-first century.

2. Which of the following is protected by the U.S. Constitution and the courts?
   a. slander
   b. libel
   c. fighting words
   d. symbolic speech

3. Teacher-led prayer in public schools is prohibited by
   a. the establishment clause.
   b. the free exercise clause.
   c. the due process clause.
   d. the equal protection clause.

4. The right to privacy was first established in the case
   a. *Griswold v. Connecticut.*
   b. *Roe v. Wade.*
   c. *Lemon v. Kurtzman.*
   d. *Miller v. California.*

5. Criminal defendants' rights to legal counsel and a jury trial are protected by the
   a. First Amendment.
   b. Second Amendment.
   c. Fourth Amendment.
   d. Sixth Amendment.

6. Critics of the USA PATRIOT Act charge that the law violates the
   a. Second Amendment.
   b. Fourth Amendment.
   c. Eighth Amendment.
   d. Tenth Amendment.

7. Police would most likely be required to use a warrant if they wanted to collect evidence from
   a. a house.
   b. the back seat of a car.
   c. a school locker.
   d. a prison cell.

8. According to the Supreme Court, burning the U.S. flag is a form of
   a. hate speech.
   b. libel.
   c. symbolic speech.
   d. treason.

9. Citizens' disagreement about how to interpret the Eighth Amendment is reflected in the current debate over
   a. school vouchers.
   b. intelligent design.
   c. "virtual" child pornography.
   d. lethal injection.

10. The Second Amendment protects U.S. citizens'
    a. free speech.
    b. freedom from self-incrimination.
    c. freedom of religion.
    d. freedom to bear arms.

FILL IN THE BLANKS.

11. _____ refers to the process by which the Supreme Court has applied to the states those provisions in the Bill of Rights that serve some fundamental principle of liberty or justice.

12. _____ set guidelines that the government must follow in investigating, bringing to trial, and punishing those accused of committing a crime.

13. Under the _____ , evidence obtained illegally cannot be used in a trial.

14. The Fifth Amendment protection against _____ ensures that criminal defendants cannot be tried again for the same crime when a court has already found them not guilty of committing that crime.

15. Speech that is likely to bring about public disorder or chaos and which may be banned in public places to ensure the preservation of public order is called _____ .

Answers: 1. c; 2. d; 3. a; 4. a; 5. d; 6. b; 7. a; 8. c; 9. d; 10. d; 11. Selective incorporation; 12. criminal due process rights; 13. exclusionary rule; 14. double jeopardy; 15. fighting words.

RESOURCES FOR RESEARCH AND ACTION

Internet Resources

Center for Democracy and Technology
www.cdt.org The effect of new computer and communications technologies on American civil liberties is the subject of this site.

Public Broadcasting Station
www.npr.org/news/specials/patriotact/patriotactprovisions.html PBS provides a summary of controversial provisions of the USA PATRIOT Act, including major arguments for and against each provision.

Internet Activism

The American Civil Liberties Union
www.aclu.org/blog/ The American Civil Liberties Union (ACLU) is a national organization with state affiliates that consistently supports the interest of liberty when challenged by security interests. Go to the Web site to follow the ACLU blog and engage in the subsequent discussion over the appropriate protection of constitutional rights from infringement by federal, state, and local governments.

Twitter
http://twitter.com/acuconservative The American Conservative Union is one of the oldest conservative interest groups in the country and engages the debate between liberty and security from a conservative perspective.

Facebook: Epic.org
www.facebook.com/group.php?gid=20774297052 The Electronic Privacy Information Center focuses public attention on the political issues surrounding privacy and civil liberties emerging from rapidly changing technologies.

Recommended Readings

Baker, Thomas E., and John F. Stack. *At War With Civil Rights and Civil Liberties.* Rowan & Littlefield Publishers, 2005. A collection of essays written by constitutional law scholars, as well as Supreme Court Justice Breyer and Attorney General John Ashcroft, that demonstrate the difficulty of balancing liberty with security in a time of war.

Bollinger, Lee C., and Geoffrey R. Stone, eds. *Eternally Vigilant: Free Speech in the Modern Era.* Chicago: University of Chicago Press, 2002. Drawing on the work of legal scholars, an examination of the philosophical underpinnings of free speech, with a highlighting of the history of contentious free speech disputes.

Carroll, Jamuna, ed. *Privacy.* Detroit, MI: Greenhaven Press, 2006. An edited volume of point-counterpoint articles exploring a wide variety of issues, including counterterrorism measures, Internet privacy, video surveillance, and employee monitoring.

Fisher, Louis. *The Constitution and 9/11: Recurring Threats to America's Freedoms.* Lawrence, KA: University Press of Kansas. This book, written by one of the nation's foremost experts on separation of powers, surveys the historic responses to threats to national security by the branches of the federal government and then evaluates the current challenges to the constitutional law of national security after 9/11.

Spitzer, Robert J. *The Politics of Gun Control,* 4th ed. Washington, DC: CQ Press, 2007. Analysis of the gun control debate in the United States, including its history, the constitutional right to bear arms, the criminological consequences of guns, citizen political action, and the role and impact of American governing institutions.

Movies of Interest

Rendition (2007)
When an Egyptian terrorism suspect "disappears" on a flight from Africa to Washington, D.C., his American wife and a CIA analyst struggle to secure his release from a secret detention (and torture) facility somewhere outside the United States.

Good Night and Good Luck (2005)
This film examines the conflict between veteran journalist Edward R. Murrow and Senator Joseph McCarthy as Murrow attempts to investigate and discredit McCarthy's tactics in investigating and destroying Communist elements in the federal government and larger society.

Enemy of the State (1998)
This film depicts the adventures of an attorney entangled in a web of national politics when a reporter friend accidentally records the murder of a senator. Unaware that he is in possession of the reporter's video, the attorney becomes the target of a National Security Agency investigation that nearly succeeds in destroying his personal and professional life.

The Siege (1998)
After the U.S. military abducts an Islamic religious leader, New York City becomes the target of escalating terrorist attacks. As the bombings continue, the U.S. government responds by declaring martial law, detaining Muslim men, and sending U.S. troops into the streets of New York City.

The People Versus Larry Flynt (1996)
This film documents the economic success, courtroom battles, and personal challenges of *Hustler* magazine publisher Larry Flynt. Flynt is obnoxious and hedonistic in ways that offend and anger "decent people," even as he fights to protect freedom of speech for all.

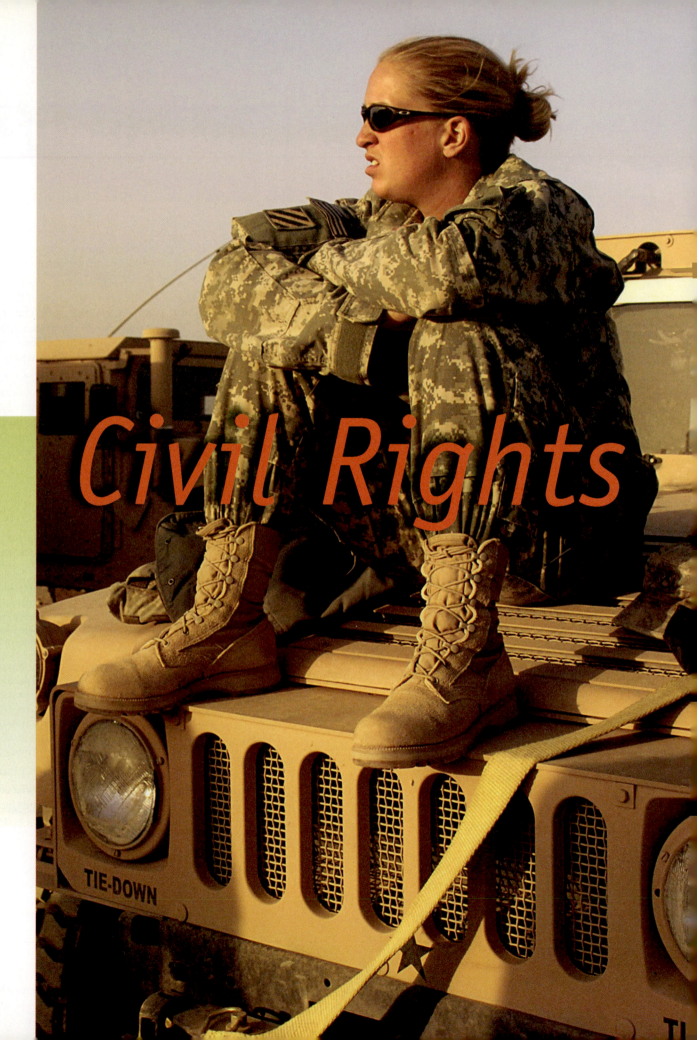

Civil Rights

THEN

African Americans, women, Native Americans, Latinos, and other groups struggled to achieve equality in the United States.

NOW

Groups of citizens continue to struggle for their civil rights, including Asian Americans, lesbians and gay men, and citizens with disabilities.

NEXT

What other groups of legally disadvantaged citizens will fight for their civil rights?

What criteria will the U.S. Supreme Court use in deciding cases concerning sex-based discrimination?

How will the state of the economy and threats of terrorism shape the issues and the demands at the forefront of future civil rights battles?

civil rights

the rights and privileges guaranteed to all citizens under the equal protection and due process clauses of the Fifth and Fourteenth amendments; the idea that individuals are protected from discrimination based on characteristics such as race, national origin, religion, and sex

inherent characteristics

individual attributes such as race, national origin, religion, and gender

Although the Declaration of

Independence claims that all men are created equal and are endowed with the natural rights of life, liberty, and the pursuit of happiness, neither the Articles of Confederation nor the Constitution as initially ratified guaranteed that the government would treat or protect all men equally. Indeed, those constitutions did *not* guarantee nonwhite men or women of all races and colors the same legal rights that they guaranteed to white men. For example, African American men and women had no legal rights and were bought and sold as property until 1865, when the Thirteenth Amendment to the Constitution made such enslavement illegal. The Constitution did not guarantee American women the right to sue, nor did it protect married women's right to own property, until well into the nineteenth century. Many Americans experienced unequal treatment under the law throughout U.S. history.

Fast-forward to today. When asked what principles or ideals they hold most dear, many Americans will mention equality. Yet, even today, not all people in the United States are treated equally under the law. Moreover, people disagree strongly on the meaning of "equal protections of the law," which has been a stated constitutional guarantee since 1868, when the states ratified the Fourteenth Amendment to the U.S. Constitution.

Disagreement about what constitutes "equal treatment" is at the heart of many past and current struggles for equality. Does equal treatment mean that the government must ensure that all people have equal opportunities to pursue their happiness? Does it bar all differential treatment by the government and its officials, or are there certain situations in which it is acceptable for the government to treat people differently to fulfill its mission (establish justice, ensure domestic tranquility, provide for the common defense, protect the general welfare, and secure the blessings of liberty)?

In this chapter, we examine the concept of equality under the law. We focus on how groups of citizens that were originally deprived of equal protection of their liberties and pursuit of happiness have been able to expand their rights in numerous areas, including voting rights and equal access to educational and employment opportunities, to housing, and to public accommodations.

The Meaning of Equality Under the Law

Although the issue of protecting civil liberties was in the forefront at the nation's founding, as we discussed in Chapter 4, the issue of guaranteeing civil rights reached the national agenda much later.[1] When we talk about **civil rights** in the United States, we mean the rights and privileges guaranteed by the government to all *citizens* under the equal protection and due process clauses of the Fifth and Fourteenth amendments and the privileges and immunities clause of the Fourteenth Amendment. These rights are based on the idea that the government should protect individuals from discrimination that results from inherent characteristics. **Inherent characteristics** are individual characteristics that are part of a person's nature, such as race, religion, national origin, and sex.

The Constitution imposes constraints (civil liberties) and responsibilities (civil rights) on governments, which includes government officials and employees, but *not* on private individuals or organizations. However, governments can write laws that prohibit private individuals and organizations from infringing on civil liberties and civil rights. For example, the national government enacted the Civil Rights Act of 1964, which prohibited private businesses and organizations from discriminating in hiring decisions based on the inherent characteristics of race, color, religion, national origin, and sex.

Most people agree that no government, private individual, or organization should treat people differently because of these inherent characteristics. The courts have determined that treating citizens differently based on their inherent characteristics is unfair, arbitrary, and in most situations illegal. However, people and even government officials, including judges, disagree about whether the list of inherent characteristics should include characteristics such as age, physical and mental disabilities, and sexual orientation. For example, should the government guarantee same-sex couples the same right to marry, and hence have the same legal benefits of marriage, as it guarantees to heterosexual couples? Moreover, there are debates over if and when the government should allow differential treatment in order for it to fulfill its mission.

As we explored in Chapter 4, no civil liberty is absolute; there are situations in which the government may infringe on an individual's liberty. For example, the government may infringe on an individual's freedom of speech if it views her speech as violating the imminent lawless action test (or incitement test); the risk of harm from the speech is

Fighting for Their Rights: How Groups and Issues Change

THEN (1960s AND 1970s)	NOW (2011)
African Americans, women, Native Americans, and Latinos fought for equal treatment under the law.	Asian citizens, citizens with disabilities, and lesbian, gay, bisexual, and transgendered citizens fight for equal treatment under the law.
Key strategies included nonviolent civil disobedience, protests, and seeking remedy through the justice system.	Protest and lawsuits remain important strategies, but today's activists also focus on petitioning Congress and state legislatures in attempts to pass legislation.
Important issues included equal access to schools, public accommodations, voting rights, and equal pay.	Important issues include spousal rights for gays and lesbians, voting rights, and immigration policy.

WHAT'S NEXT?

> What groups will begin to seek ways of achieving their civil rights?

> How will new technologies change the strategies and tactics that civil rights activists use?

> What important issues will be at the forefront of the civil rights agenda in the future?

highly likely and the harm is imminent or immediate. Civil rights are also not absolute. The national courts have established "tests" that the government uses to determine when unequal protection under the law (that is, differential or discriminatory treatment) is legal.

Today, the courts use three tests—*strict scrutiny, heightened scrutiny,* and *ordinary scrutiny*—to determine when unequal treatment is legal. Which test the court uses depends on the inherent characteristic that is the basis for differential treatment. For example, courts view race, ethnic origin, and religion to be **suspect classifications,** meaning that judges will assume that the laws treating individuals differently because of these inherent characteristics are unconstitutional and violate the equal protection clauses. When the courts hear a challenge to laws with suspect classifications, they use the **strict scrutiny test,** which means that the government must show that the differential treatment is necessary for it to achieve a compelling public interest for which it is responsible. Using the strict scrutiny test in *Loving v. Virginia* (1967), the Supreme Court determined that laws barring interracial marriage violated the Constitution because there was no compelling public interest for which the government was responsible; hence, the laws were not necessary for a compelling public interest.[2] Therefore, today it is illegal to deny interracial couples the right to marry.

The courts do not consider the inherent characteristic of sex to be a suspect classification, and therefore laws that allow differential treatment of women and men do not need

suspect classifications
distinctions based on race, religion, and national origin, which are assumed to be illegitimate

strict scrutiny test
the guidelines the courts use to determine the legality of suspect classification-based discrimination; on the basis of this test, discrimination is legal if it is a necessary means by which the government can achieve a compelling public interest

heightened scrutiny test (intermediate scrutiny test)
the guidelines used most frequently by the courts to determine the legality of sex-based discrimination; on the basis of this test, sex-based discrimination is legal if the government can prove that it is substantially related to the achievement of an important public interest

ordinary scrutiny test (rational basis test)
on the basis of this test, discrimination is legal if it is a reasonable means by which the government can achieve a legitimate public interest

to pass the strict scrutiny test when challenged. Instead, the courts apply the **heightened scrutiny** test (also known as the **intermediate scrutiny test**) in sex-based discrimination cases, which requires the government to show that the sex-based differential treatment is substantially related to an important public interest for which the government is responsible. The heightened scrutiny test is a weaker test, making it easier for the government to justify sex-based discrimination than discrimination based on race, religion, or ethnic origin. Therefore, today women in the military do not have the same opportunities in combat roles (and hence combat-related benefits) as military men do.

The weakest test the courts use when determining if a law allowing discriminatory treatment is legal is the **ordinary scrutiny test** (also called the **rational basis test**). Using the ordinary scrutiny test, courts require governments to show that the differential treatment is a rational means to achieve a legitimate public interest for which the government is responsible. State governments have established minimum ages for numerous legal rights, such as the right to marry, the right to get a driver's license, and the right to purchase alcoholic beverages. Many states have also established a retirement age (a maximum age) for state judges. These are areas of life where the courts, applying the ordinary scrutiny test, have determined age-based discrimination to be legal. Differential treatment based on age is a reasonable way to achieve some legitimate public interests. Can you determine what the public interests are in each of these age-based differential treatment situations?

For most of our nation's history, the law not only allowed unequal treatment for different racial, ethnic, and religious groups as well as for men and women, but also *required* this unequal treatment for a majority of the population. Women were not granted the right to vote until 1920, and they faced a wide variety of discriminatory practices. Ethnic and religious groups also faced widespread discrimination, some as a matter of law. For example, more than 120,000 people of Japanese ancestry were forcibly interned in camps during World War II. More recently, following the terrorist attacks of September 11, 2001, the federal government has detained thousands of Arabs and Arab Americans in prisons without providing any criminal due process protections. But probably the most blatant example of discrimination in U.S. history is slavery. This practice was protected under the law, and slaves were considered to be the property of their owners. They had no protection under the law and could be treated in any way their owners saw fit.

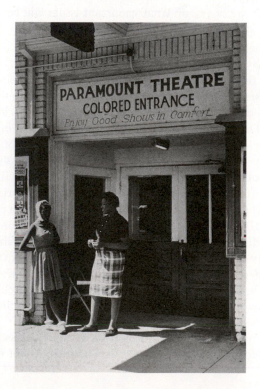

> Historically, people have encountered discrimination because of their ethnicity, race, or gender. In some places, Irish citizens were barred from applying for jobs, African Americans attending theaters were forced to use separate entrances (here with the ironic promise of "good shows in comfort"), and help-wanted ads were segregated based on gender.

Slavery and Its Aftermath

When it was first written, the Constitution implicitly endorsed the unequal and discriminatory treatment of African Americans.[3] Some of the most important provisions of the new constitution treated people of African descent as property, allowing states to continue to permit them to be enslaved. Although the movement to abolish slavery was in its early stages in 1787, the year the Constitution was completed, by the early to mid-1800s, it had gained significant momentum in the North, largely because of the activism of various religious and humanitarian groups.[4]

Slavery in the United States

Most African Americans today are the descendants of Africans who were forcibly brought to the New World. In 1619, twenty Africans arrived in Jamestown as *indentured servants,* workers with a fixed term of service. But by the mid-1600s, slavery began to replace indentured servitude.

OPPOSITION TO SLAVERY   Many chafed at the hypocrisy of those who sought freedom and equality but kept slaves. Among the first to challenge slavery were former slaves, who staged both peaceful protests and armed insurrections throughout the late 1700s and early 1800s. These activists successfully rallied support in the North for the gradual abolition of slavery by 1804. They argued forcefully against the injustice of the slave system, moving the opponents of slavery to action by their horrifying firsthand accounts of the treatment of slaves.

Despite those arguments, the U.S. Congress, wary of the divisiveness caused by the slavery issue, sought to balance the antislavery position of the abolitionist states with the pro-slavery sentiments of the slaveholding states. One such attempt was the Missouri Compromise, passed by Congress in 1820. The compromise regulated slavery in the newly acquired western territories: slavery was prohibited north of the 36°30′ north parallel, except within the state of Missouri.

The abolitionists, including organizations such as the American Anti-Slavery Society, objected to the efforts of Congress to accommodate the slaveholding states and called for the emancipation of all slaves. Members of the American Anti-Slavery Society were actively engaged in **civil disobedience,** which is nonviolent refusal to comply with laws or government policies that are morally objectionable. Specifically, American Anti-Slavery Society members actively supported the Underground Railroad, a series of safe houses that allowed escaping slaves to flee to the northern states and Canada. Between 1810 and 1850, an estimated 100,000 people escaped slavery through the Underground Railroad (see Figure 5.1 on page 152). But in 1850, the U.S. Congress—in an attempt to stall or prevent the secession, or separation, of southern states from the Union—passed the Fugitive Slave Act. The law required federal marshals to return runaway slaves or risk a $1,000 fine (over $20,000 in today's dollars); private citizens who harbored or abetted runaway slaves could be imprisoned for six months and fined $1,000. Passage of this law meant that "conductors" on the Underground Railroad operated in clear violation of the statute, risking their own livelihoods and property.

THE CIVIL WAR ERA   Abolitionists were bolstered in their efforts when Harriet Beecher Stowe's popular book *Uncle Tom's Cabin* was published in 1852. Vividly depicting the harsh reality of slavery in the United States, this work inspired many to actively challenge slavery. By the late 1850s, the widespread distribution of *Uncle Tom's Cabin,* as well as the trial and execution of John Brown, a white abolitionist who tried to ignite a slave insurrection in Harpers Ferry, in what was then Virginia and is now West Virginia, had convinced many northerners that slavery was immoral.

Yet the U.S. Supreme Court ruled otherwise. In 1857, Dred Scott, an African American enslaved by a surgeon in the U.S. Army, sued for his freedom, arguing that because he had lived in both a free state (Illinois) and a free territory (the Wisconsin Territory, now Minnesota),

civil disobedience
active, but nonviolent, refusal to comply with laws or governmental policies that are morally objectionable

standing to sue
the legal right to bring lawsuits in court

he had become a free man and as such he could not be re-enslaved when he moved to Missouri. (Figure 5.1 shows states that did and did not allow slavery at that time.) The Supreme Court rejected Scott's claim and in *Dred Scott v. Sandford* ruled that the Missouri Compromise of 1820 was unconstitutional because the U.S. Congress lacked the authority to ban slavery in the territories.[5] It also ruled that Scott was not a U.S. citizen, asserting that slaves were property rather than citizens with **standing to sue,** or the legal right to bring lawsuits in court. Although the *Dred Scott* decision appeared to be a victory for slaveholding states, it was also pivotal in mobilizing the abolitionist movement and swaying public opinion in favor of a war to prevent secession and to bring about emancipation.

Certain that their way of life was under siege and alarmed by the election of Abraham Lincoln as president in 1860, the southern states decided that they should secede from the union. By May 1861, eleven southern states had declared their independence and created the Confederate States of America. A long and bloody civil war followed as the North fought to bring the southern states back into the union.

POLITICAL INQUIRY

FIGURE 5.1 ■ ROUTES TO FREEDOM ON THE UNDERGROUND RAILROAD Why did many escaping slaves use routes that followed the Mississippi River or the Atlantic coast? Which northern cities were important "stations" on the Underground Railroad? Why was legislation such as the Fugitive Slave Act ultimately powerless to stop this movement?

One of the most important turning points of the Civil War was the Emancipation Proclamation, issued by Abraham Lincoln in April 1862. This order abolished slavery in the states that had seceded from the Union. The Union army and navy were charged with implementing the order. The proclamation had several purposes: it decreed that the abolition of slavery was a goal of the war, and by doing so it effectively prevented Britain and France from intervening in the war on the southern side, because those countries had both renounced the institution of slavery. When the South finally surrendered in April 1865, it did so knowing that its economic way of life, which depended on slave-based plantation farming, was over. At the end of the war, nearly 4 million slaves in the United States were freed. The states then ratified three constitutional amendments to codify the victories won on the battlefield:

- the Thirteenth Amendment (1865), which ended slavery throughout the United States and prohibited it in the future
- the Fourteenth Amendment (1868), which defines *citizens* as "all persons born or naturalized in the United States" and mandates the same privileges and immunities for all citizens and due process and equal protection for all people
- the Fifteenth Amendment (1870), which decrees that every man has the right to vote, regardless of color

Reconstruction and the First Civil Rights Acts

After the North won the war and Lincoln was assassinated in April 1865, members of Congress and others in government disagreed about the best way to proceed in the South. Many Republicans thought that the South should be stabilized and quickly brought back into the political fold. Like Lincoln, these moderates endorsed a plan that would enable the southern states to be quickly represented in Congress. Others, however, took a more radical view and argued that all those who had ever supported the Confederacy should be kept out of national and state politics. As the 1860s drew to a close, many of these more radical Republicans had come to power and had strictly limited the people in southern states who could participate in politics. As a result of their activities, during the **Reconstruction era** between 1866 and 1877—when the institutions and the infrastructure of the South were rebuilt—freed slaves, who could easily say they had never supported the Confederacy, made up a sizeable portion of both the electorate and the candidate pool in the southern states. Federal troops provided protection that facilitated their participation. During this decade, African American voters made the most of their position in the South and elected a substantial number of other African Americans to legislative offices in the local, state, and federal governments. In some places, such as South Carolina, African American legislators outnumbered whites, giving them a majority during the Reconstruction years.

Between 1865 and 1875, Congress passed a series of laws designed to solidify the rights and protections outlined in the Thirteenth, Fourteenth, and Fifteenth amendments. Congress needed to spell out the rights of African Americans because of the pervasiveness of **Black Codes,** laws passed immediately after the Civil War by the confederate states that limited the rights of "freemen," or former slaves. These codes prevented freemen from voting, owning property, or bringing suit. To remedy that situation, Congress passed laws that sought to negate the Black Codes. One law, the Civil Rights Act of 1866, extended the definition of *citizen* to anyone born in the United States (including freemen) and granted all citizens the right to sue, own property, bear witness in a court of law, and enter into legal contracts. The Enforcement Act of 1870 bolstered the Fifteenth Amendment by establishing penalties for interfering with the right to vote. The Civil Rights Act of 1872, also known as the Anti–Ku Klux Klan Act, made it a federal crime to deprive individuals of their rights, privileges, or immunities protected by the Constitution. Although the Reconstruction-era Congress sought to remedy the new forms of inequality that emerged after the Civil War, its efforts would be short-lived.

Reconstruction era
the time after the Civil War between 1866 and 1877 when the institutions and infrastructure of the South were rebuilt

Black Codes
laws passed immediately after the Civil War by the confederate states that limited the rights of "freemen" (former slaves)

Backlash: Jim Crow Laws

In 1877, the inauguration of President Rutherford Hayes (1877–1881) brought the Reconstruction era to a decisive end, almost immediately rolling back the gains African Americans had achieved in education and political participation. Under Hayes, the federal troops that

GLOBAL CONTEXT

MODERN FORMS OF SLAVERY

On December 10, 1948, the United Nations General Assembly adopted the Universal Declaration of Human Rights, which promoted "universal respect for and observance of human rights and fundamental freedoms." The Declaration includes the following statement: "No one shall be held in slavery or servitude: slavery and the slave trade shall be prohibited in all their forms." When Americans think of slavery, they think of our nation's own historical experience with the institution of slavery: slave ships, plantation life, and the Civil War. It surprises many that in the twenty-first century, slavery still exists. As former United Nations Secretary General Kofi Annan has observed:

What can governments do to prevent modern-day slavery?

> Nearly every day, there are shocking reports of men, women and children who are exploited, denied their basic rights and their dignity and deprived of a better future, through both ancient and modern forms of slavery.
>
> Slavery and trafficking, and related practices such as debt bondage, forced prostitution and forced labour, are violations of the most fundamental human rights: the right to life; the right to dignity and security; the right to just and favourable conditions of work; the right to health; and the right to equality. These are rights that we all possess—irrespective of our sex, our nationality, our social status, our occupation or any other characteristic.*

Women and children, particularly in Asia but also in countries of the former Soviet Union, are sometimes forced to be part of prostitution rings that operate in those countries as well as in Western democracies. In some countries, young women who respond to help-wanted ads for international work as nannies or domestic servants are essentially kidnapped and forced to work as prostitutes. Often, traffickers advertise in the help-wanted sections of local newspapers, offering high-paying jobs as models, domestic servants, hotel maids, nannies, or shop clerks in Western nations and promising to help secure the required visa applications and work permits.

Traffickers rely on people's desire for a better life as a lure. Once victims are out of their homeland, they may be raped and forced into prostitution. Frequently, traffickers will confiscate the victim's identification and travel permits (often forgeries), withhold food or shelter unless the victim complies, and use the threat of imprisonment by authorities or the threat of harm to the victim's family at home as a means of ensuring compliance. The U.S. Department of State estimates that 800,000–900,000 people annually are trafficked across international borders worldwide, including an estimated 20,000 people who are brought into the United States.

*Secretary-General Kofi Annan, message on the occasion of the International Day for the Abolition of Slavery, December 2, 2003.

Jim Crow laws
laws requiring strict separation of racial groups, with whites and "nonwhites" required to attend separate schools, work in different jobs, and use segregated public accommodations, such as transportation and restaurants

de jure segregation
segregation mandated by law

had protected African Americans from physical reprisals were withdrawn. State and local governments throughout the South mandated racial segregation by enacting what came to be known as **Jim Crow laws.** These laws required the strict separation of racial groups, with whites and "nonwhites" going to separate schools, being employed in different jobs, and using segregated public accommodations, such as transportation and restaurants. **De jure segregation,** legally mandated separation of the races, became the norm in much of the South.

The idea behind the Jim Crow laws was that whites and nonwhites should occupy separate societies and have little to do with each other. Many whites feared that racial mixing would result in interracial dating and marriage, which would inevitably lead to the decline of their superior position in society; thus in many southern states, miscegenation laws, which banned interracial marriage, cohabitation, or sex, were passed and severe penalties imposed for those who violated them. Interracial couples who married risked losing their property and even their liberty, since heavy fines and jail sentences were among the penalties for breaking those laws.

State and local governments in the South also found creative ways to prevent African Americans from exercising their right to vote. They relied on several tactics:

- The **white primary** was a primary election in which only white people were allowed to vote. Because Democrats dominated politics so heavily in the post–Civil War South, the only races that really mattered were the primary races that determined the Democratic nominees. But Southern states restricted voting in these primaries to whites only.
- The **literacy test** determined eligibility to vote. Literacy tests were designed so that few voters would stand a chance of passing the exam administered to African American voters, whereas the test for white voters was easy to pass. Typically, white voters were exempt from literacy tests because of a grandfather clause (see below).
- A **poll tax,** a fee levied for voting, often presented an insurmountable obstacle to poor African Americans. White voters were often exempt from poll taxes because of a grandfather clause.
- The **grandfather clause** exempted individuals from conditions on voting (such as poll taxes or literacy tests) if they themselves or their ancestor had been eligible to vote before 1870. Because African Americans did not have the right to vote in southern states before the Civil War, the grandfather clause was a mechanism to protect the voting rights of whites.

These laws were enforced not only by government agents, particularly police, but by nongovernmental groups as well. Among the most powerful of these groups was the Ku Klux Klan (KKK). During the late 1800s and into the 1900s, the Klan was dreaded and hated throughout the southern states, and it used its powers to threaten and intimidate those African Americans and whites who dared to question its core principle: that whites are in every way superior to African Americans. The Klan's particular brand of intimidation, the burning cross and the lynching noose, was reviled throughout the southern and border states, but few could dispute the power the Klan wielded in those areas.

Governmental Acceptance of Discrimination

The federal government too had seemingly abandoned African Americans and the quest for equality under the law. In the *Civil Rights Cases* of 1883, the Supreme Court ruled that Congress lacked the authority to prevent discrimination by private individuals and organizations. Rather, Congress's jurisdiction, the Court claimed, was limited to banning discrimination in official acts of state or local governments. The Court also declared that the Civil Rights Act of 1875, which had sought to mandate "full and equal enjoyment" of a wide variety of facilities and accommodations, was unconstitutional.

In 1896, the Court struck what seemed to be the final blow against racial equality. In 1890, Louisiana passed a law that required separate accommodations for blacks and whites on railroad trains. Several citizens of New Orleans sought to test the constitutionality of the law and enlisted Homer Plessy, who was one-eighth African American (but still considered "black" by Louisiana state law) to serve as plaintiff. The choice of Plessy, who could pass for white, was intended to show the arbitrary nature of the statute. On June 7, 1892, Plessy boarded a railroad car designated for whites only. Plessy was asked to leave the whites-only car, and he refused. He was then arrested and jailed, charged with violating the state law. In 1896, the U.S. Supreme Court heard ***Plessy v. Ferguson,*** in which Plessy's attorneys argued that the Louisiana state law violated the **equal protection clause** of the Fourteenth Amendment, which states that no state shall "deny to any person within its jurisdiction the equal protection of the laws."

In a 7–1 decision, the Court rejected Plessy's arguments, claiming that segregation based on race was not a violation of the equal protection clause. Rather, the court made this argument:

> We consider the underlying fallacy of the plaintiff's argument to consist in the assumption that the enforced separation of the two races stamps the colored race with a badge of inferiority. If this be so, it is not by reason of anything found in the act, but solely because the colored race chooses to put that construction upon it.[6]

In its decision, the Court created the **separate but equal doctrine,** declaring that separate but equal facilities do not violate the Fourteenth Amendment's equal protection clause. Under this doctrine, the Court upheld state laws mandating separation of the races in schools

white primary
a primary election in which a party's nominees for general election were chosen but in which only white people were allowed to vote

literacy test
a test to determine eligibility to vote; designed so that few African Americans would pass

poll tax
a fee for voting; levied to prevent poor African Americans in the South from voting

grandfather clause
a clause exempting individuals from voting conditions such as poll taxes or literacy tests if they or their ancestor had voted before 1870, thus sparing most white voters

Plessy v. Ferguson
1896 Supreme Court ruling creating the separate but equal doctrine

equal protection clause
the Fourteenth Amendment clause stating that no state shall "deny to any person within its jurisdiction the equal protection of the laws"

separate but equal doctrine
established by the Supreme Court in *Plessy v. Ferguson,* it said that separate but equal facilities for whites and nonwhites do not violate the Fourteenth Amendment's equal protection clause

and all public accommodations such as businesses, public transportation, restaurants, hotels, swimming pools, and recreational facilities. The only condition the Court placed on these segregated facilities was that the state had to provide public facilities for both whites and nonwhites. The Court paid little attention to whether the school systems or public accommodations were comparable in quality. As long as the state had some kind of facilities in place for both whites and nonwhites, the segregation was permitted. This doctrine would become the legal backbone of segregationist policies for more than five decades to come.

The Civil Rights Movement

In the early decades of the twentieth century, African Americans continued their struggle for equal protection of the laws. Though the movement for civil rights enjoyed some early successes, the century was nearly half over before momentous victories by civil rights activists finally began to change the status of African Americans in revolutionary ways. These victories were the result of strong leadership at the helm of the movement, the effective strategies used by activists, and a national government that was finally ready to fulfill the promise of equality embodied in the Declaration of Independence.

Fighting Back: Early Civil Rights Organizations

In the early years of the twentieth century, the political climate was open to reform, with activists in the Progressive movement calling for an end to government corruption, reforms to labor laws, the protection of children from abusive labor practices, and an expansion of rights, including the right of women to vote and the civil rights of African Americans (see Chapter 8 for more on the Progressive movement). In 1909, W. E. B. Du Bois (an influential African American writer and scholar, who is today acknowledged as the father of social science) joined with Oswald Garrison Villard (publisher of the *New York Evening Post,* an influential newspaper, and grandson of the abolitionist leader William Lloyd Garrison) to form the National Association for the Advancement of Colored People (NAACP). One of the targets of the NAACP for the next several decades was the separate but equal doctrine, which remained in place through the first half of the twentieth century.

Citing the lack of graduate schools, law schools, and medical schools for African Americans, the NAACP argued that the states had violated the equal protection clause by failing to make such schools available to African Americans. During the 1930s, lawsuits brought by the NAACP in several states ended discriminatory admissions practices in professional schools.[7] Momentum in the movement for equality continued to grow, fueled in part by the growing political activism of African American soldiers returning home after fighting against fascism abroad during World War II. Many of these soldiers began to question why they were denied freedom and equality in their own country, and they mobilized for civil rights in their communities. Though the Court had not yet overturned the separate but equal doctrine, by 1950 the U.S. Supreme Court had ruled that segregating classrooms, dining rooms, or library facilities in colleges, universities, and professional schools was unconstitutional.

Taking cues from those court decisions, by the 1950s the NAACP and other groups had changed their tactics. Instead of arguing that states had to provide equivalent schools and programs for African Americans and whites, these groups began to argue that segregation itself was a violation of the equal protection clause. But it was not until 1954 that the U.S. Supreme Court struck down the separate but equal doctrine, finding it inherently unequal and therefore unconstitutional.

The End of Separate but Equal

In the fall of 1951, Oliver Brown, a welder at the Santa Fe Railroad yard in Topeka, Kansas, sought to have his daughter Linda enrolled in the third grade in an all-white public school seven blocks from their home. The act was not accidental; it was the calculated first step in an NAACP legal strategy that would result in sweeping changes to the nation's public school system, effectively shattering the segregated school system dominant in the South.[8] The Browns lived in an integrated neighborhood in Topeka, and Topeka schools were segregated, as allowed (but not required) under Kansas state law. Oliver Brown spoke with a Topeka attorney and with the Topeka NAACP, which persuaded him to join a lawsuit against the Topeka Board of Education. Brown agreed and was directed to attempt to register Linda at the all-white public school. Linda was denied admission.

The stand taken by Oliver Brown and the other plaintiffs was not in vain. Thurgood Marshall, who would go on to become the first African American to sit on the U.S. Supreme Court, argued the case, and in a unanimous decision in 1954 the Supreme Court ruled in *Brown v. Board of Education of Topeka* that segregated schools violate the equal protection clause of the Fourteenth Amendment. In one stroke, the Court concluded that "separate but equal" schools were inherently unequal, because they stamped African American children with a "badge of racial inferiority" that stayed with them throughout their lives.

In a second case the following year (sometimes called the second Brown decision or Brown II), the court grappled with the issue of how the first *Brown* decision should be implemented—recognizing that many southern states would be reluctant to enforce the decision unless they were made to do so. In its decision, the justices called on the states to dismantle the segregated school system "with all deliberate speed" but left it to local officials to determine how to achieve a desegregated system. Many have criticized the Court's unwillingness or inability to provide more concrete guidelines to local and state officials, contending that the Court's failure to act ultimately undermined the impact of the *Brown* opinion. Nevertheless, the Court's decision in this case signaled both a new era in civil rights law and a governmental climate favorable to changing centuries-long inequalities in American society.[9]

> *Brown v. Board of Education,* the Supreme Court case that resulted in orders to desegregate all public schools, was brought by the father of Linda Brown, here shown in her segregated classroom (front, center). The strategy and plans for this monumental case were developed by the best legal and political minds of the civil rights movement.

Brown v. Board of Education of Topeka
the 1954 Supreme Court decision that ruled that segregated schools violated the equal protection clause of the Fourteenth Amendment

Rosa Parks's Civil Disobedience on a Montgomery Bus

In December 1955, a now-legendary woman named Rosa Parks was on a bus returning home from work as a seamstress at a Montgomery, Alabama, department store. In Montgomery and throughout the South, buses were segregated, with white riders boarding in the front and sitting front to back and African American riders sitting back to front.[10] The bus driver asked the 43-year-old African American woman to give up her seat for a white man; Parks refused and was arrested for violating a local segregation law. (See "Analyzing the Sources" on page 158.)

The Montgomery chapter of the NAACP, of which Parks and her husband were active members, had sought a test case to challenge the constitutionality of the state's Jim Crow laws. Parks agreed to participate in the case, and her arrest came at a pivotal time in the civil rights movement. Activists were buoyed by the *Brown* decision. Momentum favored the civil rights activists in the South, and their cause was bolstered when civil rights and religious leaders in Montgomery chose a 27-year-old preacher relatively new to the city to lead a bus boycott to protest Parks's arrest and the segregated public facilities. His name was Martin Luther King Jr.[11]

Dr. Martin Luther King Jr. and the Strategy of Civil Disobedience

The year-long bus boycott garnered national media attention and King became a national symbol for the civil rights movement. King's leadership skills were put to the test during the year-long battle: He was arrested. His home was bombed. Death threats were made against

ANALYZING THE SOURCES

A FAMOUS IMAGE FROM THE CIVIL RIGHTS ERA

Chances are you have seen this famous photograph before. It is a powerful image. Rosa Parks is the African American woman who refused to obey the law requiring her to give up her seat for a white man and move to the back of the bus. Her refusal and subsequent arrest were the catalyst for a 381-day bus boycott in Montgomery, Alabama, a boycott that ended when the Supreme Court ruled that Montgomery's segregated bus law was unconstitutional. This photo of Parks sitting on a bus in front of a white man was taken a month later.

Evaluating the Evidence

① The man sitting behind Rosa Parks is Nicholas Chriss, a reporter who was working for United Press International at the time the photograph was taken. Who do you think most people looking at this photograph assume that he is? Who did you think he was when you first saw the image?

② Journalists and civil rights advocates, who wanted to create a dramatic, lasting image of the landmark Court decision, had to talk Rosa Parks into having the picture taken. Do you think the photo's impact would be diminished if more people knew about its origin?

③ What is your opinion of the ethics of using a staged photograph such as this one? Can a staged photograph accurately depict a historic event? Why or why not?

him. But for 381 days, the buses of Montgomery remained virtually empty, representing a serious loss in revenue to the city and causing the NAACP to be banned in the state of Alabama. African Americans walked to and from work, day in and day out, for over a year. White employers drove some domestic servants to and from work. Finally, in December 1956, the U.S. Supreme Court ruled that segregated buses were unconstitutional.[12] The bus boycott was a success on many fronts: its righteousness was confirmed by the Supreme Court, the protests garnered national media attention and evoked public sympathy, and the civil rights movement had gained an articulate leader who was capable of unifying and motivating masses and who had an effective strategy for challenging the racism of American society. King advocated protesting government-sanctioned discrimination through civil disobedience and peaceful demonstrations. African American students, as well as white students and other civil rights activists from throughout the country, used the tactics of civil disobedience, including boycotts, sit-ins, and marches, to challenge the policies of segregation. One such demonstration was held in August 1963, in which hundreds of thousands of black and white Americans heard King deliver his famous "I Have a Dream" speech in the shadow of the Lincoln Memorial. (You can view the speech on YouTube at www.youtube.com/watch?v=PbUtL_0vAJk.)

One famous series of marches occurred in early March 1965 from Selma to Montgomery, Alabama. On Sunday, March 7, about six hundred civil rights activists began a march out of Selma, protesting the policies of intimidation and violence that prevented African Americans from registering to vote. The demonstrators, led by John Lewis (now a Democratic member of Congress from Georgia), walked only six blocks to the Edmund Pettus bridge, where law enforcement officials, including Alabama State Troopers and members of the sheriff's office of Dallas County, Alabama, were waiting.[13] When the peaceful protesters attempted to cross the bridge, law enforcement officers brutally attacked them, using tear gas, bull whips, and night sticks. Dubbed Bloody Sunday, the march and the beatings were televised nationally and were instrumental in swaying public opinion in favor of civil rights. The marches sparked a renewed focus on the lack of voting rights for African Americans and ultimately helped to pressure Congress to pass the Voting Rights Act in 1965.[14]

King, who was not present at the Bloody Sunday march, returned to Selma to lead another march on the following Tuesday. When law enforcement officers again confronted the marchers at the bridge, King asked his followers to kneel in prayer and then turn around and return to their starting point. Critics charged that King was giving in to law enforcement and questioned his nonviolent tactics.[15] Differences over the use of nonviolent civil disobedience generated divisions within the civil rights movement,[16] with the more militant leaders such as Stokely Carmichael and Malcolm X advocating more aggressive tactics.[17]

Although the violence used against protesters generated positive opinions of the civil rights movement, another form of violence, urban riots, eroded feelings of goodwill toward the movement. For five days in 1965, rioting in the Watts neighborhood of Los Angeles resulted in thirty-four deaths, more than 1,000 injuries, and over 4,000 arrests. Though the immediate cause of the violence was an altercation between white police officers and an African American man who had been arrested for drunk driving, the frustration and anger that spilled over had long been brewing in this poor, predominantly African American neighborhood.

On April 4, 1968, Martin Luther King was in Memphis, Tennessee, in support of African American sanitation workers who were striking for equal treatment and pay with white workers. Standing on a balcony at the Lorraine Motel, King was killed by an assassin's bullet. Heartbreak, hopelessness, and despair followed King's assassination—a feeling manifested in part by further rioting in over one hundred cities. Many Americans, both black and white, objected to the looting depicted in nightly news broadcasts. But those who sympathized with the rioters noted that because of the accumulated injustices against African Americans, the government and the rule of law had lost legitimacy in the eyes of those who were rioting.

> Dr. Martin Luther King Jr. delivers his "I Have a Dream" speech to close to 300,000 people participating in the August 28, 1963 March on Washington. The march supported proposed civil rights legislation and the end of segregation. Dr. King was awarded the Nobel Peace Prize in 1964.

The Government's Response to the Civil Rights Movement

The civil rights movement is credited not only with ending segregation in public schools but also with the desegregation of public accommodations such as buses, restaurants, and hotels and with promoting universal suffrage. As a result of the movement, Congress passed the 1965 Voting Rights Act, which aggressively sought to counter nearly one hundred years of disenfranchisement, as well as the 1964 Civil Rights Act, which bars racial discrimination in accommodations and private employment, and the 1968 Civil Rights Act, which prohibits racial discrimination in housing.

> Two young college students help a Mississippi woman register to vote during the Freedom Summer of 1964. In that summer, thousands of civil rights activists encouraged and assisted African Americans in the Deep South to register to vote. During the Freedom Summer more than 1,000 civil rights volunteers were arrested, close to 100 were beaten by angry mobs and police officers, and at least 3 black volunteers were murdered in response to their efforts to register African American voters.

The Civil Rights Act of 1964

Simultaneously expanding the rights of many Americans and providing them with important protections from discrimination, the Civil Rights Act of 1964 includes provisions that mandate equality on numerous fronts:

- It outlaws arbitrary discrimination in voter registration practices within the states.
- It bans discrimination in public accommodations, including hotels, restaurants, and theaters.
- It prohibits state and local governments from banning access to public facilities on the basis of race, religion, or ethnicity.
- It empowers the U.S. Attorney General to sue to desegregate public schools.
- It bars government agencies from discrimination, and imposes the threat of the loss of federal funding if an agency violates the ban.
- It establishes a standard of equality in employment opportunity.

The last part of the act, Title VII, which establishes the equality standard in employment opportunity, provides the legal foundation for a body of law that regulates fair employment practices. Specifically, Title VII bans discrimination in employment based on inherent characteristics—race, national origin, religion, and sex. Title VII also established the Equal Employment Opportunity Commission (EEOC), a government body that still administers Title VII today.

Other Civil Rights Legislation in the 1960s

Although the Civil Rights Act of 1964 sought to address discrimination in access to public accommodations, employment, and education, many civil rights leaders believed that further legislation was necessary to protect the voting rights of African Americans in the South because they had been so systematically intimidated and prevented from participating.[18] In some southern counties, less than a third of all eligible African Americans were registered to vote, whereas nearly two-thirds of eligible white voters were registered in the same counties.

During the summer of 1964, thousands of civil rights activists, including many college students, worked to register black voters in southern states where black voter registration was dismal. Within months, a quarter of a million new voters had been added to the voting rolls. However, because of violent attacks on thousands of civil rights activists and the murders of three black activists in Mississippi in the summer of 1964, Congress determined that it needed to enact a federal law to eliminate discriminatory local and state government registration and voting practices. The Voting Rights Act of 1965 (VRA) banned voter registration practices, such as literacy tests. Moreover, the VRA mandated federal intervention in any county in which less than 50 percent of eligible voters were registered.

One component of the VRA provided for periodic review of some of its tenets. After a specified period of time, Congress must pass and the president must sign an extension of the law to have those requirements remain in effect. In 2006, President George W. Bush (2001–2009) signed legislation extending the VRA for twenty-five years.

In 1968, in the aftermath of Martin Luther King's murder on April 4, Congress passed and President Lyndon Johnson signed an additional piece of civil rights legislation. The Civil Rights Act of 1968 sought to end discriminatory practices in housing, including mortgage lending and the sale or rental of housing. The act also banned the practice of **steering,** in which realtors would steer African American families to certain neighborhoods and white families to others. National civil rights laws enacted since the 1960s have made de jure segregation and discrimination in housing and credit opportunities illegal. However, **de facto segregation,** the segregation caused by the tendency of people to live in neighborhoods with others of their own race, religion, or ethnic group, still prevails in many communities throughout the United States today.

Impact of the Civil Rights Movement

The culmination of many acts of resistance by individuals and groups, the civil rights movement has had a momentous impact on society by working for the laws and rulings that bar discrimination in employment, public accommodations, education, and housing. The movement has also had a profound impact on voting rights by establishing the principle that the laws governing voter registration and participation should ensure that individuals are permitted to vote regardless of their race. As shown in Figure 5.2, as a result of the Voting Rights Act, in Mississippi, for example, the percentage of African Americans registered to vote jumped from 7 percent in 1965 to 72 percent in 2006, and then to 82 percent in 2008. Today, in some states, including Georgia, Mississippi, and South Carolina, a greater percentage of African Americans are registered than whites. In addition, all states, especially those in the

steering
the practice by which realtors steered African American families to certain neighborhoods and white families to others

de facto segregation
segregation caused by the fact that people tend to live in neighborhoods with others of their own race, religion, or ethnic group

Voter Registration Rates 1965, 2006, and 2008

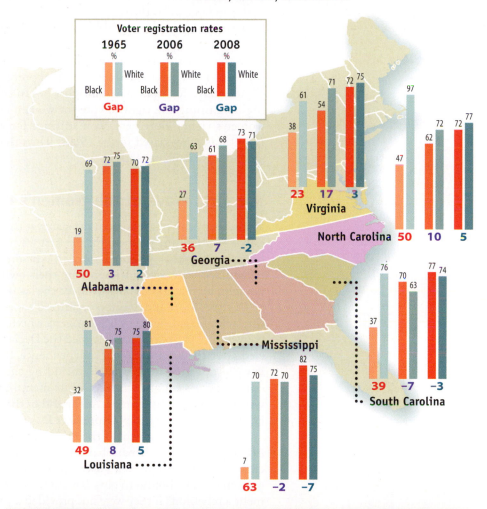

POLITICAL INQUIRY

FIGURE 5.2 ■ In view of the profound impact of the Voting Rights Act, as indicated by the data presented here, has the act outlived its usefulness? What might be some reasons for continuing the act? For discontinuing it? In which states was the voter registration for black citizens in 2008 substantially larger than it was in 2006? What might explain these large increases in black citizen voter registration in 2008?

SOURCE: www.usdoj.gov/crt/voting/intro/intro_c.htm; Table 4b, Reported Voting and Registration of the Voting-Age Population, by Sex, Race and Hispanic Origin, for States: November 2006, www.census.gov/hhes/www/socdemo/voting/publications/p20/2006/tables.html; Table 4b, Reported Voting and Registration of the Voting-Age Population, by Sex, Race and Hispanic Origin, for States: November 2008, www.census.gov/hhes/www/socdemo/voting/publications/p20/2008/tables.html.

South, have seen an increase in the number of African Americans elected to serve in offices at the state, county, and municipal levels and in school districts. Indeed, more African Americans serve in elected office in Mississippi than in any other state, and all southern states boast among the highest numbers of African American elected officials.[19]

In addition to having a profound impact on race relations and civil rights law, the civil rights movement soon came to be regarded by other groups as a model of political engagement. Ethnic minorities, women, persons with disabilities, and gays and lesbians have adopted many tactics of the movement in their own quest to secure their civil rights.

The Movement for Women's Civil Rights

As already noted, the pronouncement in the Declaration of Independence that "all men are created equal" initially applied only to white men, and usually only to those who owned property. Not only did the concept of equal protection of the laws not apply to nonwhite male citizens, until the Civil War amendments to the Constitution and subsequent pieces of national legislation such as the Voting Rights and Civil Rights acts, it also did not apply to female citizens—white or nonwhite. Like African American men, women had to wait until the Constitution was amended and civil rights legislation was adopted, in response to the women's rights movement, for equal protection of the laws.

Advocates for women's civil rights began their efforts in the mid-1800s, initially focusing on gaining the right to vote for women citizens. That endeavor, the first wave of the women's rights movement, won suffrage for women in 1920. The cause of women's civil rights was rejuvenated in the 1960s, when the second wave of the movement began. This second wave continues today.

The First Wave of the Women's Rights Movement

The segregation of the women delegates at the 1840 World Anti-Slavery Conference in London was a defining moment for the first wave of the U.S. women's rights movement. Forced to sit in the balcony behind a drawn curtain, Lucretia Mott and Elizabeth Cady Stanton recognized that without improving their own legal and political status, women were not going to be successful in fighting for the legal rights of other groups of people.

In 1848, Mott and Stanton organized a meeting at Seneca Falls, New York, to talk about the lack of legal rights of U.S. citizens who happened to be born female. At the end of the convention, the participants signed the Declaration of Sentiments. This Declaration, modeled after the Declaration of Independence, listed many rights and opportunities that the law did not guarantee women, including the right to vote, educational and employment opportunities equal to those of white men, and married women's rights to own property as well as legal standing to sue. At the end of the convention, the participants signed the Declaration of Sentiments (see Appendix D).

Clearly, John Adams and the other architects of the Constitution had ignored Abigail Adams's request to her husband and his colleagues to "remember the ladies" when they created the new system of government. Adams warned her husband that not only would women not feel bound to obey laws in which they had no say but also the ladies would "foment a rebellion" if they were not provided a voice in government.

The signatories of the Declaration of Sentiments began Adams's forecasted rebellion. The document they signed insisted "that [women] have immediate admission to all rights and privileges which belong to them as citizens of these United States." For those women and men who joined this new movement for women's civil rights, the right to vote became the focal point. They recognized that this right was the foundational right that would enable women to win the other rights and privileges of citizenship.

Because the Constitution initially reserved for the states the authority to determine who had the right to vote as well as to be employed and obtain the best possible education, many of the initial battles for women's rights took place at the state level of government. Eventually, as the national government's responsibilities expanded through court interpretations of the Constitution, especially the Fourteenth Amendment, the federal government's role in guaranteeing civil rights expanded.

STATE-LEVEL RIGHTS Even after ratification of the Fourteenth Amendment (1868) guaranteeing equal protection of the laws for all people and the same privileges and immunities to all citizens, women's educational and work opportunities were limited by social norms as well as state laws. Education for girls prepared them to be good wives and mothers, not to be economically independent. By the late 1800s, a few colleges began to admit women, and several women's colleges were established. Yet most colleges did not offer women the same educational opportunities as men, and women who graduated and aspired to a career were limited in two ways. First, by choosing a career, these educated women gave up the possibility of marriage. They were not legally banned from marriage, but societal norms prevented them from having both a career and a husband. Second, their career choices were limited: teaching, the developing professions of nursing and social work, or missionary work.

In 1873, Myra Bradwell challenged women's limited career choices when she sued the state of Illinois over its refusal to let her practice law.[20] She argued that the Fourteenth Amendment's privileges and immunities clause protected her right to earn a living in a career of her choice. In this case, the Supreme Court found that women's God-given destiny was to "fulfill the noble and benign offices of wife and mother" and that allowing women to practice law would impinge on that destiny. The *Bradwell* case established the precedent for the Court to justify allowing women to be treated differently from men (sex-based discrimination) if the different treatment was deemed a *rational* means by which the government could fulfill a *legitimate* public interest. In the *Bradwell* case, the Court applied the *ordinary scrutiny* test, deeming it legitimate for the government to protect the role of women as wives and mothers, and to accomplish that protection, it was rational to deny them equal employment opportunities.

In 1875, another women's rights case came before the Supreme Court. In this case, Virginia Minor of Missouri (actually her husband, because she, like all married women, did not have standing to sue) challenged the constitutionality of the Missouri law that guaranteed the right to vote only to male U.S. citizens. In this case, *Minor v. Happersett,* the Court acknowledged that women were citizens, yet it also decreed that state governments established voting rights, not the U.S. Constitution.[21] Therefore, the justices argued that the Fourteenth Amendment's privileges and immunities clause did not give women rights not established in the Constitution, hence it did not extend to women the right to vote. Although by 1875 some local governments (school districts specifically) had extended voting rights to women, no state other than New Jersey had ever given women the right to vote. Women who owned property in New Jersey had the right to vote for a brief period between the end of the War for Independence and 1807, when it was taken away in response to the lobbying of politicians and professional men.

THE NINETEENTH AMENDMENT TO THE CONSTITUTION The American Women's Suffrage Association (AWSA), directed by Lucy Stone, had been leading the battle to extend the right to vote to women in the states since 1869. Also since 1869, the National Women's Suffrage Association (NWSA), directed by Susan B. Anthony and Elizabeth Cady Stanton, had been fighting to extend to women all rights of citizenship, including but not limited to the right to vote. Unlike the AWSA, the NWSA focused its suffrage battle on the federal level, specifically on amending the U.S. Constitution. In 1890, frustrated by their lack of success in the battle to extend suffrage to women, the AWSA and the NWSA joined forces, creating the National American Women's Suffrage Association (NAWSA). The NAWSA focused its efforts on amending the U.S. Constitution.

In 1916, Alice Paul founded the National Women's Party, which adopted more radical tactics than the NAWSA had been willing to use in its fight for suffrage. Noting the lack of support on the part of national officials for suffrage, Paul's organization called on voters in the 1916 election not to vote for candidates who opposed women's suffrage, including President Wilson, who was running for reelection. In 1917, after President Wilson was reelected, Paul and other suffragists chained themselves to the White House fence and called

> A line of women rally for women's suffrage in New York City in 1915. After the Supreme Court determined in 1875 that the Fifteenth Amendment (1870) did not guarantee women the right to vote, suffragists mobilized to win the vote for women.

on Wilson to support the suffrage amendment. Arrested, jailed, and force-fed when they engaged in a hunger strike, the women gained media attention, which in turn brought national attention to their struggle for suffrage and the president's opposition. After several months and persistent media pressure, President Wilson called on the House and the Senate to approve the women's suffrage amendment.

By June 1919, the House and the Senate approved what was to become the Nineteenth Amendment. In 1920, Tennessee became the thirty-sixth state to ratify the amendment, and it was added to the Constitution. The Nineteenth Amendment prohibited the national and state governments from abridging or denying citizens the right to vote on account of sex. The right to vote was extended to another group of citizens in 1971 when the states ratified the Twenty-sixth Amendment. This amendment guarantees citizens 18 years of age and older the right to vote. However, college students and civil rights advocates have raised concerns about lack of equal protection of voting rights for college students living away from their parents.

> Alice Paul designed this pin and presented it to the many suffragists arrested and imprisoned for picketing in front of the White House for women's suffrage between 1917 and 1919. The pin, a replication of a prison gate, calls attention to the injustice of being "jailed for freedom."

The Second Wave of the Women's Rights Movement

After the Nineteenth Amendment was added to the Constitution, the push for women's rights ceased to be a mass movement. Women were still organized in groups and lobbied the government for women's civil rights, but the many women's organizations were no longer working collectively toward one agreed-upon goal, such as the right to vote. Another mass women's movement did not arise until the 1960s. Several factors account for the mobilization of the second wave of the women's movement in the

1960s, which focused this time on the plethora of rights related to the social, economic, and political status of women, many of the same rights originally demanded in the Declaration of Sentiments.

By the 1960s, large numbers of women were working outside the home in the paid labor force. Working women talked with one another about their work and family lives and came to recognize common concerns and problems, including discrimination in educational opportunities, employment opportunities, and pay; lack of child care; domestic violence; the problem of rape, for which *they* were often blamed; and their inability to obtain credit (borrow money) without having a male cosign on the loan. Women recognized that as a class of citizens they did not have equal protection of the laws.

In 1961, at the prodding of Esther Peterson, the director of the Women's Bureau in the Department of Labor, President John F. Kennedy (1961–1963) established a Commission on the Status of Women, chaired by Eleanor Roosevelt. In 1963, the commission reported that women in the United States were discriminated against in many areas of life, including education and employment. In its report, the commission argued that women needed to pursue lawsuits that would allow the Supreme Court to interpret properly the Fourteenth Amendment's equal protection clause, hence prohibiting discrimination against women.

By the mid-1960s, the women's rights movement was rejuvenated with a second wave of mass activity. The goal of this second wave was equal legal rights for women. The means to achieve that goal included public demonstrations, legislation, litigation, and an as yet unsuccessful attempt to enact the Equal Rights Amendment (ERA), which had been written by Alice Paul and first introduced in Congress in 1923.

FEDERAL LEGISLATION AND WOMEN'S RIGHTS In 1955, Edith Green (D-Oregon) introduced into Congress the first piece of national legislation written specifically to protect women, the Equal Pay Act. Enacted into law in 1963, the Equal Pay Act prohibited employers from paying women less than men were paid for the same job, which was the standard employment practice at the time. Indeed, beginning with school boards in the mid-1800s and the federal Mint during the Civil War, governments had hired women specifically because they could pay them less than men.

The 1964 Civil Rights Act as initially drafted prohibited discrimination in education, employment, and public accommodations based on race, ethnicity, and religion. Yet because of congressional women's efforts, Title VII of the proposed act was rewritten to

> Members of the Business and Professional Women (an advocacy and educational organization that has promoted women's equity since 1919) and Representative Catherine May (R-Washington), one of the thirteen women serving in Congress at the time, surround President John Kennedy as he signs the Equal Pay Act in 1963. President Barack Obama is surrounded by six of the ninety women serving in Congress in 2009, including Nancy Pelosi, the Speaker of the House of Representatives, as he signs the Lilly Ledbetter Fair Pay Act, which remedies loopholes in the Equal Pay Act. Ledbetter, standing to the left of the president, sued her employer after learning that—over a period of nineteen years—her pay was lower than that of her male coworkers who were doing the same job. Her failed discrimination lawsuit fueled the bill's passage.

prohibit discrimination in all personnel decisions based on *sex* as well as the other inherent characteristics. Initially, the EEOC, the federal agency responsible for monitoring Title VII implementation, did not take sex-based discrimination complaints seriously. Women serving on state committees on the status of women responded by establishing the National Organization for Women (NOW) in 1966. NOW's initial statement of purpose is modeled on the requests of the 1848 Seneca Falls Declaration of Sentiments, demonstrating the continued lack of progress toward the goal of women's equality under the law.[22]

To take advantage of Title VII's promise of equal employment opportunities, women needed to pursue educational opportunities on an equal basis with men. Yet Title VI of the 1964 Civil Rights Act does not prohibit sex-based discrimination in institutions that receive federal funds, including educational institutions. By 1972, women's rights advocates won an amendment to the 1964 Civil Rights Act, Title IX, which prohibits sex-based discrimination in educational institutions receiving federal funds.

The Equal Pay Act, Title VII, and Title IX are landmark pieces of national legislation that provide equal protection of the law for women. At the same time that Congress was enacting laws prohibiting sex-based discrimination, the courts were reinterpreting the equal protection clause of the Fourteenth Amendment.

WOMEN'S RIGHTS AND THE EQUAL PROTECTION CLAUSE   In 1971, in the case of *Reed v. Reed,* the Supreme Court for the first time in history used the equal protection clause of the Fourteenth Amendment to find a law that discriminated against women unconstitutional.[23] In the *Reed* case, the Supreme Court found that an Idaho state law giving automatic preference to men to administer the estate of a deceased person who had not named an administrator was not a rational means to fulfill a legitimate government interest. Hence, using the ordinary scrutiny test established in the 1873 *Bradwell* case, the court ruled this discriminatory treatment of women was unconstitutional.

Then, in 1976, the Supreme Court developed a new test for the legality of sex-based discrimination. Oklahoma law allowed women 18 years of age to buy beer with 3.2% alcohol content. Yet men in Oklahoma had to be 21 years of age to purchase 3.2% beer. Men challenged the law, asking the Court to decide if this sex-based discrimination was constitutional. In this case, *Craig v. Boren,* the Court established the heightened scrutiny test for sex-based discrimination cases: different treatment is legal if it is substantially related to an important government interest.[24] The Court used this test in the *Craig* case to find the Oklahoma law unconstitutional. The Court also used the heightened scrutiny test in the 1996 *U.S. v. Virginia* case.[25] In this case, the Court found the male-only admission policy of the Virginia Military Institute unconstitutional. Justice Ruth Bader Ginsburg noted in her opinion that the state of Virginia had not shown that this discriminatory admissions policy was substantially related to the important government objective of training soldiers.

Today, courts sometimes use the ordinary scrutiny test and other times the heightened scrutiny test when deciding sex-based discrimination cases as well as other non–race-based discrimination cases. Proponents of an ERA argue that the strict scrutiny test, which is used in race-, religion-, and ethnic-based discrimination cases, should also be used in sex-based discrimination cases and that this will not happen until the Constitution is amended to explicitly guarantee equality of rights under the law whether a person is a man or a woman.

THE PROPOSED EQUAL RIGHTS AMENDMENT   During the 1970s, as the Supreme Court was reinterpreting the implications of the Fourteenth Amendment for sex-based discrimination, lobbying for the Equal Rights Amendment increased. In 1972, Congress approved the ERA, which states that "equality of rights under the law shall not be denied or abridged by the United States or by any State on account of sex." Finally, forty-nine years after it was first introduced in Congress, the ERA was sent to the states for ratification.

Opponents of the ERA argued it was a duplication of the Fourteenth Amendment and therefore was not needed. Opponents also claimed that passage of the amendment would make women subject to the military draft; would lead to the integration of all single-sex institutions, including schools and public bathrooms; and would result in the legalization of and public funding for all abortions. Moreover, they argued that the ERA was not needed because Congress was passing laws that guaranteed women equal protection in employment and education. Whether or not the claims of its opponents were accurate, they were successful in defeating the ERA, which had not been ratified by enough states by the deadline of 1982.

The first wave of the women's rights movement won the vote through constitutional amendment. The second wave successfully expanded women's civil rights through litigation and legislation. Yet many women's rights advocates argue that women still battle inequities, including unequal pay, sexual harassment, and the glass ceiling (aspiring to higher-level jobs but being unable to win them). Although the situation for women has greatly improved, some argue, not all women have benefited equally from gains in women's rights. Nonwhite women have two characteristics that can lead to discriminatory treatment: gender and color, necessitating a struggle for equal protection on two fronts: the women's rights movement and the civil rights movements of their racial group. We now explore the struggles of several other groups of citizens for equal civil rights.

Other Civil Rights Movements

Today, discriminatory treatment is still a reality for many groups of citizens. The civil rights acts notwithstanding, discrimination in employment, education, housing, and due process still occurs. Moreover, battles for civil rights continue. Unfortunately, we cannot discuss all the civil rights movements that have occurred or are ongoing in the United States. Therefore, we will explore the civil rights battles of just a few groups of citizens: Native Americans; Hispanic Americans; Asian Americans; citizens with disabilities; and lesbian, gay, bisexual, and transgendered people. The hard-fought victories and aspirations of these groups offer an overview of both the history and the breadth of contemporary civil rights movements.

Native Americans' Rights

At first, the fledgling nation recognized the native residents of the land that became the United States as members of sovereign and independent nations with inherent rights. The federal government entered into more than 370 treaties with Native American tribes between 1778 and 1870.[26] Most of those treaties promised land to tribes that agreed to move, and almost all those promises were empty, with the government reneging on most of the agreements. In addition, in 1830, Congress passed the Indian Removal Act, which called for the forced relocation of all native peoples to lands west of the Mississippi. In the end, most Native Americans were dispossessed of their lands and wound up living on reservations. The federal government treated Indians as subhumans, relegating them to second-class status, as they had African Americans.

Until Congress passed the Indian Citizenship Act in 1924, Native Americans had virtually no rights to U.S. citizenship, and even the laws that allowed immigrants to become citizens did not apply to Native Americans. The Indian Rights Association, founded in 1882 and active in lobbying Congress and the state legislatures until the 1930s, was one of the most important of the early groups that actively campaigned for full suffrage for native peoples, in the belief that enfranchisement would help to "civilize" them. The early 1900s also saw the founding of the Society of American Indians and the American Indian Defense Association, both of which fought for citizenship for Native Americans and then for their civil rights. However, for more than forty years after passage of the Indian Citizenship Act, the basic rights enumerated in the Bill of Rights were not granted to Native Americans. In the 1960s, Indian activists became more radical, occupying government

> Elouise Cobell watches Deputy Secretary of the Interior David Hayes testify during a Dec. 17, 2009, Senate Indian Affairs Committee hearing in Washington, D.C., on a multi-billion dollar lawsuit in which Cobell, a member of the Blackfeet Nation of Montana was the lead plaintiff. In the suit, which took 13 years to make its way through the courts, Cobell accused the federal government of mismanaging funds held in trust for Native Americans since 1887. The settlement reached in 2009 awarded Native Americans $3.4 billion in reparations, but the Senate has yet to approve it, delaying payment to half a million Native Americans.

buildings, picketing, and conducting protests. In 1968, the American Indian Movement (AIM) was founded. In the same year, Congress passed the Indian Civil Rights Act, which ensured that Native Americans would have the full protection of the Bill of Rights both on and off their reservations. Although this law had significant symbolic impact, it lacked an enforcement mechanism, and so native peoples continued to be deprived of basic due process protections and equal education and employment opportunities. The National Indian Education Association (NIEA), founded in 1969, continues to confront the lack of quality educational opportunities for Native Americans and the loss of native culture and values.

During the 1970s, Native American organizations began a new effort to force the federal government to honor treaties granting Indians fishing and hunting rights as well as rights to the natural resources buried in their lands. Indians in New York, Maine, and elsewhere sued for land taken from them decades or even a century ago in violation of treaties. Starting with the 1975 Indian Self-Determination and Education Assistance Act, the national government has enacted laws that support greater autonomy for Indian tribes and give them more control of their assets.

The 1988 Indian Gaming Regulatory Act is the best known of the federal laws enacted to support Indian self-determination. This law authorizes Indian tribes to establish gaming operations on their property and requires them to negotiate compacts with the states in which their lands are located. The compacts typically include a profit-sharing understanding that requires the Indian tribe to give a proportion of its profits to the state government and possibly to contiguous local governments. The act mandates that the money made through gaming operations be used for education, economic development, infrastructure (for example, roads and utilities), law enforcement, and courts. By 2009, the National Indian Gaming Commission, the independent agency that regulates Indian gaming, reported that more than 240 of the federally recognized 562 Indian tribes operate more than four hundred casinos and bingo halls in twenty-eight states. The gross revenues for these gaming activities totaled $26.7 billion in 2008.[27] Clearly, one goal of the Gaming Act was to generate resources that would increase the educational and employment opportunities on Indian reservations.

Even with gaming profits, however, the prospects for many Native Americans today remain bleak. According to race and ethnic relations scholars Joe R. Feagin and Clairece Booher Feagin, "Native Americans have endured the longest Depression-like economic situation of any U.S. racial or ethnic group."[28] They are among the poorest, least educated U.S. citizens. Moreover, congressional testimony and materials submitted to support reauthorization of the Voting Rights Act in 2005 documented a pattern of continued discrimination against Native Americans in their right to vote in several states, including Arizona and South Dakota.[29] Like many other groups of U.S. citizens with characteristics that identify them as non–white European descendants, Native Americans continue to fight in the halls of government, in the courtrooms, and in the public arena for their constitutionally guaranteed rights and privileges.

Citizens of Latin American Descent

U.S. citizens of Latin American descent (Latinos) include those whose families hail from Central America, South America, or the Caribbean. Latinos are the largest minority group in the United States, making up almost 16 percent of the total U.S. population. Sixty percent of this Latino population is composed of natural-born U.S. citizens.[30] Latinos make up a large percentage of the population of several states, including New Mexico, California, Texas, Arizona, and Florida.

Sixty-three percent of the voting-age Hispanic population were citizens and 59 percent of this group were registered voters in 2008. In the 2008 presidential election, 84 percent of Hispanic registered voters voted, constituting almost 8 percent of the voters.[31] So far, the elections that have occurred in the twenty-first century have been followed by numerous lawsuits claiming that individual citizens, organized groups, and local governments have prevented eligible Latino voters from voting. For example, in 2006 the national government sued Philadelphia's city government for failing to assist voters effectively—specifically

Spanish-speaking voters—who had limited-English proficiency. Limited-English proficiency continues to cause problems with access to voting and equal educational and employment opportunities for many U.S. citizens, including Latino citizens. We focus here on U.S. citizens of Mexican origin—the largest Latino population in the United States today.

EARLY STRUGGLES OF MEXICAN AMERICANS

In 1846, because of land disputes sparked by white immigrants from the United States encroaching on Mexican territory, the United States declared war on Mexico. By the terms of the 1848 Treaty of Guadalupe Hidalgo, which ended the war, Mexico ceded territory to the United States for $15 million. The Mexican landowners living within this ceded territory had the choice of staying on their land and remaining in what was now the United States or relocating to Mexico. According to the treaty, those Mexicans who stayed on their land would become U.S. citizens, and their civil rights would be protected. Although nearly 77,000 Mexicans chose to do so, and became U.S. citizens, their civil rights were *not* protected.[32] Thus began a long and continuing history of discrimination against U.S. citizens of Mexican descent.

At the turn of the twentieth century, Mexican Americans organized to protest the various forms of discrimination they were experiencing, which included segregated schools, inequities in employment opportunities and wages, discrimination by law enforcement officers, and barriers to their voting rights such as poll taxes and English-only literacy tests. In 1929, several Mexican American organizations combined to create the League of United Latin American Citizens (LULAC).[33]

In 1945, LULAC successfully challenged the segregated school systems in California, which provided separate schools for Mexican children that were of poorer quality than the schools for white children. In this case, *Mendez v. Westminister,* the federal court set an important precedent by using the Fourteenth Amendment to guarantee equal educational opportunities.[34] In 1954, the U.S. Supreme Court followed this lower court's precedent when it ended legal race-based segregation in public schools throughout the nation in the *Brown v. Board of Education of Topeka* case.

THE CHICANO MOVEMENT

In addition to the women's rights movement and the civil rights movement for African American rights, the 1960s witnessed the birth of the Chicano Movement, the mass movement for Mexican American civil rights. The Chicano Movement was composed of numerous Latino organizations focusing on a variety of issues, including rights to equal employment and educational opportunities. One of the most widely recognized leaders in the Chicano Movement was Cesar Chavez.

Cesar Chavez began his civil rights work as a community organizer in 1952, encouraging Mexican Americans to vote and educating them about their civil rights. In the early 1960s, Chavez, along with Jessie Lopez and Dolores Huerta, founded the Agricultural Workers Organizing Committee (AWOC) and the National Farm Worker Association (NFWA). Under Chavez's leadership, the AWOC and the NFWA merged to form the United Farm Workers (UFW) in 1966. The UFW organized successful protests and boycotts to improve working conditions and pay for farmworkers.[35]

The activism of Mexican American workers inspired others to call for additional civil rights protections, including access to equal educational opportunity. In 1968, Mexican American high school students in East Los Angeles staged a walkout to protest high dropout rates of Latino students and the lack of bilingual education, Mexican American history classes, and

> Cesar Chavez began his civil rights work as a community organizer in 1952 by encouraging Mexican Americans to vote and use their civil rights. Together with Dolores Huerta, he founded the United Farm Workers. From the early 1960s until his death in 1993, Chavez was the leading voice for and organizer of migrant farmworkers in the United States. Today, Huerta is the most prominent Chicana labor leader in the country, developing leaders and advocating for the rights of immigrant workers, women, and children.

Mexican American teachers. Though the student walkout did not lead to many immediate changes in the school system, it drew national attention, empowered the students, and inspired other protests.

Until 1971, Latinos were not legally considered a racial minority group, and therefore antidiscrimination laws, such as the 1964 Civil Rights Act, did not apply to them. In the landmark case *Corpus Christi Independent School District v. Cisneros*[36] (1971), the Supreme Court upheld a lower court's ruling that Latinos are a racial minority group; therefore, they are covered by laws protecting the rights of minority groups.[37]

EMPLOYMENT DISCRIMINATION AND OTHER CIVIL RIGHTS ISSUES

Since the 1986 Immigration Reform and Control Act went into effect, organizations that work to protect the rights of Latinos and other minority citizens have been receiving increasing numbers of complaints about employment discrimination. Under this act, employers who hire undocumented immigrant workers are subject to sanctions. To comply with this law, some employers refuse to hire—and thus discriminate against—any applicants for whom English is a second language and any who look Latino under the assumption that all such people could be undocumented immigrants. This means that employers are violating the equal employment rights of Latino citizens in many cases, for they are mistakenly assuming they are undocumented immigrants.

Today, U.S. citizens of Mexican descent continue to experience violations of their civil rights. LULAC, along with the Mexican American Legal Defense and Education Fund (MALDEF; founded in 1968), and other organizations continue to fight for laws that will provide due process and equal protection, equal access to education, and other civil rights for Latino citizens and immigrants. They also work to educate Latinos about their rights and empower them to engage in the political process. Through the efforts of these and other groups, Hispanic voter registration and turnout has significantly increased in recent elections. Moreover, according to the National Association of Latino Elected and Appointed Officials (NALEO), the number of Latinos elected to local, state, and national positions has grown by almost 40 percent in the last decade. Latino elected officials are serving in all levels of government in all regions of the nation.[38]

Citizens of Asian Descent

Asian American citizens come from, or have ancestors from, a number of different countries with diverse cultures, religions, histories, and languages. Today, the largest percentage of Asian Americans have Chinese origins, followed by those of Filipino, Asian Indian, Vietnamese, Korean, and Japanese ancestry. Large numbers of immigrants from Japan came to the United States around the turn of the twentieth century, but it was not until the 1940s that the flow of immigrants from other Asian countries began to increase, beginning with the Philippines. In the 1960s, the number of immigrants from Korea and India began to increase significantly, and in the 1970s—as the Vietnam War ended—immigrants from Vietnam began to arrive in large numbers. Today, 5 percent of the U.S. population is of Asian descent. The largest Asian American populations live in California, New York, Hawaii, Texas, New Jersey, and Illinois.[39]

Like other U.S. citizens with non–white European ancestry, Asian Americans have had to fight continually for their civil rights, specifically for equal protection under the law and particularly for equal access to educational and employment opportunities as well as citizenship. Asian immigrants and Asian Americans created organizations to fight for citizenship and equal protection of the law, such as the Japanese American Citizens League (JACL; founded in the 1930s). One successful result of those efforts was the 1952 Immigration and Nationality Act, which allowed Asian immigrants to become citizens for the first time. Before passage of this law, only U.S.-born children of Asian immigrants could be citizens.

INTERNMENT OF JAPANESE AMERICANS DURING WORLD WAR II   As

noted previously, one of the most egregious violations of the civil rights of tens of thousands of Asian American citizens occurred during World War II when Americans of Japanese ancestry were forced to move to government-established camps. Under President Franklin Roosevelt's Executive Order 9066, over 120,000 Japanese Americans, two-thirds of whom were native-born U.S. citizens, were relocated from the West Coast of the United States after Japan's attack on Pearl Harbor. During that same period, the federal government also restricted the travel of Americans of German and Italian ancestry who were living on the West Coast (the United States was also fighting against Germany and Italy), but those citizens were not relocated. Many relocated Japanese Americans lost their homes and businesses.

The JACL fought for decades to obtain reparations for the citizens who were interned and for the repeal of a section of the 1950 Internal Security Act that allowed the government to imprison citizens deemed enemy collaborators during a crisis. Congress repealed the section of the 1950 law targeted by the JACL, and in 1987 President Ronald Reagan (1981–1989) signed a bill providing $1.2 billion in reparations.

CONTEMPORARY ISSUES FOR ASIAN AMERICANS During the 1960s and 1980s, the number of organizations and coalitions pressing for the civil rights of Asian Americans grew as large numbers of new immigrants from Asian countries arrived in the United States in response to changes in U.S. immigration laws. During the 1960s, Asian Americans on college campuses organized and fostered a group consciousness about the need to protect their civil rights. During the 1980s, Asian American organizations began to pay more attention to voting rights as well as to hate crimes and employment discrimination. Then in 1996, numerous organizations, each representing Asian Americans with ancestry from one country, joined to form the National Council of Asian Pacific Americans (NCAPA), which presses for equal protection of the law for all Asians.

With the exception of Korean Americans and Vietnamese Americans, Asian Americans have the highest median income compared with the population as a whole.[40] Asian Americans are also twice as likely as the population as a whole to earn a bachelor's degree or higher.[41] Moreover, Asian Americans are better represented in professional and managerial positions than any other racial or ethnic group, including white Americans. Yet like women, Asian American citizens appear to hit a glass ceiling, for they are not represented in the very top positions in the numbers that their high levels of educational achievement would seem to predict. Therefore, those advocating for Asian American civil rights are increasingly concentrating their efforts on discrimination in employment. Professor Don T. Nakanishi, an expert on Asian Americans, points out that Asian Americans are becoming "more organized, more visible and more effective as participants and leaders in order to advance—as well as to protect—their individual and group interests, and to contribute to our nation's democratic processes and institutions."[42] Today, more than 2,000 Asian Americans serve as elected or appointed officials in all levels of government throughout the nation.

> Before 1952, foreign-born Asian immigrants could not become U.S. citizens; however, children born in the United States to Asian immigrants were citizens by birth. Today, both the biological and the adopted children of U.S. citizens who are born abroad acquire automatic citizenship. For example, for children adopted from Asian countries, such as the young girl in this photo, U.S. citizenship is acquired automatically once the adoption process is completed.

Citizens with Disabilities

The civil rights movements of the 1960s and 1970s made society more aware of the lack of equal protection of the laws for diverse groups of citizens, including people with disabilities. The first law to mandate equal protection for people with physical and mental disabilities was the 1973 Rehabilitation Act, which prohibited discrimination against people with disabilities in federally funded programs. In 1990, people with disabilities achieved a

> Access to public transportation is key to education and employment opportunities, independence, and full community engagement for people with disabilities. The 1990 Americans with Disabilities Act prohibits discrimination against and sets specific requirements to accommodate transportation for people with disabilities on publicly and privately funded transportation systems.

significant enhancement of this earlier victory in their fight to obtain protection of their civil rights. The Americans with Disabilities Act (ADA), enacted in that year, extends the ban on discrimination against people with disabilities in education, employment, health care, housing, and transportation to all programs and organizations, not just those receiving federal funds. The ADA defines a disability as any "physical or mental impairment that substantially limits one or more of the major life activities of the individual." The ADA does not enumerate every disability that it covers, resulting in much confusion over which conditions it covers and which it excludes.

A series of U.S. Supreme Court rulings in the late 1990s and early 2000s narrowed the interpretation of "disability," which decreased the number of people benefiting from the ADA. For example, the Court determined that if an individual can take an action to mitigate an impairment (such as taking medication to prevent seizures), then the impairment is not a disability protected by the ADA. In response, disability advocates, including the National Coalition of Disability Rights and the ADA Watch, successfully lobbied Congress to propose an act restoring the broader interpretation of the term "disability" and, hence, increasing the number of people benefiting from the ADA. The Americans with Disabilities Act Amendments of 2008 went into effect in January 2009. The act applies to the equal protection guaranteed in the Rehabilitation Act (1973) and the ADA (1990). It does not change the written definition of "disability" that is in the ADA, but it does broaden what "substantially limits" and "major life activities" mean, and no longer considers actions taken to mitigate impairments as relevant to determining if employers and educational institutions must accommodate a person's mental or physical disability in public facilities and housing.[43]

There is no question that the ADA has enhanced the civil rights of citizens with disabilities. Before the ADA was enacted, people with disabilities who were fired from their jobs or denied access to schools, office buildings, or other public places had no recourse. Cities were under no obligation to provide even the most reasonable accommodations to people with disabilities who sought employment or the use of public transportation systems. And employers were under no obligation to make even the most minor modifications to their workplaces for employees with disabilities. For example, if a qualified job applicant was wheelchair bound, an employer did not have to consider installing ramps or raising desks to accommodate the wheelchair but could simply refuse to hire the individual. The ADA changed that situation by requiring employers and governmental organizations to make it possible for people with disabilities to participate meaningfully in their communities through reasonable accommodations.

Lesbian, Gay, Bisexual, and Transgendered Citizens

Lesbian, gay, bisexual, and transgendered people (people whose gender identity cannot be categorized as male or female)—a group often referred to with the abbreviation LGBT or GBLT—also actively seek equal civil rights. Some of the specific rights that LGBT persons have organized to fight for include employment rights, housing rights, and marriage rights. Though the 1970s and 1980s saw some successes in these civil rights battles, there was some backlash in the 1990s and early in the twenty-first century. In this section, we focus on the rights of lesbians and gay men.

THE GAY PRIDE MOVEMENT   Several LGBT civil rights organizations were founded after the Stonewall Rebellion. In June 1969, groups of gay men and lesbians clashed violently with police in New York City, in a protest over the routine harassment by law enforcement of members of the lesbian and gay community. This influential conflict, which started at the Stonewall bar, marked the first time that members of this community acted collectively and in large numbers to assert their rights. Shortly after this event, in 1970, Lambda Legal, a national organization fighting for full recognition of the civil rights of LGBT citizens, was founded. Within a few years, gays and lesbians began to hold gay pride marches throughout the country, and many new groups such as the Human Rights Campaign and the National Gay and Lesbian Task Force, began advocating for LGBT rights.

As a result of organized educational and lobbying efforts by the gay community, during the 1980s a number of state and local governments adopted laws prohibiting discrimination in employment, housing, public accommodations, and employee benefits—that is, guaranteeing equal protection of some laws—for LGBT persons. In 1982, Wisconsin was the first state to prohibit such discrimination. Yet during the same decade, numerous states had laws on the books prohibiting sex between mutually consenting adults of the same sex, typically in the form of antisodomy laws. In the 1986 case of *Bowers v. Hardwick,* the U.S. Supreme Court upheld Georgia's antisodomy law.[44] In 2003, another lawsuit challenging the constitutionality of a state antisodomy law came before the Supreme Court in the case of *Lawrence v. Texas.*[45] This time, the Court overturned the 1986 *Bowers* decision, finding that the Fourteenth Amendment provides due process and equal protection for sexual privacy and therefore the Texas law was unconstitutional.

Advocates for the rights of LGBT persons hoped this 2003 ruling would lead to federal protections of LGBT citizens' civil rights. But there is still no federal law prohibiting LGBT-based discrimination in employment, housing, or public accommodations. In contrast to the lack of federal legislation, today twenty states and the District of Columbia have antidiscrimination laws guaranteeing equal access to employment, housing, and public accommodations regardless of sexual orientation. Twelve states also prohibit gender identity discrimination.[46]

BACKLASH AGAINST THE MOVEMENT FOR LGBT CIVIL RIGHTS   On the other side of the issue, in 1992, opponents of civil rights for LGBT persons succeeded in placing on the ballot in Colorado a proposed law that would prohibit all branches of the state government from adopting any law or policy making it illegal to discriminate against gay men, lesbians, bisexuals, or transgendered people. In 1996, the U.S. Supreme Court, in *Romer v. Evans,* found the state law to be unconstitutional.[47] The parties who filed the suit challenging the law included the Boulder school district; the cities of Denver, Boulder, and Aspen; and the County of Denver.

Another civil rights battle for lesbians and gays is over the issue of marriage rights. The Hawaii state Supreme Court ruled in 1993 that it was a violation of the Hawaii state constitution to deny same-sex couples the right to marry. Opponents of same-sex marriage succeeded in their subsequent efforts to get a state constitutional amendment banning same-sex marriage on the ballot, and in 1996 the majority of Hawaiian voters approved it. The conflict over same-sex marriage that began in Hawaii quickly spread to other states. According to Lambda Legal, by early 2010, four states (Connecticut, Iowa, Massachusetts, and Vermont) and the District of Columbia allowed same-sex couples to marry. Ten states provide equal protection for some state-based rights to same-sex couples through civil union or registered domestic partnership (non–marriage status) laws. In addition, several states respected marriages and non–marriage statuses that same-sex couples enter into in the other states that allow them. The effect of these state laws is that "as of 2009, roughly one-third of the same-sex couples in the United States resided in a jurisdiction offering them at least some form of state-level legal protection."[48] However, the 1996 national Defense of Marriage Act states that the federal government does not recognize same-sex marriages, or civil unions, legalized by any state and that states do not need to recognize same-sex marriages that were legalized in other states.

> On the presidential campaign trail, Barack Obama promised to work for advances in the civil rights of gay and lesbian citizens. However, before his first year in office was over, gay rights activists marched in Washington, D.C. to protest President Obama's lack of action on their behalf.

Though the LGBT community is winning some of its civil rights battles in a growing number of states, in many areas the battle has just begun. For example, in the area of family law, issues involving adoption rights and child custody as well as divorce and property rights are now battlegrounds. In addition, hate crimes continue to be a problem for members of the LGBT community as well as for citizens (and noncitizens) with non–white European ancestry (see "Thinking Critically About Democracy").

The national government enacted its first hate crime law in 1969. Since then, it has expanded the inherent characteristics for which the law guarantees protection. Today, under federal law, a **hate crime** is a crime in which the offender is motivated in part or entirely by her or his bias against the victim because of the victim's actual or perceived race, color, religion, nationality, ethnicity, gender, sexual orientation, gender identity, or disability. Forty-five states and the District of Columbia also have hate crime laws, but the inherent characteristics covered by those laws vary. Although all the state laws cover race, religion, and ethnicity, and most cover gender, sexual orientation, and disability, only a handful also cover gender identity.[49]

> The federal government began collecting data on hate crimes in the 1990s, highlighting the increasing incidence of such crimes. Today, hate crimes motivated by racial prejudice are the most commonly reported.

Affirmative Action: Is It Constitutional?

Laws reinforcing constitutional guarantees by prohibiting discriminatory treatment are the most common objectives of civil rights battles. Nevertheless, in the 1960s the federal government also began implementing policies aimed at reinforcing equal access to employment by mandating recruitment procedures that actively sought to identify qualified minority men for government positions. This policy of **affirmative action** was extended to women in employment and then to educational opportunities. However, affirmative action policies have been and continue to be very controversial.

How Affirmative Action Works

In 1961, President John F. Kennedy (1961–1963) used the term *affirmative action* in an executive order regarding the hiring and employment practices of projects performed by private contractors that were financed with federal funds. The order did more than prohibit race-based discrimination. It required that employers receiving federal funds take affirmative action to ensure that their hiring and employment practices were free of racial discrimination. In 1965, President Lyndon B. Johnson (1963–1968) extended Kennedy's affirmative action order to include the inherent characteristics of race, color, religion, and national origin. Then in 1967, Johnson again extended affirmative action to include women.

Today, affirmative action policies cover such processes as hiring, training, and promoting. Private companies, nonprofit organizations, and government agencies that receive federal government contracts worth at least $50,000 are required by law to have an affirmative action plan for their workers and job candidates.

Affirmative action does not require organizations to hire unqualified candidates, nor does it require the hiring of a qualified minority candidate over a qualified nonminority candidate. Affirmative action does require that an organization make intentional efforts to diversify its workforce by providing equal opportunity to classes of people that have been historically, and in many cases are still today, subject to discrimination. It focuses attention on an employer's history of personnel decisions. If over the years an employer with an affirmative action plan does not hire qualified underutilized workers (women and minority men), it will appear to many that the employer is discriminating and is violating Title VII of the Civil Rights Act. However, critics of affirmative action argue that it discriminates against Caucasians, and they have questioned whether the way it is applied to personnel policies as well as to college admissions policies is constitutional.

In the 1970s, institutions of higher education began to adopt intentional efforts to expand educational opportunities for both men and women from various minority groups. In addition, colleges and universities use affirmative action to ensure a student body that is diverse in race, color, economic status, and other characteristics. These institutions believe

hate crime
a crime committed against a person, property, or society, where the offender is motivated, in part or in whole, by his or her bias against the victim because of the victim's race, religion, disability, sexual orientation, or ethnicity

affirmative action
in the employment arena, intentional efforts to recruit, hire, train, and promote underutilized categories of workers (women and minority men); in higher education, intentional efforts to diversify the student body

SHOULD HATE CRIMES BE PUNISHED MORE SEVERELY THAN OTHER CRIMES?

The Issue: In October 2009, President Obama signed the Matthew Shepard and James Byrd Jr. Hate Crimes Prevention Act. This act expands coverage of the federal hate crime laws by adding sexual orientation, gender, gender identity, and disability to the list of characteristics already covered in the laws: race, color, religion, national origin, and ethnicity. Now those found guilty of committing a crime and having been motivated by bias against their victims because of one of these characteristics will have their punishment increased. Is this type of law just? Is it constitutional?

Yes: Hate crime laws further a compelling government interest. Crimes motivated by hate for a person because of an immutable characteristic are crimes against a whole group of people, not just that individual. When a Muslim is assaulted because he or she is a Muslim, fear spreads throughout the Muslim community, for any member of the community could be next. Hate crimes are intended to intimidate the victim and incite fear in all people like the victim. Hate crimes threaten domestic tranquility in a way that other crimes do not because hate crimes breed retaliatory hate crimes. The harm to public order and tranquility caused by hate crimes requires an additional punishment that indicates society will not tolerate people acting on their biases. Increased punishment may also deter others from committing hate crimes.

No: Hate crime laws violate the principle that all people are created equal. Enhancing punishment for hate crimes sends the message that some people are worth more than other people. If you commit a crime against any person, you might find the government arguing that you were motivated by your prejudice, and therefore the crime was a hate crime and you should be punished more severely. Valuing some victims more by punishing the perpetrators of crimes against them more harshly creates—rather than heals—divisions in society. Assault is assault. Does it really matter what motivated the criminal?

Other approaches: Many states have laws that make it a punishable crime to commit a *breach of the peace:* an act or a behavior that seriously endangers or disturbs public peace and order or that results in community unrest or a disturbance. A legal act can disrupt the public peace and lead to a charge of breaching the peace. For example, although burning the American flag is legal, if you burn it during a Memorial Day Parade in clear view of war veterans and a scuffle ensues, you can be charged with the crime of breach of the peace in many jurisdictions. Any *illegal* act that creates community unrest, no matter what motivated the offender, should therefore result in the additional charge of breach of the peace.

What do you think?

① Do you think that increased punishment for those found guilty of a crime motivated by hate will deter future hate crimes? Explain.

② Some opponents of hate crime laws argue that they will lead to limits on free speech. Do you think this concern is valid? Explain.

---

that having students on campus from a wide variety of backgrounds enhances all students' educational experience and best prepares them to function successfully in a nation that is increasingly diverse. Yet like affirmative action in personnel policies, affirmative action in college admission policies has been controversial.

Opposition to Affirmative Action

In the important *Bakke* decision in 1978, the U.S. Supreme Court found unconstitutional the University of California at Davis's affirmative action plan for admission to its medical school.[50] The UC Davis plan set aside sixteen of the one hundred seats in its first-year medical school class for minorities (specifically, African Americans, Latinos, Asian Americans, and Native Americans). Justice Powell noted in his opinion that schools can take race into consideration as one of several factors for admission but cannot use it as the sole consideration, as Alan Bakke argued UC Davis had done.

Ward Connerly, chairman of the American Civil Rights Institute (ACRI) argues, "There can be no middle ground about the use of race. This is not an area where one can fudge or cheat just a little bit. Either we permit the use of 'race' in American life or we don't. I say,

'We don't!'"[51] Connerly is leading the battle against affirmative action in admissions and employment procedures. Connerly founded the ACRI in 1997, one year after his successful effort to have California voters repeal their state's affirmative action policies in college admissions and employment. After anti–affirmative action victories in Washington (1998) and Michigan (2006), the ACRI has targeted Arizona, Colorado, Missouri, Nebraska, and Oklahoma for similar efforts.[52]

Opponents have challenged affirmative action in the courts as well as through legislative processes and statewide ballot measures. In two cases involving the University of Michigan in 2003, the U.S. Supreme Court upheld the *Bakke* decision that universities can use race as a factor in admissions decisions, but not as the overriding factor. Using the strict scrutiny test, the Court said in the *Grutter v. Bollinger* case that the school's goal of creating a diverse student body serves a *compelling public interest:* a diverse student body enhances "cross-racial understanding . . . breaks down racial stereotypes . . . and helps students better understand persons of different races."[53]

In 2007, however, the Supreme Court found unconstitutional two school districts' policies of assigning students to elementary schools based on race to ensure a diverse student body.[54] The majority of justices argued that those policies violated the equal protection clause of the Fourteenth Amendment. Chief Justice Roberts, writing for the majority, argued that governments should not use laws to remedy racial imbalances caused by economic inequalities, individual choices, and historical biases (de facto imbalances). He stated that such laws put in place discrimination that the Court found unconstitutional in the *Brown* case back in 1954. The justices who dissented from the majority opinion noted that today's policies are trying to ensure inclusion of minorities, not create segregation of, and hence cause harm to, minorities. The dissenters view policies that take race into account to ensure inclusion and balance as necessary means to achieving the compelling public good gained by a diverse student body.

Are affirmative action policies aimed at ensuring equal educational and employment opportunities for women and minority men constitutional, or do they violate the equal protection clause of the Fourteenth Amendment? The answer to that question depends on

POLITICAL INQUIRY

This cartoon suggests a number of the factors that colleges consider when making admissions decisions. Why is membership in a minority group controversial, whereas other factors—such as the ability to play a certain sport or being the son or daughter of a graduate—are not? In the future, how can colleges achieve the goals of a diverse campus and a fair admissions process?

how the majority of the members of the Supreme Court interpret the Fourteenth Amendment. Today, for an affirmative action policy for minority men to be constitutional, the government must pass the strict scrutiny test by showing that affirmative action is necessary to achieve a compelling public interest. In the case of affirmative action for women, the government must pass the heightened scrutiny test by showing that the policy is substantially related to the government's achievement of an important public interest.

CONCLUSION

THINKING CRITICALLY ABOUT WHAT'S NEXT IN CIVIL RIGHTS

For most of U.S. history, the law allowed, and in some cases even required, discrimination against people based on inherent characteristics such as race, ethnicity, and sex. This discriminatory treatment meant that the U.S. government did not guarantee all citizens equal protection of their civil rights. The long and continuing battles for civil rights of African Americans, Native Americans, and women are only part of the story. Latinos, Asian Americans, citizens with disabilities, and LGBT citizens are all currently engaged in political, legal, and civic activities aimed at guaranteeing equal protection of their civil rights. Numerous other groups are working to gain their civil rights as well. These include older Americans, poor Americans, and children born in the United States to parents who are in the country illegally. (The Fourteenth Amendment extends citizenship, and hence civil rights, to these children.) What other groups of legally disadvantaged citizens will fight for their civil rights?

The courts have the final determination of what rights are granted equal protection under the Fourteenth Amendment. The courts also determine if there are situations in which government does not have to guarantee equal protection. For the latter determinations, the courts use one of three scrutiny tests—ordinary scrutiny, heightened scrutiny, or strict scrutiny. Currently, advocates for women's rights criticize the courts' use of the heightened scrutiny test in sex-based discrimination cases. They believe that the courts should apply, instead, the strict scrutiny test which they use in cases of discrimination based on race, religion, and ethnic origin. What criteria will the U.S. Supreme Court use in deciding cases concerning sex-based discrimination in the future?

History tells us that an unhealthy economy, with high levels of unemployment and inflation and without real improvements in wages, as well as perceived threats to national security that are attributed to one ethnic, religious, or racial group, often trigger increased violations of civil rights and therefore new civil rights battles. How will the state of the economy and threats of terrorism shape the issues and the demands at the forefront of future civil rights battles?

Summary

1. The Meaning of Equality Under the Law
The Fourteenth Amendment guarantees all people equal protection of the laws. However, courts use one of three tests—ordinary scrutiny, heightened scrutiny, or strict scrutiny—to determine when discriminatory treatment is a legal means by which the government can fulfill its responsibility to a public interest.

2. Slavery and Its Aftermath
One legacy of slavery in the United States was a system of racial segregation. Under that system, both the states and the federal government condoned and accepted a structure of inherent inequality for African Americans in nearly all aspects of life, and they were forced to use separate facilities, from water fountains to educational institutions.

3. The Civil Rights Movement

Through the efforts of the early and modern civil rights organizations such as the NAACP, chinks appeared in the armor of the segregationists. The strategy of using the justice system to right previous wrongs proved instrumental in radically changing the nation's educational system, especially with the key *Brown v. Board of Education* decision in 1954, in which the Supreme Court ruled against segregation. In other arenas, such as public accommodations, and housing, Dr. Martin Luther King's leadership and strategy of nonviolent civil disobedience proved instrumental in winning victories in both legislatures and the court of public opinion.

4. The Government's Response to the Civil Rights Movement

The government responded to the demands for equal rights for African Americans with an important series of laws that attempted to secure fundamental rights, including voting rights and rights to employment, public accommodations, housing, and equal pay.

5. The Movement for Women's Civil Rights

The 1848 Seneca Falls Convention, which produced the Declaration of Sentiments, was the beginning of the first wave of the women's rights movement in the United States. This first wave focused on winning for women the right to vote, which was accomplished by the ratification of the Nineteenth Amendment in 1920. The second wave of the women's rights movement began in the 1960s with women organizing and lobbying for laws guaranteeing them equality of rights. The efforts of the second wave continue today.

6. Other Civil Rights Movements

In addition to African Americans and women, numerous other groups of U.S. citizens have battled for, and continue to fight for, equal treatment under the law. These groups include Native Americans, Latino and Asian American citizens, citizens with disabilities, and lesbian, gay, bisexual, and transgendered citizens. They seek equal employment opportunities, educational opportunities, housing, voting rights, and marriage rights, among others.

7. Affirmative Action: Is It Constitutional?

Since 1866, the national government has enacted civil rights laws that have prohibited discrimination. In a 1961 executive order, President John F. Kennedy introduced the nation to a proactive policy of intentional actions to recruit minority male workers, which he labeled *affirmative action*. President Lyndon B. Johnson extended affirmative action to women. Institutions of higher education also adopted the concept of affirmative action in their admissions policies. Affirmative action has been controversial, however, and a review of recent Supreme Court cases indicates that the constitutionality of affirmative action is in question.

Key Terms

affirmative action 174

Black Codes 153

Brown v. Board of Education of Topeka 157

civil disobedience 151

civil rights 148

de facto segregation 161

de jure segregation 154

equal protection clause 155

grandfather clause 155

hate crime 174

heightened scrutiny test (intermediate scrutiny test) 150

inherent characteristics 148

Jim Crow laws 154

literacy test 155

ordinary scrutiny test (rational basis test) 150

Plessy v. Ferguson 155

poll tax 155

Reconstruction era 153

separate but equal doctrine 155

standing to sue 152

steering 161

strict scrutiny test 149

suspect classifications 149

white primary 155

For Review

1. What is meant by *suspect classification?*

2. What tactics did whites in the South use to prevent African Americans from achieving equality before the civil rights era?

3. What strategy did the early civil rights movements employ to end discrimination?

4. What civil rights did the 1964 Civil Rights Act protect for minority, male citizens but not for female citizens?

5. Why did those fighting for women's civil rights begin their work by concentrating their efforts on state governments rather than on the national government?

6. Other than color and sex, what inherent (immutable) characteristics have been used as a basis for discriminatory treatment of citizens?

7. Explain how an approach to improving access to employment and educational opportunity based on affirmative action differs from an approach based on civil rights legislation.

For Critical Thinking and Discussion

1. Is it constitutional to deny any citizen the equal protection of marriage laws; is denying gay men and lesbians the right to marry a necessary means to a compelling public interest? Explain.

2. Today, more women than men are in college pursuing their bachelor's degrees. Is it legal for schools to give preference to male applicants by accepting men with lower SAT scores and high school grade-point averages than women, to maintain sex balance in the student body? Explain.

3. Many organizations fighting for civil rights protections include in their name the phrase "legal defense and education fund." What do you think explains the common two-pronged focus of these organizations?

4. What would be the effect of using the strict scrutiny test to determine the legality of sex-based discrimination? Would sex-based affirmative action pass the test? Explain.

PRACTICE QUIZ

MULTIPLE CHOICE: Choose the lettered item that answers the question correctly.

1. The idea that individuals are protected from discrimination on the basis of race, national origin, religion, and sex is called
   a. civil liberties.
   b. civil rights.
   c. natural rights.
   d. unalienable rights.

2. Individual attributes such as race, national origin, religion, and sex are called
   a. unalienable rights.
   b. inherent characteristics.
   c. indiscriminatory qualities.
   d. civil rights categories.

3. Laws that required the strict separation of racial groups, with whites and "nonwhites" attending separate schools, working in different jobs, and using segregated public accommodations such as transportation and restaurants are called
   a. Fred Samuels laws.
   b. Sally Hemmings laws.
   c. Jim Crow laws.
   d. Abraham Lincoln laws.

4. An election in which a party's nominees were chosen but in which only white people were allowed to vote is called
   a. a general election.
   b. a run-off primary.
   c. an uncontested primary.
   d. a white primary.

5. A mechanism that exempted individuals from conditions on voting (such as poll taxes or literacy tests) if they or their ancestor had been eligible to vote before 1870 is called
   a. a poll tax.
   b. a white primary.
   c. the grandfather clause.
   d. a literacy test.

6. Unlike sex-based discrimination, race-based discrimination must pass the
   a. heightened scrutiny test.
   b. ordinary scrutiny test.
   c. strict scrutiny test.
   d. ultimate scrutiny test.

7. Initially the courts interpreted which amendment in such a way that women were told they were citizens but that they had no constitutional right to vote?
   a. Thirteenth Amendment
   b. Fourteenth Amendment
   c. Fifteenth Amendment
   d. Nineteenth Amendment

8. What right does Title IX protect for women?
   a. equal access to credit
   b. equal access to educational opportunities
   c. equal access to employment opportunities
   d. suffrage

9. In what decade was the ERA ratified and added to the U.S. Constitution?
   a. 1920s
   b. 1970s
   c. 1980s
   d. It has not been ratified and added to the U.S. Constitution.

10. Today, citizens of what descent experience the highest educational and income level compared with the nation as a whole?
    a. African
    b. Asian
    c. Mexican
    d. Native American

FILL IN THE BLANKS.

11. _____ was the period between 1866 and 1877 when the institutions and infrastructure of the South were rebuilt after the Civil War.

12. The legal right to bring lawsuits in court is called _____ .

13. To pass the strict scrutiny test, differential treatment must be _____ for the government to achieve a _____ public interest.

14. During World War II, the federal government relocated citizens of _____ descent to internment camps.

15. The ADA is the _____ .

Answers: 1. b, 2. b, 3. c, 4. d, 5. c, 6. c, 7. b, 8. b, 9. d, 10. b, 11. Reconstruction, 12. standing to sue, 13. necessary, compelling, 14. Japanese, 15. Americans with Disabilities Act.

RESOURCES FOR RESEARCH AND ACTION

Internet Resources

American Democracy Now Web site
www.mhhe.com/harrison2e Consult the book's Web site for study guides, interactive activities, simulations, and current hotlinks for additional information on civil rights.

Equal Employment Opportunity Commission
www.eeoc.gov/facts/qanda.html This federal government site offers a list of federal laws relevant to equal employment opportunities and includes answers to the most frequently asked questions regarding equal employment laws.

Leadership Conference on Civil Rights/Leadership Conference on Civil Rights Education Fund
www.civilrights.org Founded by the LCCR and the LCCREF, this site seeks to serve as the "online nerve center" for the fight against discrimination in all its forms.

Internet Activism

YouTube

Invite your friends to join you in a critique of the evolution of race relations. Begin by viewing Dr. Martin Luther King's 1963 "I Have a Dream Speech" (www.youtube.com/watch?v=PbUtL_0vAJk) and presidential candidate Barack Obama's 2008 talk on race relations (www.youtube.com/watch?v=pWe7wTVbLUU).

Twitter

http://twitter.com/lambdalegal Lambda Legal is a national organization committed to achieving full recognition of the civil rights of lesbians, gay men, transgendered people, and those with HIV through litigation, education, and public policy work.

Blog

www.splcenter.org/blog/ The Southern Poverty Law Center is a nonprofit civil rights organization dedicated to fighting hate and bigotry and is known internationally for tracking and exposing the activities of hate groups.

Facebook

www.facebook.com/NationalNOW The National Organization for Women (NOW) stands against all oppression, recognizing that racism, sexism, and homophobia are interrelated, that other forms of oppression, such as classism and ableism, work together with these three to keep power and privilege concentrated in the hands of a few.

Recommended Readings

Branch, Taylor. *Parting the Waters: America in the King Years*. New York: Simon and Schuster, 1989. A Pulitzer Prize–winning book focusing on the civil rights movement from 1954 to 1963.

Feagin, Joe R., and Clairece Booher Feagin. *Racial and Ethnic Relations*. Upper Saddle River, NJ: Prentice Hall, 2003. A comprehensive look at the immigration of Africans, Asians, Europeans, Latin Americans, and Middle Easterners to the United States and the history of relations between Native Americans and the U. S. government.

Harrison, Brigid. *Women in American Politics: An Introduction*. Belmont, CA: Wadsworth, 2003. *American Democracy Now* coauthor Brigid Harrison introduces the study of women's participation in American politics, including their historic and contemporary participation in political groups, as voters, and in government.

Herr, Stanley S., Lawrence O. Gostin, and Harold Hongju Koh. *The Human Rights of Persons with Disabilities: Different but Equal*. Oxford: Oxford University Press, 2003. A collection of essays explaining how Article I of the Universal Declaration of Human Rights defines the standard for rights for people with disabilities.

Rosenberg, Gerald. *The Hollow Hope: Can Courts Bring About Social Change?* Second ed. Chicago: The University of Chicago Press, 2008. Rosenberg supports his argument that Congress, the White House, and civil rights activists—not the courts—bring about social change by reviewing the evolution of federal policy in the areas of desegregation, abortion, and the struggle for LGBT rights.

Movies of Interest

Bury My Heart at Wounded Knee (2007)
Based on Dee Brown's book of the same name, this HBO made-for-television movie chronicles ordeals of Sioux and Lakota tribes as the U.S. government displaces them from their lands.

Iron Jawed Angels (2004)
The little-known story of the tensions between the young, militant women's suffrage advocates, led by Alice Paul, and the older, more conservative advocates, such as Carrie Chapman Catt. The details of the suffrage battle during wartime, with a popular president opposed to women's suffrage, are well presented in this made-for-television movie.

Malcolm X (1992)
Based on the book *The Autobiography of Malcolm X* (as told to Alex Haley), this Spike Lee film stars Denzel Washington as black power movement leader Malcolm X. The film depicts the struggle in the 1960s between the black nationalists, such as Malcolm X and the activists who advocated more peaceful means, such as Martin Luther King Jr.

Mississippi Burning (1989)
Gene Hackman and Willem Dafoe portray FBI agents sent into Mississippi in 1964 to investigate the disappearance of two civil rights workers.

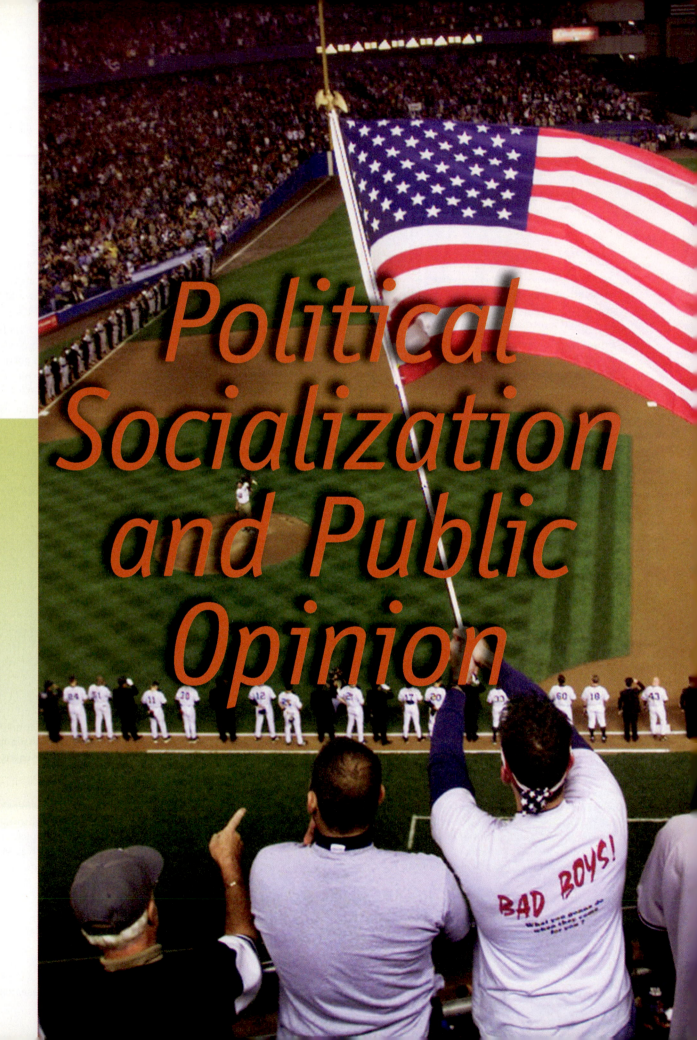

Political Socialization and Public Opinion

THEN

Families and schools were the most important influences on children as they developed their political views.

NOW

Families and schools remain influential, but the media have been enormously important in developing the political views of the Millennial Generation.

NEXT

How will technology affect the socialization of new generations of Americans?

How will polling organizations find ways to harness the power of the Internet to predict political behavior accurately?

How can pollsters measure opinions of "cell-onlys"—potential respondents who own only cell phones?

In this chapter, we consider the ways in which people become socialized to politics, and explain the influence of various agents of socialization. We consider how public opinion is measured and take a look at how Americans currently view their governmental institutions.

FIRST, we examine the process of *political socialization* and how it can lead to *civic participation.*

SECOND, we consider the different *agents of socialization,* including family, the media, schools, churches, peers, community and political leaders, and demographic characteristics.

THIRD, we look at ways of *measuring public opinion.*

FOURTH, we focus on *what Americans think about politics.*

The process of developing in-

formed opinions about issues begins with the process of political socialization. Through socialization, we acquire our basic political beliefs and values. Through political socialization, we come to value the attributes of our own political culture. We also develop our ideological outlook and perhaps even begin to identify with a particular political party. Though the process of political socialization begins in early childhood, throughout our lives, institutions, peers, and the media continue to influence our views.

Political socialization is a key component in the process of creating an engaged citizenry. Psychologist Steven Pinker once noted that ". . . no matter how important learning and culture and socialization are, they don't happen by magic."[1] Joe Zavaletta, director of the Center for Civic Engagement at the University of Texas at Brownsville, would agree with Pinker's assertion: "Democracy is not magic. Why we expect our kids to magically become engaged citizens when they turn 18 when they haven't practiced . . . doesn't make any sense."[2]

Through the process of socialization, individuals acquire the ideology and the perspective that shape their political opinions. Though seemingly simple, public opinion is a fundamental building block on which American democracy rests. When we discuss public opinion, we often do so in the context of various public opinion polls that ask respondents everything from whether they approve of the president's job performance to how many sugars they take in their skim milk lattes. Political scientist V. O. Key Jr. wrote, "To speak with precision of public opinion is a task not unlike coming to grips with the Holy Ghost."[3] Key was referring to the nebulous nature of public opinion, which changes from day to day, is sometimes difficult to pinpoint, and is open to subjective interpretation. The glut in the number of "latest polls" has perhaps made us forget that the act of voting is itself simply the act of expressing one's opinion. Indeed, the word *poll* means to gauge public opinion as well as the location where one casts a ballot.

Public opinion is one of the ways citizens interact with their government. Through public opinion surveys, people express their policy priorities ("What do you think is the country's most important problem?") and their approval or disapproval of both government officials ("Do you approve or disapprove of the way the president is handling his job?") and the policies they create ("Do you agree or disagree with President Obama's decision to increase the number of troops in Afghanistan?") Much of the literature bemoaning the decline of civic involvement is based on public opinion research. But studies of civic involvement reveal that public opinion is the starting point for many forms of informed participation—participation that begins when individuals learn about an issue and choose to express their views on it using a variety of media.

Political Socialization and Civic Participation

How do we acquire our political views? Though an infant would be hard pressed to evaluate the president's job performance, of course, children begin to acquire political opinions at an early age, and this process continues throughout adulthood. As noted above, the process by which we develop our political values and opinions is called **political socialization.** As we develop our political values, we form the bedrock of what will become our political ideology. As this ideology emerges, it shapes how we view most political subjects: what side we take on public issues, how we evaluate candidates for office, and what our opinions on policies will be.

Although many tend to think that political socialization occurs as people approach voting age, in reality this process begins at home in very early childhood. Core tenets of our belief system—including our political ideology, our beliefs about people of different races and sexes, even our party identification—are often firmly embedded before we have completed elementary school.

A key aspect of political socialization is whether children are socialized to participate in politics. Simply put, civically engaged parents often have civically engaged children. Parents who engage in active forms of participation, such as volunteering on a campaign, and passive forms, such as watching the nightly news or reading a newspaper, demonstrate to children what matters to them. Parents who change the channel to a *Monk* rerun during an important presidential news conference are also socializing their children to their values. Children absorb the political views of their parents as well: a parent's subtle (or sometimes not so subtle!) comments about the president, a political news story, or a policy debate contribute to a child's political socialization by shaping that child's views.

The Process of Political Socialization

The beliefs and values we learn early in life also help shape how we view new information. Although events may change our views, we often choose to perceive events in a way that is consistent with our earlier beliefs. For example, people's evaluation of which candidate "won" a debate often strongly coincides with their party identification. Thus, the process of political socialization tends to be cumulative.

Historically, most social scientists have agreed that family and school have the strongest influence on political socialization. Our families teach us that it is—or is not—valuable to be an informed citizen and coach us in the ways in which we should participate in the civic life of our communities. For example, if your mother is active in Republican Party politics in your town, you are more likely to be active in the party than someone whose parents are not involved in a local party. Is your father active in charitable organizations such as the local food bank? He might ask you to run in a 5K race to raise money to buy food for the upcoming holiday season. Schools also influence our political socialization by teaching us shared cultural values. And in recent times, the omnipresent role that the media play in everyday life warrants their inclusion as one of the prime agents of political socialization.

political socialization
the process by which we develop our political values and opinions throughout our lives

> Children are socialized to the views of their parents at a very early age. Here a young boy attending an environmental rally holds a placard expressing "his" views. What opinions were you socialized to as a young child?

Participating in Civic Life

Does the process of socialization matter in determining whether individuals are active in civic life? Studies indicate that socialization does matter in a number of ways. First, children whose parents are active in politics or in their community are more likely to be active themselves. Schools also play an important role in socializing young people to become active in civic life—high school and college students are more likely to participate than young

Political Socialization and Civic Participation   **185**

people of the same age who are not attending school. Research also indicates that socialization actually *generates* participation. People who have been socialized to participate in civic life are more likely to volunteer for a charitable or a political organization in their communities when they are invited to do so.

From our families and schools we also learn the value of becoming informed. Parents and schools, along with the media and the other agents of socialization that are discussed in the next section, provide us with important information that we can use to make decisions about our political actions. People who lack political knowledge, by contrast, tend not to be actively involved in their communities.[4] In fact, research indicates that when young people use any source of information regularly, including newspapers, radio, television, magazines, or the Internet, they are more likely to engage in all forms of civic participation. There is also a strong link between being informed and voting behavior. According to the results of one survey that measured civic engagement among young people, "youth who are registered to vote are more informed than their nonregistered peers. Eighty-six percent of young registered voters answered at least one of the knowledge questions (measuring political knowledge) correctly as opposed to 78 percent of youth who are not registered to vote."[5]

Agents of Socialization

agents of socialization
the individuals, organizations, and institutions that facilitate the acquisition of political views

Learning, culture, and socialization occur through **agents of socialization,** the individuals, organizations, and institutions that facilitate the acquisition of political views. Among the most important agents of socialization are the family, the media, schools, churches, peers, and political and community leaders. Our political views are also shaped by who we are: our race, ethnicity, gender, and age all influence how we become socialized to political and community life.

Family Influences on Activism and Attitudes

Family takes one of the most active roles in socializing us to politics and influencing our political views and behaviors. We learn whether our family members value civic activism by observing their actions and listening to their views. By example, parents show children whether community matters. The children of political activists are taught to be engaged citizens. They may see their parents attend city council meetings, host Democratic or Republican club meetings in their home, or help local candidates for office by volunteering to campaign door-to-door on a weekend afternoon. Other parents may teach different forms of political engagement—some young children might attend protests or demonstrations with their parents. Others might learn to boycott a particular product for political reasons. When political activists discuss their own involvement, they often observe that "politics is in my blood." In reality, political activism is passed from one generation to the next *through example.*

In other homes, however, parents are not involved in politics or their communities. They may lack the time to participate in political activities, or they may fail to see the value of doing so. They may have a negative opinion of people who participate in politics, constantly making comments like "all politicians are corrupt," "they're just in it for themselves," or "it's all about ego." Such opinions convey to children that politics is not valued and may in fact be frowned upon. A parent's political apathy need not necessarily sour a son or a daughter on politics or civic engagement permanently, however. Instead, first-generation activists often point to external influences such as school, the media, friends, and public policies, any of which can cause someone to become involved in civic life, regardless of family attitudes.

Our families influence not only whether or not we are civically active participants in the political process but also what we believe. While parents or older siblings may discuss specific issues or policies, their attitudes and outlook also shape children's general political attitudes and ideology. Children absorb their parents' beliefs—whether their parents think the government should have a larger or smaller role in people's lives, whether they value equality between the sexes and the races, whether they consider people in government to be trustworthy, and even specific opinions they have about political leaders. In fact, we can see evidence of how strongly parents' views are transmitted to their children in one of the best predictors of the results of presidential elections: each election year, the *Weekly Reader,* a current events magazine that many school districts subscribe to, conducts a nonrandomized poll of its readers. Since 1956, the first- through twelfth-grade student poll has correctly predicted the outcome of every presidential election. Children know for whom their parents will vote and mimic that behavior in their responses to the poll.

The Media's Ever-Increasing Role in Socialization

An almost ever-present fixture in the lives of young Americans today, the media contribute to the political socialization of Americans in many ways. Television, radio, the Internet, and various forms of electronic entertainment and print media help shape Americans' political perspectives. First, the media, especially television, help shape societal norms. The media impart norms and values on children's shows such as *Sesame Street, Barney,* and *Dora the Explorer,* which teach about racial diversity and tolerance. For example, Barney's friends include children with and without disabilities. These shows and others reflect changing societal standards and values. The media also reinforce core democratic values. Television programs such as *American Idol* or *The Biggest Loser,* or Sirius/XM Radio's *20on20,* incorporate the principle of voting: viewers decide which contestant stays or goes, or listeners pick which songs are played.

Second, the media also help determine the national agenda. Whether they are covering the war in Afghanistan, sex-abuse scandals, global climate change, or congressional policy debates, the media focus the attention of the American public. This attention may then have spillover effects as people demand action on a policy issue. We will see in Chapter 7, for example, how media coverage of the Tea Party movement propelled that organization's policy priorities to the forefront of the national political scene during the 2010 congressional elections.

Third, the media educate the public about policy issues. Local and national news programs, newsmagazine shows, and even comedies such as *The Colbert Report* and *The Daily Show with Jon Stewart* (yes, they really are comedies, *not* news programs) inform viewers about current events, the actions of policy makers, and public policy challenges in communities, states, and the nation.

Finally, the media, particularly television, can skew people's perception of public policy priorities and challenges. The oft-quoted saying "if it bleeds, it leads" demonstrates the attention that most local news stations focus on violence. Although crime rates have dropped since the 1970s, the reporting of crime, particularly violent crime, on nightly news broadcasts has increased. Even national news broadcasts and talk shows fall prey to the tendency to emphasize "visual" news—fires, floods, auto accidents, and plane crashes. Although these stories are important to those involved, they have very little long-term impact on society as a whole. But because they pique viewer interest more effectively than, say, a debate in Washington or in a state capital, news programs devote more time to them. Internet news sources also cover these dramatic events, but the sheer number of Internet news sites and blogs makes it more likely that at least some of them will also cover more important news, and people interested in political events and debates can find Internet news sources that cover such events and issues.

Schools, Patriotism, and Civic Participation

As early as kindergarten, children in the United States are socialized to believe in democracy and express patriotism. Schools socialize children to the concept of democracy by making the idea tangible for them. On Election Day, children might vote for their favorite snack and wait for the results at the end of the day. Or they might compare different kinds of apples or grapes, or different books, and then vote for a favorite. Lessons such as these introduce children to processes associated with democracy at its most basic level: they learn about comparing attributes, choosing a favorite, voting, and winning and losing.

Children also are taught patriotism as they recite the Pledge of Allegiance every day, sing patriotic songs, and learn to venerate the "founding fathers," especially George Washington and other American heroes, including Abraham Lincoln, Dr. Martin Luther King Jr., and

> Reciting the Pledge of Allegiance is one way schools socialize children to express patriotism.

John F. Kennedy. Traditionally, elementary and high schools in the United States have emphasized the "great men in great moments" form of history, a history that traditionally concentrated solely on the contributions of men in formal governmental or military settings. Increasingly, however, the curriculum includes contributions by women, African Americans, and other minorities.

Education also plays a pivotal role in determining *who* will participate in the political affairs of the community. Research indicates that higher levels of education are associated with higher levels of political activism. In a book on civic voluntarism, authors Sidney Verba, Kay Schlozman, and Henry Brady write, "Well-educated parents are more likely to also be politically active and to discuss politics at home and to produce children who are active in high school. Growing up in a politicized household and being active in high school are associated with political engagement."[6]

Churches: The Role of Religion

The impact of church and religion in general on one's political socialization varies a great deal from individual to individual. For some people, religion plays a key, defining role in the development of their political beliefs. For others, it is irrelevant.

For many years, political scientists have examined the impact religious affiliation—whether one is Catholic or Jewish, Protestant or Muslim—has on political preferences. For example, religion is related to how people view various issues, especially the issue of abortion. (See "Thinking Critically About Democracy.") But more recent analysis shows that a better predictor of the impact of religion on voting is not so much the religion an individual practices but, rather, how regularly he or she practices it. In general, it seems that those who regularly attend religious services are more likely to share conservative values—and support Republican candidates in general elections.

Research also shows that this relationship between frequency of church attendance and identification with the Republican Party is particularly strong among white Protestants, but less so among Catholics, who are generally more Democratic, and among African Americans. African American voters are even more likely than Catholics to vote for a Democratic candidate but are also likely to have high levels of religiosity, as measured by frequency of attending services.

Figure 6.1 shows the breakdown in party affiliation by religiosity. The results are based on respondents' assessment of the importance of religion in their lives and their frequency of church attendance. Notice in Figure 6.1 that a large proportion of highly religious people (34 percent of Americans, not shown in the figure) are Republicans or lean Republican in voting. Party identification is

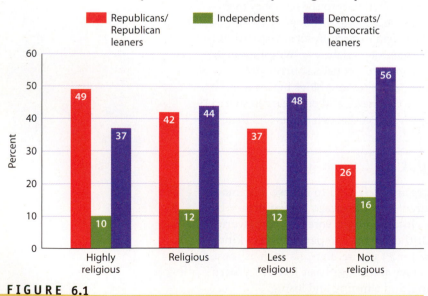

Party Identification, by Religiosity

Legend: Republicans/Republican leaners (red), Independents (green), Democrats/Democratic leaners (blue)

Category	Republicans	Independents	Democrats
Highly religious	49	10	37
Religious	42	12	44
Less religious	37	12	48
Not religious	26	16	56

FIGURE 6.1

Party Identification, by Religiosity

SOURCE: www.gallup.com/poll/124649/Religious-Intensity-Remains-Powerful-Predictor-Politics.aspx.

SHOULD ABORTION BE LEGAL?

The Issue: In the 1973 decision *Roe v. Wade,* the Supreme Court legalized abortion, essentially ruling that abortion would be legal in the first trimester of pregnancy, that states could regulate it in the second trimester (for example, by requiring that abortions be performed in a hospital), and that states had the power to ban abortion in the third trimester. Since that time, several other cases have influenced public policy on this issue, with the Court granting states more powers to regulate the circumstances surrounding abortion. Many states now require a mandatory waiting period before obtaining an abortion and/or parental consent for minors who wish to have an abortion. The Court has also struck down some proposed regulations, including a requirement that women notify their spouses before having an abortion.

Abortion is one of the most divisive issues in the United States, and public opinion on this issue has changed very little since the decision in *Roe v. Wade* was announced in 1973. About a quarter of Americans believe that abortion should be legal under any circumstances; 53 percent believe that it should be legal under certain circumstances, and 22 percent think it should be illegal in all circumstances.* As the accompanying figure shows, in 2009, for the first time a small majority (51 percent) of Americans called themselves "pro-life," while 42 percent consider themselves "pro-choice." Although individuals tend to hold very strong views on the abortion issue, very few people base their vote for a candidate solely on that candidate's position on the abortion issue. The divisiveness on this issue is heightened because those who hold different positions on the abortion issue also differ on other issues as well. Consider the stances articulated below, which typify views people express on this issue.

Yes: Women are the ones affected by a pregnancy, and they should be able to make decisions about their own bodies, without interference from the government—the "pro-choice" stance. Therefore, abortion should be legal under all circumstances until the point of viability. Women should be able to choose abortion, in consultation with their doctors, up to the time when the fetus can survive outside the womb, and there should be no restrictions on a woman's options.

No: Life begins at the moment of conception, and a fetus is another human life, as worthy of protection from the law as any other human

being—the "pro-life" stance. We need to value life at every stage. Abortion should be illegal except to save the life of the mother; no other exceptions should be allowed. Doctors and others who perform abortions should be subject to criminal prosecution.

Other approaches: Abortion should be legal, but states should be allowed to place various restrictions on abortion. Parents should be notified when their underage daughters are seeking the procedure, for example, and states can require providers to inform women about alternatives such as adoption or make them wait twenty-four hours before performing the procedure. In other words, the goal should be to make abortion "legal but rare."

What do you think?

① Do you consider your view to be pro-choice or pro-life, or do you favor another approach? Do you think that abortion should be legal or illegal under all circumstances, or legal but with restrictions?

② Have you ever based, or would you ever base, your vote solely on a candidate's position on abortion? Why or why not?

③ Think about your own socialization process—how did family, church, peers, and events shape your views on this issue?

*"Abortion: Gallup's Pulse of Democracy: Guidance for Lawmakers," www.galluppoll.com/content/?ci=1576&pg=1.

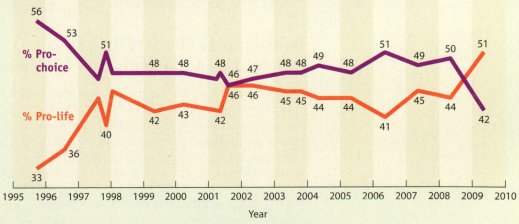

With respect to the abortion issue, would you consider yourself to be pro-choice or pro-life?

% Pro-choice: 56, 53, 51, 48, 48, 48, 46, 47, 48, 48, 49, 48, 51, 49, 50, 51, 42

% Pro-life: 33, 36, 40, 51, 42, 43, 42, 46, 46, 45, 45, 44, 44, 41, 45, 44, 51

Year: 1995 1996 1997 1998 1999 2000 2001 2002 2003 2004 2005 2006 2007 2008 2009 2010

Source: www.gallup.com/poll/118399/More-Americans-Pro-Life-Than-Pro-Choice-First-Time.aspx.

nearly evenly divided among the religious (18 percent of Americans), with 42 and 44 percent identifying themselves as Republicans/Republican leaners and Democrats/Democratic leaners, respectively. Among the less religious (32 percent of the population), a large proportion (48 percent) identify themselves as Democrats/Democratic leaners, as do a majority (56 percent) of the not religious (16 percent of the population). Though there is a strong link between religiosity and political party, the differences between the proclivities of religious and nonreligious voters are applicable only to white voters—as discussed later in this chapter, African Americans are likely to be Democrats no matter how religious they are. And although religious Latinos are more likely to be Republican, by and large, majorities of Latinos identify as Democrats. Nonetheless, the relationship between religiosity and party identification is an important factor in American politics, particularly to the extent that religiosity shapes political views on social issues—abortion, or gay marriage, say—and renders them moral imperatives for voters, rather than mere opinions.

Peers and Group Norms

Friends, neighbors, coworkers, and other peers influence political socialization. Through peers, we learn about community and the political climate and values of the area in which we live. For example, your neighbors might inform you that a particular member of the city council is a strong advocate for your neighborhood on the council, securing funds for recreational facilities or increased police protection in your area. Or a coworker might let you know what your member of Congress is doing to help save jobs in the industry in which you work. Much research indicates that the primary impact of peers is to reinforce our already-held beliefs and values, however. Typically, the people with whom you are acquainted are quite similar to you. Although diversity exists in many settings, the norms and values of the people you know tend to be remarkably similar to your own.

Political and Community Leaders: Opinion Shapers

Political and community leaders also help socialize people and influence public opinion. Positions advocated by highly regarded government leaders hold particular sway, and the president plays an especially important role in shaping Americans' views. For example, President Obama's prioritization of health care reform propelled it to become a higher priority for many average Americans. But the role of political leaders in influencing public opinion is not limited to the national stage. In your city, chances are that the views of community leaders—elected and not—influence the way the public perceives local policies. Perhaps the fire or police chief endorses a candidate for city council, or the popular football coach for the Police Athletic League makes the funding of a new football field a policy priority in your town. Often we rely on the recommendations and priorities of well-respected leaders who have earned our trust.

Demographic Characteristics: Our Politics Are a Reflection of Ourselves

Who we are often influences our life experiences, which shape our political socialization and therefore what we think. The racial and ethnic groups we belong to, our gender, our age and the events that have shaped our lives, and where we live all play a role in how we are socialized to political and community life, our values and priorities, and even whom we vote for. Demographic characteristics also shape our levels of civic involvement and may even help determine the ways in which we contribute to the civic life of our communities and our nation.

RACE AND ETHNICITY   Whites, African Americans, Latinos, and Asian Americans prefer different candidates, hold different political views, and have different levels of civic involvement. Among the most salient of these differences are the candidate preferences of African Americans, who strongly support Democratic candidates over Republicans. But

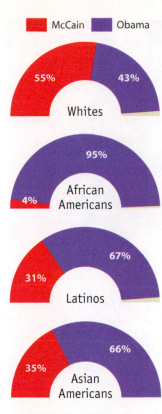

McCain   Obama

55%   43%
Whites

95%
African Americans
4%

67%
31%
Latinos

66%
35%
Asian Americans

FIGURE 6.2

Support of the 2008 Presidential Candidates by Racial Group

SOURCE: The Gallup Poll, Candidate Support by Race, www.gallup.com/poll/108040/Candidate-Support-Race.aspx, and Jane Junn, Taeku Lee, S. Karthick Ramakrishnan, and Janelle Wong, the National Asian American Survey, *Asian Americans and the 2008 Election*, www.naasurvey.com/assets/NAAS-National-report.pdf; www.cnn.com/ELECTION/2008/results/polls/USP00p1.

Figure 6.2 shows that in 2008, President Obama won majorities from Latinos, Asian Americans, and particularly African Americans, 95 percent of whom voted for President Obama. This proportion exceeds the share of the African American vote that Democratic presidential candidates have garnered in recent years, which has averaged 84 to 90 percent. The 43 percent of the white vote that President Obama won exceeds the 41 percent that John Kerry received in 2004, and the average of 39 percent of white votes that Democratic candidates have received since 1964.

This breakdown of 2008 voter preferences is not unique but, rather, reflects well-established differences in party affiliation and ideology between racial and ethnic minorities and whites. But there are also significant differences even within racial and ethnic groups.[7] Table 6.1 shows how the various categories of Latinos differ in terms of party identification. As the table shows, Latinos who identify themselves as Puerto Rican are very likely to be Democrats, while roughly half of all other ethnic Latino groups are likely to be Democrats.

Party affiliation among ethnic groups within the Asian American community also varies somewhat, as Figure 6.3 shows. In general, about 60 percent of all Asian Americans are registered Democrats. South Asians are most likely to be Democrats, and majorities of Chinese and Koreans are Democrats as well. A quarter to a third of all Korean, Southeast Asian, Filipino, and Chinese Americans are unaffiliated with either party.

White, African American, Latino, and Asian American youth also differ significantly in their levels of civic engagement as well as in how young people in these groups connect with their communities. Trends reported in *The Civic and Political Health of the Nation: A Detailed Look at How Youth Participate in Politics and Communities* include the following:

- African American youth are the most politically engaged racial or ethnic group. They are the most likely to vote, belong to political groups, make political contributions, display buttons or signs, canvass voters, and contact the media about political issues.

- Asian Americans are more likely to have been active in their communities. They are more apt to work to solve community problems, volunteer, engage in boycotts, sign petitions, and raise charitable contributions.

14%   17%
42%
28%
Japanese

28%
7%
25%
40%
Chinese

7%   21%
39%
33%
Indian Asian

18%   6%
38%
39%
Korean

29%   15%
22%
34%
Vietnamese

19%   18%
35%
28%
Filipino

Democrat
Republican
Independent
Nonpartisan

FIGURE 6.3

Asian Americans' Party Affiliation by Ethnic Group

SOURCE: Jane Junn, Taeku Lee, S. Karthick Ramakrishnan, and Janelle Wong, the National Asian American Survey, *Asian Americans and the 2008 Election*, www.naasurvey.com/assets/NAAS-National-report.pdf.

Latino Party Identification by National Origin, 2008

TABLE 6.1

	Republican	Democratic	Independent
Puerto Rican	11	61	24
Mexican	18	50	22
Cuban	20	53	26
Other	12	52	24

SOURCE: "Changing Faiths: Latinos and the Transformation of American Religion." © 2006 Pew Hispanic Center, a Pew Research Center project. <http://www.pewhispanic.org>www.pewhispanic.org

> Members of the Millenial Generation are more likely to volunteer than are members of any other age group. Here, Rice University freshman Chris Keller (center) uses a nail gun as Karen Lin (right), Larissa Ikelle (left), and Thurston Spears (far left) help assemble frames at a Habitat for Humanity warehouse that will be used to build low-cost homes in Houston.

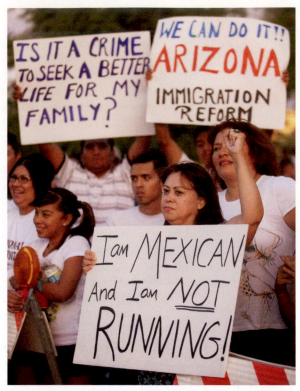

> Latinos are the most likely Millenials to engage in political protest. Susan Peralta rallies against a 2010 Arizona immigration reform bill in downtown Phoenix.

> Eleanor Smeal, president of the Feminist Majority and a former president of the National Organization for Women, coined the term "gender gap" after the 1980 presidential election. Smeal noticed that in poll after poll women favored Democratic incumbent Jimmy Carter over Republican challenger Ronald Reagan. Was there a gender gap in the 2008 presidential election?

■ Young Latinos are the least likely to be active in politics or their communities, but they are most likely to have engaged in political protests. One-quarter of Latinos (more than twice the proportion of any other group) have protested, primarily in immigration rights demonstrations. The lack of civic involvement may arise from barriers to participation—including the fact that many Latino youths in the United States are not citizens, which would bar them from voting. The slogan of many immigration reform marches, "Hoy marchamos! Mañana votamos!" (Today we march! Tomorrow we vote!) may be a promise of increased political participation among young Latinos in the future.

■ Young white people are moderately likely to engage in many community and political activities. They are more likely than other groups to run, walk, or bike for charity, and they are also more likely to be members of a community or political group. Of the groups of young people considered here, they are the least likely to protest, the least likely to contribute money to a political cause, and the least likely to persuade others to vote.[8]

GENDER   Public opinion polls and voting behavior indicate that men and women have very different views on issues, have different priorities when it comes to public issues, and often favor different candidates, particularly in national elections. This difference in men's and women's views and voting preferences is called the **gender gap,** the measurable difference in the way women and men vote for candidates and in the way they view political issues. Eleanor Smeal, who at the time was president of the National Organization for Women, first noticed the gender gap. In the 1980 presidential election, Democratic incumbent Jimmy Carter lost to Republican challenger Ronald Reagan, but Smeal noticed that in poll after poll, women favored Carter.

Since that watershed 1980 election, the gender gap has been a factor in every subsequent presidential election: women voters are more likely than men to favor Democratic candidates. President Bill Clinton, first elected in 1992, had the smallest gender gap that year, with women voters favoring him by only 4 percent. Four years later, when he ran for reelection, he had the largest gender gap to that point, with women voters favoring him by 11 percent. In the 2008 presidential election, the gender gap continued to favor the Democratic nominee, with women voters favoring Barack Obama over John McCain by 7 percent. The presence of Alaska Governor Sarah Palin as the Republican vice presidential nominee appeared not to have swayed vast numbers of women voters.

Voting turnout patterns increase the effect of the gender gap. Women in most age groups—except those under age 25—are more likely to vote than their male counterparts. In addition, on average women also live longer than men, so older women constitute an important voting bloc. The difference in women's candidate preferences and their higher likelihood of voting means that the gender gap is a political reality that any candidate seeking election cannot ignore.

Young men and women also differ in their level of civic engagement, in the ways in which they are involved with their communities, and in their perspectives on the government. While majorities of young men and women believe it is their *responsibility* (rather than their choice) to get involved to make things better for society, how they choose to get involved varies by gender. As Figure 6.4 shows, women in particular are more likely to participate in certain forms of community activism, such as volunteering and running, walking, biking, or engaging in other fund-raising activities for charity. Men and women are about equally likely to work on solving a community problem, such as volunteering for a nonprofit mediation service that helps negotiate disputes between neighbors.

Men are more likely than women to choose formal political forms of activism, such as voting, persuading others to vote, and contributing money to political campaigns.

Women's and men's opinions also differ on public policy issues, though often in unexpected ways. On the one hand, there is very little difference of opinion between men and women on the issue of abortion. On the other hand, men's and women's views on the optimal role of government vary greatly: 66 percent of young women believe that government should do more to solve problems (versus 60 percent of young men), whereas only 27 percent of women believe that government does too many things better left to businesses and individuals, as opposed to 35 percent of men.[9] Women are also more likely to believe that the United States is at risk of another terrorist attack since

> Women's formal participation in government has increased significantly in the past generation, yet there remain differences in how men and women vote and participate in politics. Hawaii state Senate President Colleen Hanabusa (D), a candidate for Hawaii's 1st Congressional District seat (left), and volunteer Sharon Worthington (right), review the phone database at Hanabusa's 2010 campaign headquarters.

gender gap
the measurable difference in the way women and men vote for candidates and in the way they view political issues

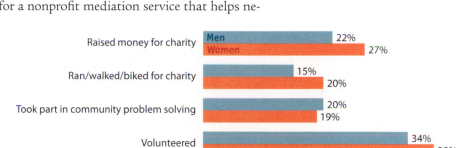

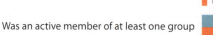

	Men	Women
Raised money for charity	22%	27%
Ran/walked/biked for charity	15%	20%
Took part in community problem solving	20%	19%
Volunteered	34%	38%
Volunteered regularly for nonpolitical groups	16%	21%
Volunteered regularly for political group	2%	1%
Was an active member of at least one group	18%	22%
Voted regularly	28%	25%
Persuaded others to vote	39%	31%
Donated money to a political campaign	9%	5%

FIGURE 6.4

Participation in Civic Activities Among Young Men and Women

SOURCE: Karlo Barrios Marcelo, Mark Hugo Lopez, and Emily Hoban Kirby, *Civic Engagement Among Young Men and Women* (College Park, MD: Circle: The Center for Information and Research on Civic Learning and Engagement, 2007).

September 11, 2001 and they are less likely to feel safe from terrorism. Women, too, are more likely to believe that going to war in Iraq was a mistake, and they were more likely to have reached that conclusion earlier than men were. When it comes to domestic priorities, men and women are equally likely to cite jobs and the economy as high priorities, but women are more likely to consider health care a priority. Men are about 10 percent more likely to favor the death penalty than are women.[10] Do the different life experiences of women and men help to explain some of their policy preferences, and hence their candidate preferences?

AGE AND EVENTS   Differences in the candidates voters prefer—party, gender, the age of the candidates themselves—are one reflection of age and political opinions. People's opinions are also influenced by the events they have lived through and by their political socialization; an epic event may lead to a widespread change in political views. The **generational effect** (sometimes called the *age-cohort effect*) is the impact of a significant external event in shaping the views of a generation. Typically, generational effects are felt most strongly by young people. As a result of the attacks that occurred on September 11, 2001, people who were under age 30 on that day might place a heightened priority on keeping the United States safe in the face of a new kind of threat, for instance. Other key events that have shaped the socialization of a generation include the Great Depression and World War II for the oldest Americans and the war in Vietnam and the changes in society that occurred during the 1960s for the Baby Boom Generation born between 1946 and 1964. The major events that occur while we grow up affect our socialization by shaping our viewpoints and our policy priorities.

One of the strongest examples of the generational effect is the Great Depression. The oldest Americans, who came of age during the era of Democratic president Franklin Roosevelt's New Deal social programs, remain most likely to vote Democratic. But often the impact of events is not immediately apparent. Political scientists continue to measure the effects of the September 11, 2001, terrorist attacks and the subsequent war on terror on the views of the generation socialized to politics during the first decade of the twenty-first century. In the 2008 presidential election, young voters strongly preferred Senator Barack Obama over Republican candidate Senator John McCain. But was this difference in candidate preference a result of the generational effect? Will the Americans who grew up in the wake of those attacks be more patriotic than their parents? Will they resist a militaristic foreign policy throughout their lifetimes? These types of questions will interest public opinion researchers in the decades to come.

GEOGRAPHIC REGION   Since the nation's founding, Americans have varied in their political attitudes and beliefs and how they are socialized to politics, depending on the region of the United States from which they come. These differences stem in part from historical patterns of immigration: Irish and Italian immigrants generally settled in the northeastern seaboard, influencing the political culture of Boston, New York, Philadelphia, and Baltimore. Chinese immigrants, instrumental in building the transcontinental railroad in the nineteenth century, settled in California and areas of the Pacific Northwest and have had a major impact on the political life of those areas.

Among the most important regional differences in the United States is the difference in political outlook between those who live in the Northeast and those in the South. The differences between these two regions predate even our nation's founding. During the Constitutional Convention in 1787, northern and southern states disagreed as to the method that should be used to count slaves for the purposes of taxation and representation. The differences between these two regions were intensified in the aftermath of the Civil War— the quintessential manifestation of regional differences in the United States. Since the Republican Party was the party of Lincoln and the North, the South became essentially a one-party region, with all political competition occurring *within* the Democratic Party. The Democratic Party dominated the South until the later part of the twentieth century, when many Democrats embraced the civil rights movement (as described in Chapter 5). Differences in regional culture and political viewpoints between North and South remain. Today, in national elections, Republicans tend to carry the South, the West, and most of the Midwest, except for large cities in these regions. Democrats are favored in the Northeast, on the West Coast, and in most major cities.

generational effect
the impact of an important external event in shaping the views of a generation

Religious Affiliation in Geographic Regions of the United States

TABLE 6.2

MOST PROTESTANT STATES		MOST CATHOLIC STATES		MOST JEWISH STATES		MOST NONRELIGIOUS STATES	
State	Percentage of Population	State	Percentage of Population	State	Percentage of Population	State	Percentage of Population
Alabama	76	Rhode Island	52	New York	7	Oregon	18
West Virginia	75	Massachusetts	48	New Jersey	6	Idaho	17
Mississippi	75	New Jersey	46	Massachusetts	4	Washington	16
Tennessee	72	Connecticut	46	Florida	4	Colorado	15
South Carolina	71	New York	40	Maryland	4	Maine	14
Arkansas	70	New Hampshire	38	Connecticut	3	California	14
North Carolina	70	Wisconsin	34	Vermont	3	New Hampshire	13
Georgia	68	Louisiana	33	California	3	Nevada	13
Oklahoma	67	New Mexico	32	Nevada	3	Arizona	12
Kentucky	65	Vermont	32				

SOURCE: Jeffrey M. Jones, "Tracking Religious Affiliation, State by State," June 22, 2004, http://www.gallup.com/poll/12091/tracking-religious-affiliation-state-state.aspx#1.

Table 6.2 illustrates one factor that contributes to these differences in regional political climate: religious affiliation. Although differences in religious affiliation are often a function of people's heritage, church membership can alter the political culture of a region through the perpetuation of values and priorities. As Table 6.2 shows, the South is much more Protestant than other regions of the United States. Not surprisingly, Republicans dominate in this area, particularly among religious Protestants, born-again Christians, and Evangelicals (see the discussion of the influence of churches on political socialization on pages 188–190). Catholics and Jews tend to dominate in the Northeast along the East Coast; both groups are more frequently supporters of the Democratic Party. People without a religious affiliation, who tend to value independence and have negative views of governmental activism, tend to live in the West and vote Republican. We can discern many of the similarities and differences between the political beliefs of members of these various demographic groups because of the increasingly sophisticated and accurate ways in which we can measure public opinion.

Measuring Public Opinion

Public opinion consists of the public's expressed views about an issue at a specific point in time. Public opinion and ideology are inextricably linked because ideology is the prism through which people view all political issues; hence their ideology informs their opinions on the full range of political issues. Indeed, the growing importance of public opinion has even led some political scientists, such as Elizabeth Noelle-Neumann, to argue that public opinion itself is a socializing agent in that it provides an independent context that affects political behavior.[11] Though we are inundated every day with the latest public opinion polls on television, on the Internet, in magazines, and even on podcasts, the importance of public opinion is not a new phenomenon in American politics.

As early as the War for Independence, leaders of the Continental Congress were concerned with what the people thought. Popular opinion mattered because support was critical to the success of the volunteer revolutionary army. As discussed in Chapter 2, after the thirteen colonies won their independence, public opinion was an important concern of political and economic leaders during the early years of the new nation. The dissatisfaction

public opinion
the public's expressed views about an issue at a specific point in time

of ordinary people troubled by debt caused Shays's Rebellion in Massachusetts in 1786–87, which led to a shift in the thinking of the elites who came together in Philadelphia the following May to draft the new Constitution. And once the Constitution was drafted, *The Federalist Papers* were used as a tool to influence public opinion and generate support for the new form of government.

Public opinion is manifested in various ways: demonstrators protesting on the steps of the state capitol; readers of the local newspaper writing letters to the editor on behalf of (or against) a proposal before the city council; citizens communicating directly with government officials, perhaps by telling their local city council member what they think of the town's plan to develop a recreational center or by calling their member of Congress to indicate their opinion of a current piece of legislation. One of the most important ways public opinion is measured is through the act of voting, discussed in Chapter 9. But another important tool that policy makers, researchers, and the public rely on as an indicator of public opinion is the **public opinion poll,** a survey of a given population's opinion on an issue at a particular point in time. Policy makers, particularly elected officials, care about public opinion because they want to develop and implement policies that reflect the public's views.[12] Such policies are more likely to attract support from other government leaders, who are also relying on public opinion as a gauge, but they also help ensure that elected leaders will be reelected because they are representing their constituents' views.[13]

public opinion poll

a survey of a given population's opinion on an issue or a candidate at a particular point in time

The Origins of Public Opinion Polls

In his book *Public Opinion,* published in 1922, political writer Walter Lippmann stressed both the importance of public opinion for policy makers and the value of measuring it accurately. Lippman's thought informed a generation of public opinion researchers, who in turn shaped two divergent areas of opinion research: marketing research, used by businesses to increase sales, and public opinion research, used to measure people's opinions on political issues.

Among the first efforts to gauge public opinion were attempts to predict the outcomes of presidential elections. In 1916, the *Literary Digest,* a popular magazine similar in format to today's *Reader's Digest,* conducted its first successful **straw poll,** a poll conducted in an unscientific manner to predict the outcome of an election. (The term comes from the use of natural straw to determine which way the wind is blowing; so too does a straw poll indicate how the winds of public opinion are blowing.) Between 1920 and 1932, *Literary Digest* correctly predicted the winner of every presidential race by relying on its subscribers to mail in postcards indicating their vote choice. The 1936 presidential election between Democrat Franklin Roosevelt and Republican governor Alfred M. "Alf" Landon of Kansas centered on one issue, however: the government's role in responding to the Great Depression. In effect, the election was a mandate on Roosevelt's New Deal policies. The *Literary Digest* poll predicted that Landon would defeat Roosevelt by 57 to 43 percent, but Roosevelt won that election by a landslide, receiving nearly 63 percent of the popular vote.

straw poll

a poll conducted in an unscientific manner, used to predict election outcomes

Where did the *Literary Digest* go wrong? The greatest error the magazine committed was to use an unrepresentative sample to draw conclusions about the wider voting public. The straw poll respondents were selected from a list of subscribers to the magazine, automobile owners, and people listed in telephone directories. At the height of the Depression, this sample excluded most members of the working and middle classes. And class mattered in the 1936 election, with Roosevelt deriving his support primarily from poor, working-class, and middle-class voters. *Literary Digest* had committed what Lippmann termed an error of the casual mind: "to pick out or stumble upon a sample which supports or defies its prejudices, and then to make it the representative of a whole class."[14] Notice the similarity between *Literary Digest*'s faulty straw poll and many of today's voluntary Internet polls—self-selected respondents often differ dramatically in their views from those of the broader public, thus resulting in poll results that sometimes do not accurately reflect public opinion.

Although the 1936 election destroyed the credibility of the *Literary Digest* poll, it was also the watershed year for a young Princeton-based public opinion researcher named George Gallup. Gallup's entry in political public opinion research was driven in part by a desire to help his mother-in-law, Ola Babcock Miller, win election as Iowa's secretary of state, the

INTERNATIONAL OPINION OF THE UNITED STATES

Many Americans' patriotism and national pride result in the unflagging view that the United States is the best country in the world, but that view is not supported by the opinions of citizens of other nations. Indeed, by and large, many throughout the world have a negative view of the United States. The British Broadcasting Company (BBC) regularly conducts international polls gauging sentiment throughout the world regarding people's views of countries' influence. Respondents are asked to evaluate whether each one of fourteen nations, including the United States, has a positive or a negative influence in the world.

Why do so many nations view the United States negatively? Why are the negatively-ranked nations viewed so poorly?

One poll of residents of twenty countries indicates predominantly negative views of the United States. So although many people's opinions of the United States improved slightly after the election of Barack Obama, more countries have predominantly negative views of America (twelve of twenty), than predominantly positive views (five of twenty). As shown in the accompanying figure, among the nations where the United States enjoys the most favorable ratings are the Philippines (80 percent favorable), Ghana (76 percent), Nigeria (65 percent), and Italy (55 percent), and the region of Central America (64 percent). The United States is most negatively viewed in Germany and Russia (at 65 percent each), Turkey (63 percent), and China (58 percent).

Which countries enjoy the most favorable status? Germany (61 percent positive), Canada (59 percent), the United Kingdom (58 percent), Japan (57 percent), and France (52 percent) all enjoy majority favorable opinions. Israel (52 percent negative), North Korea (51 percent negative), Pakistan (56 percent negative), and Iran (58 percent negative) are the least favorably viewed nations.

SOURCE: www.worldpublicopinion.org/pipa/pdf/feb09/BBCEvals_Feb09_rpt.pdf.

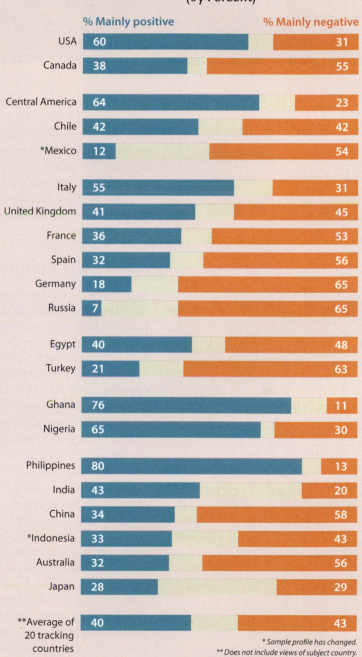

Views of the United States' Influence by Country, January 2009
(by Percent)

Country	% Mainly positive	% Mainly negative
USA	60	31
Canada	38	55
Central America	64	23
Chile	42	42
*Mexico	12	54
Italy	55	31
United Kingdom	41	45
France	36	53
Spain	32	56
Germany	18	65
Russia	7	65
Egypt	40	48
Turkey	21	63
Ghana	76	11
Nigeria	65	30
Philippines	80	13
India	43	20
China	34	58
*Indonesia	33	43
Australia	32	56
Japan	28	29
**Average of 20 tracking countries	40	43

*Sample profile has changed.
** Does not include views of subject country.
The gap between "mainly positive" and "mainly negative" in this chart represents "Depends," "Neither/neutral," and "DK/NA."

first woman elected to that position. In 1935, Gallup founded the American Institute of Public Opinion, which would later become the Gallup Organization. Gallup gained national recognition when he correctly predicted the outcome of the 1936 election, and scientific opinion polls, which rely on the random selection of participants rather than their own self-selection, gained enormous credibility during this era.

Gallup's credibility suffered a substantial setback, however, after the presidential election of 1948 between Democrat Harry S Truman and Republican Thomas E. Dewey. That year, the "big three" polling organizations, Gallup, Roper, and Crossley, all concluded their polls in October, and all predicted a Dewey victory. By ending their efforts early, the polls missed the swing of third-party voters back to Harry S Truman's camp in the final days of the campaign. The organizations didn't anticipate that many voters would switch back to the Democratic nominee, who wound up winning the presidency. During his administration, Truman would sometimes offer a good-natured barb at the pollsters who had prematurely predicted his demise, and George Gallup responded in kind: "I have the greatest admiration for President Truman, because he fights for what he believes. I propose to do the same thing. As long as public opinion is important in this country, and until someone finds a better way of appraising it, I intend to go right ahead with the task of reporting the opinions of the people on issues vital to their welfare."[15]

How Public Opinion Polls Are Conducted

In politics, public opinion polls are used for many reasons.[16] Political scientist Herbert Asher noted, "Polling plays an integral role in political events at the national, state, and local levels. In any major event or decision, poll results are sure to be a part of the news media's coverage and the decision makers' deliberations."[17] In addition, public opinion polls help determine who those decision makers will be: candidates for public office use polls to determine their initial name recognition, the effectiveness of their campaign strategy, their opponents' weaknesses, and how potential voters are responding to their message. Once elected to office, policy makers often rely on public opinion polls to gauge their constituents' opinions and to measure how well they are performing on the job.

The process of conducting a public opinion poll consists of several steps. Those conducting the poll first need to determine the **population** they are targeting for the survey—the group of people whose opinions are of interest and about whom information is desired. For example, if your neighbor were considering running for the U.S. House of Representatives, she would want to know how many people recognize her name. But she would be interested only in those people who live in your congressional district. Furthermore, she would probably narrow this population by looking only at those people in the district who are registered to vote. She might even want to narrow her target population further by limiting her survey to likely voters, perhaps those who have voted in past congressional elections.

The sponsor of any poll, whether a candidate, a political party or group, or a news organization, needs to determine what information is desired from survey respondents. Sometimes this information is relatively clear—news media organizations track presidential approval ratings each month, for example. But other times this process might be more complex. Polling organizations construct polls carefully to ensure that the questions actually measure what the client wants to know. Pollsters also recognize that many factors, including question design and question order, influence the responses. For example, this chapter's "Analyzing the Sources" provides data on how Americans identify themselves ideologically:

population
in a poll, the group of people whose opinions are of interest and/or about whom information is desired

ANALYZING THE SOURCES

EXAMINING AMERICANS' IDEOLOGY

This graph shows the trend over time regarding Americans' self-described ideology. In all the surveys, respondents were asked to describe their political views as very conservative, conservative, moderate, liberal, or very liberal. Very conservative/conservative and very liberal/liberal responses have been consolidated.

How would you describe your political views?

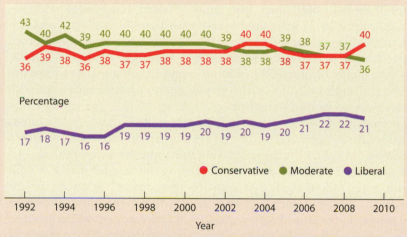

SOURCE: www.gallup.com/poll/124958/Conservatives-Finish-2009-No-1-Ideological-Group.aspx.

Evaluating the Evidence

① What does the graph indicate about how most people identify themselves now? Why do you think this is the case?

② Why do the 2009 data stand out? Are the 2009 data consistent with those of previous years?

③ The data come from a national sample of U.S. citizens. How would the data vary in your state? In your community?

5 percent of Americans identify themselves as very liberal, 16 percent as liberal, 36 percent as moderate, 31 percent as conservative, and 9 percent as very conservative. But other Gallup surveys have indicated that when pollsters changed the term "liberal" to "progressive" in half of the surveys sent to respondents, those who received the questionnaire with the "progressive" alternative responded quite differently. In general, people were more likely to identify themselves as moderates or as progressives when that terminology was used.[18] This simple change in terminology indicates that Americans may be more likely to identify themselves as "conservative" when the opposing term "liberal" is used rather than when the opposing term "progressive" is used.

SAMPLING Once the target population is determined and the survey measurement instrument, or poll, is designed, pollsters then must select a sample that will represent the views of this population. Because it is nearly impossible to measure all the opinions of any given population, pollsters frequently rely on **random sampling,** a scientific method of selection in which each member of the population has an equal chance at being included in the sample. Relying on random sampling helps to ensure that the sample is not skewed so that one component of the population is overrepresented. To demonstrate this point, suppose the dean of students asks your class to conduct a public opinion survey that will measure whether students believe that parking facilities are adequate at your school. In this case, the population you need to measure is the entire student body. But clearly how you

random sampling
a scientific method of selection for a poll in which each member of the population has an equal chance at being included in the sample

conduct the sampling will affect the responses. If you ask only students in your 8:00 a.m. American Government class, you might find that they have little trouble parking because the campus is not crowded at that hour. If you ask students who attend classes only during peak hours, you might get different, yet not necessarily representative, views as well, since these students may have more difficulty parking than average. How then would you obtain a random sample? The best way would be to ask the registrar for a list of all students, determine your sample size, randomly select every nth student from the list, contact each nth student, and ask for his or her views.

Researchers have noted, however, that one problem with polls is that even those conducted using random samples may not provide the accurate data needed to illuminate political opinions and behaviors. Part of the problem is that randomization can go only so far. One standard method for conducting telephone surveys is to use random-digit dialing of telephones.[19] Many polling organizations still exclude cellular lines from their population.[20] But even those that include cell phone subscribers face a high rate of nonresponse because of the nearly universal use of caller ID, and the transportable nature of cell phones that makes their owners unwilling to participate in surveys.[21] But today, 20 percent of the U.S. population relies exclusively on cell phones and has no landline phone.[22] How might cell phone users be different from those who use only landlines? People who rely exclusively on landlines are likely to be older than "celly-onlys." Indeed, one study found that 33 percent of young adults aged 18–29 years lived in celly-only households.[23] And some individuals who eliminate landlines from their homes do so in order to save money. In fact, in 2008, adults living in poverty were nearly twice as likely to rely on cell phones exclusively, compared with those with higher incomes.[24] So, by eliminating cell phone users from a potential sample, pollsters eliminate individuals who may be poorer or more concerned with the economy than those who pay to keep a landline.

quota sample
a method by which pollsters structure a sample so that it is representative of the characteristics of the target population

One way pollsters attempt to address these types of concerns is through the use of a **quota sample,** a more scientifically sophisticated method of sampling than random sampling. A pollster using this method structures the sample so that it is representative of the characteristics of the target population. Let's say that your mother is running for mayor of your town, and you would like to conduct a poll that measures opinions of her among various constituencies. From census data, you learn that your town is 40 percent white, 35 percent African American, 20 percent Latino, and 5 percent Asian. Therefore, at a citywide event, you structure your sample so that it reflects the proportions of the population. With a sample of 200 voters, you would seek to include 80 white respondents, 70 African Americans, 40 Latinos, and 10 Asians. Pollsters routinely rely on quota sampling, though often they may not ask participants about their demographic characteristics until the end of the poll.

stratified sampling
a process of random sampling in which the national population is divided into fourths and certain areas within these regions are selected as representative of the national population

Another method used to address problems in sampling is **stratified sampling,** in which the national population is divided into fourths and certain areas within these regions are selected as representative of the national population. Although some organizations still rely on quota sampling, larger organizations and media polls now use stratified sampling, the most reliable form of random sample. Today, nearly every major polling organization relies on U.S. census data as the basis of their four sampling regions. Stratified sampling is the basis for much of the public opinion data used by political scientists and other social scientists, in particular the General Social Survey (GSS) and the National Election Study.

SAMPLING ERROR   As we have seen, to accurately gauge public opinion, pollsters must obtain an accurate sample from the population they are polling. A sample need not be large to reflect the population's views. In fact, most national polling organizations rarely sample more than 1,500 respondents; most national samples range from 1,000 to 1,500. To poll smaller populations (states or congressional districts, for example), polling organizations routinely use samples of between 300 and 500 respondents.

The key is having a sample that accurately reflects the population. Let's say that your political science instructor offers extra credit if you attend a weekly study group. The group initially convenes immediately after your regular class session. At the conclusion of the study group, the leader asks if this is a convenient time for everyone to meet. Since everyone present has attended the study group, chances are that the time is more convenient for them than it is for those students who did not attend—perhaps because they have another class immediately after your political science class, or they work during that time period,

leaders learn what issues are important to people, which policy solutions they prefer, and whether they approve of the way government officials are doing their jobs.[30] The role of opinion polls in shaping citizens' involvement with their government is also circular: polls play a pivotal role in shaping public opinion, and the results of polls, frequently reported by the media, provide an important source of information for the American public.

The Most Important Problem

Several polling organizations routinely ask respondents to identify (either from a list or in their own words) what they view as "the most important problem" facing the country. Since April 2008, "the economy" has been most frequently cited as the most important problem, with fully 72 percent of those surveyed in 2010 identifying it as their top concern, as shown in Figure 6.5.[31] Not surprisingly, until November 2007, the war in Iraq was the top issue, with about a third of Americans—34 percent—citing it as the most important problem. By April 2008, only 23 percent named the war in Iraq as the most important problem. Until that time, Iraq had consistently been named the top problem for the four previous years. Interestingly, however, the percentage of Americans who were concerned about the situation in Iraq was not as high as it was for other wars, as reflected in the results of previous surveys conducted during earlier armed conflicts. For example, 56 percent of respondents identified the Korean War as the most important problem in September 1951, and 62 percent named the Vietnam War as the top problem in January 1967.[32] In general, other problems Americans identify as important include the state of the economy, gas prices, health care, immigration, and terrorism.

Figure 6.5 shows the proportion of people who responded "the economy" when asked "What do you think is the most important problem facing this country today?" From 2001 through 2008, comparatively smaller proportions of respondents identified the economy as the most important problem. During that time, other issues, including the wars in Iraq and Afghanistan, dominated the public psyche. But as the recession hit in 2008, increasing numbers identified the economy as important, peaking at over 80 percent in early 2009. As the recovery started in 2010, decreasing proportions were naming the economy as the most important problem, declining from 72 percent in February to 63 percent in April.

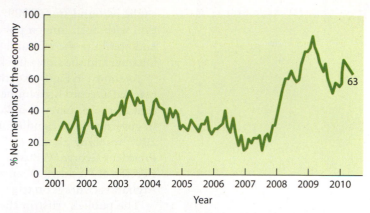

FIGURE 6.5

Percentage of Americans Mentioning the Economy as the Nation's Most Important Problem

SOURCE: Frank Newport, "U.S. Satisfaction at 15%, Lowest Since 1992," April 14, 2008, www.gallup.com/poll/106498/US-Satisfaction-15-Lowest-Since-1992.aspx.

Public Opinion About Government

Analysts of public opinion, government officials, and scholars of civic engagement are all concerned with public opinion about the government at all levels, in particular about the institutions of the federal government. For decades, public opinion researchers have measured the public's trust in government by asking survey respondents to rate their level of trust in the federal government's ability to handle domestic and international policy matters and to gauge their amount of trust and confidence in the executive, legislative, and judicial branches of government.

The responses to these questions are important for several reasons. First, although these measures indicate public opinion about institutions rather than individuals, individual officeholders nonetheless can use the data as a measure of how well they are performing their jobs. Lower levels of confidence in the institution of the presidency, for example, tend to parallel lower approval ratings of specific presidents.[33] Second, trust in government is one measure of the public's sense of efficacy, their belief that the government works for people like them, as discussed in Chapter 1. If people trust their government, they are more likely to believe that it is responsive to the needs of citizens—that it is working for people like them.

As indicated by the results of a Gallup poll that tracks trust in government over time, the public's trust in the ability of the federal government to handle both international affairs and domestic problems has in general declined over the years, but has experienced a slight rebound since 2009. Many analysts attribute the decline to widespread dissatisfaction with both foreign policy as it relates to the war in Iraq and the economic downturn, and attribute the rebound to the optimism fostered by the election of a president, Barack Obama, and the slow uptick in the economy.

As shown in Figure 6.6, the public's trust in government to handle international problems reached a record high immediately after the September 11, 2001, terror attacks, with 83 percent of those surveyed indicating a great deal or a fair amount of trust. The public's trust in government to handle international problems then steadily declined from 2004 through 2007, reaching a nadir of 51 percent in 2007, as the war in Iraq dragged on. The effect of President George W. Bush's "surge strategy" in Iraq and then the optimism generated by the election of President Obama account for a temporary increase in optimism, but as the war in Afghanistan drags on trust declines again, hitting 57 percent in late 2010.

The public's trust in the government's ability to handle domestic matters also peaked in 2001, as shown in Figure 6.7, which indicates the percentage of people who trust the government to handle domestic problems. Notably, a significant dip in the assessment of the government's ability to handle domestic matters occurred in 2005, immediately after Hurricane Katrina devastated parts of Louisiana, Mississippi, and other southern states. The drop in confidence that begins in 2005 reflects the widely perceived ability of the government to manage this crisis. By 2007, worries about the economy dominated the public's thinking, and trust in government to handle domestic problems dropped to 47 percent, a figure that rivals the record low confidence levels of 51 to 49 percent seen in the period between 1974 and 1976, following the Watergate scandal. An uptick registers in 2009, coinciding with Barack Obama's assuming the presidency. But that trust declines to 46 percent in 2010. This decline in trust was viewed by many analysts as a repudiation of both the president's handling of the economy and his health care plan.

The public's trust in specific institutions has also been affected by the September 11, 2001, terror attacks, the subsequent weariness with the war in Iraq, and the optimism following Barack Obama's election as president As Figure 6.8 shows, for example, trust in the executive branch hit a near-record mark in 2002, when fully 72 percent of Americans

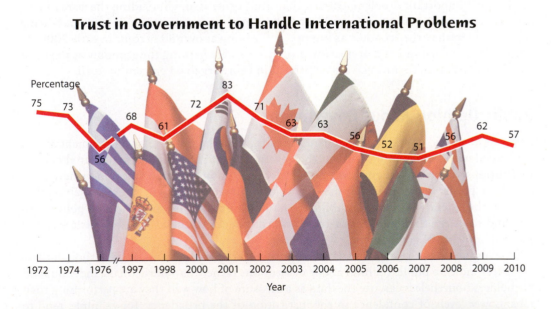

Trust in Government to Handle International Problems

Percentage

75 73   68 61   72 83 71 63 63 56 52 51 56 62 57
         56

1972 1974 1976 1997 1998 2000 2001 2002 2003 2004 2005 2006 2007 2008 2009 2010

Year

POLITICAL INQUIRY

FIGURE 6.6 ■ As you can see, public trust in the government's ability to deal with international problems has increased since 2008. Why do you think this is the case? Why was public trust comparatively low from 2003 through 2008?

SOURCE: Jeffrey M. Jones, "Trust in Government," The Gallup Poll, www.gallup.com/poll/5392/Trust-Government.aspx.

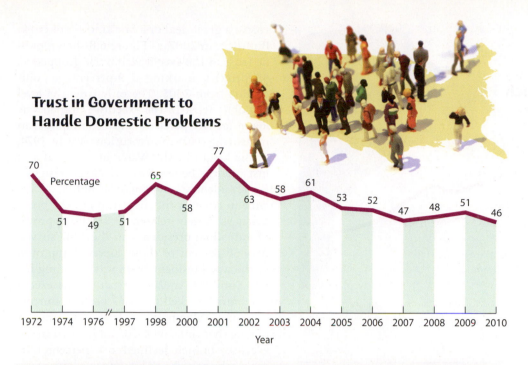

Trust in Government to Handle Domestic Problems

Percentage

70 — 1972
51 — 1974
49 — 1976
51 — 1997
65 — 1998
58 — 2000
77 — 2001
63 — 2002
58 — 2003
61 — 2004
53 — 2005
52 — 2006
47 — 2007
48 — 2008
51 — 2009
46 — 2010

Year

POLITICAL INQUIRY

FIGURE 6.7 ■ What impact does the state of the economy have on the public's trust in the government's ability to handle domestic problems? What can you infer about the state of the economy in May 1972? In September 2004? In September 2010?

SOURCE: Jeffrey M. Jones, "Trust in Government," The Gallup Poll, www.gallup.com/poll/5392/Trust-Government.aspx.

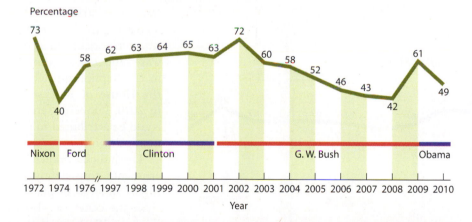

Trust in the Executive Branch of Government

Percentage

73 — 1972
40 — 1974
58 — 1976
62 — 1997
63 — 1998
64 — 1999
65 — 2000
63 — 2001
72 — 2002
60 — 2003
58 — 2004
52 — 2005
46 — 2006
43 — 2007
42 — 2008
61 — 2009
49 — 2010

Nixon   Ford   Clinton   G. W. Bush   Obama

Year

POLITICAL INQUIRY

FIGURE 6.8 ■ As the graph shows, the public's trust in the executive branch declined steeply (from 73 percent to 40 percent in two years) during the Nixon presidency as a result of the Watergate scandal. The decline during George W. Bush's presidency was more gradual, from 72 percent to 42 percent in six years. Was this decline partly to be expected for any second-term president? How has President Obama fared in trust since becoming president in 2009?

SOURCE: Jeffrey M. Jones, "Trust in Government," The Gallup Poll, www.gallup.com/poll/5392/Trust-Government.aspx.

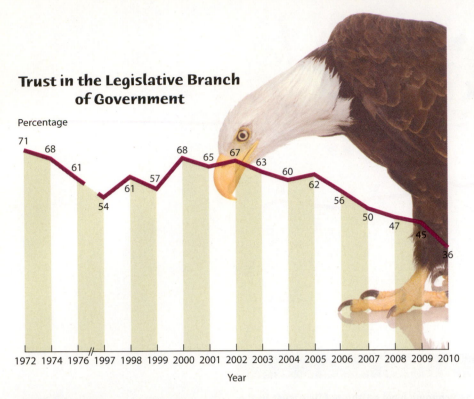

Trust in the Legislative Branch of Government

Percentage

71 68 61 54 61 57 68 65 67 63 60 62 56 50 47 45 36

1972 1974 1976 // 1997 1998 1999 2000 2001 2002 2003 2004 2005 2006 2007 2008 2009 2010

Year

POLITICAL INQUIRY

FIGURE 6.9 ■ Trust in the legislative branch plummeted from 62 percent in 2005 to 47 percent in 2010. What factors can explain that trend? Why do you believe that trust in both the executive and the legislative branches was low from 2006 to 2008, even though those branches were controlled by different political parties?

SOURCE: Jeffrey M. Jones, "Trust in Government," The Gallup Poll, www.gallup.com/poll/5392/Trust-Government.aspx.

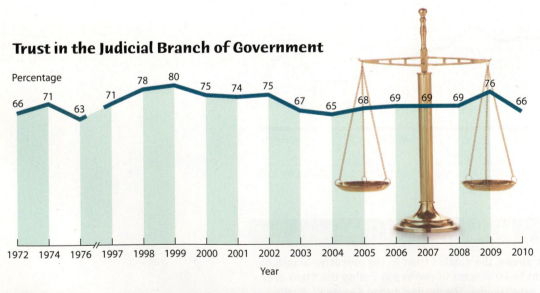

Trust in the Judicial Branch of Government

Percentage

66 71 63 71 78 80 75 74 75 67 65 68 69 69 69 76 66

1972 1974 1976 // 1997 1998 1999 2000 2001 2002 2003 2004 2005 2006 2007 2008 2009 2010

Year

POLITICAL INQUIRY

FIGURE 6.10 ■ Trust in the judicial branch is consistently high, but climbed in 2009 after a period of steady decline. What could account for this change in public trust?

SOURCE: Jeffrey M. Jones, "Trust in Government," The Gallup Poll, www.gallup.com/poll/5392/Trust-Government.aspx.

voiced a great deal or a fair amount of trust. But then, in 2007, as Figure 6.8 shows, public trust in the executive branch dropped to 43 percent, marking a 9-percentage-point decline from 2005. The only time the level of public trust in the executive branch was lower (at 40 percent) since Gallup began measuring trust in institutions was in 1974, at the height of the Watergate scandal and just months before Richard Nixon resigned the presidency.[34] As previously noted, the decline in trust in the institution of the presidency is closely related to public approval of individual presidents: in the 2007 survey, only 36 percent of those surveyed approved of the way President Bush was handling his job. Similarly, in 2009, trust in the executive branch spiked up to 61 percent, mirroring Barack Obama's higher approval ratings during that time. By 2010, public trust in the executive branch declined to 46 percent, mirroring the president's low approval rating.

For example, in 2009, 61 percent of those surveyed expressed trust in the executive branch, but only 45 percent expressed trust in the legislative branch. But this is not always the case. Take 2007, for example. As shown in Figure 6.9, trust in the legislative branch also declined to 50 percent from 62 percent in 2005. Before 2006, part of this decline of trust could be attributed to the public's dissatisfaction with the Republican Congress's consent to Bush administration policies concerning Iraq. From 2006 through 2010, increasing dissatisfaction with the Democrats in Congress was apparent, culminating in the Republican takeover of the House of Representatives in 2010. Public dissatisfaction could be attributed to the economic downturn.

The judicial branch of government consistently scores higher in levels of public trust than the other two branches. Figure 6.10 shows that confidence in the judiciary typically hovers between 65 and 75 percent, sometimes climbing into the high 70s (or even 80 percent in 1999). The judiciary's lowest rating came in 1976, when there was widespread dissatisfaction with government as a whole in the aftermath of the Watergate scandal.

The process of political socialization is quite different from what it was even a generation ago. Although some agents of socialization such as families, peers, and churches remain important, other agents, particularly the media, are more pervasive and influential than ever before. Although television and radio have played a part in socializing the average 40-year-old in 2011, today's young people are almost constantly bombarded by various forms of media, which may influence their viewpoints, priorities, behaviors, and opinions.

Technology has also drastically changed the way public opinion is measured. The advent of the computer alone—from powerful mainframes to personal computers—has revolutionized the data collection process; today computers facilitate near-instant access to polling data. They also provide the means to generate and survey increasingly representative samples to gauge the public's views with a high degree of accuracy. How will the pervasiveness of cell phones revolutionize the process of public opinion polling?

The catch-22, however, has been the pervasiveness of public opinion polls. People's opinions are solicited by every kind of survey from cheesy Internet polls to reputable polling organizations. As a result, the public has become poll weary, dubious of the value of the pollster's next set of questions. Will increasing weariness with Internet polling result in less representative samples? How might pollsters overcome this challenge?

But technology has provided—and will continue to provide—ways to solve the problems that technology itself has generated in accurately measuring public opinion. Stratified samples and other increasingly sophisticated microsampling techniques have improved the ability of reputable pollsters to gauge public opinion. And pollsters are incorporating new technologies, including text messaging and cell phone surveys, as they work to develop new ways to accurately measure and convey the public's views to candidates, to policy makers, and, through the media, to the public itself.

Summary

1. Political Socialization and Civic Participation

Political socialization begins at home in very early childhood, when our political ideology, our beliefs about people of different races and sexes, and even our party identification can be firmly embedded, and the beliefs and values we learn early help shape how we view new information as we age. One key aspect of political socialization is whether children are socialized to participate in the civic and political life of their communities. Families, schools, and media all contribute to whether and how people participate.

2. Agents of Socialization

Among the agents of socialization—including family, the media, schools, churches, peers, community and political leaders, and demographic characteristics—the most important are the family and the media. Family shapes our political values and ideology from childhood and has a strong impact on our political perspective. The media now rival the family in the influence that they have in shaping our views and informing our opinions. A person's level of religiosity is actually a more important influence than his or her actual belief structure so that, in general, very religious people of all faiths have more in common with one another than with less religious people of the same faith. Demographic characteristics—including race and ethnicity, gender, age, and geographic region—not only contribute to how we are socialized to political and community life and our values and priorities but also influence the candidates we vote for.

3. Measuring Public Opinion

The measurement of public opinion has evolved and become increasingly complex and reliable when done scientifically, though the proliferation of questionable straw polls on the Internet, similar to the initial attempts to predict presidential elections in the early twentieth century, still offers dubious results to the gullible. In measuring public opinion, reputable pollsters identify the target population, design an accurate measure, select a sample, and administer the poll. Through various methods of sampling, pollsters attempt to select a subset of the population that is representative of the population's views. Different types of polls, including tracking polls, push polls, and exit polls, are used for different purposes in political campaigns.

4. What Americans Think About Politics

Americans identify the state of the economy as the "most important problem," replacing the war in Iraq as their top concern. Polls also indicate that their overall satisfaction with the direction the country is headed in is low. Among the three branches of government, people's trust in both the presidency and Congress is at near-record lows, while trust in the judiciary remains relatively stable.

Key Terms

agents of socialization 186

exit polls 202

gender gap 193

generational effect 194

political socialization 185

population 198

public opinion 195

public opinion poll 196

push polls 202

quota sample 200

random sampling 199

sampling error (margin of error) 201

stratified sampling 200

straw poll 196

tracking polls 201

For Review

1. How are political socialization and civic participation linked?
2. Explain in detail the agents of socialization. How does each agent influence an individual's political views over a lifetime?
3. What demographic characteristics contribute to how individuals view politics?
4. How did public opinion polls evolve historically?
5. Explain how public opinion polls are conducted.
6. What factors have an impact on what Americans perceive as the "most important problem"?
7. Describe the most recent trend regarding Americans' trust in government.

For Critical Thinking and Discussion

1. Were you brought up in a family in which joining groups was important? Do your parents belong to any interest groups? Do you? If not, why do you think that is the case?
2. How have your demographic characteristics—your age, the area of the country in which you were raised—contributed to the formation of your political views? How relevant are the generalities described in the chapter to your own experience and beliefs?
3. What do you think is the "most important problem" facing the United States? Is it a problem discussed in this book? Is it one shared by your classmates?
4. What factors influence how satisfied you feel about the direction of the country?
5. Which branch of government do you trust the most? Why?

MULTIPLE CHOICE: Choose the lettered item that answers the question correctly.

1. The public's expressed views about an issue at a specific point in time are called
   a. public opinion.
   b. time frame analysis.
   c. time tracked sample.
   d. stratified sample.

2. Agents of socialization *do not* include
   a. pets.
   b. peers.
   c. churches.
   d. the media.

3. A majority of which of the following demographic groups did not support Barack Obama's candidacy for the presidency?
   a. Latinos
   b. women
   c. whites
   d. Asians

4. The impact of an important external event in shaping the views of a generation is called
   a. the age-cohort effect.
   b. the generational effect.
   c. the lifetime effect.
   d. both (a) and (b).

5. A poll conducted in an unscientific manner, used to predict election outcomes, is called
   a. an exit poll.
   b. a tracking poll.
   c. a push poll.
   d. a straw poll.

6. In a poll, the group of people whose opinions are of interest and/or about whom information is desired is called the
   a. quota sample.
   b. target sample.
   c. population.
   d. bull's-eye group.

7. A method by which pollsters structure a sample so that it is representative of the characteristics of the target population is called a
   a. quota sample.
   b. target sample.
   c. population.
   d. bull's-eye group.

8. Polls that measure changes in public opinion over the course of days, weeks, or months by repeatedly asking respondents the same questions and measuring changes in their responses are called
   a. exit polls.
   b. tracking polls.
   c. push polls.
   d. straw polls.

9. A special type of poll that both provides information to campaigns about candidate strengths and weaknesses and attempts to skew public opinion about a candidate is called
   a. an exit poll.
   b. a tracking poll.
   c. a push poll.
   d. a straw poll.

10. Polls conducted at polling places on Election Day to determine the winner of an election before the polls close are called
   a. exit polls.
   b. tracking polls.
   c. push polls.
   d. straw polls.

FILL IN THE BLANKS.

11. The process by which we develop our political values and opinions throughout our lives is called _____ .

12. The measurable difference in the way women and men vote for candidates and in the way they view political issues is called the _____ .

13. A survey of a given population's opinion on an issue or a candidate at a particular point in time is called a _____ .

14. A scientific method of selection for a poll in which each member of the population has an equal chance at being included in the sample is called _____ .

15. A process of random sampling in which the national population is divided into fourths and certain areas within these regions are selected as representative of the national population is called _____ .

Answers: 1. a; 2. a; 3. c; 4. d; 5. d; 6. c; 7. a; 8. b; 9. c; 10 a; 11. political socialization; 12. gender gap; 13. public opinion poll; 14. random sampling; 15. stratified sampling.

Internet Resources

Annenberg National Election Studies
www.electionstudies.org The ANES Web site contains a plethora of information on American public opinion as well as a valuable user guide that can help acquaint you with using the data. It also provides a link to other election studies, including some cross-national studies at www.electionstudies.org/other_election_studies.

The Gallup Organization
www.galluppoll.com You will find both national and international polls and analysis on this site.

The Roper Center
www.ropercenter.uconn.edu This Web site features the University of Connecticut's Roper Center polls, the General Social Survey, presidential approval ratings, and poll analysis.

Zogby International
www.zogby.com For a wide variety of political, commercial, and sociological data, go to this site.

Internet Activism

Twitter
@poll—demonstrates both the power and the limitations of polls relying on new technologies.

Facebook
Friend "Gallup" or search "poll application" to add an application that enables you to create polls for your Facebook page.

Recommended Readings

Bishop, George F., and Stephen T. Mockabee. *Taking the Pulse of Public Opinion: Leading and Misleading Indicators of the State of the Nation.* New York: Springer Publishing, 2010. This analytical work examines how psychology and the media influence well-established public opinion indicators.

Fiorina, Morris P. *Culture War: The Myth of a Polarized America.* New York: Pearson Longman, 2006. A critical view of the notion that the United States is divided along ideological lines. Fiorina asserts that Americans are generally moderate and tolerant of a wide variety of viewpoints.

Jamieson, Kathleen Hall. *Electing the President, 2008.* Philadelphia: University of Pennsylvania, 2008. A fascinating "insider's view" of how public opinion shaped the 2008 presidential campaigns by the director of the Annenberg National Election Studies.

Page, Benjamin I., and Robert Y. Shapiro. *The Rational Public: Fifty Years of Trends in Americans' Policy Preferences.* Chicago: University of Chicago, 1992. An analysis of the policy preferences of the American public from the 1930s until 1990. The authors describe opinion on both domestic and foreign policy.

Traugott, Michael W., and Paul J. Lavrakas. *The Voter's Guide to Election Polls,* 4th ed. New York: Chatham House, 2008. A user-friendly approach, written in question-and-answer format, that helps beginners understand the polling process and how to interpret public opinion data.

Welch, Susan, Lee Sigelman, Timothy Bledsoe, and Michael Combs. *Race and Place: Race Relations in an American City* (Cambridge Studies in Public Opinion and Political Psychology). Cambridge: Cambridge University Press, 2001. An analysis of the impact of residential changes on the attitudes and behavior of African Americans and whites.

Movies of Interest

Lions for Lambs (2007)
Directed by Robert Redford and starring Redford, Meryl Streep, and Tom Cruise, this film about a platoon of U.S. soldiers in Afghanistan demonstrates the influence educational socialization can have on individuals.

Wag the Dog (1997)
A classic Barry Levinson film featuring a spin-doctor (Robert De Niro) and a Hollywood producer (Dustin Hoffman) who team up eleven days before an election to "fabricate" a war in order to cover up a presidential sex scandal.

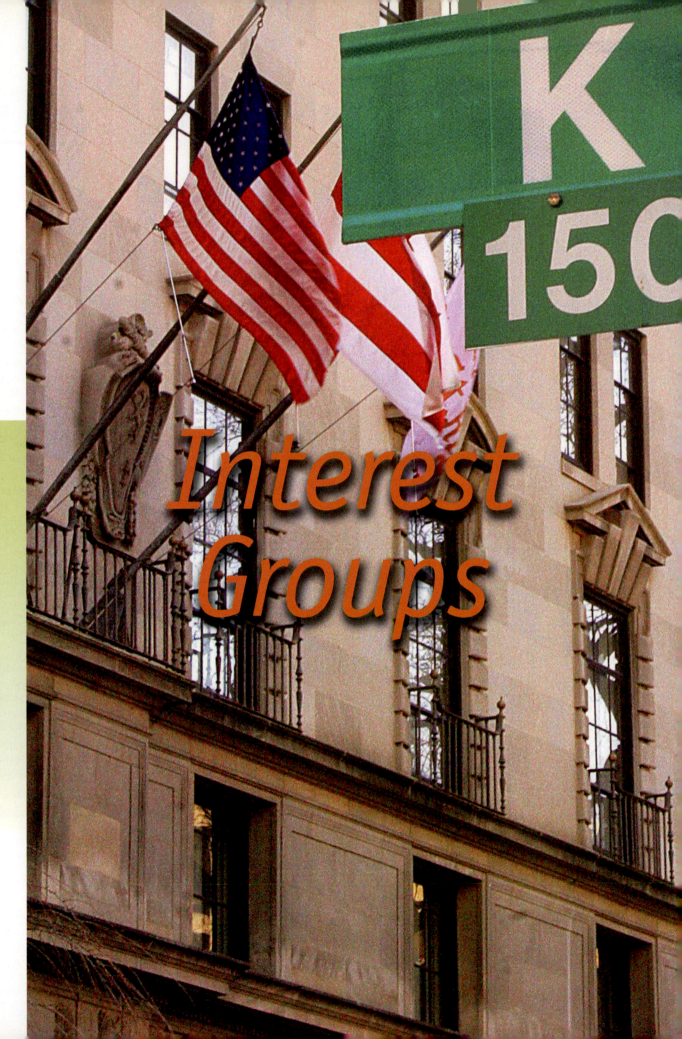

Interest
Groups

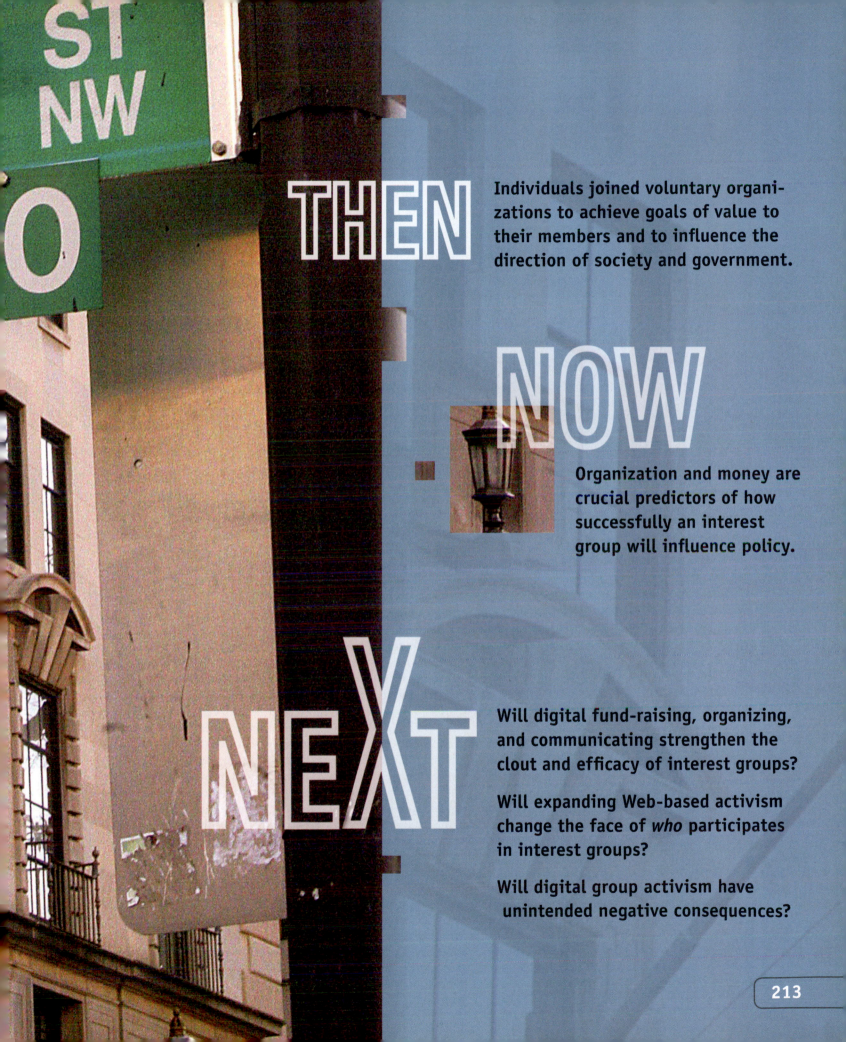

THEN

Individuals joined voluntary organizations to achieve goals of value to their members and to influence the direction of society and government.

NOW

Organization and money are crucial predictors of how successfully an interest group will influence policy.

NEXT

Will digital fund-raising, organizing, and communicating strengthen the clout and efficacy of interest groups?

Will expanding Web-based activism change the face of *who* participates in interest groups?

Will digital group activism have unintended negative consequences?

213

In this chapter, we survey the composition, power, and strategies of interest groups in the United States. We explore the development of interest groups over time and analyze what makes an interest group successful.

FIRST, we examine *the value of interest groups* as tools of citizen participation.

SECOND, we consider the questions of *who joins interest groups, and why.*

THIRD, we examine *how interest groups succeed.*

FOURTH, we look at various *types of interest groups.*

FIFTH, we focus on *interest group strategies.*

SIXTH, we probe the intersection of *interest groups, politics, and money:* specifically, *the influence of political action committees.*

interest groups
organizations that seek to achieve some of their goals by influencing government decision making

social capital
the many ways in which our lives are improved by social connections

Organizations that seek to

achieve their goals by influencing government decision making are called **interest groups.** Also called *special interests,* interest groups differ from political parties in that interest groups do not seek to control the government, as parties do. Interest groups simply want to influence policy making on issues. Interest groups are more important in the political process of the United States than anywhere else in the world.[1] Their strong role is partly due to the number of interest groups that attempt to influence U.S. policy.

Take just one issue—the environment, say—and chances are that you or someone in your class is a member of one of the almost two hundred organizations concerned with the environment, conservation, or ecology in the United States.[2] The multitude of interest groups focused on any given issue is an important component of how government policy is formulated. Interest groups shape the policy process by helping determine which issues policy makers will act on and which options they will consider in addressing a problem.

When we think of interest groups, the typical images that come to mind are of wealthy lobbyists "schmoozing" with easily corrupted politicians. Although that may sometimes be the case, interest groups do not require the leadership of the rich and well connected to be effective. But today, using new technologies such as the social networking Web sites Facebook and Twitter, the organized effort of people from all walks of life can influence policy making. Although moneyed interests may dominate politics, interest groups play a crucial role in leveling the political playing field by providing access for organized "average" people.

The Value of Interest Groups

The nineteenth-century French historian and writer Alexis de Tocqueville, author of the influential work *Democracy in America,* dubbed Americans "a nation of joiners" in 1835, and his analysis still rings true today.[3] Indeed, estimates indicate that about 80 percent of all Americans belong to some kind of voluntary group or association, although not every group is an interest group.[4] The key role interest groups would play in politics was foreseen by the founders—James Madison acknowledged the idea that people with similar interests would form and join groups to prompt government action. He believed that the only way to cure "the mischiefs of faction" was by enabling groups to proliferate and compete with one another.[5]

Yet despite this heritage, some contemporary scholars argue that Americans today are increasingly staying at home. Political scientist Robert Putnam, author of *Bowling Alone: The Collapse and Revival of American Community,* found a marked decrease in the number of people who belong to interest groups and other types of clubs and organizations. These organizations, Putnam argues, are essential sources of **social capital,** the relationships that improve our lives by giving us social connections with which to solve common problems. Putnam demonstrates that social capital improves individual lives in very concrete ways: those with a greater number of social ties live longer, happier, and healthier lives. But social capital also improves communities, and even larger polities, because it stimulates individuals to communicate and interact with their government. Efficacy increases, because when people are engaged and communicate with government officials, government responds by meeting their needs more effectively. This response in turn creates the feeling among individuals that government listens to people like them. And when government responds, it becomes more likely that those affected will try to influence government decisions again.[6]

Critics of Putnam's work have noted that although the number of people belonging to the kinds of groups Putnam analyzed may be declining, people are engaged in other types of groups and clubs and enjoy various forms of group recreation.[7] For example, it is unlikely that you are a member of a gardening club such as those that Putnam researched. (But if you are, good for you!) Yet it is likely that you belong to an online community such as MySpace or Facebook. Such communities facilitate social relationships and may even provide the opportunity for participants to solve community problems. And although people may be less likely to entertain friends and relatives in their homes

> Can a conversation over a skim latte create social capital? People may not be joining gardening clubs, but are they really less connected than in the past? Or are their connections just different?

today (another activity Putnam measured), they are *more likely* to socialize with friends and relatives over meals in restaurants. So even if Putnam is correct in his analysis that we are no longer socially engaged the way Americans used to be, we may still be engaged—but through different channels and in different settings.

Political scientist E. E. Schattschneider has written, "Democracy is a competitive political system in which competing leaders and organizations define the alternatives of public policy in such a way that the public can participate in the decision-making process."[8] One of the key types of competitive organizations Schattschneider was describing is interest groups. Schattschneider and other political scientists study and assess the value that interest groups provide in American democracy. This value centrally includes interest groups' usefulness in channeling civic participation—serving as a point of access and a mechanism by which people can connect with their government. Political scientists also explore interest groups, on the one hand, as valuable avenues by which people can influence the policy process and, on the other hand, as resources for policy makers. In this section, we consider various perspectives on the role of interest groups in a democracy, the diverse value that interest groups confer, and the drawbacks of interest groups.

Interest Groups and Civic Participation

Scholars who study civic engagement acknowledge the significant ways in which interest groups channel civic participation. Interest groups afford a way for people to band together to influence government as a *collective force*. Interest groups also seek to involve *individuals* more actively in the political process by encouraging them to vote and to communicate their views one-on-one to their elected officials. In addition, interest groups assist in the engagement of *communities* by providing a forum through which people can come together and form an association. Importantly, too, interest groups offer an alternative means of participation to individuals who are disenchanted with the two-party system. By taking part in interest groups, individuals, acting together, perform important roles in the polity not only by communicating their viewpoints to policy makers but also by providing a medium that other people can use to express their opinions.

Pluralist Theory Versus Elite Theory

An interest group can represent a wide variety of interests, as in the case of a community Chamber of Commerce that serves as an umbrella organization for local businesses. Alternatively, an interest group can restrict itself to a narrower focus, as does the Society for the Preservation and Encouragement of Barbershop Quartet Singing. Scholars who support

How Group Participation Has Changed in the United States

THEN (1960s)	NOW (2011)
Individuals joined bowling leagues, civic associations, and community service organizations.	People join Internet-based organizations and use social-networking sites to keep in touch with others who share their personal and public interests.
Many people entertained and socialized a great deal at home.	People are more likely to visit with friends and relatives in restaurants, cafés, and other public settings, as well as online through "virtual visits."
Groups used traditional activities to communicate their interests to policy makers, including letter writing and lobbying.	Groups rely on traditional activities but also increasingly use new technologies to communicate with members, to fund-raise, and to lobby policy makers.

WHAT'S NEXT?

> What new media technologies and strategies might shape how interest groups organize and mobilize members in the future?

> Are there *negative* consequences to relying on the Internet as an organizing tool? What obstacles will some Internet-based organizations face in mobilizing their supporters around a given issue?

> In what ways will technology change how policy makers are influenced in the future?

pluralist theory
a theory that holds that policy making is a competition among diverse interest groups that ensure the representation of individual interests

elite theory
a theory that holds that a group of wealthy, educated individuals wields most political power

pluralist theory emphasize how important it is for a democracy to have large numbers of diverse interest groups representing a wide variety of views.[9] Indeed, pluralists view the policy-making process as a crucial competition among diverse groups whose members attempt to influence policy in numerous settings, including agencies in the executive branch of government, Congress, and the courts.[10] Pluralists believe that interest groups are essential players in democracy because they ensure that individual interests are represented in the political arena *even if some individuals opt not to participate*. Like some of the founders, pluralists argue that individuals' liberties can be protected only through a proliferation of groups representing diverse competing interests, so that no one group dominates.

Pluralists believe, moreover, that interest groups provide a structure for political participation and help ensure that individuals follow the rules in participating in civic society. Following the rules means using positive channels for government action rather than extreme tactics such as assassinations, coups, and other forms of violence. Pluralists also stress that groups' varying assets tend to counterbalance one another. Pluralists contend that this is frequently the case with many policy debates. And so although an industry association such as the American Petroleum Institute, an interest group for the oil and natural gas industry, may have a lot of money at its disposal, an environmental group opposing the industry, such as Greenpeace, may have a large membership base from which to launch grassroots activism.

Proponents of elite theory dispute some claims of pluralist theory. In particular, elite theorists point to the overwhelming presence of elites as political decision makers. According to **elite theory,** a ruling class composed of wealthy, educated individuals wields most of the power in government and also within the top universities, corporations, the military, and media outlets. (See "Thinking Critically About Democracy.") Elite theorists claim that despite appearances that the political system is accessible to all, elites hold disproportionate power in the United States. They also emphasize that elites commonly use that power to protect their own economic interests, frequently by ensuring the continuation of the status quo. And so though nonelites represented by interest groups may occasionally win political victories, elites control the direction of major policies. But elite theorists posit that there is mobility into the elite structure. They emphasize that (in contrast to the situation in aristocracies) talented and industrious individuals from nonelite backgrounds can attain elite status in a democracy, often through education. This mobility, they say, gives the political system an even greater façade of accessibility.

Although these theories offer competing explanations for the role and motivation of interest groups in the United States, many political scientists agree that aspects of both theories are true: elites do have disproportionate influence in policy making, but that power is

THINKING CRITICALLY ABOUT DEMOCRACY

SHOULD CORPORATIONS AND LABOR UNIONS BE ABLE TO SPONSOR UNLIMITED CAMPAIGN ADVERTISEMENTS?

The Issue: During the 2008 Democratic primary, a nonprofit conservative interest group, Citizens United, produced a critical film about then–presidential candidate Hillary Clinton. The group sought to have commercials promoting its film aired on television but was prevented from doing so because a federal court ruled that the commercials violated provisions of the Bipartisan Campaign Reform Act of 2002, which banned corporations, labor unions, and other organizations from independent expenditures designed to influence the outcome of an election.

The case wound its way to the U.S. Supreme Court, which had to decide whether collective entities such as labor unions and corporations enjoy the same rights as individuals when it comes to electioneering speech—that is, do these organizations have the same right to unlimited speech (in the form of paid campaign commercials) that individuals do?

Yes: In fact, the Supreme Court ruled that corporations and labor unions do enjoy these same rights. Many conservatives argue that organizations, including corporations, consist of individuals who form associations, and that the Constitution protects not only free speech but also freedom of association.

In writing the opinion of the Court, Justice Anthony Kennedy noted, "If the First Amendment has any force, it prohibits Congress from fining or jailing citizens, or associations of citizens, for simply engaging in political speech."*

No: Critics of the decision argue that it facilitates unmitigated corporate influence in political campaigns. Saying that organizations and corporations share in the protected rights that individuals enjoy detracts from their protection as individual human rights.

In addition, many liberal critics argue that enabling these organizations to spend freely to influence campaigns will have a detrimental effect on campaigns. In his criticism of the decision, President Barack Obama called it "a major victory for big oil, Wall Street banks, health insurance companies and the other powerful interests that marshal their power every day in Washington to drown out the voices of everyday Americans."**

Other approaches: In light of the Supreme Court's ruling in *Citizens United v. the Federal Election Commission,* some groups maintain that voters need to be increasingly skeptical of claims made by organizations and corporations about political candidates. In effect, some interest groups recognize that corporations and labor unions are only as powerful as average Americans enable them to be. The availability of technology provides a medium for average citizens to get both information and their own opinions out in the public arena, thus potentially mitigating the effect of the influence of associations.

What do you think?

① Do you believe that enabling corporations and labor unions to purchase unlimited independent expenditure ads is a protected right?

② What will be the effect of this decision, in your view?

③ How can average Americans get their opinions about candidates heard? How can they find out whether allegations made by associations are accurate?

*www.nytimes.com/2010/01/22/us/politics/22scotus.html.   **Ibid.

---

checked by interest groups. Undisputed is that interest groups are an essential feature of American democracy and provide an important medium through which individuals can exercise some control over their government.

Key Functions of Interest Groups

Many Americans join interest groups, and yet interest groups have a generally negative reputation. For example, it has been said of many a politician that he or she is "in the pockets of the special interests." This statement suggests that the politician is not making decisions based on conscience or the public interest but, rather, has been "bought." This notion is closely linked to the ideas held by elite theorists, who argue that elites' disproportionate share of influence negatively affects the ability of the "average Jill or Joe" to get the government to do what she or he wants it to. Yet despite the criticisms frequently leveled by politicians, pundits, and the populace about interest groups' efforts to influence government, they serve several vital functions in the policy-making process in the United States:

- *Interest groups educate the public about policy issues.* Messages from interest groups abound. For example, thanks to organizations such as Mothers Against Drunk Drivers (MADD), most people are aware of the dangers of drinking and driving. In educating the public, interest groups often provide a vehicle for civic discourse, so that genuine dialogue about policy problems and potential solutions is part of the national agenda.

- *Interest groups provide average citizens with an avenue of access to activism.* Anyone can join or form an interest group. Although wealthy and well-educated people are most likely to do so, interest groups can speak for all kinds of people on all kinds of issues. Historically in the United States, groups have been significant forces for advocates of civil rights for African Americans[11] as well as for supporters of equal rights for women,[12] gays and lesbians, and ethnic minorities. Even you and your fellow students can form an interest group. At Swarthmore College, a small number of students formed the Genocide Intervention Network, a group concerned about the genocide in Darfur that became a full-fledged interest group.

- *Interest groups mobilize citizens and stimulate them to participate in civic and political affairs.* Some people are "turned off" by politics because they feel that neither the Democratic nor the Republican party represents their views. In these cases, interest groups, with their typically narrower area of focus, can sometimes fill the void. Moreover, interest groups nurture community involvement by encouraging the formation of local chapters of larger interest groups. They support public education activities by private citizens. And interest groups not only can facilitate the ongoing conversation of democracy between people and their government officials but also encourage voting.

- *Interest groups perform electoral functions.* By endorsing and rating candidates and advertising their positions, interest groups provide voters with cues as to which candidates best represent their views. Interest groups also mobilize campaign volunteers and voters. These activities facilitate informed civic participation.

- *Interest groups provide information and expertise to policy makers.* The private sector often has greater resources than the public sector and can be a source of meaningful data and information for policy makers on pressing social issues.

- *Interest groups can protect the common good.* The federal government is structured so that only one individual (the president) is elected from a national constituency. Interest groups can work to protect the nation's interest as a whole rather than just the needs of a specific constituency.

- *Interest groups are an integral part of the government's system of checks and balances.* Interest groups often "check" one another's influence with competing interests, and they can similarly check the actions of policy makers.

The Downside of Interest Groups

Despite the valuable functions of interest groups, certain criticisms of these organizations are valid. Interest groups do contribute to the appearance of (and sometimes the reality of) corruption in the political system. Indeed, there are various criticisms of the "interest group state." Former president Jimmy Carter bemoaned the influence of special interests, saying that they are "the single greatest threat to the proper functioning of our democratic system," and former president Ronald Reagan charged that interest groups are "placing out of focus our constitutional balance."[13]

Another criticism is that interest groups and their political action committee (PAC) fundraising arms (which we consider briefly later in this chapter and in more detail in Chapter 9) make money a vital force in American politics. By contributing large sums of money to political campaigns, interest groups' PACs make campaigns expensive and often lopsided; candidates without well-stuffed campaign war chests have a difficult, if not impossible, task in challenging those who receive large PAC contributions. Money also changes the nature of campaigns, making them less engaging for citizens on a grassroots level and more reliant on the mass media. These concerns have been exacerbated by a 2010 U.S. Supreme Court ruling that enables corporations and labor unions to spend money freely on political ads supporting or targeting candidates for federal office, and allows corporations and unions to buy issue advertisements even in the last days of political campaigns. Critics, including President Obama, say these rule changes will increase the importance of money in political campaigns and will enable corporations to exert greater influence over the electoral process.

Interest groups, moreover, are faulted with strengthening the advantages enjoyed by incumbents. Most interest groups want access to policy makers, regardless of these elected officials' party identification. Realizing that the people already in office are likely to be re-elected, interest groups use their resources disproportionately to support incumbent candidates. Doing so increases incumbency advantage even further by improving the odds against a challenger.

Finally, although the option to form an interest group is open to any and all activists and would-be activists, elites are more likely to establish and to dominate interest groups than are nonelites. This fact skews the policy process in favor of elites. Interest group activism is much more prominent among the wealthy, the white, the upper-middle class, and the educated than among the poor, the nonwhite, the working class, and the less educated. Although Internet-based interest groups have been particularly effective in attracting young people and others not traditionally drawn to such organizations, many of the most effective national interest groups remain dominated by traditional interest-group populations.

Who Joins Interest Groups, and Why?

People are not all equally likely to join or form interest groups, and this reality has serious consequences for the ability of interest groups to represent everyone's views. Political scientists agree that income and education tend to be the best predictors of interest group membership. That said, enormous diversity exists in the types of people who choose to join or form interest groups.

Patterns of Membership

Interest group participation is related to three demographic characteristics: income, social class, and education. People with higher incomes are more likely to participate in interest groups than those with lower incomes. Also, many surveys show that those who identify themselves as upper-middle or middle class are more likely to join interest groups than those who self-identify as lower-middle or working class. Similarly, higher education levels are a strong predictor of interest group participation. But interest group participation also frequently reflects one's occupation: people tend to belong to associations related to their work.

INTEREST GROUP PARTICIPATION BASED ON OCCUPATION There are several reasons for interest group membership patterns, some of which, as we shall see, are interconnected. For example, people with higher incomes have more disposable income to spend on membership dues for organizations. They are also likely to have occupations in which interest group activity is useful (or even required, as in some professional fields such as the law).

Doctors and lawyers, for example, are likely to be members of professional associations such as the American Medical Association (AMA) and the American Bar Association. These organizations give incentives for membership, such as accreditation of qualified professionals. They also confer benefits by providing various services to members and by attempting to influence government policy on members' behalf. The AMA accredits qualified physicians, promotes opportunities for continuing education to members, and lobbies the government on policy issues related to health care. For example, during the debate over the 2010 health care reform legislation, the AMA sponsored television ads opposing a 21 percent cut in Medicare payments to physicians, and urged viewers to call their senator asking them to "fix the Medicare access problem."[14]

Workers such as teachers and tradespeople are likely to belong to labor unions.[15] Many labor unions are influential in local politics, generating grassroots support for candidates through their membership base. A few of the national labor unions, especially the National Education Association (NEA), the largest teachers' union in the country, and the American Federation of Labor-Congress of Industrial Organizations (AFL-CIO), an organization of many different labor unions, are strongly influential in national politics.

Executives in business and industry are likely to be members of industry-specific and general business organizations that advocate on behalf of their members. All of these professional associations, labor unions, and business organizations are types of interest groups.

INTEREST GROUP PARTICIPATION AND SOCIAL CLASS Differentiating the influence of income from that of class can be difficult when examining the impact of social class on the likelihood of joining an interest group. But in general, people who identify themselves as working class are less likely to have been socialized to participate in interest groups, with the important exception of labor unions, which historically have been most likely to organize working-class occupations. As we considered in Chapter 6, an important predictor of political participation (and interest group participation, specifically) is whether a person learns to take part and join from a young age. If your mother participated in your town's historical preservation society, and your father attended meetings of the local Amnesty International chapter, you are likely to view those behaviors as "what people do" and do them yourself. If you come from a working-class family, you are generally less likely to see your parents engage in these participatory behaviors, rendering you similarly less likely to participate. Although scholars trace much of the lack of participation of working-class people to how they are socialized, the overlapping occurrence of working-class status and lower income is also a factor.[16] That is, working-class people are likely to have lower incomes and less job security than their middle-class counterparts. Thus they may not be able to afford membership dues and contributions to interest groups or may not have access to child care that would allow them to attend meetings. Their lower likelihood of owning a computer limits their chances of taking an active role in Internet-based groups. Or they may simply lack the leisure time to participate.

INTEREST GROUP PARTICIPATION AND EDUCATION Educational attainment also has a strong impact on whether a person will join an interest group. One recent study surveyed 19- to 23-year-olds and found that those who were college students were more than twice as likely to join a politically motivated interest group as their age-group peers who did not attend college.[17] Individuals with higher education levels are more likely to be informed about issues and more willing to invest the time and energy in joining an interest group that represents their views. They may also be more likely to understand how important interest groups are in shaping public policy.

College students are among the most avid participants in Internet-based activist groups. But "belonging" to these groups varies a great deal (not unlike the situation in "real-world" interest groups). A member of an Internet-based interest group may play a highly active role—communicating with other members regularly, attending rallies and other campus events, and taking concrete actions such as signing an Internet petition and participating in a protest. Or members may be more passive: they may limit their activity to reading the regular e-mails from the group that inform them of issues and events, and may only occasionally participate. Or they may be members of a group in name only. But this phenomenon is not unique to Internet-based groups. Many interest groups are dominated by a cadre of committed activists supported by "sometimes-activists." And nearly every group has a contingent of "members" who signed up mainly for the free T-shirt, tote bag, or umbrella.

Motivations for Joining Interest Groups

Some people may join an interest group for the benefits they can gain. Others may gravitate to a group sponsoring a particular cause. Still others may become members of a group for the simple reason that they want to meet new people. Recognizing that

solidary incentives
motivation to join an interest group based on the companionship and the satisfaction derived from socializing with others that it offers

purposive incentives
motivation to join an interest group based on the belief in the group's cause from an ideological or a moral standpoint

individuals have various motivations for joining, interest groups typically provide a menu of incentives for membership. As Figure 7.1 shows, for example, the National Association for the Advancement of Colored People (NAACP) offers a wide range of motivations for people to join the group. In doing so, the NAACP, like many other interest groups, attempts to attract as many members as possible.

SOLIDARY INCENTIVES Some people join interest groups because they offer **solidary incentives**—the feeling of belonging, companionship, friendship, and the satisfaction derived from socializing with others. Solidary incentives are closely linked to Robert Putnam's idea of social capital: both solidary incentives and social capital are related to the psychological satisfaction derived from civic participation. For example, a person might join the Sierra Club because she wants to participate in activities with other people who enjoy hiking or care deeply about wilderness protection. Your uncle might join the National Rifle Association because he likes to compete in shooting contests and wants to get to know others who do the same.

PURPOSIVE INCENTIVES People also join interest groups because of **purposive incentives,** that is, because they believe in the group's cause from an ideological or a moral standpoint. Interest groups pave the way for people to take action with likeminded people. And so you might join People for the Ethical Treatment of Animals (PETA) because you strongly object to animal abuse and want to work with others to prevent cruelty to animals. A friend who is passionately pro-life might join the National Right to Life Committee (NRLC), whereas your pro-choice cousin might join NARAL Pro-Choice America (formerly the National Abortion Reproductive Rights Action League).

The Internet is a particularly effective forum for attracting membership through purposive incentives. Accessible anyplace and anytime, the Internet provides resources for you to join an interest group even during a bout of insomnia at 3:00 a.m. Suppose a conversation earlier in the day got you thinking anew about the brutal genocidal conflict in Darfur. In those dark predawn hours, you can google "save Darfur" and within seconds have a variety of access points for becoming civically engaged by participating in an interest group. Some interest groups may ask you to contribute money; others may urge you to sign an online petition or to call the White House to make your opinions known. You may follow other interest groups on Twitter, enabling you to learn about demonstrations sponsored by other groups right on your college campus and in your community. You may even find out about state and national

POLITICAL INQUIRY

FIGURE 7.1 ■ SOLIDARY, PURPOSIVE, AND ECONOMIC INCENTIVES TO JOIN AN INTEREST GROUP What is the NAACP, and what does this interest group advocate? What solidary incentives does the membership appeal described in this figure mention? What purposive and economic incentives does it describe?

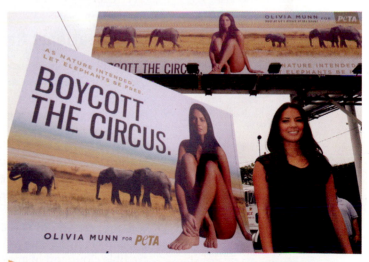

> Interest groups often rely on celebrities to advance their issue positions. Here, actor and TV host Olivia Munn stands beside her image on a PETA billboard targeting the use of elephants and other animals in circuses. Celebrities Demi Moore, Darren Aronofsky, Jennie Garth, and Kyra Sedgwick have all publicly condemned circuses that use animals.

demonstrations. The media contacts provided by online interest groups make it easy for you to write a letter to an editor, attempting to convince others of your views. Just learning about the wide variety of activities available can make you feel that you are "doing something" about a cause you believe in.

economic incentives

motivation to join an interest group because the group works for policies that will provide members with material benefits

ECONOMIC INCENTIVES   Many people join interest groups because of material or **economic incentives;** that is, they want to support groups that work for policies that will provide them with economic benefits. For example, the National Association of Police Organizations lobbies Congress concerning many appropriations measures that could affect its membership, including bills that would provide or increase funding for Community Oriented Policing Services (COPS) programs, bulletproof vests, and overtime pay for first responders to disasters.

Nearly all corporate and labor interest groups offer economic incentives to their members. They sometimes do so by advocating for policies that support business or labor in general, such as policies focused on the minimum wage, regulations concerning workplace conditions, and laws governing family leave or health coverage.

Other interest groups offer smaller-scale economic benefits to members. Many Americans over age 50 join the American Association of Retired Persons (AARP) because of the discounts members receive on hotels, airfares, and car rentals. Other organizations provide discounts on health insurance, special deals from merchants, or low-interest credit cards.

Most people join and remain in interest groups for a combination of reasons. A person may initially join an interest group for purposive incentives and then realize some solidary benefits and remain in the group because of the friendships formed. Or someone may join a professional association for the economic benefits but then develop rewarding social networks. Many individuals who join and stay in interest groups do so because of overlapping incentives.

How Interest Groups Succeed

Given that interest groups attempt to influence all kinds of policies, why are some interest groups better at getting what they want than others? Political scientists agree on various factors that influence whether an interest group will succeed. These factors include the interest group's *organizational resources,* the tools it has at its disposal to help achieve its goals; and its *organizational environment,* the setting in which it attempts to achieve those goals. (See "Global Context.")

Organizational Resources

The effectiveness of interest groups in influencing government policy often depends on the resources they use to sway policy makers.[18] Interest groups rely on two key types of resources: membership, the people who belong to a given group; and financial resources, the money the group can spend to exert influence.

HOW MEMBERSHIP AFFECTS SUCCESS   A large membership enhances an interest group's influence because policy makers are more likely to take note of the group's position. The age-old concept of "strength in numbers" applies when it comes to interest groups. The sheer number of a group's membership is often an important factor in forcing policy makers, the media, and the public to pay attention to an issue. Among the largest U.S. interest groups is the American Association of Retired Persons (AARP), which boasts a membership of more than 35 million people. This vast size gives the organization incredible clout and historically has made policy makers unwilling to take on any issue that would unleash the wrath of AARP's formidable membership. For example, for years many economic analysts have suggested increasing the age at which people become eligible to receive Social Security. They reason that the average life span has risen significantly since the eligibility age was set, and that people are working longer because they remain healthier

AMNESTY INTERNATIONAL

On many college campuses throughout the United States, you may find a college chapter of the human rights organization Amnesty International. The group strives to protect human rights by informing the public about violations of human rights, and has attempted to exert pressure on governments and on political and corporate organizations. The group especially seeks to protect those whose rights of freedom of speech and religion have been violated, and political dissidents who have been imprisoned and tortured. The organization familiar to many throughout the United States is part of a much larger international network. In fact, Amnesty International boasts 2.2 million members in 150 countries.

> **How can international organizations help protect human rights?**

In the autumn of 1960, two Portuguese students raised their wineglasses in a toast to "freedom," and were arrested and sentenced to seven years in prison. (Portugal was then under the dictatorial rule of António Salazar.) When British lawyer Peter Benenson learned of the students' plight in 1961, he wrote an article for the newspaper *The Observer*, and so began the organization that has sought to ensure the protection of human rights internationally for decades—Amnesty International. Its goals, according to the Amnesty International Web site, are as follows:

We believe human rights abuses anywhere are the concern of people everywhere.

So, outraged by human rights abuses but inspired by hope for a better world, we work to improve people's lives through campaigning and international solidarity.

Our mission is to conduct research and generate action to prevent and end grave abuses of human rights and to demand justice for those whose rights have been violated.*

In their pursuit of these goals, Amnesty International members have relied on diverse strategies. Whereas student members may conduct letter-writing campaigns, campus vigils, and protests to call attention to the violations of human rights, the organization uses other tactics, including

- sending experts to talk with victims
- observing trials
- interviewing local officials
- meeting with human rights activists
- monitoring global and local media
- publishing detailed reports
- informing the news media
- publicizing their concerns in documents, leaflets, posters, advertisements, newsletters, and Web sites**

*www.amnesty.org/en/who-we-are/about-amnesty-international.
**www.amnesty.org/en/who-we-are/faq#how-ai-works.

> Since 1961, Amnesty International has sought to protect human rights throughout the world. Here, members of the organization stage a protest in front of the Chinese Embassy in Tokyo, Japan, after China executed a Japanese man for drug smuggling in 2010. The sign at right reads "China is supposed to be a generous nation."

longer. But this potential policy solution has long simmered on the back burner. The reason? Politicians in Congress and the White House have not wanted to incur the disapproval of the AARP's members, who would widely oppose increasing the eligibility age and might respond by voting unsympathetic officials out of office. While he was Speaker of the House of Representatives, Dennis Hastert (R-Illinois) remarked that he took "the AARP very seriously"—as had Newt Gingrich when he was Speaker before—and that "Republicans had been courting AARP for some time, listening to them, engaging in a give-and-take dialogue that none of the capital's pundits even suspected was going on."[19]

But size is not the only important aspect of an interest group's membership. The *cohesion* of a group, or how strongly unified it is, also matters to participants and to policy makers.[20] For example, the Human Rights Campaign (HRC) lobbies for federal legislation to end discrimination on the basis of sexual orientation and provides research to elected officials and policy makers on issues of importance to people who are gay, lesbian, bisexual, or transgender. The HRC has a membership of about 600,000, but because the organization limits its advocacy to issues affecting gay, lesbian, bisexual, and transgender people, it is an extremely cohesive association.

Another significant aspect of an interest group's membership is its *intensity*. Intensity is a measure of how strongly members feel about the issues they are targeting. Certain kinds of organizations, including pro-life interest groups such as the National Right to Life Committee, environmental groups such as the Sierra Club and Greenpeace, and animal rights groups such as People for the Ethical Treatment of Animals (PETA), are known for sustaining high levels of intensity. These organizations are more adept at attracting new members and younger members than are older, more entrenched kinds of groups. These newer, youthful members are a significant force behind the persistence and intensity of these groups.

The *demographics* of a group's membership also may increase its success. Members who know policy makers personally and have access to them mean greater influence for the group.[21] Other demographic attributes also matter. Members who are well educated, geographically dispersed (because they can influence a broader network of policy makers than a geographically consolidated membership), or affluent tend to have more influence. Policy makers perceive these attributes as important because the groups' membership is more likely to lobby and to contribute financial resources on behalf of the organization's cause.

HOW FINANCIAL RESOURCES AFFECT SUCCESS

For an interest group, money can buy power.[22] Money fuels the hiring of experienced and effective staff and lobbyists, who communicate directly with policy makers, as well as the undertaking of initiatives that will increase the group's membership. Money also funds the raising of more money.[23] For example, the Business Roundtable represents the interests of 150 chief executive officers of the largest U.S. companies, including American Express, General Electric, IBM, and Verizon. In 2009, it spent over $13 million lobbying the president, Congress, and several cabinet departments for policies that would benefit its member corporations, their shareholders, and their member corporations' 10 million employees. Issues of concern to the Business Roundtable include policies such as Securities and Exchange Commission rules, laws concerning corporate ethics, and reform to the nation's class action lawsuit regulations. In the aftermath of the 2010 U.S. Supreme Court decision that enables corporations and labor unions to spend their resources targeting or supporting specific candidates for office, including individuals running for Congress and the presidency, many critics believe that the financial resources of an organization will play an even greater role in determining the group's success in the future.

political action committee (PAC)

a group that raises and spends money to influence the outcome of an election

Sometimes interest groups form a separate entity, called a **political action committee (PAC),** whose specific goal is to raise and spend money to influence the outcome of elections. (See Chapter 9 for a detailed discussion of PACs.) Interest groups use PACs to shape the composition of government; that is, they contribute money to the campaigns of favored candidates, particularly incumbents who are likely to be reelected.[24] That is just one specific example of the influence that interest groups' money has on politics. Interest groups representing the economic concerns of members—business, industry, and union groups—generally tend to have the greatest financial resources for all these activities.[25]

Organizational Environment

The setting in which an interest group attempts to achieve its goals is the *organizational environment.* Key factors in the organizational environment include its leadership and the presence or absence of opposition from other groups.[26]

LEADERSHIP Strong, charismatic leaders contribute to the influence of an interest group by raising public awareness of the group and its activities, by enhancing its reputation, and by making the organization attractive to new members and contributors. An example of a dynamic leader who has increased his interest group's effectiveness is James P. Hoffa, the son of powerful Teamsters Union president Jimmy Hoffa, who disappeared without a trace in 1975. He has served since 1999 as the president of the Teamsters Union, which primarily represents unionized truck drivers. The younger Hoffa—a graduate of the University of Michigan Law School—is lauded by many teamsters as an intelligent, energetic, and charismatic leader whose skills have increased the size and power of the union.

OPPOSITION The presence of opposing interest groups can also have an impact on an interest group's success. When an interest group is "the only game in town" on a particular issue, policy makers are more likely to rely on that group's views. But if groups with opposing views are also attempting to influence policy, getting policy makers to act strongly in any one group's favor is more difficult. Consider this example: Hotel Employees and the Restaurant Employees International Union supported increasing the minimum wage, but the National Restaurant Association, which advocates for restaurant owners, opposed a minimum wage hike, arguing that the higher wage would cut into restaurant owners' profits or limit its members' ability to hire as many employees as before. In the face of such opposing interests, policy makers are often more likely to compromise than to give any one group exactly what it wants.

Although each of these factors—organizational resources and the organizational environment—influences how powerful an interest group will be, no single formula determines an interest group's clout. Sometimes an interest group has powerful advocates in Congress who support its cause. Other times, a single factor can prove essential to an interest group's success.

Types of Interest Groups

A wide variety of political interest groups exercise their muscle on virtually every type of policy question, from those concerning birth (such as what is the minimum hospital stay an insurance company must cover after a woman gives birth?) to matters related to death (such as what are the practices by funeral directors that should be banned by the government?). Despite the broad range of issues around which interest groups coalesce, political scientists generally categorize interest groups by what kinds of issues concern them and who benefits from the groups' activities. For example, some interest groups focus primarily on economic decisions that affect their members. Other interest groups pursue ideological, issue-based, or religion-based goals. Yet others lobby for benefits for society at large, and still others advocate on behalf of foreign interests.

Economic Interest Groups

When economic interest groups lobby government, the benefits for their members can be direct or indirect. In some cases, the economic benefits flow directly from the government to the interest group members, as when an agricultural interest group successfully presses for *subsidies,* monies given by the government to the producers of a particular crop or product, often to influence the volume of production of that commodity. For example, in 2008 the finance, insurance, and real estate sector spent nearly $460 million on federal lobbying efforts. These same industries were among the prime beneficiaries of both federal government bailouts and the 2009 economic stimulus package.

In other instances, economic interest groups lobby for or against policies that, though not directly benefiting their members, have an indirect impact on the interest group's membership. That was the case when many unions, including the AFL-CIO, lobbied against the creation of private Social Security accounts, fearing that this privatization would result in a decrease in Social Security retirement benefits for their members.

CORPORATE AND BUSINESS INTERESTS   Large corporate and smaller business interest groups are among the most successful U.S. pressure groups with respect to their influence on government. These groups typically seek policies that benefit a particular company or industry. For example, the Motion Picture Association of America (MPAA) represents the seven major U.S. manufacturers and distributors of movies and television programs. The MPAA lobbies policy makers (often by hosting prerelease screenings of films and lavish dinner receptions) with the goal of securing the passage of antipiracy laws, which aim to prevent the illegal copying of movies and to penalize individuals who sell them. This advocacy benefits the group's members and their employees, because antipiracy laws help to ensure that any copies of movies sold are legal and thus profitable for MPAA members.

Certain industries' associations are stand-alone organizations, such as the National Association of Realtors and the National Beer Wholesalers Association. But industry and business groups also commonly advocate for policies using **umbrella organizations,** which are interest groups representing groups of industries or corporations. Examples of umbrella business organizations include the Business Roundtable, which represents the chief executive officers (CEOs) of 150 large corporations, and the U.S. Chamber of Commerce, a federation of local chambers of commerce that represents about 3 million large and small businesses.

Often corporate and business groups compete against labor groups. This rivalry is a natural result of having different constituencies. Typically, corporate interests advocate on behalf of the company owners, stockholders, and officers, whereas labor unions champion employees' interests.

LABOR INTERESTS   Like corporate interest groups, labor interest groups include both national labor unions and umbrella organizations of unions. The AFL-CIO, an umbrella organization made up of more than fifty labor unions, is among the nation's most powerful interest groups, although its influence has waned over the past several decades as union membership has declined generally. During the 1950s and 1960s, nearly 35 percent of all U.S. workers were union members. By 1983, membership had decreased to about 20 percent, and today about 12 percent of all U.S. workers belong to unions. In part, this decline stems from changes in the U.S. economy, with many highly unionized manufacturing jobs being replaced by less unionized service sector jobs. Given the drop in union membership, labor interest groups' influence has also waned, although the unions' reduced clout is in part due to a lack of cohesion among labor union members.

Like corporate and business interest groups, labor unions pursue policies that benefit their members, although these are frequently at odds with the positions of corporate and business interest groups. And like corporate and business interest groups, labor unions sometimes press for policies that primarily benefit their own members, and at other times they promote policies that benefit all union workers and sometimes even non-union workers. For example, in 2007 the AFL-CIO successfully lobbied Congress for an increase in the federal minimum wage, which benefited the members of many unions whose contracts are based on federally mandated minimum wages but also many non-union workers who are paid the minimum wage.

AGRICULTURAL INTERESTS   Of all types of U.S. interest groups, agricultural interest groups probably have the most disproportionate amount of influence given the small number of farmers and farmworkers in the country relative to the general population. And because agricultural producers in the United States are also very diverse, ranging from small farmers to huge multinational agribusinesses, it is not surprising to see divergent opinions among people employed in the agricultural sector.

umbrella organizations
interest groups that represent collective groups of industries or corporations

The largest agricultural interest group today is the American Farm Bureau Federation (AFBF), which grew out of the network of county farm bureaus formed in the 1920s. With more than 5 million farming members, the AFBF is one of the most influential interest groups in the United States, primarily because of its close relations with key agricultural policy makers. It takes stands on a wide variety of issues that have an impact on farmers, including subsidies, budget and tax policies, immigration policies that affect farmworkers, energy policies, trade policies, and environmental policies. For example, when President Obama sought to end direct subsidies to farmers with sales of over $500,000 as part of his 2010 budget proposal, the opposition by agricultural interest groups, including the AFBF, killed the proposal in Congress.

In addition to large-scale, general agricultural interest groups such as the AFBF, there is an industry-specific interest group representing producers for nearly every crop or commodity produced in the agricultural sector. Table 7.1 shows that corn producers are among the most effective groups in securing subsidies for their growers. Between 1995 and 2006, more than 1.5 million corn farmers across the United States received in excess of $56 billion in government subsidies. Table 7.1 reveals as well that the producers of several other crops—wheat, cotton, soybeans, and rice—have managed to secure subsidies of more than $10 billion each from 1995 to 2006.

TRADE AND PROFESSIONAL INTERESTS Nearly every professional occupation—doctor, lawyer, engineer, chiropractor, dentist, accountant, and even video game developer—has a trade or professional group that focuses on its interests. These interest groups take stands on a variety of policy matters, many of which indirectly affect their membership.

Public and Ideological Interest Groups

Public interest groups typically are concerned with a broad range of issues that affect the populace at large. These include social and economic issues such as Social Security reform and revision of the federal tax structure, as well as environmental causes such as clean air

TABLE 7.1

Top 10 Crops Receiving Federal Subsidies as Direct Payments to Farmers (1995–2009)

Rank	Program	Subsidy Total 1995–2009
1	Corn	$12,927,171,703
2	Wheat	$6,969,982,923
3	Soybeans	$4,133,353,401
4	Upland cotton	$3,820,779,718
5	Rice	$2,637,683,165
6	Sorghum	$1,207,917,786
7	Barley	$497,873,693
8	Peanuts	$481,060,291
9	Sunflower	$ 91,536,061
10	Canola	$34,389,538

SOURCE: The Environmental Working Group, http://farm.ewg.org/farm/region.php?fips=00000.

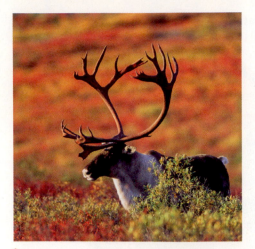

> The Sierra Club and other public interest groups that lobby Congress about environmental issues work to protect public lands such as the Denali National Wildlife Refuge, home to herds of caribou and other species.

and clean water. Examples of public interest groups include the National Taxpayers Union, Common Cause, and the Sierra Club. Usually, the results of the efforts of a particular public interest group's advocacy cannot be limited to the group's members; rather, these results are **collective goods** (sometimes called *public goods*)— outcomes that are shared by the general public. Collective goods are "collective" and "public" because they cannot be denied to people who are not group members. For example, if the Sierra Club succeeds in winning passage of an environmental bill that improves water and air quality, *everyone* shares in the benefits. Specifically, it is impossible to make pure drinking water and clean air a privilege restricted to Sierra Club members.

The nature of collective goods—the fact that they cannot be limited to those who worked to achieve them—creates a **free rider problem,** the situation whereby someone derives a benefit from the actions of others. You are probably familiar with the free rider problem. Suppose, for example, that you form a study group to prepare for an exam, and four of the five members of the group come to a study session having prepared responses to essay questions. The fifth member shows up but is unprepared. The unprepared group member then copies the others' responses, memorizes them, and does just as well on the exam. The same thing happens to interest groups that advocate for a collective good. The group may work hard to improve the quality of life, but the benefits of its work are enjoyed by many who do not contribute to the effort.

Economist Mancur Olson asserted in his **rational choice theory** that from an economic perspective it is not rational for people to participate in a collective action designed to achieve a collective good when they can secure that good without participating. So, in the study group example, from Olson's perspective, it is not economically rational to spend your time preparing for an exam when you can get the benefits of preparation without the work. Of course, taking this idea to the extreme, one might conclude that if no one advocated for collective goods, they would not exist, and thus free riders could not derive their benefit.

Current scholarship on civic engagement has focused on the free rider problem. Researchers have investigated the increased benefits of widespread citizen participation in interest groups, citing evidence that groups with higher levels of public participation may be more effective, and may provide greater collective benefits, than groups with lower rates of participation. Studies also indicate that through the act of participating in civic life, individuals derive some benefit themselves in addition to the benefits created by their work. So, if the fifth person in the study group prepares for the exam, too, *all* members of the group may perform better on the exam. And if more people are civically involved in groups, then their potential to have an impact on their government increases. In addition, civic engagement scholars cite the psychic benefit to an individual of knowing that a collective good was achieved in part because of *her* participation, and these researchers also mention the other benefits derived from collective action, including solidary and purposive benefits.

CONSUMER INTERESTS   Well before attorney and activist Ralph Nader gained nationwide attention as a Green Party candidate for the presidency in 2000, he founded numerous organizations to promote the rights of consumers. In the 1970s and 1980s, these organizations lobbied primarily—and successfully—for changes in automotive design that would make cars safer. One result was the mandatory installation of harness safety belts in rear seats, which then typically had only lap belts. In 1971 Nader founded the interest group Public Citizen, which lobbies Congress, the executive branch, and the courts for openness in government and consumer issues, including auto safety, the safety of prescription drugs, and energy policy. Each year in December, the group issues a list of unsafe toys to guide gift-buyers' holiday purchases.

ENVIRONMENTAL INTERESTS   Many groups that advocate for the protection of the environment and wildlife and for the conservation of natural resources came about as a result of a broader environmental movement in the 1970s, although the Sierra Club was founded more than a century ago, in 1892. Some environmental groups, particularly Greenpeace, have been criticized in the media and by their opponents for their use of confrontational tactics. But many environmental activists say that the power of corporate in-

collective goods
outcomes shared by the general public; also called *public goods*

free rider problem
the phenomenon of someone deriving benefit from others' actions

rational choice theory
the idea that from an economic perspective it is not rational for people to participate in collective action when they can secure the collective good without participating

terests (with which they are frequently at odds) is so pervasive that they can succeed only by taking strong, direct action to protect the natural environment, thus rationalizing their sometimes extreme tactics. And so while some environmentalists follow the conventional route of lobbying legislators or advertising to raise public awareness of their causes, others camp out in trees to attempt to prevent their removal or sit on oil-drilling platforms to halt drilling into a coral reef. In addition to stalling the undesired action, the confrontational protest tactic also has the advantage of attracting media attention, which serves to increase public awareness.[27] Such environmental groups hope that they can prevent environmental destruction by embarrassing the corporation or government involved.

RELIGIOUS INTERESTS   For a long time, organized religions in the United States were essentially uninvolved in politics, partly because they were afraid of losing their tax-exempt status by becoming political entities. But formal religions increasingly have sought to make their voices heard, usually by forming political organizations separate from the actual religious organizations. Today, religious interests are among the most influential interest groups in U.S. politics.

In the early stages of their activism, Christian organizations typically were most politically effective in the Republican presidential nomination process, when the mobilization of their members could alter the outcome in low-turnout primaries. During the 1970s, several conservative Christian organizations, most notably the Moral Majority, founded by the late Reverend Jerry Falwell, were a force in national politics. The Moral Majority helped to elect Ronald Reagan, a Republican, to the presidency in 1980 and was instrumental in shaping the national agenda of the Reagan years, particularly regarding domestic policy. In 1989, another conservative Christian organization, the Christian Coalition, took shape, marking a new era in the politicization of religious groups. The Christian Coalition advocates that "people of faith have a right and a responsibility to be involved in the world around them" and emphasizes "pro-family" values.[28] During its first decade, the Christian Coalition's influence grew gradually. During the 2000 election, the organization was an important supporter of George W. Bush's candidacy for the presidency, and with his election, the group's influence has grown considerably. In the 2004 presidential election, conservative Christian organizations proved enormously important in activities such as voter registration and get-out-the-vote campaigns, thus aiding President Bush's reelection efforts.

The Christian Coalition and other religious groups—including Pax Christi USA (the national Catholic peace movement), B'nai Brith (an interest group dedicated to Jewish interests), and the Council on American-Islamic Relations (CAIR, a Muslim interest group)—also advocate for the faith-based priorities of their members. Many of these organizations have become increasingly active in state and local politics in recent years. For example, in 2010, members of CAIR vocally advocated for the construction of an Islamic center at the site of the World Trade Center, which had been destroyed in the September 11, 2001 terrorist attacks.

Foreign Interest Groups

In the United States, advocacy by interest groups is not limited to U.S.-based groups. Foreign governments, as well as international corporations based abroad, vigorously press for U.S. policies beneficial to them. Foreign governments might lobby for U.S. aid packages; corporations might work for beneficial changes to tax regulations. Often a foreign government will rely on an interest group made up of U.S. citizens of the foreign nation's heritage to promote its advocacy efforts. Indeed, one of the more influential interest groups lobbying for foreign concerns is the U.S.-based American Israel Public Affairs Committee (AIPAC), which has 65,000 members. AIPAC lobbies the U.S. government for pro-Israel foreign policies such as the grant of nearly $2.5 billion in economic and military aid for Israel in 2007. Despite its relatively small membership, AIPAC is considered highly influential because of its financial resources and well-connected membership base, which enjoys access to many policy makers.

Sometimes it is readily apparent when foreign interests are lobbying for their own causes—as, for example, when a trading partner wants better terms. But in other cases, particularly when international corporations are lobbying, it is difficult to discern where their "American" interest ends and their "foreign" interest begins. So although only U.S. citizens and legal immigrants can contribute to federal PACs, American employees of foreign companies do form and contribute to PACs. Many people would be surprised at the large amounts of money that international corporations' PACs contribute to both of the major U.S. political parties. But because many subsidiaries of these corporations are important American businesses, their lobbying activities are not necessarily a foreign encroachment on U.S. politics.

Interest Group Strategies

Interest groups use two kinds of strategies to advance their causes. *Direct strategies* involve actual contact between representatives of the interest group and policy makers. *Indirect strategies* use intermediaries to advocate for a cause or generally to attempt to persuade the public, including policy makers, to embrace the group's position.

Direct Strategies to Advance Interests

Groups often opt for direct strategies when they seek to secure passage or defeat of a specific piece of legislation. These strategies include lobbying, entering into litigation to change a law, and providing information or expert testimony to decision makers.

lobby
to communicate directly with policy makers on an interest group's behalf

LOBBYING, ISSUE NETWORKS, AND IRON TRIANGLES Interest groups hire professionals to **lobby,** or communicate directly with, policy makers on the interest groups' behalf. President Ulysses S. Grant coined the term *lobbyist* when he walked through the lobby of the Willard Hotel in Washington, D.C., and commented on the presence of "lobbyists" waiting to speak to members of Congress.

Today, lobbying is among the most common strategies that interest groups use, and the practice may include scheduled face-to-face meetings, "buttonholing" members of Congress as they walk through the Capitol, telephone calls, and receptions and special events hosted by the interest groups. The professional lobbyists whom interest groups hire are almost always lawyers, and their job is to cultivate ongoing relationships with members of Congress (and their staff) who have influence in a specific policy area. In many situations, lobbyists help navigate access to these policy makers for industry and interest group members.

Interest groups have learned that one of the most effective ways of influencing government is to hire former government officials, including cabinet officials, members of Congress, and congressional staffers, as lobbyists. Because these ex-officials often enjoy good relationships with their former colleagues and have an intimate knowledge of the policy-making process, they are particularly effective in influencing government. Frequently, this practice creates an **issue network,** the fluid web of connections among those concerned about a policy and those who create and administer the policy.

Similarly, an interest group's efficacy often depends on its having close relationships with the policy makers involved in decisions related to the group's causes. During the rough-and-tumble policy-making process, the interaction of mutual interests among a "trio" comprising (1) members of Congress, (2) executive departments and agencies (such as the Department of Agriculture or the Federal Emergency Management Agency), and (3) organized interest groups is sometimes referred to as an **iron triangle,** with each of the three players being one side of the triangle (see Figure 7.2). Although each side in an iron triangle is expected to fight on behalf of its own interests, constituents, or governmental department, the triangle often seeks a policy outcome that benefits all parts of the triangle. Often this outcome occurs because of close personal and professional relationships that develop as a result of the interactions among the sides in an issue-based triangle. And sometimes the individual players in a triangle that is focused on a particular issue—say, military policy or subsidies for tobacco growers—share a personal history, have attended the same schools, come from the same region of the country, and have even worked together at one time. Such long-term relationships can make it difficult for opposing interests to penetrate the triangle. (See Chapter 13 for further discussion of the role of iron triangles in policy making.)

LITIGATION BY INTEREST GROUPS Sometimes, interest groups challenge a policy in the courts. For example, the 2010 U.S. Supreme Court case that resulted in a drastically altered political landscape for campaign funding came as the result of a lawsuit filed by an interest group. In *Citizens United v. Federal Election Commission,* the interest group Citizens United argued that federal bans on corporate and union expenditures to promote or target candidates for federal office violated the organization's right to free speech. A 5–4 majority of Supreme Court justices agreed with the interest group, and lifted the ban.[29]

In other instances, interest groups sue to prevent a particular public policy from being enacted or to prompt a court ruling on the constitutionality of an issue. The latter was the case in 1992, when Planned Parenthood of Pennsylvania, an abortion-rights advocacy group, sued the state's governor, claiming that the state's Abortion Control Act violated the constitutional protections on abortion outlined in the Supreme Court's decision in *Roe v. Wade* (1973). In particular, Planned Parenthood argued that the clauses in the state legislation that required a pregnant woman to notify her husband, a pregnant teen to get parental consent, and any abortion seeker to satisfy a twenty-four-hour waiting period after receiving counseling presented an undue burden and violated the spirit of *Roe v. Wade.* In *Roe,* the Supreme Court had ruled that a woman's right to abortion was essentially guaranteed in the first trimester, could be regulated by the states in the second, and could be banned by the states in the third. The Supreme Court agreed to hear the Planned Parenthood case and struck down some components of the Pennsylvania legislation, including the requirement

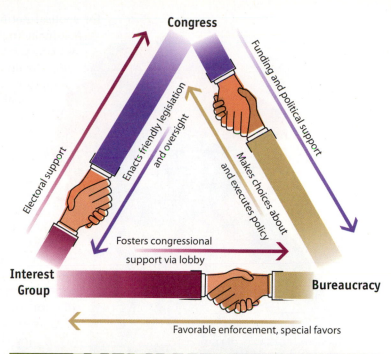

Congress

Funding and political support

Enacts friendly legislation and oversight

Makes choices about and executes policy

Electoral support

Fosters congressional support via lobby

Interest Group

Bureaucracy

Favorable enforcement, special favors

POLITICAL INQUIRY

FIGURE 7.2 ■ **AN IRON TRIANGLE** Who are the players in an iron triangle? How do interest groups benefit from their iron triangle relationships? Why do you think the triangular relationship has been described as "iron"?

issue network
the fluid web of connections among those concerned about a policy and those who create and administer the policy

iron triangle
the interaction of mutual interests among members of Congress, executive agencies, and organized interests during policy making

for spousal notification, while allowing other components not specified in *Roe,* including the parental consent requirement and the twenty-four-hour waiting period, to stand.

By litigating, interest groups can ensure that laws passed by legislatures and signed by executives are in keeping with current constitutional interpretation. By bringing their causes before the courts, they also can shape policy and encourage enforcement by executive agencies.

PROVIDING INFORMATION AND EXPERT TESTIMONY

Interest groups are one of the chief sources of information for policy makers. Interest groups have the resources to investigate the impact of policies. They have access to data, technological know-how, and a bevy of experts with extensive knowledge of the issues. Most interest groups provide information to policy makers, and policy makers understand that the information received is slanted toward the group's interest. But if competing interest groups supply information to policy makers, then policy makers can weigh the merits of the various sets of information.

Sometimes interest groups use celebrities as "experts" to testify, knowing that they will attract greater attention than most policy experts. Elmo, the furry red *Sesame Street* Muppet, testified in 2002 on behalf of a bill that would provide $2 million in federal funding to public schools for music education. The House Appropriations Subcommittee on Labor, Health and Human Services, and Education heard testimony from Elmo, who apparently is an authority on music education. Elmo told the subcommittee: "Elmo loves to sing and to dance and to make music with all his friends on *Sesame Street.* It helps Elmo learn ABCs and makes it easier for Elmo to remember things. Sometimes it makes Elmo excited, and sometimes it calms Elmo down. Elmo's teacher really likes that! My friend [American Music Conference Executive Director] Joe Lamond says some kids don't have music in school. That makes Elmo sad."[30] Other celebrities who have testified on behalf of causes important to them include Bono, the lead singer of the group U2, who testified concerning debt relief for African nations; actor Michael J. Fox, who testified about Parkinson's disease, from which he suffers; actor Goldie Hawn, who testified against granting permanent, normal trade status to China; and actor Julia Roberts, who spoke on behalf of those who suffer from Rett Syndrome, a nervous system disorder disproportionately suffered by women.

> Celebrity "experts" frequently offer testimony before Congress on many issues. School music education was the subject of Elmo's appearance before a hearing of the House Labor, Health and Human Services, and Education Appropriations Committee in 2002.

Indirect Strategies to Advance Interests

Reaching out to persuade the public that the interest group's position is right, deploying citizens as grassroots lobbyists, and electioneering are some of the indirect strategies interest groups use to pursue their public policy agendas. Indirect tactics are likely to be ongoing rather than targeted at a specific piece of legislation, although that is not always the case.

PUBLIC OUTREACH Interest groups work hard—and use a variety of strategies—to make the public, government officials, their own members, and potential members aware of issues of concern and to educate people about their positions on the issues. Some interest groups focus solely on educating the public and hope that through their efforts people will be concerned enough to take steps to have a particular policy established or changed. In doing so, the groups promote civic engagement by informing individuals about important policy concerns, even if the information they provide is skewed toward the group's views. The groups also encourage civic discourse by bringing issues into the public arena. Often they do so by mounting advertising campaigns to alert the public about an issue. NARAL

Pro-Choice America used such a strategy during the 2008 elections when the league took out ads in many traditionally Democratic states urging the election of pro-choice senators and alerting the public to the important role the U.S. Senate plays in confirming U.S. Supreme Court nominees. The ads stressed that the balance of the Court could shift in favor of an overruling of abortion protections if a sitting justice were to retire and be replaced by a pro-life justice.

Sometimes interest groups and corporations engage in **climate control,** the practice of using public outreach to build favorable public opinion of the organization or company. The logic behind climate control is simple: if a corporation or an organization has the goodwill of the public on its side, enacting its legislative agenda or getting its policy priorities passed will be easier because government will know of, and may even share, the public's positive opinion of the organization. For example, when Wal-Mart started to see opposition to the construction of its superstores in communities across the country, it relied on public relations techniques, particularly advertising, to convince people that Wal-Mart is a good corporate citizen. As critics complained about Wal-Mart's harmful effects on smaller, local merchants, the firm's ads touted Wal-Mart's positive contributions to its host communities. When opponents publicized the company's low-wage jobs, Wal-Mart countered with ads featuring employees who had started in entry-level positions and risen through the ranks to managerial posts. These ads would be viewed both by policy makers (municipal planning board members, for example) and by citizens, whose opinions matter to those policy makers. This type of climate control is designed to soften opposition and increase community goodwill.

Other groups, especially those without a great deal of access to policy makers, may engage in protests and civil disobedience to be heard. Sometimes leaders calculate that media attention to their actions will increase public awareness and spark widespread support for their cause.

ELECTIONEERING   Interest groups often engage in the indirect strategy of **electioneering**—working to influence the election of candidates who support their issues. All the tactics of electioneering are active methods of civic participation. These techniques include endorsing particular candidates or positions and conducting voter-registration and get-out-the-vote drives. Grassroots campaign efforts often put interest groups with large memberships, including labor unions, at an advantage.

Campaign contributions are considered a key element of electioneering. The importance of contributions puts wealthier interest groups, including corporate and business groups, at an advantage. Figure 7.3 shows the breakdown of contributions by incumbency status. From Figure 7.3, we can see that incumbent candidates have a significant edge in raising money from political action committees. These data indicate that most PACs recognize that incumbents—who are most likely to win reelection—are best situated to look after their interests after the election.

The issue of party affiliation also matters to political action committees. Business PACs and individuals with business interests make up the largest sources of revenue for political candidates and tend to favor Republicans over Democrats. Labor groups and individuals associated with them give overwhelmingly to Democratic candidates, but they contribute a great deal less money than do business PACs. Ideologically driven PACs and individuals are nearly evenly divided between Democrats and Republicans. (See "Analyzing the Sources" on page 234.)

Interest groups also commonly use the tactics of endorsements and ratings to attract support for the candidates whom they favor and to reduce the electoral chances of those whom they do not. Through endorsements, an interest group formally supports specific candidates and typically notifies its members and the media of that support. An endorsement may also involve financial support from the interest group's PAC. And by the technique of rating candidates,

climate control
the practice of using public outreach to build favorable public opinion of an organization

electioneering
working to influence the elections of candidates who support the organization's issues

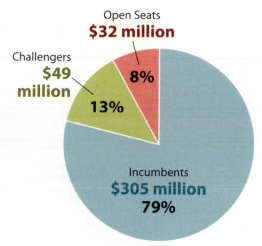

Contributions to 2008 Congressional Candidates by Political Action Committees

POLITICAL INQUIRY

FIGURE 7.3 ■ Roughly half of the congressional candidates running for office in 2008 were challengers, who netted only 13 percent of the PAC contributions donated to candidates. What are some of the reasons PACs are more likely to contribute to incumbents? What might be the effect of contributing to challengers?

SOURCE: Federal Election Commission, www.fec.gov/press/press2009/20090415PAC/20090424PAC.shtml.

ANALYZING THE SOURCES

TO WHICH CANDIDATES DO POLITICAL ACTION COMMITTEES CONTRIBUTE?

The following chart shows PAC contributions and percentages by candidates' political party over several election cycles.

PAC Contributions by Political Party
(in Millions of Dollars)

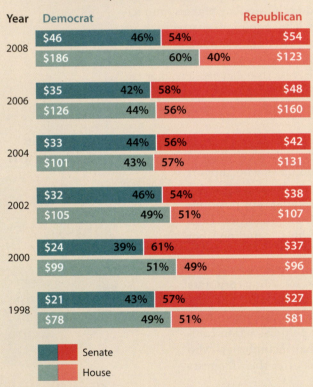

Year	Democrat		Republican
2008	$46 — 46%	54%	$54
	$186 — 60%	40%	$123
2006	$35 — 42%	58%	$48
	$126 — 44%	56%	$160
2004	$33 — 44%	56%	$42
	$101 — 43%	57%	$131
2002	$32 — 46%	54%	$38
	$105 — 49%	51%	$107
2000	$24 — 39%	61%	$37
	$99 — 51%	49%	$96
1998	$21 — 43%	57%	$27
	$78 — 49%	51%	$81

Senate
House

SOURCE: Federal Election Commission, www.fec.gov/press/press2009/20090415PAC/20090424PAC.shtml.

Evaluating the Evidence

① In general, what is the trend with regard to the amount of money PACs are contributing to congressional candidates? Are they contributing more than they used to?

② What is the trend with regard to the partisan breakdown of contributions? Do Republicans or Democrats usually receive more contributions, does it vary, or are contributions nearly evenly divided?

③ Are there differences between the level of financial support given to Democrats and that given to Republicans in the House and the Senate?

the interest group examines candidates' responses to a questionnaire issued by the group. Sometimes a group rates members of Congress on the basis of how they voted on measures important to the group. The ratings of a liberal interest group such as the Americans for Democratic Action (ADA) or a conservative interest group such as the American Conservative Union (ACU) can serve as an ideological benchmark. So, for example, as senators in 2007, both Hillary Clinton and Barack Obama had ADA ratings of 75, while Republican John McCain had an ADA rating of 10. McCain had an ACU rating of 82, and Clinton and Obama each had about an 8. Interest group ratings are used by voters and the media to evaluate candidates and also by candidates themselves, who may advertise their rating to targeted constituencies.

Interest Groups, Politics, and Money: The Influence of Political Action Committees

The influence of money on politics is not a recent phenomenon. Louise Overacker, one of the first political scientists to do research on campaign finance, wrote in 1932, "Any effective program of control must make it possible to bring into the light the sources and amounts of all funds used in political campaigns, and the way in which those funds are expended. . . . Negatively, it must not attempt to place legal limitations upon the size of contributions or expenditures."[31] Years later, Congress saw the wisdom of Overacker's analysis and enacted regulations stipulating that a group that contributes to any candidate's campaign must register as a political action committee (PAC). For that reason, most interest groups form PACs as one arm of their organization, though federal law now permits corporations and labor unions to use their financial resources to purchase advertisements for federal campaigns directly.

Whereas an interest group pursues a group's broad goals by engaging in a variety of activities, its PAC raises and spends money to influence the outcome of an election. Typically it will do so by contributing to candidates' campaigns. Funding campaigns helps an interest group in various ways. For one thing, it establishes the interest group as a formal supporter of one or more candidates. And importantly, campaign contributions are a door opener for an interest group's lobbyists. For a lobbyist, access to policy makers is crucial, and campaign contributions provide a means of contact and help ensure that a phone call will be returned or an invitation responded to, even if the policy maker does not support the group's position on every issue.

Table 7.2 on page 236 lists the PACs that contribute the most money to U.S. campaigns and highlights the party their contributions favor. As the table illustrates, many business

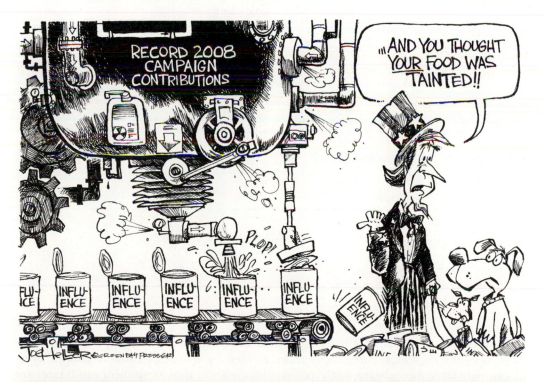

POLITICAL INQUIRY

What point does this cartoon make about the nature of 2008 political campaign contributions? Exactly what are these contributions buying, according to the cartoonist?

© Joe Heller, 2008. www.cagle.com

TABLE 7.2

Top All-Time Donors, 1989–2010

Rank	Organization	Total '89–'09	Tilt
1	AT&T Inc.	$44,214,960	On the fence
2	American Federation of State, County & Municipal Employees	$41,941,811	Solidly Democrat
3	National Association of Realtors	$35,595,518	On the fence
4	Goldman Sachs	$31,437,825	Leans Democrat
5	American Association for Justice	$31,424,029	Solidly Democrat
6	International Brotherhood of Electrical Workers	$31,407,507	Solidly Democrat
7	National Education Association	$30,097,067	Solidly Democrat
8	Laborers Union	$28,978,400	Solidly Democrat
9	Service Employees International Union	$27,933,232	Solidly Democrat
10	Carpenters & Joiners Union	$27,767,683	Strongly Democrat
11	Teamsters Union	$27,728,124	Solidly Democrat
12	Citigroup Inc.	$27,101,058	On the fence
13	Communications Workers of America	$27,025,396	Solidly Democrat
14	American Federation of Teachers	$26,282,491	Solidly Democrat
15	American Medical Association	$26,282,446	Leans Republican
16	United Auto Workers	$25,774,502	Solidly Democrat
17	Machinists & Aerospace Workers Union	$25,105,777	Solidly Democrat
18	National Auto Dealers Association	$24,344,808	Leans Republican
19	United Parcel Service	$24,183,691	Leans Republican
20	United Food & Commercial Workers Union	$24,123,333	Solidly Democrat
21	American Bankers Association	$22,414,966	On the fence
22	National Association of Home Builders	$21,864,655	Leans Republican
23	EMILY's List	$21,239,168	Solidly Democrat
24	National Beer Wholesalers Association	$21,038,345	Leans Republican
25	Time Warner	$20,041,510	Strongly Democrat

LEGEND: Republican Democrat On the fence

= Between 40% and 59% to both parties

= Leans Democrat/Republican (60%–69%)

= Strongly Democrat/Republican (70%–89%)

= Solidly Democrat/Republican (over 90%)

SOURCE: Copyright © 2010 Center for Responsive Politics. Used with permission.

and corporate PACs favor Republicans, whereas labor groups tend to support Democrats. More consistently, PACs, particularly those formed by economic interest groups, overwhelmingly favor incumbents. PACs' powers-that-be know that incumbent candidates are most likely to be reelected, and thus the PACs support their reelection bids. As we will examine further in Chapter 9, interest groups rely on political action committees to channel their support to candidates that espouse their views.

Interest groups are a powerful vehicle by which individuals can join forces and collectively persuade policy makers to take legislative action on their goals. As such, interest groups play a strong role in the policy-making process. Throughout U.S. history and continuing today, the prevalence of interest groups is testimony to people's desire to influence the pathways of their society and government.

Interest groups are one of the great leveling devices in U.S. politics. They are organizations that enable "regular Jills and Joes" to influence policy through collective action and organization. And although not all Americans are equally likely to join and form interest groups, interest groups represent an avenue of participation open to all, and with enough variety in tactics and strategies to offer appealing means of civic participation to a broad spectrum of the population. Particularly today, with the Internet providing a highly accessible medium for participation, interest groups give individuals the opportunity to increase their own social capital—to improve their own lives and the life of their community by making government more responsive to their needs and concerns and by increasing the effectiveness of the public policy-making process.

Although there are competing opinions about the role and value of interest groups in U.S. politics, their influence in policy making is unquestioned. Thus interest groups offer enormous potential for people who wish to become civically engaged. The abundance of groups for virtually every cause (and the ability of anyone to form his or her own group) means that like-minded individuals can work together to ensure that government policy represents their views. How does the number of groups available today differ from decades past? What is the result of that difference in terms of potential members?

Today, through the Internet and other digital technology, interest groups can provide individuals with instantly accessed information and organizational tools. Advances in computing, telephone communications, and television have opened the doors to participation in politics and government in ways that were undreamed of a few decades ago. Thanks to technology, the potential exists for interest groups to reach new and ever-widening audiences. As we have seen, however, the potential audience, at least in the present day, excludes many members of the working class, who may not have been socialized to take part in groups and who may lack the time and means to access computer technology. This lack of access poses a challenge to interest groups as they rely ever more heavily on digital recruiting, communicating, organizing, and fund-raising. How will new technologies continue to alter the landscape for interest groups?

In becoming increasingly dependent on relatively low-cost technological tools, interest groups also have to deal with the challenges of paying for the expertise needed to design, build, and maintain their Web sites and Weblogs. Once such issues are resolved, and once access is opened to those not currently wired, digital strategies will further strengthen the clout and efficacy of interest groups and these groups will speak for a broader swath of Americans.

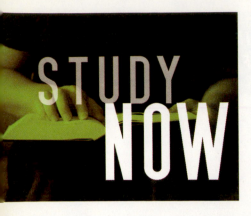

STUDY NOW

Summary

1. The Value of Interest Groups

Interest groups offer individuals a vehicle for engaging in civic actions and improving their communities and the nation as a whole. The positive impacts of improved social capital are reciprocal: as participation benefits individuals, it also benefits communities and larger governments, which in turn provide benefits to individuals, and so on. Interest groups also have some downsides: they can allow well-organized minority views to dominate over less well-organized majority viewpoints; they emphasize the role of money in politics; they strengthen the incumbency advantage of elected officeholders; and they tend to draw participants disproportionately from among society's elites.

2. Who Joins Interest Groups, and Why?

Although interest groups serve as an accessible channel for citizen participation, not everyone is equally likely to join or form an interest group. In general, people with high incomes, individuals who are upper-middle and middle class, and those with high levels of education are more likely to join interest groups than are people with low incomes, those who are lower-middle and working class, and those who have less education. In addition, some people join interest groups related to their occupation. People typically join interest groups for a variety of reasons that can be categorized as solidary incentives, purposive incentives, and economic incentives.

3. How Interest Groups Succeed

Interest groups succeed by using their organizational resources and maximizing the effectiveness of their organizational environment. Organizational resources consist of groups' membership and financial resources. The organizational environment comprises the group's leadership and the presence of opposing or competitive interest groups in the policy-making environment.

4. Types of Interest Groups

Interest groups typically fall into one of three categories. Economic interest groups, such as business, agricultural, or labor union groups, advocate for financial benefits for their members in the form of subsidies or wage policies, for example. Public and ideological interest groups lobby for policies that affect public, or collective, goods and include abortion-rights groups and environmental groups. Foreign governments and corporations also use interest groups to influence a wide variety of policies, especially trade and military policy.

5. Interest Group Strategies

Interest groups usually combine direct and indirect strategies in their attempts to influence the policy process. Direct strategies typically involve lobbying a policy maker, and indirect strategies may include using public outreach to build favorable public opinion of the organization (climate control), using campaign contributions and electioneering to influence who will be making policy, and educating the public so that they share a group's position and can convey that view to policy makers.

6. Interest Groups, Politics, and Money: The Influence of Political Action Committees

PACs are the tool by which interest groups contribute to electoral campaigns. Some PACs are partisan, but in general PACs tend to support incumbent candidates, making it difficult for nonincumbents effectively to challenge those already in office.

Key Terms

For Review

1. Explain in detail how the pluralist and elite theories differ in their views of interest groups in U.S. democracy.
2. Why do people join interest groups? Who is most likely to join an interest group? Why?
3. What kinds of interest groups exist in the United States? Which types are the most influential? Why are they most influential?
4. What resources help determine how powerful an interest group is?
5. How do political action committees attempt to influence government action?

For Critical Thinking and Discussion

1. Were you brought up in a family in which joining groups was important? Do your parents belong to any interest groups? Do you? If not, why do you think that is the case?
2. What kinds of interest groups are you and your friends most likely to be involved in (even if you are not)? Why are the issues these groups advocate important to you?
3. How has the Internet changed how interest groups operate? What kinds of groups has it made more effective? Has it made any groups less effective?
4. Select a controversial issue such as abortion or gun control, and use the Internet to search for and learn about the interest groups that represent opposing views. What tactics does each group use? Is one strategy more effective than the other?
5. The Supreme Court has ruled that political expenditures constitute a form of free speech. Do you agree? Can you think of any other ways in which "money talks"?

MULTIPLE CHOICE: Choose the lettered item that answers the question correctly.

1. The idea that a group of wealthy, educated individuals wields most political power is called
   a. pluralist theory.
   b. elite theory.
   c. rational choice theory.
   d. democratic theory.

2. The motivation to join an interest group based on a belief in the group's cause from an ideological standpoint is called a(n)
   a. solidary incentive.
   b. purposive incentive.
   c. economic incentive.
   d. organizational incentive.

3. A restaurant owner who joins a trade association interest group because it advocates for wage policies that would benefit the business is an example of someone motivated by
   a. solidary incentives.
   b. purposive incentives.
   c. economic incentives.
   d. organizational incentives.

4. A group that raises and spends money to influence the outcome of an election is called
   a. an interest group.
   b. a bundling organization.
   c. a political action committee.
   d. a social compact.

5. The phenomenon of someone deriving benefit from others' actions is called
   a. the problem of collective action.
   b. the bundling problem.
   c. the free rider problem.
   d. the slacker problem.

6. A direct strategy to advance the interest of an interest group is
   a. lobbying.
   b. public outreach.
   c. electioneering.
   d. contributing to political parties.

7. The fluid web of connections among those concerned about a policy and those who create and administer the policy is called
   a. political action committee.
   b. a congressional quorum.
   c. an issue network.
   d. a social network.

8. The interaction of mutual interests among members of Congress, executive agencies, and organized interests during policy making is called
   a. a social network.   c. a square cube.
   b. an iron triangle.   d. an issue network.

9. The practice of using public outreach to build a favorable public opinion of the organization is called
   a. climate control.   c. agenda setting.
   b. interest outreach.   d. maximizing spin.

10. Working to influence the election of candidates who support the organization's issues is called
    a. interest group bias.
    b. incumbency advantage.
    c. agenda setting.
    d. electioneering.

FILL IN THE BLANKS.

11. To social scientists, the ways in which our lives are improved by social connections is called _____ .

12. The motivation to join an interest group based on the companionship and the satisfaction derived from socializing with others is called _____ .

13. A group that represents collective groups of industries or corporations is called a(n) _____ .

14. Outcomes shared by the general public are called _____ .

15. The idea that it is not economically rational for people to participate in collective action when the resultant collective good could be realized without participating is the essence of _____ .

Internet Resources

Center for Responsive Politics
www.opensecrets.org   This nonpartisan Web site provides information on the campaign financing of candidates for federal office.

Common Cause
www.commoncause.org   This Web site features a special section on money and politics and provides links to sites related to its endorsed reform measures.

Federal Election Commission
www.fec.org   You'll find a plethora of information about campaign financing, including regulations, contributions and expenditures, specific candidates, individual donors, political action committees, and political parties.

Internet Activism

Join an online interest group that supports a cause you believe in. Google any of your interests with the term "interest group" to find groups that identify with causes you believe in. Examples might include conservative or liberal organizations, environmental groups, groups centered on demographic characteristics, and groups concerned with specific policies. After finding an organization, determine what membership requirements are, and how the group facilitates online participation.

Facebook and Twitter
You can follow or become a fan of hundreds of interest groups on Twitter and Facebook. On Twitter, search the group name. On Facebook, search the group name and click "groups."

Recommended Readings

Alexander, Robert M. *Rolling the Dice with State Initiatives: Interest Group Involvement in Ballot Campaigns.* Westport, CT: Praeger, 2001. A probing analysis of the impact of interest groups on gambling initiatives in California and Missouri that, unlike most treatments of interest group activity, focuses on interest group initiatives within states and on lobbying in a nonlegislative arena.

Berry, Jeffrey M., and Clyde Wilcox. *The Interest Group Society,* 5th ed. New York: Longman, 2008. Analyzes the proliferation of various types of interest groups in the United States, as well as the strategies interest groups use to sway policy makers.

Cigler, Alan J., and Burnett A. Loomis. *Interest Group Politics,* 7th ed. Washington, DC: CQ Press, 2007. A classic analysis, first published

in 1983, detailing the impact of interest groups in modern American politics.

Franz, Michael M. *Choices and Changes: Interest Groups in the Electoral Process.* Philadelphia: Temple University Press, 2008. A comprehensive examination of interest groups' use of electioneering tactics, especially campaign contributions, and how electioneering strategies are shaped by the campaign regulatory environment.

Hays, Richard A. *Who Speaks for the Poor: National Interest Groups and Social Policy.* New York: Routledge, 2001. An examination of how the poor gain political representation in the policy process through the efforts of interest groups.

Herrnson, Paul S., Ronald G. Shaiko, and Clyde J. Wilcox. *The Interest Group Connection: Electioneering, Lobbying, and Policymaking in Washington,* 2nd ed. Washington, DC: CQ Press, 2004. A collection of essays describing the role of interest groups on the federal level. The essays focus on elections, Congress, the president, and the judiciary.

Wright, John. *Interest Groups and Congress (Longman Classics Edition).* New York: Longman, 2002. A study of the influence of both historical and modern interest groups, asserting that interest groups' practice of providing specialized information to members of Congress increases their influence there, has an impact on the resultant policy, and shapes opinion.

Movies of Interest

Thank You for Smoking (2005)
Aaron Eckhart stars as a lobbyist in this satirical comedy about the big tobacco lobby.

Erin Brockovich (2000)
Starring Julia Roberts, this film is based on the true story of Erin Brockovich, an activist fighting for the rights of a community whose water supply has been contaminated.

The Pelican Brief (1993)
Based on the John Grisham novel of the same name, this film, starring Julia Roberts and Denzel Washington, spotlights competition between big business and the environmental movement and illuminates how interested parties can use the courts to make policy.

Paths of Glory (1957)
This Stanley Kubrick film delves into the realities of trench warfare during World War I, but through it we see how organizations may succeed or fail at motivating individuals.

2·0·1·0
Southern Republican
Leadership Conference
New Orleans

*Political
Parties*

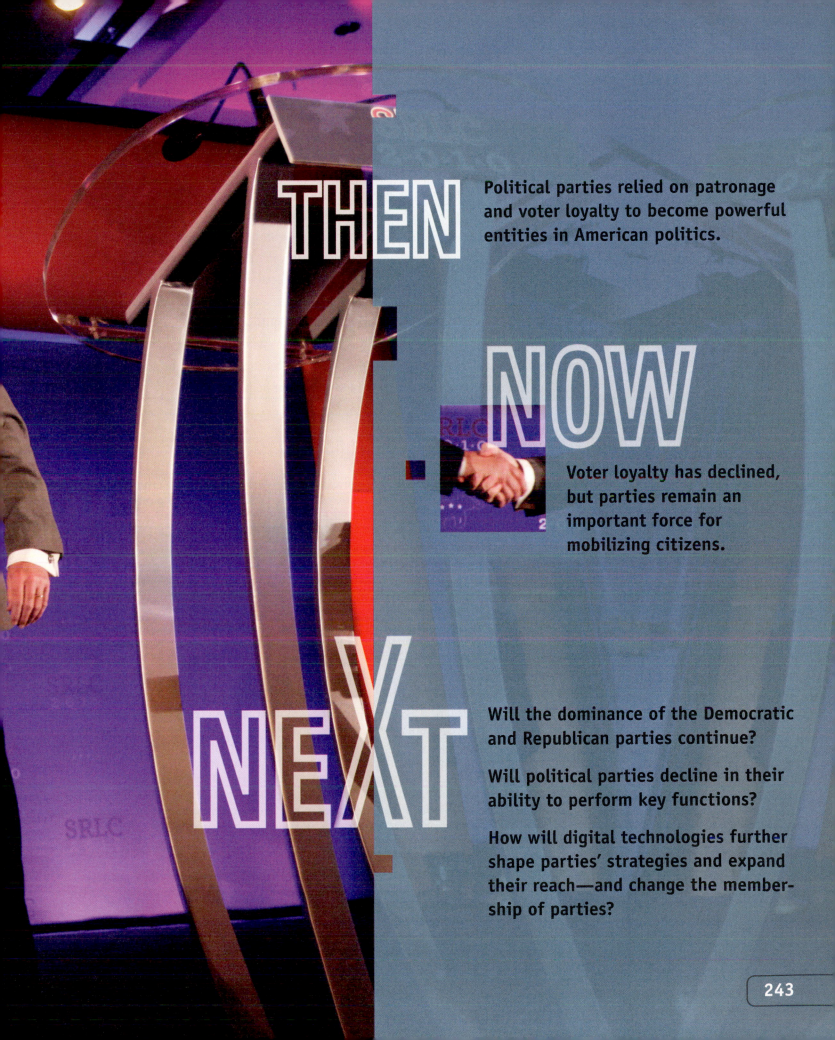

THEN

Political parties relied on patronage and voter loyalty to become powerful entities in American politics.

NOW

Voter loyalty has declined, but parties remain an important force for mobilizing citizens.

NEXT

Will the dominance of the Democratic and Republican parties continue?

Will political parties decline in their ability to perform key functions?

How will digital technologies further shape parties' strategies and expand their reach—and change the membership of parties?

political party
an organization that recruits, nominates, and elects party members to office in order to control the government

platform
the formal statement of a party's principles and policy objectives

Political parties are essential

channels for the realization of American democracy. Political parties serve the American system in many crucial capacities, from recruiting candidates, to conducting elections, to distributing information to voters, to participating in governance. One of their essential functions is to provide an open arena for participation by civic-minded individuals, while reaching out to involve those who do not participate.

Because Americans place high value on independent thought and action, some citizens view political parties with suspicion. For such observers, the collective activity of parties brings worries about corruption and control by elite decision makers. But even though party insiders sometimes do exert considerable power, parties remain one of the most accessible forums for citizens' participation in democracy. Indeed, political scientist E. E. Schattschneider, who believed that parties represented the foremost means for citizens to communicate with political decision makers—and in this way to retain control over their government—wrote that "modern democracy is unthinkable save in terms of political parties."[1]

Parties Today and Their Functions

In the United States today, two major political parties—the Democratic and the Republican parties—dominate the political landscape. Generally speaking, a **political party** is an organization of ideologically similar people that nominates and elects its members to office in order to run the government and shape public policy. Parties identify potential candidates, nominate them to run for office, campaign for them, organize elections, and govern. But given some overlapping roles, political scientists agree that parties can be distinguished from other political organizations, such as interest groups and political action committees, through four defining characteristics.

Defining a Political Party

First, political parties run candidates under their own label, or affiliation. Most candidates who run for office are identified by their party affiliation. Running a candidate under the party label requires party functions such as recruiting candidates, organizing elections, and campaigning.[2] And political parties typically are the only organizations that regularly run candidates for political office under the party label on a ballot.

Second, unlike interest groups, which hope to have individuals sympathetic to their cause elected but which typically do not want to govern, *political parties seek to govern.* Political parties run candidates hoping that they will win a majority of the seats in a legislature or control the executive branch. Such victories enable the party to enact a broad partisan agenda. For example, the Democratic victories in the 2008 presidential and congressional elections paved the way for President Obama and the Democratic leadership in the U.S. House of Representatives and the U.S. Senate to act on the party's stated agenda, particularly in reforming the nation's health care system.

A third defining characteristic is that *political parties have broad concerns, focused on many issues.* The major parties in the United States are made up of coalitions of different groups and constituencies who rely on political parties to enact their agendas. That is to say, if we were to look at a party's **platform**—the formal statement of its principles and policy objectives—we would find its stance on all sorts of issues: war, abortion rights, environmental protection, the minimum wage. These positions are one articulation of the interests of that party's coalition constituencies. Typically, interest groups have narrower issue concerns than parties do, and some focus on only a single issue. For example, we know that the National Rifle Association opposes governmental controls on gun ownership, but what is this interest group's position on the minimum wage? On the environment? Chances are high that the NRA does not have positions on those matters because its concern is with the single issue of gun ownership.

Finally, *political parties are quasi-public organizations that have a special relationship with the government.* Some functions of political parties overlap with governmental functions, and some party functions facilitate the creation and perpetuation of government (running elections, for example). The resulting special status subjects political parties to greater scrutiny than private clubs and organizations.

How Parties Engage Individuals

Political scientists who study the nature of Americans' civic engagement recognize that political parties represent one of the main channels through which citizens can make their voices heard. A fixture in the politics of American communities large and small, parties today are accessible to virtually everyone.

Historically, political parties excluded various groups from participating. For example, in many states, women were shut out of party meetings until the mid-twentieth century.[3] African Americans were formally excluded from voting in Democratic primaries in the South until the U.S. Supreme Court banned the practice in 1944, though it took decades before the party complied with that decision.[4] But in recent times, political parties have increasingly embraced and championed diversity. They have encouraged various groups beyond the traditional white European American male party establishment to get involved formally in the party organization, to participate in campaign activities, and to vote. As a result, parties today are much more inclusive of women, ethnic and racial minorities, and students, providing an important avenue for those traditionally excluded from political life to gain valuable experience as party activists, campaign volunteers, and informed voters. This increasingly diverse participation has also contributed to the parties' health, because it has caused them to recognize that to be successful, candidates must reflect the diverse identities and interests of voters.

What Political Parties Do

As we have seen, by promoting political activity, political parties encourage civic engagement and citizen participation and in that way foster democracy. Parties provide a structure for people at the **grassroots** level to volunteer on party-run campaigns, make campaign contributions, work in the day-to-day operations of the party, and run for office. During the 2010 congressional elections, Democratic and Republican activists registered, canvassed, and mobilized voters. Both parties focused their efforts on competitive districts where Democratic incumbents were at risk of being unseated. In some cases, those Democrats were vulnerable because their districts had large numbers of conservative voters; in other cases, they were vulnerable because of their comparatively short tenure in the House. In general, representatives who have served only a term or two are more likely to be defeated than their more senior counterparts.

On the local level, a political party's ability to promote citizen participation varies with its relative influence within the community. Viable political parties—those that effectively contest and win some elections—are more effective at promoting citizen participation than weak political parties. A party that typically is in the minority in a local government—on the town council, in the county legislature—will find it more difficult to attract volunteers, to bring people out to fund-raisers, and to recruit candidates. And it naturally follows that parties that are better at attracting public participation are more likely to win elections.

Political parties also foster cooperation between divided interests and factions, building coalitions even in the most divisive of times. For example, in 2010 when Democratic and Republican wrangling over health care reform reached a crescendo, a bipartisan group of

grassroots organizing
tasks that involve direct contact with voters or potential voters.

> Political parties provide an easy avenue for citizens to participate in the civic life of their communities and nation. One way to participate is to volunteer at a national political party convention, or to try to become a convention delegate.

senators joined forces to support a Clean Air bill, which would reduce the emissions of sulfur dioxide, nitrogen oxides, and mercury. The bill had the support of Senators Tom Carper (D-Delaware), Lamar Alexander (R-Tennessee), Amy Klobuchar (D-Minnesota), Jeanne Shaheen (D-New Hampshire), Judd Gregg (R-New Hampshire), Charles Schumer (D-New York), and Joseph Lieberman (I-Connecticut). The Clean Air bill was able to attract bipartisan support partially because it was considered a less controversial alternative to sweeping climate-change reform legislation. Civic engagement researchers point out that political parties' work in building coalitions and promoting cooperation among diverse groups often occurs away from the bright lights of the media-saturated public arena, where the parties' differences, rather than their common causes, often are in the spotlight.

Political parties also grease the wheels of government and ensure its smooth running. Nearly all legislatures, from town councils to Congress, consist of a *majority party*, the party to which more than 50 percent of the elected legislators belong, and the *minority party*, to which less than 50 percent of the elected legislators belong. Thus, if five of the nine members of your town council are Republicans and four are Democrats, the Republicans are the majority party and the Democrats are the minority party. The majority party elects the legislature's leaders, makes committee assignments, and holds a majority on those committees.

By serving as a training ground for members, political parties also foster effective government. This role of parties is particularly important for groups that traditionally have not been among the power brokers in the government. Historically, African Americans, Latinos, and women have gained valuable knowledge and leadership experience in party organizations—by volunteering on party-run campaigns, assisting with candidate recruitment, or helping with fund-raising endeavors—before running for office.[5] Party credentials established by serving the party in these ways can act as a leveling device that can help make a newcomer's candidacy more viable.

Perhaps most important, political parties promote civic responsibility among elected officials and give voters an important "check" on those elected officials. There is no doubt that the 2010 congressional elections were a mandate on the Obama presidency, even though the president's name was not on the ballot. When an elected leader, particularly a chief executive, is the crucial player in enacting an important policy, the existence of political parties enables voters to hold party members responsible *even if that particular elected official is not running for reelection*. The system thus provides a check on the power of elected officials, because it makes them aware that the policy or position they are taking may be unpopular.

Historically, according to one theory, political parties have also made government more effective and have provided important cues for voters. The **responsible party model,** developed by E. E. Schattschneider, posits that a party tries to give voters a clear choice by establishing priorities or policy stances different from those of the rival party or parties. Because a party's elected officials tend to be loyal to their party's stances, voters can readily anticipate how a candidate will vote on a given set of issues if elected, and can thus cast their vote according to their preferences on those issues.

The Three Faces of Parties

American political parties perform their various functions through three "faces," or spheres of operation.[6] The three components of the party include the party in the electorate, the party organization, and the party in government (see Figure 8.1).

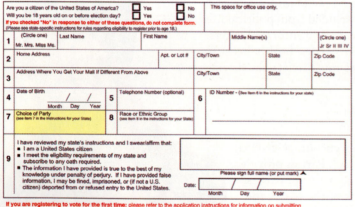

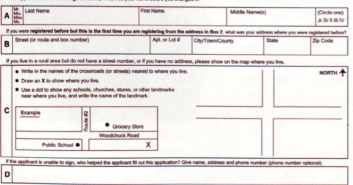

> Most states offer voters the opportunity to declare their party affiliation when registering to vote. Affiliated voters are the party in the electorate.

The Party in the Electorate

All the individuals who identify with or tend to support a particular party make up the **party in the electorate.** Several factors influence which party an individual will identify with, including personal circumstances, race, and religion, as well as the party's history, ideology, position on issues of importance to the voter, and candidates.[7]

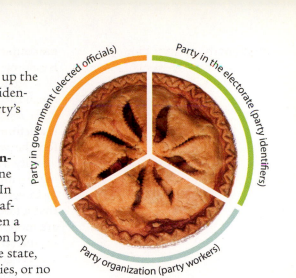

MEASURING THE PARTY IN THE ELECTORATE

The term **party identifier** refers to an individual who identifies himself or herself as a member of one party or the other; party identifiers typically are measured by party registration. In most states, party registration is a legal process in which a voter formally selects affiliation with one political party. This declaration of affiliation often occurs when a person registers to vote; the prospective voter selects his or her party identification by filling out a voter registration form or party declaration form. Depending on the state, a voter may select the Democratic or the Republican Party, a variety of third parties, or no party. When a voter does not select a party, he or she is technically an unaffiliated voter, but often analysts refer to such a voter as an **independent.**

People's party identification sometimes does not match their actual voting preferences. When we refer to the party in the electorate, we also consider those individuals who express a tendency to vote for one party or a preference for that party.

DETERMINING WHO BELONGS TO EACH POLITICAL PARTY

Although we commonly speak in terms of which groups affiliate with and "belong to" each of the political parties, those are just generalizations, with many exceptions. In general, each political party counts specific demographic groups as part of its base of support. A party will often draw party activists and leaders from the ranks of this bloc of individuals whose support can be counted on.

Although whites, men, and people with some college education are naturally found in both parties, they are more likely to be Republicans. For the Democrats, key voting blocs include African Americans, ethnic minorities, women, and people with no college education. Individuals with a college degree or more are evenly divided between the two parties. Social class also plays a role in party preference. The working class is largely Democratic; the upper-middle class is largely Republican; and the middle class, by far the largest class in the United States, is divided between the two parties. But the best predictor of a person's party identification is his or her ideology. People who identify themselves as conservative are much more likely to be Republicans; people who identify themselves as liberal are much more likely to be Democrats. (See the discussion of ideology in Chapter 1.)

DIFFERENCES BETWEEN DEMOCRATS AND REPUBLICANS

We can trace some of the differences—in both ideologies and core constituencies—between today's Democrats and Republicans to the 1930s. That was the era of the Great Depression, a time of devastating economic collapse and personal misery for people around the world. President Franklin D. Roosevelt's drive to expand the role of government by providing a safety net for the most vulnerable in society has remained part of the Democratic agenda to this day. In the past several decades, this agenda has centered on pressing for civil rights for African Americans and for the expansion of social welfare programs. Today, key components of the Democratic agenda include gay rights, environmental protection, and freedom of choice with respect to abortion.

Traditionally, Republicans have countered that position by advocating a smaller government that performs fewer social welfare functions. Many members of the Tea Party movement argue that smaller government should be the focus of the modern Republican party. But a major priority for the Republican Party today is advocacy of a stronger governmental role in regulating traditional moral values. Because of this stance, a solid voting bloc within the Republican Party comprises conservative Christians, sometimes called the Christian Right or the Religious Right, who agree with the Republicans' pro-life position on abortion (which includes support for an increased regulation of abortion) and appeals for a constitutional amendment banning gay marriage. Republicans also emphasize protection of business and business owners and generally support a decreased role for the federal government,

FIGURE 8.1

The Three Faces of Parties

party in the electorate
individuals who identify with or tend to support a party

party identifiers
individuals who identify themselves as a member of one party or the other

independent
a voter who does not belong to any organized political party; often used as a synonym for an unaffiliated voter

particularly with respect to the economy and social welfare issues, and a corresponding larger role for state governments.

More recent analysis of the differences between Democrats and Republicans reveals how much the world has changed in the past several years. Research on party identifiers between 2005 and 2010 shows how the perception of a party's level of assertiveness in foreign affairs is a defining characteristic of Democrats and Republicans.[8] Previous analyses, conducted before the wars in Afghanistan and Iraq, showed that this factor had very little bearing on party identity. The more recent research also indicates that positions on social issues, once a defining feature of the parties, have declined tremendously as a key determinant of partisanship.

In concrete terms, these differences mean that Republicans are more likely to believe that a foreign policy emphasizing military action is the right course, and that Democrats are more likely to oppose war (such as the war in Iraq) and to believe that foreign policy should stress diplomacy over military action. In general, Democrats remain committed to a larger government role in providing an economic safety net.

It is not surprising that the base constituencies of the parties are drawn from the groups that each party's platform emphasizes. The base of the Democratic Party prominently includes women, the majority of whom, since 1980, have voted for the Democratic presidential nominee. Since Franklin Roosevelt's New Deal social welfare policy during the 1930s, African Americans have been an important voting bloc within the Democratic Party, although they have faced struggles and strife in asserting and securing their rights, particularly during the civil rights movement of the 1960s. Other ethnic minorities, including Latinos and Asian Americans, also tend to support the Democratic Party (as described in Chapter 6), as do many working-class voters. The base of the Republican Party prominently includes many small-business owners, citizens who identify themselves as being very religious, and upper-middle-class voters.[9]

party organization
the formal party apparatus, including committees, party leaders, conventions, and workers

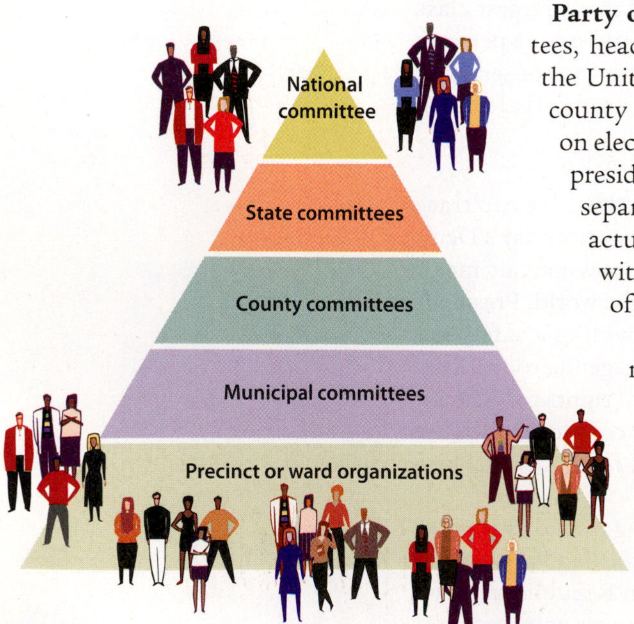

FIGURE 8.2

Theoretical Structure of Political Parties: A Hierarchical Model of Party Organizations

National committee

State committees

County committees

Municipal committees

Precinct or ward organizations

The Party Organization

Thomas P. "Tip" O'Neill (D-Massachusetts), Speaker of the House of Representatives from 1977 until 1987, is often quoted as saying, "All politics is local." In no case is that statement truer than it is for American political parties.

Party organization refers to the formal party apparatus, including committees, headquarters, conventions, party leaders, staff, and volunteer workers. In the United States, the party organization is most visible at the local level. Yet county and local parties tend to be *loosely* organized—centered predominantly on elections—and may be dormant when election season passes.[10] Except during presidential elections, state and local political parties typically function quite separately from the national party. Although the number of individuals who actually participate in the party organization is quite small when compared with the party in the electorate, on the local level, political parties offer one of the most accessible means for individuals to participate in politics.

But with respect to political *power,* county and local parties are the most important components of a party organization. Theoretically, political parties' organization resembles a pyramid (see Figure 8.2), with a broad base of support at the bottom and power flowing up to a smaller group at the state level and then to an even smaller, more exclusive group at the national level.[11] In reality, the national committees of both major U.S. political parties exist separately from the committees of the state and local parties (see Figure 8.3), and real political power can usually be found at the local or county party level, as we will see in the following discussion.

THE NATIONAL PARTIES Every four years, political party activists meet at a national convention to determine their party's nominee for the presidency. Here the delegates also adopt rules and develop a party platform that describes the party's policy priorities and positions on issues.

The national party committees (the Democratic National Committee, or DNC, and the Republican National Committee, or RNC) are the national party organizations charged with conducting the conventions and overseeing the operation of the national party during the interim between conventions. The national committee elects a national chair, who is often informally selected by the party's presidential nominee. The national chair, along with the paid staff of the national committee, oversees the day-to-day operations of the political party.

But the role of the national chair depends to a large extent on whether the party's nominee wins the presidency. If the party's nominee is victorious, the national chair has a less prominent role because the president serves as the most public representative of the party. If the party's nominee loses, however, the national chair may take on a more public persona, serving as the spokesperson for the **loyal opposition**—the out-of-power party's objections to the policies and priorities of the government in power. In recent years, regardless of whether the party's nominee has won or lost, one of the most important roles of the national chair has been to raise funds. Money donated to the national parties is often redirected to the state and local parties, which use it to help contest elections and mobilize voters.

FIGURE 8.3

Modern Structure of Political Parties: Power Diffused Through Many Party Organizations

STATE PARTIES   Both national parties have committees in each state (the Illinois State Democratic Committee, for example) that effectively *are* the party in that state. State committees act as intermediaries between the national committees and county committees. Typically, state committees are made up of a few members from each county or other geographical subdivision of a given state.

Historically, state parties were important because of their role in the election of U.S. senators, who until 1913 were elected by their states' legislatures. Since the ratification of the Seventeenth Amendment in that year, the voters of each state have directly elected their senators by popular election.

Later in the twentieth century, state political parties began a rebound of power, partly because of the U.S. Supreme Court's decision in *Buckley v. Valeo* (1976). In this case, the Court ruled that political parties are entities with special status because their functions of educating and mobilizing voters and contesting elections help to ensure democracy.[12] This ruling created the so-called **soft money loophole,** through which the political parties could raise unlimited funds for party-building activities such as voter registration drives and get-out-the-vote (GOTV) efforts, although contributions to specific candidates were limited. The Court's decision strengthened the influence of the state parties, which the national parties often relied upon to coordinate these efforts. The Bipartisan Campaign Reform Act of 2002 eliminated the soft money loophole, but until that time state parties were strengthened by their ability to channel those contributions to political parties. (See Chapter 9 for further discussion of soft money.)

COUNTY AND LOCAL PARTIES   County committees consist of members of municipal, ward, and precinct party committees. The foot soldiers of the political parties, county committees help recruit candidates for office, raise campaign funds, and mobilize voters. The importance of a given county committee's role largely depends on whether its candidates are elected and whether its party controls the government. Party success tends to promote competition for candidates' slots and for seats on the county committee.

In most major cities, ward committees and precinct committees dominate party politics. Because city council members are often elected to represent a ward, ward committees are a powerful force in city politics, providing the grassroots organization that turns voters out in city elections. Precinct committees (a precinct is usually a subdivision of a ward) also help elect city council members.

Besides fund-raising, county and local political parties still play key roles in shaping both community engagement and individual participation in the political process, as they have done historically. During election season (in most places, from the end of August through the first week in November), county and local parties recruit and rely on volunteers to perform a host of functions, including answering phones in party headquarters, registering voters, coordinating mailings, doing advance work for candidates, compiling

loyal opposition
a role that the party out of power plays, highlighting its objections to policies and priorities of the government in power

soft money loophole
Supreme Court interpretation of campaign finance law that enabled political parties to raise unlimited funds for party-building activities such as voter registration drives and get-out-the-vote (GOTV) efforts

THE PEOPLE'S OPINION OF THE PARTIES

The figure below shows the percentage of survey respondents who have a favorable view of the Republican and Democratic parties at selected dates between September 2001 and May 2010.

Evaluating the Evidence

① What is the general trend with regard to party favorability ratings? Is one political party consistently viewed more favorably than the other? What is the trend over time regarding the favorability of Democrats versus Republicans?

② Look at particular high and low points for each political party. What events may have caused people's opinions of the parties to increase or decline?

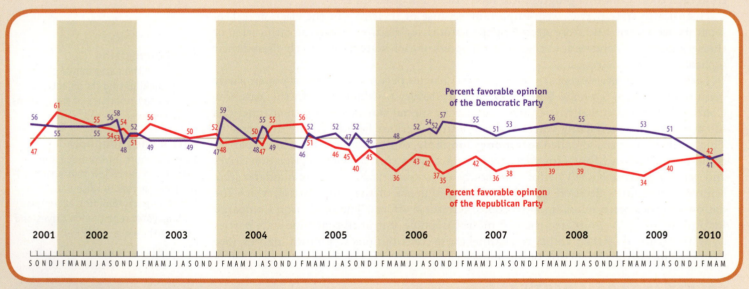

SOURCE: "Party Images," www.gallup.com/poll/24655/Party-Images.aspx.

lists for get-out-the-vote efforts, supervising door-knocking campaigns, and staffing phone banks to remind voters to vote on election day.

The Party in Government

When candidates run for local, state, or national office, their party affiliation usually appears next to their name on the ballot. After an elected official takes the oath of office, many people do not think about the official's party affiliation. But in fact, the **party in government**—the partisan identification of elected leaders in local, county, state, and national government—significantly influences the organization and running of the government at these various levels.

In most towns, the party identification of the majority of the members of the legislative branch (often called *city council* or *town council*) determines who will serve as the head of the

party in government
the partisan identifications of elected leaders in local, county, state, and federal government

legislature (sometimes called the *president of city council*). And in most towns, the president of city council hails from the majority party. In addition, paid professional positions such as city solicitor (the town's lawyer), town planner, and city engineer are often awarded on the basis of the support of the majority of council. Even though the entire council votes on appointments, the minority party members often defer to the majority, since appointments typically are viewed as a privilege of winning a majority. Other appointments might include positions on voluntary boards such as a town planning or zoning board.

On the state level, the party in government plays a similarly prominent role in organizing government work. Typically, state legislatures are organized around political party. Seating assignments and committee assignments are made by the majority party leadership and are based on a legislator's party affiliation. Figure 8.4 illustrates the partisan breakdown of state legislatures. In each state, the party with a majority (shown in the figure) in the legislature also has a majority on the legislature's committees, which decide the outcome of proposed legislation. Parties moreover are important in the executive branch of state government, since state governors typically appoint party loyalists to key positions in their administrations. Depending on the appointment powers of the governor, which vary from state to state, a governor may also appoint party members to plum assignments on state regulatory boards. In states where the governor appoints the judiciary, the governor also frequently selects judicial nominees from his or her own political party.

Parties perform a similar role in the federal government. Presidents draw from party loyalists to fill cabinet and subcabinet appointments and typically appoint federal judges from their own political party. Congress is organized based on the party affiliation of its members. When representatives or senators refer to a colleague "on the other side of the aisle," they are referring to a member of the other political party, since congressional Democrats and Republicans sit across the aisle from one another. As in state legislatures, the party with the majority in Congress essentially runs the legislative branch. From its ranks comes the congressional leadership, including the Senate Majority Leader, the Speaker of the House of Representatives, and the House Majority Leader (see Chapter 11).

Partisan control

- Democrat
- Republican
- Split
- Non-Partisan

FIGURE 8.4

Partisan Control of State Legislatures Before the Election of 2010

*Republicans control the Montana Senate 27–23, but the House is evenly divided 50–50. Republicans control the Tennessee Senate 19–14, but the House is evenly divided 49–49.

SOURCE: The National Conference of State Legislatures, www.ncsl.org/default.aspx?tabid=16507.

> Speakers of the House of Representatives are members of the party in government. Nancy Pelosi (D-California) served as Speaker from 2007–2011, and was the first woman to serve in that post. John Boehner (R-Ohio) is the current Speaker, elected after the Republican majority took control of the House in 2011.

DIVIDED GOVERNMENT   There are limits to a party's power. Probably the most important check comes from the opposition party, which can openly criticize the party in power and aggressively investigate alleged misconduct on the part of its officials. During parts of the Bill Clinton and George W. Bush administrations, for example, the president and the members of Congress functioned with a **divided government,** the situation in which one party controls Congress and the other party, the presidency.[13] Divided government emerged after the 2006 midterm elections, when the Democrats won control of both houses of Congress. Democrats in Congress alleged administration misconduct when it appeared that Bush's attorney general, Alberto Gonzales, dismissed federal prosecutors for political reasons of politics rather than competence.

divided government
the situation that exists when Congress is controlled by one party and the presidency by the other

Political Parties in U.S. History

Modern Americans' divided opinions of political parties would not be surprising to the founders, who viewed political parties with suspicion.[14] Thomas Jefferson said, "If I could not go to heaven but with a party, I would not go there at all." That sentiment was shared by George Washington, who warned of "the baneful effects of the spirit of party."[15] Despite those reservations, political parties began to emerge in the United States during the debate over ratification of the Constitution (with both Washington and Jefferson instrumental in their creation). Those who advocated ratification and a strong central government were called Federalists, and those who opposed ratification and favored states' rights were called Anti-Federalists. Thus began the first party system in the United States. **Party system** refers to the number and competitiveness of political parties in a polity[16]—for example, a government may have a two-party system in which one party is ascending in power. As we will see, the demarcation of party systems typically occurs in hindsight, when social scientists recognize points where there has been a **realignment,** a shift in party allegiances or electoral support.[17]

party system
the categorization of the number and competitiveness of political parties in a polity

realignment
a shift in party allegiances or electoral support

Although these shifting allegiances have played a pivotal role in shaping the context of politics since the country's early days, the founders generally believed that parties threatened the stability of the fledgling democracy.[18] Most thought that political parties enabled individuals and groups to pursue self-serving interests that were often contrary to the common good. Some of the founders argued that parties discouraged independence in thought and action. Some thought that parties exacerbated conflicts and disagreements among the people rather than building consensus. Yet their formation and continued evolution testifies to their important role in achieving political and policy goals for their members.[19]

The First Party System:
The Development of Parties, 1789–1828

In 1788, George Washington was elected president, but the consensus surrounding his election proved short-lived. Washington deeply opposed the idea of political parties and ruled during an era without formal parties. But he recognized that despite his popularity, he needed legislators who would push his initiatives through Congress. Washington's secretary of the treasury and close ally, Alexander Hamilton, gathered legislators into a loosely knit party, the Federalists, that favored a strong national government.

Thomas Jefferson, secretary of state during Washington's first term (1789–1793), feared a strong central government, and he and his backers opposed Hamilton's Federalists. But Jefferson's primary concern was that the new government should succeed, and so despite his opposition, he remained in Washington's cabinet during the president's first term. When Jefferson later resigned his secretarial post, in 1793, many of those who shared his apprehensions about a strong central government remained in Congress.

Although Jefferson lost to Federalist John Adams in the 1796 presidential election, he paved the way for his future electoral success by building a base of support—including partisan groups in the states and newly established political newspapers—that allowed him to get his message out.[20] This direct communication with voters marked a significant step in the civic development of the U.S. electorate. The strategy was effective: Jefferson won election to the presidency in 1800 over Adams, and Adams's defeat marked the end of the Federalist Party. Jefferson was reelected in 1804, and both of his elections demonstrated the important function that political parties would play in elections.[21] His supporters became known as Jeffersonian Republicans; later, Democratic-Republicans. The modern descendants of the Democratic-Republicans today are called Democrats.

The Jeffersonian Republicans' effective campaign tactics of communicating with voters, along with the absence of well-organized opposition, resulted in their continued dominance from 1815 to 1828. Historians call those years the Era of Good Feelings, largely because of the widespread popular support for Democratic-Republican presidents James Madison (1809–1817), James Monroe (1817–1825), and John Quincy Adams (1825–1829).

The Second Party System: The Democrats' Rise to Power, 1828–1860

By 1828, some dissension among the Jeffersonian Republicans was becoming apparent. Members of the party, including the charismatic military general and politician Andrew Jackson of Tennessee, chafed at the elitism of the party and the era. The Jacksonian Democrats—the name for the new coalition that Jackson formed—emphasized leadership through merit rather than birth.[22] They espoused **populism,** a philosophy supporting the rights and empowerment of the masses, particularly in the area of political participation, and the **spoils system,** in which political supporters were rewarded with jobs (from the phrase "to the victor go the spoils"). The Jacksonian Democrats succeeded in mobilizing the masses, sweeping Jackson to victory in the presidential election of 1828.[23] Political parties had become the medium through which many Americans were politicized, and in 1828, for the first time, more than one million Americans cast their ballots in the presidential contest.

Jackson's populism marked a critical step in opening up the civic life of the polity to many new groups of citizens who had not been involved in politics previously.[24] It redefined not only who was eligible to succeed as political leaders but also who should be eligible to participate in the selection of those leaders. Historian Richard P. McCormick noted that the Jacksonian Democrats extended voting rights to all white adult males, changed the mechanism for selecting presidential electors to popular elections by voters instead of by the state legislatures, and increased the importance of the party convention, in effect giving party members more say in candidates' selection. And although women would not gain the right to vote until 1920, the Jacksonian era saw the formal beginnings of the women's suffrage movement with the formation of the two major women's suffrage organizations and the advent of the Seneca Falls Convention (1848) in support of expanded rights for women.[25]

During the 1830s, southern plantation owners and northern industrialists became concerned about the impact the Democrats' populism would have on economic elites.[26] Their mutual interests crystallized in the formation of the Whig Party in 1836, which succeeded in electing two presidents, William Henry Harrison (succeeded by John Tyler upon his death) and Zachary Taylor.[27] But the era of the Second Party System ultimately was defined by the long-standing effects that Jacksonian principles would have on U.S. politics, namely through the politicization of a previously excluded mass of citizens—many of whom had been initiated into the rites of full citizenship and others of whom had begun the struggle to win their own status as full citizens.[28]

The Third Party System: The Republicans' Rise to Power, 1860–1896

In the 1850s, slavery became the primary concern for both the Whigs and the Democrats.[29] This highly charged issue divided the Whig Party into proslavery and abolitionist factions, and the party consequently faded away.[30] In its place, a new antislavery party, the Republicans (also called the Grand Old Party, or GOP), took shape in 1854 and gained the support

populism
a philosophy supporting the rights and empowerment of the masses as opposed to elites

spoils system
the practice of rewarding political supporters with jobs

THE CURIOUS EFFECT OF CLEAN LINEN UPON

THE DEMOCRATIC PARTY

POLITICAL INQUIRY

In this cartoon by the famous nineteenth-century caricaturist and cartoonist Thomas Nast, what does the tiger represent? What point is the cartoonist making about the "clean linen" the tiger is wearing?

of abolitionist Whigs and northern Democrats.[31] The victory of the Republican presidential nominee, Abraham Lincoln, in the election of 1860 marked the beginning of a period of dominance of the antislavery Republicans, which continued even after the Civil War.[32] During this time, the Republican Party enjoyed strong support from newly franchised African American voters. Although many African Americans in the South were prevented from exercising their right to vote through threats, intimidation, and tactics such as the white primary (see Chapter 5), African Americans in the North widely voted Republican. They would remain strong supporters of the "party of Lincoln" for decades.

During this time, political parties grew very strong, and political machines came to dominate the political landscape. A **political machine** was both a corrupt and a useful organization that dominated politics around the turn of the twentieth century, particularly in cities. Each political machine was headed by a "boss," whose power rested on a system of patronage. A party leader used **patronage** as a device to reward political supporters—rather than individuals who might demonstrate greater merit or particular competence—with jobs or government contracts. In exchange, those receiving patronage would vote for the party and might be expected to volunteer on a campaign or kick back some of their wages to the party.

Although political machines were known for corruption, they did accomplish some good. Richard Croker was political boss of Tammany Hall, New York City's Democratic Party political machine from 1886 until 1902. He explained: "Think of what New York is and what the people of New York are. One half are of foreign birth. . . . They do not speak our language, they do not know our laws. . . . There is no denying the service which Tammany has rendered to the Republic, there is no such organization for taking hold of the untrained, friendless man and converting him into a citizen. Who else would do it if we did not?"[33]

On that score, Croker was right. At the time, political machines provided the vital service of socializing a generation of immigrants to democracy and to the American way of political life. Some machines, including Tammany Hall, generated widespread political participation, and some allowed the participation of women.[34] Political machines helped integrate immigrants into the social, economic, and political fabric of the United States, usually by awarding jobs for loyalty to the party. And in an era when the federal government had not yet become a large-scale provider of social services, urban political machines also provided a safety net for the injured, the elderly, and widows.

The Fourth Party System: Republican Dominance, 1896–1932

The 1896 presidential election between populist Democrat William Jennings Bryan and Republican William McKinley marked the beginning of a new era in party politics. Bryan appealed widely to Protestants, southerners, midwesterners, and rural dwellers who were suspicious of Catholic, ethnic, working-class immigrants in the urban Northeast. McKinley emphasized economic growth and development and garnered support from industrialists, bankers, and even working-class factory workers, who saw his backing of business as being good for the economy. McKinley won the election handily, his victory ushering in an era of Republican dominance in presidential politics that would last until the election of 1912.

That year, Theodore Roosevelt (who had succeeded McKinley as president in 1901 after the latter's assassination, and who had been elected president as a Republican in 1904) ran in the presidential election as a Progressive. The Progressive Party advocated widespread governmental reform and sought to limit the power of political bosses. The Republicans'

political machine
big-city party organization that exerted control over many aspects of life and lavishly rewarded supporters

patronage
system in which a party leader rewarded political supporters with jobs or government contracts in exchange for their support of the party

split between William Howard Taft's regular Republicans and Roosevelt's Progressives powered Democrat Woodrow Wilson to the presidency with only 42 percent of the popular vote.

As Wilson's Democratic administration ended up enacting many of the Progressive Party's proposals, the power of the urban political machines declined. For example, recorded voter registration and secret ballot laws were passed, the direct party primary was established, and civil service reform was expanded. The national leaders who spearheaded those measures designed them to take political power out of the bosses' hands and give it to the electorate.

After Wilson's two terms, the Republicans continued to enjoy the support of business elites and the industrial working class. They also benefited from the backing of the many African Americans in the northern cities who continued to support the party of Lincoln, and of women voters, many of whom had been activists in the Progressive movement. With this widespread and diverse support, the Republicans retained control of the presidency throughout the 1920s.

The Fifth Party System: Democratic Dominance, 1932–1968

When the stock market crashed in 1929, the economy entered the deep downturn that history remembers as the Great Depression. In the election of 1932, a broad constituency responded to the calls of the Democratic candidate, Franklin D. Roosevelt, for an increased governmental role in promoting the public welfare. Roosevelt pressed tirelessly for a **New Deal** for all Americans, a broad program in which the government would bear the responsibility of providing a "safety net" to protect the most disadvantaged members of society.

A new alignment among American voters swept "FDR" into presidential office. In fact, the **New Deal coalition**—the name for the voting bloc comprising traditional southern Democrats, northern city dwellers (especially immigrants and the poor), Catholics, unionized and blue-collar workers, African Americans, and women—would give Roosevelt the presidency an unprecedented four times.[35]

The era of the Fifth Party System significantly opened up party politics and civic activity to a widening spectrum of Americans. Notably for African Americans and women, Franklin Roosevelt's elections marked the first time that they had been actively courted by political parties, and their new political activism—particularly in the form of voting and political party activities—left them feeling they had a voice in their government.

Vice President Harry Truman assumed the presidency on Roosevelt's death in 1945 and was elected in his own right in 1948, but subsequent Democrats were unable to keep Roosevelt's coalition together. Republican Dwight Eisenhower won the White House in 1952 and again in 1956. And although Democrats John F. Kennedy and Lyndon Johnson held the presidency through most of the 1960s, the events of that decade wreaked havoc on the

Party Politics in Flux

THEN (1889)	NOW (2011)
Powerful political parties were in their heyday, and party bosses ruled the cities with an iron fist.	The era of party politics in the United States is over, according to some scholars.
The patronage system was in high gear, and political parties derived enormous power and loyalty from the recipients of jobs and lucrative contracts.	A merit-based civil service system has largely replaced patronage, and parties are weakened because of a decline in the number of loyal members.
Elected officials toed the party line, because they depended on the party for their office.	Elected officials pride themselves on their "independence" and sometimes owe very little to their political party.

WHAT'S NEXT?

> How are advancing technologies likely to change political parties and their operations in the future? Will these weaken or strengthen the parties? Explain.

> Do you think that the voters who went to the polls in the 2008 primaries and general election remained loyal to their parties in 2010? Why or why not?

> How do parties today help voters evaluate candidates? Will they still perform this function in the future? Will the nature of this process change? Explain.

New Deal
Franklin Roosevelt's broad social welfare program in which the government would bear the responsibility of providing a "safety net" to protect the most disadvantaged members of society

New Deal coalition
the group composed of southern Democrats, northern city dwellers, immigrants, the poor, Catholics, labor union members, blue-collar workers, African Americans, and women that elected FDR to the presidency four times

> African American voters were a key constituency in electing both Franklin Roosevelt and Barack Obama to the presidency. Here, voters in New York City's Harlem wait to cast their ballots for President Roosevelt in 1936 and President Obama in 2008.

Democratic Party, with deep divisions opening up over the Vietnam War and civil rights for African Americans.[36]

A New Party System?

Political scientists have sought to determine whether the era that began when Richard Nixon was elected president in 1968 can be considered a separate party system. Barack Obama's election in 2008, particularly his strong support among young and first-time voters, points to a continuation of the trend of Democratic dominance established in the Fifth Party System. But Republican dominance of the presidency since 1968, coupled with increasing support of the Republican Party by southern whites and the increasing activism of conservative Christians in the party, gives support to the claim that a new party system has emerged.

Additional characteristics of this new party system, according to scholars, include *intense party competition,* in which the two major U.S. political parties have been nearly evenly matched and neither one has dominated; and *divided government,* where a president of one party has to deal with a Congress of the other. This fierce partisan competitiveness is clearly apparent in the outcomes of recent national elections. In particular, the 2000 presidential campaign demonstrated the ferocious rivalry of the two parties, with a presidential election so close that the outcome was in question for weeks after the voting had ended. That year, voters also evenly divided the Senate, electing fifty Democrats and fifty Republicans.

Moreover, some scholars see **dealignment,** the phenomenon in which fewer voters support the two major political parties and instead self-identify as independent, as a notable characteristic of this new party system.[37] Others view the increasing trend toward supporting candidates from both parties (**ticket splitting**) or from other parties as evidence of a new party system's emergence.

The period since 1968 has also been characterized by the growing importance of candidate-centered politics. The rise of **candidate committees,** organizations that candidates form to support their individual election as opposed to the party's slate of candidates, is one reflection of how politics has increasingly become candidate-centered. Candidate committees compete with political parties in many arenas. They raise and spend money, organize campaigns, and attempt to mobilize voters. One impact of their enhanced influence has been that elected officials, particularly members of Congress, are less indebted to their parties than in previous eras and thus sometimes demonstrate less loyalty when voting on bills in the legislature.

Some political scientists argue that these characteristics of the new party system demonstrate that the responsible party model (discussed earlier) is not as strong as it once was.

dealignment
the situation in which fewer voters support the two major political parties, instead identifying themselves as independent, or splitting their ticket between candidates from more than one party

ticket splitting
the situation in which voters vote for candidates from more than one party

candidate committees
organizations that candidates form to support their individual election

The rise of candidate committees and the increase in ticket splitting mean that parties are less helpful to voters as they assess candidates, because the differences between Republican and Democratic candidates may dissipate in the face of constituent opinion. Yet most Americans disagree: a recent Gallup poll indicated that nearly two-thirds of those surveyed believe that there are important differences between the Democratic and the Republican parties.[38] And the research of some scholars, including David Karol, Hans Noel, John Zaller, and Marty Cohen, indicates that party elites, including elected officials and former elected officials, have increased their control in selecting party presidential nominees, suggesting a potential revival of the importance of parties as players in politics today.[39]

Two-Party Domination in U.S. Politics

Since the ratification of the Constitution in 1787, the United States has had a two-party system for all but about thirty years in total. This historical record stands in marked contrast to the experience of the many nations that have third parties.[40] A **third party** is a political party organized as opposition or an alternative to the existing parties in a two-party system. Many countries even have *multi*party systems. (See "Global Context" on page 258.)

The United States' two-party system has had two contradictory influences on people's civic engagement. On the one hand, the dominance of only two strong political parties through most of American history has made it easy for individuals to find avenues for becoming civically engaged. Further, at various historical points, political parties have worked for the outright extension of political rights to groups that were excluded, although often with the foremost aim of bolstering their core supporters. On the other hand, the dominance of just two political parties that tend to be ideologically moderate discourages the political participation of some people, particularly those who are strongly ideological.

Although the grip of the United States' two-party system is frustrating to people who support a greater diversity of parties, the reasons for the two-party system are numerous and difficult to change.

The Dualist Nature of Most Conflicts

Historically, many issues in the United States have been dualist, or "two-sided." For example, the debate over ratification of the U.S. Constitution found people with two basic opinions. On one side, the Federalists supported ratification of the Constitution, which created a federal government that separated powers among three branches and shared power with state governments. They were opposed by the Anti-Federalists, who campaigned against ratification of the Constitution, supported stronger states' rights, and wanted to see states and individuals enjoy greater protections. This split provided the initial structure for the two-party system, and a multitude of issues followed that format.

Political scientists Seymour Martin Lipset and Stein Rokkan asserted that the dualist nature of voter alignments or cleavages shapes how political parties form. In particular, these alignments or cleavages concern the character of the national fabric (for example, should religious ideals or secular notions prevail?), and they are determined by function (business versus agrarian interests, for example).[41] These cleavages shaped party formation during the nineteenth century, when the dualist nature of conflict continued to be in evidence in public affairs. Some states wanted slavery; other states opposed "the peculiar institution" of human bondage. In some states, commercial and industrial interests dominated; in other states, agricultural interests held the reins of power. Immigrants, often Catholics, controlled the politics of some states, whereas native-born Protestants held sway in others.

"IT JUST WOULDN'T WORK OUT, DEREK. I'M FROM A RED STATE, AND YOU'RE FROM A BLUE STATE."

GLOBAL CONTEXT

POLITICAL PARTIES IN NORTHERN IRELAND

Although the functions and the focus of political parties in the United States today are broad and important, it may be hard to envision modern parties as institutions that can change people's everyday lives and alter the course of a nation's history. But that is exactly what happened in the mid-1990s in the six counties that make up Northern Ireland. This region, which was under the rule of the British government, had been racked by violence for decades as Catholic and Protestant paramilitary forces engaged in guerrilla warfare over a deep division among the citizenry: Catholics wanted the counties to be reunited with the Republic of Ireland, but Protestants wanted them to remain part of Great Britain.

Will Northern Ireland's bold experiment in governance by party power-sharing succeed?

Reflecting the varying preferences of the country's voters, Northern Ireland features more than a dozen political parties. Only a subset of those parties enjoys a competitive edge, however, because of their wider support among the people. In the mid-1990s, Gerry Adams and John Hume, the leaders of two of Northern Ireland's most influential political parties, began talks to explore how to end political violence in the provinces once and for all. Gerry Adams's Sinn Fein Party (pronounced "shin fane," meaning "ourselves alone" in Irish) was affiliated with the Provisional Irish Republican Army, the Catholic paramilitary group engaged in violence that sought to end British rule in Northern Ireland. John Hume's Social Democratic and Labour Party, Northern Ireland's largest political party, has a liberal ideology and has always rejected violence as a means of achieving political goals. Over the course of many months that turned into years, Adams and Hume, later joined by Ulster Unionist Party (UUP) leader David Trimble (who negotiated with Adams despite the UUP's fierce commitment to retaining British control in the region), agreed to a six-plank set of principles. Called the Mitchell Principles in honor of then-U.S. senator George Mitchell (D-Maine), who helped to broker the deal, the agreement called for the people of Northern Ireland to decide their political fate democratically

and provided for the verifiable disarmament of the paramilitary groups.

The so-called Good Friday agreement was signed by the Irish and British governments and was endorsed by nearly all major political parties in 1998. In May of that year, 71 percent of the voters of Northern Ireland approved the Good Friday agreements, a major step in the Northern Ireland peace process. The way was paved for the election of a devolved Northern Irish Assembly, a legislature that would essentially govern the territory through a power-sharing agreement among the leading political parties. Until March 2007, it appeared that all the negotiations would be undone when Democratic Unionist Party (DUP) leader Ian Paisley refused even to discuss the agreement with Adams or other Sinn Feiners. (The DUP is vehemently anti-Catholic and opposed the Good Friday agreement.) But on March 27, one day before a deadline that would have put Northern Ireland back under British control, Paisley relented and accepted the power-sharing scenario. A new era of devolved democracy thus began in Northern Ireland. By May 2007, a power-sharing agreement covering executive power was established, with Paisley and Sinn Fein's Martin McGuinness holding equal powers. Upon Paisley's retirement in 2008, DUP leader Peter Robinson replaced Paisley, and he and McGuinness continue the power-sharing executive arrangement today.

> As a testament to the power of political parties to shape policy, Northern Ireland First Minister Peter Robinson of the Democratic Unionist Party (second from the right) and Deputy First Minister Martin McGuiness of Sinn Fein (second from the left) attend a 2009 North-South Council meeting along with Minister for Foreign Affairs Michael Martin (left) and Jeffrey Donaldson, DUP member of Parliament (right).

By the twentieth century, the dualist conflict had become more ideological. Some Americans agreed with President Franklin D. Roosevelt's plan to help lift the country out of the Great Depression by significantly increasing the role of government in people's everyday lives. Others opposed this unprecedented expansion of the federal government's power. In later decades, debates over civil rights and women's rights demonstrated the continued dualist nature of conflict in American society and culture.

The Winner-Take-All Electoral System

In almost all U.S. elections, the person with the most votes wins. If a competitor gets just one vote fewer than the victor, he or she wins nothing. If a third party garners a significant proportion of the vote in congressional elections nationwide but does not win the most votes in any given district, the party will not win any seats in Congress.

Compare the **winner-take-all** system with the proportional representation system found in many nations. In a **proportional representation system,** political parties win the number of parliamentary seats equal to the percentage of the vote each party receives. So, for example, if the Green Party were to capture 9 percent of the vote in a country's election, it would get nine seats in a one-hundred-member parliament. In a proportional representation system, the 19 percent of the vote that Reform Party candidate Ross Perot won in the 1992 U.S. presidential election would have given the Reform Party about 85 seats in the House of Representatives!

In nations with proportional representation, third parties (which we consider in more detail later in the chapter) are encouraged because such parties can win a few seats in the legislature and use them to further their cause and broaden their support.[42] In addition, in proportional representation systems, third parties sometimes form a *coalition,* or working union, with a larger party so that the two together can control a majority of a legislature. And so, for example, the Green Party that won nine seats in Parliament in the example mentioned above might form a coalition with another party that had received 42 percent of the vote, together forming a majority government. In this way, a third party can get members appointed to key positions as a reward for forming the coalition. Consequently, societies with proportional representation systems can sometimes be more inclusive of differing points of view because even those winning a small proportion of the vote achieve representation, and that representation can be pivotal in the formation of coalitions.

winner-take-all
electoral system in which the candidate who receives the most votes wins that office, even if that total is not a majority.

proportional representation system
an electoral structure in which political parties win the number of parliamentary seats equal to the percentage of the vote the party receives

Continued Socialization to the Two-Party System

Another reason that the two-party system dominates in the United States is that party identification—like ideology, values, and religious beliefs—is an attribute that often passes down from one generation to the next. Hence many an individual is likely to be a Democrat or a Republican because his or her parents were one or the other. Many people first learn about government and politics at home. Around the dinner table, a child may have heard her parents rail against Barack Obama's health care proposal or criticize George W. Bush's Iraq policy. Having become socialized to their household's political culture, children are likely to mimic their parents' views.

Even children who do not share their parents' political outlook or who grow apart from it over time (as commonly occurs during the college years) have been socialized to the legitimacy of the two-party system—unless, of course, their parents routinely criticized both Democrats and Republicans or voiced dissatisfaction with the two-party system.

Election Laws That Favor the Two-Party System

At both the federal and the state level in the United States, election laws benefit the two major parties because they are usually written by members of one of those parties. Although some local governments mandate nonpartisan elections, in most cities and towns, getting on the ballot typically means simply winning the party's nomination and collecting a state-specified number of signatures of registered party members on a nominating petition. Usually, the party organization will circulate this petition for a candidate. Third parties have a much steeper climb to get their candidates in office. In the 2008 presidential election, candidate Ralph Nader, who ran as an independent, had difficulty just getting his name on the ballot in some states.

Scholars of civic engagement point to the structural impediments to the formation of third parties as key to the low level of civic engagement on the part of individuals who are dissatisfied with the two-party system. Facing seemingly insurmountable structural obstacles to the formation of successful third parties, some Americans shy away from political engagement.

The Two-Party System Today: In Decline or in Resurgence?

Given the various historical changes to the U.S. political party system that we have examined, many political scientists have inquired into what the impact of those changes will be. Do the changes signify an end to party control in American politics? Or can political parties adapt to the altered environment and find new sources of power?

The Party's Over

Some scholars argue that changes in the political environment have rendered today's political parties essentially impotent to fulfill the functions that parties performed during stronger party systems. In 1982, political scientist Gary Orren wrote, "In a world in which political scientists disagree on almost everything, there is remarkable agreement among the political science profession that the strength of American political parties has declined significantly over the past several decades."[43] Although some political scientists would subsequently challenge Orren's perspective, many agreed with him at the time.

These theorists note several key factors that have contributed to party decline. Some argue that the elimination of political patronage through the requirement of civil service qualifications for government employees has significantly hurt parties' ability to reward loyal followers with government jobs. Patronage jobs still exist, but most government positions are now awarded upon an applicant's successful performance on a civil service exam that is designed to measure qualifications based on objective criteria. Whereas the recipients of patronage jobs were among the most loyal party members in previous decades, party loyalty has decreased as political parties have lost a significant amount of control in the awarding of jobs.

Other political scientists emphasize the government's increased role over time in providing social welfare benefits as a contributor to the decline of political parties. Because of President Franklin Roosevelt's New Deal and further expansion of the government's role as the key provider of social services, the parties typically no longer perform that function. Thus changing times have brought the elimination of another source of party loyalty.

primary election
an election in which voters choose the party's candidates who will run in the later general election

Primary elections—elections in which voters choose the party's candidates who will run in the later general election—also have decreased parties' power by taking the control of nominations from party leaders and handing it to voters. In the past, when a party machine anointed nominees at nominating conventions, those nominees became indebted to the party and typically responded with loyalty if they got elected. But today's candidates are less likely to owe their nomination to the party: instead, in many cases they have fought for and won the nomination by taking their campaign directly to primary voters.

Changes in the mass media have also meant a drastically decreased role for political parties. In their heyday, political parties were one of the most important providers of news. Parties published so-called penny papers that reported information to the public. Today, political parties may still provide some information to voters at election time, but most voters rely on other, independent media outlets—newspapers, television, radio, and Internet news sources—rather than exclusively partisan sources.

The rise in candidate-centered campaigns has also weakened political parties. **Candidate-centered campaigns,** in which an individual seeking election, rather than an entire party slate, is the focus, have come about because of changes in the parties' functions, the advent of direct primaries, and trends in the mass media that have shifted the focus to individual office-seekers. Candidate-centered campaigns also must rely more heavily on paid professional campaign workers (instead of party volunteers), making it necessary for contributors to support individual candidates rather than political parties.

These changes in the nature of political parties and in their ability to perform their traditional functions have led some political scientists to conclude that the era of party rule is ending. Other players, they say—including interest groups, candidate-based organizations, and the media—will come to assume the roles traditionally performed by political parties.

candidate-centered campaign
a campaign in which an individual seeking election, rather than an entire party slate, is the focus

The Party's Just Begun

Pointing to the record-breaking turnout in the 2008 presidential primaries, other political scientists strongly disagree that U.S. parties' prime has passed.[44] While conceding that political parties' functions have changed, these theorists observe that parties have proved themselves remarkably adaptable. When the political environment has changed in the past, political parties have responded by assuming different functions or finding new avenues by which to seed party loyalty. According to this view, the parties' ability to rebound is alive and well.

These scholars also argue that the continued dominance in the United States of two political parties—through decades of threats to their survival—has demonstrated a strength and a resilience that are likely to prevail. Today's Republicans, the party of Lincoln, have endured the assassinations of party leaders, the Great Depression, the four-term presidency of popular Democrat Franklin D. Roosevelt, and the Watergate scandal during the Nixon presidency. Today's Democrats are the same party that opposed suffrage for African Americans in the aftermath of the Civil War, and that survived internal divisions over civil rights through the 1960s, to become strong supporters of African American rights in recent decades. The Democrats too have endured assassinations and scandals, and have weathered Republican control of the White House for all but twelve years since 1968. Both political parties have remained remarkably competitive despite the challenges to their success.

Scholars who argue that the two main U.S. political parties are once again rebounding cite the lack of viable alternatives to the two-party system. Yes, third parties have made a mark in recent presidential elections. But the present-day party system has not seen the emergence of a strong, viable third party with a cohesive ideology that has attracted a significant portion of the vote in more than one election. And civic education scholars agree that third parties have served an important function by encouraging the political participation of people who are disenchanted with the current two-party system. They also acknowledge, however, the continued dominance of the two main parties in creating opportunities for civic engagement within communities.

> The party organization consists of both paid staff and party volunteers. Here, Republican party volunteers in Texas make last minute calls to remind supporter to get out and vote in the 2008 election.

Third Parties in the United States

As we have seen, the absence of viable U.S. political parties beyond the Democrats and the Republicans is a source of frustration for some Americans. Despite that frustration, there has been little consensus about whether the Democratic and Republican political parties do an adequate job in representing the American people, as shown in Figure 8.5 on page 262. The figure does not show that, at different times, the proportions of conservatives, liberals, and moderates vary in their likelihood of agreeing that a third party is needed. According to pollsters, this difference may reflect the respondents' opinions of the effectiveness of their party at representing their views. And so, for example, at high points in the

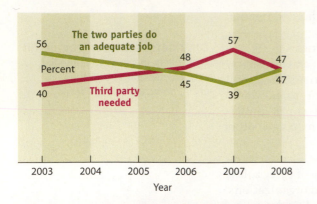

FIGURE 8.5 ■ IS A THIRD PARTY NEEDED?
What trend do the polling data in this figure show?
What factors in the political and social environments
might explain this trend?

SOURCE: The Gallup Poll, "Public Divided on Need for Third Party," www.gallup
.com/poll/110764/Public-Divided-Need-Third-Party.aspx.

George W. Bush presidency, conservatives would have been less likely to say a third party was needed, and the same would hold true for liberals during high points in Barack Obama's presidency.

Because of the differing ideological viewpoints of those who agree a third party is needed, third parties have had little success in contesting elections. In recent times, Ralph Nader was an influential candidate in 2000, not because he netted a sizeable proportion of votes but because the 3 percent that he did win was enough to change the outcome of that razor-close election. Other third-party candidacies have proved influential because of their role in focusing attention—particularly the attention of the victorious candidate—on an issue that might not otherwise have been addressed.[45] Such was the case in 1912 when Progressive Party candidate Theodore Roosevelt ran against Woodrow Wilson. Although he lost the presidency, Roosevelt succeeded in shaping public opinion so that Wilson felt compelled to enact part of the Progressives' national agenda, including sweeping changes to the nation's child labor laws.

One of the most significant obstacles to the formation of a viable third party is that people who are dissatisfied with the two dominant parties fall across the ideological spectrum: some are very liberal; others, quite conservative; still others, moderate. Thus, although many Americans are dissatisfied with the current parties, a third party would have difficulty attracting enough support from among these diversely dissatisfied party members.

Nonetheless, third parties have played, and continue to play, an influential role in American electoral politics. Third parties are particularly effective at encouraging the civic engagement of people who feel that the two dominant parties do not represent their views or do not listen to them. Third parties give such citizens a voice. And even though third parties often do not succeed electorally, their mere presence in the political arena enlivens civic discourse and frequently encourages debate about urgent policy issues that the two major parties ignore or slight.

Types of Third Parties

Third parties have existed in the United States since the early nineteenth century. Over the nation's history, third parties typically have fallen into one of three general categories: issue advocacy parties, ideologically oriented parties, and splinter parties.

ISSUE ADVOCACY PARTIES   Formed to promote a stance on a particular issue, many issue advocacy parties are short-lived. Once the issue is dealt with or fades from popular concern, the mobilizing force behind the party disintegrates. An example is today's Green Party, which promotes environmental protection as a primary issue and also emphasizes human rights, childhood poverty, globalization, health care, and corporate corruption and greed in its party platform. In the 2000 presidential election, the Green Party sought to win 5 percent of the vote for its presidential candidate, Ralph Nader. If the Greens had succeeded, they would have automatically qualified their party for federal matching funds in the 2004 campaign. The Green Party fell short, however, since it captured only 3 percent of the vote. Its share of the vote then dropped sharply in the 2004 presidential election.

IDEOLOGICALLY ORIENTED PARTIES   The agenda of an ideologically oriented party is typically broader than that of an issue-oriented party. Ideologically oriented parties are structured around an *ideology*—a highly organized and coherent framework concerning the nature and role of government in society (see Chapter 6). Such parties have broad views about many different aspects of government. For example, the Libertarian Party, which holds the ideological position that government should not interfere with individuals' social, political, and economic rights, advocates a very limited role for government: no guarantees of minimum wages or other forms of governmental regulation of the economy, including environmental regulation; no governmental interference in individuals' privacy; the legalization of prostitution and drugs; and the elimination of major governmental bureaucracies, including the Central Intelligence Agency, the Internal Revenue Service, and the Federal Bureau of Investigation.

Another ideologically oriented party is the Socialist Party, which lies at the other end of the ideological spectrum from the Libertarian Party. The Socialist Party, formed in 1901, is one of the longest-standing ideologically oriented parties in the United States. Socialists believe that government should play a large role in ensuring economic equality for all people.

SPLINTER PARTIES A splinter party is a political party that breaks off, or "splinters," from one of the two dominant parties. Often a group splinters off because of intra-party (internal, or within the party) disagreement on a particular issue. Though many Tea Party candidates sought election under the Republican Party label in 2010, the sometimes fractured relationship between the activists and more moderate Republicans caused many to wonder if the Tea Party will splinter from the Republican Party. In 1948, a group of southern Democrats who opposed the Democratic Party's support of civil rights for African Americans splintered from the Democratic Party to form the States' Rights Party, which quickly became known as the Dixiecrat Party. The party called itself the States' Rights Party because it claimed that Congress had no power to interfere with the administration of laws made by the states. It used that claim to retain the policies that created a system of racial segregation in the South. Although the States' Rights Party was a separate, formal organization, many southern Democratic elected officials and party leaders who agreed with the States' Rights Party's platform supported its views from within the Democratic Party.

The Impact of Third Parties

Despite the difficulties associated with sustaining support in American electoral politics, third parties have important effects in the political arena. First, although U.S. third parties usually do not win elections, they can influence electoral outcomes. For example, given the closeness of the 2000 presidential race, many Democrats believe that Green Party candidate Ralph Nader caused Democrat Al Gore to lose the election. They reason that Nader voters would have been more likely to vote for the liberal Gore than for the conservative George W. Bush if Nader had not been a candidate. In a state such as Florida where the electorate was evenly divided, Nader's candidacy in fact could have changed the outcome of that state's balloting and thus the results of the national election as well. Of course, many third-party advocates claim that supporters of a third-party candidate may not have voted at all if their party had not been on the ballot. (See "Thinking Critically About Democracy" on page 264.)

Second, third parties provide a release valve for dissatisfied voters. People who are disgruntled with the two major parties can join or form another political party. And although a third party's chances of electoral success are not great, such parties provide a mechanism for like-minded people to come together to try to effect change. Sometimes, these efforts result in a victory, especially on the local level. A well-known third-party victor is Jesse Ventura, a former professional wrestler who was elected governor of Minnesota in 1998 as a candidate of the Reform Party. At the national level, there have been several elections in which third parties were a release valve for discontented voters, as shown in Figure 8.6. In U.S. history, third-party presidential candidates have won more than 10 percent of the vote seven times, the latest being in 1992, when Independent Party candidate H. Ross Perot captured 19 percent of the vote. As the figure illustrates, in five of those seven cases, the incumbent party's presidential nominee lost the presidency. Thus, third parties tend to help the major out-of-power party win election.

Finally, third parties put a variety of issues on the national political agenda. When a third party, especially an issue-oriented third party, draws attention to an issue of

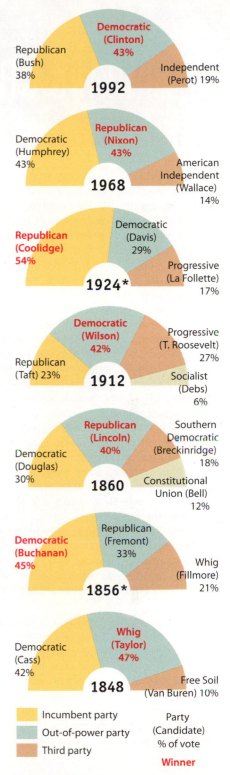

FIGURE 8.6

Third Parties Help the Out-of-Power Party

NOTE: Candidate appears in parentheses; percentage is percentage of vote won by candidate.

* Denotes election in which incumbent party retained power in face of a strong third-party challenge

ARE THIRD PARTIES BAD FOR THE UNITED STATES?

The Issue: The United States' political culture and electoral structure predispose the country to a two-party system. Historically, two parties have dominated, and when third parties have emerged, they have either been subsumed by the dominant parties or simply disappeared when their primary issue of concern was no longer relevant.

The question of whether third parties are bad or good for American democracy dates back almost as far as the democracy itself. But the question has modern implications. Third-party candidates are often seen as spoilers who siphon off votes from the majority's top candidate and thereby enable the less-favored candidate to win. Many pundits argued that was the case in the 2010 congressional elections, when Tea Party candidates challenged Democrats and Republicans for seats in the U.S. House of Representatives and the U.S. Senate. In some races that year, critics charged that conservative Tea Party candidates who had won primaries against mainstream candidates were weaker general election candidates, and paved the way for some Democratic victories. In other races, Tea Party candidates who ran as independents may have siphoned votes from Republicans, resulting in a stronger Democratic showing. Similar arguments were made in 1992, when pundits charged Reform Party candidate H. Ross Perot with taking votes away from Republican George H. W. Bush and thus ushering Democrat Bill Clinton into the White House.

Do third-party candidacies hurt American democracy by skewing elections away from the third party's major party rival? Or are they good for democracy because they bring out voters who would otherwise have stayed at home and because they help ensure that issues of crucial concern to the electorate get on the national agenda?

Yes: The presence of third-party candidates on a ballot means that the major political party—Democratic or Republican—that is closest to the third party in ideology and in base of support will be hurt. This effect occurs because if the third-party candidate were not on the ballot, many of his or her supporters would vote for the candidate (Democratic or Republican) who is ideologically closest to the third-party candidate. Thus, that major party candidate is at a disadvantage, because the third-party candidate essentially siphons off or splits the vote for the major party candidate. Democ-

racy is subverted, because often a candidate wins who is least appealing to the majority of voters (that is, those who voted for the losing major party candidate and those who voted for the third-party candidate). As a result, people are highly dissatisfied with both the political process and elected officials.

No: Only through third parties and third-party candidacies can voters get the national agenda they desire. In 2010, many citizens wanted issues such as labor law reform and corporate crime to be priorities on the federal policy agenda. Other citizens wanted serious national attention given to tort reform, the elimination of most social welfare benefits, and flat taxes. These issues were not part of the national policy debate between the two major political parties. Without third parties to spearhead such conversations of democracy, many more people will be turned off by and disaffected from the political process.

Other approaches: Third parties are a mixed blessing for the United States. Proponents of third parties are correct in asserting that they provide a safety valve for participation by those dissatisfied with the status quo. Third parties have been effective at getting specific policy concerns on the national agenda, even though frequently that has occurred because one of the major parties co-opts a third party's key issue. But supporters of third parties should realize that the electoral politics in the United States is structured to ensure the perpetuation of the two-party system, and that by supporting a third party candidate, they run the risk of spoiling the chances of their preferred major party candidate.

What do you think?

① Do you think third parties help or hurt American democracy? Why?

② What was the impact of third-party candidates in the 2010 election?

③ What kind of third party do you think would be successful in winning elections?

---

concern, sometimes government officials respond to that concern even if the third party fails in its election bid. In some such cases, the issue has not previously been given priority, and the attention the third party draws to it serves to create a groundswell of political pressure that forces action. In other cases, the policy makers might act to address the issue in order to woo the supporters of the third party who have expressed that particular issue concern.

Historically, the two major parties' co-option of issues that were first promoted by third parties has sometimes contributed to the demise of third parties. For example, as we have seen, the Progressives' presidential candidate, Theodore Roosevelt, lost to Democrat Woodrow Wilson in 1912, but Wilson enacted many elements of the Progressive Party's platform, including antitrust regulations, corporate law reforms, and banking regulations. Lacking a unique platform, and with comparatively little electoral success, the Progressives faded away. More recently, Reform Party candidate H. Ross Perot's activism concerning campaign finance reform eventually led the two major parties to pass the Bipartisan Campaign Finance Reform Act of 2002. The Reform Party's inability to sustain voter support over the long haul is also apparent: after the party's 2000 presidential nominee Pat Buchanan failed to net even 1 percent of the national vote, the party did not nominate a candidate in 2004, instead backing Green Party nominee Ralph Nader.

Tea Party movement
a grassroots, conservative protest movement that opposed recent government actions, including economic stimulus spending and health care reform

New Ideologies, New Technologies: The Parties in the Twenty-First Century

American political parties have changed dramatically in recent years. Global events such as the end of the Cold War, international and domestic terrorism, and the impact of the Internet have partly driven the changes. Within the Republican and Democratic parties, the changes have reflected an ideological shift from an era when a party's defining position was its position on social welfare policy, to a time when foreign policy issues were central, and back again. Today, much emphasis is placed on the differences between the Democrats and the Republicans, but for many citizens there are shades of "purple" between the reds and the blues (see Figure 8.7).

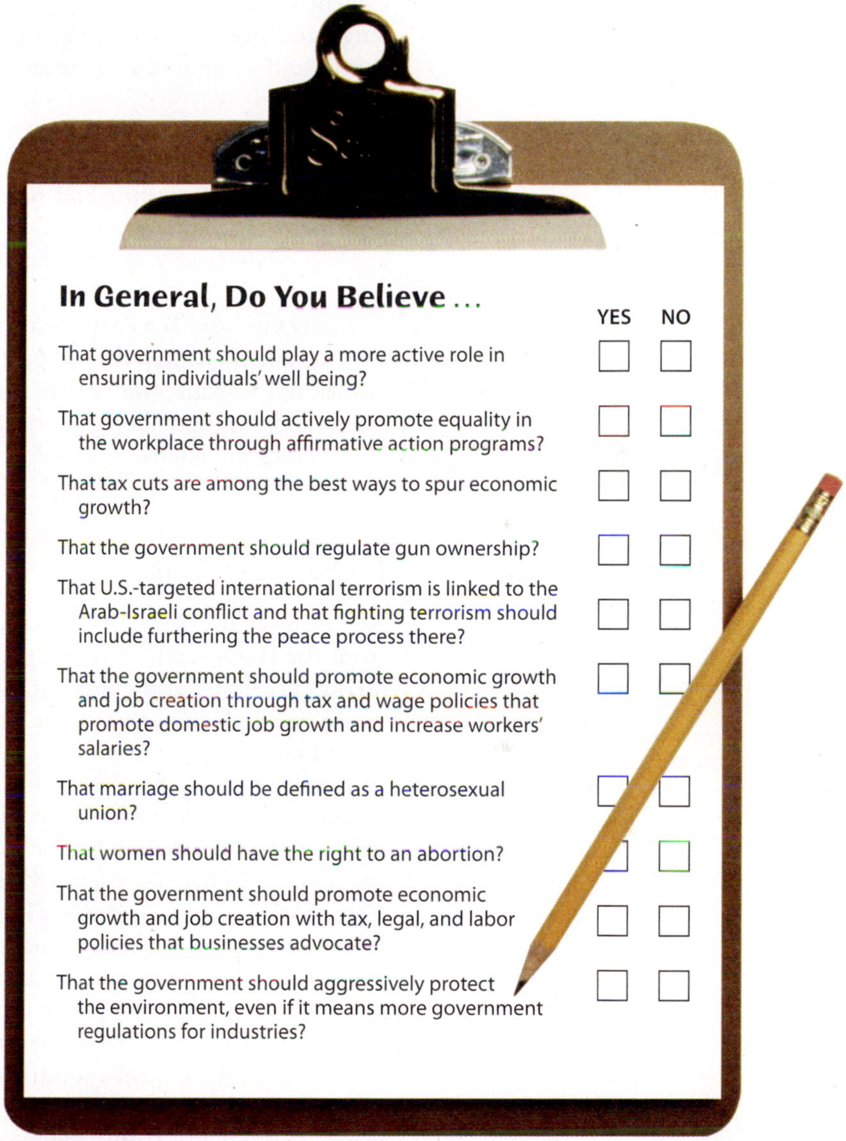

Struggling for the Heart of the Republican Party: Moderates, Neocons, and a Tea Party Movement

In the wake of the inauguration of Barack Obama in January 2009, a grassroots movement began growing in communities across the United States. Outraged by what they saw as excessive spending by the administration and the Democrats in Congress, and particularly incensed during the debates concerning health care reform, conservative activists formed the **Tea Party movement,** a grassroots, conservative protest movement that opposed recent government actions, including economic stimulus spending and health care reform. The moniker is a reference to the colonial era, when colonists dumped tea into Boston Harbor to protest taxes imposed by the British Crown, an action that contributed to the American Revolution.

Though plagued with the growing pains characteristic of virtually any large-scale political movement, Tea Partiers have identified five key principles they believe. These include

In General, Do You Believe ...

	YES	NO
That government should play a more active role in ensuring individuals' well being?	☐	☐
That government should actively promote equality in the workplace through affirmative action programs?	☐	☐
That tax cuts are among the best ways to spur economic growth?	☐	☐
That the government should regulate gun ownership?	☐	☐
That U.S.-targeted international terrorism is linked to the Arab-Israeli conflict and that fighting terrorism should include furthering the peace process there?	☐	☐
That the government should promote economic growth and job creation through tax and wage policies that promote domestic job growth and increase workers' salaries?	☐	☐
That marriage should be defined as a heterosexual union?	☐	☐
That women should have the right to an abortion?	☐	☐
That the government should promote economic growth and job creation with tax, legal, and labor policies that businesses advocate?	☐	☐
That the government should aggressively protect the environment, even if it means more government regulations for industries?	☐	☐

FIGURE 8.7

Are You Red, Blue, or Purple? News commentators use *red* and *blue* to refer to Republicans and Democrats, respectively. Although the basis for an individual's political ideology is complex (see Chapter 1), party identification in the United States often reflects differences in viewpoint on several key issues. Do you know what each party stands for? Do you know which party best represents your views? Take this brief quiz to find out which party you lean toward. Of course, before voting for candidates of that party or even counting yourself as a party identifier, you should further investigate the positions of the parties. The Web sites listed at the end of the chapter are a good place to start.

- less government
- fiscal responsibility
- lower taxes
- states' rights
- national security

Activism centering on these principles has involved a variety of tactics. Some, such as the formation of a political action committee that contributes donations to endorsed candidates who espouse the Tea Party's views, are standard for such movements. But other strategies have proven more controversial: the first candidate endorsed by the Tea Party movement was Florida Republican Marco Rubio, who challenged Florida's Republican governor, Charlie Crist, for the GOP nomination for the U.S. Senate. Faced with Rubio's strong challenge and eventually trailing in the polls, Crist effectively conceded the nomination to Rubio and announced his intention to run for the Senate as an Independent candidate.

In another controversial maneuver, a New Jersey branch of the Tea Party movement sued to recall U.S. Senator Robert Menendez because of his support of government-sponsored health care. The lawsuit had national significance because of the Tea Party movement's argument that state election law (which provided for the recall of state elected officials) applied to federal elected officials, including members of the U.S. House and Senate.

Many view the Tea Party as a splinter party, in part a backlash against the neoconservative faction of the Republican party that dominated party politics during the Bush administration. Neoconservatives are less concerned with domestic issues but are frequently defined (and distinguished from other conservatives) by their aggressive foreign policy stance, particularly in defense of Israel.[46] Neoconservatives also advocate for the proactive spread of democracy.

Democrats Today

The Democratic Party today—the party of Barack Obama—is a markedly different party from the Democratic Party President Bill Clinton molded and shaped in the 1990s. When it comes to issues and policy priorities, today's Democrats, under Obama's leadership, more resemble the Democrats of the mid-twentieth century: a party that emphasized a strong role of government. In particular, today's Democrats emphasize the need for government to provide a safety net for its most disadvantaged citizens, particularly during tough economic times. President Obama's priority of reforming health care and his desire to include a public option demonstrates the Democrats' comfort with expanding the role of the federal government. This is contrasted with Democrats during the Clinton era, sometimes called New Democrats, who were less likely to emphasize government solutions to problems, and who, during a healthy economic era, recognized that *globalization*—the continuing integration of world markets for goods, services, and financial capital—was the most significant factor in framing public policy problems and their solutions

But coupled with the Democratic Party's emphasis today on its traditional values, there also is an emphasis and a sophistication when it comes to maximizing the use of new technologies in politics. Indeed, part of President Obama's success has stemmed from the savvy use of technology—from relying on Facebook to mobilize student primary voters in early primary states in 2008 to raising millions online for his general election campaign. And so while the values of today's Democrats resemble those of Presidents Franklin Roosevelt and Lyndon Johnson more closely than those of Bill Clinton, the means by which these values and priorities are communicated is decidedly modern and technologically sophisticated.

Changing Both Parties: New Technologies

The ways in which party members and voters give and get information, as well as the methods by which parties campaign, have changed drastically in recent years. More and more people in the electorate are finding information about issues on the Internet and via their cell phones. For their part, the parties are increasingly using new technologies as tools for reaching loyalists and communicating with potential supporters. Take, for example, the way the president now communicates with the electorate. Using a medium unheard of only a decade ago, President Obama regularly relies on YouTube (his channel is http://www.youtube.com/user/BarackObamadotcom) not just as a means of disseminating information but also as a two-way tool of communicating with Americans. And throughout the 2010 congressional elections, we have seen an ever-expanding use of technology by candidates who tweet supporters, ooVoo their staff, text volunteers, organize through Facebook, and raise money online.

> Twitter offers candidates another means of communicating with their supporters and potential voters. While private individuals use Twitter to send micro-messages about their everyday lives ("standing in line @ bookstore behind a guy named Buster"), candidates can tweet about the everyday lives of their campaigns ("just got Rev. Buster's endorsement").

During the 2008 campaign, both the McCain and the Obama campaigns used their Web sites to plug their supporters into assorted outlets for their interest and activism. Both offered downloadable apps that allowed supporters to link their social-networking pages and to raise funds by linking the campaign site to their own Web sites. Both also hosted a wide variety of ways for individuals to stay connected to the campaigns, including listing candidates' favorites on del.icio.us, links to campaign videos on YouTube and to Facebook and MySpace pages, a Twitter micro-blog through which the campaign sent short, updated communications to instant messaging and e-mail accounts and to the Twitter Web site, and campaign photos available at the flickr Web site.

The Internet has also democratized the party process. Partisan activism is no longer limited to individuals who can attend meetings. Whole new forms of Internet activism have emerged. People with access to the Internet can chat, organize, plan, lobby, raise funds, contribute, and mobilize without leaving their desks.

Today, each party relies heavily on the Internet for communicating with supporters, as, for example, the Democratic Party's blog "Kicking Ass" and the Republican Party's activist arm, "The Digital Brigade," reveal. Each party's Web site gives visitors information and plenty of opportunities to volunteer. Moreover, adopting a strategy first employed by individual candidates, parties are also using the Internet as a fund-raising tool: they solicit contributions via special e-mail accounts and on party Web sites and accept donations through online credit card payments. At the end of this chapter, you will find URLs for the Web sites of the Democratic National Committee, the Republican National Committee, and a nonpartisan organization, where you can explore your own opportunities for Internet activism.

CONCLUSION

THINKING CRITICALLY ABOUT WHAT'S NEXT IN AMERICAN POLITICAL PARTIES

Despite the cynicism with which people often view them, political parties are a vital institution for the civic engagement of Americans and are essential to democracy. For many citizens, political parties are the gateway to political participation. For others, they provide cues that guide decisions at the ballot box. The role of parties in teaching individuals essential skills that may lead to elective office, in recruiting candidates, in contesting elections, and in governing—all these valuable functions often do not get the recognition they deserve.

The two major U.S. political parties have demonstrated enormous adaptability over time. The ability to change in response to constituent demands is a consistent trait of these two dominant parties. The cultural and structural forces that perpetuate the two-party system show little sign of relenting. And although groups such as the Tea Party movement and third parties such as the Green Party provide rich fodder for political pundits who speculate about their importance, in electoral terms third parties have demonstrated very little ability to win elections. Instead, third parties commonly advocate issues that eventually are co-opted by one or both of the major parties, and they sometimes play the role of spoiler in elections. What issues advocated by the Tea Party movement were incorporated into the major party stances in the 2010 elections?

In the future, the parties will be challenged to adapt. In particular, they will need to adjust continually to new circumstances, as technology changes how the party organizations identify, organize, mobilize, and communicate with the party in the electorate, as well as how the party in government governs. The contemporary faces of the two major parties demonstrate their continuing evolution and responsiveness to their identifiers and constituents.

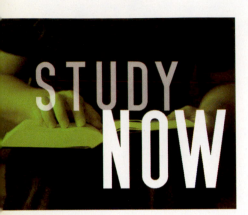

Summary

1. Parties Today and Their Functions
Political parties run candidates in elections in an effort to control government. They advance the cause of civic engagement by facilitating citizens' participation, providing unity and cohesiveness, encouraging civic discourse, and communicating important cues to voters.

2. The Three Faces of Parties
Three spheres of operation of parties are the party in the electorate (the individuals who tend to support a particular party), the party organization (the formal party apparatus), and the party in government (the partisan identification of elected leaders).

3. Political Parties in U.S. History
Political scientists have identified five U.S. party systems. Stretching back to the eighteenth century, these systems describe the evolution of party competition and dominance. Through these party systems, we see the ideological roots and political foundations of the two dominant political parties today.

4. Two-Party Domination in U.S. Politics
Explanations of why two political parties dominate include the ideas that parties reflect the dualist nature of conflict in the United States; that the winner-take-all election system creates a two-party structure; that people are socialized to the two-party system; and that election laws strengthen and perpetuate that structure.

5. The Two-Party System Today: In Decline or in Resurgence?
Some political scientists argue that recent times show a decline in the influence of the two major U.S. parties. As factors, they cite waning constituent loyalty to parties, caused by decreases in patronage, and the advent of direct primaries and candidate-centered campaigns. Other scholars assert that parties are rebounding, and they note parties' adaptability, as well as the lack of viable alternatives to the two major parties.

6. Third Parties in the United States
Third parties, which include issue advocacy parties, ideologically oriented parties, and splinter parties, sometimes act as a spoiler for one of the two major parties. Although third-party candidates typically lose elections, they do succeed in getting various issues on the national agenda.

7. New Ideologies, New Technologies: The Parties in the Twenty-First Century
Neoconservatives and Tea Party activists are important factions within the Republican Party. Whereas neocons are less concerned than traditional Republicans with constraining governmental involvement in domestic policy, Tea Party activists emphasize a staunchly conservative stance on domestic issues. New Democrats shy away from the traditional liberal advocacy of government as the chief solution to social problems and focus on globalization as a determining factor shaping public policy dilemmas and their solutions.

Key Terms

For Review

1. What functions do political parties perform? How do these functions encourage the civic engagement of Americans?

2. What are the three faces of political parties?

3. Explain the development of the five party systems in U.S. history. Why, historically, does the majority change from one party to another?

4. Why do two parties dominate in politics and government in the United States?

5. What are the arguments that political parties are in decline? What do opponents of these arguments contend?

6. What has been the impact of third parties in recent elections?

7. Describe the political philosophy of the neoconservatives, the Tea Party movement, and the New Democrats. How do these factions represent new ways of thinking about politics?

For Critical Thinking and Discussion

1. How were you socialized to the two-party system? Do your views reflect your parents' views? Were third parties even mentioned in your house when you were growing up?

2. What factors explain the demographic bases of the two major parties? How could each party expand its base of support?

3. What impact do you think the neoconservatives, the Tea Party activists, and the New Democrats will have on the two major parties over time? Why?

4. What evidence is there that a new party system is emerging? Do the 2010 election results support the claim that a new party system is taking shape?

5. In what ways beyond those discussed in the chapter might the Internet and other new technologies be used as means of communication between voters and parties? In your view, what are the most important uses for new technologies in partisan politics?

MULTIPLE CHOICE: Choose the lettered item that answers the question correctly.

1. The formal statement of a party's principles and policy objectives is called a
   a. policy memo.
   b. policy manifesto.
   c. platform.
   d. mission statement.

2. Individuals who identify with or tend to support a party are called the
   a. the party in the electorate.
   b. the party organization.
   c. the party in government.
   d. responsible party members.

3. The formal party apparatus, including committees, party leaders, conventions and workers, is called
   a. the party in the electorate.
   b. the party organization.
   c. the party in government.
   d. responsible party members.

4. The situation that exists when Congress is controlled by one party and the presidency by the other is called
   a. party disorganization.
   b. bipartisan camaraderie.
   c. divided government.
   d. executive/legislative split.

5. A philosophy supporting the rights and empowerment of the masses as opposed to elites is called
   a. neoconservatism.
   b. conservatism.
   c. New Deal philosophy.
   d. populism.

6. A significant shift in party allegiances or electoral support is called
   a. populism.
   b. dealigment.
   c. realignment.
   d. disalignment.

7. Franklin Roosevelt's broad social welfare program in which the government would bear the responsibility of providing a "safety net" to protect the weakest members of society was called
   a. the New Deal.
   b. the Grand Formula.
   c. the War on Poverty.
   d. the Social Contract.

8. The situation in which voters vote for candidates from more than one party is called
   a. populism.
   b. dealigment.
   c. realignment.
   d. ticket splitting.

9. An election structure in which political parties win the number of parliamentary seats equal to the percentage of the vote the party receives is called
   a. a first-past-the-post system.
   b. a winner-take-all system.
   c. a proportional representation system.
   d. a two-party system.

10. An election in which voters choose the party's candidates who will run in the later general election is called a
    a. primary election.
    b. recall election.
    c. general election.
    d. referendum election.

FILL IN THE BLANKS.

11. A new, grassroots, conservative protest movement that opposed recent government actions, including economic stimulus spending and health care reform, is called the _____ .

12. Political scientists' view that a function of a party is to offer a clear choice to voters by establishing priorities or policy stances that differ from those of rival parties is called the _____ .

13. The role that the party out of power plays, highlighting its objections to policies and priorities of the government in power, is called the _____ .

14. Organizations that candidates form to support their individual election are called _____ .

15. A campaign in which an individual seeking election, rather than an entire party slate, is the focus in a _____ .

Answers: 1. c; 2. a; 3. b; 4. c; 5. d; 6. c; 7. a; 8. d; 9. c; 10. a; 11. Tea Party movement; 12. responsible party model; 13. loyal opposition; 14. candidate committees; 15. candidate-centered campaign.

RESOURCES FOR RESEARCH AND ACTION

Internet Resources

Democratic National Committee
www.democrats.org The Democrats' Web site contains hotlinks for state and local party Web sites and opportunities for volunteering, internships, and employment, as well as party position papers and platforms and candidate information.

Project Vote Smart
www.vote-smart.org This nonpartisan site provides independent, factual information on candidates and elected officials of all political parties.

Republican National Committee
www.gop.com The Republicans' site also has links for state and local party sites and opportunities for volunteering, internships, and employment, as well as party position papers and platforms and candidate information.

The American Presidency Project
www.presidency.ucsb.edu/platforms.php The American Presidency Project Web site at the University of California Santa Barbara provides the party platforms of every party whose presidential candidate received electoral votes.

Internet Activism

The path to becoming a party activist begins on the Internet. Use Figure 8.7 on page 265 to help you determine your own party beliefs. Then, plan on attending a party county committee meeting. If you are a Democrat, go to www.democrats.org, click on "local," and enter your zip code. If you are a Republican go to www.gop.com, click on "our GOP," then click on "states." Enter your state in the "Search community" box and then "view state." If you are interested in volunteering for party activities, be certain to introduce yourself to the party chair and let him or her know that you would like to volunteer.

Recommended Readings

Berlatsky, Noah. *Does the U.S. Two-party System Still Work?* Belmont, CA: Greenhaven Press, 2010. Part of the "At Issue" series, this work examines the effectiveness of the U.S. party system.

Flammang, Janet. *Women's Political Voice.* Philadelphia: Temple University Press, 1997. A well-researched account of women's political participation in general and women's participation in political parties in particular.

Hershey, Marjorie Random. *Party Politics in America,* 14th ed. New York: Longman, 2010. A classic work on American political parties, analyzing the changing roles of parties in the twentieth century and the impact of the campaign finance system on political parties.

Lijphart, Arend. *Electoral Systems and Party Systems: A Study of Twenty-Seven Democracies 1945–1990.* New York: Oxford University Press, 1994. An exploration of the nature of party systems in many industrialized democracies both historically and in modern times.

Pimlott, Jamie Pamelia. *Women and the Democratic Party: The Evolution of EMILY's List.* Amherst, NY: Cambria Press, 2010. This work consists of both descriptive and quantitative analysis of the growth and impact of EMILY's List, the leading fund-raising organization that supports Democratic women candidates.

Rohde, David W. *Parties and Leaders in the Postreform House.* Chicago: University of Chicago Press, 1991. Analyzes the reasons behind the realignment and resurgence of partisanship in Congress during the 1980s.

Schattschneider, E. E. *Party Government.* New York: Rinehart, 1942. A classic work that explains the nature of political parties and their impact on party government.

Movies of Interest

Primary Colors (1998)
Starring John Travolta, and based on the anonymously written book of the same name, this popular movie—a fictionalized account of Bill Clinton's 1992 campaign—provides insight into the primary election season of a presidential nominee.

City Hall (1996)
This film starring Al Pacino and John Cusack shows the workings of a corrupt political machine—and the consequences of that corruption.

Elections, Campaigns, and Voting

THEN

Political party–dominated campaigns and grassroots activism were deciding factors in how people voted.

NOW

Candidate-centered campaigns rely on paid professionals to shape and spin candidates' messages—and on costly media buys to disseminate it.

NEXT

How will new technologies drive and change campaigns?

How will changes in the campaign finance structure affect how campaigns are conducted?

What new faces and voices will determine the campaign environment?

grassroots organizing
tasks that involve direct contact with voters or potential voters.

When Americans think about

politics, their first thought is often about elections, campaigns, and voting. In the eyes of many of us, these activities are the essence of political participation, because it is through the electoral process that we feel we participate most directly and meaningfully in our democracy. Often viewed as the pinnacle of the democratic experience, the act of voting is the culmination of a wide range of forms of political engagement. In the discussion that follows, we see the interconnectedness of many aspects of political campaigns and elections, including fund-raising, **grassroots organizing,** candidate selection, and voter mobilization. These opportunities for civic participation in the democratic process are present in such a broad variety of forms that they are accessible to everyone who wants to be engaged.

Political Participation:
Engaging Individuals, Shaping Politics

Elections, campaigns, and voting are fundamental aspects of the civic engagement of Americans and people in other democracies. These activities represent concentrated forms of civic engagement and are important both for the polity as a whole and for the individuals who participate.[1] But intensive political engagement—working on a campaign or running for office, say—rarely represents an individual's first foray into a civically engaged life. Rather, people who are engaged in the political process usually are initiated through smaller, less intensive steps. Perhaps a group of classmates who especially enjoy the political discussions in your American government class might continue their conversations of democracy over a cup of Starbucks after class. Those same classmates might begin regularly reading political blogs and daily newspapers to become better informed about candidates and issues. Some members of the informal group might decide to hear a candidate who is giving a speech on campus—and wind up volunteering on his or her campaign. Political engagement often begins with small steps such as those, but the cumulative results are large: they help to ensure that the government is representative of the people and responsive to their needs. Representative governments, which are the product of individuals' political engagement, tend to be more stable and to make decisions that best reflect the needs and the will of the people who elect them.

Direct forms of political participation such as voting, volunteering on a campaign, and running for office are of keen interest to scholars of civic engagement. Many scholarly analysts have noticed an overall decrease in levels of political participation. As discussed in Chapter 7, political scientist Robert Putnam argues that the United States is seeing a decline in its social capital, the social networks and reciprocal relationships characteristic of a community or a society. These networks are varied and include formal organizations such as clubs, fraternities, sororities, interest groups, and sports teams. But there are also informal networks, such as babysitting co-ops, car pools, and study groups. Putnam details how solitary pursuits such as watching television and using a computer have pervasively replaced group activities related to civic participation.

Some scholars have challenged Putnam's assertion that social capital has declined. They point out that new forms of social capital have arisen in the form of Internet social networks, instant messaging, and Internet activism to replace the traditional social networks that Putnam studied. Despite these differing views, there is consensus that civic participation is essential and that among its most important forms is electoral political participation.

Indeed, elections offer a wealth of opportunities for citizen involvement:

- Members of political parties recruit candidates to run for election.
- Cadres of volunteers organize campaign events, including fund-raisers, rallies, and neighborhood leafleting.
- Phone bank volunteers try to persuade other people to participate in the electoral process—for instance, by giving a campaign contribution, putting a candidate's sign on their lawn, or simply voting for the candidate.
- Other volunteers focus exclusively on **GOTV**—that is, they work to get out the vote. They register voters for both primary and general elections, and they provide absentee ballots to people who are ill or who will be out of town on election day. On Election Day itself, they remind people to vote by phoning them or knocking on their door and asking if they need a ride to the polls.[2]
- Others (who may be paid) volunteer to work at the polls on election day.

Although each volunteer effort plays a part in ensuring the success of a democracy, a key form of political participation is running for office. Electoral contests in which more than one candidate seeks to win office are a fundamental component of a democracy.

> Are more people really *"Bowling Alone"*? Political scientist Robert Putnam has argued that the United States is experiencing a decline in social capital because its citizens are participating less in civic life. But perhaps Americans are engaged in civic life in very different ways from those of previous generations. Here, a group of Wii bowling enthusiasts compete in a friendly match in an Illinois restaurant.

Elections in the United States

Every state holds at least two types of elections. A *primary election* comes first and determines the party's nominees—those who will run for office. For most political offices, there is little or no competition in the primary election. But in presidential and gubernatorial primary elections, vigorous contention is often the rule, particularly within the out-of-power party. House and Senate primary elections that lack an incumbent candidate (that is, one who has been elected to that office before) are also often highly competitive as many candidates attempt to win their party's nomination.

In a **general election,** the parties' respective nominees run against each other, and voters decide who should hold office, since the person with the most votes wins. (Presidential elections, discussed later in this chapter, are a notable exception.) The degree of competition in general elections depends on a number of factors, including the presence of and the strength of incumbency, the degree of party competition, and the level of the office. In recent times, presidential elections have been brutally competitive, as have been certain gubernatorial races and many congressional contests where no incumbent is seeking reelection. Some communities, particularly big cities, may also experience intense competition for office in general elections.

GOTV
get out the vote

general election
an election that determines which candidates win the offices being sought

Nominations and Primary Elections

In a primary election, voters decide which nominees the political parties should run in the general election. But *which* voters decide varies greatly from state to state. In some states, only registered party members are eligible to vote in primary elections, whereas in other states, any registered voter can vote in any party's primary, and in North Dakota, voters are not even required to register.

In U.S. presidential primaries, voters do not vote directly for the candidate whom they would like their party to nominate. Instead, the popular vote determines which candidate's delegates will attend the party's nominating convention and vote for that party's nominee.

> Chicago police restrained protesters during the 1968 Democratic National Convention by using tear gas, among other methods. As a result of the riots during this convention, sparked by dissatisfaction over the selection of Hubert Humphrey as the nominee by party insiders, the two major U.S. parties made major reforms to the delegate-selection process.

caucus

meeting of party members held to select delegates to the national convention

open primary

a type of primary in which both parties' ballots are available in the voting booth, and voters select one on which to register their preferences

closed primary

a type of primary in which voting in a party's primary is limited to members of that party

Super Tuesday

the Tuesday in early March on which the most primary elections were held, many of them in southern states; provided the basis for Super-Duper Tuesday in 2008

This system of selecting delegates through primary voting is different from the earlier system, when party leaders selected the presidential nominee with little or no input from the rank-and-file party members.

The two major U.S. parties made reforms to the earlier delegate selection process after the 1968 Democratic National Convention in Chicago. Anti–Vietnam War activists outside the convention protested the presumed nomination of Vice President Hubert Humphrey as the Democratic Party's presidential candidate. Humphrey had not won any primaries but was favored among the convention's delegates who had been hand-picked by party leaders. The activists instead supported the candidacy of Senator Eugene McCarthy (D-Minnesota), an outspoken war opponent. The demonstrations turned into riots when Chicago police beat the protesters. The Democratic National Committee, in an attempt to address the concerns of those complaining that they had been excluded from the nomination process, appointed the McGovern-Fraser Commission (named after its cochairs), which recommended a series of reforms to the delegate-selection process.

The reforms, many of which both the Democratic Party and the Republican Party adopted, significantly increased the influence of party voters. Voters could now select delegates to the national conventions, a power previously restricted to the party elite. Party voters today select the delegates at statewide conventions or through primary elections or **caucuses**—meetings of party members held to select delegates to the national convention. The reforms also included provisions that would ensure the selection of a more representative body of delegates, with certain delegate slots set aside for women, minorities, union members, and young party voters. These slots roughly correspond with the proportion of support the party receives from those groups.

When an individual is elected to be a delegate at the national convention, often that delegate has pledged to vote for a specific candidate. That pledge is nonbinding, however, since delegates of a losing candidate often switch their support to the apparent victor.

TYPES OF PRIMARY ELECTIONS   In an **open primary** election, any registered voter can vote in any party's primary, as can independent voters not registered with a party. In an open primary, parties' ballots are available in the voting booth, and the voter simply selects privately or publicly one on which to register his or her preferences.

In a **closed primary** election, voting in a party's primary is limited to members of that party. In some states, voters must declare their party affiliation well in advance of the primary election—sometimes as many as sixty days before. In other states, voters can declare their party preference at the polling place on the day of the election. Such restrictions on who can vote in a party's primary originated in the parties' maneuvering to have the strongest candidate nominated. For example, if a popular incumbent president were running unopposed in a primary election, members of the president's party might choose to vote in the other party's primary as a way of scheming to get a weak candidate nominated. A closed primary aims to thwart that strategy.

PRESIDENTIAL PRIMARIES   The states determine the timing of primary elections. Historically, states that held their presidential primary earlier in the year had a greater say in determining the nominee than did states with later primaries. The reason is that candidates tended to drop out if they did not win primaries, did not meet media expectations, or ran out of funds. (See "Thinking Critically About Democracy.") In general, past presidential primaries gave great sway to the agricultural states, because many of the more urban states' primaries fell later in the season.

All of that changed in 2007 when, in an attempt to increase their political clout, a number of diverse states banded together to hold their primaries on the same day so that presidential candidates would be forced to address issues of the keenest interest to those states. These states modeled their objective on **Super Tuesday,** the day in early March on which the most presidential primary elections took place, many of them in southern states. Super Tuesday had been the fruit of a successful effort in 1988 by several southern and rural

THINKING CRITICALLY ABOUT DEMOCRACY

SHOULD THE UNITED STATES HAVE A NATIONAL PRIMARY?

The Issue: The party primary process that selects each party's nominee for president was a hot-button issue in the 2008 presidential race. Historically, the primary system focused enormous attention on the states of Iowa, where the first caucus is held, and New Hampshire, where the first party primary takes place. In these states, voters have had the opportunity to gain a deep familiarity with all the candidates seeking the parties' nominations. But critics of the system have charged that these two states' political culture does not reflect the vast majority of Americans. As a result, many of the most populous states moved their primaries to the earliest day allowed by the political parties—in 2008, that day was February 5. Other states, including Pennsylvania, Texas, West Virginia, and Kentucky, held off having their primaries, in the hopes that one state could find itself in the position of kingmaker by bringing one of the party candidates over the top in the needed delegate count. Given this structure, many citizens have asked, "Is this any way to begin electing a president?"

Should states matter when it comes to selecting the parties' nominees? One potential solution to the skewed emphasis on various states is to hold a national primary so that party members throughout the country can choose their nominees on the same day. People have voiced arguments for and against the idea of a national primary.

Yes: Having a national primary will help the parties, because it will ensure that the nominee chosen in each case is the best candidate for the party. With the shift to a national primary, states that currently have late primaries will no longer be forced to accept a nominee chosen by party members who might be very different from themselves. Furthermore, if more people have a say in choosing their party's nominee, voter turnout might rise in both the primary and the general election. Holding a national primary also will shorten the election season, so that voters will be less fatigued by the length of the campaign.

No: The primary system ensures that small, agricultural states have a voice in national politics. In the general election, smaller states are overshadowed because the Electoral College, which is based on state population, determines the winner. The current primary and caucus system enables voters in those states to analyze the candidates thoroughly, without the noise and distraction that would come with a large-scale, media-saturated national primary. And because the voters in states such as Iowa and New Hampshire are, after all, party members, they naturally understand that a large part of their responsibility is to select the nominee best equipped to win the general election.

Other approaches: Some have suggested the idea of holding regional primaries instead of one national primary, with a different region holding its primary election first in each presidential election year so that no region would have the influence that Iowa and New Hampshire now enjoy. Each region would include a mix of large and small states and urban and rural areas. Candidates would need to campaign throughout each region in turn rather than the entire country, thus allowing them to focus their efforts more than they would be able to with one national primary, and with three or four regional primaries, the campaign season would still be shortened significantly, thus eliminating voter fatigue.

What do you think?

① Do you believe that we should have a national primary? Explain.

② What impact would a national primary have on your home state's say in the nomination process? How will small states fare compared with large states? Rural compared with urban?

③ What impact do you think a national primary or regional primaries would have on voter turnout? What effect might either type of primary have on how presidential campaigns are waged? Would money be more or less important? Why?

---

states to hold their primaries on the same day so as to increase their political importance and allow expression of southern voters' political will.[3] But in 2007, the Super Tuesday strategy was challenged by state legislators in some of the most populous states, including California, New York, Illinois, and New Jersey, who sought to have their presidential primaries on the earliest day that national political party rules allowed. In 2008, that day, dubbed "Super-Duper Tuesday" by the media, was February 5. In all, twenty other states jumped on the early-primary bandwagon, with the result that twenty-four states held their primaries and caucuses on February 5, 2008. Under normal circumstances, such a change would have muted the impact of other primaries because the most populous states control an enormous number of delegates to the national conventions, in 2008 that was not the case. That year, the highly competitive Democratic primary between Senator Hillary Clinton (D-New York) and Senator Barack Obama (D-Illinois) meant that states such as New Mexico and Oregon (which had late primaries, in early June) were competitive and received national media coverage.

General Elections

In a general election, voters decide who should hold office from among the candidates determined in the primary election. Most general elections, including presidential elections, are held on the first Tuesday after the first Monday in November. But because the states schedule and oversee elections, you might find that your gubernatorial election, state legislative election, or town council election occurs at a different time of the year.

General elections for Congress and most state legislatures feature a **winner-take-all** system. That is, the candidate who receives the most votes wins that office (even if that total is not a majority, or even if an opponent receives only one vote fewer than the victor). Thus, a member of the U.S. House of Representatives or Senate can be elected with less than a majority of the votes in his or her district, particularly when three or more candidates are seeking that seat.

Because electoral law varies from state to state, and counties and municipalities within those states have their own structures of governance, less common kinds of elections are possible and are used in some locales. For example, some states require a runoff election when no candidate receives the majority of the votes cast. In a **runoff election,** if no candidate receives more than 50 percent of the vote, several of the top vote-getters (usually the top two) run in another, subsequent election. Typically, the field of candidates is winnowed down until one candidate receives the requisite 50 percent plus one vote. Runoff elections often occur in *nonpartisan* municipal elections where candidates do not run on a party label.

Owing to advances in technology, runoff elections can occur immediately in some states when needed. In an **instant runoff election,** a computerized voting machine simulates the elimination of last-place vote-getters. How does this system work? In an instant runoff, voters rank candidates in order of preference (first choice, second choice, and so on). If any candidate garners more than 50 percent of all the first-choice votes, that candidate wins. But if no candidate gets a majority of first-choice votes, the candidate in last place is electronically eliminated. The voting machine computer then recalculates the ballots, using the second-choice vote for those voters who voted for the eliminated last-place finisher; in effect, every voter gets to choose among the candidates remaining on the ballot. This process is repeated until a candidate who receives more than 50 percent of the votes emerges. Today's voting machines allow this process to take place instantly.

Referendum, Initiative, and Recall

Whereas primary elections and general elections select an individual to run for and serve in office, other kinds of elections are held for the purpose of deciding public policy questions. Although no national mechanism allows all Americans to vote for or against a given policy proposal, citizens can directly decide policy questions in their states by referendum or initiative.[4]

A **referendum** is an election in which voters in a state can vote for or against a measure proposed by the state legislature. Frequently, referenda concern matters such as state bond issues, state constitutional amendments, and controversial pieces of legislation. An **initiative,** sometimes called an initiative petition, is a citizen-sponsored proposal that can result in new or amended legislation or a state constitutional amendment. Initiatives differ from referenda in that they are typically propelled to public vote through the efforts of citizens and interest groups.[5] The initiative process usually requires that 10 percent of the number of the voters in the previous election in that state sign a petition agreeing that the **proposition,** or proposed measure, should be placed on the ballot. An example of an initiative is California's Proposition 8, also called the California Marriage Protection Act, which passed

winner-take-all

an electoral system in which the candidate who receives the most votes wins that office, even if that total is not a majority.

runoff election

a follow-up election held when no candidate receives the majority of votes cast in the original election

instant runoff election

a special runoff election in which the computerized voting machine simulates the elimination of last-place vote-getters

referendum

an election in which voters in a state can vote for or against a measure proposed by the state legislature

initiative

a citizen-sponsored proposal that can result in new or amended legislation or a state constitutional amendment

proposition

a proposed measure placed on the ballot in an initiative election

with a majority of votes in the November 2008 state elections. Prop. 8 amended California's state constitution to read "Only a marriage between a man and a woman is valid or recognized in California." As a state constitutional amendment, Prop. 8 had the effect of overturning the California Supreme Court decision stating that same-sex couples have the right to marry. That decision had nullified a previous initiative, Proposition 22, in which a majority of voters had statutorily banned same-sex marriage. The validity of Prop. 8 was the subject of *Perry v. Schwarzenegger*.[6]

A third type of special election, the recall, differs from referenda and initiatives in that it is not concerned with policy-related issues. Rather, the **recall** election allows voters to cut an officeholder's term of office short. Recall elections are typically citizen-sponsored efforts that demonstrate serious dissatisfaction with a particular officeholder. Concerned citizens circulate a petition, and after they gather the required number of signatures, an election is held to determine whether the official should be thrown out of office. In 2010, a federal district court decided that Prop. 8 violated the Due Process and Equal Protection clauses of the Foureenth Amendment. The decision has been stayed pending an appeal to the U.S. Supreme Court.

> A proposition is a question placed on a ballot for voters' approval. Arizona's Proposition 100 proposed to increase the state sales tax from 5.6 cents on the dollar to 6.6 cents, for a temporary three years, to raise a projected $1 billion annually. It won passage in May, 2010.

The Act of Voting

The process of voting begins when a voter registers to vote. Voting registration requirements vary greatly from state to state. Some states require registration months in advance of an election; others allow voters to register on the day of voting. In the United States, the voters use an **Australian ballot**, a secret ballot prepared by the government, distributed to all eligible voters, and, when balloting is completed, counted by government officials in an unbiased fashion, without corruption or regard to individual preferences. Because the U.S. Constitution guarantees the states the right to conduct elections, the mechanics and methods of voting vary widely from state to state. Some states use touch-screen technology; others employ computerized ballots or punch cards that are counted by computers. Still other states use traditional lever ballots, in which voters pull a lever to register their vote for a particular candidate. Despite those differences, all ballots are secret ballots.

Although secret ballots are the norm today, that was not always the case. From the days of the early republic through the nineteenth century, many citizens exercised their right to vote using oral votes cast in public or written votes witnessed by others; some made their electoral choices on color-coded ballots prepared by the political parties, which indicated which party the voter was supporting.

The 2000 Election and Its Impact

In the 2000 presidential election between Democrat Al Gore and Republican George W. Bush, an enormous controversy erupted over the voting in Florida. Because of the closeness of the electoral vote, the outcome of the Florida election turned out to be pivotal. But the tallies in that state's election were in question, not only because of the narrow difference in the number of votes won by each candidate, but also because of the voting process itself. Florida citizens cast their vote on a punch card by poking through a **chad,** a ready-made perforation, near the name of their candidate of choice. Officials then counted the punch card ballots using a computer program that calculated votes by counting the absence of chads. But in the case of the 2000 election, thousands of ballots could not be read by the computer and needed to be counted by hand. This unexpected development put election officials in the difficult, and ultimately deeply controversial, position of gauging "voter intent." If a chad was hanging by one perforation only, did the voter intend to vote for that

recall
a special election in which voters can remove officeholders before their term is over

Australian ballot
a secret ballot prepared by the government, distributed to all eligible voters, and, when balloting is completed, counted by government officials in an unbiased fashion, without corruption or regard to individual preferences

chad
a ready-made perforation on a punch card ballot

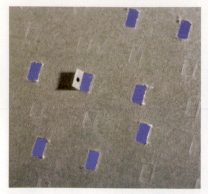

> The problems with chads: A hanging chad . . . and a pregnant chad.

candidate? What if the chad was "pregnant" (that is, sticking out but not removed; see the photo)? What if the chad was dimpled, and the voter had cast his or her entire ballot by only dimpling the chads?

In the end, the U.S. Supreme Court had the final say. On December 12, 2000, the Court halted the hand counting of ballots in Florida, with the Court's majority ruling that the differing standards of hand counting ballots from one county to the next and the absence of a single judicial officer charged with overseeing the hand counts violated the equal protection clause of the U.S. Constitution. The ruling meant that George W. Bush, who was leading in the count, was certified the winner of the Florida race, thus securing that state's twenty-five Electoral College votes and the presidency of the United States.

Indignation surrounding the 2000 election resulted in federal policy changes to the conduct of elections by the states. The key policy revision came through the passage of the Help America Vote Act of 2002 (HAVA). HAVA allocated $650 million to assist states in changing from punch card ballots to electronic voting systems and set a deadline of 2005 for states to comply, although some states have not yet done so.

Types of Ballots

party-column ballot
a ballot that organizes the candidates by political party

There are two types of ballots most commonly used in general elections in the states today. The first, the **party-column ballot,** organizes the candidates by party, so that all of a given party's candidates for every office are arranged in one column. The opposing party's candidates appear in a different column.

The impact of a party-column ballot is twofold. First, party-column ballots increase voters' tendency to vote the "party line," that is, to vote for every candidate of a given party for every office. In fact, some states provide a party lever, which allows a voter to vote for all of a given party's candidates simply by one pull of a lever or one press of a "vote party" button. Second, because they increase the tendency to vote the party line, party-column ballots also increase the **coattail effect,** the phenomenon whereby *down-ballot candidates* (candidates who are running for lower-level offices, such as city council) benefit from the popularity of a top-of-ticket nominee. Often, the composition of city councils, county legislatures, and even state legislatures changes because of a coattail effect from a popular presidential or gubernatorial candidate. Because party-column ballots strengthen political parties, parties tend to favor this type of ballot, which is the most commonly used ballot in the United States.

coattail effect
the phenomenon by which candidates running for a lower-level office such as city council benefit in an election from the popularity of a top-of-ticket nominee

office-block ballot
a type of ballot that arranges all the candidates for a particular office under the name of that office

Another type of general election ballot is the **office-block ballot,** which arranges all candidates for a particular office under the name of that office. Office-block ballots are more likely to encourage ticket splitting, where voters "split their ticket"—that is, divide their votes—between candidates from different parties.[7] Because office-block ballots deemphasize political parties by breaking up the party line, the parties do not tend to favor them.

Why Ballot Design Matters

The 2000 presidential election voting in Florida provides evidence that not only the voting process but also the design of ballots can make a difference in outcomes. Specifically, with respect to the vote in Florida's Palm Beach County, where voters push a button on their voting machine ballot to register their vote, critics charge that the ballot in use, the *butterfly ballot* (so called because candidates are listed on two "wings" with a common "spine"), was particularly confusing to voters.

Because of the lack of ballot clarity, many Democrats complained that this ballot layout put the Gore/Lieberman ticket at a disadvantage. Although supporters of Reform Party candidate Pat Buchanan in Palm Beach County projected that he should have received at best

1,000 votes there, Buchanan received over 3,400 votes. Many people, including Buchanan himself, believed that these votes were mistakenly cast for him and intended for Al Gore.[8]

In fact, an additional 19,000 votes were nullified in the Palm Beach County election because voters cast *two* votes for president, presumably with balloters realizing too late that they had pushed the wrong button. Buchanan himself addressed this issue, saying, "If the two candidates they pushed were Buchanan and Gore, almost certainly those are Al Gore's votes and not mine. I cannot believe someone would vote for Gore and say, 'I made a mistake, I should have voted for Buchanan.' Maybe a small minority of them would have done that. But I—I've got to think that the vast majority of those [votes] would naturally belong to Al Gore and not to me."[9]

Voting by Mail

One form of voting, **absentee voting,** is a long-standing tradition by which voters cast their ballots in advance by mail when disability, illness, school, work, service in the armed forces, or travel prevents them from casting a ballot in their voting precinct. To cast an absentee ballot, an individual must typically apply (before a specific state-designated deadline) to vote by absentee in the county where he or she usually votes. The superintendent of elections then mails a ballot to the voter, who votes and then mails the ballot back. The absentee ballots are counted and added to the votes cast in the voting precincts. Requirements for absentee ballots vary from state to state. Some states require a legitimate excuse, but increasingly many states accept ballot applications simply because absentee voting is more convenient for the voter.

A relatively recent development is the advent of statewide voting by mail, a practice that states have adopted in an attempt to increase voter participation by making voting more convenient. The first experiment with statewide vote by mail occurred in Oregon in 1996. In a special election there, where officials had predicted a turnout of less than 50 percent, more than 66 percent of voters cast their ballots. This experiment brought another benefit: it saved taxpayers more than $1 million. Oregon decided to continue the practice in the 2000 presidential election, in which voter turnout hit 80 percent, and in the 2004 presidential race, where the turnout approached 85 percent. Oregon has now taken the drastic step of abandoning voting in polling places on Election Day.

There are obvious advantages to voting by mail. As Oregon's experience demonstrates, more people participate when voting becomes easier. Further, increased participation may bring to office candidates who are more representative of the will of the people because more people had a say in their election.

Some scholars, however, have criticized the vote-by-mail trend. One important criticism is that voting by mail means that people vote before the final days of the campaign, thus casting their ballot before some additional last-minute information might be revealed about a candidate. Indeed, some voters may cast their ballots before the political rivals' debates occur or before candidates fully articulate their message. Consider one case in Bainbridge Island, Washington, where it was revealed just days before the election that a candidate for mayor had padded his résumé. By the time the exaggerations came to light, some voters had already cast their ballots by mail.[10]

Voting by mail also increases the chances of vote fraud. Even though states take measures to ensure the principle of "one person, one vote," voting by mail presents opportunities for corruption. Voting at the polls requires a face-to-face encounter, but voting by mail does not, so ballots could be stolen from individuals' mailboxes or intercepted after having been mailed by a voter.

Voting by mail also may eliminate the privacy associated with voting in recent times. With mail balloting, the vote occurs in a less controlled setting, and the voter might feel pressured by others to select a particular candidate. In contrast, booth voting affords privacy and secrecy that go far toward ensuring that the votes cast behind the curtain reflect the individual voter's will.

Finally, voting by mail may undermine feelings of civic engagement by eliminating a source of psychological rewards for voters. Going to a polling place, signing the voting

absentee voting
casting a ballot in advance by mail in situations where illness, travel, or other circumstances prevent voters from voting in their precinct

registry, entering the voting booth, and casting your vote can elicit feelings of patriotism, civic pride, and fulfillment of civic responsibility: the sense that you are doing your duty to help ensure the election of the best-qualified candidates. Although the results may be the same with voting by mail, some evidence suggests that voting by mail does not bring with it the same sense of civic satisfaction that voting at a polling place confers.

Running for Office: The Choice to Run

The reasons that individuals become political candidates vary almost as much as the individuals do. Yet four types of motivation are generally in play when a person decides to declare a candidacy:

- a sense of civic responsibility—the feeling on the candidate's part that he or she bears an obligation to govern
- a sense of party loyalty—of filling the need for parties to run viable candidates
- personal goals, and in particular, interest in electoral politics and officeholding as a career
- interest in increasing the candidate's name recognition and stature in the community, often for business reasons

Some people believe they have an obligation to put their experience, knowledge, and skills to work for the greater good of the community or country. Often these civically motivated people become politically involved out of concerns about specific issues. They might object to a specific policy or want to see the government take action on a given issue. For example, Representative Carolyn McCarthy (D-New York) ran for and won a seat in the House of Representatives after her husband was killed and her son was injured in a mass shooting on the Long Island Railroad. While nursing her adult son's injuries after the senseless tragedy, McCarthy decided to run when her congressman voted to repeal a ban on assault weapons.

Sometimes an individual may choose to run for office out of a sense of party duty. The candidate may run as a "sacrificial lamb" for a seat he or she has little chance of winning, mainly with the intent to ensure that the party offers an alternative to the favored candidate. Or an elected official may decide to run for another office because he or she has the best chance at winning an election and allowing the party to attain control of that office.

Other people are motivated to run for a particular office because of personal goals. Many of these individuals seek elected office as their career. Whereas presidents and governors typically serve no more than eight years, members of Congress, state legislators, county commissioners, and council members often serve for decades. Holding office is what they do—and because of the advantages of incumbency, once elected, many remain in office for years. Other candidates run for office because of political ambitions: a town council member who aspires to serve in the state legislature might run for county commissioner even if she thinks she will not win because she realizes that leading a viable campaign might help her in a later bid for the statehouse.

Finally, some people run for office because of the heightened stature that a candidacy brings to their "regular" careers. Lawyers may run for the state legislature, realtors for the city council, or insurance brokers for county commissioner because a candidacy makes them more successful in their daily occupations. Running for office enhances a person's name recognition so that, for example, the realtor sitting on the city council might get more business because people in the community know his name. Running for office also opens doors to networks of potential business contacts, as many candidates address civic groups and get to know people in the community. These networks can be useful in business as well as politics.

Many candidates, of course, run for office for a combination of reasons. They might believe, for example, that they have a responsibility to serve their country *and* that they have something valuable to contribute.

Formal Eligibility Requirements

Article I of the U.S. Constitution specifies some minimum criteria for those seeking election to federal office:

- President: A candidate for the presidency must be a natural-born citizen. Naturalized citizens, who are born citizens of another country and then choose to become American citizens such as Ileana Ros-Lehtinen (R-Florida), a member of the House of Representatives and a native of Cuba, cannot run for president. Presidential candidates also must be at least 35 years old. The youngest person elected president was the 43-year-old John F. Kennedy, but Theodore Roosevelt, who assumed the presidency after William McKinley's assassination, was the youngest to hold the office, at age 42. A presidential candidate also must have been a resident of the United States for fourteen years by the time of inauguration.
- Vice president: A vice-presidential candidate, like a contender for the presidency, must be a natural-born citizen and must be at least 35 years old; he or she must not be a resident of the same state as the candidate for president with whom he or she will serve. John Breckinridge, elected vice president in 1856 at age 35, was the youngest person to win the office.
- U.S. senator: A candidate for the Senate must have citizen status of at least nine years, must be at least 30 years old when taking office, and must be a resident of the state from which he or she is elected.
- U.S. representative: A candidate for the House of Representatives must be a citizen for at least seven years, must be at least 25 years old when taking office, and must be a resident of the state from which he or she is elected.

Typically, a state's constitution determines the minimal qualifications for the governorship and state legislature, and these vary from state to state. In general, state requirements address the same issues as federal guidelines—citizenship, age, and residency.

Informal Eligibility Requirements

In addition to the legal eligibility requirements prescribed by the federal and state constitutions, informal eligibility criteria—that is, the characteristics that voters expect officeholders to have—help to determine who is qualified to run for a particular office. By and large, the eligibility pool for elected office depends on the office—and so although your car mechanic might be considered a good candidate for your town council, he would not likely meet the informal eligibility criteria to be elected president of the United States.

Generally speaking, the higher and more prestigious the political office, the greater the informal eligibility requirements are. On the local level, particularly in smaller communities, an individual would be considered eligible to run for town council if he or she was liked and respected in the community, had lived in the community long enough to know the voters, and was gainfully employed, a homemaker, or retired.

Farther up the political office ladder, state legislative candidates in most states are expected to have some kind of professional career. Still, there is a great deal of variation from state to state, and certainly nonprofessionals occupy many state legislative seats. State legislatures tend to be dominated by lawyers and business professionals, occupations that offer the prestige to be considered part of the informal eligibility pool and that allow enough flexibility to facilitate campaigning and legislative work.

The informal eligibility requirements for federal office are even more stringent. Voters expect candidates for the House of

> Informal qualifications for Congress vary according to the political culture in the district. Openly gay members of Congress are a rarity. Representative Tammy Baldwin (D-Wisconsin), the only openly lesbian member of Congress, talks here with a constituent.

Representatives, the U.S. Senate, and the presidency to have higher qualifications than candidates for state and local offices. Among most congressional constituencies, candidates for federal office would be viewed as "qualified" to hold office if they had a college degree, considerable professional and leadership experience, and strong communication skills. But informal qualifications vary according to the political culture in a district, with some districts favoring a particular religious affiliation, ethnicity, or other characteristic. In races for the U.S. Senate and the presidency, the popular press examines the minutest details of candidates' professional and educational background. For example, sometimes it is not enough that candidates are college graduates; where they went to college, whose university is more prestigious, and who had the higher grade point average are all fodder for the media and political pundits.

The Nature of Political Campaigns Today

Campaigns today are different from the campaigns of the 1980s or even the early 1990s. The main reasons for the changes are the professionalization of campaign staffs, the dramatically expanded role of the media and the Internet, and candidates' ever-rising need for funding to keep pace with the unprecedented demands of contemporary campaigning.[11]

The Professionalization of Political Campaigns

One of the most significant changes in the conduct of campaigns is the rise in prominence of **campaign consultants,** paid professionals who specialize in the overall management of political campaigns or an aspect of campaigns, such as fund-raising or advertising. Previously, volunteers who believed in the party's ideals and in the candidate ran most campaigns. Although some volunteers may have been motivated by the expectation that they would personally benefit from the election of their candidate, their efforts focused largely on the election itself—of a single candidate or a slate of candidates.

In contrast, professional consultants dominate modern campaigns for federal offices, many state offices, and some municipal offices. Typically, these advisers receive generous compensation for their services. Although professional consultants may not be as dedicated to a single candidate as earlier grassroots volunteers were, these strategists are typically committed to seeing their candidate elected and often are quite partisan, usually working only for candidates of one party throughout their careers. For example, during the 2008 presidential campaign, Democratic strategist David Axelrod faced a difficult choice in deciding which potential Democratic nominee he would work for: five of the contenders for the nomination—Barack Obama, Hillary Rodham Clinton, John Edwards, Christopher Dodd, and Tom Vilsack—had been past clients of Axelrod.[12] Though he considered sitting 2008 out, Axelrod wound up working for Obama and now serves as Senior Advisor to the President. Similarly, Steve Schmidt, who managed the 2008 McCain-Palin presidential campaign, works exclusively for Republican candidates.

One of the top jobs in a political campaign is that of **campaign manager,** a professional whose duties comprise a variety of strategic and managerial tasks. Among these responsibilities may be the development of the overall **campaign strategy,** the blueprint for the campaign, which includes a budget and fund-raising plan, an advertising strategy, and staffing objectives. Once the campaign strategy is set, the campaign manager often hires and manages the office staff; selects the campaign's theme, colors, and slogan; and shapes the candidate's image. Another crucial campaign professional is the pollster, who conducts focus groups and polls that help develop the campaign strategy by identifying the candidate's strengths and weaknesses and by revealing what voters care about.

Other professionals round out the candidate's team. A **fund-raising consultant** works with the candidate to identify likely contributors and arranges fund-raising events and meetings with donors. Policy directors and public relations consultants help to develop the candidate's stance on crucial issues and to get the candidate's positions out to the voters, and a **media consultant** brings the campaign message to voters by creating handouts and

campaign consultant
paid professional who specializes in the overall management of political campaigns or an aspect of campaigns

campaign manager
a professional whose duties comprise a variety of strategic and managerial tasks, from fund-raising to staffing a campaign

campaign strategy
blueprint for the campaign, including a budget and fund-raising plan, advertising strategy, and staffing plan

fund-raising consultant
a professional who works with candidates to identify likely contributors to the campaign and arrange events and meetings with donors

media consultant
a professional who brings the campaign message to voters by creating handouts and all forms of media ads

brochures, as well as newspaper, radio, and television promotions. Media consultants rely increasingly on the Internet to bring the campaign to voters through e-mail campaigns, Web-based advertising, blogs, and message boards.[13]

Media and New Technologies: Transforming Political Campaigns

Today, with the presence everywhere of the media in all its forms—television, Internet news sites, blogs, Twitter, radio, podcasts, newspapers, magazines—citizens' access to information is unprecedented. Whereas our ancestors had far fewer sources of news—word of mouth and the printed newspaper dominated for most of American history—people today can choose from a wide range of information sources and a bounty of information. Today, twenty-four-hour news channels such as CNN and MSNBC compete with the Internet news outlets, satellite radio programming, and news text messages to grab audience attention. But not all of this bombardment of information is accurate.

Given the abundance of information disseminated today, and in light of its diverse and sometimes questionable sources, engaged citizens have a greater responsibility to be discerning consumers of the news, including coverage of campaigns, voting, and elections. They cannot be passive listeners and spoon-fed watchers of news as it is dished out by daily newspapers, nightly newscasts, and the occasional weekly or monthly periodical. Vivé Griffith at the University of Texas at Austin's Think Democracy Project writes, "The challenge for the contemporary citizen is to be more than an audience member. Voters have unprecedented opportunities to access information and, at the same time, myriad ways to see issues obscured. An informed polity is essential to a democracy, and it can be difficult to sort through whether our media-saturated world ultimately serves to make us more or less informed."[14] We consider media coverage of elections, campaigns, and voting in detail in Chapter 10.

PERSONALITY VERSUS POLICY In sorting through the abundance of "news," citizens must also contend with changes in how information is presented by the media. When news was less available, that is, when TV networks aired a single fifteen-minute nightly news broadcast, the content tended to be policy-oriented and hard-hitting. Today, networks have much more time to fill: in addition to their nightly thirty-minute news broadcasts, most metropolitan areas have an hour and a half of local news in the evening, with two additional half-hour broadcasts in the morning and at noon. This all-day banquet of news programming does not include national morning talk shows such as *Good Morning*

> Recognizing the enormous importance of the national media in helping to deliver his 2008 presidential campaign's message to voters, Republican candidate Senator John McCain (R-Arizona) talks to reporters while riding in his campaign bus, the Straight Talk Express, in New Hampshire.

How Political Campaigns Have Changed in the Past 30 Years

THEN (1980s)	NOW (2011)
Many campaigns were managed and staffed by volunteers.	Campaigns are increasingly managed professionally by "guns for hire" and often have an extensive staff dedicated to strategy setting, fund-raising, and media relations.
Grassroots activism was the norm in all but the largest campaigns.	*Netroots* activism—political activism driven by candidates' Web sites, tweets, blogs, and social-networking sites—uses the Internet as a complement to traditional grassroots campaign efforts.
Money was a crucial consideration in campaigns, but grassroots activism demanded fewer financial resources.	Money rules the day in most campaigns, but technology has the potential to level the campaign playing field.

WHAT'S NEXT?

> How can the Internet change the need for money in political campaigns?

> Given the extent of Web activism during the 2010 campaigns, is there still a role for grassroots activism in future campaigns? Explain.

> Will campaigns continue to be dominated by professional staffers? Why or why not?

America and the *Today Show,* nor does it include evening news magazines such as *60 Minutes, 20/20,* and *48 Hours.* Because of the many (and sometimes endless) hours that networks and twenty-four-hour cable news shows must fill, the focus has shifted more and more from the policy stances of candidates and government officials to the personalities of these individuals. Many Americans are well equipped to describe the personality traits and lifestyle preferences of elected leaders: President Barack Obama's preference for Hawaii beach vacations, his reputation as a strict but loving father, his reliance on his BlackBerry, and his battle with his pack-a-day smoking habit; former President George W. Bush's exercise routine; or former president Bill Clinton's reputation as a fast-food junkie. The reason for this shift is twofold: many viewers enjoy lighter content when watching so much television, and personality-oriented coverage is less likely to offend viewers and advertisers.

Revolutionizing the Campaign: New Technologies

New technologies have dramatically changed the conduct of political campaigns in recent years, and continuing developments promise to force campaigns to continue to evolve and adapt as technology develops new and faster ways to communicate and interact. Through texting, tweeting, and Web-chatting, candidates can use technologies to communicate with voters, mobilize supporters, and interact with the media. The Internet is among the most valuable and powerful new tools used by candidates. It serves as an efficient means by which office seekers can communicate with potential supporters, contributors, and the media. Candidates' Web sites provide a readily available forum where the electorate can find out about candidates' experiences, policy positions, and priorities. This information can be used by voters to make more informed decisions in the voting booth. In addition, the Internet is a powerful fund-raising tool. Indeed, Barack Obama's use of the Internet to raise thousands of small donations in the 2008 Democratic presidential primary was an important part of the formula for his successful campaign. In his twenty-one-month campaign for the presidency, Obama raised a half-billion (yes, billion) dollars. "Three million donors made a total of 6.5 million donations online adding up to more than $500 million. Of those 6.5 million donations, six million were in increments of $100 or less. The average online donation was $80, and the average Obama donor gave more than once."[15] In discussing the growth of campaign fund-raising on the Internet, Eli Pariser, founder of MoveOn.org's Peace Campaign, noted that "candidates are wasting their time with rubber-chicken donors,"[16] an illusion to the donors who contribute to candidates by paying to attend campaign dinners.

Using e-mail and instant messaging, campaigns can communicate quickly with the media, both informing them of positive campaign developments and spinning negative developments in the best possible light for the candidate. Through campaign blogs, candidates can also supplement the information available in more traditional news media outlets. Internet communities and social-networking sites such as Facebook also provide a powerful tool for campaigns and an important mechanism for political engagement for individuals. Some Internet communities may be dedicated to advancing the electoral chances of a candidate for a particular office—and may or may not be sponsored by that candidate. But Internet communities and social-networking sites also provide a forum for average citizens to engage in political discourse, become informed about candidates and issues, and get information that facilitates activism in their communities.

Regulating Federal Campaign Contributions

Money—lots of it—is essential in electoral races today. Money and the modern campaign are inextricably linked because of the importance of costly media advertising in modern campaigns.[17] Federal regulations require any group that contributes to candidates' campaigns to register as a political action committee (PAC), and many interest groups form PACs as one arm of their organization. PACs are a relatively recent phenomenon, but the influence of money in electoral politics goes back a long time, as do the efforts to regulate it.[18] Reformers have attempted to limit the impact of money on political campaigns for almost as long as campaigns have existed.

Those efforts started after a scandal that erupted during the administration of President Warren Harding (1921-1923). In 1921, the president transferred oil reserves at Teapot Dome, Wyoming, from the Department of the Navy to the Department of the Interior. The following year, Harding's secretary of the interior leased the oil fields without competitive bidding. A Senate investigation into the deal revealed that the lessee of the fields had "loaned" the interior secretary more than $100,000 in order to win political influence. The interior secretary was convicted and sentenced to a year in prison and a $100,000 fine. Dubbed the Teapot Dome scandal, this sordid affair led Congress to try to limit influence of money on politics through legislation.

The Federal Corrupt Practices Act of 1925 sought to prevent future wrongdoing. This act aimed to regulate campaign finance by limiting campaign contributions and requiring public disclosure of campaign expenditures, and it was one of the first attempts at campaign finance regulation. But because the act did not include an enforcement mechanism, it was a weak attempt to fight corruption, and candidates found numerous loopholes in the law.

The Political Activities Act of 1939, also known as the Hatch Act, marked another congressional attempt to eliminate political corruption. With the growth of the federal bureaucracy as a result of the New Deal programs of President Franklin D. Roosevelt, several scandals had emerged, demonstrating the problems that could arise when government employees took an active role in politics. The Hatch Act banned partisan political activities by all federal government employees except the president, the vice president, and Senate-confirmed political appointees. The act also sought to regulate the campaign finance system by limiting the amount of money a group could spend on an election and placing a $5,000 cap on contributions from an individual to a campaign committee. Although the Hatch Act was more effective than the Federal Corrupt Practices Act of 1925, it also contained a significant loophole: groups that wanted to spend more than the legislated limit of $3 million simply formed additional groups.

© N. Y. "Tribune."

> A *New York Tribune* cartoon titled "The First Good Laugh They've Had in Years" depicts the Democrats' jubilation over the Teapot Dome Scandal of 1921, which saddled Republicans with a reputation for corruption. The scandal led Congress to try to limit the influence of money on politics.

In 1971, Congress passed the Federal Election Campaign Act (FECA), the most significant attempt at overhauling the nation's campaign finance system. The law was sponsored by Democrats in Congress who were concerned about the enormous fund-raising advantage the Republicans had had during the 1968 presidential election. This law placed considerable limitations on both campaign expenditures and campaign contributions, and it provided for a voluntary tax-return check-off for qualified presidential candidates. This provision enables you, when filling out your federal income tax return, to contribute three dollars, which will go toward the matching funds that qualified presidential candidates receive.

In 1974, FECA was amended to place more stringent limitations on individual contributions and to limit expenditures by PACs, and it revamped the presidential election process by restricting spending and providing public financing for qualified candidates who abided by the limits. The act also required public disclosure of contributions and expenditures by all candidates for federal office. Most important, the act created an enforcement mechanism in the Federal Election Commission, the agency charged with enforcing federal campaign finance laws.

In the subsequent, highly significant Supreme Court case *Buckley v. Valeo* (1976), however, the plaintiffs contended that placing limitations on the amount an individual candidate could spend on his or her own campaign violated First Amendment protections of free speech. The Court agreed, ruling that "the candidate . . . has a First Amendment right to engage in the discussion of public issues and vigorously and tirelessly to advocate his own election."[19] This ruling paved the way for the subsequent explosion in the formation of PACs, by recognizing political expenditures as a protected form of speech and removing limits on overall campaign spending, on personal expenditures by an individual candidate, and on expenditures not coordinated with a candidate's campaign and made by independent interest groups. In its *Buckley* ruling, the Court boldly overturned the limitations on expenditures that to that point had been written into law.

In 2010, the Supreme Court further cleared the way for the increased presence of money in political campaigns by more broadly interpreting First Amendment protections. In *Citizens United v. Federal Election Commission*, the Supreme Court ruled that corporations and labor unions are entitled to the same free speech rights that individuals enjoy, and thus their expenditures to influence the outcome of elections cannot be limited. The controversial 5–4 decision was hailed by conservatives as a recognition of free speech rights and was decried by liberals as an avenue by which corporations could increase their stranglehold on politics and the policy process.

Regulatory Loopholes: Independent Expenditures

independent expenditures
outlays by PACs and others, typically for advertising for or against a candidate, but uncoordinated with a candidate's campaign

When the Supreme Court determined that campaign expenditures constitute free speech for individuals, it uncovered an important loophole in the Federal Election Campaign Act of 1974. Because expenditures are protected from limitations, many PACs now use the so-called independent expenditure loophole to spend unlimited sums for or against political candidates.[20] **Independent expenditures** are outlays, typically for advertising supporting or opposing a candidate, that are uncoordinated with a candidate's campaign. Although PAC contributions to a candidate are limited, a PAC can spend as much as it wants on mailings, television promotions, or other advertisements supporting (or working against) candidates for federal office. This tactic is legal if these expenditures are not coordinated with the candidates' campaigns. Until the Court's ruling in the 2010 *Citizens United* decision, these ads could not "expressly advocate" a candidate by using terms such as "Vote for . . ." or "Elect . . . ,"[21] but those restrictions were eliminated by the Court's decision.

Regulatory Loopholes: Soft Money

Another loophole in the amended Federal Election Campaign Act of 1974 proved important in the 1990s. *Soft money* constitutes contributions to the political parties that are not subject to contribution limits and are designated for use on so-called party-building activities. The soft money loophole allowed donors who had contributed the maximum to federal candidates to give even more money by contributing to the national party committees. The party committees then gave the money to state parties, which subsequently spent the funds on party-building activities under more lenient state regulations. Frequently, such soft money contributions benefited federal candidates by paying for voter registration drives, polls, and general, party-based advertisements. Then, during the 1990s, the political parties began to use soft money for television advertisements that featured the presidential candidates but did not expressly advocate their election. The Bipartisan Campaign Finance Reform Act of 2002 banned soft money contributions to political parties.

The Bipartisan Campaign Finance Reform Act of 2002

Throughout the 1980s and 1990s, campaign finance reform was a perennial topic in presidential campaigns, and candidates roundly criticized the role of "special interests" in politics. But members of Congress had little to gain from reforming the system that had brought them to office. Although various campaign finance proposals were considered, only one passed both the Senate and the House, in 1992, and President George H. W. Bush vetoed it.

Then in 2002, the world's largest energy-trading company and one of the nation's biggest corporations, Enron, collapsed after an internal accounting scandal, leaving in its wake furious stockholders, employees, and retirees whose financial health depended upon the company. Investigations revealed extensive corporate fraud, including accounting improprieties that had enabled corporate leaders to lie about profits and debt. Investigations also revealed that Enron had contributed nearly $4 million to state and federal political parties for "party-building activities" through the soft money loophole. Public indignation at the scandal flared, leading to the passage of the McCain-Feingold Act. This bipartisan campaign reform proposal, named after its two sponsors, Senator John McCain (R-Arizona) and Senator Russell Feingold (D-Wisconsin), had been making its way at a snail's pace through committees before the Enron scandal broke.

The McCain-Feingold Act, formally known as the Bipartisan Campaign Finance Reform Act (BCRA) of 2002, banned nearly all soft money contributions, although PACs can contribute up to $5,000 to state, county, or local parties for voter registration and get-out-the-vote drives. Table 9.1 on page 290 shows that the law also increased individual contribution limitations and regulated some independent expenditure advertising. Although BCRA sought to fix many of the system's problems, some of the remedies remain in dispute.

One aspect of the McCain-Feingold Act became the subject of a series of legal challenges. In 2003, Senator Mitch McConnell (R-Kentucky), an opponent of the act, and a variety of groups affected by the new law (including the National Rifle Association and the California State Democratic Party) filed *McConnell v. the Federal Election Commission.*[22] The suit alleged that McCain-Feingold was a violation of the plaintiffs' First Amendment rights. One aspect of the law to which the groups objected was a ban on independent issue ads (thirty days before a primary election and sixty days before a general election), in which a group purchases advertising targeting a particular candidate for federal office. But the Supreme Court upheld the constitutionality of McCain-Feingold in a 5–4 decision.

Then in 2007, the Court (in another 5–4 decision) did an about-face and created an exception to the ban on issue-based ads. In *Federal Election Commission v. Wisconsin Right to Life, Inc.,*[23] the justices held that advertising within the thirty- and sixty-day window could not be prohibited, thus paving the way for its extensive use in the 2008 presidential race.

Regulatory Loophole: 527s

Another loophole in the campaign finance law became apparent with the emergence of a new form of political group, the so-called 527. Named after the section of the Internal Revenue Service tax code that regulates such organizations, a **527** is a tax-exempt group that raises money for political activities, much like those allowed under the soft money loophole. If a 527 engages only in activities such as voter registration, voter mobilization, and issue advocacy, it does not have to report its activities to the Federal Election Commission, only to the government of the state in which it is located or to the IRS. Disclosure to the FEC is required only if a 527 engages in activities expressly advocating the election or defeat of a federal candidate, or in electioneering communications.

527
a tax-exempt group that raises money for political activities, much like those allowed under the soft money loophole

TABLE 9.1

Campaign Finance Rules Under the Bipartisan Campaign Finance Reform Act, 2010 Cycle

	To Each Candidate or Candidate Committee per Election	To National Party Committee per Calendar Year	To State, District, and Local Party Committee per Calendar Year	To Any Other Political Committee per Calendar Year[1]	Special Limits
Individual may give	$2,400*	$30,400*	$10,000 (combined limit)	$5,000	$115,500* overall biennial limit: • $45,600* to all candidates • $69,900* to all PACs and parties[2]
National Party Committee may give	$5,000	No limit	No limit	$5,000	$42,600* to Senate candidate per campaign[3]
State, District, and Local Party Committee may give	$5,000 (combined limit)	No limit	No limit	$5,000	No limit
PAC (multicandidate)[4] may give	$5,000	$15,000	$5,000 (combined limit)	$5,000	No limit
PAC (not multi-candidate) may give	$2,400*	$30,400*	$10,000 (combined limit)	$5,000	No limit
Authorized Campaign Committee may give	$2,000[5]	No limit	No limit	$5,000	No limit

*These contribution limits are indexed for inflation.

[1]A contribution earmarked for a candidate through a political committee counts against the original contributor's limit for that candidate. In certain circumstances, the contribution may also count against the contributor's limit to the PAC. 11 CFR 110.6. See also 11 CFR 110.1(h).

[2]No more than $45,600 of this amount may be contributed to state and local party committees and PACs.

[3]This limit is shared by the national committee and the national Senate campaign committee.

[4]A multicandidate committee is a political committee with more than fifty contributors which has been registered for at least six months and, with the exception of state party committees, has made contributions to five or more candidates for federal office. 11 CFR 100.5(e)(3).

[5]A federal candidate's authorized committee(s) may contribute no more than $2,000 per election to another federal candidate's authorized committee(s). 11 CFR 102.12(c)(2).

SOURCE: Federal Election Commission, www.fec.gov/ans/answers_general.shtml#How_much_can_I_contribute.

In 2004, two 527s—Swift Boat Veterans and POWs for Truth, which opposed the presidential bid of Senator John Kerry (D-Massachusetts), and MoveOn.org, which opposed President George W. Bush's candidacy—grabbed national attention as each ran television "issue advocacy" advertisements across the country targeting the opposing candidate. Many observers viewed the emergence of these and other 527s as attempts to get around the ban on unlimited soft money contributions to political parties. Campaign finance reform advocates note that several 527s have been partially funded by large contributions from a few wealthy individuals, a claim bolstering the charge that 527s are a way to evade the soft money ban. In 2008, 527s spent about $200 million to influence the outcome of federal elections through voter registration and mobilization efforts and through ads that, though purportedly issue based, typically criticized a candidate's record. In the 2010 elections, 527s spent more than $154 million on federal campaigns.

The Growth of PACs

The year 2010 saw one of the most dramatic episodes in U.S. campaign finance history, with the Supreme Court's decision that corporations and labor unions are entitled to the same First Amendment protections that individuals enjoy. The impact of the *Citizens United*

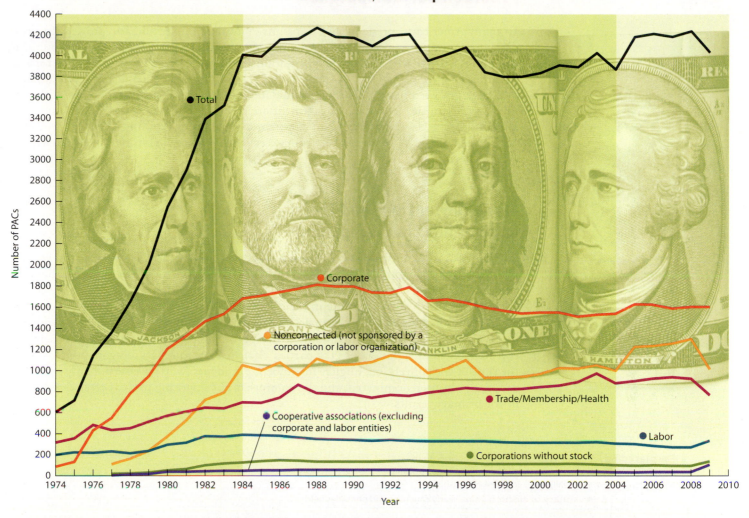

PAC Count, 1974 to present

Number of PACs (y-axis): 0 to 4400
Year (x-axis): 1974 to 2010

- Total
- Corporate
- Nonconnected (not sponsored by a corporation or labor organization)
- Trade/Membership/Health
- Cooperative associations (excluding corporate and labor entities)
- Labor
- Corporations without stock

POLITICAL INQUIRY

FIGURE 9.1 ■ **What trends does the figure show with respect to the number of political action committees since 1977? For which groups has the growth in PACs risen most steeply?**

SOURCE: Federal Election Commission, www.fec.gov/press/press2009/20090309PAC.count.shtml.

decision has been a continued expansion of political action committees, as corporations and labor unions now recognize the uncontestable influence that they may have in federal elections. In the 2010 congressional elections, PACs played an important role in creating the most expensive mid-term elections in history.

The last time that the United States saw such an important campaign finance ruling was after *Buckley v. Valeo* in 1976, when the number of political action committees shot up dramatically, as Figure 9.1 demonstrates. The figure shows that the number of corporate PACs alone nearly doubled between 1977 and 1980. Many of those PACs were formed by corporations that do business with the federal government and by associations whose members' livelihoods are significantly affected by federal regulations, including defense contractors, agricultural producers, and government employee unions.

The ballooning of the number of PACs over time is indicative of the increased power that PACs have wielded in campaigns for federal office since 1980, and, in light of the 2010 Supreme Court decision, many campaign finance analysts predict that PACs will continue to increase both in numbers and in influence.

Presidential Campaigns

To many Americans, presidential campaigns epitomize the democratic process. In presidential election years, nonstop campaigning affords ample opportunities for the public to learn about the candidates and their positions. Campaigns also provide avenues for participation by the people—for example, by volunteering in or contributing to candidates' campaigns or even just by debating candidates' views around the water cooler. Although these opportunities for citizen engagement are especially abundant during a presidential election, they arise well before, because potential candidates typically position themselves years in advance of a presidential election to secure their party's nomination and to win the general election.

Party Conventions and the General Election Campaign

As Figure 9.2 illustrates, political parties hold conventions in presidential election years to select their party's nominee for president of the United States. As discussed in Chapter 8 and as reviewed earlier in this chapter, the delegates to the national conventions are chosen by citizens in each state who vote in their party's primary election. After the conventions are over and the nominees have been decided (typically by late August or early September of the election year), the nominees and their vice-presidential running mates begin their general election campaign. Usually, the parties' choice of nominee is a foregone conclusion by the time of the convention. Eligible incumbent presidents (who have served only one term) are nearly always renominated, and the nominee of the opposing party is often determined by the primary results.

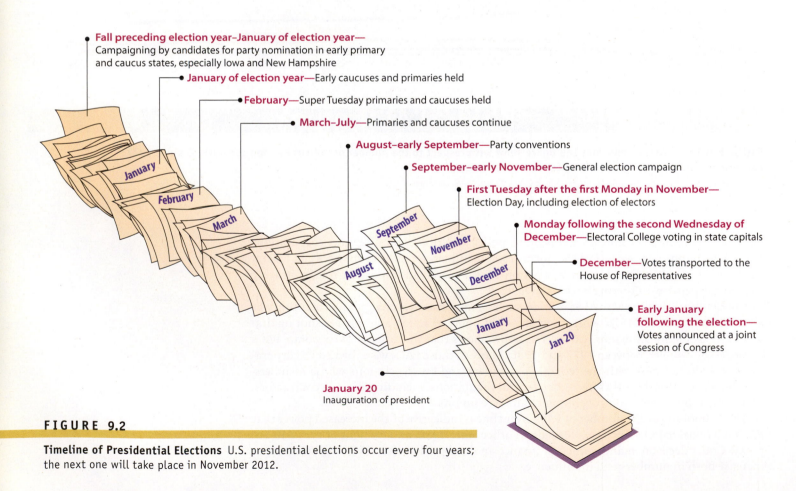

Fall preceding election year–January of election year— Campaigning by candidates for party nomination in early primary and caucus states, especially Iowa and New Hampshire

January of election year— Early caucuses and primaries held

February— Super Tuesday primaries and caucuses held

March–July— Primaries and caucuses continue

August–early September— Party conventions

September–early November— General election campaign

First Tuesday after the first Monday in November— Election Day, including election of electors

Monday following the second Wednesday of December— Electoral College voting in state capitals

December— Votes transported to the House of Representatives

Early January following the election— Votes announced at a joint session of Congress

January 20 Inauguration of president

FIGURE 9.2

Timeline of Presidential Elections U.S. presidential elections occur every four years; the next one will take place in November 2012.

The Electoral College

The votes tallied on Election Day determine which presidential candidate's slate of electors will cast their ballots, in accordance with state law. There are 538 electors in the Electoral College because the number of electors is based on the number of members of Congress—435 in the House of Representatives, 100 in the Senate—plus 3 electors who represent the District of Columbia. A presidential candidate needs a simple majority of votes (270) to win. Figure 9.3 shows the electoral votes of each state from the 2008 election.

On the Monday following the second Wednesday of December, the slate of electors chosen in each state meets in the state capital and casts their electoral votes. The results are then announced in a joint session of Congress in early January. In most presidential elections, however, the winner is known on election night, because analysts tabulate the outcome in each state and predict the electoral vote. The winner takes the oath of office as president in inaugural ceremonies on January 20. Figure 9.3 shows the electoral votes of each state from the 2008 election.

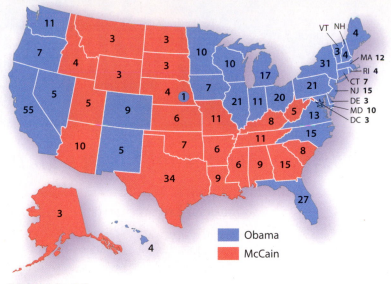

FIGURE 9.3

The 2008 Electoral College Vote In what areas of the country did President Obama get most of his support? Where did John McCain win? Which candidate won the most populous states?

Who Votes? Factors in Voter Participation

Not all people are equally likely to participate in the process of voting for the president or other government officials. Yet of all the forms of political participation, the act of voting has been analyzed perhaps more than any other.[24] (See "Analyzing the Sources" on page 294) Scholars such as Angus Campbell, Philip E. Converse, Warren Miller, and Donald Stokes have examined what factors influence who votes and how voters decide.[25] They and others have analyzed how characteristics such as education level, income, age, race, and the degree of party competitiveness in a given election influence whether a person will vote.[26] Of course, in considering demographic characteristics such as voter age and income level, we must remember that these are merely generalizations.

Education Level— the Number One Predictor of Voting

An individual's level of education is the best predictor of whether that person will vote. Table 9.2 shows that in 2008, less than one-third of U.S. citizens with less than a ninth-grade education were registered to vote, and only 23 percent actually voted. As education increases, so too does the likelihood of voting, with measurable differences even among those who have only attended college, those who have graduated, and those with advanced degrees. Among those with a college or an advanced degree, about three-quarters are registered and have voted.

TABLE 9.2

U.S. Voters' Rate of Registering and Voting by Educational Attainment, 2008

	Total Number (millions)	Percent Registered	Percent Voted
Less than 9th grade	7	30	23
Less than high school graduate	16	43	34
High school graduate or GED	65	60	51
Some college or associate degree	61	72	65
Bachelor's degree	38	76	72
Advanced degree	19	79	76

SOURCE: "Reported Voting and Registration by Educational Attainment: November 2008," www.census.gov/hhes/www/socdemo/voting/publications/p20/2008/tables.html.

ANALYZING THE SOURCES

EXPLORING VOTER TURNOUT IN THE STATES, 2008

STATE	TURNOUT RATE*	STATE	TURNOUT RATE*
United States	61.7%	Missouri	68.1%
Alabama	61.8%	Montana	66.3%
Alaska	68.3%	Nebraska	62.6%
Arizona	56.0%	Nevada	58.6%
Arkansas	53.4%	New Hampshire	71.3%
California	61.7%	New Jersey	66.2%
Colorado	69.8%	New Mexico	60.3%
Connecticut	67.2%	New York	58.0%
Delaware	66.2%	North Carolina	65.8%
District of Columbia	60.7%	North Dakota	65.0%
Florida	67.5%	Ohio	66.7%
Georgia	61.4%	Oklahoma	56.7%
Hawaii	50.5%	Oregon	67.8%
Idaho	63.3%	Pennsylvania	64.2%
Illinois	62.8%	Rhode Island	62.5%
Indiana	59.4%	South Carolina	58.6%
Iowa	69.9%	South Dakota	63.8%
Kansas	62.5%	Tennessee	57.3%
Kentucky	57.9%	Texas	54.7%
Louisiana	62.1%	Utah	53.3%
Maine	71.4%	Vermont	66.7%
Maryland	67.7%	Virginia	67.7%
Massachusetts	66.2%	Washington	67.0%
Michigan	68.9%	West Virginia	50.6%
Minnesota	78.2%	Wisconsin	72.5%
Mississippi	61.0%	Wyoming	65.4%

SOURCE: http://elections.gmu.edu/Turnout_2008G.html. Copyright © Dr. Michael McDonald.

*Turnout rate is the proportion of the voting-eligible population who cast a ballot for the highest office; that is, the vote for the highest office on the ballot (in this case, the presidency) divided by the voting-eligible population.

Evaluating the Evidence

① What states enjoy the highest voter turnout? Do these states share any common characteristics that you are aware of?

② What states have the lowest voter turnout? Do they share any common traits?

③ What is the turnout in your home state? How does it compare with that of neighboring states? Can you think of any reasons for similarities or dissimilarities in the turnout for these states?

The Age Factor

During any presidential campaign, you will hear much about age as a factor in the likelihood of voting. Despite efforts by organizations such as MTV's Rock the Vote, and despite campus-focused initiatives by presidential campaigns, young adults are less likely to vote than Americans who are middle-aged and older, though that figure has increased in re-

FIGURE 9.4 ■ **AGE AND VOTING IN THE 2008 PRESIDENTIAL ELECTION** For which age group was the percentage of people voting highest? For which age group was the voting percentage lowest? What overall pattern does the graph show? How do you explain it? In 2008, about 53 percent of individuals aged 18 to 29 voted, compared with a national average of 58 percent. Why did the youth vote matter in 2008? Was President Obama's ability to mobilize young voters a phenomenon unique to 2008?

SOURCE: U.S. Census Bureau, www.census.gov/hhes/www/socdemo/voting/publications/p20/2008/tables.html.

Percent voting

Age of voters

18–24	25–34	35–44	45–54	55–64	65–74	75+
44%	49%	55%	63%	68%	70%	66%

cent years.[27] In the 2008 election, we saw that the turnout rate among young Americans—those aged 18 to 29—continued to climb, reaching about 53 percent, the highest turnout rate for voters of that age group since 18-year-olds were first granted the right to vote in 1972. Although the turnout rate may not have broken records, the youth vote was key in President Obama's election: 66 percent of young voters favored Obama. But given the lower turnout among young people in subsequent elections, many wonder if the influence and participation of young voters peaked in 2008. Figure 9.4, which plots the percentage of people in various age groups who voted in the 2008 presidential election, shows a historic trend: as Americans age, they are more likely to vote. Whereas 44 percent of individuals aged 18 to 24 years reported that they had voted, 70 percent of people aged 65 to 74 said that they had. There are numerous reasons why young people do not vote. Among 18- to 24-year-olds, the reason most often cited is that they were too busy or had a schedule conflict, but members of this age group are also more likely to report that they forgot to vote or were out of town. Age also is related to mobility—young people might move when they leave for college or to start a new job, and mobility depresses voter turnout.

Race and Voter Participation

As the 2008 presidential contest demonstrated, race plays a significant role in voter turnout. For decades after the Voting Rights Act of 1965 ensured that African Americans could freely exercise the right to vote, turnout rates among African Americans lagged substantially behind those of non-Hispanic white Americans. Today, however, voter participation among African Americans nearly equals that of whites, as Figure 9.5 indicates. The figure also shows that voting participation among Hispanics and Asian Americans lags behind that of whites and African Americans.

Figure 9.5 shows that the percentage of non-Hispanic whites who reported they voted in the 2008 presidential election was 65 percent, and for African Americans the voting rate was 61 percent. The 2008 election saw increases in the turnout rate among all racial and ethnic groups. Importantly, in addition to increased turnout by African Americans, Barack Obama's candidacy netted him 95 percent of all votes cast by African Americans.

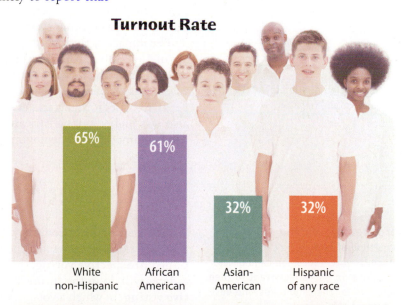

Turnout Rate

White non-Hispanic	African American	Asian-American	Hispanic of any race
65%	61%	32%	32%

FIGURE 9.5 ■ **VOTER TURNOUT IN THE 2008 PRESIDENTIAL ELECTION, BY RACE** Which demographic group had the highest turnout of the four groups shown? Which had the lowest? Which groups do you believe increased the most in the 2008 election? Why? Looking ahead to the next presidential election in 2012, what do you predict about the voting turnout rates for each of the groups shown?

Income—a Reliable Predictor of Voting

Besides education, income is one of the best predictors of whether an American will vote.[28] Typically in recent years, U.S. citizens with the lowest income level have had voter turnout levels of 50–60 percent, whereas those with the highest income level have had turnout levels above 85 percent.[29] As income increases, so too does the likelihood of voting.

The reasons for the close correlation between income and likelihood of voting are complex.[30] One possibility is that people with lower incomes may have less belief than higher-income earners that the government listens to people like them. Another factor may be that individuals with lower incomes have less leisure time in which to learn about candidates and issues and even to vote. Further, in contrast to the situation in many European democracies, U.S. political parties and political organizations tend not to be highly class based. Whereas European voters are often mobilized—by class-based trade unions and by the parties themselves—to vote on the basis of their economic interests, in the United States, the lowest-income workers are less likely to be members of organized labor unions and thus are less likely to be mobilized to vote on the basis of their own economic interests.

Party Competitiveness and Voter Turnout

Finally, researchers have found that party competitiveness in elections also influences voter turnout.[31] In tight contests, in which either party has a viable chance of winning, voter turnout typically is high because the race generates more voter interest than an election in which the winner is a foregone conclusion. Sometimes turnout is high in competitive elections because voter efficacy is higher—a voter may believe that her vote "counts" more in a close election than in a less competitive race. Voter turnout also runs high in competitive elections because the parties and other campaign organizations work harder to get out the vote when they think they have a chance at winning but know that victory is not guaranteed.

Competitive races also draw increased media attention. A tightly competitive local mayoral race might get greater than usual regional news attention, and a close race for the White House brings nearly nonstop media reports and candidate advertisements. The barrage of media coverage increases public awareness and may also boost voter efficacy by conveying the message that every vote counts.

turnout rate
the proportion of eligible voters who actually voted

The impact of this competitiveness can be seen in recent presidential elections. In 2008, about 130 million Americans voted, about 5 million more than the 126 million who voted in 2004. In both elections, the **turnout rate,** the proportion of eligible voters who actually voted, was 64 percent.[32] The 2008 election saw higher turnout rates among those in competitive battleground states, where intense party competition generated turnout. Turnout also was higher among African Americans, Hispanics, and young voters, but lower or flat turnout among other demographic groups offset those increases.

How Voters Decide

prospective voting
a method of evaluating candidates in which voters focus on candidates' positions on issues important to them and vote for the candidates who best represent their views

retrospective voting
a method of evaluating candidates in which voters evaluate incumbent candidates and decide whether to support them based on their past performance

When deciding for whom they will vote, some voters evaluate candidates on the basis of their positions on issues and then cast their ballots for those who best represent their views. Called **prospective voting,** this method of candidate evaluation focuses on what the candidates will do in the future. A more common form of candidate evaluation is **retrospective voting,** in which a voter evaluates an incumbent candidate on the basis of whether the incumbent's past decisions and actions are satisfactory to the voter.[33] If they are satisfactory, the voter will likely support the incumbent. If not, the voter will be disposed to support the incumbent's opponent. The prevalence of an incumbency advantage in election outcomes indicates that many voters have a favorable view of the decisions and actions of incumbent candidates for most offices.[34]

The most important factor that plays into how a voter decides on a candidate and perceives specific candidates, however, is the voter's party identification. Other influential determinants include those specific to a given election, such as candidates' attributes and the impact of the candidates' campaigns.

Major Factors in Voter Decision Making

The strongest bearing on voter preference is party identification, with about half of all voters basing their candidate choice on which party they identify with. Table 9.3 shows that in the 2008 presidential election, party identification was a potent influence on how voters decided among candidates. As shown in the table, among voters who identified themselves as either Democrats or Republicans, loyalty to their party's candidate was high, with 90 percent of both Democrats and Republicans voting for their party's nominee for president. President Obama's victory came in part because of his support among the nation's independent or unaffiliated voters—those who do not identify themselves as either Democrats or Republicans.

Often a significant determinant in why people vote the way they do, policy priorities are to a certain extent aligned with party identification (or, even more generally, with ideology), because the political parties usually embrace differing viewpoints on issues. National issues that top the list of concerns among voters have remained consistent over many years and include several domestic policy matters, such as the health of the economy, education, crime, health care, and Social Security. Since the terrorist attacks of 2001, homeland security and issues related to terrorism and then the wars in Iraq and Afghanistan have also ranked high in the list of issue concerns on which voters base their vote choices.

But how do voters decide which party and which candidate to support at the polls, based on the issues? First and foremost, an issue must be **salient** to voters—that is, it must resonate with them and reflect something that they care deeply about, an issue they are willing to base their vote on.[35] The ability of voters to cast an issue-based vote increases when candidates differ in their positions on an issue.

Incumbency, the situation of already holding an office or an official position, as we've seen, is also a key factor influencing how people vote. Because an incumbent is a "known commodity" with demonstrated experience to serve in office, voters are much more likely to vote for incumbents than for their challengers. Thus, for most offices, incumbents are much more likely to be reelected than their challengers are to be elected. Indeed, in congressional elections, generally more than 90 percent of incumbent U.S. senators and 95 percent of incumbent members of the House of Representatives win reelection. But incumbency is also an influence in presidential elections, gubernatorial and state legislative elections, and probably even your local city council elections. Incumbents have notable advantages over challengers, namely, greater name recognition, a track record that voters can evaluate, and access to campaign contributions that help get their message out.

Campaign Influences on Voter Choice

As we have seen, parties and candidates conduct campaigns to influence voters' choices at the polls. Campaigns today vary a great deal in how they are waged. Whereas a candidate for a small town's board of selectmen might knock on the door of every voter in the community, a U.S. Senate or gubernatorial candidate might spend most of his or her time raising money to pay for expensive television and radio advertisements. Generally, the lower the level of office, the greater the likelihood that the candidate will rely on grassroots activism.

Trends in modern campaigns, including a far deeper reliance on paid professional staffers and the prevalence of the media as a tool for communicating with voters, are catapulting the costs of campaigns sky-high. Voter choices are also affected by increasingly negative campaigns, one outcome of the modern political campaigns' reliance on paid professionals. Outside consultants typically have far fewer qualms about "going negative" than do activists in the all-community volunteer-run campaigns that were more typical of earlier times.

TABLE 9.3

Party Loyalty in the 2008 Presidential Election

	Voting for McCain (%)	Voting for Obama (%)
Democrats	10	90
Independents	45	51
Republicans	90	9

salient
having resonance, in relation to a voting issue, reflecting intense interest

incumbency
the situation of already holding the office that is up for reelection

> "Going negative" is a common feature of many modern campaigns. In 2008, as the competition for the Democratic nomination wore on, the campaigns of both Senator Hillary Clinton and Senator Barack Obama became increasingly negative. A widely publicized Clinton ad questioned Senator Obama's foreign policy experience, asking voters to consider who they wanted to answer a 3:00 a.m. phone call at the White House, while their children sleep soundly in their beds.

Consultants use negative campaign tactics for a simple reason: research shows that the approach sways voter opinion.[36] Although the candidates themselves often prefer to accentuate a positive message that highlights their background, experience, and qualifications, paid campaign consultants generally do not hesitate to sling the mud. Once a candidate establishes name recognition and credibility with voters, many consultants believe highlighting the opponent's negative qualities and actions is an effective campaign strategy.

But the impact of negative campaigning is not limited merely to swaying voters from one candidate to another. Research by political scientists shows that negative campaigning can suppress voter turnout in several ways. For example, Shanto Iyengar and Jennifer A. McGrady note that negative advertising may suppress voter turnout among the attacked candidate's supporters.[37] Other political scientists' research shows that negative campaigning undermines the democratic process by decreasing civic engagement among all voters. According to these findings, the electorate becomes disenchanted with the candidates (about whom voters get a barrage of negative information), with the campaigns (because campaigns serve as the primary messengers for delivering negative information about opponents), or with the entire electoral process that facilitates this negativity. Some voters view negative campaigning as being completely at odds with their idealized conception of the democratic process, and this may discourage them from voting.

Why Some People Do Not Vote

Negative campaigning is one reason why some people do not vote, but political scientists have proposed several others. Lack of civic engagement on the part of voters underlies many of these ideas. Other reasons have to do with the nature of campaigns and the structure of elections.

Lack of Efficacy

Some voters do not vote because they do not participate in civic affairs, either locally or at the national level. Many of these nonvoters lack efficacy.[38] They do not believe that the government listens to people like them or that their vote actually matters in determining the outcome of elections and the business of government.[39]

Scholars have determined that individuals who lack efficacy exist across the social and economic spectrums but that poorer people are more likely than better-off individuals to feel that the government does not listen to people like them. Yet although it is a common notion that people are alienated from politics or think that the government does not listen to their concerns, a recent study estimated that only about 9 percent of the U.S. population feels that way.[40] This same survey indicated that people lacking efficacy—a group that the study called the "disaffecteds"—typically had a low level of educational attainment and were less likely to follow current events than more engaged citizens.

Voter Fatigue and Negative Campaigns

Another explanation for why some Americans do not vote stems from the nature of political campaigns. In the United States, campaigns tend to be long-drawn-out affairs. For example, presidential campaigns typically last for more than a year, with some candidates positioning themselves three or four years in advance of an election. Contrast that with many parliamentary systems, including Germany's, in which an election must be held within sixty days of the dissolution of parliament because of a "no confidence" vote of the chancellor (similar to a prime minister). Some scholars say that the lengthiness of the campaigns leads to **voter fatigue,** the condition in which voters simply grow tired of all candidates by the time Election Day arrives, and may thus be less likely to vote.

American journalist and humorist Franklin Adams commented that "elections are won by men and women chiefly because most people vote against somebody rather than for somebody." The prevalence of negative campaigning compounds the impact of voter fatigue. Even the most enthusiastic supporters of a candidate may feel their advocacy withering under the unceasing mudslinging that occurs in many high-level campaigns. And so while evidence shows that negative advertising is effective in swaying voters' opinions, sometimes it also succeeds in suppressing voter turnout by making voters less enthusiastic about voting.

The Structure of Elections

Political scientists also cite the structure of U.S. elections as a reason why more Americans do not vote. For years, voting rights activists claimed that the registration requirements in many states were too complicated and discouraged people from voting by making it too difficult to register. In 1993, Congress sought to remedy that situation by passing the National Voter Registration Act, frequently called the "Motor Voter" Act, which allows eligible people to register to vote when they apply for a driver's license or enroll in a public assistance program or when they submit the necessary information by mail. Although there was enormous anticipation that the motor voter law would significantly boost voter registration and turnout, in fact its impact has been negligible.

Critics of the structure of elections also point to their frequency. In the United States, the number of elections varies from municipality to municipality, and local government charters may call for more than four elections for municipal offices alone. Although most federal offices require only two elections (a primary and a general), these elections are not always held in conjunction with state, county, and municipal elections.

The timing of elections also affects voter participation. Most general elections are held on a weekday—the first Tuesday after the first Monday in November. Moreover, although states decide when to hold primary elections, state legislative elections, and municipal and school board elections, these elections, too, typically occur on a weekday. Critics say that holding elections on weekends or over a two-day period instead, or establishing a national voting holiday, would increase voter turnout by ensuring that voters had ample opportunity to cast their ballots. (See "Global Context" on page 300.)

The Rational Abstention Thesis

A final explanation as to why some people do not vote is that they make a conscious choice that not voting is a rational, logical action. Called the **rational abstention thesis,** this theory states that some individuals decide that the "costs" of voting—in terms of the time, energy, and inconvenience required to register to vote, to become informed about candidates and elections, and actually to vote—are not worth the effort when compared with the expected "benefits," or what the voters could derive from voting.

In light of these cumulative "costs," it is perhaps surprising that so many people choose to vote.[41] One explanation for why they do is that most voters report that they derive psychological rewards from exercising this citizen's right—feelings of being civically engaged, satisfied, and patriotic. But when the costs associated with voting increase too much, turnout drops; more people choose not to vote when voting becomes too inconvenient. This drop-off occurs, for example, when municipalities shorten voting hours and during inclement weather.

The Impact of Nonvoting

From a civic engagement perspective, nonvoting is both a symptom and a result of a lack of civic involvement on the part of individuals.[42] Your roommate might not vote because she is not civically engaged—because she feels that she has little to contribute and that the

GLOBAL CONTEXT

ELECTIONS IN INDIA

Although we may think that conducting elections in the United States is a large undertaking, holding elections in India is even more challenging. India is the largest democracy in the world and the second most populous country after China. Thus, the efforts associated with organizing the general election process are enormous.

The Indian Election Commission, an independent committee that is insulated from executive interference, has authority for running elections. The commission's job is to ensure free and fair elections. Since the beginning of India's democracy in 1947, free and fair elections have taken place at regular intervals, as the Indian constitution requires.

Should the United States adopt a general election process like India's?

Indian elections today constitute the largest elections in human history. Eight hundred thousand polling stations span the country in widely varying climatic and geographic zones, giving accessibility to the vote to more than 668 million people. With such a large electorate, polling for the national elections extends to at least three days.

The entire election process takes five to eight weeks for the national election to the Lok Sabha (the House of the People), the lower house of India's Parliament, and four to six weeks for the state legislative assemblies. Elections begin with the announcement of the election schedule, usually at a press conference a few weeks before the formal election

> In the world's most populous democracy, Indian voters in Chandigarh hold their voter identity cards and wait to cast their ballots in the fifth and final phase of country's marathon elections on May 13, 2009.

process begins, and with notifications calling upon the electorate to elect members of the House. Once the notifications are made, candidates can file their nominations. Candidates then get two weeks to campaign before the voting begins.

After the minimum three days set aside for voting, a later date is set for counting the votes, and the election commission compiles a complete list of the House members elected.

For more information on India's Parliament, visit the Parliament of India's Web site: http://rajyasabha.nic.in/. For more information on elections in India, visit www.indian-elections .com/.

government does not listen to "people like her" anyway. But by not voting, she perpetuates this lack of efficacy by remaining outside the process rather than staking a claim to what is rightfully hers: the idea that every individual has the right to a voice in the composition and priorities of the government. Only by becoming civically engaged—learning about the candidates, discussing issues, and voting—can she break the cycle of inefficacy. Voting will make her pay more attention to campaigns, candidates, and issues.

Beyond the effects of nonvoting on individuals, low voter turnout affects the polity. When relatively few people vote in a given election, the outcome is likely to represent the will of only that subset of the electorate who voted. This impact is important: consider that polls indicate that the outcomes of the 2000 and 2004 presidential elections would have been different if voter turnout had been higher. In each of those elections, the Democratic nominee (Al Gore and John Kerry, respectively) was the favored candidate among several groups whose turnout falls below average, including voters under age 24, African American voters, and voters with lower incomes. The process becomes cyclical: these nonvoters who disagree with the outcome conclude that the government does not represent them, feel less efficacious, and are less inclined to vote in the future.

Moreover, some scholars assert that democracies with low voter turnout are more likely to generate threats to their own well-being.[43] In democracies with low turnout, these scholars say, charismatic, popular political figures may rise to power and become authoritarian leaders. Corruption, too, can be a problem in low-turnout democracies where government officials might feel relatively unconcerned about the disapproval of disgruntled constituents.

Other researchers, however, contend that nonvoting is not a big problem, especially in cases where large numbers in the electorate are relatively uninformed about candidates and issues.[44] A number of scholars in this camp argue that participation by the uninformed is undesirable, because it may lead to drastic changes in government. Opponents of this view counter that because of political parties' role in selecting candidates, the menu for voter choice is actually quite limited in most elections. Those who argue that nonvoting does not matter also ignore the fact that voting tends to produce more engaged citizens who, because they vote, feel a duty to be informed and involved.

Other scholars who claim that low voter turnout is not a problem argue that low voting rates are simply a function of people's satisfaction with the status quo: their nonvoting simply means that they do not seek change in government. This argument, however, does not explain why lower turnout is most likely to occur in populations that are least likely to be satisfied with their situation. For example, people with lower incomes are much less likely to vote than those with higher incomes. Whatever the reason—a lack of efficacy as argued by some, satisfaction as argued by others—nonvoters' best chances of having their views reflected in the policy process is to articulate them through voting.

CONCLUSION

THINKING CRITICALLY ABOUT WHAT'S NEXT IN ELECTIONS, CAMPAIGNS, AND VOTING

The nature of political campaigns in the United States has continuously evolved, but the changes in recent decades have been especially dramatic. An era in which political parties and grassroots activism dominated campaigns has given way to the present-day realities where money, media, and mavens of strategy are key forces in shaping campaigns, which have grown increasingly candidate-centered. Prominently driving the changes are the simultaneous *decrease* in political party clout and *increase* in the need for money—money to pay for the small army of professional staffers that run the campaigns; and money to cover the expensive media buys that candidates, especially those running for national and state office, heavily depend on for communicating with the electorate.

Technology offers the potential to bring the politics of electoral campaigns back to the grassroots—now perhaps more appropriately called the netroots. Although campaigns' use of technology certainly is not free, digital communication is cost-effective and rapid. Campaigns' and candidates' option of communicating with voters through mediums such as social-networking sites, YouTube, e-mail, and instant messaging presents an exciting alternative to high-priced "campaigning-as-usual." In what ways did congressional candidates make use of these new media in the 2010 elections? How might the use of these technologies change in the 2012 campaign?

Through the new mediums of communication, there is great potential, too, for the inclusion of a variety of new voices in the political campaigning process. Groups that want to influence campaigns and voters have at their disposal a vast arsenal of new technology that makes such influence possible.

Summary

1. Political Participation: Engaging Individuals, Shaping Polities

Active political engagement benefits both the individual and the polity. When it comes to elections, campaigns, and voting, the opportunities for civic engagement are numerous. Although some civic activities, such as working full-time on a campaign, might represent enormous commitments, others, including casting a ballot and engaging in political discourse, are less time-consuming and are manageable for even the busiest people.

2. Elections in the United States

U.S. elections include the primary election, in which a party's nominee to run in the general election is selected; the general election, in which the winning candidate attains the office being sought; and special-purpose elections such as the initiative, the referendum, and the recall, which are citizen-sponsored efforts to have a greater say in the political process.

3. The Act of Voting

Although all the states rely on the Australian (secret) ballot, the types of ballots used in states vary significantly. The type of ballot can have an impact on election outcomes, as in the 2000 presidential election.

4. Running for Office: The Choice to Run

Most offices have formal eligibility requirements, but there are also more subjective requirements by which voters view candidates as qualified to hold a given office. Often these characteristics have to do with occupation, education, and experience.

5. The Nature of Political Campaigns Today

Today's political campaigns hire a wide variety of professionals who perform the tasks that were once accomplished by volunteer staffs. Office seekers' increasing reliance on electronic media, in particular television, has drastically changed both the ways in which campaigns are conducted and the costs of those campaigns. The widespread use of the Internet, too, continues to alter the nature of campaigns.

6. Regulating Campaign Contributions

Government efforts over the years to regulate campaign contributions have led to laws with numerous loopholes. The latest attempt to curtail the influence of money on politics is the Bipartisan Campaign Finance Reform Act of 2002.

7. Presidential Campaigns

Presidential campaigns are increasing in duration. They begin with the primary process, continue through the national party conventions, proceed to the general election campaign and voting, and end with the Electoral College vote.

8. Who Votes? Factors in Voter Participation

Influences on voter participation include education, age, race, income, and party competitiveness.

9. How Voters Decide

Party identification, policy priorities, incumbency, and campaigns are factors influencing how voters decide for whom to vote.

10. Why Some People Do Not Vote

The many reasons why people don't vote include a lack of efficacy, the impact of voter fatigue and negative campaigns, the structure of elections, and the rational abstention thesis. Whatever the reason, nonvoting has a harmful impact on individuals and the government.

Key Terms

absentee voting 281

Australian ballot 279

campaign consultant 284

campaign manager 284

campaign strategy 284

caucus 276

chad 279

closed primary 276

coattail effect 280

527 289

fund-raising consultant 284

general election 275

GOTV 275

grassroots organizing 274

incumbency 297

independent
 expenditures 288

initiative 278

instant runoff election 278

media consultant 284

office-block ballot 280

open primary 276

party-column ballot 280

proposition 278

prospective voting 296

rational abstention
 thesis 299

recall 279

referendum 278

retrospective voting 296

runoff election 278

salient 297

Super Tuesday 276

turnout rate 296

voter fatigue 299

winner-take-all 278

For Review

1. What are some opportunities for civic engagement related to elections, campaigns, and voting?

2. What are the different kinds of elections in the United States? What is the difference between a primary election and a general election?

3. What is the difference between formal and informal eligibility requirements for political office?

4. Why is regulating campaign finance so difficult? Explain the various efforts to limit the impact of money on campaigns.

5. What factors influence whether a person will vote or not?

6. What factors influence how or for whom an individual will vote?

7. What is the rational abstention thesis? Is it rational? What factors might not be calculated into the costs and benefits of voting?

For Critical Thinking and Discussion

1. Why do formal and informal eligibility requirements for office differ? What are the informal eligibility requirements to run for the state legislature where you live? What are the requirements for the city or town council in your hometown or the community where your school is located? How do these differences reflect the nature of the constituency for the office being sought?

2. How has the increasing cost of political campaigns changed the nature of American politics? Why have costs escalated?

3. What has been the impact of the increasing negativity in American political campaigns?

4. Using the text discussion of factors influencing whether a person votes, assess a classmate's likelihood of voting based solely on those factors. Then ask the person if he or she votes. Was your assessment accurate?

5. In your view, what is the impact of nonvoting?

PRACTICE QUIZ

MULTIPLE CHOICE: Choose the lettered item that answers the question correctly.

1. An election that determines which candidates win the offices being sought is called a(n)
   a. blanket primary.
   b. open primary.
   c. caucus.
   d. general election.

2. A meeting of party members held to select delegates to the national convention is called a(n)
   a. blanket primary.
   b. open primary.
   c. caucus.
   d. general election.

3. A special election in which voters can remove officeholders before their term is over is called a(n)
   a. referendum.
   c. recall.
   b. initiative.
   d. proposition.

4. An election in which voters in a state can vote for or against a measure proposed by the state legislature is called a(n)
   a. referendum.
   c. recall.
   b. initiative.
   d. proposition.

5. The phenomenon by which candidates running for lower-level office such as city council benefit in an election from the popularity of a top-of-ticket nominee is called
   a. the petticoat effect.
   b. the bustle effect.
   c. the coattail effect.
   d. the bolster effect.

6. A professional who brings the campaign message to voters by creating all forms of media ads is called a(n)
   a. campaign manager.
   b. fund-raising consultant.
   c. outreach manager.
   d. a media consultant.

7. The proportion of voters who actually voted is called
   a. the turnout rate.
   b. the electoral rate.
   c. the eligibility factor.
   d. the voter sample.

8. Outlays by PACs and others, typically for advertising for or against a candidate but uncoordinated with a candidate's campaign, are called
   a. a soft money expenditure.
   b. an independent expenditure.
   c. a 527 expenditure.
   d. a 626 expenditure.

9. An issue that has resonance and intense interest among voters is said to be
   a. a divide issue.
   b. a fence-sitting issue.
   c. a salient issue.
   d. a litmus-test issue.

10. The condition in which voters grow tired of all candidates by the time Election Day arrives, making them possibly less likely to vote, is called
   a. rational abstention.
   b. absentee voting.
   c. voter ennui.
   d. voter fatigue.

FILL IN THE BLANKS.

11. A follow-up election held when no candidate receives the majority of votes cast in the original election is called a(n) _____ .

12. A special election in which the computerized voter machine simulates the elimination of last-place vote-getters to eventually decide a winner is called a(n) _____ .

13. A measure proposed by voters and placed on the ballot for their approval is called a(n) _____ election.

14. A ballot that organizes the candidates by political party is called a(n) _____ .

15. A(n) _____ is the blueprint for an election campaign, including a budget and fund-raising plan, an advertising strategy, and a staffing plan.

Answers: 1. d; 2. c; 3. c; 4. a; 5. c; 6. d; 7. a; 8. b; 9. c; 10. d; 11. runoff; 12. instant runoff; 13. initiative; 14. party-column ballot; 15. campaign strategy.

RESOURCES FOR RESEARCH AND ACTION

Internet Resources

The Living Room Candidate
www.livingroomcandidate.org   This site, maintained by the Museum of the Moving Image, provides videos of television commercials run by presidential campaigns from 1956 to 2008.

Project Vote Smart
www.vote-smart.org   This nonpartisan Web site provides independent, factual information on election procedures in each state.

Rock the Vote
www.rockthevote.org   This nonprofit, nonpartisan organization encourages political participation by young people and provides resources on policies of interest, as well as voting information.

Vote, Run, Lead
www.voterunlead.org   This is the Web site for an organization that encourages the civic engagement of young women as voters, activists, and candidates for political office.

Internet Activism

Both political parties provide processes for including young people as delegates to their national party conventions every four years, and volunteer opportunities abound at these meetings. To try to become a delegate or a volunteer at the 2012 national party conventions, go to **www.democrats.org** or **www.gop.com**.

Twitter
www.Media Bloggers.org
Follow "electionblogs" to receive coverage of U.S. elections.

YouTube
Watch and analyze the effectiveness of 2010 mid-term campaign commercials on YouTube's thehilldotcom channel (sponsored by The Hill newspaper). **http://www.youtube.com/user/thehilldotcom**.

Facebook
Search "politicians" to see a list of candidates and elected officials you can friend or fan.

Recommended Readings

Abramson, Paul R., John H. Aldrich, and David W. Rohde. *Change and Continuity in the 2008 Elections.* Washington, DC: CQ Press, 2009. The latest in this series of election analyses examines the tactics employed in the 2008 presidential and congressional elections.

Bimber, Bruce, and Richard Davis. *Campaigning Online: The Internet in U.S. Elections.* New York: Oxford University Press, 2003. Describes how voters and political campaigns are increasingly relying on the Internet as a communication, fund-raising, and organizing tool.

Burns, Nancy, Kay Lehman Schlozman, and Sidney Verba. *The Private Roots of Public Action: Gender Equality, and Public Action.* Cambridge, MA: Harvard University Press, 2003. Explores the differences in political participation between men and women.

Faucheux, Ron. *Campaigns and Elections: Winning Elections.* New York: M. Evans and Company, 2003. A collection of the "best of the best" articles from *Campaigns and Elections* magazine; a practical guide to conducting campaigns.

Herrnson, Paul S., Richard G. Niemi, Michael J. Hanmer, Benjamin B. Bederson, and Frederick C. Conrad. *Voting Technology: The Not-So-Simple Act of Casting a Ballot.* Washington, DC: Brookings Institution Press, 2008. Explains the intricacies of voting technology, including the electoral implications of how votes are cast.

Jacobson, Gary C. *The Politics of Congressional Elections.* New York: Longman, 2008. A classic work explaining the process of congressional elections and demonstrating how electoral politics reflects and shapes other basic components of American democracy.

Leighley, Jan. *Strength in Numbers: The Political Mobilization of Racial and Ethnic Minorities.* Princeton, NJ: Princeton University Press, 2001. Examines the factors that influence political participation by African Americans and Hispanic Americans.

Plouffe, David. *The Audacity to Win: The Inside Story and Lessons of Barack Obama's Historic Victory.* New York: Viking Press, 2009. Barack Obama's campaign manager writes a captivating political memoir of the 2008 campaign.

Zukin, Cliff, Scott Keeter, Molly Andolina, Krista Jenkins, and Michael X. Delli Carpini. *A New Engagement? Political Participation, Civic Life, and the Changing American Citizen.* New York: Oxford University Press, 2006. Describes the changing ways in which Americans are participating in the political life of their country and communities.

Movies of Interest

Swing Vote (2008)
Kevin Costner stars in this film in which one man—an average apolitical American—determines the outcome of a presidential election.

Bulworth (1999)
Warren Beatty stars in this offbeat skewering of the impact of money on political campaigns in the United States.

The Candidate (1972)
Robert Redford's character is convinced to run for the Senate on the premise that, with no chance at success, he can say whatever he wants. But success changes him, and his values shift as the prospect of winning becomes apparent.

The Media

THEN

The relationship between the media and consumers was one-way.

NOW

Technology has created a two-way relationship between the media and consumers, involving the exchange of a seemingly limitless amount of information of varying quality.

NEXt

Will the abundance and the reach of the media overload people with information?

Will people select media sources that serve only to confirm their views?

Will the ever-increasing speed and volume of information affect its quality?

If you are like most Americans

—and indeed like multitudes of people across the globe—the media are a fixture in your daily life. You may wake up to a radio show each morning or read a newspaper over breakfast or while commuting on a bus or train. You may watch televised news stories on the war in Afghanistan in the evening. You may receive real-time news updates on your cell phone, Internet news sites, and Weblogs or tune in to the twenty-four-hour news channels available virtually everywhere. There is no escaping that as a citizen of the twenty-first century, you are bathed in a sea of news and information. Some of what the media offer you is meant to entertain, some is meant to inform, but increasingly the lines between the two have blurred.

No one can dispute that the sheer amount of information and entertainment available courtesy of the media has increased immeasurably over the past few decades. Within a generation, the modern media have transformed American life. Where once people had to seek out news and information, today they are inundated with it, and they must develop the skill to filter the good from the bad.

Although this abundance of information at times may rise to the level of a blitz, information is empowering. It serves as the basis on which people shape well-founded opinions. Those opinions are the building blocks for meaningful civic engagement and political participation. In the discussion that follows, we see how the media continuously shape the ways we receive information and the ways we exercise the rights and privileges of our American democracy.

This chapter focuses on the role of the contemporary U.S. media as both an information source and a conduit through which individuals convey information and opinions to others, and it explores the growing, shifting influence of the media on politics and civic life over time.

FIRST, we examine what *the modern media* are.

SECOND, we consider *the political functions of the media.*

THIRD, we explore *the press and politics,* taking *a historical view.*

FOURTH, we focus on the origins and formats of the first of the electronic media with a look at *the radio and television revolutions.*

FIFTH, we examine the diverse and growing uses of the Internet as *the media revolution continues.*

SIXTH, we ponder charges that the U.S. media are *biased media.* Do most people believe that the media are too liberal or too conservative? Are they right?

SEVENTH, we consider the government's *regulation of the media* and examine how the media's rapidly continuing transformation affects government's ability to regulate new formats of communicating.

The Modern Media

On June 20, 2009, 27-year-old Neda Agha-Soltan was shot to death in the streets of Tehran, Iran, as she was about to join a demonstration to protest the outcome of the Iranian election. Agha-Soltan was killed by a bullet allegedly fired by a member of the Basij, the Iranian paramilitary organization loyal to Iranian President Mahmoud Ahmadinejad. What made Agha-Soltan's death unique was that it became the iconic representation of the antigovernment movement. The murder was captured on a cell phone video camera by a bystander. It was sent to the British newspaper *The Guardian* and to the Voice of America radio network. It was also sent to several individuals, one of whom uploaded the video to Facebook, and then to YouTube. Within hours, it was broadcast on CNN. In 2010, the anonymously recorded video won the prestigious George Polk journalism award for videography. Polk Award curator John Darnton, of the *New York Times,* noted that "this award celebrates the fact that, in today's world, a brave bystander with a cellphone camera can use video-sharing and social networking sites to deliver news."[1]

The Agha-Soltan case demonstrates a tension that now exists in defining the media. Traditionally, we have easily recognized the media: our hometown newspaper, the local television news, and the cable news networks. But defining the media today is trickier: do tweets from your mayor, blogs from your roommate, or Facebook posts from your mom count as media? Although many regard the **media** simply as tools used to store and deliver information or data (in which case, all of the above would be considered media), we must differentiate between media outlets that distribute unverifiable or opinion-based information, and those that disseminate verifiable information.

The media are present in various forms today, including print media such as newspapers and magazines; the electronic media, which traditionally means radio and television; and new media, usually thought of as being those forms associated with the Internet and cellular technology, including Web sites and social-networking sites such as Facebook, Twitter,

media
tools used to store and deliver information or data

and YouTube. In previous eras, media consumers often accepted what was broadcast or printed as fact, but today one must be a critical consumer of information. Just because information appears on a blog, or even hundreds of blogs, it is not necessarily true. How can today's media consumers be certain the information they are receiving is accurate? One good method is by relying on media outlets with a track record of providing solid information and adhering to journalistic standards. Another is to check sources independently: today, the Internet has made it possible to verify some information simply by clicking on a hotlink to the original sources. More and more, news organizations will come to rely on citizen journalists such as the videographer who filmed Agha-Soltan's death, increasing the probability that false information will be widely distributed by unscrupulous individuals. Thus today's media consumers must exercise a high level of caution when reading, listening, or viewing.

> Epitomizing how new technologies have changed the media: a frame grab from a cell-phone video shows a woman identified as Neda Agha-Soltan lying on the ground after getting shot in the chest in Tehran June 20, 2009. The footage, filmed by a citizen journalist, later won the prestigious Polk journalism award for videography.

The Political Functions of the Media

In the United States today, the media in all their forms—including print, television, radio, and the Internet—fulfill several key functions. Much of what the media do revolves around entertaining us, whether that means watching *NCIS* or reading the Sunday funnies. But the media perform important political functions as well and are a vital element of our democracy. Specifically, the media perform the following political functions:

- provide political information
- help us to interpret events and policies and are influential in setting the national policy agenda
- provide a forum for political conversations
- socialize children to the political culture

Providing Information

One long-standing function of the mass media is to serve up a steady diet of news and information to readers, viewers, and listeners. Indeed, the media, particularly the electronic media, are the primary source of information for most individuals. And today, the quantity of information available—on blogs, Web sites, and cable television stations—surpasses the volume available at any other time in history. Coverage includes everything from weather watches, to sports scores, to the latest legislative developments on Capitol Hill, to serious analysis of top domestic policy issues and international problems. From this steady diet arises the problem of information overload—the constant availability of news information to the point of excess, which may cause media consumers to ignore, dismiss, or fail to see the significance of particular events. Media critics especially fault the television networks for injecting entertainment into news shows. They dub this combination **infotainment** (a hybrid of the words *information* and *entertainment*). More recent is the trend of uniting comedy with political content, as in Jon Stewart's *The Daily Show* and Stephen Colbert's *The Colbert Report,* both of which interpret news events with a comedic slant.

infotainment
news shows that combine entertainment and news, a hybrid of the words *information* and *entertainment*

Interpreting Matters of Public Interest and Setting the Public Agenda

Besides reporting information, the media help people to comprehend and interpret matters of public interest and to make informed decisions about public policies. Political scientist Shanto Iyengar asserts that this process often begins with media **framing**—setting a context that helps people understand important events and matters of shared interest.

framing
the process by which the media set a context that helps people understand important events and matters of shared interest

ANALYZING THE SOURCES

CONFIDENCE IN THE MEDIA

The Gallup Organization has asked the following question in surveys since 1972: "In general, how much trust and confidence do you have in the mass media—such as newspapers, T.V., and radio—when it comes to reporting the news fully, accurately, and fairly: a great deal, a fair amount, not very much, or none at all?"

SOURCE: The Gallup Poll, *Media Use and Evaluation*, www.galluppoll.com/poll/1663/Media-Use-Evaluation.aspx.

The line graph illustrates survey respondents' views on that question, showing survey data at various times between May 1972 and September 2009. You can see that considerable changes have occurred in people's assessment of news organizations in this period.

Evaluating the Evidence

① Describe trends during the 1970s in people's confidence in the media, citing specific data from the graph.

② Describe trends since 2001 in people's confidence in the media, citing specific data.

③ What do the latest surveys indicate about respondents' opinions on the issue of confidence in the media?

④ What do the data say about the *overall* trends with regard to people's confidence in the media?

⑤ What factors could have contributed to the changes in people's assessment of the media over time? Explain.

Political scientist Pippa Norris has analyzed the process of framing as it relates to gender. She asserts that gender has become a common frame through which journalists provide context for different kinds of political stories.[2] Norris explains that voters, candidates, public opinion, and issues all may be viewed from a gender-based perspective. For example, in the 2008 presidential campaign, the media initially covered the race for the Democratic nomination by accentuating the gender of Senator Hillary Clinton (D-New York) and played up Clinton's potential to be the first woman president of the United States. Media reporting defined her opponent, Senator Barack Obama, as potentially the first African American president. Similarly, when Senator John McCain announced that Alaska governor Sarah Palin would be his running mate in the 2008 general election campaign, the media emphasized the gendered aspects of her nomination, particularly her role as a mother.

The media also help to shape the **public agenda**—public issues that most demand the attention of government officials. The media commonly influence the setting of the public agenda by **priming**—using their coverage to bring particular policies on issues to the public agenda.

public agenda
the public issues that most demand the attention of government officials

priming
bringing certain policies on issues to the public agenda through media coverage

Providing a Forum for Conversations About Politics

Although the media have provided an often lively forum for conversations about politics, the prominence of this role has reached new heights in the Internet era. Historically, information flowed from the media—which through the years have included everything from the political broadsides and leaflets of colonial times to modern newspapers, radio news, and television programming—to the people. The people then formed opinions based on what they read, heard, and saw. This historical one-way tradition typically featured little give-and-take between media sources and their consumers. A notable exception has been the **letter to the editor,** in which a reader responds to a newspaper story, knowing that the letter might be published in that paper.

The advent of talk radio gave listeners one of their first regular opportunities to express their views publicly. Television took note, and call-in shows such as *Larry King Live* now are common fare on cable television stations.

But no other medium has expanded the ability of people to communicate their views to the degree that the Internet has. David Weinberger, a Democratic marketing consultant and Internet adviser, describes this phenomenon: "Think of it as conversation space. Conversation is the opposite of marketing. It's talking in our own voices about things we want to hear about."[3] Weblogs facilitate this conversation by inviting an ongoing dialogue between the blog hosts and the posters. Discussion boards (even those that are "nonpolitical") are filled with political discussion and opinions. Social-networking sites such as MySpace, Facebook, BlackPlanet, MyBatanga, AsiaAve, and Faithbase allow individuals to share their stories, interests, and political viewpoints.

letter to the editor
a letter in which a reader responds to a story in a newspaper, knowing that the letter might be published in that paper

Socializing Children to Political Culture

The media also socialize new generations to the political culture. For young children, television remains the dominant medium for both entertainment and socialization. TV-viewing toddlers receive regular messages about important cultural values. Shows such as *Sesame Street* and *Barney* send powerful messages about the value of diversity in society. A song such as *Barney*'s "You Are Special" underscores the value of individualism in the culture. Young children's shows also subtly instruct watchers on the value of patriotism and of specific civic behaviors, such as voting.

TV programming for older children similarly takes on political issues. In *Arthur*, the main character comes face-to-face with censorship when adults in his town have the "Scare Your Pants Off" book series removed from the public library, thus providing a concise fifteen-minute lesson on civil liberties issues.

Even television and radio programs not specifically aimed at youth often reinforce democratic principles and practices. What is *American Idol* if not a televised election? And when the tribe speaks on *Survivor,* they do so through the process of voting. Talk radio and television call-in programs rest on the assumption that individuals' opinions matter and that they have the right to voice them. (See "Global Context" on page 312.) These various kinds of programming may not directly spur a particular political behavior on the part of viewers. Nonetheless, television and other forms of media that we often think of as pure entertainment frequently reinforce and legitimize dominant American political values.

> The media socialize individuals to key political values. On shows such as *American Idol,* principles of democracy prevail as viewers vote for their favorite contestant. What are some other popular television shows that reflect society's core political values?

TALK RADIO, SAUDI STYLE—MUBASHER FM

When you think of Saudi Arabia, one thing that probably does not pop into your mind is talk radio. But every Monday night during prime-time hours, radio host Salama al-Zaid takes calls from about twenty listeners, most of whom are seeking help in dealing with the national bureaucracy or lodging complaints of corruption against government officials.

Saudi Arabia, an oil-rich nation bordered by the Persian Gulf on the east and the Red Sea on the west, is a kingdom ruled by King Abdullah and administered primarily through an enormous network of the royal family.

Can the media open up closed societies?

The Muslim Shari'a is the basis of the nation's laws, although some secular laws have been enacted in recent years. Women do not have basic rights such as voting and driving. Although the country traditionally has enjoyed a high standard of living, poverty is a growing problem. Restrictions on the media abound, and criticism of the monarchy is especially frowned upon. It is in this environment that Zaid hosts his radio program. *Mubasher FM* ("Live FM" in Arabic) went on the air in 2006.

Zaid claims that King Abdullah views Zaid's program as a useful tool in gauging public opinion. "The media has always been a red line in this country. But the king came and said this is the way to reach the people. And he sent a message to me: 'Keep going,'" explains Zaid, who fully supports the monarchy. Callers to the program get more than a sympathetic ear. Not only do government officials try to rectify problems aired on the program, but also callers sometimes receive an audience with the king, who has issued decrees to address various issues broadcast on *Mubasher FM*.

> Radio Host Salama al-Zaid.

Zaid is highly critical of corrupt officials, whom he has challenged to phone in and explain their behavior. Moreover, he is not afraid of speaking out on some of the most controversial issues in Saudi society, including those affecting the rights of women. During one program, he took Saudi schools and universities to task for failing to hire qualified women as teachers. Calling on the royal court to address this problem, he complained that "our daughters are being wronged by our universities and places of higher learning."

The optimistic Zaid believes that Saudis are advancing toward being a more open society. He takes heart that people are increasingly willing to come forward and complain about corruption of government officials and unacceptable problems such as the sexual harassment of women. That he must sift through thousands of calls each week indicates a willingness by individuals to voice their complaints without fear of reprisals, and Zaid characterizes that as progress.

SOURCE: Hassan M. Fattah, "Challenging Saudi Arabia's Powerful, One Caller at a Time," *New York Times*, May 5, 2007, p. A4.

The Press and Politics: A Historical View

The sheer volume of information available today through the media makes the influence of the media in our times beyond dispute. Historically, too, the media have played an essential role in setting the political agenda and shaping public policy. The power of the media was evident even in pre-Revolutionary times, when, for example, newspaper owners and readers rallied against the Stamp Act's (1765) imposition of taxes on newspapers and other kinds of legal documents. Newspaper publishers sympathetic to the colonists' cause of ejecting Great Britain from American shores used their "power of the pen" to arouse public opinion, and they strongly supported the patriot cause throughout the Revolution. Taking sides in an internal conflict was a new role for the press, one that would sow the seeds of future media influence on the country's domestic and foreign policy. The early history of media development also raised issues that continue to create conflict about the media's role in society.

The Early Role of the Press

Great leaders learned early how intimately their careers were linked to favorable press coverage and influence. From the 1790s to the 1830s, the press served primarily as a vehicle for the leaders of political parties, who expressed their opinions through newspapers known to reflect their particular viewpoints in reporting the news. The circulation of these newspapers was small, but so was their audience; most people could not read and write and did not vote.

By the 1830s, the environment had changed. For openers, the average American was now able to read. New technology made possible the **penny press**—newspapers that sold for a penny. The field of **journalism,** the practice of gathering and reporting events, flourished. Circulation increased, and the working class became interested in what the newspapers had to offer. Another reason newspapers reduced their price was the advent of advertising; newspaper owners figured out that if they sold advertising, they could increase both their profits and their papers' circulation. The 1830s was the first time advertising became part and parcel of the newspaper business, and although pressures from advertisers sometimes affected coverage and editorial opinion, few readers noticed that practice, and even fewer challenged it.

Over time, the influence of advertising grew exponentially. Although today's major newspapers do not openly change their editorial opinions to please their advertisers, occasionally advertisers flex their muscles, as General Motors did when it withdrew its advertising from the *Los Angeles Times* after the newspaper recommended the firing of the company's CEO.[4]

penny press
newspapers that sold for a penny in the 1830s

journalism
the practice of gathering and reporting events

Yellow Journalism and Muckraking

Throughout the last part of the nineteenth century, newspapers competed vigorously with one another for ever-greater shares of readership. Publishers found that stories about sex, gore, violence, and government corruption sold papers faster than reports about garbage collection and school budgets. Well-known publishers William Randolph Hearst and Joseph Pulitzer established their reputations and their fortunes at that time, Hearst with the *New York Journal American* and Pulitzer with the *New York World.* Along with Hearst and Pulitzer at the beginning of the twentieth century came the practice of yellow journalism, so named after the yellow ink used in the "Yellow Kid" cartoons in the *New York World.* The term **yellow journalism** has come to signify an irresponsible, sensationalist approach to news reporting and is used to this day to criticize certain elements of the press.

yellow journalism
irresponsible, sensationalist approach to news reporting, so named after the yellow ink used in the "Yellow Kid" cartoons in the *New York World*

The most famous example of the impact of yellow journalism came with both Hearst's and Pulitzer's support of the United States' entry into the Spanish-American War (1898). This conflict is sometimes referred to as "the newspaper war" because of the major role of the press in President William McKinley's decision to invade Cuba and later the Philippines. Public sentiment in the United States, influenced by reports of Spanish cruelty toward the Cubans during and after the Cuban independence movement, strongly favored Cuba. Hearst and Pulitzer, followed by other newspapers across the country, fanned the flames of war with sensational and lurid anti-Spanish stories, dwelling on the brutality of the Spanish toward Cuban rebels. The precipitating event, the explosion of the U.S. battleship *Maine* in Havana harbor in February 1898, may or may not have been due to a Spanish torpedo according to recent evidence; but press reports, accompanied by the cry "Remember the *Maine*," galvanized the public and Congress. The president responded to

> Yellow journalism can influence the national policy agenda. When the battleship *Maine* exploded in Havana harbor in February 1898, newspaper coverage significantly molded public opinion, and in turn Congress declared war on Spain. Can you think of examples of recent media coverage of events that have influenced public opinion?

muckraking

criticism and exposés of corruption in government and industry by journalists at the turn of the twentieth century

the intensifying pressures, and Congress declared war on Spain in April. The press and the public had guided public policy.

Hard on the heels of the Spanish-American "newspaper war" came the era of **muckraking,** an about-face that placed journalists in the heroic role of exposing the dark underbelly of government and industry. The most famous of the muckrakers included Ida Tarbell, who exposed the oil industry in a series of articles running from 1902 to 1904 in *McClure's* magazine; Lincoln Steffens, who published *The Shame of the Cities* in 1904; and Upton Sinclair, whose novel *The Jungle* (1906) revealed the horrors of the meat-processing industry, leading to passage of the Pure Food and Drug Act and later to the establishment of the Food and Drug Administration.[5]

A Widening War for Readership

Yellow journalism died down after World War I, and newspapers entered a period that at least on the surface valued objectivity. Newspapers increasingly found themselves competing with the new media that were just coming into being: radio stations from 1920 to 1950; television from the 1940s to 1980; and from then on, the explosion of the **new media**— cable television, the Internet, blogs, and satellite technology.

new media

cable television, the Internet, blogs, and satellite technology

This increased competition has had several impacts on the newspaper industry. First, newspaper readership has steadily declined, particularly the audience for local newspapers. For example, Figure 10.1 shows that between 1998 and 2008, the proportion of people who read a local newspaper every day or several times a week decreased from 68 percent to 53 percent. This figure also illustrates that although readership of national newspapers increased slightly after the terrorist strikes of September 11, 2001, since that time readership has ebbed to the same level as before the attacks. Partly as a result of a long-term decline in local newspaper readership, the number of daily newspapers has decreased dramatically, with many cities that used to support three or four "dailies" now typically having only one newspaper. Second, competition has resulted in consolidation of the newspaper industry, so that today a single large parent company typically owns many local newspapers. For example, the Gannett Corporation, which publishes *USA Today,* also publishes numerous daily and weekly newspapers in towns throughout the country. Third, competition has forced nearly every newspaper to offer free online editions. Thus you can receive nearly any newspaper at no cost in your e-mail inbox each morning.

Beyond falling readership, the newspaper industry has changed as society has changed. Large cities are now likely to have smaller weekly publications targeted to specific demographic audiences—gays, women, African Americans, for example— and to publish foreign-language newspapers appealing to such diverse newcomers to the United States as Mexican, Brazilian, Vietnamese, Iranian, Nigerian, and Russian immigrants.

As the industry has changed, so, too, has the human face of the newsrooms. Figure 10.2 shows that in 2009, more than one third of all newsroom supervisors were women, as were more than

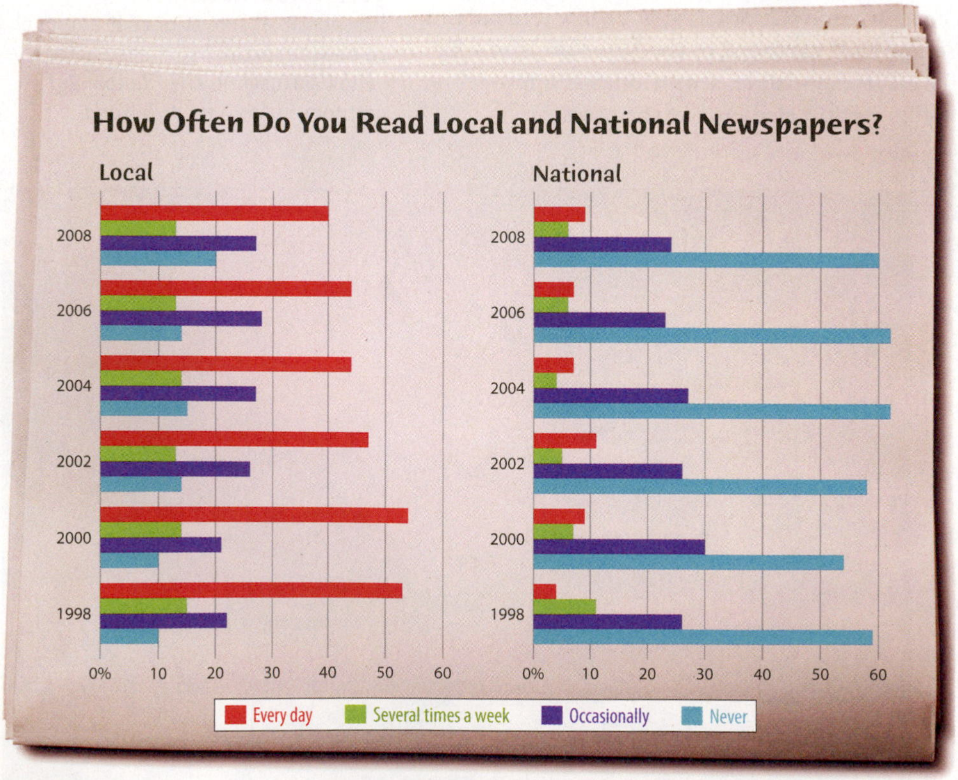

How Often Do You Read Local and National Newspapers?

Local: 2008, 2006, 2004, 2002, 2000, 1998
National: 2008, 2006, 2004, 2002, 2000, 1998

Legend: Every day / Several times a week / Occasionally / Never

FIGURE 10.1

Readership of Local Newspapers Declines, National Newspaper Readership Stagnates

SOURCE: www.gallup.com/poll/1663/Media-Use-Evaluation.aspx.

40 percent of all layout and copy editors and reporters. Those figures reflect the societal changes from the times when "newsmen" were in fact news*men*. Among all positions measured in the annual newsroom census, women were least likely to hold jobs in the visual arts, such as photographer and artist.

Table 10.1 shows another measure of how modern newsrooms have changed along with American society. The table illustrates the proportion of minority journalists working at newspapers in eight circulation categories. From Table 10.1 we can see that minority journalists are much more likely to be employed at larger-circulation newspapers, with minorities constituting one fifth of the journalists at papers having a circulation of 250,000 to 500,000. That proportion is nearly identical at the largest-circulation newspapers and steadily tapers off among newspapers with circulation of less than 250,000.

The Media Go Electronic: The Radio and Television Revolutions

It is impossible to overemphasize the transformative impact of the early electronic media. From the time of the first U.S. radio broadcasts in the early 1920s, radio allowed listeners to hear news in real time. That immediacy marked a drastic change from the standard, delayed method of receiving news, which was by reading the morning and evening editions of newspapers, plus the occasional "extra edition" published when important breaking news warranted it. Radio also altered the relationship between politicians—particularly presidents—and their constituents, because it enabled listeners to hear the voices of their elected leaders. Television further revolutionized that relationship by making it possible for people to see their leaders (though initially only in black and white).

employment

Supervisors	65% Men	35% Women
Copy/layout editors/online producers	58%	42%
Reporters	61%	39%
Photographers/artists/videographers	73%	27%
Total	63%	37%

FIGURE 10.2 ■ NEWSROOM EMPLOYMENT BY GENDER In the past, "newsmen" were in fact news*men*. What does the graph indicate about women's employment in today's newsrooms?

SOURCE: The American Society of Newspaper Editors, "Newsroom Employment Census," Table M, www.asne.org/index.cfm?id=5660.

TABLE 10.1

Minority Journalists as a Percentage of the Professional Workforce of Newspapers in Eight Circulation Categories

NEWSPAPER CIRCULATION	1980	1992	YEAR 2000	2005	2009
Over 500,000	7	16	18	18	20
250,001 to 500,000	6	13	18	21	21
100,001 to 250,000	6	10	14	16	17
50,001 to 100,000	6	9	10	12	13
25,001 to 50,000	4	6	8	10	8
10,001 to 25,000	3	6	7	8	6
5,001 to 10,000	2	5	6	6	6
5,000 and under	3	5	6	7	6

SOURCE: The American Society of Newspaper Editors, "Newsroom Employment Census," Table F, www.asne.org/index.cfm?id=5653. Copyright © 2009 The American Society of Newspaper Editors.

How Radio Has Opened Up Political Communication

Radio was the first electronic medium that brought people into direct contact with their leaders. Beginning in the 1920s, radios became a fixture in American living rooms, and families who could not afford a radio of their own would often spend evenings at the homes of friends or neighbors who could.

FDR'S FIRESIDE CHATS Franklin D. Roosevelt was the first politician to realize the value of radio as a device for political communication—and to exploit that value. As governor of New York (1928–1932), Roosevelt faced a Republican state legislature hostile to many of his liberal social welfare programs. To overcome the opposition, Roosevelt used radio addresses to appeal directly to his constituents, who would then lobby the legislators for his policies. Indeed, after some of Roosevelt's radio addresses, legislative offices were flooded with letters from constituents asking lawmakers to support a particular policy.

By the time Roosevelt became president in 1933, he had grasped the importance of radio as a tool for communicating directly with the people. FDR often began his radio addresses to the country—his **fireside chats**—with the greeting, "Good evening, friends," highlighting the personal relationship he wished to cultivate between himself and his listeners. (You can download many of Roosevelt's fireside chats in MP3 format from the Vincent Voice Library at Michigan State University.) Through the folksy fireside chats, Americans learned about presidential initiatives on the banking crisis, New Deal social welfare programs, the declaration of war on Japan after that nation's attack on Pearl Harbor, and the progress of U.S. forces during World War II. In all, Roosevelt had thirty fireside chats with Americans over his twelve years as president.

During the golden age of radio—the period from the early 1920s through the early 1960s—radio was the dominant form of electronic entertainment. Radio programming included a wide array of shows, from newscasts, to serial dramas, to comedies, to variety shows. Although political and news radio programming remained popular during the 1950s and 1960s, radio generally took a backseat to television during that era.

TALK RADIO: TALKING THE POLITICAL TALK Radio began to emerge from the shadows of television in the 1970s and 1980s. Those decades brought a renaissance of sorts for radio, as the medium saw tremendous growth in **talk radio**—a format featuring conver-

fireside chats
President Franklin Roosevelt's radio addresses to the country

talk radio
a format featuring conversations and interviews about topics of interest, along with call-ins from listeners

fairness doctrine
requirement that stations provide equal time to all parties regarding important public issues and equal access to airtime to all candidates for public office

> President Franklin Roosevelt was recognized as a master political communicator. Roosevelt relied on a folksy, conversational tone and the medium of radio to bring his message to the people.

> Some seventy-five years later, another president, Barack Obama, is widely recognized as a skilled political speaker. Unlike FDR, however, Obama uses lofty rhetoric and new technologies to drive his message home. How does a politician's ability to communicate successfully with the people influence his or her governing?

sations and interviews about topics of interest, along with call-ins from listeners. As many AM station owners switched to an all-talk format in those years, music programming migrated to the FM band.

In 1987, the Federal Communications Commission (FCC) repealed the **fairness doctrine,** which had required stations to provide equal time to all sides regarding important public issues and equal access to airtime to all candidates for public office. Since the law's repeal, partisan radio programming has grown dramatically. Today, listeners tend to tune in to radio hosts who share—many say, reinforce—their opinions, and they interact with them through call-in opportunities. Talk radio features numerous well-known personalities, including Rush Limbaugh, Sean Hannity, Mark Levin, and Laura Ingraham, whose shows are also available via the Internet and through podcasts, thus potentially reaching a significantly expanded number of listeners.

Figure 10.3 shows the rise in listenership for talk radio programs since 1995. Daily listenership of such programs nearly doubled between 1995 and 2002, increasing from 12 percent to 22 percent in that time. Since 2002, although daily listnership has dropped, the proportion of people who listen several times a week has held steady at 9 percent.

Talk radio was one of the first forums that allowed media consumers to "talk back" to the host. At its best, talk radio allows for a natural, real-time exchange of information between the host and the audience; at its worst, it has given rise to loud, angry rants and arguments. Scholars widely agree that talk radio programs promote citizen engagement in the form of civic discourse. Recall from earlier chapters that civic discourse means the sharing of viewpoints and the articulation of personal positions on public issues (along with the information gathering and reflective thinking that must accompany that expression). This information sharing is fundamental to a civic society. That is, without informed and shared opinions, people cannot be responsible, politically engaged citizens.

The appeal of talk radio, particularly as broadcast via the Internet, mirrors the allure of Internet blogs. The messages of both media have become highly personal and emotional, targeted to a narrow segment of the public. Conservative radio commentators tend to draw an audience dominated by middle-aged conservative males, while the much smaller liberal market segment tends to draw the coveted younger audience.

Television and the Transformation of Campaigns and Elections

Although radio predates television, TV nonetheless has been the centerpiece of U.S. home entertainment for a long time. Television began to make a mark on the American scene in the 1940s, when small TV sets—their screens flecked with static snowflakes—hit the market. Today, the images we view are crystal clear, as high-definition big-screen

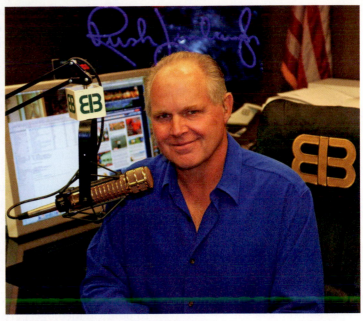

> Although political talk radio programs have been around for decades, technologies such as the Internet and podcasts expand the reach of talk radio hosts such as conservative commentator Rush Limbaugh to a significantly larger audience.

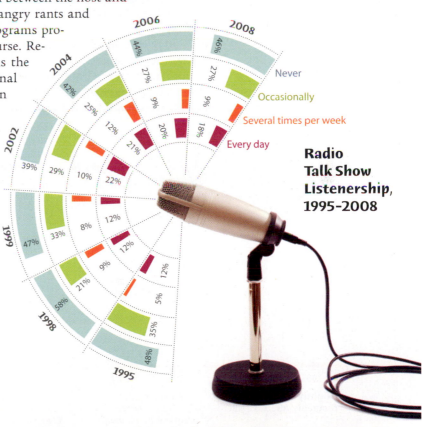

Radio **Talk Show Listenership,** 1995–2008

Never
Occasionally
Several times per week
Every day

POLITICAL INQUIRY

FIGURE 10.3 ■ What has been the trend in talk radio listenership since 1995? What factors might explain this trend?

SOURCE: The Gallup Poll, "Media Use and Evaluation," www.galluppoll.com/content/?ci=1663&pg=1.

TVs increasingly dominate households. Hundreds of channels compete for audience share, ending the previous dominance of the three major networks, ABC, NBC, and CBS.

With all the new competition, network television is rapidly losing viewers. Along with announcing in July 2004 that cable television enjoyed 52 percent of the prime-time TV-viewing audience, Nielsen Media Research, publisher of the famous Nielsen ratings for television shows, reported that network television had just 44 percent (with public television having a 4 percent market share). In addition, total viewership for the television networks had fallen by 41 percent between 1977 and 2003, from 51 million viewers to 30 million.

Figure 10.4 shows the continuation of those changes. Viewership of nightly network news broadcasts on ABC, CBS, and NBC plummeted between 1996 and 2008. In 1996, a large majority of Americans watched a nighttime network news broadcast; by 2008, only 34 percent did, and the number who never watched grew to 23 percent. Compare those figures with the data for the networks' cable news counterparts, where daily viewership has increased by 17 percent in those same years. Among the other categories of TV news (morning shows such as *Good Morning America* and the *Today* show, public television news broadcasts, and local news shows), viewership has essentially stagnated.

As cable news channels such as CNN and Fox News have increased their viewing audience, it is no wonder the word *broadcasting* has spawned the term **narrowcasting**: the practice of aiming political media content at specific segments of the public, divided according to political ideology, party affiliation, or economic interests. This winnowing of audiences has led to **media segmentation,** the breaking down of the media in general according to the specific audiences they target. Examples of segmented media include Black Entertainment Television (BET); the U.S.-based Spanish-language television network Telemundo; and the Lifestyle Network, which includes the Food Network and HGTV. Through media segmentation, advertisers can hone their advertising to the tastes of their targeted market.

Being **telegenic,** or looking good on TV, has become almost mandatory today for serious political candidates. It is unlikely that President William Howard Taft (1909–1913), who weighed over 300 pounds, would ever have been elected if he had been forced to appear on television. Nor would Abraham Lincoln, whose handlers would have marched him straight to a cosmetic surgeon to have the giant mole on his cheek removed. Richard Nixon might have won the presidency in 1960 had it not been for his nervous demeanor and the "five o'clock shadow" on his face that made him look sinister in the first-ever televised presidential candidate debates that year. His opponent, the handsome, relaxed, and articu-

narrowcasting
the practice of aiming media content at specific segments of the public

media segmentation
the breaking down of the media according to the specific audiences they target

telegenic
the quality of looking good on TV

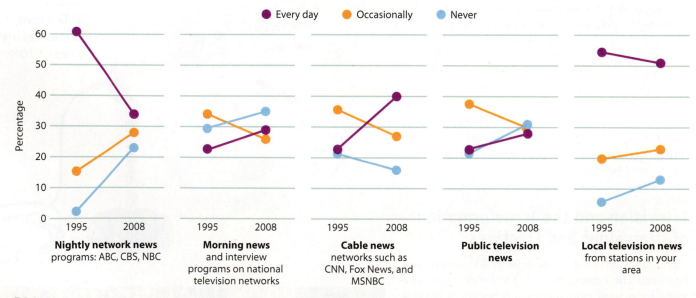

FIGURE 10.4

Where Do Americans Get Their News?

SOURCE: The Gallup Poll, "Media Use and Evaluation," www.gallup.com/poll/1663/Media-Use-Evaluation.aspx.

late John F. Kennedy, won the visual debate hands down, even though in hindsight most analysts agree that Nixon "won" the debate on its verbal merits.

The Media Revolution Continues: The Internet and Cellular Technology

The modern media revolution continued with the birth of the Internet. As a medium of communication, a source of news and information, and a tool for political engagement and grassroots organizing, the Internet has had an incalculable—and a global—impact on the way people interact.

But access to the Internet is not equal, because affluent individuals are more likely than the less affluent to have computers and Internet connections. The term for this unequal access to computer technology is the **digital divide.** Sociologist Mark Wheeler has examined the digital divide, particularly when it comes to high-speed Internet connectivity. He has noted that income and wealth affect individuals' access to high-speed Internet service, even in the world's most affluent democracies.[6]

Yet even for those without computers of their own, the Internet has broadly transformed life in the United States. How the average U.S. citizen is educated, communicates, gets news, shops, receives information about politics, and participates in the political process all have changed because of the Internet. As political scientist Michael Cornfield noted, "I can't think of anything except kissing babies that you can't do online."[7] The influence of the Internet has been both positive and negative, and it continues to evolve.

How the Media Have Shaped Entertainment and the Information Highways

THEN (1960s)	NOW (2011)
Television programming matured and revolutionized how the media entertained and provided information.	The Internet matures and revolutionizes how we are entertained and how we get information.
Television accentuated a new set of candidate qualities—including being telegenic—that had not mattered much in earlier political campaigns.	The Internet accentuates a new set of candidate qualities—including being tech savvy and Net organized—that were unheard of a generation ago.
Communication between the media and voters was one-way: people got information but could not "talk back."	Information flow is two-way, thanks to talk radio and the Internet—including blogs, YouTube, and social-networking sites.

WHAT'S NEXT?

> What new media technologies will shape campaigns and political participation in the future?

> For individuals seeking information about policy issues and political campaigns, what might be the negative consequences of the abundance of information flowing through the electronic media?

> How will technology change political participation in the future?

The Internet and Civic Engagement

Over time, the Internet has transformed the media's function as a conveyor of information and a resource for civic engagement. Communications scholar Howard Rheingold argues that the digital media in particular serve as a key avenue by which young people can use their "public voice" to consume and share information.[8]

THE EVOLUTION OF THE INTERNET In its early years, the Internet functioned in much the same way that traditional media formats such as newspapers and periodicals functioned: it provided a convenient but "one-way" means for people to get information at times determined by the publishers. As **bandwidth**—the amount of data that can travel through a network in a given time period—has increased, so, too, has the sophistication of Web content, as well as the venues and formats that serve as information sources. Today's

digital divide
the inequality of access to computers and Internet connections

bandwidth
the amount of data that can travel through a network in a given time period

news Web sites—including those of all the network and cable news stations, plus sites maintained by Internet service providers such as AOL—give Internet users news stories when they want them instead of at predetermined times. Users can selectively search for specific information about public issues that matter to them, potentially building their knowledge base with a mouse click. Moreover, many contemporary news outlets, including magazines and radio programs, are now making available downloadable podcasts of content that users can view or listen to at their convenience. These podcasts are giving individuals even greater access to information, including reports on social issues, policy initiatives, and politics. Civic participation has been facilitated by the rise of news Web sites and social-networking sites, as well as blogs that allow readers to engage in virtual civic discourse.

THE INTERNET AS A SOURCE OF INFORMATION AND COMMUNITY YouTube provides a compelling example of how the evolving Internet has worked to the benefit of civic engagement. This Web site, which debuted in February 2005, allows individuals to post and watch original videos. The success of the YouTube experiment is inconceivable in the world of the dial-up Internet connection that was the norm just a few years ago. And so, if you want to watch a political advertisement, see congressional testimony, or participate in Citizen Tube (YouTube's video Weblog, or **vblog**), today's technology makes it possible for you to do so in seconds. In fact, President Obama has his own YouTube channel, which broadcasts speeches and press conferences. The interactivity embodied in viewing, commenting, posting, and vblogging has revolutionized civic discourse.

Today's Internet technology also facilitates the formation of virtual communities. These networks of interested participants, though different from their IRL (in real life) counterparts, share features with those real-world groups. Many blogs, for example, have community leaders, regular contributors, expert commentators, and participants with established roles. Blogs promote civic engagement by disseminating information, exposing readers to the viewpoints of others, providing a forum allowing bloggers to share their own views, serving as a venue for the formation of online communities that can foster feelings of efficacy among participants, and channeling activism, both virtual and real.* In short, the Internet has led to the phenomenon of the **prosumer**—the individual who simultaneously consumes information and news and produces information in the form of videos, blogs, and Web sites.

The Internet as a Source of News

The amount of time that Americans spend on the Internet is steadily increasing: in 2005, the average time spent online was three hours daily; it is now over four.[9] Time spent online exceeds the amount of time that people spend consuming other media, including television, radio, and newspaper. Perhaps more important, the number of individuals using the Internet as a source of news continues to increase dramatically. Figure 10.5 shows that in the thirteen-year span from 1995 to 2008, the proportion of Americans who get news from the Internet has grown exponentially. In fact, by 2008 two-thirds of Americans got news from the Internet at least sometimes, and nearly one-third used the Internet as a news source daily. It is no wonder Nielsen TV ratings and newspaper subscriptions have declined.

The adage that a "week is an eternity in politics" has become an understatement in the age of the Internet and the twenty-four-hour news cycle. Things happen in the click of a mouse button, and increasingly politicians are making snap statements in front of ever-present cell phone video cameras and regretting them later.

Such was the case in 2010, when Vice President Joseph Biden used an expletive caught on an open microphone. After introducing President Barack Obama, who had just succeeded in

---

*A note about content: The authors recognize the enormous variation in the quality of information available on the Internet in general and in blogs in particular. So when you are using the Internet as a source of information, a healthy dose of skepticism can be quite useful.

vblog
a video Weblog

prosumers
individuals who simultaneously consume information and news and produce information in the form of videos, blogs, and Web sites

shepherding health care reform through Congress, the vice president turned to the president and said, "This is a big [expletive] deal." Video footage of the gaffe spread like wildfire on the Internet, and more than 1 million people watched a YouTube video of the blunder. In response (and in an effort to control damage), Robert Gibbs, the White House Press Secretary, tweeted, "And yes Mr. Vice President, you're right . . ." on Twitter.

Internet news sites could be doing some things better, though. For example, many news outlets present a news story as either an article or a video, but few major media outlets offer hotlinks to original source data that would aid interested site users in delving more deeply into the story. Instead of a synthesized news article on a Supreme Court decision, for instance, media outlets could provide links to the original opinions on the case as well as links to audio recordings of the arguments before the court, records of lower-court decisions, and briefs filed with the court, supporting or opposing one side or the other, which are available elsewhere online *if* one is willing to search for them. Instead, most outlets offer only broad coverage with links to related stories—an approach that does not make it easy for an individual to research a matter of interest more deeply.

How Often Do You Get News From the Internet?

FIGURE 10.5

Increasing Percentages of Americans Get News from the Internet

SOURCE: The Gallup Poll, "Media Use and Evaluation," www.gallup.com/poll/1663/Media-Use-Evaluation.aspx.

The Internet's Influence on Political Participation and Campaigns

Even more than talk radio, the Internet has made politics participative. People can express their preferences online on issues from health reform to term limits, from income tax credits to repealing the inheritance tax. But besides acting as a gauge for public opinion, the Internet can also be a useful tool for citizens' political activism. The traditional media have not had nearly the impact on political participation that the Internet has had. For example, the left-of-center wing of the Democratic Party has not achieved the same media dominance in radio as the conservative wing of the Republican Party. One radio station targeting liberal listeners, Air America, went on the air in 2004, but it never succeeded in attracting a competitive share of the radio audience and ceased operation early in 2010. What *has* worked in attracting the liberal wing of the youth vote are blogs and Web sites such as www.moveon.org.

USING THE INTERNET TO MOBILIZE VOTERS Jesse Ventura, a professional wrestler who served as the governor of Minnesota from 1999 to 2003, credits the Web for opening up the political process by enabling grassroots mobilization through **e-campaigning,** the practice of mobilizing voters using the Internet, which allowed an outsider like him to be elected governor. Winning half of the under-thirty vote, Ventura conducted a campaign without any physical headquarters—at least at first. Armed with a large e-mail list, he enlisted pledges of support that short-circuited the traditional doorbell ringing and telephone calls that go with the territory when running for office. His tactics gave him the final surge of voters that he needed to win. Ventura's victory testifies to the power of the Internet as a political campaign tool.

During the 2010 mid-term congressional elections, candidates updated their Facebook status and tweeted press releases. E-campaigning became fully integrated into the political communication process. For example. Sen. Pat Toomey (R-PA) tweeted "why Democrats are supporting Pat Toomey." BlogHer.com collected questions from blog readers, then posed those questions to women candidates running for Congress. The responses were then posted on the blog's site. Nearly every candidate boasted a Facebook page, and staffers often jokingly compared the numbers of candidates friends and fans.

e-campaigning
the practice of mobilizing voters using the Internet

The Internet has even changed how candidacies are announced and presidential campaigns unfold. A campaign video of former senator John Edwards announcing his candidacy in New Orleans ran on YouTube, and both Senator Barack Obama and Senator Hillary Rodham Clinton announced their candidacies via their Web sites, followed by the posting of the corresponding videos on YouTube.

HOW THE INTERNET CAN AFFECT A POLITICAL CAMPAIGN

The Internet has also changed the nature of political organizing. On the day that Senator Obama announced his bid for the presidency, Farouk Olu Aregbe, a student government adviser at the University of Missouri, logged on to www.facebook.com and announced the formation of a group called "One Million Strong for Barack." Within a month, Aregbe's Facebook group had over a quarter of a million members, and other Facebook users had formed more than five hundred groups supporting the candidate.

But the rapid expansion of Internet technology has also made it more difficult for presidential campaigns (and administrations) to manage the news.[10]

Today's Blogosphere

Clearly, the widespread use of the Internet has also contributed to the spread of blogs. A

blogosphere
a community, or social network, of bloggers

new language has sprouted to incorporate this development, beginning with **blogosphere**—the community, or social network, of bloggers. Estimates indicate that the number of blogs has doubled every five months since 2003 to a current level of over 50 million individual blogs.[11] As the number has multiplied, their variety and credibility have increased. Bloggers received press credentials at both the Democratic and the Republican conventions in 2008. Traditional television and print media outlets now host blogs as well. Many who read blogs note that they are more up to date than traditional media outlets, and bloggers themselves believe that blogs have influenced and are most likely to continue to influence the field of politics. Figures 10.6 and 10.7 show the results of a Technorati.com poll, in which the majority of bloggers (57 percent) said they thought that bloggers have influenced politics more than any other field. Fifty-one percent also said that they thought blogging will have more impact in the field of politics than in any other field in the next decade.

The blog's rise as a tool of grassroots organizing has given birth to the term **netroots** to describe Net-centered political efforts on behalf of candidates and causes. A blog makes information available to large numbers of users immediately, spreading news and energizing supporters more rapidly than any other medium. It also differs from traditional media in one important way: bloggers make no attempt to be impartial. A blog is an opinion journal, offering a specific perspective and appealing to a specific segment of the public. In that respect, it cannot replace traditional journalism, especially because there is no check on whether the facts it presents are correct. But blogs continue to change the face of political campaigning and grassroots organization—for better and for worse.

netroots
the Internet-centered political efforts on behalf of candidates and causes

> In 2008, bloggers at the national party conventions were granted press credentials. Blogs spread news—though sometimes *inaccurate* news—and opinions very quickly. Their drawbacks aside, blogs have changed the landscape of political campaigning and grassroots organizing.

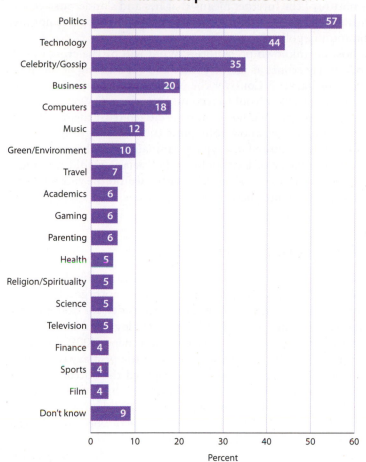

Bloggers believe blogging has influenced politics the most . . .

Field	Percent
Politics	57
Technology	44
Celebrity/Gossip	35
Business	20
Computers	18
Music	12
Green/Environment	10
Travel	7
Academics	6
Gaming	6
Parenting	6
Health	5
Religion/Spirituality	5
Science	5
Television	5
Finance	4
Sports	4
Film	4
Don't know	9

Percent

FIGURE 10.6

Looking back on the history of blogging so far, what fields do you think it has had the greatest impact on?

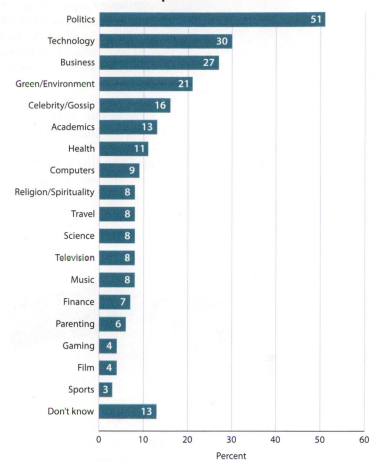

. . . and will continue to influence politics in the future.

Field	Percent
Politics	51
Technology	30
Business	27
Green/Environment	21
Celebrity/Gossip	16
Academics	13
Health	11
Computers	9
Religion/Spirituality	8
Travel	8
Science	8
Television	8
Music	8
Finance	7
Parenting	6
Gaming	4
Film	4
Sports	3
Don't know	13

Percent

FIGURE 10.7

Looking forward, what fields do you think blogging will have the greatest impact on in the next ten years?

SOURCE: http://technorati.com/blogging/article/day-5-twitter-global-impact-and/page-2/.

Media Convergence

The concept of convergence has taken hold among media observers today. **Convergence** refers to the merging of various forms of media—newspapers, television stations, radio networks, and blogs—under one corporate roof with one set of business and editorial leaders. The emergence of Politico, a multimedia start-up that debuted in Washington, D.C., in January 2007, is an example of this concept come to life. What would have been regarded in the past as a violation of antitrust laws is now considered the wave of the future. Politico's mission is to report on the daily politics on Capitol Hill and in the White House. Politico is a publication of Capital News Corp., which is financed by Allbritton Communications, which used to own a now-defunct newspaper called the *Washington Star*.

convergence
the merging of various forms of media, including newspapers, television stations, radio networks, and blogs, under one corporate roof and one set of business and editorial leaders

The Negative Political Impact of the Internet

The explosion of the Internet in politics has also opened a Pandora's box of problems. One key problem is misinformation. Unlike newspapers, magazines, and television networks, where editors and fact-checkers are responsible for ensuring accuracy, the Internet is almost entirely unmonitored. In political campaigns, misinformation can be devastating.

Another problem is that the Internet has contributed to the decline in civility in political discourse. Some bloggers and anonymous messageboard posters seek to destroy their opponents' reputations. The nature of the Internet means that lies and slanderous accusations can often be leveled with no consequence to the poster. This problem occurs not just in national politics but in community politics as well.

The Internet also poses a host of unknown possibilities. What will be the crossover effects, for example, of such present-day crimes as identity theft and the stealing of social security numbers and state secrets by hackers? Consider the problems of a national election conducted through computer terminals. How would a recount be managed? Would the outcome be fair? Would the losers view it as fair? Would the average citizen trust the results?

And although new communications tools allow politicians substantially to reduce the amount of legwork and "flesh pressing" required in a typical campaign, the absence of such glad-handing could also destroy the flavor of local politics. Politicians would no longer have to stand in front of supermarkets and kiss babies, but neither would the voters be able to get to know the candidates or to probe into their views on the issues.

The Internet and Free Speech

The rise of the Internet has occurred at a pace that has not allowed societies to digest its potential for both good and evil causes in the battle for free speech. Consider, for example, the impact the Internet and cellular technology had in the aftermath of the Iranian elections in the summer of 2009. That year, Web sites, blogs, and cell phones were the primary tools used by pro-democracy activists who disputed the outcome of the Iranian elections, in which President Mahmoud Ahmadinejad claimed victory over opposition candidate Mir-Hossein Mousavi, so that the protests came to be dubbed the "Twitter Revolution." Protesters relied on Twitter, text messages, and social-networking sites to organize rallies. In response, the Iranian government also used technology, including videos recorded on cell phones, to identify and arrest protesters.

But the use of the Internet as a dangerous tool is not limited to Iranian government officials half a world away: in the United States, there are few restrictions on the content that can be posted on the Internet. Thus hate groups throughout the world are able to register their domain name in the United States. These Web sites can be used to spew hatred and organize like-minded individuals.

The danger is that some of these activities might lead to acts of violence, including murder. In spring 2005, U.S. District Court judge Joan Humphrey Lefkow returned home from work to find the murdered bodies of her husband and her mother in the basement of her home on Chicago's North Side. Their killer, an unemployed electrician, had found Judge Lefkow's name and address posted on several hate Web sites, where readers were encouraged to take justice into their own hands. The day after the murders, Bill White, editor of one of the hate sites, posted his approval: "Everyone associated with the Matt Hale trial [over which Judge Lefkow had presided] has deserved assassination for a long time. I don't feel bad that Judge Lefkow's family was murdered. . . . In fact . . . I laughed."[12]

The availability of cheap worldwide communications technology makes the Internet an ideal tool for terrorists and other haters who hide among the world's 1.8 billion users, including

> New media has changed how politics occurs within societies. During protests in Iran in 2009, the Iranian government restricted reporters covering the events, but both journalists and private citizens used Twitter to post updates about the situation there.

SOURCE: http://travelintoaprworld.files.wordpress.com/2009/06/iran_tweets_0616.jpg.

about 220 million Americans.[13] The murder of Judge Lefkow's husband and her mother introduced a new dimension to the nation's debate over the limits of free speech. The Internet has allowed extremists to seize on new technologies to spread their messages far more effectively than the soapboxes of earlier days; it also enhances their ability to promote and recruit supporters to their causes.

The United States is wedded to the principle of freedom of speech, refusing to regulate the Internet or any other vehicle of free speech. Throughout the nation's history, speech of all kinds has been protected, with periodic exceptions for sedition in war as well as for child pornography in peacetime. Americans have great tolerance for language and believe that fringe groups can flourish freely in a democracy without risking tears in the fabric of society. But the world has changed since 9/11, and as the threat of terrorism grows, many citizens expect lawmakers to do whatever is necessary—including setting limits on free speech—to curb violence spawned by the prevalence of hate on the Internet.[14]

Biased Media?

A recent joke about how the media will cover the end of the world stereotyped the nation's major newspapers while also emphasizing their importance in reporting world events. As the story goes, the *New York Times* headline would be: "World Ends; Third World Hit Worst." The *Washington Post*'s front page would blare: "World Ends; Unnamed Source Says White House Had Prior Knowledge." In *USA Today,* a newspaper with a huge national and international circulation, the story would be titled "We're Dead; State-by-State Analysis, page 4D; Sports, page 6C." And the *Wall Street Journal*? "World Ends; Stock Market Goes Down."

Media critics today are everywhere. All of them claim that both print and electronic media exhibit bias in their reporting, in their selection of what issues to cover, and in favoring one side of an issue (or one politician) over another. One of the most common complaints is that the media have an ideological bias.

THE QUESTION OF IDEOLOGICAL BIAS   A long-standing complaint is that the media—particularly big-city newspapers—evidence a liberal bias. For example, former House majority leader Tom DeLay (R-Texas) protested the liberal leanings of two of the country's major newspapers, the *New York Times* and the *Washington Post,* for running stories about his ethics problems. Those media, he claimed, ignored the same practices when Democrats such as Nancy Pelosi (D-California), then House minority leader, engaged in them. The day after the *New York Times* published an article revealing that DeLay's congressional campaign had paid his wife and daughter more than $500,000 for their services, DeLay lashed out, stating that the article was "just another seedy attempt by the liberal media to embarrass me."

The notion that the media have a liberal bias is an often-heard criticism. In 1964, former president Dwight D. Eisenhower, in his address to the Republican National Convention, condemned a liberal media bias:

> My friends, we are Republicans. If there is any finer word in the field of partisan politics, I have not heard it. So let us particularly [scorn] the divisive efforts of those outside our family, including sensation-seeking columnists and commentators, who couldn't care less about the good of our party.[15]

Many conservatives point to studies indicating that a majority of newsroom reporters identify themselves as liberal or Democrat. Conservatives charge that the ideological bent of the journalists carries through to the topics covered and to the perspectives of the stories. But studies conducted by various political scientists, including C. Richard Hofstetter, Michael J. Robinson, and Margaret A. Sheehan, refute the idea that journalists' personal viewpoints tinge the content of the news in a liberal way.[16] Indeed, studies suggest that most news stories take the form of a debate, with the journalist presenting the various sides of an issue and leaving the conclusion to the reader's interpretation.

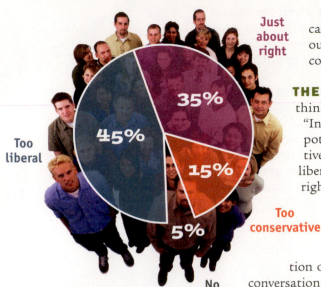

Just about right

35%

45%

Too liberal

15%

5%

Too conservative

No opinion

FIGURE 10.8

Public Opinion of Ideological Media Bias

SOURCE: The Gallup Poll, "Media Use and Evaluation," www.gallup.com/poll/1663/Media-Use-Evaluation.aspx.

Changes in the nature of the mass media have led to increasingly vocal charges, especially by Democratic elected officials, that newer media outlets, particularly talk radio and the blogosphere, are dominated by conservatives.

THE PUBLIC'S VIEW ON MEDIA BIAS What does the public think about partisan bias? Figure 10.8 shows that when asked the question "In general, do you think the news media are — ?" (the survey rotated the potential responses: "too liberal," "just about right," and "too conservative"), 45 percent responded that they thought the news media were too liberal. Thirty-five percent said they thought the media were "just about right" ideologically, and 15 percent said they believed the news media were too conservative.

Thus more than half (60 percent) of those surveyed believed that the media are biased (either liberally or conservatively). Yet research by William P. Eveland Jr. and Dhavan V. Shah into people's perception of media bias concluded that it is often linked to whether people have conversations with others whose views differ from theirs. When they do not have such dialogues, they are more likely to believe that the media are biased against their view.[17]

THE ISSUE OF CORPORATE BIAS Most professional journalists hold journalistic objectivity to be important, and that principle well serves the interests of the large corporations that dominate the U.S. media industry today. Within the giant media conglomerates, motivated as they are by the drive for profits, there is strong disincentive for ideological bias on the part of their reporters. Newspapers and television stations rely on advertisers, and advertisers want not only to attract the largest number of readers or viewers but also to avoid offending the largest numbers. Thus, given the corporate nature of today's media, neutrality is generally a guiding principle.

Critics on the left, however, argue that these corporate structures create their own bias and that this bias has altered what is considered news and how that news is covered.[18] Corporate bias—and the desire to attract, keep, and please an audience—produces skewed programming. Will corporate conglomerates be willing to report on situations that may put themselves and their advertisers in a negative light? How does the drive for profits influence what is in the news? Are viewers being fed "news" that is not particularly newsworthy? There is no doubt that profits influence the media to cover the kinds of stories that viewers and readers want. In particular, violence dominates most local news programming, so much so that the principle of "if it bleeds, it leads" now extends into the first fifteen minutes of many local news broadcasts. Fires; political, sport, and sex scandals; and celebrity-heavy news are also powerful audience attractors.

"Why don't the media report good news?" is an oft-repeated question from those who feel scarred by bad publicity. Are the media biased in favor of the negative? If the sun comes up in the morning, is that news? In fact, although many individuals bemoan the emphasis on the negative, good news typically does not attract the audience that bad news does.

Regulation of the Media: Is It Necessary?

The framers of the Constitution had to be concerned only with print media when they guaranteed freedom of the press—one of the fundamental liberties they ensured in the Bill of Rights. As the media evolved beyond print into electronic formats, so, too, did thinking about the government's role in regulating the media, especially media outlets such as radio and television stations. But technology has outpaced the ability of the government to regulate certain forms of electronic media, including the Internet and satellite radio services

> Should telecommunications giants such as Verizon and Comcast be allowed to use their market power to control information flowing over the Internet or to favor certain online clients?

such as Sirius XM. Nonetheless, television and regular radio transmissions are still subject to government regulation.

The government regulates and controls the ownership of radio and television stations through the independent regulatory agency known as the Federal Communications Commission (FCC), founded in 1934. Most of the FCC's rules have concerned ownership, such as the number of outlets a network may own.

In 1996, Congress passed the Telecommunications Act, which opened the communications markets to telephone companies. This sweeping law allowed competition in the communications industry. It presented new (often confusing) options for consumers, as individual companies began to offer a suite of services, from local and long-distance telephone service, to Internet access, to cable and satellite television.

With the combination of all of these services under single companies, large corporate conglomerates have increasingly gained control of the media. Firms such as Disney, Viacom, News Corporation, and Time Warner exert a powerful influence over what news the average American sees and reads on a given day. The advent of these media titans has given rise to concerns about whether this type of control will deter balanced reporting of the news and unbiased presentations of issues. In addition, public conversations about our democracy are questioning whether the relative lack of competition (because there are so few competitors) means that a valuable check on what the media do and how they do it has been lost.

Congress is currently considering another question of control over the business of the media. The issue, a controversial one, centers on **Net neutrality**: the idea that Internet traffic—e-mail, Web sites, videos, and phone calls—should flow through the Internet pipeline without interference or discrimination by those who own or are running the pipeline. (See "Thinking Critically About Democracy" on page 328.) *Should* these broadband behemoths be able to use their market power to control information or to favor certain clients online? Critics charge that congressional passage of legislation supporting the service providers would destroy the neutrality and openness of the Internet. Tim Berners-Lee, the inventor of the World Wide Web, says, "The neutral communications medium is essential to our society. . . . It is the basis of democracy, by which a community should decide what to do."[19] Do you agree with Berners-Lee? In what ways would you say that neutral media are the basis of a democracy?

Net neutrality
the idea that Internet traffic—e-mail, Web site content, videos, and phone calls—should flow without interference or discrimination by those who own or run the Internet pipeline

THINKING CRITICALLY ABOUT DEMOCRACY

SHOULD CONGRESS REGULATE THE INTERNET INFRASTRUCTURE?

The Issue: The technological revolution has brought ongoing, exponential growth in Internet traffic. As rising numbers of people turn to the Internet for more and more uses—from viewing videos online to sending pictures to Grandma, and from buying gifts and personal items to calling friends and relatives—the volume of information that the broadband infrastructure of the Internet must transmit is becoming overwhelming. The owners of that infrastructure—corporate giants such as AT&T, Verizon, and Comcast—seek legislation that would allow them to charge companies that produce high volumes of traffic. In effect, this legislation would set up a two-tiered system of broadband access in which one tier is an "express lane" with tolls, and the other an older, slower lane with free access. One problem is that many of today's services require the faster access to make them effective.

Yes: Congress should regulate the Internet infrastructure. We need a two-tiered system of broadband access. The telecommunications titans in command of the Internet infrastructure argue that to keep up with the increasing demand for broadband space, they will have to expand and improve the system continually. Corporate advocates of a two-tiered system of broadband access are also interested in providing premium-quality broadband service to their own clientele. Thus, for example, Verizon wants to ensure that its Internet subscribers (rather than the subscribers of its competitors) have high-quality access to the broadband infrastructure technology that Verizon owns so that its subscribers do not get caught in an Internet traffic jam.

No: "Fast lane" services are a bad idea, because they would hurt both businesses and consumers. In fact, a broad coalition of businesses and interest groups, including savetheinternet.org, oppose measures that would enable broadband providers to charge for their services. The opposing entities also include firms such as Microsoft, Google, eBay, and Yahoo and powerful citizen organizations such as the American Association of Retired People (AARP). Senator Ron Wyden (D-Oregon) has introduced legislation that would prevent broadband providers from creating for-fee "fast lane" services.

It is the very accessibility of the Internet that has fostered strong business growth. Start-ups such as YouTube and Vonage Internet phone service are examples of ventures that may not have been able to compete and survive in a tiered broadband system. A paying system could also prevent future Internet business development.

Other approaches: Without essential maintenance and expansion, the Internet infrastructure cannot keep up with soaring demand. In addition, the security of the system is crucial to continued business activity and corporate financial growth, as well as to national economic health. Broadband availability is a national security issue because if law enforcers, airports, hospitals, nuclear power plants, and first responders do not have adequate or immediate access to the information they need to perform their jobs, human lives are at risk. Because of these critical financial and security implications, a tax or user fee could be instituted that would pay for Internet infrastructure improvements.

What do you think?

① Do you believe that Congress should reject proposals to create a for-fee fast lane for Internet traffic? If so, why? Or do you think the marketplace should determine which services get faster access to broadband lines? If so, why would the latter be preferable?

② What impact would the creation of a two-tiered Internet structure have on Internet business development? On national security?

③ Should the federal government help to defray the costs of improvements to the Internet infrastructure? Why, or why not?

The surge in the number and the variety of media outlets—along with the changes in the nature of the media and in people's interactions with them—has affected politics and government in many ways. Once defined as a one-way relationship, the relationship between the media and consumers has evolved in unforeseen ways. Even the nature of the "old media" has changed, although many would ask whether the change has been for the better. On the one hand, narrowcasting and the resulting segmentation of media markets, a central feature of media growth, might raise the comfort level of many people, who no longer have to throw soft objects at their television sets in protest but can instead pick and choose what they watch. On the other hand, media segmentation also limits the exposure of many people to new ideas. Like gated communities, segmented media are also segregated media, detached environments that expose people only to viewpoints with which they agree, thus cordoning them off from society and from many of its problems. Segmented media also confuse genuine political participation with mere ranting. After all, sounding off on a radio talk show is much easier and more entertaining than attending a zoning board meeting to fight urban congestion or becoming civically engaged in other ways.

Technology has created a two-way relationship between the media and consumers, involving the exchange of seemingly limitless information in a vast conversation of democracy. The openness and easy accessibility of the new media have led to considerable criticism of them, but the good news is that almost all public—and to a lesser extent, private—institutions have become much more transparent in recent years. Supreme Court justice Louis Brandeis (1856–1941) once said that sunlight was the best disinfectant, that public scrutiny was the best step toward genuine reform. This two-way relationship has also meant that citizens are afforded greater opportunities to use their public voice to influence government and the policies it creates. How can this changing public voice be used in today's political arena?

Can we predict the future of the media by examining the past and the present? Certainly we can foretell increasing transparency because of the pervasive nature of today's media and the steady trend in that direction, but we cannot predict the forms media will take. What we can guarantee is continued change in the forms and usage of media, and steadily increasing access to information. Will this expanding access overload people with information? It appears that many of us are developing new skills to cope with the abundance of information, much in the way that our grandparents may have developed the skill of skimming a newspaper, selecting only those stories that mattered to them. The question remains as to whether we will select only information that confirms what we already think. One trend is clear: the ever-increasing volume of information and the speed of its delivery will yield an abundance of both poor-quality and high-quality information. How can media consumers use the plethora of information to ensure they are receiving verifiable information?

The modern media have opened the door more widely to citizens' direct participation in the democratic process. In light of Americans' high levels of cynicism about their elected leaders, might this powerful new opportunity to be heard make our democracy more participatory than the Constitution's framers ever intended or imagined? Will the availability of the Internet as a forum for citizens and a tool for organizing lead to a meaningful expansion of participation in civic life and in the conversation of democracy? Will citizens use the new technology productively?

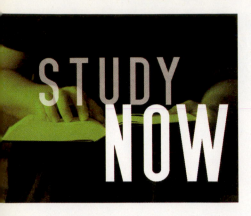
STUDY NOW

Summary

1. The Modern Media
Changing technology has meant an overabundance of information, which varies greatly in quality. The modern media is also increasingly reliant on citizen journalists. Both trends mean that consumers of the media must be cautious and consider the sources of information.

2. The Political Functions of the Media
The media perform several key political functions, including disseminating information, helping to interpret matters of public interest and to set the national policy agenda, providing a forum for political conversations, and socializing children to the political culture.

3. The Press and Politics: A Historical View
Since early in American history, the press has played a vital role in shaping the political context. As the format of the media has evolved over the centuries, so has media impact on politics and policy making.

4. The Media Go Electronic: The Radio and Television Revolutions
The advent of the electronic media marked a revolutionary change with respect to the impact of media on politics. Television has altered the nature of politics and campaigning, affecting everything from how campaigns for office are conducted to how candidates look and dress. Talk radio, too, has had a significant impact on politics and government by providing a forum for political discourse that is open to participation by virtually everyone.

5. The Media Revolution Continues: The Internet and Cellular Technology
The Internet has drastically altered the political landscape by making available, in a keystroke, an abundance of information and by serving as a powerful medium for the broad, rapid dissemination of information and opinion. The Internet has changed how political campaigns are conducted, including aspects such as fund-raising, voter mobilization, candidacy announcements, and campaign strategy.

6. A Biased Media?
In considering the question of media bias, we must consider the issues both of content bias and of ideological bias. A frequent complaint is that the media—particularly big-city newspapers—have a liberal bias. However, studies by various political scientists conclude that journalists' personal views do not color news content in a liberal way. This research stresses, rather, that most news stories take the form of a debate that presents the various sides of an issue and leaves the conclusion to the reader's interpretation.

7. Regulation of the Media: Is It Necessary?
The Federal Communications Commission is the government agency charged with regulating radio and TV stations and controlling their ownership. The Telecommunications Act of 1996 allowed competition in the communications industry and presented new options for consumers, as individual companies began to offer a suite of services. With the combination of all these services under single companies, large corporate conglomerates increasingly have gained control of the media. Thus, in an era of new media technologies, the FCC's job has become more complex.

Key Terms

bandwidth 319
blogosphere 322
convergence 323
digital divide 319
e-campaigning 321
fairness doctrine 316
fireside chats 316
framing 309
infotainment 309

journalism 313
letter to the editor 313
media 308
media segmentation 318
muckraking 314
narrowcasting 318
Net neutrality 327
netroots 322
new media 314

penny press 313
priming 310
prosumer 320
public agenda 310
talk radio 316
telegenic 318
vblog 320
yellow journalism 313

For Review

1. What has been the impact of changing technologies on the type of information available to media consumers?

2. What political functions do the media perform? How have these functions changed over time?

3. Describe the evolution of the press in the United States. How do newspapers today differ from newspapers in earlier centuries?

4. What impact has television had on how people get information? On how political campaigns are waged?

5. How have changes in technology influenced political participation? In particular, what has been the impact of the Internet and blogs?

6. What evidence is there to support claims of media bias? Is all bias ideological?

7. In what specific ways does the government regulate media? What aspects of the media and their coverage does the government not regulate?

For Critical Thinking and Discussion

1. Has the Internet changed how you personally participate in politics? Does virtual activism make real-world activism less likely or more likely? Explain.

2. What do you think are the *most important* functions the media perform? Why? Does the diversity of media outlets hinder the media's ability to serve some of their more traditional functions? Explain.

3. Compare and contrast the penny papers of the nineteenth century with today's blogs. What are the similarities and differences between the two? How will blogs evolve given the evolution of other media forms?

4. Discuss the dangers of the unchecked Internet in the political world. Can these dangers be combated? If so, how?

5. What difficulties are associated with government regulation of the media in an era of cable television, the Internet, and satellite radio?

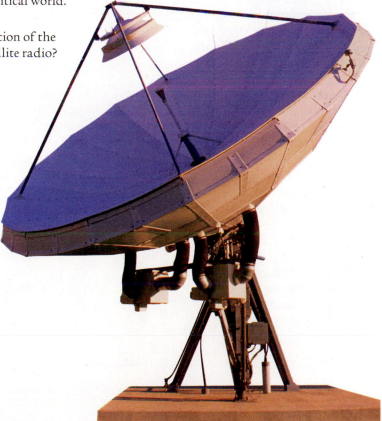

PRACTICE QUIZ

MULTIPLE CHOICE: Choose the lettered item that answers the question correctly.

1. Merging various media forms (newspapers, television stations, radio networks, and blogs) under one roof is called
   a. networking.
   b. convergence.
   c. media relations.
   d. blogosphere.

2. When it comes to content on the Internet,
   a. all information posted must be verifiable.
   b. all information posted must be opinion.
   c. consumers must exercise caution and consider the source of the information.
   d. citizen journalists do not play a role in providing information.

3. Individuals who simultaneously consume information and news and produce information in the form of videos, blogs, and Web sites are called
   a. bloggers.
   b. net audience.
   c. Web makers.
   d. prosumers.

4. President Franklin Roosevelt's radio addresses to the country were called
   a. great communications.
   b. White House communiqués.
   c. roundtable conversations.
   d. fireside chats.

5. The idea that Internet traffic—e-mails, Web site content, videos, and phone calls—can be transmitted through the Internet pipeline without interference or discrimination by those who own or run the pipeline is called
   a. Net neutrality.
   b. Internet objectivity.
   c. the neutral frontier.
   d. absolute Web domain.

6. The practice of aiming media messages at specific segments of the public is called
   a. limited media.
   b. media messaging.
   c. narrowcasting.
   d. information limitation.

7. The requirement that stations provide equal time to all parties regarding important public issues and equal access to airtime to all candidates for public office is called
   a. Net neutrality.
   b. the limited media.
   c. the fairness doctrine.
   d. information objectivity.

8. The breaking down of the media according to specific audiences they target is called
   a. media segmentation.
   b. media messaging.
   c. narrowcasting.
   d. media categorization.

9. The practice of mobilizing voters using the Internet is called
   a. I-rallying.
   b. e-campaigning.
   c. netroots.
   d. Web mobilization.

10. The inequality of access to computers and Internet connections is called
    a. narrowcasting.
    b. media inequality.
    c. the media class system.
    d. the digital divide.

FILL IN THE BLANKS.

11. Public issues that most demand the attention of government officials are called the _____ .

12. A _____ is a video weblog.

13. The journalists who criticized and exposed corruption in government and industry at the turn of the twentieth century were called _____ .

14. The amount of data that can travel through a network in a given time period is called _____ .

15. A person who looks good on TV is called _____ .

Answers: 1. b, 2. c, 3. d, 4. d, 5. a, 6. c, 7. c, 8. a, 9. b, 10. d, 11. public agenda, 12. vblog, 13. muckrakers, 14. bandwidth, 15. telegenic.

RESOURCES FOR RESEARCH AND ACTION

Internet Resources

State of the Media
www.stateofthemedia.org Run by the Project for Excellence in Journalism, this site features an annual report on the media and tracks trends in media usage and confidence in the media.

The Pew Research Center for People and the Press
http://people-press.org This site provides independent research, surveys, data sets, and commentary on the media and issues of media interest.

Media Watch
www.mediawatch.com Visit this site to learn about the initiatives of an activist group that monitors media content and seeks to combat stereotypes and violence in the media.

Internet Activism

Twitter
Follow ReadWriteWeb on Twitter to keep up with one of the most popular technology blog's coverage of the Internet industry.

YouTube
Watch the YouTube video channel Reporter's Center, which teaches aspiring citizen journalists how to cover news events.

Recommended Readings

Arnold, R. Douglas. *Congress, the Press, and Political Accountability.* Princeton, NJ: Princeton University Press, 2004. Analyzes how local newspapers cover members of Congress in their districts throughout a legislative session.

Bennett, W. Lance. *News: The Politics of Illusion.* 7th ed. New York: Longman, 2006. Offers a behind-the-scenes tour of the media in politics while grappling with the question, How well does the news, as the core of the national political information system, serve the needs of democracy?

Cavanaugh, John William. *Media Effects on Voters.* Lanham, MD: University Press of America, 1995. Explores how traditional and new media influence voting choices.

Cook, Timothy E. *Governing with the News: The News Media as a Political Institution.* Chicago: University of Chicago Press, 1998. Examines the media as the "fourth branch" of government, including how the media shape public policy and how policy makers respond to the media's agenda setting.

Crouse, Timothy. *The Boys on the Bus.* New York: Random House, 1973. A classic tale of the presidential campaign press corps.

Graber, Doris. *Media Power and Politics.* Washington, DC: CQ Press, 2006. Analyzes the influence of the media on opinions, elections, and policies, as well as efforts to shape the content and impact of media coverage.

Iyengar, Shanto, and Jennifer A. McGrady. *Media Politics: A Citizen's Guide.* New York: W.W. Norton, 2006. Surveys how politicians use the media to get elected, wield power in office, and achieve policy goals.

Jamieson, Kathleen Hall, and Paul Waldman. *The Press Effect: Politicians, Journalists, and the Stories That Shape the Political World.* Oxford: Oxford University Press, 2003. Demonstrates how the national press molds the news through its reporting, using the examples of the 2000 presidential election, the Supreme Court's decision on the Florida vote that year, and the press's response to national politics after 9/11.

Plissner, Martin. *The Control Room: How Television Calls the Shots in Presidential Elections.* New York: Free Press, 1999. Describes the effect of television news and advertising on presidential elections.

Movies of Interest

Good Night and Good Luck (2005)
Directed by George Clooney, this film tells the story of famed CBS newsman Edward R. Murrow, who takes on Senator Joseph McCarthy and the House Un-American Activities Committee's communist witch hunt during the 1950s despite pressure from corporate sponsors and from McCarthy himself.

Shattered Glass (2003)
Stephen Glass was a staff writer for the *New Republic* and was also freelancing for other prominent publications when it was discovered that he had fabricated stories. This film depicts his career and his downfall.

Veronica Guerin (2003)
Starring Cate Blanchett, this film is based on the true story of Veronica Guerin, a crime reporter for the *Dublin Sunday Independent,* who was murdered in 1996.

Live from Baghdad (2002)
This movie demonstrates the differences in tactics between twenty-four-hour news channels and network news shows, telling the story of CNN's coverage of the U.S. invasion of Iraq in 1990.

All the President's Men (1976)
Starring Dustin Hoffman and Robert Redford, this film, based on Bob Woodward and Carl Bernstein's best-selling book of the same title, tells the saga of the two *Washington Post* reporters' investigation of the Watergate scandal that rocked the Nixon White House.

Network (1976)
Faye Dunaway, Peter Finch, William Holden, and Robert Duvall star in this classic satirizing the nature of newscasting in the 1970s.

Citizen Kane (1941)
This classic, directed by and starring Orson Welles, is Welles's fictionalized version of newspaper scion William Randolph Hearst, who purportedly attempted to halt release of the film.

Resources for Research and Action   333

Congress

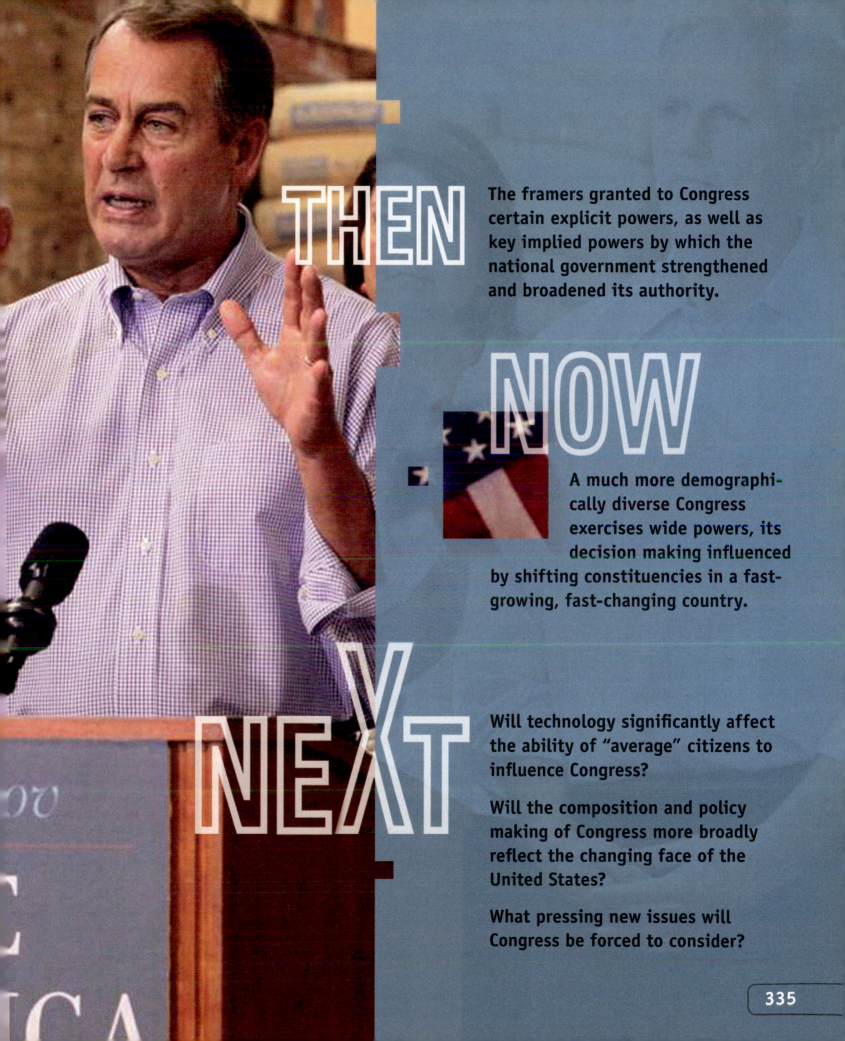

THEN

The framers granted to Congress certain explicit powers, as well as key implied powers by which the national government strengthened and broadened its authority.

NOW

A much more demographically diverse Congress exercises wide powers, its decision making influenced by shifting constituencies in a fast-growing, fast-changing country.

NEXT

Will technology significantly affect the ability of "average" citizens to influence Congress?

Will the composition and policy making of Congress more broadly reflect the changing face of the United States?

What pressing new issues will Congress be forced to consider?

335

Congress is an institution shaped

by the people elected to serve there, men and women acting as the trusted representatives of the constituents who voted them into office. Congress and the policies it sets are molded by the times; laws passed in one generation may seem antiquated to the next. And Congress and the policies it creates are influenced by many other factors, including the legislative body's institutional history, the lawmaking process, and the internal and external actors—congressional leaders, political parties, interest groups, the president, staff members, ordinary citizens, and the media, who seek to influence congressional actions.

The Constitution's framers structured the government so that Congress—more so than the two other institutions of the federal government—would be responsive to the needs and the will of the people. In representing their constituents, members of Congress provide an easily accessed point of contact for people to connect with their government and to have their voices heard.

Citizens today have countless opportunities to participate in shaping Congress's agenda and influencing how the members of Congress vote. Individuals and groups of constituents communicate through e-mail, networking sites on the Internet such as Facebook, and telephone, and meet face-to-face with members of Congress on issues that concern them. Constituents meet with congressional staff members for help in understanding how to deal with government bureaucracy. Through congressional campaigns and elections, citizens learn about issues of national importance and can participate in a variety of ways, such as volunteering in support of a candidate's run for office, contributing to the individual's campaign, becoming informed about the candidates and the issues, and casting a ballot on Election Day.

Throughout this chapter, we view Congress through the lens of civic engagement, seeing that Congress—the people's branch of the federal government—though imperfect, is structured to empower citizens to play a role in determining public policy priorities. And ultimately it is the people, through their choices at the ballot box, who decide who the creators of those policies will be.

The Origins of Congress

For the United States' founders, creating the national Congress was a crucially important task. Fearful of a powerful executive, but having endured the problems stemming from the weak national government under the Articles of Confederation, the framers of the Constitution believed that the legislature should be the key branch of the newly formed national government. In their vision, the Congress would be the institution responsible for making laws that would create effective public policy. In structuring the Congress, the framers strove to create a legislative branch that was at once powerful enough to govern and to check the power of the president and yet not so powerful that the legislature itself would exercise tyrannical rule. (See "Global Context" for an example of how a different constitution structured Japan's legislature.)

As they debated the shape of the Congress, the Constitution's framers had to balance the desires of representation of two opposing groups. The Constitution created a bicameral, or

GLOBAL CONTEXT

JAPAN'S NATIONAL DIET, 国会

Should the U.S. House of Representatives have the ultimate decision-making power in the event of policy disagreements, like the Japanese Shūgiin?

Much like the United States, Japan has a bicameral legislature. The Japanese call this body the *Kokkai,* or National Diet. Japan's post–World War II constitution created the current legislative structure, which eliminated the power held by the emperor in the previous constitution and granted the legislature the exclusive power to create laws. It also bestowed on the legislature the power to select the country's prime minister.

Japan's lower house, like that of the United States, is the House of Representatives (*Shūgiin*), which has 480 members. Of those members, 300 are elected in district elections, in which the candidate with the most votes wins the seat. If a particular candidate nets 40 percent of the vote and that is more than any other candidate receives, that candidate wins the seat. (There is no minimum percentage of the vote required; the candidate with more votes than anyone else wins.) The remaining 180 seats are elected in a proportional representation system, in which candidates in eleven separate blocs are elected in proportion to the percentage of the votes their party receives. And so, if a particular party receives 10 percent of the votes, they win 18 seats (10 percent of the 180 proportional representation seats).

Japan's upper house, the House of Councilors (*Sangiin*), is the equivalent of the U.S. Senate. Of its 242 members, 146 are elected from districts through a single nontransferable vote system. This means that each voter (in Japan the voting age is 20) may cast a vote for only one candidate and that candidate cannot transfer extra votes to other members of his or her party, but the top several candidates with the most votes win. The other 96 members of the Senate are elected in a proportional representation system, in which rank-ordered candidates are awarded seats based on the percentage of the vote their party receives in national balloting.

If the *Sangiin* and the *Shūgiin* disagree on policy matters such as the ratification of treaties, the national budget, and the designation of the prime minister, the Japanese Constitution grants the ultimate decision-making power to the House of Representatives, the *Shūgiin*. But outside those policy matters, the *Shūgiin* needs a two-thirds majority vote to override action taken by the House of Councilors, or *Sangiin*.

two-house, legislature in which one house, the House of Representatives, would be based on population, and the other chamber, the Senate, would be based on state representation.[1] The constitutionally specified duties of each house of Congress reflect the framers' views of the essential nature of the two chambers and the people who would serve in them.

The House of Representatives, with the smallest constituencies of any federal office (currently about 647,000 people reside in each congressional district), is the chamber closer to the people. As such, the framers intended the House to closely represent the people's views. The Constitution thus requires, for example, that all revenue bills (bills that would impose taxes) must originate in the House of Representatives. In the framers' eyes, unwarranted taxation was an egregious offense. By placing the power to tax in the hands of the members of the House of Representatives—the officials who face more frequent federal elections—the framers sought to avoid the types of unpopular, unfair taxes that had sparked the American Revolution. A short electoral cycle, they reasoned, would allow disfavored politicians to be voted out of office. Like all other bills, revenue bills must be passed in identical form by both the House and the Senate to become law, but requiring revenue bills to originate in the House reflected a victory by the large states at the Constitutional Convention. (Smaller states wanted taxation power to reside with the Senate.)

Although the framers viewed the House as the "people's chamber," they conceived the Senate to be a more elite, more deliberative institution, one not subject to the whims of mass politics like its lower-house counterpart. Today, because of its smaller size and because its members face elections less frequently than House members, the Senate remains a more deliberative body than the House. In addition, because of the specific constitutional duties mandated to the upper house, particularly the requirement that treaties must be ratified in the Senate, many U.S. senators have specialized in U.S. foreign policy issues. (See "The House and the Senate Compared" later in this chapter for further discussion of House-Senate differences.)

The framers' vision was to structure the Congress to embody republican principles, ensuring that in its central policy-making responsibilities, the national legislature would be responsive to the needs and the will of the people. Both historically and continuing in the present day, civically engaged citizens have exerted a strong influence on the outcome of the policy-making process. One important avenue by which individuals influence Congress and its acts is through congressional elections, a topic we now consider.

Congressional Elections

The timetable for congressional elections reflects the framers' views of the differing nature of the House of Representatives and the Senate. House members, as public servants in the legislative body that the framers conceived as closer to the people, are elected every two years, in even-numbered years (2010, 2012, and so on). But the framers also sought to check the power of the people, who they believed could be irrational and unruly, and so members of the Senate originally were chosen by state legislators. Ratification of the Seventeenth Amendment to the Constitution in 1913 shifted the election of senators to popular election within the states. Senators serve six-year terms, which are staggered so that one-third of the Senate is elected every two years. Thus, in any given congressional election year, thirty-three or thirty-four members of the Senate are up for election. Usually, the two senators from a given state will not be elected in the same cycle, unless the death or resignation of a sitting senator requires a special election. As we saw in Chapter 2, the Constitution requires that the number of seats in the House of Representatives awarded to each state be based on that state's population and that each state have two U.S. senators. On average, a successful campaign for a seat in the House of Representatives cost about $1.1 million in 2008. That is a veritable bargain compared with the price tag for a successful bid for the U.S. Senate, which averaged about $5.6 million that year. Compare this with the annual salary of $174,000 that rank-and-file members of the House and the Senate collect.

> At 84, Representative John Dingell (D-Michigan), is the longest serving member of the U.S. House of Representatives. Here he accepts a ceremonial key from Deacon Claudia Hollinger of Flint, Michigan, after speaking at the 2010 National Affordability Summit, which brought more than 200 clergy and community leaders together with members of Congress to urge the passage of health care reform. In any election year, about 95 percent of the members of the House of Representatives are reelected. Dingell has been reelected 28 times since his first election in 1955.

Incumbency

The status of already holding office—known as incumbency—strongly influences a candidate's ability to raise money and is probably the most important factor in determining success in a congressional campaign. Indeed, in any election year, about 95 percent of incumbent members of the House of Representatives running for reelection win, and about 93 percent of their Senate counterparts do. These outcomes may indicate what *individual* members of Congress are doing right: representing their own constituencies effec-

How to Contact Congressman Michael McCaul

WASHINGTON OFFICE
131 Cannon HOB
Washington, DC 20515
Phone (202) 225-2401
Fax (202) 225-2995

TOMBALL OFFICE
Rosewood Professional Building
990 Village Square, Suite B
Tomball, TX 77375
Phone (281) 255-8372

KATY OFFICE
1550 Foxlake, Suite 120
Houston, TX 77084
Phone (281) 398-1247

BRENHAM OFFICE
2000 S. Market Street, Suite 303
Brenham, TX 77833
Phone (979) 830-8497

AUSTIN OFFICE
5929 Balcones Dr. Suite 305
Austin, TX 78731
Phone (512) 473-2357

Sign up for the McCaul Minute,
my e-newsletter at
www.house.gov/mccaul

U.S. HOUSE OF REPRESENTATIVES
WASHINGTON, D.C. 20515

PUBLIC DOCUMENT

OFFICIAL BUSINESS
This mailing was prepared, published and
mailed at taxpayer expense.
It is provided as a service to
10th Congressional District constituents.

Pre Sorted Standard

TO: CURRENT RESIDENT
7512 HILLVIEW DR
AUSTIN TX 75712

> A piece of franked mail from a congressional office. Note the signature of the sending member of Congress, which serves as a postage stamp.

tively, engaging with their constituents, and listening to and addressing their needs. But voters typically think about Congress in terms of *a whole,* rather than individuals, viewing it as a body that is overwhelmingly composed of "other people's" representatives, who do not reflect their views.[2] Thus the voting public frequently attacks Congress as a collective entity.

Why do incumbents so often win reelection? Several factors make it more likely that someone already in office will be returned to that office in a reelection bid:

- **Stronger name recognition.** Having run for election before and served in government, incumbents tend to be better known than challengers.
- **Easier access to media coverage.** Media outlets routinely publicize the activities of elected congressional officials, rationalizing that they are covering the institution of Congress rather than the individuals. Nonincumbent challengers face an uphill battle in trying to get coverage of their campaigns.
- **Franking.** The privilege of sending mail free of charge is known as *franking.* Federal law allows members of Congress free mailings to every household in their state or congressional district. These mailings make it easy for members of Congress to stay in touch with their constituencies throughout their tenure in office.
- **Campaign contributions.** Political action committees and individuals are interested in supporting candidates who will be in a position to help them once the election is over. Because donors are aware of the high reelection rates of incumbent candidates, incumbents garner an enormous proportion of contributions, sometimes as much as 80 percent in any given congressional election year.
- **Casework.** When an incumbent personally helps constituents solve problems with the federal bureaucracy, the resulting loyalty and good-word-of-mouth reputation helps to attract support for that candidate during a run for reelection.

Thus incumbency is a powerful obstacle for outsiders who seek to unseat an elected member of Congress. Despite the incumbency advantage, in each congressional election, many individuals challenge incumbent members of Congress, often doing so knowing that the odds are stacked against them but believing in giving voters a ballot choice. Others run because they seek to bring attention to a particular issue or to shape the policy agenda—or sometimes because they simply underestimate the power of incumbency.

Reapportionment and Redistricting

Sometimes the advantages of incumbency can be diminished, as in election years after reapportionment and redistricting. **Reapportionment** is the reallocation of seats in the House of Representatives on the basis of changes in a state's population since the last

reapportionment
reallocation of seats in the House of Representatives to each state based on changes in the state's population since the last census

redistricting
redrawing of congressional district boundaries within each state, based on the reapportionment from the census

census. Every ten years, in the year ending in zero (2010, 2020, and so on), the federal government counts the number of people in the country as a whole. If the census indicates that a state's population has changed significantly, that state may gain or lose seats in the House of Representatives. **Redistricting,** the redrawing of congressional district boundaries within a state, is based on the reapportionment from the census.

Because the composition of a given congressional district can change as a result of reapportionment and redistricting, this process can mitigate the impact of incumbency. Frequently, the greatest shifts in the composition of the House of Representatives occur in election years ending in 2 (2002, 2012, and so on), when the first elections take place that incorporate the changes from reapportionment and redistricting. As a result of reapportionment in 2002, for example, New York and Pennsylvania each lost two House seats. Five states in the Midwest lost one House seat each, while several states in the South and the Southwest gained seats. Reapportionment and redistricting following the 2010 census does not occur until 2012, but on the basis of U.S. Census Bureau projections, demographers have projected that Texas will probably gain the largest number of House seats, perhaps as many as four, while Arizona and Florida could each gain two additional seats. Other states whose congressional delegations may increase in size include Georgia, Nevada, South Carolina, and Utah, which probably will each gain one seat. States whose slow population growth may mean the loss of one seat include Illinois, Iowa, Louisiana, Massachusetts, Michigan, Minnesota, Missouri, New Jersey, New York, and Pennsylvania, while Ohio could lose two representatives.[3] When a state loses a seat, the result is that an incumbent member of Congress is likely to lose a seat. When a state gains a seat, a new member of Congress can be elected to the open seat.

In some states, the goal of congressional redistricting is to protect House incumbents. The redrawing of congressional boundaries for the purpose of political advantage is a form of **gerrymandering,** the practice of drawing legislative district boundaries to benefit an incumbent, a political party, or some other group. The term was coined in reference to Massachusetts governor Elbridge Gerry after a district shaped like a salamander was created to favor his party in 1811. The illustration shows the first gerrymander.

Most forms of gerrymandering are legal. The U.S. Supreme Court ruled in 1986 that a gerrymandering plan is unconstitutional only when it eliminates the minority party's influence statewide.[4] Because of the strict standards, only one partisan gerrymandering plan filed after the 1990 census was successfully challenged.

State legislatures have attempted to address the issue of racial imbalance in the House of Representatives by constructing a kind of gerrymander called a majority-minority district. A **majority-minority district** is composed of a majority of a given minority community—

gerrymandering
the drawing of legislative district boundaries to benefit an incumbent, a political party, or another group

majority-minority district
a legislative district composed of a majority of a given minority community—say, African Americans—the intent of which is to make it likely that a member of that minority will be elected to Congress

THE GERRY-MANDER.

say, African Americans—and the creators' intent is to make it likely that a member of that minority will be elected to Congress. The Supreme Court has ruled that such racial gerrymandering is illegal unless the state legislature redrawing the district lines creates majority and minority districts at the expense of other redistricting concerns. Typically, those concerns include preserving the geographic continuity of districts, keeping communities within one legislative district, and reelecting incumbents.

POLITICAL INQUIRY

> The term *gerrymander* originated from this Gilbert Stuart cartoon of a Massachusetts electoral district. To Stuart, the district looked like a salamander. A friend christened it a "Gerry-mander," after Massachusetts governor Elbridge Gerry, a signer of the Declaration of Independence and the politician who approved redrawing district lines for political advantage. What point does this famous historical cartoon of 1812, representing Massachusetts legislative districts, make about the nature of a gerrymander? What do people today mean when they talk about gerrymandering? What are your own views on the practice?

Powers of Congress

The primary source of congressional authority is the U.S. Constitution. As shown in Table 11.1, the Constitution enumerates to Congress a number of different powers. The nature of these responsibilities reveals that the Constitution is both very specific in describing congressional powers (as in punishing illegal acts on the high seas) and at the same time quite vague (as in its language establishing the federal court system). Many of the specific duties of Congress reflect Americans' bitter experience in the colonial era, in that the framers granted powers to Congress that they did not want to place in the hands of a strong executive. For example, the economic powers granted to Congress, including the ability to tax and spend, to establish tariffs, and to borrow money, all limit the power of the president.

Powers specifically granted to Congress still have a distinct impact on our everyday lives. For example, Congress regulates currency, establishes weights and measures, and administers post offices. As we have seen, the connection between Congress, particularly the House, and the people was crucial to the framers, and so the Constitution requires that all taxation and spending measures originate in the House because the framers believed this chamber would be nearer to the people—and that House members would therefore ensure that the people's will was done.

The Constitution moreover imbues the Congress with an additional source of power, one that has proved very important in the expansion of legislative authority over time. As discussed in Chapter 2, the necessary and proper—or elastic—clause states that the Congress shall have the power to "make all Laws which shall be necessary and proper for carrying into Execution the foregoing powers, and all other Powers vested by this Constitution in the Government of the United States, or in a Department or Officer thereof." This clause has been responsible for

TABLE 11.1

Enumerated Powers of the Congress

JUDICIAL POWERS

Establish the federal court system

Punish counterfeiters

Punish illegal acts on the high seas

ECONOMIC POWERS

Impose taxes

Establish import tariffs

Borrow money

Regulate interstate commerce

Coin and print money, determine the value of currency

NATIONAL SECURITY POWERS

Declare war

Raise and regulate national armed forces

Call up and regulate state national guard

Suppress insurrections

Repel invasions

REGULATORY POWERS

Establish standards of weights and measures

Regulate copyrights and patents

ADMINISTRATIVE POWERS

Establish procedures for naturalizing citizens

Establish post offices

Govern the District of Columbia

> The Constitution's necessary and proper clause has resulted in the expansion of congressional authority into policy areas not specifically mentioned in the Constitution, including health care. Here, Senate Minority Leader Mitch McConnell (left), then-House Minority Leader John Boehner (now Speaker of the House of Representatives, center), and Republican Senator Jon Kyl of Arizona (right), prepare for a 2010 bipartisan summit on health care with President Barack Obama.

Congress's ability to legislate in many matters not described in the enumerated powers. Reforming our nation's health care system, determining the powers of law enforcement in investigating terrorism, and regulating stem cell research are all examples of powers not enumerated in the Constitution but that Congress exercises because of the broad scope of authority provided by the necessary and proper clause.

In addition to the Constitution, Congress derives power from Supreme Court decisions, the media, and the people. Supreme Court decisions often uphold the constitutionality of a law, in a sense verifying Congress's ability to create policy on a given subject. The media grant Congress power by providing members with a forum in which to communicate with constituents, sway public opinion, and create a favorable climate for the passage of legislation. The people are a key source of congressional power through civic participation in the electoral and legislative processes. Citizens communicate their views and priorities to their representatives, who then can claim public support in their endeavors to enact policy.

Functions of Congress

The Constitution is far more explicit in defining the responsibilities of the national legislature than it is in describing the function of the other branches of the government.[5] In its shaping of congressional functions, the Constitution's concerns with limited government, checks and balances, the separation of powers, and the creation of a federal system are all readily apparent.

Representation Comes in Many Forms

In delineating the composition of the federal legislature and the procedures for electing its members, the Constitution shapes the congressional function of representation in several ways. Representation traditionally involves a House or Senate member's articulating and voting for the position that best represents the views of his or her constituents.[6] But sometimes a member of Congress may speak for other constituencies as well. For example, a feminist legislator might "represent" feminists nationwide,[7] just as a gay legislator might "represent" the collective interests of gays across the United States.

Often, Congress's policy-making function is at odds with its representation function. A legislator may be pressured—by his or her political party or own conscience—to vote for a policy that clashes with constituents' interests or views. In representing constituents, legislators frequently follow one of two models of representative behavior.

trustee model
a model of representation in which a member of the House or Senate follows his or her own conscience when deciding issue positions

MODELS OF REPRESENTATION According to the **trustee model** of representation, a member of the House or the Senate follows his or her own conscience when deciding issue positions and determining how to vote. Sometimes a legislator relying on the trustee model will act contrary to the views of his or her constituents. This model was espoused by British political theorist Edmund Burke (1729–1797), who served in Parliament as a representative of Bristol, England. Explaining his conception of representation, Burke emphasized to his constituents, however, that a member of Parliament "is not a member of Bristol, he is a member of Parliament."[8] Burke accordingly argued that a member of Parliament should follow his conscience when making decisions in the legislature: "Your representative owes you, not his industry only, but his judgement [sic]; and he betrays, instead of serving you, if he sacrifices it to your opinion."[9] In this trustee view, a legislator may act in opposition to the clear wishes of his or her constituents, such as in cases where an action is "for their own good" or the good of society.

instructed delegate model
a model of representation in which legislators, as representatives of their constituents, should vote in keeping with the constituents' views, even if those views contradict the legislator's personal views

Another model of representation is the **instructed delegate model,** the idea that a legislator, as a representative of his or her constituents, should vote in keeping with the constituents' views, *even if those views contradict the legislator's personal views.* This model of representation conceives of legislators as the agents of their constituents. A legislator hewing to the instructed delegate model faces a dilemma when his or her constituency is evenly divided on an issue.

Given these two different models of representation, which one do legislators typically follow? Most analyses of representation indicate that legislators are likely to combine the approaches. Specifically, with regard to many important or high-profile issues, legislators act as instructed delegates, whereas for more mundane matters about which their constituents are less likely to be aware or to hold a strong position, they rely on the trustee model.

PORK BARREL AND EARMARKS   Members of Congress also represent their constituencies through pork barrel politics. **Pork barrel** (also called simply *pork*) refers to legislators' appropriations of funds for special projects located within their congressional district. Because pork brings money and jobs to a particular district, legislators who are seeking reelection work aggressively to secure monies for their states or districts—to "bring home the bacon."[10] Members frequently use transportation bills as a means of creating pork barrel projects for their districts. One analysis estimates, for example, that every $1 billion spent on highway and mass transit projects creates about 47,500 jobs, and members of Congress are happy to take credit for the jobs and for highway and mass transit improvements when running for reelection.[11] In 2010, Congress appropriated about $16.5 billion for pork barrel projects. Hawaii received the most pork per capita at $259.78. Wyoming took home the least, $12.28 per capita.[12] Table 11.2 lists the top ten recipients.

Members of Congress also use **earmarks** as a means of representing constituent interests: a designation within a spending bill that provides for a specific expenditure. And so, for example, in 2009 Representative Lynn Woolsey (D-California) helped ensure that the Sonoma County Integrated Emergency Operations Center (EOC) Information and Communication System was granted a $190,000 earmark in the federal budget for police and emergency communications. But many critics of the earmark process complain that earmarks are a way for members of Congress to reward supporters. Sonoma County had spent $320,000 lobbying federal lawmakers.

CASEWORK   A special form of representation called **casework** refers to providing representation in the form of personal aid to a constituent or a group of constituents, typically by getting the government to do something the constituent wants done. Members of Congress and their staffs commonly assist constituents in dealing with bureaucratic agencies. In doing so, they serve in the capacity of an **ombudsperson,** an elected or appointed representative who acts as a citizens' advocate by listening to their needs and investigating their complaints

pork barrel
legislators' appropriations of funds for special projects located within their congressional district

earmark
a designation within a spending bill that provides for a specific expenditure

casework
personal work by a member of Congress on behalf of a constituent or a group of constituents, typically aimed at getting the government to do something the constituent wants done

ombudsperson
a role in which an elected or appointed leader acts as an advocate for citizens by listening to and investigating complaints against a government agency

Top 10 States: Pork per Capita
(National Average: $27.36 per Person)

TABLE 11.2

2010 Rank	State	2010 Pork	Population	Pork/Capita
1	Hawaii	$326,099,850	1,295,178	$251.78
2	North Dakota	$127,743,350	646,844	$197.49
3	West Virginia	$265,728,000	1,819,777	$146.02
4	Alaska	$92,072,850	698,473	$131.82
6	Mississippi	$321,643,000	2,951,996	$108.96
5	South Dakota	$87,874,150	812,383	$108.17
7	Montana	$102,400,450	974,989	$105.03
8	District of Columbia	$62,318,500	599,657	$103.92
9	Vermont	$61,733,280	621,760	$99.29
10	Rhode Island	$71,937,000	1,053,209	$68.30

SOURCE: Citizens Against Government Waste, *2010 Congressional Pig Book Summary*, p. 63, www.cagw.org/assets/pig-book-files/2010/2010-pig-book-summary.pdf.

with respect to a particular government agency. For example, a member of Congress might intervene with the Immigration and Naturalization Service (INS) to request that a constituent's relative in a foreign country be granted a visa to travel to the United States.

According to political scientist Morris Fiorina, casework is a valuable tool for legislators. Fiorina points out that serving constituents is relatively easy for members of Congress, because bureaucrats—who depend on Congress for their funding—typically respond quickly to the requests of legislators.[13] The loyalty derived from assisting constituents is one aspect of the incumbency advantage that makes incumbent members of Congress more likely to be elected than their challengers, who do not enjoy that source of constituent loyalty.

Casework benefits constituents when, for example, a member of Congress's staff works with a local branch of a Veterans' Administration clinic to secure services for a retired veteran, whose family members derive a sense of efficacy—a feeling that they can get things done and that the government works for people like them. They perceive that their individual member of Congress genuinely represents them and protects their interests, with the result that these constituents not only feel engaged but also are likely to advocate for their member's reelection bid.

But casework is not without its costs, as noted by Walter F. Mondale. Mondale, who served as a member of both the House and the Senate, as well as vice president of the United States, warns that casework can take a legislator's time away from his or her legislative responsibilities:

> Good constituent service is, of course, necessary—and honorable—work for any member of Congress and his [sic] staff. Citizens must have somewhere to turn for help when they become victims of government bureaucracy. But constituent service can also be a bottomless pit. The danger is that a member of Congress will end up as little more than an ombudsman between citizens and government agencies. As important as this work is, it takes precious time away from Congress' central responsibilities as both a deliberative and a law-making body.[15]

In describing the constituent service dilemma, Mondale raises questions worthy of citizens' reflection. For example: Is the national interest served when a congressional staff member has to track down your grandma's Social Security check? Does doing so result in a missed opportunity for government officials to create policy with broad, significant implications? And is the use of congressional staff members as ombudspeople a prudent application of taxpayers' money?

Policy Making: A Central Responsibility

Each year, Congress passes laws determining everything from incentives for the creation of alternative energy sources, to what restrictions should govern gun purchases, to what law enforcers can do when they suspect someone of being a terrorist. The Constitution invests Congress with other policy-making powers as well, including the authority to tax and spend, to declare war, to establish courts, and to regulate the armed forces. This policy-making function is the central responsibility that the Congress carries out, and nearly all its other functions are related to its policy-making role. Congressional policy-making power also extends to the operations and priorities of governmental departments and agencies. For example, Congress has directed the State Department to select a domestic secure production facility to create ePassports, next-generation passports with an embedded microchip.

Oversight: A Check on the Executive Branch

In creating a system of checks and balances in the Constitution, the framers established the key congressional function of oversight.[14] **Oversight** is the process by which Congress "checks" the executive branch to ensure that the laws Congress passes are being administered in keeping with legislators' intentions. Congressional oversight is a check on the executive branch because the federal bureaucracy that implements laws is part of the executive branch.

In carrying out their oversight function, members of Congress use a variety of tools, some of which are listed here:

oversight
the process by which the legislative branch "checks" the executive branch to ensure that the laws Congress has passed are being administered in keeping with legislators' intent

- congressional hearings, in which government officials, bureaucrats, and interest groups testify as to how a law or a policy is being implemented and examine the impact of its implementation
- confirmation hearings on presidential appointees to oversee executive departments or governmental agencies
- investigations to determine whether a law or a policy is being implemented the way Congress intended it to be, and inquiries into allegations of wrongdoing by government officials or bureaucrats
- budgetary appropriations that determine funding of an executive department or a government agency

These tools ensure that Congress has some say in how the executive branch administers the laws that Congress creates. Members of Congress increasingly have viewed their role of checking the executive branch as crucially important.

Agenda Setting and Civic Engagement

Congress engages continuously in **agenda setting**: determining which public policy issues the federal legislature should consider.[16] Indeed, political scientists such as Cox and McCubbins assert that agenda setting relieves the pressure parties face in getting their members to vote with the party.[17] At the beginning of a congressional term, House and Senate leaders announce their goals for the coming session. Those goals reflect the issues and positions that predominated during the electoral campaign and that congressional leaders perceive to represent the people's priorities.

In setting the national agenda, Congress serves as a key agent in molding the scope of civic engagement and discourse, as people learn about, discuss, and form positions about issues. Frequently, agenda setting is itself influenced by public discourse, as when constituents complain to a member of Congress about a problem that needs to be solved or when an interest group contacts a legislator about a policy its membership would like to see implemented. For example, in 2010, pressure from gay rights activists led Congress to eliminate the "Don't Ask, Don't Tell" policy on gays in the military as part of a defense spending measure. Though elimination of the policy was narrowly defeated, its inclusion demonstrates how the public shapes the congressional agenda.

> One function of Congress is to provide oversight—to examine how a law or policy is being implemented. Here Toyota President and CEO Akio Toyoda (center) and North American President and CEO Yoshimi Inaba (right) and their official interpreter (left) are sworn in before they testify at the U.S. House of Representatives committee hearing "Toyota Gas Pedals: Is the Public at Risk?" on February, 2010. The hearing focused on the U.S. government's response to the recall of millions of Toyota vehicles due to reports of malfunctioning gas pedals.

agenda setting
determination by Congress of which public issues the government should consider for legislation

Managing Societal Conflict

Congress also has a significant influence in managing the societal conflict inherent in a divided society such as the United States. Some citizens want policies benefiting rural areas, and others give higher priority to urban areas. Some want more money for programs for senior citizens; others seek funding for children's programs. With respect to abortion policy, some people are pro-life, and others are pro-choice. In addition, there are divisions related to social class, race, geography, gender, sexual orientation, religion, and so on. Congress manages these conflicts by representing a wide range of views and interests.

The House and the Senate Compared

Although the House of Representatives and the Senate share numerous functions, the two chambers of Congress differ in significant ways. As President Woodrow Wilson remarked, the "House and Senate are naturally unalike."[18] Constitutionally, the two houses are

TABLE 11.3	Differences Between the House and the Senate	
	House	**Senate**
	Larger (435 members)	Smaller (100 members)
	Shorter electoral cycle (two-year term)	Longer electoral cycle (six-year term)
	Narrow constituency (congressional districts)	Broad constituency (states)
	Less prestigious	More prestigious
	Originates all revenue bills	Ratifies treaties; confirms presidential nominees
	Less reliant on staff	More reliant on staff
	Power vested in leaders and committee chairs	Power more evenly distributed

bill
a proposed piece of legislation

hopper
a wooden box that sits on a desk at the front of the House of Representatives, into which House members place bills they want to introduce

> California senators must balance the views not only of surfers and Hollywood stars but also of farmers and ranchers. They must take into account the concerns of liberal urban coastal dwellers along with the more conservative views of those who live in the state's heartland to the east, including the significant agricultural interests in those areas. Agribusiness interests and farmers often lobby for government support of irrigation programs, for example. Here, sprinklers irrigate a cotton field at pre-bloom stage.

conceived as unique organizations, and the framers designated their duties to match the strengths and expertise of the people who would come to hold office in each chamber. Table 11.3 highlights these major differences. As discussed earlier in this chapter, the Constitution empowers the House of Representatives, as the legislative body closer to the people, with initiating any bills that result in taxes; whereas it empowers the Senate, as the more deliberative house, to give the president advice and consent on appointments and the ratification of treaties. The differences between the House and the Senate are not limited merely to their functions, however. The electoral and legislative structures are also sources of differences between the two houses.

Each of the 435 current members of the House of Representatives represents a legislative district determined by the reapportionment and redistricting process that occurs every ten years, as described earlier in this chapter. In more populated areas, these congressional districts are often homogeneous, cohesive units in which a House member's constituency is likely to have fairly unified positions on many issues.[19] Senators, however, are elected by the population of an entire state, and although the political culture in some states is somewhat cohesive (for example, Vermont voters are more liberal on most issues than are Kansas voters), in many states there are notable differences in constituents' views, ideology, and policy priorities. For instance, senators Barbara Boxer and Dianne Feinstein both represent the entire state of California, and both are Democrats. Although California is generally viewed as a very liberal political culture, Boxer and Feinstein also must represent the interests of both liberal voters in the western coastal areas of the state and more conservative voters inland to the east. At times, moreover, the interests of a senator's constituents divide over a given issue: in California, for example, environmental activists and fishers have argued against programs that divert water from lakes and streams so that it can be used for irrigation on commercial farms, whereas affluent agribusinesses advocate water diversion. A U.S. senator must balance such conflicting positions when making policy decisions.

The differing length of representatives' and senators' terms of service affects how members of each chamber of Congress relate to their constituents. Given their short two-year terms, members of the House of Representatives naturally are reluctant to defy the will of the electorate on a given issue because of the likelihood that their opposition will be used against them during their reelection campaign. As the framers structured it, the House remains "the people's house," the chamber in which civically engaged individuals can effectively have their interests represented. And although U.S. senators naturally also want to please their constituents, they recognize that voting against their constituents' will on a particular issue might be less significant than such an action would be for a House member, especially if the issue arises early in their term and is not important enough for people to hold against them six years down the road.

The size of the chambers and the length of terms also affect the relative prestige of each chamber. In general, the smaller Senate is considered more prestigious than the House of Representatives, although some individual House members may enjoy more prestige than some senators.

Although the House and the Senate differ in their constitutionally determined duties, both must pass any piece of legislation before it can become law. But the way in which legislation is considered and voted upon differs in each house of Congress.

The larger size of the House of Representatives, with its 435 members, necessitates a more formal legislative structure to prevent unruliness.

The House, for example, generally has more, and more formal, rules guiding debate than the Senate. Despite the differences between the two chambers, the legislative process is remarkably similar in both.

joint referral
the practice, abolished in the 104th Congress, by which a bill could be referred to two different committees for consideration

The Legislative Process

Article I, Section 1, of the Constitution states, "All Legislative Powers herein granted shall be vested in a Congress of the United States, which shall consist of a Senate and House of Representatives." A **bill** is a proposed piece of legislation. As shown in Figure 11.1, every bill must be approved by *both houses* (the House and the Senate) *in identical form*. In general, bills must pass through five steps to become law:

1. **Introduction.** A member of the House of Representatives or the Senate formally proposes the bill.

2. **Committee review.** Subgroups within the House and the Senate, composed of legislators who have expertise in the bill's subject matter, review the bill.

3. **House and Senate approval.** If the bill makes it out of committee, a majority of members in the House and the Senate must approve it.

4. **Conference Committee reconciliation.** The Conference Committee reconciles the bill when different versions have passed in the House and the Senate.

5. **Presidential approval.** If the president signs the bill, it becomes law. But even after this arduous process, a presidential veto can kill the bill.

Introducing a Bill

Bills are introduced differently in each chamber of Congress. In the House of Representatives, a member of a legislator's staff drafts the proposed legislation, and the House member puts the bill into the **hopper,** a wooden box that sits on a desk at the front of the House chamber. Upon introduction, a bill is referred to as "H.R.," meaning House of Representatives, followed by a number that indicates the order in which it was introduced in a given legislative session, for example, "H.R. 207."

In the Senate, the process is less formal. Here, senators can announce proposed legislation to colleagues in a speech on the Senate floor. (See "Analyzing the Sources" on page 348.) Alternatively, a senator can submit a written draft of the proposed legislation to an official known as the Senate clerk, or sometimes a senator will propose legislation simply by offering it as an amendment to an already pending piece of legislation. Once a bill is introduced in the Senate, it is referred to as "S.," or "Senate," followed by its number reflecting the order in which it was introduced in a given legislative session—for example, "S. 711."

Before 1995, a bill introduced in the House of Representatives could be subject to **joint referral,** the practice of referring the bill simultaneously to two different House committees for consideration. But the 104th Congress abolished joint committee referrals. Today, bills introduced in the

POLITICAL INQUIRY

FIGURE 11.1 ■ Where are there similarities between the House and the Senate in the legislative process? How do the Senate and the House resolve differences in versions of a bill passed in each chamber? What outcomes are possible once a bill goes to the president for approval?

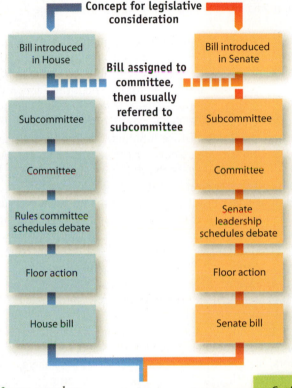

The Legislative Process

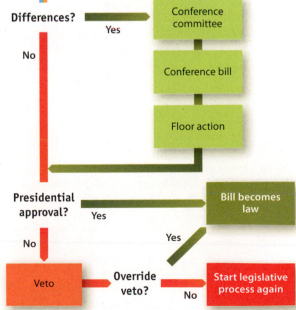

NAVIGATING CONGRESS

When we think of Congress, we typically picture the gleaming white dome of the Capitol. This image is appropriate, because the Capitol Rotunda is a highly important place for members of Congress and the people whom they represent. The Capitol is home to the House and Senate chambers where issues are debated on the floor and where votes are cast.

As shown in the map, however, a large part of Congress's work takes place in the office buildings surrounding the rotunda that are considered part of "Capitol Hill." Members of the House of Representatives are typically assigned an office in one of three buildings on the south side of the Capitol Rotunda: the Cannon Office Building, the Longworth Office Building, and the Rayburn Office Building. Senators work out of an office in one of the three office buildings located on the north side of the rotunda: the Russell Office Building, the Dirksen Office Building, and the Hart Office Building. The Cannon and Russell buildings share essentially the same design. The House office buildings are named after former Speakers of the House of Representatives, and the Senate office buildings are named after prominent U.S. senators.

Many of the buildings boast beautiful architecture and amenities such as gymnasiums, post offices, kitchens, and recording studios. In the Rayburn Office Building, members can travel to the Capitol via a subway tunnel with two cars, and pedestrian tunnels join it to the Longworth Building. A double-track subway system connects Dirksen, Russell, and the Capitol, and tunnels beneath the Cannon and Russell buildings connect to the Capitol. Immediately east of the Capitol Rotunda is the Library of Congress, and the U.S. Supreme Court Building sits just south of the Senate office buildings.

Although office space and layout are not something that political scientists typically analyze, the proximity of members of Congress to their office neighbors, along with the common facilities they share, surely has an impact on the legislative process. In the Capitol Hill office buildings, just as in any other kind of office or group setting, senators and representatives of diverse backgrounds become familiar with colleagues whom they see regularly in the hallways, elevators, gyms, kitchens, and subway trains between buildings.

Evaluating the Evidence

① Like a member of Congress, you also have a network of relationships based on your daily activities. What people do you see regularly because of your work or school schedule? What unlikely relationships have you formed because of your daily activities?

② In what ways might the time spent in their Capitol Hill offices and common facilities breed familiarity among federal legislators? What different kinds and backgrounds of people might this daily contact bring together?

③ In what specific ways do you think legislators' interactions in their office buildings might affect their political decision making in the chambers of the House and the Senate?

Legend

HOB: House Office Building
LOC: Library of Congress Building
SOB: Senate Office Building
USBG: United States Botanic Garden

SOURCE: www.aol.gov/cc/cc-map.cfm

House are referred to one committee, called the **lead committee.** Occasionally, when the substance of a bill warrants additional referrals to other committees that also have jurisdiction over the subject of the bill, the bill might be subsequently referred to a second committee.[20] In the Senate, bills typically are referred to only one committee.

The Bill in Committee

After introduction by a member of the House or the Senate, a bill is read into the *Congressional Record,* a formal record of all actions taken by Congress. Because of the large number of bills introduced, both chambers rely on an extensive committee structure that facilitates the consideration of so high a volume of bills.[21] Most bills that are introduced "die" in committee. That is, a committee does not consider the bill (sometimes because the committee does not have the time in a legislative session to take up the measure) or declines to forward the bill to the full chamber.

Each congressional committee and subcommittee is composed of a majority of members of the majority party in that chamber. For example, if 218 or more members (a majority in the House) elected to the House of Representatives are Republicans, then every committee and subcommittee in the House has a majority of Republicans. The parties in each chamber decide members' committee and subcommittee assignments.

Though the selection of committee chairs varies between chambers and parties, committee chairs are often chosen using the **seniority system,** by which the member with the longest continuous tenure on a standing committee receives preference when the committee chooses its chair. The committee chairs run committee meetings and control the flow of work in each committee. Although the seniority system is an institution in Congress, it is an informal system, and seniority does not always determine who will be the committee chair.[22] Chairs are chosen by a secret ballot, and in recent years junior members sometimes have won out over senior committee members.

Standing committees are permanent committees with a defined legislative jurisdiction. The House has twenty-four standing committees, and the Senate has twenty. The House Committee on Homeland Security and the Senate Armed Services Committee are examples of standing committees.

Select committees are specially created to consider a specific policy issue or to address a particular concern. In 2005, the House formed a select committee, the Select Bipartisan Committee to Investigate the Preparation for and Response to Hurricane Katrina, which examined what went wrong in the preparations for and response to that killer storm. Other select committees have focused on such issues as homeland security and terrorism, aging, and transportation.

Joint committees are bicameral committees composed of members of both chambers of Congress. Sometimes these committees offer administrative or managerial guidance of various kinds. For example, one joint committee oversees the presidential inauguration, and another supervises the administration of the Library of Congress.

In addition to the congressional committees, the House has more than ninety subcommittees, and the Senate has sixty-eight. **Subcommittees** typically handle specific areas of the committees' jurisdiction. For example, the House Committee on Foreign Affairs is a standing committee. Within the committee there are seven subcommittees: the Subcommittee on Africa and Global Health; the Subcommittee on Asia, Pacific, and the Global Environment; the Subcommittee on Europe; the Subcommittee on the Middle East and South Asia; the Subcommittee on International Organizations, Human Rights, and Oversight; the Subcommittee on Terrorism, Nonproliferation, and Trade; and the Subcommittee on the Western Hemisphere. Each subcommittee handles bills relevant to its specified jurisdiction.

When a committee or a subcommittee favors a measure, it usually takes four actions:

- **Agency review.** During **agency review,** the committee or subcommittee asks the executive agencies that would administer the law for written comments on the measure.
- **Hearings.** Next the committee or subcommittee holds **hearings** to gather information and views from experts, including interest groups, concerned citizens, and celebrities involved with the issue.

lead committee
the primary committee considering a bill

seniority system
the system in which the member with the longest continuous tenure on a standing committee is given preference when the committee chooses its chair

standing committee
permanent committee in Congress, with a defined legislative jurisdiction

select committee
congressional committee created to consider specific policy issues or address a specific concern

joint committee
bicameral committee composed of members of both chambers of Congress

subcommittee
a subordinate committee in Congress that typically handles specific areas of a standing committee's jurisdiction

agency review
part of the committee or subcommittee process of considering a bill, in which committee members ask executive agencies that would administer the law for written comments on the measure

hearings
sessions held by committees or subcommittees to gather information and views from experts

markup

the process by which members of legislative committees "mark up" a bill with suggested language for changes and amendments

report

a legislative committee's explanation to the full chamber of a bill and its intent

discharge petition

a special tactic used to extract a bill from a committee to have it considered by the entire House

Rules Committee

one of the most important committees in the House, which decides the length of debate and the scope of amendments that will be allowed on a bill

unanimous consent

an agreement by every senator to the terms of debate on a given piece of legislation

filibuster

a procedural move by a member of the Senate to attempt to halt passage of or change a bill, during which the senator can speak for an unlimited time on the Senate floor

■ **Markup.** During **markup,** the committee "marks up" the bill with suggested language changes and amendments. The committee does not actually alter the bill; rather, members recommend changes to the full chamber. In a typical bill markup, the committee may eliminate a component of the proposal or amend the proposal in some way.

■ **Report.** After agreeing to the wording of the bill, the committee issues a **report** to the full chamber, explaining the bill and its intent. The bill may then be considered by the full chamber.

In the House of Representatives, a special measure known as a **discharge petition** is used to extract a bill from a committee to have it considered by the entire House. A discharge petition requires the signature of a majority (218) of the members of the House.

Debate on the House and Senate Floor

Table 11.4 compares the legislative process in the House and the Senate. For example, if a House bill is "discharged," or makes it out of committee, it then goes to the **Rules Committee,** one of the most important committees in the House, which decides on the length of debate and the scope of amendments that will be allowed on a bill. The Rules Committee sets the structure for the debate that ensues in the full House. For important bills, the Rules Committee tends to set strict limits on the types of amendments that can be attached to a bill. In general, the Rules Committee also establishes limits to floor debate in the House.

The Senate does not have a committee to do the work of the Rules Committee, but the Senate's small size allows members to agree to the terms of debate through **unanimous consent** agreements. Unanimous consent must be just that: every senator needs to agree to the terms of debate (including time limits on debate), and if even one senator objects, unanimous consent does not take effect. Senators do not look favorably on objections to unanimous consent, and so such objections are rare. Objecting to unanimous consent agreements can potentially undermine a senator's ability to get legislation passed by provoking the ire of other senators.

If the Senate does not reach unanimous consent, the possibility of a **filibuster** arises—a procedural move that attempts to halt passage of the bill.[23] Sometimes the mere threat of a filibuster is enough to compel a bill's supporters to alter a bill's content. During a filibuster, a senator can speak for an unlimited time on the Senate floor. Filibustering senators do

TABLE 11.4

Differences in the Legislative Process in the House and Senate

House	Senate
Bill introduced by member placing bill in hopper	Bill introduced by member
Relies on Rules Committee to schedule debate on House floor and to establish rules for amendments	Relies on unanimous consent agreements to determine rules for debate and amendments
Has a rule barring nongermane amendments	No rule banning nongermane amendments
Does not allow filibusters	Allows filibusters
Discharge petition can be used to extract a bill from a committee	No discharge petitions allowed

not need to restrict themselves to speaking only on the subject of the bill—they just need to keep talking. Some senators have read the Bible, cookbooks, and even the Nynex Yellow Pages into the *Congressional Record*. In the 1930s, Senator Huey P. Long (D-Louisiana) filibustered many bills, once speaking for fifteen hours to block one that he viewed as "helping the rich get richer and the poor get poorer." Long, viewed as a character by many of his Senate colleagues, was a favorite among visitors to the Senate galleries, where he would entertain onlookers with New Orleans recipes for "pot-likkers" and with his articulations of Shakespeare in a Louisiana drawl. Former Republican South Carolina senator Strom Thurmond holds the Senate record for the longest filibuster. In an attempt to block passage of the Civil Rights Act of 1957, Thurmond filibustered for twenty-four hours and eighteen minutes. A filibuster can end by a vote of **cloture,** in which a supermajority of sixty senators agrees to invoke cloture and end debate. Cloture is initiated if sixteen senators sign a cloture petition. In 2010, when Senator Scott Brown (R-Massachusetts) was elected in a special election to replace the late Democratic senator Edward M. Kennedy, the specter of filibusters in the Senate became more likely as Brown's election as the forty-first Republican in the Senate meant that Democrats had lost the sixty-member filibuster-proof majority they had held.

cloture
a procedural move in which a super-majority of sixty senators agrees to end a filibuster

After a bill is debated by the full chamber, the members vote on it. Before a bill can become law, identical versions of the bill must pass in both the House and the Senate. If only one chamber passes a bill during a congressional term, the bill dies. If both the House and the Senate pass bills on the same topic but with differences between the bills, the bills are then sent to a **conference committee,** a bicameral, bipartisan committee composed of legislators whose job is to reconcile the two versions of the bill. Typically, the legislators appointed to the conference committee will be members of the standing committees that considered the bill in their chambers. After the committee develops a compromise version of the bill, the bill then goes back to both chambers for another vote. If the bill does not pass in both chambers during a congressional term, the bill is dead, although it can be reintroduced in the next session. If both chambers approve the bill, it then goes to the president for signature or veto.

conference committee
a bicameral, bipartisan committee composed of legislators whose job is to reconcile two versions of a bill

Presidential Action

When both the House and the Senate manage to pass a bill in identical form, it proceeds to the president, who may take one of three actions. First, the president may sign it, in which case the bill becomes a law. Second, the president may choose to do nothing. If the president does nothing and Congress is in session, the bill becomes law after ten days without the president's signature. A president may take this route if he or she does not support the bill but knows that Congress would override a veto. If, however, the Congress has adjourned (that is, the bill was passed at the end of a legislative session), the president may exercise a pocket veto. A **pocket veto** occurs when Congress has adjourned and the president waits ten days without signing the bill; the president effectively "puts the bill in his pocket," and the bill dies. Finally, a president may exercise the executive power of a *veto:* rejecting the bill and returning it to Congress with a message explaining why the bill should not become law. Congress can vote to override the veto by a two-thirds vote in both houses, in which case the bill becomes law. But overriding a presidential veto is a difficult and rare achievement.

pocket veto
a special presidential veto of a bill passed at the conclusion of a legislative session, whereby the president waits ten days without signing the bill, and the bill dies

Congressional Leadership

The House and the Senate alike choose the majority and minority leaders for their adept negotiating skills, their finely honed ability to guide compromise, and their skills of persuasion. A majority leader nurtures compromise in the legislative process by knowing the members' positions on legislation well enough to recognize which issues are negotiable and which are deal-breakers; by engineering trade-offs between players; and by convincing committee chairs that a negotiated compromise is the best outcome they can expect.

In earlier eras, forceful leaders rose to the position of majority leader in both houses and strongly influenced congressional priorities and legislation.[24] But as political parties

> Rep. Nancy Pelosi, former Speaker of the House of Representatives, proved to be a lightning rod for critics in the 2010 mid-term elections, with Republican candidates urging voters to "Fire Pelosi" by electing a Republican majority. They did, and John Boehner was selected by the Republican caucus as her replacement.

Speaker of the House
the leader of the House of Representatives, chosen by the majority party

House majority leader
the leader of the majority party, who helps the Speaker develop and implement strategy and works with other members of the House of Representatives

have come to play a less important role in the election of members of the House and the Senate, allegiance to party leaders in these institutions has dwindled.[25] The era has long passed in which individuals could essentially control what Congress did through their assertive personalities.[26] Today's congressional power brokers face members whose loyalty to the party and the leadership is tempered by the need to please constituencies that themselves are less loyal to the parties than in bygone times.[27] Nonetheless, despite the evolution in the role of congressional leader, partisanship remains a strong aspect of congressional politics, particularly since 1994.

Leadership in the House of Representatives

Although Article I, Section 2, of the Constitution states, "The House of Representatives shall choose their Speaker and other Officers," and all members of the House vote for the Speaker, it is really the members of the majority party who select their **Speaker of the House.** Second in the line of presidential succession (after the vice president), the Speaker serves as the presiding officer and manager of the House. In this capacity, the Speaker chairs floor debates, makes majority party committee assignments, assigns members to the powerful Rules Committee, negotiates with members of the minority party and the White House, and guides legislation through the House.[28] But the Speaker is also the leader of his or her party in the House, and a key duty associated with this role is helping party members get reelected. Finally, the Speaker is himself or herself an elected member of the House.

The House leadership—which, in addition to the Speaker, includes the majority leader, the minority leader, and the party whips—is chosen at the beginning of each session of Congress through a conference also known as a *caucus*. During a caucus, all the members of the political party meet and elect their chamber leaders, approve committee assignments, and elect committee chairpersons. Party leaders also may call a party caucus during a legislative session to shore up support on an issue being voted upon or to formulate the party's position on an issue on the agenda.[29] One issue before Congress is the problem of controlling greenhouse gas emissions, which is considered in "Thinking Critically About Democracy."

In 2010, Republicans won a majority in the House of Representatives, ousting Rep. Nancy Pelosi (D-CA), who had served as speaker since 2006. Pelosi proved to be a lightning rod for critics in the 2010 mid-term elections, with Republican candidates urging voters to "Fire Pelosi" by electing a Republican majority. Voters, many of whom objected to President Obama and the Democratic Congress's handling of the economy and health care reform, listened and the Republican majority swept into office.

Pelosi, the first woman to serve as speaker, was an unabashed liberal who had railed against many of the George W. Bush administration's policies during her first two years as speaker. Her posturing resulted in a lack of cooperation by many Republicans in her chamber, and then the loss of the Democratic majority in the 2010 elections paved the way for the election of John Boehner (pronounced BAY-ner) as Speaker of the House.

As speaker, Boehner's priority is repealing the Affordable Healthcare Act, President Obama's healthcare reform package that had been passed during Pelosi's tenure. Boehner, who enjoys respect and loyalty among his colleagues, is also a vocal critic of the Obama administration, much in the way that Pelosi opposed the Bush administration during her tenure. As speaker, Boehner will be forced to herd the various elements of the Republican party in House of Representatives, including those members ascribing the Tea Party positions, to a cohesive position. He will need to unify liberal, moderate, and conservative Republicans, build coalitions composed of representatives from different districts, generations, ethnicities, and sexes. These skills are essential attributes for the Speaker of the House.

The Speaker relies on the **House majority leader** to help develop and implement the majority party's legislative strategy, work with the minority party leadership, and encourage unity among majority party legislators. In this last task, the Speaker and the House

THINKING CRITICALLY ABOUT DEMOCRACY

SHOULD CONGRESS LIMIT GREENHOUSE GAS EMISSIONS?

The Issue: One policy issue taken up in several recent sessions of Congress is emissions of carbon dioxide (CO_2), a "greenhouse gas" believed to contribute to global warming. These emissions, produced by public utilities, industries, and motor vehicles' burning of fossil fuels, have been an increasingly hot-button issue since the Democrats took control of Congress in 2006. After former vice president Al Gore won the Nobel Peace Prize for his contributions to raising public awareness about global climate change, many members of Congress felt pressure from their constituents to address the problem of carbon dioxide emissions. Should Congress limit greenhouse gas emissions?

Yes: The United States generates 22 percent of the world's CO_2 emissions, excluding gases that are the by-product of foreign countries' production of goods for U.S. consumption. Given this volume of consumption, Americans should take responsibility for protecting the global environment. Failure to curb greenhouse gas emissions will have terrible long-term consequences for the environmental and the economic health of not only the United States but also the wider world. Failure to reduce CO_2 emissions promotes global warming, resulting in the melting of the polar ice caps, higher tides throughout the world, and drastic changes in weather patterns and ecology, all of which can have a devastating impact on humans' as well as other species' ability to survive and thrive.

No: There is no need to create a massive regulatory structure to compel industry to reduce CO_2 emissions. Some political leaders maintain that carbon dioxide is not a pollutant and does not threaten public health. Furthermore, Senator James Inhofe (R-Oklahoma) has said that global warming is a hoax and has faulted environmental groups for duping the American public.* Forcing regulations on industry will significantly harm the U.S. economy. Regulating CO_2 emissions will drive up costs for gasoline, utilities, and various products we use every day.

Other approaches: Instead of mandating curbs directly, Congress could take a cue from states such as California and use the federal government's role as an energy customer to encourage companies to curb emissions and become more green. For example, it could require national parks or other federally owned properties to purchase electricity from sources that meet certain emissions standards. It should also further encourage the development of alternative, renewable sources of energy—such as wind, solar, and geothermal energy—by continuing to extend tax credits for these promising industries.

What do you think?

① Do you support legislation that would limit industrial output of carbon dioxide? Why or why not?

② What businesses and industries could be hurt by such legislation? Would you be willing to pay more at the pump to curb greenhouse emissions?

③ If limiting the production of greenhouse gases is crucial, what role should other countries play? What are some challenges of getting other countries to reduce their emissions of carbon dioxide?

*www.usatoday.com/news/world/2009-12-13-copenhagen_N.htm?loc=interstitialskip.

---

majority leader are assisted by the **majority whip,** who acts as a go-between with the leadership and the party members in the House. The term *whip* comes from the English hunting term *whipper-in,* a hunter whose job is to keep the foxhounds in the pack and to prevent them from straying during a fox hunt. Similarly, the job of the party whip is to keep party members together, encouraging them to vote with the party on issues and preventing them from straying off into their own positions. The minority party in the House also elects leaders, the **House minority leader** and the **minority whip,** whose jobs mirror those of their majority party colleagues but without the power that comes from holding a majority in the House.

Leadership in the Senate

In the Senate, the vice president of the United States serves as the president of that body, according to the Constitution. But in actual practice, vice presidents preside over the Senate only rarely. Vice presidents, however, have one power in the Senate that, although rarely exercised, is enormously important. If a vote in the upper house of Congress is tied, the

majority whip
a go-between with the majority leadership and party members in the House of Representatives

House minority leader
the leader of the minority party, whose job mirrors that of the majority leader but without the power that comes from holding a majority in the House of Representatives

minority whip
go-between with the minority leadership, whose job mirrors that of the majority whip but without the power that comes from holding a majority in the House of Representatives

Congressional Leadership

353

vice president breaks the tie. Such a situation occurred in 2005 when Vice President Dick Cheney cast the tie-breaking vote on a major budget bill that slashed federal spending by nearly $40 billion by allowing states to impose new fees on Medicaid recipients, cutting federal funds that enforce child-support regulations, and imposing new federal work requirements on state welfare recipients.

The majority party in the Senate elects a Senate leader called the **president pro tempore.** Meaning "president for the time," this position is often referred to as "president pro tem." The job of the president pro tem is to chair the Senate in the vice president's absence. Historically, this position has been honorary, with the majority party senator who has the longest record of continuous Senate service being elected to the office. Although the position is honorary, the Senate's president pro tem is third in the line of presidential succession (following the vice president and the Speaker of the House). Following the death of Senator Robert Byrd (D-West Virginia) on June 28, 2010, Senator Daniel Inouye (D-Hawaii) was sworn in as the current president pro tem.

The real power in the U.S. Senate is held and wielded by the **Senate majority leader,** whose job is to manage the legislative process so that favored bills are passed; to schedule debate on legislation in consultation with his or her counterpart in the minority party, the **Senate minority leader;** and to act as the spokesperson for the majority party in the Senate. The majority and the minority leaders both play crucial roles in ushering bills through the Senate, and the majority leader facilitates the numerous negotiations that arise when senators bargain over the content of a given piece of proposed legislation.[31]

Senate majority leader Harry Reid (D-Nevada) was elected after the Democrats won a majority of seats in the 2006 Senate elections. Reid is a soft-spoken politician who was elected partly because of his talent at building consensus, a necessary skill given his desire to tackle some highly partisan and controversial issues when he assumed his leadership role, including ethics reform, funding for stem cell research, and an increase in the federal minimum wage.

president pro tempore
(also called *president pro tem*) theoretically, the chair of the Senate in the vice president's absence; in reality, an honorary title, with the senator of the majority party having the longest record of continuous service being elected to the position

Senate majority leader
the most powerful position in the Senate; the majority leader manages the legislative process and schedules debate on legislation

Senate minority leader
the leader of the minority party in the Senate, who works with the majority leader in negotiating legislation

Decision Making in Congress: The Legislative Context

When deciding whether to "toe the party line" on a legislative vote, members of Congress do not operate independently and in isolation. Throughout the legislative process, they face a variety of external pressures that influence their views. Some of these influences are subtle; others are more pronounced. Moreover, the impact of the influence varies according to the timing and type of legislation being considered. For example, political scientist Barry C. Burden has noted that the personal experiences of legislators sometimes have a bearing on their policy stances on issues.[32] Among the most important influences on members of Congress with respect to the legislative process are political parties, members' colleagues and staff, interest groups, the president, and of course their constituents—the people who elected them to serve as their representatives in our system of republican government.

Political Parties and Partisanship in Decision Making

Figure 11.2 shows the party breakdown in Congress since 1985. The data show that 1994 was a pivotal year, ending Democratic control in the House and the Senate. For nearly all of the next twelve years, Republicans retained control over both the House and the Senate. (Re-

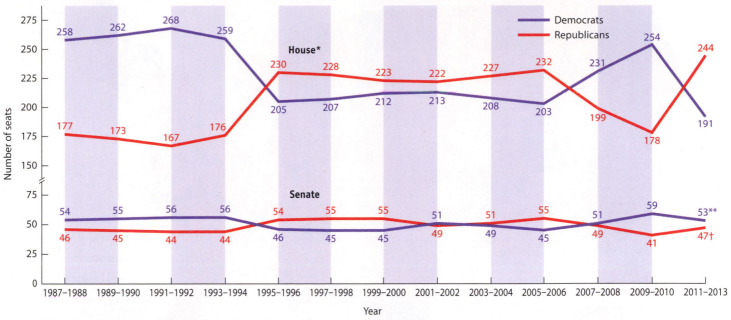

Party Breakdowns in the House and Senate, 1987–2013

Democrats
Republicans

House*

Democrats: 258, 262, 268, 259, 205, 207, 212, 213, 208, 203, 231, 254, 191

Republicans: 177, 173, 167, 176, 230, 228, 223, 222, 227, 232, 199, 178, 244

Senate

Democrats: 54, 55, 56, 56, 46, 45, 45, 51, 51, 45, 51, 59, 53**

Republicans: 46, 45, 44, 44, 54, 55, 55, 49, 49, 55, 49, 41, 47†

Years: 1987–1988, 1989–1990, 1991–1992, 1993–1994, 1995–1996, 1997–1998, 1999–2000, 2001–2002, 2003–2004, 2005–2006, 2007–2008, 2009–2010, 2011–2013

Number of seats (y-axis)

Year (x-axis)

* Based on projected outcomes at press time.

** Two Independent members of the Senate typically vote Democratic.

† Sen. Lisa Murkowski appeared to be the winner of Alaska's U.S. Senate election. Murkowski lost a primary to Tea Party candidate Joe Miller, but Murkowski launched a write-in campaign against Miller and Democratic candidate Scott McAdams. At press time, "write-in candidate" (presumed to be Murkowski) held 41 percent of the vote to Miller's 34 percent and McAdams' 24 percent.

POLITICAL INQUIRY

FIGURE 11.2 ■ **What trends does this graph show with respect to party representation in the House of Representatives since 1987? What trends does it indicate for the Senate? Generally speaking, do the patterns for the House resemble those for the Senate?**

publicans lost their narrow majority in the Senate in 2001 when one Republican senator switched parties, but they regained control in the 2002 elections.) But in 2006, the balance of power shifted back to the Democrats, who won majorities in both houses, squeaking out a majority in the Senate with a one-member lead. That year, Democratic candidates benefited from President George W. Bush's unpopularity and public weariness with the war in Iraq. As shown in Figure 11.3 (on page 356), in 2008 the Democrats continued to increase their majorities in both houses, as a result of voters' continuing dislike of Bush's policies, and—for some Democratic congressional candidates—from Barack Obama's coattails. But this trend was reversed in 2010, with Republicans winning a majority of seats in the House of Representatives and increasing their numbers in the U.S. Senate.

The partisan breakdown of Congress is important because most major legislative votes cast are "party votes," meaning that most members of one political party vote one way, and most members of the other party vote the other way. In some cases, this divide is due to the differing ideologies. In other instances, party voting is simply pure partisanship: Democrats vote against something because Republicans vote for it and vice versa. For example, in 2009, when Congress voted to overhaul the nation's health care system, all 60 Democrats in the Senate voted for the bill, and all 39 Republicans voted against it (Senator Jim Bunning, a Republican, did not vote). Similarly, in the House of Representatives, only one of 216 Republicans supported the measure, whereas all 219 Democrats voted for it.

Partisan voting increased after the Watergate scandal in the 1970s and rose again after the 1994 congressional elections, in which Republicans took control of Congress. Partisan voting tends to be particularly acrimonious immediately before congressional and presidential elections. It occurs more often when members are voting on domestic policy issues, such as environmental or economic regulatory policy and entitlement programs, that tend

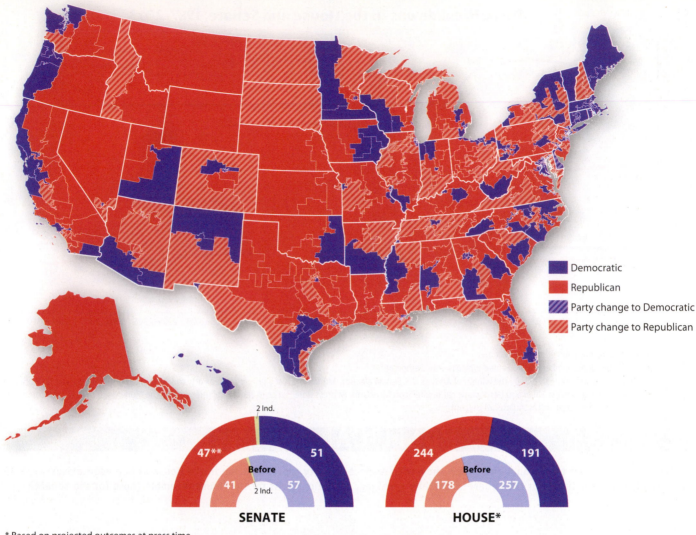

Democratic

Republican

Party change to Democratic

Party change to Republican

SENATE

2 Ind.

47** | 51

Before

41 | 57

2 Ind.

HOUSE*

244 | 191

Before

178 | 257

* Based on projected outcomes at press time.

** Senator Lisa Murkowski appeared to be the winner of Alaska's U.S. Senate election. Murkowski lost a primary to Tea Party candidate Joe Miller, but Murkowski launched a write-in campaign against Miller and Democratic candidate Scott McAdams. At press time, "write-in candidate" (presumed to be Murkowski) held 41 percent of the vote to Miller's 34 percent and McAdams' 24 percent.

POLITICAL INQUIRY

FIGURE 11.3 ■ PARTY REPRESENTATION IN THE HOUSE OF REPRESENTATIVES, 2011 How many seats in the house do the Republicans have as a result of the 2010 election? How many seats do the Democrats have? Which party has the majority? Given the party of the president, how do you think the new House composition might affect lawmaking?

to crystallize ideological differences between the parties, as the health care bill did. But often, partisan votes are politically motivated, plain and simple. One of the most partisan votes on record in Congress was the 1998 vote on whether President Bill Clinton should be impeached. In that vote, 98 percent of all members of Congress voted the party line—Republicans for impeachment, Democrats against.

Scholars believe that changes in how congressional district maps are drawn partly explains increased partisan voting in the House of Representatives. In earlier times, redistricting occurred through a simple redrawing of the lines of a congressional district to accommodate population changes. But today, with the widespread use of computer-driven mapmaking technology, congressional seats can be configured to ensure a "safe seat"—one in which the party identification of the majority of a district's voters makes it likely that a candidate from a given party will win election. Sometimes, for example, more than 60 percent of a district's population identifies with one political party. A House member holding a safe seat generally can be partisan with immunity because his or her constituency often agrees with the representative's partisan stance. In contrast, when congressional districts were more competitive, a House member typically would have to temper partisan impulses to placate the sizeable proportion of his or her constituency that identified with the opposing party. Today, that is no longer the case, and it appears that Republicans in the House of Representatives have become more conservative and their Democratic counterparts have become increasingly liberal. Consequently, House members are less likely to compromise or to be moderate in their positions in negotiating issues with the opposition.

Many scholars assert that a similar bifurcation of political ideology has not occurred in the Senate. They claim that because state populations as a whole tend to be more ideologically diverse and less homogeneous than House districts, U.S. senators often must temper their views to reflect the wider range of their constituents' perspectives. Thus senators tend to be more willing to compromise and to take a more moderate stance in negotiating with the opposing party than their House counterparts. Nonetheless, on some issues, other scholars note that the Senate is increasingly dividing along strongly partisan lines.[33] In the 2006 Senate confirmation hearings for Supreme Court nominee Samuel Alito, Democrats opposed Alito's nomination, fearing that the conservative judge would provide the swing vote to overturn the landmark Supreme Court ruling *Roe v. Wade,* which legalized abortion in the United States. In the Senate's vote to confirm Alito, forty out of forty-four Democratic senators voted against Alito's confirmation, whereas all but one of the fifty-four Republicans (Rhode Island senator Lincoln Chafee) voted for Alito's confirmation.

Partisanship in Congress

THEN (1980s)	NOW (2011)
Congress was divided; Democrats controlled the House of Representatives, and Republicans controlled the Senate.	Congress is divided; Republicans control the House of Representatives and Democrats control the Senate.
Although incumbents enjoyed a considerable advantage, many congressional districts were a mix of constituents of both major parties.	Fewer congressional districts are competitive. Many districts are more homogeneous because district boundaries can be drawn with sophisticated computer programs.
Partisan voting was evident, but legislators were often forced to base their positions on constituent preferences in addition to their own party loyalty.	With the advent of less competitive districts, legislators are more partisan than their predecessors.

WHAT'S NEXT?

> Has the outcome of the 2010 elections increased or decreased party tensions, in your view? Why?

> In recent years, partisanship has increased when there has been a president of one party and a Congress of another. Does such a scenario exist today? What implications does that have for the future of partisanship in Congress for the next several years?

> Increases in technological sophistication could make redistricting an even more exact science. What impact would this have on partisanship in Congress?

Colleagues and Staff: Trading Votes and Information

Congressional colleagues provide cues for members of the House and the Senate in their decision making over whether to vote for a pending piece of legislation. Members may seek the opinions of like-minded colleagues in determining how to vote on a proposed bill. In addition, legislators may consult with peers who are policy experts, such as Senator Tom Harkin (D-Iowa) and Senator Mike Enzi (R-Wyoming), both of whom are recognized as health care policy experts.

Members of Congress also engage in **logrolling,** the practice of trading votes between members. Logrolling is a reciprocal tactic by which a member agrees to vote on one piece of legislation in exchange for a colleague's vote on another.

logrolling
the practice in which members of Congress agree to vote for a bill in exchange for their colleague's vote on another bill

In addition, House and Senate members rely on their staffs to inform their decision making on legislation.[34] Staff members frequently have policy expertise that can guide a legislator's decision on an upcoming vote. They also figure in the legislative voting process by communicating with legislators about the desires of constituents and interest groups with respect to a pending piece of legislation.

Interest Groups: Influence Through Organization

In various ways, interest groups also influence congressional elections. They can affect electoral outcomes, for example, through an endorsement process by which a group notifies its members that it backs a certain candidate in the hope that members get on the bandwagon and express their support at the polls. In addition, through their political action committees, interest groups make financial contributions to congressional campaigns. And interest groups whose memberships are mobilized to support or oppose a candidate often provide grassroots activists to political campaigns.[35]

As we considered in Chapter 7, interest groups also shape the legislative process. They make their mark by influencing congressional campaigns, by providing information to members of Congress as they try to decide whether to vote for a particular piece of legislation, and by lobbying members of Congress to support or oppose legislation.[36]

The President's Effect on Decision Making

As we have seen, the president determines whether to sign or to veto legislation that reaches his desk. But often, before a bill reaches the signing stage, the president's position on it carries enough influence to sway members of Congress, particularly members of his political party, to vote for or against the proposed legislation.

The president can compel congressional action on an issue. Consider, for example, the issue of health care. President Obama challenged the Congress in 2009 to reform the nation's health care system, and it was this initiative that spurred Congress to consider overhauling this structure.

Constituents: The Last Word

Of all the players with a voice in the legislative process, congressional constituents—the people whom the members of Congress represent—wield perhaps the strongest, if indirect, influence with respect to congressional decision making. Most members of Congress want to be reelected, and representing constituents' views (and being able to convince voters that their views are represented well) is a major avenue to reelection to Congress. Thus constituents influence the legislative process by ensuring that their representatives in Congress work hard to represent their perspectives and policy interests, whether those concerns are over environmental pollution, crime, or the soaring cost of higher education.

In fact, some research shows that the public's "potential preferences" can motivate legislators to espouse a policy position likely to be embraced by constituents.[37] But other research shows that most voters are not espe-

TABLE 11.5

Demographic Characteristics of the 111th Congress Compared to the U.S. Population

	House (%)	Senate (%)	Population (%)
PARTY			
Democrat	58	57	34
Republican	42	41	29
Independent Unaffiliated	0	2	37
AVERAGE AGE	57 years	63 years	37 years
SEX			
Male	83	83	49
Female	17	17	51
RACE			
White	85	95	81
Black	9	1	13
Hispanic (any race)	6	1	14
Asian/Pacific Is.	2	2	3.5
Native American	.22	0	0.7
EDUCATION			
Bachelor's degree	94	99	27
Master's degree	20	17	7
Law degree	39	57	1
PhD	6	0	1
MD	4	3	2

SOURCES: Jennifer E. Manning, *Membership in the 111th Congress: A Profile* (Washington, DC: Congressional Research Service), www.senate.gov/CRSReports/crs-publish.cfm?pid=%260BL) PL%3B%3D%0A, U.S. Census Bureau, *The Statistical Abstract of the United States*.

cially vigilant when it comes to monitoring their elected officials in Congress. In fact, only a very small percentage of voters, sometimes called the **attentive public,** pay careful attention to the public policies being debated by Congress and to the votes cast by their representatives and senators. But the fact that the attentive public is a relatively small minority does not mean that votes taken in Congress are insignificant as far as constituents' opinions go. Indeed, if a member of Congress should disregard constituents' views in voting on a major issue, it is quite likely that an opposing candidate or political party will bring this misstep to the public's attention during the individual's next congressional campaign.

The People and Their Elected Representatives

Although members of Congress may make it a priority to represent the viewpoints and interests of their constituents, demographically speaking, they do not represent the American public at large. As Table 11.5 shows, Congress, especially the Senate, is older, whiter, more educated, and more likely to be male than the population as a whole. That said, Congress is not designed to be a perfect sampling of American demographics.[38] It is logical that the leaders of government would more closely resemble individuals who have achieved leadership positions in other realms, such as the corporate world and academia.

Yet importantly, Congress is more diverse today than at any other point in history. Figure 11.4 shows that most states have women as part of their congressional delegation. But the proportion of women in Congress is not nearly equal to their proportion in the national population. In 2010, at least 70 women were elected to the House of Representatives (with the races of four additional women too close to call at press time), including 12 new women.

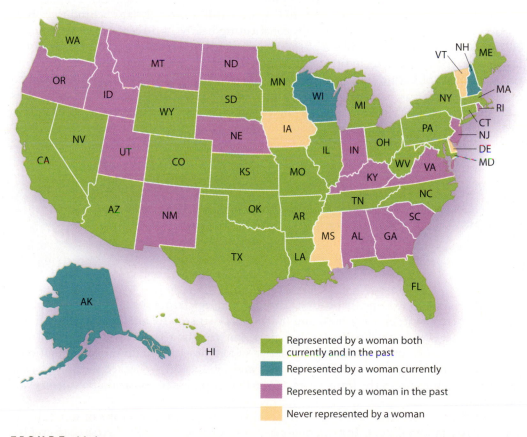

FIGURE 11.4

States Represented by Women in the U.S. Congress

African Americans in the House of Representatives

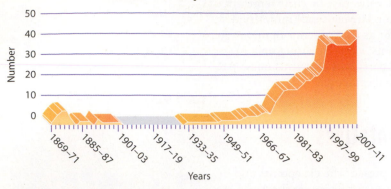

POLITICAL INQUIRY

FIGURE 11.5 ■ What explains the rise in African American representation in the House from 1871 through 1887? Why did blacks' representation fall after 1877? What pattern do you see since the late 1960s, and what political and social changes explain it?

Despite this upward trend, the United States lags behind many industrialized democracies with respect to the proportion of women serving in the national legislature.

Similarly, African Americans have historically been underrepresented in Congress. To date, only five African Americans have served in the Senate, including two, Hiram Revels and Blanche Bruce, who served during the Reconstruction era that followed the Civil War. After Bruce left the Senate in 1881, no other African American would be elected to the Senate until 1967, when Senator Edward Brooke (R-Massachusetts) was elected for one term. More recently, Senator Carol Moseley Braun (D-Illinois) was elected in 1992 and served for one term, and Barack Obama was elected from the state of Illinois in 2004. Today, the only African American in the U.S. Senate is Senator Roland Burris (D-Illinois). Burris's controversial appointment to the Senate seat, formerly held by Barack Obama, came in the wake of a major corruption scandal involving the man who appointed Burris to the seat, then Illinois governor Rod Blagojevich.

Figure 11.5 (on page 360) traces the increasing success of African Americans in getting elected to the House of Representatives. The figure shows that as in the Senate, African Americans' initial service in the House came about in the Reconstruction period. But the successes of that era were short-lived, and the numbers of African Americans in Congress would not match those of the immediate post-Reconstruction period until after the civil rights movement of the 1960s. Today, as in the case of women, more African Americans serve in Congress than at any other point in U.S. history.

Latinos' success at winning election to Congress still drastically lags behind their proportion of the population, with Latinos constituting nearly 14 percent of the population but just 6 percent of the members of the House of Representatives and 1 percent of the Senate. But many states, including New Mexico, California, Texas, and Arizona, are seeing rising numbers of Latinos elected to state legislatures, providing a pool of candidates who could move on to run for Congress. As women, African Americans, and ethnic minorities take up an increasing proportion of the eligibility pool—the group of people deemed qualified for office—diversity in Congress is sure to grow.

CONCLUSION

THINKING CRITICALLY ABOUT WHAT'S NEXT IN CONGRESS

Congress is an ever-evolving institution. The national legislature is shaped by the framers' vision that created it; by the groups and individuals that seek to, and do, influence it; and by the broader electorate who vote for the representatives who serve in it. The Constitution's framers ingeniously created a strong legislative system designed to dominate the national government. In doing so, they simultaneously—and significantly—checked the power of the executive. Do the checks the framers created enable Congress to constrain presidential action today?

The framers ensured that the legislative branch of the federal government would be responsive to changing times. Today, Congress is more demographically diverse than ever before in history. It has also responded to modern challenges by exercising a wider scope of powers, concerned with issues that were unimaginable even two decades ago, let alone more than two centuries ago. Congressional decision making today is influenced by shifting constituencies in a country that is rapidly growing more diverse. How will continued increasing diversity affect congressional decision making in the future?

With Congress well structured to respond to constituents' needs, ongoing technological advances and the spread of cheap technology to more and more citizens mean that members of Congress and their staffs should be increasingly accessible to the people. And representatives' district offices will continue to provide constituents another easily accessed channel through which to convey their needs and interests to their representatives—and through which their representatives, in turn, can monitor the opinions of their constituents so that they may better represent them.

Congress has proved itself to be a remarkably flexible institution, responding to changes in society, shifting constituencies, and increasingly diverse members, particularly in recent times. That Congress will become even more diverse is relatively assured.

Summary

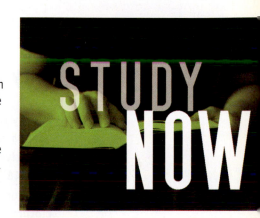

1. The Origins of Congress

The Constitution's framers intended Congress to be the strongest and most important branch of the federal government, a body both representative and deliberative. They structured the national legislature in such a way as to ensure both a check on the power of the executive and a voice for the people. The Constitution provided a flexible framework for the evolution of Congress to meet changing times. That framework continues to this day to shape the structural and procedural differences between the House of Representatives and the Senate, including the two houses' respective sizes, rules, and processes.

2. Congressional Elections

One of the most important factors shaping congressional elections is incumbency, which confers numerous advantages to those already serving in elective office. Congressional elections are also shaped by the processes of reapportionment and redistricting, which occur every ten years.

3. Powers of Congress

The Constitution enumerates certain powers for Congress, including judicial, economic, national security, regulatory, and administrative powers. Other powers of the federal legislature have evolved through national legislators' interpretation of the Constitution's necessary and proper clause, which has been a mechanism for the expansion of congressional authority.

4. Functions of Congress

The primary functions of Congress are public policy making, popular representation, oversight of the executive branch to ensure the proper administration of laws, civic education, and management of societal conflict. In their representation function, members of Congress may follow the instructed delegate model or the trustee model of representation.

5. The House and the Senate Compared

Members of the House of Representatives and the Senate serve different constituencies for different terms of office. House members are elected for a two-year term from a congressional district, and senators serve for a six-year term and represent an entire state. With respect to the legislative structure and environment, the House, with its larger size (435 members today), is more formal, and the Senate (100 members) is less formal.

6. The Legislative Process

A member of the House or the Senate can introduce a bill, the precursor to a law. Once proposed, the bill is then referred to a committee, where it is debated, reviewed, and amended. If it passes out of committee, it is debated by the full chamber; if it passes in both the House and the Senate, the president may sign the bill, veto it, or take no action. By far, most bills introduced do not become law.

7. Congressional Leadership

House leadership consists of the Speaker of the House of Representatives and the House majority and minority leaders, plus the majority and minority whips. In practice, the Senate majority leader wields the power in the upper chamber of the national legislature. Frequently, the skills demonstrated by various leaders in Congress reflect the needs of their chambers—quiet fortitude in some circumstances, adept partisanship in others.

8. Decision Making in Congress: The Legislative Context

Political parties, congressional colleagues, interest groups, the president, and constituent viewpoints all influence members of Congress. In recent years, partisanship has increased in Congress, making legislators' debates more rancorous and divisive.

9. The People and Their Elected Representatives

Although Congress is not demographically representative of the United States, it is more demographically diverse than the leadership structure of other institutions. Nonetheless, Congress is becoming increasingly diverse, with higher proportions of women, African Americans, and Latinos serving today than ever before.

Key Terms

agency review 349
agenda setting 345
attentive public 358
bill 346
casework 343
cloture 351
conference committee 351
discharge petition 350
earmark 343
filibuster 350
gerrymandering 340
hearings 349
hopper 346
House majority leader 352
House minority leader 353

instructed delegate model 342
joint committee 349
joint referral 347
lead committee 349
logrolling 357
majority whip 352
majority-minority district 340
markup 350
minority whip 353
ombudsperson 343
oversight 344
pocket veto 351
pork barrel 343

president pro tempore 354
reapportionment 339
redistricting 340
report 350
Rules Committee 350
select committee 349
Senate majority leader 354
Senate minority leader 354
seniority system 349
Speaker of the House 352
standing committee 349
subcommittee 349
trustee model 342
unanimous consent 350

For Review

1. Why was Congress created in the way it was?

2. What impact does incumbency have on congressional elections?

3. What is the difference between reapportionment and redistricting?

4. Historically, what has been the impact of the necessary and proper (elastic) clause?

5. Describe the two types of congressional powers.

6. What impact do the constitutionally enumerated duties of the House and the Senate have on the expertise of each chamber?

7. Outline the basic steps of the legislative process.

8. What factors influence the legislative process? How?

9. Why are so many bills introduced but so few passed?

10. How do the qualities of congressional leaders differ today from those needed in earlier eras?

11. Why has party-line voting increased in Congress in recent years?

For Critical Thinking and Discussion

1. If you were serving in Congress, would you tend to follow the instructed delegate model of representation or the trustee model? Why? What might be the likely outcome of your choice?

2. How does the legislative process differ in the House and the Senate? In which chamber is the process more streamlined? More deliberative? Why?

3. What do you and the people you know think about the work and contributions of Congress? Would you give Congress high or low approval ratings as an institution, or something in between? Who is your own congressional representative, and what rating would you give her or him? Why?

4. Log on to the Library of Congress Web site (http://thomas.loc.gov/) and read about issues currently on the floor of the House of Representatives. Can you see the impact of any of the external influences mentioned in this chapter on the legislative process? Describe those influences and discuss how they are shaping the process.

5. Why do you think so few women and racial and ethnic minorities have been elected to Congress? Why is this situation changing? What do you imagine that Congress will look like, demographically speaking, in the year 2050?

PRACTICE QUIZ

MULTIPLE CHOICE: Choose the lettered item that answers the question correctly.

1. Reallocation of seats in the House of Representatives to each state based on changes in the state's population since the last census is called
   a. earmarking.
   b. reapportionment.
   c. gerrymandering.
   d. redistricting.

2. Redrawing congressional district boundaries within each state is called
   a. earmarking.
   b. reapportionment.
   c. gerrymandering.
   d. redistricting.

3. A model of representation that says that a member of Congress should vote for the position that best represents his or her constituents' view even if the legislator does not share those views is called
   a. the instructed delegate model.
   b. the logrolling model.
   c. the trustee model.
   d. the pork barrel model.

4. The process by which the legislative branch checks the executive branch to ensure that the laws Congress passed are being administered in keeping with the legislature's intent is called
   a. oversight.
   b. earmarking.
   c. gerrymandering.
   d. agenda setting.

5. Differences between the House and the Senate do not include
   a. the Senate being more prestigious than the House.
   b. the Senate being larger than the House.
   c. the Senate being more reliant on staff than the House.
   d. the Senate having broader constituencies than the House.

6. A primary committee considering a bill is called
   a. a standing committee.
   b. a subcommittee.
   c. a select committee.
   d. a lead committee.

7. The system in which the member with the longest continuous tenure on a standing committee is given preference when the committee chooses its chair is called
   a. the spoils system.
   b. the patronage system.
   c. the seniority system.
   d. the last man standing principle.

8. A congressional committee created to consider specific policy issues or address a specific concern is called
   a. a standing committee.
   b. a subcommittee.
   c. a select committee.
   d. a joint committee.

9. A special tactic used to extract a bill from a committee to have it considered by the entire House is called
   a. a report.
   b. markup.
   c. filibuster.
   d. a discharge petition.

10. A procedural move in which a supermajority of sixty senators agrees to end a filibuster is called
    a. cloture.
    b. unanimous consent.
    c. a discharge petition.
    d. senatorial courtesy.

FILL IN THE BLANKS.

11. A designation within a spending bill that provides for a specific expenditure is called a(n) _____ .

12. A role in which an elected or appointed leader acts as an advocate for citizens by listening to and investigating complaints about a government agency is called a(n) _____ .

13. A proposed piece of legislation is called a _____ .

14. A legislative committee's explanation to the full chamber of a bill and its intent is called a _____ .

15. _____ is an agreement by every senator to the terms of debate on a given piece of legislation.

RESOURCES FOR RESEARCH AND ACTION

Internet Resources

Congressional Quarterly
www.cq.org *Congressional Quarterly (CQ)* is an important provider of news and analysis for Washington insiders, but its Web site is a subscriber site. Nonetheless, free trial subscriptions are available. Its job opportunities site, www.cq.com/corp/show.do?page=corp _hilljobs, is not password protected.

C-Span
www.c-span.org The cable television network C-Span provides a plethora of information on Congress, including Internet video, audio, and podcast programs of congressional hearings, committee meetings, C-Span video series, and a wide variety of public affairs information.

Library of Congress
http://thomas.loc.gov (note the absence of www) Thomas (named for Thomas Jefferson) is the Web site for the Library of Congress, the most important clearinghouse for information about Congress, legislation, hearings, votes, and other federal matters.

Roll Call
www.rollcall.com This Web site for *Roll Call,* the "newspaper of Capitol Hill since 1955," offers an insider's look at the world of Capitol Hill, including issue analysis, politics, and opinions.

U.S. Senate and U.S. House of Representatives
www.senate.gov and **www.house.gov** These Web sites for the Senate and the House provide information about members of Congress, votes, pending legislation, committees, and session schedules, plus information about the Capitol and information for visitors.

Internet Activism

Twitter
Follow HouseFloor and SenateFloor for congressional proceedings. Go to www.congressional140.com/tweeting.php for a list of all members of Congress on Twitter.

YouTube
YouTube's househub and senatehub channels provide an organized platform for citizens to access YouTube videos from members of Congress.

Recommended Readings

Ahuja, Sunil. *Congress Behaving Badly: The Rise of Partisanship and Incivility and the Death of Public Trust.* Santa Barbara, CA: Praeger, 2008. This analysis examines the causes and the results of increased party cleavages in Congress.

Dodd, Lawrence C., and Bruce J. Oppenheimer. *Congress Reconsidered,* 8th ed. Washington, DC: CQ Press, 2008. The most recent edition of a classic series providing comprehensive coverage of the evolution of the American Congress.

Fenno, Richard F., Jr. *Home Style: House Members in Their Districts.* New York: Longman, 2009. Fenno traveled the United States observing members of Congress at home in their districts and explains how constituent interaction affects congressional decision making.

Loomis, Burdett, and Wendy J. Schiller. *The Contemporary Congress.* Belmont, CA: Wadsworth, 2005. A concise yet comprehensive analysis of Congress, particularly the legislative context that influences the legislative process.

O'Neill, Thomas P. *Man of the House: The Life and Political Memoirs of Speaker Tip O'Neill.* New York: Random House, 1987. The political memoir of a long-term Speaker of the House of Representatives, providing a fascinating glimpse into the "real world" of Capitol Hill politics from the 1960s through the 1980s.

Sulkin, Tracy. *Issue Politics in Congress.* New York: Cambridge University Press, 2005. An examination of the issue of representation through the rubric of issue politics—that is, why legislators adopt the issue stances they do.

Thomas, Sue. *How Women Legislate.* New York: Oxford University Press, 1994. Groundbreaking analysis of the differences and similarities between how men and women approach the task of legislating.

Waxman, Henry. *The Waxman Report: How Congress Really Works.* Amazon Kindle edition, 2009. One of the liberal icons of the U.S. House of Representatives shares experiences from his 35-year tenure in Congress.

Movies of Interest

The Congress (1988)
This Ken Burns documentary provides a fine introduction to the U.S. Congress (both the institution and the Capitol building). Burns traces the history of the institution and the people who have served in it, including nineteenth-century statesmen Henry Clay and Daniel Webster and continuing to Congress's modern leaders.

The Ugly American (1963)
This drama stars Marlon Brando as Harrison Carter MacWhite, who, after surviving an acrimonious Senate confirmation hearing, becomes ambassador to a Southeast Asian nation on the brink of civil war.

Mr. Smith Goes to Washington
(1939) This classic Frank Capra movie features Jimmy Stewart as Jefferson Smith, who, after the death of a senator, is appointed to serve in the U.S. Senate despite his political naïveté. Stewart's depiction of a filibuster informs most Americans' perception of this political maneuver.

The Presidency

THEN

Presidential power grew over the centuries to "imperial" proportions and then ebbed in the late twentieth century in the wake of scandals.

NOW

The power of modern presidents varies, and is affected by congressional actions and public opinion.

NEXT

Will future presidents continue down the path of an imperial presidency?

What checks will constrain future presidents' exercise of power?

How will the relationship between presidents and the people change in the future?

In this chapter, we survey the election, functions, and powers of American presidents and analyze the complex relationship between presidents and the people. We also examine the evolution of presidential powers over time, including the idea of an "imperial presidency."

FIRST, we look at the process of *presidential elections.*

SECOND, we focus on *presidential roles in the domestic sphere.*

THIRD, we study *presidential roles in the foreign policy sphere.*

FOURTH, we consider points of *overlap in the president's domestic and foreign policy roles.*

FIFTH, we turn attention to *the president and the executive branch* and consider the key offices that influence the president in making and carrying out public policy.

SIXTH, we review the formal procedures in place for *presidential succession.*

SEVENTH, we explore the *sources of presidential power,* including constitutional, statutory, and emergency powers; executive privilege; and the power to issue executive orders.

EIGHTH, we examine *the people as a source of presidential power.*

NINTH, we trace *the evolution of presidential power* from the administration of George Washington to the present day, analyzing in particular the development of what some analysts have called the imperial presidency.

TENTH, we shift the focus to *evaluating presidential leadership.*

ELEVENTH, we probe the various roles of *women in the White House* and anticipate the likelihood that a woman will be elected president in the future.

Each presidency is shaped not

only by the person who holds the office but also by the support of constituencies within the public, the support of Congress for presidential policy priorities, and the societal context of the day. Each presidential term can be molded and manipulated in many ways, with the result that one president may appear strong, and the next, weak—or a president may be both effective and ineffectual during the course of just one term. Compare, for example, the early days of Barack Obama's presidency, when he enjoyed strong support for his policy agenda both in the Congress and among the public, with the period leading up to the 2010 midterm congressional elections, when some Democrats in Congress were hesitant to support presidential initiatives because of his lower public approval ratings. In looking at the roles presidents play in conducting their office, as well as the sources of their power, we consider in this chapter why some presidents are more effective than others.

The presidency is constantly evolving. The institution of the presidency that Barack Obama has is not the one that George Washington left behind. In the discussion that follows, we examine the development of the presidency to gain historical perspective on how the individuals who have served as president have changed the nature of the institution over time and what the impacts of those changes are for presidents today.

The presidency has changed in part because of the way this institution—which for many Americans embodies their government—has evolved.[1] We consider that even within this most "imperial" of the American institutions of government, the people play a vital part in determining not only who serves as president but also how effective and successful the president is in exercising the executive power.[2]

Presidential Elections

The relationship between Americans and their president begins well before a president takes the oath of office. In presidential election years, nonstop campaigning provides ample opportunities for the public to learn about presidential candidates and their positions on issues. Campaigns also present many avenues for participation by the people—for example, by volunteering in or contributing to candidates' campaigns or even just by debating candidates' views around the water cooler. Although these opportunities for citizen engagement are especially abundant during a presidential election year, similar chances to get involved arise well before, because potential candidates typically position themselves years in advance of Election Day to secure their party's nomination and to win the general election.

As discussed in Chapter 8, citizens in each state who vote in their party's primary election choose the delegates to the national conventions. After the nominees have been decided, typically by late August, they and their vice-presidential running mates begin their general election campaign. Usually, the parties' choice of nominee is a foregone conclusion by the time of the convention. Eligible incumbent presidents (that is, those who have served only one term) are nearly always renominated, and the nominee of the opposing party is chosen at the National Party Convention, many of the delegates to which are chosen based on the outcome of caucuses and primary elections held in the states.

The votes tallied on Election Day determine which presidential candidate's slate of electors will cast their ballots, in accordance with state law. There are 538 electors in the

SHOULD WE ABOLISH THE ELECTORAL COLLEGE?

The Issue: The 2000 presidential election saw a historically unlikely but obviously possible occurrence: the candidate with the most popular votes, Democrat Al Gore, lost the presidential election to his opponent, Republican George W. Bush. In every other election for federal office, the candidate with the most popular votes wins that seat. But instead of the direct election of the president, the Constitution requires that the president be elected by the Electoral College. Essentially, the winner is determined by the cumulative results of fifty-one separate elections, one conducted in each state plus the District of Columbia, with the number of electoral votes determined in proportion to the size of the state's congressional delegation.

Is the Electoral College system unfair? Should we abolish it?

Yes: The Electoral College is exclusive and undemocratic. The Electoral College system demands that candidates focus nearly exclusively on key swing states that will be pivotal to their election and on populous states that carry the most electoral votes. The system is undemocratic because of its reliance on plurality elections within the states. In a plurality, the candidate with the most votes wins, even if that candidate does not receive a majority of the votes. The ultimate victory in the 2000 presidential election by the candidate (George W. Bush) whom the most people did not prefer highlights the undemocratic nature of the Electoral College. The Electoral College should be abolished.

No: The constitutionally mandated Electoral College system provides a crucial check on what would otherwise be the unchecked will of the people. In structuring the Electoral College as they did, the Constitution's framers devised a way of representing the views of both the *people* who elect the electors and the *states* because of the state-based nature of the elections. Other checks on the will of the people include staggered senatorial elections (in which one-third of that body is elected every two years) and appointed Supreme Court justices, and these are evidence of the framers' view that the will of the people needed to be tempered. If the Electoral College were abolished, the most populous geographical regions would dominate in presidential elections. Urban areas would have tremendous clout in presidential elections, and less densely populated rural areas would be virtually ignored. The current structure strengthens the power of the states and in this way ensures that our federal system remains strong.

Other approaches: Because of the difficulty of abolishing the Electoral College, various schemes have been proposed that would make it almost impossible for the loser of the popular vote to win the presidency, including awarding a state's electoral votes proportionally instead of on a winner-take-all basis, dividing electoral votes by congressional district (currently done in Maine and Nebraska), and awarding extra electoral votes to the winner of the popular vote. Legislation recently passed in Maryland, Hawaii, Illinois, and New Jersey would commit those states' electors to vote for the winner of the popular vote if states representing a 270-vote majority in the Electoral College enact similar legislation.

What do you think?

① Do you think that the Electoral College should be abolished, should remain the same, or should be reformed? Why? If your answer is "should be reformed," what changes would you implement?

② If the Electoral College were abolished, what impact would the change likely have on voters in your home state? Does that scenario influence your view?

③ Americans revere the Constitution as a near-sacred document. Typically, citizens are reluctant to advocate amending the "supreme law of the land." What is your view concerning amending the Constitution?

Electoral College because the number of electors is based on the number of members of Congress—435 in the House of Representatives, 100 in the Senate—plus three electors who represent the people of the District of Columbia. (See "Thinking Critically About Democracy.") A presidential candidate today needs a simple majority of votes (270) to win the presidency. On the Monday following the second Wednesday of December, the slate of electors chosen in each state meets in their respective state capitals and casts their electoral votes. The results are then announced in a joint session of Congress in early January. In most presidential elections, however, the winner is known on election night because analysts tabulate the outcome in each state and predict the electoral vote. The winner takes the oath of office as president in inaugural ceremonies on January 20.

Presidential Roles in the Domestic Sphere

A newly elected president quickly discovers that the presidential office requires the performance of a variety of functions each day. Many of these roles involve leadership in domestic policy issues,[3] whether it is Barack Obama's desire to overhaul health care, George W. Bush's priority of reforming schools, or all presidents' need to keep the economy sound and growing strongly. As leaders in the domestic sphere, presidents must interact with Congress, manage the economy, and serve as the leader of their party.[4]

Chief Legislator

Although the separation of powers precludes the president from actually creating laws, presidents nonetheless have significant legislative power.[5] Presidents can influence Congress by lobbying its members to support or oppose pending legislation and by defining the congressional agenda in the annual presidential State of the Union message, a constitutionally required address to Congress. Presidents also "legislate" when they submit the budget for the entire federal government to Congress annually, although Congress ultimately passes the spending plan.

Today, one of the most important legislative tools at a president's disposal is the authority either to sign legislation into law or to veto it,[6] as described in Chapter 2. Although a veto allows the president to check the power of Congress, it also provides Congress with the opportunity to check presidential power by overriding the veto with a two-thirds majority vote.[7] In giving the president the right to veto laws, the Constitution essentially integrates the executive into the legislative process.[8]

As discussed in Chapter 11, there are several variations on the veto. During a regular legislative session, if the president does not sign or veto a bill within ten days after receiving it from Congress, the bill becomes law even without the president's consent. But if the president receives a congressional bill for his signature and Congress is scheduled to adjourn within ten days, the president can exercise a pocket veto by taking no action at all. Further, during the presidency of Bill Clinton, Congress statutorily equipped the president with a new kind of veto power: the **line-item veto** allowed the president to strike out specific line items on an appropriations bill while allowing the rest of the bill to become law. In 1997, however, the Supreme Court declared the line-item veto unconstitutional, asserting that it violated the separation of powers because the Constitution grants Congress the inherent power to tax and to spend.

Figure 12.1 shows that the use of the veto varies widely from president to president. Modern presidents are generally much more likely to veto legislation than their predecessors were. A primary determinant of whether a president will regularly exercise veto power is whether the president's party has a majority in Congress.

An exception to this trend was the presidency of Franklin D. Roosevelt. As Figure 12.1 shows, during Roosevelt's twelve-year term in the White House, he issued 372 vetoes, or 12 percent of all presidential vetoes. Roosevelt chalked up this exceptional record despite having strong Democratic majorities in Congress throughout his tenure. But Roosevelt used the veto much differently than most presidents do. Because he was such a strong president, he exercised his veto power to prevent the passage of even small pieces of legislation with which he disagreed. Most presidents save the veto for important legislative matters, because they are unwilling to offend members of Congress over smaller laws that they do not favor.

President George W. Bush vetoed relatively few (fifteen) pieces of legislation during his two terms of office. His first veto came in 2006, when a congressionally passed measure that would have eased restrictions on federal funding for stem cell research reached Bush's desk. One explanation for Bush's scant use of vetoes is that while the Republicans controlled Congress, Bush did not need to veto legislation often because he effectively persuaded Congress to act on his legislative priorities. (See "Analyzing the Sources") Indeed, ten of President Bush's eleven successful vetoes occurred after the Democrats took control of Congress in 2006.

But President Bush used a different tactic—the signing statement—to put his mark on the way policies were to be administered during his tenure of office. A presidential **signing**

line-item veto
power of the president to strike out specific line items on an appropriations bill while allowing the rest of the bill to become law; declared unconstitutional by the Supreme Court in 1997

signing statement
a written message that the president issues upon signing a bill into law

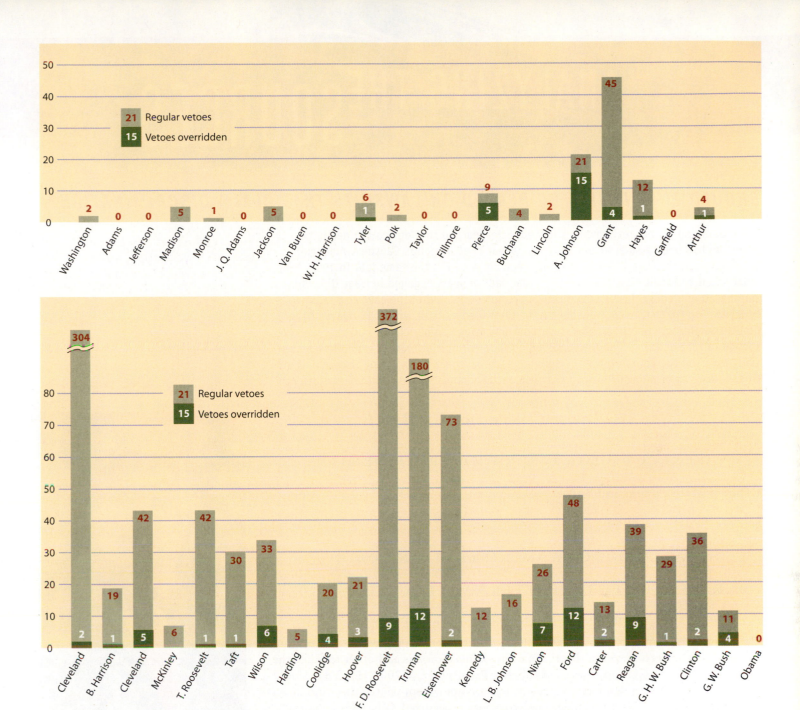

FIGURE 12.1 ■ PRESIDENTIAL VETOES, 1789–2010 What does this graph generally indicate about the use of the presidential veto over time? What trend is evident in presidents' use of the veto from the administration of Franklin Roosevelt to the present? Why do you think a president is more likely to veto legislation when one party controls Congress and the other controls the presidency?

statement is a written message that the president issues upon signing a bill into law. A presidential signing statement may, for example, direct executive departments in how they should implement a law, taking into account constitutional or political considerations. Controversy arose over the perception that the president used the tool of the signing statement to modify the intent of the laws. Critics, including the American Bar Association, complained that by using signing statements, President Bush was asserting unconstitutional legislative authority, and some critics compared the presidential directives to

ANALYZING THE SOURCES

SHOULD TIME LIMITS BE PLACED ON LAWSUITS THAT CLAIM DISCRIMINATION?

While planning for her retirement, Lilly Ledbetter learned that during the nearly twenty years she had been a salaried worker in Goodyear Tire Company's Gadsden, Alabama, plant, she had received less pay than had men employed in the same job. In 1998, Ledbetter filed a lawsuit claiming that Goodyear had for years engaged in wage discrimination based on gender. In 2007, the U.S. Supreme Court ruled in the case *Ledbetter v. Goodyear Tire Co.* that because Ledbetter had not filed her suit within 180 days of the first discriminatory paycheck, the statute of limitations on her claims had passed. In response to that decision, Congress in 2008 considered legislation that would have essentially reversed the Court's ruling by defining each paycheck as an act of discrimination. What follows are the positions of two presidential administrations on this legislation:

President George W. Bush

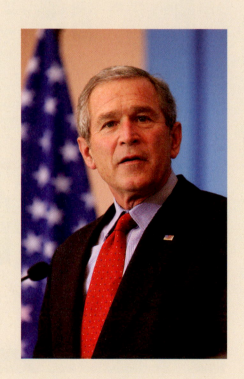

EXECUTIVE OFFICE OF THE PRESIDENT

Office of Management and Budget   Washington, D.C. 20503

July 27, 2007 (House Rules)

STATEMENT OF ADMINISTRATION POLICY

H.R. 2831–LILLY LEDBETTER FAIR PAY ACT OF 2007

(Rep. Miller (D) CA and 31 cosponsors)

The Administration supports our Nation's anti-discrimination laws and is committed to the timely resolution of discrimination claims. For this and other reasons, the Administration strongly opposes the Ledbetter Fair Pay Act of 2007. H.R. 2831 would allow employees to bring a claim of pay or other employment-related discrimination years or even decades after the alleged discrimination occurred. H.R. 2831 constitutes a major change in, and expanded application of, employment discrimination law. The change would serve to impede justice and undermine the important goal of having allegations of discrimination expeditiously resolved. Furthermore, the effective elimination of any statute of limitations in this area would be contrary to the centuries-old notion of a limitations period for all lawsuits. If H.R. 2831 were presented to the President, his senior advisors would recommend that he veto the bill.

. . . H.R. 2831 purports to undo the Supreme Court's decision of May 29, 2007, in *Ledbetter v. Goodyear Tire & Rubber Co.* by permitting pay discrimination claims to be brought within 180 days not of a discriminatory pay decision, which is the rule under current law, but rather within 180 days of receiving any paycheck affected by such a decision, no matter how far in the past the underlying act of discrimination allegedly occurred. As a result, this legislation effectively eliminates any time requirement for filing a claim involving compensation discrimination. Allegations from thirty years ago or more could be resurrected and filed in federal courts. . . .

President Barack Obama

January 29, 2009

It's . . . fitting that we're joined today by the woman after whom this bill is named—someone who Michelle and I have had the privilege to get to know ourselves. And it is fitting that we are joined this morning by the first woman Speaker of the House of Representatives, Nancy Pelosi. . . .

Lilly Ledbetter did not set out to be a trailblazer or a household name. She was just a good hard worker who did her job—and she did it well—for nearly two decades before discovering that for years, she was paid less than her male colleagues for doing the very same work. . . .

. . . [S]he set out on a journey that would take more than ten years, take her all the way to the Supreme Court of the United States, and lead to this day and this bill which will help others get the justice that she was denied.

Because while this bill bears her name, Lilly knows that this story isn't just about her. It's the story of women across this country still earning just 78 cents for every dollar men earn—women of color even less—which means that today, in the year 2009, countless women are still losing thousands of dollars in salary, income and retirement savings over the course of a lifetime. . . .

That is what Lilly Ledbetter challenged us to do. And today, I sign this bill not just in her honor, but in the honor of those who came before—women like my grandmother, who worked in a bank all her life, and even after she hit that glass ceiling, kept getting up and giving her best every day, without complaint, because she wanted something better for me and my sister.

And I sign this bill for my daughters, and all those who will come after us, because I want them to grow up in a nation that values their contributions, where there are no limits to their dreams and they have opportunities their mothers and grandmothers never could have imagined. . . .

So thank you, Lilly Ledbetter.

Evaluating the Evidence

① How does the Bush administration shape—and justify—its threatened rejection of the Ledbetter Fair Pay Act? What is your opinion of the argument for vetoing the bill?

② How does the Obama administration frame its advocacy for the Ledbetter Fair Pay Act? What is your opinion of the argument presented in Obama's speech?

③ In his remarks upon signing the bill, President Obama refers to his wife, his grandmother, his daughters, and House Speaker Nancy Pelosi. What is the desired impact of referring to these women in his life in this speech? How might the Bush administration answer this type of appeal?

---

invoking the line-item veto in some pieces of legislation.[9] In all, President Bush issued more than 750 signing statements during his two terms of office.

Chief Economist

Although the Constitution makes no mention of presidential responsibilities with respect to the economy, submitting a budget to Congress reflects what has become another key presidential role: the manager of the economy. Of course, the president does not exert a great deal of control over the enormous national economy, but presidents have numerous tools at their disposal that powerfully influence the country's economic performance. For example, in 2009 President Obama persuaded Congress to pass a $787 billion program intended to stimulate the U.S. economy. Obama's plan came on the heels of Bush administration policies, which urged Congress in 2008 to allocate funds to bail out banking, mortgage, insurance, and financial services corporations that were at risk of failing. By submitting a budget to Congress, presidents shape where federal tax dollars are spent, and

> One way presidents try to affect the nation's economy is through the appointment of the "Fed Chief," who oversees the board that plays a crucial role in managing the economy. Federal Reserve chair Ben Bernanke, who was appointed by President Bush in 2005, was reappointed by President Obama in 2009. Bernanke is frequently called on to testify before Congress on the state of the economy and monetary policy.

thereby set the economic priorities of the legislative agenda. Presidents also help to establish the regulatory and economic environment in which businesses must operate, and in that way they can influence economic growth and employment levels.

Central in presidents' oversight of economic performance is the appointment of the Federal Reserve Board ("the Fed") and its chair, who play a crucial role in managing the economy. The position of Fed chair tends to be less partisan than many other appointments, and a given chair often serves under presidents of both political parties. In 2005, President Bush named Ben Bernanke as Fed chair, replacing Alan Greenspan, who had served for eighteen years under both Democrats and Republicans. President Obama reappointed Bernanke to a second four-year term in 2009, despite criticism that Bernanke was slow to recognize the severity of the economic crisis.[10] But many lauded Obama's reappointment of Bernanke, arguing that appointing a new, inexperienced Fed chair would be destabilizing to already-bruised markets.

The appointment of a Fed chair has a lot to do with consumer confidence, as well as with support from economically influential individuals on Wall Street, including investment bankers, stockbrokers, and mortgage lenders. The fact that reaction to a Fed action (such as increasing the interest rate that banks charge one another for loans, which affects other interest rates charged to private individuals and businesses) can send the stock market plummeting sheds light on why presidential appointments to the Fed are watched so closely.

Party Leader

One of the most important domestic roles for the president is political: the function of party leader. As chief of one of the two main parties, the president is a symbolic leader for the party members and asserts influence in the party's operations by selecting the national party chair and serving as the party's premier fund-raiser. The presidential function of party leader has become even more significant in recent White House administrations, with presidents working ever more aggressively to promote the reelection of candidates from their party by ensuring that enough money is available for their campaigns.

The president also acts as party head in the day-to-day operations of the executive branch, because many of the staff appointments to the White House Office, cabinet, subcabinet, ambassadorships, and judiciary typically come from party ranks. Finally, at the end of a president's term, he likely campaigns on behalf of his party's presidential nominee.

> In the president's role as party leader, President Barack Obama endorsed former U.S. senator Arlen Specter of Pennsylvania. Specter had switched to the Democratic party after serving as a Republican senator for decades to increase his chances of reelection in 2010. Despite the president's endorsement, Specter lost his primary bid.

Presidential Roles in the Foreign Policy Sphere

Presidential responsibilities also extend to setting and executing foreign policy. The president's foreign policy powers are for the most part constitutionally derived.[11] Specifically, the Constitution gives the pres-

GLOBAL CONTEXT

PARLIAMENTARY SYSTEMS

In the many nations of the world that have parliamentary systems, the country's chief executive—the *prime minister* or *premier*—is elected not by the people but by the members of the majority political party in the legislature. Parliamentary systems distinguish between the head of government and the head of state. The *head of government* is the prime minister or premier, the individual who leads the government in its work. The *head of state* is frequently a constitutional monarch whose duties are primarily ceremonial and symbolic. In Great Britain, Prime Minister David Cameron is the head of government, and Queen Elizabeth II is the head of state.

When compared with a presidential system such as that of the United States, parliamentary systems are viewed as being more responsive to the will of the people. Although the people do not directly elect the prime minister, the desire of members of a parliament to serve the needs of their constituents ensures that the prime minister remains responsive as well.

Although the United States' presidential system has not yet produced a woman president, female members of many parliaments around the world have succeeded in getting elected to the chief executive post—prime minister. This is the case even in nations where the political culture places less emphasis on women's equality than Americans do. Women have served as prime minister in Sri Lanka, India, Israel, the Central African Republic, Great Britain, Portugal, Bolivia, Dominica, Norway, Yugoslavia, Netherlands Antilles, New Zealand, Bermuda, Guyana, Bangladesh, Haiti, Turkey, Rwanda, Canada, Burundi, France, Nicaragua, Lithuania, and Pakistan.

Parliamentary systems lack the separation of powers between the legislative and executive branches that characterizes presidential systems. In addition, parliamentary systems are seen as more unstable than presidential systems because the governments they form often depend on coalitions made up of members of two or more parties. When those parties disagree, the coalition sometimes disintegrates.

✳ What are the trade-offs between presidential and parliamentary systems?

---

ident the authority with which to carry out the roles of chief diplomat and commander in chief of the U.S. armed forces.

Chief Diplomat

Serving in the capacity of chief diplomat, the president (along with advisers) shapes and administers the nation's foreign policy. Supported by a wide array of foreign policy resources, including the State Department, the National Security Council, the Central Intelligence Agency, and the various branches of the U.S. military, the president creates and administers foreign policy. In setting foreign policy, the president can act more unilaterally than with most domestic policies. Members of Congress, who, in reflection of their constituents' main interests, tend to be concerned primarily with domestic policy issues, are much less likely to challenge presidents in the foreign policy arena.

As chief diplomat, the president, in conjunction with his or her staff, negotiates treaties and other international agreements with foreign nations and represents the United States at international summits. The president also has the authority to enter into an **executive agreement,** a kind of international agreement. Executive agreements are based on the constitutional authority vested in the president, and, unlike treaties, they may not be binding on future presidents nor do they require Senate approval.

The Constitution also empowers the president to appoint ambassadors to other nations. As high-ranking diplomats, ambassadors are the official representatives of the United

executive agreement
international agreement between the United States and other nations, not subject to Senate approval and only in effect during the administration of the president who negotiates the agreement

States in their host nation. Ambassadors' duties vary widely, depending upon the locale of their appointment. Some ambassadors play an influential, highly visible role in carrying out U.S. foreign policy, but others remain in the background.

The president, acting in the role of chief diplomat, is the leader of the diplomatic corps. In the capacity of chief diplomat, the president also hosts state dinners at the White House and formally receives the ambassadors of other nations.

Commander in Chief

As commander in chief, the president is the supreme military commander of the U.S. Army, Navy, Air Force, Marines, and Coast Guard. Counseled by advisers, the president decides when to send troops into battle (although only Congress can formally declare war) and sets military strategy in times of both peace and war.[12] Advisers have played an important part in shaping how President Obama carries out the role of commander in chief:

> [C]ircumstances made Obama commander in chief of a nation fighting two wars. Consciously or not, he prepared himself for the transition by his choice of associates. He picked a vice president, Joe Biden, who visited the battlefronts repeatedly as chairman of the Senate Foreign Relations Committee; a secretary of state, Hillary Clinton, who immersed herself in defense issues as a member of the Senate Armed Services Committee; and a defense secretary, Bob Gates, who ran the wars for Bush. Then, most strikingly, as his national security adviser he chose not another of the academics who have customarily filled that role but a very tough retired Marine general, James L. Jones.[13]

Journalist David S. Broder argues that, shaped by the views of his advisers, Barack Obama's actions as commander in chief, including his decision to increase the number of troops in Afghanistan, vary drastically from the positions Obama espoused as a candidate. Broder also cites Obama's opposition to releasing photos of detainees abused in custody and retention of military tribunals as evidence that Obama's positions as commander in chief do not vary drastically from those of his predecessor, George W. Bush.

But a key difference between Obama and Bush has been Obama's position on the "don't ask, don't tell" policy regarding gays in the military. In his January 2010 State of the Union address, President Obama urged Congress to repeal the policy so that gays might serve openly

> In modern times, the president's role as commander in chief is particularly important. In that role, President Barack Obama has had to decide where to send troops, and how many troops should be sent. Here, Obama waves to U.S. troops during a rally at Osan Air Base in Songtan, South Korea.

in the military. But when repealing the measure was proposed as part of a larger defense bill in September, 2010, Senate Democrats failed to win the votes necessary to repeal the policy.

The role of commander in chief is often a difficult one for presidents. In 2009, President Obama announced that he would send an additional 34,000 troops into Afghanistan in an effort to secure the nation so that Afghani forces could retain control of the nation after U.S. forces leave. When asked what the most difficult decision of his presidency had been so far, Obama answered, "Ordering 17,000 additional troops into Afghanistan. There is a sobriety that comes with a decision like that because you have to expect that some of those young men and women are going to be harmed in the theater of war."[14]

Overlap in the Domestic and Foreign Policy Roles: Chief Executive and Chief of State

Some presidential functions overlap the domestic and foreign policy spheres. This spillover notably exists in the president's role as chief executive—in which the president, as head of the executive branch, appoints advisers and staff—and the role of chief of state, the ceremonial function of the president.

Chief Executive

As the nation's leader in domestic and foreign policy initiatives, the president serves as chief executive. In this capacity, the president appoints the *secretaries* (top administrators) of the cabinet—the fifteen departments of the federal government—as well as the heads of other federal government agencies charged with developing and implementing the administration's policy. As chief executive, the president also appoints other staff members and numerous advisers, including staff in the Executive Office of the President. In the capacity of chief executive, the president determines how the bureaucracy will implement the laws Congress has passed and which policies—those concerning education, crime, social welfare, and so on—will be emphasized.[15]

Chief of State

The president's role as chief of state reflects the chief executive's embodiment of the values and ideals of the nation, both within the United States and abroad. The function of chief of state is similar to the ceremonial role played by the constitutional monarch in parliamentary systems such as Great Britain's (see "Global Context" on page 375). In the United States, the role of symbolic leader of the nation enhances the president's image and authority and promotes national unity. We may experience this sense that we are one indivisible nation, for example, when the president, as chief of state, makes a formal state visit to another nation, hosts Olympic medalists at the White House, and visits the sites of national tragedies such as Ground Zero after the terrorist attacks of September 11, 2001.

The President and the Executive Branch

Because daily news reports so often showcase the president acting as head of state and chief diplomat, it is easy to overlook one of the president's primary responsibilities—administering the federal government. As chief executive, the president is constitutionally charged with ensuring that the "laws be faithfully executed." Today, this responsibility means that the president oversees a bureaucracy of more than 4 million government employees, including the members of the military, while presiding over an astonishing annual federal budget of nearly *$4 trillion*. In addition, as we now consider, the president is the leader of the executive branch of government, which includes the vice president, the cabinet, the offices within the White House, and the entire federal bureaucracy.

The Vice President's Role

John Nance Garner, Franklin D. Roosevelt's vice president from 1933 to 1941, vulgarly commented that "the vice presidency isn't worth a pitcher of warm piss."[16] This insider's observation on the vice-presidential office matches the perceptions of many Americans fairly well. But although the media and the public tend to ignore the vice presidency and to marginalize the responsibilities of the second-in-command, vice presidents have an enormously important function. They are first in the line of succession to the presidency if the president should die or become incapacitated. Only eight presidents have died while in office, and although presidential succession may not be the foremost consideration in selecting a running mate for many presidential candidates, it can be an issue. Bill Clinton, in describing his selection of Tennessee senator Al Gore as his running mate, explained that his choice of Gore in part reflected Clinton's belief that Gore would make a good president "if something happened to me."[17]

THE VICE PRESIDENT'S JOB Many vice presidents serve a largely ceremonial function, performing such activities as attending state dinners, visiting foreign nations, and attending the funerals of foreign dignitaries. But vice presidents may have more substantive responsibilities, depending upon their skills and the needs of the administration. Sometimes, for example, a vice president acts as legislative liaison with Congress, particularly if the vice president has more experience in dealing with the legislative branch than the president. Such was the case with Al Gore, who had served eight years in the House of Representatives and eight years in the Senate, whereas the president under whom he served, Bill Clinton, lacked Washington experience. In other instances, vice presidents' policy expertise is a crucial resource for the administration. In the case of Vice President Dick Cheney, experience in foreign policy and national security determined the pivotal role he played in developing the foreign policy of George W. Bush's administration.

Although vice presidents are only "a heartbeat away" from the presidency, their own election to the presidency (should they decide to run) is not ensured when their term as second-in-command has ended. It is true that several vice presidents—among them, George H. W. Bush and Lyndon B. Johnson—have won election to the presidency in their own right; but many other former vice presidents have failed.[18] Notably, Al Gore, Walter Mondale, and Gerald Ford (the vice presidents of Bill Clinton, Jimmy Carter, and Richard Nixon, respectively) all went down to defeat at the polls in their bid for the White House.

balanced ticket
the selection of a running mate who brings diversity of ideology, geographic region, age, gender, race, or ethnicity to the slate

> Presidential candidates often choose a running mate who complements their attributes. Vice President Joe Biden, who served thirty-six years in the U.S. Senate, brought experience to Democratic President Barack Obama's ticket in 2008.

CHOOSING A VICE PRESIDENT In selecting a vice-presidential running mate, presidential candidates weigh several considerations. Would-be presidents strive for a **balanced ticket;** that is, to broaden their appeal to the electorate and increase their chances of getting elected, they select a running mate who brings diversity of ideology, geographic region, age, gender, race, or ethnicity to the slate.

Or they may base their vice-presidential selection on their own shortcomings, whether in policy expertise or in governing experience. For example, as a candidate vying for the presidency against Senator John McCain, an older and respected member of the U.S. Senate, Barack Obama chose Senator Joe Biden, who was thought to complement Obama in terms of age (Biden was 65 years old, compared with Obama's 47); experience (Biden had served in the Senate since 1972, Obama since 2000); and expertise (Biden was chair of the Senate Foreign Relations Committee, Obama had faced criticism in the media about his lack of foreign policy experience). In naming Alaska governor Sarah Palin as his running mate, Senator McCain also sought to bring youth, vigor, and enthusiasm to the Republican ticket to complement his experience and expertise. McCain's selection was also designed to attract the votes of women and cultural conservatives.

The Cabinet

Since George Washington's presidency, every president has depended upon the advice of a **cabinet,** the group of experts chosen by the president to serve as advisers on running the country. These advisers serve as the heads of each of the executive departments. Figure 12.2 shows the fifteen departments of the cabinet. Each cabinet member except the head of the Department of Justice is called the *secretary* of that department. The head of the Department of Justice is called the attorney general.

Figure 12.2 shows cabinet departments and their respective Web sites. President George W. Bush created the newest department, the Department of Homeland Security, in 2002. This department is charged with increasing the nation's preparedness, particularly with respect to catastrophic events such as terrorist attacks and natural disasters. George Washington's cabinet consisted of the heads of only four departments—justice, state, treasury, and war. (The last is now called the Department of Defense.) Subsequent presidents added other departments.

Each president may also designate cabinet rank to other advisers whose agencies are not permanent cabinet departments. Typically, presidents have specified that their national security adviser, director of the Office of Management and Budget, and administrator of the Environmental Protection Agency be included in their administration's cabinet.

Today, presidents and the public scrutinize presidential cabinet appointments to determine whether, in the words of Bill Clinton, they "look like America." As the data in Table 12.1 (see page 381) confirm, this is a relatively new gauge, since only three women and two members of ethnic minority groups had served in presidential cabinets until the Carter administration. Increasingly, however, as the table shows, presidential cabinets have become more diverse, with significant strides made during the Clinton administration.[19] President Clinton became the first president to appoint a woman to any of the "big four" posts when he named Janet Reno attorney general and Madeleine Albright secretary of state. George W. Bush named Colin Powell the first black secretary of state, and when Powell resigned, Bush replaced him with Condoleezza Rice, an African American woman who had served previously as national security adviser. Female members of President Obama's cabinet include Hillary Rodham Clinton as secretary of state; Labor Secretary Hilda Solis, who is Latina; Secretary of Homeland Security Janet Napolitano; Secretary of Health and Human Services Kathleen Sebelius; Environmental Protection Agency Administrator Lisa Jackson, who is African American; and United Nations Ambassador Susan Rice, who is African American. Other African Americans in Obama's cabinet include Attorney General Eric Holder and U.S. Trade Representative Ron Kirk. Latinos also include Interior Secretary Ken Salazar. And three Asian Americans, Secretary of Commerce Gary Locke, Secretary of Veterans' Affairs Eric Shinseki, and Energy secretary Stephen Chu, serve in the Obama cabinet.

cabinet
the group of experts chosen by the president to serve as advisers on running the country

The Executive Office of the President

Whereas the cabinet usually functions as an advisory board for the president, the **Executive Office of the President (EOP)** typically is the launch pad for the implementation of policy. The offices, counsils, and boards that compose the EOP help the president to carry out the day-to-day responsibilities of the presidency and similarly assist the First Lady and the vice president in their official activities. The EOP also coordinates policies among different agencies and departments.

Among the EOP offices, several are particularly important, including the White House Office, the National Security Council, the Office of Management and Budget, and the Council

Executive Office of the President (EOP)
offices, counsils, and boards that help the president to carry out the day-to-day responsibilities of the office

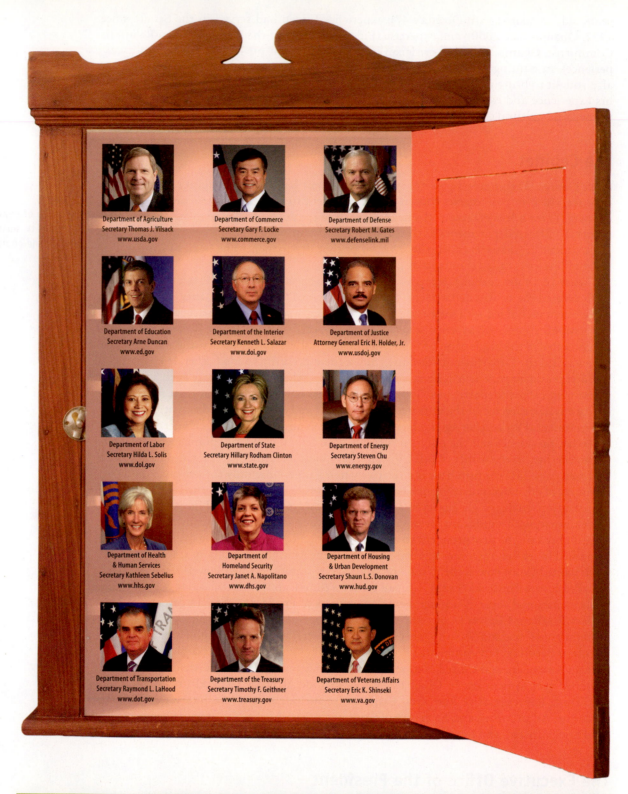

POLITICAL INQUIRY

FIGURE 12.2 ■ THE DEPARTMENTS OF THE PRESIDENT'S CABINET The presidential cabinet consists of the heads of the fifteen departments shown in the figure. Which department is concerned with finding alternatives to the use of fossil fuels? Which one addresses the problems of the dedicated service men and women who serve in Afghanistan and Iraq? Which department arose as a result of the 9/11 terrorist strikes?

of Economic Advisers. These offices are crucial not only because of the prominent issues with which they deal but also because of their strong role in developing and implementing policy in these issue areas.[20]

THE WHITE HOUSE OFFICE

Playing a pivotal role in most presidential administrations, the **White House Office (WHO)** staff members develop policies favored by the presidential administration and protect the president's legal and political interests. They research policy and keep the president informed about policy issues on the horizon. WHO staffers also regularly interact with members of Congress, their primary goal being to get presidential policy priorities enacted into law. They strive to ensure that those policies, once passed into law, are administered in keeping with the president's expectations.

Because of the enormous influence of staff members in the White House Office, presidents take pains to ensure their loyalty and trustworthiness. Among the top staff members of the White House Office is the **chief of staff,** who serves as both an adviser to the president and the manager of the WHO. Other staff members with clout include the **press secretary,** the president's spokesperson to the media, and the **White House counsel,** the president's lawyer. The president's secretary and appointments secretary are also influential WHO employees; they act as gatekeepers by controlling access to the president by other staffers and by members of Congress and the cabinet.

NATIONAL SECURITY COUNCIL

The president consults members of the **National Security Council (NSC)** on domestic and foreign matters related to national security. Since its creation in 1947 during the Truman administration,[21] the NSC has advised presidents on key national security and foreign policy decisions and assisted in the implementation of those decisions by coordinating policy administration among different agencies. For example, once the president has decided on a specific policy, the NSC might coordinate its implementation among the Department of State, the Central Intelligence Agency, various branches of the military, and diplomatic officials.

The president officially chairs the National Security Council. Its other regular members include the vice president, the secretary of defense, the secretary of state, the secretary of the treasury, and the assistant to the president for national security affairs, who is responsible for administering the day-to-day operations of the NSC and its staff. Other administration officials serve the NSC in advisory capacities or are invited to meetings when matters concerning their area of expertise are being decided.

OFFICE OF MANAGEMENT AND BUDGET

Once part of the Department of the Treasury, the **Office of Management and Budget (OMB**—originally called the Bureau of the Budget) has been a separate office within the EOP since 1939. Its chief responsibility is to create the president's annual budget, which the president submits to Congress each January. The budget outlines all of the anticipated revenue that the government will receive in

TABLE 12.1

Women and Minorities Appointed to Presidential Cabinets

President	Number of Women* Cabinet Members	Number of Minority** Cabinet Members	Tenure
Obama	7	9	2009–
G. W. Bush	7	10	2001–2009
Clinton	13	11	1993–2001
G. H. W. Bush	4	3	1989–1993
Reagan	4	2	1981–1989
Carter	4	1	1977–1981
Ford	1	1	1974–1977
Nixon	0	0	1969–1974
Johnson	0	1	1963–1969
Kennedy	0	0	1961–1963
Eisenhower	1	0	1953–1961
Truman	0	0	1945–1953
F. Roosevelt	1	0	1933–1945

*Includes cabinet and cabinet-level appointments.
**Includes African American, Latino/a, and Asian Americans.

SOURCES: Brigid C. Harrison, *Women in American Politics: An Introduction* (Belmont, CA: Wadsworth Publishing, 2003); the Center for the American Woman and Politics, *National Information Bank on Women in Public Office,* Eagleton Institute of Politics, Rutgers University; www.whitehouse.gov, and various presidential library Web sites.

White House Office (WHO)
the office that develops policies and protects the president's legal and political interests

chief of staff
among the most important staff members of the WHO; serves as both an adviser to the president and manager of the WHO

press secretary
the president's spokesperson to the media

White House counsel
the president's lawyer

National Security Council (NSC)
consisting of top foreign policy advisers and relevant cabinet officials, this is an arm of the EOP that the president consults on matters of foreign policy and national security

Office of Management and Budget (OMB)
office that creates the president's annual budget

the next year, usually from taxes and fees paid by businesses and individuals. The budget also lists the anticipated expenditures for the coming year, detailing how much money the various departments and agencies in the federal government will have available to spend on salaries, administrative costs, and programs. The OMB is among the president's most important agencies for policy making and policy implementation.

The director of the Office of Management and Budget, a presidential appointee confirmed by the Senate, has a staff of about six hundred career civil servants. In recent decades, the OMB director has figured prominently in presidential administrations and typically has been designated a member of the cabinet. The director's job is complex. He or she interacts intensively with Congress, trying to ensure that the budget that passes resembles the president's proposed budget as closely as possible. The director also lobbies members of Congress with the goal of ensuring that the key provisions of the budget that are important to the president remain intact in the congressionally approved version.

Once Congress approves the budget, the director of the OMB turns attention to its implementation, since it is the job of the OMB staff to manage the budget's execution by federal departments and agencies—to ensure that monies are spent on their designated purposes and that fraud and financial abuse do not occur. This managerial responsibility of the Office of Management and Budget was the reasoning behind the change in the office's name (from the Bureau of the Budget) in 1970.

Presidential Succession

No examination of the executive branch would be complete without considering the question, What happens if the president dies? Presidential succession is determined by the Presidential Succession Law of 1947. But sometimes incapacitation other than death prevents presidents from fulfilling their duties. In such cases, the Twenty-Fifth Amendment, ratified in 1967, determines the course of action.

When the President Dies in Office

When the president dies, the course of action is clear in most cases: the vice president assumes the presidency. Such was the situation when Harry Truman became president upon Franklin D. Roosevelt's death from natural causes in 1945 and when Lyndon Johnson was sworn in as president after the assassination of John F. Kennedy in 1963. Vice presidents sometimes fill the unexpired term of their president for reasons other than the president's death, as when Gerald Ford acceded to the presidency upon the resignation of Richard Nixon after the Watergate scandal.

The Presidential Succession Law of 1947 determines presidential succession if the vice president also dies or is unable to govern. Table 12.2 shows that after the vice president, the next in line for the presidency is the Speaker of the House of Representatives, then the president pro tem of the Senate, followed by a specified order of the members of the cabinet. Notice that as new cabinet departments have been established, their secretaries have been added to the bottom of the line of succession. As a precaution, at the State of the Union address each year, one cabinet member is chosen not to attend the president's speech before Congress but, rather, to stay behind at the White House. This measure ensures that if

> When a president dies in office, the line of presidential succession is clear. Crowds watched the funeral procession for President Franklin D. Roosevelt, who died in office in 1945 and was succeeded by his vice president, Harry S. Truman (1945–1953).

a catastrophe should occur in Congress during the address, someone in the line of succession will be able to assume the duties of the president.

When the President Cannot Serve: The Twenty-Fifth Amendment

What happens when a president is alive but unable to carry out the responsibilities of the office? Until the ratification of the Twenty-Fifth Amendment in 1967, the course of action was not clear. Such was the case in 1881, when an assassin shot President James Garfield, and Garfield lived two and a half months before succumbing to his injuries. In another such instance, President Woodrow Wilson was so ill during his last months in office that he was incapacitated. First Lady Edith Wilson assumed some of his responsibilities and decision making. Questions about presidential health also arose toward the end of Franklin D. Roosevelt's tenure; and during the Eisenhower administration, the president authorized Vice President Richard Nixon to determine whether Eisenhower, who was battling a series of illnesses, was competent to govern. President Kennedy, who suffered from a host of physical ailments including severe, chronic back pain and Addison's disease, similarly empowered Vice President Lyndon Johnson: in an informal agreement, the men arranged that if Kennedy was physically unable to communicate with Johnson, Johnson was authorized to assume the presidency.

After Kennedy's assassination, the ratification of the Twenty-Fifth Amendment (1967) finally put codified procedures in place for dealing with an incapacitated president. According to the Twenty-Fifth Amendment, if a president believes he or she is unable to carry out the duties of the office, the president must notify Congress, and the vice president becomes the acting president until the president can resume authority. The amendment would apply in the case when a president is anesthetized for surgery, for example, or perhaps recuperating from a debilitating illness.

In other situations, a president might be incapable of carrying out the duties of office and incapable of notifying Congress. In such a case, the Twenty-Fifth Amendment requires that the vice president and a majority of the cabinet notify Congress, and the vice president becomes the acting president. If a question arises as to whether the president is fit to reassume the duties of office, a two-thirds vote of Congress is required for the acting president to remain.

Sources of Presidential Power

The presidency that Barack Obama assumed on January 20, 2009, scarcely resembled George Washington's presidency in the 1790s. From the late eighteenth century to today, the powers of the president have evolved, reflecting the expansion of the federal government, changes in public attitudes about the proper role of government, and the personalities and will of those who have served as president.

TABLE 12.2

The Line of Presidential Succession

1. Vice president
2. Speaker of the House of Representatives
3. President pro tem of the Senate
4. Secretary of state
5. Secretary of the treasury
6. Secretary of defense
7. Attorney general
8. Secretary of the interior
9. Secretary of agriculture
10. Secretary of commerce
11. Secretary of labor
12. Secretary of health and human services
13. Secretary of housing and urban development
14. Secretary of transportation
15. Secretary of energy
16. Secretary of education
17. Secretary of veterans affairs
18. Secretary of homeland security

In describing the powers that would guide presidents for centuries to come, the framers of the Constitution created a unique office. These visionary authors had lived through a repressive era in which an authoritarian monarch had exercised absolute power. They subsequently had witnessed the new American nation's struggles under the ineffectual Articles of Confederation, in which the federal government had too little power and the states too much. Thus the framers sought to establish an office that would balance the exercise of authority with the preservation of the rights and the will of the people.

Given their colonial experience, it was no surprise that the framers granted the presidents both *expressed powers* and *inherent powers* in the Constitution. Congress grants presidents additional powers, called *statutory powers,* through congressional action. We consider these various powers in this section.

Additional presidential powers have emerged over time. These newer authorities reflect both changes in the institution of the presidency and shifts in popular views on the appropriate role of government and the president. These powers include emergency powers granted in Supreme Court decisions and powers that, though not formalized, are given to presidents by the public through election mandates, presidential popularity, or unified public opinion on a particular issue or course of action.

The Constitution: Expressed Powers

expressed powers
presidential powers enumerated in the Constitution

The primary source of presidential power comes from the Constitution in the form of the **expressed powers,** which are those enumerated in the Constitution. Article II, Sections 2 and 3, list the following powers:

- serve as commander in chief of the armed forces
- appoint heads of the executive departments, ambassadors, Supreme Court justices, people to fill vacancies that occur during the recess of the Senate, and other positions
- pardon crimes, except in cases of impeachment
- enter into treaties, with two-thirds consent of the Senate
- give the State of the Union address to Congress
- convene the Congress
- receive ambassadors of other nations
- commission all officers of the United States

The expressed powers outlined in the Constitution provide a framework for presidential responsibilities and an outline of presidential power. They also shape how presidents themselves develop their authority.

The Constitution: Inherent Powers

take care clause
the constitutional basis for inherent powers, which states that the president "shall take Care that the Laws be faithfully executed"

inherent powers
presidential powers that are implied in the Constitution

One of the principal ways by which the Constitution provides for presidents themselves to assert additional powers, beyond those expressed in the Constitution, is the **take care clause,** which states that "the executive Power shall be vested in a President of the United States of America" and that "he shall take Care that the Laws be faithfully executed." On the basis of that clause, presidents throughout U.S. history have asserted various **inherent powers,** which are powers that are not expressly granted by the Constitution but are inferred.

President Thomas Jefferson exercised inherent powers in his far-reaching Louisiana Purchase in 1803. Jefferson authorized this $15 million purchase of 800,000 square miles of land, even though the Constitution did not authorize any such action on the part of a president. Interestingly, in the civic discourse over the Constitution, Jefferson, an Anti-Federalist, had argued for states' rights and against a strong central government and a powerful presidency. Jefferson had believed that the powers enumerated in the Constitution defined the powers of the government. But Jefferson thought that the purchase of the Louisiana Territory was of crucial strategic and economic importance. He believed that the deal was key to the United States' averting war with France and to securing the port of New Orleans, which was essential for the new American republic's fortunes in trade. Jefferson could not wait for a constitutional amendment to authorize the transaction, and so he forged ahead with the purchase. Congress and many Americans of the day agreed with his actions, and so there were no negative consequences to them.

More recently, in the 1930s, President Franklin D. Roosevelt drew on the inherent powers when he expanded the size of the federal government to administer his New Deal programs, designed to relieve the economic and human distress of the Great Depression. Beginning in 2002, President George W. Bush used the inherent powers when he suspended the civil liberties of foreign nationals being held in a military prison at the U.S. naval base at Guantánamo Bay, Cuba, as part of the administration's war on terror. The individuals at Guantánamo Bay have been detained indefinitely for questioning about their possible terrorist activities. These instances of presidents' exercise of inherent powers generated varying degrees of controversy among Americans of the times.

Statutory Powers

The Constitution's expressed and inherent powers provided a foundation for presidential power that has evolved over time. Those powers have been supplemented by additional powers—**statutory powers**—explicitly granted to presidents by congressional action.

An example of such a grant of statutory powers is the 1996 Line Item Veto Act, discussed earlier, which gave the president the power to strike down specific line items on an appropriations bill while allowing the rest of the bill to become law. As noted, in 1997 the Supreme Court declared the line-item veto unconstitutional on the grounds that the congressional action violated the separation of powers.

statutory powers
powers explicitly granted to presidents by congressional action

Special Presidential Powers

Presidents also have special powers that have evolved from various sources, including the Constitution, Supreme Court decisions, and congressional statutes. These powers, which numerous presidents have exercised, have come to be regarded as accepted powers and privileges of the presidency. They include *executive orders, emergency powers,* and *executive privilege.*

EXECUTIVE ORDERS   The president has the power to issue **executive orders** that have the force of law. Executive orders carry the same weight as congressional statutes and have been used in a variety of circumstances to guide the executive branch's administrative functions.[22] In general, executive orders:

executive order
power of the president to issue orders that carry the force of law

- direct the enforcement of congressional statutes or Supreme Court rulings
- enforce specific provisions of the Constitution
- guide the administration of treaties with foreign governments
- create or change the regulatory guidelines or practices of an executive department or agency

Executive orders can be an important strategic tool, because they convey the president's priorities to the bureaucracy that implements the laws. For example, in 1948 President Harry Truman signed Executive Order 9981, which states, "It is hereby declared to be the policy of the President that there shall be equality of treatment and opportunity for all persons in the armed services without regard to race, color, religion, or national origin."[23] This executive order effectively banned segregation in the U.S. military. Why would Truman issue an executive order instead of working for congressional passage of a statute that would desegregate the military? Many analysts think the reason is that Truman, who ardently believed that the military should be desegregated, not only doubted that Congress would pass such a measure but also faced pressure from early civil rights activists who had pledged an African American boycott of military service if the military was not desegregated.

Executive orders have very few limitations and stipulations. One limitation is that presidents cannot use them to create new taxes or appropriate funds, because the Constitution reserves those powers for Congress. But although there are few limitations on executive orders, an order itself is sometimes not sufficient to ensure that the president's will is followed. Take the case of President Obama, who two days into his tenure as president issued an executive order declaring that the detention facilities at Guantánamo Naval Base in Cuba be closed by January 2010. Because of the complexity of the Guantánamo situation—the need to determine the status of all prisoners and to relocate them—the detention facility will remain open until at least 2011.

EMERGENCY POWERS   Broad powers that a president exercises during times of national crisis have been invoked by presidents since Abraham Lincoln's claim to **emergency powers** during the Civil War. Lincoln used emergency powers during the war to suspend the civil liberties of alleged agitators, to draft state militia units into national service, and to federalize the governance of southern states after the war.

In 1936, the U.S. Supreme Court acknowledged the existence of presidential emergency powers in *United States v. Curtiss-Wright Export Corp.*[24] In this case, the U.S. government charged the Curtiss-Wright Corporation with conspiring to sell fifteen machine guns to Bolivia, in violation of a joint resolution of Congress and a presidential proclamation. Without congressional approval, President Franklin D. Roosevelt had ordered an embargo on the machine gun shipment. The Court supported Roosevelt's order, ruling that the president's powers, particularly in foreign affairs, are not limited to those powers expressly stated in the Constitution. The justices also stated that the federal government is the primary actor in foreign affairs and that the president in particular has inherent powers related to his constitutional duties in foreign relations.

EXECUTIVE PRIVILEGE   Presidents also can exercise **executive privilege,** the authority of the president and other executive officials to refuse to disclose information concerning confidential conversations or national security to Congress or the courts. In invoking executive privilege, presidents draw on the idea that the Constitution's framework of separation of powers justifies the withholding of certain information from Congress or the judiciary,[25] a claim initially asserted when George Washington refused to grant Congress access to all documents pertaining to treaty negotiations. Typically, presidents claim executive privilege so they can get advice from aides without fear that such conversations might be made public or scrutinized by members of Congress or the judiciary. Presidents also have invoked executive privilege when negotiating foreign policies with other heads of state, to shield these leaders from having sensitive negotiations examined by the other branches of the federal government.

On occasion, the judicial branch of the federal government has successfully challenged executive privilege. For example, when President Richard Nixon refused to turn over tapes of Oval Office conversations to a special prosecutor investigating the Watergate scandal in 1974, the Supreme Court intervened. In *United States v. Richard M. Nixon,* the Court asserted that although executive privilege does exist, it was not applicable regarding the tapes because President Nixon's claim of executive privilege concerning the tapes was too broad.[26] (See pages 390–391 for more on Watergate.)

More recent cases in which a president has invoked executive privilege are notable. President Bill Clinton attempted to do so to prevent White House aides from testifying before special prosecutor Kenneth Starr during the Monica Lewinsky scandal. (Clinton was accused of having extramarital relations with Lewinsky, a White House intern.) Clinton's maneuver failed, and his aides were compelled to testify. In 2007, President George W. Bush asserted executive authority in a showdown with Congress over the politically motivated firing of nine U.S. attorneys. Bush invoked executive privilege to prevent White House Counsel Harriet Miers and presidential adviser Karl Rove from testifying before Congress. The congressional inquiry continued without Miers's and Rove's testimony, however, and eventually Attorney General Alberto Gonzales stepped down as a result of the scandal.

In general, the courts have allowed executive privilege in cases where a clear issue of separation of powers exists—as with respect to international negotiations and conversations regarding matters of policy or national security. The courts have tended to limit the use of executive privilege when presidents have exercised it in an effort to prevent the revelation of misdeeds by members of the executive branch.

The People as a Source of Presidential Power

One of the most important sources of presidential power today comes from the people. Although one president generally will have the same formal powers as the next, presidents' ability to wield their power, to control the political agenda, and to get things done typically is a function of political skill, charisma, and what political scientist Richard Neustadt has called "the power to persuade."[27]

The President and the Bully Pulpit

Modern presidents work to persuade the public on a virtually continuous basis. They know that if they win popular support for their views and political agenda, they will have an easier time getting their policy priorities through Congress. In their efforts to persuade the people, they exploit the power of their office, using the presidency as a forum from which to speak out on any matter—and to have their views listened to. This ready access to the public ear and broad power of the president to communicate led President Theodore Roosevelt to exclaim, "I have got such a bully pulpit!"[28]

In using their bully pulpit, presidents seek to communicate that their stances on important issues are the right choices and that their actions, particularly controversial decisions, should be supported. Presidents also strive to persuade the public that they are doing a good job on key policy fronts such as economic and foreign policy. Sometimes presidents seek to mobilize the public to take specific actions or to adopt certain beliefs. For example, President Barack Obama attempted to use the bully pulpit to convince the American public that the health care system was in need of reform—and that Congress should enact his proposals to change the system.

The reason why presidents work so tirelessly to win public support for their agenda is that they understand that getting Congress to act on policy priorities, to approve budgets, and to pass favored legislation depends heavily on the perception that the public supports presidential initiatives. Indeed, political scientist Richard Neustadt argues that the modern institution of the presidency is weak and that presidents in fact must rely on public and congressional support in order to enact their agendas.[29] Getting Congress to do what the president wants is more difficult when a president faces a divided government, the situation in which the president belongs to one political party and Congress is controlled by a majority of members of the other party. For example, when the Republicans lost control of both the House and the Senate in the 2006 congressional elections, President Bush's chances of enacting his legislative priorities, such as privatizing Social Security, decreased significantly because the new Democratic majorities in Congress did not share those priorities.

But beyond partisan differences, presidents' ability to get things done in Congress also is a function of their popularity with the people. A popular president can use that clout to persuade members of Congress that his positions are the right ones; an unpopular president will face greater obstacles to having his legislative agenda enacted.

The President and Public Approval

When Barack Obama was sworn in as president, fully 67 percent of the American people approved of the way he was handling his job as president. He enjoyed a strong **honeymoon period,** a time early in a new president's administration characterized by optimistic approval by the public. As his presidency progressed, however, the president's approval rating steadily declined, reaching a low point of 43 percent in August 2010, as shown in Figure 12.3 on page 388. Americans grew increasingly wary of the president's proposal to reform the nation's health care system and increasingly frustrated at the sluggish rate of economic recovery.

The flow and ebb of presidential popularity during the administration of George W. Bush illustrates how essential the people's support is to the success of a chief executive's initiatives. After the September 11, 2001, terrorist attacks and President Bush's rapid and dignified response to them, Bush enjoyed record high approval ratings. **Approval ratings** are the percentage of survey respondents who say that they "approve" or "strongly approve"

honeymoon period
a time early in a new president's administration characterized by optimistic approval by the public

approval ratings
the percentage of survey respondents who say that they "approve" or "strongly approve" of the way the president is doing his job

Job Approval Ratings for Presidents
George W. Bush and Barack Obama

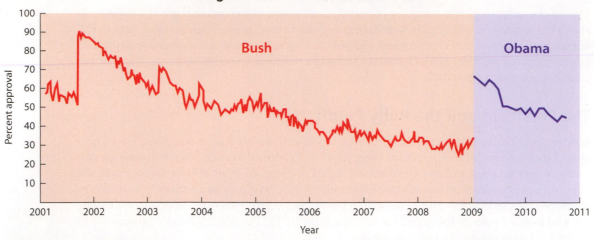

POLITICAL INQUIRY

FIGURE 12.3 ■ **GEORGE W. BUSH'S APPROVAL RATINGS (2001–2009) COMPARED TO BARACK OBAMA'S APPROVAL RATINGS (2009–2010)** What could cause Obama's approval ratings to reach their former levels? To decline further? How important is the economy in determining his approval ratings? What other issues or circumstances might have an impact on presidential approval ratings in the future?

SOURCE: www.gallup.com/poll/116500/Presidential-Approval-Ratings-George-Bush.aspx; www.gallup.com/poll/113980/Gallup-Daily-Obama-Job-Approval.aspx.

of the way the president is doing his job. Immediately after September 11, President Bush's approval ratings hovered in the high 80s, occasionally reaching 90 percent, meaning that 90 percent of those surveyed indicated that they approved of the way the president was handling his job. (In contrast, the average presidential approval rating since the Franklin D. Roosevelt administration was 56 percent.) During this time, Bush had enormous legislative successes. These included the passage of the USA PATRIOT Act of 2001, which gave law enforcement officers greater authority in handling suspected terrorist acts, and the congressional declaration of a "war on terror." When Bush's popularity subsequently waned because of the people's dissatisfaction with the rate of progress in the war in Iraq, the high number of casualties in the war, and continued weakness in the American economy, so too did support decrease for the continuation of the war, the president's economic policies, and a proposed extension of the USA PATRIOT Act.

In general, presidential approval ratings reveal that some presidents are simply more popular than others. For example, presidents Reagan and Clinton tended to enjoy high approval ratings, with President Clinton's second-term ratings running particularly high, especially in light of the Monica Lewinsky scandal and the subsequent impeachment proceedings against him.

When the United States engages in a short-term military action or is the subject of an attack by terrorists, we see similar peaks of approval ratings, sometimes referred to as the **rally 'round the flag effect.**

rally 'round the flag effect
peaks in presidential approval ratings during short-term military action

A president rarely sustains high public approval continuously. Once achieved, however, high ratings help the chief executive to achieve his goals by demonstrating the people's support of the presidential agenda.[30]

The Media as a Tool of Presidential Influence

Modern presidents rely heavily on the mass media to convey their message to the people. As presidential candidates, they hire media consultants to assist them in preparing for televised debates. Teams of consultants create sophisticated media strategies that aim to integrate the presidential campaign's use of television, radio, and the Internet.

Once a president takes office, the expertise of the White House communications office kicks in to "spin" news in a favorable light for the administration. In particular, the White House communications director forges relationships with the most prominent media outlets by providing access, exclusive interviews, and scoops on breaking stories to reporters considered friendly to the administration. And today, the president relies on YouTube, Facebook, and Twitter to communicate directly with the American people.

Important national speeches and the State of the Union address are televised and made available on YouTube, just as press conferences are. Interestingly, before the advent of television, presidential press conferences occurred more frequently than they do today, providing the best opportunity for the president to "talk to the people" and for reporters and their audiences to learn about presidential priorities.[31]

Although the nature of presidential press conferences and other media forums has evolved over time, the mass media have served as a key avenue by which modern presidents have communicated directly to the population at large. And because the nature of the president's relationship with his constituency is constantly evolving, so too is presidential power.

> Today, the president relies on technology to communicate directly with the American people. On the White House's Online Town Hall Web site, viewers can submit questions to President Obama.

The Evolution of Presidential Power

Although the constitutional powers of the presidency have changed little over time, the power of the presidency has evolved a great deal.[32] In part, this development stems from some presidents' skillful use of powers not granted by the Constitution, such as the powers to persuade and to assert more authority. But the political environment within which presidents have governed has also contributed to the evolution of presidential power.[33]

The history of the early republic saw an incremental expansion of the power of the presidency, whereas the Great Depression of the 1930s and the election of Franklin D. Roosevelt in 1932 spawned an enormous growth of presidential authority.[34] As successor presidents inherited the large bureaucracy that Roosevelt built, presidential powers have further expanded—gradually creating what historian Arthur Schlesinger Jr. has called the "imperial presidency."

Early Presidents and the Scope of Presidential Power

Thomas Jefferson's election to the presidency in 1801 marked one of the earliest expansions of presidential power. Jefferson broadened the powers of the office despite his Anti-Federalist reluctance to delegate too much power to the national government. Jefferson increased presidential power in two significant ways. First, as we have seen, Jefferson established the principle of inherent powers of the presidency by undertaking the Louisiana Purchase. Second, Jefferson's tenure of office witnessed the first time that a president had to act as party leader. Jefferson had no choice but to assume this role: if he had not, he would not have been elected president given the dominance of the Federalist Party during this era (see Chapter 8).

Twenty-five years later, Andrew Jackson would also adopt the role of president-as-party-leader, but he would add a new twist. Jackson's emphasis on *populism,* a political philosophy that emphasizes the needs of the common person, spawned a new source of presidential power, because Jackson was the first president to derive real and significant power from the people. Whereas earlier politics had mostly emphasized the needs of the elite, Jackson's populism mobilized the masses of common people who traditionally had not been civically engaged. This populism augmented the power of the presidency by increasing the popularity of the president and investing him with power that came from the people's goodwill.

In the twentieth century, the nature and scope of presidential power changed as a consequence of the prevailing political environment. One of the most extraordinary shifts in the nature of the presidency occurred during Franklin D. Roosevelt's administration, which lasted from 1932 until his death in 1945. (Roosevelt was elected to an unprecedented four terms; the Twenty-Second Amendment to the Constitution, which allows only two elected presidential terms, was ratified six years after his death.)

Having come to power during the Great Depression, Roosevelt engineered a significant change in the function of the federal government. He called for a New Deal for the American people, a series of social welfare programs that would provide employment for many of the nation's unemployed workers. Roosevelt's New Deal was based on the ideas of economist John Maynard Keynes, who argued for temporary deficit spending by the government (that is, going into debt) to spur the economy during economic downturns.

Works Progress Administration (WPA)
a New Deal program that employed 8.5 million people at a cost of more than $11 million between 1935 and 1943

Roosevelt's primary weapon in his New Deal arsenal was the **Works Progress Administration (WPA),** a federal government program that employed 8.5 million people at a cost of more than $11 million between 1935 and 1943. The idea was that government-funded employment would create economic growth in the private sector because those employed by the government would have the money to buy goods and services, thus creating spiraling demand. The rising demand for goods and services would mean that the private sector could then employ more people, and the cycle of recovery and growth would continue. For example, if during the 1930s, the government employed your great-grandfather to work on a road-building project in his town, he might have put his paycheck toward buying more bread and other baked goods than he previously could have afforded. If enough people in town could have similarly patronized the bakery, then the baker might have had to hire an assistant to keep up with demand, and consequently the assistant would have had money to spend on, say, new shoes for his children. In that way, the increased demand for products and services would continue, creating additional economic growth.

Roosevelt's New Deal was important to the presidency for two reasons. First, it dramatically changed people's views of the role of the federal government. People now tend to think of the federal government as the provider of a "safety net" that protects the most vulnerable citizens—a safeguard that did not exist before the New Deal, when those needing assistance had to rely on the help of family, friends, churches and private charities. Second, this popular perception and the programs that emerged—the Works Progress Administration, unemployment insurance, Social Security—meant that the federal government would have to grow larger in order to administer these programs. As a result, the president's role as chief executive would become much more important to modern presidents than it had been to those who served before Roosevelt.[35]

> **William Frazee, the chief of the presses for the *Washington Post*, makes the victory sign after learning of the Supreme Court's decision allowing newspapers to publish the *Pentagon Papers*. Applause broke out in the press room as the first print run began rolling.**

The Watershed 1970s: The *Pentagon Papers*, Watergate, and the "Imperial Presidency"

Americans' penchant for strong presidents modeled after Roosevelt diminished drastically in the 1970s. In 1971, an employee of the Department of Defense named Daniel Ellsberg leaked a classified, top-secret 7,000-page history of the nation's involvement in and thinking on Vietnam dating from the Truman administration in 1945 to the Nixon administration then installed in the White House. Called the *Pentagon Papers,* the work first appeared as a series of articles in the *New York Times.* When the Nixon administration in 1971 successfully petitioned the Department of Justice to prevent the publication of the remainder of the articles, the *Washington Post* assumed publication of them. When the Department of Justice sued the *Post,* the *Boston Globe* resumed their publication. Two weeks later, in an expedited appeals process, the U.S. Supreme Court ruled in *The New York Times Co. v. The United States* that the government "carries a heavy burden of showing justification for the imposition of such a restraint" and that the government had failed to meet that burden, thus allowing the continued publication of the papers.[36]

The *Pentagon Papers* tainted the public's view of the presidency. The published work revealed miscalculations by policy makers in presidential administrations from Truman's to Nixon's, as well as arrogance and deception on the part of policy makers, cabinet members, and presidents. Specifically, the *Pentagon Papers* revealed that the federal government had repeatedly lied about or misrepresented the fact of increasing U.S. military involvement in Southeast Asia. In particular, the analysis in the *Pentagon Papers* indicated not only that U.S. marines had conducted offensive military maneuvers well before the public was informed, but also that the U.S. military had engaged in other actions, including air strikes, over Laos and military raids throughout the North Vietnamese coastal regions. The Nixon administration's legal wrangling to prevent release of the *Pentagon Papers* cast a dark cloud over the public's perception of the presidency.

Cynicism about the presidency continued to grow in light of the **Watergate** scandal that took place a year later. In 1972, men affiliated with President Nixon's reelection campaign broke into the headquarters of the Democratic National Committee (located in the Watergate Hotel in Washington, D.C.) to retrieve wiretaps that they had previously installed to monitor their opponents. *Washington Post* reporters Bob Woodward and Carl Bernstein, in a groundbreaking series of stories, traced the burglaries and the subsequent cover-up to high-level officials in the Nixon administration. This crime and the Nixon administration's attempts at cover-ups became known as the Watergate scandal. A Senate investigation revealed that President Nixon had secretly taped conversations in the Oval Office that would shed light on "what the president knew [about the break-in] and when he knew it."[37] Nixon claimed executive privilege and refused to turn the tapes over to a special prosecutor who had been appointed to investigate the scandal. When the U.S. Supreme Court ruled in *United States v. Richard Nixon* that Nixon must provide the tapes to the special prosecutor, one key tape was found to have a gap of almost twenty minutes where someone, reportedly his secretary, Rosemary Woods, had erased part of the recording.

Meanwhile, all the Watergate burglars had pleaded guilty and been sentenced, and only one refused to name the superiors who had orchestrated the break-in. But the testimony of burglar James W. McCord Jr. linked the crime to the Committee to Re-Elect the President (CREEP), Nixon's campaign organization, and to high-ranking Nixon White House officials. The disclosure prompted John Dean, Nixon's White House counsel, to remark, "We have a cancer within, close to the presidency, that is growing."[38] With indictments handed down for many of Nixon's top aides, and with a Senate investigation and a special prosecutor's investigation in progress, the House Judiciary Committee took up the matter of impeachment. The committee handed down three articles of impeachment against Nixon— one for obstruction of justice, a second for abuse of power, and a third for contempt of Congress. When a newly released tape documented that Nixon had planned to block the investigations by having the Federal Bureau of Investigation and the Central Intelligence Agency falsely claim that matters of national security were involved, the tape was referred to as a "smoking gun."[39] Nixon lost the support of his few loyalists in Congress and on August 8, 1974, announced that he would resign from office the following day.

Watergate might seem like a relatively insignificant event in the history of the American presidency, but the impact of the Watergate scandal on the presidency has been enormous. Watergate badly wounded the trust that many Americans held for their president and for their government. Combined with the unpopularity of the Vietnam War and the release of the *Pentagon Papers,* it created a deep cynicism that pervades many Americans' perception of their government even today—a pessimistic attitude that has passed from generation to generation.

Watergate also dramatically demonstrated how enormously the presidency had changed. Modern presidents had supplanted Congress as the center of federal power and in so doing had become too powerful. Historian Arthur Schlesinger Jr. and other presidential scholars have decried the problem of the growth of the executive branch and, in particular, the imperial "courts"—the rising number of Executive Office of the President staff members, many of whom are not subject to Senate confirmation and share a deep loyalty to the person who is president rather than to the institution of the presidency. In juxtaposition with an attitude like that expressed by Richard Nixon in his comment that "when the president does it, that means it is not illegal,"[40] the imperial presidency left much room for abuse.

Watergate

during the Nixon administration, a scandal involving burglaries and the subsequent cover-up by high-level administration officials

Evolution of the Modern Presidency

THEN (1970s)	NOW (2011)
The presidency had become an increasingly powerful institution, shaped by the predecessors of Richard Nixon, who assumed office in 1969.	Congress continues to attempt to "check" the power of modern presidents.
The presidency supplanted Congress as the epicenter of power in the federal government.	Presidential exercise of authority in the foreign policy realm serves to limit Congress's ability to rein in presidential power.
Backlash against abuses of executive power in the Nixon administration paved the way for the election of Jimmy Carter, a comparatively weak president.	Voter backlash against the Obama administration's economic policy propels a Republican majority to the House of Representatives, providing a check on presidential power in the domestic policy realm.

WHAT'S NEXT?

> How do you anticipate that the congressional election of 2010 will further shape the institution of the presidency?

> What public policy issues will likely dominate in the months and years to come? How will these issues influence the ways presidential power is exercised?

The Post-Watergate Presidency

With the election of Jimmy Carter to the White House in 1976, many observers believed that the era of the imperial presidency had passed. Carter, the mild-mannered governor of Georgia and thus a Washington outsider, seemed to be the antidote the nation needed after the display of power-run-amok during Nixon's tenure. But given the significant challenges Carter faced during his term, many people believed that he did not exercise *enough* authority—that he acted weakly when faced with various crises.

Ronald Reagan's election in 1980 in some ways represented a return to a more powerful, "imperial" presidency. Reagan, a former actor, was Hollywood swagger personified, speaking tough talk that many Americans found appealing. His administration was not unlike an imperial court, featuring a group of advisers with deep loyalties to Reagan. Although the era of unchecked presidential power was gone for good, many would argue that the George W. Bush administration was best at re-creating a form of an imperial presidency. Bush was able to exercise strong authority because of the fear created both among the citizenry and in Congress after the September 11, 2001, terror attacks. And given President Bush's activist foreign policy, he exercised great authority in that realm, with Congress having little ability to check him. Ironically, many critics of the Bush administration would assert that he was assisted in creating a modern imperial presidency by many of the same staff members who were part of the Nixon administration. But administration supporters would note that a strong presidency was necessary at this critical juncture in the nation's history.

Impeachment: A Check on Abuses of Presidential Power

Although presidential powers are flexible and can be shaped by the individuals holding the office, these powers do not go unchecked. One crucial check on presidential power is **impeachment,** the power of the House of Representatives to formally accuse the president (and other high-ranking officials, including the vice president and federal judges) of crimes. The Constitution specifically refers to charges of "Treason, Bribery, or other high Crimes and Misdemeanors," an appropriately vague description of the potential offenses a president could commit. An impeachment can be thought of as an indictment: If a majority of the members of the House of Representatives vote to impeach the president, they forward the charges against the president, called the **articles of impeachment,** to the Senate. The Senate then tries the president and, in the event of conviction for the offenses, determines the penalty. In convicting a president, the Senate has the authority to punish the president by removing him from office.

Although the Senate can force a president to step down, it has never done so in practice, and only two presidents have been impeached by the House of Representatives. The first was Andrew Johnson, who succeeded Abraham Lincoln as president in 1865 upon the latter's assassination. When he assumed the presidency, Johnson faced not only a divided

impeachment
the power of the House of Representatives to formally accuse the president (and other high-ranking officials, including the vice president and federal judges) of crimes

articles of impeachment
charges against the president during an impeachment

nation but also a government in turmoil. The eleven articles of impeachment against him had to do primarily with his removal of the secretary of war, Edwin Stanton, who was working with Johnson's congressional opponents to undermine Johnson's reconstruction policies in the South. The so-called Radical Republicans in the House believed that Johnson's policies were too moderate, and they sought to treat the Confederate states as conquered territories and to confiscate the land of slaveholders. Those same House members wanted to protect their ally Stanton and prevent him from being removed from office. The Senate ultimately recognized the politically motivated nature of the articles of impeachment against Johnson and acquitted him on all counts.

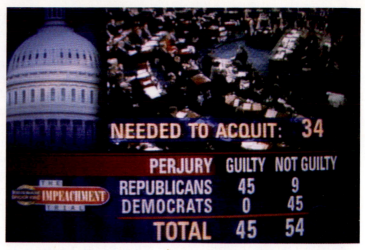

> On the basis of an investigation by special prosecutor Kenneth Starr, the House impeached President Bill Clinton for committing perjury by lying to a grand jury about his relationship with White House intern Monica Lewinsky and for obstructing justice. The Senate voted to acquit Clinton on those perjury charges.

The most recent occurrence of the impeachment of a president was in 1998, when the House of Representatives approved two articles of impeachment against President Bill Clinton. On the basis of an investigation by a special prosecutor, the House impeached Clinton for lying to a grand jury about his relationship with White House intern Monica Lewinsky and for obstructing justice. The Senate acquitted Clinton on both counts.

During the Watergate scandal that rocked Richard Nixon's presidency, the House Judiciary Committee approved articles of impeachment against the president and sent them to the full House for a vote. Republican members of Congress convinced Nixon that the House would vote to impeach him and that the Senate would convict him and remove him from office. Faced with the inevitable, Nixon became the first president to resign from office before the House could vote to impeach him.

Evaluating Presidential Leadership

In 1998, while President Clinton was mired in impeachment hearings in Congress, his public approval ratings stood at 60 percent. Despite the Monica Lewinsky scandal and the risk that the president might be removed from office for lying about his relationship with the White House intern, a healthy majority of Americans separated Clinton's personal moral failings from his ability to govern successfully.

While a president is in office, people evaluate the president's performance on the basis of specific criteria. These include questions such as these: Does the president prioritize the same issues that I do? Is the president effectively managing the economy? Is the United States respected around the world? Is the president a strong leader, unafraid to exercise power? Does the president have a vision for the nation and for his administration? Is the president able to communicate that vision to the people? If presidents are successful in these areas, they tend to have generally high approval ratings. As we have seen, however, high approval ratings are difficult to sustain over the course of an administration.

In general, the average American's criteria for presidential greatness differ substantially from assessments by scholars of the presidency. The American public at large tends to emphasize recent presidents with strong communication skills, citing Ronald Reagan, John F. Kennedy, and Bill Clinton among the top four presidents in one survey (with Abraham Lincoln number three). Scholarly rankings tend to be more historically inclusive, with George Washington, Abraham Lincoln, Franklin D. Roosevelt, and Thomas Jefferson leading the list of the greatest presidents.

Women in the White House

Of the three branches of government, the executive branch has been the most challenging for women to gain entry into as formal participants. As we saw earlier in this chapter, no woman served as a cabinet member until the twentieth century, and to date, a woman has not been elected president. Yet cabinet positions are not the only place where women's influence in the executive branch has been felt. Historically, the women who have served as First Lady have influenced both presidents and policy.

Some recent First Ladies, among them Nancy Reagan and Hillary Clinton, have exercised undisguised public power. Following President Obama's election, many Americans wondered whether First Lady Michelle Obama would take up the reigns as policy leader, but that has not been the case. And with women becoming an increasing proportion of the pool of candidates deemed eligible to be president, a woman's election to the presidency in the near future becomes nearly assured. Indeed, Senator John McCain's selection of Alaska Governor Sarah Palin was seen by many analysts as an acknowledgment of the importance of women voters and the inevitability of a woman president. As President Richard Nixon remarked, "Certainly in the next 50 years we shall see a woman president, perhaps sooner than you think. A woman can and should be able to do any political job that a man can do."[41]

The First Lady

Much like the presidency itself, the office of the First Lady has been defined by the individuals who have occupied it. That women as different as Barbara Bush, the wife of President George H. W. Bush, and Hillary Clinton, the wife of President Bill Clinton, could consecutively and successfully serve as First Lady demonstrates the open-mindedness with which the American people view the role. First Lady Michelle Obama has shunned the policy-oriented role that Hillary Rodham Clinton forged, though Obama did show her activist side in the aftermath of the devastating earthquake in Haiti in January 2010. By and large, though, Obama has instead preferred to focus on raising the Obamas' young daughters, Malia and Sasha, and on the more ceremonial aspect of serving as First Lady.

Other First Ladies have used their proximity to the chief executive to influence policy concerns more broadly and more forcefully. Some have acted "behind the scenes," as was the case with Edith Wilson, the wife of Woodrow Wilson. Others have taken a more public role. Eleanor Roosevelt, the wife of Franklin D. Roosevelt, fought for many causes during her husband's administration, including human rights and civil rights for African Americans. Hillary Clinton transformed the office of First Lady by serving, at her husband's appointment, as the chair of a presidential task force on health care reform. Her role in the task force, and indeed throughout the Clinton administration, proved to be a lightning rod for critics who thought that a First Lady should not be so prominent. Laura Bush by contrast was a more reserved and less public First Lady.

When a Woman Is Elected President

As First Lady, Barbara Bush speculated about the election of a woman president. She wryly commented, "Somewhere out in this audience may even be someone who will one day follow my footsteps, and preside over the White House as the president's spouse. I wish him well!"[43]

Over a period of time, pollsters have explored the possibility that Americans would vote for a qualified woman for president. Figure 12.4 shows that since 1937, when only 33 percent of Americans said they would cast their presidential ballot for a qualified woman, that figure has steadily risen. By 1999, the number rose to 92 percent of respondents who said they would vote for a female presidential candidate. Yet by 2005, that figure had declined to 89 percent. One explanation for this drop could be that Senator Hillary Clinton was frequently mentioned at the time of the poll as a likely 2008 presidential candidate and that respondents unwilling to support her candidacy responded that they were unwilling to vote for a woman for president.

Though Senator Clinton's bid for the White House was unsuccessful, inevitably, the United States will have to face the issue of the role of the First Gentleman. We can wonder about the dilemmas that might arise for the men who pioneer in this new role. Will the ceremonial functions of the first spouse remain the same? Will the First Gentleman choose the White House china; will he assist in the organization of state dinners and other social functions? Will he work in a private-sector job outside the White House? Will he have a voice in influencing administration policy?

We will learn the answers only when a married woman becomes president. In all likelihood, people's fascination with the role of First Gentleman will wane when the novelty of the office wears off. And similarly to the various interpretations of the role that First Ladies have created, it is likely that the role of First Gentleman will be flexible and adaptable, responding to the inclinations and the personalities of the men who occupy it, as well as to public preferences.

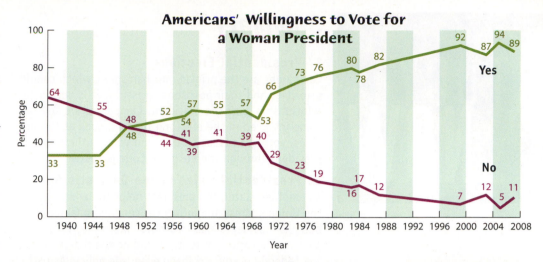

POLITICAL INQUIRY

FIGURE 12.4 ■ What has been the trend since the late 1930s in the American electorate's willingness to vote for a woman president? What factors do you think explain this shift?

SOURCE: The Gallup Poll, www.galluppoll.com/content/?ci=8611&pg=1, Please move the entire title "Americans' Willingness..." 1p above the top edge of the vertical blue bars. (To match all other figures of this style.)

WWW.GALLUP.COM/POLL/18937/, and www.gallup.com/poll/26875/ Analysis=Impact=Personal=characteristics=Candidate=Support. aspx.

CONCLUSION

THINKING CRITICALLY ABOUT WHAT'S NEXT IN THE PRESIDENCY

The American presidency is a dynamic institution, one that is molded by the individuals who serve as president and by the American people—by their changing interests, viewpoints, struggles, and needs. The presidency has a symbiotic relationship with the larger culture in which it exists; it is at once shaped by, and shapes, the culture.

The executive branch of the federal government is also flexible, incorporating the needs of diverse constituencies and participants, particularly in recent times. The continued evolution of the presidency as a more diverse institution is relatively assured. How will this evolution take place in the next several decades? In your view, what is the likelihood of a woman being elected president in the next twenty years?

The presidency is a product of both the design of the framers and the desires of the citizenry. As the country's need for stronger presidents has increased, the resources and authorities of presidents have grown to accommodate new powers. But at what point does the presidency become, in the minds of Americans, *too* powerful?

Since the activist administration of Franklin D. Roosevelt, the characterization of the presidency as an "imperial" institution has dogged numerous presidents, most recently former president George W. Bush. Looking ahead, how will the citizens of the future view the scope of presidential power? The answer will depend in large part on the people themselves, particularly those who vote. It will depend on whom citizens elect to the highest office in the land; on how the people's opinions shape (or, in some cases, fail to shape) presidential actions; and on how the people's relationship with their presidents develops. For although the Constitution created a system in which presidential powers can institutionally be checked, the framers did not foresee the most significant checks on modern presidents: the will of the people and a ruthlessly investigatory media, both of which ensure that presidential power is not unrestrained.[44]

STUDY NOW

Summary

1. Presidential Elections

Campaigns are the primary mechanism by which candidates for the presidency outline their priorities and their positions on issues. It is during campaigns that the people forge their relationship with the president. Campaigns are key avenues by which individuals can become involved in the electoral process, such as through participating in nominating conventions, voting on Election Day, and voicing their opinions about the formal selection of the president through the Electoral College system.

2. Presidential Roles in the Domestic Sphere

As chief legislator, the president helps to define Congress's agenda through the annual State of the Union address and influences congressional legislation, particularly concerning the federal budget. Presidents also "legislate" when they veto legislation. As chief economist, the president uses a variety of tools, including the federal budget and the appointment of the chair of the Federal Reserve, to shape economic policy. As party leader, the president acts as the chief of his own party and helps party members get elected to federal, state, and local offices.

3. Presidential Roles in the Foreign Policy Sphere

As chief diplomat, the president and his administration shape the foreign policy of the United States. As commander in chief, the president is the leader of all branches of the armed forces.

4. Overlap in the President's Domestic and Foreign Policy Roles

The president's roles of chief executive and chief of state encompass both domestic and foreign policy spheres. The responsibility as chief executive includes the job of chief administrator of the entire executive branch of government, including the cabinet departments. As chief of state, the president is the ceremonial head of state, a function that is carried out by a separate officeholder in many other nations.

5. The President and the Executive Branch

Leading the executive branch of the federal government is among the president's top responsibilities. Key executive branch offices are the vice president, the cabinet, and the Executive Office of the President (EOP). The EOP includes the White House Office, the Office of Management and Budget, the National Security Council, and the Council of Economic Advisers. Each office assists the president in devising and implementing policy.

6. Presidential Succession

A president who dies in office is succeeded by the vice president, the Speaker of the House, the president pro tem of the Senate, and then by a specified order of cabinet officials, according to the Presidential Succession Act of 1947. When a president becomes incapacitated in office, the Twenty-Fifth Amendment to the Constitution prescribes the course of action.

7. Sources of Presidential Power

Article II, Sections 2 and 3, of the U.S. Constitution enumerate the expressed powers of the president. Inherent powers emanate from the "take care" clause of the Constitution and have been asserted by presidents as constitutionally implied. Statutory powers include powers that the Congress grants presidents, and special presidential powers include emergency powers, executive privilege, and the power to issue executive orders.

8. The People as a Source of Presidential Power

Because the people are a major source of presidential power, presidents continuously seek to secure public support. To that end, presidents exploit their easy access to the "bully pulpit" and the media. High public approval ratings can be an important source of presidential power and are of particular help in getting Congress to enact popular presidential proposals.

9. The Evolution of Presidential Power

The presidential powers of George Washington contrast strikingly with the powers of contemporary presidents. Presidential power first expanded during the administration of Thomas Jefferson, and this authority continued to grow through Andrew Jackson's tenure of office. Franklin D. Roosevelt's administration witnessed the greatest expansion in executive power to date, to the point that modern presidencies have been characterized as "imperial presidencies." The Watergate scandal in 1973 significantly damaged the notion of the imperial presidency. Since then, presidents have fought hard to secure the public trust while often facing a media skeptical of their integrity and motivations.

10. Evaluating Presidential Leadership

Scholarly assessments of presidents differ significantly from the views of the general population. Nonacademics tend to name modern presidents who are effective communicators as among the greatest, whereas scholars cite a number of earlier presidents as most effective.

11. Women in the White House

Traditionally, the most prominent role for women in the White House has been that of First Lady. Some First Ladies, among them Eleanor Roosevelt and Hillary Clinton, have been much more powerful and visible public figures than others. As the pool of potential female presidential candidates increases, there is a growing likelihood that a woman will be elected president.

Key Terms

approval ratings 387

articles of impeachment 392

balanced ticket 378

cabinet 379

chief of staff 381

emergency powers 386

executive agreement 375

Executive Office of the President (EOP) 379

executive order 385

expressed powers 384

executive privilege 386

honeymoon period 387

impeachment 392

inherent powers 384

line-item veto 370

National Security Council (NSC) 381

Office of Management and Budget (OMB) 381

press secretary 381

rally 'round the flag effect 388

signing statement 371

statutory powers 385

take care clause 384

Watergate 391

White House counsel 381

White House Office (WHO) 381

Works Progress Administration (WPA) 390

For Review

1. Explain the process of presidential elections. What role do states play in the process?
2. List the various roles of the president, and provide an example of each.
3. What are the sources of presidential power?
4. How has presidential power evolved over time?
5. Explain the organization and the functions of the Executive Office of the President.
6. Discuss Americans' willingness to vote for a qualified woman for president.

For Critical Thinking and Discussion

1. What do you think are the most important roles for presidents today? Why do these roles matter more than others?
2. Who do you think has been the greatest president in U.S. history? What characteristics do you admire about the president you choose?
3. What factors affect how frequently presidents veto legislation? Does vetoing legislation signify presidential strength or weakness? Explain.
4. What impact did Watergate have on people's perception of the presidency and of government? Have there been lasting effects from this scandal? Explain.
5. Would people you know vote for a woman for president? Which demographic groups do you think would be more willing? Which groups would be less willing? Why?

MULTIPLE CHOICE: Choose the lettered item that answers the question correctly.

1. A written message that the president issues upon signing a bill into law is called
   a. a veto message.
   b. a presidential resolution.
   c. a signing statement.
   d. an executive decree.

2. Appointing the Fed chair and submitting a budget to Congress are part of the president's responsibilities as
   a. party leader.   c. chief legislator.
   b. chief economist.   d. chief diplomat.

3. Appointing the cabinet and determining how the bureaucracy will implement the laws are part of the president's responsibilities as
   a. chief executive.   c. chief legislator.
   b. chief economist.   d. chief diplomat.

4. The office that develops policies and protects the president's legal and political interests is
   a. the Executive Office of the President.
   b. the Chief Executive's Office.
   c. the Office of Management and Budget.
   d. the White House Office.

5. The office that creates the president's annual budget is
   a. the Executive Office of the President.
   b. the Chief Executive's Office.
   c. the Office of Management and Budget.
   d. the White House Office.

6. Presidential powers that are implied in the Constitution are called
   a. enumerated powers.
   b. inherent powers.
   c. expressed powers.
   d. statutory powers.

7. Presidential powers granted to presidents by congressional action are called
   a. enumerated powers.
   b. inherent powers.
   c. expressed powers.
   d. statutory powers.

8. The right of the president to withhold information from Congress or the courts is called
   a. emergency powers.
   b. executive privilege.
   c. expressed powers.
   d. statutory powers.

9. A time early in a new president's administration characterized by optimistic approval by the public is called
   a. the rose-colored-glasses period.
   b. the honeymoon period.
   c. the benefit-of-the-doubt period.
   d. the goodwill period.

10. During the Nixon administration, a scandal involving burglaries and the subsequent cover-up by high-level administration officials was called
    a. Watergate.
    b. Iran-Contra.
    c. Whitewater.
    d. Newport.

FILL IN THE BLANKS.

11. The _____ is the group of experts chosen by the president to serve as advisers on running the country.

12. The executive staff member who serves as both an adviser to the president and manager of the White House Office is the _____ .

13. The _____ consists of the top foreign policy advisers and relevant cabinet officials who advise the president on matters of foreign policy and national security.

14. The constitutional basis for inherent powers is the _____ .

15. A(n) _____ is the power of the president to issue orders that carry the force of law.

Answers: 1. c; 2 b; 3. a; 4. d; 5. c; 6. b; 7. d; 8. b; 9. b; 10. a; 11. cabinet; 12. chief of staff; 13. National Security Council; 14. take care clause; 15. executive order.

RESOURCES FOR RESEARCH AND ACTION

Internet Resources

270 to Win
www.270towin.com This interactive Web site demonstrates how the Electoral College outcome is determined; users can experiment with altering the results of elections. It also contains past voting information for all states.

Center for the Study of the Presidency
www.thepresidency.org This research center analyzes presidential leadership and offers seminars and symposia for presidential researchers, including the Center Fellows program for undergraduate students.

Presidential Libraries
You can find the Web sites of the libraries of recent presidents, which typically include a wealth of information about individual presidencies and archival resources, by searching "[President's name] Presidential Library."

The White House
www.whitehouse.gov You can visit the White House Web site for information about current issues and news, the text of presidential speeches, links to cabinet departments, the EOP, and information about the First Lady and the vice president.

Internet Activism

Twitter
Follow President Obama's White House spokesman Robert Gibbs on Twitter. Follow: PressSec.

YouTube
Subscribe to the White House's YouTube channel at www.youtube .com/user/whitehouse.

Recommended Readings

Borrelli, MaryAnne. *The President's Cabinet: Gender, Power, and Representation*. Boulder, CO: Lynne Rienner, 2002. Analysis of the evolution of presidential cabinets in terms of gender representation.

Ehrenhalt, Alan. *The United States of Ambition: Politicians, Power and the Pursuit of Office*. New York: Times Books, 1991. Interesting account of the importance of personal drive and ambition in catapulting would-be presidents to the White House.

Halberstam, David. *The Best and the Brightest*. Fawcett Books, 1993. Riveting analysis of how the Kennedy and Johnson administrations entrenched the United States in the war in Vietnam.

Neustadt, Richard E. *Presidential Power and the Modern President*. New York: The Free Press, 1990. Update of the author's classic 1960 volumes, explaining the evolution of power in the modern presidency and probing, in particular, presidents' ability to persuade.

Schlesinger, Arthur M., Jr. *The Imperial Presidency*. Boston: Houghton Mifflin, 1973. Classic volume describing how the presidency has become a rarely checked, "imperial" institution.

Suskind, Ronald. *The Price of Loyalty: George W. Bush, the White House, and the Education of Paul O'Neill*. New York: Simon & Schuster, 2004. Critical account of decision making in the George W. Bush White House.

Woodward, Bob, and Carl Bernstein. *All the President's Men*, 2nd ed. New York: Simon & Schuster, 1994. Classic work that launched investigative journalism, particularly concerning the presidency, in which the authors describe their investigation of the Watergate scandal that led to President Richard Nixon's resignation.

Movies of Interest

Recount (2008)
This movie chronicles the 2000 presidential election, focusing on the controversy surrounding ballot counting in Florida that culminated in the U.S. Supreme Court case *Bush v. Gore*.

Air Force One (1997)
In this suspense thriller, the president of the United States, played by Harrison Ford, is forced to do battle with terrorist hijackers aboard Air Force One.

The American President (1995)
Rob Reiner directed this comedic drama about an unmarried male president (portrayed by Michael Douglas) and a lobbyist (Annette Bening), who fall in love.

All the President's Men (1976)
In this 1976 film adaptation of the book by the same name, Robert Redford and Dustin Hoffman star as *Washington Post* reporters Bob Woodward and Carl Bernstein (respectively), who uncover the details of the Watergate scandal that led to President Nixon's resignation.

In addition, there are numerous biographical movies of American presidents, including many that air on the A&E network's *Biography* series. You can find these programs at www.biography.com.

The Bureaucracy

THEN

The federal bureaucracy under President George Washington had three departments and two offices serving a national population of 4 million.

NOW

Almost 3 million civilian federal bureaucrats—plus 35 to 40 million state, local, private for-profit, and non-profit bureaucrats—serve a national population of over 300 million.

NEXT

Will the bureaucracy remain a target of criticism from citizens, candidates, and elected officials?

Will the best and the brightest respond to the call to serve as a large proportion of federal employees retire in the next decade?

Will the volume of public service outsourced to private organizations continue to increase?

Citizens turn to the government

to solve their problems and provide services. Through policy-making processes, Congress and the president determine which problems the national government will address and what services it will provide. After Congress and the president approve policies, millions of public servants put them into action. The daily implementation of policy by public servants is the key to citizens' satisfaction with government.

President Barack Obama (2009–present) estimated the cost of providing national public services in his proposed 2011 budget to be $3.7 trillion.[1] This staggering sum amounts to $10.2 billion per day, $425 million per hour, or $7 million per minute. Almost 3 million national civilian bureaucrats and 1.5 million military personnel provide public services. Beyond the legions of federal public servants, almost 20 million state and local bureaucrats assist in implementing national public policies. In addition, through grants and contracts with the national government, millions of employees in private for-profit businesses and in nonprofit organizations help to do the work of the national government.

Americans expect these millions of government and nongovernment employees to provide public services and benefits efficiently and effectively. In our democracy, citizens also expect accountability. They want assurance that their tax dollars are spent properly for the public good. But such accountability is hindered by the complexities of public service delivery. Moreover, assessing performance is difficult when the services bureaucrats provide include ensuring justice and domestic tranquility, defending the nation, and promoting the general welfare.

Bureaucrats and Bureaucracy

Most people think of government agencies when they hear the word *bureaucracy*, and they think of government employees when they hear the word *bureaucrat*—and their thoughts are often negative. They typically focus on a large government organization with inefficient, dehumanizing procedures that require tedious paperwork. They visualize long lines at the Department of Motor Vehicles as uncaring workers (who they believe cannot be fired) slowly process mounds of forms.

Taxpayers are not the only people who think and speak negatively of the bureaucracy. Even our presidents—who rely on bureaucrats and bureaucracies to implement their policy promises—historically have not hesitated to criticize bureaucrats. In an April 2009 radio and Internet address, President Barack Obama stated that with the leaders he had placed in the bureaucracy, in the positions of chief performance officer, chief information officer, and chief technology officer, "I am confident that we can break our bad habits, put an end to the mismanagement that has plagued our government and start living within our means."

Are the negative images and the criticisms of bureaucrats and bureaucracies fair? Before we can answer, we must understand who the bureaucrats are, what they are hired to do, and how they are expected to accomplish their work.

Who Are the Bureaucrats?

Who was the last government employee with whom you had a face-to-face interaction? Who was the last government worker to make a decision that directly affected you? Chances are it was not an elected official such as the president or a member of the Senate. It was probably not an appointed federal judge. Rather, the government employees that you (and the people around you) interact with and are affected by on a daily basis are those individuals who are hired into executive branch agencies to implement public policy—that is, **bureaucrats.** Bureaucrats include government employees such as the administrator who reviews college students' Pell Grant applications, the Food and Drug Administration (FDA) inspector who monitors food and drug quality, and the Equal Employment Opportunity Commission (EEOC) lawyer who argues that an employer allowed sexual harassment of its workers. Bureaucrats provide the public services that elected officials authorize, and in doing so they make decisions that affect people daily.

Because elected officials and ordinary citizens perpetually criticize bureaucrats and bureaucracies, individuals working in the national bureaucracy do not take being called a bureaucrat as a compliment. Bureaucrats prefer the term *public servant,* because that phrase captures how they see themselves and their essential job goal.[2] Even as people love to bash bureaucrats, data from the International Social Survey Programme (ISSP) indicate that 63.9 percent of U.S. respondents agreed that "public service" in the United States is "somewhat committed" to serving the people, and an additional 11.6 percent agreed that public service is "very committed" to serving the people.[3] See "Global Context" on page 404 for a cross-national look at citizens' perceptions of the public service commitment of the bureaucracy in their country.

Charles Goodsell, a respected scholar of public administration and public policy, notes that studies show government employees to be very hard workers who are motivated by the recognition of the importance of public service. This public service motivation is distinct from the motivation of private-sector employees, for whom salary levels and shorter work hours provide key incentives.[4] Compared with private-sector employees, public servants have higher levels of formal education, must comply with more stringent codes of behavior, and express a greater concern for serving the public.[5] In addition, government bureaucrats tend to report somewhat higher levels of job satisfaction than do their private sector counterparts.[6]

Very few children say that they want to be bureaucrats. Yet millions do aspire to careers as public servants, including teachers, police officers, lawyers, and health care professionals. National, state, and local governments hire professionals such as these to implement public policy—to do the business of government. Chances are, whatever your major in college, you can get a job as a public servant. In fact, approximately 40 percent of federal civilian public servants and almost 50 percent of both state and local public servants have at least a bachelor's degree. In comparison, only about 25 percent of private-sector workers have at least a bachelor's degree.[7] Figure 13.1 presents a comparison of the distribution of employment by major occupational groups for the federal government and for all industries in the United States.

Joining the 23 million national, state, and local bureaucrats are the so-called **shadow bureaucrats**—employees on the payroll of private for-profit businesses and private nonprofit organizations with government

bureaucrats
people employed in a government executive branch unit to implement public policy; public administrators; public servants

shadow bureaucrats
people hired and paid by private for-profit and nonprofit organizations that implement public policy through a government contract

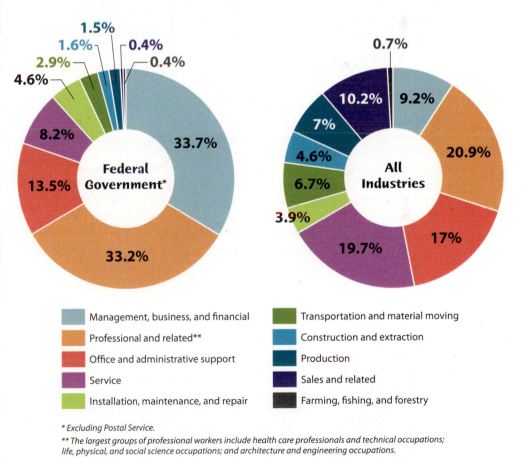

Management, business, and financial
Professional and related**
Office and administrative support
Service
Installation, maintenance, and repair
Transportation and material moving
Construction and extraction
Production
Sales and related
Farming, fishing, and forestry

Excluding Postal Service.

** *The largest groups of professional workers include health care professionals and technical occupations; life, physical, and social science occupations; and architecture and engineering occupations.*

FIGURE 13.1

Percent Distribution of Employment in Federal Government and All Industries by Major Occupational Group in 2008

SOURCE: U.S. Bureau of Labor Statistics, "Career Guide to Industries, 2010–11 Edition," http://data.bls.gov/cgi-bin/print.pl/oco/cg/cgs041.htm.

GLOBAL CONTEXT

PUBLIC SERVICE COMMITMENT TO SERVING THE PEOPLE

Criticism of bureaucrats in the private and public sectors is widespread. Yet research by political scientists David J. Houston and Lauren K. Harding reveals that the majority of citizens in European countries, Canada, and the United States think that the public service in their own country is at least somewhat committed to, if not very committed to, serving the people.*

The research results reveal certain patterns. In most countries—the United States being an exception—there is a significant positive correlation between a person's being employed as a public servant himself or herself and thinking that public service is committed to serving the public. In addition, younger and older citizens are generally more likely than middle-aged citizens to perceive that their national bureaucracies have a distinct public service motivation. But most important to thinking that one's national bureaucracy is committed to public service is a person's overall attitudes about government. Citizens with a relatively greater sense that they have the ability to influence government report higher trust in public service, as measured by their belief that the bureaucracy is committed to public service. Moreover, those who think that democracy is working well in their nation are more likely to report that their public servants are committed to serving the public.

So, although bureaucrat-bashing is common, research indicates that at least in the majority of European nations, Canada, and the United States, the majority of people believe that public servants have a public service motivation—in other words, that bureaucrats are committed to serving the public.

COUNTRY	PERCENTAGE OF CITIZENS WHO THINK THE PUBLIC SERVICE IN THEIR COUNTRY IS SOMEWHAT OR VERY COMMITTED TO SERVING THE PEOPLE
Austria	80.3%
Ireland	77.1%
United States	**75.4%**
Switzerland	71.8%
Canada	69.9%
Great Britain	68.9%
Norway	67.9%
Belgium	66.5%
Germany-West	63.9%
Denmark	60.3%
Germany-East	59.5%
Netherlands	56.7%
France	56.1%
Finland	55.6%
Sweden	55.0%
Spain	50.3%
Portugal	39.3%

*David J. Houston and Lauren K. Harding, "Trust in the Public Service: A Cross-National Examination," presented at the 66th Annual National Conference of the Midwest Political Science Association, Chicago, April 3–6, 2008, p. 24.

contracting-out
also called *outsourcing* or *privatizing*; a process by which the government contracts with a private for-profit or nonprofit organization to provide public services, such as disaster relief, or resources needed by the government, such as fighter planes

contracts. Through a process of **contracting-out** (also called *outsourcing* or *privatizing*), the government signs work contracts with these organizations to assist in the implementation of national policy. In other words, shadow bureaucrats do the work of government, but they do not receive a government paycheck.

In summary, today, a mix of national, state, and local bureaucrats, as well as shadow bureaucrats, deliver national public services. In addition to having in common the delivery of public services, public and shadow bureaucrats share a similar work environment. That is, they work in bureaucratic organizations.

Bureaucracy: An Organizational Structure

Max Weber (1864–1920), the "father of sociology," coined the word *bureaucracy* to describe large organizations, such as government, with the following features: a division of labor, specialization of job tasks, hiring systems based on worker competency, hierarchy with a vertical chain of command, and standard operating procedures. Weber argued that those features enhance the performance and accountability of large organizations. In our discussion, **bureaucracy** is any organization with a hierarchical structure, although the term is most commonly used to designate a government agency or the collection of all national executive branch organizations.

Organizations with those bureaucratic features are not unique to government. For example, colleges and universities are also bureaucratic organizations. They have a division of labor with specialization of tasks. (Consider the various academic departments, each specializing in a different discipline.) They hire employees (such as professors, computer technicians, and student affairs staff) with the knowledge, skills, and abilities essential to doing their jobs well. Colleges and universities also have a hierarchy with a chain of command (faculty members report to chairpersons, who report to a dean, who reports to the vice president for academic affairs, who reports to the president, who makes final decisions). University employees implement standardized procedures to register students for classes, determine financial aid eligibility, and punish violations of the conduct code.

So, although most people think of government when they hear the word *bureaucracy*, a bureaucracy is *any* organization with Weber's bureaucratic structure. Yet in this chapter, as is appropriate to our study of American government, we focus on the departments and agencies that compose the national government bureaucracy. And even though most people think of government employees when they hear the term *bureaucrat*, nongovernment employees, as we have seen, may also be paid with taxpayer money to serve the public, and so it is appropriate that we consider them, too.

Federal Bureaucrats

Political scientists distinguish among national bureaucrats according to several factors, including the process by which they are hired, the procedures by which they can be fired, and the grounds for which they can be fired. On the basis of these factors, we can differentiate among three categories of national civilian bureaucrats: political appointees, civil servants, and senior executive service employees.

Political Appointees

In 1863, President Abraham Lincoln, suffering from smallpox, told his secretary to "send all the office seekers in here. I finally have something I can give to them all." Indeed, before the creation of the civil service system in 1883, presidents had the authority to hire bureaucrats, selecting whomever they wanted and establishing whatever qualifications they desired, in a noncompetitive hiring system known as *patronage*. Under the patronage system, hordes of men seeking government jobs presented themselves to the president after each election.

Every four years, after the presidential election, the federal government publishes the **plum book,** which lists thousands of top jobs in the bureaucracy to which the president will appoint people through the patronage system. As we've seen, there is no standard process for assessing the knowledge, skills, and abilities needed for appointive positions, nor is there open competition for these patronage jobs. Further, because citizens expect presidents to be responsive and accountable to them, and presidents rely on their political appointees to support their efforts to meet those expectations, presidents tend to appoint people who support their policy preferences to these top positions.

Patronage positions come with a downside for the appointees: no job security. The president not only hires but also can fire political appointees at his pleasure. More common than firing is the resignation or retirement of appointees who no longer enjoy presidential approval.

Civil Servants

During the first century of U.S. history, all national bureaucrats got their jobs through patronage. Then in 1883, mobilized by the assassination of President James Garfield (whose brief administration lasted from March to September 1881) by an unsuccessful seeker of a

bureaucracy

any organization with a hierarchical structure; most commonly used to designate a government agency or the collection of all national executive branch organizations

plum book

a publication that lists the top jobs in the bureaucracy to which the president will appoint people through the patronage system

> This engraving depicts President James Garfield's assassination. Shot in July 1881, Garfield died two and a half months later of a fatal heart attack brought on by his doctors' attempts to find the assassin's bullet in his body.
What was President Garfield's assassin's motivation? How did the tragedy change the process of choosing civil servants?

patronage position, Congress and President Chester Arthur (1881–1885) approved the Pendleton Civil Service Act. This law introduced a merit-based civil service system to the national government. The hiring principles of the **merit-based civil service** system are open competition, competence, and political neutrality. **Civil servants** are bureaucrats hired through the merit-based personnel system. The 1978 Civil Service Reform Act reinforced these merit principles and legislated the right to unionize for many federal civil servants.

OPEN COMPETITION AND COMPETENCE

Today, merit-based civil service jobs, which compose at least 85 percent of the national bureaucracy, are open and accessible to all who wish to compete for a position. The competition requires that candidates prove their competence to do the job (their merit). Jobs covered by the merit-based civil service system are analyzed and ranked on the basis of the knowledge, skills, and abilities needed to do the job competently. A job's rank determines its salary. The pay scales offer equal pay for jobs of equal worth, as determined by the job analysis. (See Table 13.1 for the pay scales and education requirements for white-collar government jobs.)

Several national laws have helped to make today's civil servants, as a group, look more like the U.S. pop-

TABLE 13.1

Education Requirements and Salary Ranges for White-Collar Federal Civil Service Positions* (2009)

Level	Salary Range	Qualifying Education
GS-1	$17,540–21,944	No high school diploma required
GS-2	$19,721–24,815	High school graduation or equivalent
GS-3	$21,517–27,970	One academic year above high school
GS-4	$24, 156–31,401	Two academic years above high school, or associate's degree
GS-5	$27,026–35,135	Four academic years above high school leading to a bachelor's degree, or a bachelor's degree
GS-7	$33,477–43,521	Bachelor's degree with superior academic achievement or one academic year of graduate education or law school
GS-9	$40,949–53,234	Master's (or equivalent graduate degree) or two academic years of progressively higher level graduate education
GS-11	$49,544–64,403	PhD or equivalent degree or three academic years of progressively higher level graduate education
GS-12	$59,383–77,194	Completion of all requirements for a doctoral or equivalent degree (for research positions only)
GS-13	$70,615–91,801	Appropriate specialized experience.
GS-14	$83,445–108,483	Appropriate specialized experience.
GS-15	$98,156–127,604	Appropriate specialized experience.

* Table shows the amount and level of education typically required for each grade for which education alone can be qualifying.

SOURCES: www.opm.gov/flsa/oca/09tables/html/gs.asp (salary data); www.govcentral.com/benefits/articles/1757-what-determines-where-you-stand-on-the-gs-scale (education level data).

ulation at large than they did in the past. Title VII of the 1964 Civil Rights Act, as amended, prohibits employers, including the government, from making personnel decisions based on factors irrelevant to job competence, such as sex, race, color, ethnicity, age, and disabilities that can be reasonably accommodated. The merit principles of the 1978 Civil Service Reform Act (CSRA) reiterate this prohibition against discrimination in personnel practices. The bans against discrimination in Title VII and the CSRA do not apply to the positions of elected officials or political appointees.

Title VI of the 1964 Civil Rights Act prohibits discrimination based on race, color, religion, and ethnicity in educational opportunities offered by institutions receiving federal funding. Title IX, which was added to the act in 1972, extended this prohibition to sex-based discrimination. Enforcement of these laws has increased the diversity of people who are able to gain the education and experience needed to do government jobs competently. The interaction of Titles VI, VII, and IX has fostered greater *descriptive representation* among civil servants than among any other category of government worker. This means that the people serving resemble the larger population whom they serve in demographic characteristics such as race, age, ethnicity, sex, religion, and economic status. "Analyzing the Sources" on page 408 considers the influence these laws have had on the national civil service.

POLITICAL NEUTRALITY Merit-based civil servants cannot be fired merely because someone with different political beliefs is elected or appointed to supervise them. They can be fired for poor quality of work (misfeasance), or for nonperformance of their work (nonfeasance), or for violating the rules or regulations that guide their work (malfeasance). The system thus gives civil servants job protection and does not require them (unlike political appointees) to adhere to the president's policy preferences. Hence the civil service system supports political neutrality to ensure efficient and effective public service delivery.

In 1939, Congress approved the Hatch Act, limiting civil servants' rights to engage in political activity. The rationale behind this law's passage was that if civil servants stayed out of politics, they would be less inclined to allow party loyalty to influence their job performance. Over time, however, civil servants have contested the constitutionality of the legal limits on their political engagement. As a result, the Hatch Act has been modified in the last few decades to loosen the restrictions on civil servants' political activities. This easing of limits on political engagement has allowed civil servants to exercise their First Amendment rights of expression, including political expression, more freely and fully.

CIVIL SERVICE REFORM ACT (1978) "There is widespread criticism of federal government performance. The public suspects that there are too many government workers,

THEN NOW NEXT

Characteristics of Federal Bureaucrats

THEN (1970)*	NOW (2011)**
30% female	44% female
Average age: 41	Average age: 47
Average length of service: 13 years	Average length of service: 16 years
20% minorities (included "Negroes, American Indians, Orientals, and persons with Spanish surnames")	32% minorities (includes "black, Hispanic, Asian/Pacific Islander, and American Indian/Alaska Native")
80% in white-collar positions	89% in white-collar positions
91% in competitive, civil service positions	72% in competitive, civil service positions

WHAT'S NEXT?

> Will the percentage of female and minority bureaucrats continue to increase? Why or why not?

> Will the percentage of white-collar positions continue to increase with continuing changes in technology? Explain.

> How might the health of the economy affect the retirement decisions of the many bureaucrats who become eligible for retirement in the next few years, and hence affect the average age of bureaucrats as well as the average length of service?

> How will demands for new or expanded government services affect the proportion of white-collar positions in the federal bureaucracy? Explain your answer.

* U.S. Department of Commerce, Bureau of the Census, *Statistical Abstract* 1972.
** Office of Personnel Management, *Federal Civilian Workforce Statistics, The Fact Book* 2007 Edition.

merit-based civil service
a personnel system in which bureaucrats are hired on the basis of the principles of competence, equal opportunity (open competition), and political neutrality; once hired, these civil servants have job protection

civil servants
bureaucrats hired through a merit-based personnel system who have job protection

ANALYZING THE SOURCES

EQUAL EDUCATIONAL AND EMPLOYMENT OPPORTUNITY AND STRATIFIED OCCUPATIONAL SEGREGATION

Laws prohibit race-based and sex-based discrimination in educational and employment opportunities. In addition, affirmative action requires most governments (as employers) and private businesses with government contracts to adopt and implement personnel plans detailing how they will actively recruit qualified women and minorities for open positions.

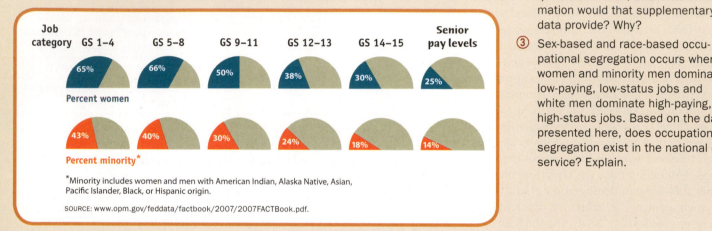

Job category	GS 1–4	GS 5–8	GS 9–11	GS 12–13	GS 14–15	Senior pay levels
Percent women	65%	66%	50%	38%	30%	25%
Percent minority*	43%	40%	30%	24%	18%	14%

*Minority includes women and men with American Indian, Alaska Native, Asian, Pacific Islander, Black, or Hispanic origin.

SOURCE: www.opm.gov/feddata/factbook/2007/2007FACTBook.pdf.

COLLEGE DEGREES CONFERRED BY SEX AND RACE/ETHNICITY

DEMOGRAPHIC	BACHELOR'S	MASTER'S	DOCTOR'S*
Men	42.5%	41.2%	52.9%
Women	57.5%	58.2%	47.1%
White	70.0%	60.3%	56.2%
Black	8.7%	7.8%	5.1%
Hispanic	6.3%	4.4%	3.2%
Asian/Pacific Islander	6.2%	4.8%	4.9%
Native American	0.7%	0.5%	0.4%

* Doctor's degrees are the highest degree a student can earn for graduate study and include EdD, JD, PhD.

SOURCE: U.S. Department of Education, National Center for Education Statistics, http://nces.ed.gov/fastfacts/display.asp?id=72.

Evaluating the Evidence

① Review the accompanying chart and table. Do equal educational and equal employment laws work? Explain.

② Are there additional data you would want to review before answering question 1? If so, what kind of information would that supplementary data provide? Why?

③ Sex-based and race-based occupational segregation occurs when women and minority men dominate low-paying, low-status jobs and white men dominate high-paying, high-status jobs. Based on the data presented here, does occupational segregation exist in the national civil service? Explain.

that they are underworked, overpaid, and insulated from the consequences of incompetence."[8] With those words, President Jimmy Carter (1977–1981) announced proposed civil service reforms in 1978. The resulting Civil Service Reform Act of 1978 (CSRA) reaffirmed and expanded the merit principles established by the Pendleton Act and reorganized the management of the national civil service. Carter's reforms also eliminated the Civil Service Commission (CSC), the central personnel office created by the Pendleton Act.

Three new independent administrative agencies—the Office of Personnel Management (OPM), the Merit System Protection Board (MSPB), and the Federal Labor Relations Authority (FLRA)—replaced the old Civil Service Commission. Today, the OPM is the central personnel office, responsible for developing and implementing merit-based civil service personnel policies and procedures. The MSPB ensures proper implementation of the merit system. The CSRA also legislated for the collective bargaining rights (unionization rights) of national civil servants and created the FLRA to monitor the relations between unionized bureaucrats and the federal government.

UNIONIZED CIVIL SERVANTS Twenty-eight percent of U.S. federal civil servants belong to labor unions.[9] The American Federation of Government Employees (AFGE) is the largest such union, representing 600,000 national bureaucrats. The level of union membership varies dramatically from agency to agency. Whereas about 90 percent of U.S. Postal Service employees are union members (not AFGE members but members of one of several unions for postal employees), the level of union membership among bureaucrats in the State Department is close to zero. Part of the explanation for the range of unionization levels across national agencies is the percentage of each agency's workers that is composed of blue-collar workers. In general, blue-collar workers are likelier to be union members than are white-collar workers.

Unionized civil servants have leverage to negotiate certain conditions of work. For example, they may bargain for improved training opportunities and enhanced due process protections in disciplinary matters. National civil service employee unions cannot negotiate salaries or work hours, however. And unlike private-sector unions, national civil servant unions do not have the legal right to strike. The prohibition of strikes by national civil servants is typically justified by the fact that these workers provide essential services that are vital to public safety. A strike by these workers would therefore threaten public safety and health.

THE SENIOR EXECUTIVE SERVICE One additional CSRA-mandated change to the national bureaucracy was the creation of a new category of civil servant, the **senior executive service (SES)** bureaucrat. SES positions are hybrids of political appointee and civil service positions. The SES includes most of the top managerial, supervisory, and policy positions that are not patronage positions.

senior executive service (SES) a unique personnel system for top managerial, supervisory, and policy positions offering less job security but higher pay than the merit-based civil service system

> First Lady Michele Obama greets employees at the Department of Housing and Urban Development as she arrives to make remarks. Mrs. Obama visited with public servants from numerous departments and agencies during the first few months of President Barack Obama's administration to thank them for their service to the nation.

At least 90 percent of SES bureaucrats are career civil servants (hired through an open competition based on competence) who have given up some job security for positions with higher pay. These employees can be moved from job to job and from agency to agency (less job security), but they are immune from firing except for proven misfeasance, nonfeasance, or malfeasance. The remaining SES bureaucrats are typically hired from outside the merit-based civil service system. Appointed with approval of the OPM and the White House Office of Presidential Personnel, these SES noncareer bureaucrats do not face open competition and do not have the job protection of merit-based civil servants.[10]

Supplementing the work of national political appointees, civil servants, and SES bureaucrats are armies of state, local, and shadow bureaucrats. The volume of national public policy executed by these non-national bureaucrats has been increasing dramatically since the 1960s because of devolution and a rise in contracting-out.

State, Local, and Shadow Bureaucrats

Today, the overwhelming majority of the almost 20 million state and local bureaucrats, and possibly as many as 15 million shadow bureaucrats, provide various national public services. Through devolution and contracting-out, the national government relies on these non-national bureaucrats to serve the people's daily needs. National bureaucrats monitor these state, local, and shadow bureaucrats' compliance with the rules and regulations that come with devolution and outsourcing.

As you may recall from Chapter 3, devolution is the federal government's shifting of greater responsibility for financing and administering public policies to state and local governments, putting the implementation of national policy in the hands of state and local bureaucrats. Mandates in federal laws require state and local governments to implement national policies. In cases where national law preempts (takes precedence over) state and local law, state and local bureaucrats have to implement federal policy instead of state or local programs. Preemption is common, for example, in the area of environmental protection, where state and local officials must ensure private- and public-sector compliance with federal air, water, and landfill standards.

As we've seen, the national government also contracts with shadow bureaucracies—private for-profit and nonprofit organizations—to provide vital services as well as to produce certain resources needed to serve the public. Outsourcing, for example, includes the federal government's contracting-out with Lockheed Martin and Boeing for the production of defense resources such as helmets, fighter planes, and laser-guided missiles. Traditionally, too, the government undertakes large capital projects such as the construction of roads and government buildings through contracts with private businesses. Further, the federal government outsources medical as well as social research to cure disease and address the ills of society. And through government contracts, the Red Cross has dispensed disaster relief for decades. The federal government's contracts totaled more than $523 billion in its 2009 budget.[11]

The national government expects that contracting-out will reduce the expense of government by eliminating the overhead costs (including employee benefits and basic operating costs) of producing public goods and services. Outsourcing also provides a means by which the government can hire experts and specialists when they are needed and keep them off the payroll at other times. The government can eliminate these contracted personnel and their costs more easily than it can fire civil servants, who have job protection. The expectation is that the private- and nonprofit-sector employees and organizations will be more efficient and effective than government bureaucracies.

Some government contracts and grants-in-aid flow to faith-based organizations (FBOs). This development has sparked concerns about the preservation of the constitutionally mandated separation of church and government. (See "Thinking Critically About Democracy.")

Even with the increased use of state, local, and shadow bureaucrats, the national bureaucracy itself is neither small nor streamlined. It is composed of thousands of bodies with a

SHOULD FAITH-BASED ORGANIZATIONS RECEIVE PUBLIC FUNDING TO DELIVER SOCIAL SERVICES?

The Issue: The federal government provides more than $3 billion of grants-in-aid to thousands of faith-based organizations (FBOs) each year to provide social services. For example, the Young Men's Christian Association (YMCA) and the Salvation Army both receive federal funds to support their housing, counseling, and after-school programs. The amount of public funding going to FBOs has been on the rise since the 1990s. However, the courts have interpreted the First Amendment of the Constitution, which establishes religious freedom, to mean that there must be a separation between religious organizations and government support, including financial support. So the question is, should faith-based organizations be receiving public funds?

Yes: Faith-based hospitals, nursing homes, and children's institutions, as well as the YMCA and the Salvation Army, have received government funds for decades. These FBOs provide vital services to those in need and in some cases do a superior job at distributing these services. People in need of assistance for housing, food, and clothing—and individuals seeking treatment for an addiction—feel more comfortable turning to a familiar local religious organization than to a complex government bureaucracy. In addition, because volunteers compose a large percentage of the FBO labor force, providing social services through FBOs is cheaper than paying government workers.

No: First, it is unconstitutional for the government to support a religion. Providing funding to any FBO flagrantly does exactly this.

Further, we cannot ensure that the FBO employee who has a strong faith will not include religious education or preaching in delivering services. Nor can we prevent such an individual from using a religious test to determine whom he or she will serve. Government bureaucrats who monitor the grant rules will have difficulty ensuring that public money is not supporting religious activities.

Other approaches: The law prohibits FBOs from spending public funds on religious activities. Therefore, FBOs should be required to keep separate accounts for the public funds they receive. Such separate accounts would make it easier to ensure that FBOs are not spending public funds on religious activities.

What do you think?

① Reflecting back on the discussion in Chapter 4 of the First Amendment's religious freedom guarantee, do you think the public funding of social services delivered by faith-based organizations violates the Constitution? Explain.

② Just as opponents of public funding of FBOs claim that FBO employees may push their religious beliefs on clients or use a religious test to deny services to some clients, do you think that some government employees may also behave this way? How might the government prevent such behavior among its bureaucrats as well as publicly funded FBO employees?

---

variety of names and organizational structures. The national bureaucracy, an evolving organism, continues to grow in complexity even as it privatizes and devolves more of its work.

The Evolution and Organization of the Federal Bureaucracy

Four million people resided in the United States in 1789, the year George Washington was sworn in as the first president. Most of them lived off the land and were self-sufficient; they expected few services from the national government. The federal bureaucracy consisted of the Department of War, Department of Foreign Affairs, Treasury Department, Attorney General's Office, and Postal Services Office. Those three departments and two offices handled the core functions demanded of the national government at that time: respectively, providing defense; managing foreign affairs; collecting revenues and paying bills; resolving lawsuits and legal questions; and delivering mail. Initially, other than for military personnel, the work of public servants was mostly clerical in nature.

Today, as the U.S. population tops 300 million, more than 2,000 executive branch units, employing 4 million bureaucrats (2.7 million civilian bureaucrats and about 1.5 million military personnel), implement volumes of national policies. The number of bureaucrats is equal to the nation's population in 1789. Figure 13.2, the organizational chart of the federal government, provides a window on the breadth of the federal bureaucracy today. Figures 13.3 and 13.4 show the growth in size and cost of the national bureaucracy since the 1940s.

Political scientists distinguish among five categories of executive branch organizations based on their structure and the type of work they perform: (1) departments, (2) indepen-

FIGURE 13.2

U.S. Government Organizational Chart

SOURCE: www.gpoaccess.gov/gmanual/browse-gm-08.html.

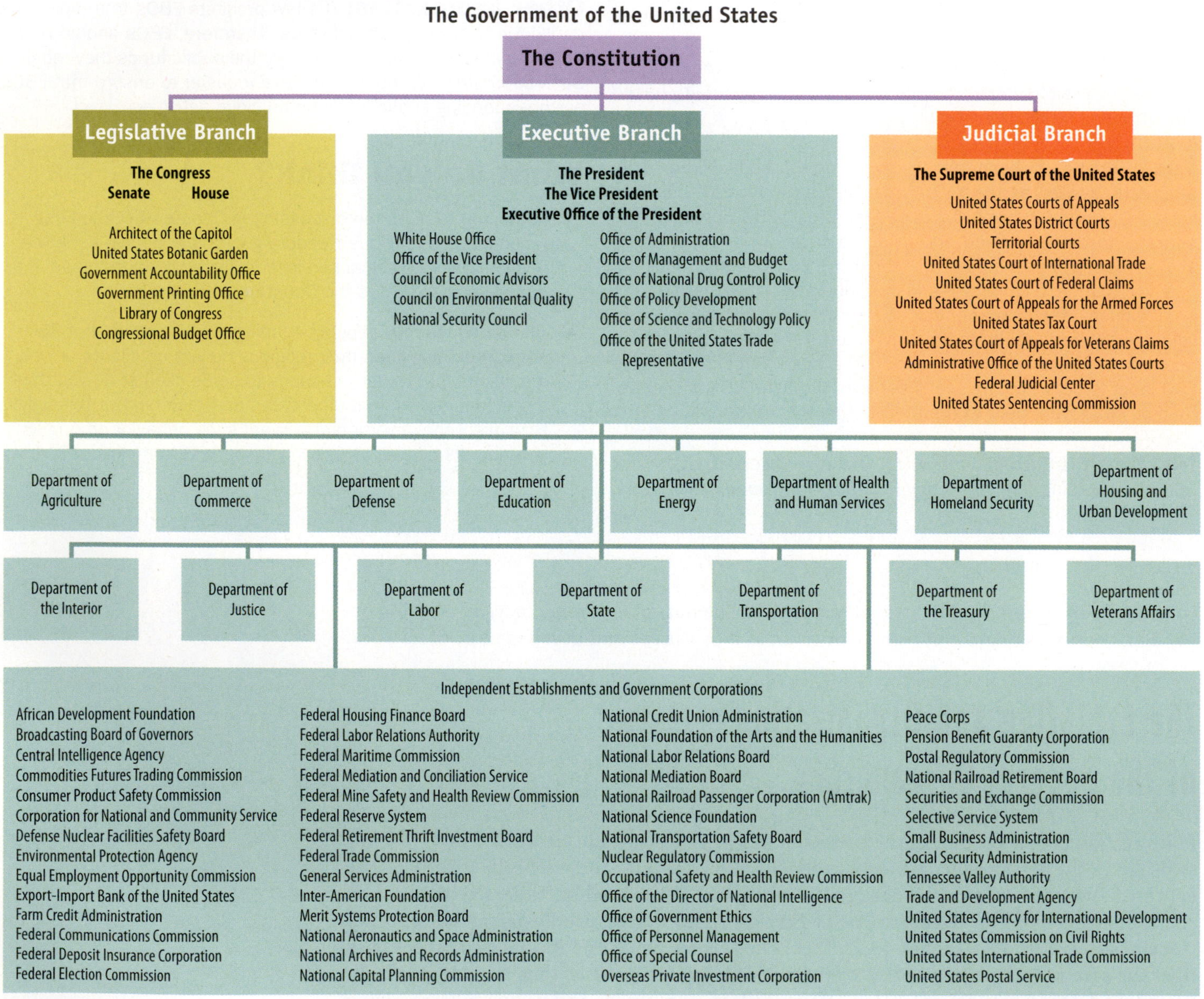

The Government of the United States

The Constitution

Legislative Branch

The Congress
Senate   House

Architect of the Capitol
United States Botanic Garden
Government Accountability Office
Government Printing Office
Library of Congress
Congressional Budget Office

Executive Branch

The President
The Vice President
Executive Office of the President

White House Office
Office of the Vice President
Council of Economic Advisors
Council on Environmental Quality
National Security Council

Office of Administration
Office of Management and Budget
Office of National Drug Control Policy
Office of Policy Development
Office of Science and Technology Policy
Office of the United States Trade
Representative

Judicial Branch

The Supreme Court of the United States

United States Courts of Appeals
United States District Courts
Territorial Courts
United States Court of International Trade
United States Court of Federal Claims
United States Court of Appeals for the Armed Forces
United States Tax Court
United States Court of Appeals for Veterans Claims
Administrative Office of the United States Courts
Federal Judicial Center
United States Sentencing Commission

Department of Agriculture
Department of Commerce
Department of Defense
Department of Education
Department of Energy
Department of Health and Human Services
Department of Homeland Security
Department of Housing and Urban Development

Department of the Interior
Department of Justice
Department of Labor
Department of State
Department of Transportation
Department of the Treasury
Department of Veterans Affairs

Independent Establishments and Government Corporations

African Development Foundation
Broadcasting Board of Governors
Central Intelligence Agency
Commodities Futures Trading Commission
Consumer Product Safety Commission
Corporation for National and Community Service
Defense Nuclear Facilities Safety Board
Environmental Protection Agency
Equal Employment Opportunity Commission
Export-Import Bank of the United States
Farm Credit Administration
Federal Communications Commission
Federal Deposit Insurance Corporation
Federal Election Commission

Federal Housing Finance Board
Federal Labor Relations Authority
Federal Maritime Commission
Federal Mediation and Conciliation Service
Federal Mine Safety and Health Review Commission
Federal Reserve System
Federal Retirement Thrift Investment Board
Federal Trade Commission
General Services Administration
Inter-American Foundation
Merit Systems Protection Board
National Aeronautics and Space Administration
National Archives and Records Administration
National Capital Planning Commission

National Credit Union Administration
National Foundation of the Arts and the Humanities
National Labor Relations Board
National Mediation Board
National Railroad Passenger Corporation (Amtrak)
National Science Foundation
National Transportation Safety Board
Nuclear Regulatory Commission
Occupational Safety and Health Review Commission
Office of the Director of National Intelligence
Office of Government Ethics
Office of Personnel Management
Office of Special Counsel
Overseas Private Investment Corporation

Peace Corps
Pension Benefit Guaranty Corporation
Postal Regulatory Commission
National Railroad Retirement Board
Securities and Exchange Commission
Selective Service System
Small Business Administration
Social Security Administration
Tennessee Valley Authority
Trade and Development Agency
United States Agency for International Development
United States Commission on Civil Rights
United States International Trade Commission
United States Postal Service

Growth in National Civilian Bureaucrats and State and Local Bureaucrats

Year	Federal bureaucrats (thousands)	State and local bureaucrats (thousands)
1940	1,033	1,928
1945	3,496	3,140
1950	2,052	4,258
1955	2,376	5,054
1960	2,496	6,387
1965	2,496	7,696
1970	2,944	9,822
1975	2,848	11,937
1980	2,821	13,375
1985	3,008	13,519
1990	3,067	15,219
1995	2,858	16,484
2000	2,639	17,925
2005	2,636	19,078
2007	2,636	19,538

Legend:
- Federal bureaucrats (thousands)
- State and local bureaucrats (thousands)

POLITICAL INQUIRY

FIGURE 13.3 ■ **What has been the trend in the growth of the national civilian bureaucracy since 1965? What has been the pattern for the growth of state and local bureaucracies over the same period? What explains the patterns?**

SOURCE: Table 17.5 in *Fiscal Year 2009 Historical Tables*, www.whitehouse.gov/omb/budget/fy2009/pdf/hist.pdf; Statistical Abstracts of the United States, 1941, 1946 1961, 1981.

Growth in Federal Expenditures, 1940–2011

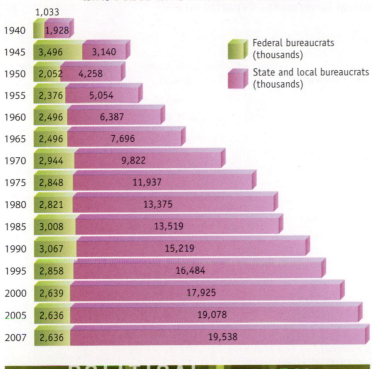

Year	Budget in billions of current dollars (rounded to nearest billion)
1940	$10
1945	$93
1950	$43
1955	$68
1960	$92
1965	$118
1970	$196
1975	$332
1980	$591
1985	$946
1990	$1,253
1995	$1,516
2000	$1,789
2005	$2,472
2011	$3,755 (estimate)

Budget in billions of current dollars (rounded to nearest billion)

POLITICAL INQUIRY

FIGURE 13.4 ■ **What has been the overall trend in the growth of federal government spending since 1940? What would you say about the pattern since 2000? What political factors—domestic and international—explain the trend in federal spending over the past decade?**

SOURCE: http://www.whitehouse.gov/sites/default/files/omb/budget/fy2011/assets/tables.pdf.

dent administrative agencies, (3) independent regulatory commissions, (4) government corporations, and (5) agencies in the Executive Office of the President.

Within each category there is much variation in size, structure, and function. When Congress and the president authorize a new policy, they must decide whether they will assign its implementation to an existing agency or create a new agency. If they choose the latter option, they must determine which type of agency to create.

Departments

The Department of Homeland Security, established in 2002, is the newest of fifteen federal **departments,** each responsible for one broadly defined policy area. The president holds the fifteen departments accountable through the appointment of a head official. *Secretary* is the title of this top political appointee in all departments except the Department of Justice, where the head is the attorney general. Although the Senate must confirm them, these top appointees serve at the president's pleasure. In addition to appointing the department secretaries, the president names bureaucrats to positions in several levels of the hierarchy below the secretaries. These political appointees have titles such as *deputy secretary, assistant deputy secretary, agency director,* and *deputy director.* Table 13.2 lists the fifteen departments and gives the number of employees and budget outlay for each in 2008.

department
one of fifteen executive branch units responsible for a broadly defined policy area and whose top administrator (secretary) is appointed by the president, is confirmed by the Senate, and serves at the discretion of the president

TABLE 13.2

Evolution of Federal Government Departments

Department and Year Created	Civilian Employees (July 2008)	Budget Outlay in Billions of Dollars (2008)
State, 1789	35,724	$17.5
Treasury, 1789	112,366	$548.8
Interior, 1849	68,414	$9.9
Justice, 1870 (attorney general's office 1789; department status 1870)	107,790	$26.6
Agriculture, 1889	97,584	$90.8
Commerce, 1913 (separated from Department of Commerce and Labor, which had been created in 1903)	41,217	$7.7
Labor, 1913 (separated from Department of Commerce and Labor, which had been created in 1903)	16,267	$58.8
Defense, 1947 (previously, Department of War, created 1789; Army Department and Navy Department, created 1798)	680,025	$640.5
Housing and Urban Development, 1965	9,559	$49.1
Transportation, 1966	54,547	$70.0
Energy, 1977	14,782	$21.4
Health and Human Services, 1979 (created from Department of Health, Education and Welfare, established in 1953)	62,097	$700.5
Education, 1979 (created from Department of Health, Education and Welfare, established in 1953)	4,281	$66.0
Veterans Affairs, 1988	263,620	$84.8
Homeland Security, 2003	164,592	$40.7

SOURCES: Civil employee statistics from www.opm.gov/feddata/html/2008/july/table3.asp; budget information from www.whitehouse.gov/omb/budget/Historicals/, Table 3.1.

independent administrative agency
an executive branch unit created by Congress and the president that is responsible for a narrowly defined function and whose structure is intended to protect it from partisan politics

Independent Administrative Agencies

Whereas each executive branch department has authority for a broadly defined policy area, a host of **independent administrative agencies** are each responsible for a more narrowly defined function of the national government. Congress and the president create these agencies to fulfill one of several purposes. Some of them, such as the Smithsonian Institution, were established to handle new governmental functions that did not easily fall within the purview of existing departments. Other independent administrative agencies support the work of existing departments and agencies, including recruiting and training employees (Office of Personnel Management) and managing government properties and records (General Services Administration). Still others, such as the National Science Foundation and the National Aeronautics and Space Administration, focus on research and preservation of national resources.

Structurally independent administrative agencies look like cabinet departments, with a single head appointed by the president. However, these agencies are "independent" because Congresses and presidents place them outside of the cabinet departments. In addition, these agencies have a varying level of independence from the president. Some independent administrative agency heads serve fixed terms, making their agencies independent from the president. In other agencies, the heads serve at the pleasure of the president, but the president must have a cause (misconduct or malfeasance) to remove them. In yet other agencies, the president can remove the head without specifying a cause. Although the structures of independent administrative agencies are expected to make them "independent" of patrician politics, ultimately such agencies still need to earn the support of those who authorize the spending of money and who have authority to restructure the agency or its mission—Congress or the president.

Independent Regulatory Commissions

Over time, Congress and presidents have recognized the need for expertise in regulating the country's diverse economic activities and their impact on the overall economy, workers, consumers, and the environment. Acknowledging their own lack of such expertise, they have created numerous **independent regulatory commissions,** bureaucracies outside of the cabinet departments with the authority to develop standards of behavior for specific industries and businesses, to monitor compliance with these standards, and to impose sanctions on those it finds guilty of violating the standards.

independent regulatory commission
an executive branch unit outside of cabinet departments responsible for developing standards of behavior within specific industries and businesses, monitoring compliance with these standards, and imposing sanctions on violators

Initially, such government regulation centered on *economic regulation*—matters such as setting the prices of goods and services and ensuring competition in the marketplace. The first independent regulatory commission, the Interstate Commerce Commission (ICC, 1887), was set up to oversee the prices and services of the railroad industry. Beginning in the 1960s, Congress turned more in the direction of *social regulation*, establishing regulatory commissions that focused on how business practices affected the environment, and the health and safety of consumers and workers. For example, legislation created the Consumer Product Safety Commission (CPSC) in 1972.

Independent regulatory agencies are under the direction of bipartisan boards whose members do not need to be loyal to the president's preferences. Typically, the president nominates and the Senate confirms an odd number of board members. Board members serve staggered fixed terms. This structure allows the agency to make decisions based on the expertise of its board members, not on the preferences of the president or Congress. Still, the agencies need both presidential and congressional support to survive.

Government Corporations

Like private businesses, **government corporations** sell a service or a product; but unlike private businesses, they are government owned. Congress and the president create government corporations when they believe it is in the public interest for the national government to engage in a commercial activity, such as selling stamps to pay for the cost of delivering mail. (In fact, the best-known U.S. government corporation is the United States Postal Service.) Unlike the other categories of bureaucracies, government corporations are expected to make enough money to cover their costs.

government corporation
an executive branch unit that sells a service and is expected to be financially self-sufficient

A bipartisan board typically directs each government corporation. The president appoints the board members to serve for staggered fixed terms. Typically, the Senate is not required to confirm the board members. Like regulatory commissions and administrative agencies, government corporations are structured to be independent.

Executive Office of the President

By 1939, the national bureaucracy for which the president serves as chief executive officer had grown tremendously in size and diversity of structure and functions. Acknowledging that the president needed help to manage this constellation of departments, independent administrative agencies, independent regulatory commissions, and government corporations, President Franklin Roosevelt (1933–1945) and the Congress created the Executive Office of the President (EOP).

The EOP is composed of dozens of offices and councils that assist the president in managing the complex and sprawling executive branch of the bureaucracy. The EOP has evolved into the locomotive of the national government—the engine driving the development and implementation of presidential policies and programs. The president appoints the top-level bureaucrats in EOP agencies, and the majority of these appointments are not subject to Senate confirmation. The president has the authority to fire these appointees at his pleasure. Therefore the EOP serves the president; it is in fact the presidential bureaucracy. (See Chapter 12 for a detailed discussion of the EOP.)

Hybrids

Although political scientists commonly talk about five categories of bureaucracies, not all bureaucracies fit neatly into a given category. In addition to the five categories of bureaucracy we have considered, the executive branch features hybrid agencies that have characteristics of more than one category. The Food and Drug Administration (FDA) is one such hybrid. The FDA regulates the food and pharmaceutical industries to ensure the safety of food and drugs on the market and hence is a regulatory agency. Yet it is not an independent regulatory commission, because it is housed within the Department of Health and Human Services.

In this section, we took stock of the executive branch organizations in which national bureaucrats implement policy. We next consider the nature of the essential roles bureaucrats play in all stages of public policy.

Federal Bureaucrats' Roles in Public Policy

Although the primary work of bureaucrats is implementation—putting public policy into action—bureaucrats play an active, vital role in all six stages of the public policy cycle. These stages are (1) agenda setting, (2) policy formulation, (3) policy approval, (4) resource allocation, (5) policy implementation, and (6) policy evaluation.

politics-administration dichotomy

the concept that elected government officials, who are accountable to the voters, create and approve public policy, and then competent, politically neutral bureaucrats implement the public policy

According to the **politics-administration dichotomy,** there is a clear line between *politics* (the formulation and approval of public policy, and the allocation of resources to put the policy into effect) and the *administration* of public policy (the real-world implementation of the policy). The dichotomy says that elected officials (whom citizens hold accountable through the ballot box) have authority for politics and that competent bureaucrats (hired through merit-based civil service) have authority for policy administration. Theoretically, this arrangement fosters not only responsive government but also efficient and effective public services.

The politics-administration dichotomy may sound good, but the reality of public policy processes does not allow for such a clean separation between those who "do politics" and those who administer policy. Although bureaucrats are hired to implement policy made by elected officials, those officials tap the expertise of bureaucrats throughout the other five stages of the policy process, allowing bureaucrats to influence and even make policies themselves, as we now shall see.

Agenda Setting

In the first stage of the public policy cycle, elected officials place issues on their agendas to discuss, if not to address by formulating a *policy*—a plan of government action to deal with a particular public concern. Bureaucrats play an instrumental role in setting the policy agenda. Because their focus is to implement public policy at the street level, bureaucrats have a clear view of the societal problems that citizens expect the government to address and strong views on how best to address those problems. Political scientists use the term *iron triangle* to describe long-term collaborative efforts among bureaucrats in a government agency, the members of an interest group, and the members of a legislative committee to get their mutual concerns on the agenda and then to formulate the policies they deem necessary to address those concerns. *Issue networks,* which are temporary collaborations among bureaucrats, elected officials, and the members of several interest groups, also engage in lobbying to set the agenda, as well as to influence policy formulation. Bureaucrats who want to get their concerns and proposed programs on the agenda may work to create issue networks as well as iron triangles. For more about iron triangles and issue networks, see Chapter 7.

Policy Formulation

The second stage of the policy process, policy formulation, involves defining a problem that has made it to the agenda and setting a plan of action (a policy) to address the problem. (Note, however, that not all concerns that reach an elected official's agenda—or even the agendas of numerous elected officials—go further in the policy process.) Although anyone can formulate a public policy, only elected officials can officially introduce policy proposals into the lawmaking process. Thus individuals and groups outside government, as well as bureaucrats, must identify members of Congress to introduce policy proposals for legislative action. The president can also make policy by issuing an executive order, an authority that lies outside the legislative process (see Chapter 12).

Because bureaucrats often have specialized knowledge of societal problems, elected officials rely on bureaucrats when formulating policies. House and Senate committees frequently call on bureaucrats to review and comment on bills that, if approved, they will implement and to testify in the hearings in which congressional members investigate and study problems. Thus bureaucrats regularly take part in policy formulation, whether at their own impetus or at the request of elected officials.

In recognition of bureaucrats' expertise, Congress often includes vague or ambiguous language in bills and relies on bureaucrats to fill in the program details after a bill is passed, during the policy implementation stage. Vague legislative language may also reflect the congressional sponsors' need to win majority votes in both the House and the Senate and to secure presidential approval of the policy. Fuzzy language means that if the bill becomes law, bureaucrats will need to discern what the policy is directing them to do before they can implement it.

Policy Approval

When Congress and the president vote to approve or reject the formulated policy, which is in the form of a proposed piece of legislation—a bill— they have reached the third stage, policy approval. Bills detailing the government's plan to address a problem are called authorization bills; when

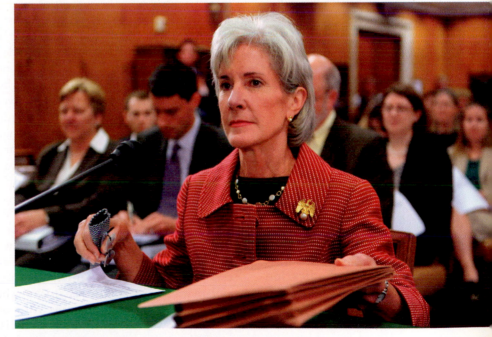

> Kathleen Sebelius, secretary of the Department of Health and Human Services, testifies in front of the Senate Appropriations Committee on the proposed budget estimates for her department in June of 2009. As secretary of health and human services, she oversees the formulation of bills relevant to her department, including the department's budget request, and the department's implementation of policy.

authorization law
a law that provides the plan of action to address a given societal concern and identifies the executive branch unit that will put the plan into effect

Congress and the president, or Congress alone over a president's veto, approves such bills, the laws thus created authorize government action. **Authorization laws** not only provide the plan of action to address a given societal concern but also identify the executive branch unit that will put the plan into effect. The law may authorize an existing executive unit to carry out the policy, or it may establish a new unit to do the job. Presidential executive orders, another form of public policy, direct bureaucrats in how to implement policy. Yet bureaucracies cannot implement a public policy until they have legal authority to spend money.

Resource Allocation

In the next phase of the policy process, resource allocation, Congress and the president specify how much money each bureaucracy will be authorized to spend during the budget year. Through the budget process (see Chapter 15), Congress and the president formulate appropriation bills, which are plans for the distribution of government revenue to government entities, including bureaucracies, legislative bodies, and judicial bodies. Approved appropriation bills—**appropriation laws**—give bureaucracies the legal authority to spend money.

appropriation law
a law that gives bureaucracies and other government entities the legal authority to spend money

Bureaucrats play three key roles in the budget process. First, at the request of the president, bureaucrats develop an annual budget request for their agencies. Second, before Congress approves the appropriation bills that distribute government revenues to the agencies, it calls on bureaucrats to justify their budget requests. In turn, bureaucrats lobby members of Congress to allocate to their agencies the funds they requested. With limited money available, bureaucracies typically do not receive all the funding they request. Therefore bureaucracies compete with one another for their piece of the limited budget pie. Once Congress and the president approve the appropriation bills, bureaucrats take on their third role in the budget process; they spend money to put the public policy into action.

Policy Implementation

Bureaucrats are at the center of the second-to-last stage of the policy cycle, policy implementation. In this phase, bureaucrats must first interpret the law and then carry it out. Congress and the president delegate to bureaucrats the authority to determine the best way to implement the policy; this authority is called **administrative discretion.** Applying administrative discretion, bureaucrats make the day-to-day decisions related to executing policy programs and enforcing the necessary rules and standards. Elected officials risk the loss of control over the content of public policy when they delegate administrative discretion to bureaucrats. However, they have numerous tools to limit this risk, which we discuss later in this chapter's section on federal bureaucratic accountability.

administrative discretion
the authority delegated to bureaucrats to use their expertise and judgment when determining how to implement public policy

Bureaucrats, specifically those in independent agencies, use administrative discretion to establish programs, rules, regulations, and standards necessary for the effective and efficient implementation of policy. The process by which bureaucrats translate vague law into concrete plans of action is a quasi-legislative ("as-if legislative") process. It is "quasi-legislative" because bureaucrats in the executive branch, not legislators, make policy as they fill in the details needed to implement legislation. **Administrative rule making** is the name of this process by which upper-level bureaucrats use their administrative discretion and their expertise in the policy area to create rules, regulations, and standards that the bureaucracy will then enforce. For example, recognizing its lack of expertise in the specifics of how to prevent air and water pollution, Congress delegated to the Environmental Protection Agency (EPA) the authority to establish policy. The EPA sets specific pollution emissions standards to implement the Clean Water and Clean Air acts. Although Congress does not approve these EPA administrative standards, importantly, the standards have the force of law.

administrative rule making
the process by which an independent commission or agency fills in the details of a vague law by formulating, proposing, and approving rules, regulations, and standards that will be enforced to implement the policy

Agencies involved in administrative rule making also have a quasi-judicial ("as-if judicial") role. Through **administrative adjudication,** they determine when their rules are violated, and they impose penalties on the violators. Citizens who disagree with an agency's application of its administrative rules or those whom an agency finds guilty of violating its rules may challenge the agency's decisions through a lawsuit. Indeed, several states successfully sued the EPA in 2007 for its failure to set carbon dioxide emissions standards and

administrative adjudication
the process by which agencies resolve disputes over the implementation of their administrative rules

hence its inadequate implementation of the Clean Air Act. Claiming that the EPA was still not properly implementing the law, Massachusetts attorney general Martha Coakley, along with the attorneys general of seventeen other states, as well as two cities and eleven environmental interest groups, successfully sued the EPA in April 2008.[12]

Policy Evaluation

The last stage of the policy process is policy evaluation—the assessment of the intended and unintended effects of policy implementation. People do not assess government success by the number of laws passed or by the promises made in the language of the laws. Rather, the effectiveness and the efficiency of public service delivery are what matter to the public. The implementation of policy by bureaucrats is thus the key to citizens' satisfaction with government—and the key to government success.

Since the 1970s, U.S. taxpayers have called for increased transparency in government, including evaluations of public policy implementation to determine how effectively government is using their tax dollars. The corruption of the administration of President Richard Nixon—which featured Nixon's misuse of the Internal Revenue Service to collect information on opponents, as well as the infamous White House cover-up of the break-in at the Democratic Party headquarters in the Watergate Building—partially explains the call for greater transparency in government. The publication in 1973 of political scientists Jeffrey L. Pressman and Aaron B. Wildavsky's study of a federally funded economic development program also fueled outcries for increased transparency and evaluations.[13] Their landmark research concluded that it is "amazing that federal programs work at all" given the hurdles that policy implementers encounter.

As a result, policy evaluation has become a larger component of the workload of legislators and bureaucrats in recent decades than it ever was before. Because elected officials and citizens want proof of the efficiency and the effectiveness of implemented policies, agencies must document what they do and its impact. Because citizens do not elect bureaucrats, they do not have the opportunity to fire civil servants whose performance is unsatisfactory. Therefore citizens defer the responsibility for bureaucratic accountability to members of Congress, the president, and the judges who preside over the courts because these elected and appointed government officials have legal means to monitor bureaucrats' work and to hold them accountable.

Federal Bureaucratic Accountability

When it comes to public service, everyone is watching. The courts, through the mechanism of lawsuits, review the actions of the executive and legislative branches to ensure that they are constitutional and legal. Congress and the president, as the creators and funders of bureaucracies, can threaten to revamp or eliminate any bureaucracy, or to decrease its funding, if its performance falls short of expectations. Congress and the president not only structure bureaucracies to foster efficient, effective, and accountable public service but also pass laws to increase self-policing by bureaucrats.

People outside government, including many ordinary citizens, also keep a close eye on bureaucracies. National **sunshine laws** open up government functions and documents to the public, ensuring transparency and the public's right to know about government business and decision making. But these laws are effective only if citizens know about them and take advantage of them.

sunshine laws
legislation that opens up government functions and documents to the public

Accountability to the People

One of the first national sunshine laws for the enhancement of bureaucratic accountability to the people was the Administrative Procedure Act (APA) of 1946. The APA responded to citizens' and interest groups' concerns about the fast growth in the number of agencies involved in administrative rule making and about the lack of transparency and accountability of the bureaucratic rule makers. The APA, which applies to all federal agencies except those specifically excluded by legislation, standardized rule-making procedures and requires bureaucracies to publicize their proposed rules in the *Federal Register,* a daily national government publication. They also must publish an invitation for people to offer comments on the agency's proposals.

Once the agency collects and reviews the people's comments, it must publish its approved rules in the *Federal Register.* To facilitate this open process, the national government Web site www.regulations.gov posts proposed administrative rules and accepts electronically submitted comments on the rules. In this way, people can have a voice in administrative rule making. Such citizen input is essential to democracy, because bureaucrats propose and approve more administrative rules each year than the pieces of legislation proposed and approved by Congress and the president.

The Freedom of Information Act (FOIA) is a 1966 amendment to the APA. The FOIA requires national agencies to give citizens access to government documents upon request and at a reasonable cost. After the terrorist attacks on September 11, 2001, however, the national government denied an increasing percentage of such requests in the name of national security. The decreased access to government documents has heightened tensions between people advocating government confidentiality on the one hand, and individuals cherishing democratic openness and those dedicated to holding the national bureaucracy accountable on the other hand. The American Society of Newspaper Editors was so concerned about the diminished access that it established Sunshine Week (first held March 13–20, 2005) to educate citizens about their right to know and to request information about what the bureaucracy is doing.

Another law that aims to make the federal bureaucracy open and responsive to the people is the Government in the Sunshine Act of 1976. This act of Congress requires all multiheaded national agencies, except those in the Executive Office of the President (EOP), to conduct open, public meetings where citizens can testify and present their concerns about these agencies' actions (past, current, and potential) and the procedures by which they make decisions.

National agencies are now also using the Internet to make government more transparent. In September 2000, the General Services Administration (GSA) of the national government launched its FirstGov Web site, the national government's one-stop portal to national, state, local, and tribal government agency Web sites. This portal puts government information and services at your fingertips. In 2007, the GSA renamed the Web site USA.gov (www .usa.gov) in response to feedback from users who wanted a name that was easier to remember.

Strongly supporting the use of the Internet as a means to enhance citizen access to government information and services, Congress approved and President George W. Bush signed into law the E-Government Act of 2002. This law established a Federal Chief Information Officer within the Office of Management and Budget. Moreover, it requires national agencies to use Internet-based information technology. President Barack Obama promised that under his administration the federal government will provide Americans with an "unprecedented level of openness, collaboration, and efficiency and effectiveness through the use of information technology."[14]

Private organizations that monitor and evaluate the activities of bureaucrats have certainly taken advantage of sunshine laws and e-government. For example, in 2007, Congress passed legislation to establish an independent, bipartisan commission to investigate U.S. wartime contracting in Iraq and Afghanistan. Senator Claire McCaskill (D-Missouri), the bill's cosponsor, praised "POGO's [the Project on Government Oversight] work in supporting these provisions, along with the support of other watchdog groups including Taxpayers for Common Sense, the Government Accountability Project, OMBWatch, Common Cause, U.S. PIRG and Iraq and Afghanistan Veterans of America."[15] In addition to taking advantage of their right to government documents under the FOIA, watchdog groups are more likely than the average citizen to use government Web sites to track bureaucratic activities.

In a democracy, bureaucrats, like elected officials, operate in a fishbowl. Working face to face, or computer screen to computer screen, with the people whom they serve, they are in full view of anyone interested in monitoring them. Sunshine laws and e-government provide citizens with the means to find out what is going on in the bureaucracy. When citizens or watchdog groups identify a problem with bureaucratic operations, they frequently turn to the media to bring public attention to the issue, because the media are always ready to report on bureaucratic inefficiency and impropriety. A more expensive option for citizen and interest group action against bureaucratic waste and misconduct is the filing of a lawsuit.

Accountability to the Courts

As bureaucratic agencies implement policy, they must comply with constitutional guarantees of due process and equal protection of laws. A citizen believing that bureaucrats have violated those rights can challenge bureaucratic actions through the agency's quasi-judicial processes, discussed earlier. If the citizen is not satisfied with the result of this quasi-judicial recourse, he or she can sue the agency through the courts.

Through the litigation process, the U.S. judicial system seeks to ensure that administrative agencies conduct their quasi-legislative and quasi-judicial functions in compliance with the constitutional guarantees of due process (in the Fifth and Fourteenth amendments) as well as the Administrative Procedure Act of 1946. In 2006, for example, federal district judge Richard Leon ruled that the Federal Emergency Management Agency (FEMA) procedures and notices to Hurricane Katrina victims were so difficult to understand that evacuees were deprived of due process because they were unable to determine what the process was. According to ACORN, a housing advocacy group that brought the lawsuit, as many as 11,000 families may have been wrongfully denied long-term housing assistance by the lack of due process in FEMA procedures.[16]

Accountability to Congress

Bureaucrats must always keep in mind the preferences and the agenda of Congress if they want to survive, for Congress approves the legislation that creates, regulates, and funds bureaucracies. The Senate has an additional mechanism for promoting bureaucratic accountability, in that more than one-quarter of the president's appointees are subject to Senate confirmation. The confirmation process for top bureaucrats gives senators a degree of influence over the leadership and direction of executive departments and agencies.

Another means by which Congress encourages bureaucratic accountability is the monitoring of bureaucracies' policy implementation, a form of legislative oversight. When the media, citizens, or interest groups bring concerns

> Individual citizens and interest groups frequently pressure the government to investigate scandals and disasters to find out what went wrong and what the government can do to prevent future misbehavior and disasters. Sally Regenhard, founder of the Skyscraper Safety Campaign, participates in a vigil in front of the White House urging the formation of an independent commission to investigate the terrorist attacks of September 11, 2001. Ms. Regenhard's son, a probationary New York City firefighter, perished in the World Trade Center collapse.

about a bureaucracy's policy implementation to the attention of legislators, Congress might launch an investigation. If, consequently, Congress and the president are dissatisfied with that bureaucracy's performance or behavior, they can cut its budget, modify its legal authority, or even eliminate the agency.

In most cases, oversight does not occur unless citizens, interest groups, and the media push for congressional action, as occurred in the aftermath of September 11, 2001, when public pressure forced Congress to create the 9/11 Commission to investigate the terrorist attacks on the World Trade Center in New York City and on the Pentagon in Arlington, Virginia. An evaluation of bureaucratic performance can also be required in the authorization legislation by a **sunset clause,** which forces the expiration of the program or policy after a specified number of years unless Congress reauthorizes it through new legislation.

sunset clause
a clause in legislation that sets an expiration date for the authorized program/policy unless Congress re-authorizes it

Accountability to the President

The president also has several tools for holding bureaucracies accountable. Like Congress, the president can use the authorization and appropriation processes to ensure accountability. In addition, because most top political appointees serve at the president's pleasure, they are responsive to the president's policy preferences—and in this way, they and their agencies are accountable to the president.

Today, the Office of Management and Budget, an EOP agency, is the key lever in the president's efforts to hold the bureaucracy accountable. The OMB evaluates bureaucratic performance for the president. On the basis of OMB performance assessments, the president proposes budget increases or decreases, agency growth or elimination, or even a reorganization of the executive branch in which agencies are consolidated.

In addition to overseeing performance evaluations of bureaucratic agencies, the OMB spearheads the development of the president's budget, controls the implementation of appropriation laws, and regulates administrative rule making. Through its Office of Information and Regulatory Affairs (OIRA), the OMB ensures that regulations created by executive branch agencies are not "unnecessarily costly"[17] and support the president's policy preferences.

> Peter Orszag, President Obama's first Office of Management and Budget director, reviews documents in his office in February 2009. Upon his announced resignation from the OMB in June 2010, President Obama credited Orszag with helping to identify more than one hundred programs for elimination because they had outlived their purpose.

Internal Accountability

The president, Congress, the courts, and ordinary citizens have multiple means by which to hold bureaucrats accountable. But bureaucrats, who themselves are taxpayers, also worry about inefficiency and waste in public service. Legislated codes of behavior and whistle-blower protections help to foster accountability from within bureaucracies.

CODES OF BEHAVIOR AND THE ETHICS IN GOVERNMENT ACT To ensure the best public service, bureaucracies have codes of behavior. These codes specify guidelines for ethical, efficient, and effective behavior on the part of bureaucrats. Each government agency has its own such code. In addition, in 1992, the Office of Government Ethics published a comprehensive set of ethical standards for national bureaucrats. Moreover, many of the professions in which bureaucrats are members (lawyers, doctors, nurses, accountants, engineers, and so on) also have established codes of behavior. Importantly, however, codes of behavior are just guidelines. They do not stipulate what a bureaucrat should do in a given situation. Thus bureaucrats must use discretion when applying such codes to their daily work of providing public service.

The Ethics in Government Act of 1978 established the United States Office of Government Ethics (OGE), which is charged with preventing conflicts of interest by bureaucrats (political appointees, SES bureaucrats, and civil servants). A **conflict of interest** arises when a public servant is in a position to make a decision or take an action from which he or she can personally benefit. In such a situation, the public servant's private interest is in conflict with his or her responsibility to serve the public interest. A key to the prevention of conflicts of interest is the requirement that top government officials must disclose their finances.

conflict of interest
in the case of public servants, the situation in which they can personally benefit from a decision they make or an action they take in the process of doing their jobs

WHISTLE-BLOWER PROTECTIONS AND INSPECTORS GENERAL Whistle-blower laws offer an additional means of internal accountability in the national bureaucracy. The 1978 Civil Service Reform Act provided some protections to civil servant **whistle-blowers**—employees who disclose government misconduct, waste, mismanagement, abuse of authority, or a threat to public health or safety. The CSRA established the Office of Special Counsel to protect whistle-blowers' job security. Then in 1986, thanks to the lobbying efforts of many groups, including the Project on Government Oversight, Congress approved the False Claims Act. This law allows for a monetary reward for government whistle-blowers who expose fraud that harms the U.S. government.

whistle-blower
a civil servant who discloses mismanagement, fraud, waste, corruption, and/or threats to public health and safety to the government

In another attempt to improve internal accountability, Congress approved the Inspector General Act in 1978. This law aims to ensure the integrity of public service by creating government watchdogs, called **inspectors general,** appointed by the president and embedded in government agencies to monitor policy implementation and investigate alleged misconduct. The law requires the appointment of the inspectors general without regard to their political affiliation and strictly on the basis of their abilities in accounting, auditing, or investigation. "We're supposed to check our politics at the door and call things as we see them. If we uncover things that reflect badly on the government, we're legally and morally obliged to report it. We're obliged to do that for the good of the country." So explained Clark Ervin, who held the position of inspector general at the State and Homeland Security departments.[18]

inspectors general
political appointees who work within a government agency to ensure the integrity of public service by investigating allegations of misconduct by bureaucrats

In summary, whistle-blower protection laws and inspectors general enhance the ability of the bureaucrats themselves to police the agencies in which they work, and sunshine laws give government outsiders various instruments for monitoring the bureaucracy. But many citizens and government officials believe that more needs to be done to improve bureaucrats' record of performance.

Can Bureaucratic Performance Be Improved?

In the United States, bureaucrats perform every job imaginable. They generally do their job so well that we rarely think about how their work positively affects us around the clock. We and our elected officials are nevertheless quick to bash the bureaucracy at the slightest hint of inefficiency. Similarly, the media seize upon any opportunity to report on problems with bureaucrats and bureaucracies. Our public discourse infrequently covers bureaucrats' *good* performance. When was the last time you heard a news report or were a party to a friendly conversation that praised a public servant?

Yet the U.S. Postal Service delivers hundreds of millions of pieces of mail six days a week, and rarely is a letter or a package lost. Thousands of planes safely take off from and land at U.S. airports every hour, guided by federal bureaucrats in the person of air traffic controllers. Millions of senior citizens receive a monthly Social Security check on time every month. Even more people travel the interstate highway systems without incident each day.

Public administration and policy scholar Charles Goodsell has found that two-thirds to three-fourths of Americans report their encounters with government bureaucrats and bureaucracy as "satisfactory."[19] However, research consistently shows that some national agencies perform better than do others.

The Best-Performing Bureaucracies

Political scientists William T. Gormley and Steven Balla reviewed national performance data and summarized the characteristics of national agencies that perform well.[20] They found that numerous factors correlate with better-performing bureaucracies—factors that individual bureaucrats have little control over. They include legislative language that clearly states the goal of the legislation and provides high levels of administrative discretion, allowing bureaucrats to determine the best way to achieve the goal. Better-performing bureaucracies tend to be those with easily measured goals, especially goals that include providing resources to citizens (such as Social Security checks) as opposed to taking resources (tax collection). Another factor correlated with good performance is high levels of support from elected officials, the media, and diverse groups of citizens for the legislated goal and the implementing agency. High levels of support typically result in an agency receiving ample resources. Effective leaders who develop and maintain high levels of support from government officials and interested parties outside government are also important to well-performing bureaucracies.

Does Contracting-Out Improve Performance?

In addition to analyzing citizen satisfaction with public bureaucracies, Charles Goodsell has analyzed the body of research that assesses the efficiency of public policy implementation by government bureaucrats compared with the efficiency of private organizations. He has found that "the assumption that business always does better than government is not upheld."[21] In fact, Goodsell reports that "despite antigovernment rhetoric to the contrary, the federal government achieves essentially the same degree of satisfaction for its services as corporate America does for its products."[22] Nevertheless, many commentators and elected officials argue that private businesses are more efficient than are governments and therefore that more public service should be outsourced to private businesses.

Contracting-out to private businesses certainly decreases the number of bureaucrats on the national payroll. But does outsourcing foster more efficient and effective public service? Does it save taxpayer dollars? The evidence strongly suggests otherwise.

Outsourcing government work can lead to waste, fraud, overpricing, and corruption. In its evaluation of contract waste and fraud in Hurricane Katrina relief, the House of Representatives Government Reform Committee reported that "the main problems were no-bid contracts, layers of subcontracting that inflated costs, and a lack of oversight on the completion of work."[23] What causes these inefficiencies?

First, for-profit organizations must make a profit to survive. As contract law experts note, for many private government contractors, overestimating the costs of the work and then reaping illegally high profits are a common reality. Second, holding bureaucrats accountable for their performance is not easy in general, and determining whom to hold accountable for delays, cost overruns, and quality issues is complicated when policy implementation occurs through the shadow bureaucracy.[24] Unlike government bodies, private businesses can legally function behind closed doors—unless and until concerned citizens,

> In August 2007, the I-135W bridge in Minneapolis collapsed, killing thirteen people. Barely one year after the collapse, the new replacement bridge opened to traffic. The private construction firm contracted by the state of Minnesota to design and build the new bridge completed the job three months earlier than the state's deadline and less than 2 percent over budget—unusual for a project of this magnitude. The success of this $234 million contract can be attributed to cooperation among local, state, and federal bureaucracies, all moving with record speed, as well as an innovative arrangement with the private contractor.

watchdog groups, the media, and government officials force the doors open through congressional investigations or lawsuits.

Citizens' Role in Bureaucratic Performance

Citizens turn to the government to provide services and solve problems. As we have discussed, the government's success in serving the people well depends on many factors. Ultimately, even if all other factors correlated with a well-performing bureaucracy are in place, the bureaucracy will fail without the participation and compliance of the people it serves. The effectiveness of public policies depends on people's knowledge of and compliance with the law. It depends on their applying for the government programs for which they qualify and their conformity to the rules, regulations, standards, and directions of bureaucrats. This symbiotic relationship is essential to the success of government.

CONCLUSION — THINKING CRITICALLY ABOUT WHAT'S NEXT IN THE BUREAUCRACY

Candidates, elected officials, and the media perpetually criticize government bureaucrats and bureaucracies. At the same time, they do not typically bring attention to or compliment bureaucrats for work satisfactorily or well done. In reality, citizens take for granted the overwhelming majority of public services because they are provided day-in and day-out without problem. And although citizens typically use the terms *bureaucrat* and *bureaucracy* to insult public servants and government agencies, 61 percent of respondents to a summer 2009 Gallup poll indicated they were satisfied with their most recent interaction with a federal government agency.[25]

Numerous groups, including the Partnership for Public Service, are working to improve the image of public service and to inspire quality college graduates to work as public servants. Will such efforts succeed, or will the bureaucracy remain a target of criticism from citizens, candidates, and elected officials? Will the best and the brightest respond to the call to serve as a large proportion of federal employees retire in the next decade?

Many critics of the bureaucracy argue that private-sector for-profit and nonprofit organizations can provide better-quality public services for less money. However, studies done to support that theory have produced mixed findings. Moreover, several private organizations with government contracts have been involved in scandals regarding their provision of services and materials to victims of natural disasters and man-made disasters both on U.S. soil and abroad. Given these realities, will the volume of public service outsourced to private organizations continue to increase?

Summary

1. Bureaucrats and Bureaucracy
Traditionally, bureaucrats are defined as employees in the executive branch of government who are hired to deliver public services. Today, however, many private-sector employees—the so-called shadow bureaucrats—also implement public policy. Although most people think of government agencies when they hear the word *bureaucracy*, a bureaucracy is any large, hierarchical organization featuring a division of labor, specialization of tasks, standard operating procedures, and a chain of command.

2. Federal Bureaucrats
The national government hires almost 3 million civilians into the executive branch to administer public policies. The president appoints a small percentage of these bureaucrats. The government hires the overwhelming majority of national bureaucrats on the basis of merit, using a hiring process that includes open competition and equal opportunity. As a result, the national bureaucracy features a more diverse representation of the people than do the elective institutions of the federal government.

3. State, Local, and Shadow Bureaucrats
The overall number of national bureaucrats has been stable over the past few decades. However, the number of state, local, and shadow bureaucrats has grown significantly because of the proliferation of grants-in-aid and the practice of contracting-out more and more public service.

4. The Evolution and Organization of the Federal Bureaucracy
The federal bureaucracy has grown tremendously in size, scope, and complexity since 1789. Political scientists typically put government agencies in one of five categories—departments, independent administrative agencies, independent regulatory commissions, government corporations, and Executive Office of the President agencies. But this categorization oversimplifies the diversity of structure, size, and function of the thousands of national bureaucracies.

5. Federal Bureaucrats' Roles in Public Policy
Federal bureaucrats do much more than implement policy. Bureaucrats lobby elected officials in all stages of the policy cycle to get their concerns, and the concerns of the citizens who are their clients, addressed. Elected officials frequently defer to the expertise of bureaucrats when it comes to determining the detailed programs, rules, and standards that are needed to serve the people. Citizen satisfaction with government is deeply dependent on the efficient and effective work of bureaucrats.

6. Federal Bureaucratic Accountability
Elected officials delegate administrative discretion to bureaucrats. Interested parties inside and outside government closely scrutinize bureaucrats' use of this discretion. Taxpayers, clients, the media, and interest groups, as well as the president, Congress, and the courts, hold bureaucrats accountable. In addition to sunshine laws and ethics codes, the structure of national bureaucracies lends itself to accountability.

7. Can Bureaucratic Performance Be Improved?

All those who scrutinize bureaucracies are quick to find fault and slow to offer praise. Certainly, not every agency is evaluated as performing well, but for the most part, citizens report that their interactions with government bureaucrats are at least satisfactory.

Key Terms

administrative adjudication 418

administrative discretion 418

administrative rule making 418

appropriation law 418

authorization law 418

bureaucracy 405

bureaucrats 403

civil servants 407

conflict of interest 423

contracting-out (privatizing, outsourcing) 403

department 413

government corporation 415

independent administrative agency 414

independent regulatory commission 415

inspectors general 423

merit-based civil service 407

plum book 405

politics-administration dichotomy 416

senior executive service (SES) 409

shadow bureaucrats 403

sunset clause 422

sunshine laws 419

whistle-blower 423

For Review

1. List and describe the structural characteristics of bureaucratic organizations.

2. Compare and contrast the following categories of bureaucrats: political appointees, civil servants, senior executive service bureaucrats, and shadow bureaucrats.

3. What accounts for the fact that the national budget and the scope of its responsibilities have continued to grow in recent decades, yet the number of its civilian employees has remained stable?

4. Differentiate the five categories of national bureaucracies by discussing differences in their structures and the type of services they provide.

5. Describe the role that bureaucrats play at each stage of the policy process.

6. Distinguish between internal and external means of bureaucratic accountability and give some examples of each.

7. According to Gormley and Balla, what are three or four characteristics of bureaucracies that perform well?

For Critical Thinking and Discussion

1. Do citizens expect too much from government and hence from bureaucrats and bureaucracies? Explain your answer.

2. Does the profit motive of private businesses threaten the efficient use of taxpayer money when public services are contracted-out? Why or why not?

3. Identify at least one public service that you believe the national government should not contract-out to private-sector organizations, and defend your choice(s).

4. How often do you interact with national bureaucrats? What about state bureaucrats? Local bureaucrats? Give some recent examples of each interaction. Can you identify some shadow bureaucrats that have provided you with public services?

5. Compose a list of public services provided to you since you woke up this morning. Were you satisfied with the services? Which of those services do people generally take for granted?

MULTIPLE CHOICE: Choose the lettered item that answers the question correctly.

1. The number of federal civilian bureaucrats is
   a. almost 3 million.
   b. almost 5 million.
   c. almost 13 million.
   d. almost 20 million.

2. The youngest department in the national bureaucracy is the department of
   a. energy.
   b. homeland security.
   c. state.
   d. veterans affairs.

3. The demographics of what category of federal employee are most comparable to those of the population as a whole?
   a. elected officials
   b. civil servants
   c. political appointees
   d. senior executive service employees

4. The legislation that created the federal merit-based civil service system was the
   a. Civil Rights Act (1964).
   b. Civil Service Reform Act (1978).
   c. Pendleton Act (1883).
   d. Title IX (1972).

5. The independent administrative agency that is the central personnel office for the federal bureaucracy today is the
   a. EOP.   c. MSPB.
   b. FLRA.   d. OPM.

6. In what category of federal bureaucracies are secretaries the top appointed officials?
   a. department
   b. independent administrative agency
   c. independent regulatory commission
   d. government corporation

7. Bureaucracies in which category are expected to make enough money to cover their costs?
   a. department
   b. independent administrative agency
   c. independent regulatory commission
   d. government corporation

8. Bureaucrats make policy, using the administrative discretion that Congress delegates to them, at the stage of the policy process that is called
   a. policy formulation.
   b. policy approval.
   c. policy implementation.
   d. policy evaluation.

9. All of the following are merit principles except
   a. competence.   c. political neutrality.
   b. open competition.   d. Senate confirmation.

10. Political appointees who work within a government agency to ensure the integrity of public service by investigating allegations of misconduct by bureaucrats are
    a. inspectors general.
    b. shadow bureaucrats.
    c. watchdogs.
    d. whistle-blowers.

FILL IN THE BLANKS.

11. A _____ is an organization with the following characteristics: a division of labor; workers hired based on competence to do a specialized task; standard operating procedures; and a vertical chain of command.

12. The hiring system initially used by the federal government, which allowed the president to hire anyone he wanted based on whatever qualifications he decided on, is the _____ system.

13. People hired and paid by private for-profit and nonprofit organizations that implement public policy through a government contract are _____ .

14. _____ is the authority delegated to bureaucrats to use their expertise and judgment when determining how to implement public policy.

15. Laws that force the government to be transparent by holding open meetings and providing citizens with requested information at a reasonable cost are collectively known as _____ .

Answers: 1. a; 2. b; 3. b; 4. c; 5. d; 6. a; 7. d; 8. c; 9. d; 10. a; 11. bureaucracy; 12. patronage; 13. shadow bureaucrats; 14. Administrative discretion; 15. sunshine laws.

RESOURCES FOR RESEARCH AND ACTION

Internet Resources

Office of Management and Budget
www.whitehouse.gov.omb This Web site provides access to the current and previous federal budget documents and historical budget tables.

Regulations.gov
www.regulations.gov You can review proposed and approved rules, regulations, and standards of federal executive agencies and submit your comments about them.

U.S. Government Printing Office
www.gpoaccess.gov/gmanual/browse This Web site allows you to view the most current U.S. Government Manual as well as several older editions of the manual.

USA.gov
www.usa.gov Use this site as a one-stop portal to national, state, and local government officials, agencies, and documents.

Internet Activism

Like the U.S. population as a whole, the bureaucracy is "graying." More than 40 percent of the national workforce is now eligible for retirement. That means growth in job opportunities, especially for college graduates looking for secure jobs with good compensation (pay and benefits). To find out more about government job opportunities as well as apprenticeships, fellowships, and internships, visit the Web site of the Office of Personnel Management (OPM): www.usajobs.gov

YouTube
www.youtube.com/RecoveryBoard Recovery Board Chairman Earl Devaney explains how citizens can use the recovery.gov Web site to hold the federal government accountable for its spending by becoming a "citizen inspector general."

Blog
http://blog.usa.gov/roller/govgab Federal bureaucrats from the Office of Citizen Services and Communications at the U.S. General Service Administration encounter on a daily basis a staggering amount of information about the government and its services. Go to the blog to learn about services from which you can benefit.

Facebook
www.facebook.com/partnershipforpublicservice The Partnership for Public Service's mission is to revitalize the federal government by inspiring a new generation to serve and by transforming the way government works.

Recommended Readings

Goodsell, Charles T. *The Case for Bureaucracy: A Public Administration Polemic,* 4th ed. Washington, DC: CQ Press, 2004. A review of the common myths and criticisms of bureaucracy, with evidence to show that they are indeed unsupported.

Gormley, William T., Jr. and Steven J. Balla. *Bureaucracy and Democracy: Accountability and Performance.* Washington, DC: CQ Press, 2004. Uses case studies and examples to illustrate what the national bureaucracy does and why it is important, and draws on social science theories to describe how bureaucracy works and the complex and conflicting demands put on it.

Kettl, Donald F. *System Under Stress: Homeland Security and American Politics.* Washington, DC: CQ Press, 2004. Analysis of the environmental factors that led to the creation of the newest cabinet-level department, the Department of Homeland Security, with an examination of the intergovernmental nature of the endeavor to protect homeland security.

Stillman, Richard. *The American Bureaucracy: The Core of Modern Government.* Chicago: Nelson-Hall Publishers, 1996. A comprehensive introductory textbook in public administration, with excellent description and analysis of bureaucracies (national, state, and local) in the United States.

Wilson, James Q. 1989. *Bureaucracy: What Government Agencies Do and Why They Do It.* New York: Basic Books, 1989. A classic treatise on what government agencies do and why they function as they do, with analysis on how they might become more responsible and efficient.

Movies of Interest

Pentagon Papers (2003)
In this made-for-TV movie, a Department of Defense bureaucrat, Daniel Ellsberg, has access to classified documents that he decides should be brought to the public's attention. The documents detail the secret history of U.S. involvement in Vietnam, which includes bureaucrats misinforming decision makers and the public. Ellsberg risks his career and his freedom to try to get the truth to the public. Based on a true story.

Mississippi Burning (1989)
Two committed FBI agents, with very different personal styles, investigate the disappearance of three civil rights workers during the 1960s. Based on a true story.

Serpico (1973)
The story of a New York City police officer who is living his dream of being a cop. His dream job turns life threatening when he blows the whistle on corruption in the police force, the existence of which shows that not all of Serpico's coworkers are as committed to public service as he is. Based on a true story.

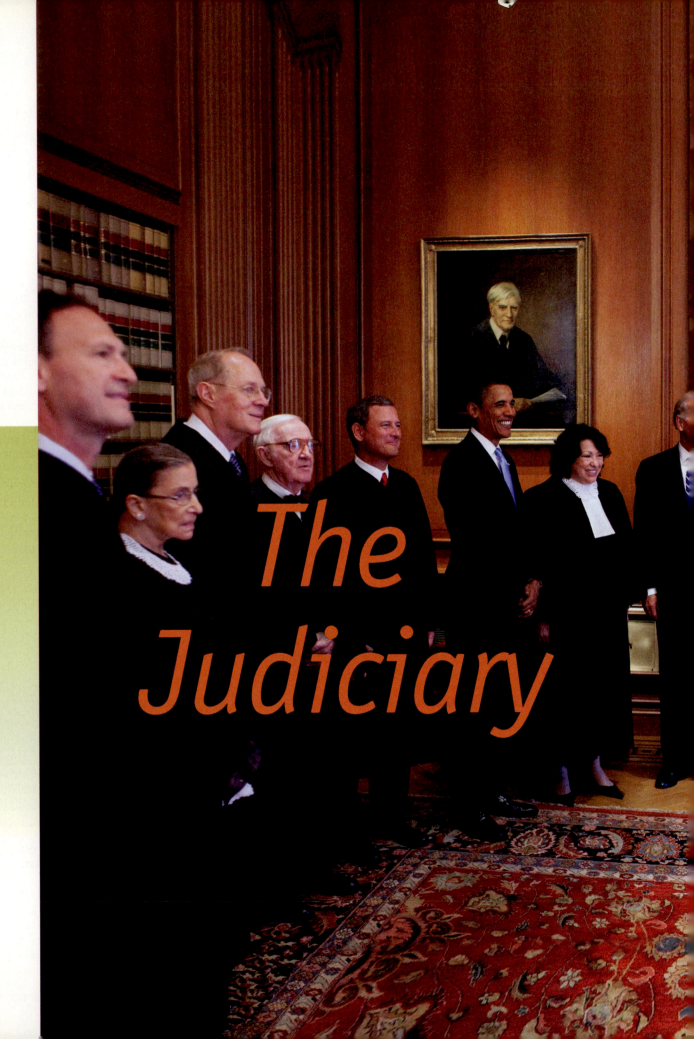

CHAPTER

14

The Judiciary

THEN

A common-law tradition imported from England dominated in the U.S. legal system.

NOW

Through code law and further interpretation of common law, the courts respond to unprecedented developments, from a torrent of technology to a continuing terrorist threat.

NEXT

Will new laws successfully address the complexities of issues including technological advances and the terrorist menace?

Will shifting Supreme Court ideology influence government actions in response to the ever-present threat of terrorism?

Will courts with specific policy expertise supplant legislatures' policy making in areas such as technology?

431

PREVIEW

judiciary
the branch of government comprising the courts and the judges who preside over them

We think of the courts primarily

as places where citizens turn when they have a dispute that they need to resolve. We venture into a courtroom when we encounter some difficult legal issue with either the government or a private individual or group. The resolution of disputes is indeed the primary function of the courts in the United States. But courts and judges are concerned with other, more significant and far-reaching endeavors. In this chapter, we consider how the judiciary, consisting of the federal and state court systems, provides one of the most important defenses that citizens have against abuses of power by the executive and legislative branches. In recognition of the judiciary's role as protector of civil liberties and civil rights, the American people typically award courts higher approval ratings than the other institutions of government.[1]

In *Federalist* No. 78, Alexander Hamilton explains that the Constitution intentionally structures the judiciary to be the weakest branch of government. But the judiciary has evolved significantly, to the point that it shares an equal role with the other two branches. Today, the courts play a central role in ensuring that power remains in balance among the three branches of government on the federal level, as well as between the federal government and the states.

Judges have powers that go well beyond the immediate case they are considering. This authority allows them to make law for future generations. In fact, on both the national and the state level, lawmaking is a shared enterprise among the three branches—legislative, executive, and judicial. Although the Constitution created a government characterized by a separation of powers, lawmaking is far less compartmentalized.[2] It is simplistic to think that legislatures make law, executives enforce it, and courts interpret it; rather, lawmaking is a part of what all three branches are empowered to do.

The Origins of the U.S. Judiciary

The foundations of the U.S. **judiciary**—the branch of government comprising courts and the judges who preside over them—reach back to American colonial history and the early years of the republic that took shape after the colonies broke with England. The U.S. Constitution created the framework for the judiciary. The structure and the authority of the federal judiciary have evolved further, and continuously, through compromises forged over the last 200-plus years.

The Constitution and the Judiciary Act of 1789: Establishing the Supreme Court and the Federal District Courts

During the debates over the ratification of the Constitution, the Anti-Federalists and the Federalists had sparred over what the powers of the national judiciary should be. The Anti-Federalists had warned that a too powerful national judiciary would erode states' rights. For their part, the Federalists had contended that a strong national court would be necessary to moderate conflicts between the states. Ultimately, the Constitution named the **U.S. Supreme Court** as the high court of the land, but the framers intentionally did not make the Court's powers specific. Only by saying little about the specific powers of the Supreme Court were they able to reach agreement on the judiciary.

One of the most important of the framers' compromises was to establish only one national court, the Supreme Court, and to empower Congress to create all lower national courts. Congress accordingly set up these inferior courts in the earliest days of its first session, when it passed the Judiciary Act of 1789, creating the federal district courts.[3] The federal district courts' geographic jurisdictions matched state boundaries, with at least one federal court in every state. Congress intended that these courts would have strong ties to the states in which they were located and expected that in many cases federal judges would apply state, not federal, law. These federal district courts drew strength from their ties to the states, but the federal judiciary was quite weak, with little authority.

Marbury v. Madison and the Principle of Judicial Review

Shortly after his election in 1800, President Thomas Jefferson barred the Supreme Court from meeting in the 1801–1802 term. Jefferson was concerned about the out-of-power Federalists' potential use of the federal judiciary to maintain control in the national government. Jefferson was perhaps right to worry, because in the following term, in the landmark case *Marbury v. Madison* (1803), the Federalist-led Supreme Court grabbed for itself the power of judicial review.[4] **Judicial review** is the Court's authority to review and to strike down laws passed by the other branches of the national government (see Chapter 2).

In the *Marbury* case, the Court argued something that it had never argued before: that it had the power not only to review acts of Congress and the president but also to decide whether those laws were consistent with the Constitution, and to strike down those laws that conflicted with constitutional principles. Legal scholar Joel B. Grossman observes that in *Marbury*, "[John] Marshall made it abundantly clear that the meaning of the Constitution was rarely self-contained and obvious and that those who interpreted it—a role he staked out for the federal courts but one that did not reach its full flowering until the mid-twentieth century—made a difference."[5] Judicial review is the most significant power the Supreme Court exercises. Over time, the Court has extended this power to apply not only to acts of Congress and the chief executive but also to laws passed by state legislatures and executives, as well as to state court rulings.[6]

The Judiciary Act of 1891: Expanding the Federal Courts

The middle level in the federal court structure, the courts of appeals, also known as **circuit courts** of appeals, were created some one hundred years after the *Marbury* decision, through the Judiciary Act of 1891. This law sought to relieve the heavy caseload that the U.S. Supreme Court faced after Congress had gradually expanded the jurisdiction of the federal courts to include criminal cases during the nineteenth century.

Until the advent of separate circuit courts of appeals, federal district court judges and even Supreme Court justices had needed to ride by horseback around the circuits to hear intermediate-level appeals cases. They sometimes traveled thousands of miles in a year in the practice, which became known as **circuit riding.** Over time, they began to bitterly bemoan the hardships they faced in serving the geographically expanding country and the increasing case docket. But it took a long time for the states and their representatives in Congress to become convinced of the necessity of **courts of appeals**—courts that review previous decisions made by courts in the federal or state judicial

U.S. Supreme Court
high court with a limited original jurisdiction whose decisions may not be appealed; it serves as the court of last resort in the U.S. judiciary

Marbury v. Madison
the 1803 Supreme Court case that established the power of judicial review

judicial review
court authority to determine that an action taken by any government official or governing body violates the Constitution

circuit courts
also known as *courts of appeals;* the middle level in the federal court structure, the courts of appeals

circuit riding
the practice of traveling around the circuits by early Supreme Court justices and district court judges to hear appeals cases

courts of appeals
intermediate appellate courts in the federal system that review the application of law in previous decisions made by courts in the federal or state judicial system

> Historically, federal district court judges and even Supreme Court justices rode by horseback around their geographic circuit to hear cases. The harsh demands placed on judges by circuit riding spurred the creation of federal courts of appeals that would review the application of the law in previously-decided cases.

system. These courts were charged exclusively with reviewing the application of law in previous court decisions rather than reviewing evidence or facts of the cases.

The Judiciary Act of 1891 divided the courts of appeals into nine geographic units, with each unit number corresponding to a circuit. The assumption in carving out these units was that each state should be grouped with states likely to have similar political cultures. Today, there are twelve courts of appeals covering designated regions, and the thirteenth hears specific kinds of cases, among them cases involving international trade, governmental contracts, and patents. By creating these separate courts of appeals, Congress significantly reduced the Supreme Court's workload: in 1890, 623 cases were filed with the Court, but just two years later, after passage of the Judiciary Act, that number fell by more than half, to 275. The act also eliminated the requirement of circuit riding, thus easing the burden on Supreme Court justices. Significantly, in using statutes rooted in the common-law tradition, the Congress itself was creating a relatively new form of law: code law.

The Basis of U.S. Law

U.S. law combines two kinds of law: *common law,* which is made principally by judges reaching decisions in cases, and *code law,* enacted primarily by legislators (and often referred to as *statutory law*) and by chief executives.[7] Although the U.S. legal system has roots in a common-law system, most legal disputes today center on disagreements involving the interpretation of code law.

civil law
the body of law dealing with the rights of private citizens

criminal law
the body of law dealing with conduct so harmful to society as a whole that it is prohibited by statute, and is prosecuted and punished by the government

Civil law is the body of law dealing with the rights of private citizens. In civil law cases, there is a conflict between private individuals in which one party alleges that some action or inaction by the other party, the defendant, has caused harm to him or her. **Criminal law** is the body of law dealing with conduct considered so harmful to society as a whole that it is prohibited by statute, and is prosecuted and punished by the government. Criminal law cases are always filed by the government against the defendant.

Because criminal cases are concerned with the breach of an obligation owed by the individual to the larger society, criminal cases always involve either a state government or the national government (though sometimes civil cases can involve a government entity). For example, when the baseball legend and home run–record breaker Barry Bonds was indicted for allegedly having lied to federal authorities investigating the sale of steroids, the criminal case was filed as *The United States of America v. Barry Lamar Bonds*. In contrast, civil cases typically pit individual against individual, as in *Dawn Simorangkir* (also known as the "Boudoir Queen") *v. Courtney Love*, a case in which Simorangkir alleged that celebrity Love used Twitter and other online platforms to publish "delusional accusations and lies" and "threats of harm" concerning the fashion designer.[8] Civil cases typically center on the breach of some obligation owed by one individual to another. The most common civil cases are concerned with the family, a contractual matter, or a negligent injury to a person or property (known as a **tort**).

tort
a wrongful act involving a personal injury or harm to one's property or reputation

Common Law

common law
law made by judges who decide cases and articulate legal principles in their opinions; based on the British system

Law created by courts through the cases they decide is called **common law,** and it binds all courts considering similar cases in the future. To understand how common law functions in the American legal system, consider the 2005 case of Terri Schiavo, the woman at the center of a very controversial debate about an individual's right to die. When Schiavo became ill and collapsed in 1990, her brain lost oxygen and she lapsed into what doctors call a persistent vegetative state, or PVS. A person in a PVS can breathe on his or her own but has very limited brain activity and requires artificial food and hydration. Terri remained in this terrible state for years. Then in 1998, Terri's husband, Michael Schiavo, asked a Florida state court to issue an order that would allow the discontinuance of artificial food and hydration. When the state court issued the order, Terri's family filed a motion to block the removal of the feeding tube. Over the next seven years, the disputing parties battled out the case of Terri Schiavo in the state and federal courts. The courts had to determine whether Terri would have wanted to terminate life support. That determination must have been difficult for the judges, who had to puzzle out Terri's intent by listening to her loved ones'

testimony on Terri's comments, before her accident, about how she would have wanted to live if she were ever in such a state.

Competent individuals have a right to discontinue food and hydration without government interference. The Supreme Court recognized this right in the case *Cruzan v. Missouri Department of Health* (1990). The *Cruzan* case concerned Nancy Cruzan, who also was in a persistent vegetative state and for whom the family sought to discontinue food and hydration. The state of Missouri had intervened, arguing that the family had not provided sufficient evidence that Ms. Cruzan would have wanted this termination. Ultimately, however, the family prevailed.

The *Cruzan* case is important because it created new law. The Supreme Court's decision in this case established that the Constitution's due process clause, which states, "No state shall make or enforce any law which shall abridge the privileges or immunities of citizens of the United States; nor shall any state deprive any person of life, liberty, or property, without due process of law," protected the right to discontinue food and hydration. This right was assumed in the *Schiavo* case. The courts were not trying to puzzle out whether Terri Schiavo had the right to discontinue food and hydration, since *Cruzan* had already established this right. Instead, the judicial deliberations focused solely on whether this was a choice that Terri herself would have made if she had been competent.[9] The court decision that established the right to discontinue food and hydration is now part of U.S. common law.

HISTORICAL BASIS OF COMMON LAW

England began using the common law as a means of unifying the country in the 1100s, when local courts began to write down this national, or "common," law to make it easy to use. Nobles soon realized that the law might be applied to limiting the power of the king and could protect them against unfair and arbitrary actions by the monarchy. Most significant in the creation of common law was the Magna Carta ("Great Charter") of 1215, the first document to list the rights and protections granted to individuals in England. The Magna Carta is one of the core documents in the evolution of constitutional law.

In the common-law system, the jury provides a key check on the powers of the government. The English colonists of North America and later the framers of the Constitution embraced the right to a jury trial. This right rests on the belief that a jury of one's peers is best able to place itself in the shoes of the accused and to make a determination about whether a wrong has been committed. Serving on a jury, like voting in an election or volunteering for an interest group, is an important form of citizen engagement.

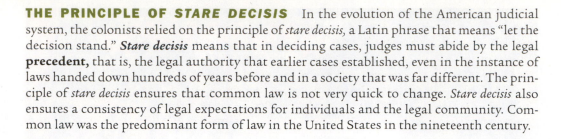

THE PRINCIPLE OF *STARE DECISIS* In the evolution of the American judicial system, the colonists relied on the principle of *stare decisis,* a Latin phrase that means "let the decision stand." ***Stare decisis*** means that in deciding cases, judges must abide by the legal **precedent,** that is, the legal authority that earlier cases established, even in the instance of laws handed down hundreds of years before and in a society that was far different. The principle of *stare decisis* ensures that common law is not very quick to change. *Stare decisis* also ensures a consistency of legal expectations for individuals and the legal community. Common law was the predominant form of law in the United States in the nineteenth century.

Code Law

By the early twentieth century, rapid changes in society and the economy demanded much faster responses in the law than what common law could provide. Legislators in Congress and the states responded to those changes by creating laws to regulate the behavior of individuals and organizations and to deal with a vast array of new issues. The kind of law they developed is known as **code law.** Code law differs from common law in that it traditionally is formulated by legislators through statutes, whereas common law is created through judicial decisions.

A similar, continuously changing social environment prevails today. Because of the steady flow of change and the fast pace of contemporary life, particularly due to nonstop technological advances, the prior body of law has become inadequate to deal with unprecedented developments in commerce, communication, and even crime. In creating code law responsive to these new realities, legislators have had to become more knowledgeable and specialized about the topics of the laws they write. They have had to rely heavily on experts—police attempting to enforce laws; business and industry leaders; other specialists—to help shape how laws are written. Code law functions very differently from common law. When legislatures or executives make law, they can move quickly in response to some pressing crisis or problem. They can decide to change course and even take a totally unprecedented approach to a situation.

Sources of U.S. Law

We have seen that code law and common law coexist in the United States and that judges, legislators, and presidents all contribute to lawmaking. What's more, these officials often cooperate in the lawmaking enterprise, interacting to clarify ambiguous provisions in the code law or to apply the common law to more specific situations. These lawmakers collectively create law that is distinct, but they do so in different ways, as we consider in this discussion.

In this section, we examine the five sources of laws in the United States:

- the U.S. and state constitutions
- statutes
- judicial decisions
- executive orders
- administrative and regulatory law

These sources differ not only in who makes the law but also in their place in the hierarchy of the U.S. legal system. Moreover, lawmakers create law not only at the national level but in all fifty state governments as well.

The Federal and State Constitutions

Atop the hierarchy of the sources of U.S. law are constitutions—the U.S. Constitution and the constitutions of the fifty states. Constitutions are the highest form of law, taking precedence over all other laws, and they are the primary organizational blueprint for the fed-

stare decisis
from the Latin "let the decision stand," the principle that binds judges to rely upon the holdings of past judges in deciding cases

precedent
legal authority established by earlier cases

code law
laws created by legislators to regulate the behavior of individuals and organizations

eral and state governments. Constitutions delineate the powers of the government and the limitations on those powers. They also establish the structure and the function of each of the branches—executive, legislative, and judicial—and define the relationship between the federal and state governments and between the government and the individual.

The body of law that comes out of the courts in cases involving constitutional interpretation is known as **constitutional law.** In cases concerning a provision of the federal Constitution, the high court is the U.S. Supreme Court, and its decisions bind all Americans, including Congress and the president.

If the president or the members of Congress do not like the outcome of a particular case, they may test the Supreme Court's ruling by passing a law challenging the decision. (In the instance of state high court cases, a governor or the state legislature can take a similar action.) Legislatures and executives also may try to circumvent a Court decision by changing the law through a constitutional amendment. For example, since 1963, some members of Congress have sought to blunt the impact of a series of Supreme Court decisions establishing that prayer in public schools violates the Constitution's separation of church and state. These legislators have introduced into the House and the Senate various constitutional amendments that would allow vocal prayer or mandate a "moment of silence" in public schools. None of these proposed amendments has garnered the two-thirds supermajority vote in Congress necessary to move the amendment to the next stage in the ratification process. Yet some representatives in Congress continue to seek to negate the Court's decision by amending the Constitution.

Statutes

Laws written by legislatures are called **statutes.** Statutory lawmaking is the hallmark of any code-law system. In such a system, legislative law reflects the core principles of the government system. For example, the **U.S. Code** is a compilation of all the laws ever passed by the U.S. Congress, and it reflects that body's priorities and concerns. The U.S. Code has fifty sections spanning a range of issues including agriculture, bankruptcy, highways, the postal service, and war and defense.

Judicial Decisions

When a judge or a panel of judges decides a case, they sometimes write an opinion that justifies their decision and explains how they have applied principles of *stare decisis.* These judicial opinions then become part of the common law.

Under what circumstances do judges write an opinion? To answer that question, we must consider the resources for appealing cases on the federal and state levels. The federal court system comprises two levels of appeals, or appellate, court: the circuit courts of appeals, previously described, and the U.S. Supreme Court, which has the final say in cases. The state systems generally feature two appeals levels, and the final appellate court is the court of last resort, performing much the same function as the U.S. Supreme Court.[10] Judges serving in *courts of last resort*—that is, the U.S. Supreme Court and the state high courts—almost always write opinions in cases, and those opinions have the force of law. The Supreme Court's decisions govern all similar cases heard in all the federal courts and become the law of the land; a state high court's decisions become law in that state.

Executive Orders

Article II, Section 1, of the U.S. Constitution states that "the executive power shall be vested in [the] president of the United States." This power has been interpreted to allow the president to issue orders that create and guide the bureaucracy in implementing policy. Because executive orders have the force and effect of law, they represent a crucial tool in the president's lawmaking toolbox. Historically, presidents have sometimes used executive orders to create policy that may not have garnered sufficient legislative support. For example, Chapter 12 describes President Harry Truman's use of executive orders to desegregate the military in 1948.

constitutional law
the body of law that comes out of the courts in cases involving the interpretation of the Constitution

statute
a law enacted by Congress or by state legislatures to deal with particular issues or problems, sometimes more detailed and comprehensive than the common law

U.S. Code
a compilation of all the laws passed by the U.S. Congress

dual court system
a two-part judicial system such as that of the United States, which has both federal and state courts

trial court
the court in which a case is first heard and which determines the facts of a case

jurisdiction
the power of a court to hear a case and to resolve it, given to a court by either a constitution or a statute

federal question
a question of law based on interpretation of the U.S. Constitution, federal laws, or treaties

diversity of citizenship
the circumstance in which the parties in a legal case are from different states or the case involves a U.S. citizen and a foreign government

A president or a governor can enact an executive order without input from the other branches of government, though executive orders are subject to judicial review and depend on Congress for funding. As described in Chapter 12, President Bush used executive orders extensively to address a wide range of issues. These included prohibiting new investment in Burma to punish that nation's repressive regime and improving the coordination and effectiveness of bureaucracies administering youth programs in the United States.[11]

Administrative Law

In addition to the executive order, presidents and governors have another source of lawmaking power: they head a vast bureaucracy of agencies that have their own lawmaking authority. As we saw in Chapter 13, bureaucrats get their power directly from the Congress or the state legislatures. By delegating significant power to bureaucratic administrators with expertise in specific policy areas, Congress and the state legislatures help to ensure the effective implementation of the laws they pass.

Why, specifically, must legislators delegate such power? The reason is that lawmakers typically write vague or ambiguous bills. They do so to increase the chances that representatives and senators with differing ideologies will find a given bill acceptable for passage into law. But the result of vague or ambiguous wording might be that the law, once passed, is difficult to implement. Thus legislators must turn to bureaucrats with expertise and specialized knowledge to help them to administer the law.

This delegation of authority gives administrators substantial power. It allows them to act as quasi- ("as if") legislators in creating administrative rules, implementing them, and interpreting those rules as well. Administrative rule making fleshes out the broad principles in the statutory law, much of which is interpreted by the federal courts.

The Federal Court System

Article III of the Constitution created only one court—the Supreme Court—and left it to Congress to create any additional federal courts that the country might need. As we saw earlier in this chapter, Congress responded with a series of laws that created inferior (or lower) courts in the form of federal district courts and federal appellate courts (or courts of appeals).

In addition to these constitutionally and legislatively created courts, each state has its own independent state court system structured by state constitutions. Because the U.S. judicial system has both federal and state courts, it is said to be a **dual court system.** Figure 14.1 shows that nearly every case, whether tried in a federal or a state court, originates in a **trial court**—the court in which a case is first heard and which determines the facts of a case.[12]

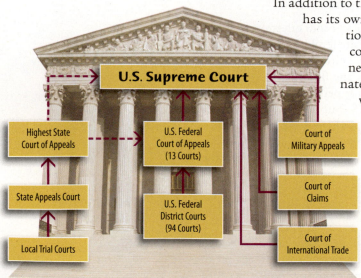

FIGURE 14.1

The U.S. Court System

Jurisdiction of Federal Courts

The ability of a court to hear a case depends on whether that court has **jurisdiction**—the authority of a court to hear and decide a case. Federal jurisdiction is strictly defined by Article III, Section 2, of the Constitution. In this passage, federal courts are empowered to hear only cases involving a federal question or a diversity of citizenship. A **federal question** is a question of law based on interpretation of the U.S. Constitution, federal laws, or treaties. **Diversity of citizenship** means that the parties in the case are individuals from different states or that the case involves a U.S. citizen and a foreign government. It may also mean that the suit centers on the complaint of one or more states against another state or states.

When a court has **original jurisdiction** over a case, that court is the first court to hear the case—no other court has yet considered the legal issues in this case. In instances of original jurisdiction, the court must decide what happened in the case and must apply the existing law to resolve the dispute. In contrast, **appellate jurisdiction** empowers a court to review the decision of the court that has already heard a case. Usually, the appellate court is called upon to decide not what happened but, rather, whether the first court correctly applied or interpreted the law.

In the federal courts, the federal district courts have original jurisdiction in most cases. The U.S. courts of appeals handle first-level appeals of decisions made in those federal district courts. Most cases that reach the Supreme Court come to it under its appellate jurisdiction.

The Structure of the Federal Courts

The U.S. court system is a dual system in two ways. First, as noted above, parallel federal and state court systems operate largely independently of each other and make law in specific areas. Second, each of these systems has both trial courts and appellate courts. In the brief discussions that follow, we consider the different kinds of courts in the federal system.

FEDERAL DISTRICT COURTS   The federal judiciary is structured hierarchically, similar to a pyramid. There are ninety-four federal district courts at the bottom of this pyramid. These are the trial courts in this system, and they do much of the work of the federal judiciary. The function of trial courts is straightforward: judges or juries decide what happened in a case and then apply the law. For example, in a terrorism case, the judge or the jury assesses whether the defendant is guilty of committing acts of terror as defined by federal law. If the defendant is found guilty, the court then looks to the law to impose a penalty. Federal district courts operate throughout the United States; every state must have at least one.

U.S. COURTS OF APPEALS   At the middle level of the federal judicial pyramid are thirteen courts of appeals. As Figure 14.2 on page 440 shows, twelve of these courts cover specific regions (circuits) plus the Federal Circuit located in the District of Columbia. The thirteenth court of appeals covers specific kinds of cases, involving such matters as international trade, government contracts, and patents. Congress has authorized 179 judgeships for these courts of appeals, though typically there are vacancies.

The size of each circuit varies depending on the size of the court's constituency and its caseload. Today, the smallest circuit is the First Circuit, which consists of six judgeships; the largest, the Ninth, has twenty-eight.[13] Each circuit court of appeals is supervised by a chief judge. The chief judge is the individual on the bench who has the most seniority but is under age 65. The judges who hear a case typically include a three-judge panel made up of the courts of appeals judges. They are sometimes joined by visiting judges (usually from the corresponding federal district of the court of appeals) and retired judges. In deciding cases, the judges read briefs submitted by lawyers, which argue their clients' case, and then may hear oral arguments. During this process, no new facts are admitted into evidence; instead, the court of appeals focuses on questions of procedure or the application of law that occurred in a decision of the lower court.

The Judiciary Act of 1891 carved out only nine geographic units for the courts of appeals. The increased number of circuit courts to the thirteen of the present day (see Figure 14.2) occurred through a process by which Congress split up existing circuits. Each new division has typically reflected Congress's desire to keep together states with similar legal and political cultures.

Courts of appeals have no original jurisdiction—that is, these courts do not decide the facts of a case. Rather, as appellate courts, they review the legal procedures of a preceding case and decide whether the law was applied appropriately given the facts already admitted into evidence. Courts of appeals are the courts of last resort for most federal cases,

original jurisdiction
the power of a court to hear a case first, before other courts have decided it

appellate jurisdiction
the authority of a court to review the the application or interpretation of the law in previous decisions reached by another court in a case

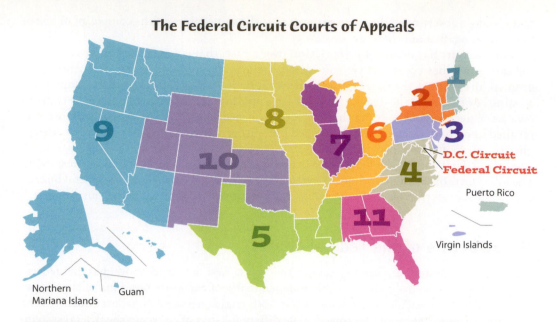

The Federal Circuit Courts of Appeals

D.C. Circuit
Federal Circuit

Puerto Rico

Virgin Islands

Northern Mariana Islands

Guam

POLITICAL INQUIRY

FIGURE 14.2 ■ How many U.S. circuit courts of appeals are there today? What are the circuits (regions) they cover, and what determines the size of each circuit? What kinds of cases does an additional, special court of appeals (not shown in the map) cover?

because after a case has been decided by the appellate court, there is no automatic right to an appeal. Although some cases may be appealed to the U.S. Supreme Court, the Court ultimately chooses to hear only a small fraction of those.

SPECIAL COURTS   In addition to the federal district courts and the courts of appeals, Congress, acting under Article I of the Constitution, created several specialized courts. These include the Court of International Trade, the U.S. Court of Military Appeals, the U.S. Tax Court, and the U.S. Court of Veterans' Appeals.

In recent years, media coverage has highlighted the activities of another kind of specialized court, the Foreign Intelligence Surveillance Act (FISA) court. It was established by Congress in a 1978 act that spells out the procedures for the collection of human and electronic intelligence.[14] During the George W. Bush administration, FISA courts were charged with determining whether an individual could be subject to warrantless surveillance of his or her communications (see Chapter 4).

FISA courts are evidence of a notable trend in how the judicial branch is coping with the growing complexity of the types of cases that come before the courts. This trend involves increasing specialization, both by law, as in the creation of special courts such as FISA courts, and by practice, as when judges develop an "informal" expertise in a policy area—say, DNA testing or software patent law. Legal scholar Lawrence Baum assesses this trend as an effort by the courts to gain and apply the kind of expertise characteristic of the administrative agencies of the government:

> Whether judicial specialization is established by law or develops in practice, it reflects an effort to gain the perceived strengths of administrative agencies while retaining the form and name of the courts. The efficiency and expertise that are ascribed to specialization can help courts keep up with their caseloads and perhaps improve the quality of decision-making.[15]

Although this specialization may occur in both state and federal courts, it is not possible for the highest court in the land, the U.S. Supreme Court, to limit its expertise.

THE U.S. SUPREME COURT WITHIN THE FEDERAL SYSTEM   At the top of the federal judicial pyramid sits the U.S. Supreme Court. Although this court has a very limited original jurisdiction (which we examine later in this chapter), it hears appeals from both the federal and the state courts when cases decided there concern a federal constitutional question or when federal law is involved.

Nine judges, called **justices,** sit on the Supreme Court. One of these justices has been specially selected by the president to serve as the **chief justice,** the judge who provides both organizational and intellectual leadership on the Court. The chief justice has the same voting power as the other justices, called the associate justices. But he or she has an important, distinctive role in the decision-making process. When the chief justice agrees with the majority, he or she chooses whether to write the majority opinion or assign it to another justice. The current chief justice is John Roberts, whom President George W. Bush appointed in 2005.

Selecting Judges for the Federal Bench

In both 2009 and 2010, President Barack Obama faced one of the most important decisions of his presidency, a decision that would have implications for policy decades after his presidency had ended. In May 2009, Obama announced Sonia Sotomayor as his nominee for the seat that had been occcupied by Supreme Court Justice David Souter, who had retired at the end of the Court's 2008–2009 term. The following year, he selected Elena Kagan as his nominee to replace retiring Associate Justice John Paul Stevens. Obama's selections of Sotomayor and Kagan illustrate the differing characteristics presidents might emphasize when selecting judges for the federal bench.

In selecting Sonia Sotomayor, who had sat on the second circuit of the U.S. Court of Appeals since 1998, Obama sought a competent individual who would win Senate confirmation. Obama also wanted to make his mark on a Supreme Court whose ideology has been greatly shaped by the appointments of his predecessor, President George W. Bush, who had appointed two conservatives—Chief Justice John Roberts and Associate Justice Samuel Alito—to the Court. Finally, following his election, President Obama had been pressured by both Latino constituents and interest groups to appoint the Court's first Latino member.

Obama's selection of Kagan was perhaps more surprising. Kagan, who served as the Dean of the Harvard Law School, had never served as a judge. Though there was precedent for nonjudges being appointed to the Court, that career path was not the usual one. But in Kagan, many analysts believe that Obama saw traits that far outweighed her lack of experience on the bench. Throughout her career, Kagan had gained a reputation as a conciliator—a peacemaker who could bring divergent ideological sides together, a characteristic that could prove important given the often divided nature of the Court. In addition to her impeccable

Changing Caseloads: Fraud on the Internet

	THEN (2001)*	NOW (2009)**
Number of complaints processed by the federal government's Internet Fraud Complaint Center and referred to law enforcement agencies	16,775	275,284
Cumulative losses by victims of cybercrimes whose cases were processed by the federal government's Internet Fraud Complaint Center	$17.8 million	$265 million
Top three reported offenses	Internet auction fraud (43%) Nondelivery of merchandise and payment (20%) Nigerian letter fraud (10%)	Nondelivery of merchandise and/or payment (33%) Internet auction fraud (25%) Credit/debit card fraud (9%)

WHAT'S NEXT?

> Have you been, or do you know anyone who has been, a victim of Internet fraud?

> Will cyberfraud continue to grow, in keeping with the present trend? What will be the impact of any growth on the court system?

> What new forms might Internet crime take in the future?

* www.ic3.gov/media/annualreport/2001_IFCCReport.pdf.
** www.ic3.gov/media/2009/090331.aspx.

justice
any of the nine judges who sit on the Supreme Court

chief justice
the leading justice on the Supreme Court, who provides both organizational and intellectual leadership

> With her mother holding the Bible and her brother looking on, Sonia Sotomayor is sworn in by Chief Justice John Roberts. President Obama's 2009 appointee to the Supreme Court was the Court's first Latino member.

academic credentials, because she had not served as a judge, Kagan was not saddled with an enormous record of judicial opinions that could have been used against her during the confirmation process. Kagan is the fourth woman to serve on the Court (three women sit today, and Associate Justice Sandra Day O'Connor retired from the bench in 2006), the first member in forty years appointed without a judicial background (the last being the late Chief Justice William Rehnquist). Kagan is the eighth Jewish person to serve on the Court, which currently has three Jewish members. The criteria important for Obama's selections are typical for presidents faced with the nomination of a member of the U.S. Supreme Court.

Once Supreme Court and other federal court judges are confirmed by the Senate, they serve for life, as long as they do not commit any impeachable offense. While lifetime tenure is controversial (see "Thinking Critically About Democracy"), it also means that such appointees often are the longest-lasting legacies of the presidents who appoint them. Chief Justice John Roberts, who was appointed to the Court at age 50, and Associate Justices Sonia Sotomayor and Elena Kagan, who were 55 and 50, respectively, when appointed, will each likely serve on the Court for about thirty years.

The Senate's Role in Appointment and Confirmation

The president and the Senate share power in the selection of federal court judges and Supreme Court justices. In this way, the nomination and confirmation process serves as a check on the respective powers of the presidency and the Senate.

In the case of the federal district court judges, a custom known as **senatorial courtesy** gives senators—though only those who are of the same political party as the president—a powerful voice in choosing the district court judges who will serve in their state. Under this tradition, a senator from the same political party as the president can block the president's choice of a federal district court judge in the senator's state.

Because circuit courts of appeals judges and Supreme Court justices serve more than one state, the individual senators from any one state play a far less powerful role in the appointment of these judges than they do in the selection of district court judges. Rather, in the selection procedure for circuit court judges and U.S. Supreme Court justices, the Senate Judiciary Committee, composed of eighteen senators, takes the lead. Committee members are charged with gathering information about each nominee and providing it to the full Senate. The Senate Judiciary Committee also typically votes on the nominee, and the full Senate uses this vote to signal whether the nominee is acceptable. Sometimes the judiciary committee does not make a recommendation about a candidate, as when members split their vote 7-7 on the nomination of Clarence Thomas to be a U.S. Supreme Court justice in 1991.

Judicial Competence

Competence is of central concern for nominees to the circuit courts of appeals and the Supreme Court. Appeals court judges and Supreme Court justices first and foremost must be qualified, and some nominees in recent decades have been rejected because of senatorial doubts about their qualifications. The Senate rejected two nominees of President Richard Nixon because of such concerns. And when President George W. Bush nominated his White House counsel Harriet Miers as an associate Supreme Court justice in 2005, he was forced to withdraw his nomination because of concerns about Miers's lack of qualifications. Those objections strongly indicated that Miers would face a steep uphill climb in achieving

senatorial courtesy

A custom that allows senators from the president's political party to veto the president's choice of federal district court judge in the senator's state

SHOULD THERE BE A CONSTITUTIONAL AMENDMENT MANDATING A RETIREMENT AGE FOR SUPREME COURT JUSTICES?

The Issue: Some states require top judges to retire at age 70 or 75, but a Supreme Court justice has a lifetime tenure. Thus a Supreme Court justice can potentially serve well beyond the age at which most people retire from their professional lives. In 2006, Justice Sandra Day O'Connor stepped down from the Court at age 76. But O'Connor was an exception. Justice John Paul Stevens sat on the bench until 2010, when, at age 90, he retired. Chief Justice William Rehnquist presided until his death at age 80 in 2005. Such precedents—given the cognitive and physical problems generally associated with old age—have given rise to questions about the wisdom of allowing justices to serve on the Supreme Court for life. Some Americans believe that the country needs a constitutional amendment to mandate a specific retirement age for the justices. Others disagree, although some of these naysayers propose alternative means of ensuring judicial competence.

Should there be a constitutional amendment mandating a retirement age for Supreme Court justices? Here is what the various camps have to say.

Yes: The country needs a constitutional amendment that modifies the framers' specification of a life term for Supreme Court justices. Relevant is the work of legal scholar David J. Garrow. His research on Supreme Court justices' "mental decrepitude" has emphasized that many former Supreme Court justices themselves, including Earl Warren and Potter Stewart, did not oppose a constitutional amendment limiting tenure to age 75—*if* such an age limit were imposed on members of Congress and the president as well. Moreover, in *Gregory v. Ashcroft* (1991), which addressed the constitutionality of a mandatory retirement age of 70 for state court judges, Justice Sandra Day O'Connor opined that a mandatory retirement age of 70 could be in the public interest.*

No: A constitutional amendment requiring a mandatory retirement age for Supreme Court justices constitutes age discrimination. Such an amendment violates the framers' intentions, because the Constitution explicitly states that justices may serve for life. Through such an amendment, the United States would lose the expertise, wisdom, and perspective of older jurists. Thus the Constitution should not be amended to set a specific age for retirement from the Court.

Other approaches: A constitutional amendment that would apply across the board to all Supreme Court justices, regardless of their health status, denies citizens the invaluable experience of some older justices whose health may not be in decline. Society can address the challenge of ensuring competence on the Court by other means. For example, the ever-watchful media could publicize the behaviors of justices whose health seems to be impeding their ability to perform their duties. In addition, or alternatively, Congress could aggressively monitor the mental and physical health of Supreme Court justices by requiring the justices to provide health information to a special congressional monitoring committee.

What do you think?

① Do the potential advantages of preventing an elderly, mentally diminished Supreme Court justice from serving outweigh the benefits (wisdom, experience, and so on) that might come from the continued service of this jurist or other aging justices? Explain.

② Should the country pass a constitutional amendment setting a mandatory retirement age for Supreme Court justices? Why or why not?

③ What alternative solutions beyond those proposed here might address the problem of ensuring competence on the Court?

* *Gregory v. Ashcroft,* 501 U.S. 452 (1991).

> Born in 1920, Associate Justice John Paul Stevens retired from the U.S. Supreme Court in 2010, at age 90.

Senate confirmation. (Some in the media argued, however, that the questions about Miers's competence were in part a political smoke screen—a ploy by certain conservative Republican senators who would be voting on her nomination to reject the Republican nominee because her ideological outlook may not have been conservative enough for them.)[16]

Ideology and Selection to the Bench

Once the Senate establishes the competence of a circuit court or Supreme Court candidate, attention shifts to the nominee's ideology—his or her worldview. Mindful that federal judges typically serve far beyond their own tenure, presidents often regard these nominations as a way of cementing their own legacies. They give the nod to judges, and more significantly, to Supreme Court justices, with whom they are ideologically compatible. When President Barack Obama chose Sonia Sotomayor to serve on the Court, he chose a person who held liberal views consistent with his own. In Elena Kagan, he found a nominee who, though holding liberal views, could build bridges with the conservative members of the Court. At the same time, it appeared that Kagan was on the record as someone who "supported assertions of executive power."[17] When George W. Bush nominated John Roberts, he chose an individual who shared the president's own policy views, particularly with regard to issues such as abortion, church and state relations, and criminal due process protections.

A Supreme Court justice's (and a circuit court judge's) ideology can shift over time, however. President Richard Nixon selected Justice Harry Blackmun to serve on the Supreme Court because of Blackmun's conservative record in deciding cases involving civil rights and civil liberties. But Blackmun, who wrote the Court's opinion in *Roe v. Wade*—the decision guaranteeing a woman's right to abortion—and who was a vocal critic of capital punishment once seated on the Court, was a serious disappointment to Nixon. Still, in most instances, a justice's worldview remains fairly constant. Justices' ideologies are reinforced by the presence of stable ideological blocs on the Supreme Court, which may bolster long-held beliefs and discourage the rethinking of issues from a completely new perspective. This reality underscores why the nomination and confirmation process is so important: the president and the Senate are banking on their assumption that the nominee's demonstrated ideology or perspective will color how he or she sees issues and cases that come before the Court in the future.[18]

Representation of Demographic Groups

Faced with the prospect of appointing a successor to replace the retiring Associate Justice David Souter, President Barack Obama encountered significant pressure from constituents and from interest groups (which created expectation in the media) to appoint the first Hispanic justice to the Court. (See "Analyzing the Sources.") Obama obliged, selecting Sonia Sotomayor, who sat on the second circuit of the U.S. Court of Appeals and is of Puerto Rican descent. In selecting Sotomayor, Obama named the first Hispanic and third woman to the Court. Other presidents have faced similar expectations: when Thurgood Marshall, the Supreme Court's first African American jurist retired in 1991, political analysts and the media expected President George H. W. Bush to appoint another African American to the seat. Bush obliged and appointed Clarence Thomas to the Court. Even though the federal courts effectively underrepresent the population at large, because judges are overwhelmingly male, white, Protestant, and upper middle class, the current Supreme Court has a relatively diverse composition. In recent decades, an informal demographic composition of the Court has evolved with an African American seat (currently occupied by Associate Justice Clarence Thomas), a Jewish seat (now there are three Jewish associate justices: Stephen Breyer, Ruth Bader Ginsburg, and Elena Kagan), a Roman Catholic seat (now actually several such seats, with Chief Justice John Roberts and Associate Justices Anthony Kennedy, Antonin Scalia, Clarence Thomas, and Samuel Alito all being Catholic), a woman's seat (held exclusively for over a decade by Sandra Day O'Connor, who served on the Court from 1981 to 2006; she was joined on the Court by Ruth Bader Ginsburg in 1993; Ginsburg was joined by Sotomayor in 2009 and Kagan in 2010), and now a Hispanic seat (occupied by Sotomayor).

ANALYZING THE SOURCES

THE DEMOGRAPHIC BALANCE ON THE SUPREME COURT

> In this cartoon by Ed Fischer, a Republican senator considers the nomination of U.S. Supreme Court Justice Sonia Sotomayor while voters, representing 40 million Hispanic voters, look on.

Evaluating the Evidence

① Why would the cartoon specify that Republican legislators might be cautious in considering Hispanic voters when considering the Sotomayor nomination?

② What does the size of the Hispanic man and woman indicate about the strength of the Hispanic vote in shaping the outcome of some elections?

③ As it turned out, only 9 Republican U.S. Senators voted for Sotomayor's confirmation. Republican senators from both Texas and Arizona (where Hispanics constitute a sizeable proportion of the electorate) voted against her nomination. Among those voting for Sotomayor was Senator Mel Martinez of Florida. Do you think Hispanic voters will consider their senators' position on the Sotomayor nomination in future Senate elections? Why or why not?

The impulse to recognize specific seats that reflect major groups in the population serves the goal of **symbolic representation,** which is the representation on the Court of the country's leading demographic groups. There is an implicit assumption that a justice occupying one of these seats will best serve the concerns of the racial, ethnic, gender, or other group to which he or she belongs. That is, the Latino justice will take the perspective of Latinos, the female justice will consider the policy preferences of women, and so on. In fact, however, the representation may be more symbolic than real because the issues of importance to Latinos, women, or any other group are hardly monolithic. These issues are so multidimensional that no one person could speak for all the members' concerns. Nevertheless, many public figures and citizens say that the Court should mirror as closely as possible the main contours of the national demographic profile.

Clearly, the nomination and confirmation of federal judges does not take place in a vacuum. Beyond presidents' and senators' concerns about judicial qualifications, ideology, and demographic representation, these players are acutely aware of what their constituencies will think of any nominee and of what might happen at the confirmation hearings. For that reason, they continuously gauge public opinion throughout the nomination and confirmation process. In addition to being mindful of the voters, the president and the senators calculate how interest groups, particularly those that helped to put them in office, will view the nominee. In nominating John Roberts, George W. Bush sought to ensure that his nominee would be acceptable to one of his core constituencies, conservative voters.

symbolic representation
the attempt to ensure that the Supreme Court includes representatives of major demographic groups, such as women, African Americans, Jews, and Catholics

Interest groups often have a significant voice in the confirmation hearings. Some groups almost always participate in the hearings, among them the American Bar Association, labor and civil rights organizations, law enforcement groups, and business interests. These groups do not hesitate to let the members of the Senate Judiciary Committee know clearly whether they support or oppose a given candidate.

The U.S. Supreme Court Today

collegial court
a court made up of a group of judges who must evaluate a case together and decide on the outcome; significant compromise and negotiation take place as members try to build a majority coalition

The decisions of the U.S. Supreme Court's nine justices are binding on all other courts in the country, and no other court may overturn them. Decision making on the Court is a multistep process that provides many opportunities for conflict and compromise. As a **collegial court,** which means it is made up of a panel of justices, Supreme Court justices must work closely together as they navigate the process. The need for compromise on the Court is especially intense because of the sheer number of cases it hears and the fact that its decisions are final.

The Supreme Court's Jurisdiction

In the vast majority of cases, the Supreme Court is reviewing a decision made by a lower court rather than exercising original jurisdiction. The framers limited the Supreme Court's original jurisdiction to only those cases that concern ambassadors, public ministers, and consuls, and those involving two or more states. But over time, Congress, in cooperation with the Court, has decided that the Court should retain original jurisdiction only in cases involving suits between two or more states.

Choosing Cases for Review

Approximately 7,000 petitions are filed with the Court each year, each asking for the review of a case already decided. Each case is one that a party or parties are appealing from

> The current U.S. Supreme Court. Front from left are Associate Justices Clarence Thomas and Antonin Scalia, Chief Justice John Roberts, and Associate Justices Anthony Kennedy and Ruth Bader Ginsburg. Top from left are Associate Justices Sonia Sotomayor, Stephen Breyer, Samuel Alito, and Elena Kagan.

some other court because one or both sides dispute the decision in the case. Ultimately, the justices write decisions in only eighty to ninety cases, however. How do they decide which cases to hear? Like the other stages of the decision-making process, "deciding to decide," as Supreme Court scholar H. W. Perry puts it, is a joint activity.[19]

The decision to place a case on the Supreme Court's agenda is a collaborative one. Important in this process is the role of Supreme Court clerks. These young lawyers, who are recommended for the positions by certain "feeder professors" at selective law schools, are charged with drafting a **pool memo,** a description of the facts of the case, the pertinent legal arguments, and a recommendation as to whether the case should be taken.

The chief justice distributes a list of selected cases, the **discuss list,** to the other justices before a regularly scheduled conference. A chief justice's decision as to whether to include a given case on the discuss list is based primarily on review of the Supreme Court clerks' pool memos. On Fridays throughout the Court's term, which lasts from October to June, the justices meet in conference to discuss the cases on the list.[20] At this point, they vote on whether to issue a writ of *certiorari*—a Latin term roughly translated as "a request to make certain"—for specific cases. The **writ of *certiorari*** is a higher court's order to a lower court to make available the records of a past case so that the higher court can determine whether mistakes were made during the lower-court trial that would justify a review of the case.[21] The writ of *certiorari* falls within the Court's discretionary jurisdiction, meaning that the Court can choose whether to hear such cases (unlike those cases that have a mandatory appeal to the U.S. Supreme Court).

The justices determine whether they will consider a case according to a practice known as the **Rule of Four,** under which the justices will hear a case if four or more of nine justices decide they want to hear it. They do not need to give reasons for wanting or not wanting to hear a case—they simply must vote. The vast majority of the cases the Court hears reach the justices through a writ of *certiorari*, reflecting its role as primarily an appellate court.

On the Docket: Considering the Case

When a case makes its way onto the Court docket, the parties in the litigation shift into high gear (see Figure 14.3). The petitioner (the party that sought the Court's review in the first place) usually has forty-five days to file a written **brief**—a document detailing the legal argument for the desired outcome—with the Court. After the filing of this brief, the opposing party (the respondent) has thirty days to file its own brief with the Court.

Today, *amicus curiae* briefs are a common part of Supreme Court litigation. Filed within a specified time period by a person or group that is not party to the lawsuit, an ***amicus curiae* brief,** or **"friend of the court" brief,** is a document that aims to influence the Court's decision. Some cases trigger the filing of many *amicus* briefs; the largest number of such briefs (ninety) ever filed in a Supreme Court case came in two cases involving affirmative action at the University of Michigan.[22]

Amicus curiae briefs seek to provide information that jurists need to resolve cases and can be very influential. In the University of Michigan cases, a wide variety of interested parties, ranging from the MTV network to the Law School Admissions Council, filed

Cases on the U.S. Supreme Court's docket

Applications for review by appeal or writ of *certiorari* from federal and state courts (justices use Rule of Four to determine docket)

Original jurisdiction

1 — Briefs submitted by both sides; amicus curiae briefs filed by interested parties

2 — Oral arguments presented by attorneys for each side

3 — Justices' conference: cases discussed; nonbinding votes taken; opinion writing assigned

4 — Justices' opinions drafted and circulated for comment

5 — Court's final decision announced

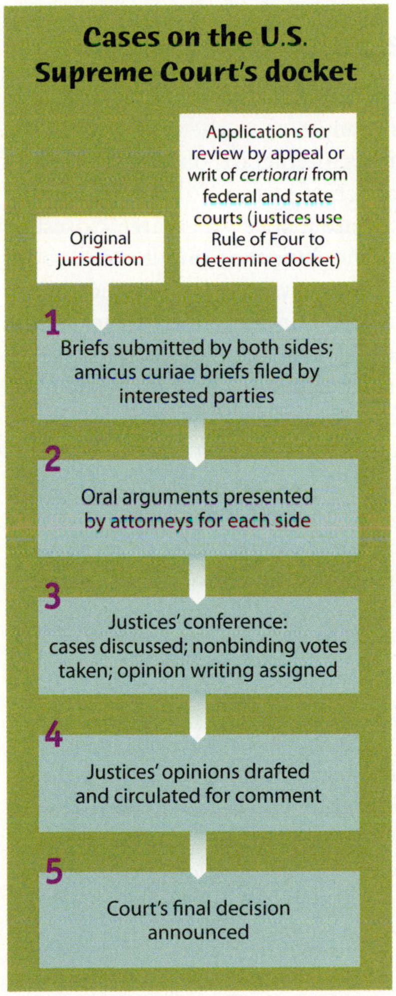

FIGURE 14.3

Decision Making on the Supreme Court

pool memo
description written by Court clerks of the facts of a case filed with the Court, the pertinent legal arguments, and a recommendation as to whether the case should be taken

discuss list
compiled by the chief justice, the list of cases on review that he thinks may be appropriate for the Court to hear

writ of *certiorari*
Latin for "a request to make certain"; this is an order to a lower court to produce a certified record of a case so that the appellate court can determine whether any errors occurred during trial that warrant review of the case

Rule of Four
practice by which the Supreme Court justices determine if they will hear a case if four or more justices want to hear it

brief
a document detailing the legal argument for the desired outcome in a court case

***amicus curiae* brief ("friend of the court" brief)**
document submitted by parties interested in a certain case or issue in an attempt to provide the Court with information that may be used to decide the case

briefs describing their views on how racial equality has been and can be achieved in various settings. Judges often use the information or the legal arguments contained in *amicus curiae* briefs to decide cases.[23] The use of these briefs democratizes the judicial system by opening it up to lobbying that is similar to lobbying in the other branches of government. And the participation of interest groups and other organized interests in the judicial decision-making process provides an avenue for citizen engagement and civic discourse.[24] But the playing field for these groups is not level: like lobbyists in the other branches of government, some groups are more influential than others. Elite interest groups, benefiting from members' influence and richer resources, are likelier to have their views heard in a court case than groups with less privileged members.[25]

oral arguments
the stage when appeals court judges or Supreme Court justices meet with the petitioner and the respondent to ask questions about the legal inter-pretations or information contained in their briefs

In docketing a case, the clerk of the court selects a date for **oral arguments**—attorneys' formal spoken arguments that lay out why the Court should rule in their client's favor. Heard in the Supreme Court's public gallery, oral arguments give the justices the opportunity to ask the parties and their lawyers specific questions about the arguments in their briefs. In typical cases, each side's lawyers have thirty minutes to make a statement to the Court and to answer the justices' questions. Although the public gallery is very grand, and the mood is often somber and formal, the justices can sometimes be less than polite toward one another and the lawyers during the oral arguments. The justices frequently interrupt the attorneys during their opening statements and responses to questions and sometimes seem to ignore the lawyers entirely, instead talking with one another. This discourse takes place entirely within public view, and transcripts (and sometimes even tapes) are readily available to the public.

Meeting in Conference: The Deliberative Stage

After the justices have listened to the oral arguments in the case, they meet in conference to deliberate. At this point, each justice will signal his or her likely vote on the case and discuss the legal issues in play. We have few clues as to how the justices interact in conference, because those proceedings are entirely closed to the public. The late chief justice William Rehnquist once described conferences in which the most junior associate justice was seated closest to the door and was charged with answering any knocks on the door that might come about during deliberation.[26] But other than the anecdotal descriptions we have from justices, once a case enters this phase, it is in a kind of black box. We can only guess about how the justices deliberate and make their decisions, because there is no public record of the proceedings.

We do know that the justices must work together at the deliberation stage if they hope to reach a decision that a majority of them will sign. Because cases are decided by majority rule, there is a strong incentive to cooperate. The chief justice plays a vital role in this process. After the likely votes of the other justices are tallied in the conference, the chief justice decides whether he is with the majority. If he is, he chooses whether he wants to write the majority opinion. If he declines, he can assign the task to one of the other justices in the likely majority. If the chief justice is not with the majority, the senior member of this majority decides whether to write the opinion or assign the opinion to another justice. By the time the justices have finished with the conference, they will have already read the briefs in the case, heard the oral arguments, and listened to one another's views. In assigning the majority opinion, the senior member is effectively giving a stamp of approval to the view of the case that either he or she or some other member of the Court has articulated.

The assignment of the opinion is a crucial stage. The justice who writes the opinion must consider the positions of the other justices, especially those who are likely to vote with him or her in the majority. No justice who is assigned with writing the majority opinion can afford to ignore the policy views of the other justices. At the opinion-writing stage, the justices must cooperate and try to hammer out a decision that at least five of them will agree to. Their discussion about the case often centers on the legal arguments that the parties have advanced or on the underlying factual issues.

Deciding How to Vote: Voting Blocs on the Court

How does each justice decide how to vote in a particular case? Frequently, the justices vote in blocs—those with similar views tend to vote together, especially in similar cases. By the late 1990s and early 2000s, Supreme Court watchers could predict with a great deal of certainty how specific justices would line up to vote in cases involving abortion restrictions, for example.

These voting blocs work as a kind of shorthand for the justices, who often look to other, like-minded justices to decide how they should vote in certain cases.[27] In cases involving broad areas of the law, such as civil rights and civil liberties, and in cases concerned with the separation of powers, the justices are remarkably predictable.[28] Their decision making follows patterns, with many justices voting together term after term. For example, in case after case brought before the Rehnquist Court (from 1986 to 2005, when William Rehnquist was chief justice), four of the nine justices lined up on each side and Justice Sandra Day O'Connor cast the swing vote that determined the outcome in those closely divided cases.[29]

In terms of political stance, we tend to talk about the justices as either conservative or liberal, with conservative justices tending to favor the state and state interests in cases involving civil liberties or civil rights, and liberal justices tending to favor the individual in these cases. The justices are arrayed in groups on a kind of spectrum, and Justice O'Connor occupied the central position for many years. Because the Court was so closely divided, she exercised significant power in the decision-making process.

Writing the Opinion

At the opinion-writing stage, give-and-take comes into play among the justices, especially if the case is particularly close so that the justice writing the majority opinion must lock in all the available votes. This is an important consideration because at this point the justices are still free to change their minds about how they will vote or whose opinion they will join.[30] Although there are no records of the justices' deliberations, it is likely that the first draft of most majority opinions is modified to reflect the desires of at least some of the justices who agree to sign it.

There are significant incentives for the author of the draft opinion to take into account the perspectives not only of the justices who agree with his or her conclusions but also of those who disagree. The reason is that the majority draft may not be the only draft circulating among the justices. When the justices disagree about a decision, it is likely that other drafts also circulate. Some of these drafts may become concurring opinions; others may become dissenting opinions. **Concurring opinions** agree with how the majority opinion decides the case but disagree with at least some of the legal arguments or conclusions reached in this majority opinion. **Dissenting opinions** not only disagree with these arguments and conclusions but also reject the underlying decision in the case.[31]

As drafts of the majority, concurring, and dissenting opinions circulate, the justices continue to gauge the level of support for each. It does not appear to be unusual for majority opinions to become concurring opinions and vice versa. Again, the ability of the justices to persuade their colleagues on the Court is the primary indicator of which opinion will prevail as the majority decision.

After the opinions are written and signed off on, the Court announces the decision by publishing it. On rare occasions, the justices read their majority opinions, and sometimes their concurring and dissenting opinions, from the bench.

concurring opinion
judicial opinion agreeing with how the majority decides the case but disagreeing with at least some of the legal interpretations or conclusions reached by the majority

dissenting opinion
judicial opinion disagreeing both with the majority's disposition of a case and with their legal interpretations and conclusions

The Supreme Court Today: The Roberts Court

Many legal scholars say the Roberts Court, particularly in the absence of the strong moderate voice of Sandra Day O'Connor and with the addition of the conservative Alito, has been tilting more conservatively than the Rehnquist Court, in which O'Connor played the pivotal balancing role.[32] But President Obama's 2009 appointment of Sonia Sotomayor, considered more liberal than the justices appointed by President George W. Bush, seems to have altered public opinion concerning the Supreme Court's ideology. Figure 14.4 (on page 450) shows the shifts in public opinion that have accompanied these changes in the composition of the court.

Today, half of all Americans consider the ideology of the Court "about right," while an increasing number (from 21 to 28 percent between 2008 and 2009) believe the Court is too

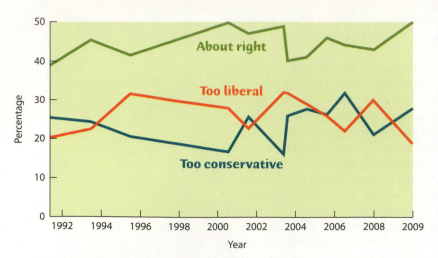

FIGURE 14.4

Citizens' Views on Supreme Court Ideology

SOURCE: Gallup News Service, www.gallup.com/poll/4732/Supreme-Court.aspx.

conservative. Paralleling this trend is a decreasing percentage (30 to 19 percent) who believe the Court is too liberal.[33] Despite the evidence that increasing numbers of Americans believe the Court is too liberal, the short track record established by the Roberts Court thus far indicates that the outcome of many cases undertaken by the Court have had a decidedly conservative flavor; for example, the 2007 decision regarding affirmative action in which the Court ruled that judicial decisions concerning the use of racial criteria in higher education do not apply to public high school admission policies.[34] This decision illuminates a distinct trend of the Court today: the justices' willingness to limit the authority of the states and the other branches of government. In another example, the Roberts Court weakened a key provision of a landmark campaign finance law, the Bipartisan Campaign Finance Reform Act of 2002, by loosening restrictions on campaign television ads. The Court's recent conservatism is also evident in a case in which the justices upheld a federal ban on partial birth abortion, a procedure in which labor is induced and suction is used to remove a fetus.[35]

Many other important cases that the Roberts Court has chosen to hear deal with the balance of power between individuals and government, often reaching a conservative decision by a slim (5–4) margin. Though not divisive, one important case involved a 13-year-old suing her school district after being strip-searched when school officials suspected that she had provided over-the-counter ibuprofen to a classmate. In an 8–1 decision, the court ruled that although it was reasonable to search a student's backpack and outer garments, a strip search violated the student's right to privacy and was unreasonable.[36] Another more closely divided case dealt with when federal courts may act to enforce federal mandates on states. By a 5–4 decision, the Court made it easier for state schools to shed federal supervision of their English-language education program, a decision that will affect other state institutions, including prisons.[37] In another 5–4 decision, the Court dealt a blow to the criminal justice system in forty states by requiring that crime lab analysts testify in criminal proceedings, instead of allowing reports written by the analysts to substitute as evidence.[38] At the time of the ruling, laws in only ten states complied with the ruling.

Figure 14.5 shows the ideological distribution of the Supreme Court today and highlights its slight tilt toward the conservative side, with Justices Clarence Thomas, Antonin Scalia, and Samuel Alito, and Chief Justice Roberts, reflecting a conservative viewpoint and Justices Sonia Sotomayor and Ruth Bader Ginsburg taking a more liberal stance on many issues. In the center are Justice Anthony Kennedy, a moderate conservative, and Justices Stephen Breyer and Elena Kagan, moderate liberals.

Judges as Policy Makers

Courts make law—common law—by deciding cases and establishing legal principles that bind future litigants and judges. The lawmaking function of courts ensures that judges have a powerful role as public policy makers.[39] This is particularly true of judges who serve in appellate courts such as the state supreme courts, the federal circuit courts of appeals, and the U.S. Supreme Court.

Because of their policy-making role, judges participate in a larger political discourse that goes far beyond the concerns of individual litigants. As we consider in this section, judges are not free to act completely independently of the other branches of the government, but they *are* able to weigh in on some of the country's most important issues. Supreme Court Justice Antonin Scalia has colorfully described the crucial role that judges play in using the law to create policy. As Scalia sees it, the ideal judge is "one who has the intelligence to

POLITICAL INQUIRY

FIGURE 14.5 ■ **THE IDEOLOGICAL DISTRIBUTION OF THE SUPREME COURT TODAY** In what direction does today's supreme court tilt with respect to ideology? How could that slant change? Given the current presidential administration, what is the likelihood that it will?

discern the best rule of law for the case at hand and then the skill to perform the broken-field running through earlier cases that leaves him free to impose that rule: distinguishing one prior case on the left, straight-arming another on the right, high-stepping away from another precedent about to tackle him from the rear, until (bravo!) he reaches the goal—good law."[40] Most recently, the courts have been called upon to resolve issues related to the war on terror, the death penalty (see "Global Context"), the powers of the chief executive, freedom of speech, abortion, euthanasia, and affirmative action.

What does it mean to be a policy maker? Recall from Chapter 13 that policy makers are individuals who have authority to influence, or to determine, solutions—public policies—that address the issues and problems a society faces. After choosing a policy, the policy maker must stand ready to adapt it to changed situations or new challenges.

judicial activism
an approach to judicial decision making whereby judges apply their authority to bring about specific social goals

Activism Versus Restraint

When considering the courts' role as policy makers, legal analysts often categorize judges and justices as exercising either judicial activism or judicial restraint. **Judicial activism** refers to the courts' practice of applying their authority to bring about particular social goals. It reflects the notion that the role of the courts is to check the power of the federal and state executive and legislative branches when those governmental entities exceed their authority.

> In May 1954, in a landmark decision, the U.S. Supreme Court ruled unconstitutional segregation in American public schools.

GLOBAL CONTEXT

JUDGES AS POLICY MAKERS: THE DEATH PENALTY WORLDWIDE

The United States is the only industrialized Western democracy that executes its citizens as punishment for crimes committed. In nations where the death penalty is legal, an argument often heard in favor of the death penalty is that it deters crime. But surveys undertaken by the United Nations indicate that "it is not prudent to accept the hypothesis that capital punishment deters murder to a marginally greater extent than does the threat and application of the supposedly lesser punishment of life imprisonment."

In 2008, the executions performed in China, Iran, Saudi Arabia, the United States, Pakistan, and Iraq accounted for more than 95 percent of executions worldwide. According to Amnesty International, in 2008, nearly 2,400 people were executed in 25 countries around the world and 8,864 people were sentenced to death in 52 countries. Amnesty International reports that in 2008, executions almost doubled from 1,252 in 2007 to 2,390. As shown in the accompanying table, the United States ranks fourth, behind only China, Iran, and Saudi Arabia in the number of executions it carried out.

While several international human rights treaties—including the International Covenant on Civil and Political Rights, the American Convention on Human Rights, and the Convention on the Rights of the Child—prohibit death sentences for minors (under 18 years of age) who commit crimes, seven countries—China, the Democratic Republic of Congo, Iran, Nigeria, Pakistan, Saudi Arabia, and Yemen—execute individuals who were minors when they committed the crime for which they were sentenced to death. The U.S. Supreme Court ruled that the execution of juveniles was unconstitutional in 2005, but between 1990 and the Court's ruling, the United States executed 19 people for crimes they committed as juveniles, some of whom were still juveniles when executed.

Opponents of the death penalty mainly cite humanitarian reasons, but concerns also have emerged about the execution of innocents. Since 1973, states have released more than 107 prisoners from death row after evidence of their innocence was presented to the courts. The problem of the potential execution of innocent convicts became so acute that Illinois Governor George Ryan declared a moratorium on the implementation of the death penalty after 13 death row inmates were exonerated in that state. Currently, more than 3,300 prisoners sit on death row in the United States.

COUNTRIES WITH THE MOST CONFIRMED EXECUTIONS IN 2008

1. China (1,718)	4. United States (37)
2. Iran (346)	5. Pakistan (36)
3. Saudi Arabia (102)	6. Iraq (34)

COUNTRIES WITH A DEATH PENALTY FOR ORDINARY CRIMES

Afghanistan	Guinea	Qatar
Antigua and Barbuda	Guyana	Saint Christopher & Nevis
Bahamas	India	Saint Lucia
Bahrain	Indonesia	Saint Vincent & Grenadines
Bangladesh	Iran	Saudi Arabia
Barbados	Iraq	Sierra Leone
Belarus	Jamaica	Singapore
Belize	Japan	Somalia
Botswana	Jordan	Sudan
Burundi	Kazakstan	Syria
Cameroon	Korea (North)	Taiwan
Chad	Kuwait	Tajikistan
China	Lebanon	Thailand
Comoros	Lesotho	Trinidad and Tobago
Congo (Democratic Republic)	Libya	Uganda
Cuba	Malaysia	United Arab Emirates
Dominica	Mongolia	United States of America
Egypt	Nigeria	Viet Nam
Equatorial Guinea	Oman	Yemen
Ethiopia	Pakistan	Zimbabwe
Guatemala	Palestinian Authority	

SOURCE: Death Penalty Information Center, http://www.deathpenaltyinfo.org/death-penalty-international-perspective.

During the Warren Court (the tenure of Chief Justice Earl Warren, from 1953 to 1969), the Supreme Court took an activist stance, most notably in rejecting the constitutionality of racial segregation. By barring southern states from segregation in a variety of contexts—including schools and other public facilities—the activist Warren Court powerfully bolstered the efforts of civil rights activists. The activism of the Warren Court was also instrumental in shaping the modern rights of the accused. During Warren's tenure, the Supreme Court established *Miranda* rights for individuals accused of a crime[41] and mandated that states provide counsel to such defendants when they cannot afford an attorney.[42] The Warren Court's activism also shaped modern definitions of the privacy rights of individuals,[43] which would later form the framework for the Court's thinking about abortion rights. (See Chapter 4 for further discussion of those cases.) Supported by presidents who enforced its rulings, the Warren Court took on a leadership role in changing the nature of U.S. society.

Some judges reject the idea that the courts' role is to actively check legislative and executive authority. Noting that officials in those branches are elected to carry out the people's will, these judges observe **judicial restraint**—the limiting of their own power as judges. Practitioners of judicial restraint believe that the judiciary, as the least democratic branch of government, should not check the power of the democratically elected executive and legislative branches unless their actions clearly violate the Constitution.[44]

By tradition, judicial activism and judicial restraint are linked, respectively, with the liberal and conservative ideologies. That neat categorization, however, breaks down when one tries to apply it to recent courts. The Rehnquist Court (1986–2005) was both conservative and activist.[45] That Court chose to hear a case, *Planned Parenthood of Southeastern Pennsylvania v. Casey* (1992), that checked the authority of the state of Pennsylvania to implement a state law that limits access to abortion. In its decision, the Court laid the framework for the tightening of abortion laws in many states by clarifying what measures the states could take in restricting abortions.

judicial restraint
an approach to judicial decision making whereby judges defer to the democratically elected legislative and executive branches of government

Competing Legal Interpretations

When judges and lawyers consider a case, the common-law tradition—specifically, the principle of *stare decisis*—means that they must consider past cases with similar facts and legal questions. They must be guided by how courts in those cases have interpreted the underlying legal issues. As we have seen, the legal principles that come out of those cases constitute case law.

But even though *stare decisis* binds jurists and attorneys to prior case law, this does not mean that judges, in ruling on new cases, simply apply previous decisions to new circumstances. Rather, in interpreting the legal precedent, they typically choose among several cases related to the legal issues at stake, and their choice often determines the outcome of the present case. For that reason, law school students become skilled at identifying the line of cases that might help them to succeed in making a particular argument. They must assume, however, that the lawyer on the other side of the courtroom will also select cases that best support that attorney's chances for success.

Checks on the Courts

The U.S. judiciary is a powerful institution. It operates as the equal of the legislative and executive branches of government yet is insulated from the influence of those other institutions. Nonetheless, judges and justices face checks and constraints that limit how they decide cases, make law, and act as policy makers. Among the most important checks on the judiciary's power are the other branches of government. But the law enforcement community, lawyers, interest groups, and individual citizens also check the courts and constrain their activism, as we next consider.

The Inner Ring: Legislatures and Chief Executives

Formidable checks on the judiciary come from what some analysts call the *inner ring*—the other core institutions of the government, namely, the legislative and executive branches.

> Congress and the president can check the courts' power of judicial review by enacting new laws. In 1976, Congress passed the Pregnancy Discrimination Act, which amended Title VII of the 1964 Civil Rights Act to state explicitly that sex discrimination encompassed pregnancy discrimination, after the Supreme Court had narrowly interpreted Title VII's bans on sex discrimination.

Article II of the Constitution explicitly gives the legislative and executive branches crucial checks on the structure of the courts. It grants Congress the power to create all federal courts other than the Supreme Court and gives both the president and the federal legislature important powers in determining who sits on all federal courts. Indeed, the procedures for choosing the judges who will serve on the federal bench afford both of these branches significant control over the judiciary. Executives check the judiciary through their appointment authority, and the legislature does so through the confirmation process.

Beyond giving the president a check on the judiciary by specifying the executive's power to appoint judges, the Constitution also empowers the chief executive to grant pardons to individuals for violations of the law. A further check on judges results from the courts' reliance on the executive branch for the enforcement of their decisions. Specifically, if presidents fail to direct the bureaucracy to carry out judicial decisions, those decisions carry little weight. Frequently, it is executive implementation that gives teeth to the judiciary's decisions.

The Constitution also creates a legislative check on the judiciary because the framers established only the Supreme Court and left it up to Congress to create the lower federal courts. In addition, Article I allows Congress to control the Supreme Court's appellate docket and even to remove whole categories of cases from the Court's consideration. Congress also can control the number of judges or justices who serve in the federal judiciary and can increase this number to get a majority of judges or justices to choose a preferred policy outcome. The two houses of Congress moreover have a central role in deciding whether to impeach federal judges. The House issues the articles of impeachment, and the Senate conducts the impeachment trial. Finally, Congress initiates the process of constitutional amendment. In fact, in several cases Congress has embarked on such amendment procedures in direct response to a Court decision with which members of Congress or their constituencies have disagreed. For example, the Twenty-Sixth Amendment, which standardized the voting age to 18 years of age, came about after the Supreme Court ruled that states could set their own age limits for state elections.[46]

Additional constitutional checks also limit the power of the judges. So although the courts can check the lawmaking power of the legislative and executive branches by exercising judicial review (which, to recap, is the courts' power to decide whether the laws passed by the other branches are constitutional), the legislature and the executive can check the courts' power of judicial review through the creation of new laws. For example, Title VII of the 1964 Civil Rights Act bars sex discrimination in employment. In decisions reached in 1974 and 1976, the Supreme Court interpreted this prohibition narrowly, concluding that Congress did not mean to bar discrimination on the basis of pregnancy when it passed Title VII. Many legislators were angered by those decisions. Consequently, in 1976, Congress passed the Pregnancy Discrimination Act, which amended Title VII to state explicitly that sex discrimination encompassed pregnancy discrimination. The Court could do nothing to respond to this new law because Congress used the law specifically to clarify the Civil Rights Act. Only if the new act had been in conflict with the Constitution could the Court have taken action.

The Gatekeepers: Participants in the Judicial Process

Participants in the judicial process—especially law enforcement officers and interest groups concerned with issues of law—also provide checks on how judges and justices decide cases, make law, and act as policy makers.

LAW ENFORCERS' CHECKS ON THE JUDICIARY
One way in which law enforcement officials check the judiciary is through the exercise of *discretion*. Every day, police officers face situations in which they must decide whether to investigate wrongdoing and whether to arrest suspects engaged in illegal acts. The use of discretion by the police and others who are in the front line of law enforcement means these citizens are effectively deciding how and whether to enforce the laws made by courts, legislatures, and chief executives.

For many years, local law enforcement agents closed their eyes to spousal abuse, for example. If they investigated domestic violence, they often treated the perpetrator much more leniently than they would have if the person had not been married to the victim. That decision to be less aggressive in enforcing the law against assault and battery in such cases made some sense, because police knew that entering a home where spousal abuse was occurring was dangerous and that the victim would be unlikely to cooperate in prosecuting his or her attacker. Police often acted on their own, disregarding what the lawmaking institutions, including the courts, required them to do. Only when victims or their families successfully sued police departments for their failure to act did agencies throughout the country begin to treat spousal abuse cases more seriously.

INTEREST GROUPS' CHECKS ON THE JUDICIARY   Legal scholar Andrew Jay Koshner argues that interest groups have transformed how the judiciary operates.[47] Often, lawyers and law firms assist interest groups in bringing their concerns to the judiciary. For example, when lawyers for the National Association for the Advancement of Colored People (NAACP) hit a roadblock in their attempts to persuade state legislatures to eliminate segregation in public schools, they pressed civil rights advocacy groups to go to court. The result was the landmark Supreme Court ruling in *Brown v. Board of Education* (1954), which established that segregation in public schools violated the equal protection guarantees in the Fourteenth Amendment.[48]

Experienced and trusted interest groups also constrain the courts by providing them with essential information. Courts need such information, especially in highly complex or technical cases involving issues far outside judges' expertise. Depending on what information and arguments they provide, these groups can constrain the courts' options in a case. When a court decides, for example, to rely on information detailed in the brief of the American College of Obstetrics and Gynecology, a mainstream physicians' group, and virtually to ignore information provided by the pro-life group Physicians for Life, the court is legitimizing one group over the other and giving special access to the preferred group. This favored group's lawyers can provide information that helps them to advance their legal argument and that, in so doing, can limit the court's options and effectively constrain the judges in their decision making.

Intra-Court Constraints

Confirmed judges and justices also face powerful internal constraints on their judicial actions. For lower-court judges, the higher courts, or those courts' decisions in previous cases, impose limitations. Federal district court and appeals court judges, for example, do not diverge far from Supreme Court precedent because if they did so, they would risk having their decisions overturned.

Even the Supreme Court faces substantial constraints, some of which arise from dynamics inside the Court itself. The relationships and interactions among the justices seem to place serious restrictions on their decisions. We have seen, for example, that compromise and negotiation are a central part of the Court's decision making, particularly at the opinion-writing stage. Justices who can persuade others to sign their opinions exercise significant power. This power takes a different form than it does in the other branches. Whereas in the executive and legislative branches the players exercise the power of the purse and engage in overt forms of vote trading, in the judiciary this power is based on legal reasoning and persuasion.

The Outer Ring: The Users

In addition to these various other influences on the courts, an "outer ring" of *users*—the people whom a law directly affects—can considerably constrain the actions of judges. In the many cases where these users are the general public, the courts must consider how this public will receive their decisions and interpretations.

Indeed, public opinion seems to have a distinct impact on what the courts do, especially appellate courts such as the U.S. Supreme Court. The Court rarely issues a decision that is completely out of step with the thinking of the majority of the population. This trend is confirmed by the comparatively high levels of approval of the Court among Americans, illustrated in Figure 14.6 on page 456. In fact, most cases seem to follow public opinion. When

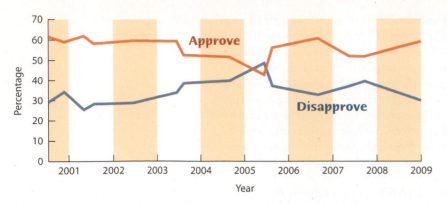

FIGURE 14.6

The Supreme Court's high approval ratings indicate that while the Constitution may be the foremost determinant of Court decisions, often these decisions reflect public opinion.

SOURCE: Gallup News Service, June 19, 2009.

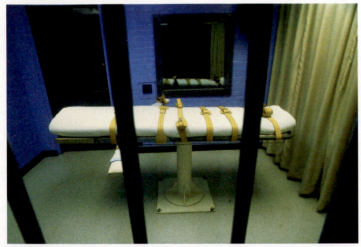

> In the many capital punishment cases decided since *Gregg v. Georgia* (1976), the justices have upheld capital punishment in general but have barred states from imposing it on juveniles and people with mental disabilities, using public opinion polls to justify their rulings. The lethal injection death chamber in the prison in Huntsville, Texas, shown here, is one of the most active in the nation.

the Court does break with public opinion, as it has in prohibiting prayer in the public schools, it opens itself up to harsh criticism by the president, Congress, interest groups, and the general public.

But sometimes in the case of a landmark decision that is out of touch with public sentiment, the Court's ruling and people's opinions align over time. This shift can occur either because later courts adjust the original, controversial decision or, less commonly, because the Supreme Court's decision changes public opinion. One example of the interplay between public opinion and judicial decisions can be seen in Court rulings concerning the death penalty. In the case of *Furman v. Georgia* (1972), the Supreme Court prohibited capital punishment as it was practiced at the time, finding that it violated the Eighth Amendment prohibition against cruel and unusual punishment. The *Furman* decision evoked a public outcry that led many state legislatures to modify their laws governing capital punishment. In 1976, the Court upheld this new generation of laws in *Gregg v. Georgia*, and public opinion has continued to be central to how the Court handles cases involving capital punishment. In the many cases brought to trial since *Gregg*, the justices have used the public opinion polls to justify the Court's decision to uphold capital punishment in general but to bar states from imposing it on juveniles and people with mental disabilities.

Users can also constrain the courts by threatening to ignore their rulings. When members of the public disagree with judicial decisions, or with any law for that matter, they can engage in civil disobedience. In acts of civil disobedience, individuals or groups flout the law to make a larger point about its underlying unfairness. Keep in mind that the courts have little ability to enforce their decisions, and if people refuse to recognize those decisions and the other branches of the government fail to enforce them, the courts risk losing their authority and power. Fear of losing authority may partly explain why judicial decisions rarely fall out of step with the larger public stance on an issue. Like the inner ring and the gatekeepers, the outer ring imposes significant constraints on courts and probably limits how judges handle cases and interpret laws. These constraints may not be written into the U.S. Constitution as the checks are, but they are nonetheless very powerful and probably have a significant impact on how judges decide cases.

CONCLUSION

THINKING CRITICALLY ABOUT WHAT'S NEXT FOR THE JUDICIARY

Rooted in a common-law tradition and framed by the Constitution, the American judiciary in its early form strongly reflected its English heritage, with its emphasis on law made by judges. Over the past two-plus centuries, the judiciary has evolved powerfully to accommodate a broad spectrum of societal changes in a continuously growing country.

The judiciary has proved remarkably responsive to the sweeping societal changes that have occurred since those early beginnings. Specifically, the judicial branch has expanded to reflect both the rising population and citizens' increased use of courts to settle disputed matters. At the same time, the body of law that the courts interpret and apply has developed well beyond its common-law origins into a system based heavily on more explicit code law.

In the coming years, the judicial system will face questions that are likely to grow in number and complexity. Future courts will be challenged to interpret new laws addressing a host of thorny issues, including many currently unresolved dimensions of technology and terrorism. For example, how can the courts effectively apply laws—dealing with everything from child pornography to hate speech—given the anonymity and global reach of the Internet? How will the courts balance issues of privacy with the urgent need to provide common security? Furthermore, *entirely new* problems, arising from forces in play today and to come in the future, will require the wisdom of the best and brightest judges. Deciding cases centered on these currently unknown issues also will vitally involve the input of experts and well-informed citizens. These issues may include, for example, new legal questions emerging as a result of the tide of new immigrants, related demographic shifts, and the country's mounting energy problems.

We can anticipate how the judicial branch will meet these and other new demands by examining the strategies the courts have brought to bear in the past. We can see that the judiciary has responded to societal changes in incremental ways, through both revisions in code law and increased judicial specialization. Today, special FISA courts are determining whether the domestic wiretapping of personal communications is warranted. Perhaps it will come to pass that activist courts with expertise in the technology of terrorism will play a more central role in policy making. A key question is, will the incremental change in judicial specialization that has thus far characterized the courts be sufficient in a world that is rushing forward at so high a rate of speed? And another important question is, how will shifting Supreme Court ideology figure into the mix?

Despite the uncertainties, the courts will remain a bastion in defense of individual liberties and rights. And public opinion of the judiciary will likely continue to run high, particularly when this institution is compared with the other branches of the government.

Summary

1. The Origins of the U.S. Judiciary

The Constitution and the Judiciary Act of 1789 created a weak judiciary. The Constitution specified only the Supreme Court and left it to Congress to establish lower courts. In the landmark case *Marbury v. Madison* (1803), the Court asserted the principle of *judicial review,* which empowered the courts to check the democratically elected branches of government. The Judiciary Act of 1891 expanded the federal court system by creating federal appellate courts.

2. The Basis of U.S. Law

The American legal system has its basis in both common law and code law. Common law is created when judges reach decisions and write opinions in cases. Code law is made by the legislative and executive branches when they pass statutes or create regulations. There are advantages and disadvantages to both common law and code law. Common law has the advantage of stability over time, but it is also slow to change when social, political, or economic conditions shift. Code law has the advantage of being quickly amendable to meet the needs of a rapidly changing society, but the resulting instability can undercut well-established principles.

3. Sources of U.S. Law

There are five sources of law in the American system: the federal and state constitutions, statutes, judicial decisions, executive orders, and administrative law. Constitutions take precedence over all other laws, in that when a conflict arises between a constitutional provision and some other law, the constitutional provision prevails and the other law is struck down. Both the federal government and the fifty state governments take part in the lawmaking enterprise. There are also fifty-one legal systems in operation: the federal court system and the systems in place in the fifty states.

4. The Federal Court System

The Constitution expressly established only the Supreme Court, and Congress created the appeals and district courts in a series of laws, beginning in 1789. The Supreme Court has almost total control over the cases it will hear, and compromise and negotiation mark deliberations among the justices. This Court is the United States' highest court, and its decisions are binding on both the lower federal courts and all the state courts.

5. Selecting Judges for the Federal Bench

Federal judges and justices are nominated by the president and confirmed by the Senate. In evaluating nominees, senators examine the nominee's competence and ideology and consider how the nominee's demographic characteristics might represent the population at large.

6. The U.S. Supreme Court Today

Although the Supreme Court has limited original jurisdiction, it is the highest court in the land. The justices choose to hear only a fraction of cases that come before them. The cases they select tend to have broad repercussions in their application. To date, the current Supreme Court, headed by Chief Justice John Roberts, has been conservative in its ideology and activist in its willingness to check the states and other branches of government.

7. Judges as Policy Makers

Judges are influential actors in the policy-making enterprise. They choose among several policy options in deciding cases. Although U.S. legal culture encourages the view that there is only one way for a case to be decided, the reality is that judges often draw from multiple legal interpretations in deciding cases and weigh these options in determining which best promotes the goal or social good that they think should receive priority.

8. Checks on the Courts

Powerful constraints limit what judges and justices in the U.S. legal system may do. The influences that can constrain policy making come from both outside and inside the judiciary. Outside influences include an inner ring consisting of legislatures and executives, a ring of gatekeepers comprising law enforcers and interest groups, and an outer ring of users, the people whom the laws directly affect. Within the judicial system, on the Supreme Court itself, legal precedent and the need to build coalitions restrict the justices' actions. Even in light of these various constraints, however, U.S. courts and judges play a crucial role in lawmaking and policy making.

Key Terms

amicus curiae brief ("friend of the court" brief) 447

appellate jurisdiction 439

brief 447

chief justice 441

circuit courts 433

circuit riding 433

civil law 434

code law 436

collegial court 446

common law 434

concurring opinion 449

constitutional law 437

courts of appeals 433

criminal law 434

discuss list 447

dissenting opinion 449

diversity of citizenship 438

dual court system 438

federal question 438

judicial activism 451

judicial restraint 453

judicial review 433*

judiciary 432

jurisdiction 438

justice 441

Marbury v. Madison 433*

oral arguments 448

original jurisdiction 439

pool memo 447

precedent 436

Rule of Four 447

senatorial courtesy 442

stare decisis 436

statute 437

symbolic representation 445

tort 434

trial court 438

U.S. Code 437

U.S. Supreme Court 433

writ of *certiorari* 447

*Judicial review and *Marbury v. Madison* were introduced in Chapter 2.

For Review

1. What is the basis of the American legal system? Why is it unusual for a nation-state to blend the two traditions that are the core of this system? What are the advantages and disadvantages of these two traditions?

2. What are the five sources of law in the U.S. legal system? What is the relationship among these five sources?

3. What is the structure of the federal court system? Does this system have more or less power than the state court system? Explain.

4. How are federal judges chosen? Who tends to be chosen? How does the selection process differ for federal district court judges, circuit court judges, and Supreme Court justices? In what ways do conflict and compromise characterize the selection process for all these judges?

5. Outline the stages by which the Supreme Court decides cases. Why do we say that negotiation and compromise are a part of every one of these stages?

6. In what ways do federal judges participate in civic discourse as policy makers? Outline the ways in which this participation is either checked by the Constitution or constrained by internal and external actors.

For Critical Thinking and Discussion

1. How did the American legal system come to be a blend of the common law and code law traditions? Which tradition better suits today's political, social, and economic realities? Why?

2. What is your view on the shared lawmaking by the three branches of American government? Are you satisfied that this shared system benefits the country? Can you think of some negatives to the U.S. system?

3. The Supreme Court has the power of judicial review, that is, the power to strike down federal and state laws that it views as in conflict with the U.S. Constitution. Can you think of any reasons why it would not be a good thing to allow the Court to overturn laws passed by the democratically elected branches?

4. When a president nominates a prospective federal judge, a number of factors are at play, and the nominee's qualifications are only one of these. What are these other factors? Should they be in play? Why or why not? In what ways do these factors reinforce or undermine democratic principles?

5. Which do you think impose greater limitations on policy making by federal courts: constitutional checks or intra-court and external constraints? Why?

MULTIPLE CHOICE: Choose the lettered item that answers the question correctly.

1. The notion that it is the role of the Court to check the power of the federal and state executive and legislative branches when those governmental entities exceed their authority is called
   a. judicial review.
   b. judicial constraint.
   c. judicial restraint.
   d. writ of *certiorari*.

2. The high court with a limited original jurisdiction whose decision may not be appealed is called:
   a. the U.S. Court of Appeals.
   b. the U.S. Supreme Court.
   c. federal District Court.
   d. the U.S. Superior Court.

3. The middle level of the federal court structure is
   a. circuit courts.
   b. courts of appeals.
   c. the U.S. Supreme Court.
   d. (a) and (b).

4. *Stare decisis* means
   a. "I have decided."
   b. "The king has decided."
   c. "Decided by God."
   d. "Let the decision stand."

5. Law created by legislators to regulate the behavior of individuals and organizations is called
   a. common law.
   b. code law.
   c. constitutional law.
   d. judicial law.

6. Federal courts are empowered to hear only cases
   a. involving a federal question.
   b. involving diversity of citizenship.
   c. involving statutory law.
   d. (a) or (b).

7. Legal authority established by earlier cases is called
   a. precedent.
   b. statutory law.
   c. tort law.
   d. oral law.

8. A wrongful act involving personal injury or harm to one's property or reputation is called
   a. administrative law.
   b. statutory law.
   c. tort law.
   d. oral law.

9. The practice by which the Supreme Court justices determine if they will hear a case is called
   a. the Rule of Two.
   b. the Rule of Four.
   c. the Rule of Six.
   d. the Rule of Eight.

10. The list of cases on review that the Chief Justice thinks may be appropriate for the Court to hear is called
    a. an *amicus curiae* brief.
    b. a pool memo.
    c. a discuss list.
    d. an opinion.

FILL IN THE BLANK.

11. The practice of traveling around the circuits by early Supreme Court justices and district court judges to hear appeals cases is called _____.

12. The description written by Court clerks of the facts of the case filed with the Court, the pertinent legal arguments, and a recommendation as to whether the case should be taken is called a _____.

13. A judicial opinion agreeing with how the majority decides the case but disagreeing with at least some of the legal interpretations or conclusions reached by the majority is called a _____.

14. A custom that allows senators from the president's political party to veto the president's choice of federal district court judge in the senator's state is called _____.

15. An approach to judicial decision making whereby judges apply their authority to bring about specific goals is called _____.

Answers: 1. a; 2. b; 3. d; 4. d; 5. b; 6. d; 7. a; 8. c; 9. b; 10. c; 11. circuit riding; 12. pool memo; 13. concurring opinion; 14. senatorial courtesy; 15. judicial activism.

RESOURCES FOR RESEARCH AND ACTION

Internet Resources

FindLaw
www.findlaw.com This Web site provides a wealth of information about lawmaking in the federal and state judiciaries, as well as ongoing cases in the news. It allows users easy access to federal and state code law, case law, and regulatory law. It also helps pre-law and law students stay connected to helpful information about legal education and practice.

Oyez
www.oyez.org/oyez/frontpage This interactive Web site allows you to access recordings of the oral arguments in a select group of cases. You can also visit the site to take a virtual tour of the Supreme Court building and to learn interesting trivia about the Court, including a list of the most active lawyers before the Court.

Legal Information Institute (LII)
http://straylight.law.cornell.edu This is a valuable resource for doing research not only on the U.S. Supreme Court but also on the other courts in the federal and state judiciaries. The site provides an excellent catalog of statutory, regulatory, and administrative laws, as well as executive orders. It also allows you to search for all sources of law in a particular area of the law, including not only federal and state court decisions but laws coming out of the other branches as well.

U.S. Supreme Court
www.supremecourtus.gov The official Web site of the U.S. Supreme Court is an excellent resource for doing research on the Court. You can access the briefs and oral argument transcripts for cases currently before the Court, as well as cases recently decided. The site also allows easy access to nearly all cases that the Court has decided, including historical decisions.

Internet Activism

Twitter
Follow **@SCOTUSOpinions** for links to the latest opinions from the U.S. Supreme Court.

Recommended Readings

Friedman, Leon. *Justices of the United States Supreme Court*. 2010. This chronological biography of Supreme Court justices examines each Supreme Court justice's education and legal background.

McGuire, Kevin T. *Understanding the Supreme Court: Cases and Controversies*. New York: McGraw-Hill, 2002. A book that uses real cases to examine the selection of justices, the Supreme Court's decision-making procedures, the influence of interest groups, and the impact of Court rulings.

Samuels, Suzanne U. *Law, Politics and Society: An Introduction to American Law*. Boston: Houghton Mifflin, 2006. A comprehensive survey of the foundations of the American legal system, lawmaking by institutions and groups, and law and public policy.

Savage, David G. *Guide to the U.S. Supreme Court*. Washington, DC: Congressional Quarterly, 2010. This volume contains a thorough description of the U.S. Supreme Court, including its origins, its functions, and its impact.

Tarr, G. Alan. *Judicial Process and Judicial Policymaking*. Belmont, CA: Thomson/Wadsworth, 2006. A broad outline of the institutions and main actors in the U.S. judicial system, explaining both judicial decision making and policy making.

van Geel, T. R. *Understanding Supreme Court Opinions*. New York: Pearson/Longman, 2005. An introduction to Supreme Court opinions and to the justices' use of different schools of legal argument and interpretation in those opinions.

Movies of Interest

The Runaway Jury (2003)
This film provides critical examination of the role of the jury in the American judicial system.

Monster's Ball (2001)
Probing the issues of capital punishment and racism in a personal way, this film explores the relationships among a white executioner, his African American prisoner, and their families.

A Civil Action (1998)
Based on a real-life story, this engrossing film takes the viewer through the pitfalls of civil litigation in a series of cases involving the pollution of a Massachusetts town's water supply by several corporations and businesses.

Gideon's Trumpet (1980)
This classic film starring Henry Fonda traces the true story of Clarence Gideon's fight to have a counsel appointed to his case at the expense of the state. *Gideon v. Wainwright* was the 1963 Supreme Court's decision that extended state-appointed attorneys to all criminal defendants.

12 Angry Men (1957)
Henry Fonda starred in and produced this classic drama depicting the acrimonious deliberations of a jury in a death penalty case.

DON'T LET YOUR JOB SEARCH
BECOME A WAITING GAME

Experience the Industries highest
standard of client care. Discover a
better way to advance your career.
Don't let your job search become a
waiting game, be pro-active and
take control.

UNPARALLED RESOURCES
ALL SEGMENTS OF BUSINESS AND INDUST

AA-CAREERS

Associated offices in most major U.S. Cities

AA-CARE

AA -
CAREERS

FREE

RESUME
CRITIQUE

CHAPTER

15

Economic
Policy

THEN

The federal government played a limited role in the economy, and there was consensus about the need for a balanced federal budget.

NOW

The federal government makes policy to achieve national economic health, and borrowing to balance the federal budget is the norm.

NEXT

Will continuing globalization impede the government's ability to maintain a healthy national economy?

Will the national government enact major tax, spending, or regulatory reforms in the wake of the Great Recession?

Will your generation and future generations achieve the American dream?

economic policy
a government's body of diverse policies geared toward promoting the nation's economic health

American dream
the belief that in the United States hard work and persistence will reap a financially secure, happy, and healthy life, with upward social mobility

Every government has an

economic policy, a body of diverse policies geared toward promoting its nation's economic health. Since World War II, the United States' economic policy has made it the dominant force in the global economy. But participants in the 2008 World Economic Forum—an annual meeting of thousands of corporate chief executive officers, government officials, and intellectuals—came to some sobering conclusions. The consensus was that the United States has fallen from its pedestal as the world's economic leader because of its colossal national debt and its deep reliance on imported oil, as well as the serious problems within its financial institutions.[1]

From President George Washington's terms in office to the current administration, the involvement of the national government in the nation's economy has evolved dramatically. Today, the national government enacts a variety of laws that seek to ensure economic prosperity. These laws include tax laws, laws that regulate economic activity in the domestic and international marketplaces, laws that protect the health and safety of workers and consumers, and spending policies that encourage economic growth as well as provide for the public good. In addition, the Federal Reserve—the United States' central banking system—makes policy decisions that affect the amount of money in circulation and hence consumer prices and employment rates.

Debates about the proper role for the national government in creating and maintaining a healthy economy have been ongoing since the birth of the American republic. The economic downturn experienced by the United States beginning in 2007 intensified the tone and the volume of debates about U.S. economic policy among elected and appointed officials at the national and state levels, economists, corporate leaders, and taxpayers. As these debates raged, and the global economy faltered, the U.S. national debt continued to grow, surpassing $12.4 trillion.

Economic Health and the American Dream

The American national government seeks a healthy economy so that it can raise the revenue it needs to serve the people in compliance with the mission laid out in the Preamble to the Constitution: to establish justice, ensure domestic tranquility, provide for the common defense, promote the general welfare, and secure the blessings of liberty today and in the future. On a more personal level, many U.S. citizens desire a healthy economy so that they can achieve the **American dream**—a financially secure, happy, and healthy life, with upward social mobility, attained through an individual's hard work and persistence.

Despite its name, the American dream's promise is not limited to Americans: people around the globe widely aspire to these same ideals. Hundreds of thousands of foreigners immigrate to the United States each year—most legally, some illegally—in search of the American dream. The primary cause of immigration is poverty. Foreign peoples come to the United States to get jobs that will provide more for them and their families than the jobs that their home country can provide. U.S. immigration policy (see Chapter 16) accommodates immigration on a limited basis, imposing an annual cap on the number of immigrants allowed legal entrance and giving preference to immigrants with family members living permanently in the United States, as well as those with high-level job skills needed in select segments of the U.S. economy.

The desire for enough money to buy not only what we require to meet our basic needs (food, shelter, and clothing) but also what many people would consider luxuries seems natural to most Americans. In developed countries such as the United States, "luxuries" typically include owning a home instead of renting, owning a car or two, dining at a nice restaurant now and then, taking vacations, and sending children to good schools. The American dream includes sustaining this middle-class lifestyle through retirement and expecting our children's lives to be even better than our own.

Clearly, it takes money to live the American dream. For some, being born into a wealthy family or just dumb luck (winning the lottery!) may provide the means to live the American dream. For most individuals, however, the ability to earn enough money to attain the American dream is the product of several factors, including their education level, their work ethic, and the availability of well-paying jobs.

Why are you attending college? Are you taking classes to develop your intellectual capacities? To better understand yourself and the world around you? To get a better-paying job so you can live the American dream? If you read your college's mission statement, you will find that your institution hopes to facilitate all those accomplishments. Probably the easiest accomplishment to measure is gaining a well-paying job, and personal income is a logical measure of a well-paying job. Table 15.1 shows that personal income is positively correlated with educational attainment; generally, the more education you acquire, the higher your personal income will be. In addition, Table 15.1 shows that race and sex—two factors that you cannot control—are also correlated with personal income. So earning a college degree is the best step you can take in your quest to live the American dream. However, for women and nonwhite men, the income benefits of a college education are muted.

Although you may be able to increase your level of education, and you have some control over your work ethic, the availability of well-paying jobs commensurate with your level of education is not within your control. The health of the national economy determines the availability of jobs and their compensation (pay and benefits). So, although achieving the American dream depends on individual attributes and opportunities to develop those attributes, the health of the national economy also plays a major role.

A healthy national economy—with low unemployment, stable prices, and high productivity—supports a nation's ability to raise sufficient revenue to serve its people. The better the economy's performance, the greater the **tax base:** the overall wealth (income and assets, such as property) of citizens and corporations that governments tax to raise revenue.

tax base
the overall wealth (income and assets of citizens and corporations) that the government can tax to raise revenue

economy
a system for producing, distributing, and consuming goods and services

Education, Race, Sex, and Mean Personal Income

TABLE 15.1

	High School	Associate's Degree	Bachelor's Degree	Master's Degree	Doctoral Degree
All groups	$31,286	$39,746	$57,181	$70,186	$ 95,565
Female	$24,234	$33,276	$43,127	$54,772	$ 69,251
Male	$36,839	$47,190	$70,898	$86,966	$108,941
Black	$27,179	$36,445	$46,502	$56,398	$ 96,092
Female	$24,724	$34,774	$41,560	$51,695	$*
Male	$29,640	$38,921	$53,029	$63,801	$*
Hispanic	$27,604	$35,348	$44,696	$68,040	$*
Female	$22,283	$29,884	$38,584	$54,263	$*
Male	$30,932	$42,140	$50,805	$81,069	$*
White	$32,223	$40,373	$58,652	$71,321	$ 97,254
Female	$24,276	$33,223	$42,846	$54,532	$ 69,778
Male	$38,214	$48,444	$73,477	$89,678	$110,480

* Too few earning PhDs to meet statistical standards for reliability.

SOURCE: U.S. Census Bureau, *Statistical Abstract of the United States: 2010*, 129th Ed. (Washington, DC: 2009), Table 227, www.census.gov/statab/www/.

The American Economy

In the United States and other countries, national government policies influence the **economy,** a system for producing, distributing,

POLITICAL INQUIRY

On average, do women or men make more money? Does this pattern hold for blacks, Hispanics, and whites? On average, people of which racial/ethnic background earn the most money? Which group earns the least? Do these patterns hold for all levels of education? What are some of the possible explanations for these patterns?

and consuming goods and services. Economic policies are those aimed at creating and/or maintaining a healthy economy. Economists view a healthy economy as one in which unemployment is low, the prices of consumer goods are relatively stable, and the productivity of individual workers, and of the economy as a whole, is increasing.

Although labeled as a capitalist economy, the U.S. economy is not an example of pure capitalism. In a **pure capitalist economy,** private individuals and companies own the modes of producing goods and services, and the government does *not* enact laws aimed at influencing the marketplace transactions that distribute those goods and services. In other words, a pure capitalist economy has a government-free marketplace. Although private ownership of the modes of production dominates the U.S. marketplace, it is not a government-free marketplace. National government policies in some cases encourage, and in other cases mandate, certain business practices that the government deems essential to sustain a healthy economy, as well as a clean environment and a safe and productive citizenry. Because of the many national policies enacted to influence the economy, the U.S. economy is an example of a **regulated capitalist economy (mixed economy),** not a pure capitalist economy.

People around the world want their governments to engage in actions that ensure a healthy economy. Yet the actions a government takes to ensure a healthy economy depend on the economic theories its lawmakers follow. In the United States, Democrats and Republicans traditionally disagree on economic policies, each justifying their policy preferences with different economic theories. Next, we survey several economic theories that have influenced U.S. national economic policy in various historical periods.

pure capitalist economy

an economy in which private individuals and companies own the modes of producing goods and services, and the government does not enact laws aimed at influencing the marketplace transactions that distribute those goods and services

regulated capitalist economy (mixed economy)

an economy in which the government enacts policies to influence the health of the economy

Economic Theories That Shape Economic Policy

Today's debates about the proper role of the national government in the economy are nothing new. It was the lack of an economic role for the national government and the poor health of the economy under the Articles of Confederation that sparked the call for a constitutional convention in 1787. The framers of the new system of government established by the Constitution envisioned a national government much more involved in the economy. Moreover, although citizens initially supported a very limited role for the government in the economy—a *laissez-faire* economic policy—as the national economy evolved and experienced ups and downs, citizens and corporations sought greater government involvement in the economy, and economists developed new theories about the proper role for governments in creating and maintaining a healthy economy: Keynesian economics, supply-side economics, and monetarism.

Laissez-Faire Economics: An Unrealized Policy

laissez-faire

hands-off stance of a government in regard to the marketplace

Until the late 1800s, a majority of the American people believed that the national government should take a relatively **laissez-faire,** or "hands-off," stance with regard to the marketplace. That is, they thought that the government should neither encourage nor discourage (through its laws) business practices that affected economic health. In his *Wealth of Nations* (1776), economist Adam Smith described the principles underlying the theory of laissez-faire. Smith's classical capitalist argument emphasized that the most effective means of supporting a strong and stable economy in the long term is to allow unregulated competition in the marketplace. According to Smith, people's pursuit of their self-interest in an unregulated marketplace would yield a healthy economy. Although it supported a hands-off approach in general, the national government became involved in economic activity as early as 1789, when Congress approved and President George Washington (1789–1797) signed the first import tariff (tax on imported goods).

As a manufacturing economy replaced the farming-dominated economy during the nineteenth century, the general laissez-faire stance of the national government disappeared. Technological advances fueled industrialization and the movement of workers from farms to manufacturing jobs in the cities. As immigrants flocked to the United States in search of the American dream, the supply of cheap labor ballooned. Giant corporations formed, and individuals with money to invest accumulated great wealth. Monopolies and trusts also developed, limiting competition in a variety of industries. **Income inequality,** the gap in the proportion of national income held by the few at the top of the income ladder compared with the many on the lower rungs, grew. At the same time, the quality of life for most working-class citizens deteriorated as additional family members, including children, needed to work to pay for life's basic necessities. As fewer and fewer people achieved the American dream, even with all family members working, many Americans began to look to the federal government to improve working and living conditions.

In the late nineteenth century, the federal government began to respond to workers' demands for better wages and working conditions and to business owners' calls for uniform (national) rules and regulations for business practices to replace the existing hodgepodge of state-imposed regulations. Moreover, by the early twentieth century, the national government took steps to protect public health by passing laws regulating the processing of foods and drugs, and the cleanliness and safety of manufacturing plants. Though not directed at the health of the economy, such regulations increased the costs of doing business, hence affecting the economy. In addition to regulating working conditions, the national government began to use the tool of immigration policy to bolster the national economy and the wages of American-born workers. For example, the Chinese Exclusion Act of 1882 disallowed immigrants from China, who were willing to work to build the railroads for lower wages than American-born workers. The contemporary public debate about the impact of immigrants on the U.S. economy—in terms of wages, working conditions, and the cost of health, education, and welfare policies—is discussed in Chapter 16.

Clearly, the national government never fully implemented laissez-faire. Moreover, as the national economy grew with industrialization, Americans accepted and even called for a mixed economy featuring regulated capitalism. Today, consensus continues on the need for some level of government involvement in the marketplace to ensure a healthy and sustainable economy, environment, and standard of living. But debate continues over how much government involvement is appropriate and what specific policies the government should enact.

> In the late eighteenth and early nineteenth centuries, income inequality forced many American families to rely on the income brought home by their children to help pay the bills. By 1900, large numbers of children worked in mines, glass factories, textiles, agriculture, canneries, and home industries such as cigar making. Here two little girls work in a hosiery mill in 1910.

income inequality
the gap in the proportion of national income held by the richest compared to that held by the poorest

Keynesian Economics

Before the Great Depression of the 1930s, government officials and economists believed that a **balanced budget,** a budget in which the government's expenditures (costs of doing business) are equal to or less than its revenues (money raised from taxes), was important for a healthy economy. Yet officials and economists recognized that during wartime the government might need to engage in **deficit spending,** spending more than is raised through taxes, to pay for the military effort.

During the Great Depression, when unemployment rates soared to 25 percent, President Franklin D. Roosevelt (1933–1945) and Congress supported deficit spending to address the severe economic depression that engulfed the nation. The Roosevelt administration implemented numerous economic regulations and a number of innovative work and public

balanced budget
a budget in which the government's expenditures are equal to or less than its revenues

deficit spending
government expenditures costing more than is raised in taxes, leading to borrowing and debt

Keynesian economics
theory that recommends that during a recession the national government should increase its spending and decrease taxes, and during a boom, it should cut spending and increase taxes

recession
an economic downturn during which unemployment is high and the production of goods and services is low

depression
a long-term and severe recession

economic boom
rapid economic growth

fiscal policy
government spending and taxing and their effect on the economy

assistance programs. Those policies drove up government spending at a time of shrinking government revenues. A key objective of the government's increased spending was to trigger economic growth by lowering unemployment rates, thereby increasing demand for goods (because more employed people means more people with money to spend), thus boosting the national economy. Deficit spending, Roosevelt said, would provide the solution to the American people's economic woes.

The new economic theory of John Maynard Keynes supported Roosevelt's unprecedented peacetime deficit spending. **Keynesian economics** recommends that during a **recession**—an economic downturn during which unemployment is high and the production of goods and services is low—the national government should increase its spending (to create jobs) and decrease taxes (so that people have more money to spend) to stimulate the economy. Based on this theory, during a **depression,** which is a long-term and severe recession, deficit spending is justified. During times of rapid economic growth—an **economic boom,** which is the opposite of a recession/depression—Keynesian theory recommends cutting government spending and possibly increasing taxes. In the long term, deficit spending during recessions and collecting a surplus when the economy is booming should lead to a balanced budget. Hence Keynesian economic theory advocates using **fiscal policy,** the combination of tax policy and spending policy, to ensure a healthy economy.

In February 2008, following the tenets of Keynesian economics, Congress and President George W. Bush (2001–2009) approved tax refunds for citizens totaling $168 billion and tax cuts for select businesses. In September 2008, Congress and the president pledged to spend $300 billion to rescue two top mortgage companies (Fannie Mae and Freddie Mac) and the American International Group (AIG), a major international insurance and financial services organization. The Bush administration continued these fiscal policies in the fall of 2008 by winning approval from Congress for $700 billion to bail out faltering Wall Street financial institutions.

President Barack Obama (2009–present) and Congress continued to use fiscal policy to stimulate the sagging economy by enacting the American Recovery and Reinvestment Act (ARRA), which authorized $787 billion in combined tax cuts and federal spending, in February 2009. The ARRA tax cuts and increased federal spending compose what the media and government officials refer to as a "stimulus package." The goals of the ARRA were to create and save jobs, jump-start the nation's economy, and build the foundation for long-

> Created in 1935 as one component of President Roosevelt's effort to end the Great Depression, the Works Projects Administration (WPA) put millions of unemployed people to work on public works projects such as highway and building construction. In his efforts to address the growing U.S. unemployment rate during the severe global recession of 2007–2009, President Obama signed into law the American Recovery and Reinvestment Act (ARRA), aimed at creating 3.5 million jobs, in February 2009. By June 2009, ARRA stimulus funds were being spent on hundreds of construction projects throughout the country.

term economic growth. Whereas Keynesian economics has shaped the economic policies of Democratic and Republican administrations from Roosevelt to Bush to Obama, President Ronald Reagan (1981–1989) implemented a different economic theory in his efforts to deal with the economic downturn that began during the late 1970s.

Supply-Side Economics

President Reagan introduced the nation to a competing economic theory, **supply-side economics,** which advocates tax cuts and a decrease in government regulation to stimulate the economy in times of recession. Supply-siders argue that the government collects so much money in income taxes from workers that they are discouraged from working more than they absolutely need to (because any extra effort will just mean they pay more in taxes). In addition, high taxes drain the economy because they diminish people's ability to save and corporations' ability to invest to increase productivity. Therefore, the theory goes, if the government cuts taxes, workers will be more productive and people will have more money to save and invest, thus stimulating economic growth. Supply-siders also argue that because government regulation increases the cost of producing goods, **deregulation**—reducing or eliminating restrictions on business—will contribute to increased production at the same cost, thus increasing the supply of goods.

Republican President George H. W. Bush (1989–1993) initially continued the supply-side economic policies of Reagan, but before the end of his presidency, Bush broke his promise not to raise taxes in an attempt to begin to address the growing **national debt**—the total amount of money owed to others due to borrowing. In addition to increasing taxes, he signed into law new regulations. Democratic President Bill Clinton (1993–2001) battled a Republican-dominated Congress for most of his presidency. Clinton's proposed spending increases were muted by Congress, and Congress pushed for tax cuts. As a result of those policies and economic growth, by the end of the 1990s, the national government was no longer engaging in deficit spending.

President George W. Bush (2001–2009), working with a Republican-dominated Congress for most of his presidency, initially pursued supply-side economics by cutting taxes and deregulating. However, as the recession that began in 2007 persisted, the Bush administration and Congress approved increased spending to prevent the collapse of numerous financial institutions.

Monetarism

Economist Milton Friedman, a onetime supporter of Keynesian economics, is today best known for yet another economic theory, **monetarism,** which advocates that the government's proper role in promoting a healthy economy is the regulation of the money supply to ensure that the rate of inflation remains low. **Inflation** refers to a rising price level for consumer goods, which decreases the purchasing power of money. The Bureau of Labor Statistics provides an inflation calculator (www.bls.gov/data/inflation_calculator.htm) that allows you to determine what yesterday's dollar is worth today because of inflation. For example, according to the calculator, $1.25 in 2009 bought what $1.00 in 2000 could buy.

Monetarists believe that *too much* money in circulation leads to a high inflation rate, which slows economic growth as people spend less because of higher prices. In addition, as the rate of inflation increases, investors begin to worry about the health of the economy, and investments may decline as a result, ultimately limiting economic growth. On the flip side, the monetarists say, *too little* money in circulation means there is not enough for new investments and that consequently new jobs are not created; this situation, too, retards

> April 15th is tax day, the day that citizens must pay their federal income taxes. Anti-tax protests are common on tax day. Critics of President Obama marked tax day 2009 with "tea party" protests across the country, including this one in Staten Island, New York. Tea Party protests are reminiscent of the 1773 Boston Tea Party revolt against British colonial taxes.

supply-side economics
theory that advocates cutting taxes and deregulating business to stimulate the economy

deregulation
reduction or elimination of regulatory restrictions on firms and industries

national debt
the total amount of money the national government owes to its creditors

monetarism
theory that says the government's proper economic role is to control the rate of inflation by controlling the amount of money in circulation

inflation
the decreased value of money as evidenced by increased prices

economic growth. Today, monetarists target an inflation rate of 1–3 percent per year to ensure an adequate money supply for a healthy economy. They believe that the national government must use its monetary policy to maintain this level of inflation.

Should One Economic Theory Predominate?

Although economists, government officials, and citizens broadly agree that the government should act to ensure a healthy economy, there is perpetual debate over how involved the government should be in the economy and what specific policy actions it should take. Where people stand in this debate depends on which economic theory they advocate. Each theory supports the use of different government policies to promote a healthy economy. Before we discuss these various policies that theoretically promote economic health, we consider how governments measure economic health. Once we know what a healthy economy looks like, we can then consider the effects that various policies have on the performance of the economy.

Measuring Economic Health

Economists and government officials describe a healthy economy as one that has the following characteristics: expanding gross domestic product (GDP); increasing level of worker productivity; low unemployment rate; low inflation rate.

These traditional measures of economic health together provide a useful snapshot of how the national economy is doing. Other measures of economic health focus on the general well-being of the people by accounting for factors such as rates of poverty and literacy and the financial situation of households. These less traditional measures include the United Nations Human Development Index, real median household income, income inequality, and the poverty rate.

Traditional Measures of Economic Health

gross domestic product (GDP)
the total value of all goods and services produced within a country's borders

Most economists assume that growth in the gross domestic product translates into a prosperous nation with improving living standards—hence progress toward living the American dream. **Gross domestic product (GDP)** is the total market value of all goods and services produced within a country's borders. Another assumption made by most economists is that high productivity, or output per worker, also fosters improved living standards. Rising GDP and productivity are signs of an expanding economy, which means the production of more goods and services—and thus the availability of more goods and services for consumers.

Economists also expect a healthy economy to correlate with a low level of inflation. When inflation rises, consumers' purchasing power falls and they cannot buy as much this year with the same amount of money they spent last year. The government agency known as the Bureau of Labor Statistics publishes the **consumer price index (CPI),** which measures the average change in prices over time of a "market basket" of goods and services, including food, clothing, shelter, fuel, transportation costs, and selected medical costs. The CPI is the most commonly used measure of inflation's impact on people. According to economists, when the economy is healthy, the inflation rate (measured by the change in CPI) ranges between 1 and 3 percent.

consumer price index (CPI)
the most common measure of inflation, it gauges the average change in prices over time of a "market basket" of goods and services including food, clothing, shelter, fuels, transportation costs, and selected medical costs

A low unemployment rate, 5 percent or less, is also characteristic of a healthy economy, according to economists. When more people are working, the financial situation of families overall should improve. In addition, in a growing economy with falling unemployment, government revenues should increase (since there is more corporate and personal income to tax), and government spending for social welfare programs should decrease (because fewer people should need public assistance). These trends create a healthier financial situation for government. (For a closer look at what the GDP and unemployment rates measure, see "Analyzing the Sources.")

ANALYZING THE SOURCES

GDP AND UNEMPLOYMENT RATES: WHAT DO THEY MEASURE?

Traditionally, no measure of economic health has been as widely accepted as gross domestic product (GDP), although some economists argue that a more accurate economic assessment would add a quality-of-life measure to the value of GDP. Employment status clearly correlates with a person's quality of life, but some economists and government officials have also questioned the current means by which the government measures this indicator.

The Gross Domestic Product

The U.S. Commerce Department calculates the *gross domestic product (GDP),* which it defines as the total value of all goods and services produced within a country's borders for a specified period, usually one year. The GDP is calculated from the following formula:

$$GDP = C + G + I + NX$$

where

C is the total amount of *consumer spending* to purchase goods and services

G is the total amount of *government spending* to purchase goods and services

I is the total amount of money *businesses invest* in new capital resources (such as equipment, computers and software, automobiles, and facilities)

NX is the nation's total net exports, which is the difference between the value of all its exports and the value of all its imports

The Unemployment Rate

Every month, the Bureau of Labor Statistics of the Department of Labor reports the *unemployment rate,* which is the percent of people who are actively looking for work but who do not have jobs. To calculate the unemployment rate, each month more than 2,000 trained Census Bureau employees (the Census Bureau is within the Department of Commerce) interview people in 60,000 households that are representative of the households across the United States. Collectively these interviews are called the Current Population Survey (CPS).

The Census Bureau classifies individuals as employed if they did any work at all for pay or profit during the survey week, including part-time and temporary work. The Bureau also counts as employed people who have a job but did not work during the survey week because they were on vacation, ill, experiencing child-care problems, taking care of some other family or personal obligation, on maternity or paternity leave, involved in an industrial dispute, or prevented from working by bad weather.

The CPS classifies persons as *unemployed* if they meet the following criteria:

1. They do not have a job.
2. They have actively looked for work in the preceding four weeks.
3. They are currently available for work.

Therefore, people who do not have a job and have stopped looking for work are not counted as unemployed.

Evaluating the Evidence

① The GDP does not include the value of unpaid work done in the home, such as home-cooked meals, child care, adult care, house cleaning, and clothes cleaning. Should it include those costs? Why or why not?

② Does the fact that the "unemployment" rate does not account for people who have given up hope of finding a job and therefore have stopped looking for work call into question the rate's accuracy? Justify your answer.

③ What measure, or combination of measures, would you argue provides citizens with the most accurate picture of the health of the economy? Explain your answer.

In sum, a high or rising GDP, high or increasing rate of productivity, low inflation rate, and low unemployment rate suggest a healthy national economy. Yet as the U.S. Department of Commerce's Bureau of Economic Analysis points out, "While the GDP is used as an indicator of economic progress, it is not a measure of well-being."[2] Therefore we next describe other measures that attempt to assess the well-being of the people, which most people expect is a product of a healthy economy.

Other Measures of Economic Health

The United Nations (UN) created the **Human Development Index (HDI)** to measure the standard of living of the people of various nations. As discussed in the "Global Context" box, the HDI assesses three components of human development that people in prosperous nations should be able to enjoy: a long and healthy life, educational opportunities, and a decent standard of daily living. These measures of economic health shed light on the ability of people to earn enough to *enjoy a decent quality of life*. Thus they are probing into something quite different from the traditional measures of national economic health that we have just discussed.

With an HDI score of .956 (1.0 is the highest score possible), the United States ranked thirteenth out of 182 countries in the *Human Development Report 2010*.[3] How do we know what this rank means to American households and their ability to live the American dream? Additional measures—looking at household income, income inequality, and the level of poverty within the population—can help us answer this question.

Real median household income is an important measure of the financial well-being of American households. **Real income** is income adjusted for inflation so that it can be compared across years. **Household income** is the total pretax earnings of all residents over the age of 15 living in a home. **Median household income** is the income level in the middle of all household incomes; 50 percent of the households have incomes less than the median and 50 percent have incomes greater than the median. An increase in real median household income should characterize a healthy, expanding economy if we assume that increases in workers' productivity will translate into increases in workers' incomes.

To determine whether people at all income levels are benefiting from a healthy economy, the government calculates changes in the percentage of the total national income possessed by households in five income groups. Specifically, the government divides U.S. households into five *quintiles,* each composed of 20 percent of the households in the nation, based on total household income. The bottom group (bottom quintile) is composed of the 20 percent of households with the lowest incomes, and the top quintile comprises the 20 percent of households with the highest incomes. The government then determines the percentage of the total national income possessed by each quintile. Changes in the percentage of the total income held by each quintile over time indicate whether income inequality is growing or shrinking. The ideal is to see a shrinking of income inequality as the national economy expands.

The ideal healthy economy would also ensure that all workers earn enough to stay out of **poverty**—the condition of lacking sufficient income to purchase the necessities for an adequate living standard. The **poverty rate** is the percentage of the population with income below the nationally designated poverty level. The U.S. Census Bureau calculates the poverty rate by using its **poverty thresholds**—an annually updated set of income measures (adjusted for family size) that define who is living in poverty. According to the poverty thresholds for 2008, a family of four, with two children under the age of 18 years, earning less than $21,834 was living in poverty.[4] A family of the same size and makeup earning $21,835 was not living in poverty.

So we have seen that not only traditional economic measures such as GDP, productivity, inflation, and employment serve as indicators of national economic health, but also other measures shed light on the quality of life of people in the United States. With this context in mind, we next explore the way the national government uses fiscal policy to promote a healthy national economy that provides benefits to individuals and households.

Human Development Index (HDI)
UN-created measure to determine how well a country's economy is providing for a long and healthy life, educational opportunities, and a decent standard of living

real income
earned income adjusted for inflation

household income
total pretax earnings of all residents over the age of 15 living in a home

median household income
the middle of all household incomes—50 percent of households have incomes less than the median and 50 percent have incomes greater than the median

poverty
the condition of lacking sufficient income to purchase the necessities for an adequate living standard

poverty rate
proportion of the population living below the poverty line as established by the national government

poverty thresholds
an annually updated set of income measures (adjusted for family size) that defines who is living in poverty

NATIONAL ECONOMIES AND HUMAN DEVELOPMENT

The United Nations Development Programme (UNDP) focuses on the question, How does the economic development of a country translate, or fail to translate, into improved well-being for its inhabitants? In an effort to understand the complex relationships between a country's economic development, its inhabitants' incomes, and their well-being, the UNDP created the Human Development Index (HDI). The HDI uses three components to assess the most fundamental aspects of people's lives. The UNDP maintains that the HDI provides a more complete picture of a country's development than do traditional measures of economic development, such as the GDP.

The first component of the HDI is a long and healthy life, as measured by life expectancy at birth. The second component is knowledge, measured by adult literacy rates and enrollment in primary, secondary, and tertiary schools. The third component is a decent standard of living, which is measured by GDP per capita (per person inhabiting the country). The closer to 1 a country's HDI score is, the better the living standard in the country. The accompanying table compares the top five and the bottom five nations, based on their HDI scores in 2009.

✳ How will the global recession affect the pattern of improvement in HDI scores?

TOP FIVE NATIONS	BOTTOM FIVE NATIONS
1. Norway (.971)	178. Mali (.371)
2. Australia (.970)	179. Central African Republic (.369)
3. Iceland (.969)	180. Sierra Leone (.365)
4. Canada (.966)	181. Afghanistan (.352)
5. Ireland (.965)	182. Niger (.340)

Between 1990 and 2009, HDI scores in all regions of the world have increased, in part because of improvements in health and education. Progress is slower in some years and regions, however, and incomes in the poorest countries have been problematic. In addition, many countries have experienced setbacks from regional economic downturns, civil wars and other conflict-related causes, and epidemics. Indeed, inequality in the distribution of the world's income persists.

SOURCE: http://hdr.undp.org/en/.

Fiscal Policy and Economic Health

As noted earlier, fiscal policy comprises a government's spending and tax policies. The national government, through its budget process, annually approves a twelve-month plan for raising revenue and spending revenue. The twelve-month accounting period for revenue raising and spending is a **fiscal year (FY)**. The national government's fiscal year runs from October 1 through September 30 of the following calendar year, and is named for the calendar year in which it ends. Therefore the federal FY 2011 began on October 1, 2010 and ends on September 30, 2011.

National government expenditures accounted for 25 percent of the GDP of the United States in 2009—unquestionably, a substantial percentage of national economic output.[5] Although government spending certainly can create jobs, its primary goal is to provide the services necessary to fulfill the Constitution's mission. The other side of the coin, tax policy, raises revenue needed by the national government to serve the people. Although the main goal of tax policy is to collect revenue, taxation also decreases the amount of money taxpayers have to spend in the marketplace and corporations have to invest. Hence, taxation may

fiscal year (FY)
the twelve-month accounting period for revenue raising and spending, which for the national government begins on October 1 and ends on September 30 of the following year

reduce consumer demand for goods and services, with possible effects on the unemployment rate as well as company profits. It may also affect investment, which contributes to economic growth. Thus tax policy, like spending policy, powerfully affects the economy.

To understand fiscal policy, we look next at the sources of the funds the federal government uses to run the nation, as well as the spending decisions that Congress and the president must make.

Tax Policy

The Constitution delegates the power of the purse to Congress. By the authority of the Constitution, Congress formulates and approves *tax laws* to raise money along with *appropriation laws*—legislation that authorizes the spending of government money for a fiscal year. The Constitution specifies that the House must introduce revenue-raising bills before the Senate can consider them. The House Ways and Means Committee and the Senate Finance Committee are the congressional standing committees from which tax bills emerge.

Figure 15.1 presents the tax mix proposed in the FY 2011 budget. Today, the national tax on individual income is the largest revenue source for the national government. The federal individual income tax is imposed on each individual's *earned income* (salaries and wages) and *unearned income* (profits made from investments).

The second-largest revenue category, social insurance, includes taxes collected for Social Security and Medicare. Because employers deduct from workers' paychecks the amount they owe for social insurance taxes, these taxes are referred to as *payroll taxes*. The federal government's third-largest revenue source is corporate income taxes. The national government also collects *excise taxes,* which are taxes levied against a specific item such as gasoline or liquor, *estate and gift taxes,* and *customs duties* (import taxes).

Taxes levied by the federal government do not affect the income of all taxpayers in the same way. The national income tax is a **progressive tax** because it takes a larger percentage of the income of wealthier taxpayers and a smaller percentage of the income of less-well-off taxpayers. Most taxpayers view a progressive tax, theoretically based on a person's ability to pay, as fair. Some people believe that a **proportional tax (flat tax),** which takes the same percentage of each taxpayer's income, is fairer than a progressive tax. A flat tax of 10 percent would equal $3,500 for a person earning $35,000 and $13,500 for a person earning $135,000. Although these two taxpayers pay a different amount of money in taxes, the *proportion* of their income collected is the same—hence the name proportional tax. Taxes can also be regressive. A **regressive tax** takes a greater percentage of the income of lower-income earners than of higher-income earners. States' sales taxes are the prime example of a regressive tax.

Taxes may affect various taxpayers differently because the government grants **tax expenditures** (better known as *tax breaks* or *tax loopholes*). These are government financial supports to individuals and corporations to encourage behaviors that ostensibly enhance the public good. Tax breaks and loopholes allow taxpayers to pay lower taxes on their income than they would otherwise pay. For example, to encourage home ownership, the government gives tax breaks to individuals paying interest on a home mortgage. The government also offers tax breaks to businesses for job creation and worker retraining.

State and local governments, as well as nonprofit organizations that provide a public service, pay no federal taxes. Thus we say that they are exempt from federal taxes. Included in this group of tax-exempt organizations are the overwhelming majority of colleges and universities, which are public or nonprofit institutions. They are tax exempt because they provide the public good of higher education without making a profit; they must invest any surplus money back into the institution.

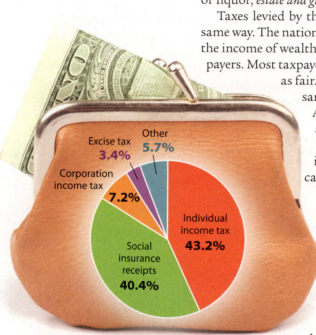

FY 2011 Executive Budget Revenue

Excise tax **3.4%**
Other **5.7%**
Corporation income tax **7.2%**
Individual income tax **43.2%**
Social insurance receipts **40.4%**

POLITICAL INQUIRY

FIGURE 15.1 ■ **What is the government's top source of revenue in the FY 2011 executive budget? Do you project that the revenue from this source will remain high in future budgets? Why or why not? What are the other two main sources that provide national revenue? How do you think they may change in future budgets?**

Tax expenditures and tax cuts would not be such a big concern if the government raised enough money to balance its budget. Unfortunately, deficit spending is the norm for the national government. How is the government spending all this money?

Spending Policy

Decisions the federal government makes about spending significantly affect both the national economy and the ability of individuals to achieve their American dream. Although setting the budget is an annual process, with Congress and the president approving a spending plan one fiscal year at a time, not all national government spending is approved annually.

For the government to spend money, Congress and the president must enact laws that establish **budget authority,** which is the legal authority for agencies to obligate government spending. Programs granted budget authority through annual appropriation acts are **discretionary spending** programs. There are two categories of discretionary spending programs: security programs and nonsecurity programs. As Figure 15.2 indicates, security spending is a bigger piece of the budget pie than is nonsecurity spending. Security program spending includes expenditures for the Department of Defense, the Department of Homeland Security, and international affairs. Nonsecurity spending covers an array of activities and programs, including the administration of justice, agriculture, education, energy, environment, health, housing, income security for the poor and disabled, and transportation.

Congress and the president deliberate each year over how much budget authority to include in annual appropriation acts for these discretionary spending programs. Typically, Democrats and Republicans differ on their priorities for discretionary spending programs. As the share of the budget spent on discretionary spending has been shrinking, because of the growing share that goes to *mandatory spending,* the partisan battles between Democrats and Republicans become even more intense.

Figure 15.2 shows that the largest share of the national budget pays for **mandatory spending,** which includes programs whose budget authority is provided in laws other than annual appropriation acts. The budget authority for mandatory spending is established in the authorization legislation that created the program, and is *open ended* because it obligates the government to pay for the program every year, whatever the cost may be, as long as the program exists. Social Security (income security for retired Americans and people with certain disabilities), Medicare (health insurance for the elderly), and Medicaid (health insurance for low-income individuals) are prime examples of mandatory spending programs. Because the government is legally obligated to pay back money it borrows, payments for the national debt also fall within the category of mandatory spending.

In the annual budget process, Congress and the president do not make annual decisions about most of the money spent by the national government because most expenditures are mandatory. Other than interest payments on the debt, mandatory spending could be controlled by Congress and the president by rewriting the legislation that established these open-ended budget obligations. Recent attempts to rewrite the legislation that created the Social Security retirement program have shown that many mandatory programs are politically difficult to change. This is partly because elected officials fear the impact such changes would have on their reelection prospects, and partly because of partisanship. Not only do Democrats and Republicans disagree on the proper reforms, but also members of both parties disagree among themselves on specific reforms. Hence mandatory spending continues to grow as a percentage of the federal budget.

Creating Fiscal Policy Through the National Budget Process

The federal government creates its programs through authorization legislation that specifies the program's goals and establishes whether its budget authority is obligated for the life of the program

budget authority
authority provided by law for agencies to spend government funds

discretionary spending
payment on programs for which Congress and the president must approve budget authority each year in appropriation legislation

mandatory spending
government spending for debt and programs whose budget authority is provided in legislation other than annual appropriation acts; this budget authority is open ended, obligating the government to pay for the program as long as it exists

Discretionary nonsecurity spending — 13.6%   Discretionary security spending — 23.3%   Mandatory spending — 63.1%

FIGURE 15.2

Federal Expenditures by Budget Categories: FY 2011 Executive Budget

SOURCE: Table S-4 at www.whitehouse.gov/omb/budget/fy2011/assets/tables.pdf.

(mandatory spending) or must be set annually (discretionary spending). In an annual appropriation process, Congress and the president establish yearly funding for discretionary spending programs and possibly change tax policy to increase revenue raised—to pay the bills—or to cut taxes in an effort to stimulate the economy. This process begins in the executive branch.

THE PRESIDENT'S EXECUTIVE BUDGET

The budget process officially starts about a year and a half before the beginning of the fiscal year for which budget authority will be obligated. For example, work on the budget for FY 2011 began during the spring of 2009. The process begins when the Office of Management and Budget (OMB) sends the president's budget priorities (policy and financing preferences) to the executive branch agencies. Executive branch agencies use the president's guidelines to formulate their funding requests. Typically, these requests are incremental changes (small increases) to their current fiscal year's budget authority.

The budget requests work their way back up the executive branch hierarchy to the OMB. The OMB reviews the budget requests, conducts hearings in which the agencies justify their requests, and analyzes the requests in light of economic forecasts. The OMB then submits its budget recommendations to the president, who works with the OMB to create a proposed fiscal plan for the entire national government for the upcoming fiscal year. The OMB drafts a budget document and a budget message, collectively labeled the **executive budget,** which explains the president's fiscal plan. The president is required by law to submit the executive budget to Congress by the first Monday in February, eight months before the fiscal year begins.

CONGRESSIONAL ACTION

Once Congress receives the president's executive budget, the Congressional Budget Office (CBO), the legislative branch's counterpart to the OMB, swings into action. The CBO analyzes the executive budget in light of economic forecasts and predicted government revenues. The House Budget Committee and the Senate Budget Committee use the CBO's analysis, along with reports from other congressional committees, to develop the **concurrent budget resolution,** which establishes a binding expenditure ceiling (the maximum amount that can be spent) and a binding revenue floor (the minimum amount that must be raised) as well as proposed expenditure levels for major policy categories. The House and the Senate must both agree to the concurrent budget resolution. This agreement is to occur by April 15, less than six months before the fiscal year begins.

After approval of the concurrent budget resolution, the House and the Senate Appropriations Committees each draft appropriation bills to provide budget authority for discretionary programs. To comply with the concurrent budget resolution, Congress may also need to revise the legislation that authorized selected government programs. For example, the House and Senate may have to agree to change the open-ended budget authority in existing legislation to comply with the expenditure ceiling in the concurrent budget resolution. Or they may have to agree to changes in tax legislation to meet the revenue floor specified in the concurrent resolution. **Budget reconciliation** is the annual process of rewriting authorization legislation to comply with the concurrent budget resolution. The deadline for completion of the reconciliation process is June 15, less than four months before the fiscal year begins.

Congress has until the end of June to approve the twelve appropriation bills that fund the national government for the upcoming fiscal year. This timetable leaves two months for the president to approve the bills so that by October 1 the national government can begin the new fiscal year with budget authority for discretionary spending programs. If Congress and the president fail to approve one or more of the appropriation bills by October 1, Congress must approve a **continuing resolution** to authorize agencies not covered by approved appropriation laws to continue to spend money within their previous budget year's levels.

The nature of the annual budget process is such that, at any given time, some government body in the executive or legislative branch is preparing a future budget, even as the executive branch is implementing the current budget. At the same time, the Government

> Congress received President Barack Obama's 2011 executive budget on Capitol Hill on February 1, 2010. The executive branch's work on the 2011 budget began in the spring of 2009 when the OMB sent President Obama's budget priorities to the government agencies.

executive budget
the budget document and budget message that explains the president's fiscal plan

concurrent budget resolution
document approved by the House and Senate at the beginning of their budget process that establishes a binding expenditure ceiling and a binding revenue floor as well as proposed expenditure levels for major policy categories

budget reconciliation
the annual process of rewriting authorization legislation to comply with the expenditure ceiling and revenue floor of the concurrent budget resolution for the upcoming fiscal year

continuing resolution
an agreement of the House and Senate that authorizes agencies not covered by approved appropriation laws to continue to spend money within their previous budget year's levels

Accountability Office (GAO) is evaluating the implementation of the previous fiscal year's budget. Thus budgeting is a perpetual government activity, one that takes up a great deal of national officials' time.

Deficit Spending, Debt, and Economic Health

Most Americans highly value the ideal of a balanced budget, in which, as we have seen, the government spends no more than the revenues that it raises. Although the nation had a **budget surplus** (money left over when all expenses are paid) for several years at the end of the 1990s, **budget deficits** (more money spent than collected through revenues) recurred as the first decade of the twenty-first century unfolded. Indeed, deficit spending has become the norm, not the exception (see Figure 15.3). In February 2010, President Obama estimated the FY 2010 deficit would be $1.6 trillion. What impact does fiscal policy dominated by deficit spending have on the nation's economic health?

A government that engages in deficit spending borrows money and hence goes into debt. Even as politicians, some economists, and many concerned citizens call for a balanced budget—with some people even proposing a constitutional amendment mandating this objective—deficit spending continues, and so the national debt grows. The long-term impact of debt is the legal obligation to pay back not only the money initially borrowed (the *principal*) but also *interest*, an additional amount of money equal to a percentage of the amount initially borrowed. In the case of government borrowing, future generations

budget surplus
money left over after all expenses are paid

budget deficit
more money spent than collected through revenues

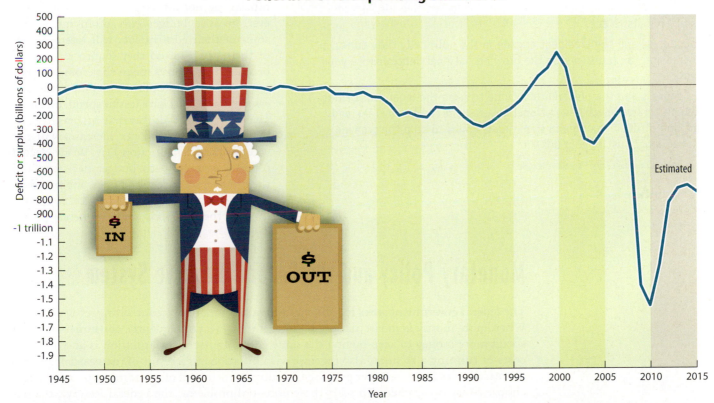

Federal Deficit Spending Since 1945

POLITICAL INQUIRY

FIGURE 15.3 ■ What do we mean by a budget deficit and a budget surplus? What trend in deficit spending does the graph indicate? In what recent years has there been a surplus rather than a deficit? What government expenditures do you think explain the rise in deficit spending since 2002?

SOURCE: Table 1.1, www.whitehouse.gov.omb/budget/Historicals.

The Federal Government's Financial Status

THEN (FY 2000)	NOW (FY 2010)
$1.7 trillion total budget outlay	$3.7 trillion total budget outlay*
$409 billion Social Security outlay	$722 billion Social Security outlay*
$236 billion surplus	$1.6 trillion deficit*
$5.6 trillion national debt	$13.8 trillion national debt*
$6 trillion legal debt ceiling	$14.3 trillion legal debt ceiling

WHAT'S NEXT?

> Will Congress and the president engage in the politically risky endeavor of cutting spending to stop the growing national debt? Explain what discretionary spending you think it is politically feasible for elected federal officials to cut.

> Will Congress and the president engage in the politically risky endeavor of increasing tax rates to stop the growing national debt? Justify your answer.

> Will Congress and the president continue to raise the legal debt ceiling (the limit on how much the national government can borrow) instead of making difficult taxing and spending changes to stop the growing national debt? Justify your answer.

* These are estimates from the FY 2011 Executive Budget.

must pay back the debt of their parents and grandparents. Today, to pay off the $12.4 trillion national debt, each citizen would have to chip in about $40,176.[6]

Public debate is ongoing about the economic impact of long-term deficit spending and the colossal national debt, which is more than three times the amount of money the national government spends in one year. Some economists argue that the more money the national government borrows, the less money businesses can borrow to invest and expand the economy. In addition, many citizens grow increasingly concerned that today's deficit spending will burden future generations with the bill for current policies. Complicating the picture, as the debt incurred from decades of deficit spending accumulates, the debt payment is becoming a larger proportion of the annual federal budget, increasing the percentage of the budget that pays for mandatory spending.

For the government to stop its deficit spending and ultimately reduce its debt, it must increase taxes, cut expenditures, or both. Elected officials do not like to reduce spending, however, because budget cuts often mean that some of their constituents will lose a service or their jobs. Nor do they like to raise taxes, because higher taxes mean that some citizens must give even more of their income to the government and thus have less to spend, invest, or save. Elected officials fear that citizens harmed by spending cuts and tax increases will not vote for them on Election Day. While elected officials struggle with budget decisions and their impact on reelection hopes, appointed officials, whom citizens cannot hold accountable through the ballot box, make monetary policy.

Monetary Policy and the Federal Reserve System

The federal government seeks to influence the value of money by controlling its availability. When more money is in circulation, it is lower in value; consequently, consumers need to spend more money to keep buying the same goods and services. Inflation is at work. The costs of running a business also increase with inflation. As a result of increased costs and decreased sales (because fewer people can maintain their level of spending), businesses may choose to lay off workers. To avert these potential problems, the Federal Reserve, the nation's central banking system, works to maximize employment, ensure stable prices (keep inflation low), and moderate long-term interest rates.

Congress and President Woodrow Wilson (1913–1921) established the Federal Reserve System (the Fed) in 1913. The Fed is composed of the Board of Governors (a government agency whose members the president nominates and the Senate must confirm), twelve Federal Reserve Banks, and the Federal Open Market Committee (FOMC). The Board of Governors, the president of the Federal Reserve Bank of New York, and the presidents of four other

Federal Reserve Banks, who serve on a rotating basis, make up the FOMC. Today, the Fed's responsibilities include (1) setting **monetary policy**—the body of government policies aimed at maintaining price stability; (2) supervising and regulating banking institutions; (3) maintaining the stability of financial markets; and (4) providing financial services to depository institutions, the national government, and foreign official institutions—central banks of other nations, and international organizations such as the International Monetary Fund.

The Fed has three primary tools for setting monetary policy. It can raise or lower the *reserve requirement*—the amount of money that financial institutions must keep out of circulation. In times of high inflation, the Fed may raise the reserve requirement to decrease the amount of money available through credit, hence decreasing the money supply. The Fed can also raise or lower the *discount rate*—the interest charged to financial institutions that borrow money from the Federal Reserve bank—and thereby make it more or less costly to borrow money. The Fed action that most influences the money supply, however, is its decision to buy or sell Treasury Securities (bills, notes, and bonds, which represent loans of money to the government to meet expenditures not covered by tax revenues). The Fed sells Treasury Securities when it wants to decrease the money supply and buys them to increase the supply.

Beyond its authority to set monetary policy, the Fed exerts supervisory and some regulatory authority over about 3,000 banks that are members of the Federal Reserve System (including all commercial banks chartered by the national government and those state-chartered banks that choose to join the Federal Reserve System), companies that control banks, and the U.S. activities of foreign banks. However, the Fed is not the only federal agency supervising and regulating the banking and financial industries. For example, the Office of the Comptroller of the Currency (OCC)—created in 1863 as a bureau within the Treasury Department—also charters, supervises, and regulates national banks. The Federal Deposit Insurance Corporation (FDIC)—an independent agency established in 1933—supervises state-chartered banks that are not members of the Federal Reserve System. Since the mid-1800s, the national government has created numerous regulatory agencies charged with ensuring the safety and soundness of the nation's banking and financial industries and systems, with the ultimate goal of promoting a healthy national economy.

monetary policy
the body of government policies, controlled by the Federal Reserve System, aimed at influencing the supply of money in the marketplace to maintain price stability

Regulatory Policy

As stated by Adam Smith in 1776, in theory, the competition that characterizes a free, unregulated market serves the public good by producing the range of high-quality and affordable products and services that citizens need or demand. Free-market advocates assume that competition provides for the public good. Yet at times, the competition of a free, unregulated market may harm consumers, workers, and the environment.

Indeed, competition among private entities, each trying to make a profit, may threaten public safety and health. Consider, for example, the unsafe products, including dangerous food and drugs, that may be manufactured and sold to make a profit. Think about production and manufacturing processes that may pollute the air, water, and land, creating conditions that are injurious to public health. Competition may also lead firms to cut salaries and benefits to ensure their profits, or their very survival. Such cuts decrease workers' ability to earn wages and benefits that keep them in the middle class, or even out of poverty. Unsafe and unhealthful working conditions may be another "cost" that workers "pay" so that firms can hold down or reduce production expenses. Moreover, if marketplace competition results in a few firms driving out their competition, they then have the power to raise prices or produce goods of lower quality, harming consumers.

Recently, the United States experienced a failure in the financial market to channel funds from savers to borrowers because of risky decisions by numerous financial and banking institutions. Loans and credit lines extended to people without the means to repay the borrowed money sparked an increase in the number of people who could not pay their mortgages and therefore lost their homes. Hundreds of billions of dollars worth of mortgage-related investments went bad by the fall of 2008, and several large, prominent financial and banking companies collapsed. President Bush and Congress began discussions about the need for new regulations for the banking and financial industries to prevent similar market failures in the future. Congress and President Obama's administration continued those discussions, focusing on protecting consumers of the banking and financial industries. In the summer of 2010, President Obama signed legislation establishing the Bureau of Consumer Financial Protection, an independent unit within the Fed. The Bureau of Consumer Financial Protection has the authority to regulate a wide range of financial products, including mortgages and credit cards, and to collect and monitor consumer complaints about the financial and banking industries, and a responsibility to educate consumers about financial products and services.

In the U.S. economy today, the government regulates marketplace practices to protect the public. This regulation occurs in two broad categories: business regulation and social regulation. **Business regulation** includes government policies that aim to preserve competition in the marketplace. **Social regulation** refers to government policies directed at protecting workers, consumers, and the environment from the harm caused by marketplace competition. In Chapter 13, we surveyed the administrative rule-making process by which executive branch agencies establish business and social regulations. In this discussion, we trace the evolution of these two types of regulatory policy.

Business Regulation

The federal government created the first agency for the purpose of regulating business, the Interstate Commerce Commission (ICC), in 1887. The ICC initially regulated the prices of and services provided by the railroad industry to protect the livelihood of farmers who relied on the nation's rail lines to transport their goods to distant markets. Next, in 1914, the federal government established regulations to prevent large corporations from engaging in business practices that harmed marketplace competition and established the Federal Trade Commission (FTC) to oversee these regulations.[7]

In 1934, during the Great Depression, the government created the Securities and Exchange Commission (SEC) to regulate and make transparent the nation's stock markets and financial markets. Another regulation of the Depression era, the National Labor Relations Act of 1935 (commonly known as the Wagner Act), authorized the national government to

business regulation
government rules, regulations, and standards directed at protecting competition in the marketplace

social regulation
government rules and regulations aimed at protecting workers, consumers, and the environment from market failure

> Women carry their belongings from the headquarters of Lehman Brothers in New York in September 2008 after the 158-year-old investment bank filed for bankruptcy. Because of the credit crisis and devalued real estate market that devastated banking and financial institutions such as Lehman Brothers, the federal government proposed new regulations for these institutions.

regulate interactions between management and labor unions. The Wagner Act empowered union members by guaranteeing the right of workers to unionize and elect representatives to bargain collectively with management for improved wages and working conditions. Moreover, the Wagner Act outlawed certain management practices that Congress considered unfair to labor—and hence a potential threat to the economy. Then in 1947, Congress overrode President Harry Truman's (1945–1953) veto and passed the Labor-Management Relations Act (Taft-Hartley Act), which identified and outlawed labor practices Congress deemed unfair and restricted the right to unionize to nonsupervisory employees only.

Thus within fifty years of the creation of the first regulatory agency, the ICC, the national government had put in place a full range of business regulations. From regulating prices and standards in industries, to criminalizing business practices that restrict marketplace competition, to making stock transactions transparent, to regulating labor-management relations—today, the government regulates the marketplace in a wide variety of ways in the interest of creating and maintaining a healthy economy.

Social Regulation

The national government also uses social regulatory policy—which aims to protect the public's health and safety—to safeguard workers, consumers, and the environment from the potential harm created by the competitive quest for profits in the marketplace. Like business regulation, social regulation has an economic impact because it increases the costs of doing business.

EARLY SOCIAL REGULATION Scholars see precedents for social regulation in two 1906 laws that protected *public* health—the Pure Food and Drug Act and the Meat Inspection Act. Upton Sinclair's descriptions of the dangerous and unsanitary conditions in the Chicago meatpacking industry in his novel *The Jungle* motivated President Theodore Roosevelt (1901–1909) to sign those two laws. The Pure Food and Drug Act created the Food and Drug Administration (FDA) and charged it with testing all foods and drugs produced for human consumption. It also requires individuals to present prescriptions from licensed physicians to purchase certain drugs and mandates the use of warning labels on habit-forming drugs. The Meat Inspection Act requires government inspection of animals that are slaughtered and processed for human consumption and establishes standards of cleanliness for slaughterhouses and meat processing plants.

The federal government first addressed working conditions that jeopardized *workers'* health when it enacted the Fair Labor Standards Act (FLSA) in 1938. The FLSA established standards for a legal workweek, overtime pay for those working more than the standard workweek, minimum wages, record keeping of workers' hours, and limits on child labor. President Franklin D. Roosevelt characterized the law as the "most far-reaching, far-sighted program to the benefit of workers ever adopted."[8]

CONSUMER AND ENVIRONMENTAL PROTECTION In the 1960s, the government focused anew on growing concerns about product quality and safety. In his 1965 book *Unsafe at Any Speed,* attorney and consumer advocate Ralph Nader warned that "a great problem of contemporary life is how to control the power of economic interests which ignore the harmful effects of their applied science and technology."[9] Although Nader's book targeted the unsafe cars rolling off the assembly lines of the U.S. auto industry, his warning was equally relevant to the countless American industries that were discharging chemicals and toxins into the environment. Nader's book ignited a consumer safety movement, and a related environmental movement was born with the first Earth Day in 1970.

Lobbying by concerned citizens and interest groups led to passage of the Environmental Protection Act of 1970 and the Consumer Product Safety Act (CPSA) of 1973. These far-reaching federal laws aimed to regulate business practices that threatened consumers' health and safety as well as the environment. The federal Consumer Product Safety Commission (CPSC), created through the CPSA, is charged by law with protecting the public from unreasonable risk of injury associated with more than 15,000 consumer products,

> Employee Raul Quecada places a "No Sale" sign on a Toyota a day after Toyota Motor Corporation announced it would stop sales of some of its top-selling vehicles to fix a sticking gas pedal problem. This action followed several voluntary safety recalls Toyota announced (September 2007, October 2009, January 2010) after the number of gas pedal problems sparked media attention and concerns among the public. In February 2010, the National Traffic and Safety Administration, the regulatory agency to which automakers must report defects, initiated an investigation to determine if Toyota conducted the three recalls in a timely manner.

including toys, products for children, products for inside and outside the home, and products made for sports and recreation. The CPSA can recall such products if it deems them unsafe, just as the FDA can recall food and prescription medicines it judges to be unsafe. The CPSC and the FDA post recall information on their Web sites (www.cpsc .gov/; www.fda.gov/opacom/Enforce.html).

The financial and economic free fall that began in 2007 sparked a national conversation about the need for additional regulation of the financial and banking industries. In 2009, President Obama and Treasury Secretary Timothy Geithner proposed restructuring the numerous existing federal agencies that regulate the financial banking industries. In addition, they proposed the creation of a new agency to oversee financial products sold to consumers to protect consumers and the economy. In 2010, Congress and President Obama created the Bureau of Consumer Financial Protection.

THE COSTS OF REGULATION Market regulation has unquestionably lowered the risk of harm to citizens and the environment caused by marketplace competition. It also has cushioned economic downfalls. But the burden of government regulations has driven up the cost of doing business, and in the end, consumers pay for this cost. In many industries, this increased cost poses greater problems for smaller firms than for larger ones. The higher costs caused by regulation may also put U.S. industries and firms at a competitive disadvantage in the global marketplace, because many other countries do not impose regulations. Therefore the production costs of firms in other countries are often lower than those in the United States.

The lack of regulations imposed by governments in other nations is a growing concern in the United States. The FDA and the CPSC are recalling numerous products manufactured in foreign countries, and even some products manufactured in the United States that use ingredients or components from foreign sources. Because of these concerns, trade policy and the interdependence of the global economy are prominent contemporary issues.

Trade Policy in the Global Economy

The next time you are shopping, try to purchase only American-made products. Is it possible? Stores in the United States offer products that are domestic (that is, American-made) as well as imported (made overseas by American or foreign companies). Moreover, many American-made products have imported components and ingredients. For example, U.S. International Trade Commission data show that ingredients for food products are imported from more than one hundred countries.[10] Today, marketplaces in every country offer products grown and produced in countries from throughout the world. Hence national economies are integrated and interdependent—holistically forming the **global economy.**

To navigate in this global economy, each nation has its own **trade policy**—a collection of tax laws and regulations that support the country's international commerce. In addition, international organizations whose mission is to establish trade rules for all nations to follow have created a global trade policy. The goal of trade policy, like the other economic policies we have discussed, is ostensibly to promote prosperous economies.

global economy
the worldwide economy created by the integration and interdependence of national economies

trade policy
a collection of tax laws and regulations that supports the country's international commerce

Trade Policy: Protectionist or Free Trade?

A government's trade policy takes one of two basic forms: free trade or protectionism. **Protectionist trade policy** aims at protecting domestic producers and businesses from foreign competition through tariffs and nontariff trade barriers. A **tariff** is a special tax on imported goods. **Nontariff trade barriers** include government social and business regulations as well as government **subsidies**—tax breaks or another kind of financial support that encourages behaviors the government deems beneficial to the public good. Most subsidies are given to producers or distributors of goods to promote economic growth. Proponents of national government subsidies to U.S. farmers argue that to decrease these subsidies would place the farmers at a competitive disadvantage because European farmers receive even larger subsidies from their governments. Regulations include restrictions such as limits on the number of imports allowed into the country and bans on the sale of imports that the government deems unsafe. For example, in 2007 the national government blocked imports of wheat gluten from a company in China after the FDA recalled a brand of pet food manufactured in Canada that contained this wheat gluten. The pet food caused cats and dogs throughout the United States to become ill and even to die.

From the 1790s until the 1930s, protectionism was the aim of U.S. trade policy. As the first secretary of the treasury, Alexander Hamilton argued successfully that taxes on imported goods could be set high enough to protect American-made products in the domestic marketplace. In 1930, even as the American economy was failing, Congress hiked tariffs 20 percent—so high that it set off an international tariff war. This tariff hike fueled the Great Depression, whose economic toll was global in scope.

After World War II, the United States and its international partners gradually shifted toward a **free trade policy,** which aims at lowering or eliminating tariffs and nontariff barriers to trade. Free trade policies decrease the costs of bringing products to markets throughout the world and, in this way, open markets to a greater diversity of products and brisker competition. When other nations eliminate tariffs, American companies can participate in the global marketplace at a lower cost. These opportunities encourage an increase in the supply of U.S. goods and thus lead to an expansion of the U.S. economy. By the same token, when the United States eliminates its tariffs, more foreign products make their way into the American marketplace, increasing the diversity of consumer goods and producer competition and decreasing consumer prices in the United States.

International Trade Agreements

In 1947, the United States and twenty-three other nations signed the General Agreement on Tariffs and Trade (GATT). This multilateral agreement on guidelines for conducting international trade had three basic objectives. First, the signatory countries would not discriminate against one another in trade matters. Second, the signatory countries would work toward eliminating all tariff and regulatory barriers to trade among their countries. Third, the signatory countries would consult and negotiate with one another to resolve any trade conflicts or damages caused by trading activities of another signatory country. Through multilateral negotiations, the GATT established the guidelines for international trade and resolved trade disputes from 1947 to 1995.

Then in 1995, the World Trade Organization (WTO) came into being. The WTO continues the GATT's advocacy of free trade and punishment of protectionism. Specifically, the WTO monitors adherence to international trade rules and resolves charges of rule violations raised by any of its over 130 member countries. The WTO Ministerial Conference meets every two years to discuss and deliberate on international trade rules. The meetings have become magnets for massive and sometimes violent demonstrations by protesters from around the world who believe that free trade is harming the environment, impeding human development in developing countries, and hurting the poor in all countries.

protectionist trade policy
establishment of trade barriers to protect domestic goods from foreign competition

tariff
a special tax on imported goods

nontariff trade barriers
business and social regulations as well as subsidies aimed at creating a competitive advantage in trade

subsidy
a tax break or another kind of financial support that encourages behaviors the government deems beneficial to the public good

free trade policy
elimination of tariffs and nontariff trade barriers so that international trade is expanded

Opponents of free trade argue that the deregulation of nontrade barriers has exacerbated deplorable working conditions, child labor problems, and poverty. (See "Thinking Critically About Democracy.")

In the 1990s, bipartisan support for free trade in the U.S. Congress produced regional trade agreements such as the North American Free Trade Agreement (NAFTA), which the United States, Canada, and Mexico signed in 1993. NAFTA eliminated barriers to trade and financial investments across the economies of the three nations. Yet by the beginning of the twenty-first century, congressional legislators' concerns about possible damage to living standards and the health of the global environment, which many argue are caused by free trade, were growing, as was the nation's **trade deficit** (a negative balance of trade in which imports exceed exports).

trade deficit
a negative balance of trade in which imports exceed exports

Activists throughout the world are advocating policies to limit some of the harms they ascribe to free trade. Environmental groups fight for environmental protections to be included in international trade agreements. The International Labor Organization—a United Nations agency that promotes internationally recognized human and worker rights—advocates for bans on forced labor and child labor, prohibitions against discrimination in personnel decisions and policies, and safeguards for the rights of workers to organize and bargain collectively with employers, all of which are forms of social regulation. Groups concerned about human development worry that free trade agreements ignore the economic status of small family farmers, artisans whose goods are sold in local markets, and poor people in general. In addition to these global concerns, American activists look closer to home, concerned about the impact of free trade on American living standards.

The U.S. Economy, the Global Economy, and the American Dream Today

Between 2000 and 2006, according to traditional measures of economic health—GDP, unemployment rates, and rates of inflation—the U.S. economy was expanding; however, it was the weakest economic expansion since World War II.[11] During the same period, in American households, the real median household income decreased[12] and the poverty rate crept up to 12.3 percent.[13] Moreover, income inequality grew. According to the U.S. Census Bureau, by 2007 the bottom quintile (20 percent of the population) possessed just 3.4 percent of the total national income, while the top quintile held 50.5 percent, the largest share of the national income held by the top quintile since 1967.[14] Alan Greenspan, the renowned economist who chaired the Federal Reserve from 1987 to 2005, testified to Congress's Joint Economic Committee in 2005 about this paradox of a growing economy that disproportionately benefits those at the top: "This is not the type of thing which a democratic society—a capitalist democratic society—can really accept without addressing." He even suggested that this income gap seriously threatened the stability of the U.S. economy.[15]

Indeed, in 2007 the economy began to stagnate. The Fed used monetary policy to try to stimulate the economy, cutting interest rates six times between September 2007 and March 2008. However, by February 2008, some in the media and the government were forecasting an economic downturn as consumer prices increased at the same time that economic growth (as measured by change in the GDP) was stagnating.[16] Senator Christopher Dodd (D-Connecticut), chairman of the Senate Banking Committee, stated, "The current economic situation is more than merely a 'slowdown' or a 'downturn.' It is a crisis of confidence among consumers and investors."[17] This "crisis in confidence" sparked a call for the Fed to increase its regulation of the banking and financial investment industries in spring 2008.

President George W. Bush and Congress attempted to use fiscal policy to address this economic situation. In February 2008, they approved tax rebates totaling $168 billion and tax cuts for select businesses. Then in October 2008, as we have seen, President Bush signed the $700 billion Emergency Economic Stabilization Act, allowing the federal government to buy assets from the biggest banks to shore them up and restore confidence in the financial system.

THINKING CRITICALLY ABOUT DEMOCRACY

IS FREE TRADE MERELY A RACE TO THE BOTTOM?

The Issue: Since World War II, world powers—including governments and influential nongovernmental organizations (NGOs)—have worked to expand international trade. Although the founders of this globalization movement envisioned a "race to the top" with respect to living standards, today a global debate rages on the pros and cons of free trade. Supporters of free trade argue that it is the path out of poverty. Opponents insist that free trade has set off a brutal "race to the bottom" because of market failures.

Yes: Free trade sets off a race to the bottom. Free trade encourages today's corporations to move their jobs to countries where business and social regulation is weak or nonexistent. Consequently, the workers in producer nations lose jobs to lower-paid foreign workers toiling in deplorable conditions. Foreign plants, with weak or nonexistent environmental regulations to follow, also create major environmental hazards that spill across national borders.

No: Free trade spreads wealth. Free trade opens new markets for products from all countries. New markets increase demand for products, hence creating jobs in the producing countries. As consumers enjoy a greater variety of products at lower costs, the standard of living improves, especially for lower-income households. History shows that in the long term, this type of economic transition—economic development—improves the quality of life for workers as everyone benefits financially.

Other approaches: Creative capitalism can ameliorate a race to the bottom. Under creative capitalism, governments, businesses, and nonprofit organizations work together to ensure that current global economic forces benefit profit-making corporations while also addressing societal problems. For example, the (RED) Campaign is a coordinated effort in which corporations have pledged a percentage of their profits from select products to purchase medications needed to fight AIDS in Africa. Creative capitalism does not tinker with free trade, but it does encourage corporations to develop a social consciousness for which consumers reward them. The profits of free trade benefit the poor as well as the corporations.

What do you think?

1. Are U.S. companies that create jobs in foreign countries interested in improving those countries' working conditions and pay and in protecting the environment? Explain.

2. In the long term, what effect will a global laissez-faire policy have on the quality of life of the world's population as a whole?

3. How can the benefits of global economic development decrease income inequality?

In his FY 2010 executive budget (published in February 2009), President Barack Obama summarized the economic status of the nation and the actions his administration planned to take in response to it: "We start 2009 in the midst of a crisis unlike any we have seen in our lifetime. Our economy is in a deep recession that threatens to be deeper and longer than any since the Great Depression. . . . The time has come to usher in a new era—a new era of responsibility in which we act not only to save and create new jobs, but also to lay a new foundation of growth upon which we can renew the promise of America." Obama then highlighted the planned investments in clean energy, education, health care, and infrastructure (such as roads, bridges, schools, and broadband lines) that are part of the American Recovery and Reinvestment Act (2009). The hope was that these investments would maintain and create jobs. He also discussed the need for government to be more transparent and accountable to the people, beginning with the necessity of cutting deficit spending.

In February 2010, a year after the enactment of the ARRA, while Congress was debating the content of proposed new stimulus packages, economists, government officials, and citizens were assessing the effect of the 2009 stimulus package. Because most people worry about being employed during poor economic times, many people focused on the national unemployment rate, which was close to 10 percent. Critics of the ARRA claimed this high rate of unemployment was proof that the stimulus package did not work—it did not save or create jobs. However, others argued that without the ARRA's tax cuts and increased

TAKE YOUR CHILD TO WORK DAY 2009

UNEMPLOYMENT

Source: Chan Lowe/South Florida Sun-Sentinel.

spending, the unemployment rate would have been even higher. In addition, by the end of 2009, even though salaries and wages on average had decreased, consumer spending was up. Corporate spending had surged by the end of 2009, as tax credits for corporate investment were expiring. Clearly, the Great Recession was not over, but there was little doubt among most economists that the U.S. economy would have declined even further without the 2009 ARRA.[18]

The recession, which began in 2007 and deepened throughout 2008 and 2009, was a global phenomenon. Rising unemployment, shrinking confidence in financial institutions, decreasing availability of credit and hence decreasing investment, and slow economic growth were economic realities in countries throughout the world. In November 2008, leaders of twenty countries met in Washington, D.C., for an emergency economic summit and agreed to work together to address the global recession. Central banks in European and Asian countries took actions to encourage investment and to shore up financial institutions. Many nations also put in place stimulus packages—taxing and spending plans—to combat the worst global economic crisis since the Great Depression.

It was during the Great Depression that historian James Truslow Adams coined the term "American dream." In his book *The Epic of America* (1931), Adams argued that what made America a unique nation was its inhabitants' "dream of a better, richer, and happier life" for all citizens based on equal "opportunity for each according to his [or her] ability or achievement."[19] For many, the American dream has come to mean owning a home, providing their children with good educational opportunities so they can advance in life, and saving for retirement. For others, it means being rich. Today, Americans tell pollsters that they are living better than their parents did. At the same time, Americans tell pollsters that today's children will *not* be able to live better than *their* parents did.[20] Indeed, *New York Times* columnist Bob Herbert summarized several studies of the millennial generation (those born between 1980 and 2000) by stating that it "is in danger of being left out of the American dream—the first American generation to do less well economically than their parents."[21] Is the American dream doing better economically than your parents? Is it being rich? Or is the American dream living in a nation that has a stable, healthy economy and an equal opportunity to achieve (measured by home ownership, high levels of education, and comfortable retirement) according to your ability and effort? If the American dream is the last, can government policies—fiscal, monetary, regulatory, and trade—ensure a healthy national economy in today's interdependent global economy? In addition, can government domestic policies—which we discuss in Chapter 16—ensure equal opportunity for citizens to achieve according to their ability and effort?

CONCLUSION

THINKING CRITICALLY ABOUT WHAT'S NEXT IN ECONOMIC POLICY

Governments throughout the world seek to maintain healthy economies using economic policy. U.S. economic policy comprises taxing and spending policies (fiscal policy), monetary policy, regulatory policy, and trade policy. Today, the economic decisions made by the president, Congress, and the Fed are influenced by the realities of the global economy. Just as the economic policy decisions made in other countries throughout the world can affect the economic health of the United States, the economic policies made by the U.S. national government can affect the economic health of nations all over the globe. What impact will continuing globalization have on the U.S. government's ability to maintain a healthy national economy?

The global recession that began in 2007 has reinvigorated long-standing debates on the proper role of government in maintaining a healthy economy. As the recession developed, the national government attempted to address its immediate effects with limited tax cuts and spending increases to shore up unemployment and health benefits, and to protect and create jobs. In addition, taxpayers became partial owners of some businesses when the government bought assets of collapsing businesses. However, many politicians, economists, and citizens argue that the nation needs major changes to current fiscal, monetary, and regulatory policies to ensure long-term economic health. People are again beginning to call for a constitutional amendment mandating a balanced budget. Will national elected and appointed officials enact major tax, spending, and regulatory reforms in the wake of the Great Recession?

The viability of the American dream depends on a healthy national economy. Even before the current recession began, income inequality was growing. The gap between those who have the largest share of the nation's wealth and everyone else has expanded in the last few decades. Will your generation and future generations be able to achieve the American dream?

Summary

1. Economic Health and the American Dream
Though work ethic and education level influence personal income, a healthy national economy is essential to the ability of people to live a financially secure, happy, and healthy life—to realize the American dream. The health of the economy influences the availability of jobs with adequate levels of compensation (salaries and benefits).

2. The Nature of the American Economy
The national government's economic policy is aimed at establishing and maintaining a healthy economy so that it can raise the money necessary to fulfill its mission of serving the people. Because the government implements many policies that encourage, and sometimes mandate, certain business practices in the interest of creating and maintaining a healthy economy, the United States has what is known as a regulated capitalist economy.

3. Economic Theories That Shape Economic Policy
The national government's efforts to achieve and maintain a healthy economy have expanded as lawmakers have embraced various economic theories, among them Keynesian economics, supply-side economics, and monetarism. The specific policies implemented by the government depend on the particular economic theories government officials adopt. In recent decades, Democrats and Republicans have followed different economic theories, with the result that taxing, spending, and regulatory policies have frequently shifted.

4. Measuring Economic Health
Traditional measures of economic health include worker productivity, GDP, rate of inflation, and rate of unemployment. Other measures include real median household income, income inequality, rate of poverty, and the Human Development Index. Together, they can be used to assess how well a prosperous national economy enables its citizens to live the American dream. Unfortunately, many times this diversity of measures yields conflicting assessments of economic health: the nation's economy may be growing at the same time that the financial status of households is stagnating or even declining.

5. Fiscal Policy and Its Impact on the Health of the Economy
Taxing and spending decisions by the president and Congress influence how much money consumers have to spend, save, and invest; how much profit firms make and how much they have to invest in expanding business; and how much the government has to spend in order

to serve the people. Deficit spending is a persistent reality of U.S. fiscal policy, creating economic problems in the long term.

6. Monetary Policy and the Federal Reserve System

The Fed, directed by a group of appointed officials, works to keep inflation and unemployment low by regulating the amount of money in circulation in the economy. Aimed at creating and maintaining price stability, monetary policy is a component of U.S. economic policy.

7. Regulatory Policy

By the late 1800s, the laissez-faire ideal concerning government regulation of marketplace competition and business practices was clearly not the reality. Today, business regulation (to ensure competition) and social regulation (to protect workers, consumers, and the environment) are pervasive components of the U.S. economy, despite ongoing calls by business, some economists, and politicians (more apt to be Republicans than Democrats) to deregulate.

8. Trade Policy in the Global Economy

Protectionist trade policy dominated the United States until after World War II. Then free trade policy became the goal of international agreements and U.S. trade policy. Today, debate continues over the domestic and global effects (positive and negative) of free trade policy in the global economy.

9. The U.S. Economy, the Global Economy, and the American Dream Today

The recent global recession, the worst since the Great Depression of the 1930s, has sparked conversations about the nature of the American dream and whether or not it is achievable in the global economy.

Key Terms

American dream 464

balanced budget 467

budget authority 475

budget deficit 477

budget reconciliation 476

budget surplus 477

business regulation 480

concurrent budget
  resolution 476

consumer price index
  (CPI) 470

continuing resolution 476

deficit spending 467

depression 468

deregulation 469

discretionary spending 475

economic boom 468

economic policy 464

economy 465

executive budget 476

fiscal policy 468

fiscal year (FY) 473

free trade policy 483

global economy 482

gross domestic product
  (GDP) 470

household income 472

Human Development Index
  (HDI) 472

income inequality 467

inflation 469

Keynesian economics 468

laissez-faire 466

mandatory spending 475

median household income 472

monetarism 469

monetary policy 479

national debt 469

nontariff trade barriers 483

poverty 472

poverty rate 472

poverty thresholds 472

progressive tax 474

proportional tax
  (flat tax) 474

protectionist trade policy 483

pure capitalist economy 466

real income 472

recession 468

regressive tax 474

regulated capitalist economy
  (mixed economy) 466

social regulation 480

subsidy 483

supply-side economics 469

tariff 483

tax base 465

tax expenditures 474

trade deficit 484

trade policy 482

For Review

1. What is the American dream? Describe one impact each of the following national policies can have on the American dream: tax policy, spending policy, business regulation, social regulation, monetary policy, trade policy.

2. What distinguishes a pure capitalist economy from a regulated capitalist economy?

3. Differentiate among Keynesian economics, supply-side economics, and monetarism.

4. Explain at least four measures of economic health.

5. What is fiscal policy and who makes it?

6. What is monetary policy and who makes it?

7. Distinguish between business regulation and social regulation. Indicate how each type of regulation affects the economy.

8. Differentiate between the goals as well as the techniques of free trade policy and protectionist trade policy.

9. What is the health of the U.S. economy as well as the American dream at the beginning of the twenty-first century?

For Critical Thinking and Discussion

1. If you were president of the United States and wanted to balance the annual budget, what programs' cost cuts do you think you could get American taxpayers to support? What tax increases or new taxes do you think you could get American taxpayers to support? Explain your choices.

2. Consider your family's financial situation. What economic policy would you propose the national government implement to improve your family's financial situation? Explain.

3. Which type of tax do you think is the most fair, progressive, proportional, or regressive? Explain your choice.

4. If the national government deregulates with regard to environmental protection, product safety, and/or working conditions, would there be negative consequences? Give some examples, or explain why there would not be any.

5. Some politicians have suggested that a flat income tax of about 17 percent could raise about the same amount of revenue for the national government as the current progressive income tax and should replace it. Politically speaking, who would support such a proposal, and who would oppose it?

PRACTICE QUIZ

MULTIPLE CHOICE: Choose the lettered item that answers the question correctly.

1. The economic theory that advocates the use of fiscal policy to create and maintain a healthy economy is called
   a. Keynesian economics.
   b. laissez-faire economics.
   c. monetarism.
   d. supply-side economics.

2. Which of the following is *not* included in the mandatory spending category of the national government?
   a. debt payments
   b. education
   c. Medicare
   d. Social Security

3. The officials that approve fiscal policy are
   a. Congress (on its own).
   b. Congress and the president.
   c. Congress, the president, and the Fed.
   d. the Fed (on its own).

4. The officials that approve monetary policy are
   a. Congress (on its own).
   b. Congress and the president.
   c. Congress, the president, and the Fed.
   d. the Fed (on its own).

5. The policy that decreases the costs of bringing products to markets throughout the world by lowering or eliminating tariffs and deregulating is called
   a. free trade policy.
   b. monetary policy.
   c. protectionist trade policy.
   d. regulatory policy.

6. The policy in which the national government engages to protect consumers, workers, and the environment from the harm of marketplace competition is called
   a. business regulation.
   b. deregulation.
   c. protectionist trade policy.
   d. social regulation.

7. Based on its impact on taxpayers' income, what type of tax is the state sales tax?
   a. flat
   b. progressive
   c. proportional
   d. regressive

8. The largest revenue source for the national government is
   a. corporate income taxes.
   b. import taxes.
   c. individual income taxes.
   d. social insurance taxes.

9. During what president's administrations did the national government first adopt Keynesian economic principles to create and maintain a healthy national economy?
   a. George Washington
   b. Franklin Delano Roosevelt
   c. Ronald Reagan
   d. George W. Bush

10. During what president's administration did the national government adopt the American Recovery and Reinvestment Act to address a great recession?
    a. Franklin Delano Roosevelt
    b. Ronald Reagan
    c. George W. Bush
    d. Barack Obama

FILL IN THE BLANKS.

11. When it spends more money than it collects in taxes, the government is engaging in _____ .

12. _____ refers to the rising prices of consumer goods, which means the value of the dollar has decreased.

13. The date on which the national 2011 fiscal year (FY 2011) began is _____ .

14. The _____ is a nongovernmental organization that advocates for free trade policy, monitors adherence to international trade rules, and resolves charges of trade rule violation raised by its member countries.

15. The collection of national tax policies and spending policies is referred to as _____ policy.

RESOURCES FOR RESEARCH AND ACTION

Internet Resources

American Enterprise Institute (AEI)
www.aei.org The AEI sponsors research on government policy and economic policy and advocates limited government involvement in the marketplace.

American Institute for Economic Research
www.aier.org This nonprofit research and educational organization provides studies and information on economic and financial issues.

Bureau of Economic Analysis (BEA)
www.bea.doc.gov The BEA, an agency in the Department of Commerce, produces and disseminates data on regional, national, and international economies.

Economic Policy Institute
http://epinet.org This nonprofit organization aims to broaden public debate on strategies to achieve a prosperous and fair economy.

Office of Management and Budget (OMB)
www.whitehouse.gov/omb The OMB's site has links to the most recent executive budget and historical budget documents.

U.S. Census Bureau
www.census.gov The Census Bureau, a bureau in the Department of Commerce, collects and disseminates data about the people and economy of the nation.

Internet Activism

Public Citizen, founded by Ralph Nader in 1971, is a national, nonprofit, public interest organization engaged in research and advocacy on a multitude of issues, including reform of the financial system, protections for consumers and workers, equitable trade, and globalization. To learn more about these economic issues and the role you can play in Public Citizen's lobbying efforts, visit **www.facebook.com/publiccitizen** or **www.citizen.org**.

Twitter
http://twitter.com/OnSafety Get notified about U.S. Consumer Product Safety Commission's safety alerts and recalls.

YouTube
www.youtube.com/watch?v=6_7jaEO3pPs The landmark National Debt Clock in New York City is running out of room as the debt expands to fourteen-digit numbers.

Facebook
www.facebook.com/taxfoundation The Tax Foundation is a non-partisan, nonprofit research institution founded in 1937 to educate Americans about sound tax policy at all levels of government. Its economic and policy analysis is guided by the principles of neutrality, simplicity, transparency, and stability.

Recommended Readings

Derber, Charles. *People Before Profit.* New York: Picador, 2003. A disturbing analysis of globalization to date with a blueprint for a new form of globalization that will lead to a more stable and just global community.

Lieberman, Carl. *Making Economic Policy.* Englewood Cliffs, NJ: Prentice Hall, 1991. A concise yet comprehensive overview of economic policies, including spending policy, tax policy, monetary policy, economic regulation, and economic subsidies.

Schick, Allen. *The Federal Budget.* Washington, DC: Brookings Institute, 2000. A comprehensive, in-depth consideration of the national budget process.

Woodward, Bob. *Maestro: Greenspan's Fed and the American Boom.* New York: Simon & Schuster, 2000. A probing look into how the Fed operated under the leadership of Alan Greenspan from 1987 to 2000. The effect of the evolving global economy on the economic health of the United States is an intriguing part of Woodward's account.

Movies of Interest

Cinderella Man (2005)
Based on the life of prizefighter Jim Braddock, this film movingly depicts the common person's struggle to survive the Great Depression and the hopes and inspiration that one person's rise from the bottom can evoke in the population at large.

Enron: The Smartest Guys in the Room (2005)
Based on the best-selling book of the same title, this documentary spotlights the human drama of Enron's fall—the biggest corporate scandal in American history—including the company's collapse, the elimination of thousands of jobs, and the loss of $60 billion in market value and $2 billion in pension plans.

Commanding Heights: The Battle for the World Economy (2002)
This documentary exploration of the political side of today's global economy looks at the people, ideas, and events that fostered the liberalization of trade policies around the globe.

CHAPTER

16

Domestic
Policy

THEN

In the 1930s, radical new federal government policies created a safety net that enabled economically distressed citizens to provide for their basic needs.

NOW

The federal government faces a host of domestic policy issues, from the high cost of maintaining the safety net to environmental degradation, scarce energy supplies, homeland security threats, and calls for immigration reform.

NEXT

Will global warming and worldwide environmental degradation force U.S. policy makers to sign international treaties?

Will the perpetually increasing costs of income security programs and health care force U.S. policy makers to enact major legislative reforms?

Will demographic change owing to high immigration today bring new issues to tomorrow's domestic policy agenda?

In this chapter, we survey national domestic policies that are most directly related to the basic needs of a sustainable, safe country where citizens can live healthy lives in pursuit of their happiness.

FIRST, we review the role of *citizen engagement* in establishing *domestic policy.*

SECOND, we consider the *tools of domestic policy,* the array of public programs by which the government provides for citizens' basic needs.

THIRD, we look at *environmental policy,* the government's efforts to preserve the environment, conserve scarce resources, and control pollution.

FOURTH, we examine *energy policy,* specifically looking at the problems of rising energy consumption and Americans' reliance on nonrenewable fossil fuels.

FIFTH, we consider *income security programs*—in particular, safety-net policies for citizens in financial need.

SIXTH, we probe *health care policy,* where soaring costs are prompting ongoing research and experimentation with new models.

SEVENTH, we discuss *homeland security* policy, which is directed at preventing and responding to natural and man-made disasters.

EIGHTH, we examine legislators' efforts at reforming *immigration policy* to address citizens' concerns over the masses of unauthorized immigrants streaming into the country.

safety net
a collection of public policies ensuring that the basic physiological needs of citizens are met

According to the Declaration of

Independence and the U.S. Constitution, American government must ensure a just and safe society in which citizens can live their lives freely, in pursuit of their happiness. Essential to the achievement of these goals are the preservation and protection of the natural environment so that future generations can enjoy a quality of life comparable to today's. And implicit in these founding documents is that government policy makers must recognize the long-term impact of their policies, as well as their lack of policies, on citizens, their communities, and the nation at large.

In our federal system, when citizens bring societal problems to the attention of government officials, the ensuing legislative and public debates typically revolve around several key questions. First, government officials must decide whether the problem is one that government should address. If the answer to that fundamental question is yes, then additional questions follow. What level of government has legal authority to address the problem? What level of government has the financial resources? What is the most cost-effective means to deal with the problem? Beyond the expected positive effects of a policy's implementation, what unexpected costs and negative consequences might occur?

Citizen Engagement and Domestic Policy

The Constitution established a government that is by and for the people. Previous chapters have explored the many ways in which individuals and groups engage with government officials and political processes to influence what government does and does not do. Yet a widespread national affliction is *NIMBY,* or "not-in-my-backyard" syndrome. People with NIMBY syndrome decline to participate in politics until a government action or inaction threatens them directly. Lobbying government officials is a common first step in citizen engagement, and it may be as basic as making a phone call, sending an e-mail, or writing a letter. Citizens may also use lawsuits to press government officials to focus on issues of concern and to address them through policy making.

Complicating the work of U.S. policy makers, the diversity of citizens' needs and expectations for government action means that almost every call for government action sparks a call for either a different action or no action. The plurality of citizens' needs, individuals' constantly changing priorities, and their range of political ideologies make for an ongoing public conversation and legislative debate over which policies warrant government spending and who will pay the taxes to cover the bills. Democrats and Republicans frequently disagree on these matters. Democrats typically are liberal in inclination and tend to support **safety nets**—programs ensuring that every citizen's basic physiological needs (food, water, shelter, health care, and a clean environment) are met. Republicans more commonly have a conservative ideology and focus more on public safety and national security issues. Ultimately, elected officials—whose career goal, after all, is to get reelected—find it much easier to add new policies and programs, and consequently to drive up government expenses, than to eliminate programs or to decrease program costs.

As we have seen in preceding chapters, the government makes policy in several ways. For one, Congress and the president set policy by approving *authorization bills,* which establish a policy and identify who will implement it, and *appropriation bills,* which authorize the spending of national revenue. Federal, state, local, and shadow bureaucrats also make policy, through both the administrative rule-making process and their daily use of administrative discretion. In addition, the presidential power of the executive order amounts to making policy, because it gives the president the authority to tell bureaucrats how to carry out a national policy. Finally, the federal judiciary, through the various cases that come before the courts, has policy-making power by virtue of its authority to declare unconstitutional the laws made by the legislative and executive branches of national, state, and local government (the authority of judicial review). The courts also resolve conflicts over the meaning and proper implementation of laws. In summary, each of the three branches of the national government has policy-making authority that it uses to fulfill the government's constitutionally established mission to serve present and future generations.

Since 1788 (when the states ratified the U.S. Constitution), the national government's scope of responsibility for addressing domestic matters has gradually expanded as citizens and groups have lobbied to press for their interests. Federal authority now covers a diverse collection of public policies. Today's national budget lists seventeen superfunctions of the federal government (see Table 16.1).[1] The numbers in the table show that most federal government functions and most government spending are directed at *domestic* policy matters: 72.5 percent for domestic policies and 21.0 percent for foreign and defense policies. The remaining percentage pays the interest on the national debt incurred by past borrowing to cover deficit spending.

Because it would be impossible for us to examine every domestic policy program, we limit our focus in this chapter to a subset of national homeland policies. Specifically, we concentrate on policies that address the most basic of human needs and are essential to sustaining life, liberty, and opportunities to pursue happiness: environmental, energy, income security, health care, and homeland security policies. We also look at the controversial policy

TABLE 16.1

National Budget Superfunctions and Expenditures: Total Proposed National Budget Authority, 2011—$3,833,861 million ($3.8 trillion)

Defense and Foreign Policy ($803,940 million; 21.0% of budget outlays)*	National defense ($749,748 million; 19.5%)
	International affairs ($54,192 million; 1.4%)
Domestic Policy ($2,779,212 million; 72.5%)	General science, space, and technology ($31,554 million; 0.8%)
	Energy ($24,863 million; 0.6%)
	Natural resources and environment ($42,537 million; 1.1%)
	Agriculture ($25,590 million; 0.7%)
	Commerce and housing credit ($22,127 million; 0.6%)
	Transportation ($104,189 million; 2.7%)
	Community and regional development ($31,973 million; 0.8%)
	Education, training, employment, and social services ($126,399 million; 3.3%)
	Health ($400,661 million; 10.5%)
	Medicare ($497,341 million; 13.0%)
	Income security ($595,005 million; 15.5%)
	Social Security ($736,284 million; 19.2%)
	Veterans benefits and services ($124,539 million; 3.3%)
	Administration of justice ($57,280 million; 1.5%)
	General government ($27,670 million; 0.7%)
Net Interest ($250,709 million; 6.5%)	

*Numbers in parentheses represent (1) total outlay for each function and (2) percentage of total budget outlay, rounded to the nearest tenth of a percent.

SOURCE: Budget of the United States Fiscal Year 2011, Historical Tables, Table 3.1, www.whitehouse.gov/omb/budget/Historicals/.

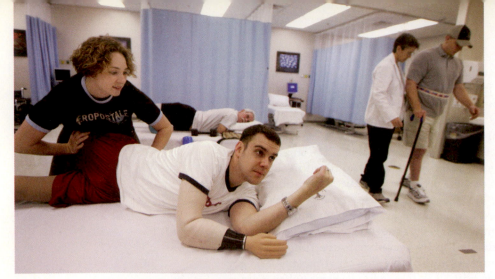

> Jayme Bozik assists her husband, U.S. Army Sargeant Joey Bozik, with his physical therapy at Walter Reed Army Medical Center in Washington, D. C. The national government hires doctors, nurses, physical therapists, and other health professions to work in military hospitals, providing medical services to injured military personnel.

area of immigration, defined by some as a national security concern, by others as an economic issue, and by still others as a humanitarian cause reflecting the United States' roots and highest ideals.

Tools of Domestic Policy

The national government attempts to address citizens' problems and to provide benefits and services to the people by using various policy tools. Domestic policy tools include laws and regulations, direct provision of public goods, cash transfer payments, loans, loan guarantees, insurance, and contracting-out the provision of public goods to nongovernmental entities.

Laws and Regulations

At the federal, state, and local levels alike, government strives to accomplish its domestic policy goals by creating laws with which individuals and organizations must comply. These include environmental laws, national narcotics laws, and laws addressing work standards and conditions. Many laws assign administrative agencies the authority to establish the specific rules, regulations, and standards that are essential to effective implementation of the laws.

The overwhelming majority of people and organizations comply with most laws and regulations. But because some individuals and organizations fail to do so, the government must monitor compliance. For example, the government hires inspectors to monitor adherence to rules that limit industrial plants' emissions of pollutants, and hires police officers to monitor compliance with laws that prohibit narcotic drug use. The government counts on citizens, interest groups, and the media to assist in overseeing compliance—and in reporting violators.

Direct Provision of Public Goods

direct provision
the policy tool whereby the government that creates a policy hires public servants to provide the service

In addition to creating rules of behavior through law and regulations, governments provide services and benefits. Using the domestic policy tool of **direct provision,** governments hire public servants—bureaucrats who receive a government paycheck—to dispense the service. For example, veterans hospitals hire doctors, nurses, and physical therapists to administer health care to veterans; the U.S. Postal Service hires mail carriers, postal clerks, and postal processing machine operators to deliver billions of pieces of mail each week. To provide for the country's common defense, the national government employs millions of military personnel. The workers hired by the national government to provide these services directly are on the payroll of the national government.

Cash Transfers

cash transfer
the direct provision of cash (in forms including checks, debit cards, and tax breaks) to eligible individuals or to providers of goods or services to eligible individuals

in-kind assistance
a cash transfer in which the government pays cash to those who provide goods or services to eligible individuals

Another instrument of government policy is the **cash transfer**—the direct provision of cash (in various forms) to eligible individuals or to the providers of goods or services to eligible individuals. **In-kind assistance** is a form of a cash transfer in which the government pays cash to those who provide goods or services to eligible individuals. Approximately 60 percent of the money spent by the national government goes toward cash transfers to citizens. Today, the majority of U.S. citizens receive cash payments of some kind from the federal government at some time during their lives.

Examples of cash transfers include unemployment and Social Security checks, Pell grants to college students, grants-in-aid to state and local governments (see Chapter 3), and tax breaks and subsidies to individuals and corporations (see Chapter 15). Medicaid, the government program that provides health care for the poor, is an example of an in-kind assistance, cash transfer program. The Medicaid recipient receives medical care at no cost or at a reduced cost because the government pays health care providers for their services. The Supplemental Nutrition Assistance Program (SNAP), the new name for the food stamp program created in 1964, is another example of in-kind assistance. The government provides cash to the stores that accept SNAP vouchers or debit cards for food purchases.

The main cash transfer programs are of two kinds, depending upon their sources of revenue. For **noncontributory programs,** the general revenues collected by the government pay for the program. This means that a proportion of the money collected from all taxpayers funds the cash transfer. Temporary Assistance to Needy Families, the income security program for families with children who have no or very low income, is an example of a noncontributory cash-transfer program. In contrast, **contributory programs,** or **social insurance programs,** are funded by revenue collected specifically for these programs, and they benefit only those who have paid into the programs. Social insurance programs are **entitlement programs,** meaning the government guarantees the program's benefits to all who meet the eligibility criteria. Thus workers who pay the payroll tax for Social Security will receive Social Security checks when they retire.

With a **direct subsidy,** another type of cash transfer, the government provides financial support to specific persons or organizations that engage in activities that the government believes benefit the public good. Individual farmers and agricultural corporations, for example, receive money from the government to grow specified crops or to limit how much they grow. College students receiving Pell grants, which do not need to be paid back, are also recipients of direct subsidies funded through the federal government's general revenue.

Loans, Loan Guarantees, and Insurance

In addition to using tax breaks and grants to encourage behaviors that accomplish its goals, the national government lends money to individuals and organizations, and it guarantees loans made by private businesses. Some examples are government loan programs to assist individuals in purchasing homes, reflecting the widespread belief that home ownership promotes the general welfare and domestic tranquility, and Perkins loans, which pay some of the college expenses of students from very-low-income families. In addition, the government guarantees banks that it will repay the loans they provide to college students if the students cannot repay the loans themselves; these guaranteed loans are called Stafford loans. If the government did not guarantee them, it is unlikely that banks, which are profit-making organizations, would lend thousands of dollars to unemployed young people to pay for college costs.

The national government is also in the insurance business. The Federal Deposit Insurance Corporation (FDIC) is one example of a national insurance program. The FDIC insures bank deposits in member banks to encourage people to save money not only for their own sake but also for the good of the national economy.

> The federal government assists college students through cash transfers such as Pell grants, student loans, and loan guarantees. College financial aid offices play a role in administering these grant and loan programs.

noncontributory program
a benefit provided to a targeted population, paid for by a proportion of the money collected from all taxpayers

contributory program (social insurance program)
a benefit provided only to those who paid the specific tax created to fund the benefit

entitlement program
a government benefit guaranteed to all who meet the eligibility requirements

direct subsidy
a cash transfer from general revenues to particular persons or private companies engaged in activities that the national government believes support the public good

THEN

NOW

32 DAYS	0.85	%	0.85	%
MONEY MARKET SAVINGS	0.40	%	0.40	%
MINIMUM DEPOSIT $ 1,500 TO OBTAIN APY				
MONEY MARKET NOW	0. 40	%	0.40	%
MINIMUM DEPOSIT $ 1,000 TO OBTAIN APY				
PASSBOOK SAVINGS	0.35	%	0.35	%
MINIMUM DEPOSIT $500.00				
MINIMUM DEPOSIT $ 5 00.00 TO OBTAIN APY			FDIC	

INTEREST PENALTY IS REQUIRED FOR EARLY WITHDRAWAL OF TIME DEPOSIT. ANNUAL PERCENTAGE YIELD ASSUMES INTEREST REMAINS ON DEPOSIT. WITHDRAWAL OF INTEREST WILL R

> Depositors, fearful that the money they had deposited had been lost, besieged banks such as this one in Passaic, New Jersey, after Wall Street crashed and the Great Depression began in 1929. To protect depositors' money, in 1933 the federal government created the Federal Deposit Insurance Corporation (FDIC), which insures bank deposits. During the Great Recession that began in 2008, the federal government temporarily increased the insurance limit from $100,000 to $250,000. The limit is scheduled to revert to $100,000 on January 1, 2014.

Contracting-Out

The government also contracts with private and nonprofit organizations to produce essential resources or to deliver services historically provided by the government. One example of contracting-out, or outsourcing (see Chapter 13), is its contracts with corporations such as Lockheed Martin and Boeing to build the planes and missiles it needs to defend the country.

By means of contracting-out and the other various tools we have surveyed, the government delivers goods and services to its citizens now and in the future. In the rest of this chapter, we examine how government uses these tools to implement overall policy in several domestic policy areas, including the environment, energy, income security, health care, homeland security, and immigration.

Environmental Policy

At the most basic level, providing for the general welfare means ensuring that people have the basic necessities for sustaining life. These needs include clean and drinkable water, breathable air, and unpolluted land on which to grow food safe for consumption. No one argues against a clean environment. Yet there is no consensus on how to achieve and maintain one. In addition, appeals for environmental protection often conflict with demands for ample supplies of energy and for economic development. For example, the extraction of coal and oil from the earth, as well as the development of nuclear energy, poses immediate as well as long-term threats to the environment. They also create jobs.

Environmental protection includes conserving natural resources and limiting the pollution emitted into the air and water and onto the land. By the late 1960s and 1970s, several environmental crises had brought the harm humans had caused to the natural environment, plants, animals, and people into stark view.

Environmental Degradation

Since the 1940s, farmers have used chemicals to destroy insects, weeds, fungi, and other living organisms that harm their crops. The threats such pesticides pose to air, water, and land became the focus of public concern and political debate after the publication of Rachel Carson's eye-opening best seller *Silent Spring* in 1962. Carson's book documented how pesticides were contaminating the environment and getting into human food. The use of chemicals, she warned, threatened the existence not only of birds—whose extinction would mean a silent spring—but of humankind itself. Although the chemical industry tried to discredit Carson's findings, President John F. Kennedy (1961–1963) established a special panel to investigate them, and the panel found support for Carson's concerns.

Then, in 1969, those growing apprehensions became a spectacular reality when the heavily polluted Cuyahoga River in northeastern Ohio caught fire (again!). Around the same time, arsenic was found in the Kansas River, and millions of fish went belly-up in major waterways such as Lake Superior, killed by the chemicals and untreated waste emitted by industrial plants and local sewage systems. In response, state and local governments banned fishing in many waterways, including Lake Erie, because of their excessive pollution.

The mounting environmental crises and additional governmental studies brought amplified calls to action from both citizens'

> In April 2010, more than one billion people around the world celebrated the 40th anniversary of Earth Day by engaging in teach-ins, clean-ups, and lobbying efforts. In Washington, D. C., members of the Washington Nationals professional baseball team, including infielder Ronnie Belliard, collaborated with students from the Charles E. Smith Jewish Day School to clean up the banks of the Anacostia River, which flows along side the Nationals' baseball stadium.

groups and elected officials during the 1960s and 1970s. U.S. Senator Gaylord Nelson (D-Wisconsin) responded by founding Earth Day. He later recollected that "all across the country, evidence of environmental degradation was appearing. . . . The people were concerned, but the politicians were not. . . . Suddenly, the idea occurred to me—why not organize a huge grassroots protest over what was happening to our environment?"[2]

Nelson's vision of a day of educational rallies in Washington, D.C., became a reality on April 22, 1970, when more than 200,000 people gathered on the National Mall. Millions more congregated across the country to draw attention to environmental concerns. Earth Day 1970 was so successful at bringing attention to the environmental cause that many consider it the beginning of the environmental movement. Celebrated every year with rallies and teach-ins involving millions of people worldwide, Earth Day keeps concerns about environmental degradation on the public policy agenda.

Environmental Protection

A cascade of groundbreaking national legislation followed the first Earth Day. The Environmental Protection Act of 1970 established the Environmental Protection Agency (EPA) to oversee the implementation of laws protecting the quality of air, water, and land. The Environmental Protection Act mandates that all construction projects receiving federal funding begin with an environmental impact study analyzing the project's effects on the environment and on endangered species. The act also has a sunshine component requiring the government to invite citizens' comments on proposed projects. Under these provisions of the law, environmental interest groups frequently bring lawsuits challenging the quality and accuracy of environmental impact studies and developers' lack of compliance with the sunshine provisions. Developers and parties probing into new energy sources view such lawsuits as a waste of time and money. But in fact, this litigation, combined with the broader work of various environmental groups, has become a driving force in environmental protection today.

CLEAN AIR The landmark Clean Air Act of 1970 delegates authority to the EPA to set air quality standards while giving state governments enforcement responsibility. Today, states in turn typically delegate some of their enforcement responsibilities to local governments. If states and their local governments do not enforce compliance with the national standards, the EPA can take over.

To bolster compliance with the Clean Air Act, the law gives citizens the right to sue those who are violating the standards. Citizens also have the right to sue the EPA if it does not enforce the Clean Air Act. Citizens and environmental interest groups have availed themselves of their right to sue, pushing the government and industries to comply with the law. For example, in 2007, Massachusetts and eleven other states, three cities, and several environmental groups successfully challenged the EPA and President George W. Bush's interpretation of the law, when the U.S. Supreme Court determined that carbon dioxide is a pollutant that the EPA has the authority to regulate.[3]

CLEAN WATER   The Clean Water Act is actually the 1972 Federal Water Pollution Control Act as amended over the years. This law, which has the goal of making waterways clean enough to swim in and to eat fish from, authorizes the EPA to set water quality standards and to require permits for anyone discharging contaminants into any waterway. However, the direct discharge of pollutants into waterways is not the only source of water pollution. Runoff from farms, which carries animal waste and pesticides into waterways, also contributes heavily to the problem. The Department of Agriculture joins forces with the EPA to prevent this indirect source of pollution.

Under the Clean Water Act, state and local governments must monitor water quality, issue permits to those discharging waste into waterways, and enforce the national standards. If states and localities fail to carry out these mandated responsibilities, the EPA can step in and do the job. The law also provides for federal loans to local governments, funneled through state governments, for building wastewater treatment plants.

The Safe Drinking Water Act of 1974 authorizes the EPA to establish purity standards for drinking water. Because states or localities typically operate water systems, this act effectively requires the EPA to regulate state and local governments. The act provides for national grants to state and local governments for research and for improving their water systems.

Water problems extend far beyond U.S. borders. For insight into international efforts to address water issues, see "Global Context."

CLEAN LAND   The United States produces more solid waste—from household garbage to toxic by-products of manufacturing—per person than any other country. If not properly disposed of or treated, all waste has the potential to harm the environment, as well as plants, animals, and people. Some toxic by-products, such as the radioactive nuclear wastes produced in manufacturing nuclear weapons and generating nuclear power, cannot be treated or disposed of, but they dissipate over time—from one hundred years for low-level radioactive waste to hundreds of thousands of years for high-level radioactive waste.

Citizens with resources, including money and the time to organize or to join an existing organization, are able to fight the location of undesirable land uses in their communities. Lower-income communities are more likely than more affluent cities and towns to bear the burden of housing waste storage facilities. **Environmental racism** is the term used to describe the higher incidence of environmental threats and subsequent health problems in lower-income communities, which frequently are also communities dominated by people of color.[4]

The Resource Conservation and Recovery Act of 1976, administered by the EPA, regulates the disposal of solid and hazardous wastes and encourages recycling. Although this act authorized the cleanup of toxic waste sites, and the government identified thousands of such sites in the 1970s, no national funding was made available for the cleanup. Then in 1980, as Congress was debating how to address potential harm caused by toxic waste sites, an abandoned site for the storage, treatment, and disposal of hazardous waste in Elizabeth, New Jersey, exploded.[5] Shortly thereafter, Congress approved the Comprehensive Environmental Response, Compensation and Liability Act of 1980 (known as the Superfund law) to pay for cleanup of the nation's most toxic waste dumps.

Because U.S. air quality and water quality have improved tremendously since the 1970s, many citizens and government officials have shifted their attention to other societal concerns. At the same time, U.S. industries have become more resistant to legislative proposals

environmental racism
the term for the higher incidence of environmental threats and subsequent health problems in lower-income communities, which frequently are also communities dominated by people of color

CLEAN WATER FOR A HEALTHY WORLD

Clean water is necessary for life. It is necessary for drinking, growing safe and healthy food (crops and domestic animals, including fish), preparing food, preventing illness (through personal hygiene, cleaning, washing, and waste disposal), and caring for the sick. Most people in North America and Europe take for granted their access to toilets and drinkable water, and are not aware of the spreading water crisis. But more than one out of six people in the world lack access to drinkable water. More than one in three people worldwide do not have access to toilets or latrines. As a result, diseases related to unsafe drinking water, inadequate sanitation, and poor hygiene cause more than 2 million global deaths a year, most of them children under 5 years of age.*

What are some of the potential barriers to providing millions more people around the globe with clean water, the essential ingredient for life?

Currently, the water crisis is limited to certain countries and regions in the world, with the populations of Asia and Africa particularly hard-hit. Yet with the world's population poised to grow by at least 40 percent over the next fifty years, and with increased economic development and urbanization, the demand for clean water to drink and to grow healthy food has the potential to develop into a worldwide crisis.**

Recognizing as crucial the need to protect and manage water resources for a healthy world, the United Nation's General Assembly established the UN International Decade for Action on Water, 2005–2015. UN member states agreed to reduce by half the proportion of people without clean drinking water by 2015. To achieve this goal, in each year of the Decade for Action on Water, 100 million additional people (or 274,000 people each day) will need to gain access to clean, drinkable water.† With the efforts of governments, nongovernmental organizations, and activists throughout the world, the United Nations International Children's Emergency Fund (UNICEF)—an organization dedicated to the protection, survival, and development of children and mothers—predicts that this target will be met.§

> More than one out of six people in the world lack drinkable water, and so they drink water from polluted wells or wells infested with parasites, such as this one in the Ivory Coast. The lack of safe drinking water results in more than 2 million global deaths each year caused by water-related diseases.

*www.un.org/waterforlifedecade/pdf/waterforlifebklt-e.pdf.
**Ibid.
†Ibid.
§www.unicef.org/voy/explore/wes/explore_2711.html.

to stiffen environmental standards and are increasingly challenging the implementation of environmental laws. In addition, a growing private property rights movement is challenging restrictions on land use that have been put in place in the name of environmental protection. Although no one is arguing against a clean environment, tensions persist between the need for environmental protection and other policy areas. The increasing demand for cheap energy is one such area.

The environmental threats and damage created by energy production, accidents during the extraction of energy sources such as coal and oil, and energy consumption are evident worldwide. In April 2010, the United States witnessed the deaths of twenty-nine coal miners in West Virginia and eleven oil rig workers in the Gulf of Mexico. In both cases, explosions occurred as private companies extracted natural resources, killing the workers. In addition to the loss of life, the oil rig explosion created an environmental disaster whose total damage to wildlife, the livelihoods of thousands of people, and the economy of numerous communities we will not know for decades. The national government began investigating the causes of these accidents immediately, and calls for better government oversight and increased regulation of the coal mining and oil industries followed quickly.

International, national, state, and local policies are focusing on limiting the threats to the environment posed by energy production and consumption. An additional energy concern for the United States is its reliance on nonrenewable energy sources, as we next consider.

Energy Policy

Energy creation—the production of electricity and heat, as well as fuels to power automobiles, trucks, planes, trains, and other transport vehicles—is essential to the prosperity of the U.S. economy and to the American way of life. The United States uses more energy than any other country in the world, and its demand for energy continues to rise. What underlies this increasing demand? Industrial and commercial expansion, the construction of larger houses, and soaring computer use all have contributed to the ballooning demand for electricity. Robust sales of trucks for personal use, as well as of gas-guzzling sport utility vehicles (SUVs), have driven up consumers' demand for gasoline. Moreover, the transportation system in the United States relies more heavily on passenger cars than is the case in other countries, where public transportation links cities to one another and to suburbs more effectively. The ever-rising energy demands of the U.S. economy and the lifestyle of U.S. residents are problematic for several reasons, as we shall see.

Energy and Global Warming

greenhouse effect
the heating of the earth's atmosphere as a result of humans' burning of fossil fuels and the resultant buildup of carbon dioxide and other gases

global warming
rising temperature of the earth as a result of pollution that traps solar heat, keeping the air warmer than it would otherwise be

Most energy consumed in the United States is produced by burning fossil fuels—oil, coal, and natural gas. Burning fossil fuels pollutes the air. The pollution produced from burning fossil fuels is not just a national problem; it is a global problem. Mounting evidence indicates that pollution from burning fossil fuels has increased temperatures worldwide, creating a **greenhouse effect**—so-called because in a greenhouse, the walls and roof trap solar heat, keeping the temperature inside warmer than it is outside. **Global warming,** the gradual average increase in the earth's temperature, is the result of pollution that traps solar heat in the earth's atmosphere.

International fears about the potential harm of global warming led to a treaty called the Kyoto Protocol of 1997. Countries that ratify the Kyoto Protocol agree to work toward eliminating the greenhouse effect by reducing their emissions of carbon dioxide and other gases believed to cause it. Although 184 countries have ratified the treaty, the United States has not.

Even though the federal government has opted not to ratify the Kyoto Protocol, many state and local governments are collectively working to meet its provisions, with the goal of showing the national government the benefits of abiding by it. Currently, ten Northeast and mid-Atlantic states have agreed to the Regional Greenhouse Gas Initiative (RGGI). The RGGI commits those states to capping emissions from power plants and to reducing emissions by 10 percent by 2018.

President Barack Obama (2009–present) came into office with the reduction of global warming as one of his top priorities. With his support, the House of Representatives approved the American Clean Energy and Security Act in June 2009. In July 2009, the Senate Energy and Natural Resources Committee approved the Clean Energy and Leadership Act. Both the House and the Senate bills propose a change in the direction of the nation's energy policy by imposing the first-ever federal limits on carbon dioxide and other pollutants

> In response to their disappointment over the perceived weakness of the U.S. House's American Clean Energy and Security Act, environmentalists draped a banner over South Dakota's Mount Rushmore in July 2009 to urge President Obama and other world leaders meeting in Italy to develop a strong global strategy for reducing greenhouse emissions.

linked to global warming. Al Gore, who won a Nobel Peace Prize in 2007 for his work on global warming, posted a statement on his Web site declaring this bill "an essential first step towards solving the climate crisis."

National Energy Policy

Today, energy policy debates focus on the nation's reliance on *nonrenewable energy sources*—crude oil, natural gas, coal, and nuclear power—and calls to increase the use of *renewable energy sources*—solar, geothermal, wind, hydropower, and biomass. Figure 16.1 on page 504 shows the current mix of U.S. energy sources. Those who advocate the use of renewable energy cite the environmental threats that result from burning fossil fuels, the nonrenewable nature of fossil fuels as an energy source, and the nation's reliance on imported petroleum.[6]

According to the U.S. Energy Information Administration, in 2008, 93 percent of U.S. energy came from nonrenewable sources. Petroleum is the largest U.S. energy source, providing close to 40 percent of U.S. energy. In 2008, the United States imported almost 60 percent of the petroleum that it consumed.[7] This heavy reliance on foreign oil concerns citizens and government officials because of the volatile political environments in some oil-producing countries in the Middle East and South America, and because of conflicts between U.S. policies and the policies of some of those countries.

THE OPEC EMBARGO AND CARTER'S RESPONSE In 1973, for example, the Arab members of the Organization of Petroleum Exporting Countries (OPEC) implemented an embargo on oil supplies. This embargo was a reaction to U.S. support of Israel in that nation's Yom Kippur War of 1973 against Egypt and Syria over disputed lands. Outraged by what they saw as U.S. interference, OPEC member nations refused to sell oil to the United States and western European nations that supported Israel in the war. This

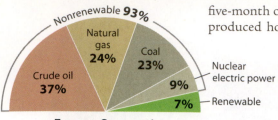

Energy Sources*

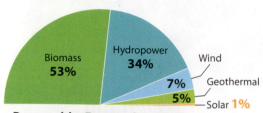

Renewable Energy Sources*
(7% of energy sources)

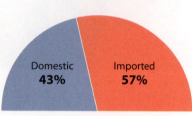

Sources of U.S. Crude Oil**

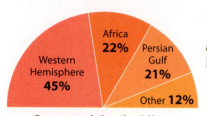

Imported Crude Oil**

FIGURE 16.1 ■ U.S. ENERGY SOURCES
Should U.S. citizens be concerned about the proportion of energy coming from nonrenewable sources? Explain your answer. What might explain why the proportion of energy coming from renewable sources is so low? From what part of the globe does the majority of U.S. petroleum (crude oil) come?

*HTTP://TONTO.EIA.DOE.GOV/ENERGYEXPLAINED/INDEX_CFM?PAGE=ABOUT_HOME
**http://tonton.eia.doe.gov/energy_in_brief/foreign_oil_dependence.cfm.

five-month oil embargo, followed by OPEC production limits that kept oil prices high, and produced hours-long waits in gas station lines, forced the United States to set national energy policies.

In 1975, the national government established the Strategic Petroleum Reserve, a growing supply of crude oil stored away in case of a future energy emergency or an interruption in the U.S. supply of imported oil. That same year, Congress also set fuel-efficiency standards for passenger cars and light trucks, the Corporate Average Fuel Economy (CAFÉ) standards. In 2007, more than thirty-five years after establishing CAFÉ, Congress significantly increased the fuel-efficiency standards for the first time. Automobile producers must meet the new 35-miles-per-gallon standard, up from 25 miles per gallon, by the year 2020.[8] However, it was not until May 2009, during President Barack Obama's administration, that the Department of Transportation finalized the rules needed to enforce the new CAFÉ standards.

In 1976, the federal government established the Department of Energy to develop and oversee a comprehensive national energy plan. In 1977, President Jimmy Carter (1977–1981) declared an "energy crisis" and announced energy conservation measures such as the regulation of temperature settings in public buildings and tax incentives to insulate homes. In addition, government regulation of oil and natural gas prices was curtailed during Carter's presidency.[9] Although the government had historically regulated the prices of those energy resources, the expectation was that if prices rose on the basis of supply and demand, people would conserve. Carter's energy policies also included increased financial support for research and development of alternative energy sources such as solar, wind, geothermal, and renewable biomass.

With deregulation, oil prices jumped by 1980 to more than ten times their 1972 level. But by 1986, oil prices began to fall. With lower prices through the 1990s came reduced federal government support for research and development of alternative energy sources. The public, too, lost interest in energy conservation, and the demand for energy grew, as did the production of gas-guzzling automobiles.

AN ENERGY POLICY FOCUSED ON FOSSIL FUELS In 2001, Secretary of Energy Spencer Abraham sounded an alarm: "America faces a major energy-supply crisis over the next two decades. The failure to meet this challenge will threaten our nation's economic prosperity, compromise our national security, and literally alter the way we live our lives."[10] In response, President George W. Bush appointed Vice President Dick Cheney—a former oil company executive—to preside over a task force charged with formulating a new national energy policy. The result was an energy policy emphasizing the increased production of fossil fuels. This policy was in stark contrast to the conservation approach developed in the 1970s. Moreover, Bush's 2002 budget drastically cut funding for conservation initiatives and for research on alternative, renewable energy sources.

By the winter of 2005, government officials and citizens were increasingly concerned over the price and availability of oil. Hurricane Katrina had taken a toll on domestic oil production. The Iraq War and tensions with Iran jeopardized the stability of imports from the Middle East. President Hugo Chavez of Venezuela, the number 3 U.S. oil supplier, was also threatening to limit the availability of his country's oil.

In response, President Bush emphasized in his 2006 State of the Union address how essential affordable energy is to the United States' success in the world economy. He stressed that Americans' "addiction" to oil must be reduced. Bush called for a 22 percent increase in funding for research in alternative renewable energy sources such as solar and wind, as well as in nuclear energy, and recommended increased use of coal. The president also called for expanded research in alternative means to power automobiles, including electricity, hydrogen, and ethanol (produced from corn, wood chips, and switchgrass).

FUTURE DIRECTIONS   In 2009, the U.S. House and Senate worked on clean energy bills. Under the proposed policies, energy companies would pay a price for the greenhouse pollution they create through the purchase of pollution allowances, or they could shift to using cleaner, renewable energy, including solar, wind, and geothermal power, or to cleaner nuclear energy. Automakers would be required to make more fuel-efficient cars. Members of Congress who supported the bills and President Obama argued that another outcome would be creation of new green jobs—such as making or installing solar panels and wind turbines, developing equipment to harness carbon emissions, and producing energy-efficient lightbulbs, washing machines, and other home appliances. President Obama called on all Americans to support clean energy legislation, which, he argued, would "open the door to a clean energy economy and a better future for America."[11]

Today, limited supplies and high costs of traditional energy sources, along with the environmental impact of the continuing use of fossil fuels, threaten the quality of life of Americans and people around the globe. Americans are looking to national and state government for public policy solutions to these energy-related and environmental concerns. In a similar way, during the 1930s, Americans had turned to the national government to address the economic downturn that was impeding millions of Americans' ability to enjoy a decent quality of life, as we next consider.

Income Security Programs

Before the Great Depression of the 1930s, Americans who could not provide for their basic needs relied on relief from family, friends, charities, and, in some cases, local or state government. During the Depression, however, the excessively weak economy left one-quarter of the U.S. labor force unemployed. Families lost jobs, savings, and homes. Charities were overwhelmed. State and local governments lacked the resources to assist the millions of people without incomes. Citizens, as well as state and local governments, looked to the federal government for assistance.

Within his first one hundred days in office, President Franklin D. Roosevelt (1933–1945) proposed a sequence of revolutionary bills to stimulate and regulate sectors of the depressed economy and to provide income to the needy. His administration's radical proposals placed the national government at the center of issues it had historically left to local and state governments. Those and the subsequent New Deal policies approved in Roosevelt's first few years in office created jobs, established a more regulated capitalist economy (see Chapter 15), and provided income security for retired citizens and a safety net for people in financial need. Many of the New Deal programs are still in place today, though in modified form.

Noncontributory safety-net programs, which are funded through general tax revenues, engender a good deal of debate. Conservatives typically oppose these programs on the grounds that hard work, not government handouts, should be the source of the income individuals need to sustain themselves. Liberals are more inclined to support noncontributory safety-net programs. They make the case that systemic factors, not individual characteristics, prevent many people from earning enough income to sustain themselves. Although you would be hard pressed to find someone who argues against contributory safety-net programs (also called *social insurance programs*), there is an ongoing debate over the best means of funding such programs and the proper level of benefits. The largest contributory income security program, in cost and people served, is the Old-Age and Survivors component of Social Security.

Social Security

The Social Security Act of 1935, a centerpiece of the New Deal, established a range of landmark income security programs. To this day, these programs provide financial assistance to the elderly, disabled, dependent, and unemployed.

The Future of Old Age and Survivors Insurance (OASI)

	THEN (1937)	NOW (2010)
Percentage of workers covered*	60%	97%
Payroll tax collected from employee to fund OASI*	1% on wages up to $3,000	6.2% on wages up to $106,800
Payroll tax collected from employer to fund OASI*	1% on wages up to $3,000	6.2% on wages up to $106,800
Number of workers paying into OASI per retiree*	16	3
Normal retirement age*	65	67 (for those born after 1959)
Total receipts**	$747 million	$695,462 million (end of 2008)
Total benefit payments**	$ 1 million	$509,337 million (end of 2008)
Assets at end of year**	$766 million	$2,202,886 million (end of 2008)

WHAT'S NEXT?

> With only three workers paying into the system for every one retiree and retirees living longer, the system is not sustainable. What can the government do to bring more money into the system to pay benefits to future retirees?

> Currently, all workers who pay into the system can apply for OASI benefits at their normal retirement age, even workers who continue to work and those earning money through investments, including millionaires and billionaires. Will government officials have the political will to cut the benefits of millionaires and billionaires to ensure security income to other beneficiaries? Explain your answer.

> The Social Security Trustees report indicates that within 30 to 75 years, the OASI trust fund will be depleted. Is there a particular Social Security reform, or combination of reforms, that you believe most U.S. citizens would support? Explain.

*www.newyorklife.com/cda/0,3254,5786,00.html.
**www.ssa.gov/OACT/STATS/table4a1.html.

indexed benefit
a government benefit with an automatic cost of living increase based on the rate of inflation

OLD-AGE AND SURVIVORS INSURANCE The Social Security Act established the Old-Age and Survivors Insurance (OASI) Program, which initially provided income to individuals or families when a worker covered by the program retired. This contributory cash transfer program is the traditional retirement insurance component of Social Security; most people are aware of it and anticipate benefiting from it in retirement. OASI is a social insurance entitlement program, funded by contributions that employees as well as employers make. Each year, the federal government establishes the amount of earnings subject to the Social Security tax, which is called the *covered income*. Employees and employers each pay 6.2 percent (for a total of 12.4 percent) of the employee's covered income for Social Security. In 2010, income up to $106,800 was subject to the tax.

A formula that accounts for how much individuals paid into Social Security over their years of employment determines the amount of each beneficiary's monthly Social Security check. The more money invested, the greater the check. Because OASI is an **indexed benefit,** the government makes regularly scheduled, automatic cost of living adjustments (COLAs), increasing the benefit based on the rate of inflation. The 1937 Federal Insurance Contribution Act (FICA) established the pay-as-you-go funding mechanism for OASI. Through FICA contributions, current workers and employers deposit money in the Social Security Trust Fund, and the government uses the money contributed today to pay today's beneficiaries. The money left over after today's payments are made is invested so that the trust fund will grow; income from investments will be combined with future FICA revenues to pay for future Social Security checks.

Because Social Security is an entitlement, and because the government cannot predict how long a Social Security recipient will live—and therefore how many checks the recipient will receive during his or her lifetime—the government cannot control or predict the annual cost of Social Security.

Most people collect more from Social Security than they pay into the fund, and the number of retirees is growing. With the increasing number of retirees and with those retirees living longer lives, the pay-as-you-go system will eventually reach the point of not covering the full costs of OASI. The surplus money in the Social Security Trust Fund is already shrinking. This situation generates intense public debate over what the national government should do to ensure that Social Security funds are available for workers who are currently contributing to the program.

AMENDMENTS TO THE SOCIAL SECURITY ACT Congress amended the Social Security Act in 1939 to provide benefits to the dependents and surviving spouse of a deceased worker. In 1956, the act was further amended to assist workers who, because of physical or mental disabilities, had to stop working after age 50 but before the OASI-designated retirement age. The new benefit program thus created, called Social Security Disability Insurance (SSDI), provides income to those covered by the Social Security program and to their families if they meet the guidelines for disability. Similarly to OASI, SSDI is a contributory (social insurance) program.

In 1972, Congress again amended the Social Security Act by establishing the Supplemental Security Income (SSI) program, a noncontributory program. Recipients of SSI include low-income elderly people whose Social Security benefits are so low they cannot provide for themselves, individuals with disabilities, and blind people. Unlike other Social Security programs, SSI is a **means-tested benefit,** meaning that the eligibility criteria to receive the benefit include a government-specified income level, which is very low.

The Social Security Act of 1935 created other income security programs, including unemployment compensation and Aid to Dependent Children. Three years after passage of the Social Security Act, the Roosevelt administration also enacted a minimum wage, and several decades later, in 1975, Congress established an additional income security program known as the Earned Income Tax Credit. We now turn to these other income security programs.

means-tested benefit
a benefit for which eligibility is based on having an income below a specified amount, typically based on a percentage of the poverty guideline

Unemployment Compensation

Together, employees, employers, the federal government, and state governments fund the unemployment compensation program created by the Social Security Act of 1935. Through this program, employees who lose their jobs through no fault of their own can collect unemployment compensation for up to twenty-six weeks. An employee fired for cause (not doing the job, doing it poorly, or violating work rules or the law) cannot receive unemployment compensation.

During economic recessions, the national government has sometimes extended the twenty-six-week benefit period if the unemployment rate remains high for a long time. For example, in February 2009, the federal government approved a new, temporary unemployment program to provide up to twenty additional weeks of unemployment benefits to certain workers. This extension was added to a 2008 extension that provided up to thirteen additional weeks of benefits to workers in states with unemployment rates of at least 6 percent. The federal government paid for these additional thirty-three weeks of extended benefits.[12]

Minimum Wage

In addition to guaranteeing some income for workers who lose their jobs through no fault of their own, Congress in 1938 enacted the Fair Labor Standards Act, which established a minimum wage. The aim was to guarantee most employed workers a **living wage**—a wage high enough to keep them out of poverty. The federal government has amended this law several times to expand minimum wage coverage to additional job categories, yet there are still many exceptions to it. Workers not guaranteed the federal minimum wage include full-time students, youths under 20 years of age for the first ninety days of their employment, workers who earn tips, commissioned sales employees, farm laborers, and seasonal and recreational workers. (Why do you think these workers are excluded from the minimum wage?) For workers guaranteed the minimum wage, employers must pay overtime (equal to one and a half times an employee's regular hourly rate) for all hours over 40 worked during a workweek.

In 1938, the government set the federal minimum wage at twenty-five cents per hour. Unlike the Social Security retirement program, OASI, the minimum wage benefit is not indexed to other economic factors and so does not automatically receive a COLA to keep up with inflation. Congress and the president must approve new legislation if the minimum wage is to increase. (Why do you think OASI is indexed to receive automatic COLAs and the minimum wage is not?)

Proposals to raise the minimum wage are always controversial, as revealed by the intense debate that preceded legislation in May 2007 that increased the national minimum wage

living wage
a wage high enough to keep workers and their families out of poverty and to allow them to enjoy a basic living standard

from $5.15 (the wage set in 1997) to $7.25 per hour. Senate Democrats, led by the late Senator Edward Kennedy (D-Massachusetts), included the provision for the minimum wage hike in a bill to continue funding for the Iraq War. In that way, they won needed votes from those who did not support the wage increase but did support the war funding. Speaker of the House Nancy Pelosi (D-California) said of the increase, "We are raising wages for the hardest-working Americans."[13]

State and local governments can establish a minimum wage higher than the federal minimum for covered workers, and they can extend a minimum wage to workers not covered by the federal minimum wage. In 2009, thirteen states and the District of Columbia had minimum wages higher than the new national $7.25 an hour.[14] But even in instances of these more generous benefits, the harsh reality is that many minimum wage workers, as well as many people earning several dollars over the national minimum wage—whom we collectively call the working poor—are still living in poverty. Hence, today's minimum wage is not a living wage. To reduce the financial hardship of minimum and low-wage workers, the national government established the Earned Income Tax Credit program.

Earned Income Tax Credit

In addition to providing cash transfers and regulating wages, the government supports income security through programs offering tax breaks. One of these is the Earned Income Tax Credit (EITC) program, established in 1975.

Citizens with low to moderate earned income from employment or from self-employment who file an income tax return are eligible for EITC benefits. Working parents are eligible for larger tax credits than are workers without children. The amount of the tax credit decreases (eventually reaching zero) as earned income increases.

According to the Center on Budget and Policy Priorities (CBPP), a research organization concerned with the status of poor people, in 2009 the EITC kept an estimated 6.6 million people out of poverty, including 3.3 million children. The CBPP claims, "There is broad bipartisan agreement that a two-parent family with two children with a full-time, minimum-wage worker should not have to raise its children in poverty. At the minimum wage's current level, such a family can move out of poverty only if it receives the EITC as well as food stamps."[15] Yet the antipoverty program with which many Americans are most familiar began in 1935 as Aid to Dependent Children.

Temporary Assistance to Needy Families

The Social Security Act established Aid to Dependent Children (ADC), which evolved into Aid to Families with Dependent Children (AFDC) and was then replaced by Temporary Assistance to Needy Families (TANF). Initially supporting stay-at-home single widows with children, the ADC program evolved into TANF, with its emphasis on assisting needy single-parent and two-parent families with children. The focus moreover has changed from one of encouraging women to stay home with their children to one of requiring recipients to work (those in single- and dual-parent households) and requiring fathers (particularly those not living with their children) to take on greater financial responsibilities for their children.

Federal grants and state funds paid for the ADC and AFDC noncontributory cash transfer, entitlement programs, and a formula in the national law determined what percentage of each state's annual program cost the federal government would cover. The federal law also gave each state discretion to determine the level of benefits as well as the eligibility criteria for program recipients in that state. (See "Analyzing the Sources" for data on the level of state benefits.) However, as mandated by federal law, eligibility criteria for AFDC in every state included the presence of children under the age of 18 and a means test indicating no or very low family income.

Beginning in the late 1950s, the number of households headed by women with children living in poverty began to increase, a development referred to as the **feminization of poverty.** Although the overwhelming majority of AFDC beneficiaries were children, myths

feminization of poverty
the phenomenon of increasing numbers of unmarried, divorced, and separated women with children living in poverty

ANALYZING THE SOURCES

DO TANF MONTHLY BENEFITS KEEP FAMILIES OUT OF POVERTY?

Each state establishes the TANF benefit levels for its recipients. The map indicates the 2008 TANF per-month benefit levels in each state for a family of three (one adult and two children) with no income.

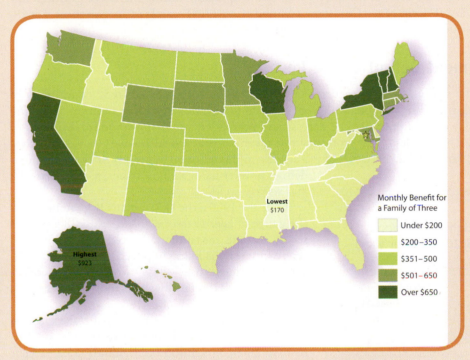

Lowest $170

Highest $923

Monthly Benefit for a Family of Three

- Under $200
- $200–350
- $351–500
- $501–650
- Over $650

SOURCE: Liz Schott and Zachary Levinson, "TANF Benefits Are Low and Have Not Kept Pace with Inflation" (Washington, DC: Center on Budget Policy and Priorities, November 24, 2008).

Evaluating the Evidence

① On the basis of the information in the map, determine the annual income provided to a family of three in your home state; in the state with the highest benefit; and in the state with the lowest benefit. How does your home state's benefit compare with the highest and lowest state benefits?

② Compare the annual incomes you identified in item 1 with the data supplied in Table 16.2 on page 510 to determine whether the family of three in these three states would be defined as living in poverty according to the Department of Health and Human Services (HHS) poverty guidelines. Report your findings.

③ Do a second comparison to see whether the families in these states would be eligible for programs available to families based on 185 percent of the income in the HHS poverty guidelines, found in Table 16.2. Report your findings.

about a poor work ethic and irresponsible sexual practices on the part of their typically single mothers fueled many calls for reform.

With passage of the Family Support Act (FSA) of 1988, the federal government adopted the objective of cultivating self-sufficiency in AFDC recipients. The FSA drove up the expense of the aid programs substantially, because it required states to provide job training, child care, and health benefits. In the long-term, the FSA was expected to decrease in cost as welfare recipients became self-sufficient workers. The short-term cost spike, however, led to calls for further welfare reform. In response, the federal government offered states waivers from some of the AFDC grant conditions to encourage experimentation with new forms of income security for low-income families with children.

On the national level, in 1996, President Bill Clinton (1993–2001) signed the Personal Responsibility and Work Opportunity Reconciliation Act (PRWORA), which radically

Income Security Programs **509**

changed both the nature and the provision of income security for low-income families with children. PRWORA replaced the AFDC entitlement program and several other grant assistance programs for low-income families with one grant, Temporary Assistance to Needy Families (TANF). Unlike AFDC, TANF is not an entitlement program.

Although PRWORA gives state governments a great deal of flexibility in determining TANF eligibility, benefits, and programs, it comes with several very specific regulations. For example, a family can receive benefits only for two consecutive years and a lifetime maximum of five years. Moreover, program beneficiaries must work or be enrolled in an educational or a training program that prepares them for work. In addition, female TANF recipients must identify their children's fathers so that these men can be required to provide financial support for their children. Ultimately, the success of this radical approach to welfare reform depends on the availability of jobs that pay well and offer benefits; hence its success depends on the overall health of the U.S. economy.

Congress included $5 billion in the 2009 American Recovery and Reinvestment Act (ARRA) for a temporary TANF Emergency Contingency Fund. The ARRA contained tax breaks and new spending aimed at stimulating the national economy as the Great Recession that began in 2007 continued. A state could apply for additional TANF grant money from the TANF Emergency Contingency Fund if its TANF caseload increased or if it increased the benefits provided to TANF recipients.[16]

poverty guidelines
a simplified version of the Census Bureau's poverty thresholds developed each year by the Department of Health and Human Services; used to set financial eligibility criteria for benefits

Government Definitions of Poverty

Despite the various income security programs we have considered, tens of millions of Americans, including millions who work full-time, live in *poverty*—the condition of lacking sufficient income to purchase the necessities for an adequate living standard. Millions of others are one problem away from poverty, meaning that a health emergency, significant car repair, family relations issue, or job layoff could land them in poverty. The government defines poverty using two measures: *poverty thresholds* and *poverty guidelines*.

Since the 1960s, the U.S. Census Bureau has used the gauge of *poverty thresholds*—an annually updated set of income measures (adjusted for family size) that define who is living in poverty (see Chapter 15). The government uses these thresholds to collect data on how many families and individuals are living in poverty.

Using 100 percent of the poverty threshold as the definition of poverty, according to the Census Bureau, in 2009, 39.8 million individuals (13.2 percent of the U.S. population) were living in poverty. There were 14.1 million children below the age of 18 years (19 percent) living in poverty, and almost 3.7 million people over the age of 64 (9.7 percent) in the same situation. The poverty rate among blacks was 24.7 percent; Hispanics, 23.2 percent; Asians, 11.8 percent; and non-Hispanic whites, 8.6 percent.[17]

Government agencies that offer additional safety-net programs beyond those we have considered so far do not use the Census Bureau's poverty thresholds to determine eligibility. Instead, many use the Department of Health and Human Services' (HHS) **poverty guidelines,** a version of the poverty thresholds simplified for administrative use. Table 16.2 presents the HHS Poverty Guidelines for 2009/2010.

Most (in-kind assistance) safety-net programs allow families with incomes of a certain percentage above the HHS poverty guidelines (say, 185 percent)

TABLE 16.2

Poverty Guidelines for the Forty-Eight Contiguous States and Washington, D.C., 2009/2010 ($ per year)

Persons in Household	100 Percent of Poverty	185 Percent of Poverty
1	10,830	20,036
2	14,570	26,955
3	18,310	33,874
4	22,050	40,793
5	25,790	47,712
6	29,530	54,631
7	33,370	61,550
8	37,010	68,469
For each additional person add	3,740	

SOURCE: http://liheap.ncat.org/profiles/povertytables/FY2010/popstate.htm.

POLITICAL INQUIRY

What quality of life could you, as a single person, achieve at the income of 100 percent of the poverty guideline? What quality of life could you, as a single person, achieve at the income of 185 percent of the poverty guideline?

to receive benefits. Administrators recognize that families with even those income levels experience difficulties in meeting their basic needs. Programs that use the HHS poverty guidelines as the basis for determining eligibility include the Supplemental Nutrition Assistance Program (SNAP) and the National School Lunch Program. These programs target the problem of **food insecurity,** the situation in which people have limited or uncertain ability to obtain, in socially acceptable ways, enough nutritious food to sustain a healthy and active life.

Housing insecurity—the condition in which people have limited or uncertain ability to obtain, in socially acceptable ways, housing that is affordable, safe, of decent quality, and permanent—is another problem for a growing proportion of the U.S. population. According to the Joint Center for Housing Studies at Harvard University, "The nation's housing challenges are escalating. Affordability is worsening, inadequate conditions persist, and crowding is more common."[18] The National Coalition for the Homeless estimates that more than 3 million people (1 percent of the entire U.S. population) experience homelessness in a given year.[19] About 40 percent of the homeless are children under the age of 18. Forty-nine percent are African American (compared with 11 percent of the general population). Twenty-three percent are veterans (compared with 13 percent of the general population).

Today, most federal revenue spent on housing assistance is in the form of tax breaks to homeowners, developers, and property owners who rent to low-income householders. But the programs that are most in the public eye are means-tested public housing and housing voucher (Section 8 rent subsidy) programs for which low-income households can apply. According to the Department of Housing and Urban Development (HUD), the availability of these forms of housing assistance is very limited, not close to meeting the demand.[20]

food insecurity
situation in which people have limited or uncertain ability to obtain, in socially acceptable ways, enough nutritious food to live a healthy and active life

housing insecurity
situation in which people have limited or uncertain ability to obtain, in socially acceptable ways, affordable, safe, and decent-quality permanent housing

Health Care Policy

Lack of health insurance is an additional problem for low-income households. Further, it is a growing challenge for middle-income households because the number of employers providing medical insurance for their employees (at no cost or a shared cost) has decreased in recent years as the cost of medical care has skyrocketed.

According to the U.S. Census Bureau, in 2008, 46.3 million people in the United States (15.4 percent) were without health insurance. Among those uninsured, 7.3 million (9.9 percent) were under 18 years of age. Approximately 67 percent of those with insurance had private insurance; 58.6 percent of people were covered by employer-provided insurance. Twenty-nine percent of those insured were covered by government health programs, just over 14 percent were covered by Medicaid, and another 14 percent were covered by Medicare.[21] These two programs were established in 1965 as part of President Lyndon Johnson's (1963–1969) "Great Society" plan, which included government programs to address the effects of poverty during a time of national economic prosperity. Medicare and Medicaid are part of today's safety net.

Medicaid

Title XIX, added to the Social Security Act in 1965, created Medicaid—a joint federal-state entitlement program providing health care to people meeting the means test. Because the national legislation delegates substantial discretion to state governments regarding eligibility and benefits, there are really fifty different Medicaid programs.

In this cash transfer program, state governments pay health care providers, and then the national government reimburses the states for a percentage of those bills. The national government's share of each state's cost is based on a formula that takes into account the state's wealth. The national government pays as little as 50 percent of the Medicaid bill in the fourteen wealthiest states and as much as 77 percent in the poorest state, Mississippi.[22]

Medicaid beneficiaries fit into one of five broad categories: (1) pregnant women and children under 6 with family income at or below 133 percent of the federal poverty guideline; (2) children ages 6 to 19 with a family income at or below 100 percent of the poverty guidelines; (3) low-income adults who care for children under age 18; (4) low-income adults who are blind, disabled, or living in a nursing home or a long-term care facility; (5) individuals who receive Supplemental Security Income. States have discretion to provide Medicaid to some additional groups, as defined by the national government. Many states cover children up to age 21 who are living on their own.[23]

The State Children's Health Insurance Program (SCHIP), established in 1997, covers medical costs for low-income uninsured children under the age of 19 who are not eligible for Medicaid. In this joint federal-state cash transfer program, eligibility is based on a family income that is generally less than 200 percent of the HHS poverty guideline. States participating in SCHIP can expand their current Medicaid program to cover these children, or they can create a new program that provides the standard coverage mandated by the national government.

Although most of those who benefit from Medicaid are women and children, the bulk of Medicaid spending covers the health care costs of the elderly. The largest percentage of Medicaid spending pays for nursing home and long-term care services, which Medicare does not cover.

Medicare

In 1965, President Lyndon Johnson signed legislation enacting Medicare, a program that provides health insurance to persons over age 65 and those under 65 who have been receiving SSDI for at least two years. Today, Medicare has four components.

Part A, Medicare's Hospital Insurance Program, is a social insurance program funded by a 1.45 percent tax paid by employees and employers that helps to pay for hospital stays. (This tax and the Social Security tax make up the "FICA" deduction from your paychecks.) All who pay into Medicare are eligible for Part A benefits when they reach the age of 65. Also eligible for Part A are persons under age 65 who have been receiving SSDI for at least two years.

All persons eligible for Part A and any persons over age 65, even if they are not eligible for Part A, can opt into *Part B*, Medicare's Supplemental Medical Insurance. Part B covers a percentage of physician costs and other outpatient health care expenses, such as laboratory fees and ambulance services.

In 1997, Congress established a third Medicare component, *Part C*, Medicare + Choice. This component allows Medicare beneficiaries to choose private health plans that provide them with the same coverage found in Medicare Parts A and B.

Under pressure from the American Association of Retired Persons (AARP) and other senior citizen interest groups, Congress proposed and President George W. Bush signed the Medicare Prescription Drug, Improvement, and Modernization Act in 2003. This act established Medicare *Part D*, the core of which is a prescription drug plan that took effect in 2006. A complicated program, Part D requires Medicare beneficiaries to choose a prescription drug plan provided by a private insurer if they do not already have prescription coverage through another health plan.

> On March 23, 2010, nearly a century after President Teddy Roosevelt first called for health care reform, and thirteen months after stating that "health care reform cannot wait, it must not wait, and it will not wait another year." President Barack Obama signed into law the Patient Protection and Affordable Care Act. Joining the president at the signing were Democratic congressional members and Vice President Joe Biden. Not present at the signing is even one Republican. The partisan battle over passage of this major health care reform did not end with its signing. It is ongoing as the national government attempts to implement the act.

The Patient Protection and Affordable Care Act

In February 2009, as he began his presidency, President Barack Obama staked out health care reform as one of his top priorities. Of the anticipated battle over health care reform, President Obama stated, "I suffer no illusions that this will be an easy process. It will be hard. But I also know that nearly a century after Teddy Roosevelt first called for reform, the cost of our health care has weighed down our economy and the conscience of our nation long enough. So let there be no doubt: health care reform cannot wait, it must not wait, and it will not wait another year."[24]

SHOULD ALL PEOPLE BE REQUIRED TO HAVE HEALTH INSURANCE?

The Issue: People who claim that U.S. health care is second-to-none support their claim by pointing to quick adoption of new medical technologies, patient participation in treatment decisions, prompt care, and the fact that the United States spends more per person on care than any other country. However, critics of U.S. health care point out that the United States has shorter life expectancy and higher infant mortality rates than most other wealthy industrialized countries. There is consensus that these are the two most reliable factors to compare health care systems. Critics also note that the United States is the only wealthy industrialized country in the world without some form of universal health care to ensure that everyone has access to some level of medical care. Moreover, approximately 45 million individuals in the United States do not have health insurance at some point each year. Should all people be required to have health insurance?

Yes: People without health insurance experience poorer health and die younger. The nation's economy is also harmed by reduced employment and job productivity, higher costs of public health programs, and diminished public health from lack of access to preventive care for those without insurance. Ultimately, people who pay health insurance premiums and taxpayers are burdened with paying the costs of health care for the uninsured through higher premiums and taxes, respectively. Those who can afford health care should be legally required to purchase it so as not to be a burden on the rest of us. The government should provide health insurance for those who cannot afford it.

No: First, it is unconstitutional to force individuals to purchase health insurance. The freedom to choose how they spend their money is a foundational right of American citizens. In addition, if the government has to insure all those who cannot afford insurance, we will experience further loss of personal freedom because the government will increase taxes on smoking, fast food, soda, and so on to pay for it. Moreover, uninsured Americans *do* have access to health care through nonprofits and public hospitals. Current law makes it illegal for any hospital to refuse emergency medical services because of a lack of insurance.

Other approaches: The national government requires employees and employers to pay into income security programs (Social Security and unemployment compensation). It also requires employers and employees to pay into the Medicare system (health insurance for retired citizens). Therefore, there is legal precedent for the national government to require employees and employers to pay into a health insurance system. The government could extend Medicaid coverage to nonemployed Americans who cannot afford to purchase their own health insurance.

What do you think?

① Is health care a right? Is it a privilege? Explain your answer.

② Do you think the lack of universal health insurance coverage is a large enough threat to public health that the national government should ensure that every individual has coverage? Explain your answer.

③ Is there a particular health care reform, or combination of reforms, that you believe the majority of U.S. citizens would support? Explain.

On March 23, 2010, President Barack Obama signed into law the Patient Protection and Affordable Care Act. However, the battle over health care reform did not end with the president's signing of this act. Congressional Republicans vowed to repeal the law. Attorneys general in more than a dozen states filed lawsuits against the federal government, contending that some provisions in the new law are unconstitutional. What is in this controversial, landmark legislation? The law's goal is to expand coverage to 32 million Americans who are currently uninsured through modifications to current government programs, new regulations imposed on the insurance industry and employers, and a requirement that all individuals acquire insurance. At the same time, the law attempts to contain health care costs.

The law expands Medicaid coverage to families earning 133 percent of the federal poverty level. It also requires states to expand Medicaid coverage to childless adults starting in 2014. Another means by which the law expands coverage is by making illegal (by 2014) the current insurance industry practice of denying coverage to people with preexisting conditions. In addition, insurance companies must now allow children to stay on their parents' insurance plans until age 26.

The law mandates that by 2014, everyone (with some exceptions for low-income people) must purchase health insurance, if it is not provided through their employer or a government program, or face an annual fine. The federal government will make subsidies available to individuals with income between 133 percent and 400 percent of the federal poverty level to help them purchase insurance. The law also calls for the establishment of health insurance exchanges in which uninsured and self-employed individuals will be able to purchase health insurance with federal subsidies. Moreover, employers with more than fifty employees will have to provide health insurance or pay annual fines for each of their employees who receive federal subsidies to purchase insurance.

For seniors participating in the Medicare Part D prescription program, the new law closes a gap in prescription coverage by providing rebates and discounts on brand-name drugs. To pay for the new government-provided benefits, the law imposes a new tax on indoor tanning services, on insurance companies that provide expensive, high-end insurance plans, and on investment income of higher-earning individuals and families.

After signing the Patient Protection and Affordable Care Act, President Obama said it "enshrines the core principle that everybody should have some basic security when it comes to their health care."[25] However, controversy continues over how the new law implements this core principle. (See "Thinking Critically About Democracy.")

Homeland Security

The government's responsibility does not stop with ensuring basic necessities such as a clean environment, affordable energy, a secure income, sufficient food, shelter, and health care. Federal, state, and local governments also cooperate to prevent threats to personal safety, home, and health. Such threats may come from natural disasters such as hurricanes and earthquakes or from human-made calamities such as terrorist attacks.

President George W. Bush and Congress established the Department of Homeland Security in 2002 in response to the September 11, 2001, terrorist attacks. The department's mission is to improve the coordination of efforts to prevent and respond to disasters, both human-made and natural, within U.S. borders. Homeland security is a central theme in contemporary U.S. domestic policy and an ever-present concern in Americans' daily lives.

Four Challenges for Policy Makers

Four significant challenges present themselves in homeland security policy deliberations. The first is how much intrusion into citizens' lives, in the name of prevention, is acceptable. The second challenge is the appropriate level and distribution of national grants-in-aid to state and local governments for improved communication systems and response capabilities. A third challenge has to do with the intergovernmental aspect of homeland security. The issue is, how much discretion should state and local governments have in administering the federal grants-in-aid? Although this is a common concern with respect to intergovernmental efforts for any policy area, the stakes can be very high and the finger-pointing and blaming can be especially vigorous when homeland disasters arise.

The fourth challenge for policy makers is how to ensure that national, state, and local bureaucrats, as well as other first responders, are able to coordinate their efforts to prevent and respond to homeland disasters. Communication, leadership, authority, and cooperation have all proven to be problematic during homeland disasters.

The Importance of Intergovernmental Coordination

Homeland security can succeed only as an intergovernmental effort. The prevention of attacks relies on intelligence collected by local and state law enforcement as well as federal agencies such as the Central Intelligence Agency (CIA), the National Security Agency (NSA), and the Federal Bureau of Investigation (FBI). Typically, the first responders to attacks and natural disasters are police officers, firefighters, emergency medical technicians, and other public servants hired by local governments. Federal and state agencies, when necessary, support first responders. The Department of Homeland Security agencies that back up first responders are the Federal Emergency Management Agency (FEMA), the Office of Domestic Preparedness, and the National Biological Warfare Defense Analysis Center.

Hurricane Katrina and its aftermath in September 2005 presented the first real test of the response capacity of the Department of Homeland Security. The department failed the test according to citizens living in the states damaged by the hurricane, along with local and state government officials, the media, and Bush administration investigators. According to the Bush administration's *Fact Sheet: The Federal Response to Hurricane Katrina: Lessons Learned,* the hurricane and the subsequent flooding of New Orleans "exposed significant flaws in our national preparedness for catastrophic events and our capacity to respond to them."[26] The report highlights the crucial need for the integration of homeland security plans across national, state, and local government, as well as across organizations in the private and nonprofit sector.

Clearly, intergovernmental efforts are essential if we are to have secure homes, health, and opportunities to pursue happiness within the borders of the United States—the mission of domestic policy. The efforts of individual citizens are also vital.

Another facet of the Department of Homeland Security's work is the implementation of immigration policy and border security. Continuing concerns about potential acts of terrorism on U.S. soil, as well as debates over the economic effects of the increasing number of immigrants coming to the United States, have placed immigration policy reform high on the national agenda.

Immigration Policy

The majority of immigrants to the United States are young people seeking two goals: reunification with family members residing here and work that will provide a better quality of life than they are able to achieve in their home countries. U.S. immigration policy, the collection of laws that specify which people the government will authorize to immigrate to the United States, allows approximately 1 million immigrants, in four categories, to immigrate legally each year. Figure 16.2 shows that these legal immigrants come from around the globe. In addition to the legal newcomers, about 500,000 unauthorized immigrants come into the United States annually. After the events of 9/11, citizens and their elected representatives, concerned about the impact of both authorized and unauthorized immigrants, began to analyze immigration policy anew. Debate on immigration policy reform has been ongoing ever since.

Authorized and Unauthorized Immigration

Federal immigration policy determines who may immigrate to the United States as permanent residents and as temporary visitors (such as tourists, students, and guest workers). Since the Immigration and Nationality Act of 1965, the largest category of immigrants authorized to come to the United States permanently are those seeking to reunify with family members who are either U.S. citizens or authorized permanent residents. The second-largest category comprises individuals welcomed for their employment skills; this group includes highly skilled professionals and wealthy entrepreneurs expected to invest in job creation. Persons to whom the United States offers humanitarian protection from persecution (or likely persecution) because of race, religion, nationality, membership in a particular social group, or political views compose the third-largest category of authorized immigrants. The smallest category of permanent authorized immigrants gain entry through the country-quota system, which allows up to 25,000 people per country per year (selected by lottery) to

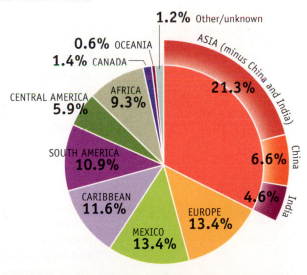

FIGURE 16.2 ■ GLOBAL SCOPE OF U.S. IMMIGRATION What world region is the source of most U.S. immigrants today? With respect to the Americas, what country or larger geographical unit is the source of most immigrants to the United States?

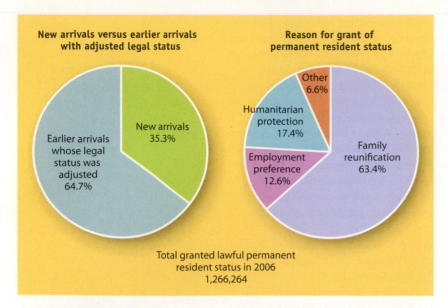

New arrivals versus earlier arrivals with adjusted legal status

Earlier arrivals whose legal status was adjusted 64.7%

New arrivals 35.3%

Reason for grant of permanent resident status

Other 6.6%

Humanitarian protection 17.4%

Employment preference 12.6%

Family reunification 63.4%

Total granted lawful permanent resident status in 2006 1,266,264

POLITICAL INQUIRY

FIGURE 16.3 ■ LEGAL IMMIGRATION TO THE UNITED STATES For immigrants who were granted lawful permanent residence in 2006, what percentages, respectively, were (1) new arrivals and (2) earlier arrivals whose legal status was adjusted? What factor accounted for the most grants of permanent status?

enter the United States legally.[27] Figure 16.3 presents the breakdown of authorized and unauthorized immigrants for 2006.

Who is *not* eligible for permanent authorized immigration to the United States? In addition to foreigners who do not fall within one of the categories described above, foreign nationals perceived to be anarchists or political extremists have been excluded since 1901, when a Polish anarchist assassinated President William McKinley (1897–1901). More recently, in 2002, the USA PATRIOT Act established new criteria for denying entry to the United States. Today, the national government can deny authorized immigration to foreigners who are perceived as a security or terrorist threat, have a criminal history, have previously been removed from the United States, or present a health risk.[28]

Why do half a million immigrants enter the United States without authorization each year? There are several answers to that question. One is that economic opportunities are better than those available in the home country. Yet unless an individual fits into one of the four categories for authorized immigration, he or she has no basis on which to apply for permanent, legal entry into the United States. Another reason for the large volume of unauthorized immigration is that individuals applying for immigration under the family reunification category or through their country's quota system come up against the annual U.S. quota of 25,000 per country. There is a wide gap between the number allowed under this quota and the number of applications. The result is a backlog of millions of applications that may mean up to a twenty-year wait for authorized immigration.[29] These are just some of the obstacles that explain why approximately 500,000 unauthorized immigrants enter the United States each year.

Proposed Immigration Policy Reforms

The flood of unauthorized immigrants creates financial and other stresses and strains that have prompted calls for immigration reform. Although unauthorized immigrants are not eligible for safety-net benefits such as programs for income security and food security, all children born on U.S. soil—even those born to unauthorized immigrants—are citizens and hence are eligible for these benefits. Moreover, the government guarantees a public education to all children, citizens and unauthorized immigrants alike. State and local governments cover approximately 92 percent of the cost of public education, and the national government funds the remaining 8 percent. And with respect to legal rights, the Fourteenth Amendment to the Constitution guarantees all people, not just citizens, due process before the government can infringe on their life, liberty, or pursuit of happiness, as well as equal protection of the law. Typically, the costs of these constitutional guarantees fall to state and local governments. Most unauthorized immigrants *do* pay taxes and so are contributing to government revenues collected to pay these bills. Yet their tax contributions do not cover these costs, just as the taxes collected from low-income citizens and authorized immigrants do not cover the costs of their safety-net benefits.

Given the financial burden of supporting the 10 million unauthorized immigrants residing in the United States in 2005, and in light of concerns about the ease with which terrorists (posing as well-intended immigrants) might gain entry into the country, Congress and President Bush worked intensively, yet unsuccessfully, to reform immigration policy. Without immigration reform, the federal government increased spending to install fencing along the U.S.-Mexico border and to post additional border patrol agents on the border.

Responding to the lack of national government immigration reform, numerous state and local governments began enacting their own immigration laws. According to the National Conference of State Legislatures, during 2007, state lawmakers introduced at least 1,100 immigration bills. That was double the number of state immigration bills submitted in 2006. Local governments also enacted laws pertaining to immigrants. Immigration reform was an issue in the 2008 presidential campaign as well, with Barack Obama saying he would work on it in his first year as president. However, by April 2010, the national government still had not taken up the issue of immigration reform. Then on April 23, 2010, Arizona governor Jan Brewer signed an immigration law that sparked protests and lawsuits. Civil rights organizations argued that the law would lead to racial profiling. The federal government sued Arizona claiming portions of the law were unconstitutional because they abridged the federal government's authority over immigration policy. In July 2010, a federal District Court judge blocked the implementation of several provisions of the law while allowing other provisions to go into effect. Arizona appealed this decision to the Ninth U.S. Circuit Court of Appeals, which scheduled a hearing for early November 2010. Ultimately, Arizona's immigration law forced national lawmakers to move immigration reform up on their policy agenda.

> Members of the U.S. Army install part of the fence along the border near Puerto Palomas, Mexico. The federal government is building a 745-mile fence along the U.S.-Mexico border to reduce the flow of illegal migrants into the United States.

CONCLUSION

THINKING CRITICALLY ABOUT WHAT'S NEXT IN DOMESTIC POLICY

A healthy environment is essential to human health, happiness, and survival. Reliance on nonrenewable energy sources, specifically fossil fuels, as well as the volumes of waste produced by the world's growing population, harm the global environment. Pollution and environmental degradation do not recognize the borders between countries. Emission caps in the northeastern United States do not compensate for the lack of caps elsewhere in the country, or in the world. Will worldwide environmental degradation force U.S. policy makers to sign international treaties?

Ensuring a healthy and safe society in which citizens can live their lives freely, in pursuit of their happiness, means more than protecting air, water, and land quality. During the Great Depression, the national government established income security programs to ensure at least a minimum quality of life for U.S. citizens. During the economic boom of the 1960s, the national government continued its efforts to ensure at least a minimum quality of life by creating national health care programs for the elderly, persons with disabilities, and very-low-income families. Today, the ever-increasing costs of ensuring a just and safe society in which citizens can live their lives freely, in pursuit of happiness, is forcing U.S. policy makers to take a hard look at income security and health care programs. Will the perpetually increasing costs of income security programs and health care force U.S. policy makers to enact major legislative reforms?

Each year, millions of immigrants enter the United States, some legally and others illegally, to take advantage of the quality of life in the United States. Throughout U.S. history, immigrants have been essential to the workforce and hence the economic health of the nation. High levels of immigration since the early 1990s have produced a U.S. population that is much more diverse in race, ethnicity, religion, and languages. Will demographic change owing to high immigration today bring new issues to tomorrow's domestic policy agenda?

STUDY NOW

Summary

1. Citizen Engagement and Domestic Policy

U.S. domestic policy addresses internal problems that threaten the people's well-being, domestic tranquility, and civil liberties, and a decent standard of living. The exponential growth in the number and range of domestic policies since the Constitution's ratification in 1788 is the product of the responses of elected representatives to citizens' and interest groups' lobbying efforts as well as national crises.

2. Tools of Domestic Policy

The national government uses various policy tools to accomplish its domestic goals. These include laws, regulations, direct provision of public goods, cash transfers, loans, loan guarantees, insurance plans, and contracting-out.

3. Environmental Policy

Since the 1970s, the federal government has assumed the primary role in formulating environmental policy. Through its regulatory policy, supplemented with grants-in-aid and loans, the national government has devolved the implementation of environmental protection to state and local governments. The tensions between the competing goals of environmental protection, economic development, and ensuring an ample supply of affordable energy are ongoing.

4. Energy Policy

Economic development and the high standard of living that is the American way have driven up energy demand. Given U.S. reliance on imported oil, much of it from politically unstable foreign nations, the internal situation of other countries strongly affects U.S. energy supplies and hence prices. Most U.S. energy is produced by the burning of nonrenewable fossil fuels, which harms the natural environment. This damage has led to an energy policy that includes funding for research and the development of alternative, renewable energy sources for the long term and conservation efforts for the short term.

5. Income Security Programs

The idea that the government should provide a safety net for citizens in financial need took shape through key components of President Franklin D. Roosevelt's New Deal. The government expanded that safety net with President Lyndon Johnson's Great Society programs. The national government meets its responsibility to provide a safety net through income security, food security, and housing security policies.

6. Health Care Policy

Health care costs are rising steadily for all. Even with the protections of Medicare and Medicaid, and even with the recent expansion of these programs, millions of people, including many employed adults, do not have health insurance. Given the steeply rising national and state expenditures for health care, and the large percentage of citizens lacking health insurance, research into and experimentation with new health care policies is ongoing.

7. Homeland Security

The Department of Homeland Security's mission is to prevent terrorist attacks and to respond to domestic disasters (human-made and natural). To accomplish this mission, the national government uses the policy tools of direct provision and grants-in-aid, working in collaboration with state and local governments.

8. Immigration Policy

Approximately 1.5 million authorized and unauthorized immigrants come to the United States each year seeking family reunification, asylum from persecution, and a better quality of life. Concerns over taxpayer costs to provide for immigrants and over the ease with which terrorists might gain entrance into the United States have sparked new efforts for immigration policy reforms.

Key Terms

cash transfer 496

contributory program (social insurance program) 497

direct provision 496

direct subsidy 497

entitlement program 497

environmental racism 500

feminization of poverty 508

food insecurity 511

global warming 502

greenhouse effect 502

housing insecurity 511

indexed benefit 506

in-kind assistance 496

living wage 507

means-tested benefit 507

noncontributory program 497

poverty guidelines 510

safety net 494

For Review

1. Explain the NIMBY syndrome.

2. Describe four or five of the domestic policy tools used by the federal government.

3. Discuss how the federal policy tools used for environmental protection make intergovernmental relations a key component of environmental policy.

4. Explain how concerns about environmental protection, as well as the political situation in oil-producing countries, influence national energy policy.

5. Use the following terms to distinguish between OASI and TANF: contributory program, noncontributory program, means-tested program, and entitlement program.

6. Differentiate between Medicaid and Medicare in terms of who benefits from each program.

7. What is the mission of the Department of Homeland Security?

8. For what reasons do hundreds of thousands of foreigners come to the United States as unauthorized immigrants each year?

For Critical Thinking and Discussion

1. Many critics of current environmental policy argue that government regulation of pollution amounts to ineffective policy. Some claim that using cash transfer tools, including tax expenditures, grants, and direct subsidies, would be more effective. Explain how the government could use at least one of the cash transfer tools to protect the environment.

2. Which cash transfer programs (including tax expenditures) will the majority of Americans benefit from at some point in their lives? Explain.

3. Explain how at least two of the programs discussed in this chapter are important to a sustainable community.

4. What might explain why Social Security and Medicare are entitlements but TANF is not an entitlement? Keep in mind the nature of the programs (contributory or noncontributory) and the populations each program targets.

5. Frequently, a crisis or a disaster is the catalyst for revolutionary, new public policies. Discuss one or two crises or disasters that have occurred in your lifetime and that led to major changes in public policy.

PRACTICE QUIZ

MULTIPLE CHOICE: Choose the lettered item that answers the question correctly.

1. The largest national cash transfer program is
   a. SNAP.
   b. Social Security.
   c. Temporary Assistance to Needy Families (TANF).
   d. unemployment compensation.

2. The largest component (in cost and number of people served) of Social Security is
   a. COLA.   c. SSDI.
   b. OASI.   d. SSI.

3. Pell grants and financial support to farmers for growing or limiting the growth of crops are two examples of the policy tool of
   a. contributory cash transfer.
   b. direct subsidy.
   c. insurance.
   d. loan guarantee.

4. All of the following safety-net programs were created during President Franklin D. Roosevelt's administrations *except*
   a. Medicaid.
   b. the minimum wage.
   c. Social Security's Old-Age and Survivors Insurance.
   d. unemployment compensation.

5. The environmental movement began in the
   a. 1890s.   c. 1970s.
   b. 1930s.   d. 1990s.

6. What is the current national minimum wage?
   a. $5.50.
   b. $6.75.
   c. $7.25.
   d. $8.00.

7. The disaster that prompted the national government to establish the Department of Homeland Security is
   a. the Great Depression.
   b. Hurricane Katrina.
   c. Love Canal.
   d. the terrorist attacks on 9/11.

8. The largest category of immigrants to the United States consists of
   a. authorized immigrants seeking family reunification.
   b. authorized immigrants with professional skills and/or wealth.
   c. authorized immigrants seeking humanitarian protection from persecution.
   d. unauthorized immigrants.

9. The entitlement retirement income program created in 1935 is
   a. EITC.
   b. OASI.
   c. SSDI.
   d. TANF.

10. The income security program that is subject to a regular COLA is
    a. minimum wage.
    b. OASI.
    c. TANF.
    d. unemployment compensation.

FILL IN THE BLANKS.

11. _____ is the national program that provides health insurance to the elderly.

12. _____ is the national program that provides health insurance to low-income citizens.

13. A (An) _____ program guarantees a benefit to all who meet the program's eligibility criteria, regardless of the total cost to the government.

14. An indexed benefit is one that automatically increases to keep up with inflation. The increase is a COLA, which stands for _____ .

15. A (An) _____ benefit has a government-specified income level (typically based on the poverty guidelines) as one of its eligibility criteria.

RESOURCES FOR RESEARCH AND ACTION

Internet Resources

Center for Budget and Policy Priorities
www.cbpp.org The center focuses on the impact of public policies on low-income households. On the Web site, you will find links to numerous reports elaborating on the effects of public policies on such households.

Environmental Protection Agency
www.epa.gov/history/topics This section of the EPA's Web site provides historical overviews of toxic waste sites that the government has worked to clean up.

USA Government Information
www.usa.gov This easy-to-use first stop for government information offers links to government agencies and their programs.

Internet Activism

Is there an issue you are passionate about? Do you want the government to address it? If your answer is yes, then visit **www.freethechildren.com/youthzone/media/sevensteps**. This Web site provides a step-by-step guide to political engagement, from researching an issue, through developing the agenda for and running a meeting of peers, to creating a blueprint for social action.

Blog
www.offthechartsblog.org The Center on Budget and Policy Priorities is a nonprofit, nonpartisan policy organization working at the federal and state levels on fiscal policy and public programs that affect low- and moderate-income families and individuals.

Facebook
www.facebook.com/pages/Ecological-Footprint-Quiz-Myfoot printorg/111090025594739?ref=ts Take the Ecological Footprint quiz to determine how your lifestyle affects the environment.

Youtube
www.youtube.com/watch?v=Q3JToii4Aq4 For a quick overview of the history of immigration to the United States through 2007, the last year that the U.S. House or Senate passed an immigration bill, watch this video.

Recommended Readings

Carson, Rachel. *Silent Spring.* New York: Houghton Mifflin, 1962. Thorough and alarming description of how the pesticide DDT harmed the food chain, caused cancer and genetic damage, and threatened the world as we know it.

Ehrenreich, Barbara. *Nickel and Dimed: On (Not) Getting By in America.* New York: Henry Holt, 2001. Documentation of the author's experiences when she joined the millions of Americans working full-time, year-round, for wages higher than the minimum wage ($6 to $7 per hour) in jobs with no benefits.

Gore, Al. *Earth in the Balance: Ecology and the Human Spirit.* Boston: Houghton Mifflin, 1992. Comprehensive assessment of the major post–Cold War threat to the United States and the world: planetary destruction due to overpopulation, deforestation, soil erosion, air pollution, and water pollution. Written before his more popularly known *An Inconvenient Truth,* Gore recommends far-reaching and specific governmental and corporate actions.

Kettl, Donald. *System Under Stress: Homeland Security and American Politics,* 2nd ed. Washington, D.C.: CQ Press, 2007. Comprehensive presentation of the massive bureaucratic reorganization that created the Department of Homeland Security. The effectiveness of this reorganization is assessed in light of the disastrous governmental response to Hurricane Katrina.

Movies of Interest

An Inconvenient Truth (2006)
A rallying cry for citizens and government to address the problem of global warming, this documentary presents the science of global warming as it follows Al Gore's environmental advocacy from his college years to today.

United 93 (2006)
An account of the fate of United Flight 93—the fourth plane hijacked on September 11, 2001—this fact-based film documents the plight of the passengers (who had become aware of the other hijackings) and their struggle to prevent another catastrophe. It also reveals the national government's lack of preparedness for the emergency.

A Civil Action (1998)
This movie highlights the enormous expense (financial and emotional) of proving in a court of law that a large corporation's chemical waste pollution caused the leukemia that killed children from eight families.

The Grapes of Wrath (1940)
The winner of two Academy Awards, this movie, set during the Great Depression, tells the story of the Joad family (and their acquaintances) as they struggle to meet their basic needs, first in the Oklahoma Dust Bowl and later in California.

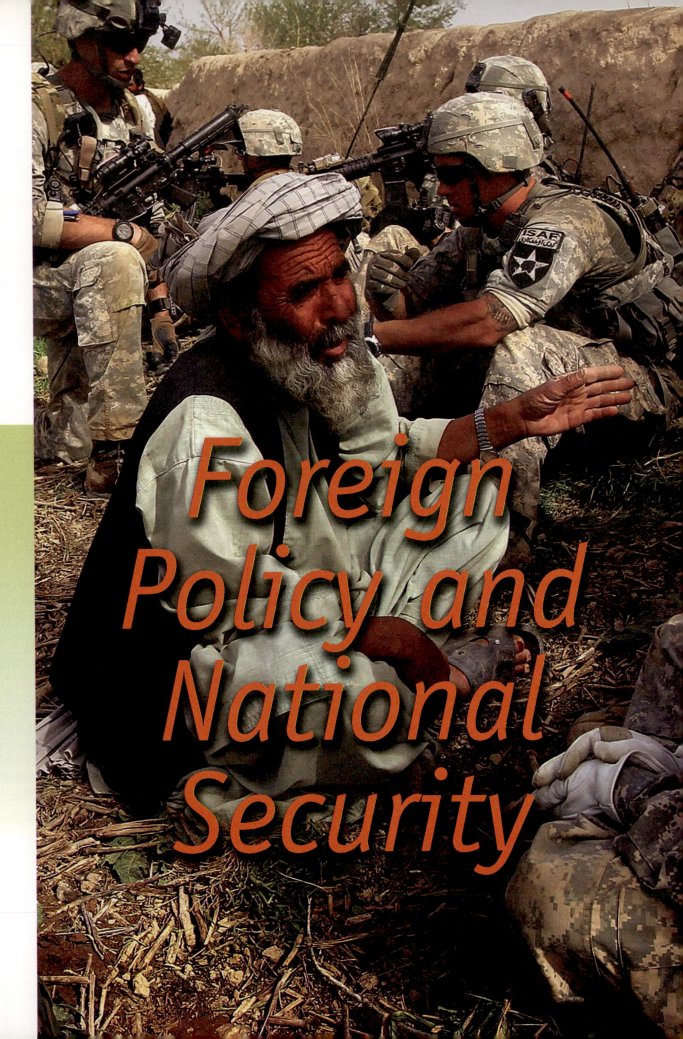

Foreign Policy and National Security

THEN

The emergence of the United States as a superpower and the Cold War dominated U.S. foreign policy in the aftermath of World War II.

NOW

The war on terror defines U.S. foreign and national security policy.

NEXT

What long-term repercussions will the wars in Afghanistan and Iraq and ongoing tensions with Iran and North Korea have on the future of U.S. foreign policy and the United States' role as world leader?

How will the continuing threat of terrorism against the United States influence foreign and national security policy in the future?

Will U.S. foreign policy in the coming years increasingly reflect a clash of civilizations between Western democracies and fundamentalist Islamic states?

This chapter provides a framework for your study of foreign policy and national security.

FIRST, we examine *the tools of U.S. foreign policy.*

SECOND, we analyze the question of *who decides: the creators and shapers of foreign policy.*

THIRD, we look at *U.S. foreign policy in historical context,* tracing its development from the ratification of the Constitution until World War II.

FOURTH, we analyze *the postwar era* and the status of *the United States as superpower.*

FIFTH, since it has become clear that Cold War policies are no longer relevant, we consider *U.S. foreign policy after 9/11.*

SIXTH, we take a look at *future challenges in American foreign policy.*

diplomacy
the conduct of international relations, particularly involving the negotiation of treaties and other agreements between nations

foreign service officers
the diplomatic and consular staff at U.S. embassies abroad

normal trade relations (NTR) status
the international trade principle holding that the least restrictive trade conditions (best tariff rates) offered to any one national trading partner will be offered to every other nation in a trading network (also known as *most favored nations*)

The conventional view is that

foreign policy is all about wizened old statesmen negotiating treaties and about sophisticated ambassadors clinking wine glasses at chic cocktail parties. It is true that top government officials in Washington, D.C., formulate foreign policy—the politics and the programs by which the United States conducts its relations with other countries and furthers American interests around the globe. But the broader, everyday reality of U.S. foreign policy is that individual American citizens play an important part in shaping and implementing the programs decided upon by foreign policy makers. Citizens play their part by staying informed about policy makers' decisions on war, peace, trade issues, and policies that ensure national security in the post-9/11 world, and expressing their personal views to their representatives in government and through the ballot box.

Of all the country's policy arenas, the foreign policy arena is the most volatile. During the past sixty years, the goals of U.S. foreign policy have shifted significantly, from preventing the spread of communism in the post–World War II era, to redefining the national foreign policy agenda as the world's only superpower in the 1990s, to responding to the terrorist attacks of September 11, 2001. As the objectives and the worldviews of policy makers have changed in concert with unprecedented world developments, so too have their priorities and the instruments available to them in implementing U.S. foreign policy.

The Tools of U.S. Foreign Policy

Government officials use a variety of instruments to shape foreign policy. Among these are diplomacy, trade and economic policies, and military options.

Diplomacy

Covering a gamut of situations, diplomacy is often foreign policy makers' tool of choice. **Diplomacy** can be generally defined as the conduct of international relations, particularly involving the negotiation of treaties and other agreements between nations. It can include an occurrence as mundane as the communication between two embassies when a citizen of one country commits a crime in another. Or it can involve an event as significant as a major summit attended by world leaders. When diplomacy works, we typically do not hear about it.

Among the central figures in the diplomatic arena are **foreign service officers,** the diplomatic and consular staff at American embassies abroad. Foreign service officers, who are employees of the Department of State, conduct formal communications among nations. They are frequently responsible for negotiating many types of international agreements, including economic and trade policies.

Trade and Economic Policies

U.S. foreign policy makers rely on trade policies, economic aid (foreign aid), and economic penalties to compel foreign governments to conform to the United States' will. Consider the example of most favored nation status. In international trade, conferring **normal trade relations (NTR) status** means that a country grants to a particular trading partner the same, least restrictive trade conditions (that is, the lowest tariff rates) that the country offers to its other favored trading partners—its "most favored nations." U.S. foreign policy makers can bestow most favored nation status on a country to influence it to enact policies the United States prefers. Conversely, they can withhold this status to punish a nation that does not institute policies supportive of the United States' goals. For example, the United States withheld most favored nation status from Vietnam for many years, in an attempt to get the Vietnamese to account for American prisoners of war and soldiers missing in action in the Vietnam War.

Governments also use trade agreements as a tool of foreign policy. Among the most important of these agreements in the United States is the North American Free Trade Agreement (NAFTA), whose members include the United States, Mexico, and Canada. NAFTA eliminated barriers to trade and financial investments across the economies of the three nations.

Beyond trade policy, American diplomats frequently use economic enticements in the form of foreign aid to pressure other countries into enacting and enforcing policies that the United States supports. After the terrorist attacks of September 11, 2001, for example, the George W. Bush administration sought the cooperation of the Pakistani government in Operation Enduring Freedom, the U.S. military offensive in neighboring Afghanistan. The United States sought to overthrow the Islamic fundamentalist Taliban regime, which had harbored and provided training grounds for terrorists, and to capture 9/11 mastermind Osama bin Laden, who was believed to be hiding in Afghanistan. Before the 9/11 terrorist strikes on domestic U.S. targets, Pakistan had received comparatively little aid from the United States. In fact, the United States had imposed sanctions on Pakistan because of its pursuit of nuclear weapons, its history of domestic coups, and its track record of defaulting on international loans. But after 9/11 and because of Pakistan's proximity to Afghanistan (they share a 1,500-mile-long border), Pakistan became a focal point of the U.S. war on terror. To encourage (and finance) the country's cooperation, the Bush administration waived the sanctions on Pakistan.[1] Moreover, whereas Pakistan had received only about $3.4 million in aid from the United States in the year before the terrorist attacks, in 2002 the country was the beneficiary of over $1 billion in U.S. aid. Although aid levels tapered off to between $400 million and $600 million annually between 2003 and 2007, the Bush administration requested $785 million for Pakistan in 2008.[2] The Obama administration continued the policy of relying on economic enticements to compel compliance. In 2009, the administration sought and won congressional approval for a $7.5 billion aid bill, to be disbursed over five years. The bill includes prohibitions against the use of the funds for nuclear proliferation, to support terrorist groups, or to pay for attacks in neighboring countries. And it reserves the right to end aid to the Pakistanis if they fail to crack down on militants.[3] The aid has proven effective in paving the way for warmer Pakistani-U.S. relations: the United States regularly uses Pakistani air bases to launch attacks into Afghanistan, and it continues to rely on Pakistani intelligence for information about terror network activity.

sanctions
penalties that halt economic relations

American foreign policy makers also rely on economic strategies to punish countries whose policies or behavior the U.S. government disapproves of. In February 2010, President Barack Obama announced that the United States and its allies were developing a host of **sanctions**—penalties that halt economic exchanges (and that may include boycotts and a suspension of cultural exchanges)—on Iran. The Obama administration and its western European allies object to Iran's pursuit of nuclear weapons. Obama's announcement came after Iranian state media reported that the nation had begun the uranium enrichment process. Iran stated that the uranium would be used for medical research, but the administration

rejected that claim. However, as former Senator Christopher Dodd (D-Connecticut), who chaired the Banking, Housing, and Urban Affairs Committee, noted, "Economic sanctions are a critical element of U.S. policy toward Iran. But sanctions alone are not sufficient. They must be used as effective leverage, undertaken as part of a coherent, coordinated, comprehensive diplomatic and political strategy which firmly seeks to deter Iran's nuclear ambitions and other actions which pose a threat to regional stability."[4]

Almost a century ago, President Woodrow Wilson made this observation:

> A nation that is boycotted is a nation that is in sight of surrender. Apply this economic, peaceful, silent, deadly remedy and there will be no need for force. It does not cost a life outside the nation boycotted, but it brings a pressure upon the nation which, in my judgment, no modern nation could resist.[5]

globalism
the interconnectedness between nations in contemporary times

But others argue that sanctions actually may worsen conditions, particularly for the poorest people in a sanctioned nation.[6] And given the high levels of **globalism,** or interconnectedness, among the world's countries today, a nation on which boycotts or sanctions are imposed often has recourse—sometimes in the form of aid from allies—to withstand the pressure of the economic penalty.

The Military Option

Since September 11, 2001, the United States has been involved in a multifront war that prominently features military actions in Afghanistan and Iraq. The September 11 terrorist strikes and subsequent U.S. government actions demonstrate how the creators of foreign policy use the military option as an instrument of foreign policy. Hungry for an enemy after the deadly attacks on American soil, the United States targeted Afghanistan's Taliban regime. The Taliban had supported and harbored members of **al-Qaeda,** the radical international Islamic fundamentalist terror organization that took credit for the 9/11 bloodshed. Foreign intelligence had pointed to Osama bin Laden, a Saudi millionaire living in Afghanistan, as the engineer of the attacks. U.S. military action in Afghanistan continues today.

al-Qaeda
a radical international Islamic fundamentalist terror organization

But the bases of world terrorist activity today transcend national borders. The nineteen 9/11 terrorists themselves were not citizen-soldiers of any one country but, rather, nationals from Saudi Arabia, the United Arab Emirates, Egypt, and Lebanon. They had trained in various nations, including Afghanistan, and had been supported by citizens of still other countries. Thus no single, clear nation-state was the enemy. Without a concrete enemy (over which a victory could be defined and declared), the Bush administration requested, and Congress passed, a formal declaration of a "war on terror."

Then–Secretary of State Colin Powell subsequently made a case to the United Nations and to the American people alleging that U.S. intelligence indicated that the Saddam Hussein regime in Iraq was harboring **weapons of mass destruction (WMDs)**—nuclear, chemical, and biological weapons.[7] In response to what at the time appeared to be a credible threat, on March 18, 2003, American troops invaded Iraq. The military strike toppled the Hussein regime, which the United States had supported for years through foreign aid.[8] Following the invasion, weapons inspectors conducted a thorough search of suspected weapons sites, but no WMDs were ever found, leaving many critics of the Bush administration to question the administration's motives and to ask whether the intelligence community had been pressured by administration officials to find intelligence rationalizing the war in Iraq.[9] Nonetheless, the military effort continues today.

weapons of mass destruction (WMDs)
nuclear, chemical, and biological weapons

When they use the military as an instrument of foreign policy, policy makers send a strong signal. When military conflict occurs on a grand scale—for the United States, that would include today's wars in the Mideast, as well as the Gulf War (1990–1991), the Vietnam War (1965–1975), the Korean War (1950–1953), and the two world wars (1914–1918 and 1939–1945), the goal often is **regime change,** the replacement of a country's government with another government by facilitating the deposing of its leader or leading political party. That is, rather than attempting to change another nation's policies, the wars are fought to end the reign of the enemy nations' leaders. On the other hand, most military action by the United States in the past century has occurred on a smaller scale, as policy mak-

regime change
the replacement of a country's government with another government by facilitating the deposing of its leader or leading political party

ers have sought to change the policy in another country or perhaps to protect U.S. interests or allies. For example, in 1999 during the Clinton administration, the United States took military action in Kosovo in the former Yugoslavia to halt ethnic cleansing in that region. Other military actions—in Somalia (1992–1994), Bosnia (beginning in 1993), and Panama (1989)—have also been on a limited scale with specific and smaller goals than those of the major conflicts.

Who Decides? The Creators and Shapers of Foreign Policy

In the United States, the executive and legislative branches are the primary foreign policy makers, with the president and the executive branch playing the dominant role. That said, a wide variety of interests—from the media, to interest groups, to other nations, and even private individuals—provide the context of the foreign policy process and contribute to shaping the policy outcomes of that process.

The President and the Executive Branch

The president of the United States is the foremost foreign policy actor in the world. This vast power partially derives from the constitutionally prescribed duties of the president, particularly the role of commander in chief of the U.S. armed forces. But presidents' foreign policy powers also have roots in the way the institution of the presidency has evolved and continues to evolve. Other government institutions, especially the U.S. Congress, have some ability to rein in the foreign policy authority of the president. But presidential resources such as cabinet departments and the national intelligence community, as well as the executive prestige that supplements presidents' legal and administrative powers, mean that U.S. presidents in the twenty-first century are the central figures in the foreign policy arena.

THE DEPARTMENTS OF STATE AND DEFENSE In the executive branch, the departments of State and Defense take the lead in advising the president about foreign and military policy issues. Specifically, the Department of State, headed by the secretary of state, has more than 30,000 employees located both within the United States and abroad. (State Department employees work at more than three hundred U.S. consular offices around the world.) These staff members are organized according to topical specialty (trade policy, environmental policy, and so on) and geographic area specialty (the Middle East or Southeast Asia, for example). Political appointees hold many of the top ambassadorial posts. These ambassadors and the career members of the foreign service who staff each **country desk**—the official operation of the U.S. government in each country with diplomatic ties to the United States—help to shape and administer U.S. foreign policy in that country.

country desk
the official operation of the U.S. government in each country that has diplomatic ties to the United States

The Department of Defense, often referred to as the Pentagon for its five-sided headquarters, is headed by the secretary of defense. The modern Department of Defense traces its history to the end of World War II, although it is the successor of the Department of War established at the nation's founding. The Defense Department is the cabinet department that oversees all branches of the U.S. military. Thus, although the Army, Navy, Marines, Air Force, and Coast Guard operate independently, administratively they are part of the Department of Defense. The commanding officers of each branch of the military, plus a chairperson and a vice chairperson, make up the Joint Chiefs of Staff, important military advisers to the president. Increasingly, both the State and the Defense departments rely on private contractors to perform some functions typically associated with these respective departments, particularly overseas.

THE NATIONAL SECURITY COUNCIL AND THE INTELLIGENCE COMMUNITY
As discussed in Chapter 12, the National Security Council, consisting of the vice president, the secretary of state, the secretary of the treasury, the secretary of defense, and the national

> The national security advisor has traditionally competed with the secretary of state for influence over foreign policy. Here, National Security Advisor James Jones chats with Secretary of State Hillary Clinton. Competition between the two advisors often stems from the differing time frames emphasized by each agency, with the NSC focusing more on short-term crises while the State Department emphasizes a long-term strategic view of global affairs.

director of national intelligence (DNI)
the person responsible for coordinating and overseeing all the intelligence agencies within the executive branch

security adviser, advises and assists the president on national security and foreign policy.

Through the input of the National Security Council, the president's administration considers the country's top security matters. The NSC also coordinates foreign policy approaches among the various government agencies that will implement them. A recent addition to the foreign policy apparatus, the national security adviser has traditionally competed with the secretary of state for influence over foreign policy—and for influence over the president as well. The tension between the two advisers also stems from the differing approaches each agency takes in shaping foreign policy. Frequently, the State Department has a long-term view of world affairs and advocates for foreign policies in keeping with long-term goals. In contrast, the National Security Council focuses more on short-term crises and objectives. These competing viewpoints have at times sparked media wars between the leaders of these foreign policy bureaucracies. Perhaps none of these battles was more contentious than the one between President Jimmy Carter's (1977–1981) secretary of state Cyrus Vance and Zbigniew Brzezinski, his national security adviser. Brzezinski publicly attacked Vance because he disagreed with Vance's push for increased diplomacy with the Soviet Union, advocating instead a tougher, more hawkish strategy.

A key resource in presidential foreign policy making is the intelligence community. Chief among the agencies in this community is the Central Intelligence Agency (CIA). This independent agency of the federal government is responsible for collecting, analyzing, evaluating, and disseminating foreign intelligence to the president and senior national policy makers. The CIA's roots are the World War II–era Office of Special Services. Like the NSC, the modern CIA was created by the National Security Act of 1947 at the dawn of the Cold War to monitor the actions of the expansionist Soviet Union. Since that time, the CIA has expanded its mission, using agents to penetrate the governments of foreign countries, influence their politics, and foment insurrections when the president has deemed such tactics necessary to promote American interests.

The clandestine nature of the CIA's activities prompted some members of Congress to raise questions about the agency's operations abroad. In 1975, the Select Committee to Study Governmental Operations with Respect to Intelligence—called the Church Committee after its chair, Senator Frank Church (D-Idaho)—began investigations into whether the CIA and the FBI had engaged in illegal activities while gathering intelligence. Those probes led to a series of reforms aimed at increasing Congress's oversight of the CIA's activities. Primary among the reforms was creation of the Senate Select Committee on Intelligence. Today, this committee and the House Intelligence Committee are the congressional watchdogs that oversee intelligence operations. Then, in the mid-1990s, following the collapse of communism, members of Congress again challenged the CIA's mission and operations. These critics complained that the agency was behind the times in remaining focused on an enemy that no longer existed. Evidence that operatives working for foreign governments had infiltrated the CIA led to even louder congressional demands for reform of the agency's operations.

These calls for reform gained strength in the aftermath of the 9/11 attacks. Congress, the media, and the independent 9/11 Commission pointed fingers at both the domestic intelligence service—the Federal Bureau of Investigation (FBI)—and the Central Intelligence Agency for failing to anticipate and to avert the terrorist strikes. Congress scrutinized both agencies for lapses in intelligence and apprehension. Because the CIA and the FBI had been seriously understaffed in Arabic translators, neither agency had had the means to interpret intercepted messages that might have enabled them to prevent the tragedy.

Spurred by the 9/11 Commission's findings, in 2005 President Bush announced the appointment of a national intelligence czar, called the **director of national intelligence (DNI).** This individual is responsible for coordinating and overseeing all the intelligence agencies within the executive branch.

DO THE GENEVA CONVENTIONS APPLY WHEN TERRORISTS HAVE SO DRASTICALLY ALTERED THE RULES OF WAR?

The Issue: The Geneva Conventions are a set of four treaties signed in Geneva, Switzerland, in 1949, in the aftermath of World War II. The conventions established standards for the protection of humanitarian concerns under international law. They apply to injured or ill members of the armed forces, prisoners of war, and civilians. Article 13 of the Third Geneva Convention, which specifically guides the treatment of prisoners of war, states that "prisoners of war must at all times be humanely treated. Any unlawful act or omission by the Detaining Power causing death or seriously endangering the health of a prisoner of war in its custody is prohibited, and will be regarded as a serious breach of the present Convention. In particular, no prisoner of war may be subjected to physical mutilation or to medical or scientific experiments of any kind which are not justified by the medical, dental or hospital treatment of the prisoner concerned and carried out in his interest. Likewise, prisoners of war must at all times be protected, particularly against acts of violence or intimidation and against insults and public curiosity. Measures of reprisal against prisoners of war are prohibited."*

Beginning in 2002, U.S. military authorities at the United States' Guantánamo Bay Naval Base in Cuba have detained about 775 "enemy combatants." Captured primarily in Afghanistan, these individuals were transported to Guantánamo for questioning. Although authorities in the Bush and Obama administrations have released nearly two-thirds of the prisoners, over 200 remain. As designated enemy combatants, the prisoners have not enjoyed the legal rights granted to individuals charged with a crime in the United States. In effect, the detainees at Guantánamo do not have the legal rights that those charged with a crime in the United States typically enjoy—no right to a lawyer, a trial, or *habeas corpus* (which, as you may recall, is a petition that allows a prisoner to go to a court where a judge will determine whether he or she is being held illegally).

Yes: The Geneva Conventions clearly apply in this situation. As many human rights organizations, including Amnesty International, argue, the detention of prisoners at Guantánamo amounts to a violation of the Geneva Conventions. Specifically, as these critics cite, there have been emphatic allegations of torture by individuals who have been released. Furthermore, the indefinite nature of the detentions—combined with the captors' acknowledged practices of sleep deprivation and constant light exposure, plus the disrespect of the Muslim religion on the part of some—constitutes the abuse of their human rights in violation of the Geneva Conventions. The moral high ground usually occupied by the United States is at stake, and if the United States does not accord these prisoners' rights consistent with the Geneva Convention, our own soldiers will be at risk of having their rights denied when they are captured by enemy forces.

No: The Geneva Conventions do not apply when the rules of engagement of war have changed so drastically. The Bush administration convincingly argued that the Geneva Conventions apply only to "prisoners of war" (POWs) and not to "unlawful combatants." Because the nature of the war on terror and of the tactics used by terrorists is in stark contrast to accepted international conventions of war, the treatment of combatants in that war should also vary. The Supreme Court has thus far agreed with the Bush administration's assessment that holding enemy combatants is legal.**

Other approaches: The Geneva Conventions do not apply to detainees at Guantánamo because they are not conventional enemy combatants, but the detainees should be afforded their human rights. In times like these, when international terrorist organizations do not follow centuries-old rules of engagement in warfare, the United States cannot follow antiquated rules and expect to keep its citizens safe. Therefore, detention can prevent further terrorist attacks if potential terrorists are prevented from carrying them out. Nevertheless, the detainees are entitled to humane treatment and to a hearing before an impartial judge to determine if they are truly a threat.

What do you think?

① Are the prisoners held at Guantánamo different from the prisoners of war held in other wars? If so, how?

② Are the Geneva Conventions, drafted soon after the conclusion of World War II, still applicable in the post-9/11 world, in which terrorism is such an urgent problem in international affairs?

* You can read the rules and explore other topics at this International Committee of the Red Cross site: www.icrc.org/ihl.nsf/7c4d08d9b287a42141256739003e636b/6fef854a3517b75ac125641e004a9e68.
** *Hamdi v. Rumsfeld*, 542 U.S. 507 (2004).

Congress

Along with the president, Congress enjoys significant constitutional authority in foreign policy making. The constitutional provisions that outline congressional authority with respect to foreign relations include, prominently, Congress's power to declare war. In modern times, however, presidential administrations have circumvented this congressional power by using U.S. troops without a formal congressional declaration of war. Such was the case in the Vietnam War, for example.

In response to this presidential tactic, Congress in 1973 passed the **War Powers Act.** This law limits presidential use of military forces to sixty days, with an automatic extension of thirty additional days if the president requests such an extension. But the nature of modern warfare has quickly made the War Powers Act less effective than in the days of traditional warfare, since most modern warfare (the Iraq War being an exception) is measured in weeks rather than months. Thus it has been possible for modern presidents to wage full-scale wars without congressional involvement. Because of this reality, some critics have argued that designating war powers to the president is a cowardly decision. Representative Ron Paul (R-Texas), a conservative Republican presidential candidate in 2008, observed that "Congress would rather give up its most important authorized power to the President and the [United Nations] than risk losing an election if the war goes badly."[10] Other critics contend that the war powers law itself violates the constitutional provision for the separation of powers by mitigating both the president's power as commander in chief and Congress's authority to declare war.

But Congress's ability to shape foreign policy does not rest merely with its authority to declare war. Congressional powers with respect to foreign relations also include the authority of the U.S. Senate to ratify treaties, as well as to confirm presidential appointees to ambassadorial posts and to cabinet positions (including those of the secretaries of defense and state). Furthermore, one of Congress's greatest powers is its national legislature's control of the purse strings. This control means that although the president can order troops into action, the members of Congress must authorize spending for such an operation. This tension between Congress and the president is plainly evident in the numerous congressional votes to allocate funds for the war in Iraq, particularly after the Democratic Party won control of Congress in the midterm elections of 2006. Although the Democrats in Congress would have preferred not to allocate as much money to the war effort, their hands were tied because they did not want to relinquish their obligations to the troops already deployed in Iraq, nor did they want to alienate constituents in the military or defense communities who were benefiting from the increased expenditures.

The Military-Industrial Complex

In his farewell address, President Dwight D. Eisenhower (1953–1961), Supreme Allied Commander of Europe during World War II, warned the nation of the influence of the expanding military-industrial complex. Eisenhower stressed that the American people and their representatives in government must "guard against the acquisition of unwarranted influence" and noted that "only an alert and knowledgeable citizenry can compel the proper meshing of the industrial and military machinery of defense with our peaceful methods and goals so that security and liberty may prosper together."[11]

Eisenhower was describing the mutually advantageous—and potentially corrupting—collusion among the U.S. armed forces, the defense industry, and Congress. These three entities have the potential to develop "unwarranted influence" over foreign policy in general and defense spending in particular, for several reasons. First, the goals of the military and the goals of the defense industry often intersect. Consider, for example, the military's need to supply soldiers with the appropriate equipment to fight wars. Both the military complex and the defense industry benefit from doing so: the military wants to protect its troops and help ensure their success on the battleground, and the defense industry seeks to sell such goods to the military—and reap a healthy profit.

A second reason that the military-industrial complex has the potential to be so highly influential is the close personal and professional relationships that flourish between the

---

War Powers Act
law that limits presidential use of military forces to sixty days, with an automatic extension of thirty additional days if the president requests such an extension

> Governments attempt to shape public opinion, especially in wartime. During World War II, posters urged Americans to buy war bonds, but during the Vietnam War, journalists—especially television reporters—allowed Americans to see a harsher image of war. In an indelible 1972 image of that war, 9-year-old Kim Phuc, who had stripped off her burning clothes, flees an aerial napalm attack. Kim Phuc is now a Canadian citizen, and her spoken essay, "The Long Road to Forgiveness," was broadcast on National Public Radio in 2008.

individuals in the military and their counterparts in the defense industry. These relationships are similar to the associations that develop in the case of iron triangles (see Chapter 13). Indeed, many retired military personnel often put their military expertise to work in "retirement jobs" with defense contractors or as congressional lobbyists.

For many congressional districts throughout the United States, spending by the federal government for military bases, personnel, and defense contracts represents an important infusion of money into the local economy. When this economic influence is combined with the clout members of the military, veterans, their interest groups, and their families can wield, we can see why many members of Congress support the military-industrial complex.

The Media

Because of the pervasiveness and reach of the media, foreign policy decisions provide prime fodder for news reporting. But the media go well beyond monitoring and reporting on foreign policy; they also frequently play a role in shaping the country's foreign policy and in influencing the conduct of that policy.

Since the beginning of the twentieth century, the U.S. government has used the news media in an organized way to promote its foreign policy priorities. During World War I, newspapers ran ads calling on Americans to take all kinds of actions to help the war effort, from cleaning their plates and planting "victory gardens" (to conserve food supplies for soldiers) to buying war bonds to help finance the war. By World War II, filmmakers spurred Americans to action, from enlisting in the armed services to conserving food fats and saving scrap metal for the war effort. In those various wartime initiatives, the media worked hand in hand with the government and generally took a highly patriotic and supportive stance. By the era of the Vietnam War, however, journalists, particularly television reporters stationed among U.S. troops in the faraway Asian country, painted a grimmer, more realistic canvas, focusing on the ravages of war that most Americans had never before seen.

> The media play an important role in keeping tabs on those who carry out foreign policy on the ground. In April 2004, the news magazine program *60 Minutes II* broadcast an investigation of prisoner abuses at the Abu Ghraib prison in Baghdad, Iraq. Among the images shown was this one from late 2003 showing Pfc. Lynndie England holding a leash attached to an Iraqi detainee. England and several other soldiers serving at the prison were convicted by the Army courts-martial. England served 521 days for inflicting sexual, physical, and psychological abuse on Iraqi prisoners of war. Though the soldiers claimed they were instructed by superiors to engage in the abuse, no commanding officers were convicted.

As for the news media's influence over the conduct and substance of foreign policy, it can take a variety of forms, including the following:

- *Agenda setting and public awareness.* By focusing public attention on policy makers in a certain area of the world or on a particular aspect of foreign policy, the media have an impact on setting the policy agenda. During the current conflict in Afghanistan, for example, the news media highlight the war's casualties. Newspapers report the names and sometimes print the photographs of soldiers killed in action; TV news specials scroll the names and hometowns of fallen U.S. troops and civilians. This coverage reminds policy makers and the American public alike about the human costs of war and can have an effect on subsequent policy-making decisions.
- *Investigations.* The media play a powerful role in determining that U.S. foreign policy is being implemented in a way that the policy makers intended. The news media also help to ensure that the men and women who carry out foreign policy "in the trenches" of real life cease to commit or rectify any abuses they may be committing. Consider the media coverage surrounding U.S. soldiers' scandalous abuse of enemy prisoners at the Abu Ghraib prison in Iraq. Graphic photos published in print and online of American soldiers tormenting naked captives reached readers all over the world. These photos heightened public awareness of the culture that appeared to be prevalent at the prison and led to the court-martial of twelve soldiers.

Public Opinion

Hot-button foreign policy issues such as the abuse of prisoners and the fighting of costly wars generate high levels of media coverage. The public might voice strong opinions on these issues in the wake of the saturated media reporting. Yet when it comes to foreign policy matters, public opinion is rarely the strong force that it can be in setting the domestic policy agenda. In general, people tend to be less concerned, less informed, and less interested in foreign policy matters than in domestic issues. Thus the public at large is likely to accept the views and actions of the individuals who make their country's foreign policy.

Public opinion plays a comparatively small role in shaping foreign policy for several reasons. First, foreign policy is made incrementally, over years and decades, and keeping up with international developments in different parts of the world is not something that many individuals or even news organizations do. Often, international issues must reach crisis proportions before media coverage becomes significant and exerts an impact on public opinion.

Many Americans also feel less connected to foreign policy decisions than they do to domestic policy issues. Individuals may feel empathetic toward Chinese citizens who endure human rights violations at the hands of their government or may express sympathy toward North Korean famine victims. Yet their compassion goes only so far, because those incidents have less bearing on their own lives than, say, whether their mortgage payments will increase because of Federal Reserve policy or whether more student loans will be available to pay their tuition. Despite the disconnect between most people's everyday lives and pressing issues in foreign policy, individuals nonetheless can and do influence foreign policy decisions, as we now consider.

public diplomat
an individual outside government who promotes his or her country's interests and thus helps to shape international perceptions of that nation

Private Citizens

Individuals can have an impact on the foreign policy process. Consider the various educational exchange programs that arrange for students from one country to visit another. In effect, such visitors act as **public diplomats**—individuals who promote their country's interests by shaping the host country's perception of their homeland, not only through educational but also through business or entertainment initiatives that advance mutual understanding.

A world conflict can become an influence in American foreign policy, too, when individuals take personal causes that are related to their ethnic origins to the White House and Congress. The influence of domestic interests on foreign policy, called **intermestics,** plays a distinct part in foreign policy making.

Among the most powerful examples of intermestics is the importance of large numbers of Cuban immigrants in Florida, many of them refugees or descendants of refugees from the regime of Fidel Castro. This influential group has swayed U.S. policy toward the imposition of an embargo against the Castro government since 1962, as well as encouraged tightened travel and currency restrictions between the United States and Cuba.

> Individuals can have an impact on the foreign policy process. Here, Music Director Lorin Maazel conducts the New York Philharmonic Orchestra near a North Korean flag during a rehearsal at the East Pyongyang Grand Theater in Pyongyang, North Korea, in 2008. The Philharmonic was the first major American cultural group to visit North Korea and the largest delegation from the United States ever to visit that isolated nation.

U.S. Foreign Policy in Historical Context: Isolationism and Intervention

As those who make and shape U.S. foreign policy continue to confront the challenges of a new century, they can look back on two broad historical traditions with respect to American foreign relations: isolationism and intervention. Historically, an initial policy of **isolationism,** a foreign policy characterized by a country's unwillingness to participate in international affairs, gave way to **interventionism,** the willingness of a country to take part and intervene in international situations, including another country's affairs.

The Constitutional Framework and Early Foreign Policy Making

In drafting the Constitution, the founders sought to remove the United States from international affairs. They reasoned that it was best for the new American republic to stay out of the deadly wars that had plagued Europe for centuries and because of which many Americans had left their native lands. Because of that isolationist outlook, the founders structured the Constitution so that responsibility for conducting foreign affairs rests exclusively with the national government rather than with the states.

THE CONSTITUTION AND FOREIGN POLICY POWERS The Constitution provides for shared responsibility for foreign policy making in the national government between the executive and the legislative branches. The Constitution grants the president very specific powers. These include powers related to the role of commander in chief, to making treaties, and to appointing and receiving ambassadors. In comparison, Congress's powers in foreign policy making are broader. Moreover, the Constitution structures executive and legislative powers as complementary. Note that the Constitution provides for checks and balances: although the president is commander in chief, Congress declares war and raises and supports an army and navy. Political scientist Roger Davidson has termed the give-and-take between presidential and congressional power "an invitation to struggle," reflecting the founders' attempt to ensure that neither entity dominates the process.[12]

EARLY ISOLATIONISM In keeping with the founders' emphasis on isolationism, President George Washington's Farewell Address in 1796 warned the young government against involving the United States in entangling alliances. Washington feared that membership in such international associations would draw a war-weary people and a

intermestics
the influence of domestic interests on foreign policy

isolationism
a foreign policy characterized by a nation's unwillingness to participate in international affairs

interventionism
a foreign policy characterized by a nation's willingness to participate and intervene in international situations, including another country's affairs

war-weakened nation into further conflicts. He refused to accept the advice of either his secretary of state, Thomas Jefferson, who favored an alliance with France, or his treasury secretary, Alexander Hamilton, who wanted stronger ties to Great Britain. As a general who knew firsthand about the ravages of war and who also was the first American leader to connect foreign and defense policy, Washington set the tone for the United States' role in the world for the next two hundred years.

> *Burning of the Frigate Philadelphia in the Harbor of Tripoli, February 16, 1804,* a painting by Edward Moran (1829–1901), shows the USS *Philadelphia* aflame in Tripoli Harbor during the Barbary Wars.

impressment

the forcible removal of merchant sailors from U.S. ships on the spurious grounds that the sailors were deserters from the British Navy

FOREIGN TRADE AND THE EROSION OF U.S. ISOLATIONISM

During Washington's tenure as president and in successive administrations, the United States' primary activity in the international arena was trade. Rich in natural resources and blessed with an industrious labor force, the United States sought to increase its wealth by selling raw materials and supplies to all sides in the Napoleonic wars (1792–1815), the latest in the never-ending series of European conflicts. The French empire took exception to the United States' provision of supplies to its enemies, and when France captured ships that it alleged were bound for enemy ports, the United States was forced into an undeclared naval war with France in the 1790s.

Neutral international trade was a difficult feat to accomplish in the American republic's early years. American ships had to cross sea lanes where neutrality was not the governing principle; instead, pirates, warring nations, and the allies of warring nations controlled the seas, and nationality counted for little. When pirates off the Barbary Coast of Africa seized ships and their crews, which they held for ransom, the United States fought the Barbary Wars (1801–1805 and 1815) against the North African Barbary states (what are now Morocco, Algeria, Tunisia, and Libya).

Throughout the early part of the nineteenth century, the seas proved a difficult place for American sailors. During that time, the British Navy began the practice of **impressment,** or forcing merchant sailors off U.S. ships—in effect, kidnapping them—on the spurious grounds that American sailors were "deserters" from the British Navy. In protest of this policy, Congress passed the Embargo Act of 1807, which forced U.S. ships to obtain approval from the American government before departing for foreign ports. But the British continued impressments, and the Embargo Act seriously curtailed the amount of U.S. goods being exported. Overall, the Embargo Act harmed the U.S. economy, as the decline in trade spurred more economic woes.

The tensions between the United States and Great Britain escalated as the practice of impressment continued. When the United States sought to increase its territory northward into Canada (then still part of the British Empire), the United States and Great Britain fought the War of 1812 over the United States' desire to annex portions of Canada and to put a halt to the practice of impressments. The war was relatively short-lived, ending with the signing of the Treaty of Ghent in 1814, when the British decided that their military resources could be better used against France in the Napoleonic wars.

Hegemony and National Expansion: From the Monroe Doctrine to the Roosevelt Corollary

After the conclusion of the War of 1812 in 1814 and of the Napoleonic wars in 1815, peace settled over the United States and Europe. Still, some American politicians feared that European nations—especially France, Spain, and Russia—would attempt to assert or reassert their influence in the Western Hemisphere. Thus, the view arose in American foreign policy-making circles that the United States should establish hegemony over its own hemisphere. In 1823, President James Monroe declared that "the American continents by the free and independent condition which they have assumed and maintain, are henceforth not to be considered as subjects for future colonization by any European power." Known as the **Monroe Doctrine,** this declaration sounded more like bravado than policy, because the United States was still too weak militarily to chase a European power away from South America, Central America, or the Caribbean. But the United States' interest in preventing the colonization of the Americas was consistent with the interest of the British, who did not want to see European rivals dominating in the Americas. Thus Monroe's doctrine had the backing of the still-formidable British fleet.

With the Americas out of play, European countries were expanding their colonial empires in Africa and the Middle East during the first half of the nineteenth century. Meanwhile, the United States also extended its territories westward and solidified its borders. Supporters of the theory of **manifest destiny**—the idea that it was the United States' destiny to expand throughout the North American continent—used this concept to rationalize the spread of U.S. territory. As the philosophy of manifest destiny took hold on the popular imagination, the United States expanded west to the Pacific Ocean, as well as south and southwest.

During this era, too, the United States became increasingly active in profitable international trade, particularly with China and Japan. To facilitate this Pacific trade—which was a primary goal of American policy makers—the United States acquired the islands of Hawaii, Wake, and Midway and part of Samoa in the 1890s. In 1898, on the pretext of ending Spanish abuses in Cuba and instigated by a jingoistic (extremely nationalistic and aggressive) President William McKinley and press, the United States decided to fight Spain, which by then was the weakest of the colonial powers. The United States won the Spanish-American War handily, and the victory increased the country's international prestige.

Theodore Roosevelt, who later became president, achieved enormous national popularity during the Spanish-American War for his leadership of the Rough Riders, a cavalry regiment. Their charge up San Juan Hill in Cuba in 1898 was the war's bloodiest and most famous battle. As spoils, the United States obtained the Philippines, Guam, Puerto Rico, and—temporarily—Cuba from Spain. Roosevelt supported the United States' entry into the war and later, as president (1901–1909), added his own famous dictum to the Monroe Doctrine: the **Roosevelt Corollary.** He announced that to ensure stability in the region, the United States had the right to act as an "international police power" and intervene in Latin America—and indeed, the entire Western Hemisphere—if the situation in any country warranted the intervention of a "civilized society."

After Roosevelt became president, the United States intervened in Panama, where U.S.-backed revolutionaries won independence from Colombia in 1903. The United States then immediately began construction on the Panama Canal in 1904. The canal improved the flow of trade by reducing the length of time ships took to travel between the Atlantic and Pacific oceans. It also accomplished one of Roosevelt's more cherished dreams: to show off U.S. naval power. At one point, Roosevelt decided to send the navy around the world strictly for public relations reasons, as a "show of force." Congress protested the cost of this endeavor, however. To outsmart Congress, Roosevelt, who had

Monroe Doctrine
President James Monroe's 1823 declaration that the Americas should not be considered subjects for future colonization by any European power

manifest destiny
the idea that it was the United States' destiny to spread throughout the North American continent; used to rationalize the expansion of U.S. territory

Roosevelt Corollary
the idea, advanced by President Theodore Roosevelt, that the United States had the right to act as an "international police power" in the Western Hemisphere to ensure stability in the region

> **The Panama Canal improved the flow of international trade by reducing the length of time ships took to travel between the Atlantic and Pacific oceans. This is an aerial view of the Gatun Locks.**

enough funds in the treasury for half the trip, sent the troops as far as Tokyo Bay. To "bring the boys home," Congress had to ante up the rest of the money.

World War I and the End of U.S. Isolationism

Encouraged by its successful efforts at colonization and strong enough by this time to ignore George Washington's admonition about avoiding foreign entanglements, the nation became embroiled in two major European wars in the twentieth century: World War I and World War II. The United States' isolation from the world ended with these two wars, even though strong isolationist forces in Congress and the White House continued to play a role during the first half of the twentieth century.

World War I came about primarily because of the balance of power system that dominated the world's foreign policy decisions from the end of the Napoleonic wars in 1815 until the conclusion of World War I in 1918. The **balance of power system** was a system of international alliances that, in theory, would balance the power of one group of nations against the power of another group and thus discourage war. For nearly a century, that attempt to bring order to international relations worked, and Europe enjoyed a long period of peace. But a flaw of the balance of power system was that a relatively small skirmish could escalate into a major international incident because of agreements for **collective defense**—the idea that allied nations agree to defend one another in the face of invasion—that were inherent in the system. Such was the case in 1914 in Sarajevo when a young Bosnian Serb student assassinated Archduke Ferdinand, heir to the Austro-Hungarian throne. The assassin was a member of a group seeking Bosnia's independence from the Austro-Hungarian empire. The empire demanded that Serbia respond to the assassination, and when it determined that Serbia had not so responded, it declared war. Austria-Hungary's declaration of war led to a sweeping domino effect that had the European continent in full-scale war within weeks of that initial declaration because of those alliances and collective defense obligations between nations.

The United States entered World War I in 1917, three years after the conflict began and largely at the behest of Britain. U.S. participation led President Woodrow Wilson to formulate the first conceptual framework for world governance that had ever been articulated. The most effective way to maintain peace, Wilson believed, was through **collective security**—the idea that peace could be achieved if nations agreed to collectively oppose any nation that attacked another country. By using this approach, nations at peace could prevent war by working together to restrain the lawlessness inherent in more unstable parts of the world.

Internationalism and the League of Nations

In negotiating the end of World War I at the Paris Peace Conference, Wilson sought to organize a **League of Nations,** a representative body that would ensure the collective security of nations. Wilson was successful in convincing representatives at the Paris meetings of the need for such an organization. But he was less successful in convincing Congress of the merits of the League of Nations. In 1918, the Republican-controlled Senate—Wilson was a Democrat—refused to ratify the Treaty of Versailles, which included among the terms for ending World War I the formation of the League of Nations. Without the United States, the League died a natural death before being replaced near the end of World War II by the United Nations.

In the dawning days of World War I, the United States was still heeding George Washington's call to avoid entangling alliances. At the war's conclusion, isolationism remained a key tenet of U.S. foreign policy. In the years immediately following the war, trade reasserted itself as the key component of U.S. foreign policy. The industrial revolution was in full swing, and the United States depended upon the import of raw materials and the export of manufactured goods to grease the wheels of its prosperous economy in the 1920s. During this time, however, Europe was healing from the ravages of World War I, and growth in its manufacturing sector meant serious competition for American industry.

The U.S. economy suffered another blow in 1929 when the stock market crashed, marking the beginning of the Great Depression. To protect American industry from interna-

balance of power system
a system of international alliances that, in theory, would balance the power of one group of nations against the power of another group and thus discourage war

collective defense
the concept that allied nations agree to defend one another in the face of an invasion

collective security
the idea that peace could be achieved if nations agreed to collectively oppose any nation that attacked another country

League of Nations
a representative body founded in the aftermath of World War I to establish the collective security of nations

tional competition, in 1930 Congress passed the Smoot-Hawley Tariff, which imposed a significant tax on imported goods. Confronted with this measure, other nations responded in kind, placing tariffs on American goods imported into their countries. The result? International trade dropped dramatically, and the economies of various nations, burdened by lower demand for the goods they produced, faltered. Industrialists, as well as citizens who saw the economic impact of an isolated United States, began to question the isolationism that had characterized U.S. foreign policy to date—from the era of Washington to the era of Smoot-Hawley.

World War II: U.S. Foreign Policy at a Crossroads

World War I was supposed to be the "war to end all wars." In hindsight, however, many observers believed that the victors only sowed the seeds of World War II (1939–1945). By impoverishing the defeated Germany through the imposition of huge reparations (compensation paid by a defeated nation to the victors for war damages) and the loss of 13 percent of its territory, the Treaty of Versailles (1919) created the environment that gave Adolf Hitler, the fascist leader of Germany, the opportunity to succeed politically. With his aggressive foreign policy, Hitler aimed to expand the German homeland at the expense of non-Germanic populations.

Influenced by a strong isolationist group in Congress, the United States waited until two years after the official start of the war in 1939 to declare war. Following a deadly Japanese attack on the U.S. naval base at Pearl Harbor, Hawaii, in December 1941, the United States declared war first on Japan and then on the other Axis powers (Germany and Italy) after those countries declared war on the United States. Following years of fighting on multiple fronts, in August 1945 the United States dropped two atomic bombs on the Japanese cities of Hiroshima and Nagasaki. Those devastating attacks ended the war.

The question remains whether the United States would have joined the efforts of the Allies (the United States, England, France, China, and the Soviet Union) sooner had policy makers known about the **Holocaust**—the murder by Hitler and his subordinates of 6 million Jews, along with political dissidents, Catholics, homosexuals, the disabled, and gypsies. Newspapers did not report the genocide until 1943, well after the war was under way. The experience of fighting World War II and dealing with its aftermath forced U.S. policy makers to reassess the country's role in the world, as well as the policies that governed its entire approach to foreign affairs.

Holocaust
the genocide perpetrated by Adolf Hitler and the Nazis against 6 million Jews, along with political dissidents, Catholics, homosexuals, the disabled, and gypsies

The Postwar Era: The United States as Superpower

The post–World War II era saw the emergence of two of the Allied victors, the United States and the Soviet Union, as **superpowers**—leader nations with dominating influence in international affairs. The United States' role as superpower in a new international system, and the relationship between these superpowers, would shape America's foreign policy for the remainder of the twentieth century. Increasingly important in this new era was the role that **multilateral** (many-sided, or supported by numerous nations) organizations and agreements would play.

superpowers
leader nations with dominating influence in international affairs

multilateral
many-sided; having the support of numerous nations

International Agreements and Organizations

In the aftermath of World War II, the United States was intent on avoiding the mistakes of the Treaty of Versailles, which many policy makers felt had led directly to the conditions that produced the war. They proceeded to address those mistakes one by one, often forming international organizations equipped to respond to the public policy challenges confronting the postwar world.

A key component of the postwar recovery effort was the **Marshall Plan.** Named for Secretary of State George Marshall, the program provided the funds necessary for Western

Marshall Plan
the U.S. government program that provided funds necessary for Western European countries to rebuild after World War II

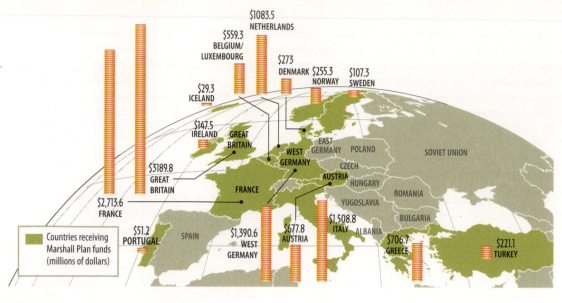

FIGURE 17.1

Recipients of Marshall Plan Aid, 1948–1951

SOURCE: www.cnn.com/SPECIALS/cold.war/episodes/03/maps.

European countries—even the United States' enemies from World War II—to rebuild. War-ravaged nations, including defeated (West) Germany, soon became economic powerhouses, thanks to initial help from the Marshall Plan. Ironically, by forcing the Germans to demilitarize as a condition of their surrender, the Allies freed Germany from spending large amounts of its own tax money on defense, thus enabling the German people to devote more of their resources to economic development. Other countries impoverished by war also benefited from the Marshall Plan (see Figure 17.1), creating new markets for U.S. products. Eastern European nations, now securely under Soviet influence, were prevented from participating. Because of the plan's success in Western Europe, the United States recognized that economic development and peace were intertwined, that economic stability was critical if future wars were to be prevented, and that an international approach was preferable to isolationism in foreign policy.

THE UNITED NATIONS   The Allied victors of World War II recognized the need for a structure to ensure collective security. In that spirit, U.S. officials organized a meeting in San Francisco in 1945 with fifty U.S. allies, all of whom agreed to create the **United Nations (UN)**. Participants hoped that this international body, through collective security, would develop the capacity to prevent future wars. The charter of the United Nations created these components:

- A Security Council with eleven members, five of which—including the United States, the Soviet Union (now Russia), China, Great Britain, and France—are permanent members with the power to veto any action taken by the council. Today, the Security Council consists of fifteen members, with the permanent members and their veto power remaining unchanged.
- A General Assembly consisting of all the member nations, each with a single vote (in 1945, there were 51 member nations; today there are 192).
- A Secretariat headed by a secretary-general with a staff at UN headquarters in New York. The secretary-general in 2010 is Ban Ki-moon of South Korea.
- Several specialized organizations to handle specific public policy challenges, including the Economic and Social Council, the Trusteeship Council, and the International Court at The Hague.

The United Nations' mission includes the promotion of economic and social development. Since its founding, it has added peacekeeping to its functions and has had some lim-

United Nations (UN)
established in 1945, an international body intended to prevent future wars by achieving collective security and peace

ited success in that endeavor in areas of the former Yugoslavia, the Middle East, and Africa. But in the immediate post–World War II era, the ability of the United Nations in general, and of the Security Council in particular, to provide for collective security was seriously undermined by the presence of the Soviet Union on the Security Council. Because the Soviet Union was a permanent member with veto power, any attempt by the Security Council to thwart Soviet aggression was blocked by the Soviets' veto.

NATO   It did not take long for the United States and the Western democracies to be disappointed by the inability of the United Nations to provide for collective security. The UN's failure to halt the militaristic expansion of the Soviet sphere of influence particularly troubled them. Their frustrations led the United States and its Western allies to attempt to bring order to international relations through the creation of regional security alliances. **Regional security alliances** typically involve a superpower and nations that are ideologically similar in a particular area of the world.

The first regional security alliance was the **North Atlantic Treaty Organization (NATO)**. Established in 1949, NATO created a structure for regional security for its fifteen member nations through a declaration that "an armed attack against one or more NATO nations . . . shall be considered an attack against them all."[13] Through the formation of NATO, the United States made a specific commitment to defend Western Europe in the event of a Soviet attack. In response to the creation of NATO, the Soviet Union and its seven satellite states in Eastern Europe formed a similar regional security alliance, the **Warsaw Pact,** in 1955.

The success of NATO at holding Soviet expansion into Western Europe at bay motivated the creation of the **Southeast Asia Treaty Organization (SEATO),** whose goal was to prevent communist encroachment in Southeast Asia. SEATO was a decidedly weaker organization than NATO; decisions had to be reached unanimously and rarely were. For example, SEATO was unable to agree to intervene in Cambodia, Laos, or Vietnam because member nations, including France, Pakistan, and the Philippines, objected to intervention.

Both NATO and the Warsaw Pact reflected the tensions and the rivalry that existed between the United States and the Soviet Union. They also reflected the failure of the United Nations to provide for collective security, that is, the security of *all* nations. Instead, the regional security alliances more closely resembled the balance of power alliances established after the Napoleonic wars.

INTERNATIONAL FINANCIAL ORGANIZATIONS

In addition to establishing the United Nations and NATO for the purposes of conflict management and security, the United States recognized the need to relinquish a great deal of its own economic power in exchange for the economic stability that would come from international financial institutions. Doing so would benefit the global economy in general but also the U.S. economy in particular.

To that end, in 1944, an international agreement made in Bretton Woods, New Hampshire—the Bretton Woods Agreement—established the International Monetary Fund. The delegates to the meeting charged the **International Monetary Fund (IMF)** with regulating the monetary relationship among nations, including the establishment of exchange rates for major currencies around the world. To the present day, IMF member states provide the resources the IMF needs to operate through a formula by which nations pay amounts roughly proportional to the size of their economies. Based on these IMF contribution quotas, nations are allocated votes proportional to their contributions. Thus the IMF perpetuates the dominance of the high-contributing economic powerhouses. Today, the United States has nearly 20 percent of the IMF votes. The Bretton Woods agreement also established the institution that would become the **World Bank,** which initially focused on lending money to countries devastated in World War II. Today, the World Bank lends money to developing nations to help them become self-sufficient.

Still reeling from the effects of high tariffs on international trade during the Depression, the United States also encouraged an international agreement that would heal the economies of nations by lowering tariffs and promoting international trade. In 1948, twenty-three nations signed the General Agreement on Tariffs and Trade (GATT). The GATT is based on the most favored nation principle.

In 1995, the **World Trade Organization (WTO)** replaced the GATT. Whereas the GATT was a series of agreements among nations, the WTO is an actual organization that

regional security alliance
an alliance typically between a superpower and nations that are ideologically similar in a particular region

North Atlantic Treaty Organization (NATO)
an international mutual defense alliance formed in 1949 that created a structure for regional security for its fifteen member nations

Warsaw Pact
regional security structure formed in 1955 by the Soviet Union and its seven satellite states in Eastern Europe in response to the creation of NATO

Southeast Asia Treaty Organization (SEATO)
regional security agreement whose goal was to prevent communist encroachment in the countries of Southeast Asia

International Monetary Fund (IMF)
institution charged with regulating monetary relationships among nations, including establishment of exchange rates for major world currencies; established in 1944 by the Bretton Woods Agreement

World Bank
international financial institution created by the Bretton Woods Agreement of 1944 and charged with lending money to nations in need

World Trade Organization (WTO)
organization created in 1995 to negotiate, implement, and enforce international trade agreements

FIGURE 17.2

Membership in the World Trade Organization, 2010

- Member
- Member: European Communities
- Observer: ongoing accessions
- Observer
- Non-member: negotiations pending
- Non-member

negotiates, implements, and enforces international trade agreements. Today, the WTO consists of 153 member nations (see Figure 17.2). Although it has a one-nation, one-vote policy, this policy is moot because the largest economies have the greatest say. The organization's goal—to remove all types of trade barriers, including obstacles to investment—is more ambitious than that of the GATT.

The Cold War: Superpowers in Collision

During World War II, the United States, Great Britain, and the Soviet Union were allies against the Nazis. But events at the wartime Yalta Conference in 1945—the second of three wartime conferences among British, U.S., and Soviet leaders—sowed the seeds of what would become known as the Cold War. The **Cold War** refers to the political, ideological, and military conflict that lasted from 1945 until 1990 between communist nations, led by the Soviet Union, and Western democracies, led by the United States. Each leader came to the Yalta Conference with an agenda. The United States' Franklin Roosevelt needed Soviet help in battling Japan in the naval wars of the Pacific. England's Winston Churchill sought democratic elections in Eastern Europe. And Soviet Premier Joseph Stalin wanted Eastern Europe as a Soviet sphere of influence, arguing that the Soviet Union's national security depended on its hegemony in the region.

At the conference, Stalin agreed to allow free elections in the region, but he later broke that promise. In response, former British prime minister Churchill warned Americans in a 1946 speech that the Soviets were dividing Europe with an "Iron Curtain." Churchill's characterization was accurate, because Stalin's brutal dictatorship, combined with the force of the Soviet Red Army, would install a communist government in every Eastern European nation. When Stalin also refused to cooperate in the planned cooperative allied occupation of Germany, the result was the division of Germany into separate zones, one administered by the Soviet Union and the other three by the United States, Great Britain, and France. In 1948, when the Soviets backed communist guerillas who were attempting to take over Greece and Turkey, U.S. president Harry Truman (1945–1953) committed the United States to "support free people who are resisting attempted subjugation by armed minorities or by outside pressures."[14] This policy—the United States' foreign policy commitment to assist efforts to resist communism—was called the **Truman Doctrine.**

Cold War
the political, ideological, and military conflict that lasted from 1945 until 1990 between communist nations led by the Soviet Union and Western democracies led by the United States

Truman Doctrine
articulated by President Harry Truman, a foreign policy commitment by the United States to assist countries' efforts to resist communism in the Cold War era

POLITICAL INQUIRY

U.S. Efforts to Contain Communism: Korea, Cuba, and Vietnam

The Truman Doctrine reflected the ideas of George F. Kennan, the State Department's Soviet expert at the time. Specifically, Kennan advocated the principle of **containment,** the policy of preventing the spread of communism, mainly by providing military and economic aid as well as political advice to beleaguered countries that were vulnerable to communist takeover. Kennan argued, "It is clear that the main element of any United States policy toward the Soviet Union must be that of a long-term vigilant containment of Russian expansive tendencies."[15] The idea of containment would spur the United States to fight in two protracted wars, the Korean War and the Vietnam War, to contain communism.

containment
Cold War-era policy of preventing the spread of communism, mainly by providing military and economic aid as well as political advice to countries vulnerable to a communist takeover

THE KOREAN WAR, 1950–1953   The first military effort the United States engaged in to check the spread of communism occurred in 1950. In June of that year, North Korea, with the backing of Stalin and the Soviet Union, invaded South Korea in an attempt to reunify the Korean peninsula under communism. During that summer, the United States sent in forces as part of a United Nations force to help the South Koreans repel the attack. The defensive strategy quickly succeeded, but by October the United States changed military strategy. Instead of merely containing the spread of communism, the United States sought to reunify North and South Korea—and, in doing so, to depose the communists from North Korea. But as U.S. and South Korean forces edged north, they also came closer and closer to the North Korea–China border.

That October, China, wary of a potential invasion, came to the aid of fellow communists in North Korea. The two countries' combined forces repelled the United Nations forces back to the 38th parallel, the original border between North and South Korea. Over the next two years, U.S. forces (as part of the UN contingent), North and South Koreans, and Chinese soldiers would continue to do battle, with very little territory changing hands. When an armistice was reached in July 1953, the border established was the 38th parallel—exactly what it had been before the war—although a demilitarized zone (DMZ) was created. Today, U.S. and South Korean troops still patrol one side of the DMZ, while North Korean troops patrol the other.

The Korean War marked an escalation and expansion of the Cold War. Not only was the war the first occasion in which the two superpowers clashed militarily, but it also brought

limited war
a combatant country's self-imposed limitation on the tactics and strategy it uses, particularly its avoidance of the use of nuclear weapons

brinkmanship
Cold War-era practice of fooling the enemy by going to the edge (the brink), even if the party using the strategy had no intention of following through

domino theory
the principle that if one nation fell to communism, other nations in its geographic vicinity would also succumb

the Cold War outside the boundaries of Europe. Significantly, the outbreak of the Korean War also gave rise to the concept of **limited war**—a combatant country's self-imposed limitation on the tactics and strategy it uses, particularly its avoidance of the deployment of nuclear weapons. The idea of limited war would set the stage for subsequent conflicts.

THE CUBAN MISSILE CRISIS, 1962   Another tactic of U.S. foreign policy during the Cold War was brinkmanship, a term coined by John Foster Dulles, the secretary of state under President Dwight D. Eisenhower (1953–1961). In essence, **brinkmanship** meant fooling the enemy by going to the edge (the brink), even if the party employing brinkmanship had no intention of following through to its logical conclusion.

The Cuban Missile Crisis in October 1962 turned out to be a perfect example of brinkmanship, even though that was not the intention of President John F. Kennedy (1961–1963). Reacting to Soviet premier Nikita Khrushchev's decision to put ballistic missiles in Cuba, Kennedy imposed a naval blockade around that island nation and warned the Soviet Union to withdraw its missiles, or else—never specifying what he meant by "or else." Although this confrontation seemed like brinkmanship, it was no bluff; rather, it was an act of bravado that could easily have led to nuclear war. Luckily for the United States and the rest of the world, the Soviets backed down, withdrew their missiles, and entered a period of improved relations with the United States.[16]

THE VIETNAM CONFLICT, 1965–1975   The United States' involvement in the war in Vietnam was motivated in large part by policy makers' acceptance of the **domino theory,** the principle that if one nation fell to communism, other nations in its geographic vicinity would also succumb. As described by President Dwight Eisenhower, "You have broader considerations that might follow what you would call the 'falling domino' principle. You have a row of dominoes set up, you knock over the first one, and what will happen to the last one is the certainty that it will go over very quickly. So you could have a beginning of a disintegration that would have the most profound influences."[17]

And so the United States again sought to contain the spread of communism in Southeast Asia. Although Vietnam was not of particular strategic importance to the United States, it represented the second "domino" in the faraway region. U.S. involvement in Vietnam started in the late 1950s, and by 1963, the United States became enmeshed in an all-out ground, naval, and air war there. The United States supported the South Vietnamese against the North Vietnamese in the decade-long civil war that would take the lives of almost 60,000 U.S. soldiers and at least 3 million Vietnamese soldiers and civilians. On April 29, 1975, when the South Vietnamese capital, Saigon, fell to the North Vietnamese Vietcong forces, the event marked the first military failure by the United States in its efforts to contain communism.

> A widow is comforted as she watches a stoneworker carve the name of her husband on the Vietnam Veterans Memorial in Washington, D.C., in 2005. Names appear on the wall according to the date the service member was killed in action.

Détente: A Thaw in the Cold War Chill

Richard M. Nixon (1969–1974) was elected to the presidency in 1968, largely on his promise to conclude the war in Vietnam. Although several years would pass before the war ended, Nixon's approach to the top foreign policy issues of the day marked a departure from that of his predecessors. Specifically, the **Nixon Doctrine** emphasized the responsibility of U.S. allies to provide for their own national defense and security and sought to improve relations with the two communist world powers, the Soviet Union and China. As early as 1970, his administration sought **détente,** or the easing of tensions between the United States and its communist rivals. In keeping with this idea, the Nixon administration normalized diplomatic relations with China and began a series of nuclear arms control talks that would occur throughout the 1970s. Critics of the Nixon Doctrine argued that President Nixon's approach to foreign policy was accommodationist—that it sought the easy solution and ignored the moral and philosophical implications of improving relations between the Western democracies and their communist rivals.

Part of the motivation for détente was the recognition that any escalation of tensions between the superpowers would increase the probability of nuclear war. Since the early 1960s, the United States and the Soviet Union had engaged in a nuclear arms race in which each country attempted to surpass the other's nuclear capability. According to the doctrine of **mutual assured destruction (MAD),** if one nation attacked another with nuclear weapons, the other would be capable of retaliating, and *would* retaliate, with such force as to assure mutual annihilation. The advent of intercontinental ballistic missiles (ICBMs) meant that both the United States and the Soviet Union were capable of sending nuclear warheads through space to targets in their rivals' homelands. The goal of the arms race (which would continue through the 1980s) was first-strike capability, meaning that each nation sought the ability to use nuclear weapons against another nation and eliminate the possibility of that nation's retaliating in a second-strike attack.

Many foreign policy makers in both the United States and the Soviet Union believed in the power of **deterrence,** the idea that nations would be less likely to engage in nuclear war if the adversaries each had first-strike capability. But Nixon and his primary foreign policy adviser, Henry Kissinger (who served first as Nixon's national security adviser and then as his secretary of state), sought negotiations with the Soviets that would dampen the arms race.

SALT I AND SALT II   In 1972, the United States and the Soviet Union concluded two and a half years of **strategic arms limitation talks (SALT talks)** that focused on cooling the superheated nuclear arms race between the two superpowers. The resulting treaty, **SALT I,** limited the two countries' antiballistic missiles (ABMs) and froze the number of offensive missiles that each nation could have at the number they already possessed, plus the number they had under construction.

The SALT II strategic arms limitation talks, begun during the Nixon administration and continuing through the Jimmy Carter presidency (1977–1981), resulted in the signing of the SALT II treaty in 1979. The **SALT II** treaty set an overall limit on all strategic nuclear launchers, including ICBMs, submarine-launched ballistic missiles (SLBMs), and cruise missiles. SALT II also limited the number of missiles that could carry multiple independently targeted reentry vehicles (MIRVs) with nuclear warheads, and limited each nation to the development of only one new type of ICBM.

Later in 1979, however, the Soviet Union invaded Afghanistan, sparking a new round of U.S-Soviet tensions. In response, President Jimmy Carter withdrew the SALT II treaty from consideration for ratification by the Senate. Nevertheless, Carter announced (as did his successor, Ronald Reagan) that the United States would abide by all the terms of SALT II as long as the Soviet Union complied as well. During his one term in office, Carter also sought to engage the world in a campaign for human rights, while at the same time attempting to convert the vast U.S. military apparatus to peacetime functions—a policy known as **defense conversion.**

The Reagan Years and Soviet Collapse

Ronald Reagan's presidency (1981–1989) marked a pivotal time in U.S.-Soviet relations. On the one hand, the Reagan administration pushed for a *reduction* in missiles and nuclear warheads, not merely a limitation on increases. Because of this new direction, Reagan named

Nixon Doctrine
policy emphasizing the responsibility of U.S. allies to provide for their own national defense and security, aimed at improving relations with the communist nations, including the Soviet Union and China

détente
easing of tensions between the United States and its communist rivals

mutual assured destruction (MAD)
the doctrine that if one nation attacked another with nuclear weapons, the other would be capable of retaliating and would retaliate with such force as to assure mutual annihilation

deterrence
the idea that nations would be less likely to engage in nuclear war if adversaries each had first-strike capability

strategic arms limitation talks (SALT talks)
discussions between the United States and the Soviet Union in the 1970s that focused on cooling down the nuclear arms race between the two superpowers

SALT I
treaty signed in 1972 by the United States and the Soviet Union limiting the two countries' antiballistic missiles and freezing the number of offensive missiles that each nation could have at the number they already possessed, plus the number they had under construction

SALT II
treaty signed in 1979 by the United States and the Soviet Union that set an overall limit on strategic nuclear launchers, limited the number of missiles that could carry multiple independently targeted reentry vehicles (MIRVs) with nuclear warheads, and limited each nation to the development of only one new type of intercontinental ballistic missile (ICBM)

defense conversion
President Jimmy Carter's attempt to convert the nation's vast military apparatus to peacetime functions

strategic arms reduction talks (START talks)

talks between the United States and the Soviet Union in which reductions in missiles and nuclear warheads, not merely a limitation on increases, were negotiated

strategic defense initiative (SDI, or "Star Wars")

a ballistic missile defense system advocated by President Ronald Reagan

these arms reduction talks the **strategic arms reduction talks (START talks).** Despite this overture, the Reagan administration was passionate in the pursuit of a ballistic missile defense system, called the **strategic defense initiative (SDI, or "Star Wars").** In protest of the development of this system, the Soviet Union walked out of the START meeting in 1983. The two superpowers would return to the table in 1985, after Reagan won reelection with a resounding victory.

In 1987, the United States and the Soviet Union signed the Intermediate-Range Nuclear Forces Treaty (INF), the first agreement that resulted in the destruction of nuclear weapons. It eliminated an entire class of weapons—those with an intermediate range of between 300 and 3,800 miles. A pathbreaking treaty, the INF shaped future arms control talks. It provided for reductions in the number of nuclear weapons, established the principle of equality because both nations ended up with the same number of weapons (in this case, zero), and, through the establishment of on-site inspections, provided a means of verifying compliance.

In retrospect, many analysts credit the Soviet Union's eventual collapse to President Reagan. During his tenure, Reagan ratcheted up the rhetoric with his many speeches referring to the Soviet Union as "the Evil Empire." Under his administration, the U.S. defense budget also doubled, with much of the expenditure going toward the SDI. The Soviets reacted with fear and a surge in spending. These developments all came at a time when the Soviet Union was dealing with dissatisfied nationalities within its borders, as the fifteen republics that eventually would break away pressed for secession. The last straw, however, was the country's troubled economy, because to compete with the U.S. ballistic missile system, the Soviet Union had to increase its military budget to the point where its economy collapsed—and with it, the government.

Post-Soviet Times: The United States as Solo Superpower in an Era of Wars

The START talks, which had resumed in 1985, resulted in a long-awaited agreement that reduced the number of long-range strategic nuclear weapons to 3,000 for each side. In 1991, the agreement was signed by U.S. president George H. W. Bush and Soviet president Mikhail Gorbachev, whose tenure had ushered in the ideas of *glasnost* (openness) and *perestroika* (economic restructuring) in the Soviet Union. That same year, after an attempted coup failed, the Soviet Union ended and Russia had its first democratically elected president, Boris Yeltsin.

Upon Yeltsin's election, in another series of talks called START II, Yeltsin agreed to even deeper cuts in nuclear weapons. Importantly, he also assented to the eventual elimination of all land-based missiles with multiple warheads (MIRVs). The START II agreement of 1992 between the superpowers was fully implemented in 2003 and significantly decreased the likelihood of a massive nuclear attack.

The 1990s proved to be a novel time in U.S. foreign relations. For the first time in over half a century, the United States was without an enemy, and it found itself the world's lone superpower. The tumult following the collapse of communism ushered in an era of wars—many of them fueled by long-standing ethnic rivalries or disputes—and the creation of new borders and new nations. By the start of the new century, fourteen wars were going on around the globe. Some, such as the decades-long conflict in Northern Ireland, now seem to be resolved. Others seemed intractable, such as the conflict in the Middle East over the Palestinian question. Still others, such as the tribal wars in Africa, were all too often manipulated by foreign interests and by corrupt indigenous leaders who were reluctant to give up their power. And other events—such as fighting that erupted between UN and U.S. forces against Somali militia fighters loyal to warlord Mohamed Farrah Aidid in 1993; the 1998 attacks on U.S. embassies in Nairobi, Kenya, and Dar es Salaam, Tanzania; and the 2000 suicide bombing of the U.S. Navy guided missile destroyer USS *Cole* in the port of Aden, Yemen—were harbingers of clashes to come. It was as if a giant hand had lifted a rock at the end of the Cold War, freeing long-submerged problems to crawl out and presenting new challenges for U.S. foreign policy makers as the United States assumed its role as the world's leader.

U.S. Foreign Policy After 9/11

American foreign policy makers' challenges in the 1990s pale in comparison with those they have faced since the terrorist attacks of September 11, 2001. The incidents on that day have profoundly defined and determined recent American foreign policy.

The Bush Doctrine: A Clash of Civilizations

One prism for viewing the 9/11 attacks is that posited by political scientist Samuel P. Huntington. He asserts that "the clash of civilizations will be the battle lines of the future."[18] Huntington's **clash of civilizations thesis** asserts that bitter cultural conflict will continue and escalate between modern Western democracies and fundamentalist Islamic states. Huntington, whose thesis remains controversial, argues that the ideological divisions that characterized the twentieth century—the clash between communism and democratic capitalism, for example—will be replaced by an older source of conflict: cultural and religious identity. Huntington initially posited his ideas in 1993, and his theories seemed particularly relevant during the 1990s when ethnic and religious warfare broke out in Bosnia and in parts of Africa. After 9/11, Huntington's neoconservative theory appeared to have significantly shaped the foreign policy of the George W. Bush administration.

Huntington's clash of civilizations thesis provides one explanation of *why* contemporary U.S. foreign policy has focused on the areas that it has. President George W. Bush himself articulated his views on the *how* of that policy's implementation. According to the **Bush Doctrine,** unilateral action (action by the United States alone) directly targeted at enemies is both justifiable and feasible. The Bush Doctrine also asserted that the United States should use its role as the world's only remaining superpower to spread democracy and to create conditions of security that will benefit itself and its allies.

WAR IN AFGHANISTAN The United States' first response to the 9/11 attacks was based on the connection of Osama bin Laden and the al-Qaeda terror network to the masterminding and execution of those attacks. For several years before 9/11, the fundamentalist Taliban regime in Afghanistan had allowed al-Qaeda training camps to operate in that country. In retaliation for the 9/11 strikes, in late 2001 the United States, a coalition of allies, and anti-Taliban rebels from within Afghanistan attacked the training camps and the Taliban government itself. Within weeks the Taliban government fell. By toppling the Taliban as the leaders of Afghanistan, the United States fulfilled the policy goal of regime change.

The multilateral forces worked to create first an interim government in Afghanistan and then, in 2004, a democratically elected government. Nonetheless, U.S. forces and those of its allies must still deal with continued attacks from Taliban forces, and Osama bin Laden, believed to have escaped to the mountains of neighboring Pakistan, remains at large.

Defining U.S. Foreign Policy

THEN (1984)	NOW (2011)
The Cold War was the defining feature of U.S. foreign policy.	The U.S. presence in Afghanistan and Iraq is the defining feature of the nation's foreign policy.
The United States and the Soviet Union competed as the two world superpowers.	The United States is the world's only superpower.
The arms race resulted in unprecedented military spending.	A multifront war and national security needs result in unprecedented defense spending.

WHAT'S NEXT?

> What new realities will shape U.S. foreign and national defense policy?

> Will the United States continue as the world's only superpower? How will a superpower be defined in the future? Will the term refer to military or economic might or a combination of these (and/or other) factors?

> What impact will continued spending have on the U.S. and global economy?

clash of civilizations thesis
Samuel Huntington's idea that bitter cultural conflict will continue and escalate between modern Western democracies and fundamentalist Islamic states

Bush Doctrine
the argument, articulated by President George W. Bush, that unilateral action directly targeted at an enemy is both justifiable and feasible

> One impact of the war in Afghanistan has been increased educational opportunities for women. Here Afghan girls listen to their teacher during language class in an open-air classroom after space ran out in their school. Shortages of supplies and overcrowded classrooms are commonplace, since the nation's girls, who had been prohibited from attending school under the Taliban regime, now may receive an education, though they are often still at great risk.

preventive war
the strategy of waging war on countries regarded as threatening in order to avoid future conflicts

Although the U.S. invasion of Afghanistan occurred largely in response to the Taliban's support of al-Qaeda, the invasion also demonstrated the potential consequences for nations that support terrorism against the United States.

WAR IN IRAQ After the Taliban's fall, President Bush set his sights on changing another regime: that of Iraq's Saddam Hussein. During the presidency of Bush's father, George H. W. Bush (1989–1993), the United States had gone to war with Iraq when that country invaded Kuwait, an ally of the United States. During the younger Bush's 2003 State of the Union address, the president claimed that Iraq possessed weapons of mass destruction (WMDs) and said that the Iraqis were attempting to purchase the components of nuclear weapons. In the ensuing weeks, the Bush administration made a case for going to war with Hussein's regime to both the UN Security Council and the American people. In doing so, Bush introduced the concept of **preventive war,** the strategy of waging war on countries regarded as threatening to the United States in order to avoid future conflicts.

The concept of preventive war represents a shift in policy from responding to attacks to anticipating attacks. The idea of preventive war is in part an outgrowth of the drastically altered nature of warfare. The biological, chemical, and nuclear weapons of today can cross borders with far deadlier efficiency than troops, ships, or aircraft. In addition, U.S. enemies no longer declare themselves as openly as they did before. The national defense policy makers who advocate preventive war thus argue that the only way to defend the country against these various new threats is to invade *before* the fact, in hopes of deterring another attack.

The invasion of Iraq in March 2003 was initially successful in toppling Saddam Hussein's regime. Despite insurgency violence that prevented peace from taking root, elections were finally held in 2004 and 2005, and power officially passed to an elected government. In the face of continued violence, the Bush administration enacted a military surge policy, resulting in the addition of more than 20,000 troops in Baghdad and Al Anbar province. Though not ending the conflict, the surge strategy was credited with quelling much of the insurgent violence in these areas.

In addition to the violence that has continued to plague Iraq, political turmoil has been characteristic of this nation. In March 2010, parliamentary elections were held—and large numbers of Iraqis defied the threat of violence and actual attacks to cast their ballots in one of the most open and competitive elections Iraq has had. The results were so close that only two seats separated the top two political parties, which then had to form a coalition with other parties to acquire the requisite number of seats to govern. Despite those challenges, the election was widely viewed as a success.

Nation building in Iraq proved troublesome—far more so than the rebuilding of Japan after World War II, for example. There, U.S. general Douglas MacArthur undertook the task of reconstructing the nation and creating a system of democratic self-governance. It took four years, but when MacArthur left for duty in Korea, Japan was as close to democracy as any Far Eastern country. Japan's feudal aristocracy was abolished, the country had a new constitution that empowered the legislature to make laws, civil liberties and collective bargaining were guaranteed, the legal equality of the sexes was established, and citizens had been given the right of *habeas corpus*. MacArthur also suspended banks that had financed the war, destroyed (at least temporarily) the giant monopolies, and refused to allow "war profiteers" to invade Japan at the expense of local businesses.

Fifty years later, as the United States sought to rebuild Iraq's war-torn infrastructure and feed its people after toppling Hussein's regime, a powerful insurgency thwarted American efforts. Unlike MacArthur, the U.S. military had allowed widespread looting in the early days of the occupation, including the looting of munitions warehouses. These munitions later helped to arm the insurgents. Also unlike MacArthur, who had some familiarity with Japanese culture, few commanders knew either the Arabic language or Iraqi culture and rituals. Even fewer knew how to stem the war profiteering of the multinational corporations that had also "invaded" the country.

The Obama Doctrine: A New Tone in U.S. Foreign Policy

With the election of President Barack Obama, it seemed that a new era in U.S. foreign policy had begun. As a candidate, Obama had called for an end to U.S. presence in Iraq and a change in the tenor of U.S. foreign policy. Of particular note was Obama's position that he would meet with Iranian leader Mahmoud Ahmadinejad to pressure the Iranian leader to give up Iran's efforts to develop a nuclear weapon. (See "Global Context.") Obama's position was controversial because Ahmadinejad has used strong rhetoric against Israel, a key ally of the United States. Throughout his tenure both as a candidate and as president, Obama has used language that would seem to reject Huntington's clash of civilizations thesis, which was instrumental in shaping Bush administration policy. For example, in what was billed as an "address to the Muslim world," given in Egypt in 2009, Obama referred to the differences between his worldview and those of his predecessors:

> Violent extremists have exploited these tensions in a small but potent minority of Muslims. The attacks of September 11th, 2001, and the continued efforts of these extremists to engage in violence against civilians has led some in my country to view Islam as inevitably hostile not only to America and Western countries, but also to human rights. This has bred more fear and mistrust.
>
> So long as our relationship is defined by our differences, we will empower those who sow hatred rather than peace, and who promote conflict rather than the cooperation that can help all of our people achieve justice and prosperity. This cycle of suspicion and discord must end.
>
> I have come here to seek a new beginning between the United States and Muslims around the world; one based upon mutual interest and mutual respect; and one based upon the truth that America and Islam are not exclusive, and need not be in competition. Instead, they overlap, and share common principles—principles of justice and progress; tolerance and the dignity of all human beings.

From his rhetoric, it appears that President Obama has rejected the idea that the United States and Islamic nations are destined to clash, instead seeking to build bridges between the United States and the Muslim nations. Nonetheless, many are surprised at how similar Obama and Bush administrations policies are, despite the change in rhetoric. For example, some analysts say that the success of President Bush's "surge strategy" in Iraq was the guiding principle behind President Obama's troop surge in Afghanistan. While ramping up the United States' involvement in Afghanistan, though, the Obama administration continues to scale back involvement in Iraq and has pledged to withdraw military forces from Iraq by 2011.

Future Challenges in American Foreign Policy

The volatility and the complexity of events in the global arena show no sign of abating. In the foreseeable future and beyond, U.S. foreign policy makers will undoubtedly continue to face a number of pressing issues. Certainly among the most urgent of these problems is the ongoing, acute threat of further terrorism directed at domestic and foreign targets. Issues such as the environment, human rights, and technology promise to remain a fixture on the U.S. foreign policy agenda in the years to come.

The Ongoing Threat of Terrorism

As the terrorist attacks of 9/11 tragically demonstrated, foreign affairs can be unpredictable. There are nonetheless some clear challenges that U.S. foreign policy makers are certain to confront in the years to come. First among these is the continued threat of terrorism. As a tactic, terrorism has proven enormously effective in accomplishing the goals of the attackers. Specifically, terrorism breeds terror—it has disrupted economies, created instability, and acted as a polarizing force.

The increasing availability of chemical and biological weapons to both nations and terror groups also promises to be a tough challenge for U.S. and other foreign policy makers. The potential, enormous damage of these weapons of mass destruction cannot be underestimated.

GLOBAL CONTEXT

THE UNITED STATES AND IRAN—A COMPLEX HISTORY

We can trace today's tense and complex relations between the United States and Iran back to 1951. That year, the democratically elected prime minister of Iran, Mohammed Mossadegh, nationalized the country's oil reserves, meaning that the government took over ownership of reserves that had been held by private corporations. Mossadegh's bold stroke set off a furious reaction by then–British prime minister Winston Churchill. Churchill and President Dwight Eisenhower, who was concerned about the increasing Soviet influence in Iran, agreed to enlist the Central Intelligence Agency in orchestrating a coup to depose Mossadegh in 1953.* The coup attempt eventually succeeded, and Mohammad Reza Pahlavi, Iran's monarch (Shah), installed as prime minister Fazlollah Zahedi, the choice of Great Britain and the United States.

Are Western democracies and fundamentalist Islamic states such as Iran destined to clash?

With continued British and U.S. support, the Shah modernized Iran's infrastructure. His autocratic rule, however, opened him to criticism by Ayatollah Ruhollah Khomeini, an influential Islamic Iranian cleric. Khomeini was exiled from the country but remained a vocal critic of both the Shah and the United States, which he characterized as "the Great Satan."

In early 1978, individuals from a broad coalition of Iranians—including students, Marxists, and pro-democracy activists—took to the streets protesting the Shah's oppressive government and calling for Khomeini's return. The demonstrations evolved into what became known as the Iranian revolution and forced the Shah to flee Iran in January 1979. When a victorious Khomeini returned to Iran shortly after, many Iranians embraced the stern cleric. And although various groups had sought to depose the Shah, the Iranian people at large soon voted to make Iran an Islamic republic with Khomeini as its leader.

During the Iranian uprisings in 1979, students had seized control of the U.S. embassy in Tehran and taken its personnel as hostages. The students claimed that the diplomats were CIA agents plotting a coup against the Khomeini government, as indeed had occurred in 1953. During this time, tensions between the United States and Iran were sky-high, and fifty-two Americans were held hostage for 444 days. Khomeini supported the students' actions. Part of the American response was to freeze more than $12 billion in Iranian assets in the United States. Although the United States later returned a sizeable portion of those assets, other parts remain frozen as the United States awaits the resolution of property disputes that arose out of the revolution. To the present day, this issue is a point of sharp contention between the two countries.

Closely monitoring the bitter relations between the United States and its allies and Iran, Saddam Hussein, the president of neighboring Iraq, decided to exploit the ill will that Westerners felt for the Khomeini regime and the chaos that had accompanied the Iranian revolution. Hussein's Iraqi army invaded Iran in 1980, setting off the Iran-Iraq War. The United States backed Iraq in this six-year war, in which Hussein used chemical weapons against Iranian soldiers and civilians.

Over the next fifteen years, relations between the United States and Iran remained contentious. The United States denounced Iran's support of terrorist organizations and its pursuit of nuclear weapons. In 1995, the Clinton administration imposed economic sanctions on Iran. These sanctions were expanded with the passage of the Iran-Libya Sanctions Act of 1996, which penalized foreign corporations that invested in Iran's energy industry. This measure was a severe blow to the Iranian economy. In 1997, reformist Mohammad Khatami was elected president of Iran with a platform of strengthening democracy in Iran. Khatami made overtures to the United States, and for several years, the icy American-Iranian relations seemed to be thawing. When the terrorist attacks of September 11 occurred, young Iranians took to the streets in spontaneous demonstrations of support for the U.S. victims of the attacks.

That the good will had dissolved, however, was apparent when George W. Bush characterized Iran as part of an "axis of evil" in his 2002 State of the Union speech. Relations chilled primarily because of Iran's pursuit of nuclear weapons. Since that time, the harsh rhetoric has continued between the United States and Iran, with President Barack Obama seeking sanctions against Iran in response to its continuing pursuit of nuclear weapons.

> Iranian women light candles in Mother Square in Tehran on September 18, 2001, in memory of victims of the September 11th terrorist attacks on the United States.

* www.nytimes.com/library/world/mideast/041600iran-cia-index.html.

ANALYZING THE SOURCES

INTERNATIONAL APPROVAL OF U.S. LEADERSHIP

The graphs below show the percentage approving and disapproving of U.S. leadership worldwide, and in Europe, Africa, the Americas, and Asia from 2006 through 2009.

Do you approve or disapprove of the job performance of the leadership of the United States?

● % Approve   ● % Disapprove   ● % Don't know/Refused

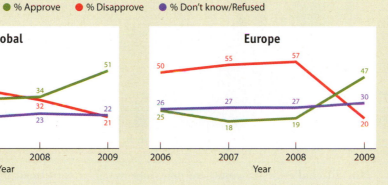

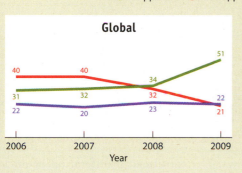

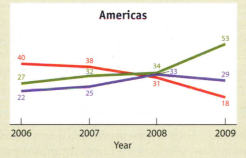

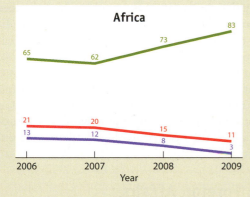

Evaluating the Evidence

① What is the overall trend regarding approval rating of U.S. leadership? What accounts for changes in the overall trend?

② Where specifically is U.S. leadership viewed most favorably? Least favorably?

③ Where have views of leadership changed the most? Why do you think this is the case?

FIGURE 17.3 ■ THE NUCLEAR CLUB What, if anything, do most or all of the countries that gave up or ended their nuclear programs have in common, either among themselves or with the countries that have nuclear capability? What do most or all of the countries that have nuclear capability—either declared or undeclared—have in common? What conclusions can you draw about these commonalities?

● **Declared nuclear capability**
United States
Russia
China
India
Pakistan
Britain
France
North Korea

● **Undeclared capability**
Israel

● **Seeking capability**
Iran
Syria

● **Gave up**
Belarus
Ukraine
Kazakhstan
South Africa

● **Ended**
Brazil
Argentina
Algeria
Libya
Sweden
Iraq
South Korea
Taiwan

Not all challenges to come are new, however. The continued proliferation of nuclear weapons presents a serious problem to foreign policy makers throughout the world. Figure 17.3 shows that eight nations have a declared nuclear weapons capability, including India and Pakistan; that another, Israel, has the undeclared potential; and that yet another, Iran, is seeking such potential. The fact that dangerous WMDs are in such wide distribution increases the likelihood of their use—either accidentally or intentionally.

Environmental Issues

In 2007, former vice president Al Gore won the Nobel Peace Prize for his work in raising public awareness of the critically important issue of rapid global climate change. This problem and other environmental concerns that by their very nature are worldwide challenges promise to remain on the United States' foreign policy agenda deep into the future. Specifically, the failure of the United States to ratify the Kyoto Protocol—an international agreement whose objective is to reduce global warming by lowering the amount of greenhouse gas emissions—makes it likely that the warming of Planet Earth will be a continuing and increasingly urgent focus of U.S. foreign policy makers. Other environmental concerns that are sure to have a secure place in foreign policy makers' agendas for the future include the enormous world consumption of fossil fuels, the deterioration of the oceans, worldwide deforestation, and ongoing air and water contamination.

Technology's Potential in Foreign Affairs

Although there are many uncertainties about what's next in the foreign policy arena, one certainty is that the impact of technology—as a tool in foreign policy and in citizens' efforts to influence the policies and institutions of government—will continue to increase. The impact of new technologies could be seen in 2009, when activists protesting Iranian elections initially relied on cell phones and the

Internet to spread word of demonstrations. During the protests, citizens and journalists photographed, videoed, and transmitted images of the massive demonstrations. Because such technologies enable citizens to see how governments in other countries work, a number of countries have thrown off the shackles of one-person or one-party rule. Finding Western democracy preferable to their own form of government, in 2004, 48 million voters in the Ukraine overturned dubious election results and ousted the first victor, Prime Minister Viktor Yanukovych, installing in his stead another Viktor: Viktor Yushenko. The electronic media broadcast the "orange revolution" in the Ukraine—so called for the orange flags and orange garments of the protesters—for viewers around the world to see. The increasing inability of countries, including China and North Korea, to limit access to technology and information from around the world will prove empowering to people everywhere.

CONCLUSION

THINKING CRITICALLY ABOUT WHAT'S NEXT IN FOREIGN POLICY

In retrospect, the development of the United States' foreign policy over time seems to have followed a natural progression as the nation itself grew and changed. The nation's initial isolationism, spawned by a healthy suspicion of foreign powers and their motives, gave way to international relations in the limited sphere of trade. Then, in both World War I and World War II, the importance of global alliances in helping to shape U.S. foreign policy became evident. With the end of World War II, the United States emerged as a superpower whose foreign policy came to be defined largely by its relations with its chief rival in the global arena, the Soviet Union. After the collapse of the Soviet empire in the 1990s, the foreign policy arena was murky as U.S. and world policy makers searched for a new prism through which to view the nations of the world. Could policy makers have anticipated the threat of terrorism that was to come?

On September 11, 2001, U.S. foreign policy instantly acquired a new focus. Their morning hardly going according to their daily planners, a shaken president and his aides scrambled to respond appropriately to the unforeseen and unprecedented terrorist attacks on U.S. soil. They asked the same question that the millions of Americans who watched the unbelievable events unfold on television asked: Why? Ultimately, the administration's responses to the terrorist strikes showed that significant cultural and political differences separate the United States and the other Western democracies on the one hand, and fundamentalist non-Western states that harbor terrorists on the other hand. The attacks crystallized perceptions both among U.S. policy makers and in the general public that no longer could the terrorist states be viewed simply as potential threats or as insignificant to the United States' interests. Do those perceptions remain widely held by the public and policy makers today?

Since assuming the presidency in January 2009, the Obama administration has signaled a departure from the tenor of the Bush administration. But it remains unclear whether Obama's more conciliatory approach will prove effective in building relations with Arab and Muslim nations. It also remains to be seen whether national security measures put in place by both Bush and Obama administrations will effectively deter future terror attacks on the United States.

Given the distinctive nature of those who practice terrorism—their lack of geographic boundaries and their refusal to abide by the conventional rules of war—such a conflict surely would differ starkly from the last major clash of ideologies, the Cold War. In view of the unique qualities of terrorism, it is difficult to anticipate how the continued threat of terrorist acts will shape U.S. foreign policy. The randomness of terrorism confounds policy makers and other experts and prevents them from making accurate predictions and determining adequate modes of defense. Nonetheless, given the high stakes of another potential attack, the threat of terrorism—and the imperative to prevent it—clearly will remain a defining characteristic of U.S. foreign policy in the decades to come.

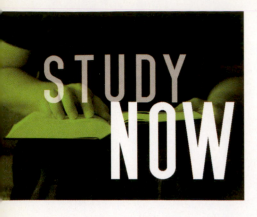

Summary

1. The Tools of U.S. Foreign Policy

The government officials who formulate U.S. foreign policy rely on diplomacy, by which nations conduct political negotiations with one another and settle disagreements. They also rely on economic policy to cajole other nations into enacting policies that the United States supports, and on military force, if needed, to force other countries to align with U.S. interests.

2. Who Decides? The Creators and Shapers of Foreign Policy

Because the Constitution grants important foreign policy-making powers to the president, the president along with the executive branch is the primary foreign policy maker in the United States. Congress also plays an important role in creating foreign policy, particularly through its decision making with respect to declaring war and appropriating funds. Interest groups, the media, and private individuals also influence the foreign policy process.

3. U.S. Foreign Policy in Historical Context: Isolationism and Intervention

The conduct of foreign policy was at first influenced by a suspicion of foreign affairs. As the U.S. economy developed, government and business interests primarily concentrated on maximizing profits through international trade. In the twentieth century, the balance of power system drew the United States into global conflict in World War I. Although the United States retreated into an isolationist position during the Great Depression, an alliance with the British and Japan's attack on the U.S. naval base at Pearl Harbor, Hawaii, precipitated U.S. entry into World War II.

4. The Postwar Era: The United States as Superpower

After the Second World War, the United States and the Soviet Union emerged as competing superpowers locked in a Cold War of clashing ideologies. This rivalry defined U.S. foreign policy for half a century. During this period, international organizations charged with ensuring security and facilitating economic relations among nations were established. During the Cold War, the United States also attempted to curb the spread of communism on the Korean peninsula, in Cuba, and in Vietnam. President Richard Nixon initiated a period of détente; President Ronald Reagan outspent the Soviets and forced the collapse of the Soviet economy. The end of communism in the Soviet Union and Eastern Europe meant drastic changes in the context of international relations.

5. U.S. Foreign Policy After 9/11

With the terrorist attacks of September 11, 2001, a new era in U.S. foreign policy commenced, seeming to reflect acceptance of the theory that a clash of civilizations—warfare over cultural and religious differences—was inevitable. In espousing the tenets of the Bush Doctrine, administration officials promoted the strategy of preventive war. After 9/11, foreign policy officials also pursued a program of regime change in both Afghanistan and Iraq, while also setting their sights on the regimes in Iran and North Korea. Though striking a different rhetorical tone, the Obama administration has continued many of the Bush administration's foreign policy practices.

6. Future Challenges in American Foreign Policy

Among the greatest challenges for the United States in the foreign policy arena are the continued threat of terrorism and the accumulation of nuclear, chemical, and biological weapons. Environmental challenges and the impact of technology will also serve as focal points in the future.

Key Terms

al-Qaeda 526
balance of power system 536
brinkmanship 542
Bush Doctrine 545

clash of civilizations
thesis 545
Cold War 540
collective defense 536

collective security 536
containment 541
country desk 527
defense conversion 543

For Review

1. What are the primary tools that policy makers use in the foreign policy process?

2. Why is the president the primary foreign policy maker in the United States? What tools do presidents have to assist them in creating foreign policy? Who are the other actors in foreign policy decision making?

3. How did the United States evolve from a nation that emphasized isolationism in its early years to internationalism in the post–World War II era? What factors spurred this transformation?

4. How did the Cold War between the United States and the Soviet Union affect U.S. foreign policy? How did it influence relations between the United States and other nations?

5. September 11, 2001, led to a significant shift in how the United States viewed itself and the world. What theories best explain how the United States now sees itself in the post-9/11 global context?

6. What specific, major challenges will U.S. foreign policy makers face in the years to come?

For Critical Thinking and Discussion

1. How have the 9/11 terrorist attacks changed the structure of the foreign policy-making apparatus in the executive branch?

2. How did World War II change the way the United States was perceived by other nations around the world? How did the war alter U.S. policy makers' perceptions of what the international order should look like?

3. In retrospect, was the theory of containment an accurate description of how the United States should have attempted to stem the tide of communism during the Cold War? Why or why not?

4. Does Samuel Huntington's clash of civilizations theory accurately reflect the current state of world affairs? Explain. What present-day realities are in keeping with Huntington's theory? What other realities defy it?

5. What additional challenges, beyond those we examined in the text, are likely to face the makers of U.S. foreign policy in the next decade?

MULTIPLE CHOICE: Choose the lettered item that answers the question correctly.

1. The conduct of international relations, particularly involving the negotiation of treaties and other agreements between countries, is called
   a. brinkmanship.
   b. diplomacy.
   c. counterintelligence.
   d. intermestics.

2. _____ is a radical international Islamic fundamentalist terror organization.
   a. GATT
   b. The IRA
   c. Al-Qaeda
   d. The WTO

3. The replacement of a country's government with another government by facilitating the deposing of its leader or leading political party is called
   a. regime change.
   b. bilateralism.
   c. brinkmanship.
   d. globalism.

4. The official operation of the U.S. government in each country that has diplomatic ties to the United States is called the
   a. American seat.
   b. nation's chair.
   c. country desk.
   d. capital consul.

5. Since 2005, the person responsible for coordinating and overseeing all the intelligence agencies within the executive branch has been
   a. the Director of Homeland Security.
   b. the Director of the Federal Bureau of Investigation.
   c. the Director of the Central Intelligence Agency.
   d. the Director of National Intelligence.

6. The law that limits presidential use of military forces to sixty days, with an automatic extension of thirty additional days if the president requests such an extension, is
   a. the Gulf of Tonkin Resolution.
   b. the War Powers Act.
   c. the Defense Authorization Act.
   d. the Executive Military Control Act.

7. An individual outside government who promotes his or her country's interests and thus helps to shape international perceptions of that nation is called a
   a. professional diplomat.
   b. public diplomat.
   c. a foreign service officer.
   d. a foreign advocate.

8. The influence of domestic interests on foreign policy is called
   a. globalism.
   b. domestic influence peddling.
   c. domestic engineering.
   d. intermestics.

9. A foreign policy characterized by a nation's unwillingness to participate in international affairs is called
   a. isolationism.
   b. interventionism.
   c. bilateralism.
   d. globalism.

10. A foreign policy characterized by a nation's willingness to participate and intervene in international situations, including another country's affairs is called
    a. isolationism.
    b. interventionism.
    c. bilateralism.
    d. globalism.

FILL IN THE BLANKS.

11. _____ are the diplomatic and consular staff at U.S. embassies abroad.

12. _____ is the international trade principle holding that the least restrictive trade conditions offered to any one national trading partner will be offered to every other nation in a trading network.

13. The interconnectedness between nations in contemporary times is called _____ .

14. Nuclear, chemical, and biological weapons are known as _____ .

15. The _____ is an organization created in 1995 to negotiate, implement, and enforce international trade agreements.

RESOURCES FOR RESEARCH AND ACTION

Internet Resources

American Democracy Now Web site
www.mhhe.com/harrison2e Consult the book's Web site for study guides, interactive activities, simulations, and current hotlinks for additional information on American foreign policy.

Central Intelligence Agency
https://www.cia.gov This is the official Web site of the CIA. Its *World Factbook,* available online at this site, is an excellent resource for research on various nations. The site also hosts news and information, history, and career opportunities.

North Atlantic Treaty Organization
www.nato.int This site hosts an informative eLibrary as well as an impressive multimedia collection of documentation about NATO-related events and history.

State Department and Defense Department
www.state.gov and www.defenselink.mil These government sites offer a plethora of information from these two cabinet departments. Included are news and information, policy statements, career opportunities, virtual tours, and reports.

World Bank
www.worldbank.org This site explains the World Bank's policy priorities and offers data, research reports, and a wide variety of related international news.

Internet Activism

Visit www.un.org/en to learn about United Nations' priorities and activities concerning peace and security, development, human rights, humanitarian affairs, and international law, as well as the UN structure.

Twitter
senatorlugar Follow Sen. Richard Lugar, the ranking member of the Senate Foreign Relations Committee.

YouTube
www.youtube.com/watch?v=6BlqlwCKkeY Watch President Obama's watershed speech to the Muslim world in Cairo, Egypt.

Facebook
www.facebook.com/home.php#!/foreign.policy .magazine?ref=ts Like *Foreign Policy* magazine.

Recommended Readings

Allison, Graham. *Nuclear Terrorism: The Ultimate Preventable Catastrophe.* New York: Times Books, 2004, and *The Essence of Decision: Explaining the Cuban Missile Crisis,* Boston: Little Brown, 1971. This key scholar of U.S. foreign policy making uses the Cuban Missile Crisis as a model to explain foreign policy making. In his more recent work, he analyzes the foreign policy dilemma of nuclear terrorism.

Cameron, Fraser. *U.S. Foreign Policy after the Cold War.* New York: Routledge, 2002. This introduction to U.S. foreign policy looks at some aspects of U.S. foreign policy from the perspective of their domestic origins. Critical of the United States' unilateralism, Cameron also details relations between the United States and the European Union.

Huntington, Samuel P. *The Clash of Civilizations and the Remaking of World Order.* New York: Simon & Schuster, 1998. Huntington asserts that Western democracies are engaged in a clash of civilizations, particularly with Islamic societies.

Jervis, Robert. *American Foreign Policy in a New Era.* New York: Routledge, 2005. A noted foreign policy scholar explains the issues and influences on American foreign policy in today's international circumstances.

Keohane, Robert. *Neo-Realism and Its Critics,* New York: Columbia University Press, 1986. This classic work explains neorealism, a theory that emphasizes the power of state actors in international affairs.

Movies of Interest

The Hurt Locker (2008)
This 2009 Oscar-winning film follows the story of a U.S. Army Explosive Ordnance Disposal (EOD) team during the war in Iraq.

The Good Shepherd (2006)
Directed by Robert De Niro and starring Matt Damon, Alec Baldwin, and Angelina Jolie, this film traces the creation of the CIA and its evolution through the Cold War.

The Killing Fields (1984)
Based on a true story, this film tells the story of an American journalist and his Cambodian guide during the vicious genocide by Cambodia's Khmer Rouge regime during the Vietnam War.

Breaker Morant (1980)
Based on a true story, this courtroom drama tells the story of three Australian soldiers who are court-martialed for shooting prisoners during the Boer War in South Africa (1899–1902).

Dr. Strangelove or: How I Learned to Stop Worrying and Love the Bomb (1964)
This Stanley Kubrick film probes the dangers of the Cold War when an insane army general tries to start a nuclear war over the objections of political leaders and other generals.

The Mouse That Roared (1959)
This Peter Sellers comedy takes a satirical look at how the United States used foreign aid to ensure the support of allies. It features a fictional impoverished European nation that invades the United States with the goal of losing so that it can receive foreign aid.

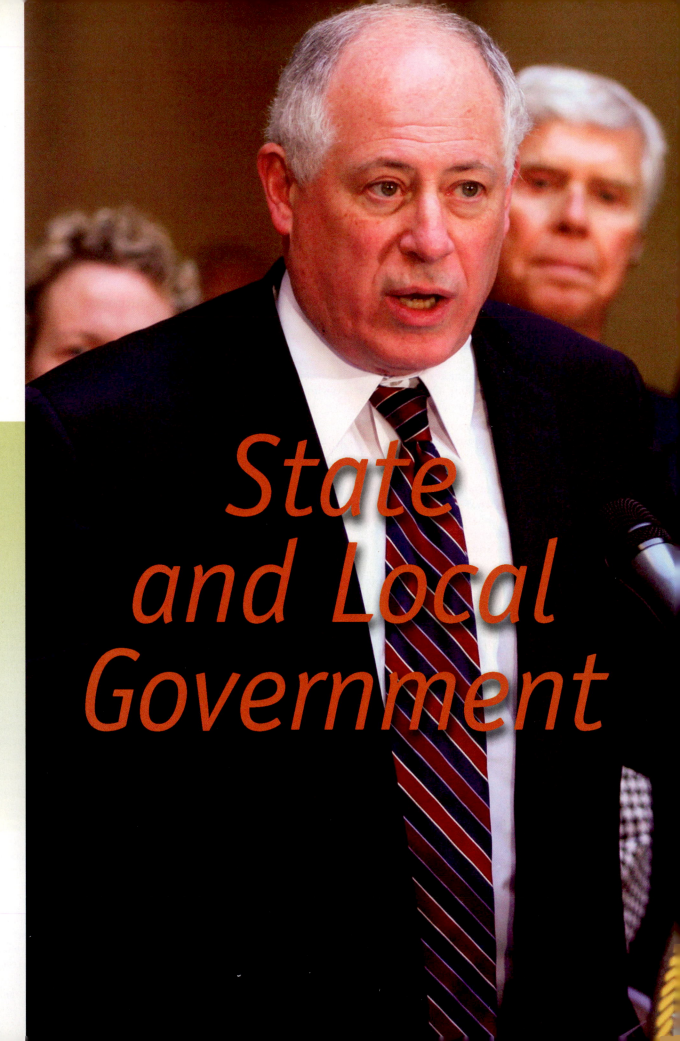

State
and Local
Government

THEN

Responding to calls to give citizens a stronger voice in their government, state and local governments adopted processes that facilitate direct democracy.

NOW

Citizens are increasingly using initiatives and referenda to constrain taxing and spending by state and local governments and to bypass legislators.

NEXT

As the U.S. population becomes ever more diverse, what new services and benefits will citizens call on state and local governments to provide?

Will states continue to experiment with public policies that address nationwide problems?

Will the success of initiatives and referenda at the state and local levels lead to a movement to adopt these processes at the national level?

This chapter surveys the institutions and policies of state and local governments. We also look at the roles of state government in national politics.

FIRST, we examine citizen engagement in state and local government by way of the exercise of *direct democracy* at the state and local levels.

SECOND, we review the constitutional documents of state and local government, specifically the common principles and constructs of *state constitutions and local charters.*

THIRD, we consider the *diversity in political cultures, people, environments, and resources* that affect the processes and policy making of state and local governments.

FOURTH, we focus on *state and local government budgets* to understand what goods and services they provide to citizens and how they pay for them.

FIFTH, we look at the *responsibilities of state and local governments in national politics:* both the formal and the informal responsibilities that have developed over the years.

SIXTH, we focus on the *institutions of state government,* examining the commonalities and differences from state to state and contrasting state and federal institutions.

SEVENTH, we survey *local governments* and differentiate among general-purpose and single-purpose local governments.

open meeting laws
laws requiring legislative bodies and executive agencies of government to conduct policy-making meetings in public

The founding fathers created a

federal system of government with dual sovereignty. In 1789, one newly created national government shared sovereign power with twelve state governments. (The thirteenth state, Rhode Island, joined the union in 1790.) The Constitution of the United States distributed powers and responsibilities among those governments. The Constitution delegated enumerated and implied powers to the national government. The Tenth Amendment, ratified by the states in 1791, reserved for the states and the people all powers that the Constitution did not delegate to the national government. State governments created local governments with whom they shared their reserved powers. Over the course of U.S. history, the differentiation between enumerated, implied, and reserved powers has proven to be murky. Although dual sovereignty still exists, intergovernmental relations is pervasive as national, state, and local governments work together to provide for and protect Americans.

Today, 1 national government, 50 state governments, and 89,527 local governments serve the people living in the United States. There is great diversity among these tens of thousands of governments. There are differences in government structures and processes, revenue-raising strategies, services and benefits, and rights guaranteed to and responsibilities imposed on the citizens by the numerous governments in whose jurisdictions they live. Yet with all this diversity, there also exist many commonalities across the tens of thousands of governments.

This chapter explores similarities and differences among the national, state, and local governments in the United States. We begin with a discussion of direct democracy, a form of democracy that exists in state and local governments but not in the national government. We then review similarities and differences between the U.S. Constitution and state constitutions. Following an examination of the diversity in political cultures, people, environments, and resources that affect processes and policies of state and local governments, we survey state and local fiscal policies, responsibilities to national politics, and institutional structures.

Direct Democracy: Letting the People Decide

In the United States, governments at the national, state, and local levels are all representative democracies in which citizens elect officials to create and approve public policies for them. To verify that representative democracy functions properly, governments have enacted sunshine laws that open their processes to public view and participation. For example, national, state, and local governments all have **open meeting laws** requiring legislative bodies, as well as executive agencies, to conduct their policy-making meetings in public. Open meeting laws typically require advance public notice of the meetings of policy-making bodies in a general circulation newspaper.

Many state and local governments couple representative democracy with *direct democracy*—a system of procedures that allow citizens to vote directly to approve or reject proposed public policies or to force an elected official from office before the completion of his or her term (see Chapter 1). In contrast to states and localities, the U.S. national government does not provide for direct democracy.

Although many local governments have provided for direct democracy since their creation, South Dakota in 1898 became the first state to adopt direct democracy. Subsequently, between 1898 and 1918, twenty-four states adopted some form of direct democracy as a result of the Progressive movement, a mass movement that called for changes in state and local government processes to expand citizens' ability to have a voice in policy making and to hold their elected officials accountable. Progressives argued that these reforms would force government at all levels to be more responsive to the people and less beholden to well-funded special interest groups. The benefit, the Progressives said, would be a more democratic government. President Theodore Roosevelt (1901–1909) argued that direct democracy should be used to "correct [representative government] whenever it becomes misrepresentative."[1]

Referenda and Initiatives

Direct democracy takes various forms. Whatever the form, the final stage involves citizens' voting on a **ballot measure**—a proposed piece of legislation, a constitutional amendment, or some other policy proposal placed on the Election Day ballot for voters to approve or reject. The various forms of direct democracy differ in who formulates the proposed law and what process is required for getting it on the ballot.

The *referendum* is a ballot measure that gives citizens veto power by allowing them to vote to approve or reject legislation or a constitutional amendment that the state legislature has proposed. All fifty states allow for a **legislative referendum**, a ballot measure whereby voters approve or reject a law or an amendment *proposed* by state officials. States use the legislative referendum (among other procedures), for example, to amend their constitutions. In this process, proposed amendments to a state constitution must appear on the ballot for citizens to approve or reject (in all states except Delaware, where legislators, not citizens, approve constitutional amendments). Twenty-four states also use the **popular referendum,** a measure that allows citizens, by collecting signatures in a petition drive, to put before voters specific legislation that the legislature has *previously approved*. In effect, the popular referendum allows voters to repeal laws that their legislators already have passed.

The *initiative* is a ballot measure, formulated by an individual or a group, that allows citizens themselves to propose legislation or state constitutional amendments through petitions signed by a specified number of registered voters. By using the tool of the initiative, citizens in twenty-one states and in almost 60 percent of U.S. cities can write legislative bills and force their state or local governments to place the bills on the ballot for citizens to approve or reject on Election Day. Twenty-four states allow their citizens to use the initiative process to place proposed state constitutional amendments on the ballot. Through the initiative procedure, citizens can bypass their elected officials to create and approve laws. Figure 18.1 on page 560 identifies the states that have initiative and/or referendum processes.

Referenda and initiatives are a large (and growing) factor in state policy making, and citizens use them even more frequently in local policy making. State ballots featured about 500 initiatives in the eighty years between 1900 and 1980, or an average of about 6 per year.[2] The success of California's Proposition 13 (1978) ignited tremendous growth in ballot measures. Between 1980 and 2009, 998 initiatives were placed on ballots, or an average of 34 initiatives per year.[3] The People's Initiative to Limit Property Taxation (Proposition 13) amended California's constitution. It set a cap on local property tax increases and required a supermajority vote of state legislators to approve increases in tax rates, thus making it more difficult for lawmakers to raise revenues.

In 2009, 32 ballot measures were on ballots in seven states. Although that number was far short

ballot measure
any proposed policy that, as the result of an initiative or a referendum, wins a place on the ballot for voters to approve or reject

legislative referendum
a ballot measure whereby voters approve or reject a law or an amendment proposed by state officials

popular referendum
a measure that allows citizens, by collecting signatures in a petition drive, to put before voters specific legislation that the legislature has previously approved

> A student volunteer for Tuition Relief Now collects signatures on a petition to place the College Affordability Act on California's 2008 ballot.

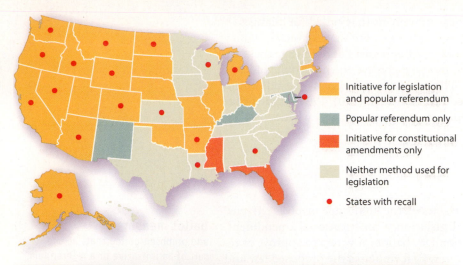

FIGURE 18.1 ■ STATES WITH INITIATIVE, REFERENDUM, AND RECALL PROCESSES In what part(s) of the country do states tend to allow their citizens the most options for participating in the political process by affecting legislation or amending their state constitutions? Where do citizens have the least ability to do so? How might the history of these areas of the country have influenced these policies?

NOTE: All states except Delaware have referenda on state constitutional amendments.

Legend:
- Initiative for legislation and popular referendum
- Popular referendum only
- Initiative for constitutional amendments only
- Neither method used for legislation
- ● States with recall

of the more than 150 ballot measures in 2008, there are always fewer measures in odd-numbered-year elections because many states do not hold elections in those years, and in states that allow initiatives, the state law typically prohibits initiatives in odd-numbered years. The headline issues among the 2009 ballot measures were same-sex marriage rights, tax limits, expenditure limits, and medical marijuana.[4]

Clearly, citizens are increasingly using initiatives and referenda as means to participate personally and to influence public policy making. Some scholars attribute the rising use of direct democracy to citizens' growing frustration with government and to their willingness to take policy matters into their own hands. Others note that an "initiative industry" has arisen, featuring professionals whom citizens and interest groups can hire to collect signatures and coordinate media campaigns in support of or opposition to initiatives. Although they come with a high price tag, such professionals make it easier for citizens to initiate ballot measures and may even encourage them to attempt to influence their state and local governments by exercising their right to direct democracy.[5]

The increased use of direct democracy is not limited to the United States. European nations also have direct democracy provisions in their laws. However, the procedures typically used in Europe differ from those used by state and local governments in the United States. (See "Global Context.")

Proponents of direct democracy applaud the growing use of these various means of increasing government responsiveness. They say that the availability of these tools fosters citizen engagement in policy making and that this trend is good for democratic government. Election Day ballot measures stimulate public conversations on public issues and mobilize voters, as indicated by higher voter turnout rates. Opponents of direct democracy note that citizens' drives to get signatures on petitions, as well as the campaigns to persuade voters to approve or reject ballot measures, are very costly, making it a tool for well-funded, well-organized special interests and wealthy individuals to influence government. Moreover, opponents argue that on Election Day, voters cannot discern from the brief statement they read on the ballot the intricacies of proposed policies, and therefore they cannot cast an educated vote. The job of elected officials is to understand complex policy issues and to make the best decisions for their constituents. If voters do not like the decisions of their elected officials, they can turn them out of office by not reelecting them and, in some states, by recalling them.

Recall of Elected Officials

Another instrument of direct democracy in the United States is *recall*—a procedure allowing citizens to remove an elected official from office before the end of the individual's term. The recall is unique to about one-third of the states and 60 percent of cities; Figure 18.1 indicates which states have recall. Recall requires a legally specified number of signatures on a petition to force a vote. The number of signatures required is typically a percentage of the number of registered voters who participated in the last election for that office; 25 percent is the most common requirement.[6]

GLOBAL CONTEXT

DIRECT DEMOCRACY IN EUROPE

Direct democracy in European nations looks quite different from direct democracy in the United States. Unlike the U.S. Constitution, which does not provide for the use of either an initiative or a referendum, the constitutions of at least thirty European countries contain provisions for national direct democracy. (Some European countries, among them Switzerland, have had national direct democracy since the early 1800s.) Moreover, in the United States, state and local governments have exercised various forms of direct democracy since before ratification of the U.S. Constitution, whereas in Europe, direct democracy is relatively new among local governments. Beyond these differences, the direct democracy processes that local governments in Europe use contrast notably with those used by state and local governments in the United States.

What issue will be the next common concern addressed by local referenda in Europe and in state and local ballot measures in the United States?

In European nations, a common component of direct democracy at the local level is the requirement that local governing councils must approve any ballot measure—whether it is initiated by citizens or formulated by a legislature—before the measure can appear on the ballot. There is no citizen initiative in European nations comparable to the U.S. initiative, which allows American citizens to bypass the local or state legislature by collecting the legally required number of signatures on a petition to place a proposal on the ballot. Direct democracy in Europe more closely resembles the U.S. referendum process, in which voters approve or reject legislation or a constitutional amendment proposed or passed by the state or local legislature.

In recent years, environmental protection and conservation have become issues of common concern in U.S. state and local government ballot measures (initiatives and referenda) and local referenda in European countries. Citizens and interest groups on both continents are using direct democracy to encourage environmental protection and sustainability.

SOURCE: Michael Smith, "Is Direct Democracy Good for the Environment? A Re-examination of the Link from the Perspective of Central and Eastern Europe," presented at the When Voters Make Laws: How Direct Democracy Is Reshaping American Cities Symposium at the University of Southern California, April 7, 2007.

States vary as to how they handle the recall procedure and how they replace a recalled official. For example, in Wisconsin when citizens vote to recall an elected official, the state holds a subsequent primary election for the position and, later, a general election. In contrast, in California, on the same day that citizens cast their ballot in the recall election, they also vote to elect an official to replace the incumbent if the majority of voters approve the recall.

In 2003, more than 1.5 million Californians (well over the state-required minimum of 12 percent of the 2002 turnout, or 900,000 signatures) signed a recall petition.[7] The recall petition charged Governor Gray Davis with "gross mismanagement of California finances by overspending taxpayers' money, threatening public safety by cutting funds to local governments, failing to account for the exorbitant cost of energy, and failing in general to deal with the state's major problems until they get to crisis stage."[8] On the same day that California voters approved Davis's recall, they selected former actor Arnold Schwarzenegger of *Terminator* fame from a field of 135 candidates to replace Davis.[9]

The 2003 recall of Governor Davis was the first gubernatorial recall since North Dakotans recalled Governor Lynn J. Frazier in 1921, and only the second recall of a governor in U.S. history.[10] In September 2009, the Ingham County Election Commission approved a petition to recall Michigan Governor Jennifer Granholm. The recall effort failed to get the

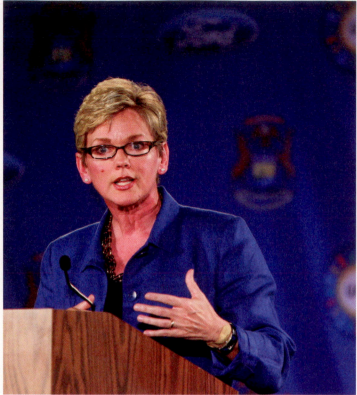

> Arnold Schwarzenegger was sworn in as the governor of California in 2003, after Californians recalled Governor Gray Davis and elected Schwarzenegger from a field of 135 candidates. In 2009, the campaign to recall Michigan Governor Jennifer Granholm failed to garner the 950,000 signatures required to place the recall question on the ballot.

950,000 signatures required to place the recall question on the ballot.[11] At the local level, the volume of recalls is growing. In 2009, citizens initiated close to three hundred recall campaigns. Most local recall efforts make it to the ballot.[12]

State Constitutions and Local Charters

Recalls, referenda, and initiatives occur in state and local governments because state constitutions allow for these forms of direct democracy. Each state's constitution, and the state laws written in compliance with it, defines that state's governing processes and legal authority. This legal basis includes the state's authority to create local governments, which the U.S. Constitution does not mention at all. In this section, we first look at the basic components of state constitutions and their differences with respect to the U.S. Constitution. We then examine local **charters**—the constitutional documents approved by state governments to establish local governments.

charter
the constitution of a local government

The Elements of State Constitutions

Similarly to the U.S. Constitution, state constitutions include

- an enumeration of fundamental rights (bill of rights)
- a division of powers among three branches of government
- an impeachment process
- a constitutional amendment process

Unlike the U.S. Constitution, the majority of state constitutions also contain

- allowances for direct democracy
- provisions for the creation of local governments
- provisions for public education
- a balanced budget requirement
- guidelines for conducting elections

State law (constitutional law and statutes) frequently offers broader fundamental rights than the U.S. Constitution and national law guarantee. For example, although the U.S. Constitution does *not* guarantee a right to "clean air, pure water, and to the preservation of the natural, scenic, historic and esthetic values of the environment," the state constitution of Pennsylvania does. Twenty state constitutions provide that equal rights under the law shall not be denied because of sex, but the U.S. Constitution has no comparable equal rights amendment. According to the U.S. Supreme Court, the rights established by the U.S. Constitution are the minimum rights that governments must guarantee. Therefore state and local governments can establish additional rights.

State constitutions are generally longer than the U.S. Constitution. The reason is that the U.S. Constitution presents only broad foundational principles and procedures, whereas the state constitutions spell out not only fundamental rights but also details of policy matters—the latter, for example, in sections on educational policy and business regulation. In addition, state constitutions discuss local governments, which the U.S. Constitution does not mention at all.

Local Charters: How Much Local Discretion?

When a state government establishes a local government, the state government specifies the local government's structures, institutions, and responsibilities in a constitutional document called a charter. Traditionally, state governments wrote and approved local government charters that specified not only the structures but also the functions of local government. Following **Dillon's Rule,** a principle articulated by Iowa Supreme Court judge John Forrest Dillon in 1868 and employed in hundreds of U.S. court decisions, local governments are creatures of the state that created them, and as such, they have only the powers expressly mentioned in their state-written and approved charters and those necessarily implied by the formally expressed powers.

In recent decades, however, most states have allowed for **home rule** by giving their citizens the opportunity to write, adopt, and amend local government charters at the city and county levels. A citizens' commission typically drafts these so-called **home rule charters,** which voters then accept or reject. These charters typically give the local government greater discretion in its activities than do state-developed charters. In comparison with local governments based on Dillon's rule, localities with home rule have discretion to determine the extent of their powers and responsibilities, as long as they comply with limits imposed by their state and by the U.S. Constitution.

In 1973, Congress enacted the District of Columbia Home Rule Act. This act devolved certain congressional powers for the governance of Washington, D.C., the federal district that is the nation's capital city, to local government. The federal law includes the District Home Rule Charter, which provides for the citizens living in DC to elect a mayor and thirteen members to a city council. Under the District Home Rule Charter, Congress maintains its constitutionally granted authority over the city, with authority to veto laws enacted by the city government and over the city's budget. In 1980, DC citizens passed an initiative calling for a constitutional convention. In 1982, the citizens ratified a constitution for a new state, New Columbia. The battle over statehood for Washington, D.C., continues today and is debated in this chapter's "Thinking Critically About Democracy" feature (see page 564).

Dillon's rule
the ruling articulated by Judge John Forrest Dillon in 1872 that local governments are creatures of the state that created them, and they have only the powers expressly mentioned in the charters written and approved by the state and those necessarily implied by the formally expressed powers

home rule
the opportunity provided by state government for citizens to write, adopt, and amend local government charters at the city and county levels

home rule charter
local government constitution written and approved by citizens following state-mandated procedures, including a referendum

SHOULD WASHINGTON, D.C., BECOME THE FIFTY-FIRST STATE OF THE UNION?

The Issue: The residents of Washington, D.C.—who are a larger population than the state of Wyoming—use the rallying cry of "taxation without representation" in their movement for statehood. Washington, D.C., is a city (Washington) and a federal district (the District of Columbia). Since the national government enacted the DC Home Rule Act of 1973, DC residents elect a local government composed of a mayor and a thirteen-member city council, but Congress can veto any laws made by the local government and maintains authority over DC's budget. The residents of Washington, D.C., pay the highest federal taxes per capita, but they have no voting representatives in either the House or the Senate. Before the Twenty-Third Amendment (1961), they also had no vote in presidential elections. Should Washington, D.C., become the fifty-first state?

Yes: Statehood would give the almost 600,000 citizens living in DC the same representation in Congress that citizens elsewhere in the nation have. It would eliminate the undemocratic policy of federal taxation without representation. In addition, it would give the DC citizens a government whose constitutional responsibility and primary focus is to attend to the day-to-day matters that affect their lives, liberties, and pursuit of happiness. Citizens in all other locations in the country have a state government that can focus all its attention on state residents. Congress would be out of the business of overseeing the legislation and administration of a city—one less concern on the overflowing congressional agenda.

No: The Constitution established a federal district as the permanent location for the nation's capital. To grant Washington, D.C., statehood would violate the intent of the founding fathers. In addition, if DC became a state, Congress, whose members meet and many of whom live in DC almost year-round, would be inclined to favor New Columbia (the name proposed for DC when it gains statehood). Moreover, because the citizens of DC vote overwhelmingly Democratic, DC statehood would likely add two Democratic Senators to a very partisan and closely divided Senate.

Other approaches: Congress could redraw the city lines so that the federal district included only the National Mall (including the U.S. Capitol, the White House, and the Supreme Court building). Then the state of Maryland could reclaim the remaining city land, which it had given to the national government to establish the capital city. DC residents would become citizens of the state of Maryland, with all rights of national and state citizenship, including full representation in Congress.

What do you think?

① Should U.S. citizens living in Washington, D.C., be guaranteed the same right to elect voting members to the House of Representatives and the Senate as citizens living elsewhere throughout the nation? Justify your answer.

② Is the fact that DC residents vote overwhelmingly Democratic relevant to the debate over statehood? Explain your answer.

③ Is there another approach that would address the complaint of "taxation without representation"?

Today, fifty state governments, each with its own constitution, and tens of thousands of local governments serve the diverse expectations and day-to-day needs of more than 300 million Americans.

Diversity in Political Cultures, People, Environments, and Resources

The Constitution of the United States distributes power and responsibilities to the national and state governments. According to this constitutional distribution, the national government is responsible for defense, foreign relations, interstate and foreign commerce, and promoting the general welfare—matters that affect the nation as a whole. By comparison, states and their local governments bear responsibility for the distinct day-to-day needs and demands of the people who live within their jurisdictions. Between 1789 and the 1960s, the national government became more and more involved in day-to-day domestic matters. Since the late 1970s, the federal government has relinquished much of its involvement in domestic issues, leaving state and local governments to step into the gap. The breadth of state and local policies, along with the size of their budgets and bureaucracies, is evidence of their increasingly central role in the lives of Americans.

The particular needs and demands each state and local government must address are the product of many factors, including residents' demographics (characteristics such as age, ethnicity, religion, income level, and educational attainment), the local environment, and resources. A state's resources (natural and financial resources alike), as well as its political culture, influence its capacity and willingness to meet the needs and demands of the people dwelling within its borders. The great diversity in people, environments, resources, and political cultures both within and across states affects the structures and public policies of state and local governments.

Political Culture and Its Effect on Governing

The dominant shared views among the people of a community concerning what the appropriate purposes and roles of government are, as well as who should participate in government, make up the *political culture*. Political scientist Daniel Elazar distinguished among three types of political culture to explain state and regional differences in "political processes, institutional structures, political behavior, and policies and programs of state and local government."[13] The three political cultures Elazar identified are traditionalistic, individualistic, and moralistic.[14]

In a **traditionalistic political culture,** government's primary purpose is to preserve the status quo—to keep things as they currently are. Further, the expectation is that the participants in government should come from among society's elite, not from the population at large. States where a traditionalistic political culture dominates tend to have relatively lower voter turnout and lower levels of mass participation than other states. These states are also less likely to have provisions for direct democracy.

In an **individualistic political culture,** citizens view politics as a means by which an individual can improve his or her economic and social status. Those who participate in politics do so for their own benefit. In areas where an individualistic political culture dominates, the primary purpose of government depends on the goals of those who get involved. These states also tend not to allow for direct democracy.

Concern for the collective good of society is the impetus for government action according to the **moralistic political culture.** In states dominated by this political culture, people feel an obligation to participate in government and to ensure that government is serving those who cannot provide for themselves. Mass political participation is common in such states, as are the processes of direct democracy. Voter turnout tends to be higher in states with a moralistic political culture than in those with traditionalistic or individualistic cultures.

Political scientist Joel Lieske extended Elazar's study of political culture to local governments. He identified ten subcultures that help to explain differences in political behaviors, policy preferences, and political institutions created by local governments. Lieske argued that the following socializing agents influence the political culture of a community of people: racial and ethnic kinship ties, value systems, and lifestyles.[15] In addition to these socializing agents, the local economy, distribution of income, life cycle, and environmental constraints, which include natural resources and climate, influence political culture.[16]

A community's political culture influences its governing processes, its people's political behavior and preferences, and ultimately public policy decisions. Therefore demographic and environmental differences throughout the country yield a variety of public policies across states as well as within them.

People: Dealing with Demographics

Demographic differences from state to state and from locality to locality place varying demands on state and local governments. In Mississippi, 20 percent of the population live in poverty; in New Hampshire, about 6 percent do.[17] The greater the percentage of a state's

traditionalistic political culture
the view that the purpose of government is to maintain the status quo and that participants in government should come from society's elite

individualistic political culture
the view that the decision to take part in government is an individual choice, and those who choose to participate determine the purpose of government and personally benefit from their participation

moralistic political culture
the view that the purpose of government is to serve the public good, including providing for those who are disadvantaged, and that all citizens should participate in government

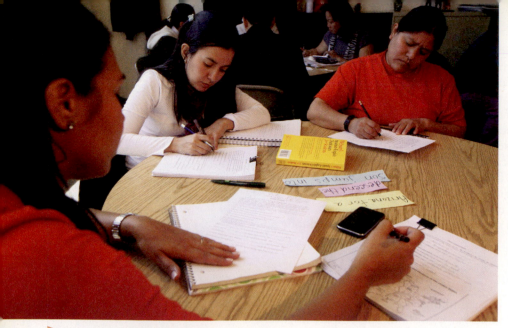

> State and local governments fund English as a Second Language (E.S.L) classes in elementary and secondary schools in localities where a large portion of the student body speak a language other than English at home. State and local governments also assist in funding E.S.L. programs for adults in community centers such as this one in Queens, New York.

population living below the poverty line, the greater the demand on state and local government budgets for safety-net provisions such as school lunch programs and subsidized housing. Similarly, the larger the proportion of children living in a state, the higher the demand for public elementary and secondary education. And the greater the proportion of a state's population that is elderly, the more extensive the need for Medicaid (the joint federal-state health insurance program for low-income citizens, which includes coverage for nursing home care).

Another demographic difference that affects governmental expenditures can be seen in California, where about 40 percent of the residents speak a language other than English at home. This places demands on state and local governments to provide English as a Second Language (ESL) programs in public schools.[18] Because of this intrastate diversity, some school districts in California must cope with as many as forty different primary languages, whereas others need to handle two or three primary languages. Moreover, California residents need multilingual police officers, hospital workers, social workers, and emergency medical workers. West Virginia, where only about 3 percent of the residents speak a language other than English at home, does not have the same need for multilingual public servants and services.[19]

Environment and Resources: Variations in Needs and Tax Capacity

Climate significantly influences the demands citizens place on state and local governments and the services governments must provide for their citizens. States vulnerable to blizzards, tornadoes, and hurricanes all face unique demands, whether these be plowing and salting roadways in a snowstorm or alerting residents to a fierce approaching windstorm. State and local governments can address these localized problems more efficiently than the national government, but when climatic emergencies spread across state borders, the national government may need to step in.

Similarly, a region's natural resources affect public policies, the types of jobs available in the economy, and a government's ability to raise revenue (tax capacity). Oil is a natural resource that positively affects the economies of Texas and Alaska by creating jobs. Because the government can tax those who extract oil from the land, oil reserves also influence the tax policies in these states. A tax on the extraction of any natural resource, from fish in streams, to lumber in forests, to oil in the land, is a *severance tax*. Texas and Alaska raise so much revenue from their oil severance taxes that they are among the seven states that do not need to impose an individual income tax on their citizens to balance their budgets.

Many other examples illustrate the influence of climate and natural resources on a state's political and economic profile. The climate and natural resources of Hawaii have made tourism a vital industry there. The midwestern Plains states (Ohio, Indiana, Illinois, Michigan, Minnesota, and Wisconsin) are called America's breadbasket owing to the agricultural enterprise and related industries (such as food processing) that dominate the economies of those states. Compared with other states, Indiana has the greatest percentage of its labor force employed in manufacturing. The state policies needed to regulate and support each type of economic activity vary considerably, depending on whether farming, tourism, or manufacturing is the dominant industry.

Climate, natural resources, and the demographic profile of residents also affect a jurisdiction's *tax base*—its wealth, in the form of personal income, property, and other assets, that the government can tax. The financial resources of a government are a product of the tax base. Given the diversity of people, climate, and natural resources, as well as the diversity of political cultures that influences decisions about taxing and spending, it is not surprising that some states and localities have more money to spend than others do, which means that taxes and public services differ from state to state.

State and Local Government Budgets

A government's budget is its central policy document. It reveals how the government is spending its financial resources and where it is getting the money to pay the bills. The constitutions of all states except Vermont require state legislators to achieve a balanced budget. How do they approach this challenge? On what do state and local governments spend their money? Where do they get the revenue to balance their budgets?

Balanced Budgets

For forty-nine states and their local governments, the balanced budget requirement means that they must balance their **operating budgets,** which include all the costs of day-to-day government operations. That is, the government must raise enough money during the budget year, without borrowing, to pay for these expenses. In the case of governments, typical examples of operating budget expenditures include salaries and benefits, utility bills, office supplies, and rent.

Although state and local governments cannot borrow money to pay for their day-to-day operations, they can borrow money (go into debt) for *capital projects*. These include expensive building projects and purchases from which citizens will benefit for many years. Because a state or local government typically cannot raise enough money through its taxes, user fees, and grants-in-aid in one year both to balance its operating budget and to build new highways, or to purchase new computer systems, states' laws allow them to borrow money to pay for these expensive projects. Such capital project expenditures and revenues are included in the **capital budget,** to which the annual balanced budget mandate does not apply.

operating budget
a budget that accounts for all the costs of day-to-day government operations and covers such items as salaries and benefits, utilities, office supplies, and rent

capital budget
a budget that accounts for the costs and revenues for expensive building and purchasing projects from which citizens will benefit for many years and for which governments can borrow money

State and Local Expenditures on Day-to-Day Domestic Matters

On what goods and services do state and local governments spend their money? Figure 18.2 shows the total expenditures of state and local governments in selected policy areas. This figure illustrates the diversity of services provided by state and local governments, most of them related to daily domestic matters, for these are the matters reserved to the states (and the local governments they create) by the Tenth Amendment of the U.S. Constitution.

State and local governments spend most of their money paying the salaries and benefits of their employees. The fifty state governments employ about 5 million people, and the 89,000-plus local governments employ more than 14 million.[20] These millions of state and local employees serve in just about every occupation imaginable, with many of them involved in providing **essential services,** the everyday work required to prevent chaos and hazardous conditions in society. As long as they receive these services, citizens seldom think about them; but if they experience an interruption in even one essential service, they become alarmed, outraged, or seriously endangered or inconvenienced. Essential service providers include elementary and secondary schoolteachers, police officers, firefighters, sanitation workers, medical care personnel, and road and bridge maintenance crews. Table 18.1 presents data on state and local government spending per capita on selected services. Let's take a close-up look at just a few of the essential services state and local workers provide: public education, public health, and public safety.

essential services
public services provided by state and local governments on a daily basis to prevent chaos and hazardous conditions in society

PUBLIC EDUCATION State constitutions guarantee equal and effective education, and states typically create school districts (a type of local government) to provide elementary and secondary education. All states have a compulsory education law, which means that children must go to school until they achieve the age or grade level specified by their state government. The overwhelming majority of U.S. children attend public schools, with only about 10 percent in private schools and about 2 percent homeschooled.[21] In view of the fact that almost 17 percent of the U.S. population is enrolled in public elementary and secondary schools at any given time, it is no wonder that the majority of local government employees are dedicated to providing elementary and secondary education.[22]

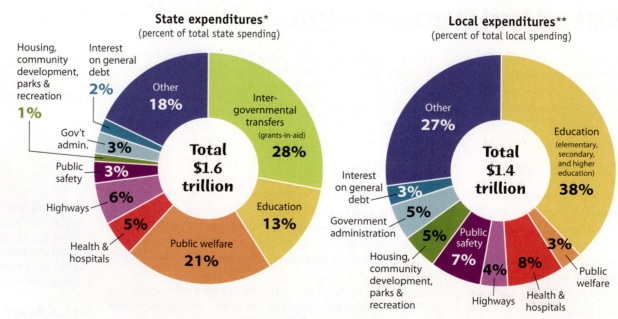

*CALCULATED from U.S. Census Bureau, *Statistical Abstract of the United States: 2010* (Washington DC: U.S. Government Printing Office, 2010), Table 442.

**CALCULATED from U.S. Census Bureau, *Statistical Abstract of the United States: 2010* (Washington DC: U.S. Government Printing Office, 2010), Table 444.

FIGURE 18.2

Expenditures of State and Local Governments

State and Local Government Spending Per Capita on Selected Services

TABLE 18.1

Service	Highest per capita state	Lowest per capita state
Fire protection	Rhode Island ($230)	Pennsylvania ($46)
Health and hospitals	Wyoming ($1,753)	North Dakota ($158)
Highways	Alaska ($1,925)	Georgia ($291)
Parks and recreation	Colorado ($221)	Maine ($51)
Police protection	Delaware ($489)	West Virginia ($131)
Welfare	New York ($2,239)	Nevada ($719)

SOURCE: *Governing State & Local Sourcebook*, http://sourcebook.governing.com/index.jsp.

According to the National Center for Public Policy and Higher Education, in 2006, state and county governments provided higher education in 1,520 public colleges and universities, educating 78 percent of enrolled undergraduates.[23] The majority of these institutions (944) were two-year colleges. California had the highest number of public colleges and universities, with 110 two-year institutions and 34 four-year institutions. Rhode Island had the fewest, with 2 four-year public institutions and 1 two-year public institution.

In a comparison of policy costs, on average, educational policy makes up the largest proportion of state and local budgets. States vary widely, though, with respect to both the amount of money and the proportion of their budgets that they spend on public education. In the 2005–2006 school year, New Jersey spent the most—$13,781 per elementary and secondary school pupil. In that same year, Utah spent the least—$5,347 per pupil. Per-pupil state support of higher education in 2006 ranged from a high of $9,733 in Hawaii to a low of $2,361 in Colorado.[24]

Since the 1970s, lawsuits challenging state elementary and secondary school financing systems have become common. State courts have ruled intrastate inequities in spending between school districts to be in violation of state constitutions. More recently, state courts are determining whether states are providing an adequate education to all children. While courts focus on the results, states may need to increase their funding in order to provide the resources needed to offer an adequate educational experience.[25]

PUBLIC HEALTH AND SAFETY Another major responsibility of state and local governments is to ensure public health and safety, which involves a broad range of state and local government activity. Medicaid, for example, competes with education as the most expensive item in state budgets. Although rising Medicaid costs are ballooning state expenditures for public health, fewer state employees provide health services than education services.

Other public health- and safety-related protections funded at the state and local levels include the provision of safe drinking water and the proper disposal of garbage and sewage to prevent disease. State and local governments also establish building codes to ensure the safe construction of homes and other structures. They pass codes related to the use of smoke detectors, handrails on staircases, functioning fire escapes in high-rise buildings, and sanitary conditions in restaurants. They regulate personal behavior by means of criminal laws, speed limits, legal drinking ages, and laws specifying the blood alcohol content that defines "driving under the

> State and local governments are responsible for essential services, including elementary and secondary education and the protection of public health and safety. One means of ensuring public safety is the regulation of individual behavior, such as the enforcement of state laws that prohibit driving under the influence of alcohol.

influence." State laws requiring the immunization of children before they are allowed to attend school also promote public health and safety.

Since the terrorist attacks of 9/11, public safety—often referred to as homeland security now—has warranted increased attention from the national government. This attention has meant both new national policies and additional federal grant moneys for state and local governments, which employ first responders. The Department of Homeland Security, established in 2003, relies on the work of state and local police, firefighters, and emergency medical technicians to ensure domestic safety and security.

State Government Revenues

How do state and local governments raise the money needed to balance their operating budgets? Figure 18.3 shows the sources of state and local government revenues.

Other than grants-in-aid from the federal government, the largest revenue source for state governments (as a group) is the sales tax, although not all states impose a sales tax. Among the forty-five states that do collect a sales tax, the tax most commonly falls on purchases of goods, not on the costs of hiring someone—such as a lawyer, an accountant, or a hairdresser—to provide a service. Yet the states that tax purchased goods do not all tax the same goods or use the same tax rate. Take groceries, for example. Mississippi has a 7 percent sales tax on all groceries purchased. Virginia's sales tax on groceries is only 2.5 percent. Pennsylvania does not collect a sales tax on unprepared food purchased, but it does impose a 6 percent sales tax on ready-to-eat store- and restaurant-prepared foods.

Today, debate continues over the collection of sales taxes on Internet and online purchases. According to federal law, states can require only companies that have a physical presence in the state to collect sales taxes. So, if the vendor from which you make an Internet purchase is located in another state, your state government cannot force the vendor to collect a sales tax on the purchase. (Did you know that you, the purchaser, are legally obligated to pay this uncollected sales tax when you file your state taxes?) As the volume of Internet purchases continues to increase, and as citizens buy relatively fewer goods in local stores, many states are losing urgently needed sales tax revenue—and thus are vigorously lobbying for changes in the federal law.

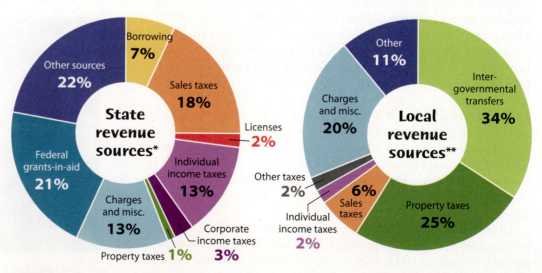

FIGURE 18.3

State and Local Revenue Sources

*CALCULATED from U.S. Census Bureau, *Statistical Abstract of the United States: 2010* (Washington, DC: U.S. Government Printing Office, 2010), Table 439.

**CALCULATED from U.S. Census Bureau, *Statistical Abstract of the United States: 2010* (Washington, DC: U.S. Government Printing Office, 2010), Table 443.

State governments also raise money through excise taxes. These taxes on the purchase of gasoline, tobacco, alcohol, and other items aim not only to raise revenue but also to reduce consumption of these products. In addition, state governments typically tax inheritances, large monetary gifts, and, as noted, the extraction of natural resources (severance taxes). Moreover, all but seven states—Alaska, Florida , Nevada, South Dakota, Texas, Washington, and Wyoming—collect personal income taxes.[26]

Beyond the variety of taxes they impose, states raise revenue by charging fees for some of the services they provide, such as higher education (through tuition at state colleges and universities) and hospital care. Some states, such as Pennsylvania and New Hampshire, even make money on the sale of liquor because they own the liquor stores in the state.

Local Government Revenues

How do local governments raise funds? A major revenue source for local governments is grants from their state government. The primary source of local government tax revenue, however, is the property tax. The property tax is imposed on the value of property a person owns (typically land and buildings, although some states also place a property tax on the value of household furnishings, clothing, and jewelry).

Unfortunately for local governments, the property tax is the most criticized tax, for several reasons. First, unlike the income tax, which (as a percentage of income) people view as based on their ability to pay, the property tax depends on the value of a person's property, which may not correlate with income and hence with that person's ability to pay. For people on a fixed income (such as Social Security), increases in property taxes mean they must pay a larger proportion of their income to hold on to their home. Further, unlike sales and income taxes, property taxes go up almost annually.

Owing to inflation, the operating costs of local governments rise every year. This increase occurs even when they are providing the same services as in the preceding year. Thus they need to raise more money each year if they are to balance their budgets. One way local governments collect more money is by increasing the property tax rate. Increases in the property tax rate take place through an annual vote (either by local government officials or by citizens in a referendum). Upon approval of the new tax rate, citizens receive a bill for their full property tax obligation and then write a check to pay the bill. This process makes the property tax a more "visible" burden to taxpayers than the sales tax, which people typically pay without much thought and do not track on an annual basis. It is also more visible than the income tax, which the government automatically deducts from individuals' paychecks, frequently without their close monitoring.

Recognizing that property taxes alone sometimes do not cover localities' full financial needs, state governments are increasingly allowing local governments to collect revenues through additional channels. Some state governments have given selected local governments the authority to collect sales taxes, and at least thirteen states allow some local governments to collect income taxes. The majority of states have authorized their local governments to collect fees for goods and services such as sewerage service and utilities.

State and local governments differ with respect to the value of their available taxable resources, as well as in their decisions about which resources to tax, and at what rate. Because the governments of the fifty states and of the tens of thousands of U.S. localities have unequal financial capacities to provide for their citizens, they sometimes compete with one another for resources. For example, state and local governments vie with one another to attract new companies because the arrival of new firms means job creation, which expands the tax base. Newly created jobs mean more people working and thus more revenue raised through income taxes—and perhaps also through sales taxes because employed people usually have more money to spend than unemployed people do. To bring in new companies, state and local governments may provide tax breaks for businesses, or they may spend money on schools, parks, and improved public safety to enhance the quality of life in their communities. State and local governments also compete for national grant money that they can put toward balancing their budgets.

The Federal Government as a Fiscal Equalizer

The federal government offers state and local governments grants-in-aid to implement national policy preferences. It also provides grants to balance the interstate (among states) and intrastate (within a state) differences in financial capacity to meet the needs of the population at large. Through grant programs, which typically distribute more money to states and localities with the greatest mismatch between their resources and their citizens' needs, the federal government acts as a fiscal equalizer. Through its grants, the national government tries to ensure that all states can adequately serve their citizens.

For example, the national government distributes Medicaid grants to the states on the basis of a formula that ensures the greatest assistance for states with the lowest per capita income. Accordingly, in 2008, the federal budget covered 76 percent of Mississippi's Medicaid cost, based on data indicating that Mississippi had the lowest per capita income and the largest percentage of people in poverty among all the states. This was the highest national cost sharing for Medicaid among all the states. Twelve states received the lowest national cost sharing—50 percent—for Medicaid: California, Colorado, Connecticut, Delaware, Illinois, Maryland, Massachusetts, Minnesota, New Hampshire, New Jersey, New York, and Virginia.[27] Table 18.2 presents data on federal grant spending.

The ability of the federal government to be a fiscal equalizer for state and local governments is limited. The great recession that began in 2007 hit state and local governments hard. Typically, job losses during a recession create revenue shortfalls for state governments that rely on sales and individual income taxes for a large proportion of their revenues, and employment is one of the last parts of the economy to bounce back. Even though the 2009 economic stimulus package (the American Recovery and Reinvestment Act)[28] provided state and local governments with $280 billion in federal grants—$48 billion of which was intended to stabilize fiscally stressed state budgets[29]—states may face budget deficits as high as $350 billion in 2010 and 2011.[30]

Even though the national economy was showing signs of growth by the end of 2009, state and local governments usually experience their worst budget years in the two years after a recession ends.[31] Therefore, state and local governments have not seen the worst of the recession. Moreover, because state constitutions require state and local governments to balance their budgets, state and local governments will have to either raise more revenue (with increases in taxes or user fees) or cut spending (which means decreases in services). As

TABLE 18.2

Federal Aid to State and Local Governments

	Highest	Lowest
Total in millions	California ($56,402)*	Delaware ($1,241)**
As percent of total revenue	Mississippi (30.7%)	Virginia (11.6%)
Per capita	Wyoming ($3,988)	Virginia ($934)

*$1,556 per capita.
**$2,120 per capita.

SOURCE: *Governing State & Local Sourcebook*, http://sourcebook.governing.com/index.jsp.

POLITICAL INQUIRY

Why does California have the highest total of federal grant dollars but a per capita amount that is more than half of Wyoming's federal aid per capita? Keeping in mind the federal government's role as a fiscal equalizer, what does the comparison of Mississippi's federal aid as a percent of total revenue with Virginia's indicate about the tax base of Mississippi compared with that of Virginia?

Vermont Governor Jim Douglas warned in February 2010, for state and local governments "the worst probably is yet to come."[32]

Responsibilities of State and Local Governments in National Politics

The U.S. Constitution describes certain state obligations to the national government, and hence these are formal responsibilities. Other state responsibilities to the federal government have developed informally over time. In this section, we explore the main formal and informal responsibilities of state and local governments to the national government.

States in National Politics: Formal Roles

The U.S. Constitution established state government authority in several areas of national import (all of which have been discussed in previous chapters):

- conducting national elections
- determining the process by which electors for the Electoral College are selected
- redrawing House districts (redistricting) after congressional reapportionment
- ratifying amendments to the U.S. Constitution

These are the formal roles of state governments in national politics. Today, most states delegate to local governments the responsibility of conducting elections, including those for national offices. In many states, there are ongoing efforts to reform the process of choosing electors for the Electoral College and redistricting.

States in National Politics: Informal Functions

In addition to those constitutionally based roles for state governments, the states, by tradition, perform various informal functions in national politics and government. Two such functions are serving as a training ground for federal government officials and acting as a laboratory for innovative and experimental public policies.

TRAINING GROUNDS FOR NATIONAL OFFICE
Since 1921, the overwhelming majority of members of Congress have had prior local or state government experience, or both. Presidents also develop experience serving in state government.

Political scientists have identified three common pathways to the presidency over the course of U.S. history: the Senate, the vice presidency, and a governorship. Four of the last six presidents—Jimmy Carter, Ronald Reagan, Bill Clinton, and George W. Bush—used their position as governor as a steppingstone to the White House. President Reagan said that being governor "was the best training school for" the presidency.[33] Reagan's vice president, George H. W. Bush, successfully ran for the presidency in 1988, but before his success, no sitting vice president had been elected to the presidency since Martin Van Buren in 1836. Yet Americans widely view their vice president as in training for the presidency because the second-in-command is only "a heartbeat away" from the office. Since 1960, only two sitting U.S. senators have been elected to the presidency—John F. Kennedy and Barack Obama. Therefore, for the last four decades, governorships have served as the primary training ground for presidents.

Although career politicians typically advance from local to state to national positions, sometimes the movement occurs in the other direction—from national to state office. In 2008, ten sitting governors had previous experience serving in Congress.[34] That national officials are running for governor suggests a growing prestige for the gubernatorial office.

LABORATORIES FOR NEW PUBLIC POLICIES State and local governments are worth watching if you are looking for innovative public policies. States and localities develop creative policies to deal with domestic matters that are reserved to them by the Constitution, as well as to carry out the authority for policy making that the national government devolves to them through mandates and grants (as discussed in Chapter 3). State and local governments also set policies for domestic problems they believe the national government is not addressing appropriately. In particular, state governments are leading the way with innovative programs for environmental protection and health care.

Dissatisfied with the national government's response to various environmental concerns of national and global context and scope, state and local governments have taken matters into their own hands. Through both legislative action and citizen initiatives, states and localities, deeply concerned about the lack of national action to address global warming, have enacted laws requiring or encouraging utilities to increase their use of alternative energy, including solar and wind power.[35] The city government of Boulder, Colorado, became the first government in the United States to impose a tax on the use of electricity generated by the burning of fossil fuels. Voters in Boulder approved the tax in a 2006 ballot measure, expecting that the tax would promote conservation and consequently decrease the carbon emissions that scientists link to global warming.[36]

States have also taken the lead in health care policy making, stepping in when the national government failed to deliver. While serving as First Lady (1993–2001), Hillary Rodham Clinton worked diligently, but unsuccessfully, for a national universal health care plan. The plan was to institute publicly funded, national medical services that would cover most or all of the health care expenses of citizens who do not have their own, private health insurance. In 2006, Massachusetts and Vermont passed legislation aimed at providing health care to all their states' residents. In addition, with support from federal Medicaid funding, state governments across the country have experimented with programs that provide health insurance specifically to children.

States monitor one another's experiments closely. When policy makers in a given state see an innovative program working effectively, they often adopt it, making the necessary adjustments to meet the distinct needs of their own citizens. In turn, the national government sometimes adopts successful state programs, as in 1996 when Congress passed the Personal Responsibility and Work Opportunity Reconciliation Act, a national welfare reform bill that combined components of several experimental state welfare programs.

> Wind energy is among the world's fastest growing sources of energy. In the United States, the state of Texas is leading the way in wind energy growth. Many Texas landowners have leased their lands to wind turbine developers. In Texas, and other states where wind power development is occurring, state and local laws regulate its development. Moreover, state-government tax incentives are one of the driving forces behind the growth in wind energy.

In summary, as the national government has placed ever-greater demands on state and local governments without always providing sufficient funding to address crucial policy issues, the states have become more creative in devising appropriate public policy solutions. States are also addressing problems when concerned citizens are not satisfied with the remedies provided—or not provided—by the national government. Finally, when an innovative policy works in one state, other states, and even the national government, are often inclined to adopt it.

Having surveyed the constitutional basis of state and local governments, as well as their responsibilities to their citizens and the nation, we now examine the structures and institutions by which state and local governments exercise their authority. Because no two states and no two local governments are identical, we will focus on the most common structures and institutions.

Institutions of State Government

The state constitutions in effect at the time of the ratification of the Articles of Confederation (1781) and the U.S. Constitution (1789) had all established three branches of government with a system of checks and balances. This state government structure became the model for the national government created by the U.S. Constitution. Although the constitutions of all the states have been amended numerous times over the centuries, and many have been totally replaced several times, the basic structures of state governments have not changed. Each state government's structure is unique, but the legislative, executive, and judicial institutions of all the states share several common characteristics that we now consider.

Legislative Branch: Formulating and Approving Policy

The basic functions of state legislatures resemble those of their federal counterpart, Congress. The primary functions of state legislatures are policy formulation and policy approval. In addition, state legislatures monitor the executive branch's implementation of policy. Further, individual state legislators, like members of Congress, assist their constituents in solving problems they may be experiencing with the various levels of government.

The state legislature, typically called the General Assembly, is bicameral (two chambered) in all states except Nebraska, which has a unicameral (single chamber) legislature. A state with a bicameral legislature commonly calls the chamber that has more members the House, and the smaller chamber the Senate. Nebraskans call their unicameral legislature the Senate. The number of legislators in each state legislature varies widely. The figure in "Analyzing the Sources" on page 576 presents the number of legislators per million people, for each state. As you can see from the graphic, the number of state legislators does not correlate with the state population.

State senators usually serve a four-year term of office; state representatives, a two-year term. Fifteen states have set term limits for legislators—incumbents can run for reelection for the same position only a set number of times. Not surprisingly, citizens (not state legislators) took the lead in establishing most of these term limits, using the state's initiative processes.

There is generally more diversity of gender, ethnicity, and race among state legislators than among national legislators. In 2010, for example, 24 percent of the total number of state legislators (7,382) were women (1,799 legislators). In New Hampshire, 38 percent of the legislators were women, but in South Carolina, only 10 percent of the lawmakers were women.[37] The predominance of a moralistic political culture (see page 565) appears to correlate with higher proportions of women elected to state legislatures, as does the presence in the population of relatively high numbers of educated, professional women—women who are more likely to have a sense of political efficacy and are more willing and able to run for office.

The racial and ethnic diversity within a state's population generally correlates with the diverse composition of its state legislature. For example, in 2009 Mississippi had the highest proportion of African Americans in its state legislature (29 percent) as well as the highest

ANALYZING THE SOURCES

HOW REPRESENTATIVE IS EACH STATE'S LEGISLATURE?

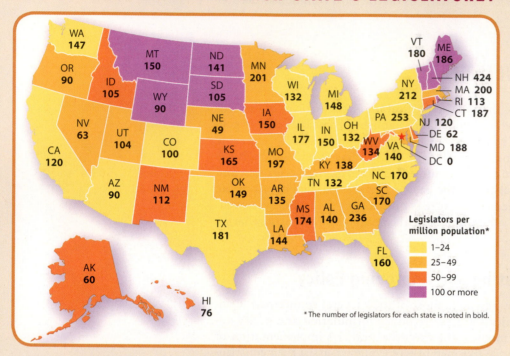

Legislators per million population*

- 1–24
- 25–49
- 50–99
- 100 or more

* The number of legislators for each state is noted in bold.

States on the map:
WA 147, OR 90, ID 105, MT 150, ND 141, MN 201, WI 132, MI 148, NY 212, VT 180, ME 186, NH 424, MA 200, RI 113, CT 187, SD 105, WY 90, NE 49, IA 150, IL 177, IN 150, OH 132, PA 253, NJ 120, DE 62, MD 188, DC 0, NV 63, UT 104, CO 100, KS 165, MO 197, KY 138, WV 134, VA 140, CA 120, AZ 90, NM 112, OK 149, AR 135, TN 132, NC 170, SC 170, TX 181, LA 144, MS 174, AL 140, GA 236, FL 160, AK 60, HI 76

As the map shows, the state's population does not determine the number of state legislators. In the case of New Hampshire residents, 324 legislators represent every 1 million people. For Californians, only 3 legislators represent every 1 million people.

Evaluating the Evidence

① After you examine the map, review Figure 18.1. Assuming that you are interested in having your voice heard by your elected officials, which state would you rather live in? Why?

② Considering all the figures in this chapter, discuss the geographic pattern of states that provide greater levels of democracy—as in government by and for the people.

③ On the basis of the figures in this chapter, which states would you characterize as having a moralistic political culture? Explain.

proportion of African Americans in its state population (37 percent). Nine states—Hawaii, Idaho, Iowa, Maine, Montana, North Dakota, South Dakota, Utah, and Wyoming—had no African American state legislators. All of these states are in the bottom fifteen states when ranked by the proportion of African Americans in their population. In 2009, 9 percent of the legislators from all fifty states were African American. As for Latino state lawmakers, in 2009 New Mexico's legislature had the largest representation, with 44 percent in the legislature. New Mexico is also the state with the largest proportion of Latino residents, with 45 percent. Overall, 3 percent of state legislators were Latino.[38]

Unlike members of the U.S. House and Senate, the overwhelming majority of state legislators (85 percent) serve on a part-time basis. Most state legislatures convene annually from January to May or June. Seven state legislatures convene only every other year.

Regardless of the variations from state to state with respect to the number of legislators, their terms of office, their demographic characteristics, and whether the job is full- or part-time, all state legislatures have the same primary function: to formulate public policy. Further, they all share with their states' governors the authority to approve public policy as part of the system of checks and balances that accommodates the separation of basic governing functions. Approved state policy is put into action by employees of the executive branch.

Executive Branch: Putting Policy into Action

The executive branch of state government implements public policy. Approximately 5 million people work in the executive branches of the fifty state governments. In addition to those who directly implement policy, states have numerous appointed and elected executive branch officials who assist in formulating policy and supervising its implementation.

Unlike citizens voting in the national presidential election, who elect individuals to only two executive branch positions (the presidency and the vice presidency), citizens in almost all states have the opportunity to elect people to *several* of the state executive branch positions. **Plural executive system** refers to a government structure in which citizens elect more than two officials to the executive branch (Figure 18.4). Whereas the average number of statewide elected executive officials is seven, North Dakota elects the most (twelve). Each statewide elected executive branch official oversees a specific policy or functional area of state government, with the governor bearing responsibility for the remaining areas. The more elected statewide executive officials, the more people with whom the governor must share authority—and hence the weaker the governor.

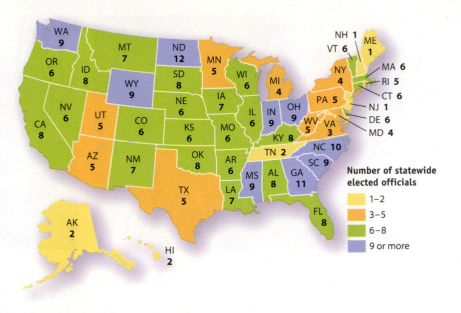

FIGURE 18.4

Total Number of Statewide Elected Officials for Each State, Executive Branch

SOURCE: State totals from Kendra A. Hovey and Harold A. Hovey, *CQ's State Fact Finder 2007* (Washington, DC: CQ Press, 2007), p. 113.

Number of statewide elected officials

- 1–2
- 3–5
- 6–8
- 9 or more

plural executive system
a state and local government structure in which the citizens elect more than two people to top positions in the executive branch of government

GOVERNOR   The best-known elected official in state government is the governor. (Can you name your governor? What about your state legislators?) Unlike the majority of state legislators, the governor is a full-time official. Moreover, the governor gets more media coverage than do legislators. Thus citizens can more easily learn about and track the governor's positions and actions than they can the work of their elected state legislators. Once the majority of legislators approve a bill, the governor can sign it into law or reject it with a veto. The governor's one vote—to approve or to reject a bill—draws more media attention than does the vote of any individual legislator.

Just as the president launches the budget process by presenting Congress with a proposed budget, the majority of governors begin the state budget procedure by drafting an executive budget they put before the state legislature. Compared with Congress, state legislatures typically have more limits on their authority to modify the executive budget. On the basis of the modified executive budget, the legislature writes specific appropriation bills that allocate spending by state departments and agencies. Most governors can use a line-item veto, the authority to eliminate one or more funding lines in appropriation bills while approving the remainder of the bill. The line-item veto is a tool that governors can and do wield to balance the state budget.

Once a bill becomes law, the governor must ensure its efficient, effective, and legal implementation. To that end, governors have the authority to appoint numerous people to top positions in the executive branch. In addition, governors can reorganize the departments and agencies in the executive branch to improve their efficiency and performance in implementing the law. Governors can also mandate specific activities and procedures on the part of executive branch bureaucrats by issuing executive orders.

In another responsibility of gubernatorial office, the governor serves as commander in chief of the state's National Guard. In this capacity, the governor can call on the National Guard to respond to state emergencies and crises, including natural disasters (for example, floods, blizzards, landslides, and hurricanes), civil unrest (such as riots), and terrorist attacks (such as those on September 11, 2001).

> Although governors are commander-in-chief of their state's National Guard, the president can supersede the governors' authority over the National Guard by federalizing troops and deploying them on behalf of the federal government. In 1957, Arkansas Governor Orval Faubus called on the Arkansas National Guard to prevent nine African American students from entering Little Rock's Central High School. In response, President Eisenhower federalized the National Guard troops, ordering them to protect the civil rights of the students as they integrated Central High. Today, National Guard troops are deployed worldwide, including in Kabul, Afghanistan, as part of the war on terrorism.

Whereas the nation elected its first minority male president in 2008, and has never elected a woman to serve as president, a diversity of gender, race, and ethnicity is evident among the nation's governors. In 2010, six of the fifty governors, and nine of the forty-two lieutenant governors were women.[39] In addition, there were two African American governors, one Latino, one Asian American, and one Arab American. Because of the plural executive structure of state government, there are many more opportunities for citizens to get elected to executive positions on the state than on the national level.

OTHER STATEWIDE ELECTED EXECUTIVES   States vary with respect to both how many elected executive branch officials they have and what positions those officials hold. All but seven states elect lieutenant governors, and many elect other statewide officials.

The lieutenant governor is in line to succeed the governor if the latter is unable to complete the term of office. States without the lieutenant governor position designate some other elected official to succeed a governor who cannot complete his or her term. Lieutenant governors also typically act as the president of their states' senates, presiding over Senate meetings and casting tie-breaking votes.

More than forty states have plural executive systems, which typically include the state attorney general, secretary of state, treasurer, and auditor. What are the responsibilities of these officials? The attorney general is the chief law enforcement officer in the state and represents the state in lawsuits. The secretary of state is the official record keeper. In addition to maintaining the legislative records, administrative rules, executive orders, and constitutional changes, the secretary of state keeps records of information relevant to elections, such as campaign finance reports, petitions by candidates to get on the Election Day ballot, and lists of registered voters. The state treasurer pays the state's bills, and the auditor reviews state spending to ensure that it is legal, efficient, and effective.

The statewide executive officials elected by citizens do not serve under the governor. Elected independently of the governor, they may even be members of a political party other than the governor's party. Because they serve for fixed terms (usually four years) and must satisfy the voters, not the governor, if they are to win reelection, these officials need not be loyal to the governor's priorities. The majority of state executives elected statewide, including governors, have term limits—usually a limit of two consecutive terms.

Judicial Branch: Resolving Questions of Law

In addition to electing state legislators and (on average) seven state executive branch officials, citizens in most states elect judges to serve in the state court system. Each of the fifty states has its own court system that is independent of the national judicial system. State judges must uphold both their state's constitution and the U.S. Constitution. Lawsuits that involve state and local laws are resolved in state courts. If such cases also involve questions of federal law or the U.S. Constitution, they may move into the federal court system.

State courts hear thousands more criminal and civil cases than do the national courts. In the process of resolving these cases, state judges may have to interpret the meaning of laws and previous court decisions. State judges also have the authority of judicial review; that is, they can declare acts of the state and local legislative and executive officials to be unconstitutional.

STRUCTURE OF STATE COURT SYSTEMS Although the primary responsibilities of the courts across the fifty states are the same, judicial structures and procedures differ from state to state. Here, we look briefly at certain commonalities in judicial organization and process.

State *trial courts* have *original* jurisdiction: they are responsible for determining whether the accused person is guilty or not guilty based on the evidence presented in court. All states have two levels of trial courts. The lower-level trial courts hear less serious cases than do the upper-level trial courts. In contrast to trial courts, *appellate courts* have *appellate* jurisdiction: they review the legality and fairness of trial and lower appellate court procedures and decisions in the cases brought to them through an appeal. Thus appellate courts do not determine guilt. Rather, they ensure due process through their review of judges' decisions made in lower courts—decisions on issues such as what evidence lawyers can submit for jurors to consider and what questions lawyers can ask of witnesses. The appellate judges review trial transcripts and lawyers' arguments to determine whether the judges made the correct decisions. The majority of states have two levels of appellate courts: the intermediate-level court and the court of last resort. Figure 18.5 summarizes the structure of and the selection process for the state court systems.

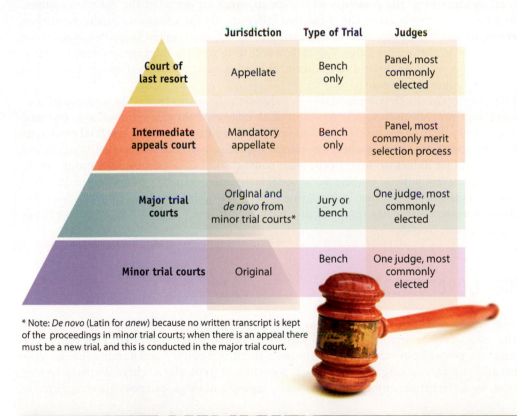

	Jurisdiction	Type of Trial	Judges
Court of last resort	Appellate	Bench only	Panel, most commonly elected
Intermediate appeals court	Mandatory appellate	Bench only	Panel, most commonly merit selection process
Major trial courts	Original and *de novo* from minor trial courts*	Jury or bench	One judge, most commonly elected
Minor trial courts	Original	Bench	One judge, most commonly elected

* Note: *De novo* (Latin for *anew*) because no written transcript is kept of the proceedings in minor trial courts; when there is an appeal there must be a new trial, and this is conducted in the major trial court.

POLITICAL INQUIRY

FIGURE 18.5 ■ STRUCTURE OF STATE COURT SYSTEMS How does the structure of the typical state court system differ from the structure of the federal court system? How does the selection of federal judges differ from the selection of state judges? What are the advantages and disadvantages of each type of judicial selection process?

Judges decide what laws mean and ensure due process. How are judges selected to ensure that they have the proper qualifications for this essential role in our democracy?

JUDGES Whereas the president appoints and the Senate confirms federal judges, the states use a variety of methods to select their judges. Some states use one selection process for trial judges and a different procedure for appellate judges. State judges may be (1) elected, (2) appointed, or (3) chosen through a process that combines an initial appointment with a subsequent retention election. Each state's law specifies the judicial selection procedure(s) the state will follow.

In states that grant judgeships through an electoral process, voters typically select judges through a nonpartisan election, a type of election not used at the national level of government. In a **nonpartisan election,** the candidates are not selected by a political party, and party affiliations do not appear on the ballot. In contrast, in a **partisan election,** political parties select candidates, and the ballot lists each candidate's party affiliation. State governments adopted nonpartisan judicial elections during the Progressive Era of the late 1800s and early 1900s—the same era when state governments were adopting direct democracy. Progressive reformers maintained that nonpartisan elections would encourage voters to pay greater attention to the candidates' qualifications than to their party affiliations and limit the influence of party organizations on both election outcomes and public policy.

Debates over appointing rather than electing judges, and over partisan rather than nonpartisan judicial elections, have led more and more states to adopt a **merit selection process,** which combines an initial appointment with a subsequent election. Proponents of this selection method believe that it combines the best of the electoral and appointive processes. Although merit selection procedures vary from state to state, they have some common elements. The process usually begins with the governor appointing citizens to a nonpartisan nominating committee. The nominating committee sends a list of qualified judicial candidates to the governor, who then appoints judges from the list of nominees. After a one- or two-year term, the appointed judge stands for a noncompetitive **retention election,** in which the judge runs unopposed and voters vote "yes" to keep the judge on the bench or "no" to remove the judge. Typically, a vote to retain the judge means a second term of eight or ten years. At the end of the term, the judge must again go through a retention election to remain on the bench.

The question of which government each judge actually works for can be a source of confusion for citizens. Even though voters elect trial judges to hear cases that arise in one city, borough, township, or county, the state government typically funds all the trial courts, as well as the appellate courts, in the state. Hence individuals who appear to be city or county judges are in fact judges working in the state court system at large. Local governments do not have a separate judicial branch. Some local governments do not even have distinct legislative and executive branches. Instead, one governmental body (a council, a commission, a board, or an authority) has responsibility for both the legislative and the executive functions, as we next consider.

Local Governments

Scholars categorize local governments as either *general-purpose* or *single-purpose* governments on the basis of the variety of services they dispense. Most citizens live within the borders of at least two general-purpose local governments (such as a county and a municipal government) and at least one single-purpose local government (typically a school district). In this section, we differentiate among these general-purpose and single-purpose governments.

General-Purpose Local Governments

As the term suggests, **general-purpose government** provides numerous and varied services, in multiple policy areas, to the people living within its borders. The fifty states have 39,044 such governments, yet not all states have all varieties of general-purpose govern-

nonpartisan election
an election in which candidates are not nominated by political parties and the ballot does not include party affiliations

partisan election
an election in which candidates are nominated by political parties and the ballot lists each candidate's political party affiliation

merit selection process
a process for selecting judges in which a nonpartisan committee nominates candidates, the governor or legislature appoints judges from among those candidates to a short term of service, and then the appointed judges face a retention election at the end of the short term

retention election
a noncompetitive election in which an incumbent judge's name is on the ballot and voters decide whether the judge should be retained

general-purpose government
a government providing services in numerous and diverse policy and functional areas to the residents living within its borders

municipal government
self-governing general-purpose government—including city, borough, and town governments—created by states to provide goods and services within a densely populated area

ments.[40] Municipal, township, and county governments are three forms of general-purpose governments.

Municipal governments are self-governing political jurisdictions created by states to provide goods and services to a densely populated area within the state. Municipal governments include city, borough, and town governments. These governments provide day-to-day services and benefits to citizens. **Townships,** which also deliver day-to-day services, are units of government that serve people living outside municipalities, in rural areas where the population is more dispersed than in areas served by municipal governments.

Day-to-day services provided by municipal and township governments include public safety, zoning regulations for land use, road maintenance, parks and recreation, and libraries. The larger the population of a municipality or township, the more numerous and diverse the services its government provides. Very large cities may have their own mass transportation systems, colleges, hospitals, and jails. Townships and smaller municipalities typically do not provide such services. Instead, county governments may provide these services in the less densely populated areas in which townships and smaller municipalities are located.

Most states initially created **county governments** to assist with the implementation of state policy in geographic subdivisions of the state. Although historically county governments were not self-governing and did not make many of their own public policies, the picture is changing. Today's county governments are taking on increased responsibilities and engaging in more policy making than in years past. County governments provide a growing list of services and benefits, including law enforcement, corrections, highway maintenance, property assessment, tax collection, the recording of legal documents (from voter registration to land transactions), higher education, nursing home care, parks and recreation, and land use planning. Because a single county typically contains numerous municipalities and townships, the services rendered by each of these general-purpose local governments somewhat depend on what services the other local governments with jurisdiction over some of the same geographical area are providing.

There are three basic structures of general-purpose governments: the commission form, the council-mayor form, and the council-manager form. These forms are differentiated by the way the executive and legislative functions are distributed among elected and appointed government officials.

In the **commission** form, which is more common in county and township governments than in other general-purpose governments, voters elect a body of officials who collectively hold the legislative and executive reins of the government. In this form of general-purpose government, there is no independently elected chief executive, and so the commission oversees day-to-day government affairs.

The **council-mayor** form of municipal government is comparable to the **council-executive** form of county government, with both composed of a legislative body, elected by voters, and an independently elected chief executive. Within the council-mayor form of government, political scientists differentiate strong mayors from weak mayors. **Strong mayors** have the traditional powers delegated to elected chief executives (veto power, power to formulate the budget, and power to appoint many executive branch officials). **Weak mayors** have fewer, if any, powers traditionally delegated to elected chief executives.

The **council-manager** (also called **commission-administrator**) form of government, found in many counties and the majority of cities, features an elected body with legislative and executive powers; this council, or commission, hires a professional manager/administrator to oversee the government's daily operations. The appointed manager has no authority to vote on policy but does advise the elected council members on policy matters.

As national and state governments have devolved more responsibilities to general-purpose local governments, and as citizens' demands for services have mounted, general-purpose governments have sought to lighten their workload and decrease their spending. One approach they have used is to establish collaborative working relationships with one or more other local governments in their region. One type of collaborative relationship is a **Council of Governments (COG),** which is a regional agency composed of representatives from several local governments that are sharing resources to address one or more mutual problems. Another type of collaboration is the consolidation of services. In this case, two or more local governments provide services to their communities through one unit, such as

township
a unit of government that serves people living outside municipalities, in rural areas where the population is more dispersed than in areas served by municipal governments

county government
a general-purpose local government created by states to assist them in implementing policy in geographic subdivisions of the state

commission
a form of local government that is more common in county and township governments than in other general-purpose governments and for which voters elect a body of officials who collectively hold legislative and executive powers

council-mayor (council-executive)
a form of general-purpose local government comprising (1) a legislative body elected by voters and (2) an independently elected chief executive

strong mayor
an elected municipal government executive who holds the powers traditionally delegated to elected chief executives (veto power, power to formulate the budget, and power to appoint many executive branch officials)

weak mayor
an elected municipal government executive who holds few, if any, of the powers traditionally delegated to elected chief executives

council-manager (commission-administrator)
a form of general-purpose local government found in many counties and the majority of cities; it is composed of an elected body with legislative and executive powers whose members hire a professional manager to oversee the government's day-to-day operations

Council of Governments (COG)
a regional agency composed of representatives from several local governments who share resources to address one or more mutual problems

Growth in State and Local Governments

	THEN (1957)*	NOW (2010)**
National	1	1
State	48	50
County	3,047	3,033
Municipalities and townships	34,381	36,011
School districts	50,446	13,051
Special districts	14,405	37,381

WHAT'S NEXT?

> Will the conditions that encourage general-purpose governments to create new single-purpose governments change any time in the near future?

> If the number of single-purpose governments continues to grow, what might cause citizens to become more aware of them and to pay more attention to them?

> Will cost concerns encourage citizens to support the consolidation of more local government services, and even consolidation of local governments?

> Will the movement to gain statehood for the District of Columbia win congressional approval, increasing the number of states to fifty-one?

* U.S. Census Bureau, *Statistical Abstract of the United States: 1959*, 80th ed. (Washington, DC: U.S. Government Printing Office, 1959), Table 502.

** U.S. Census Bureau, *Statistical Abstract of the United States: 2010*, 129th ed. (Washington, DC: U.S. Government Printing Office, 2010), Table 416.

a joint police department. In some cases, two local governments have also been consolidated into one. However, voters in most states must approve the consolidation of existing local governments through a referendum, and in the majority of cases, voters do not approve such consolidations because they do not want to lose the local government they know. Voters also fear consolidation will mean poorer-quality services.[41]

In contrast to these collaborative approaches to lightening their burden, general-purpose governments (individually or collectively) can create a new government and delegate to it one specific responsibility, such as fire protection or the management of the sewer system. The newly created local government, with one specific responsibility—known as a single-purpose government—is an independently functioning entity.

Single-Purpose Local Governments

Tens of thousands of general-purpose local governments exist, but there are even more single-purpose governments, and the number keeps growing. A **single-purpose government** provides one service or function to the people living within its borders. The most visible of these governments are school districts. Political scientists usually discuss school districts separately from other single-purpose governments because there are so many of them and because state, not local, governments created them. The number of school districts varies tremendously from state to state; Texas has 1,089, and Virginia has only one. In addition to the 13,051 school district governments in the United States, there are 37,381 other single-purpose governments.[42]

Single-purpose governments typically have a structure comparable to the commission form of general-purpose government and fall into two types: districts and authorities. The most common distinction between a district and an authority is that a district can impose and collect taxes to pay for its services, but an authority cannot do so. Instead, the authority must raise money by selling or renting its services or resources. For example, a water authority sells water, a sewer authority charges for the use of sewers, and a parking authority charges for the use of its parking spaces. In addition, because authorities do not have to deal with the same personnel and financial constraints that general-purpose governments must confront, they have more flexibility in their operations.

Most people are aware of the general-purpose local governments under which they live. Few, however, know much about the single-purpose governments in their community, other than the school district. Moreover, because the NIMBY (not-in-my-backyard) syndrome is alive and well, people rarely take advantage of the open meetings conducted by government—national, state, general-purpose local government, or single-purpose local government—until or unless an action (or a proposed action) of government negatively af-

single-purpose government
a government providing one service or function for residents living within its borders

fects them. Yet democratic governments rest on the principle that government is *by* and *for* the people. For many citizens, the *by* dimension creates an obligation to participate at least reactively, if not proactively. State and local governments provide countless, rich opportunities for citizen participation.

CONCLUSION

THINKING CRITICALLY ABOUT WHAT'S NEXT IN STATE AND LOCAL GOVERNMENT

Contemporary migration of people from locality to locality and from state to state, as well as immigration of people from other countries, fuels intrastate and interstate diversity. Intrastate and interstate diversity in cultures, resources, climate, and demographics produces different political processes and a large variety of public policies as state and local governments respond to the demands of their residents. As the U.S. population becomes ever more diverse, what new services and benefits will citizens call on state and local governments to provide?

State and local governments have always served as laboratories for innovative policies to address long-existing problems as well as for creative policies to address new problems. Over the last half century, the national government has devolved to the states responsibility for many societal problems that have a nationwide affect. Moreover, during economic downturns, state and local governments become even more innovative as they must continue to serve their citizens while experiencing decreased revenues. The economic forecast for state and local governments in the near future is grim. Will states be able to continue to experiment with public policies that address nationwide problems in dire economic times?

At the state and local levels of government, citizens have been successful in reining in tax increases and spending increases through their use of initiatives and referenda. They have also used these modes of direct democracy to enact policies that their elected officials were unable or unwilling to enact. At the same time, citizen displeasure with gridlock in national policy making has been growing. Will the success of initiatives and referenda at the state and local levels lead to a movement to adopt these processes at the national level?

Summary

1. Direct Democracy: Letting the People Decide
State and local governments give U.S. citizens opportunities for direct democracy that are not available in the national government. All states provide for some form of referendum, and about 40 percent of the states also provide for citizen initiatives. In addition, about one-third of the states allow citizens to recall elected state officials with whom they are dissatisfied.

2. State Constitutions and Local Charters
Each state has its own constitution, which authorizes state legislators to create local governments through the process of approving local government charters. According to Dillon's rule, the responsibilities of local governments are limited to only those specified in their charters. In recent decades, state governments have expanded their use of home rule charters, approved by local voters, that provide local governments with greater discretion.

3. Diversity in Political Cultures, People, Environment, and Resources
The great diversity in the fifty states affects the demands placed on state and local governments. It also influences the political processes and the policy choices of these

governments, as well as their financial capacity. The more than 89,000 state and local governments operating in the United States can better address this diversity than could one national government.

4. State and Local Government Budgets

Although the U.S. Constitution does not require the national government to balance its budget, state constitutions do mandate balanced state and local operating budgets. The ability of state and local governments to provide the day-to-day services for which they are responsible, many of which are essential to public safety and health, depends on their tax base. Because some states and localities have smaller tax bases than do others, the federal government takes on the role of fiscal equalizer to support those with weaker financial capacities.

5. Responsibilities of State and Local Governments in National Politics

The Constitution delegates to state governments a role in national elections, in the redistricting of national House districts, and in the ratification of amendments to the U.S. Constitution. In addition, state and local governments provide future national officials with government experience, and they test innovative public policies that, if successful, other state and local governments, and even the federal government, might adopt.

6. Institutions of State Government

Although the institutions of the fifty states share certain commonalities, such as a system that balances power among three branches of government, each state government is unique. In addition, state governments differ from the national government in that most states have a plural executive system and most elect rather than appoint state judges.

7. Local Governments

One useful way to differentiate among local governments in the United States is to categorize them as either general-purpose or single-purpose governments. General-purpose governments, which include cities, counties, boroughs, and townships, dispense a variety of services to their citizens. Single-purpose governments, such as school districts that provide elementary and secondary education, deliver one specific service to their citizens.

Key Terms

ballot measure 559

capital budget 567

charter 562

commission 581

Council of Governments (COG) 581

council-manager (commission-administrator) 581

council-mayor (council-executive) 581

county government 580

Dillon's rule 563

essential services 568

general-purpose government 580

home rule 563

home rule charter 563

individualistic political culture 565

legislative referendum 559

merit selection process 580

moralistic political culture 565

municipal government 580

nonpartisan election 580

open meeting laws 558

operating budget 567

partisan election 580

plural executive system 577

popular referendum 559

retention election 580

single-purpose government 582

strong mayor 581

township 580

traditionalistic political culture 565

weak mayor 581

For Review

1. How does direct democracy differ from representative democracy?

2. Differentiate between Dillon's rule and home rule.

3. Explain how diversity in political culture, people, and resources puts different demands on state and local governments and therefore leads to different policies.

4. What essential services do state and local governments provide?

5. Describe two informal functions of the states in national politics.

6. Identify some differences between the three branches of national government and the three branches of state governments.

7. Differentiate between general-purpose governments and single-purpose governments, and give examples of each.

For Critical Thinking and Discussion

1. Which of the many governments that you have interacted with has had the biggest impact on your life to date? What government will have the greatest impact on you after you graduate from college? In your retirement years?

2. Think about the distinctions the text makes among traditionalistic, individualistic, and moralistic political cultures. What would you say is the dominant political culture on your college campus? What is it in your home community? Do you think it would be possible to change these political cultures? Explain.

3. What would be the impact on state and local governments, as well as citizens, if the national government stopped acting as a fiscal equalizer?

4. Given the growth of the international direct democracy movement, do you think Congress would approve, and the states would ratify, an amendment to the U.S. Constitution that authorizes the use of direct democracy (initiative, referendum, and recall) at the national level of government? Explain why or why not.

5. Because the U.S. Constitution establishes minimums in terms of civil rights, states can establish additional rights, such as a voting age lower than 18. Some have called for states to lower the voting age to 16 years old for school board elections. Present an argument in support of this proposal. Present an argument against this proposal.

6. Given the fiscal stress that all governments (national, state, and local) are experiencing, note one national, one state, and one local public service that you are willing to have eliminated. Discuss the negative impacts of your proposed cuts.

7. Voter participation in state and local elections is lower than in national elections. What do you think explains this phenomenon? Discuss one proposal for local government action that you think might increase voter participation in local elections.

MULTIPLE CHOICE: Choose the lettered item that answers the question correctly.

1. All of the following are direct democracy processes except
   a. electing government officials.
   b. initiative.
   c. recall.
   d. referendum.

2. The direct democracy process that includes *citizens* drafting public policy, which is then placed on the Election Day ballot, is called
   a. initiative.   c. popular referendum.
   b. legislative referendum.   d. recall.

3. Higher levels of voter turnout occur in states dominated by a(n)
   a. individualistic political culture.
   b. moralistic political culture.
   c. traditionalistic political culture.
   d. libertarian political culture.

4. A state's capital budget can include the costs for all the following items except
   a. bridge and highway construction.
   b. computer systems purchases.
   c. state office buildings construction.
   d. salaries and benefits.

5. The primary source of tax revenue for state governments is
   a. excise taxes.
   b. personal income taxes.
   c. property taxes.
   d. sales taxes.

6. The primary source of tax revenue for local governments is
   a. excise taxes.
   b. personal income taxes.
   c. property taxes.
   d. sales taxes.

7. On average, citizens elect people to the greatest number of positions in
   a. the national executive branch.
   b. the national legislative branch.
   c. the state executive branch.
   d. the state legislative branch.

8. All of the following are examples of general-purpose local governments except
   a. boroughs.
   b. cities.
   c. counties.
   d. school districts.

9. The fastest-growing category of government is
   a. municipal government.
   b. single-purpose government.
   c. state government.
   d. township.

10. Three branches of government are clearly identifiable in
    a. national, state, and local governments.
    b. national and state governments.
    c. state and local governments.
    d. only the national government.

FILL IN THE BLANKS.

11. The California tax-reform ballot measure known as _____ is credited with sparking an increase in citizen use of ballot measures that began in the 1980s and continues today.

12. In forty-nine states, the _____ budget, which covers the costs of day-to-day government functions, must be balanced.

13. The everyday public services provided by state and local governments that are required to prevent chaos and hazardous conditions are collectively labeled _____ services.

14. The overwhelming majority of states have a _____ system that allows voters to elect, on average, seven state executive officials.

15. In a _____ election, candidates are not selected by political parties and the Election Day ballot does not list the candidates' party affiliations.

Answers: 1. a; **2.** a; **3.** b; **4.** d; **5.** d; **6.** c; **7.** c; **8.** d; **9.** b; **10.** b; **11.** Proposition 13; **12.** operating; **13.** essential; **14.** plural executive; **15.** nonpartisan.

RESOURCES FOR RESEARCH AND ACTION

Internet Resources

Census Bureau's Quick Facts
http://quickfacts.census.gov This site is your one stop for state-by-state statistics.

Council of State Governments
www.csg.org A resource for state governments, this site offers training for state leaders and information on the best innovative approaches to the problems confronting states. This Web site also offers current news regarding government in all fifty states.

The National Council of State Legislators
www.ncsl.org This site is a resource for state governments and individuals interested in improving state government operations and understanding state issues, as well as issues of federalism and intergovernmental relations.

The National Governors Association
www.nga.org This site is a source of information on governors, collaborative lobbying efforts of governors, and the impact of national laws on state governments.

Internet Activism

Blog
To join a conversation about your state's government, review the state-by-state list of blogs at **www.stateline.org/live/resources/State_blogs.** To join a conversation about a specific state policy issue of concern to you, review the list of policy blogs at **www.stateline.org/live/resources/Issue_blogs.**

Twitter
http://twitter.com/NCSLCOMM The Communications Division of the National Council of State Legislators (NCSL), the bipartisan organization that serves legislators and staff of states, commonwealths and territories, tweets about state governing bodies, proposed and newly enacted legislation, reports and surveys.

Facebook
www.facebook.com/governing GOVERNING connects America's governors, mayors, state legislators, local council members, other senior governmental officials, and students of state and local government by providing intelligence and analysis on management, policy, and politics to help guide and inspire innovative leaders across state and local government.

YouTube
www.youtube.com/watch?v=6JI4orbn1Nk President Obama addressed the National Governors Association in February 2010 discussing his administration's cooperative work with state governments during the current economic downturn.

Recommended Readings

Beyle, Thad L. *State and Local Government: 2007–2008.* Washington, DC: CQ Press, 2007. The most recent edition of a collection of news articles on the problems and concerns that state and local governments are confronting. Each section begins with an analysis of the most important issues relevant to that section's topic. Topics include politics, media, state institutions, and local governments.

Elazar, Daniel J. *American Federalism: A View from the States,* 2nd ed. New York: Harper & Row, 1972. The seminal work on the political cultures of states.

Maddex, Robert L. *State Constitutions of the United States,* 2nd ed. Washington, DC: CQ Press, 2006. A comprehensive overview of the constitutions of all fifty states, U.S. territories, and Washington, D.C. Covers constitutional history, fundamental rights, branches of government, amendment procedures, special provisions such as direct democracy, and trends in constitutional reforms.

Van Horn, Carl. *The State of the States,* 4th ed. Washington, DC: CQ Press, 2005. A collection of readings that provide a solid overview of the important issues confronting state governments and the behavior of state governmental institutions in the 1980s and early 1990s.

Movies of Interest

The Town That Was (2007)
This film tells the story of the battle in the 1980s between the people of Centralia, Pennsylvania, and the state government over the state's decision to raze the town and relocate its 1,600 citizens. State officials argued that these drastic measures would cost less than the estimated half-billion dollars needed to extinguish the coal mine fire burning below the town since 1962. The film centers on John Lokitis, the youngest of the eleven remaining Centralia residents.

All the King's Men (2006)
Based on a novel by Robert Penn Warren, this film follows the career of Willie Stark, a southern politician running for governor, who woos the citizens of Louisiana with promises of policies to support the lower economic classes. The novel loosely re-creates aspects of the life of Louisiana governor Huey Long.

Jaws (1975)
This popular super-thriller traces the battle between the new, yet experienced, police chief and the mayor over how to handle the crisis posed by a great white shark feasting in the waters off their small island resort town as the Fourth of July approaches. The chief, hired to protect the town's people and tourists, wants to close the beach. The mayor puts tourism and the needed revenue it will bring to the town above the people's safety.

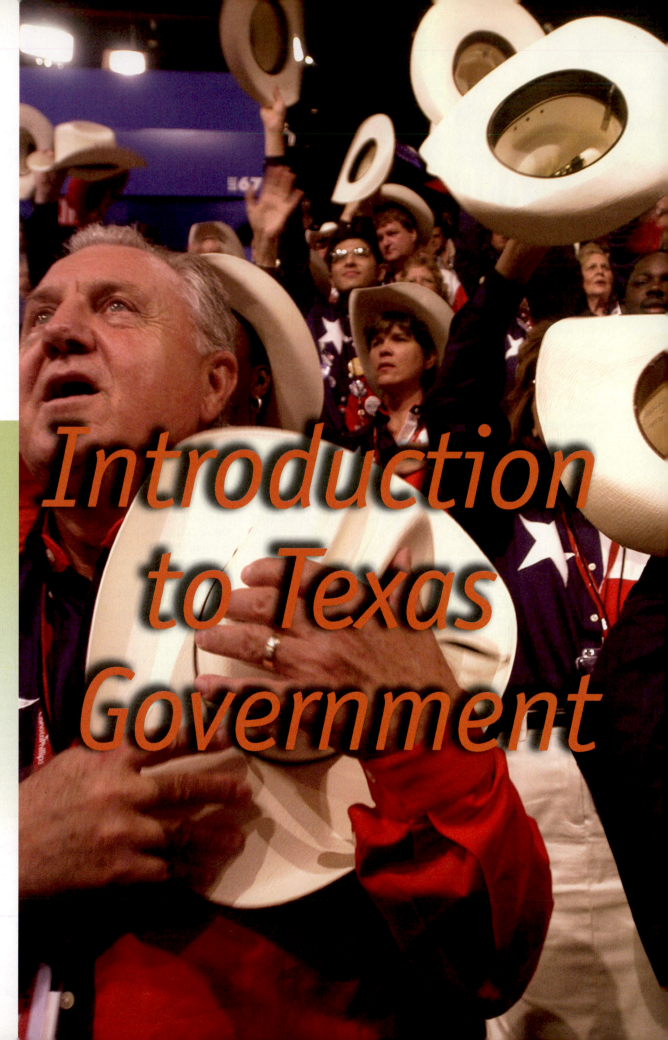

CHAPTER

19

Introduction to Texas Government

THEN

Anglos made up the majority of the population in Texas.

NOW

Texas is a majority-minority state, and minority groups make up a larger proportion of the population than Anglos.

NEXT

What population groups will grow the fastest?

How will population changes affect Texas politics?

How will economic changes affect Texas demographics?

This chapter explores how the diverse population and rapidly changing economy of Texas shape the state's politics.

FIRST, we consider the diverse character of *Texas society,* with a look at settlement patterns in Texas history and the urban and rural contrasts that are key to Texas politics.

SECOND, we examine *population growth and the changing political climate,* including the emergence of Texas as a majority-minority state as the Latino population rises.

THIRD, we evaluate *the political culture of Texas,* in particular how the ethnic mix has established a culture that is both traditionalistic and individualistic.

FOURTH, we look at *the economy of Texas,* comparing the land-based economy of the old Texas with the new emerging center of international trade and technology.

settlement patterns
the many origins of first settlers to the state

In the past half century, Texas

has changed greatly. Today, although the white, conservative society continues to thrive in a land first settled by the Spanish, social and economic diversity has turned Texas into a state of growing contrasts. Minorities have become a majority of the population, and urban professionals have built high-tech industries in the major cities. If Texas is still "a nation in every sense of the word,"[1] then it is a different nation, and these changes are having a profound impact on the politics of the state.

Texas Society

Several years ago, Texas state tourism promotion literature used the theme "Texas, a Land of Contrasts." Texas is very much a land of contrasts, and this is reflected in its government and politics. Texas is rural and urban, southern and western, Anglo, African American, and Latino. A southern state with a southern heritage, Texas is also a western state with a western heritage and a very strong Spanish and Mexican heritage.

The diversity of Texas history is reflected in the name of a popular theme park in the Dallas/Fort Worth area—Six Flags over Texas. Texas has been a Spanish colony, partially under French control; a Mexican state; an independent republic; a state in the United States; and a Confederate state. Each of these periods of its history has influenced what the state is today.

Settlement Patterns in Texas History

The contrasts in Texas society are better understood and take on meaning if we examine the history of **settlement patterns** in the state. The many origins of first settlers to the state have a significant impact on Texas politics today. This large state (268,601 square miles) has been a crossroads where the cultures of Mexico, the Old South, the West, and the Midwest have met and clashed (see Figure 19.1).

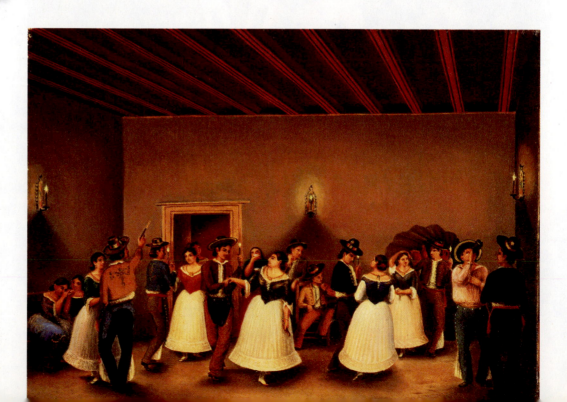

> The Tejanos, European settlers from Mexico, dance the fandango in the Spanish governor's house in San Antonio in 1844.

FIGURE 19.1

Settlement Patterns in Texas

THE TEJANOS, OR MEXICAN SETTLERS   The Rio Grande Valley was the first area of the state to be settled by Europeans. In the late 1600s, Spaniards developed settlements along the Rio Grande and as far north and east as San Antonio. Of the Spanish settlements in other parts of the state, only Nacogdoches lasted for more than a few years. Although permanent Spanish settlements did not penetrate much beyond San Antonio, the influence of Spain extends throughout the state. Most of the major rivers have Spanish names. Many other geographic features and a number of cities and counties also have Spanish names. Texas state laws are still very much influenced by past Spanish law, especially laws on land ownership and rights.

ANGLO SETTLERS   Southern Anglos and African Americans began settling East Texas in the 1820s. The southern white Protestant settlers were decidedly different from the resident Spanish Catholic settlers. These two groups clashed in 1836 during the Texas Revolutionary War, with many of the Spanish remaining loyal to Mexico while the Anglos formed the Republic of Texas (1836–1845).

The settlements of Anglo southerners did not extend west much beyond a line running from the Red River to present-day Fort Worth and south through Waco and Austin to San Antonio. This line is a natural geological feature, known as the Balcones Escarpment, which separates the Coastal Plain and pine forest regions of Texas from the middle and High Plains (Llano Estacado, which translates as "staked plains") regions of the state.

> The Company E Frontier Battalion of the Texas Rangers poses in Alice, Texas. Formed from a volunteer corp in 1835, the Rangers protected Texans from both external and internal threats. Today, the Rangers are the oldest statewide law enforcement agency in the United States.

For two reasons, most of the areas west of this line were not settled until after the Civil War. First, Comanche, Lipan Apache, Kiowa, and Tonkawa Indians inhabited this region. In the 1850s, the U.S. Army attempted to control this region by constructing a series of forts on the edge of the Cross Timbers area. The forts were Belknap, Cooper, Phantom Hill, Chadborne, McKavett, and Terrett. During the Civil War, the U.S. government abandoned these forts, and the Indian presence in this region reemerged. Indian domination of the area did not end until 1875, when Chief Quanah Parker was captured in Palo Duro Canyon near present-day Amarillo. The second reason for the lack of settlement was that the southern wood, water, and plantation culture was not adaptable to the dry, arid, treeless plains west of the Balcones Escarpment.

Settlement in this area increased after 1875 and took the form of large ranches and, later, small farms. Many of these settlers migrated from northern states, mostly from the Midwest, and from foreign countries. These settlers lacked the southern culture and traditions that dominated East Texas.

GERMAN IMMIGRANTS

One other early immigrant group also contributed to the character of Texas politics. Owing to the efforts of the Adelsverein Society (established to promote German immigrants), Germans began to immigrate to Texas in the 1840s. By 1847, the society had brought more than 7,000 Germans to Texas, most settling in and around the town of Fredericksburg.[2] By 1850, German settlers made up 5.4 percent of the state population.[3]

These German immigrants were not slave owners and objected to that institution. They lived apart from and often shunned contact with non-Germans. During the Civil War, many young German men refused to fight, and some fled to Mexico. From Reconstruction until the 1960s, a majority of the votes for Republicans in Texas were cast in areas settled by Germans.

Thus, Texas has four distinct and contrasting settlement periods and regions: Spanish South Texas, antebellum East Texas, frontier West Texas, and the German Fredericksburg Hill Country area. As we will see later, these regional differences still have an influence on Texas politics today.

Urban and Rural Contrasts

Texas is the second most populous state, and over 80 percent of its 24.8 million people live in 53 urban counties.* The remaining 20 percent live in the other 201 counties. Texas has three of the ten largest cities in the United States (Houston, Dallas, and San Antonio). Texas is also a rural state. One does not have to travel far from an urban center to see the contrast. The young urban professional living in Dallas has very little in common with someone working in a sawmill in Diboll.

These contrasts often frame the conflicts of Texas politics. East Texas Anglos demanding English-only amendments to the state constitution view demands for bilingual education by South Texas Latinos with contempt. High Plains Republicans from Amarillo often clash with East Texas traditional Democrats. The urban legislator from Austin might see things quite differently than a colleague from Muleshoe in West Texas does.

*U.S. Census Bureau, Population Estimate—2009, www.census.gov.popest/states/tables.

HOW TEXAS COMPARES

COMPARISON OF GROWTH RATES OF THE FIFTEEN MOST POPULOUS STATES

In the past thirty years, Texas has experienced tremendous growth in its population due both to birthrates and to the immigration of citizens from other states and countries. The fastest-growing segment of the population is Mexican Americans. The growth in Texas's population is also due to a movement of the U.S. population from northeastern states to southern states.

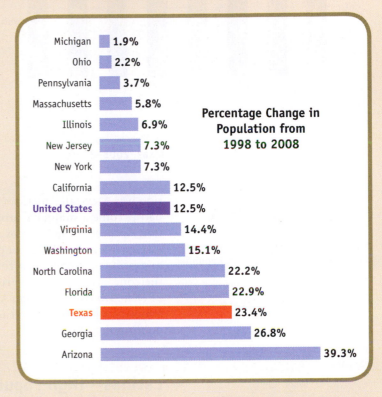

Percentage Change in Population from 1998 to 2008

State	%
Michigan	1.9%
Ohio	2.2%
Pennsylvania	3.7%
Massachusetts	5.8%
Illinois	6.9%
New Jersey	7.3%
New York	7.3%
California	12.5%
United States	12.5%
Virginia	14.4%
Washington	15.1%
North Carolina	22.2%
Florida	22.9%
Texas	23.4%
Georgia	26.8%
Arizona	39.3%

SOURCE: U.S. Census Bureau.

These regional, urban, and rural contrasts are less severe today than they were twenty-five years ago, but they are still important for understanding the unique character of politics in the Lone Star State.

Population Growth and the Changing Political Climate

In the past several decades, Texas has experienced tremendous growth in its population. This growth is due both to birthrates and to immigration of citizens from other states and countries. The largest-growing segment of the population is the Mexican Americans. Also, many northeastern states are losing population while southern states are gaining rapidly. The bar graph in "How Texas Compares" shows how Texas ranks among the fourteen other most populous states.

For the last several decades, Texas has experienced a migration of people from other states, owing partly to its strategic location in the Sunbelt and its proximity to Mexico. The 1970s Texas oil boom also contributed to this migration. Some people migrated out of the state in 1987–1989, but by 1990 the population had increased to almost 17 million,

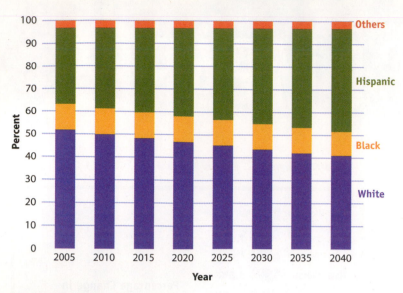

FIGURE 19.2

Historical and Projected Population in Texas, 2005–2040, as a Percentage of Total Population

SOURCE: U.S. Census Bureau.

changing political climate
changing national politics and immigration are changing the politics of the state from Democratic to Republican domination

majority-minority state
a state in which minority groups make up a majority of the population; a change from Anglos being the majority

up from 11.2 million in 1970. In 1996, the population of Texas was estimated to be 18.6 million, and today it stands at 24.8 million.

Many of these newcomers to Texas have caused a **changing political climate** in significant ways. From the end of Reconstruction until the mid-1970s, the Democratic Party dominated Texas politics, with only one person (U.S. Senator John Tower) winning statewide office as a Republican. The term Yellow Dog Democrat was used to describe the voting habits of many Texans ("He would vote for a yellow dog if it ran as a Democrat"). From the 1880s until the 1960s, straight ticket party voting was also necessitated by the absence of meaningful competition from Republicans in the November general election. Many new immigrants to the state, however, brought with them their Republican traditions and strengthened the Republican Party in the state. That, coupled with changing national politics, made it respectable to vote Republican.

Minority groups have played a significant role in changing the political climate in Texas. By the early twenty-first century, the majority of the state's population was Mexican American and African American, and Anglos became a minority: Texas had become a **majority-minority state** (see Figure 19.2). According to the Texas Education Agency, in 1987 Anglos made up 52.5 percent of all school attendees in Texas. In 2010, Anglos made up 34 percent of the school population. Higher birthrates for minorities and migration to urban areas, coupled with white migration to suburban areas, contributed to the concentration of minority groups in major cities of the state. Corpus Christi, Dallas, El Paso, Houston, and San Antonio have majority-minority populations. These changes in majority and minority status will have many implications for the politics of the state and public policy decisions.

Latinos—High Population Growth and Increasing Political Clout

Immigration of Latinos from Mexico to Texas has been a factor in population increases and in state politics. In 1960, Latinos were 15 percent of the total population of Texas. Their percentage increased to 18 percent by 1970, to 25 percent in 1990, and was a little over 36.5 percent in 2010. With liberalized voter registration procedures, Latinos began to dominate politics in the border areas, in some sections of the Gulf Coast, and in the San Antonio area. They have been successful in electing local officials to city and county government and school boards, to the state legislature, and to Congress. Dan Morales was elected the state's attorney general in 1990 and served until 1999. Raul Gonzales was appointed to serve on the Texas Supreme Court in 1984 and served until 1999.[4] Victor Morales, a newcomer to politics, won the Democratic Party nomination for the U.S. Senate in April 1996 to run against Sena-

> **Rep. Richard Raymond (D-Laredo) talks with Sen. Judith Zaffirini (D-Laredo) during a Senate session. Hispanic office holders are playing an increasingly important role in state politics.**

tor Phil Gramm. In the 2002 governor's race, Tony Sanchez was the first Latino candidate for governor in a major party. The expectation was that Sanchez would produce a great increase in Latino votes. That did not happen, and he was soundly defeated. In fact, there is some evidence that Anglo voters, who would normally vote for Democratic candidates, failed to vote for Sanchez.

Despite Sanchez's loss, Latino voters remain a potential force in Texas politics in the years ahead. By 2036, they will outnumber Anglos and should be a major force in Texas politics.

African Americans—Steady Population and Political Participation

Unlike the Latino population, which has steadily increased as a percentage of the total population since the 1960s, the African American population has remained at about 10 to 12 percent since 1950. At the time of the Civil War, African Americans made up about 30 percent of the population, and that percentage declined to about 20 percent by the turn of the twentieth century. Originally located in rural areas, African Americans moved to the cities. Today, they tend to be concentrated in three metropolitan areas—Houston, Dallas/Fort Worth, and Austin. They have had some political success at electing officials to local offices (school boards, city councils, and county offices), to the state legislature, and to a few seats in the U.S. Congress. In 1990, Democrat Morris Overstreet became the first African American to be elected to statewide office. Judge Overstreet served on the Texas Court of Criminal Appeals, the Supreme Court for criminal matters in the state until 1999. By 2010, three African Americans were serving in statewide office: Texas Supreme Court Chief Justice Wallace Jefferson, Texas Supreme Court Justice Dale Wainwright, and Railroad Chairman Michael Williams. All three are Republicans.

In 2002, Ron Kirk, a popular mayor of Dallas, ran for the U.S. Senate seat. Although polls showed Kirk to be in a dead heat with John Cornyn, he lost this race. Voting among African Americans was low, and some Anglos, who normally support Democrats, voted for Republican Cornyn. With their smaller population and low voter turnout, African Americans have not yet become as powerful a political force as the Latinos. Currently, three of Texas's thirty-two members of the U.S. House of Representatives are African American.

Asian Americans— Moderate Population Growth and Political Inroads

In 1980, Asian Americans constituted less than 1 percent of the population of Texas; by 2010, they were 2.6 percent. Projections are that by the year 2020, the Asian American population of Texas will increase to 4.5 percent. Most Asian Americans are concentrated in the Houston area. One section of Houston has such a large concentration of Chinese Americans that the City of Houston has placed Chinese writing on some of the street signs there. Asian Americans in the Houston area have had some success in electing local officials, including one city council member and a judge. In 2002, voters in the Houston area elected Martha Wong as a representative to the Texas state House of Representatives. She was only the second Asian to serve in the Texas House and the first Republican of Asian background. In 2004 and 2008, voters elected a Vietnamese, Hubert Vo, to the Texas House of Representatives.

> Asian Americans in Texas rally in support of Hubert Vo, a Democratic member of the Texas House of Representatives.

POLITICAL CULTURE IN THE STATES

The accompanying map shows how the states compare based on the concept of political culture. What political culture dominates the South? Is Texas an exception? What political culture dominates in other regions of the United States?

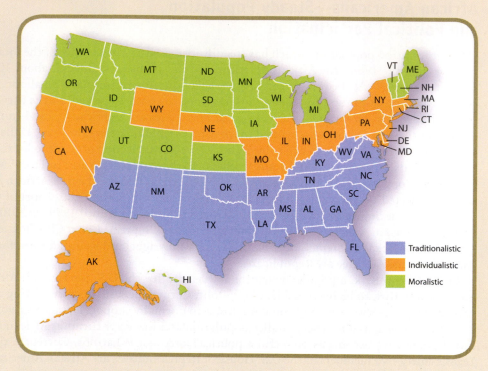

SOURCE: Daniel J. Elazar, *American Federalism: A View from the States*, pp. 124–125. Copyright © 1984 by Harper & Row Publishers, Inc. Reprinted by permission of Pearson Education, Inc.

The Political Culture of Texas

Thus far, we have discussed the historic settlement patterns, the changing makeup of the current population, and the ethnic mix of the population in the state. These factors have had a profound impact on the *political culture* of the state. As discussed in Chapter 1, political culture is the people's collective beliefs and attitudes about government and political processes. It determines the values people expect the government to support and the role they think government and ordinary citizens should play in the political process.

Daniel J. Elazar, in his book *American Federalism: A View from the States*, developed a system for applying the idea of political culture to the fifty states. Elazar found that there were three distinctive political subcultures in the United States—moralistic, individualistic, and traditionalistic.[5] (See "How Texas Compares.")

moralistic subculture
a political subculture that expects the government to act as a positive force to achieve a common good for all citizens

In the **moralistic subculture,** politics "is considered one of the great activities of [people in their] search for the good society . . . an effort to exercise power for the betterment of the commonwealth."[6] Government is a positive instrument for change and a means of promoting the general welfare of all citizens. Politics becomes the responsibility of all citizens, who have an obligation to participate in government. People serve in government, not for personal gain, but out of a sense of serving the public. The government in turn has a right, an obligation, to intervene in the private affairs of citizens when it is necessary for the "public good or the well-being of the community."[7]

The **individualistic subculture** "emphasizes the conception of the democratic order as a marketplace. In its view, a government is created for strictly utilitarian reasons, to handle those functions demanded by the people it is created to serve."[8] Government is not concerned with the creation of a "good society," and government intervention in the private sector should be kept to a minimum. Politics is viewed not as a profession of high calling but as something that should be left to those willing to dirty their hands. Participation is a necessary evil but not an obligation of each citizen.

The **traditionalistic subculture** has as its primary function the maintenance of the existing political order, and participation is confined to a small, self-perpetuating elite. The public has limited power and influence. Policies that benefit the public are enacted only when the elite allows them to be. Most policies enacted by government benefit the ruling elite and not the public. Political participation by the public is discouraged. A class-based social structure helps to maintain the existing order.

Most of the old southern states have traditionalistic or individualistic political cultures. Southern Anglo settlers of East Texas brought with them a strong traditionalistic culture. Settlers in West Texas in the late nineteenth century and early twentieth century were from midwestern states where the individualistic political culture predominates. The German settlers reinforced this individualistic perception while the Mexican American and African American populations contributed to the strong traditionalistic view of government.

These two political cultures (traditionalistic and individualistic) coexist and blend in the state. They share some common views regarding the role of government. Both see a limited role for government and discourage broad-based citizen participation in political processes. The two share a conservative view of government: Individuals should do for themselves whenever possible, and government should do only those things that individuals cannot do for themselves—such as pave the roads, keep the peace, and put out fires—and leave the rest to the private sector. Government should keep taxes low, limit social services, and limit the advancement of civil rights. However, most government institutions and political processes are much more consistent with the traditionalistic political culture than with the individualistic political culture.

Patterns of political culture are slow to change, and they persist for very long periods of time. For example, these were the primary planks of the **party platform** of the Democratic governors in the 1940s and 1950s:

1. Opposition to expanding civil rights
2. Limits on the role of the federal government in state affairs

Changes to the Population and Economy of Texas

THEN (1980)	NOW (2010)
Anglos made up over 65% of the population in Texas.	Anglos make up less than 50% of the population.
The Texas economy relied heavily on agriculture and oil.	Texas develops a high-tech industry and becomes an international center of trade. People from out of state, mostly loyal Republicans, settle in Texas to work in this industry.
To Texans, the state should preserve the status quo while playing a minimal role in social and economic spheres.	Texans continue to embrace these values, yet the state faces increasing challenges due to rapid population growth and economic development.

WHAT'S NEXT?

> How will the eventual attainment of majority status by Latinos affect the state's politics?

> Will population changes result in any shift in the political values of Texans? Why or why not?

> Will Texas's economic development continue, and if so, what political problems might emerge from this development?

individualistic subculture
a political subculture that expects government to handle functions demanded of it by the people and to intervene in individuals' lives as little as necessary

traditionalistic subculture
a political subculture that expects government to maintain the existing political order for the benefit of a small elite

party platform
statement of the primary beliefs and goals of a political party

3. Opposition to federal control over natural resources (oil and gas)

4. Opposition to organized labor unions

5. No new taxes[9]

Except for minor differences, most of these planks would fit well into the platforms of former Republican Governor George W. Bush in 1994 and 1998 and Governor Rick Perry in 2002, 2004, and 2010. Also, a review of the platform of the Republican Party in Texas in 2004 showed support for all these points (www.texasgop.org). The party in control of the governor's mansion and most statewide offices has a different name; the political culture has not changed. Texas has gone from a state dominated by the Democratic Party to a state dominated by the Republican Party with no change in philosophy, ideology, or policy.

The basic structure of state government in Texas fits the traditionalistic-individualistic model quite well. Government is limited. Power is divided among many elected officials. Executive authority is weak, and most power rests with the state legislature. Few state regulations are placed on business, and many of those that exist benefit specific businesses. Regulation of the environment is modest. Despite the repeal of the poll tax, intervention by the federal government, and the passage of the Voting Rights Act, voter participation in Texas is still quite low, ranking near the bottom of the fifty states in the percentage of the population voting. Political corruption is often tolerated as the necessary cost of doing business.

Except on rare occasions, the state legislature protects the status quo and places few restrictions on lobbying and other activities of interest groups. The office of the governor is formally very weak. The state bar and business interest groups heavily control the selection of the state judiciary in partisan elections. State finances reflect the philosophy of limited government; Texas often ranks near the bottom of the fifty states on expenditures. Limited state expenditures are financed with a regressive tax system that relies on property taxes and sales taxes. Thus, the political culture of Texas helped establish a conservative, limited government.

The Economy of Texas

The economy of a state also plays a role in its politics. The economy of Texas has changed greatly in the past several decades. Texas is no longer a rural state with an economy dominated by cattle, cotton, and oil, although these are still important elements in the economy. The Texas economy has experienced rapid growth, as large cities become centers of international trade and technological innovation. The state's economy has significantly outperformed the U.S. economy since the 1970s. This transformation has facilitated the rise of the Republican Party, spurred debate, and placed many new issues on the political agenda.

Land has always been an important factor in Texas's economy and politics. Many settlers were lured to Texas by offers of free land. The Spanish and later the Mexican government provided generous grants of land to any family that settled in the state. Each family could receive one *sitio*, or *legua* (Spanish for "league")—about 4,428 acres of land. A single person could receive 1,500 acres of land. In the 1820s, it took such a generous incentive to get people to live in Texas, given the hardships of travel and simple survival. General P. H. Sheridan, best known for his remark "The only good Indian I ever saw was dead," said in a letter from Fort Clark, Texas, dated 1855, "If I owned Hell and Texas, I'd rent out Texas and live in Hell."[10] Other people may have come to Texas from more comfortable environments to escape the law. "GTT" (Gone to Texas) was supposedly a common sign left by those escaping the long arm of the sheriff.

Land issues drove the Texas revolution in 1836 and the annexation of Texas by the United States in 1845. When Texas entered the Union, it kept its public debt and its public lands. The U.S. government had to purchase from Texans all land that was to be federal land. The U.S. government also

> Farm workers harvest wheat on the high plains near Amarillo in the 1920s.

purchased lands that were formerly the west and northwest parts of Texas and that now make up much of present-day New Mexico and some of Colorado, Utah, and Wyoming.[11]

For most of its history the Lone Star State has had a **land-based economy.** Cotton farming dominated from the 1820s to the 1860s. After the Civil War, cattle became the economic mainstay. In the early twentieth century, abundant oil was discovered in East Texas. Only in the past forty to fifty years has the economy begun to diversify and become less dependent on the land and its cotton, cattle, and oil. Some regions of the state remain more dependent on land economies than others, and vast differences can be found from one region to another.

land-based economy
an economic system in which most wealth is derived from the use of the land

Economic Regions

The State of Texas Comptroller's Office has divided Texas into a number of **economic regions,** based on their dominant economic activity, as a convenient way to collect data for a wide variety of purposes. For our discussion, we have combined them into six regions, shown in Figure 19.3.

The East Texas, or Piney Woods, region was traditionally dominated by agriculture, timber, and oil. Today, agriculture is less important and oil is declining. Timber is still important. Some diversification has occurred, with manufacturing becoming a more important element in the economy.

The Plains region of the state, with Lubbock and Amarillo as the major cities, was dominated by agriculture (especially cotton, wheat, and maize) and by ranching and cattle feedlots. In recent years, the economy of this region has become more diversified and less dominated by agriculture.

The Gulf Coast region, extending from Corpus Christi to Beaumont/Port Arthur/Orange, and including Houston, is dominated by petrochemical industries, manufacturing, shipping,

economic regions
divisions of the state based on dominant economic activity

FIGURE 19.3

Economic Regions of Texas

and fishing. In recent years, this area has diversified into manufacturing and high-tech industries. It is also the area with the highest concentration of organized labor unions in the entire state.

The border area of South Texas and the Rio Grande Valley, stretching from Brownsville to El Paso, is noted primarily for its agricultural production of citrus fruits and vegetables. In recent years, trade with Mexican border cities has diversified the economy of this region, and this process has increased with the passage of the **North American Free Trade Agreement (NAFTA)**—an act passed by Congress in 1993 that established closer trade relations with Mexico and Canada. Some writers would distinguish the El Paso area and the border area as separate economic units because the two regions are several hundred miles apart, and their economic contact is limited. Many citizens of El Paso often feel that they are not a part of Texas and feel more closely associated with New Mexico.

The Metroplex, or Dallas/Fort Worth area, is considered the financial center of the state. This economic region is the most diversified in the state, with a combination of banking, manufacturing, high-tech, and aerospace industries.

The Central Corridor, or midstate region, is an area stretching roughly from College Station in the east to Waco in the north and Austin and San Antonio in the southwest. This economic area is dominated by two large state universities (Texas A&M University and the University of Texas at Austin), high-tech industries in Austin and San Antonio, and major military bases in the Waco/Temple/Killeen and San Antonio areas.

Economic Sectors

During the 1970s and early 1980s, the state economy experienced tremendous growth because of the increase in the price of oil. In the mid-1980s, the price of oil declined, and as a result, the economy of the entire state fell into a deep recession. To many, the economic recession of the early 1980s showed a need for more **economic diversity** for the state. An economy based on many types of economic activity, rather than the old land-based economy, would be needed to carry the state into the twenty-first century. Since 1988, there has been significant restructuring of the state economy. Today, the service industry dominates the Texas economy. In 2007, this industry employed nearly 80 percent of the private-sector

North American Free Trade Agreement (NAFTA)
an act passed by Congress in 1993 that established closer trade relations and economic cooperation between the United States, Canada, and Mexico

economic diversity
an economy based on many types of economic activity rather than one or a few activities

> Today, Texas plays a leading role in IT. Here, an IBM manager demonstrates how to use "smart" medical tools in a mock hospital room at the tech giant's laboratories in Austin.

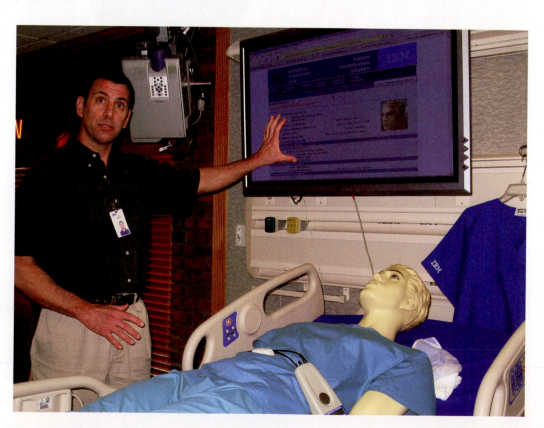

ANALYZING THE SOURCES

TEXAS EXPORTS TODAY

Texas exports a wide variety of commodities. The following bar graph shows the dollar value of the state's top five exports.

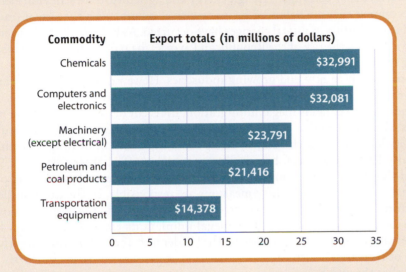

Commodity	Export totals (in millions of dollars)
Chemicals	$32,991
Computers and electronics	$32,081
Machinery (except electrical)	$23,791
Petroleum and coal products	$21,416
Transportation equipment	$14,378

SOURCE: "Texas: Crossroads of the World," Texas Ahead, 2010, Issue 3, www.texasahead.org/economic
_developer/downloads/1313-3TexasAhead_Global.pdf.

Evaluating the Evidence

① How would this graph have looked in the oil and agriculture economy of the 1970s?

② How are the top exports today different from those of forty years ago?

③ How will the changing nature of Texas exports affect the state's economy in the future? Will it strengthen Texas economically?

workforce. Moreover, the industry accounted for 63 percent of output. The state's location, its proximity to Mexico, and its centrality within the continental United States has pushed the growth of this sector. Trade has expanded rapidly because of both NAFTA and globalization. Texas has become a transportation hub. Increased trade has also fueled the growth of professional and business services in areas such as accounting, legal, and computer services, as well as construction, engineering, and management. Meanwhile, the population expansion has also produced a marked increase in the need for health care and education services. Simultaneously, the rise in both trade and population has sparked the growth of the leisure and hospitality industry.[12]

By the turn of the twenty-first century, Texas had become a major international trading power. The passage of NAFTA in 1993 had promised significant economic growth for Texas because its border with Mexico held the potential for increased trade. Within a few years, that promise was fulfilled. Since 2001, Texas has been the leading U.S. exporter. ("Analyzing the Sources" shows the state's top exports.) In 2009, Texas exported $163 billion in goods, whereas California, in second place, exported $134 billion.[13] Texas's major trading partners are Mexico and Canada, followed by countries in Asia. Texas has become a portal to Latin America, with Mexico accounting for over 34 percent of all exports in 2009.[14]

Like the rest of the United States, Texas has been transformed by the information technology revolution. New high-tech industries, especially in Austin, Dallas, and Houston, have significantly influenced the Texas economy. Whereas Texas Instruments helped turn the calculator into a common household item in the 1970s, the Texas of today boasts a thriving software, equipment, telecommunications, and semiconductor industry. To support this industry, Texas has become a leader in scientific and technological research and development. The number of international patents applications filed under the Patent Cooperation Treaty is a good indicator of technological innovation. In 2006, Texas ranked fourth in the U.S. in the number of patents filed, trailing California, New York, and Massachusetts.[15]

Although high oil prices have allowed Texas to skirt three of the United States' six most recent recessions, Texas followed the nation into the economic downturn resulting from the 2008 global financial crisis. Texas reported its highest unemployment rate in over twenty years. The weak conditions did not affect the Texas's economy overall, with employment rates in the service sector showing far less volatility than those in the goods sector.[16]

Consequences of Economic Changes

In the first decade of the twenty-first century, the economy of the state is far more diverse than it was even twenty years ago. Though energy and agriculture are still vital elements in the state's economy, they are balanced by many new elements. With the rise of trade, technology, and urbanization, political changes have occurred. As we have seen, these economic changes have spurred the rise of the Republican Party as the party acquired increasing support among the business community and as professionals from other states came to Texas to become part of these new and growing industries. However, economic transformation has also given rise to a host of political issues for the Texas government to address.

Chief among these issues is illegal immigration. In recent decades, the number of illegal immigrants who have come in the United States to work has been rising (see Figure 19.4). Because of its long border with Mexico, Texas bears the brunt of dealing with this issue. Since the early 1990s, fences have been built across high-traffic border areas. In 1996, Congress passed legislation authorizing increased funds for border patrols and stiffer penalties for smugglers. Some argue that these measures are responsible for the drop in illegal immigration from 2008 to 2010, but others attribute this decrease to the economic downturn. Despite the drop, approximately 300,000 illegal immigrants entered the country between these two years and many did so by crossing the border into Texas. Texas also has the financial burden of increased health care and education costs. A recent study in Harris County determined that the number of undocumented immigrants in the county's health care system had increased 44 percent in three years. Their care accounted for approximately 14 percent of the health care system's total operating costs.[17] In addition, many financially

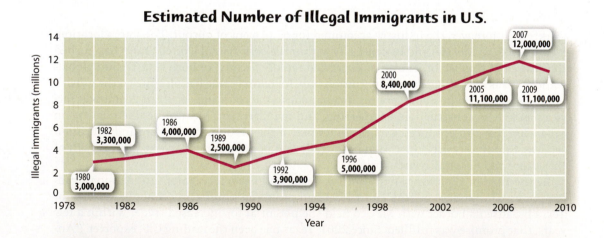

Estimated Number of Illegal Immigrants in U.S.

POLITICAL INQUIRY

FIGURE 19.4 ■ How has the number of illegal immigrants coming into the U.S. changed since 1990? How has this influx affected Texas? What do you think accounts for the drop in the number of illegal immigrants between 2007 and 2009?

SOURCE: Jeffrey S. Passel and D'Vera Cohn, "A Portrait of Unauthorized Immigrants in the United States," a Pew Research Center Project, http://pewhispanic.org/reports/report.php?ReportID=107; "Unauthorized at New High—Details of Trend Uncertain" from *Background Brief Prepared for Task Force on Immigration: America's Future* by Jeffrey S. Passel. a Pew Research Center Project, http://pewhispanic.org/files/reports/46.pdf; data for 2007 and 2009 from Jeffrey S. Passel and D'Vera Cohn, "U.S. Unauthorized Immigration Flows Are Down Sharply Since Mid-Decade," a Pew ResearchCenter Project, http://pewhispanic.org/files/reports/126.pdf.

SHOULD SOME U.S. CITIES DECLARE SPANISH THEIR OFFICIAL LANGUAGE?

The Issue: In 2007, the Texas border town of El Cenizo became a center of national attention when CNN's Anderson Cooper reported on two controversial ordinances that the city had passed several years before. The city has about 7,000 residents with a median family income of approximately $14,500. The overwhelming majority of city residents are Latino, and many are the first generation to settle in the United States from across the Rio Grande. One of the ordinances Cooper reported on was a safe haven law for illegal immigrants, forbidding city officials from inquiring into a person's immigration status. At the time it was passed, the ordinance affected only the city's one paid official and two volunteer staff members. However, the city council hoped to send a reassuring message to El Cenizo's large population of undocumented workers. The safe haven law put El Cenizo into the same category as New York City, San Francisco, and other major cities that have become "sanctuary cities." Therefore, El Cenizo's safe haven ordinance did not set any precedent.

The other ordinance did, however. It established Spanish as the city's official language, to be used during city council meetings and in conducting city business. Ordinances passed by the council would be published in both Spanish and English, but memos, contracts with businesses that provide municipal services, and other daily communication would be carried out in Spanish. The action spurred a national debate that continues to this day.

Yes: Many who support the ordinance argue that it has increased participation in city government. The mayor at the time it was enacted, Rafael Rodriguez, explained that the move was an effort to combat apathy and encourage political participation. "The community wants to know what is going on. They don't speak English," the mayor told reporters.* City officials insist that they must do what is best for the residents of El Cenizo, and that the ordinance was passed for practical rather than political reasons. They say that they are proud to be American, and since 2005, the city has organized a large, traditional July 4 celebration with a parade, hot dogs, and lemonade.

No: Those who oppose El Cenizo's ordinance establishing Spanish as the official language argue that the law discourages chil-dren from learning English. One local elementary school teacher explained that if Spanish is the official language, students will ask why they need to learn English.** Others point to immigrants who have lived in the United States most of their lives and don't speak a word of English. Some fear that immigrants and children of immigrants will face greater obstacles than English speakers within American society, and so will not have equal opportunities. Others worry that the precedent endangers American values, since the Latino community is a large and growing minority within the United States. While declaring Spanish as the official language might be more convenient for local government, it has wider implications for American society and culture.

Other approaches: To increase participation, the city government could stipulate that all city business be conducted in both languages. The city could provide Spanish translations for all formal communication. Although this solution would cost money that the city doesn't have, it could seek grants or state or federal funding for translations. Alternatively, the city could seek funding for English-language programs and gradually make the transition to English.

What do you think?

① What values are promoted by those on each side of this issue?

② Should cities in the United States with a large number of residents who speak Spanish or another language be allowed to declare Spanish—or another language—the official language for that city? Why or why not?

③ What additional alternatives might city, state, or federal governments pursue on this issue?

*Eddie Zavala, "El Cenizo Gets Wide Attention," *Laredo Morning Times*, August 13, 1999, http://lmtonline.com/news/archive/0813/pagea1.pdf.
**Lynda Gorov, "Texas Town Makes Spanish Official, Stirs War of Words," *The Boston Globe*, August 28, 1999, www.englishfirst.org/elcenizo/elcenizoglobe.htm.

strapped school districts serve the children of illegal immigrants, offering programs for those with limited English proficiency. Yet illegal immigration also serves an important function within the Texas economy, providing a cheap workforce for its growing industry. "Thinking Critically About Democracy" discusses a controversial proposal to make Spanish the official language in a small border town.

In addition to grappling with illegal immigration, the Texas government must come to terms with a number of controversies regarding how to accommodate a growing population and economy. Growth has placed new demands on the state's energy and transportation infrastructure and other public services. Issues such as the Trans-Texas Corridor and the granting of permits to build more coal-burning power plants have incited heated debate. The Trans-Texas Corridor has been especially controversial. The corridor is intended to be a vast network of toll roads, railroads, and utility lines built in part upon existing infrastructure. The government and those who support the corridor argue that it will relieve heavy traffic congestion, facilitate economic growth, and improve road safety. Some oppose it because they are anti-NAFTA, and the corridor will connect Texas and Mexico. Others worry that it will divert money from local governments. Still others argue that it will push pollution to rural areas and disrupt wildlife habitat, or that it will provide a soft target for terrorists. Governor Rick Perry and other politicians who support the corridor have been accused of accepting large campaign contributions from construction companies who will likely be awarded contracts from the Department of Transportation. As these economic changes create demands on infrastructure, the Texas government must try to find solutions that are acceptable to all.

CONCLUSION

THINKING ABOUT WHAT'S NEXT FOR THE TEXAS POLITICAL CULTURE AND ECONOMY

The settlers who came to Texas in the nineteenth and twentieth centuries shared similar views on politics. They feared powerful government and felt that the state should not interfere in the social or economic spheres. An Anglo elite held the reigns of government and preserved the status quo. Following the recession in the 1980s, Texas began to diversify economically. People from other states and Mexican immigrants helped fuel economic growth, which centered on high tech, trade, and industry. Although the population shift contributed to the rise of the Republican Party, Texans' political values appear to have changed little. Texas is still one of the lowest-ranking states in areas such as school expenditures and levels of voter participation. The legislature continues to meet only once every two years, and the government remains weak and divided. As these factors indicate, Texans still share a traditionalistic-individualistic political culture.

As the Latino population increases and the urban professional sector also grows, will they change the political values of the state significantly? Immigrants from Mexico and Central America tend to hold traditionalistic views of government. However, urban professionals are accustomed to governments that provide a broader range of services.

Even if the influx of new populations does not fundamentally shift political values, economic development is creating new political problems that the state has been and will be forced to confront. For example, the state must meet the demand of these new industries for improved transportation, increased energy supplies, and a larger workforce. These new demands may force the government to take on greater responsibilities than it has in the past.

Summary

STUDY NOW

1. Texas Society
From its early history, Texas has been a land of contrasts, as waves of Mexican, Anglo, African American, and German settlers arrived. Each group settled different parts of the state, giving rise to regional differences. Today, over 80 percent of the population lives in urban areas, adding to the diversity of political interests.

2. Population Growth and the Changing Political Climate
The population is growing rapidly as people from Mexico and from other states arrive. Minorities now outnumber the Anglo population. Partly as a result of these new arrivals from

other states, the Democratic Party has been pushed aside, if not supplanted, by the Republican Party.

3. The Political Culture of Texas
While the political climate is changing, the political culture is slower to respond to demographic change. Early settlers brought with them a political culture that was both individualistic and traditionalistic, giving rise to expectations of a minimalist government that serves the elite interests. The demographic changes have had little or no effect on that political heritage.

4. The Economy of Texas
Texas is also no longer a rural backwater state dependent on a land-based economy. It is now a large urban industrial state and a center of international trade. The rise of trade and industry has opened the door to political issues that include an impending energy crisis, illegal immigration, and the need for modernization of transportation.

Key Terms

changing political climate 594

economic diversity 600

economic regions 599

individualistic subculture 597

land-based economy 599

majority-minority state 594

moralistic subculture 596

North American Free Trade Agreement (NAFTA) 600

party platform 597

settlement patterns 590

traditionalistic subculture 597

For Review

1. Why is Texas a land of contrasts? What influence do these contrasts have on Texas politics?

2. What factors account for the recent population boom? How has this boom affected Texas politics?

3. What are the three types of political culture? How does each perceive the role of government?

4. How have the different ethnic groups shaped the political culture of the state?

5. How has the Texas economy changed over the past forty years?

6. How has Texas's economic transformation affected state politics?

For Critical Thinking and Discussion

1. How have you experienced the contrasts within Texas society? What impact have they had on you personally?

2. Describe a recent example in which the interests of diverse social or economic groups have clashed. What was the political outcome?

3. As the population continues to grow and change, do you think the political culture of the state will change? If so, how?

4. Think about one way you have interacted with the Texas state government, such as voting or registering for a driver's license. How does the way Texas handles this process conform to or contradict the state's political culture?

5. Choose a political problem that has resulted from the rise of industry and trade, and describe your solution.

PRACTICE QUIZ

MULTIPLE CHOICE: Choose the lettered item that answers the question correctly.

1. Before Europeans settled in Texas, it was populated by which Indians?
   a. Lipan Apache, Kiowa, Cherokee
   b. Comanche, Cherokee, Hopi
   c. Comanche, Lipan Apache, Tonkawa
   d. Kiowa, Comanche, Navajo

2. How were the German immigrants of the nineteenth century similar to other settlers of the time?
   a. They were slave owners.
   b. Many fought in the Civil War.
   c. They voted in line with the other settlers.
   d. They contributed to the character of Texas politics.

3. Of the three political subcultures described by Daniel Elazar, Texas is best described as
   a. moralistic and traditionalistic.
   b. individualistic and traditionalistic.
   c. moralistic and traditionalistic.
   d. idealistic and traditionalistic.

4. Which population(s) contributed to Texas's strong traditionalistic view of government?
   a. Mexican Americans
   b. African Americans
   c. Southern Anglos of East Texas
   d. All of the above

5. By the year 2020, the three largest ethnic groups in Texas, in descending order, will be
   a. Anglos, Latinos, and African Americans.
   b. Latinos, African Americans, and Anglos.
   c. Latinos, Anglos, and Asian Americans.
   d. Latinos, Anglos, and African Americans.

6. The population of African Americans in Texas
   a. is concentrated in selected areas of the state.
   b. is rising because of migration from other states.
   c. has decreased because of migration to northern states.
   d. has stood at 30 percent since the Civil War.

7. Since the 1970s, Texas has experienced staggering population growth as a result of

a. high birthrates among native Latinos.
b. high birthrates among native Anglos.
c. migration from other states and immigration from Mexico.
d. immigration from Europe and Asia.

8. How has the political culture of Texas influenced the structure of the state?
   a. Many regulations are placed on businesses.
   b. Power is concentrated in the hands of a few elected officials.
   c. Most power resides with the state legislature.
   d. The governor holds most of the political authority.

9. Since 1988, the Texas economy has been significantly restructured from _____ to _____.
   a. land-based, service-based
   b. trade-based, energy-based
   c. land-based, goods-based
   d. service-based, goods-based

10. The growth of the service sector within the Texas economy is fueled primarily by which of the following?
    a. gambling   c. trade
    b. agriculture   d. oil

FILL IN THE BLANKS.

11. _____, established by Congress in 1993, has helped Texas become a center for international trade.

12. Texas is a _____ state because Anglos no longer make up the majority of the population.

13. Even though Texas is the _____ most populous state in the nation, it is still considered a rural state.

14. A growing _____ has placed new demands on the state's public services, such as energy, transportation, and education.

15. The _____ political culture views the government as responsible for maintaining the existing political order.

Answers: 1. c; 2. d; 3. b; 4. d; 5. a; 6. a; 7. c; 8. c; 9. a; 10. c; 11. NAFTA; 12. majority-minority; 13. second; 14. population; 15. traditionalistic.

RESOURCES FOR RESEARCH AND ACTION

Internet Resources

Comptroller of Public Accounts
www.window.state.tx.us For information on state expenditures and economic regions, visit this site.

The Texas Fact Book
www.lbb.state.tx.us This site gives information on Texas past and present and is a valuable source of data on the state budget.

The Texas Handbook
www.tsha.utexas.edu/handbook/online Published online by the Texas Historical Society, this site is a fund of information on the history of the state and its people.

Texas Newspapers
www.usnpl.com/txnews.php This site provides links with information on Texas newspapers.

Texas Online
www.texasonline.com This "Official Portal of Texas" provides links to state agencies and popular online services.

Internet Activism

Texas Oral History Association provides resources for oral historians who interview people to collect eyewitness reports about important events and to give a glimpse into the culture and the mood of a particular people at a particular time. To learn how to research and conduct an interview and find out what legal documents you may need to have in place, visit www.baylor.edu/toha/.

Twitter
http://twitter.com/txinstruments Get updates about new gadgets and tech support from Texas Instruments.

YouTube
www.youtube.com/watch?v=Tvkstp6N-is Goliad State Park is the official venue of Cinco de Mayo and houses Texas's largest ranching operation from the eighteenth century.

Facebook
www.facebook.com/pages/Texas-State-Historical-Association/162122016600?ref=search#!/pages/Texas-State-Historical-Association/162122016600?v=wall&ref=search The Texas State Historical Association was founded in 1897 as a private, nonprofit educational organization. Its mission is to inform the public about the rich and unique history of Texas through its teaching, research, and publications.

Recommended Readings

Calvert, Robert A., and Arnold DeLeon. *The History of Texas.* Arlington Heights, IL: Harland Davidson, 1990.

Davidson, Chandler. *Race and Class in Texas Politics.* Princeton, NJ: Princeton University Press, 1976.

Elazar, Daniel J. *American Federalism: A View from the States.* New York: HarperCollins, 1984.

Fehrenbach, T. R. *Lone Star: A History of Texas and Texans.* New York: Collier, 1980.

Jordon, Terry G. *German Seed in Texas Soil: Immigrant Farmers in Nineteenth Century Texas.* Austin: University of Texas Press, 1966.

Soukup, James R., Clifton McCleskey, and Harry Holloway. *Party and Factional Division in Texas.* Austin: University of Texas Press, 1964.

Movies of Interest

Border (2007)
This film documents illegal border crossings, civil unrest, and drug trafficking along the U.S.-Mexican border.

The Great Debaters (2007)
Denzel Washington stars in this film relating the experiences of the debate team at all-black Wiley College in Marshall, Texas, in the 1930s as they compete nationally.

Juárez City of Dreams (2007)
This documentary explores the town of Ciudad Juárez, located just across the Rio Grande from El Paso.

Glory Road (2006)
Based on a true story, this film covers the 1966 NCAA Men's Division Basketball Championship in which an all-black lineup from Texas Western College beat the all-white Wildcats from the University of Kentucky.

Selena (1997)
Jennifer Lopez plays Tejana singer Selena Quintanilla-Pérez, a Grammy-Award winner who was murdered in 1995, in this film about her life.

Waco: The Rules of Engagement (1997)
This documentary presents an account of the FBI's fifty-one-day siege of a compound run by the Branch Davidians. It is highly critical of the siege, which ended in a fire that left most of the Davidians dead.

Lonesome Dove (1989)
The TV series and its all-star cast won six Emmy awards for their portrayal of the Pulitzer Prize–winning novel that tells the tale of retired Texas rangers heading out on the last cattle drive to Montana.

The State Constitution

PROTEC

THEN

Texans adopted a constitution that grants weak powers to the state government and sets up biennial sessions of the legislature.

NOW

As Texas takes a leading role in high tech, research and development, industrial development, and trade, the state government faces many new challenges.

pNEXt

How will Texas's government deal with its new challenges?

Will Texans have to change their constitution to provide more powers to the state government?

How will the need for a stronger state government be viewed by Texans with traditionalistic-individualistic views?

609

This chapter examines the history of Texas constitutions and how changes come about in the current state constitution.

FIRST, we compare and contrast the *Texas constitutions* that have been enacted throughout the state's history.

SECOND, we evaluate the interaction between *political culture and constitutions*, specifically the culture and constitution of Texas.

THIRD, we explore the *principles of state constitutions* and reflect on the Texas constitution within this context.

FOURTH, we analyze *the structure of state constitutions*, asking the questions, What makes them successful? and Where does Texas stand in comparison with other states?

FIFTH, we take a look at the process of *revising state constitutions* and what the prospects are for changes to the Texas constitution in the future.

> A painting of the meeting at Washington-on-the-Brazo, where Texans wrote the 1836 constitution.

All states and the national gov-

ernment have written constitutions that provide the broad outlines of government. These constitutions are contracts between the government and the people, and they stand as a measure against which governments must act. State constitutions are also a product of the political culture of a state. The Texas Constitution is very much an embodiment of its traditionalistic-individualistic political culture. It reflects the conservative nature of the state, the distrust of government, the desire to limit the government's ability to act, and the desire to protect some special interests.

Texas Constitutions

An examination of the several constitutions that have governed Texas helps us understand the importance of political culture and its impact on the formal structure of government. Texas has been governed by seven constitutions, five since it entered the Union in 1845.

Constitutions Under the Republic of Mexico

The first constitution to govern Anglos in Texas was the Republic of Mexico's constitution of 1824. This constitution was federalist in concept and a clear break with the Spanish centralist tradition.[1] Under the 1824 national constitution, Texas was governed by a provincial constitution of the state of Coahuila y Tejas that was approved in 1827. The 1827 constitution provided for a unicameral legislature, and Texas elected two representatives to the provincial legislature. This constitution, which lacked a bill of rights, provided a government structure with which the Anglos were comfortable. Texans ignored sections of the constitution of 1827, most notably those that required Catholicism as the state religion and those that did not recognize slavery.

Suspension of the Mexican national constitution of 1824, and with it the provincial constitution of 1827, by President Santa Anna of Mexico was a factor that led to the Texas Revolution. One of the early Texas flags, reportedly flown at the Alamo, had the numbers 1824 superimposed on a red, green, and white emblem of the Mexican flag. This was a demand that the constitution of 1824 be restored.[2]

The Republic of Texas Constitution of 1836

In 1836, when Texas declared itself a republic independent of Mexico, a new constitution was adopted (see Figure 20.1). This document was a composite of the U.S. Constitution and the constitutions of several southern states. It provided for a unitary, rather than federal, form of government. Signs of the distrust of government by the traditionalistic southerners who wrote the document are evident. They limited the term of the president to a single three-year term with prohibitions against consecutive reelection. The president was also prohibited from raising an army without the consent of the congress. There were other features, such as freedom of religion and property rights protection, that had been absent in the 1824 and 1827 constitutions. Slavery, which had been ignored by the Mexican government, was legalized.[3]

FIGURE 20.1

The Republic of Texas From 1836 until 1845, Texas was an independent nation known as the Republic of Texas. In the treaty forced on Mexico by Texas, Mexico ceded land stretching to the headwaters of the Rio Grande. Though it never fully occupied this land, Texas claimed parts of modern-day New Mexico, Oklahoma, Kansas, Colorado, and Wyoming.

Statehood Constitution of 1845

When Texas joined the Union in 1845, a state constitution was adopted. This document also reflected the traditionalistic southern culture, with a few notable exceptions that were adaptations of Spanish law. Women were granted property rights equal to those of men, especially in marriage, where women were given half the value of all property acquired during the marriage (community property). In addition, a person's homestead was protected from forced sale to pay debts. These ideas were later adopted by many other states.

The 1845 constitution also provided for limited executive authority, biennial sessions of the legislature, and two-year terms for most officials. Most of these features were included in later constitutions.

The Civil War and Reconstruction Constitutions of 1861, 1866, and 1869

In 1861, when Texas joined the Confederacy, another constitution was adopted. It was essentially the same as the 1845 document, with the exception of a prohibition against the emancipation of slaves, a provision to secede from the Union, and a provision to join the Confederacy.

In 1866, a third state constitution was approved as a condition for rejoining the Union following the Civil War. This document abolished slavery, nullified the ordinances of secession, renounced the right of future secession, and repudiated the wartime debts of the state. This constitution of 1866 was short-lived and overturned by Reconstruction acts of the U.S. Congress.

Military rule was again imposed on Texas, and a new constitution was adopted in 1869. This fourth state constitution, which was approved under the supervision of the federal government's military rule, is called the Reconstruction constitution, or the "carpetbagger's constitution." It represented a radical departure from past and future documents and reflected the centralization aspirations of the national Republicans. A four-year term was provided

> In this painting, a representative of the Freedmen's Bureau tries to prevent an armed conflict between whites and African Americans. The Freedmen's Bureau, created by the War Department to help freed slaves and refugees after the Civil War, was underfunded but nevertheless managed to provide needed services to many former slaves.

A Constitution in Flux—or Set in Stone?

THEN (2000)	NOW (2010)
The Texas legislature rejected a major reform of the the Texas Constitution proposed by two highly respected members.	No major political figures have backed fundamental changes to the constitution during the past ten years.
Texas's gross state product was just under $712 billion.*	Texas's gross state product nearly doubles in a ten-year period to roughly $1,266 billion.*
Few states enacted more amendments to the state constitution than Texas. Few Texans participated in voting for or against these proposed amendments.	Proposals for amendments to the Texas Constitution have increasingly become a way for Texans to express their views on gay marriage, cancer research, frivolous lawsuits, eminent domain, and other political issues.

WHAT'S NEXT?

> How will Texans view proposed constitutional changes that grant the government greater power?

> Do recent amendments signal a willingness on the part of Texans to grant the government more power?

> Will the process of proposing and approving amendments become a means by which Texans debate important social and economic issues?

*Fall 2007 Economic Forecast, Texas Comptroller of Public Account's Web site: Texas Ahead, www.texasahead.org/economy/fcst07fall/fall07-rgsp-fiscal.html; 2009–2010 Economic Forecast, Texas Comptroller of Public Accounts Web site: Texas Ahead, www.texasahead.org/economy/forecasts/fest0910/ngspfiscal.html.

for the governor, who was also given strong appointive authority. The governor could appoint most state and many local officials. County courts were abolished, and much local authority and control were removed from the planter class. Public schools were centralized under state control and funded with a poll tax and the sale of public lands. African Americans were given the right to vote, and whites who had participated in the "rebellion" (Civil War) were disenfranchised.[4]

The Constitution of 1876

The current constitution was written in 1875, at the end of Reconstruction, and approved by the voters in 1876. The constitutional convention was assembled in 1875. "Not one man who had written the constitution of 1869 sat in this delegation." As T. R. Fehrenbach put it, these men were

mostly old Texans: John Henry Brown, Sterling C. Robertson, sons of empresarios, Rip Ford (Texas Ranger), John H. Reagan (Ex-Postmaster General of the Confederacy), and a bevy of generals who [had] worn the grey. Of the ninety members, more than twenty held high rank in the C.S.A. This was a restoration convention. . . . It was a landowners' group, including forty members of the Grange. . . . This was an antigovernment instrument: too many Texans had seen what government could do, not for them but to them. It tore up previous frameworks, and its essential aim was to try and bind all state government within tight confines.[5]

These men were landowners who had objected strongly to the centralist government under Reconstruction. The document reflected the antigovernment sentiments of the traditionalistic-individualistic political culture of the state. The new document reimposed shorter terms of office, reestablished many statewide and local elected offices, and severely restricted the ability of government to act. The powers of both the legislature and the governor were restricted.[6]

None of these changes were especially controversial. The controversial issues were the poll tax payment for the right to vote, women's suffrage, and public schools. The centralized state school system was abolished and replaced by local control of schools with some state funding provided. In addition, provisions were made for a state-funded university system.[7]

Thus Texas has been governed by a number of constitutions since the early 1800s: The Spanish constitutions contributed several key elements, including community property rights for women, which was a clear departure from English laws. The 1845 constitution provided for limited government with little centralized power. The constitutions of 1861 and 1866 continued these principles of limited government. The present constitution, approved in 1876, not only reinstated but also expanded the ideas of limited government. Only the Reconstruction constitution of 1869, which provided for a strong, centralized government, was a departure from these ideas. Its swift repeal at the end of Reconstruction indicates how utterly the southern whites rejected these concepts. Many Texans today would still not accept these concepts. In 1999, voters rejected two amendments that would have expanded the power of the governor to appoint and remove minor state officials.

Political Culture and Constitutions

To a large degree, political culture drives institutions. The Reconstruction constitution of 1869 was a fundamental departure from earlier constitutions and in conflict with the political culture of the state. This document centralized power in state government and reduced the authority of local governments, provided for four-year terms for many officeholders, and gave the governor the power to appoint most state and many local officials, including the state judiciary. In addition it provided for annual sessions of the legislature, gave African Americans the right to vote, and provided for state-controlled schools and a state police system. Most of these provisions are not supported by a traditionalistic-individualistic political culture that calls for decentralized, weak government while discouraging political participation and nonelite involvement in government.

Except for the four-year terms for governor and other statewide officials, most of these ideas (gubernatorial appointment of state and local officials, annual sessions of the legislature, and state control of local affairs) have little support in Texas today. The voters have rejected annual sessions of the legislature on several occasions, and despite widespread decentralization of local schools, there is demand for even greater decentralization of decisions down to the local level. Culture drives institutions by influencing the basic structure and organization of government. Thus the current constitution is very compatible with the political culture of the state.

> Six of the delegates to the Constitutional Convention of 1875 were African Americans. They fought to maintain their voting rights. Although the constitution did not restrict voting rights by race, none of the six delegates participated in later sessions of the state legislature.

Principles of State Constitutions

We have looked at the overall impact of history, culture, and traditions on constitutions, but several important principles specifically underpin the general idea of constitutional government. As discussed in Chapter 1, constitutions are established on the principles of self-government, or *popular sovereignty,* and *limited government.* Popular sovereignty is the idea that all power rests with the people.[8] Constitutions are written by a popularly elected convention of citizens and not by state legislatures. Thus the citizens must also approve any changes in state constitutions—except in Delaware, where the state legislature can amend the state constitution. The current Texas Constitution supports this idea very strongly in its preamble and bill of rights.

Second, constitutions are a contract, or compact, between the citizens and the government and cannot be violated. The laws passed by legislatures and carried out by the executive branch must fit within the framework of the constitution. Hence, constitutions are a limitation upon the power of government. Like the U.S. Constitution, state constitutions limit the scope of government by **grants of power**—explicitly listing the powers that governments may use—and **denials of power**—explicitly listing those they may not use.

grants of power
a way to limit the power of government by explicitly listing the powers that governments may use

denials of power
a way to limit the power of government by explicitly listing the powers that governments may not use

The current (1876) Texas Constitution is very much an example of limitations upon the power of state government. When the current constitution was drafted in 1875, Governor Richard Coke said to the assembled constitutional convention:

> The accepted theory of American constitutional government is that State Constitutions are limitations upon, rather than grants of power: and as a rule, not without its exceptions, that power not prohibited exists in State government. Therefore, express prohibitions are necessary upon the power of state government . . . these restrictions . . . have multiplied in the more recently created instruments of fundamental law.

The current constitution heavily reflects those values, which are also a product of the state's individualistic-traditionalistic political culture.

In addition to the ideals of popular sovereignty, compact (or contract) theory, and limited government, other common characteristics of state constitutions serve to limit and clarify the authority of state governments.

Separation of Powers in State Constitutions

All state constitutions embrace the idea of *separation of powers* provided in the U.S. Constitution. Power is divided among an elected executive, an elected legislature, and the judiciary. The separation of powers provides a check on the actions of government. Fear of concentration of power in a single person led the framers of the U.S. Constitution to separate powers. Fragmented power was safer. All state constitutions embrace this idea. Fear of strong executive authority, experienced in Texas under Governor Edmund J. Davis and the Radical Republicans, led the framers of the 1876 document to fragment executive power. The voters elect a governor, a lieutenant governor, a comptroller, an attorney general, a commissioner of the land office, and, at that time, a state treasurer. The agricultural commissioner, railroad commissioners, and a state board of education were added later. The office of treasurer was abolished in 1995.

Bill of Rights in State Constitutions

Like the U.S. Constitution, most state constitutions have strong statements on civil liberties that grant basic freedoms. Most civil liberties protections in state constitutions duplicate those found in the U.S. document, but many state constitutions are more generous in the granting of liberties than is the U.S. Constitution. The Texas Constitution is no exception in this regard. The average citizen, upon reading the "Bill of Rights" section of the Texas Constitution, might well conclude that it is a very liberal document. Besides those rights provided by the federal document, the Texas Constitution grants equalities under the law to all citizens regardless of "sex, race, color, creed or national origin."[9] This is almost the exact wording of the failed Equal Rights Amendment to the U.S. Constitution. Citizens often have more freedoms provided in their state constitutions than in the national constitution, but most citizens are unaware of that. Attention often focuses on the national Bill of Rights and not the state bill of rights.

Supreme Law of the State

Article VI of the U.S. Constitution contains the supremacy clause, which makes the U.S. Constitution the supreme law of the land. Most state constitutions have a similar statement that makes the state constitution superior to state law and actions by local governments. Any state or local law that conflicts with the state constitution is invalid.

A recent example of local laws potentially conflicting with a state law involves the state's issuing of permits to citizens to carry concealed handguns. Many local governments (cities, counties, and metropolitan transit authorities) passed regulations prohibiting the carrying of concealed handguns in some public places. Supporters of the "concealed carry law" have charged that these local regulations violate the state law. The state court system determined that these local regulations did not violate the concept of "supreme law of the state." Recently, the issue of carrying guns has become a topic on college campuses, as you can read in this chapter's "Thinking Critically About Democracy."

The Structure of State Constitutions

Although they have common characteristics, state constitutions also have some vast differences. According to legal experts and political theorists, there are some ideal characteristics that constitutions should possess and against which constitutions can be compared. Ideally, a constitution should be brief and explicit, embody only the general principles of government, and provide the broad

> Independent consultant Delia Pompa testifies in 2004 during the *West-Orange Cove v. Neeley* case, which challenged the school finance system. The Texas constitution guarantees all students the right to a public education. The Texas system had previously been found to be unconstitutional by the Texas Supreme Court. The decision in this case forced the legislature to propose a solution to the funding crisis.

outlines of government subject to interpretation, especially through the court's power of judicial review. Constitutions should not be detailed and specific but broad and flexible. Furthermore, constitutions should provide broad grants of power to specific agencies and hold government officials accountable for their actions. Last, formal amendments to the constitution should be infrequent, deliberate, and significant.

The U.S. Constitution meets these ideals. There are only 4,300 words in the original document. It broadly outlines the basic principles of government and has been amended only twenty-seven times. All but eight of these amendments involve questions of civil liberty, voting, and electoral issues. Very few of these amendments have altered the basic structure of the federal government. The U.S. Constitution is flexible enough to allow for change without altering the basic document.

Few state constitutions can meet these standards of brevity and few amendments. This is especially true of the Texas Constitution. "Analyzing the Sources" and "How Texas Compares" include information about all fifty state constitutions. If we compare the Texas Constitution with the "average" state constitution, we find that it is longer than most, at 93,000-plus words, and has more amendments. Texas currently has 456 amendments.[10] Only five states have drafted more constitutions. One can easily conclude that most state constitutions, including the one used in Texas, do not meet the criteria outlined previously for an ideal constitution. Most are lengthy, detailed documents that require frequent alteration. Most state constitutions might be more accurately described as statutory or legislative acts rather than constitutional law. This is especially true of the document that governs Texas.

Several other generalizations can be made about state constitutions. First, most create weak executives and strong legislatures. This will be discussed in Chapter 24. Second, all state constitutions contain articles on taxation and finance that limit how funds can be spent. Taxes are often **earmarked taxes**—established for specific purposes. (A common example is the gasoline tax for state highways.) Third, all but a few constitutions prohibit deficit expenditures unless approved by voters in the form of a bond election. Finally, most state constitutions contain large amounts of trivia. For example, the original Texas Constitution contained a detailed list of items protected by the homestead protection provisions from forced sale for payment of debts. The list included the number of chickens, ducks, cows, pigs, dogs, and horses exempt from forced sale for payment of debt.

earmarked taxes
taxes dedicated to a specific expenditure

SHOULD STUDENTS BE ALLOWED TO CARRY HANDGUNS ON CAMPUS?

The Issue: In April 2006, college student Seung-Hui Cho shot thirty-three people dead at Virginia Tech in Blacksburg, Virginia. He killed two people at a coed residence hall in the morning, returned to his dorm room, and then, after packing two semi-automatic handguns and ammunition into a backpack, headed off toward Norris Hall, a building filled with laboratories, offices, and classrooms. Cho chained the three main entrances shut. His shooting spree lasted no longer than twelve minutes, and by the time police reached Cho, he had shot himself. One professor died while barricading the door to allow his students time to climb out of the classroom window to safety. But for many others, there was no escape.

Since this shooting, college students around the nation have been advocating for gun control, while others have advocated for the right to carry a handgun on campus. Students for Concealed Carry on Campus now boasts 30,000 members. Chapters of this organization are located at twenty-four institutions across Texas, and students in Texas have begun making headway on this issue. In July 2008, Texas legislators met with university students and staff to hear their sentiments and ideas. A 1995 Texas law allows Texans to carry concealed weapons if they take an eight-hour course, pass a proficiency test, and obtain a license. Students such as 22-year-old Cameron Schober at Texas State University have joined the record-high number of Texans in registering for a license. The 1995 law bans concealed weapons in a list of places, however, including campuses. After the July 2008 meeting, however, the chairman of the House Law Enforcement Committee, Joe Driver, agreed to sponsor a law that will remove campuses from the list of prohibited places.

The Texas Constitution gives Texans the right to bear arms, while allowing the legislature to limit this right in order to reduce crime. Section 23 of Article I states: "Every citizen shall have the right to keep and bear arms in the lawful defense of himself or the State; but the legislature shall have power, by law, to regulate the wearing of arms, with a view to prevent crime."

Yes: Schools are no longer safe havens, and disarming law-abiding citizens who have been trained and who have passed handgun proficiency tests only prevents them from protecting themselves and others. If the police cannot arrive at the scene until after a shooter has killed thirty-one people, then students and staff must be allowed to arm themselves rather than die while trying to barricade a door. "How horrible would that be to have to sit under a desk and wait for the cops to come," says Schober.* Students for Concealed Carry on Campus also argue that colleges and universities throughout the nation would rather deal with dozens of deaths for which they are not liable than many smaller gun-related accidents for which they might be liable. The Texas legislature has the right to regulate the wearing of arms for the purpose of preventing crime, not accidents.

No: In trying to solve one problem, the state will be creating an even bigger one if it passes this new legislation. Student drinking and suicide are two good reasons why students should not be allowed to carry concealed handguns. In one recent incident, for example, an angry Arizona State University student used a gun to murder two young women and then himself. In addition, a mere eight-hour training course is insufficient to guarantee the safe use of such weapons, and students should certainly not be expected to do the job of law enforcement agents after passing the proficiency test. Students are much more likely to be hurt in gun-related accidents than in killing sprees, which are rare, though well publicized. For these reasons, similar bills have failed to pass in fifteen of the seventeen state legislatures where they have been introduced. The Texas Constitution guarantees Texans the right to bear arms, but the framers very wisely inserted a clause giving legislators the right to create restrictions.

Other approaches: State legislation could allow professors and staff at the university to carry concealed weapons on a voluntary basis, after appropriate training. Students who wanted to carry a concealed weapon could also undergo more extensive training and a battery of psychological tests to determine if they were at risk for suicide or were likely to act irresponsibly. In addition, schools could post additional guards who could conduct weapons inspections.

What do you think?

① How secure do you feel on your campus? Would you feel more or less secure if you knew that students on your campus were allowed to carry concealed handguns? Explain.

② Do you think students should be allowed to carry concealed weapons? Under what conditions, if any, would you agree with this idea?

③ Should university and college staff be allowed to carry concealed weapons? What other measures do you think should be taken to improve safety on campus?

*Janet Elliott, "Targeting Campus Gun Laws," *Houston Chronicle*, July 12, 2008, www.chron.com/disp/story.mpl/headline/metro/5885119.html.

CONSIDERING THE STATE CONSTITUTIONS

We can draw several conclusions from examining these figures. First, most states have had several constitutions. Only nineteen states are still operating under their first constitution, most of them newer states in the western part of the United States.

Second, most state constitutions are very lengthy documents; Alabama's is the longest with 365,000 words, including the amendments. The mean word count for state constitutions is 19,300, compared with only 4,300 for the U.S. Constitution. Finally, state constitutions have a limited life span when compared with the U.S. Constitution. The average life span for a state constitution is ninety-five years.*

Evaluating the Evidence

① What do you notice about states that have had multiple constitutions? What do these states have in common?

② What factors beyond those cited in the text might have led Texas and other states to change their constitutions?

③ What patterns, if any, do you see among states that have changed their constitutions most recently?

*In Delaware the legislature amends the state constitution without voter approval.

SOURCE: *The Book of the States 2007*, vol. 38 (Lexington, KY: Council of State Governments 2007), table 1.1, p. 10. © 2008. Reprinted with permission from the Council of State Governments.

Number of State Constitutions and Dates of Most Recent Ones

Number of constitutions
- 1
- 2–3
- 4–7
- 10 or more

Lengths of State Constitutions

Approximate word length
- Less than 10,000
- 10,000–24,999
- 25,000–49,999
- 50,000–74,999
- 75,000–100,000
- Over 300,000

CONSTITUTIONAL AMENDMENTS AMONG THE STATES

The map shows the number of amendments to state constitutions. Some western states have a lot of amendments because of initiative provisions in their constitutions. Most state constitutions have been amended more often than the U.S. Constitution. Alabama is the leader with 807. How does Texas compare?

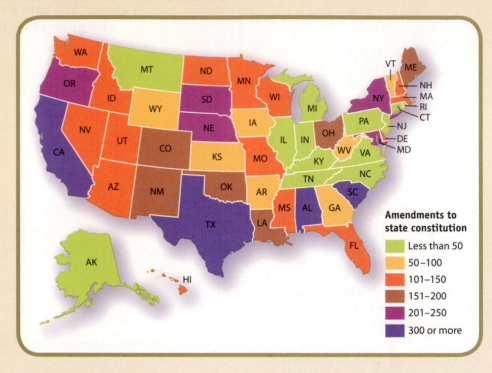

Amendments to state constitution

- Less than 50
- 50–100
- 101–150
- 151–200
- 201–250
- 300 or more

SOURCE: *The Book of the States 2010* (Lexington, KY: Council of State Governments, 2010), table 1.1, p. 11. © 2010. Reprinted with permission from the Council of State Governments. http://knowledgecenter.csg.org/drupal/system/files/Table_1.1_1.pdf.

Revising State Constitutions

All state constitutions provide procedures for amending and revising the document. Except in the state of Delaware, changing constitutions involves two steps: proposing amendments and citizen approval. In Texas, two-thirds of each house of the legislature must propose amendments, and a majority of the voters who vote on the amendment must approve.

Some states provide a variety of methods for proposing or recommending changes to the constitution. All state constitutions allow the legislature to propose changes. Most states require an extraordinary majority vote of both houses of the legislature to propose an amendment.[11]

A second method of proposing amendments to constitutions is by voter **initiative,** which requires the collection of a prescribed number of signatures on a petition within a set time. Seventeen states allow initiative. Most states with initiative are western states that entered the Union in the late nineteenth century or early twentieth century when initiative was a popular idea. Only four states with initiative are east of the Mississippi River. Texas does not have initiative. The Texas Republican party pushed the idea of initiative for many years, but in 1996 it was dropped from the party platform.

Most states, including Texas, allow the legislature to submit to the voters the question of calling a **constitutional convention** to propose amendments. This method is normally used for general revision and not for single amendments. Fourteen states have some provision for automatically submitting the question of a general convention to the voters period-

initiative
a process that allows citizens to propose changes to the state constitution through the use of petitions signed by registered voters; Texas does not have these procedures at the state level

constitutional convention
an assembly of citizens who may propose changes to state constitutions for voter approval

ically. If the voters approve, a convention is elected, assembles, and proposes amendments for voter approval.

Constitutional commissions are most often created by acts of the legislature, although other methods are provided. These commissions usually submit a report to the legislature recommending changes. If the legislature approves, the proposed amendments are submitted to the voters. In Florida, the commission can bypass the legislature and go directly to the voters. Texas last used a commission in 1973 when the legislature created a thirty-seven-member commission.[12] This commission submitted recommendations to the Texas legislature, which acted as a constitutional convention.

Except for Delaware, where the state legislature can unilaterally amend the constitution, voters must approve amendments to the constitution in an election. Most states require a majority of those voting on the amendment to approve. Some states require a majority of the voters voting for some office (usually the governor) to approve. New Hampshire requires that two-thirds of the voters approve all amendments. Texas requires that a majority of those voting on the amendment approve.

Patterns of Amending

If we examine the amendment processes discussed previously, several patterns of state constitutional change can be observed. The first pattern involves the frequency of change. State constitutions are amended more frequently than the U.S. Constitution. One reason is that state constitutions deal with a wider range of functions. About 63 percent of the state amendments deal with issues not covered in the U.S. Constitution, such as education. However, even if we remove issues not covered in the U.S. Constitution, the rate of amendment is still three and a half times the national rate. Change is also related to length. Longer state constitutions are more likely to be amended.[13]

The second pattern involves the method used to amend. As indicated, most amendments (90 percent) are proposed by state legislatures. States that require large legislative majorities for initiation have fewer amendments proposed and approved. Most amendments proposed by legislatures also receive voter approval. About 63 percent of all amendments proposed since 1970 have been approved by the voters.[14]

In the seventeen states that allow voters to initiate amendments, two patterns emerge: More amendments are proposed, and the voter approval success rate for initiative-generated amendments is about half the rate for those proposed by state legislatures (32 percent versus 64 percent).[15] This tells us that the initiative process does not screen out amendments that lack broad public support. Proposal by legislature does. Amendments that gain support from super majorities are more likely to be politically acceptable. The legislature screens out unacceptable amendments.

Process of Amending

As noted, all amendments to the Texas Constitution have been proposed by a two-thirds vote of each house of the legislature. Since 1975, the legislature has proposed 280 amendments for voter approval. Of these, the voters have approved 238 and rejected 42 (84 percent approved).[16]

Most amendments appear on the ballot in November of odd-numbered years when no statewide offices are up for election. Since 1960, the Texas legislature has proposed 355 amendments to the constitution. Of these, 288 were voted on in odd-numbered years, and 97 were approved in even-numbered years. Voter turnout for odd-year elections is lower than for even-year elections, as shown in Table 20.1. In odd-year elections, only

TABLE 20.1

Voter Turnout in Odd-Year Constitutional Amendment Elections in Texas

Year	Percentage of Voting-Age Population Voting
2009	5.90
2007	8.49
2005	13.80 (gay marriage amendment)
2003	9.30
2001	5.60
1999	6.69
1997	5.32
1995	5.55
1993	8.25
1991	16.6 (school tax reform)
1989	9.33
1987	18.6 (school tax reform)
1985	8.24
1983	6.19

SOURCE: Texas Secretary of State, www.sos.state.tx.us/elections/historical/70-92.shtml.

about 10 percent of the voting-age population participates.[17] This means that as few as 5 percent (plus one voter) could approve an amendment to the constitution.

Spikes in voter turnout generally indicate that a controversial amendment has been placed on the ballot, as shown in Table 20.1. In 1987, turnout doubled when a school tax amendment was placed on the ballot. In 2005, turnout rose almost 14 percent when the public was asked to consider an amendment prohibiting gay marriage. The amendment was a response to court rulings in other states that declared that limiting marriage to opposite-sex couples was unconstitutional. The Texas amendment passed with a large majority.

ballot wording

description of a proposed amendment as it appears on the ballot, which can be noninstructive and misleading to voters

BALLOT WORDING Ballot wording can also contribute to voter confusion and to voter support for amendments. The state legislature dictates the ballot wording of all amendments. Sometimes this wording can be misleading or noninstructive unless the voter has studied the issue before the election. This example from the 1978 election provides an illustration:

> For or against the constitutional amendment providing for tax relief for residential homesteads, elderly persons, disabled persons, and agricultural land; for personal property exceptions; truth in taxation procedures, including citizen involvement; for a redefinition [sic] of the tax base; for limitations on state spending; and for fair property tax administration.[18]

Whatever the merits of this amendment, most voters probably found the wording irresistible. Could any voter not favor tax exemptions for the elderly, the handicapped, homeowners, and farmers? Does any citizen oppose fair tax administration or citizen involvement? The amendment passed by an overwhelming majority. Another example of ballot wording bias occurred in an amendment exempting personal property in Texas ports—the "freeport" amendment, which failed in 1987. The ballot in 1987 read as follows: "rendering to the exemption from ad valorem taxation, certain tangible personal property temporarily located within the states." In 1989, the ballot read this way: "The constitutional amendment promoting economic growth, job creation and fair tax treatment for Texans who export goods." The amendment passed by a large majority. Ballot wording is apparently a significant factor in the passage or rejection of amendments.

Confusing wording can also lead to unintended consequences. In 2009, the national media had a field day when Democratic candidate for state attorney general Barbara Ann Radnofsky pointed out that the Texas amendment prohibiting gay marriage may have accidentally banned all marriage. Radnofsky pointed to a phrase in Subsection B stating, "This state or a political subdivision of this state may not create or recognize any legal status identical or similar to marriage." Having previously defined marriage as a union between one man and one woman, Radnofsky argued that "you do not have to have a fancy law degree to read this and understand what it plainly says."[19]

THE ROLE OF INTEREST GROUPS Several other observations can be made regarding the amendment processes in Texas. Most amendments pass and face little opposition. Texans have approved 470 amendments and rejected 173.[20] Most are supported by an organized interest group willing to spend money, gain support, and get the amendment passed. Interest groups attempt to protect their interests in the constitution because it is more difficult to alter than a state law, which can be easily changed in the next session of the legislature. The process of constitutional change requires a two-thirds vote of the legislature plus electoral approval. An old Texas saying goes, "Neither man nor property is safe as long as the legislature is in session."

An example of such a protection in the constitution is the Permanent University Fund (PUF). The University of Texas and Texas A&M University are the only state schools benefiting from this fund, which has a value of approximately $11 billion. Other state universities have long felt that they deserved a share of this protected fund. Texas A&M and the University of Texas wanted to protect their funds and formed a coalition with non-PUF schools to support an amendment that created the Higher Education Assistance Fund (HEAF). This fund provides money to non-PUF universities. In the end, higher education funding for all state universities became protected in the state constitution.

Odd-year elections, confusing or noninstructive ballot wording, issues that interest few voters, and voter ignorance all contribute to low voter turnout. A very small number of voters, stimulated by personal interests and supported by an active interest group, can amend the constitution without a majority of the voters becoming involved. Many voters are not even aware that an election is being held.

Prospects for Amending

Many legal scholars have pointed out the need for a general revision of the current Texas Constitution, which was written in 1876 and has been amended many times over the years. In the 1970s, a serious effort at total revision was unsuccessful.

In 1999, two prominent members of the Texas legislature introduced a bill calling for general revision of the Texas Constitution. Bill Ratliff, who was the Republican senator from East Texas at the time, and Representative Robert Junell, Democrat from San Angelo, were the chairs of budget-writing committees in the Senate and the House in that session. Ratliff served as lieutenant governor of the state from 2000 to 2003. Their bill called for substantial changes in the current constitution. They proposed to increase the power of the legislature by lengthening the terms of state senators to six years and of house members to four years, raising the salary of the legislators, and giving the legislature the power to reconvene in a special fifteen-day session to override the governor's vetoes. They also augmented the power of the governor, making only the lieutenant governor, the comptroller, and the attorney general independently elected offices. This proposal also reduced the size of the current constitution, which has 93,000 words contained in 376 sections, to some 19,000 words in 150 sections. This proposal died in committees in both houses.

Hence, the piecemeal process of amending the constitution every two years will likely continue. The political culture of the state and the conservative nature of state politics stand in the way of broad-scale change. The current constitution supports the traditionalistic-individualistic political culture of the state, carefully limiting the powers of the executive and legislative branches. Texans may also feel uncomfortable with reform that may lead to unintended consequences.

Another reason generally cited for this piecemeal amendment process is a lack of support for reform by significant political forces in the state. Strong political leadership from someone like the governor would be necessary, but powerful lobby groups whose interests are currently protected by the document would make change difficult, if not impossible.

Yet at least one recent amendment indicates that Texans may be willing to place more power in the hands of their government. In the spring of 2007, the Texas legislature passed a bill proposing an amendment to the Texas constitution that would authorize the state government to issue $3 billion in bonds to support cancer research. Many who espouse the traditionalistic-individualistic political culture of the state objected to it. The Young

> World-class cyclist Lance Armstrong campaigns for an amendment to the state constitution that would allow the state to issue $3 billion in bonds to support cancer research.

Conservatives of the Texas Coalition, for example, toured university and college campuses warning of the enormous debt that future Texas taxpayers would have to pay off. Others argued that the amendment would put too much power over research in the hands of bureaucrats. However, Texas-born, world-class cyclist Lance Armstrong spearheaded the efforts to pass the amendment, driving across the state, visiting children and adults at cancer clinics and research centers. In the end, the amendment passed with 61 percent of the vote.

CONCLUSION

THINKING ABOUT WHAT'S NEXT FOR THE STATE CONSTITUTION

The current constitution of the state of Texas was written and adopted by people who wanted minimalist government. Yet today's economic development is placing ever greater demands on the state. Will Texans be forced to give their state government greater, more centralized powers?

Those who argue against the current constitution and amendment process not only lament the weak governor but also point to a legislature so constrained by amendments and laws that responding to crises is difficult. During the budget shortfall of 2003, the legislature could not pull money from a single nonessential service to pay for an essential service. As we shall see in Chapter 26, a large portion of state revenue is earmarked for specific purposes. Some argue that these types of constraints only contribute to crises and should be removed and that a short, general constitution that provides greater power to the executive and legislative branches is the remedy the state needs.

Those who support the current constitution argue that the amendment process gives the people a say in government. Elected officials can choose to heed or ignore the opinions of their constituents; the amendment process establishes a more direct democracy. This point is valid only if a significant portion of the population votes on propositions to amend the constitution. As we have seen in this chapter, this is not usually the case. If the Texas legislature continues to pass propositions that inspire passion and debate, however, more Texans may turn out at the polls.

Senator Ratliff and Representative Junell may well have been ahead of their time in proposing changes to the constitution. As Texas emerges not only as one of the leading economies in the country but also as one of the leading economies in the world, its political culture and political system may be forced to adapt. But this change is likely to happen slowly, with an amendment on frivolous lawsuits here and an amendment on cancer research there.

STUDY NOW

Summary

1. Texas Constitutions
Texas has been governed by five state constitutions since entering the Union in 1845. Except for the constitution of 1869, which granted broad powers to the Reconstruction government, all have provided for a government with very limited powers.

2. Political Culture and Constitutions
The limitation on government is very much in keeping with the traditionalistic-individualistic political culture of the state. Texans want a government that is limited rather than broad and expansive in its power and authority.

3. Principles of State Constitutions
Like the U.S. Constitution, state constitutions are contracts that limit the scope of government by grants of power and denials of power. They are established on the principle of pop-

ular sovereignty, and most contain a bill of rights, granting civil liberties to their citizens. In addition, most state constitutions have supremacy clauses that place state laws above regulations enacted by local governments.

4. The Structure of State Constitutions

In theory, constitutions should be clear, flexible, and brief, including only general principles of government that can be interpreted over time. Formal amendments should be infrequent and significant. In practice, the U.S. Constitution meets these ideals, but state constitutions tend not to. The current Texas Constitution, written in 1876, has been amended over four hundred times.

5. Revising State Constitutions

Each session of the legislature sees many amendments proposed to the voters. These amendments are voted on in off-year (odd-numbered years) November elections. Unless an amendment is very controversial, such as the anti–gay marriage amendment in 2005, only 10 percent or less of qualified voters will bother to vote. A very small number of voters can effectively amend the constitution. Often, these amendments are designed to protect special interests or to provide advantages to some group.

Key Terms

ballot wording 620

constitutional
   convention 618

denials of power 613

earmarked taxes 615

grants of power 613

initiative 618

For Review

1. Why has Texas had seven constitutions since 1824? Describe each very briefly.
2. How does the political culture in Texas influence the type of state government established by the constitution?
3. What are the general principles on which most constitutions are established?
4. What is the purpose of the supremacy clause?
5. What qualities does the ideal constitution possess? In practice, how do most state constitutions compare?
6. Why does the Texas Constitution have so many amendments?
7. How can the Texas Constitution be amended?

For Critical Thinking and Discussion

1. Compare and contrast the current Texas state constitution with earlier Texas constitutions.
2. In what ways and to what extent does the Texas state constitution represent your own political values?
3. If the political culture in Texas became moralistic, how would this affect its constitution?
4. Why do you think most states fail to create structurally sound constitutions?
5. What changes or amendments would you make to the Texas Constitution? What could you do to try to get these changes passed?

MULTIPLE CHOICE: Choose the lettered item that answers the question correctly.

1. Ideally, a constitution should be
   a. brief and explicit.
   b. broad and flexible.
   c. specific and unquestionable.
   d. both a and b.

2. Passage of a proposed constitutional amendment in Texas requires
   a. approval by two-thirds of the house and senate and adoption by the citizens with a majority vote.
   b. approval by three-fifths of the house and senate and adoption by the citizens with a majority vote.
   c. approval by two-thirds of the house and senate and adoption by the citizens with a two-thirds vote.
   d. approval by a majority vote of the house and senate and adoption by the citizens with a majority vote.

3. Generally, most state constitutions do all of the following except
   a. contain provisions pertaining to taxation and finance.
   b. prohibit deficit spending without voter approval.
   c. require only infrequent alteration.
   d. create weak executives and strong legislatures.

4. What does the supremacy clause in the Texas Constitution establish?
   a. the supremacy of the Texas Constitution over the U.S. Constitution
   b. the supremacy of the U.S. Constitution over the state constitution
   c. the supremacy of the state constitution over state and local laws
   d. the supremacy of local laws over state laws

5. Most state constitutions, including the Texas Constitution, differ from the U.S. Constitution in that they
   a. have not established a supremacy clause.
   b. lack a bill of rights.
   c. are not based on the principle of separation of powers.
   d. grant more generous liberties to citizens.

6. The percentage of voters who participate in constitutional amendment elections in Texas is usually no higher than
   a. 10 percent   c. 30 percent
   b. 20 percent   d. 40 percent

7. Voter turnout rates for approving amendments to state constitutions can be positively influenced by
   a. odd-year elections.
   b. controversial amendments.
   c. ballot wording.
   d. interest group involvement.

8. Suspension of the Mexican national constitution of 1824 by President Santa Anna was a factor that led to
   a. the extension of slavery past the Civil War.
   b. the Texas Revolution.
   c. a unicameral legislature.
   d. all of the above.

9. When Texas joined the Confederacy in 1861, the new constitution adopted included all of the following except
   a. a prohibition against the emancipation of slaves.
   b. a provision to secede from the Union.
   c. a provision to acquire wartime debt.
   d. a provision to join the Confederacy.

10. The current state constitution, approved in 1876, did which of the following?
    a. It expanded the powers of the legislature and the governor.
    b. It abolished the centralized state school system.
    c. It abolished the state-funded university system.
    d. It abolished the poll tax.

FILL IN THE BLANKS.

11. The _____ allows citizens to propose changes to the state constitution through the use of petitions signed by registered voters.

12. Taxes are often _____ for specific purposes, such as the gasoline tax for state highways.

13. A _____ is a way to limit the power of government by explicitly listing the powers that governments may use.

14. _____ wording can mislead the voters when they are deciding whether to support a proposed amendment to the constitution.

15. The current Texas Constitution provides for _____ powers of state government.

RESOURCES FOR
RESEARCH
AND ACTION

Internet Resources

Center for State Constitutional Studies
www-camlaw.rutgers.edu/statecon/ This site contains general information on state constitutional revisions among the states.

The Secretary of State's Web site
www.sos.state.tx.us/ The votes in all elections and recent votes on constitutional amendments can be found here.

The State Bar of Texas
www.texasbar.com/ This is the Web site of one of the many state organizations that favor constitutional revision in Texas.

The Texas Constitution
http://tlo2.tlc.state.tx.us/txconst/toc.html You can read the Texas Constitution in full here on the Texas legislature's Web site.

Internet Activism

The Legislative Reference Library of Texas maintains a collection of materials on legislative bills, state documents, and legal statutes and administrative code to satisfy the research needs of legislators, the legislative staff, state agencies, and the public. To learn more about amendments to the Texas Constitution, visit www.lrl.state.tx.us/legis/constAmends/lrlhome.cfm.

Twitter
http://twitter.com/TPPF Get updates from the Texas Public Policy Foundation about pressing political, social, and economic issues.

YouTube
www.youtube.com/watch?v=04_-VWsfrt0 Watch an intriguing coverage of the eminent domain issues in Texas that sparked the passage of a recent constitutional amendment.

Facebook
www.facebook.com/pages/The-Portal-to-Texas-History/4814850619?ref=search#!/pages/Texas-Eminent-Domain-Reform-Association/231662784500?v=wall&ref=search The Texas Eminent Domain Reform Association supported the passage of the recent amendment limiting municipal use of eminent domain.

Recommended Readings

Chandler, Davidson. *Race and Class in Texas Politics.* Princeton, NJ: Princeton University Press, 1976.

Lutz, Donald S. "Toward a Theory of Constitutional Amendments," *American Political Science Review* 88 (June 1994): 355–70.

May, Janice C. "State Constitutional Development in 2004," in *The Book of the States 2005,* vol. 37, pp. 3–9.

Movie of Interest

The Alamo (2004)
An account of the 1836 battle for the Alamo in which a group of Anglos and Tejanos confront the army of Mexican dictator Santa Anna. The film features well-known actors, with Dennis Quaid as Sam Houston, Billy Bob Thornton as Davy Crocket, and Emilio Echevarria as Santa Anna.

Participation and Interest Groups in Texas Politics

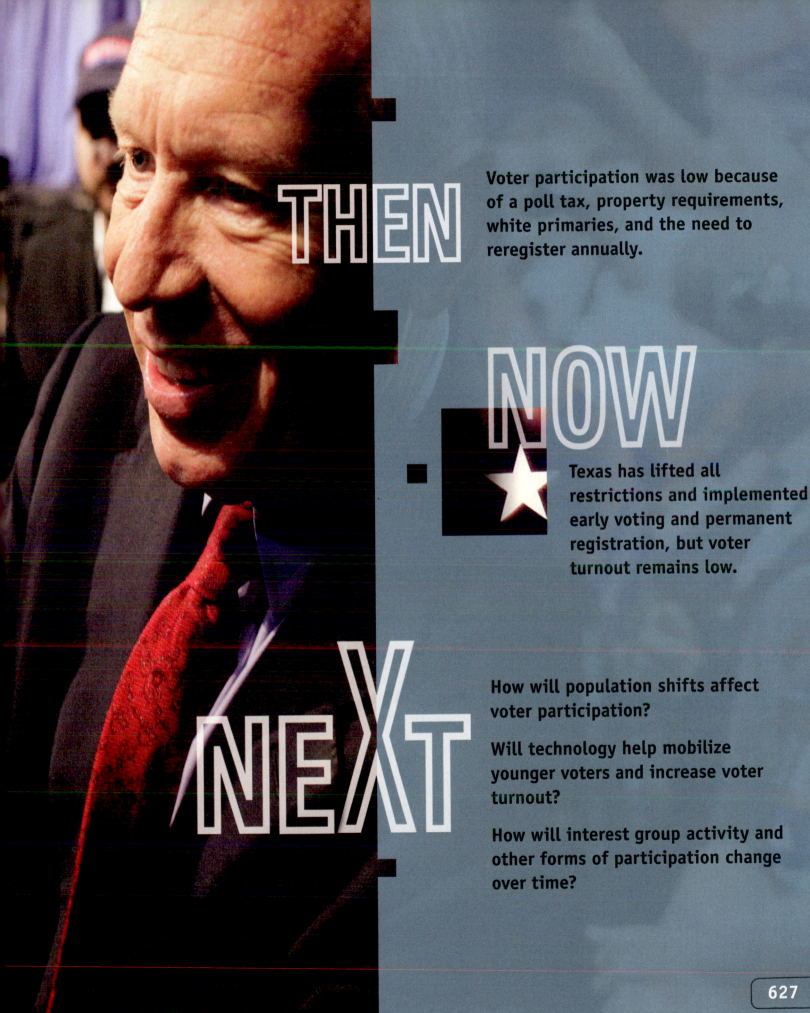

THEN

Voter participation was low because of a poll tax, property requirements, white primaries, and the need to reregister annually.

NOW

Texas has lifted all restrictions and implemented early voting and permanent registration, but voter turnout remains low.

NEXT

How will population shifts affect voter participation?

Will technology help mobilize younger voters and increase voter turnout?

How will interest group activity and other forms of participation change over time?

This chapter explores past and present voter participation in Texas and the role of interest groups in Texas government.

FIRST, we consider *opportunities for participation* in the political process and why large numbers of citizens do not take advantage of them.

SECOND, we take a look at Texas's *legacy of restricted ballot access,* connecting this history to lower voter participation today.

THIRD, we analyze *factors that affect voter participation today* and discover which groups are more likely to participate in the electoral process.

FOURTH, we categorize the *types of interest groups* in Texas and consider the purposes they serve within the state's economy, society, and government.

FIFTH, we investigate *interest group tactics* and consider *their regulation* by the government.

SIXTH, we assess *the strength of interest groups in Texas* and examine the reasons interest groups play such a prominent role in state politics.

voting-age population
all citizens who meet the formal requirements to register to vote; in Texas, you must be 18 years of age and a resident of the state for thirty days before the election

Aristotle, an early Greek philos-

opher, said that people are political animals. By this he meant that we are, by our very nature, predisposed to participate in politics. Some would say that Aristotle was an optimist. Many U.S. citizens do not choose to participate in state politics. This chapter reviews the opportunities that are available for participation, explores the reasons U.S. citizens in general—and Texans in particular—choose not to participate in state politics, and considers the influence of interest groups on Texas politics.

Opportunities for Participation

As discussed throughout this book, the term *political participation,* or *political engagement,* refers to taking part in activities related to governance. Table 21.1 lists some of these activities and the percentages of people who participate in them. As you can see from the table, and as discussed in Chapter 9, many people do not take an active part in politics, even in national elections. Voting at the national level is lower than in most other industrialized nations. Participation in state politics is lower than at the national level and still lower at the local levels. Texas ranks below all but a few states in voter participation in both national and state elections, as shown in the table in "Analyzing the Sources."

What can explain the low levels of voting among Texans? Many factors are involved. The political culture discourages participation, and there is a legacy of restricted access to the ballot for many groups within the **voting-age population**—all citizens who meet the formal requirements for voter registration. In addition, other social, economic, and political factors play a role.

Legacy of Restricted Ballot Access

Like other southern states, Texas has a history of restrictive voter registration laws. In the past, those laws made it difficult to qualify to vote and limited avenues of political participation. Largely because of actions by the federal government, most legal restrictions to voter registration have been removed. Although the past restrictions have been removed

TABLE 21.1

Political Participation by American Citizens

Run for public office	<1%
Work for a party or candidate	4%
Attend a political meeting	7–8%
Wear a button or put a bumper sticker on the car	10–11%
Vote	65–70%

Note: The data in this table are average levels of participation over several years, from 1952 to 2006. For example, the percentage for the activity "Vote" is a composite for voting in several elections.

SOURCE: The NES Guide to Public Opinion and Political Behavior, www.electionstudies.org/nesguide/gd-index.htm#6; Institute for Social Research, American National Election Studies (1952–2000), Ann Arbor: University of Michigan, Inter-University Consortium for Political and Social Research. Used with permission.

ANALYZING THE SOURCES

WHY DON'T MORE TEXANS VOTE?

Even though Texas makes it very easy to register to vote, Texans are not big voters. As can be seen in the table shown here, Texas ranks very low among all states in voter turnout. During elections held in November of odd-numbered years, voting levels decline even more, often below 10 percent of the voting-age population. In March party primary elections, participation might fall below 10 percent. In local elections for city council and school board, which are most frequently held in May, voting can decline to below 5 percent of the voting-age population.

Texas Rank as a Percentage of Voting-Age Population Voting in National Elections, 1976–2008

YEAR	TEXAS RANK*	NATIONAL TURNOUT[+]	TEXAS TURNOUT[++]
PRESIDENTIAL ELECTION YEARS			
1976	44	53	47
1980	44	52	44
1984	45	53	47
1988	46	50	45
1992	46	55	49
1996	47	52	41
2000	47	50	43
2004	47	58.3	46.1
2008	47	57	46
CONGRESSIONAL/STATEWIDE OFFICE ELECTIONS			
1978	46	35	24
1982	46	38	26
1986	45	33	25
1990	42	33	27
1994	45	36	31
1998	47	38	24
2002	46	38	26
2006	49	42	26

*Texas ranking compared with the other forty-nine states.
[+]Average turnout for all fifty states as a percentage of voting-age population voting in the election.
[++]Percentage of voting-age population in Texas elections.
SOURCES: *Statistical Abstracts of United States*, 1976, 1978, 1980, 1982, 1984, 1985, 1991, 1993, 1995, 1998, 2004, 2006, and 2008 (Washington, DC: U.S. Government Printing Office).

Evaluating the Evidence

① What factors might have affected the turnout of Texas voters in recent presidential elections? In recent congressional/statewide office elections?

② During which years was voter turnout higher? What factors might have been at work during those years?

③ What might Texas do to increase voter turnout in the future?

from law, they still have an effect today. Political behavior does not change quickly. The following are a few examples of the many restrictions common in southern political cultures.

Poll Tax and Annual Registrations

In 1902, the Texas legislature adopted, with voter approval, the payment of a poll tax as a requirement for voting. This law was aimed primarily at the Populist movement, which had organized low-income white farmers into a political coalition that threatened the

Legacy of Restricted Ballot Access

HOW TEXAS COMPARES

PERCENTAGE OF ELIGIBLE VOTERS VOTING IN THE 2008 PRESIDENTIAL ELECTION

Less than half the voting-age population of Texas went to the polls in 2008, compared with 58 percent of all Americans. Of the fifty states, only Hawaii had a lower percentage of voters that year.

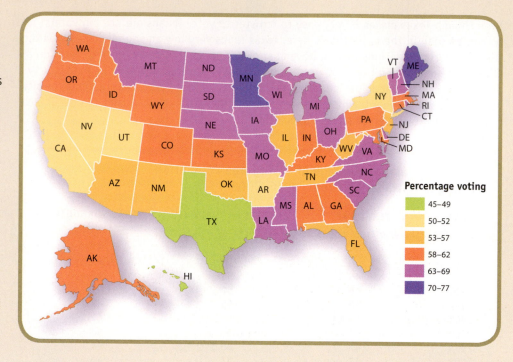

Percentage voting
- 45–49
- 50–52
- 53–57
- 58–62
- 63–69
- 70–77

establishment within the Democratic Party.[1] This tax ($1.75) was a large amount of money for poor farmers in their predominantly barter economy in the early 1900s. The poll tax also restricted ballot access for African Americans, as well as Latinos, who were disproportionately poor.

In 1964, the poll tax was eliminated as a requirement for voting in federal elections by the passage of the Twenty-Fourth Amendment to the U.S. Constitution; however, Texas kept the poll tax as a requirement for voting in state elections.[2] In 1966, the poll tax as a requirement for voting was abolished by a decision of the U.S. Supreme Court.[3]

The poll tax had the intended effect of reducing qualified voters—2.4 million Texans paid the tax in order to vote in 1964–1965. In 1968, the first election cycle after the poll tax was abolished, voter registration rose to over 4 million, an increase of about 41 percent.[4]

Even after the 1966 elimination of the poll tax as a voter requirement, Texas retained a very restrictive system of **annual voter registration,** requiring citizens to reregister every year. This was eliminated in 1971, and in 1972, the first year that Texas used a **permanent registration system,** which allows citizens to remain registered if they vote regularly, voter registration increased by almost 1.4 million.[5] All states now use some form of permanent registration.[6]

White Primary

Another past practice used by many southern states, including Texas, to eliminate participation by African Americans was the white primary. Beginning in 1923 and continuing until 1945, the Texas legislature passed bills prohibiting African Americans from participating

annual voter registration
a system that requires citizens to re-register every year

permanent registration system
a system that allows citizens to remain on the voter registration list if they continue to vote at prescribed intervals

in the Democratic Party primary election. The U.S. Supreme Court declared those legislative acts unconstitutional.[7] In 1932, the state Democratic Party passed rules that prohibited African Americans from participating in any activity of the party, including voting in the Democratic Party primary. That action led to another U.S. Supreme Court ruling.[8] The issue before the court was whether or not a political party was an agent of government or a private organization. The Supreme Court ruled in 1935 that political parties are private organizations and can decide who may participate in primary elections. That effectively prevented African Americans from participating in the Democratic Party primary. Because there was no opposition by Republicans at that time in the general election, the primary became the "general election." Thus, from 1932 until 1945, African Americans in Texas were denied the right to vote by the rules of the Democratic Party and not by state law.

In 1944, the U.S. Supreme Court outlawed all white primaries in southern states in the case *Smith v. Allwright*.[9] That ruling overturned earlier rulings that political parties were private organizations. The Supreme Court ruled that political parties are agents of the state and cannot exclude people from participating in primary elections because of race.

> Texans vote on the campus of the University of Texas, Austin. Changes in Texas law since the 1960s and 1970s have made voting easier for all citizens in Texas, yet the turnout remains low compared with that of other states.

Property Ownership Restrictions

As was common in many states, Texas used property ownership to restrict the right of people to vote. Those restrictions applied mostly to local elections, especially bond elections. The reason for restricting voting by property ownership was that local governments are financed primarily with property taxes, and supposedly renters did not pay property tax. However, renters might pay property tax, because landlords, when market conditions are favorable to them, do shift property taxes to renters as higher rents. Property ownership requirements were eliminated in the 1970s when permanent registration became effective in Texas. There was no way to effectively enforce the property ownership requirement.

Gender Discrimination in Voting

Women's access to voting was also restricted in Texas until 1920, when the Nineteenth Amendment to the U.S. Constitution was approved. By 1914, eleven states had granted women the right to vote.[10] In 1915, the Texas legislature considered granting women the right to vote, but the measure failed. In 1918, women were given the right to participate in primary elections, and in 1919, Texas became the first southern state to approve the Nineteenth Amendment.[11]

Gender discrimination along with all the other restrictions combined to produce the state's tradition of discouraging participation. The elimination of those restrictions and today's easy access to voter registration have increased the number of registered voters in

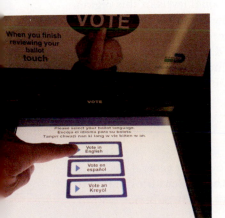

Texas, but that has not translated into a significant increase in the level of participation. Texas today still ranks near the bottom on voter turnout in elections. In time, the residual effect of restrictive practices may decline.

Factors That Affect Voter Participation Today

The increasing presence of minority candidates in elections is one factor in increasing voter participation by minorities. The 2002 election, in which the Democratic candidates for governor and U.S. senator were minorities, saw increased turnout by African Americans and Latinos. Other factors that influence voter turnout include socioeconomic status, party competition, regional differences, and timing of elections.

Effects of Social and Economic Status on Voting

On both the national and the state levels, variation in participation is strongly affected by socioeconomic factors, such as educational level, family income, and minority status. High-income, well-educated citizens are more likely to vote than are lower-income, less-well-educated citizens. People of higher socioeconomic status are likely to be more aware of elections and to perceive themselves as having a higher stake in the outcomes of elections; therefore they are more likely to vote. They are also more likely to contribute financially to political campaigns and become actively involved in elections and party activity.

Race is also a factor in voter turnout—African Americans and Latinos are less likely to vote than whites. Large minority populations in Texas may help explain the lower levels of voter participation among Texans compared with other states. Voting by Latinos is lower for a variety of reasons, but in Texas, they are disproportionately younger than Anglos, and many are not citizens. (See "Thinking Critically About Democracy" for a discussion of the controversy surrounding *politiqueras,* who have helped to get out the vote among Latinos in South Texas.) As with Latinos, voter turnout among African Americans is lower in part because of lower income and educational levels and because of a high percentage of young people in these population groups.[12]

Party Competition and Voter Turnout

Although **party competition** in Texas—the condition of having two active parties—has increased in recent years, the state has a long history of being a one-party state, which partially accounts for the state's lower voter turnout. Studies have shown that party competition is a significant factor in voter turnout. In states where there are two strong, competitive political parties, voter turnout is much higher than in those with one strong and one weak party. Competition increases voter interest in the election because of campaign activities and because of a perception by voters that their vote counts.

Party competition also increases grassroots political organizations that stimulate participation and turn people out to vote.[13] Texans elected Republicans to all statewide offices from 2002 to 2008. It remains to be seen if this domination of state politics will be permanent.

Regional Variations in Voter Turnout

Some writers have suggested that region is the most reliable factor in predicting voter turnout. This is supported by an examination of voter turnout in the states of the Old South, where voter participation is the lowest. Region alone, however, does not explain individual voting behavior. The states of the Old South, including Texas, have a history of repressed voting activity for the reasons discussed earlier—the poll tax, white primaries, annual registrations, and lack of party competition. Also, income and educational levels in this region have historically been lower than in the rest of the country. These factors, combined with traditionalistic-individualistic political cultures, historically reduced political participation.

In recent years, voter turnout in southern states has increased.[14] This is due in part to the elimination of many of the past restrictions. Income and educational levels have also increased, as has immigration from other regions of the country by people from other political cultures.

Timing of Elections

As discussed in Chapter 20, voter turnout in Texas is higher in November general elections than in odd-year elections when we do not elect a president or other statewide or national offices. Also, local elections for city councils and school boards are generally not held in

DO POLITIQUERAS PLAY A BENEFICIAL ROLE IN TEXAS POLITICS?

The Issue: In May 2008, the *New York Times* published an article accusing Hillary Clinton of hiring "electoral soldiers of fortune" in the Texas primary. Along border towns, these campaign workers are known as *politiqueras,* people paid to go door to door distributing flyers and helping people get to the polls to vote. They guarantee votes for the candidate who has hired them at the going rate of $100 to $200 a day.* *Politiqueras* are mostly women with a ready network of friends, family, and neighbors. A big factor in local elections in South Texas, experienced *politiqueras* can "deliver" over two hundred votes on or by Election Day. However, *politiqueras* are attracting an increasing amount of criticism. Some Texas candidates have even pledged not to use them.

This practice, however, is not unique to South Texas. In cities across the United States, campaigns give out "street money" or "walk around money," and in northern states, paid campaign workers can earn considerably more than *politiqueras* do. In Philadelphia, the rate can be as high as $400 per day.**

The controversial practice of hiring campaign workers is safeguarded by the First Amendment right to freedom of speech. Yet some media reports have characterized *politiqueras* as aggressive women who cross the line between what is legal and what is not by stealing mail-in ballots and sometimes even paying people for their votes. In 2005, Republican Attorney General Greg Abbott led a crackdown on voter fraud. Over the course of two years, twenty-six arrests were made. In eighteen of these instances, the campaign workers were charged with mishandling mail-in ballots. Of the twenty-six people arrested, all were Democrats and almost all were Latino or African American.[†]

Yes: Election turnout for the Latino population falls well below the turnout for Anglo voters. Campaign workers are needed to reach out to low-income, elderly, and non-English-speaking populations and involve them in the political process. These campaign workers should be paid enough to cover their expenses for food and gasoline as they canvass neighborhoods and help voters without transportation get to the polls. If campaign workers are not paid, only higher-income individuals will be able to afford to "get out the vote."

No: Elderly, handicapped, and non-English-speaking voters are easily influenced and manipulated by *politiqueras*—they do not really involve these people in the political process in a meaningful way. The *politiqueras* use undue influence and questionable techniques to get out the vote. Local leaders rely on *politiqueras* to help win elections, and so they are motivated to turn a blind eye to any voter fraud the *politiqueras* may commit. These campaign "workers" corrupt our democratic system.

Other approaches: *Politiqueras* play an important role in getting out the vote, but the Texas legislature should create laws that prevent them from participating in voter fraud. For example, the legislature could pass a law that prohibits payment tied to the number of ballots a campaign worker has mailed in for people or for the number of voters driven to the polls. The state government could also distribute a pamphlet that explains voter fraud and lists best practices for campaign workers.

What do you think?

① What role do *politiqueras* play in the political system? Is it beneficial?

② What experiences have you had or events have you witnessed that might inform your viewpoint on this issue?

③ Should political parties be allowed to pay campaign workers? If so, should the government regulate this payment? Why or why not?

④ What other measures can be used to get out the vote in rural areas and among non-English-speaking citizens?

*Mike McIntire and Michael Luo, "A Usually Legal Practice That Wears Black Eyes," *New York Times,* May 13, 2008, www.nytimes.com/2008/05/13/us/politics/13streetcash.html?_r=2&adxnnl=1&oref=slogin&adxnnlx=1216307215-uoiW43ldORQ/TWOhgysBHg.
**Ewen MacAskill, "The High Price of 'Street Money' in Philadelphia Campaigns," *The Guardian,* April 21, 2008, www.guardian.co.uk/world/2008/apr/21/uselections2008.barackobama.
†Wayne Slater, "Texas AG Fails to Unravel Large-Scale Voter-Fraud Schemes in His Two-Year Campaign," *Dallas Morning News,* May 18, 2008, www.txcn.com/sharedcontent/dws/news/localnews/tv/stories/DN-votefraud_18tex.ART.State.Edition2.46e18c2.html.

conjunction with general elections; the common time for these in Texas is in May. Turnout in local elections is always lower than in other elections. Because they are less visible and receive less attention by the media, voters do not perceive these elections as being important, and many of these races are not contested. In 1995, a constitutional amendment allowed cities and school boards to cancel elections if all races are uncontested. The governing body certifies the uncontested candidates as "winners."

Types of Interest Groups

The lack of citizen involvement in elections increases the importance and the influence of interest groups in Texas politics. Being an active member of an interest group is another form of political participation and a way to increase one's influence on government. Frequently, it is not the individual, or the more broadly defined "public opinion," that influences government officials, but the opinions of these attentive publics, organized in interest groups, who often have the ear of public officials. Involvement in interest groups is a more influential form of participation than the simple act of voting, especially in Texas where these groups wield considerable power. Interest groups in Texas can be divided into economic, citizens', and government groups.

Economic Organizations—Promoting Business and Professionalism

A few different types of economic interest groups are active in Texas politics. **Peak business organizations** are interest groups that represent statewide interests, such as the state Chamber of Commerce, the Texas Association of Manufacturers, and the National Federation of Independent Business Owners. These groups advocate for their members' interests and present a united front against policies that do not promote a "good business climate" in the state. They are often the most active at the state level and are generally well financed.

Texas business groups also include nonmembership organizations, which do not have active members and generally represent a single company, organization, corporation, or individual. These form the largest category of interest groups. Examples include Chili's Grill and Bar in Dallas, El Chico Corporation, and H. Ross Perot.

Trade associations differ from peak business organizations in that they represent more specific business interests. In Texas, examples of these groups abound. Two trade associations that are often classified as among the more powerful are the Mid-Continent Oil and Gas Association, representing oil and gas producers, and the Good Roads Association, which represents highway contractors. Some groups represent more specific economic interests.

Examples of retail trade groups are the Texas Apartment Association, the Texas Automobile Dealers Association, the Texas Restaurant Association, and the Association of Licensed Beverage Distributors. The primary goal of these groups is to protect their trades from state regulation deemed undesirable by the groups and to support regulation favorable to the groups' interests.

Agriculture groups are prominent because of the importance of agriculture to the Texas economy. There are three types of **agricultural associations.** First are those that represent general farm interests. The Texas Farm Bureau represents large agricultural producers in the state. The Texas Farmers Union represents family farms and ranches. Second are organizations that represent commodity groups, such as cotton growers, cattle raisers, chicken raisers, and mohair producers. The third type of agriculture interest group represents suppliers of services to agriculture producers. Such groups represent cotton ginners, seed and fertilizer producers, and manufacturers and sellers of farm equipment.

Professional associations differ from trade associations in two ways: (1) there is generally a professional license issued by the state, and (2) the state controls their scope of practice. They represent such professions as physicians (the Texas Medical Association) and attorneys (the Texas Trial Lawyers Association, which represents some attorneys). There are also organizations representing the interests of architects, landscape architects, engineers, surveyors, plumbers, accountants, librarians, barbers, hairdressers, cosmetologists, funeral directors, dentists, nurses, chiropractors, optometrists, pharmacists, podiatrists, clinical psychologists, veterinarians, and many other professional groups.

peak business organizations
interest groups that represent statewide business organizations, such as a state's Chamber of Commerce

trade associations
interest groups that represent specific business interests, such as oil producers and highway contractors

agricultural associations
interest groups that represent different types of farmers and businesses that provide farming supplies

professional associations
organizations of people in professions such as teaching, medicine, law, architecture, cosmetology, and many others that generally require a license, have an element of state control, and lack the right to collective bargaining

In Texas, public employees are not granted the right of **collective bargaining**—the right to negotiate wages, hours, and other working conditions with their employer—as they are in many states. In collective bargaining, the government must enter negotiations with an organization representing government workers, and both sides must reach an agreement. State law in Texas does not grant this right to state or local employees.

Because of this lack of collective bargaining in Texas, public-sector employee organizations are professional associations rather than labor unions. In other states, such groups are classified as public-sector labor unions.

The Texas State Teachers Association (TSTA) is the largest professional group in the state. Affiliated with the National Education Association, TSTA is generally considered the more liberal teachers' group. TSTA is well organized and sometimes presents a united front. At other times, TSTA members have been known to fight among themselves. The Association of Texas Professional Educators is a more conservative organization that represents some teachers in the state. It was formed to counter the TSTA and has strong associations with the Texas Republican Party.

Labor unions in Texas exist only in the private sector, are not powerful, and represent a small fraction of the workers. Strong labor unions are anathema to the traditionalistic-individualistic political culture of Texas. In many industrialized states, organized labor unions are important and powerful interest groups, although their influence has been declining in recent years. Except in a few counties on the Texas Gulf Coast, where organized labor represents petrochemical workers and longshoremen, organized labor in Texas is very weak. In 2010, only 9.6 percent of the total Texas workforce belonged to labor unions.[15] As in most of the South, strong anti-union feelings are very much a part of the political culture. Texas is one of twenty-two states with "right-to-work" laws. These laws prohibit union shops where all workers, based on a majority vote of the workers, are forced to join the union within ninety days of employment to retain their jobs.

Citizens' Groups—Promoting Ideas and Causes

Ideological interest groups in Texas consist largely of both ethnic and religious groups. African Americans and Latinos are the two most active ethnic groups in the state. Latinos are represented by a variety of groups that are sometimes at odds with one another. The League of United Latin American Citizens (LULAC) is the largest such group in the state. Other such organizations include Mexican American Democrats (MAD), the Mexican

collective bargaining
negotiations on wages, hours, and other working conditions between employers and employees

> Austin teachers protest budget cuts at the Capitol. The Texas State Teachers Association, the largest professional group in Texas, represents teachers but lacks the right to collective bargaining under Texas law.

> The National Firearms Association demonstrates against gun control in Austin. Public interest groups such as this one represent a range of causes that are important to Texans.

Influences on Elections in Texas

THEN (1996)	NOW (2010)
After two decades of decline, the turnout of voters aged 18 to 29 reached an all-time low of 40% in the presidential election.*	The turnout for young voters climbs steeply, tripling the rate in 2000 for the 2008 primary election, as students use the Internet to organize and support candidates.
About 65,000 charities and other nonprofit organizations were active in Texas.**	The number of nonprofit organizations in Texas has increased by roughly 55%.‡
Business associations spent twice as much money on political campaigns as did ideological and single-issue groups.†	Business associations still spend more money on political campaigns, but ideological and single-issue groups are catching up.

WHAT'S NEXT?

> Will technology raise the turnout of young voters to an all-time high?

> Will the influence of single-issue interest groups grow as that of business associations declines?

> Will interest groups and elected representatives become increasingly diverse?

*Alexandra Marks, "For Election '08 Youth Voter Turnout Swells," *Christian Science Monitor*, January 16, 2008, www.csmonitor.com/2008/0116/p01s03-uspo.html?page=1.
**Urban Institute, National Center for Charitable Statistics, http://nccsdataweb.urban.org/PubApps/profile1.php?state=TX.
†Texas PACs: 2006 Cycle Spending, http://www.tpj.org/reports/txpac06/chapter2.html.
‡National Center for Charitable Statistics, Number of Nonprofit Organizations in Texas, 1998–2008, http://nccsdataweb.urban.org/PubApps/profile1.php?state=TX.

American Legal Defense and Education Fund (MALDEF), and the Political Association of Spanish-Speaking Organizations (PASSO). The National Association for the Advancement of Colored People (NAACP) and the Congress of Racial Equality (CORE) represent African Americans in Texas.

These groups are primarily concerned with advancing civil rights, ending discrimination, improving government services, and gaining political power. Although they do not always share common interests, gaining economic and political equality is an interest they do share.

Texas has a history of active religious groups. As in the rest of the Old South, Protestant churches fought to eliminate the sale of alcoholic beverages in the state. Even today, large sections of the state are "dry," meaning that alcohol is not sold there. In areas where alcohol can be sold, only beer and wine can be sold on Sunday, and only after the noon hour.

The Catholic Church is also active in state politics. This activity, primarily among Latino Catholics, is driven by concerns about economic advancement, local services, and the abortion issue. In San Antonio, the Catholic Church was a driving force for the creation of Communities Organized for Public Service (COPS). This organization successfully challenged the Good Government League, which had dominated city elections for decades.[16] In the Rio Grande Valley, the Catholic Church was a driving force in the formation of the Interfaith Alliance. In the El Paso area, the Inter-Religious Sponsoring Organization was created to advance Latino interests.

In recent years, fundamentalist religious groups have increased their activities on the national level and in Texas. In 1994, they gained control of the Republican Party State Executive Committee in Texas and maintain control today. Organizations such as the Christian Coalition attempt to promote antiabortion campaigns, abstinence-based sex education, homeschooling, a school voucher system, prayer in school, and, of course, "family values." These groups have had some success at electing local school boards and now control the Texas State Board of Education, which governs some aspects of school policy statewide.

In 2010, these conservatives drew national attention when they overhauled the Texas grade school curriculum standards to deemphasize the civil rights movement, religious freedoms, and hundred of other topics. They removed Thomas Jefferson as one of the great political thinkers introduced in world history. The decision sparked intense criticism nationwide because some feared that textbook companies, catering to the new Texas standards, would make these changes in new editions of their social studies textbooks that were slated to be used by other states.[17]

Public interest groups represent causes or ideas rather than economic, professional, or governmental interests. Many of these Texas organizations have national counterparts—for instance, Mothers Against Drunk Driving (MADD), the National Organization for Women

(NOW), the National Right to Life Association, the Sierra Club, the American Civil Liberties Union (ACLU), Common Cause, the League of Women Voters, and Public Citizen. These groups usually limit their support or opposition to a narrow range of issues.

Government Organizations—Promoting Local Interests

On the state level, government organizations include **state and local interest groups (SLIGs)** consisting of government employees and officials who organize to protect and advance their interests. Examples of these groups are the Texas Municipal League, the Texas Association of Police Chiefs, the Combined Law Enforcement Association of Texas, the Texas Association of Fire Fighters, the City Attorneys Association, the Texas Association of County Officials, and the Texas School Board Association. These groups have in common the goals of protecting local government interests from actions of the state legislature, the governor, and state agencies.

state and local interest groups (SLIGs)
interest groups that represent state government employees, such as the Texas Association of Police Chiefs, and local governments, such as the Texas Association of County Officials

Interest Group Tactics and Their Regulation

Most states have laws that regulate two kinds of activities of interest groups: lobbying and making financial contributions to political campaigns. Lobby regulations generally consist of requiring organizations that have regular contacts with legislators to register and provide reports on their activities. Often, this requirement is weak, and the reports might not reflect the true activities of such organizations.

Texas first required the registration of interest groups in 1907. This statute prohibited "efforts to influence legislation 'by means other than appeal to reason' and provided that persons guilty of lobbying were subject to fines and imprisonment."[18] The act was never enforced. In 1957, a new law was passed that required lobbyists to register and disclose information about their activities; however, the law had many loopholes and was ineffective. In 1973, a new law was passed that called for more stringent reporting. The act was again amended in 1983. Under current law, three kinds of persons must register as lobbyists: individuals who lobby as professionals; "individuals who receive more than $200.00 in one calendar quarter as pay for lobbying"; and individuals who spend more than $200 for gifts, awards, or entertainment to influence legislation.[19] Each year about 1,500 groups and persons register. Government officials who lobby for state agencies and universities are exempt from registration. Also, some lawyers do not register because they claim they are representing clients and are not lobbying. Thus the total number of persons who actually lobby the legislature is much higher.

Interest groups attempt to gain influence by lobbying government officials, launching grassroots campaigns, and galvanizing voters and financial support for candidates. The type of technique depends on the type of group and the resources available to that group.

Lobbying

In Texas, the legislature meets every two years for 140 days, and the most intense lobby activity is concentrated during the regular session (see Figure 21.1). Lobbying does not stop when the legislature adjourns. Most legislation requires a signature by the governor. Persuading the governor to either sign or veto a bill is an important part of lobbying activity.

If the governor signs a bill, an administrative agency must enforce it. Administrative discretion in enforcement of a law can also be the object of lobbying. Interest groups devote great efforts to influencing how agencies interpret and enforce laws, and they try to secure appointments to governing boards and commissions of people who favor their interests.

Lobbying tactics have changed in recent years. In the past, the process was described primarily as "booze, bribes, and broads." There is much less of that today. Lobbyists emphasize information and public relations over the old tactics, but entertaining members of the legislature is still very much a part of the process.

> A lobbyist communicates by e-mail in the "owner's box" in the Texas House of Representatives. Lobbyists provide information to legislators and the governor, and they also attempt to influence administrative agencies once legislation is passed.

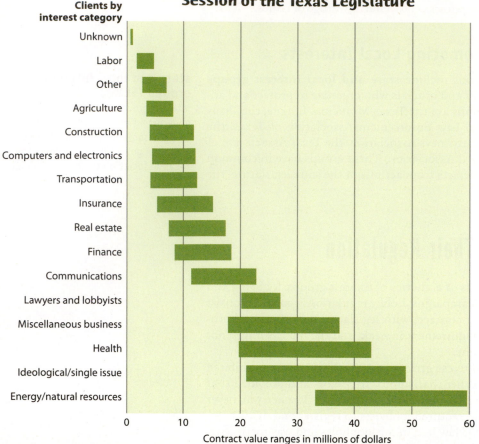

Money Spent for Lobby Activity in the 2007 Session of the Texas Legislature

Clients by interest category

- Unknown
- Labor
- Other
- Agriculture
- Construction
- Computers and electronics
- Transportation
- Insurance
- Real estate
- Finance
- Communications
- Lawyers and lobbyists
- Miscellaneous business
- Health
- Ideological/single issue
- Energy/natural resources

0   10   20   30   40   50   60

Contract value ranges in millions of dollars

POLITICAL INQUIRY

FIGURE 21.1 ■ Each year, lobbyists spend money during the legislative session to have their issues presented to the members. Ideological and single-issue clients account for 15 percent of all spending. Business interests spend most of the money. Does this kind of money buy legislation that is slanted toward business and against consumers?

SOURCE: Texans for Public Justice, *Austin's Oldest Profession: Texas' Top Lobby Clients and Those Who Serve Them*, September 2008, www.tpj.org.

Texas Ethics Commission
state agency responsible for enforcing requirements to report information on money collected and activities by interest groups and candidates for public office

Electioneering

Interest groups devote considerable time and effort trying to influence the outcome of elections through political action committees (PACs). Most states require some formal registration of PACs. In Texas, a PAC created by corporations or labor unions must be formed exclusively to support or oppose a ballot issue and may not be created to support or oppose a candidate for office. "However, employees, members or families of corporation employees, unions and associations may form a PAC and make individual donations."[20] PACs must register with the **Texas Ethics Commission,** the agency that enforces regulations for interest groups and candidates, and they must designate a treasurer and file periodic reports. These reports must give the names of persons donating more than $50 to campaigns. PACs are also prohibited from making a contribution to members of the legislature during the period beginning thirty days before the start of a regular session and ending thirty days after the regular 140-day session. In Texas, except for voluntary limits in judicial campaigns, state law does not limit how much an individual or a PAC may contribute to a candidate.

The process of electioneering is much broader than making a monetary contribution to a campaign. It begins with candidate recruitment. Interest groups work to recruit candidates for office many months before the election. They encourage individuals who will be sympathetic to their cause to seek nominations in party primaries. This encouragement takes the form of promises of support and money in the election. Some interest groups might cover their bets by encouraging both Democratic and Republican candidates to seek nomination in their respective parties. No matter which candidate wins, they win.

After the primary election, interest groups often give money to candidates in the general election. They might give money to both Democratic and Republican candidates, hoping to have access and influence regardless of who wins the general election. Some writers have observed that PAC money has undermined party loyalty and weakened political parties in this country. Candidates no longer owe their loyalty to the party that helped elect them but to interest groups. Political action committees buy access in

an intricate, symbiotic relationship involving trust, information exchange, pressure and obligations. The inescapable fact is that resources, and especially money, are at least three-fourths of the battle in building and maintaining good relations and in securing the other essential elements that lead to access and influence.[21]

Interest groups might also become directly involved in campaigns. The amount of spending on campaigns doubled between 1998 and 2006 and continues to escalate. This can involve running television and newspaper ads explaining the record of officials or the virtues of a nonincumbent, or working in voter registration drives and get-out-the-vote campaigns. Interest groups might also aid candidates by helping to write speeches and organize rallies, and by staging political events such as fund-raisers. Some groups keep track of legislators' voting records and circulate "good guy/bad guy score cards" to members of the organization, instructing members to vote for or against candidates.

Grassroots Lobbying

Interest groups also attempt to influence public policy through public education and public relations activities. These efforts portray the organization in the best possible light by creating a favorable public image of the group. Obviously, much of this information can be very self-serving and can be called propaganda. Not all such information is wrong, but some filtering of the information by public officials is necessary. Competing interest groups often counter the information provided by another interest group. In a mass media society, with much public scrutiny, an interest group's credibility can be compromised if it frequently provides inaccurate or misleading information.

Interest groups often provide research information to members of the Texas legislature. This information can be self-serving but is often accurate and can be a valuable source for state legislators. An interest group that provides high-quality research and information can have an impact on public policy. Over the years, several business-sponsored groups in Texas have developed a reputation for producing quality research and information to the Texas legislature.[22]

Besides presenting a favorable opinion of themselves to the public, interest groups curry favor with public officials. Inviting public officials to address organizational meetings is another technique to advance the group's standing in the eyes of public officials. Giving awards to public officials at such gatherings, thanking them for their service to the public, is also a common technique.

The Strength of Interest Groups in Texas

The strength and influence of interest groups vary among the states. Most writers explain this variation based on four factors: economic diversity, party strength, professionalism of the legislature, and government fragmentation.[23]

Economic Diversity

States that are highly industrialized and have a great variety of industries will have a multitude of interest groups. Because of the diversity and the complexity of the state's economy, no single industry or group can dominate. The many interests cancel each other out. In other states with less diversity, a single or a few industries dominate the economy.

In the past, the Texas economy was dominated by a few industries: cotton, cattle, banking, and oil. Today, the Texas economy is more diversified, and the number of interest groups has grown accordingly. It is much more difficult for one or a few interests to dominate state politics.

Political Party Competition

The strength of the political parties in the state can influence the strength of the interest groups. States with two strong competitive parties that recruit and support candidates for office can offset the influence of interest groups. Members of the legislature in competitive party states might owe their election to the political party and be less influenced by interest groups. In Texas, a history of weak party structure has contributed to the power of interest groups.

HOW TEXAS COMPARES

CLASSIFICATION OF STATES BASED ON THE OVERALL IMPACT OF INTEREST GROUPS

Clive S. Thomas and Ronald J. Hrebenar have classified interest group patterns in the fifty states according to their degree of influence. In Texas, interest groups are dominant but must negotiate with state agencies and the legislature.

Classification based on impact of interest groups

- Dominant
- Dominant/Complementary
- Complementary
- Complementary/Subordinate

SOURCE: Clive S. Thomas and Ronald J. Hrebenar, "Interest Groups in the States," in *Politics in the American States: A Comparative Analysis* (8th ed.), ed. Virginia Gray and Russell L. Hanson (Washington, DC: Congressional Quarterly Press, 2004). Reprinted by permission.

Professionalism of the State Legislature

A professional legislature is one that has a full-time staff, is well paid, serves full-time, and has high-quality research and advisory services. Full-time, well-paid legislators with a professional staff are less dependent upon information supplied by interest groups, and the exchange of information between the lobbyist and the legislator is reduced. The Texas legislature has improved the quality of its staff in recent years; most members have full-time staff in Austin and in local offices. In addition, committee staff has increased. The Texas legislature now provides more money than any other state for staff salaries. The Texas Legislative Council also provides excellent staff assistance in research and information.

Fragmented Government Structure

fragmented government structure

a government structure in which power is dispersed to many state agencies with no central control

The degree to which interest groups succeed in influencing the administration of state laws depends upon the structure of the state government. If the government is centralized under a governor who appoints and removes most of the heads of departments, interest groups will find it necessary to lobby the governor directly and the agencies indirectly. Texas has a **fragmented government structure** with power dispersed to many agencies and little central control. The governor of Texas makes few significant appointments of agency heads.

Each interest group tries to gain access to and influence the state agency that deals with its area of interest. Often, these agencies are created to regulate the industry that the interest group represents. For example, the Texas Railroad Commission, originally created to regulate railroads, also regulates the oil industry in Texas. Historically, the oil industry lobby groups have dominated the three members who serve on the Railroad Commission and the decisions of that commission.[24]

Similar relationships exist between many state agencies and interest groups. Until the Texas Sunset Commission was created in 1977 to review most state agencies every ten years, the members of most state licensing boards (such as the Texas State Bar, State Board of Medical Examiners, State Board of Morticians) were professionals in that field. Members of the profession still dominate these boards. These licensing boards were created to "protect the public interest," but they often spend most of their time protecting the profession by limiting the number of persons who can be licensed and by making rules favorable to the group. For example, in Texas when a person dies, he or she must be dead for seventy-two hours before cremation. However, if the body is not buried within twenty-four hours, it must be embalmed. According to authorities, the reason for embalming before cremation is to protect the public from the spread of diseases. Others have suggested the procedure is unnecessary and demonstrates the degree to which interest groups control rule making and influence the amount of money a group makes.

When the relationship between the state agency and the interest group becomes very close, it is referred to as **capture:** The interest group has "captured" the agency. However, capture of the agency by the interest group is probably more the exception than the rule. Competing interest groups often vie for influence with the agency and reduce the likelihood of capture by a single interest group. The iron triangle model shown in Figure 21.2 provides a more accurate explanation of the policy-making process in Texas. In this model, which is similar to the iron triangle shown in Figure 7.2, the interest group, the state agency, and the legislative committee (with oversight of the agency) share in the process of making policy.

In Texas, the fragmented nature of the state government, the many independent boards and commissions, and the separately elected state agency heads all increase the strength and influence of interest groups on state government.

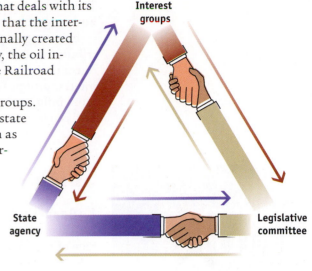

FIGURE 21.2

THE IRON TRIANGLE There is often a close relationship between the state agency created to regulate an industry, the legislative oversight committee, and interest groups.

capture

the situation in which a state agency or board falls under the heavy influence of its constituency interest groups

CONCLUSION

THINKING CRITICALLY ABOUT WHAT'S NEXT IN PARTICIPATION IN TEXAS POLITICS

Although voting restrictions such as poll taxes, white primaries, and annual registration once limited political participation in Texas, the lifting of these restrictions as well as changing populations and values are affecting the political landscape. Minorities, women, and youth, who have historically been underrepresented in both voter turnout and government office, have made inroads in twenty-first-century Texas politics. Young voters use new technologies to organize, and members of minority groups have gained increasing political clout because of population growth.

Although possibilities for participation have expanded, many continue to view interest groups with suspicion and fear the influence of rich or powerful groups. In some campaigns, the availability of PAC money has replaced the political party as the determining factor in nominating and electing a candidate for office. And there is no doubt that PAC money influences legislation. Others argue, however, that these groups balance one another and foster participation in a democratic society. In Texas, the dominance of business associations is increasingly being challenged by ideological and single-issue interest groups.

The First Amendment to the U.S. Constitution protects free speech and association, and interest groups can be seen as a necessary part of the political process.

Interest groups gain access to political candidates primarily through campaign contributions. But groups are using new technology to launch grassroots campaigns both to communicate values and to exert influence on state politicians. As a result, the role of interest groups in state politics is changing. Will these changes affect which groups have more influence? Certainly, changes in their tactics that lead to improved communication between legislators and their constituents are likely to strengthen the democratic process.

Summary

1. Opportunities for Participation
A number of citizens in the United States, and particularly in Texas, do not take advantage of the opportunities for participation that are available to them. Turnout rates in national and statewide elections, in particular, are low in Texas when compared with rates nationwide.

2. Legacy of Restricted Ballot Access
Political participation is affected by many factors. Some states, mostly southern and including Texas, have a legacy of restricted access to the ballot through poll taxes, annual registration, property requirements, and the white primary. Even when those restrictions are removed, participation does not immediately increase, however. It can take generations to change political behavior.

3. Factors That Affect Voter Participation Today
Social and economic factors also play a role in participation. Higher-income, well-educated, older people and Caucasians are more likely to vote. Large minority populations within the state, the traditional lack of party competition, and the individualistic-traditionalistic political culture help explain lower turnouts in Texas compared with other states.

4. Types of Interest Groups
Interest groups in Texas can be categorized into three broad groups: economic organizations, which include both professional/trade and business associations; citizens' groups such as the League of United Latin American Citizens; and state and local interest groups.

5. Interest Group Tactics and Their Regulation
Interest groups attempt to affect the passage of legislation favorable to their causes. Texas interest groups win influence through the traditional approaches of lobbying, electioneering, and grassroots activities. Texas checks this influence by forcing most lobbyists to register.

6. The Strength of Interest Groups in Texas
The fragmented structure of the state government and a long history of little to no party competition have allowed interest groups to play a prominent role in state government. Interest groups seek to "capture" executive branch organizations by getting people sympathetic to their cause placed on the boards that make decisions on policies that affect their interests.

Key Terms

agricultural associations 634

annual voter registration 630

capture 641

collective bargaining 635

fragmented government
    structure 640

party competition 632

peak business
    organizations 634

permanent registration
    system 630

professional associations 634

state and local interest
    groups (SLIGs) 637

Texas Ethics Commission 638

trade associations 634

voting-age population 628

For Review

1. What groups were targeted by the poll tax, annual registration, property restrictions, and the white primary?

2. What factors explain lower voter turnout in Texas relative to other states?

3. Explain the categories of interest groups, and give at least one specific example within each category.

4. What role do interest groups play in the electoral process?

5. How do interest groups today gain influence within Texas politics?

6. How strong are interest groups in Texas relative to other states? What factors explain this?

For Critical Thinking and Discussion

1. How might restrictions on voting, such as poll taxes, annual registration, property requirements, and the white primary, affect voter turnout today? What evidence can you give to support your answer?

2. Who is more likely to vote: a 43-year-old doctor or a 21-year-old mechanic? Explain your answer.

3. What steps could be taken to increase voter participation in Texas?

4. Give a recent example of an activity by an interest group that you have read about, learned about on a news program, or observed. What was the purpose of this activity, and did it achieve its end?

5. Do you feel that interest groups have too much, too little, or about the right amount of power in Texas politics? Explain your answer.

PRACTICE QUIZ

MULTIPLE CHOICE: Choose the lettered item that answers the question correctly.

1. All of the following were restrictions that once limited voter participation in Texas elections except
   a. political affiliation.
   b. the white primary.
   c. the poll tax.
   d. annual registration.

2. Which of the following groups was not negatively affected by the poll tax adopted by Texas legislature in 1902?
   a. Latinos
   b. African Americans
   c. poor white business owners
   d. poor white farmers

3. Which of the following is not a factor that affects voter participation today?
   a. socioeconomic status
   b. poll taxes
   c. regional differences
   d. timing of elections

4. Which of the following individuals does not have the right to vote in Texas today?
   a. anyone under the age of 21
   b. any citizen who does not register annually
   c. any person who cannot afford to pay the poll tax
   d. convicted felons who are serving their sentence

5. Interest groups in Texas can be divided into
   a. economic, citizens', and government groups.
   b. trade associations, economic groups, political factions.
   c. categories based on the amount of money they raise.
   d. religious, racial, and gender-based groups.

6. Interest groups wield considerable power in Texas because of
   a. tight limitations on campaign contributions.
   b. the fragmented structure of state government.
   c. the absence of a well-paid and professional legislative staff.
   d. a long history of intense two-party competition.

7. An ideological interest group that is active in Texas is
   a. the Texas Farm Bureau.
   b. the Texas Association of Fire Fighters.
   c. the Texas State Teachers Association.
   d. the Christian Coalition.

8. A group that is more likely to vote because its members are more likely to be aware of elections, to believe that they have a higher stake in election outcomes, and to contribute money, effort, and time to campaigns is
   a. Latinos.
   b. 18- to 22-year-olds.
   c. high-income professionals.
   d. blue-collar workers.

9. How does Texas restrict interest group participation in elections?
   a. The state prevents PACs from contributing to all campaigns.
   b. The state restricts PACs to supporting or opposing ballot issues, not candidates for office.
   c. The state requires interest groups to contribute to both candidates running for a particular office.
   d. The state does not limit PAC contributions at all.

10. How do professional associations differ from trade associations in Texas?
    a. There is generally a professional license issued by the state.
    b. The state controls the scope of their practice.
    c. The state limits the amount of funds they can raise to $2,000.
    d. Both a and b.

FILL IN THE BLANKS.

11. An _____ exists when the relationship between a state agency and the interest group that agency was created to regulate becomes too close.

12. _____ associations represent specific business interests, such as oil production and highway contractors.

13. In _____, the government must enter negotiations with an organization representing government workers, and both sides must reach an agreement.

14. _____ is a system that keeps citizens on the voter registration list if they continue to vote at prescribed intervals.

15. _____ includes all activities engaged in by interest groups to try to influence the outcome of elections.

RESOURCES FOR RESEARCH AND ACTION

Internet Resources

The National Rifle Association
www.nraila.org This Web site presents information to the public regarding the group's positions.

The Secretary of State
www.sos.state.tx.us This site has information on current ballot issues, where to vote, and election dates.

Texans for Public Justice
www.tpj.org This advocacy group compiles information on many aspects of Texas state government, including lists of lobbyist and campaign contributions by PACs and money contributed to judicial candidates.

The Texas Ethics Commission
www.ethics.state.tx.us This site lists information on campaign contributions and interest group registrations.

Internet Activism

The Texas Legislature Online is a gateway to a multitude of information on the leader and members of the legislature, the calendar, bills and amendments, journals, and news and research organizations. To learn more about current legislation or your representatives, visit **www.capitol. state.tx.us.**

Twitter
http://twitter.com/equalitytexas Get updates from an interest group that advocates for the elimination of discrimination by gender and sexual orientation.

YouTube
www.youtube.com/watch?v=4u55MCEdeWs The executive director of The Nature Conservancy of Texas discusses the results of an insightful poll her interest group conducted.

Facebook
www.facebook.com/search/?flt=1&q=texas&o=65&s=160#!/youngconservativestx?ref=search Young Conservatives of Texas is a nonpartisan conservative youth organization that is active among Texas's university campuses. Its members participate in Texas politics by educating students and the public, campus activism, and campaigning for political candidates, among other things.

Recommended Readings

Chavez, Linda. *Out of the Barrio: Toward a New Politics of Hispanic Assimilation.* New York: Basic Books, 1992.

Davidson, Chandler. *Race and Class in Texas Politics.* Princeton, NJ: Princeton University Press, 1990.

Leighley, Jan. *Strength in Numbers: The Political Mobilization of Racial and Ethnic Minorities.* Princeton, NJ: Princeton University Press, 2001.

Movie of Interest

Plutonium Circus (1995)
In a nuclear weapons plant in Amarillo, Texas, where workers once assembled weapons, they are now taking them apart. This film about the nuclear weapons plant looks at how the plant has affected the lives of the people of Amarillo and their attitudes toward the Cold War, illustrating how personal experiences shape public opinion on political matters.

Political Parties and Elections in Texas

THEN The Democratic Party, which included both a conservative and a liberal faction, dominated all three branches of the Texas state government.

NOW The Republican Party, dominated by conservatives, controls all three branches of state government, with the Democratic Party still split between the two factions.

NEXT How will population changes, such as the increase in the Latino vote, influence the Texas party system?

Will the Latino population continue its strong support of the Democratic Party?

Will new families arriving in Texas as a result of economic development help keep the reigns of government in the hands of the Republican Party?

This chapter examines the evolution of the party system in Texas, the state's political parties, and the process by which candidates from these parties are elected to office.

FIRST, we consider *state party systems* and compare Texas with the other forty-nine states.

SECOND, we differentiate between *state party ideologies* and national party ideologies, using this distinction to help explain how Texas governors of different party affiliations have pursued similar policies.

THIRD, we explore the history of *political parties in Texas,* including third-party movements and political party organization and party strength within the state.

FOURTH, we take a look at permanent *party organization in Texas* and evaluate factors that have weakened the role of parties in state politics.

FIFTH, we review *primary elections* and discuss the significance of cross-over voting.

SIXTH, we analyze *campaigns and elections* and the role of professional consultants and money in elections.

two-party competitive state
a state in which parties switch control of the statewide elected offices and control of the state legislature

modified one-party state
a state in which one party regularly wins elections

State party systems vary widely,

and often the only common link is the name Democrat or Republican. Although state-elected officials might carry common party labels—Democratic and Republican—there is little interaction between these officials and two U.S. senators and thirty-two U.S. representatives. The national and state party organizations often act independently of each other.

Texas holds general elections every two years. During nonpresidential years, voters elect candidates to statewide offices: governor, lieutenant governor, attorney general, land commissioner, agricultural commissioner, comptroller, some members of the Texas Railroad Commission and the Texas State Board of Education, and some members of the two supreme courts in the state. Before 1976, all nonjudicial officeholders served two-year terms. In 1977, the state constitution was amended, and four-year terms were first used in 1978. Every two years, voters also elect all 150 members of the Texas House of Representatives (for two-year terms), half of the members of the Texas Senate (for four-year terms), many judges to various courts, and local county officials.

Texas election results have sharply demonstrated the independence of state and national party systems. Throughout the twentieth century, Democrats dominated statewide elections. In the 1950s, however, the national Republican Party began drawing conservatives away, and Texas became a state that voted Republican in presidential elections but Democratic in all statewide elections. After the turn of the twenty-first century, Republicans for the first time captured all statewide offices. The Republican Party's ability to keep control of the state will depend in large part on the vote of Texas's growing minority population.

State Party Systems

States can be classified according to the strength of each party within the state. States in which parties switch control of the statewide elected offices and control of the state legislature are called **two-party competitive states.** States in which one party generally wins elections are called **modified one-party states.** The term *modified* is used to differentiate between the political system of these states and one-party systems in which only one party is allowed to participate in elections.

Most studies of competition between the parties, including the ones used to construct the map provided in "How Texas Compares: Party Competition in the United States," rely on several measures: (1) the percentage of votes won by each party in races for governor and the state legislature; (2) the length of time each party controls the legislature and the office of governor; and (3) the frequency with which parties divide control of the governorship and the legislature. These studies do not rely on voting for the president of the United States. The vote for presidential candidates is not a valid measure of party strength within a state.

The map in "How Texas Compares" shows current party competition in the fifty states, but since 1946, state-party competitive patterns have changed. Three patterns emerge. First, one-party Democratic states have disappeared and are now classified as modified one-party Democratic, two-party competitive states, or modified one-party Republican states. Second, modified one-party Republican states have increased slightly in the past five years. Third, the number of two-party competitive states has increased from twenty-five to twenty-six in 2006. From 1946 to 1994, thirteen states remained two-party competitive

PARTY COMPETITION IN THE UNITED STATES

This map shows party competition in the fifty states. Where are the Democratic strongholds? Where are Republican strongholds? How do you explain this pattern?

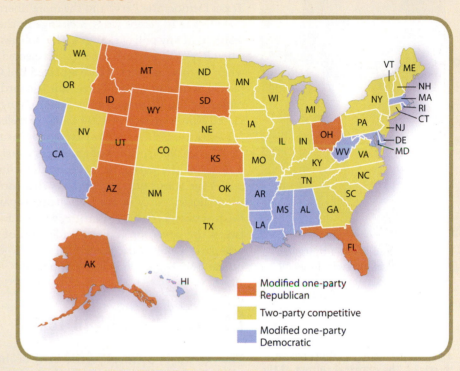

SOURCE: Thomas M. Holbrok and Raymond La Raja, "Parties and Elections," *Politics in the American States: A Comparative Analysis,* 9th ed., ed. Virginia Gray and Russell L. Hanson (Washington, DC: Congressional Quarterly Press, 2009), Table 3.4, p. 84.

states, while others began to change. Most of those changes in party competitive patterns are explained by changes in southern states, where one-party Democratic states have become two-party competitive states or modified one-party Republican states. In most other parts of the country, changes in party competitiveness have been less dramatic.

In Texas and other southern states, the Democratic Party dominated state politics from Reconstruction in the 1870s until the 1960s. Few Republicans placed their names on the ballot. The Republican Party in Texas has been gaining strength for the past thirty years. It now controls both houses of the Texas legislature, and it has captured the governor's office seven times in the last eight elections. Republicans hold all statewide elected offices. These victories have changed the classification for Texas from a modified one-party Democratic state, to a two-party competitive state, to a modified one-party Republican state.

State Party Ideologies

The party labels *Democratic* and *Republican* do not necessarily indicate ideology. **Party ideology** is the basic belief system that guides the party. The Democratic Party in one state can be quite different ideologically from the Democratic Party in another state. For many years in Texas, the Democratic Party has had very strong conservative leanings. The Democratic Party in Massachusetts has a liberal orientation. The conservatism of Texas Democrats

party ideology
basic belief system that guides a political party

shows in voter support for presidential candidates. Since the end of World War II, Texans have most often supported Republican candidates. Texas supported Dwight Eisenhower in 1952 and 1956, Richard Nixon in 1972, Ronald Reagan in 1980 and 1984, George H. W. Bush in 1988 and 1992, Bob Dole in 1996, George W. Bush in 2000 and 2004, and John McCain in 2008. Since 1960, Texas has voted Democratic only four times; in two of those cases, a native-son Democrat was on the ballot. Texans voted Democratic in 1960 and 1964 for Lyndon Johnson, and for Hubert Humphrey, vice president under Johnson, in 1968. Texans supported Jimmy Carter in 1976, in part because he was a southerner and in part because of the backwash from the Watergate scandal. This strong support for Republican presidential candidates results from ideological differences between the more conservative Texas Democratic Party and the more liberal national Democratic Party organization.

In Texas in recent years, a change in the person holding the office of governor has not resulted in any policy changes. The policies under Democrat Dolph Briscoe did not change when Republican Bill Clements was elected governor in 1976, nor did policies change much when Democrat Mark White replaced Bill Clements in 1982, or when Clements in turn replaced White in 1986. When Ann Richards was elected governor as a Democrat in 1990, replacing Bill Clements, a few policy changes occurred. George W. Bush, a Republican, defeated Ann Richards in 1994 and was reelected in 1998. In 2001, Rick Perry continued the conservative policies of the past. A close examination of the actions in the 1995, 1997, 1999, 2001, and 2003 sessions of the Texas legislature shows little change from the conservative policies of the past. The traditionalistic-individualistic political culture of the state preserves the status quo and protects elite interests, regardless of the party of the governor or the majority party in the legislature. Bipartisan cooperation, so evident during the three Bush sessions of the legislature, was made easier because of philosophical agreements between the governor and the leadership of the House and Senate. Texas has gone from a one-party Democratic-controlled state to one dominated by the Republicans with no significant change in philosophy or policy.

> When asked about a concealed weapons bill being considered by the state legislation, former Texas Democratic Governor Ann Richards, an avid hunter, remarked, "Well I'm not a sexist, but there is not a woman in this state who could find a gun in her handbag, much less a lipstick." The political culture of the state drives most politicians to take a conservative stance on gun laws.

Political Parties in Texas

The two major political parties in Texas have had a long and varied history, with periods of weakness and strength for both. In this section, we trace their history and discuss third-party movements as well.

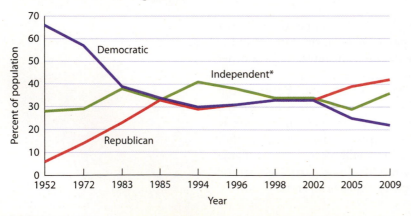

FIGURE 22.1

Party Realignment in Texas, 1952–2009

*Data on independents include those identified as "other party" and "don't know."

SOURCES: Data for 1952–1985 from James A. Dyer, Arnold Vedlitz, and David B. Hill, "New Voters, Switches and Political Party Realignment in Texas," in *The Western Political Quarterly 41*: 156, March 1988. Data for 1994 from The Texas Poll, 1994, Harte-Hanks Communications. Figures for 1996 and 1998 from Texas Poll data, Scripps Howard Inc., University of Texas at Austin. Figures for 2002 and 2005: Texas Poll Data, Scripps Howard Inc. Data for 2009 from Earl Survey Research Laboratory, Texas Tech University, Spring 2009, www.orgs.ttu.edu/earlsurveyresearchlab/data.php.

Democratic and Republican Party Strength in Texas

Texas's movement from a one-party Democratic state to a modified one-party Republican state is reflected in public opinion polls, as shown in Figure 22.1.[1] The question is, why did this change occur, and who supports each party today? To understand this, we need to examine the traditional areas of support for the Democratic and Republican parties in Texas.

The One-Party Era in Texas

From the end of Reconstruction in 1874 until the 1960s, Texas was a one-party Democratic state. This anti-Republicanism can be traced to the Civil War and Reconstruction. Following the Civil War and the experiences of Reconstruction, southerners felt a strong resentment toward the rest of the nation. That resentment bonded the South together as a unit, and they voted against all Republicans.[2] From the end of Reconstruction until at least the 1950s, Republicans were held in disrespect and were the subject of jokes. Calling someone a Republican was an insult. Some termed the Republican Party the "party of Yankee aggression." While living in Austin in the 1890s, the famous writer O. Henry once said, "We have only two or three laws [in Texas], such as against murder before witnesses and being caught stealing horses and voting Republican."

Several second-party movements developed during the last three decades of the nineteenth century, and the conservative Democrats who controlled the party effectively destroyed all opposition. In 1877, the Greenback Party (initially, Greenback Clubs) formed in the South and the West in reaction to declining farm prices. In Texas, the Greenbackers were recruited from the more radical farmers. They demanded currency expansion ("greenbacks") to drive up agricultural prices, an income tax, the secret ballot, direct election of U.S. senators, better schools, and reduced railroad freight rates. In the governor's race in 1880, the Greenback Party's candidate received about 12 percent of the vote. By 1884, the organization had faded out of existence. Also formed at that time was the Texas Farmers' Alliance, which became known as the Grange. This organization also represented small farmers and made an uneasy alliance with African Americans, who were the primary supporters of the Republican Party.[3] The large landowners and businesses of Texas controlled the state Democratic Party and successfully destroyed these party movements, allowing the Democratic Party to dominate state politics from the late 1880s until the 1960s.

Party Realignment in Texas

Until the late 1960s, Texas politics revolved almost exclusively around personality and economic issues. Race issues, which dominated many southern states, were less important in Texas.[4] The period from 1940 to 1960 might even be characterized as an era of nonpartisan politics, with domination by the conservative business community. Factional issues within the party, between liberals and conservatives, were driven by economics.

Businesspeople, oilmen, wealthy farmers, and cattle ranchers formed the backbone of the conservative element.

> The liberal element in Texas was also based on economic consideration. Liberalism in Texas encouraged welfare spending by means of deficit spending if necessary; promoted equal treatment for Negroes, Latin Americans, and other minorities; increased government regulation of business in accordance with the preceding aims, the expansion of the national government powers; trade union organization; and taxes on business—especially on large, interstate corporations—rather than on sales or individuals. Furthermore, liberals in Texas at this time made loyalty to the national Democratic Party a part of their creed.[5]

From 1940 to 1960, political conflicts and competition were confined to the Democratic Party. Party primary elections replaced November general elections because there was no competition from Republicans. On the few occasions when Republicans mounted a challenge to Democrats in the November general election, most Texans still voted a **straight ticket.** The old saying "I would vote for a yellow dog before I'd vote for a Republican" summarizes the attitude of many voters, who came to be known as **Yellow Dog Democrats.** Yellow dogs ranked above Republicans.

THE BEGINNING OF CHANGE   In the 1952 and 1956 presidential elections, many Yellow Dog Democrats broke with tradition and voted for Eisenhower. Democratic governor Allan Shivers, of the conservative faction of the party, led this movement. This faction chose to dissociate themselves from the New Deal/Fair Deal element of the national Democratic Party and any of its candidates.

The Republican state party convention also nominated Shivers and most statewide Democratic candidates as the Republican Party's nominees. Thus, Shivers and most statewide office seekers were candidates for both political parties in 1952. This group became known as the **Shivercrats.** The liberal faction of the Democratic Party became known as the "Loyalists" and were associated with the national Democratic Party.[6]

straight ticket voting
casting all votes for candidates of one party

Yellow Dog Democrats
people who voted straight ticket for Democrats—they would vote for a yellow dog if it ran as a Democrat

Shivercrats
Democrats who followed Governor Allan Shivers's example and voted for Eisenhower in 1952 and 1956

This action began the Texas tradition of supporting Republican presidential candidates while retaining Democratic Party dominance over state offices. Presidential politics in 1952 broke the tradition of voting a straight ticket, at least for the top of the ticket.

THE ELECTION OF JOHN TOWER   In a special election in 1961, John Tower was elected U.S. senator to fill the seat formerly held by Lyndon Johnson and became the first Republican statewide officeholder since the 1870s. The election was originally heralded as the beginning of a new era of two-party politics in the state. In the 1962 elections, Republicans managed to field candidates for many statewide, congressional, and local races. There were few successes.

THE ELECTION OF BILL CLEMENTS   The election of Bill Clements as governor in 1978 marked the real beginning of two-party politics in Texas. Governor Clements used his power to make appointments to boards, commissions, and judgeships and to recruit people who would publicly declare their Republicanism. Some referred to these new converts as "closet Republicans" who had finally gone public. These appointments helped build the Republican Party in Texas, the start of **party realignment** in the state.

The loss of the governorship by Clements in 1982 to Democrat Mark White was a blow to the Republicans because the party also had little success in gaining other statewide offices. In 1986, Republican fortunes improved when Bill Clements returned to the governor's office. He defeated Mark White in what many termed a "revenge match."

THE "CONVERSION" AND ELECTION OF PHIL GRAMM   In 1983, John Tower announced that he would not seek reelection to the U.S. Senate in 1984. Phil Gramm, the Democratic representative from the sixth Congressional District, used Tower's retirement to advance from the U.S. House to the Senate. Gramm had first been elected as a Democrat in 1976. By early 1981, Gramm had gained some national prominence by helping President Reagan "cut the federal budget."[7] Gramm, who served as a member of the House Budget Committee, was accused of leaking Democratic strategy to the White House budget office. David Stockman, budget director under Ronald Reagan, confirmed that he had.[8] Because of his disloyalty to the party and because of House rules, Gramm was not reappointed to another term on the Budget Committee.

In a smart political move, Gramm used this loss of his committee seat as an excuse to convert to the Republican Party. In 1983, Gramm resigned his seat in the U.S. House. Outgoing Republican Governor Clements called a special election, which was held thirty days after Gramm's resignation. Since no other candidate could possibly put together a successful campaign in so short a time, Gramm easily won reelection to Congress as a Republican. In 1984, "fully baptized" as a Republican, Gramm won election as U.S. senator, pulled along on the coattails of President Ronald Reagan. The Republican Party retained the seat in the U.S. Senate. Gramm easily won reelection in 1990 and 1996 but chose not to run for reelection in 2002, thus ending a long political career in Texas politics.

THE MOVE TOWARD PARITY, 1988–1994   In 1988, the Republicans made significant gains, aided by Bill Clements's return in 1987 and George H. W. Bush's election to the presidency. The party won four statewide offices. Three Republicans won election to the Texas Supreme Court, and Kent Hance was elected to the Texas Railroad Commission.

In 1990, Republicans captured the offices of state treasurer and agricultural commissioner and another seat on the state supreme court. The big setback for the Republicans in 1990 was the loss of the governor's office. Bill Clements did not seek reelection. Clayton Williams, a political newcomer, used his considerable wealth to win the Republican nomination. His campaign for governor was something of a disaster, and he managed to lose to Democrat Ann Richards.

In 1992, Democrat Lloyd Bentsen, after serving as U.S. senator from Texas for twenty years, resigned to become secretary of the treasury under President Clinton. His resignation allowed Republicans to capture their second seat in the U.S. Senate with the election of Kay Bailey Hutchison. In 1996, Republican Phil Gramm was elected to a third term as U.S. senator from Texas.

party realignment
the change from a state dominated by one political party to the two-party system operating today

In 1994, the Republicans captured all three seats on the Railroad Commission and a majority of the seats on the state supreme court, and they retained control of the agriculture commissioner's office. In addition, Republicans captured three additional seats on the state board of education, for a total of eight seats. More important, George W. Bush was elected governor. When the dust cleared, Republicans controlled a total of twenty-three statewide offices. Those wins, coupled with additional seats in the Texas House and Senate, substantially changed Texas party structure. Texas had moved to a two-party competitive system.

GOVERNOR BUSH AND REPUBLICAN DOMINANCE, 1995–2001

In 1994, the son of former President George H. W. Bush ran for governor of Texas and beat the Democratic incumbent, Ann Richards. Governor George W. Bush, to a large degree, won because of family name recognition rather than political experience. Governor Bush had no statewide electoral experience before running for governor. In 1976, he ran for Congress in his "hometown" of Midland. He lost to Kent Hance, who later changed parties and won a seat on the Texas Railroad Commission as a Republican.

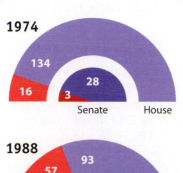

> Democratic Representative Steve Wolens and Republican Senator David Sibley look on as Texas Governor George W. Bush signs a bipartisan bill to deregulate the state's energy industry in 1999.

During the 1995 and 1997 sessions of the Texas legislature, Governor Bush developed a reputation as a bipartisan leader. This was in part due to the rather noncontroversial nature of his programs and prosperous economic times in the state. The legislature was faced not with the need to raise taxes but with the decision about what to do with a surplus.

1974

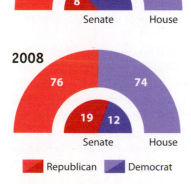

134
16
3
28
Senate
House

1988

57
93
8
23
Senate
House

2008

76
74
19
12
Senate
House

■ Republican ■ Democrat

FIGURE 22.2

Republican and Democratic Party Strength in the Texas Legislature, 1974, 1988, and 2008

In 1998, Governor Bush won reelection. His popularity also helped down-ballot candidates win election for all statewide executive offices and many judicial offices. For the first time in over 120 years, Texas voters elected Republicans to all but one statewide elected office. Figure 22.2 illustrates the gradual shift in power from the Democrats to the Republicans since the 1970s.

REPUBLICAN DOMINANCE AFTER BUSH

With the election of Governor George W. Bush as president, some speculated that his absence from state politics could make it easier for Democrats to regain some offices. Bush had received 67 percent of the popular vote in 1998. Rick Perry, who as lieutenant governor had succeeded Bush as governor in December 2000, had limited success filling the void left by Bush's departure. In 2002, Perry won the governorship in his own right with 57 percent of the vote. Facing conflict and controversy over issues such as school financing, redistricting, environmental issues, and the trans-Texas corridor, Perry's first term proved rocky. In 2006, with one Democratic and two independent challengers garnering significant electoral support, Perry won reelection with only 39 percent of the vote.

Speculations about the decline of the Republican Party proved false, however, with the party instead securing its dominant position in the state during this period. In the 2002 election, the Republican Party captured all statewide elected offices, controlled the Texas Senate, and, for the first time in 125 years, controlled the Texas

Total County Offices Held by Republicans, 1974–2008

TABLE 22.1

Year	County Office*
1974	53
1976	67
1978	87
1980	166
1982	270
1984	377
1986	504
1988	608
1990	717
1992	814
1994	900
1996	950
1998	973
2000	1,231
2002	1,327+
2004	1,390
2006	1,410
2008	1,345

*Estimates by the author. 2008 data were estimated by author on the basis of Democratic gains in Harris and Dallas counties.

SOURCES: *Houston Chronicle,* November 13, 1994, 16A. Copyright © 1994 Houston Chronicle Publishing Company. Reprinted with permission. All rights reserved. Figures for 1996 and 1998 from own sources. Data for 1996–2000 generated by the author. Data for 2002, 2004, and 2006 from the secretary of state's Web page.

ballot form
the forms used by voters to cast their ballot; in Texas, each county, with approval of the secretary of state, determines the form of the ballot

House. In both the 2004 and the 2006 elections, Republicans have maintained control over statewide offices and the legislatures.

In addition to electing statewide officeholders, the Republicans have made inroads into controlling locally elected offices, especially at the county level. As shown in Table 22.1, in 1990, Republicans controlled 717 local offices; by 2006, that number had increased to approximately 1,410.

Straight Ticket Voting

Each county in Texas decides the **ballot form** and method of casting ballots. In 2008, all counties in Texas used electronic voting systems. Formerly, paper ballots usually used a *party column format,* which lists candidates by party and by office. This type of ballot encouraged straight ticket voting and was strongly advocated by the Democratic Party for many years. Most computer ballots are *office block.* This ballot form lists the office (for example, president), followed by the candidates by party. The office block format is often advocated as a way of discouraging straight ticket voting. However, Texas law allows computer-readable ballots to enable voters to vote a straight ticket. By marking a single place on the ballot, the voter can vote for all candidates for that party. In recent years, straight ticket voting has worked to the advantage of the Republicans in some elections.

Democrats have increasingly been ousted through straight ticket voting. In Harris County in 1994, sixteen contested Democratic incumbents for district and county judges were replaced by straight ticket voting for Republican judges. By 2000, not one Democratic judge remained in office in Harris County. Straight ticket voting for the Republican Party continued to unseat even long-standing, experienced Democratic judges until 2006, when voters in Dallas County replaced most countywide elected officials with Democrats. Harris County followed suit in 2008, in part because of straight ticket voting.

Socioeconomic Factors in the Political Parties

Party realignment in Texas is in part the result of regional and national trends. There is more support nationally for Republicans, and this has an impact on Texas. Texas voters, like voters elsewhere in the Old South, have switched from the Democratic to the Republican Party. Immigration to Texas from other states has also helped the growth of the Republican Party. In addition, socioeconomic factors contribute to the dominance of the party.

In the 1950s and 1960s, Republicans began to gain strength in the suburban areas of Dallas and Houston, in oil-producing counties in East Texas, and in the Midland-Odessa area of West Texas. Voters in oil-producing areas supported Republican candidates largely because of national Republican Party policies that favored the oil industry. The suburban areas of Houston and Dallas contained many people who relocated from states with Republican loyalties.

Republican support is found today in the traditional areas and among young professionals and new immigrants to the state who have settled in the suburbs of Dallas/Fort Worth, Houston, and San Antonio. These new residents are not socialized into voting a straight Democratic ticket as older native Texans were. Republicans also draw disproportionately from young voters (see Table 22.2). The profile of the average Republican supporter in Texas would include the following: young, high income, well educated, Anglo, professional, living in the suburbs of a large metropolitan area. In addition, Republican voters are likely to be newcomers to the state. One study concluded that about one-fourth of Texas Republicans are new arrivals in the state.[9]

By contrast, the Democratic Party draws support from older residents, native Texans, the lower-income groups, the less educated, and minority groups, especially Mexican Americans in South Texas and African Americans in urban areas and East Texas. There is also some variation among religious groups, with Catholics, especially Catholic Mexican Americans, showing strong support for the Democratic Party and Protestant fundamentalists showing more support for the Republican Party.

Some Texans are concerned that party realignment will produce race-based political parties. The Republican Party's appeals to whites, especially appeals that have racial overtones, could drive most Mexican Americans and African Americans into the Democratic Party. According to Dick Murray, a political scientist at the University of Houston, in past elections, Democrats managed to get about 35 percent of the white vote. In 2002, Ron Kirk, the Democratic candidate for senator (who is black) received 31 percent of the white vote, and gubernatorial candidate Tony Sanchez received 27 percent of the white vote. Murray estimates that for every Latino voter the Democrats gain, they lose one white one.[10]

In the 1998 election, Governor Bush seemed to realize that Republicans must appeal to minority voters in order to remain the dominant party. He especially made appeals to Mexican American voters, and that effort may have paid off. He received about 40 percent of the Mexican American votes. That was not a significant change in how Mexican Americans vote, however. It was more a vote for Bush; to some degree the percentage Bush received was magnified by low voter turnout. Voter turnout will remain an issue as Texans debate the merits of requiring a voter ID card—the topic of this chapter's "Thinking Critically About Democracy."

As Texas becomes ever more a majority-minority state, these new participants (Latinos, African Americans, and Asians) may help Democratic candidates challenge the dominance of the Republican Party. Though Republicans claim to have made strong inroads into the Latino community, most Latinos and African Americans still show strong support for Democratic candidates. Historically, these groups have not voted in large numbers; yet in 2006, Latino and African American support allowed Democrats to capture most countywide offices in Dallas County for the first time in twenty years. Although some blamed a poor Republican turnout that was due to anger over immigration issues, Democratic straight ticket voting had been growing 2 to 3 percent every two-year election cycle since 1994. Whether Dallas County represents the beginning of a Democratic revival remains to be seen.

TABLE 22.2

Party Identification Among Texans by Socioeconomic Factors

	Republican, 39%	Democrat, 25%	Independent, 23%	Other, 10%
AGE				
18–29	41	25	22	7
30–39	43	23	19	13
40–49	43	21	18	15
50–59	39	24	26	9
60 and older	36	30	26	7
RACE/ETHNICITY				
Hispanic	26	34	29	8
Anglo	47	21	22	9
Black	8	58	17	12
GENDER				
Male	40	20	27	10
Female	29	30	18	10
REGION				
East	39	23	26	9
West	43	25	27	5
South	34	31	22	11
North	42	24	22	9
Gulf	47	28	18	7
Central	33	27	30	8
INCOME				
Less than $10,000	27	42	22	7
$10,001–$20,000	27	38	19	12
$20,001–$30,000	33	34	26	7
$30,001–$40,000	33	27	25	14
$40,001–$50,000	40	22	23	11
$50,001–$60,000	41	32	16	9
$60,001 and above	52	16	21	9
EDUCATION				
Some high school	29	40	20	8
High school grad	34	30	22	9
Some college	43	25	16	14
College grad	45	18	29	7
Graduate school	40	22	26	11

SOURCE: Texans poll, Scripps Howard News Service. Reprinted by permission.

THINKING CRITICALLY ABOUT DEMOCRACY

SHOULD TEXAS PASS A VOTER ID CARD LAW?

The Issue: Until the mid-1970s, Texas was known for its restrictive voter registration laws and policies. In the past, poll taxes, grandfather clauses, and other tactics have been used to keep citizens from voting. (See Chapters 5 and 21 for more on these methods.) In 1971, however, the state went from an annual to a permanent registration system. Today, Texas has a very open registration system. Voters can register "off site," meaning they do not have to appear in person at a courthouse or before some public official to register. They can simply fill in a postcard form and mail it, postage paid, to the local voter registrar. Because of these changes, Texans enjoy easy access to the ballot.

Some claim, however, that a new method to curtail voter fraud would restrict voter access: voter ID cards. Voter ID card laws require citizens who do not possess a government-issued photo ID, such as a driver's license or a passport, to purchase a digital voter ID card. The stated purpose of this requirement is to reduce voter fraud. In 2005, the Georgia legislature passed the first such law. Although the U.S. Justice Department approved the law, ruling that it did not violate the Voting Rights Act, the law was struck down by the U.S. Court of Appeals. In April 2008, however, the U.S. Supreme Court approved an Indiana voter ID card law, giving new life to the issue.

In the past two sessions of the Texas legislature, bills that would require voters to produce a photo ID with their voter registration card before they would be allowed to vote have cleared the House and stalled in the Senate. The legislature erupted in shouting matches and walkouts during debates over the voter ID law during the 2007 session. In the end, the Texas House had an interim committee studying the issue of voter fraud. During the 2009 legislative session, the Democrats successfully blocked Republican attempts to pass voter ID legislation.

Yes: Texas has long lacked the ability to detect in-person voter fraud. With the number of noncitizens living in Texas on the rise, the problem of voting fraud may increase significantly. These laws would inconvenience very few voters. In fact, in Indiana and Georgia, voter turnout actually increased following the passage of similar laws in those states.

No: Requiring photo IDs effectively disenfranchises the elderly, the homeless, the urban poor, and the disabled, who are less likely to have government-issued photo IDs such as driver's licenses. Requiring citizens to travel to government offices and pay for ID cards creates a barrier to voting. It would likely cause a significant drop-off in the number of citizens voting for Democratic candidates in state and national elections.

Other approaches: The state government could provide a free government-issued photo ID card to low-income individuals who cannot afford the cost of the ID. In addition, this service can be made available to individuals when they register to vote. The state government could also institute measures that prevent fraud resulting from off-site voter registration and mail-in ballots.

What do you think?

① What instances of voter fraud have you heard of or encountered yourself? Based on your personal experience, is voter fraud a significant problem?

② What solutions can you think of to the problems you know of? What solutions can you think of to problems with mail-in ballots and off-site voter registration?

③ Do you think requiring voter IDs is a good solution to the problem of voter fraud? Explain.

The Death of the Yellow Dog Democrat?

In 1995, Rick Perry, the Republican governor who was then state agricultural commissioner, pronounced, "Yellow Dog Democrats are dead."[11] Some Democrats disagree. Ed Martin, executive director of the Texas Democratic Party at that time, said, "Anybody who thinks Yellow Dogs are dead may be looking for tooth marks." Martin attributes much of the success of the Republicans in the Democratic stronghold of East Texas to hot-button issues: "They focus on hot-button issues, get Texans to look the other way while picking their pockets. The old saw is that Republicans have successfully used guns, gays, and God as polarizing wedges to define themselves. We have nothing equally emotional to define ourselves."[12]

If the Republican efforts to encourage straight ticket voting are successful, especially with younger Texans, perhaps Yellow Dogs are not so much dead as changed from Yellow Dog

Democrats to **Yellow Pup Republicans**— a nickname for younger voters who tend to vote straight ticket for Republicans. In the final analysis, this might not mean much in terms of a change in state policy. The traditionalistic-individualistic political culture has not changed and will not change any time soon. Texas is experiencing party realignment while maintaining continuity of political ideology.[13] The change can be described as a change in party label rather than change in ideology or policy.

An alternative view of party realignment, known as **party dealignment,** holds that the growing number of voters who do not identify with either party, but instead call themselves independent, indicates the low esteem for political parties and politics in general among American voters.[14] Many citizens do not see any difference in the two major parties and do not identify with either one.

Third-Party Movements in Texas

To date, third parties have not had much impact on Texas politics. The rules governing elections in Texas, as in many other states, do not make it easy for third parties to gain access to the ballot. To appear on the November general election ballot, candidates must meet criteria established by state law. These criteria prevent the lists of candidates from being unreasonably long. The Texas Election Code specifies three ways for names to be on the ballot through petitions, minor-party caucuses, and major-party conventions. Independents and third-party candidates either file petitions or are members of a minor party.

The Evolution of the Two-Party System in Texas

THEN (1960s)	NOW (2010)
One major party dominated Texas politics, and primary elections were more important than general elections.	Two major parties, one minor party, and independent candidates often compete in general elections.
Third parties were short-lived because their non-mainstream values were co-opted by one of the two major parties.	The Libertarian Party has grown in strength as a minor party, making gains chiefly at the local level. Its platform appeals to Texas's individualistic political culture.
The party organization played a significant role in the selection of candidates and the electioneering process.	The role of the party has declined as money and professional public relations become increasingly important in elections and interest groups have gained influence.

WHAT'S NEXT?

> Will the Republican Party face its major challenge from the Democratic Party, or will independent candidates and minor parties gain ground in the state?

> Will the Libertarian Party continue to grow as it appeals to Texans who embrace an individualistic political culture?

> Will digital fund-raising, groups that monitor government, and new laws limiting campaign contributions increase the role of individual citizens in the process of selecting candidates and electing them to office in Texas?

PETITIONS TO RUN FOR OFFICE To  run as an **independent candidate,** with no party affiliation, a person must file a petition with a specified number of signatures. For statewide office, signatures equal to 1 percent of the votes cast for governor in the last general election are required. For example, in the 2002 governor's race, a total of 4.5 million votes were cast. An independent candidate for statewide office in 2004 would have to collect 45,000 signatures. For multicounty offices, such as state representative, signatures equal to 5 percent of the votes cast for that office in the last election are needed. On the average, 30,000 to 40,000 votes are cast in House races.[15] For county offices, signatures equal to 5 percent of votes cast for those offices are needed. That may seem like a large number of signatures, but the process is intended to weed out people who do not have a serious chance of getting elected. Few candidates file for statewide office as independents. However, it is not uncommon for independents to run for Texas House and Senate races.

Getting signatures on a petition is not easy. Each signer must be a registered voter and must not have participated in the primary elections of other parties in that electoral

Yellow Pup Republicans
younger voters who tend to vote straight ticket for Republican candidates

party dealignment
the change from identifying with either major political party to identifying as independents

independent candidate
a person who has collected a required number of signatures on a petition to have her or his name appear on the ballot without a political party designation

cycle. For example, persons who voted in either the Democratic or the Republican Party primary in 1996 were not eligible to sign a petition to have Ross Perot's Reform Party on the ballot. Signing a petition is considered the same as voting. This provision of state law makes it all the more difficult for independents to get signatures and get on the ballot.

The 2006 governor's race in Texas was an exception to this. Both Carole Keeton Strayhorn, the current comptroller, and Kinky Friedman, a country-western singer and mystery writer, qualified for positions on the ballot as independents. Friedman and Strayhorn suffered the same fate as most independent and third-party candidates: They pulled enough votes away from the major-party candidates to upset the election outcome. Governor Perry won with a plurality of 38.1 percent, whereas Friedman had just 12.6 percent and Strayhorn, 18 percent. Chris Bell, the Democratic candidate, did better than expected with 30 percent. The role of the independent candidates was to help reelect an unpopular governor who, after six years in office, managed to get less than 40 percent of the votes.

Candidates defeated in the primary election may not file as independents in that year's general election. This is the "sore loser" law. In 2006, rather than run against Governor Perry in the Republican primaries, Carole Keeton Strayhorn chose to run as an independent.

Though they are sometimes confused with candidates who file and are listed on the ballot as independents, **write-in candidates** are not listed on the ballot, and the process of filing is a separate procedure. To be "official" write-in candidates, individuals must file their intention before the election. This is true for all elections, including local, city, and school board elections. If a person does not file before the election, votes for that person are not counted. For some state offices, a filing fee may be required to have a candidate's name listed on the ballot. The amount varies from $3,000 for statewide office to as little as $300 for local justices of the peace. People sometimes write in things like "Mickey Mouse" and "None of the above." These are recorded but not counted. In 1990, nineteen write-in candidates filed for governor. Bubbles Cash, a retired Dallas stripper, led the pack with 3,287 out of a total of 11,700 write-in votes.[16]

write-in candidate
a person whose name does not appear on the ballot; voters must write in the name, and the person must have filed formal notice before the election that she or he is a write-in candidate

MINOR-PARTY CAUCUS   The state election code defines a **minor party** (sometimes called a third party) as any political organization that receives between 5 and 19 percent of the total votes cast for any statewide office in the last general election. In the last fifty years, there have been three minor parties: the Raza Unida Party in South Texas in the 1970s,[17] the Socialist Workers Party in 1988, and the Libertarian Party in recent decades. Parties that achieve minor-party status must nominate their candidates in a party caucus or convention and are exempt from the petition requirement discussed previously.

Founded in 1971, the Libertarian Party of Texas has grown over the years to become a fairly stable third party. Over the past fifteen years, Libertarian candidates have served locally as city mayors and on city councils as well as other boards and commissions. In 2006, several statewide candidates received over 20 percent of the vote, securing their minor-party status for 2008. In 2008, the Libertarians once again secured their minor party status by receiving 18.1 percent of the vote in a statewide race for the Court of Criminal Appeals, as shown in Figure 22.3.

minor party
a party that receives 5 to 19 percent of the vote in any statewide election; candidates from minor parties are not required to file petitions to get on the ballot

The success of the Libertarian Party may be due in part to alignment of its platform with the individualistic political culture of the state. Libertarians oppose government spending and support the legalization of "open carry" firearms. However, the party's advocacy of other issues, such as the legalization of gambling, may not appeal to socially conservative Texans.[18]

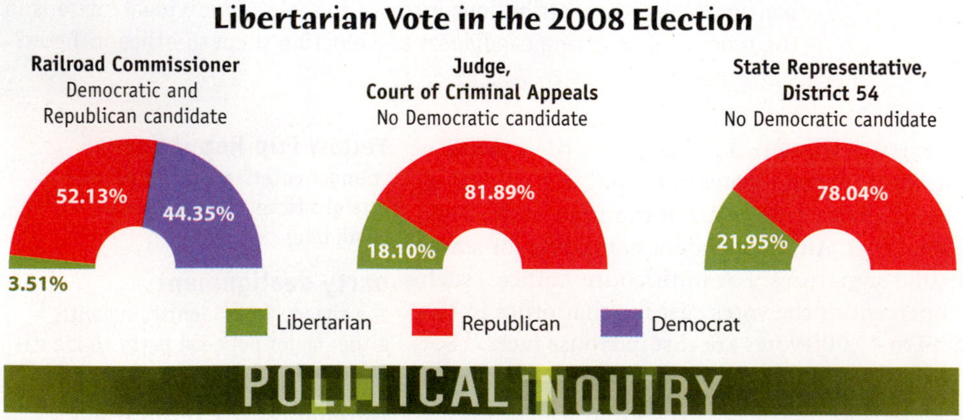

Libertarian Vote in the 2008 Election

Railroad Commissioner
Democratic and
Republican candidate

52.13%   44.35%   3.51%

Judge,
Court of Criminal Appeals
No Democratic candidate

81.89%   18.10%

State Representative,
District 54
No Democratic candidate

78.04%   21.95%

Libertarian   Republican   Democrat

POLITICAL INQUIRY

FIGURE 22.3 ■ In the competitive race for Railroad Commissioner, the Libertarian candidate only received 3.1 percent of the vote. In races where Democrats and Republicans competed, Libertarians received between about 2 percent and 5 percent of the vote. But in many races in which only one candidate from a major party competed, Libertarians sometimes garnered 20 percent or more of the vote. Why do you think this is so?

SOURCE: Office of the Secretary of State, Race Summary Report, 2008 General Election, http://elections.sos.state.tx.us/elchist.exe.

Party Organization in Texas

Political parties in all states have formal organizations. Their organizational structure is partly determined by state law, but parties have some discretion in deciding specific arrangements. Additionally, rules established by the national Democratic and Republican Party organizations might dictate state party actions in selected areas, such as the number of delegates to the national convention and how they are selected. In Texas, the Texas Election Code decides many aspects of party activity, especially the conduct of primary elections. Aside from these variations from state to state, party organization is basically the same for the Democratic and Republican parties.

In the past, the state executive committees of both parties were likely to be part-time organizations with limited staff. Today, both parties have a permanent headquarters, a full-time paid professional staff, and financial resources to help party development. They are actively engaged in organizing and building the party through voter identification and registration, candidate recruitment, candidate education, and get-out-the-vote drives, and in supporting candidates during the general election.

In all states, party organization falls into two broad categories: the permanent party organization and the temporary party organization. The **temporary party organization,** for both parties, consists of a series of conventions (caucuses) held in even-numbered years. We will examine this in the discussion of elections later in the chapter.

The **permanent party organization** consists of elected party officers. At the lowest level is the **precinct chair.** Each county in Texas is divided into voting precincts, or polling places. When voters register, they are assigned to a precinct-based polling place near their home.

The precinct chair is elected for a two-year term during the party's primary election. Any registered voter may file for precinct chair, and his or her name will be placed on the ballot. Occasionally, these races are contested, but more often the precinct chair is reelected without opposition. Write-in votes are allowed with no pre-election filing notice required. It is not uncommon for a person to win election by writing in his or her name. In 1976, Paul Van Riper, a professor of political science at Texas A&M, was elected precinct chair in Brazos County with one write-in vote, his own. In 1978, his name appeared on the ballot, and he was reelected with three votes.

Ideally, the role of the precinct chair is to organize the precinct, identify party supporters, make sure they are registered to vote, turn out voters on Election Day, and generally promote and develop the interests of the party at this level. In the one-party Democratic era in Texas, few precinct chairs performed those duties; generally their only duty was to serve as election judge during primary and general elections. As Texas developed into a two-party state, the role of the precinct chair changed from election judge to party organizer at the grassroots level in some counties; but neither party is well organized at the grassroots level. Precinct chairs often remain vacant.

The next office in the party hierarchy is **county chair.** This position is also filled during the primary election, and the person elected serves a two-year term. Any registered voter may file for the office. In large urban counties, this office is usually contested. Informally, the county chair's duties consist of representing the party in the county, serving as the official spokesperson for the party, maintaining a party headquarters (in some counties), and serving as a fund-raiser. Formally, the county chair is responsible for receiving formal filings from persons seeking to have their names placed on the party's primary election ballot, conducting the primary election, filling election judge positions, and officially counting the ballots in the primary election.

In large urban counties, the county chair is often a full-time paid employee whose job is to

temporary party organization
the series of conventions, or caucuses, that occur every two years at the precinct, county, and state levels

permanent party organization
the series of elected officers in a political party who keep the party organization alive between elections

precinct chair
party official elected in each voting precinct who organizes and supports the party

county chair
party official elected in each county to organize and support the party

> The role of precinct chair can sometimes lead in unexpected directions. In the March 2008 Democratic primary, for example, an angry group of Barack Obama supporters chased Dallas Precinct Chairwoman Sandra Crenshaw, who sought refuge in a police station. The crowd claimed Crenshaw was making off with sign-in sheets to the precinct convention. Crenshaw said she had been trying to make sure they were filled out correctly.

organize the party at the county level. This involves voter registration, fund-raising, candidate recruitment and education, and aiding in the election of candidates in the general election.

county executive committee
committee made up of the county chair and all precinct chairs in the county; serves as the official organization for the party in each county

The **county executive committee** is the next level in the permanent party organization. It is composed of all precinct chairs and the county chair. The degree of organization of this committee varies greatly from county to county. In some counties, the executive committee is an active organization that works to promote the party's interests. In many counties, especially in rural areas, this committee is more a paper organization that fulfills the formal duties of canvassing the election returns and filling vacancies in party offices when they occur.

Many large metropolitan counties use, instead of the county executive committee, a district executive committee for some functions. This is an organizational convenience because these counties have such large county committees. District committees are organized around the state senatorial districts.

state executive committee
a committee that is made up of one man and one woman elected from each state senatorial district and functions as the governing body of the party

The next level of permanent party organization is the **state executive committee.** From each of Texas's thirty-one senatorial districts, each party, by tradition, elects one man and one woman to serve on the state executive committee. Their election usually occurs during the state convention, which is traditionally held in June of even-numbered election years. Delegates to this convention caucus by senatorial district and elect their representative to the state executive committee; the state convention, as a whole, ratifies these choices.

Being selected to serve on the state executive committee is considered an honor, usually reserved for those who have strong political ties and who have supported the party for many years. Occasionally, a maverick group will surface and take control of the party, electing their people, who might not be the longtime party faithful. The Texas Republican Party experienced this type of insurgency from 1994 to 2002, when the Christian Right took control of the party; it has maintained that control for the last decade.

The state convention also elects a state party chair and vice chair; one must be a woman. Traditionally in the Democratic Party, the governor or gubernatorial candidate chose the state chair and vice chair, and the state chair office was often filled by the governor's campaign manager. With the rise of the Republican Party, the state chair is not the automatic choice of the governor; however, the party candidate for governor still has influence in deciding who the state party chair will be.

At the state level, the functions of the state chair and the state executive committee are very similar to those of the county chair and the county executive committee. They have similar informal duties of organizing the party and formal duties of conducting primary elections. Both parties in Texas have permanent, full-time, paid professional staffs that do most of the work at the state level. The state chair and executive committee are policy-making positions. Their main function should be to provide leadership for the party.

Party Strength

As discussed in Chapter 8, party strength has plummeted over the past century. In Texas, neither party has a strong party organization or a strong grassroots organization. Candidates can operate independently of any party and capture a nomination without party support. One high-profile example of this independence came in 1996 when unknown Dallas schoolteacher Victor Morales gained the Democratic Party nomination for the U.S. Senate without support from party officials. Crisscrossing the state in his beat-up pickup truck, he presented a serious challenge to Republican Senator Phil Gramm. Despite his loss in this race and a few that followed, in 2008 Morales ran unsuccessfully for a seat in the Texas House of Representatives. Morales's case points to the role of media attention in the Texas electoral system.

A number of factors contribute to the reduced role parties play today in state politics. The primary system and changes in this system have weakened the parties. Not only do parties no longer control candidate selection, but parties also no longer perform traditional functions pertaining to campaigning, fund-raising, and elections. Other institutions, such as interest groups, professional campaign managers, and the media, have assumed those functions. This changing nature of parties in Texas is not unique to the state but part of a much larger national change in the role played by political parties. ("Analyzing the Sources" looks at the role of institutional donors in comparison with parties in helping to pay for political campaigns.)

ANALYZING THE SOURCES

TOP DONORS TO POLITICAL CANDIDATES

Institutional donors of all types are playing an increasingly important role in financing political campaigns. In the 2008 elections, Republican and Democratic parties accounted for only 11.8 percent of donations by large institutional donors of $150,000 or more. A large portion of the rest of the campaign money from institutional donors came from political action committees (PACs) representing various interest groups. The pie chart shows the overall percentage of donations from the two parties and donations from large institutional donors. The table shows the top ten institutional donors for that year.

Evaluating the Evidence

① Among the large institutional donors, what type of interest group has donated the most to the candidates? Why do you think this group has done so? What issues do you think these interest groups might want legislatures to address? What reforms do you think they want to see passed by the legislature?

② How do you think the parties' relatively small contributions to their campaigns will affect their influence on the candidates?

③ Some powerful legislators have helped organize PACs that contribute to the campaigns of other candidates of their party. How might this practice affect the party itself? Would it strengthen or weaken the party?

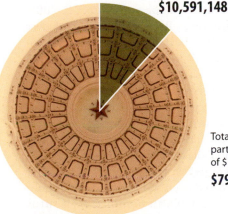

Donations by Republican or Democratic parties:

$10,591,148

Total donations by non-party institutional donors of $150,000 or more:

$79,197,525

Total donations by institutional donors of $150,000 or more:

$89,788,673

RANK	TOTAL	CONTRIBUTOR	CITY	INTEREST GROUP
1	$8,682,460	Texas Assn. of Realtors (TREPAC)	Austin	Real Estate
2	$7,962,096	Kay Bailey Hutchison for Senate	Austin	Other
3	$4,170,072	Texas Democratic Trust	Austin	Ideological/ Single Issue
4	$3,928,268	Texans for Lawsuit Reform (TLR)	Austin	Ideological/ Single Issue
5	$2,804,667	Republican Party of Texas	Austin	Ideological/ Single Issue
6	$2,389,828	Texans for Insurance Reform	Austin	Lawyers & Lobbyists
7	$2,007,357	Tom Craddick Campaign	Midland	Other
8	$1,757,872	AT&T	Austin	Communications
9	$1,536,025	Texas Medical Association (TEXPAC)	Austin	Health
10	$1,326,493	Texas Friends of Time Warner Cable	Houston	Communications

SOURCE: Texans for Public Justice, "Money in PoliTex, A Guide to Money in the 2008 Texas Legislative Elections," http://info.tpj.org/reports/politex08/donors08.html#topinstitutionaldonors.

Primary Elections

major party
any organization receiving 20 percent or more of the total votes cast for governor in the last election

The Texas Election Code defines a **major party** as any organization receiving 20 percent or more of the total votes cast for governor in the last election. Obviously, only the Democratic and Republican parties hold this status today. By law, these party organizations must nominate their candidates in primary elections. Chapter 9 discussed open primaries, in which all registered voters can vote regardless of party affiliation, and closed primaries, which are closed to all voters except those who have registered as a member of the party holding the primary. In addition, **semiclosed primaries** allow voters to register or change their party registration on Election Day. Registration as a member of a party is required on Election Day. Texas holds a **semiopen primary,** in which the voter may choose to vote in the primary of either party on Election Day. Voters are considered "declared" for the party in whose primary they vote. If you vote in the Republican Party primary, you are in effect declaring that you are a member of that party. You may not participate in any activity of any other party for the remainder of that election year.

semiclosed primary
a primary that allows voters to register or change their party registration on Election Day; registration as a member of a party is required on Election Day

semiopen primary
a nominating election in which registered voters can choose which primary to vote in on Election Day

In the past, Alaska, California, and Washington used a blanket primary, which allowed voters to switch parties between offices. A voter might vote in the Republican primary for the races for governor and U.S. House, and in the Democratic primary for the U.S. Senate race. The U.S. Supreme Court has ruled such primaries unconstitutional. Alaska currently uses a closed primary with voter registration by party, and California has adopted an open primary system. Washington has adopted Louisiana's system of a nonpartisan primary for all statewide and U.S. House and Senate races. Under this system, all candidates are listed on the ballot by office. The voter can choose one candidate per office. If no person receives a majority, the top two candidates face each other in a runoff. "How Texas Compares" shows the different types of primaries held in the fifty states.

Crossover Voting

The primary system used in a state may affect the party system in the state. Advocates of the closed primary system say that it encourages party identification and loyalty, and therefore helps build stronger party systems. Open primary systems, they say, allow participation by independents with no loyalty to the party, which weakens party organization. There is no strong evidence that this is the case.

crossover voting
a voting pattern in which voters from one party vote in the primaries of another party

Open primaries do allow voters to leave their party and vote in the other party's primary—a practice known as **crossover voting.** Occasionally, voters in one party might vote in the other party's primary in hopes of nominating a candidate from the other party whose philosophy is similar to their own. For example, Republicans have been accused of voting in the Democratic primary in Texas to ensure that a conservative will be nominated. In 2008, well-known right-wing radio host Rush Limbaugh urged Texas Republicans to cross over and vote for Democratic presidential candidate Hillary Clinton. Exit polls showed that approximately 9 percent of voters in the Democratic primary were Republican; however, 53 percent of them favored Democratic presidential candidate Barack Obama, not Clinton.[19]

From 1996 to 2002, more Texans voted in the Republican primaries than in the Democratic primaries. Republicans claimed that this was evidence that their party was the majority party. Democrats suggest that these differences in turnout are explained by the low levels of opposition in the Democratic primaries. For instance, President Clinton did not have any opposition in his primary election, whereas Bob Dole and Pat Buchanan were still actively seeking the Republican nomination; some Democratic Party leaders claim that many traditional Democratic Party voters, therefore, crossed over and voted in the Republican primary in an attempt to affect who would be the Republican nominee. As it turns out, the Democrats' explanation may be the more accurate. In the 2002 primary election, 400,000 more people voted in the Democratic Party primary than in the Republican Party primary. The difference is due almost entirely to the lack of contested races in the Republican primary and the highly contested races for U.S. Senate and governor in the Democratic primary. Governor Perry had no opponents, and John Cornyn had little opposition for the

HOW TEXAS COMPARES

PRIMARY SYSTEMS USED IN STATE ELECTIONS

The map shows the different types of primary elections used by the states. Southern states tend to have open or semiopen primaries because of their history of modified one-party systems in which winning the primary election was tantamount to winning the general election. How does Texas compare with other southern states?

Closed Primary:
Party registration required before election day

Semiclosed Primary:
Voters may register or change registration on election day

Semiopen Primary: Voters required to request party ballot

Open Primary: Voters may vote in any party primary

Nonpartisan: Voters may switch parties between races

SOURCE: "Primary Election Systems," National Conference of State Legislatures, June 2010, www.ncsl.org/Documents/legismgt/elect/Primary_Types_Table_2010.pdf.

U.S. Senate seat. Elections since that time have shown this same tendency: Crossover voting seems to be caused by voters' attraction to competitive races.

Conventions—Election of Delegates, from Precinct to State Level

As discussed earlier, the temporary party organization, for both parties, consists of a series of conventions (caucuses) held in even-numbered years. The precinct convention is held on the same day as the party primary. Any voter who has voted in that party's primary is eligible to attend the precinct convention. This primary/precinct convention has been dubbed "the Texas two-step," essentially giving voters a chance to vote twice. Usually, the precinct chair is elected permanent chair of the convention, and her or his temporary appointees for vice chair and secretary are usually selected as permanent officers. Sometimes, especially during presidential election years, control of the convention's officers becomes an issue.

After officers are elected, the most important function of the convention is the selection of delegates to the county convention, or the district convention in large metropolitan counties. The number of delegates a precinct sends to the county convention is based on party support in that precinct—the higher the turnout in previous elections, the larger the number of delegates. If a candidate is represented by a larger number of convention attendees than her or his rival, more delegates will be pledged to that candidate. During presidential election years, many people are interested in attending the county convention, and the seats can be hotly contested. In 2008, Hillary Clinton won nearly 51 percent of the popular vote in the primary, yet Barack Obama's supporters managed to capture 56 percent of the

state's precinct convention delegates. The Clinton campaign contested the results, citing over 2,000 complaints of violations and requesting that the eligibility of the 1 million attendees be double-checked.[20]

The county or district convention is a replay of the precinct convention. Selection of delegates to the state convention is its most important function. The state convention is normally held in June of even-numbered years. Normally, the convention is held in a major city and moved around to different cities for political reasons. At the state convention during presidential election years, the most important event is the selection of delegates to the national convention that nominates the party's candidate for president. Texas uses a **presidential preference primary,** held in March. The primary decides the presidential preference of most, but not all, of the delegates from Texas at the national convention. Without presidential preference primary elections, all delegate preferences would be decided at the state convention.

In addition to the state party officers chosen at these state conventions, during presidential election years these conventions also elect the representatives (electors) who will serve in the Electoral College if their party candidate wins the popular vote in Texas. By tradition, Texas Democratic delegates caucus by senatorial districts at the state convention and choose their elector. Republicans caucus by U.S. congressional districts. These decisions are ratified by the convention as a whole.[21] Those chosen to serve in the Electoral College are generally longtime party supporters. The electors of the party winning the popular vote meet in Austin, in the Senate Chamber, on the first Monday after the second Wednesday in December following their election, and cast their vote.[22]

Runoff Primary Elections

Eleven southern and border states, plus South Dakota, hold **runoff primaries,** which are required if no candidate receives a majority in the first primary. Until recently in the South, winning the Democratic Party primary was the same as winning the general election, and the runoff primary became a fixture, supposedly as a way of requiring the winner to have "majority" support. In reality, voter turnout in the runoff primary is always lower than in the first primary, sometimes substantially lower. The "majority" winner is often selected by a small percentage of the electorate, those who bother to participate in the runoff primary.

Racial and ethnic minority candidates have challenged the runoff primary system in these eleven states. They charge that because voter turnout decreases in the runoff and mi-

presidential preference primary

election held every four years by political parties to determine the preferences of delegates for presidential candidates

runoff primary

election required if no person receives a majority in the primary election; primarily used in southern and border states

norities are less likely to vote in runoff elections, the system is racially biased. The only evidence available suggests that this might not be the case. A study in Georgia examined 215 runoff elections between 1965 and 1982 and found no support for racial bias in runoff primary elections.[23]

Delegate Selection Systems

For the past seven presidential elections, Texas has used a primary system to determine the preferences of most, but not all, of the state delegates to the national convention. In states without presidential preference primaries, such as Iowa, precinct conventions (also called caucuses) take on greater significance. Delegates selected at the precinct level go to the county level and eventually to the state and national conventions. A well-organized group, such as the Moral Majority, can take control of these caucuses. In 1988, Republican presidential hopeful Pat Robertson used his organization and worked with local churches to win more delegates than any other candidate in the Iowa caucuses. Republican presidential candidate Pat Buchanan also benefited from these organizations in the 1996 Iowa caucuses. Churches become a rallying point before the evening caucus. Potluck dinners, child care services, and church buses that help deliver voters to precinct conventions produce a turnout that exceeds the candidate's actual support among the voting population. By contrast, the Iowa media campaign of Buchanan's Republican rival, Steve Forbes, had little effect in 1996.

> Bill White shakes hands with a supporter in Waco after winning the primary to become the democratic candidate in the 2010 governor's race.

Thus, a caucus system can be an effective way to win delegates to conventions. However, it requires an organization of active volunteers to produce results. Win enough delegates to enough precinct conventions, and you can take over the county. Win enough counties, and you control the state. Control the state, and you select the delegates to the national convention. Control enough states, and you might win the nomination for president.

If Texas were to change from a preference primary to a caucus system, different campaign organization and strategies would be required. Preference primaries are mass media events that require big money and professional organizations. Caucus systems require grassroots organizations and dedicated volunteers. In Texas, during a number of Republican state conventions, some Christian organizations have called for an end to preference primaries and a return to a caucus system of selecting delegates to the national convention. Obviously, the caucus system is in their best interest and would allow them to control most of the delegates to the national convention. If the Texas caucus were held early enough in the election process, it might affect the direction of the Republican presidential race or, at least, give the winner some early exposure.

The Administration of Primary Elections

In the past, primary elections were considered functions of private organizations, and the state did not regulate them. As we discussed in Chapter 21, courts have ruled that political parties are not private organizations and their functions are subject to control by state law. The Texas Election Code governs primary elections. Technically, elections are administered by the local county chair and executive committee and by the state party officials at the state level; however, the Texas Election Code and the secretary of state oversee administration of elections to ensure that rules are followed, and the party has only limited discretion in these elections.

Although voter fraud is a significant concern for many Texans, few individuals have been charged with violating the Texas Election Code. In early 2006, an election held in Duval County for county judge attracted statewide concern: A whopping 55 percent of voters had turned out for the local election. A high voter turnout is usually welcomed in democratic systems, but this large turnout was not. A highly contested sheriff's race in Nueces County had recently inspired only 11 percent of registered voters to go the polls.[24] Voting fraud was suspected, and eventually, four women in Duval County were charged with mail-in ballot fraud.

Campaigns and Elections

Campaign activity in Texas has changed considerably in the past two or three decades. These changes are not unique to Texas but are part of a national trend. Norman Brown, in his book on Texas politics, describes the form of political campaigning that once took place in the state as "local affairs."[25] Candidates would travel from county seat to county seat and give "stump" speeches to political rallies arranged by local supporters. Brown devotes special attention to the campaigns of Governors Jim and Miriam Ferguson ("Ma" and "Pa" Ferguson). Jim Ferguson, when campaigning for himself and later for his wife, would travel from county to county, telling each group what they wanted to hear—often saying different things in different counties. Brown contends that Ferguson and other candidates could do this because of the lack of a statewide press to report on these inconsistencies in such political speeches.

The Role of the Media

In modern-day Texas, the media play a significant role in political campaigns. Reporters often follow candidates for statewide office as they travel the vast expanses of Texas. Political rallies are still held but are most often used to gain media attention and convey the candidate's message to a larger audience. Candidates hope these events will attract media attention and convey a favorable image of them to the public.

Heavy media coverage can have its disadvantages for the candidates. For instance, in 1990 Clayton Williams, the Republican candidate for governor, held a media event on one of his West Texas ranches. He and "the boys" were to round up cattle for branding in a display designed to portray Williams as a hardworking rancher. Unfortunately for Williams, rain spoiled the event and it had to be postponed. Resigned to the rain delay, Williams told the reporters, "It's like rape. When it's inevitable, relax and enjoy it." The state press had a field day with that remark, and it probably hurt Williams's chances with many voters. The fact that his opponent was a woman (Ann Richards) helped to magnify the significance of the statement. In June 2008, Republican presidential candidate John McCain hastily canceled a fund-raiser that was to be hosted by Williams after learning of the remark.

In 1994, George W. Bush was the Republican candidate for governor running against incumbent Ann Richards. In Texas, the opening day of dove season is in September, and the event marks the beginning of the fall hunting season. Both Bush and Richards participated in opening-day hunts in an attempt to appeal to the strong hunting and gun element in the state. Unfortunately for Bush, by mistake he shot a killdeer rather than a dove. Pictures of Bush holding the dead bird appeared in most state papers and on television. He was fined for shooting a migratory bird. A Texas Democratic group in Austin produced bumper stickers reading "Guns don't kill killdeer. People do." In 1998, Governor Bush did not have a media event for the opening day of dove season. He was so far ahead in the polls that even opening the issue could result in nothing but a painful reminder.

TELEVISION ADS   Most campaign events are not as disastrous as the cattle-branding and dove-hunting incidents. Some gain attention and free media coverage for the candidate; however, free media attention is never enough. Candidates must purchase time on television and radio and space in newspapers. In a state as large as Texas, this can be quite costly. Candidates try to make the most of the expensive time they purchase by conveying simple messages. This has led to the **sound-bite commercial,** a thirty-second message that the candidate hopes will be remembered by the voters. This is not unique to Texas but occurs nationwide.

These sound bites can be classified into at least five types. The feel-good spot lacks substance or issues and is designed to make the public feel good about the candidate or the party. In 1988, President George H. W. Bush

sound-bite commercial
a brief, usually thirty-second, TV political advertisement that conveys a simple and memorable message about the candidate or the opponent

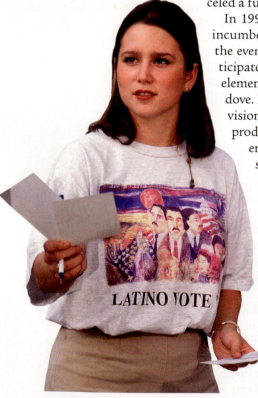

told us he saw "a thousand points of light." Others, including Clayton Williams, say, "Share my vision." In 1998, Governor George W. Bush ran a number of TV spots that asked voters to support his effort to have every child read and become a productive member of society.

Sainthood spots try to depict the candidate as having saintly qualities:[26] "Senator Smith is a Christian family man, Eagle Scout, Little League coach, Sunday School teacher, involved, concerned, committed, community leader who fights the people's fights. Let's keep him working for us."

Good ol' boy (or good ol' girl) spots are testimonials from other citizens about the candidate. In a staged "person on the street" interview, the citizen says something like, "Senator Smith is the most effective leader this state has seen since Sam Houston. He's so effective it's frightening. He is committed to his job, and we need him to fight the coming battles with the liberals." In Texas, cattle and horses in the background provide a down-to-earth backdrop for ranchers' good ol' boy testimonials.

NOOTS ("No one's opposed to this") commercials are also common. In these ads, candidates take courageous stands on issues everyone supports: sound fiscal management, planned orderly growth, good schools, open government, getting tough on crime, no new taxes, and so on.

Basher spots are the last type. In these, candidates play on voters' emotions by painting their opponent in a very unfavorable light. If the opponent is a lawyer, the candidate can point out that he or she defends criminals. Candidates can point out that their opponent has received money from controversial organizations. Governor Rick Perry, running for secretary of agriculture in 1990, defeated Democratic incumbent Jim Hightower. In one of his commercials, Perry claimed that Hightower had once visited the home of Jane Fonda, often used as a symbol for the radical war protesters of the 1960s because of her visit to Hanoi during the Vietnam War. When pressed for details on the visit, Perry said that Hightower had visited Los Angeles and that Los Angeles was the home of Jane Fonda.

Basher spots have developed into a fine art. Newt Gingrich, former speaker of the U.S. House, extended the art when he used his GOPAC political action committee to help "train local Republican candidates." In 1990, GOPAC mailed a 131-word glossary to over 4,000 state Republican candidates. This glossary included a list of "optimistic positive governing words" that Republican candidates should use to describe themselves and a list of "contrasting negative words" they should use to describe their opponents. Republicans are described as having common sense and Democrats as big-spending liberals, for example.

These types of advertisements are used because most often they work to the advantage of the candidate. Occasionally, basher spots can backfire on the candidate. These ads plant in the voter's mind a simple message that they carry into the voting booth. Most citizens do not spend much time studying issues or candidates' backgrounds. They often depend entirely on advertisements for information. Though the news media often denounce such ads, the media (which receives most of the money spent in campaigns) do not refuse to run them.

THE INTERNET Texas candidates have been increasingly turning to the Internet to raise funds and widen their base of support. When Democrat Mark Strama ran for the Texas House of Representatives in 2004, he started a summer program directed primarily at high school and college students called Mark Strama's Campaign Academy. Strama attracted students by organizing luncheons with prominent speakers involved in different aspects of local, state, and national politics. In exchange, students campaigned for Strama, utilizing the Internet to galvanize support. They came up with campaign slogans such as "No Drama with Strama: Mark Represents ALL of District 50!" and posted them on their blog. They figured out how to use social-networking Web sites such as FaceBook and MySpace to spread the word. Strama's Campaign Academy has been a key factor in his success in subsequent elections.

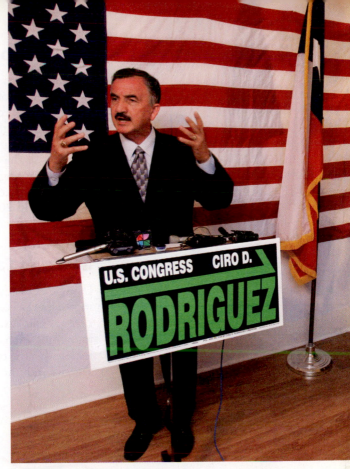

> In a 2003 runoff election, U.S. Representative Henry Bonilla charged Democratic challenger Ciro Rodriguez with meeting with and taking contributions from Islamic radicals. In a surprising upset, Rodriguez won the election. Here, Rodriguez responds to Bonilla's charges. How does Rodriguez make use of symbols in his response?

Political Consultants

As discussed in Chapter 9, the use of professional campaign consultants, or "hired guns," is becoming more common both nationally and in Texas. Most candidates find it necessary to have such professionals help run their campaigns. If their opponents use professionals, candidates might be at a disadvantage without one. Among the many techniques professional campaign consultants use are public opinion polls, which measure voter reaction to issues so the candidate knows what stands to take. They run **focus groups,** in which a panel of "average citizens" is asked to react to issues or words. Consultants also help the candidate in the design of written and visual advertisements, "packaging" the candidate to the voters. In 2002, David Dewhurst filmed a TV spot for his consulting firm in which he praised its effectiveness in making him look professional during his campaign.

focus group

opinion research technique in which a panel of "average citizens" is asked to react to issues or words

Money in Campaigns

Using media advertisements, professional consultants, and a full-time paid campaign staff increases the cost of running for state office. The cost can run into the millions even for a race for the Texas House of Representatives. The amount of money spent in campaigns is increasing each election cycle. Most of this money comes from PACs. Figure 22.4 shows the increase in the total amount of money contributed by PACs from 1996 to 2008. As you can see, the amount more than doubled during this twelve-year period.

Money supplied by PACs obviously has an impact on elected officials. At the least, PAC money buys the group access to the official. At the worst, PAC money buys the vote of the elected official. Distinguishing between the two is almost impossible. Most states, including Texas, have passed laws designed to regulate campaign finances. Many other states have passed laws limiting the amount of money that could be spent on campaigns, but these laws have been invalidated by the U.S. Supreme Court.

Statewide races can be so costly that few candidates have the resources to self-finance their campaigns. One notable exception is Tony Sanchez, the Democratic candidate for governor in 2002. In that year, Sanchez self-financed $27 million (89 percent of his total campaign costs) and received campaign contributions totaling $3.5 million.[27] In that same election year, Governor Rick Perry raised almost $31.5 million from PACs.[28]

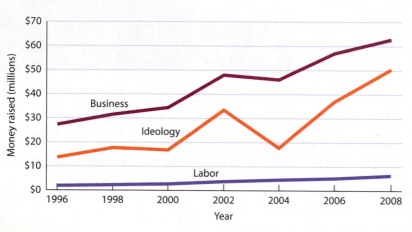

FIGURE 22.4

Total Money Raised by PACs, 1996–2008

SOURCE: Texans for Public Justice, "Texas PACs: 2008 Election Cycle Spending," www.tpj.org.

Candidates sometimes lend themselves money that they can later repay with what are sometimes called "late train" contributions. Special interest groups will seldom retire the debt of losers. The law limits the amount of money that a candidate can collect to retire personal campaign debts for each election (primary, runoff, general) to $500,000 in personal loans. In 2002, several candidates far exceeded this amount in personal loans. The leaders were gubernatorial candidate Tony Sanchez with $22,262,662 in personal loans and lieutenant governor-elect David Dewhurst with $7,413,887 in outstanding debt.[29]

All elected officials hope to keep part of the money they raise in a war chest, which can have the effect of forcing likely opponents to think twice before running against them. Also, candidates without opponents for many years, such as speaker of the house, may contribute part of their war chests to House candidates in hope of getting or keeping their support.

Today, the regulation of campaign finances in Texas is limited to requiring all candidates and PACs to file reports with the Texas State Ethics Commission. All contributions of over $50 must be reported with the name of the contributor. An expenditure report must also be filed. These reports must be filed before and after the election. The idea behind the reporting scheme is to make public the sources of the funds received by candidates and how the candidates spend their funds. Sometimes these reports are examined closely by the news media

HOW TEXAS COMPARES

LIMITATIONS ON CAMPAIGN CONTRIBUTIONS BY PACs IN STATEWIDE RACES

Texas places no limit on the amount of money PACs can spend for statewide races, but many states do. The map shows these spending limitations.

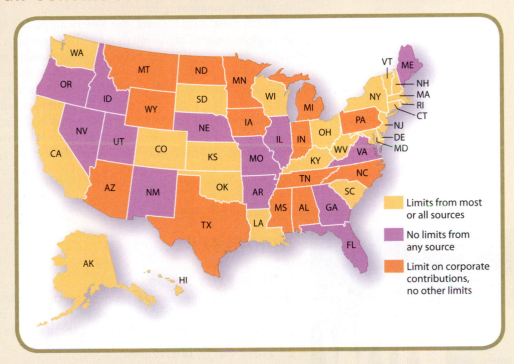

Limits from most or all sources

No limits from any source

Limit on corporate contributions, no other limits

SOURCE: National Conference of State Legislatures, Limits on Contributions to Political Parties, updated February 5, 2008, www.ncsl.org/default.aspx?tabid=16552.

and are given significant media coverage, but this is not common. Citizens mostly are left to find out such information on their own, which is difficult for the average citizen. Texas has no limit on the amount of money candidates can spend for statewide races, but many states do. The "How Texas Compares" feature here shows state limitations. Compare this map with "How Texas Compares: Political Culture in the States" in Chapter 19.

CONCLUSION

THINKING CRITICALLY ABOUT WHAT'S NEXT IN ELECTIONS IN TEXAS

Although the Republican Party has gained control of all three branches of state government in Texas, it has not attained the complete control over the system that the Democratic Party enjoyed throughout most of the twentieth century. The future of each party in the state depends on demographic changes and the Latino vote. George W. Bush was able to pull Latinos into the Republican camp by emphasizing socially conservative values. If Rick

Perry and future Republican leaders are not as successful in this regard and Latino turnout increases, the Democratic Party could well experience a revival. However, economic development in trade and industry is attracting a large population from other states that represents conservative business interests. Since this group tends to have a high voter turnout, it could counteract any gains the Democratic Party makes because of the minority vote.

As the Democratic Party lost ground, minor parties also arose to challenge its hold on power—at least at the local level. Since the 1970s, the Libertarian Party has established increasingly strong roots in Texas. The party's ideology appeals to those who espouse an individualistic political culture. But unlike the two major parties, the Libertarians do not accept assistance from special interests. Hence, they face both financial and political obstacles in campaigning for statewide elections.

In the past several years, the American public has begun to demand that federal and state governments cap campaign contributions as a means of limiting the influence of special interests. Texas is not a leader in this movement, but other states have enacted regulations. As more candidates use the Internet to appeal to individual voters for smaller campaign contributions, will elected officials become more responsive to the electorate and less beholden to large interest groups? What impact will the use of the Internet have on party organization? Will political parties continue to wane as candidates solicit funds through political blogs and Web sites? Or will individuals use new technologies to strengthen party organization? Whatever the impact of these new regulations and technology, it will likely be felt first in other states before it reaches Texas.

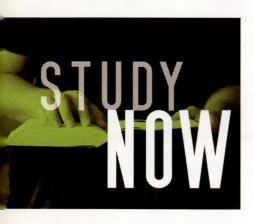

Summary

1. State Party Systems
State party systems can be classified as either two-party competitive systems, in which both parties vie for control of the legislature and statewide offices, or modified one-party systems, in which one party dominates those offices.

2. State Party Ideologies
Great differences can exist between national parties and state parties. For several decades, many southern states have voted for the Democratic Party in state elections while supporting the Republican Party nationally. The Democratic Party in Texas has traditionally contained both conservative and liberal elements.

3. Political Parties in Texas
After the Civil War, the Democratic Party controlled all important positions in the government. In response to the New Deal and Republican policies that favored the oil industry, Texas voters began to support Republican candidates in presidential elections. Newcomers from other states, Protestant fundamentalists, and young people provided the socioeconomic basis for the growth of the Republican Party. By the late 1980s, Texas had become a two-party state, with each party vying for control of statewide offices. In 2002, Republicans captured all statewide elected offices, and Texas became a modified one-party Republican state.

4. Party Organization in Texas
Parties are organized hierarchically from the precinct to the county to the state level. Control of party organization is left to the few active elites of the party. However, any citizen can become active in party activities.

5. Primary Elections
Because historically there was no party competition, primary elections became more important than general elections. In Texas, the primary consists of a general popular election and a series of conventions, starting with the precinct convention. Both the popular vote in the election and the participants in the precinct conventions determine the number of delegates a candidate receives.

6. Campaigns and Elections

Texas has a two-year election cycle. Unlike other states, most important positions within the executive branch and much of the judiciary are elected rather than appointed. As in other states, campaigns in Texas have become media affairs dominated by political consultants, sound-bite ads, and money.

Key Terms

ballot form 654

county chair 659

county executive committee 660

crossover voting 662

focus group 668

independent candidate 657

major party 662

minor party 658

modified one-party state 648

party dealignment 657

party ideology 649

party realignment 652

permanent party organization 659

precinct chair 659

presidential preference primary 664

runoff primary 664

semiclosed primary 662

semiopen primary 662

Shivercrats 651

sound-bite commercial 666

state executive committee 660

straight ticket voting 651

temporary party organization 659

two-party competitive state 648

write-in candidate 658

Yellow Dog Democrats 651

Yellow Pup Republicans 657

For Review

1. How has the party system in Texas changed since the Civil War?

2. How is it possible that the Republican Party took control of the legislature and all statewide offices without instituting significant changes in public policy?

3. Why did the Democratic Party maintain control of Texas politics until the 1980s?

4. What factors account for the rise of the Republican Party in Texas?

5. What role have minor parties played in Texas politics?

6. What is the permanent party organization?

7. What type of primary elections does Texas have? Explain how this type of electoral system works.

8. What is the role of money in political campaigns in Texas, and why has it become increasingly important?

For Critical Thinking and Discussion

1. Do you think that Texas will become a two-party competitive state in the near future? Cite trends that support your point of view.

2. What effect has straight ticket voting had on elections and the party system? What would happen if Texans were not given the option of straight ticket voting?

3. What are the advantages and disadvantages of requiring independent candidates to gather signatures on a petition before they are allowed to run? Do you agree with this practice?

4. What do you think would be the best primary system for Texas? Justify your answer.

5. Design a sound-bite commercial for your favorite political candidate. What approach would you use to persuade voters to support your candidate?

PRACTICE QUIZ

MULTIPLE CHOICE: Choose the lettered item that answers the question correctly.

1. In which region of the United States have recent changes in party competitive patterns been most drastic?
   a. northeastern   c. southern
   b. midwestern   d. west coast

2. Which of the following describes the Texas political system from the 1880s to the 1960s?
   a. modified one-party Democratic state
   b. modified one-party Republican state
   c. two-party competitive state
   d. none of the above

3. How has Texas's move from a one-party Democratic-controlled state to one dominated by the Republicans affected its general philosophy and policies?
   a. no change
   b. slight move to the right
   c. strong move to the right
   d. strong move to the left

4. Texas's period of anti-Republicanism can be traced back to which period(s)?
   a. the American Revolution
   b. the Civil War and Reconstruction
   c. the Great Depression
   d. the civil rights movement

5. The national policy that first led Texas voters to vote for Republican presidential candidates is
   a. the Civil War.
   b. the New Deal.
   c. the civil rights movement.
   d. Reaganomics.

6. In the late 1980s, Republicans made significant gains in Texas politics. Which of the following is not an example?
   a. Bill Clements's return as governor
   b. John Tower's election to the U.S. Senate
   c. George H. W. Bush's election to the presidency
   d. Kent Hance's election to the Texas Railroad Commission

7. Texas has a _____ primary system.
   a. semiclosed   c. closed
   b. blanket   d. semiopen

8. Most of the funding for political campaigns in Texas is provided by
   a. political consultants.
   b. political parties.
   c. special interest groups.
   d. the candidates themselves.

9. Which of the following lists the levels of permanent party organization from highest to lowest?
   a. county chair, county executive committee, precinct chair, state executive committee
   b. state executive committee, county executive committee, county chair, precinct chair
   c. precinct chair, county chair, county executive committee, state executive committee
   d. state executive committee, county chair, county executive committee, precinct chair

10. In the Texas primary, the mechanism that determines the number of delegates each candidate will receive is
    a. the results of a popular election.
    b. voting that takes place at precinct conventions.
    c. voting that takes place at precinct conventions and in popular elections.
    d. voting that takes place at the state convention.

FILL IN THE BLANKS.

11. _____ receive 5 to 19 percent of the vote in any statewide election. Candidates from these parties are not required to file petitions to get on the ballot.

12. _____ were Democrats who followed Governor Allan Shivers's example and voted for Eisenhower in 1952 and 1956.

13. A _____ is a party official elected in each voting precinct to organize and support the party.

14. Most computer ballots are _____, a ballot form that lists the office, followed by the candidates by party.

15. In _____, members of one party vote in the primary of another party.

Answers: 1. c; **2.** a; **3.** a; **4.** b; **5.** b; **6.** b; **7.** d; **8.** c; **9.** b; **10.** c; **11.** Minor parties; **12.** Shivercrats; **13.** precinct chair; **14.** office block; **15.** crossover voting.

RESOURCES FOR RESEARCH AND ACTION

Internet Resources

The Center for Voting and Democracy
www.fairvote.org   This slightly Republican-leaning organization promotes alternate election systems.

Texans for Public Justice
www.tpj.org   This site provides information on campaign spending and lobbying.

The Texas Democratic Party
www.txdemocrats.org   This is the official Web site of the Texas Democratic Party.

The Texas Ethics Commission
www.ethics.state.tx.us   This site has information on campaign contributions reported by candidates for office and interest groups.

The Texas Republican Party
www.texasgop.org   This is the official Web site of the Texas Republican Party.

Texas Secretary of State
www.sos.state.tx.us   For information on election laws and voter turnout, go to this site.

Internet Activism

Poll watchers observe voting activities at polling places both before the election and on Election Day. They are allowed to be present while voting machines are being inspected, while votes are being counted, and while the results are being delivered. They report irregularities to the election judge. To learn how to become a poll watcher, read the poll watcher's guide for the state of Texas at www.co.fort-bend.tx.us/upload/images/elections_administration/pwguide.pdf.

Twitter
http://twitter.com/opensecretsdc   Get updates from the Center for Responsive Politics, a good source for nonpartisan information on money in politics.

YouTube
www.youtube.com/watch?y=D0UqBZaPKGo   Dr. Matthew Burbank explains how residents over the age of 18 can register to vote in the state of Texas.

Facebook
www.facebook.com/TexasDemocraticParty   This is the Texas Democratic Party's official Facebook page to learn about candidates, news, and issues in Texas. The Web site is independent of any candidate or candidate's committee.

Recommended Readings

Anderson, James E., Richard W. Murray, and Edward L. Farley. *Texas Politics: An Introduction.* New York: Harper & Row, 1989.

Key, V. O. Jr. *Southern Politics in State and Nation.* New York: Knopf, 1949.

Key, V. O. Jr. *Politics and Pressure Groups,* 4th ed. New York: Thomas Y. Crowell, 1958.

Soukup, James R., Clifton McCleskey, and Harry Holloway. *Party and Factional Division in Texas.* Austin: University of Texas Press, 1962.

Weeks, Douglas O. *Texas Presidential Politics in 1952.* Austin: University of Texas, Institute of Public Affairs, 1953.

Movie of Interest

Charlie Wilson's War (2007)
This film depicts the real-life efforts of Texas Democratic Congressman Charlie Wilson to help Afghan fighters defeat the Soviet Union. Charlie Wilson, played by Tom Hanks, was first elected to the U.S. House of Representatives in 1972 during the Yellow Dog Democratic era, and served in that position for twenty-four years.

The Texas Legislature

THEN

Conservative Democrats dominated a part-time legislature with a low-paid, minimal staff.

NOW

Republicans control a part-time legislature with a better-paid, more abundant staff.

NEXT

Will a more professional staff be enough to meet the needs of a growing population and an expanding economy?

How will the new technologies adopted by staff and legislators facilitate the legislative process?

As the legislature becomes more professional, will legislators rise above local concerns and focus on statewide issues?

This chapter examines how the legislature is elected and how—once elected—legislators go about creating laws.

FIRST, we evaluate the different *methods of election* that are used to elect representatives and the impact of controversial attempts to change district boundaries.

SECOND, we discuss the process of *getting elected*, including the qualifications candidates must have and the obstacles they must overcome to get elected and remain in office.

THIRD, we consider *legislative procedures*, specifically, how a bill becomes a law, and explore the roles played by leaders and committees.

FOURTH, in *rating the Texas legislature*, we compare it with other state legislatures to analyze its strengths and weaknesses.

Although the office of governor,

the courts, and state agencies all have their purpose, the legislature is the most important agency in state government. Many things cannot happen without legislative actions: Money cannot be spent, taxes cannot be levied, state laws cannot be enacted or changed, and finally, as in most states, the constitution cannot be amended without the approval of the legislature. Simply put, without actions by the legislature, most state governments would soon come to a halt. In recent years, the federal government has shifted more responsibility to state governments, and this has resulted in even more emphasis on state legislatures as policy-making bodies.

The Texas Constitution literally makes the legislature the most important decision-making body in the state. The framers of the 1876 constitution distrusted government generally, but they were especially leery of executive authority and gave more power to the legislature than to the executive.

The Texas legislature consists of two houses. The Texas Senate has 31 members elected for four-year overlapping terms; half the membership is elected every two years. The Texas House of Representatives now consists of 150 members elected for two-year terms. The size of legislatures raises several issues. Large bodies might promote the representation of diverse interests within the state; however, statewide interests might go unrepresented. Large legislatures can become inefficient at decision making or, in part because of their inefficiency, become dominated by a few members. There is no doubt that decision-making dynamics depend on the size of the legislative body. The smaller Texas Senate is generally regarded as more sedate and genteel in its proceedings than the House of Representatives. Historically, few people have dominated the Senate, and members act more independently. Although the lieutenant governor is powerful, the power of the office comes from the Senate rules. The House, on the other hand, is generally more "disputatious" in its proceedings, and historically the speaker of the house dominates.

Methods of Election

single-member district
district having one member elected to the legislature

Members of legislative bodies most often are elected from **single-member districts.** Under this system, each legislative district has one member in the legislative body. In Texas, there are 31 senatorial districts and 150 House districts (see Figures 23.1 and 23.2). The voters living in these districts elect one House and one Senate member to represent the district. This system allows for geographical representation—all areas of the state get to choose representatives to the state legislature.

multimember district
district having more than one member elected to the legislature

Some states use **multimember districts** for some legislative elections. Methods of electing representatives in multimember districts vary widely, but the most common method is to elect two or three members per district. Voters get one vote for each seat in the multimember district, so more than one state representative represents each voter. Under a single-member-district system, districts can be drawn to the advantage of ethnic and political minorities within the county. Multimember districts promote majority representation or domination.

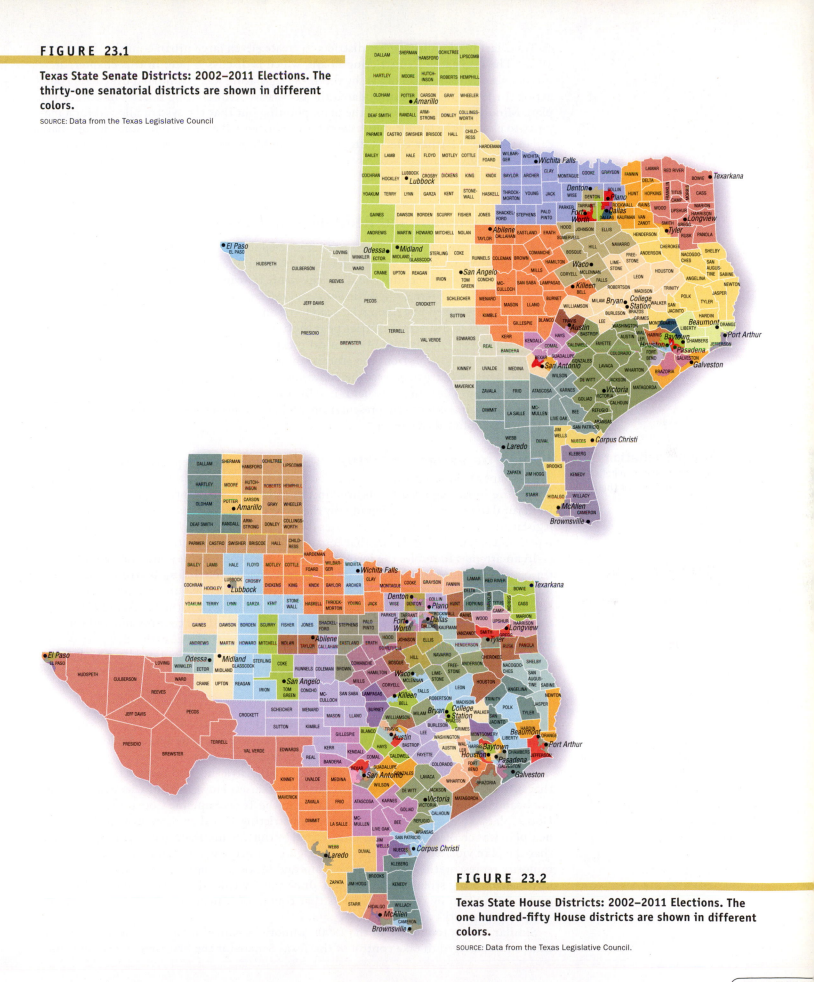

FIGURE 23.1

Texas State Senate Districts: 2002–2011 Elections. The thirty-one senatorial districts are shown in different colors.

SOURCE: Data from the Texas Legislative Council

FIGURE 23.2

Texas State House Districts: 2002–2011 Elections. The one hundred-fifty House districts are shown in different colors.

SOURCE: Data from the Texas Legislative Council.

Texas last used multimember districts to create eleven large urban counties during the 1970s. The Legislative Redistricting Board, which is discussed later in this chapter, drew up this plan after the plan drawn by the Texas legislature was invalidated by federal court action. In 1971, the courts invalidated the Legislative Redistricting Board's multimember plan. Minority groups contested the plan, pointing out that the system allowed for a majority to elect all the representatives and for minorities to be frozen out. Some writers have called this the "Matthew effect" after the words of Matthew 13:12: "For whoever has to him more will be given, and he will have abundance; but whoever does not have, even what he has will be taken away from him."[1]

Reapportionment and Redistricting Issues

The U.S. Constitution requires that Congress reapportion the seats in the U.S. House of Representatives among the states following each federal census (every ten years). The Texas Constitution likewise requires the state legislature to reapportion the seats following each federal census.[2] The terms *reapportionment* and *redistricting* are usually used to describe this process. As discussed in Chapter 11, reapportionment refers to the process of allocating representatives to districts; redistricting is the drawing of district lines. Apportioning seats in any legislative body is a highly political process. Each interest within the state tries to gain as much as possible from the process. Existing powers, such as the majority party in the legislature, will try to protect their advantages. Incumbent legislators will try to ensure their reelection. The primary issues raised by reapportionment and redistricting are equity of representation, minority representation, and gerrymandering (drawing district boundary lines for political advantage).

equity of representation
situation in which each member of a legislature represents about the same number of people

EQUITY OF REPRESENTATION   The issue of **equity of representation** is not new; it is perhaps as old as legislative bodies. Thomas Jefferson noted the problem in the Virginia legislature in the eighteenth century.[3] In the early twentieth century, population shifted from rural to urban areas, and gradually the rural areas were overrepresented in many state legislatures. In the 1960s, only two states (Wisconsin and Massachusetts) had rural/urban representation in the legislature that equaled population distributions in the state.[4]

In an attempt to resolve the inequality of representation in the state, the Texas Constitution was amended in 1948 to create the **Legislative Redistricting Board (LRB),** which was given the authority to redistrict the seats in the Texas House and Senate if the legislature failed to act. The LRB is made up of the lieutenant governor, the speaker of the house, the attorney general, the comptroller of public accounts, and the commissioner of the general land office.[5] Although the LRB was not able to resolve the issue early on, equity of representation is no longer an issue today. With advancements in computers, drawing districts with approximately the same number of people is easy. Other issues, just as contentious, have replaced the equity issue.

Legislative Redistricting Board (LRB)
state board composed of elected officials that can draw new legislative districts for the House and Senate if the legislature fails to act

minority representation
requirement that in drawing legislative districts, the legislature should create districts that give members of minority groups an opportunity to be elected

MINORITY REPRESENTATION   The second issue raised by reapportionment is **minority representation.** Not only should legislative districts be approximately equal in population, they should also allow for minority representation.

The 1981 session of the legislature produced a redistricting and reapportionment plan that advanced minority representation in both houses. However, Bill Clements, the Republican governor, vetoed the Senate plan, and the Texas Supreme Court invalidated the House plan. That forced the Legislative Redistricting Board to draw new districts. The new plan was challenged in federal courts and by the U.S. Justice Department, which ruled that the plan violated the federal Voting Rights Act because it did not achieve maximum minority representation. African Americans and Mexican Americans felt that the plan diluted their voting strength. A new plan, drawn up by federal courts, maximized minority representation by creating districts that contained a majority of ethnic minorities—"majority-minority" districts.

Similar battles took place in the 1990s. Minorities gained many seats, as did Republicans, who managed to take control of the Texas Senate for the first time in over one hundred years. In the 2001 session of the legislature, minorities did not gain significantly. Later in this chapter, the effects of this redistricting are discussed in detail.

POLITICAL AND RACIAL GERRYMANDERING   As noted in Chapter 11, the practice of gerrymandering dates to the early days of the Republic. Political parties drew legislative districts to achieve the political advantage of one party over another. The term has also been applied to the practice of creating minority districts—racial gerrymandering.

With the rise of the Republican Party, political gerrymandering in Texas has intensified. Until 2003, Republicans repeatedly charged that the Democrats have reduced the number of potential Republican districts, especially in suburban areas. In the 1980s, the Republicans forged alliances with minority groups. Republicans support the creation of **racially gerrymandered majority-minority districts,** and minority groups support the Republican efforts. As we shall see, the creation of majority-minority districts aids both groups.

In 1996, the U.S. Supreme Court reviewed a legal challenge to the practice of creating majority-minority districts.[6] In ruling against three majority-minority districts, the Court determined that these districts "are ultimately unexplainable on grounds other than the racial quotas established for these districts," resulting in "unconstitutional racial gerrymandering."

In April 2001, the U.S. Supreme Court placed further limitation on the use of racial gerrymandering in drawing legislative districts.[7] The Court said that although race can be a factor, it must not be the primary factor in determining the makeup of legislative districts. Partisan makeup can be a primary factor, but race cannot. This court ruling reduced the practice of racial gerrymandering but makes it possible to pack minority Democrats into districts so long as the intent is not based on race.

> **racially gerrymandered majority-minority districts**
> legislative districts that are drawn to the advantage of a minority group

Redistricting in the 1990s and 2001

Redistricting efforts in the 1990s increased the number of majority-minority districts, and this concentration of minority populations in districts also had the effect of increasing the number of legislative districts that are majority Anglo and that vote Republican.

In the 2001 session of the legislature, several issues surfaced. Both parties hoped to gain seats through the redistricting process. Texas gained two U.S. congressional seats, for a total of thirty-two, and the fight over these seats between Democrats and Republicans added to the controversy in the legislature. The Texas House and Senate adjourned without approving new redistricting plans. As a result of this inaction by the Senate, the Legislative Redistricting Board had to establish new districts for the Texas legislature. Only one member of this board was a Democrat—Speaker Laney, who was effectively frozen out of the discussion. Lt. Governor Ratliff objected to the proceeding. The remaining three members, Attorney General Cornyn, Land Commissioner Dewhurst, and Comptroller Rylander, proceeded to draw districts that greatly favor Republicans. Because of these redistricting efforts by the LRB, in 2003 Republicans gained control of both houses of the Texas legislature for the first time in over one hundred years.

Re-redistricting in 2003

Normally, redistricting takes place every decade following the new federal census. In the 2003 session, Republicans used their new control over the Texas legislature to redistrict the state's thirty-two congressional districts. This mid-decade redistricting, or re-redistricting, was unprecedented.

In 2001, the LRB drew districts that greatly favored Republicans in both House and Senate elections. This board cannot in fact redistrict congressional districts, and Governor Perry refused to call a special session in 2001 to consider the issue. Instead, he stated that the matter was best left to the courts.

The congressional district map used in the 2002 election cycle was drawn by a special three-judge federal court. Though this map may have favored Republicans in a majority of the districts, Democrats managed to win election in seventeen of the thirty-two districts, leaving the Republicans with fifteen districts. Five districts that heavily favored Republicans were won by Democrats. With these unexpected results, U.S. House Majority Leader Tom DeLay, a Republican from Sugarland, forwarded a plan to the Texas legislature in the 2003 session to redraw the 2001 court-ordered congressional district map.

The Texas House, under the direction of newly elected Speaker Tom Craddick, took up the cause, and a new congressional district map was reported out of committee. The Democrats were incensed, but they did not have enough votes to block the passage of the bill. Instead, they decided to deprive the Texas House of a quorum. The Texas House rules state that a quorum, two-thirds of the whole membership—one hundred representatives— must be present for the House to act. During the last week of the regular session in 2003, fifty-two Democrats crossed the border and took up residence at a Holiday Inn in Ardmore, Oklahoma. The Democratic exodus infuriated state and national Republican leadership. Texas Rangers were sent to get the renegades back to Austin, but to no avail. The absence of these Democrats effectively prevented the House from passing the redistricting legislation and the bill died.

Meanwhile, the Texas Senate, under the direction of newly elected Lt. Governor David Dewhurst, did not debate the issue during the regular session because of the Senate's two-thirds rule, which required that twenty-one members of the Senate agree to allow a bill to be considered by the whole Senate. Senate Democrats, with twelve members, refused to consider any bills.

THE FIRST SPECIAL SESSION
Despite much statewide opposition to continuing the re-redistricting battle, on June 19, 2003, Governor Rick Perry called a special session of the legislature, to begin June 30, to reconsider the re-redistricting proposal. Despite many misgivings, on July 8, 2003, the Texas House quickly passed a new congressional map by a highly partisan vote of eighty-three to sixty-two. The battle now moved to the Texas Senate.

In this first special session, Lt. Governor Dewhurst left in place the two-thirds rule required to consider a bill on the Senate floor. As long as the Democrats held twelve seats, they could block the House-passed bill from being considered by the Senate; however, several Democrats at first withheld their support for blocking the legislation. Some minority Democratic senators were offered passage of legislation favorable to their districts. Others were offered "safe" congressional seats in exchange for favoring re-redistricting. On July 15, 2003, Senator Bill Ratliff, a Republican from Mount Pleasant, joined ten Democrats in blocking the re-redistricting bill.

Great pressure was applied to Lt. Governor Dewhurst to drop the two-thirds rule; however, many senators, both Democratic and Republican, opposed the change. Newspapers

> Senator Leticia Van de Putte arranged for the two private planes that secretly flew the Texas Eleven to New Mexico. Standing with the ten other Democratic senators, she speaks to reporters during a press conference in August 2003.

across the state urged Dewhurst to hold the line and not change the rules. Statewide polls showed Governor Perry losing support over the redistricting issue.

On July 28, 2003, eleven Texas senators (the "Texas Eleven") fled to Albuquerque, New Mexico. Two things prompted this action. First, they anticipated that the governor was going to adjourn the first special session early and call a second special session immediately thereafter (which he did). The rumor was that the Senate sergeant-at-arms had been ordered to lock the senators in the Senate chamber as soon as the session was called to prevent them from busting a quorum. Second, Lt. Governor Dewhurst had stated he would suspend the two-thirds rule for future sessions.

The Texas governor and lieutenant governor were livid at the actions of these Democratic senators, but the Democratic governor and lieutenant governor of New Mexico were delighted and welcomed the eleven to the state. Republicans and Democrats held dueling press conferences, each accusing the other of wrongdoing. Governor Perry at one point blamed the absent senators for preventing consideration of a bill to fund Medicaid benefits for child health care. Perry had earlier vetoed part of the state budget that would have allowed this funding.

THE SECOND SPECIAL SESSION

A few hours after the second special session began and a quorum was present, the House passed the same redistricting bill passed in the first special session. The quick passage of the bill led some Democrats to question the fairness of the process, since no debate or discussion was allowed.

The Republican senators in Austin attempted to force the return of the eleven Democrats by imposing fines. In the end, the fines amounted to $57,000 for each of the stray senators. The Republicans also took away the parking spaces of the boycotting senators. Some have questioned the legality of that action, since a quorum was not present and technically the Senate could not take action. The fines were later removed on the condition that there would be no more boycotts until the end of the term in January 2005.

The eleven Democratic senators stayed in New Mexico until the thirty-day special session expired on August 26, 2003. They did not immediately return to the state because they thought they would be arrested and taken to Austin for a third special session call. On September 3, 2003, however, the stalemate was broken when Senator John Whitmire, Democrat from Houston, broke the boycott and returned to the state. The Texas Senate now had a quorum.

THE THIRD SPECIAL SESSION

On September 10, 2003, Governor Perry called a third special session of the legislature to consider redistricting. Some were surprised that a third session was called, since a state poll by Montgomery and Associates, an independent research firm, found that most Texans were opposed to redistricting. In fact, 47.9 percent of self-identified Republicans

> Democratic Senator John Whitmire (left) speaks with colleagues. Whitmire caved in to Republican pressure to return from New Mexico in September 2003, enabling the Republican-controlled Senate to pass the redistricting bill.

supported redistricting. The poll also showed the governor with a negative rating on job performance.

The House and the Senate quickly passed different redistricting bills, which went to a conference committee. These differences quickly led to infighting among the Republicans, with the main issue being congressional districts in West Texas. House Speaker Tom Craddick wanted a district dominated by his hometown of Midland, but Senator Robert Duncan, Republican from Lubbock, wanted to keep Midland in a district with Lubbock.

The fight over the West Texas districts became so intense that Governor Perry and U.S. Congressman Tom DeLay became involved. In the end, an entirely new map, shown in Figure 23.3, unseen before DeLay's arrival, was produced by the conference committee and accepted by both houses in mid-October 2003.

OUTCOME OF THE REDISTRICTING WRANGLE Although many predicted that the DeLay redistricting map would be found in violation of the federal Voting Rights Act because it split minority voters rather than concentrating them into majority-minority districts, they were wrong. U.S. Attorney General Ashcroft issued a one-sentence letter saying that he did not object to the new map. At the time, Democratic Texas House members claimed that the professional staff of the U.S. Justice Department objected to the map, and they asked that the report be made public, but it was not released. When it was later released, they were proved right.

A three-judge special court consisting of two Republicans and one Democrat approved the map, voting along party lines. The logic that prevailed in essence sets aside the Voting

FIGURE 23.3

U.S. Congressional Districts. The thirty-one congressional districts are shown in different colors.
SOURCE: Data from the Texas Legislative Council.

Rights Act by allowing minority voters to be divided into many congressional districts so long as the intention is to divide Democrats and not to divide minority voters. Partisan gerrymandering is considered legal. Since most minorities vote for Democrats, they can be split into many districts so long as the gerrymandering is partisan in intent. This established a new standard for redistricting. The U.S. Supreme Court later forced a change in four of these districts because the redistricting plan had diluted the voting strength of minorities.

Governor Perry, Congressman Tom DeLay, and the Republicans were successful in their redistricting efforts. In the 2004 election, the Republicans gained five congressional seats and now control the Texas delegation to Congress, with twenty-one Republicans to eleven Democrats. Democrats entered the decade with a seventeen-to-fifteen majority. All targeted Democrats either were defeated or chose not to run. Only Congressman Chet Edwards won reelection in District 17.

In July 2006, the U.S. Supreme Court heard an appeal to the DeLay redistricting and ruled that nothing in the Constitution prohibited redistricting at mid-decade. However, they did order the redrawing of three congressional districts because of concerns over minority representation.

On the national level, Republicans increased their control of the U.S. House of Representatives in 2004 by six seats. Five of these came from the redistricting effort in Texas. Without this redistricting, the Republicans might not have retained control of the House of Representatives in the 109th Congress.

The Texas mid-decade redistricting con-

The Changing Legislature

THEN (1961)	NOW (2010)
Four women, five Latinos, and no African Americans served in the legislature.*	During the past few legislative cycles, approximately one out of every five members of the Texas legislature is a woman, one out of every five is a Latino, and one out of ten is African American.**
Two members of the state legislature were Republican.	Both the Texas House and the Texas Senate are controlled by the Republican Party.
Federal courts eventually forced states to redraw districts based on the "one person, one vote" law.	Power is shifting from rural to urban areas. The invalidation of multi-member districts in urban areas and redistricting plans have increased minority representation.

WHAT'S NEXT?

> Will the state return to a two-party system? Why or why not?

> Will the Republican Party maintain its stronghold in urban legislative districts? Explain your reasons.

> What factors might influence whether the legislators continue to pursue local interests at the expense of statewide interests?

*TEXAS Handbook Online, The Texas Legislature, www.tshaonline.org/handbook/online/articles/TT/mkt2.html.
**Legislative Reference Library, www.lrl.state.tx.us/legis/leaders/.

tributed to a nationwide controversy that eventually led some states to move away from allowing state legislatures to develop new redistricting maps. Instead, this responsibility has been handed over to independent commissions. In 2008, California voters passed an initiative creating the Citizen's Redistricting Committee. The committee consists of five Democrats, five Republicans, and four independents or third-party members that are selected from a pool of individual applicants by the state auditor's office. In ten states, the redistricting commissions cannot include members of the state legislature, state employees, or elected officials. It is doubtful, however, that Texas will move in that direction anytime soon.

Getting Elected

Formal qualifications for state office include age, citizenship, state residency, district residency, and qualified voter status. Among the states, the lowest minimum age for House membership is 18 years and the upper minimum age is 25. Most states require U.S. citizenship, residency in the state from one to five years, and district residency for a year or less.

Characteristics of Members of the Texas Legislature (2009)

TABLE 23.1

	House	Senate
Sex		
Male	113	25
Female	37	6
Race		
Anglo	105	22
Hispanic	30	7
African American	14	2
Asian	1	0
Longevity		
Incumbent	128	29
Freshman	20	2
Party		
Democrat	74	12
Republican	76	19

SOURCE: www.capitol.state.tx.us/.

"birthright" characteristics
social and economic characteristics of legislators that match certain demographic characteristics of many people in their district

A Texas House member must be a U.S. citizen, a registered voter, and at least 21 years of age, and must have lived in the state for two years and in the district for one year. To be a Texas state senator, a person must be at least 26 years of age and reside in the district for one year preceding her or his election and have resided in the state for five years before the election.

The Impact of Informal Qualifications

Formal requirements are minimal and keep few citizens from serving. More important are informal qualifications that limit many people's ability to serve. These include income, education, occupation, ethnicity, and gender. On these dimensions, state legislators tend not to represent the general population. Similar to members of the U.S. Congress, state legislators tend to be male, well educated, and professionals (often lawyers). (See Table 23.1.)

Other dimensions, sometimes called **"birthright" characteristics,** include race, ethnicity, religion, and national background. On these dimensions, representatives tend to represent their district.[8] If the legislative district is predominantly Mexican American, the representative will likely be Mexican American; the same is true for African American districts. Even though legislators generally represent their constituents on these characteristics, they are usually better educated and from selected occupational groups.

An African American legislator, for example, is generally better educated than his or her constituents and is drawn from a selected occupational group. In the 2001 session of the Texas House, nine of the fourteen African Americans were attorneys, and sixteen of the thirty-one Mexican Americans were attorneys. All had a higher level of education than their constituents.[9] The same is true for Anglo legislators.

In the case of women, in 2010, 24.3 percent of all state legislators nationwide were women. Few women served until the early 1970s. The number of women increased steadily until 2000 but has remained at about that level since then, as shown in Figure 23.4. In Texas, the number of women legislators has increased from one in each chamber in 1971 to forty-three in 2009. Six are senators and thirty-seven are state representatives.

The numbers of Latinos and African Americans have also increased in legislatures across the nation, in part because of reapportionment. Both ethnic groups are underrepresented in the Texas legislature when compared with their numbers in the population. In 2009, Latinos made up 36.5 percent of the population of Texas and held 20 percent of the

FIGURE 23.4

Women in State Legislatures
SOURCE: Center for American Women and Politics, Eagleton Institute of Politics, Rutgers University, www.cawp.rutgers.edu.

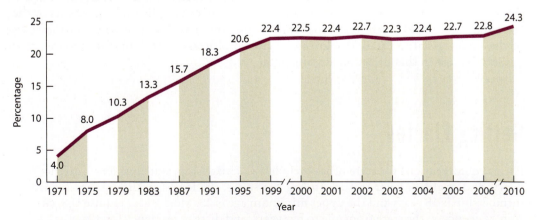

ANALYZING THE SOURCES

COMPETITION IN TEXAS HOUSE AND SENATE RACES

The graph shown here depicts the number of competitive races in recent general elections. It should be noted that only half of the Senate (16 or 15) members are up for election every two years. In the House, all 150 members are up for election every two years.

Evaluating the Evidence

① What trend does this graph illustrate?

② Do you think this trend will continue in the future? Explain your answer.

③ If this trend continues, what impact might increased competition have on the length of tenure in the legislature, party strength, and third parties in the future?

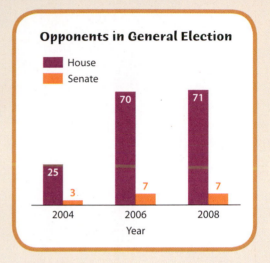

House seats and 22.5 percent of the Senate seats. African Americans made up 13.4 percent of the Texas population and held 9.3 percent of the seats in the legislature.

Even with the changes in apportionment, most legislators are upwardly mobile white males. Most are from old, established, often very wealthy families. The legislature is a good place to begin a political career. Having family and money helps launch that career. In addition, some professions, especially law, allow a person time to devote to legislative duties. As we shall see later, most states do not pay their legislators well, and having other sources of income is essential. Also, unlike the U.S. Congress, most state legislatures are part-time bodies, meeting for a set number of days annually or biennially.

The percentage of attorneys in the Texas legislature (35 percent in 2009) is much higher than in the average legislature (16.5 percent). In addition, Texas has fewer who identify themselves as full-time legislators. Texas legislators are not well paid ($7,200 per year), and this might contribute to their feeling that their legislative jobs are only part-time. There is a higher-than-average percentage of businessmen and women in the Texas legislature, and a lower-than-average percentage of schoolteachers. In some states, state employees can serve in the state legislature and keep their jobs as teachers. This is prohibited in Texas. A Texas state employee may not hold an elective and an appointive office and receive pay for both.

Competition for Office

As noted in earlier chapters, in the one-party Democratic era in Texas, most of the competition for offices was in the Democratic Party primary. Today, competition is more likely to be in the general election. (See "Analyzing the Sources.")

Historically, most candidates for the House and Senate races faced little opposition in either the primary or the general election. This lack of competition in Texas legislative races is the result of several factors, but the major reason is the degree to which districts are politically and racially gerrymandered, creating **safe election districts** for both parties. This can be seen by comparing two characteristics of Texas legislative districts in 2004: the

safe election districts
noncompetitive districts that can be won only by the party with 55 percent or more of the votes in the district

Texas House of Representatives Party Competition in 2002–2010

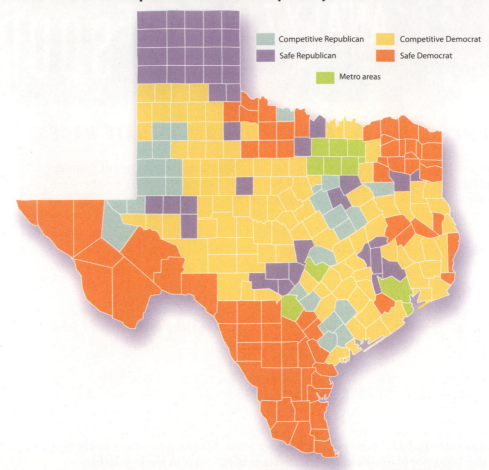

POLITICAL INQUIRY

FIGURE 23.5 ■ **This map shows the districts based on 2000 Census and voting data. Since 2000, both the demographics and the voting patterns have changed, and some districts have become more competitive, especially for Democrats in South Texas and in inner-city districts. What might this mean for future races and the composition of the Texas House?**

strength of party voting in the district and the percentage of minority population in the district. As Figures 23.5 and 23.6 clearly show, House and Senate seats are clustered into safe Democratic and safe Republican districts with only a few competitive seats.

Party voting is a measure of the strength of a political party in the legislative district based on voter support for the party's candidates in previous elections. This is also a measure of party competition. Studies of party competition in the U.S. House and Senate seats define noncompetitive as any district in which either party receives 55 percent or more of the votes. Thus, a district in which the party vote is between 44 and 54 percent is considered competitive.[10] The measure used here to gauge party competitiveness is the combined vote received by either party for all offices/candidates in the district in the 2000 general election. This is the composite party vote. Thus, a House or Senate district in which the Republican Party candidates for statewide office collectively received 55 percent or more of the votes is considered a safe Republican district.

The second variable is the racial composition of the district. This is simply the percentages of minority and nonminority population of the district. If we compare these two characteristics (party competition and minority population in the district) using some simple statistics, we can see that most Texas House and Senate seats fall into two categories—noncompetitive Republican Anglo districts and noncompetitive Democratic minority dis-

Texas Senate Party Competition in 2002–2010

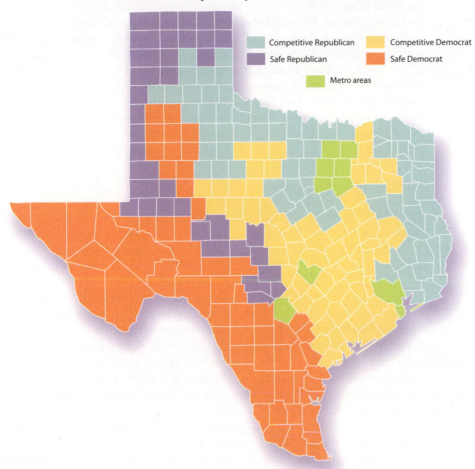

Legend:
- Competitive Republican
- Safe Republican
- Competitive Democrat
- Safe Democrat
- Metro areas

POLITICAL INQUIRY

FIGURE 23.6 ■ **This map shows the districts based on 2000 Census and voting data. Since 2000, both the demographics and the voting patterns have changed, and some districts have become more competitive, especially for Democrats in South Texas and in inner-city districts. What might this mean for future races and the composition of the Texas Senate?**

tricts. Since minority support for Democratic candidates is always very high, concentrating minorities in districts also concentrates Democratic party support in these districts. Many remaining districts are noncompetitive Republican districts. Other studies have found the same is true for U.S. congressional districts.[11]

Safe Democratic districts exist primarily in two places: South Texas, where there are concentrations of Mexican Americans, and East Texas, the traditional stronghold of Democrats. Republicans are strong in the Panhandle and the German Hill Country. Metropolitan areas of the state also contain both safe Democratic and safe Republican districts—Democrats in the inner city and Republicans in the suburbs.

Thus, one reason for the low competition in Texas legislative races is racial and political gerrymandering. In addition, members of the legislature get money from PACs because they are incumbents. They face little opposition in either the primary or the general elections. Having a war chest of money keeps competition at a low level. Competition in districts is most likely to occur at the primary level and when there is no incumbent.

In the last eight years, however, there has been an increase in the level of competition in the Republican Party primary elections. Some of this competition is related to House Speaker Craddick, who has been known to seek opponents for those members who oppose his agenda and may threaten his continuation as speaker.

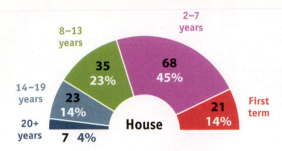

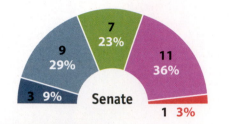

FIGURE 23.7

Years of Service of the Members of the 2009 Legislature

SOURCE: Legislative Reference Library, www.lrl.state.tx.us/legis/members/roster.crm?leg=81.

turnover

the number of new members of the legislature each session

term limits

limits on the number of times a person can be elected to the same office

Even when candidates do not face opposition, they are likely to collect large amounts of money from various groups, especially from PACs. In the 2006 races for the legislature, House winners collected an average of $208,000, and Senate winners collected an average of $917,000. Most money comes from contributors who live outside the senator's or representative's district. The upper right gallery of the Texas House chamber, looking toward the speaker's podium, is "reserved" for the most powerful members of the lobbies. Some lobbyists are almost always there when business is being conducted on the floor. They watch members of the House, and the House members know they are being watched. Members are sometimes contacted by these lobbyists and are "encouraged" to vote in the right way. Members of the House call this space the "Owners' Box."

Legislative Turnover

One could conclude from the relatively low level of competition for Texas legislative seats that there would be low turnover of the membership. This is not the case. **Turnover**—the number of new members of the legislature each session—is high in all state legislatures, and normally it is higher for the lower house than for the upper chamber.[12]

Figure 23.7 shows the number of years of service for members of the Texas legislature. Over time, turnover rates in Texas are very high. Turnover is not due mainly to electoral defeat; most members voluntarily retire from service. Retirement is prompted by poor pay, the lack of professional staff assistance, redistricting, the requirements of the job, the demands upon one's family, fund-raising demands, and the rigors of seeking reelection.[13] Some use the office as a stepping-stone to higher office and leave to become members of Congress or take statewide office.

The high turnover rate has a political fallout. If 20 to 25 percent of the members are new each session, these new members are learning the rules and finding their way. This allows a few "old-timers" to control the legislative process. Even with only nine new members in the House, a few "old-timers" can still control the process, as we shall see later in this chapter.

Though turnover in state legislatures nationwide is quite high, in recent years voters have supported formal **term limits** for state legislators, limiting the number of times they can be elected to the same office. From 1990 to 1996, twenty-one states approved term limits for both House and Senate seats. Fourteen of those states have imposed these limits with constitutional amendments and seven by statutes.[14] These limits were approved despite the fact that self-limiting of terms was working for many years. The Texas legislature has self-imposed term limits.

Legislative Procedures

All legislatures have formal rules of procedure that govern their operations. These rules prescribe how bills are passed into law and make the process of passing laws more orderly and fair. These rules also make it difficult to pass laws. A bill must clear many hurdles before it becomes a law. Rules that make it difficult to pass bills have two results: They prevent bills from becoming law without careful review, and they preserve the status quo. In the traditionalistic-individualistic political culture of Texas, these rules protect the ruling elite and enable them to control the legislative process. Thus, it is more important to understand the impact of rules on legislation than to have a detailed understanding of the actual rules. We use this basic approach here to explain how laws are made in Texas.

Leadership Roles

In any legislative body, those holding formal leadership positions possess considerable power to decide the outcome of legislation. In the Texas legislature, power is very much concentrated in the hands of two individuals: the speaker of the House and the lieutenant governor. These two individuals control the output of legislation.

SPEAKER OF THE HOUSE The members of the House elect the speaker of the Texas House of Representatives by majority vote to preside over the House. The election of the **speaker of the house** is the first formal act of the members. The secretary of state presides over the election. Only occasionally is the outcome of this election in doubt. Who the speaker will be is generally known far in advance of the beginning of the session, and this individual spends considerable time lining up supporters before the session begins. In all but a few cases, the person elected is a longtime member of the House and has support from current members. When a third of the members are new, the person elected speaker may also have to gain support from some of these new members. It is illegal for candidates for speaker to formally promise members something in exchange for their vote, but key players in the election of the speaker often receive choice **committee assignments,** since the speaker decides which members sit on which committees.

Many feel that speaker of the house is the most powerful position in Texas government. There is no doubt that the speaker is extremely powerful. Generally, speakers have the power to direct and decide what legislation passes the House. The speaker gains power from the formal rules adopted by the House at the beginning of each session. These rules allow the speaker to do the following:

- Appoint the chairs of all committees.
- Appoint most of the members of each standing committee. About half of these committee seats are assigned according to a limited seniority system. In reality, the backers of the speaker often use their seniority to choose a committee assignment, thus freeing up an appointment for the speaker.
- Appoint members of the calendar and procedural committees, conference committees, and other special and interim committees.
- Serve as presiding officer over all sessions. This power allows the speaker to recognize members on the floor who wish to speak, generally interpret House rules, decide when a vote will be taken, and decide the outcome of voice votes.
- Refer all bills to committees. As a rule, bills go to subject matter committees. However, the speaker has discretion in deciding what committee will receive a bill. Some speakers used the State Affairs Committee as a "dead bill committee." Bills assigned to this committee usually had little chance of passing. Also, the speaker can assign a bill to a favorable committee to enhance its chances of passing.

These rules give the speaker control over the House agenda. The selected chairs are members of the "speaker's team." Few bills pass the House without the speaker's approval. For example, in the 2005 session of the legislature, House Bill 1348, which would have limited campaign contributions from corporations and labor unions, was being cosponsored by two-thirds of the members of the House, both Democrats and Republicans. The bill was not given a hearing by the Elections Committee because of the influence of Speaker Tom Craddick.

For many years, the Texas House of Representatives operated on a bipartisan basis. In the 2001 session of the legislature, Democrats controlled the House and Democrat Pete Laney was speaker. Bipartisanship was much more apparent in committee assignments and the overall tone of the session. In the 2003 session, much of this bipartisanship disappeared when the Republicans held a majority of the seats in the House and Tom Craddick became speaker. Dawnna Dukes (Democrat from Houston) stated that the Republicans did not feel the need to compromise on issues, since they controlled a majority of the seats. As we have seen, this was especially evident on the issue of the redistricting of the U.S. House seats.

Incumbent speakers are almost always reelected. A new speaker is chosen only after the death, retirement, or resignation of a sitting speaker. Traditionally, speakers served for two terms and retired or moved to higher offices. From 1951 to 1975, no speaker served more than two terms. In 1975, Billy Clayton broke with that tradition and served four terms. Gib Lewis, who succeeded Clayton, served five terms, as did Pete Laney.[15] Tom Craddick was elected speaker for the 2003 session. He was the first Republican speaker since Reconstruction.

In the 2007 session, an attempt was made to remove Tom Craddick as speaker, in large degree because of his partisanship and actions that many felt were arbitrary. Several attempts were made to advance a motion to vacate the chair, but Craddick exercised his power as speaker and refused to recognize anyone wanting to make that motion. When

speaker of the house
member of the Texas House, elected by the other House members, who serves as presiding officer and generally controls the passage of legislation

committee assignments
decisions by the speaker of the house on which members of the House sit on each committee; some committees, such as appropriations, are more powerful than others

Craddick was overruled by the two **parliamentarians,** the experts in legislative procedure, he forced them to resign and brought in two former House members and colleagues to act as parliamentarians. These two upheld the speaker's decision not to recognize any member wanting to vacate the chair.

In the 2009 session, Democrats and Republicans finally succeeded in ousting Craddick, replacing him with a less autocratic, compromise speaker, Joe Straus. Straus was elected with the backing of sixty-two of the seventy-four Democrats. In November 2010, Republicans increased their majority in the House from 78 to 99, and althrough most analysts predicted that Straus would continue as speaker in the 2011 legislative session, his reelection to the post was not a sure thing.

Many regarded the battle over voter ID cards as the first real test of the new speaker. Republicans strongly supported a bill that would institute voter ID cards; Democrats opposed it. The Republican-dominated House Calendars Committee scheduled a debate on the bill for May 23, 2009—the day before a debate on reforming the Texas Department of Insurance, a major goal of the House Democrats. The idea was to entice the Democrats to work out a compromise. Instead, Democrats stalled the voter ID debate. They spent ten minutes discussing each of the two hundred noncontroversial local bills that would normally be passed without delay. Neither voter ID nor insurance reform was addressed during the session. Joe Straus and the Republicans could have rushed through and voted down the local bills. However, Straus would have alienated Democrats whose support he needed in an almost evenly divided House.

> As Speaker of the House in the Texas state legislature, Joe Straus has moved away from the autocratic leadership style of his predecessor, Tom Craddick.

LIEUTENANT GOVERNOR Unlike the speaker of the house, the **lieutenant governor** is elected by the voters for a four-year term in the general election. The lieutenant governor does not owe his or her election to the legislative body, is not formally a senator, and cannot vote except in cases of a tie. One might assume that the office is not a powerful legislative office. In most states, that is true; however, the lieutenant governor in Texas possesses powers very similar to those of the speaker. Lieutenant governors can do the following:

- Appoint the chairs of all Senate committees.
- Select all members of all Senate committees. The Senate has no formal seniority rule.
- Appoint members of the conference committees.
- Serve as presiding officer and interpret rules.
- Refer all bills to committees.

On the surface, it appears that the lieutenant governor is more powerful than the speaker. Lieutenant governors do not owe their election to the Senate, and they have all powers possessed by the speaker. The reality is different. The powers of the lieutenant governor are assigned by the formal rules of the Senate, which are adopted at the beginning of each session. What the Senate gives, it can take away. Lieutenant governors must play a delicate balancing role of working with powerful members of the Senate and often compromising in the assignment of chairs of committees and committee membership. The same is true for all other powers held by the lieutenant governor: He or she must forge an alliance with key senators to use those powers effectively.[16]

From 1876 to 1999, the Democrats controlled the lieutenant governor's office. They controlled the Senate from 1876 to 1997. Until recently, party control was not a factor. It is often suggested that if the lieutenant governor and the Senate are ever of opposite parties, the powers of the lieutenant governor could be diminished. Such concerns have been voiced in the past few years, and given the pattern in other states, this development seems quite likely. Having such a powerful lieutenant governor is unusual among the states. Only five other states (Alabama, Georgia, Mississippi, South Carolina, and Vermont) give the lieutenant governor the power to appoint committee members and assign bills to committees.[17]

Most lieutenant governors are figureheads, who stand in when the governor is out of state. In states where the lieutenant governor is a figurehead, or when there is no lieutenant governor, the Senate elects one of its members to be the presiding officer, called the pro tempore, president of the Senate, or speaker of the senate.

Thus, the office of lieutenant governor in Texas is quite different from the office in most other states, but this has not always been true. J. William Davis, in his book *There Shall Also Be a Lieutenant Governor,* traces the concentration of power in this office to the actions of Allen Shivers and Ben Ramsey during the 1940s and 1950s. Over a period of several years, the office gained power in the Senate.[18]

The speaker and the lieutenant governor also have other significant powers outside the legislature. They appoint members of other state boards, or they serve as members of such boards. For example, they appoint the members of the Legislative Budget Board, which writes the state budget, and they serve as the chair and the vice chair, respectively, of this board. The budget determines what agencies and programs will be funded and in what amounts.

The Role of Committees

Similar to the U.S. Congress, most of the work of the legislature is done in standing committees established by House and Senate rules. Besides the standing committees, there are subcommittees of the standing committees, conference committees to work out differences in bills passed by the two houses, temporary committees to study special problems, and **interim committees** to study issues between sessions of the state legislature.

Of these, the standing committees are the most important. In the 2007 session, there were seventeen standing committees in the Senate and forty-four in the House. These are listed in Table 23.2.

The chairs of these standing committees have powers similar to those of the speaker and the lieutenant governor, but at the committee level. They decide the times and the agendas for meetings of the committee. In doing so, they decide the amount of time devoted to bills and which bills get the attention of the committee. A chair that strongly dislikes a bill can often prevent the bill from passing. Even if the bill is given a hearing, the chair can decide to give that bill to a subcommittee that might kill the bill.

Thus, as in most legislative bodies, in Texas the power is concentrated in a few powerful individuals who control the agendas and the actions of the legislature. Few bills can pass the legislature without the support of these individuals.

How a Bill Becomes a Law

Figure 23.8 lists the formal procedures in the Texas House and Senate for passing a bill. Each bill, to become law, must clear each step. The vast majority of bills that are introduced fail to pass. Few bills of major importance are passed in any given legislative session. Most bills make only minor changes to existing law. At each stage in the process, the bill can receive favorable or unfavorable actions. At each step, a bill can die by either action or inaction. There are many ways to kill a bill, but only one way to pass a bill. To pass, a bill must clear all hurdles.

The rules of the Texas Senate in effect provide a number of constraints on legislation. Before the sixtieth day of the legislative session, a bill can clear the Senate with a simple majority vote. Few bills pass before the sixtieth day. After the sixtieth day, before a bill can be considered on the floor of the Senate, a two-thirds vote is required. Technically, after the sixtieth day, Senate rules state that bills must be considered in the order they are reported out of committees. If bills are not considered in the order reported out of committees, a two-thirds vote is required to consider a bill. By design, bills are never considered in the order reported out of committee. If two-thirds of the senators agree to consider the bill, it can pass by a simple majority. Because of these rules, few bills clear the Senate that are not supported by more than a simple majority of the senators.

In some cases, the formal rules can be used to hide actions of the legislature. It is not uncommon in legislative bodies to attach riders to appropriations bills. A **rider** can be a

interim committees
temporary committees of the legislature that study issues between regular sessions and make recommendations on legislation

rider
provision attached to a bill that may not be of the same subject matter as the main bill

Standing Committees of the Texas House and Senate, 2009 Session

TABLE 23.2

Senate Committees	House Committees
Administration	Agriculture & Livestock
Agriculture & Rural Affairs	Appropriations
Business & Commerce	Border & Intergovernmental Affairs
Committee of the Whole Senate	Business & Industry
Criminal Justice	Calendars
Economic Development	Corrections
Education	County Affairs
Finance	Criminal Jurisprudence
Government Organization	Culture, Recreation & Tourism
Health & Human Services	Defense & Veterans' Affairs
Higher Education	Elections
Intergovernmental Relations	Emergency Preparedness, Select
International Relations & Trade	Energy Resources
Jurisprudence	Environmental Regulation
Natural Resources	Federal Economic Stabilization Funding, Select
Nominations	Federal Legislation, Select
State Affairs	Fiscal Stability, Select
Transportation & Homeland Security	General Investigating & Ethics
Veteran Affairs & Military Installations	Government Efficiency & Accountability, Select
	Higher Education
	House Administration
	Human Services
	Insurance
	Judiciary & Civil Jurisprudence
	Land & Resource Management
	Licensing & Administrative Procedures
	Local & Consent Calendars
	Natural Resources
	Pensions, Investments & Financial Services
	Public Education
	Public Health
	Public Safety
	Redistricting
	Rules & Resolutions
	Special Purpose Districts, Select
	State Affairs
	Technology, Economic Development & Workforce
	Transportation
	Transportation Funding, Select
	Urban Affairs
	Ways & Means

SOURCE: Texas Legislature Online, www.capitol.state.tx.us.

Basic Steps in the Texas Legislative Process

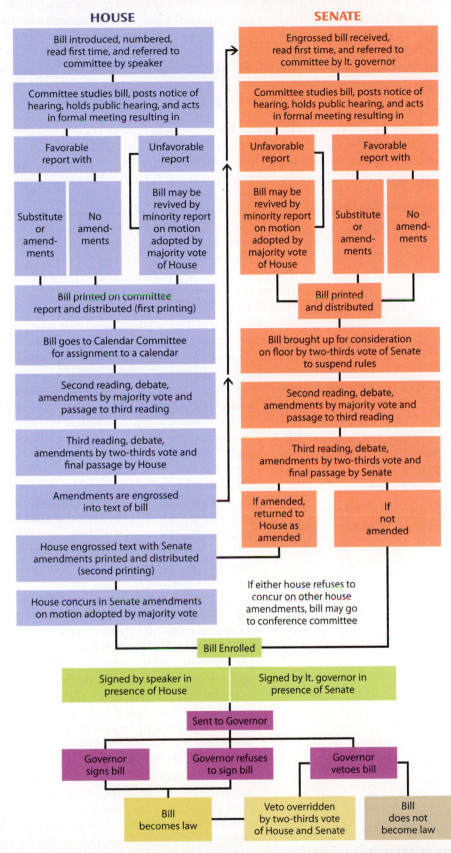

HOUSE

SENATE

Bill introduced, numbered, read first time, and referred to committee by speaker

Engrossed bill received, read first time, and referred to committee by lt. governor

Committee studies bill, posts notice of hearing, holds public hearing, and acts in formal meeting resulting in

Committee studies bill, posts notice of hearing, holds public hearing, and acts in formal meeting resulting in

Favorable report with

Unfavorable report

Unfavorable report

Favorable report with

Substitute or amendments

No amendments

Bill may be revived by minority report on motion adopted by majority vote of House

Bill may be revived by minority report on motion adopted by majority vote of House

Substitute or amendments

No amendments

Bill printed on committee report and distributed (first printing)

Bill printed and distributed

Bill goes to Calendar Committee for assignment to a calendar

Bill brought up for consideration on floor by two-thirds vote of Senate to suspend rules

Second reading, debate, amendments by majority vote and passage to third reading

Second reading, debate, amendments by majority vote and passage to third reading

Third reading, debate, amendments by two-thirds vote and final passage by House

Third reading, debate, amendments by two-thirds vote and final passage by Senate

Amendments are engrossed into text of bill

If amended, returned to House as amended

If not amended

House engrossed text with Senate amendments printed and distributed (second printing)

House concurs in Senate amendments on motion adopted by majority vote

If either house refuses to concur on other house amendments, bill may go to conference committee

Bill Enrolled

Signed by speaker in presence of House

Signed by lt. governor in presence of Senate

Sent to Governor

Governor signs bill

Governor refuses to sign bill

Governor vetoes bill

Bill becomes law

Veto overridden by two-thirds vote of House and Senate

Bill does not become law

POLITICAL INQUIRY

FIGURE 23.8 ■ This diagram displays the sequential flow of a bill from the time it is introduced in the Texas House of Representatives to final passage and transmittal to the governor. A bill introduced in the Senate follows the same procedure, flowing from Senate to House. How does this procedure compare with the route a bill follows through the U.S. House of Representatives and Senate (see Chapter 11)?

closed rider

provision attached to appropriations bills that is not made public until the conference committee meets

calendars

procedures in the House used to consider different kinds of bills: Major bills and minor bills are considered under different procedures

Local and Consent Calendars Committee

committee handling minor and non-controversial bills that normally apply to only one county

Calendars Committee

standing committee of the House that decides which bills will be considered for floor debate and to which committee they will be assigned

subject matter item (creation of a new state regulatory board) or a money item (money for a park in a legislator's district). In the Texas legislature, the practice adds a new twist. **Closed riders** can be attached to appropriations, and they are closed to public inspection and appear only after the appropriation bills have passed the House and the Senate and go to conference committee. In the conference committee, the cloak is removed, and they appear for public inspection for the first time. At this stage, which is always near the end of the session, the likelihood of change is remote. Unless the governor vetoes the bill, these closed riders become law without public comment.

A recent example of a closed rider dealt with the Bush School at Texas A&M University. In the 1999 session of the legislature, the Bush School was separated from the College of Liberal Arts and made a separate school within the university, and its budget was increased by several million dollars. This was done at the request of Governor George W. Bush.

CALENDARS AND BILLS   To fully understand the legislative process, we must distinguish between major and minor bills, because state legislators treat them very differently. State legislatures use different **calendars** to distinguish between major, controversial bills and minor or local bills. By using different calendars, legislatures can better manage their limited time and devote attention to important matters. Texas is one of thirty-six states that use both a local and a consent calendar in both chambers.[19]

The Texas House uses the local and consent calendars for minor bills. To be assigned to these calendars, a bill must meet tests established by House rules. Local bills must not have an effect upon more than one of the 254 counties in the state. Bills for the consent calendar must be minor, noncontroversial bills. To be placed on either the local or the consent calendar, bills must meet two further criteria. First, they must receive unanimous support in the substantive House committee handling the bill. Second, the **Local and Consent Calendars Committee,** the committee that handles minor bills, must approve them. If this committee does not approve the bill, it is sent to the **Calendars Committee** (which decides which bills will be considered for floor debate) for assignment to another calendar. A bill may be removed from the local or consent calendar if five members object during floor debate. Also, if debate exceeds ten minutes, the bill is withdrawn and effectively killed.[20] These procedures safeguard against important bills being approved without adequate review by the whole House.

Figure 23.9 demonstrates the fate of bills in the eighty-first session of the Texas legislature. As can be seen, only about 25 percent of all bills introduced in the House and Senate make it into law. Most bills are introduced in the House. Most make it to a committee for deliberation but die at the committee level. Some bills are introduced to satisfy a constituency, and the member has no intention of working to pass the bill.

There are three calendars for major bills: the emergency calendar, the major state calendar, and the general state calendar. The Calendars Committee only has the authority to assign bills to these calendars. This power is rarely challenged. The distinction among the major calendars is not important until the final days of the legislative session, when time is limited.

There are a few similarities and differences between major and minor bills. The bills are identical in three ways:

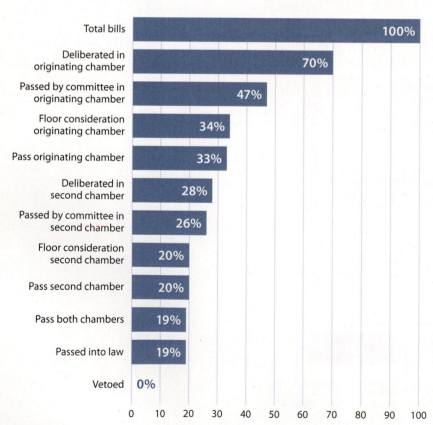

FIGURE 23.9 ■ **Bill Survival Rate in the Eighty-first Session of the Texas Legislature (2009)**

SOURCE: Adapted from Harvey J. Tucker, "Legislation Deliberation in the Texas House and Senate." Paper presented at Annual Meeting of Midwest Political Science Association, Chicago, April 15–18, 2004. Data updated for the 2009 session by Harvey J. Tucker.

1. They originate in either chamber.
2. They are equally likely to be vetoed.
3. They receive final action toward the end of the legislative session.

Major and minor bills are treated differently in six ways:

1. Major bills are introduced earlier in the session than minor bills.
2. Companion bills are introduced in the other chamber more frequently for major bills than for minor bills.
3. Major bills are more evenly distributed across committees; minor bills are more concentrated in a few committees.
4. Major bills are amended more frequently than minor bills.
5. Major bills are more likely to be killed; minor bills are more likely to be passed by the legislature.
6. Final actions to kill major bills occur later in the session than final actions to kill minor bills.[21]

WORKLOAD AND LOGJAMS According to much of the literature on state legislatures, most bills pass the legislature in the final days of the session. This scenario suggests that the legislature "goofs off" for most of the session and then frantically passes bills just before adjournment, producing laws that are given only "hasty consideration, of poor quality and are confused and inferior."[22]

In Texas, it is true that most legislation is passed in the final two weeks of the session. In 1985, almost 80 percent of all bills passed in this time period. The question remains, Does this result in poor quality and inferior legislation? The answer is, Probably not. One must understand the process of setting the agenda in the Texas legislature.

First, bills may be introduced at any time before the session and up until the 60th day of the 140-day session. After the 60th day, only local bills, emergency appropriations, emergency matters submitted by the governor, and bills with a four-fifths vote of the House may be introduced. Thus, for the first 60 days, the agendas for both houses are being set. After the 60th day, the legislature begins to clear those agendas. As indicated, most bills die in committees and are never assigned to a calendar. Killing a bill in committee is an action by the legislature, and it occurs at a regular rate during the session.[23] The bill is dead if it does not make it out of committee. That leaves only about a third of all bills for further consideration late in the session.

Thus, the image of the legislature as goofing off for 120 days is not accurate. The nature of the legislative process requires the passage of major legislation near the end of the session. Also, about half the bills that pass toward the end of the session are minor bills, and they are cleared late for different reasons than are major bills.

We have seen that the formal rules of the House and the Senate govern how and what kind of legislation gets passed. These rules have the effect of preserving the status quo because killing a bill is easy and passing one is very difficult. Although the Texas legislature is not remarkably different from most other legislatures in this respect, in Texas these rules protect the traditionalistic-individualistic political culture of the state.

Rules, Roles, and Styles

In addition to the formal rules regarding procedures, such as how bills become laws and how legislators are appointed to committees, informal rules, expected roles, and leadership styles come into play within legislative procedure. **Informal rules** are legislative norms that all state legislators must learn if they are to be successful. Examples include the following:

Do not:
    conceal the real purpose of a bill.
    deal in personalities in floor debate.

informal rules
set of norms or values that govern legislative behavior

be a thorn in the side of the majority by refusing unanimous consent.
speak on issues you know nothing about.
seek publicity from the press to look good to the people back home.
talk to the press about decisions reached in private.[24]

Each legislature will have a different set of norms and place different value on them. In Texas, dealing in personalities during floor debate has been viewed as acceptable behavior by a large number of Texas legislators, whereas in the other states, only a few members usually view this as acceptable behavior.[25] Legislators must learn the norms of their legislature and adhere to them, or they might find themselves isolated and ineffective. The informal rules are as important as the formal rules governing the legislature.

STYLES OF LEADERSHIP Each speaker approaches the job in different ways. Historically, most speakers have exerted tight control over the House. This was true of Billy Clayton, speaker from 1975 to 1983. However, Gib Lewis, who followed Clayton, exerted much less control. He allowed the members of his team—namely, committee chairs—to control the process, and he took a much more "laid-back" attitude. Pete Laney was more like Billy Clayton in that he controlled the House. Tom Craddick, speaker from 2003 to 2009, followed a style similar to that of Speakers Laney and Clayton.

Lieutenant governors can also differ greatly in their leadership styles. For instance, Bill Hobby, the son of a former governor, served as lieutenant governor for eighteen years (1972–1990). A soft-spoken, low-key person, Hobby seldom forced his will on the members of the Senate. He preferred to work behind the scenes and forge compromises.

Hobby chose not to run for reelection in 1990, and Bob Bullock succeeded him. Bullock had served for sixteen years as the state comptroller and had developed a reputation for strong, effective leadership, but he often went out of his way to make enemies. Bullock's leadership style as lieutenant governor is almost the opposite of Hobby's. Stories have circulated of shouting matches and angry behavior, sometimes even in open sessions of the Senate. The Senate seemed to adjust to Bullock's style of leadership, and he managed to get much of his agenda passed. Hobby and Bullock illustrate very different ways to be effective leaders of the Senate.

Rick Perry, while serving as the Texas agricultural commissioner, did not have the reputation of a compromiser; however, as lieutenant governor, he performed quite effectively in the 1999 session. Lt. Governor Dewhurst was something of a political unknown, having served only four years as land commissioner before his election. Dewhurst's performance received mixed reviews. He was an effective leader in the regular sessions and was partisan in the three special sessions. Powerful Republican leaders have ensured that he will keep the broad powers normally given to lieutenant governors.

Leadership in legislative bodies can take many forms. In addition to formal leadership roles, some members develop reputations as experts in some areas of legislation, and others look to them as leaders in those areas. Being recognized by other members as the expert in some area of legislation obviously increases one's influence. For instance, a person who is a recognized expert on taxation issues can use this reputation to forge coalitions and pass tax legislation.

> After being elected for the first time to the House of Representatives, Democrat Patrick Rose received a good deal of publicity when PBS chronicled his experience during the 2002 election in the documentary *Last Man Standing: Politics Texas Style.* Here, he sits on Republican senator Jeff Wentworth's wastebasket during a Senate discussion.

REPRESENTATIONAL ROLES Constituencies have expectations about their legislators' roles. As noted in Chapter 11, for centuries members of legislatures have argued about the representational role of a legislator. Are they *delegates,* sent by the voters to represent the voters' interests, or are they *trustees,* entrusted by the voters to make decisions based on their best judgment? The delegate role is perceived as being more democratic—as doing what the people want. The trustee role can be characterized as elitist—as doing what one thinks is best.

In reality, members may play both the delegate and the trustee role, depending upon the issue before them. For example, in 1981 the Texas legislature passed a bill prohibiting the catching of redfish by commercial fishermen in some waters in the Gulf of Mexico. The bill was written and advanced by sport fishermen. Representatives from coastal communities in Texas voted as delegates—with the commercial fishermen and against the bill. Representatives from the Panhandle, however, were free to vote as trustees. In matters affecting the livelihood of Panhandle ranchers but not coastal fisheries, these representatives would reverse their voting roles. Which role representatives play is largely dependent on how the issues affect their district. The problem with this is that local interests can take the forefront, leading legislators to neglect long-term statewide or larger public interests.

Rating the Texas Legislature

How does the Texas legislature compare with legislatures of other states? Making comparisons is always difficult, but several political scientists have developed indexes to measure the "professionalism" of state legislatures. Most of these indexes of professionalism rely on several measures. Two important measures are annual salary and number of days the legislature is in session. A third measure that is often employed is the amount of money available for staff assistance. Of these three measures, the last, salary and staff assistance, is most significant.

Other writers have also used "percent metropolitan" as a factor in explaining professional development of state legislatures. The argument goes that large, metropolitan states will cause an increase in the number of bills introduced because of the increased problems that come with urban growth. More bills require more time, which results in longer sessions. When sessions become longer, lasting most of the year, pay and staff assistance tend to increase.[26]

Given these criteria, how does the professionalism of the Texas legislature stack up when compared with that of legislatures in other states? Texas is a mixed bag when judged on these criteria.

Staff Assistance

Texas provides more money for legislative staff than any other state. Most members keep open offices on a full-time basis in their district, and many do in the state capital as well. The recent renovations of the state capitol building have provided each senator and House member with excellent office and committee hearing space. Texas senators receive $25,000 per month for staff salary support plus office expenses. House members each receive $8,500 per month for staff salary plus office expenses. In addition, standing committees have staff salary support during and between legislative sessions. California provides $20,000 to both House and Senate members. New York provides staff support similar to Texas for its legislature. The Texas Legislative Council has a large, professional staff to assist the legislature. It has produced one of the best Web pages of any of the states and provides easy access to the citizens during and between legislative sessions. The House also has the House Research Organization, which produces professional assistance to the legislature.

Salary and Building Facilities

As a result of the renovations to the state capitol building, the members of the Texas legislature have excellent facilities for their staff, committee hearings, and legislative work. In this area, the Texas legislature compares favorably with other state legislatures. Salaries,

HOW TEXAS COMPARES

LEGISLATIVE SALARIES IN THE TEN MOST POPULOUS STATES

Texas currently pays members of the state legislature $600 per month. Among the fifteen large states, Texas has the lowest pay. Should members of the legislature be paid a living wage?

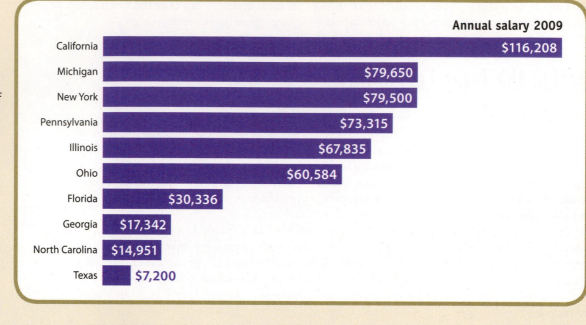

Annual salary 2009

State	Salary
California	$116,208
Michigan	$79,650
New York	$79,500
Pennsylvania	$73,315
Illinois	$67,835
Ohio	$60,584
Florida	$30,336
Georgia	$17,342
North Carolina	$14,951
Texas	$7,200

SOURCE: Council of State Governments, *The Book of the States 2009* (Lexington, KY: Council of State Governments, 2009), Vol. 41, 99–100, table 3.9.

however, are considerably lower than those in other states, and on this important indicator of professionalism, Texas does not score well.

Some citizens feel that because the legislature meets for only 140 days every two years, it is part-time and members should be paid accordingly. The pay reflects that attitude. Texas pays the 181 members of the legislature $7,200 a year plus an additional $139 per day for the first 140 days the legislature is in session. In years when the legislature meets, the total compensation is $26,600. In years when the legislature is not in session, legislators receive their $7,200 in salary and may receive some additional per diem pay for off-session committee work.

The salary of Texas legislators has not been increased in the past thirty years. Several attempts to change the state constitutional limit have been rejected by the voters. The current pay qualifies legislators who have no other income for food stamps and other federal assistance. Obviously, most legislators have other sources of income. Many are attorneys or successful businessmen and businesswomen. Lack of compensation is very much in keeping with the traditionalistic political culture of the state, according to which only the elite should serve in the legislature. Also, note in "How Texas Compares" that other southern states (Florida, Georgia, and North Carolina) also have low salaries.

Most citizens are excluded from being legislators because they would not be able to devote the large amount of time to legislative work and still earn a living. Service in the Texas legislature is possible only for the independently wealthy, "political consultants," and

SHOULD THE TEXAS LEGISLATURE MEET ANNUALLY AND BE BETTER PAID?

The Issue: In May 2008, the Texas Commission on Environmental Quality (TCEQ) granted Waste Control Specialists (WCS) a license to dump nuclear waste in Andrews County in West Texas. Some of the waste hadn't even originated in Texas. WCS had secured a contract to bury waste from a weapons processing plant in Ohio. TCEQ made the decision despite a warning from a group of geologists and engineers who believe that the dump site is too close to a water table that is "highly likely" to become contaminated.

So why was this license granted? Some say campaign dollars. Between 2001 and 2005, WCS and individuals with connections to the company spent millions of dollars in campaign contributions, lobbying, and gifts for members of the Texas legislature. In 2003, the legislature passed a bill that allowed WCS to manage low-level nuclear waste, with a portion of WCS's revenue siphoned off to Andrews County and to the state. This initial move established a cozy relationship between the company, lawmakers, and county officials. Yet Texans for Public Justice concludes, "Rarely have so few given away so much for so little."*

This case is perhaps a prime example of the powerful impact of lobby money on decision making in Austin. Many argue that when legislators are paid less than minimum wage, corruption is simply unavoidable. After serving a brief term in the legislature, lawmakers frequently benefit from enormous pay raises when they accept a job with a lobbying firm whose interests they then promote in the state House or Senate.

Chris Bell, former Democratic candidate for governor, argues that it is absurd to pay state legislators less per year than a cook earns working at McDonald's and expect them to meet only a few months every other year to run the $157 billion "corporation" that is the state of Texas. He has suggested annual sessions for the legislature, a salary increase to $100,000 a year, and rules to limit additional sources of income.

Yes: State senators and representatives must leave their regular jobs for many months every other year. Since most jobs do not allow that kind of flexibility, this requirement limits the type of candidates who can run for office. Furthermore, state legislators must compensate for their low salaries by finding additional sources of income. This situation makes them especially vulnerable to "big money" interests. Creating a professional legislature will provide Texans with a cleaner, better-run state.

No: By increasing their own salaries and meeting annually, the legislature would gain far more power than this governmental body should have. The interest groups that interact with the legislators to create policy represent the people. If the people support or oppose a policy, they organize to express their views. The interaction between interest groups and legislators should be closely monitored, but giving government more power over the people would only increase corruption, not reduce it.

Other approaches: The state can increase each legislator's pay and limit campaign contributions, but the legislature can continue to meet every other year. If lawmakers earned approximately $50,000 a year, a wider pool of candidates would be able to run for office and would be able to spend their time off building grassroots support, investigating issues that are important to their constituencies, and interacting with a wider range of organized groups—not primarily those groups that spend large sums of money on their campaigns.

What do you think?

① What can be done to mitigate the negative effect of interest groups while maintaining their positive role in the democratic system?

② What are the benefits of having a legislature that meets annually and is well paid? What are the costs?

③ Do you agree with Chris Bell's proposal? Explain your answer.

*"Texas Becomes the Nation's Lone-Star Nuclear Dump," Lobby Watch, Texans for Public Justice, March 14, 2005, www.tpj.org/publication_view.jsp?pubid=568.

people who can find a person or a group to support them while they are in the legislature. In Texas, attorney-legislators who have cases in courts while the legislature is in session can have their cases delayed until the legislature adjourns. Some attorney-legislators receive cases from people who want to delay court action. Unlike many other states, Texas does not have a financial disclosure law that forces members to disclose their sources of income. This leaves the sources of members' income an open question. Some might receive income as "consultants" to businesses with interests in current legislation. The objectivity of members under these circumstances is questionable. "Thinking Critically About Democracy" looks at this potential issue, along with the controversy over biennial versus annual sessions.

Annual Sessions

biennial session

meeting of the legislature every two years

Texas is one of five states that do not meet in annual sessions. Also, sessions are limited to 140 days, and the legislature cannot call itself into special session. The Texas legislature meets in **biennial sessions** (every two years) of 140 days in odd-numbered years, beginning in January. Texas is one of only five states that still meet in biennial sessions. Montana, Nevada, North Dakota, and Oregon are the others. In recent years, the trend has been toward annual sessions. At the end of World War II, only four states held annual sessions. There were twenty meeting annually by 1966 and forty-two by 1974.[27]

Voters in Texas rejected a move to annual sessions in 1969 and again in 1972. In keeping with the traditionalistic-individualistic political culture of the state, there is some concern that the more often the legislature meets, the more damage it can do. One political wag once remarked that there was a typographical error in the original Texas Constitution, and the founders had intended the legislature to meet for two days every 140 years.

sine die

adjourned; the legislature must adjourn at end of its regular session and cannot continue to meet

extraordinary session

legislative session called by the legislature, rather than the governor; not used in Texas

At the end of the 140-day session, the Texas legislature must adjourn (**sine die**) and cannot call special or longer sessions (known as **extraordinary sessions**). In recent years, many state governments have placed limits on the number of days a legislature can stay in session. Thirteen states do not place a limit on the length of legislative sessions.[28] The inability to call itself into special session, which Texas shares with seventeen other states, makes the limit on the regular session even more meaningful. The legislature must finish its work in the prescribed time and leave.

special session

session called by the governor to consider legislation proposed by the governor only

In Texas, only the governor may call **special sessions,** of not more than thirty days each. There is no limit on the number of special sessions the governor may call. Also, in Texas, the governor decides the subject matter of the session, thus limiting the range of topics the legislature can consider. This gives the governor tremendous power to set the agenda of the legislature during special sessions and a bargaining chip to get the legislature to do what the governor wants.

The Texas legislature's inability to call itself into special session also gives the governor stronger veto powers. If the governor vetoes a bill and the legislature has adjourned, the veto stands. This in part helps to explain why so few vetoes of the governor are overridden.

States such as Texas that limit the number of days of regular sessions are often forced to resort to special sessions. Budgetary problems, reapportionment issues, school finance, and prison funding have forced the Texas legislature to have many special sessions in the past decades. Many critics of the Texas biennial sessions point to the frequency of special sessions as evidence that the state needs to go to annual sessions. Budgeting for two years is extremely difficult, since it involves predicting state revenues.

In 1994, the National Conference of State Legislatures produced a professionalism ranking based on four factors: full-time or part-time, pay, staff size, and turnover. In this ranking, Texas was classified as a moderate professional/citizen legislature.[29] Texas is a large urban state with many problems, and many bills are introduced each session. Annual sessions have been considered by past legislatures and rejected by the voters. This situation is not likely to change any time soon. Texas will continue to be a low-pay, part-time legislature with a very professional staff. It is interesting to note that when voter approval is required for a constitutional amendment to raise pay and have annual sessions, the voters reject those changes.

Author and scholar Thomas R. Dye has observed that state legislatures tend to mirror the socioeconomic conditions within their states.[30] As Texas's economy has expanded, the level of professionalism within the legislature and the amount of interest group activity have risen. A larger, better-paid staff and the renovations to the state capitol building, which included introducing high-tech hardware and software applications, certainly point to an increasing level of professionalism within the Texas legislature. Dye also noted that state legislatures tend to represent local interests rather than statewide interests. Legislators are recruited, elected, and reelected locally. Local interests will always be the dominant factor in determining how legislators vote on proposed legislation. As a result, frequently no one represents statewide interests, which often get lost in the zeal to protect and promote local interests. As the Texas legislature becomes more professional, will legislators start to rise above local interests? Dye also concluded that the degree of party cohesion and the competition between the parties increases as the socioeconomic level of the state rises. As Texas's economy booms, will the Democratic Party regain parity within the legislature?

As the Texas legislature redraws district boundaries, the membership shifts. The federal "one person, one vote" law increased the power of urban areas at the expense of rural districts. As new residents flowed into urban areas from out of state, the Republican Party rose to power within the legislature. Minority representation increased as well, particularly after redistricting in 1981. As this trend continues, the state legislature will better reflect the contrasts within Texas society.

Summary

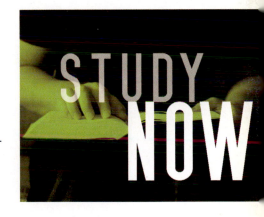

1. Methods of Election
The Texas legislature consists of the House of Representatives and the Senate, both of which are elected from single-member districts. Redistricting takes place every ten years and is based on the federal census with the aim of achieving equity of representation and minority representation. In 2001 and 2003, redistricting efforts became extremely controversial as Democrats attempted to stop the Republican majority in both houses from redrawing district lines in ways that favored Republicans.

2. Getting Elected
In general, district lines tend to be drawn to create safe party districts that reduce competition for political office. Despite relatively low competition for legislative offices, Texas has high turnover in both houses. This is because of poor pay relative to the high demands of the job. High turnover can lead to legislatures controlled by a few individuals.

3. Legislative Procedures
The speaker of the house and the lieutenant governor (who presides over the Senate) are the two most powerful positions in the Texas legislature. They appoint legislators to committees and refer all bills to committees. The process by which a bill becomes a law is similar to the federal system, with bills being placed on calendars and sent to committees. Most bills die

in committee. A distinction is made between minor, noncontroversial bills and major bills, which ensures that major bills receive adequate review. Both legislative houses have a legislative schedule that guarantees that most bills are passed in the final days of the session.

4. Rating the Texas Legislature
Because of the low pay and the biennial nature of the Texas legislature, it rates lower on the scale of "professionalism" than other state legislatures do. However, in the area of staff assistance, Texas ranks favorably.

Key Terms

biennial sessions 700

"birthright" characteristics 684

calendars 694

Calendars Committee 694

closed rider 694

committee assignments 689

equity of representation 678

extraordinary session 700

informal rules 695

interim committees 691

Legislative Redistricting Board (LRB) 678

lieutenant governor 690

Local and Consent Calendars Committee 694

minority representation 678

multimember district 676

parliamentarian 690

racially gerrymandered majority-minority districts 679

rider 691

safe election districts 685

sine die 700

single-member district 676

speaker of the house 689

special session 700

term limits 688

turnover 688

For Review

1. What is the difference between single-member and multimember districts, and what impact does using each of these in the electoral process have on minority representation?

2. How has recent redistricting in Texas affected minority representation and party dominance?

3. What are the formal and informal requirements for holding legislative office in Texas?

4. How does a bill become a law? What is the role of calendars in this process?

5. What are the powers and the duties of the speaker of the house and the lieutenant governor?

6. What are the strengths and weaknesses of the legislature in Texas compared with legislatures in other states?

For Critical Thinking and Discussion

1. What do you think is the effect of the creation of safe party districts on minor or third parties in Texas?

2. Do you feel that high turnover in the legislature is beneficial for democratic government? Explain your answer.

3. Propose a bill that you would like to see pass in the legislature. Describe the steps it would have to go through and what you would do to make sure it did not die in committee.

4. If you were in the legislature, what committees would you like to become a member of? Why?

5. Do you feel that it is necessary to improve the professionalism of the Texas legislature? If so, how would you go about accomplishing this goal?

MULTIPLE CHOICE: Choose the lettered item that answers the question correctly.

1. All of the following are true about sessions of the Texas legislature except
   a. the governor may call special sessions.
   b. the legislature may call extraordinary sessions.
   c. sessions occur biennially.
   d. the duration of a regular session is 140 days.

2. What must be present for the Texas House to act on a bill?
   a. a quota
   b. a quagmire
   c. a quorum
   d. a simple majority

3. Which of the following is *not* a power shared by the Texas speaker of the house and the lieutenant governor?
   a. appointing chairs of committees
   b. voting on all bills after the third reading
   c. serving as presiding officer
   d. referring all bills to committees

4. The Texas legislature rates favorably compared with other state legislatures in
   a. annual salary and length of sessions.
   b. length of session and staff assistance.
   c. building facilities and annual salary.
   d. staff assistance and building facilities.

5. Which of the following must a person be to become a Texas state senator?
   a. a resident of the district for more than one year
   b. at least 21 years of age
   c. a Texas resident for at least two years
   d. a registered voter

6. An area where a Democrat would be least likely to be voted in to office would be
   a. South Texas
   b. the Panhandle
   c. East Texas
   d. inner city metropolitan areas

7. Redistricting efforts during the 2003 session favored
   a. Republicans and minorities.
   b. Democrats and minorities.
   c. Republicans only.
   d. minorities only.

8. Political and racial gerrymandering in Texas has created safe party districts for
   a. Republicans.
   b. Democrats.
   c. both Republicans and Democrats.
   d. neither Republicans nor Democrats.

9. In general, about how many bills are passed by the Texas legislature and made into state law?
   a. 10 percent
   b. 25 percent
   c. 60 percent
   d. 95 percent

10. Minor, noncontroversial bills are assigned to the
    a. regular calendar.
    b. local calendar.
    c. consent calendar.
    d. local calendar or consent calendar.

FILL IN THE BLANKS.

11. When each member of a legislature represents about the same number of people, there is _____.

12. A _____ is a session called by the governor to consider legislation proposed by the governor only.

13. The _____ is more powerful in Texas than in other states, and holds powers similar to those of the speaker, but still must forge an alliance with key senators to use those powers effectively.

14. Texas compares favorably with other state legislatures in many areas except members' _____.

15. _____ are noncompetitive districts that can be won only by the party with 55 percent or more of the votes in the district.

RESOURCES FOR RESEARCH AND ACTION

Internet Resources

The National Conference of State Legislatures
www.ncsl.org   This site has information on state legislatures.

Texas Legislative Council
www.tlc.state.tx.us/research/redist/redist.htm   At this site, you can access redistricting plans as well as maps and reports.

Texas Legislative Reference Library
www.lrl.state.tx.us   This Web site has an excellent collection of information about the current and past legislatures.

The Texas Legislature
www.capitol.state.tx.us   At this site, you can find your state representative or senator if you know your postal zip code. You can also look up bills by subject matter or by bill number, author, and session.

Internet Activism

The Texas Legislative Council Web site (www.tlc.state.tx.us) contains Internet resources that allow you to view your home district, find your representatives, and learn about legislation. Find out who your senator and representatives are. Then start lobbying!

Twitter
www.twitter.com/dewhurst4texas   Get updates from Lieutenant Governor David Dewhurst about pressing political issues.

YouTube
www.youtube.com/watch?v=aRH1H7DJOJ4&feature=related
A bill that would allow students to carry concealed weapons recently passed the Texas House of Representatives. This report examines the implications of the bill while waiting for the Senate's approval.

Facebook
www.facebook.com/pages/Texas-Legislature/109146599104226?v=desc&ref=search   The Texas Legislature Facebook community page is your source for information about current issues facing the legislature today. Join the group, and become more involved in the political process.

Recommended Readings

Hamm, Keith E., and Gary F. Moncrief. "Legislative Politics in the States," in *Politics in the American States: A Comparative Analysis* (8th ed.), ed. Virginia Gray and Russell L. Hanson. Washington, DC: CQ Press, 2004.

Jewell, Malcolm E., and Samuel C. Patterson. *The Legislative Process in the United States.* New York: Random House, 1985.

Movies of Interest

State Legislature (2007)
A documentary that explores the Idaho legislature. The film offers a unique look into the daily operations of legislative committees and representatives.

Last Man Standing: Politics—Texas Style (2004)
A P.O.V. documentary that aired on PBS chronicling the 2002 race for the Texas House of Representatives in which Democrat Patrick Rose beat Republican Rick Green. Interviews with former Governor Ann Richards, Bush adviser Karl Rove, and writer Molly Ivins analyze Texas politics at a time when Anglos were losing their majority status and Republicans were capturing all statewide offices.

The Office of Governor and State Agencies in Texas

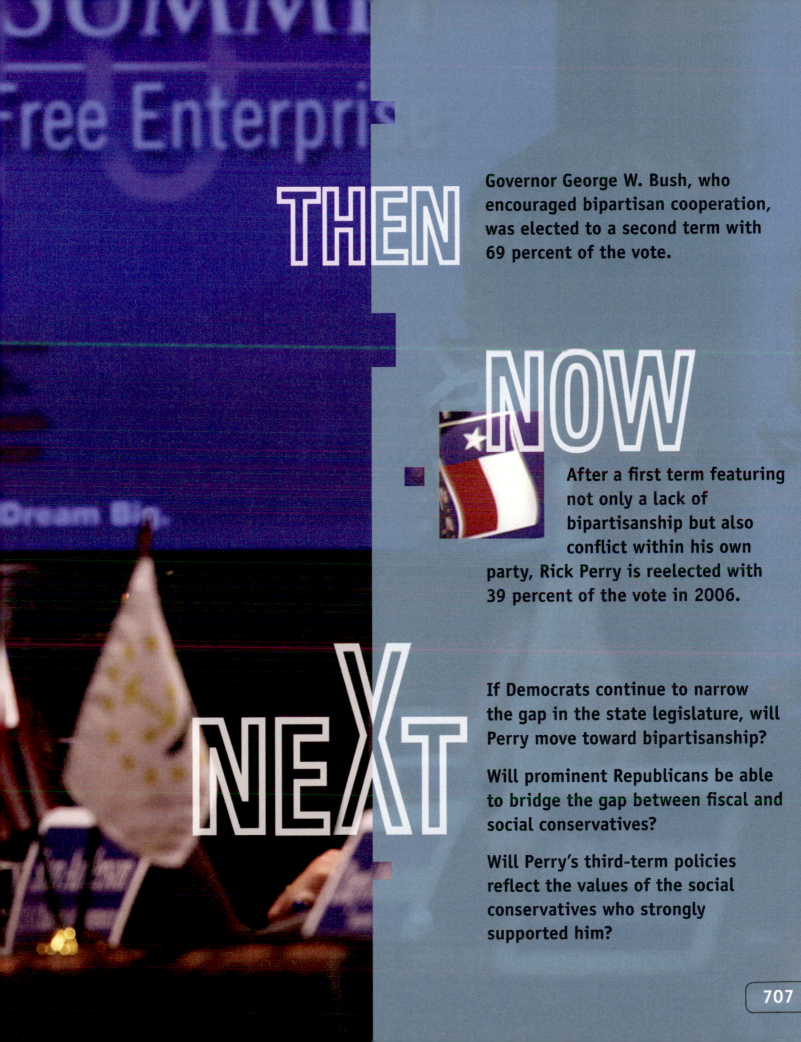

THEN

Governor George W. Bush, who encouraged bipartisan cooperation, was elected to a second term with 69 percent of the vote.

NOW

After a first term featuring not only a lack of bipartisanship but also conflict within his own party, Rick Perry is reelected with 39 percent of the vote in 2006.

NEXT

If Democrats continue to narrow the gap in the state legislature, will Perry move toward bipartisanship?

Will prominent Republicans be able to bridge the gap between fiscal and social conservatives?

Will Perry's third-term policies reflect the values of the social conservatives who strongly supported him?

This chapter examines the structure and the functions of the offices and agencies within the executive branch.

FIRST, we investigate *the roles of the governor* within the Texas political system.

SECOND, we explore *the governor's powers,* both formal and informal. The governor has formal executive, legislative, judicial, and military authority as well as informal influence as party leader and head of government.

THIRD, we analyze the *administrative agencies of state government* in Texas and compare their structure with the structures of executive branches of other states.

The governor is the most salient

political actor in state government. Whether the true power center of the state is embodied in the occupant of the office or somewhere else, the office is the focal point of state government and politics. The governor is expected to perform many tasks and is blamed for not doing others, even if the office is formally very weak. The expectation is that governors will be leaders in their state.

The power and respect accorded to governors have varied greatly over time. During the colonial period, little power or respect was afforded the office—some have argued that the American Revolution was a war against colonial governors. The experiences of southern states following Reconstruction led to a return of weak governors in the South. There is an old Texas saying: "The governor should have only enough power to sign for his paycheck." In recent times, the power and prestige of the office have increased, as evidenced by recent presidential politics. In both Democratic and Republican parties, many presidential candidates have been former governors. In the past twenty-seven years, only former President George H. W. Bush and President Barack Obama had not served as governors before becoming president. Today, the office of governor has assumed new significance because of a change in attitude toward the role of the federal government. The Republican Congress of the 1990s promised to return power and responsibility to state governments and to allow states more flexibility in administering programs funded by the federal government. Even without the renewed significance of the office, and even though many governors have little formal power, governors are important players in state politics.

The Roles of the Governor

Citizens expect governors to play many roles. They should be the chief policy makers, formulating long-term goals and objectives. This requires selling the program to state legislators and coordinating with state agencies that administer the programs.

The governor is also expected to act as **chief legislator.** Governors do not formally introduce bills, but because they need the support of significant members of the legislature who will carry their program, they must spend considerable time and energy developing those relationships. If the governor is a member of one party and the other party dominates the legislature, getting legislation passed can be difficult. The governor might have to spend considerable resources to accomplish his or her goals.

The governor must also act as **party chief.** As the most important party official in the state, the governor helps legislators and other elected officials in their reelection efforts, raises money for the party, and creates a favorable image of the party in the state.

The governor also serves as the ceremonial leader of the state. The demands of **ceremonial duties** are extreme. "Where two or more are gathered together," there also is the governor expected to be. The governor will receive many invitations to speak, make presentations, and cut ribbons. Some governors become trapped in the safe, friendly environment of ceremonial duties and neglect or avoid the other duties of their office. For governors with an agenda for action, ceremony is a diversion from more important and difficult objectives.

Governors can use ceremonial duties as communication opportunities to promote their programs. They must wisely choose which invitations to accept and which to delegate to

chief legislator
a role of governors in which they spend time and energy presenting an active agenda of legislation to the legislature and working to pass that agenda

party chief
a role of governors that calls for them to aid their fellow party members in their reelection efforts, raise money for the party, and create a favorable party image

ceremonial duties
a governor's duties to attend many functions and represent the state

others or decline. Ceremonial appearances, such as graduation speaker, provide an opportunity to generate favorable press coverage and support for programs. Former Governor Bush used these opportunities both to promote his state programs and as an avenue to promote his run for the presidency.

The governor is also the chief **intergovernmental coordinator,** working with federal officials and officials in other states. The governor must work with congressional delegations of U.S. senators and representatives, the president, and cabinet officials to promote the interests of the state.

Thus, many roles are assigned to governors. In Texas, the formal powers of the governor are very weak, and this complicates things. The governor cannot rely on formal authority but must develop and use the power and prestige of the office to persuade others to accept his or her program. This informal leadership trait, the power to persuade others, is perhaps the most necessary "power" of all.

intergovernmental coordinator
a role of governors in which they coordinate activities with other state and federal officials

Rules of the Gubernatorial Office

The rules of the Texas governor's office include both formal and informal qualifications as well as regulations regarding salary, succession to office, removal from office, and tenure.

QUALIFICATIONS   In most states the formal qualifications to be governor are minimal. All but six states set a minimum age requirement, and most require a candidate to be a resident of the state for five to ten years preceding election. Also, most states require governors to be U.S. citizens and qualified voters.

In Texas, the formal qualifications are simple: One must be at least 30 years of age, a citizen of the United States, and a resident of the state for five years preceding election. There is no requirement to be a registered voter. In the 1930s, W. Lee O'Daniel ran for governor stressing that he was not a "professional politician." To prove this, he made a point of not being a registered voter.

Informal qualifications are more important than formal qualifications. Nationwide, most governors have held elected office before becoming governor. An examination of the 933 people serving as governor between 1900 and 1997 reveals that the most common career path to that office is to begin in the legislature, move to statewide office, and then move to the governor's office.[1] Others who are elected governor have served as U.S. senator or representative, and a few have served in local elected offices (such as mayor). Thus, having held elected office emerges as an informal qualification for becoming governor. Some governors gain experience as appointed administrators or as party officials. Between 1970 and 1999, only 10 percent of all people elected governor had no prior political office experience.[2]

These observations about governors generally apply to Texas governors. Table 24.1 lists those who have served as governor in Texas since 1949 and their prior office experience. Most had served in elected of-

TABLE 24.1

Previous Office Experience of Texas Governors, 1949–Present

Governor	Terms of Office	Previous Offices
Allan Shivers	1949–1957	State Senate, lieutenant governor
Price Daniel	1957–1963	U.S. Senate
John Connally	1963–1969	U.S. secretary of the navy*
Preston Smith	1969–1973	Texas House and Senate, lieutenant governor
Dolph Briscoe	1973–1979	Texas House
Bill Clements	1979–1983 1987–1991	Assistant U.S. secretary of defense*
Mark White	1983–1987	Attorney general
Ann Richards	1991–1995	County office, state treasurer
George W. Bush	1995–2001	None
Rick Perry	2001–present	State legislature, agricultural commissioner, and lieutenant governor

*Appointive offices. No electoral experience before becoming governor.
SOURCE: James Anderson, Richard W. Murray, and Edward L. Farley, *Texas Politics: An Introduction*, 6th ed. (New York: HarperCollins, 1992), 166–88. Governors Bush and Perry from other sources.

ANALYZING THE SOURCES

WOMEN GOVERNORS

Whereas Miriam Ferguson and Lurleen Wallace were stand-in governors for husbands ineligible for re-election, an increasing number of women besides Wyoming's Nellie T. Ross have been elected in their own right. The map at right shows which states have current or past women governors.

Evaluating the Evidence

① What factors contributed to the thirty-year gap when there were no women governors?

② How many states have had women governors? Are there any regional patterns?

③ What factors might lead to an increase or a decrease in the number of women governors in the future?

SOURCE: Center for Women and Politics, Rutgers University, www.cawp.rutgers.edu/.

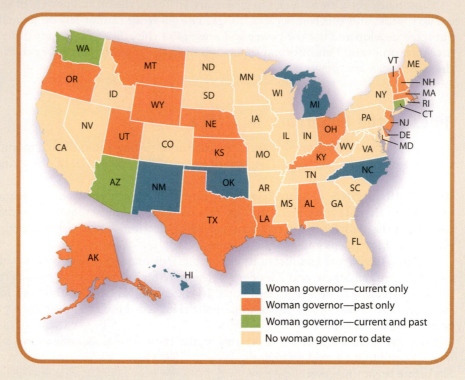

Woman governor—current only
Woman governor—past only
Woman governor—current and past
No woman governor to date

fice, five in statewide offices. Only two had not held elected office. The current governor, Rick Perry, followed a rather typical pattern before becoming governor. He served in the state legislature, as agricultural commissioner, and as lieutenant governor before becoming governor when George Bush resigned to assume the office of president of the United States. He was elected governor in his own right in 2002.

Besides electoral experience, many informal qualifications play a role in winning a governor's seat. Nationwide, most people who have served as governors have been white, male, Protestant, well-educated, wealthy individuals. Four African Americans and several Latinos have served as governors. The number of women governors has increased in recent years. In 1924, Wyoming elected the first woman governor, Nellie T. Ross, who served one term. She succeeded her husband, who died in office. Later in 1924, Texas elected Miriam A. Ferguson governor, and she was reelected in 1932. Mrs. Ferguson was a "stand-in" for her husband, Jim Ferguson, who had been impeached, removed from office, and barred from seeking reelection. Similarly, in 1968, Lurleen Wallace was elected governor of Alabama as a stand-in for her husband, George Wallace, who could not be reelected because of term limits. "Analyzing the Sources" looks at the subject of women governors.

Historically, the men who have served as governor of Texas have generally had one thing in common—wealth. A few, such as Dolph Briscoe and Bill Clements, were very wealthy. If not wealthy, most have been successful in law, business, or politics before becoming governor. Ann Richards was an exception to these informal qualifications. She was not wealthy or from a wealthy family and had no business or law experience. Governor Perry, while claiming the status of a sharecropper's son, came from a family with a moderate, middle-class background.

SALARY   Governors receive much higher pay than state legislators. As of 2010, salaries ranged from a low of $70,000 in Maine to a high of $179,000 in New York. The Texas salary of $150,000 per year is above the mean salary of $90,000.[3] In addition, Texas provides the governor with a home in Austin, an automobile with a driver, an airplane, and reimbursement for actual travel expenses. Texas governors also receive a budget for entertaining and maintaining the Governor's Mansion. Compared with members of the state legislature, the governor in Texas is extremely well paid. Given the demands and responsibilities of the job, however, the governor is not overpaid compared with executives of large corporations, who receive many times this amount.

SUCCESSION TO OFFICE   Most states provide for a successor if the governor dies or leaves office for any reason. Forty-three states have lieutenant governors who advance to the office if it is vacant for any reason. In the seven states without lieutenant governors, another officeholder, usually the leader of the state Senate, succeeds to the governor's office. In some states, the lieutenant governor and the governor are separately elected. In others, the governor and lieutenant governor run as a "team," much as candidates for president and vice president do. In these cases, the candidate for governor picks the lieutenant governor.

When the governor leaves the state, the lieutenant governor becomes **acting governor.** This is unlike the office of vice president of the United States, who does not become acting president if the president leaves the country. Some governors have experienced problems with their lieutenant governor when they have left the state. For instance, in 1995 Jim Guy Tucker of Arkansas had problems with Senate President Pro Tem Jerry Jewell, who was acting as governor in the absence of the lieutenant governor. Jewell "granted two pardons and executive clemency to two prison inmates."[4] Also, the Arkansas lieutenant governor, Republican Mike Huckabee, "signed a proclamation for a Christian Heritage Week after Tucker declined to do so earlier."[5]

acting governor
the position held by the lieutenant governor, who performs the functions of the office of governor when a governor leaves a state

REMOVAL FROM OFFICE   All states except Oregon have a procedure for removing governors by a process generally called impeachment. In this procedure, the lower House of the legislature adopts articles of impeachment, and then the Senate holds a trial on these articles of impeachment. If the Senate finds the governor guilty, he or she is removed from office. Sixteen governors have had impeachment trials, and eight have been removed from office.[6]

Technically, impeachment is a judicial process, but it is also a very political process. Impeached governors have generally been guilty of some wrongdoing, but they are often removed for political reasons. For example, one of the eight impeached governors was Jim Ferguson of Texas (1915–1917). Ferguson was indicted by the Texas House, technically for misuse of state funds, and was convicted and removed from office by the Senate. In reality, he was impeached because of his fight with the University of Texas board of regents. When the governor could not force the board of regents to terminate several professors who had criticized the governor, or force the resignation of board members, he line-item vetoed the entire appropriations bill for the University of Texas.[7] This veto led to his removal from office.

Ferguson tried to prevent his impeachment by calling the legislature into special session. Since only the governor may decide the agenda of a special session, Governor Ferguson told the legislature it could consider any item it wanted, except impeachment. That ploy did not work, and he was removed from office. Courts later upheld Ferguson's impeachment.

A few years after the Ferguson affair in Texas, Oklahoma impeached two consecutively elected governors. These two impeachments were as political as the one in Texas. In 1921, there were several race riots, in which many African Americans were killed. The most noted of these was in the Greenwood area of Tulsa, Oklahoma. Thirty-five square blocks of this segregated African American community were burned and destroyed, and over forty people were killed. In 1922, John C. Walton was elected governor as a member of the Farmer-Laborite party. Walton tried to break up the Ku Klux Klan in the state, and that led to his impeachment.

The lieutenant governor, Martin Trapp, served out the remainder of Walton's term but was unable to run for reelection because Oklahoma had a limit of one term at that time. Henry S. Johnson was elected governor in 1926 as a pro-KKK candidate and refused to use his office to quell Klan activity in the state. Johnson used the National Guard to try to prevent the legislature from meeting to consider his impeachment. The legislature was kept out of the state capitol building and had to meet in a hotel in Oklahoma City. Johnson was convicted and removed from office. He had been indicted on eighteen counts and found not guilty on all but on "general incompetence" for which he was impeached.[8]

The impeachment of Evan Mecham in Arizona in 1988 was equally political. Mecham made a number of racist remarks and had become a source of embarrassment in the state. Technically, he was impeached for misuse of state funds during his inaugural celebration.

Fifteen states also allow **recall of the governor.** Texas does not provide for recall of state officials. Many Texas home-rule cities do allow recall of city councils and mayors. Recall involves getting petitions signed by some number of voters, followed by an election in which, if a majority approves, the governor can be recalled or removed from office. Two governors have been recalled: Lynn J. Frazier of North Dakota was recalled in 1921, the same time when governors were being impeached in Texas and Oklahoma. In 1988, Governor Mecham of Arizona was spared a recall election when he was impeached by the legislature.[9] In 2003, Gray Davis of California was recalled.

TENURE   The legal ability of governors to succeed themselves in office and the length of their term is known as **tenure of office.** Historically, the tenure of governors has been less than that for most other statewide elected state officials, in part because of term limits.[10] Term limits for governors have been a fixture since the beginning of the Republic. Ten of the governors in the original thirteen states had one-year terms. States first moved to two-year terms, then four-year terms. In the 1960s, states borrowed from the federal Constitution the idea of limiting governors to two four-year terms.[11] Southern states were the last to move to longer terms. Many southern states once prohibited the governor from serving consecutive terms in office. Today, only Virginia retains that provision. (See "How Texas Compares: Term Limits for Governors.")

Tenure is an important determinant of power. If governors can be continually reelected, they retain the potential to influence government until they decide to leave office. Only fourteen states do not limit how long a person can serve as governor. When prevented from being reelected by term limits, governors suffer as "lame ducks" toward the end of their terms. Long tenure also enables governors to carry out their programs. Short terms (two years) force governors to continually seek reelection and make political compromises. Only two states retain the two-year term—Vermont and New Hampshire.

Length of tenure also influences the governor's role as intergovernmental coordinator. Building up associations with officials in other states and in Washington, D.C., takes time. Short tenure makes it difficult for governors to gain leadership roles in this area and has the effect of shortchanging the state that imposes it.[12] The map in "How Texas Compares: Term Limits for Governors" details state term limits. The Texas governor has the strongest tenure—four-year terms with no limit on the number of terms.

Still, few Texas governors have served more than four years in office. Governor Perry is the first governor to serve two consecutive four-year terms. The length of his service has raised calls for new limits. During the contentious 2010 Republican primary, Governor Perry's main opponent, U.S. Senator Kay Bailey Hutchison, unveiled a plan to limit Texas governors to two terms. A poll conducted less than a month after Senator Hutchison's proposal reported that 75 percent of Texans surveyed do support term limits. Perry's campaign, however, retorted that Hutchison's proposition lacked credibility, since she herself was serving a third term in the U.S. Senate after pledging to step down after two.[13] Hutchison lost to Perry in the March 2010 primary. Governor Perry is Texas's longest-serving governor. At the end of his current term, he will have served a total of fourteen years as governor.

recall of the governor
the removal of the governor (or another elected official) by a petition signed by the required number of registered voters, followed by an election in which a majority votes to remove the person from office

tenure of office
the legal ability of governors to succeed themselves in office and the length of their term

TERM LIMITS FOR GOVERNORS

Although term limits for legislators are a recent phenomenon, historically governors have always been limited in the number of terms they could serve. Most states limit the governor to two terms, just like the president. How does Texas compare?

Legend:
- Two-year term, no limit of terms
- Four-year term, no limit of terms
- Four-year term, limited to two terms in lifetime
- Four-year term, non-consecutive reelection
- Four-year term, no more than two terms in sixteen years
- Eight out of twelve years

SOURCE: Council of State Governments, The Book of the States 2009 (Lexington, Ky.: Council of State Governments, 2004), Vol. 41, Table 4.1, 185–186.

The Governor's Powers

As indicated previously, most governors do not have great formal powers. Nevertheless, many duties fall under the formal executive, legislative, judicial, and military powers of the office. How governors use their informal powers can contribute to their success in office.

Executive Powers

Governors exercise executive powers by appointing and removing officials and shaping the budget. In addition, like the U.S. president, governors can issue executive orders, which facilitate the operations of officials and agencies within the executive branch or implement measures specified by laws enacted by the legislature. These orders in effect become law, and hence they provide the executive branch with a degree of legislative authority. Governor Perry, for example, has issued executive orders that have ensured schools be paid on time, detailed hurricane evacuation procedures, and reorganized Adult Protective Services, a division of Health and Human Services that is part of the executive branch. Occasionally, presidents or governors overstep their authority by issuing orders that create regulations that would not have been passed by the legislature. In 2007, Governor Perry issued an executive order requiring preteen girls to receive a vaccine against a virus that causes cervical cancer. In the uproar that followed, both Republicans and Democrats in the House and Senate voted to revoke the order less than three months after it was signed. Texans acted to curtail executive powers of the governor and keep them largely within the confines of budget recommendations and the appointment and removal of officials within the executive branch.

APPOINTIVE AND REMOVAL POWERS

appointive power
the ability of a governor to appoint and remove important state administrators

Jacksonian statehouse democracy
a system in which most of the major department heads in state government are chosen by the voters at the ballot box

plural executive structure
system in which voters elect many statewide officeholders to serve as heads of departments

APPOINTIVE AND REMOVAL POWERS   More important than tenure of office is the **appointive power** of the governor to make appointments and control the agencies of state government. By appointing and removing the heads of most state agencies, the governor gains some control over the administration of programs. But we will see that control is often mitigated by the way government is structured.

Historically, governors have not had strong appointive powers. For most of the nineteenth century, the traditional method of selecting the heads of state agencies was by election. This is called **Jacksonian statehouse democracy.** President Andrew Jackson expressed ultimate faith in the ballot box for selecting administrators. Toward the end of the nineteenth century, there was a proliferation of agencies headed by appointed or elected boards and commissions. The governor was just one of many elected state officials and had little formal control over state administration.[14] Governors often share power with many other elected individuals. Such arrangements are known as **plural executive structures.**

The ability of the Texas governor to control administrative functions through formal appointive and removal powers is exceptionally weak because of Texas's plural executive structure. Voters elect a lieutenant governor, an attorney general, a comptroller of public accounts, a state land commissioner, an agricultural commissioner, the Railroad Commission, and the Texas State Board of Education.[15]

The governor does appoint a few agency heads, the most significant being the secretary of state, who serves as the chief record keeper and election official for the state. The governor also appoints the executive directors of the Departments of Commerce, Health and Human Services, Housing and Community Affairs, and Insurance, the Office of State-Federal Relations, and the Fire Fighters Pension Commission. The governor appoints the head of the Texas National Guard and appoints the executive director of the Texas Education Agency from recommendations made by the elected Texas State Board of Education. The governor also appoints the chief counsels for the Public Utility Commission, the Insurance Commission, and the State Office of Administrative Hearings. This leaves significant portions of state government beyond the control of the governor, because several agency heads are elected.

Most agencies are controlled by independent boards and commissions. These independent state agencies are usually governed by three-, six-, or nine-member boards or commissions appointed by the governor for six-year, overlapping, staggered terms. Usually, one-third of the membership of boards is appointed every two years. In total, the number of governing and policy-making positions filled by gubernatorial appointment is about 2,600.[16] If the governor stays in office for two terms (eight years), she or he will have appointed all members of these agencies and boards and might therefore have indirect influence over them. The governing board chooses the heads of these agencies. As an example, the president of a state university is selected by the board of regents, who are appointed by the governor. The governor often exercises influence with his or her appointees on the board of regents.

The governor also appoints a number of persons to non-policy-making and governing boards that recommend policy and programs to the governor or other state officials. Many of these non-policy-making boards recommend changes in policy and programs. Others are simply window dressing and allow the governor to reward supporters. Most often, these non-policy-making boards do not require Senate approval.

Some gubernatorial appointments are subject to approval by a two-thirds vote of the Senate. In these cases, the governor must clear his or her appointments with the state senator from the appointee's home district. This process, known as senatorial courtesy, limits the discretion of the governor. If the senator from an appointee's home district disapproves of the appointment, the Senate might not confirm the appointee.

Other factors limit the discretion of the governor. For example, some boards require geographic representation. Members of river authority boards, such as the Trinity River Authority and the Lower

Colorado River Authority, must live in the area covered by the river authority. Other boards require specified professional backgrounds. Membership on the Texas Municipal Retirement Board, for instance, is limited to certain types of city employees—such as firefighters, police, and city managers.[17]

Of course, there are always political limits placed on the governor's ability to appoint people. Interest groups pay close attention to the governor's appointments to these boards and commissions and try to influence the governor's choices. The governor may have to bend to demands from such groups.

Equally important to the appointive power is the power to remove administrators. Without the power of removal, the appointive powers of the governor are greatly diminished. U.S. presidents may remove many of their appointees, but state governors are often very restricted by the state constitution, or statutes creating the agency, or term limits set for appointees. Some states allow the governor to remove a person only for cause. This requires the governor to make a case for wrongdoing by the individual. The governor can force the resignation of a person without formal hearings, but the political cost of such forced resignations can be quite high and beyond what the governor is willing to pay.

Beginning in the early twentieth century, the powers of the governor to appoint and remove officials were increased in some states. This expansion of executive authority has increased in the last three decades in many states.[18] This has not been the pattern for much of the South or for the office of governor in Texas. In 2001, the voters in Texas even rejected an amendment that would have made the adjutant general of the Texas National Guard subject to removal by the governor. The traditionalistic culture does not support the idea of strong executive authority even for relatively minor offices.

As with other powers, the removal power of the Texas governor is very weak. Before 1981, Texas state law was silent on the issue of removal. In 1981, the constitution was amended to allow governors to remove any person they personally appointed, with a two-thirds vote of the Senate. Governors may not remove any of their predecessors' appointees. To date, no person has been formally removed from office using this procedure, but it does provide the governor with some leverage to force an appointee to resign. It might also be used to force a policy change that the governor wants. It does not, however, allow the governor to control the day-to-day administration of state government.

In Texas, the appointive power of the governor, even with these formal limitations, allows him or her to indirectly influence policy. A governor is unlikely to select men and women to serve on these boards and commissions who do not agree with him or her on major policy issues. Ann Richards used her appointive powers to increase the number of women and minorities serving on these boards and commissions. This broad appointive power allows the governor to influence policy even after leaving office, since some of the appointees will remain on these boards and commissions. Richards's successor, George W. Bush, appointed some women and minorities, but tended mainly to appoint businessmen to these positions. Governor Perry, for the most part, appoints business leaders as well.

Thus, the governor exerts indirect, not direct, control over policy by appointing people with similar policy views. This influence will continue for some time after the governor leaves office, since her or his appointee will remain in office for four to six years after the governor's term ends.

Governors have also been known to appoint people to governing boards and commissions who were supporters in their campaigns. Loyal supporters, especially those giving big campaign contributions, are often rewarded with appointments to prestigious state boards and commissions. University governing boards are especially desired positions. Table 24.2 lists the contributions given by individuals appointed to state boards and commissions by then Governor Bush.

TABLE 24.2

Campaign Contributions and Appointment to Boards and Commissions by Governor Rick Perry (Top Five)

State Body	Total Contributions	Number of Appointments
Commission for Women	$159,978	13
Higher Education Coordinating Board	$162,943	11
Historical Commission	$194,010	10
Texas Tech Board of Regents	$515,664	9
Rock Crushers/Quarries Adv. Com.	$103,779	9

SOURCE: "Governor Perry's Patronage," Texans for Public Justice, April 2006, http://info.tpj.org/docs/pdf/perrypatronagereport.pdf.

BUDGETARY POWERS Along with tenure of office and appointive/executive authority, the budgetary powers determine the extent of executive authority. Control over how money is spent is at the heart of the policy-making process. Some writers define a budget as a statement of policy in monetary terms. If the **budgetary powers** allow the governor to control budget formation and development (the preparation of the budget for submission to the legislature) and budget execution (deciding how money is spent), he or she can have a significant influence on state policy. There are four kinds of constraints that can undercut the governor's budgetary authority:

- The extent to which the governor must share budget formation with the legislature or with other state agencies
- The extent to which funds are earmarked for specific expenditures and the choice on how to spend money is limited by previous actions
- The extent to which the governor shares budget execution authority with others in state government
- The limits on the governor's use of a line-item veto for the budget

In forty states, the governor is given "full" authority over budget formation and development.[19] In those states where the governor is given authority for budget formation, agencies must present their requests for expenditures to the governor's office, which then combines them and presents a unified budget to the legislature. In some states, the governor is limited in how much he or she can reduce the budget requests of some state agencies. If the governor can change the requests of agencies, this gives the governor tremendous control over the final form of the budget submitted to the legislature. A common practice of state governments is to earmark revenue for specific purposes. For example, funds received through the gasoline tax are commonly earmarked for state highways. This also limits the discretion of the governor. In Texas, many funds are earmarked by the previous actions of the legislature. One estimate is that more than 80 percent of all funds are earmarked for specific expenditures, such as highways, teachers' retirement, parks, and schools.

Budget execution authority is more involved. Governors and others control budget execution in a variety of ways. If the governor controls the appointment of the major department heads of state government, he or she will have some discretion in how money is spent. The governor may decide not to spend all the money appropriated for a state park. Administrative discretion over how money is spent is a time-honored way to expand executive authority over the budget.

In Texas, the governor's budgetary powers are exceptionally weak except in the area of the line-item veto, discussed below. The governor is not constitutionally mandated to submit a budget. This power is given to the **Legislative Budget Board (LBB)**, an agency governed by the speaker of the house and the lieutenant governor. Agencies of the state must present budget requests to the LBB, and the LBB produces a budget that is submitted to the legislature. Historically, governors have submitted budget messages to the legislature, often in the form of reactions to the LBB's proposed budget. Someone once said that the "governor's budget" has the same effect as a letter to Santa Claus, since it has little effect on the final budget form.

During the 2003 financial crisis in which Texas faced a $10 billion shortfall, Governor Perry presented a budget with all zeros. In 2003–2004, spending for Health and Human Services (HHS) stood at $38.7 billion. For 2004–2005, Perry recommended an HHS budget of $0, an education budget of $0, and so forth for all state spending categories. In creating this "zero-based" budget, Perry argued that all agencies had first to justify their expenditure before any money was allocated. Some critics had a good laugh, but others argued that it was an

budgetary powers
the ability of a governor to formulate a budget, present it to the legislature, and execute or control it

Legislative Budget Board (LBB)
Texas state agency that is controlled by the leadership in the state legislature and writes the state budget

> In 2003, the $10 billion state budget deficit pitched Governor Rick Perry and Texas Comptroller Carole Keeton Strayhorn against each other. Perry wanted to make good on his promised tax cuts. Strayhorn wanted to balance the budget and keep Texas out of debt. Here, they share a rare moment of cordiality during the budget crisis—just before their battle divided the social and fiscal conservatives within the Republican Party.

attempt to depart from the tradition of basing budgets on current services. Perry and other prominent Republicans insisted that it was a gesture meant to call attention to the need for increased accountability. In the meantime, the LLB quietly submitted its own budget.

The Texas governor also has very limited authority over budget execution, but it does extend to cases of fiscal crisis. A constitutional amendment approved in 1985 created the Budget Execution Committee, composed of the governor, the lieutenant governor, the comptroller, the speaker of the house, and chairs of the Finance and Appropriations Committees in the Senate and House. The Budget Execution Committee can exercise restraints over the budget if there is a fiscal crisis such as a shortfall in projected revenue.

Another way the Texas governor influences budget decisions is with the line-item veto. The governor can veto part of the appropriations bill without vetoing the entire bill. The legislature determines what a line item is. It can be a department within an agency, or the entire agency. Rick Perry used the line-item veto to reduce the 2008–2009 state budget by $288.9 million, although some claimed that most of those cuts were due to technical corrections.

The legislature can override this veto by a two-thirds vote of each house. However, appropriations bills generally pass in the last days of the session, so the legislature has adjourned by the time the governor vetoes items. Since the legislature cannot call itself back into session ("extraordinary" sessions), overriding a line-item veto is in practice almost impossible.

Legislative Powers

The governor's **legislative powers** include the right to veto and to call special sessions of the legislature. Before exercising these powers, the governor can use them as a threat to pressure the legislature to forward his or her agenda. In addition, the governor presents a State of the State address at the beginning of each legislative session in which he or she requests that the legislature address specific issues.

legislative powers of governors
the formal powers, especially the veto authority and power to call special sessions, of the governor to force the legislature to enact his or her legislation

VETOES AND THE THREAT OF A VETO   Although the line-item veto can be viewed as a budgetary power, it is also a legislative power. There are also other types of vetoes. All governors possess some form of veto authority, but this varies among the states (see Table 24.3). Forty-three states have formalized **partial vetoes,** whereby the legislature can recall a bill from the governor so that objections raised by the governor can be changed and a veto avoided.[20] Texas does not have a formal partial veto process; however, the governor can still state objections to a bill before it is passed and thus seek to effect changes in legislation. Formalizing the process would shift some power to the office of governor and give the governor more say in the legislative process.

partial veto
a veto that allows the legislature to recall a bill to answer a governor's objections to it; Texas does not have a formal partial veto process

Requirements for overriding a governor's veto also vary widely among the states. Most states require a two-thirds vote to override, although a few allow a simple majority.[21] In Texas, the governor has very strong veto authority. The office possesses a general veto and line-item veto, with a two-thirds vote of each house required for override. Very few vetoes have been overturned. From 1876 to 1968, the legislature overrode 25 of 936 vetoes. Most of those vetoes occurred before 1940. This low number of veto overrides is primarily due to late passage of bills and adjournment of the legislature. Only one veto has been overturned in recent years, and

TABLE 24.3

Veto Authority of State Governors with Override Provisions

Type of Veto	Number of Governors
General veto and item veto: two-thirds needed to override	37
General veto and item veto: majority elected needed to override	6
General veto, no item veto: special legislative majority to override*	6
General veto, no item veto: simple majority to override	1

*Most common is three fifths vote. Data change slightly.
SOURCE: Thad L. Beyle, "Governors: The Middlemen and Women in Our Political System," in *Politics in the American States* (8th ed.), ed. Virginia Gray and Russell L. Hanson (Washington, DC: Congressional Quarterly Press, 2004). Copyright © 2004. Reprinted by permission.

it was not a significant bill. In 1979 during his first term, Bill Clements vetoed fifty-two bills. The legislature, in an attempt to get the governor's attention, overrode the veto on a bill that limited the ability of county governments to prohibit hunters from killing female deer.[22] Since 1979, no votes have been overridden by the legislature.

Some governors have a pocket veto, meaning that they can veto a bill by not signing it. The governor just "puts the bill in a pocket" and forgets about it. The Texas governor does not have a pocket veto. If the legislature is in session, the governor has ten days to sign a bill or it becomes law without his or her signature. If the legislature has adjourned, the governor has twenty days to sign a bill or it becomes law without a signature. Sometimes governors do not like a bill but do not want to veto it for some reason. Letting the bill become law without a signature can be a way of expressing displeasure short of an actual veto.

More important than the actual veto is the threat of a veto. Typically, governors do not veto many bills. Historically in Texas, governors have used the threat of a veto to discipline the legislature. It is not uncommon for the governor to threaten to veto a local line item, such as an item creating a new state park in a legislator's district. This threat to veto local appropriations can be used to gain legislative support for items important to the governor but unrelated to the park.

SPECIAL SESSIONS   The governor may call a special session of the legislature and prescribe its agenda. The session lasts thirty days. During the long period of bipartisan cooperation in Texas, from 1993 to 2001, no special sessions were called. That period ended in 2003 when Governor Perry called special sessions to deal with the budget shortfall, redistricting, and educational reform.

The fact that the governor can call a special session but the legislature cannot increases the governor's veto power. In states where legislatures can call "extraordinary" sessions, the legislature has the power to reconvene to override the governor's vetoes. Governor Perry has set a new record by vetoing eighty-two bills in one session. If the Texas legislature could have called an extraordinary session, there is little doubt that it would have happened and that some vetoes would have been overridden.

Judicial Powers

judicial powers of governors
the ability of a governor to issue pardons, executive clemency, and parole for citizens convicted of a crime

Governors also have limited **judicial powers** to grant pardons, executive clemency, and parole. Historically, governors have misused this power, which has led to the creation of checks on this authority. James "Pa" Ferguson was accused of misusing judicial powers by selling pardons and paroles to convicted felons during the second term of his wife, Miriam Amanda "Ma" Ferguson (1933–1935).[23] Those charges led to the creation of the state Pardons and Paroles Board. This eighteen-member board, appointed by the governor, recommends the actions the governor can take and serves as a check on the process. Independent of board action, the governor may grant only one thirty-day stay of execution for any condemned prisoner. This board recommends all other actions by the governor.

In the Fergusons' defense, many of the pardons were given to people who were in prison because they had violated the Prohibition laws. Laws prohibiting the use of alcoholic liquor were the "war on drugs" of several generations ago. Former Lt. Governor Hobby put it this way: "Prohibition's laws filled the prisons and ruined lives then just as marijuana laws do now. The Fergusons may have rightly concluded that the state was better served by these men being home supporting their families."[24]

Military Powers

military powers of governors
the governor's authority to use the National Guard in times of natural disaster or civil unrest

The **military powers** of the governor are quite limited and come into play only in times of natural disaster or civil unrest. The governor appoints the adjutant general of the National Guard and can direct the Guard to protect the lives and property of Texas citizens. The most common use of this power is during natural disasters, when the Guard is employed to help evacuate people, protect property, and supply food and water to victims.

HOW TEXAS COMPARES

POWERS OF THE GOVERNOR

If we take six indexes of power—election of other statewide executives, tenure of office, governor's appointive powers, governor's budgetary powers, veto powers, and governor's control over party—we can compare the Texas governor with the other forty-nine governors. The higher the score, the stronger the powers. The Texas office is comparatively weak in formal powers because of the limitations placed on administrative and budgetary powers. The office is strong on tenure and veto authority. This formal weakness in the office of governor is very much in keeping with the traditionalistic-individualistic political culture of the state. Compare this map with the map of political culture in Chapter 19. Do states with a traditionalistic or individualistic political culture grant their governors less power than states with a moralistic political culture?

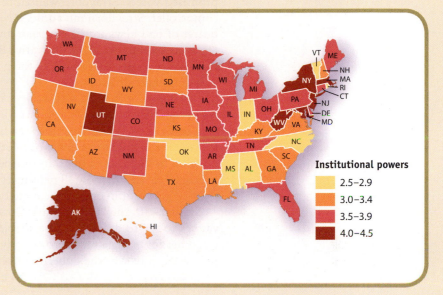

Institutional powers

- 2.5–2.9
- 3.0–3.4
- 3.5–3.9
- 4.0–4.5

SOURCE: Thad L. Beyle, "Governors," in *Politics in the American States* (9th ed.), ed. Virginia Gray and Russell L. Hanson (Washington, DC: Congressional Quarterly Press, 2004). Copyright 2008. Reprinted by permission.

Informal Powers

Although the office of Texas governor is formally very weak, the office can be strong politically. The governor's primary political resource is the ability to exert influence. The governor is the most visible officeholder in the state and can command the attention of the news media, holding press conferences and announcing new decisions on policy issues. Such news conferences are usually well covered and reported by the press and other media. This enables the governor to have an impact on the direction of state government. The governor can also stage events that are newsworthy to emphasize things she or he is interested in changing.

The popularity of the governor in public opinion polls is another aspect of informal leadership. Governors who consistently rank high in popularity polls can use this fact to overcome opposition to their policies and reduce the likelihood of opposition, to both policies and electoral challenges. A governor who is weak in public opinion polls becomes an easy target for political opponents.

In very general ways, governors are judged on their leadership abilities. Some governors develop reputations as being indecisive, and others become known as effective, decisive leaders. The characterization attached to the governor will in turn affect his or her ability to be effective. The press will begin to repeat the description of the governor's reputation, and if that happens often enough, the reputation will become "fact." Therefore, image is a factor in how much power a governor has. In addition to these informal powers, governors can make use of their staff and position as party leader to forward their agenda.

The Governor's Powers   719

PARTY LEADERSHIP   As indicated earlier, governors are expected to be leaders of their political party and in most states are in fact recognized as the leader of the party. In the one-party era in Texas, the Democratic candidate for governor picked the state party chair and controlled the state party organization. Today, party chairs are elected, and although the governor still fulfills a vital role, the parties have experienced increasing division within their ranks. The Republican Party is increasingly divided between the social conservatives who recently wrestled control from the fiscal conservatives.

In 2003, the $10 billion state budget deficit pitched two of the major Republican players in Texas politics against each other: Governor Rick Perry and Texas Comptroller of Public Funds Carole Keeton Strayhorn. Perry wanted to make good on the tax cuts he had promised voters. Strayhorn wanted to balance the budget and keep Texas out of debt. As comptroller, Strayhorn ran audits on executive branch agencies and frequently became the bearer of bad news to the governor, but the core of their conflict was much deeper. Perry represented the socially conservative Republican newcomers, whereas Strayhorn stood for the fiscally conservative wing of the party that was intent on downsizing government and reducing expenditures.

In what some called a retaliation for Strayhorn's position on the deficit, Republican leaders in the Texas legislature stripped the comptroller's office of two high-profile duties. Perry also reneged on his support for Strayhorn's proposal to fund two years of community college for Texas students. For her part, Strayhorn became an increasingly vocal critic of Perry's policies. In 2006, she ran as an independent candidate against Perry. Although Strayhorn managed to capture only 18 percent of the vote, Perry suffered a pyrrhic victory: He became the first governor in over a century to be elected with less than 40 percent of the vote.

Similarly, in the 2010 primary, Governor Perry reached for the support of social conservatives to try to defeat the formidable opponent Senator Kay Bailey Hutchison. He criticized her for being a weak pro-life advocate. By rallying the support of Tea Party activists, he managed to win the gubernatorial nomination with 48 percent of the vote to Hutchison's 27 percent.

THE GOVERNOR'S STAFF   In Texas, the trend in recent years has been to expand the staff of the governor's office. When John Connally became governor in 1963, he made the first use of a professional staff of advisers. Previous governors often appointed only a handful of individuals who were loyal to them politically, but not necessarily highly professional. Other governors since Connally have added to the governor's staff. Today, an organizational chart is necessary to maintain lines of authority and responsibility. Currently, the governor has a staff of about two hundred.

Each governor makes different uses of her or his staff. In recent years, most governors have used their staff to keep track of state agencies over which the governor has little or no direct control. The staff also gathers information and makes recommendations on changes in policy that affect most areas of state government. A message from a member of the governor's staff to a state agency is taken seriously. A report issued by the governor's office automatically attracts the attention of significant state leaders and the news media. Often the governor must use the information gathered to wage a public relations war with the legislature or state agencies. In Texas, the increases in the size, professionalism, and complexity of the governor's staff have become necessary to offset the limited formal control the governor has over state government, a situation considered in this chapter's "Thinking Critically About Democracy."

Administrative Agencies of State Government

In addition to the office of governor, a number of other state agencies make up what might be called the state bureaucracy. The term *bureaucracy* often implies a hierarchy of offices with levels of power leading to a centralized controlling authority. This term does not describe the overall structure of state government in Texas, since there is no overall central governing, controlling authority. Government authority in Texas is much decentralized

SHOULD TEXAS ELIMINATE THE PLURAL EXECUTIVE?

The Issue: When Governor Rick Perry signed Senate Bill No. 11 creating a Border Security Council in June 2007, he expressed his reservations about the provision allowing the Department of Public Safety to issue enhanced driver's licenses (EDLs). The Western Hemisphere Travel Initiative (WHTI), which was to go into effect on January 31, 2008, requires that individuals provide more documentation than just a driver's license and an oral declaration of citizenship when crossing a border into the United States by land or by sea. This change in the law was expected to cause massive delays at border crossings. EDLs, which would contain computer chips that could be scanned by machines, would speed up the process considerably. Expressing his belief that EDLs might violate federal law, Perry requested that Attorney General Gregg Abbott issue an opinion clarifying their legality.

Although EDL advocates such as the Democratic senator from El Paso, Eliot Shapleigh, and the Texas Border Coalition pointed out that the U.S. Homeland Security Secretary himself was promoting the EDL system, Abbott waited until January 22, 2008, to issue his eight-page opinion that EDLs did not violate federal law. Perry responded with more reservations. The EDL program would be a waste of taxpayer money, Perry's spokeswoman explained. The federal government was also considering issuing passport cards and REAL IDs to be used when crossing the border to Mexico or Canada. Perry didn't want to implement EDLs only to have them become outdated later in the year. Meanwhile, in Washington State, an EDL program went into operation well before the WHTI changes, while Texans continued to line up at the border with paper documents.

When Texans adopted the 1876 constitution, they opposed a strong central government and established a plural executive. The most important offices in the executive branch are elected, and so the most important officers do not depend on the governor's support. Today, many people have suggested that Texas might be better off if governors appointed these officers, who would then be more responsive to them.

Yes: When governors are elected to office, people expect them to be able to carry out their promises to the people of Texas. Yet Texas governors have such weak authority that they must often take the back seat and simply say yes or no to policies put forth by the part-time legislature. They must rely on fellow executive branch officers who might undermine their agenda. As a result, too often Texas governors are unable to craft policies themselves and get the job done. In addition, a plural executive is not as effective in implementing laws once they are passed. Texas today is one of the leading states in population, size, technology, and trade. It needs a strong and effective government to be responsive to the changing needs of the economy and the population.

No: A democratic government does not simply represent the majority of the people. By creating a plural executive and placing the bulk of lawmaking powers in the legislature, Texas has ensured that its government represents all the people. The other elected officers in the executive branch act as a check on the governor's authority. If Texas governors were allowed to appoint the most important officers in the executive branch, the minority would have less power to defend itself against the majority.

Other approaches: Texans do not need to change the constitution to create a more efficient and responsive government. The legislature simply needs to study the issue carefully and propose laws that transfer necessary responsibilities to the governor's office.

What do you think?

① Do you think the governor should appoint the most important officers within the executive branch?

② Does your opinion change depending on how much you like the current governor? How would your opinion on this issue change if a different governor were in office?

③ What do you think are the most important responsibilities that a governor should have that the Texas governor today does not have?

and resides within many independent state agencies. As we have seen, in the plural executive structure, the governor is not the only executive; she or he must share power with other elected officials. In addition, many independent boards, commissions, and agencies operate independently of the governor.

There are three basic kinds of state agencies in Texas, as illustrated in Figure 24.1. First are the agencies headed by an elected official; second are the appointed single-head agencies; and finally, and the most numerous, are those headed by a multimember appointed board or commission. The governor obviously has little or no authority over agencies headed by

Agency Heads	Boards and Commissions	

VOTERS IN STATE ELECT	Agency Heads	Boards and Commissions	
Lieutenant Governor	Secretary of State	General Government	Licensing and Professional Examining Boards
Attorney General	Adjutant General of the National Guard	Health and Human Services	Public Safety and Criminal Justice
Comptroller of Public Accounts	Director of Housing and Community Affairs	Higher Education Boards of Regents	Natural Resources
Commissioner of the General Land Office	Director of Office of State-Federal Relations	Other Education	Employee Retirement Boards
Commissioner of Agriculture	Executive Director of Texas Education Agency	Business Regulation	Interstate Compact Commissions
Railroad Commission (three members)	Commissioner for Health and Human Services	Business and Economic Development	Water and River Authorities
State Board of Education (fifteen members)	Eight other minor agencies	Regional Economic Development	Judicial

FIGURE 24.1

The Administrative Structure of State Government in Texas

Note: The governor makes about 1,000 appointments to task forces or ad hoc advisory committees whose members make recommendations to the governor or other state officials. They are not governing or policy-making bodies.

SOURCES: *Guide to Texas State Agencies,* 9th ed. (Austin: University of Texas, LBJ School); Legislative Budget Board, "Fiscal Size-up," 1999–2000 Biennium; Legislative Budget Board, Austin; some information supplied by Governor's Appointments Office.

other elected officials who are responsible to the voters who elected them. As indicated earlier, although the Texas governor appoints citizens to these 300-plus state boards and commissions, he or she has very limited removal authority. Each state board and commission operates independently from the others, and there is no central controlling authority. The governor's greatest authority is over the single-head agencies that he or she appoints, but except for the secretary of state, these are of limited significance.

Most of the work of state government is conducted by agencies controlled by either elected officials or boards and commissions that operate independently of the governor. Only the legislature, through oversight and budgetary authority, exercises control over all state agencies. Figure 24.2 illustrates the growth, decline, or stability in employment in the top five state agencies from 1998 to 2003.

Agencies with Elected Officials

Some agencies in Texas government are headed by elected officials, who are accountable to the voters.

attorney general
chief counsel to the governor and state agencies; the attorney general has limited criminal jurisdiction

OFFICE OF THE ATTORNEY GENERAL   The **attorney general** serves as the legal counsel to the governor, the legislature, and most of the other agencies, boards, and commissions in state government. Most of the work of the attorney general involves civil law and not criminal law. Criminal functions of the office are primarily limited to those cases appealed to federal courts. The most common example of these criminal cases is death penalty appeals. Occasionally, the attorney general's office may assist local criminal prosecutors when invited to do so.

Most of the resources of this office are devoted to collection of child support payments, collection of delinquent state taxes, administration of the Crime Victims Compensation program, and investigation of Medicare fraud. Despite this rather "mundane" list of functions, the office has political functions that can have an impact on the course of legislation. The most important of these is to issue so-called AG opinions on legal questions. Often when the legislature is in session, the attorney general (AG) will be asked for an opinion on a pending piece of legislation. A negative AG opinion can kill a bill's chances of passing.

In 2007, the ultraconservative chairperson of the House State Affairs Committee, David Swinford, surprised Texans by killing a series of anti-immigration bills. Swinford had sought the advice of Attorney General Greg Abbott, who suggested that these bills, which would have deprived illegal aliens and their American-born children of certain rights, were unconstitutional. Swinford decided that the bills were a waste of money because the courts would strike them down.

COMPTROLLER OF PUBLIC ACCOUNTS
The **comptroller of public accounts** has been assigned many additional duties over the years and currently functions as the chief fiscal and revenue forecasting officer. Generally in government, the controller has a preaudit responsibility for ensuring that funds can be spent for specific functions. In Texas, the comptroller not only has the preaudit responsibility but also serves as the chief tax collector (a function normally associated with the office of treasurer), revenue forecaster, and investor of state funds.

Former Governor Bob Bullock served as comptroller for many years. During his tenure, the office expanded the information and management functions and developed a fiscal forecasting model essential to projecting revenues in a two-year budget cycle. John Sharp, who followed Bob Bullock as comptroller, continued and expanded the information management programs of the office. Also under Sharp, the office developed the Texas Performance Review teams to evaluate the effectiveness of government operations and ensure the most efficient use of state funds. These reviews were estimated to have saved the state over $1.3 billion in the 1998–1999 biennium fiscal years. Similar management information and efficiency audits are available to assist local governments. Most of these programs have been kept in place.

The office also assists the private sector through the provision of information. The State of Texas Econometric Model is used to forecast state economic growth, keep track of business cycles, and generally provide information on the health of the economy of the state.

COMMISSIONER OF THE GENERAL LAND OFFICE
Texas is one of only four states to have a **land commissioner** to administer state-owned land.[25] When Texas entered the Union in 1845, the agreement between the former republic and the U.S. government was that Texas would keep its public debt and its public land. When Texas became a state, most of the land was state owned. Today, the state of Texas owns and manages 20.3 million acres of land, including open beaches and submerged land 10.3 miles into the Gulf of Mexico.[26]

The land commissioner's office is responsible for leasing state lands and generating funds from oil and gas production. The office is also responsible for overseeing the Veterans Land Board and Veterans Land Fund. This fund lends money to Texas veterans to purchase rural land. Finally, the land office is responsible for maintaining the environmental quality of the state's open beaches along the Gulf Coast.

Employment for the Top Four State Agencies

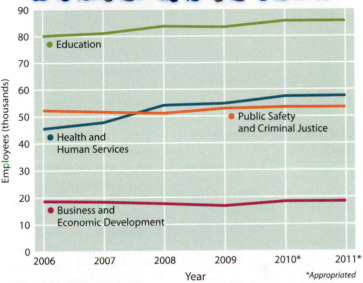

POLITICAL INQUIRY

FIGURE 24.2 ■ Approximately 76 percent of Texas state employees work in the five major areas of state government: corrections, highways, public welfare, hospitals, and higher education. Among the fifteen most populous states, Texas ranks tenth in the number of state employees per 10,000 population. Still, the state of Texas is the largest single employer in Texas. What is the fastest-growing agency in state government? What areas are losing jobs?

SOURCE: Legislative Budget Board, "Fiscal Size-up, 2010–2011," www.lbb.state.tx.us/Fiscal _Size-up/Fiscal%20Size-up%202010-11.pdf.

comptroller of public accounts

chief tax collector, revenue forecaster, and investor of state funds; the comptroller does not perform financial audits

land commissioner

elected official responsible for administration and oversight of state-owned lands and coastal lands extending 10.3 miles into the Gulf of Mexico

COMMISSIONER OF AGRICULTURE Elected by the voters in a statewide election, the commissioner of agriculture heads the Texas Department of Agriculture (TDA). The agency has the dual, and sometimes contradictory, roles of promoting agriculture products and production and regulating agricultural practices, while protecting the public health from unsafe agricultural practices. For example, the TDA must promote cotton production and sales in the state while regulating the use of pesticides.

The TDA has six major functions: marketing of Texas agriculture products, development and promotion of agricultural businesses' production, pesticide regulation, pest management, product certification and safety inspection, and inspection and certification of measuring devices (including gasoline pumps, electronic scanners, and scales).

Although the TDA and the agricultural commissioner are not as publicly visible as the other statewide agencies with elected officials, the office is vital to a large section of the state's economy—those engaged in agriculture. The economy of Texas has become more diversified in recent years, but agriculture is still a significant player in the state's economy. Major agribusinesses and others in agriculture in the state pay close attention to who serves as the agricultural commissioner.

Texas Railroad Commission (RRC)

state agency, with a three-member elected board, that regulates some aspects of transportation and the oil and gas industry of the state

THE TEXAS RAILROAD COMMISSION The three-member **Texas Railroad Commission (RRC)** was created in 1891 to regulate the railroad monopolies that had developed in the state. The commission's authority has expanded greatly since that time. In the 1920s, when oil and natural gas production developed in the state, the task of regulating the exploration, drilling, and production of oil and natural gas was assigned to the RRC in part because it was the only regulatory agency in the state at the time. When motor truck transport developed in the state, regulation of the trucking industry was also assigned to the RRC. In part because of federal rules and regulations, the original role of regulating railroads and the later role of regulating trucking have diminished to a minor role of the agency, reduced primarily to concern with safety issues. The regulation of the oil and gas industry is its primary function today.

Many have been critical of the RRC over the years because of close ties between the elected commissioners and the oil and gas industry they regulate. Large campaign contributions from oil and gas PACs have raised questions about the commission being co-opted by the industry it regulates. Also, like the agricultural commissioner, the RRC board has the dual role of promoting oil and gas production in the state and regulating the safety and environmental aspects of the industry (for example, promoting the development of pipelines to carry petroleum products as well as the safety of such pipelines). A similar conflict may exist between the RRC's task of regulating and promoting mining of minerals (especially lignite coal) in the state.

The role of the RRC that most directly affects Texas citizens is that of setting the rates charged by local natural gas companies. Natural gas companies must get RRC approval for the rates they charge residential and commercial customers. The RRC also regulates the safety of natural gas systems.

THE STATE BOARD OF EDUCATION Unlike the other offices discussed in this section, the governing body for public elementary and secondary education in the state has varied greatly in form and structure over the years. In 1986, the board was changed from appointed to elected from districts. The current board, called the State Board of Education (SBOE), nominates one of its members to be commissioner of education.

In recent years, the authority of the board has been greatly reduced by actions of the state legislature. The political battle over the power of the board revolved around the social conservatives' (Christian Right) success in electing members to the board and the actions taken in setting curriculum standards and textbook selection issues. Public infighting among members of the board diminished its effectiveness. The legislature has removed several functions, most significantly the selection of textbooks, from the Board of Education in part because of the infighting and control by this faction. In 2010, the SBOE's revision of Texas curriculum standards drew national criticism when the board removed Thomas Jefferson from the list of philosophers studied in world history courses—and attempted to push through over two hundred amendments that introduced conservative values into the curriculum.

Single-Head Agencies

In some states, an individual appointed and serving at the pleasure of the governor heads most agencies. The structure is much like that of the federal government in which the president appoints his own cabinet, whose members serve at the president's pleasure. Only a handful of state agencies in Texas meet this model, and few are of great importance.

SECRETARY OF STATE   Appointed by the governor with approval of the state Senate, the **secretary of state (SOS)** heads an office with duties assigned by the constitution and state statutes. Duties can be lumped into three broad categories: elections, records keeping/information management, and international protocol. As the chief election official, the SOS is responsible for overseeing voter registration, preparation of election information, and supervision of elections. The SOS issues rules, directives, and opinions on the conduct of elections and voter registration. These duties allow the secretary some latitude in the interpretation and application of the state Election Code. For example, the SOS has some latitude in how vigorously she or he encourages citizens to register and vote.

A second duty of the SOS is to serve as the official keeper of state records. This includes records on business corporations and some other commercial activities. The office also publishes the Texas Register, which is the source of official notices or rules, meetings, executive orders, and opinions of the attorney general that are required to be filed by state agencies. Through the protocol functions of the office, the SOS provides support services to state officials who interact with representatives of foreign countries.

COMMISSIONER FOR HEALTH AND HUMAN SERVICES   This office was created in 1991 to coordinate a number of health-related programs and agencies. The governor appoints the commissioner for a two-year term with the approval of the state Senate. The commissioner has oversight and review functions, but not direct responsibility, for eleven separate health and welfare programs, which are directed by boards, councils, or commissions. The programs include aging; alcohol and drug abuse; the blind, deaf, and hard-of-hearing; early childhood intervention; juvenile probation; mental health and retardation; rehabilitation; and departments of Health, Human Services, and Protective and Regulatory Services. This office has little direct administrative control, but it can and often does have an impact on policy. The commissioner serves as a spokesperson for the governor in health and welfare matters.

secretary of state (SOS)
chief election official and keeper of state records—appointed by the governor

> Programs coordinated by the Commissioner for Health and Human Services include drug abuse prevention programs such as this one for at-risk kids.

Curbing State Agencies in Texas

THEN (1990–2000)	NOW (2010)
The state government had 222,685 employees as of 2000.*	The state government has 238,404 employees.**
The Sunset Commission's recommendations resulted in the elimination of twenty-eight executive branch agencies by 2000.	The Sunset Commission's recommendations are responsible for reorganizing twenty-five executive branch agencies, saving Texans almost $1 million in the next two years alone.†
The Sunset Commission survived an attempt to eliminate it during Ann Richards's administration.	Some critics argue that the Sunset Commission is so crippled by the legislature that it cannot carry out its original mandate.

WHAT'S NEXT?

> Will the Sunset Commission be able to check the growth of the bureaucracy and increase the efficiency of the executive branch?

> Will the executive branch be able to meet the needs of a growing population and an expanding economy effectively?

> Should the powers of the executive branch be centralized under the governor so that the state can meet the needs of its people more efficiently?

*"Fiscal Size-up," The Legislative Budget Board, 2002–2003, www.lbb.state.tx.us/Fiscal_Size-up_Archive/Fiscal_Size-up_2002-2003_0102.pdf.
**"Texas Fact Book," Legislative Budget Board, 2010, www.lbb.state.tx.us/Fact_Book/Texas_FactBook_2010.pdf.
†Summary of Sunset Legislation, Sunset Reports for 2008–2009, www.sunset.state.tx.us/81streports/sumleg09.pdf.

OFFICE OF STATE-FEDERAL RELATIONS The governor appoints the executive director of the Office of State-Federal Relations. As the name suggests, this office coordinates relations between state and federal officials. The office has existed since 1971 and is the primary liaison between the governor's office and federal officials. To some degree, this office becomes an advocate (lobbyist) for the state in dealing with the Texas congressional delegation and federal agencies.

ADJUTANT GENERAL OF THE NATIONAL GUARD This office is created by the Texas Constitution and is responsible for directing the state military force under the direction of the governor. The governor serves as commander in chief of the Guard. The size of the National Guard (nationwide and in Texas) is determined and funded by Congress as a reserve force to the regular army. The Guard also provides emergency aid and protection of property and persons in times of natural disaster.

In the November 1999 election, Texas voters rejected a constitutional amendment that would have allowed the governor to appoint and remove the head of the National Guard. As with other appointees, the governor may appoint the head of the National Guard, but not remove him or her except on approval of the state Senate.

Boards and Commissions

In addition to the elected and appointed officials, about 2,800 people are appointed by the governor for fixed terms to about three hundred **state boards and commissions.** These administrative units carry out most of

state boards and commissions administrative units for many state agencies that carry out most of the work of state government; members are appointed by the governor for fixed terms

the work of state government. The board or commission usually appoints the head of the agency (for example, chancellor of a university or executive director of a state agency) and in varying degrees is responsible for policy and administration of the agency. Most operate quite independently from other agencies of state government, except the legislature.

Given the lack of central control and the decentralized nature of state government in Texas, it is surprising that things work as well as they do. For example, there are thirty-one agencies that provide health and welfare services. In addition to the Department of Agriculture, the General Land Office, and the Railroad Commission—all having some control over environmental and natural resources—at least seven other agencies with independent boards or commissions have some authority in this area. These include the Texas Commission of Environmental Quality, the Texas Parks and Wildlife Department, the Soil and Water Conservation Board, and the Water Development Board.

In this conservative state with a strong belief in the free market, there are, nonetheless, no fewer than thirty-eight professional licensing and examining boards. Think of a profession, and there is probably a state agency that licenses and regulates it. Just a few examples are accountants, architects, barbers, chiropractors, cosmetologists, dentists, exterminators, funeral directors, land surveyors, medical doctors, two kinds of nurses, pharmacists, physical therapists, podiatrists, and veterinarians. Most often, the professional group asks for regulation by the state. When such groups advocate government regulation and licensing, they claim they are primarily interested in protecting the public from incompetent or dishonest practitioners. This may be partially true; however, regulation also has the added benefits of limiting entry into the profession and allowing the development of rules favorable to the group. Two professions that have benefited from regulation are the water well drillers and landscape architects. Also, professionals frequently argue that the people appointed to the boards by the governor should be knowledgeable about the profession they are governing. Although knowledge is one factor, the danger is that these boards and commissions, dominated by members of the profession, will be more inclined to make rules and regulations that favor the group rather than the public. Because of that fear, in recent years, the appointment of at least some members of the board from outside the profession has become the norm—for example, nonphysicians on the State Board of Medical Examiners.

Twelve college governing boards oversee the institutions of higher education in the state. These boards are required to coordinate their activities and gain approval for some activities and programs from the State Higher Education Coordinating Board. Within these broad guidelines, each governing board is relatively free to set policy, approve budgets, and govern its university. Once again, governance is decentralized, with only a minimum of control from the state and almost none from the governor.

Legislative Agencies

In addition to the previous executive agencies, there are several legislative agencies. These are units controlled by the leadership in the Texas House and Senate. Their purpose is to provide legislative oversight of the "executive" agencies and to assist the legislature in its lawmaking functions.

LEGISLATIVE BUDGET BOARD (LBB) As discussed earlier in the chapter, this agency is primarily responsible for preparing the state budget. It is composed of the lieutenant governor, the speaker of the house, four senators, and four state representatives. All agencies that receive state funds from the state budget must submit their requests for appropriations to the LBB. The LBB reviews these requests and proposes a budget to the state legislature. As indicated before, unlike most other states, in Texas the governor plays a very limited role in budgeting.

TEXAS LEGISLATIVE COUNCIL The speaker, the lieutenant governor, four senators, and four state representatives control this agency. They appoint the executive director. This agency was created in 1949 to assist the legislature in drafting bills, conducting research on legislation, producing publications, and providing technical support services. This is a highly professional agency that produces information for the legislature that is made available to the public in various ways.

LEGISLATIVE AUDIT COMMITTEE AND STATE AUDITOR'S OFFICE The **Legislative Audit Committee** consists of the lieutenant governor, the speaker of the house, and the chairs of the Senate Finance Committee and State Affairs Committee, and the House Appropriations Committee and Ways and Means Committee. This committee appoints the state auditor, who is responsible for auditing state agencies and assisting the legislature in its oversight functions.

Legislative Audit Committee
legislative agency that performs audits on all state agencies

LEGISLATIVE REFERENCE LIBRARY This organization assists the legislature in doing research and serves as a depository of records for the legislature. The library, located in the state capitol, is open to members of the public who wish to do research on the Texas legislature.

Other Agencies

Other agencies in Texas government handle judicial matters, oversee redistricting and budgetary matters, and deal with ethics issues.

JUDICIAL AGENCIES   There are several agencies that can be called judicial agencies and are under the supervision of the State Supreme Court (civil matters). Except for budgeting of money by the legislature, these agencies are relatively free of legislative oversight. The State Bar, which licenses attorneys, receives no state appropriations. The remaining agencies are responsible for court administration (Office of Court Administration), operations of the state law library, and certification of legal licenses and specializations.

EX OFFICIO BOARDS AND COMMISSIONS   A number of state agencies are headed by boards whose membership is completely or partially made up of designated state officials who are members because of the position they hold. Examples of these officials are the statewide elected officials—governor, lieutenant governor, speaker of the house, attorney general, and land commissioner. Examples of these agencies are the Bond Review Board, the Legislative Redistricting Board, and the Budget Execution Committee.

MULTIAPPOINTMENT BOARDS   Finally, there are some state agencies that have governing boards whose members are appointed by more than one elected official. The reason for this is to prevent one individual from dominating the selection process and the outcome of decisions. Examples of these agencies are the Texas Ethics Commission and the Criminal Justice Policy Council. For example, the Texas Ethics Commission has four members appointed by the governor and two each by the lieutenant governor and the speaker of the house.

Citizen Control and the Sunset Review

Part of the concept of democracy requires that state agencies be responsible to the people—that is, that state agencies respond to demands placed on them by citizens. With Texas state administrative agencies operating independently of one another and overall administrative control being absent from state government, agencies are often able to respond only to clientele groups they serve and not the public generally. Thus, most state agencies are accountable only to small groups of attentive citizens. See Chapter 21 on interest groups for a more complete discussion of agency capture.

State government in Texas is so fragmented and responsibility so divided that holding anyone responsible for state government is almost impossible. Although citizens may blame the governor when things go wrong, and governors may claim credit when things go right, in truth the governor is responsible for very little and deserves credit for much less than most claim.

Given the lack of overall central control in state government and the limited and weak authority of the governor, in 1977 the Texas legislature created the ten-member **Sunset Advisory Commission** to review most state agencies every twelve years and recommend changes. This commission consists of five state senators, five members of the House of Representatives, and two public members.

The sunset process is basically the "idea that legislative oversight of government operations can be enhanced by a systematic evaluation of state agencies."[27] The process works by establishing a date when an agency is abolished if the legislature does not pass a law providing for its continuance. The act does not apply to agencies created in the Texas Constitution or to some exempt agencies, such as state universities. Sunset asks this basic question: "Do the policies carried out by an agency need to be continued?"[28]

As Table 24.4 shows, in more than thirty years of sunset review, very few state agencies have been abolished. Most were minor state agencies with few functions. Most notable were the Boll Weevil Commission, the Battle Ship Texas Commission, and the Stonewall Jackson

Sunset Advisory Commission
agency responsible for making recommendations to the legislature for change in the structure and organization of most state agencies

TABLE 24.4

Agencies Abolished by Sunset Review, 1979–2009

Year	Number of Agencies Abolished
1979	8
1981	2
1983	3
1985	6
1987	1
1989	3
1991	3
1993	1
1995	0
1997	0
1999	1
2001	1
2003	3
2005	6
2007	2
2009	1
Total	**41**

Memorial Board. More important than abolition is the review process. By forcing a review of an agency every twelve years, the legislature has the opportunity to recommend changes to improve the efficiency and effectiveness of state government. In many cases, functions of state agencies are transferred to other agencies, and agencies are combined or merged.

Sunset review has also forced public evaluation of many agencies that operate out of the public eye. This is especially true of those agencies that license professions. Sunset review resulted in the appointment of nonprofessionals to these agencies in an effort to promote the broader interests of the public over the narrow interests of the agency and its clientele.

CONCLUSION

THINKING CRITICALLY ABOUT WHAT'S NEXT FOR THE TEXAS GOVERNOR AND STATE AGENCIES

Even though governors in most states do not have much formal power, the office has great importance in state politics. In recent years, the office has grown in stature. Four of the last six U.S. presidents have been former governors, and the office has become increasingly visible in both state and national politics. The need for strong leadership in this office will continue to increase.

Texas, whose previous governor served as president from 2001 to 2009, is now the second-largest state in population and one of the leading states in industrial growth. Because the governor lacks formal power, however, the task of governing this large, diverse, and economically vital state is challenging. Reform of the governor's powers is still needed, but whether such changes will occur is doubtful, because the political culture of the state does not support increasing the authority of the governor's office. Leadership will have to come from force of will and personality rather than from formal changes in structure. Governor Perry has so far not worked to foster bipartisan cooperation and has faced divisions within his own party.

The Sunset Commission has led the reform of the executive branch. But as the size of the economy and population increases, the executive branch will have to take on even greater responsibility. Will the commission have enough power to ensure the effective implementation of state regulations and services? The informal powers of the governor, the cohesion of the top executive branch officers, and the efficiency of executive agencies will determine the extent to which the government can meet Texans' future needs.

Summary

1. The Roles of the Governor
Although citizens expect governors to play many roles and hold them responsible for the successes and failures of the state, many governors, including the governor of Texas, enjoy very limited power. In Texas, the governor's position is weakened by the plural executive, an executive branch in which most of the important offices are elected rather than appointed. There are formal and informal qualifications for the office—most governors have been white, male, Protestant, and well educated. Texas places no term limits on governors, yet few have served longer than four years.

2. The Governor's Powers
Formal powers of the governor consist of executive, legislative, judicial, and military authority. Leadership skills, personality, and manipulation of media attention are informal

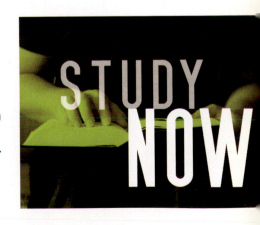

STUDY NOW

powers that the governor can use to persuade the legislature to follow his or her agenda. The governor can also make use of veto power and the right to call special sessions as threats to coerce the legislature into bargaining and reaching compromises.

3. Administrative Agencies of State Government

In Texas, there are three main types of administrative agencies: agencies with elected heads, agencies with a single appointed head, and multimember boards and commissions. These agencies carry out much of the work of state government. The governor has little authority over these agencies, and each state board and commission operates independently from the others, with no central controlling authority. Interest groups are not supportive of transferring power from state agencies they can dominate to agencies under the control of a single individual appointed by the governor. However, the Sunset Advisory Commission has had a positive impact on some agencies.

Key Terms

acting governor 711

appointive power 714

attorney general 722

budgetary powers 716

ceremonial duties 708

chief legislator 708

comptroller of public accounts 723

intergovernmental coordinator 709

Jacksonian statehouse democracy 714

judicial powers of governors 718

land commissioner 723

Legislative Audit Committee 727

Legislative Budget Board (LBB) 716

legislative powers of governors 717

military powers of governors 718

partial veto 717

party chief 708

plural executive structure 714

recall of the governor 712

secretary of state (SOS) 725

state boards and commissions 726

Sunset Advisory Commission 728

tenure of office 712

Texas Railroad Commission (RRC) 724

For Review

1. What roles is the governor expected to fulfill?
2. What are the formal and informal qualifications for the position of governor in Texas?
3. What are the executive powers of the governor?
4. What are the legislative powers of the governor?
5. What are the judicial powers of the governor?
6. How can the governor use these formal powers to coerce legislators to pursue his or her political agenda?
7. What are the informal powers of the governor?
8. What are the different types of administrative agencies?
9. What measure has Texas enacted to try to create an efficient and responsive bureaucracy?

For Critical Thinking and Discussion

1. Give a recent example of an expectation the public had of the governor. Explain whether that expectation was reasonable given the governor's limited powers of office.
2. What steps, if any, do you think should be taken to reduce the informal qualifications for getting elected governor of Texas?
3. What formal powers does the Texas governor have to resolve a crisis caused by flooding that has left thousands of people homeless?
4. If you were the governor of Texas, what steps would you take to address a shortage of qualified teachers in rural areas?
5. Using examples from your own experience, explain whether you think that the Texas bureaucracy is efficient and responsive to the people of the state. What changes would you make to improve it?

PRACTICE QUIZ

MULTIPLE CHOICE: Choose the lettered item that answers the question correctly.

1. Citizens expect governors to play many roles. Which of the following is not a role in which the governor must act?
   a. chief legislator
   b. party chief
   c. chief justice
   d. chief intergovernmental coordinator

2. The line-item veto can be viewed as a(n) _____ power.
   a. executive
   b. legislative
   c. judicial
   d. military

3. Which of the following does not limit the appointive power of the governor?
   a. appointments that are subject to two-thirds approval by the Senate
   b. requirements of racially even representation
   c. requirements of geographically based representation
   d. political influence by special interest groups

4. A state executive officer who is appointed by the Texas governor is the
   a. attorney general.
   b. secretary of state.
   c. comptroller of public accounts.
   d. commissioner of agriculture.

5. The tenure of the Texas governor is
   a. a two-year term with a two-term limit.
   b. a two-year term with no term limit.
   c. a four-year term with a two-term limit.
   d. a four-year term with no term limit.

6. The basis of the governor's legislative powers is
   a. veto power and the right to call special sessions.
   b. control of the National Guard.
   c. powers of appointment and removal.
   d. authority to pardon prisoners.

7. According to the Texas Constitution, who is responsible for submitting the state budget?
   a. the governor
   b. both the legislature and the governor
   c. the House appropriations committee
   d. the Legislative Budget Board

8. The Texas executive branch is
   a. a plural executive.
   b. a weakly unitary executive.
   c. a strongly unitary executive.
   d. a nonunitary executive.

9. The two types of veto the governor is authorized to use are
   a. the partial veto and the general veto.
   b. the line-item veto and the general veto.
   c. the pocket veto and the general veto.
   d. the partial veto and the line-item veto.

10. Review by the Sunset Advisory Commission has resulted in
    a. the abolishment of nearly one hundred state agencies, including the Boll Weevil Commission.
    b. the appointment of nonprofessionals to state agencies in an effort to promote the public's interests.
    c. decreased public evaluation of agencies that operate outside the public eye.
    d. optional reviews of agencies every twelve years to improve the efficiency of state government.

FILL IN THE BLANKS.

11. _____ is an important determinant of gubernatorial power because it determines how much time a governor has to carry out his or her programs.

12. A _____ is a system whereby voters elect many statewide officeholders to serve as heads of departments.

13. Texas is one of only four states to have a _____ to administer state-owned land.

14. The _____ is the state agency that regulates some aspects of transportation and the oil and gas industry of the state.

15. The _____ is the chief tax collector and investor of state funds.

RESOURCES FOR RESEARCH AND ACTION

Internet Resources

Council of State Governments
www.csg.org This site features up-to-date information on state governments and governors.

Governors Guide
www.nga.org/governors Look for useful information on governors in other states, including background and biographical information.

Legislative Budget Board
www.lbb.state.tx.us Check this site for information on budget proposals.

National Governors Association
www.nga.org This site has extensive resources for and about governors, including an overview of the governor's office, state-by-state staff listing, and a center for best practices.

Texas Governor's Office
www.governor.state.tx.us The governor's agenda and activities are available at this site.

Internet Activism

The Office of the Governor's Web site, **http://governor.state.tx.us,** contains a contact page where you can contact the governor with your ideas and suggestions. If you feel strongly about an issue, let the governor know!

Twitter
http://twitter.com/TexGov Get updates from Governor Rick Perry on official news from the office of the Texas governor.

YouTube
http://www.youtube.com/watch?v=ClllaXPgTE0 Watch news coverage of the Texas Attorney General protecting citizens from misleading advertising campaigns—a great example of an elected official at work for the people.

Facebook
www.facebook.com/pages/Sunset-Advisory-Commission/138608756163963?ref=search The Sunset Advisory Commission was created in 1977 to make recommendations to the Texas Legislature on the continued needs for other state agencies. Under the 2009 legislative session, all state agencies will expire after a certain amount of time unless specific legislation has been passed that allows for their continued existence.

Recommended Readings

Anderson, James, Richard W. Murray, and Edward L. Farley. *Texas Politics: An Introduction,* 6th ed. New York: HarperCollins, 1992.

Beyle, Thad. "Governors: The Middlemen and Women in Our Political System," in *Politics in the American States* (8th ed.), ed. Virginia Gray and Russell L. Hanson. Washington, DC: Congressional Quarterly Press, 2004.

Brown, Norman D. *Hood, Bonnet and Little Brown Jug: Texas Politics 1921–1928.* College Station: Texas A&M Press, 1983.

Gantt, Fred Jr. *The Chief Executive in Texas: A Study in Gubernatorial Leadership.* Austin: University of Texas Press, 1964.

Movie of Interest

Journeys with George (2003)
This Emmy-winning documentary tracks Texas Governor George W. Bush during his 2000 bid for the presidency. The documentary offers unique insight into the relationship between political candidates and the media.

Case for Innocence (2000)
This *Frontline* documentary chronicles the cases of four men who were sentenced to death, but DNA evidence later proved their innocence. The case of Roy Criner provides insight into the pardoning process in Texas.

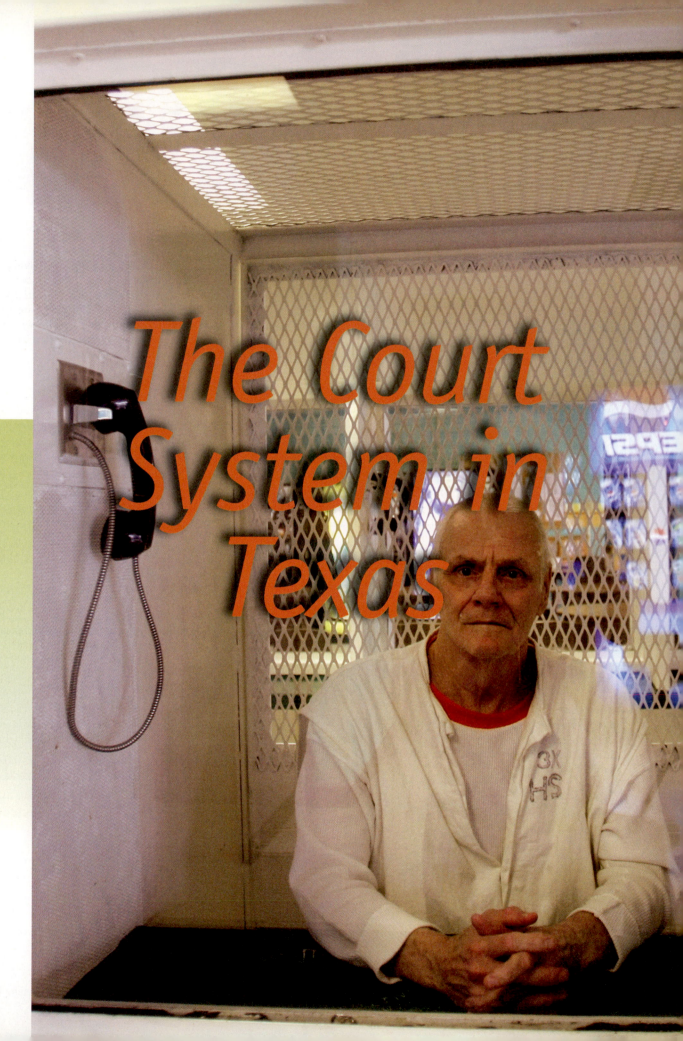

The Court System in Texas

THEN

Courts sentenced about 40 people to death each year, while approximately 10,000 people received prison sentences.

NOW

The number of people sentenced to death has decreased, while the number sentenced to prison has doubled.

NEXT

Will the economic downturn spark prison reform across the state?

What alternatives to prison will the state develop, especially for juveniles and those held on drug-possession charges?

How will policies such as tort reform affect the number and the types of cases heard by the state court system?

ing views of the appropriate role of courts in a democratic society. First, citizens think the court system should be above politics. Courts are expected to act in nonpolitical ways. Justice is often portrayed as a "blindfolded woman holding the scales of justice in her hand. Most Americans firmly believe that courts should be blind to political bias: fairness, it would seem, requires neutrality."[1] Second, Americans also want state courts to be responsive to the electorate, "especially if they play prominent roles in molding and implementing public policy."[2] But obviously, courts cannot be both above politics and responsive to the electorate.

Most citizens do not see a conflict between these two ideas. They think that courts should both dispense pure justice and do so according to the wishes of the electorate. Courts are placed in this position because they make decisions on matters ranging from domestic and family law to criminal law, and they serve as the final arbitrator of highly political decisions. In playing the dual roles of decision maker and policy maker, courts function very differently from other institutions.

The courts' approach to decision making is quite different from how the executive and legislative branches make decisions.[3] Courts must maintain a **passive appearance.** Unlike the legislature or the governor, who can initiate policy changes, courts must wait for a case to come to them. Second, courts have **strict rules of access.**[4] Whereas any citizen may approach the legislature or the governor, courts have rules that limit access to them. They must also uphold **strict procedural rules** regarding the evidence they can consider, confine their decisions to the specifics of the cases before them, and maintain the appearance of objectivity. By doing that, courts help to reinforce the legitimacy of their decisions and their place as the final arbitrators of conflict. This in turn reinforces the concept that the rule of law, and not the rule of arbitrary actions by individuals, governs.

The Structure of State Courts

Like the federal system, most state court systems provide for three levels of courts: trial courts, appellate courts, and a supreme court. Texas has several levels of trial courts and appellate courts. Figure 25.1 illustrates their structure and main characteristics. Trial courts differ from appellate courts in several important ways. First, they are localized. Jurisdiction is limited to a geographic area, such as a county.[5] Second, one judge presides over a trial court, and each court is considered a separate court. Third, citizens participate in trial court activity. They serve as members of juries and as witnesses during trials. Fourth, trial courts are primarily concerned with establishing the facts of a case (such as a determination that a person is guilty). Fifth, trial courts announce decisions immediately after the trial is finished.[6] In Texas, trial courts are the justices of the peace, municipal courts, county courts, district courts, and special-purpose courts such as probate, juvenile, and domestic relations courts.

Appellate courts decide whether proper procedures have been followed, and they are centralized, often at the state level. More than one judge presides; citizen participation is virtually absent. Texas has fourteen intermediate appellate courts and two "supreme" appellate courts: one for civil cases (Supreme Court) and one for criminal cases (the Court of Criminal Appeals).

In this chapter, we study the structure of the judiciary branch of state government, the authority of different courts and juries, and the major political issues within the justice system.

FIRST, we examine *the structure of state courts* and describe the role and authority of each type of court.

SECOND, we evaluate the process of *judicial selection and removal* in Texas, determining the advantages and disadvantages of this system relative to those used in other states.

THIRD, we consider the role played by grand and petit *juries* in the court system.

FOURTH, we explore *issues in the justice system,* such as tort reform, the death penalty, and the effect of punishment on crime rates.

---

passive appearance
the procedure followed by courts in not initiating cases but waiting for cases to be brought to them

strict rules of access
the limited access to courts because of special rules that determine whether the court will or can hear the case

strict procedural rules
the tight rules of courts regarding how cases must proceed and what evidence can be presented in court

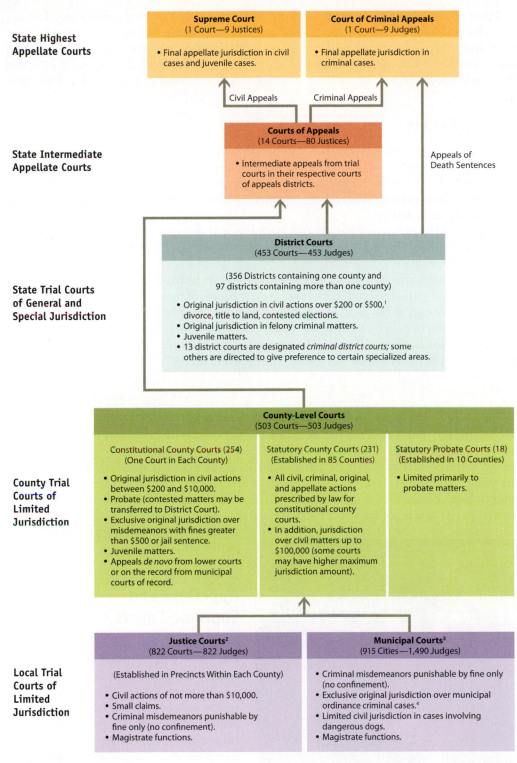

State Highest Appellate Courts

Supreme Court
(1 Court—9 Justices)
• Final appellate jurisdiction in civil cases and juvenile cases.

Court of Criminal Appeals
(1 Court—9 Judges)
• Final appellate jurisdiction in criminal cases.

Civil Appeals   Criminal Appeals

State Intermediate Appellate Courts

Courts of Appeals
(14 Courts—80 Justices)
• Intermediate appeals from trial courts in their respective courts of appeals districts.

Appeals of Death Sentences

State Trial Courts of General and Special Jurisdiction

District Courts
(453 Courts—453 Judges)

(356 Districts containing one county and 97 districts containing more than one county)
• Original jurisdiction in civil actions over $200 or $500,[1] divorce, title to land, contested elections.
• Original jurisdiction in felony criminal matters.
• Juvenile matters.
• 13 district courts are designated *criminal district courts;* some others are directed to give preference to certain specialized areas.

County Trial Courts of Limited Jurisdiction

County-Level Courts
(503 Courts—503 Judges)

Constitutional County Courts (254)
(One Court in Each County)
• Original jurisdiction in civil actions between $200 and $10,000.
• Probate (contested matters may be transferred to District Court).
• Exclusive original jurisdiction over misdemeanors with fines greater than $500 or jail sentence.
• Juvenile matters.
• Appeals *de novo* from lower courts or on the record from municipal courts of record.

Statutory County Courts (231)
(Established in 85 Counties)
• All civil, criminal, original, and appellate actions prescribed by law for constitutional county courts.
• In addition, jurisdiction over civil matters up to $100,000 (some courts may have higher maximum jurisdiction amount).

Statutory Probate Courts (18)
(Established in 10 Counties)
• Limited primarily to probate matters.

Local Trial Courts of Limited Jurisdiction

Justice Courts[2]
(822 Courts—822 Judges)

(Established in Precincts Within Each County)
• Civil actions of not more than $10,000.
• Small claims.
• Criminal misdemeanors punishable by fine only (no confinement).
• Magistrate functions.

Municipal Courts[3]
(915 Cities—1,490 Judges)
• Criminal misdemeanors punishable by fine only (no confinement).
• Exclusive original jurisdiction over municipal ordinance criminal cases.[4]
• Limited civil jurisdiction in cases involving dangerous dogs.
• Magistrate functions.

FIGURE 25.1

Court Structure in Texas, 2010

SOURCE: http://www.courts.state.tx.us

Local Trial Courts

All states provide for some type of minor or magistrate court, usually called the justice of the peace. These courts hear cases involving misdemeanors, most often traffic violations and minor civil cases. In Texas, there are two courts at this level: justices of the peace (JPs) and municipal courts. Municipal courts hear cases involving violations of city ordinances, most often, traffic tickets.

These courts also have **magistrate functions,** involving preliminary hearings for persons charged with a serious offense. These persons are informed of the charges against them and told of their rights, and bail is set. As magistrates, municipal judges and JPs can also issue search-and-arrest warrants. JP courts also serve as small claims courts in Texas. Municipal courts do not.[7] Jurisdiction in small claims is limited to a maximum of $15,000.

County Courts

In Texas, there are two kinds of county courts: constitutional county courts and county courts at law. County courts at law are created in large urban counties. In those counties, the constitutional county court ceases to function as a court, and the "county judge" becomes the administrative officer or county executive but retains the title of judge and some limited judicial functions.

County courts primarily hear intermediate criminal and civil cases. Most criminal cases are misdemeanors. The most common types of cases are DWI, worthless check, and drug and traffic appeals.

County courts also serve as appellate courts for cases heard by JP and municipal courts. All JP and most municipal courts in Texas are not courts of record but **trial *de novo* courts,** in which no record of the proceeding is kept and cases may be appealed for any reason. It is common practice in Texas to appeal traffic tickets to the county court, where, because of heavy caseloads, they get buried. If a person has the resources to hire a lawyer, there is a good chance the ticket will be "forgotten" in case overload.

District Courts

In most states, major trial courts are called district or superior courts. These courts hear major criminal and civil cases. Examples of major criminal cases (felonies) are murder, armed robbery, and car theft. Whether a civil case is major is generally established by the dollar amount of damages claimed in the case. Large urban counties generally have several district courts. In rural areas, one district court may serve several counties. The jurisdiction of these courts often overlaps with that of county courts, and cases may be filed in either court. Other cases must begin in district courts.

> Justice Wallace Jefferson, here shown at his investiture at the state capitol in Austin in November 2004, is the first African American to serve as chief justice of the Supreme Court of Texas, which has final jurisdiction in civil and juvenile cases.

Appellate and Supreme Courts

Ten states do not have courts of appeals, and twenty-three states have only one court of appeals. The other states, primarily large urban states, have several courts of appeals.[8] Texas has fourteen courts of appeals, with eighty judges elected by districts in the state. Only California has more judges and courts at this level. These courts hear all civil appeals cases and all criminal appeals except those involving the death penalty, which go directly to the Court of Criminal Appeals. All states have a supreme court, or court of last resort. Texas has two supreme courts, one for civil matters and one for criminal cases. Each court consists of nine judges elected statewide for six-year overlapping terms.

Judicial Selection and Removal

Different states use a variety of methods to select judges. Some allow certain judges to be appointed by the governor and serve for life. Some allow the legislature to elect judges.[9] Some states use partisan elections and nonpartisan elections to select certain judges. Last, some states use the **merit system,** or **Missouri system.** Under this plan, the governor appoints judges from a list submitted by a screening committee of legal officials. After appointment, a judge serves for a set term and is then subjected to a retention election in which the voters decide whether the judge stays in office.

The method of selection also varies between courts within some states. For example, appellate court judges are chosen by a merit system, and the voters elect trial court judges. Figure 25.2 shows the number of states using each selection method for appellate and trial courts. Most states have moved away from partisan election of judges and use either a nonpartisan election or a merit system.

In Texas, trial court judges are elected in **partisan elections** for four-year terms, and all appellate court judges are elected in partisan elections for six-year terms. The only exceptions to this are municipal court judges. Most municipal judges are appointed by the mayor or the city council (1,435 are appointed, and 16 are elected). Some have argued, however, that Texas really has an **appointive-elective system,** because the governor can fill any seat for district or appellate court that becomes vacant due to death or resignation or any new district court position created by the legislature. Vacancies in the county courts and justice of the peace courts are filled by the county governing body, the County Commissioners Court. Persons appointed to fill vacancies serve until the next regular election for that office, when they must stand for regular election.

Historically, many judges in Texas initially receive their seats on the courts by appointment. Although not complete for all time periods, enough data are available to show that this is a common practice. Between 1940 and 1962, about 66 percent of the district and appellate judges were appointed by the governor to their first term on the court. In 1976, 150 sitting district court judges were appointed.[10] Table 25.1 shows data on appointments of sitting judges in 2010. As you can see, many judges in all state courts get an initial appointment to serve.

Issues in Judicial Selection

In Texas, the question of judicial selection has been an issue for the last fifteen to twenty years. Several highly political issues have driven demands for change in the way Texas selects its judges. Voting based on name recognition and party label has resulted in the election of persons of questionable qualifications. Campaign contributions from groups with vested interests in cases before the courts have raised the specter of judicial bias, or "justice for sale." This issue has attracted much attention and will be discussed later in the chapter. Last, in large urban counties, minority representation on state district and county courts is affected by at-large elections at the county level. As we shall see, the legislature has not acted to correct any of these problems.

VOTING FOR FAMILIAR NAMES Several events have brought the issue of judicial selection to the forefront in Texas today. The first of these is electoral problems. Although elections are at the heart of any democracy, they are imperfect instruments for deciding the qualifications of the persons seeking office. This is especially true for judicial offices, for which qualifications are extremely important. The average voter in Texas will be asked to vote for judges for the Texas Supreme Court and the Court of Criminal Appeals, and, in large urban counties, several district judges, county judges, and JPs. Most voters go to the election booth with scant knowledge about the qualifications of judicial candidates, and they often end up voting by name familiarity. This happened in Texas in the 1976 election, when voters elected Don Yarbrough to the Texas Supreme Court. Yarbrough was

merit system (Missouri system)
a system of selecting judges in which the governor appoints judges from a list submitted by a screening committee, and after appointment, a judge serves for a set term and is then subjected to a retention election in which the voters decide whether the judge stays in office

partisan election of judges
method used to select all judges (except municipal court judges) in Texas by using a ballot showing party identification

appointive-elective system
the Texas system in which many judges are initially appointed to a seat on the court and later must stand for election

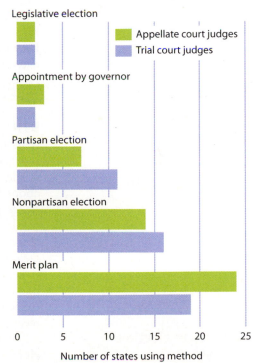

FIGURE 25.2

Methods of Selecting Judges

Note: The number of states does not add up to fifty because some states use more than one method to select judges. For example, district judges are elected; appellate judges are appointed.

SOURCE: *The Book of the States 2006* (Lexington, KY: Council of State Governments, 2006), 256–58, table 5.9.

TABLE 25.1 — Texas Judges Serving in 2010 Who Were Appointed to Their Initial Seat

	APPOINTED		ELECTED	
	Number	Percentage	Number	Percentage
Supreme Court	5	56	4	44
Court of Criminal Appeals	1	11	8	89
Courts of appeals	44	56	35	44
District courts	168	38	272	62
County courts at law	72	32	156	68
Probate courts	8	44	10	56
Constitutional county courts	48	19	203	81
Justice of the peace courts	235	29	586	71
Municipal courts	1,435	99	16	1

Note: Appellate and district court judges are appointed by the governor. County court judges and JPs are appointed by the county commissioners.

SOURCE: "Profile of Appellate and Trial Judges," Office of Court Administration, www.courts.state.tx.us.

an unknown attorney from Houston who won nomination as the Democratic candidate and claimed after the election that God had told him to run. Many voters had thought he was Don Yarborough, who had run unsuccessfully for governor. Still others thought he was Ralph Yarbrough, who had served in the U.S. Senate for two terms. Judge Yarbrough was forced to resign after about six months because criminal charges were filed against him. He was later convicted of perjury and sentenced to five years in jail, but jumped bond. He then attended medical school in Grenada, which refused extradition to the United States. He was arrested on St. Thomas, Virgin Islands, while attending medical school classes and returned to Texas, where he was eventually sentenced to five years in prison.[11]

STRAIGHT TICKET VOTING   Another electoral problem that has surfaced in recent years is straight ticket voting. Texas is one of fourteen states that allow straight ticket voting. Straight ticket voting allows a voter to vote for all candidates in a party by making a single mark. A study by Richard Murray at the University of Houston demonstrated that about 54 percent of the votes cast in Harris County in both 1998 and 2002 were straight ticket votes. A Republican running for countywide office had a 14,000-vote head start.[12]

Many incumbent judges have lost their seats in large urban counties to unknown challengers because of straight ticket voting. In Harris County in 1994, only one incumbent Democrat was reelected, and Republicans defeated sixteen Democrats because of straight ticket voting. Many of the Republican replacements lacked judicial experience, and one had no courtroom experience. In the 2006 elections in Dallas County, straight ticket voters turned the tables on Republicans, placing many inexperienced Democrats in office. This reversal occurred again in 2008—this time in Harris County.

These recent cases of straight ticket voting have caused some to call for **nonpartisan election of judges**—changing the ballots to show no party identification. Yet another suggestion is to prohibit straight ticket voting in judicial races, which has been considered in past sessions of the legislature. This would force voters to mark the ballot for each judicial race.

nonpartisan election of judges
election of judges in which party identification does not appear on the ballot

COSTLY CAMPAIGNS AND CAMPAIGN CONTRIBUTIONS   Under the Texas partisan election system, judges must win nomination in the party primary and then win in the general election. Two elections, stretching over ten months (January to November), can be a costly process. In 1984, Chief Justice John L. Hill spent over $1 million to win the chief

justice race. The cost of that race and other experiences caused Hill and two other Democratic justices to resign from the Supreme Court in 1988. They called for a merit system to replace partisan elections. Those resignations, along with other openings on the court, resulted in six of the nine seats on the Supreme Court being up for election. The total cost of the six races exceeded $10 million. One candidate spent over $2 million.[13] Races for district judgeships can also be very costly.

Money often comes from law firms that have business before the judges who receive the money. Other money comes from interest groups such as the Texas Medical Association, which has an interest in limiting malpractice tort claims in cases before the courts. In the 2002 election cycle, five of nine seats on the Supreme Court were up for election, including the chief justice. Close to $5 million had been raised by November 2002. Many of these contributions came from large law firms that had cases before the court.

The basic question raised by these contributions is their impact on judicial impartiality. Do these contributions influence the decisions made by judges? According to a poll by the Citizens for Public Justice, the average Texan thinks this money influences judges (73 percent). Even court personnel (69 percent) felt that the money influences judges. Lawyers were even more certain (77 percent), and since they contribute about 40 percent of the money, they may be in a position to know. About half of the judges (47 percent) thought the money influences their decisions. When people lose confidence in courts, respect for the law declines, and this should be of concern to all citizens.

In June 1995, the Texas legislature passed a law that aimed to reduce abuses of campaign contributions. This law limits the amount of money that individuals, PACs, law firms, and political party organizations can contribute to judicial races. Under this act, corporations are prohibited from making campaign contributions.

The amount of money an individual, PAC, law firm, or party organization can contribute is proportional to the population of the district or county from which the judge is seeking election and is highest for statewide offices. Unlike state representatives and senators, judges are elected from districts that vary greatly in the number of people voting. Judges in Dallas County must run countywide and appeal to several hundred thousand potential voters. Judges in rural counties might have only a few thousand voters in their district. The total amount of money a candidate may spend in seeking office is also limited. The limits are as follows:

- $2 million for candidates for statewide judicial office
- $500,000 for candidates for courts of appeals where the population is more than a million

- $350,000 for candidates for chief justice of courts of appeals where the population in the district is less than a million
- $200,000 for candidates for district or county courts where the population of the district or county is between 250,000 and a million
- $100,000 for candidates for district or county courts where the population is less than 250,000

All provisions of this law are voluntary. A candidate may file a declaration of intention not to comply with the provisions of this act. Candidates who file such a declaration must place a notice of noncompliance on all their campaign literature and advertisements. Candidates who comply may state in their literature that they are complying. Noncompliance by an opponent would supposedly become an issue in the campaign, and this is the intent of the act. However, the effect of this act has been marginal at best. Since the law went into effect, no one has made an issue of noncompliance. It has had no effect on campaign contributions or expenditures. Unless these provisions are made mandatory, this law will have no effect.

minority representation in judgeships
election of judges from single-member districts in major urban counties to allow minority judges to be elected

MINORITY REPRESENTATION   A fourth electoral issue is **minority representation in judgeships,** which some feel would require election of judges from single-member districts. District and county court judges all run for election on a countywide basis. Countywide races for judgeships create the same problem for minorities as multimember legislative districts do. Minority judges have not been successful in races for these at-large, countywide offices. The problem is especially difficult in nine urban counties (Harris, Dallas, Bexar, Tarrant, Jefferson, Lubbock, Ector, Midland, and Travis). In 1989, the League of United Latin American Citizens (LULAC) sued, claiming that at-large election of judges in these counties was a violation of the Voting Rights Act. In 1989, the federal district court in Midland ruled the Texas system in violation of the Voting Rights Act. On appeal, the Fifth Federal Circuit Court, in 1994, reversed that decision, and the U.S. Supreme Court refused to hear the case, thus upholding the federal circuit court.[14]

Opponents of single-member-district elections in urban counties claim that partisan voting was more significant than ethnicity in these judicial elections. The two are obviously related. One could make the same argument that if all twenty-four delegates from Harris County to the Texas House of Representatives were elected at large, few minorities would be elected, because of straight ticket voting. The issue of minority representation in the state judiciary remains politically active but as a legal matter is dead. Any change would have to come from the legislature.

IS THERE A BEST SYSTEM FOR SELECTION OF JUDGES?   Reformers, who include some of the best legal minds in the state, are calling for change from the current partisan election system. In every session of the legislature since 1995, bills have been introduced that called for the nonpartisan election of district judges and a merit system for appellate judges. In 2001, seven bills were introduced that call for the appointment or nonpartisan election of some judges in Texas. None passed. And in 2003, six such bills were introduced, and none passed. In the 2005 session, four bills were filed to move to nonpartisan elections, and none passed.

Judicial selection revolves around three basic issues. Citizens expect judges to be (1) competent, (2) independent and not subject to political pressures, and (3) responsive, or subject to democratic control. Each method used by the states to select judges has strengths and weaknesses regarding each of these issues.

When judicial selection is by appointment by the governor, there is great potential for the selection of judges who are competent, but it does not ensure competence. Governors can use judicial appointments to reward friends and repay political debts. All U.S. presidents, some more than others, have used their judicial appointive powers to select federal judges with political philosophies similar to their own. Governors do the same thing. In such cases, questions of judicial competence are sometimes raised.

Governors are not likely to select unqualified people for judicial appointments; however, governors might not be able to persuade the best candidates to agree to serve. The appointive system probably rules out the complete incompetents, but it does not necessarily result in the appointment of the most competent people to serve as judges. Once appointed, judges are not responsive to voters and can exercise great independence in their decisions.

Election by the legislature is a system left over from colonial America, when much power rested with the state legislature. It is used only in South Carolina and Virginia. This system tends to result in the selection of former legislators as judges. In South Carolina, the number of judges who formerly were legislators is very close to 100 percent. Appointment is viewed as a capstone to a successful legislative career.[15]

Nonpartisan election is one system being given serious consideration in Texas. It would reduce the cost of campaigns and the problem of straight ticket voting. Voters would be more likely to base their decisions on something other than party label. It would not necessarily result in the selection of more competent judges, but it would prevent the kind of large-scale changes in judgeships that happened in Harris County in 1994. As indicated earlier, it has also been suggested that Texas prohibit straight ticket voting for judicial candidates, requiring voters to mark the ballot for each judicial race.

The merit, or Missouri, plan is also being considered as a method of selecting judges. Under this system, the governor would appoint judges from a list of acceptable (and, it is hoped, competent) candidates supplied by a judicial panel and perhaps ranked by the state bar association. Once appointed, the judge would serve for a set term and stand for retention in an election. In this retention election, voters could vote to either retain or remove the judge. The system is used by twenty-one states for appellate judges and fifteen for trial judges.

The merit plan seems strong on the issues of competency and responsiveness; however, there is little evidence that it results in the selection of more competent judges.[16] There is also evidence that it is weak on responsiveness. In retention elections, the judge does not have an opponent.[17] Voters vote to retain or remove. Several writers have pointed out the difficulty of defeating someone with no one.[18] In the states that use this system, most judges are retained; less than 1 percent are ever removed.[19] One study showed that between 1964, when the system was first used, and 1984, only 22 of 1,864 trial judges were defeated.[20] When judges are removed, it is usually because of either an organized political effort to remove them or gross incompetence.

Some variations on these plans are worth considering in Texas. In Illinois, judges are elected using a partisan ballot, but they must win 60 percent of the vote in a retention election to remain in office. In Arizona, judges in rural counties are elected in nonpartisan elections, but judges in the most populous counties are appointed.

In short, there is no best, or perfect, system for selecting judges. All methods have problems. Also, there is no evidence that compared with the other methods, any one of these judicial selection methods results in the selection of judges with "substantially different credentials."[21] The only exception to this is that in the states where the legislature elects judges, more former legislators serve as judges.

> Supreme Court Justice Nathan Hecht arrives at a meeting of the Texas Ethics Commission in 2008, where he defended himself against charges that he broke campaign finance laws by accepting $16,000 from homebuilder Bob Perry's HillCo PAC to help pay his legal fees to fight charges that he abused his office. Would another system of selecting judges—such as nonpartisan elections or the Missouri system—help to avoid such situations?

Removing and Disciplining Judges

Most states provide some system to remove judges for misconduct. Impeachment, a little used and very political system, is provided for in forty-three states, including Texas. Five states allow for recall of judges by the voters.[22] One state, New Hampshire, allows the governor to remove a judge after a hearing. In five states, the legislature can remove judges by a supermajority vote (a two-thirds vote is most common). In recent years, the trend in the states has been to create a commission on judicial conduct to review cases of misconduct by judges and remove them from office. To date, forty-nine states have established judicial

THEN NOW NEXT

The Rising Caseload

THEN (2000)	NOW (2010)
The number of civil cases added to county-level court dockets was almost 500,000. The number of criminal cases was over 200,000.	Although the number of civil cases has dropped, the number of criminal cases has increased sixfold.
The number of motor vehicle and injury cases heard at the district and county level was approximately 50,000.	The number of motor vehicle and injury cases has dropped by about 20 percent.
Civil cases were resolved within 8.8 months on average.	Civil cases are resolved within 8.9 months on average.

WHAT'S NEXT?

> Will the state increase the number of courts as the caseload rises?

> How will Texas courts find a way to dispense fair judgments as the system becomes increasingly clogged?

> What new technologies can be used to make the system more efficient?

SOURCE: Texas Judicial System Annual Report, Fiscal Year 2000, www.courts.state.tx.us/pubs/AR2000/toc.htm; Annual Report for the Texas Judiciary, Fiscal Year 2009, www.courts.state.tx.us/pubs/ar2009/AR09.pdf.

grand jury
a jury of citizens that determines whether a person will be charged with a crime

information (administrative hearing)
a hearing before a judge who decides whether a person must stand trial; used in place of a grand jury

conduct commissions. Also, the method of removal of judges can depend on the level of the judgeship—for instance, trial judges versus appellate judges.

In Texas, the state Supreme Court may remove any judge from office. District judges may remove county judges and justices of the peace. The State Commission on Judicial Conduct may recommend the removal of judges at all levels. This twelve-member commission conducts hearings and decides whether "the judge in question is guilty of willful or persistent conduct that is inconsistent with the proper performance of a judge's duties."[23] The commission can privately reprimand, publicly censure, or recommend that the state Supreme Court remove the judge. The use of review commissions to reprimand, discipline, and remove judges acts as a check on the actions of judges.

Juries

In general, Texas convenes two types of juries: grand juries and petit juries. Every defendant in a criminal case has the right to a trial by jury. However, defendants can choose to waive this right.

Grand Jury

Any citizen may file a civil suit in court, but a screening body must review criminal cases. The U.S. Constitution requires the use of a **grand jury** to serve as a screening mechanism to prevent arbitrary actions by federal prosecutors. Some states use the grand jury system for some criminal cases, although in recent years the use of a formal hearing before a judge, called an **information,** or an **administrative hearing,** has become more common. The judge reviews the facts and decides whether there is enough evidence to try the case.

Texas uses both grand juries and administrative hearings. A citizen may waive his or her right to review by a grand jury and ask that a judge review the charges. In Texas, grand juries consist of twelve citizens chosen by district judges in one of two ways. The district judge may appoint a grand jury commission that consists of three to five people.[24] Each grand jury commissioner supplies the judge with three to five names of citizens qualified to serve on a grand jury. From these names, the judge selects twelve citizens to serve on a grand jury. In the other method, the district judge can have twenty to seventy-five prospective grand jurors summoned in the same manner used for petit juries. From this group, the district judge selects twelve citizens who are called grand jurors.[25]

Most grand juries serve for six months. They often screen the major criminal cases to decide whether enough evidence exists to go to trial. Grand juries are supposed to serve as filters to prevent arbitrary actions by prosecuting attorneys, but they do not always serve that function. The district attorney often dominates grand juries. Most grand jury members are laypeople who have never served before, and they frequently follow the advice of the prosecuting attorney. Although grand juries may conduct investigations on their own, few do. Those that do conduct investigations are sometimes termed "runaway grand juries" by the media.

A study by the *Houston Chronicle* presented evidence that some judges in Harris County had been given names of citizens for the grand jury by prosecutors from the district attorney's office. The study also demonstrated that many of the same citizens serve on grand juries year after year. Judges justified the repeated use of the same people for grand juries based on the difficulty of getting people to serve. Often, older, retired citizens volunteer to serve.[26]

Thus, a grand jury might not always serve the function of protecting the citizen from arbitrary action by prosecutors. For that reason, a person may ask for an administrative hearing before a judge. During grand jury proceedings, the accused is not allowed to have an attorney present during the hearing; during an administrative hearing, the attorney is present and can protect the accused.

In Texas, the prosecuting attorney files minor criminal cases in county courts. The county court judge, who determines whether the case should proceed to trial, holds an "administration" hearing. Criminal cases in the county court are generally less serious than those filed in district courts. They consist of DWI/DUI, minor theft, drug, assault, and traffic cases.

Petit Jury

Both criminal and civil cases can be decided by a petit (pronounced "petty") jury. Members of a **petit jury** are randomly selected from voter registration lists or, more recently in Texas, lists of licensed drivers. In criminal and civil cases, the defendant has the right to a trial by jury but may waive this right and let the judge decide the case.

Very few cases involve jury trials. In 2009, Texas county courts heard 611,231 cases, and 2,818 were jury trials. In district courts, 280,059 cases were disposed of, and 2,670 were jury trials. The lack of jury trials in criminal cases is often the subject of concern to some citizens. In a process known as plea bargaining, most people charged with crimes agree to plead guilty in exchange for a lesser sentence agreed to by the accused and the prosecuting attorney. The judge hearing the case can accept or reject the agreement.

If all criminal cases were subject to jury trials, the court system would have to be greatly expanded. Many additional judges, prosecuting attorneys, and public defenders would be needed. In addition, many more citizens would have to serve on juries. The cost of this expanded process would be excessive, and even though citizens support "getting tough on criminals," they would balk at paying the bill.

Issues in the Justice System

The Texas justice system hears three types of cases: civil, criminal, and juvenile. Civil cases are those between individual citizens and are brought to court when a lawsuit is filed. Criminal cases are those brought against individuals for violating laws. Juvenile cases resemble criminal cases but involve children aged 10 to 17, and thus are considered civil in nature. Children cannot be tried as adults in Texas. Figure 25.3 illustrates the percentage of cases in each category.

Texas laws and judicial policies have a powerful impact on the number of cases, the types of cases, and the types of punishments. Many ordinary citizens advocate for victims' rights (see this chapter's "Thinking Critically About Democracy") or against the death penalty. Texans have voted on a constitutional amendment fast-tracking tort reform in the state. As a result, the number of motor vehicle and personal injury cases has dropped. The values and the attitudes of juries and justices also affect who is sentenced and how long they serve.

Racial Disparity

Racial disparities within the criminal justice system are readily apparent both in Texas and in the United States in general. Minorities are significantly overrepresented among the group of individuals who are arrested each year in Texas. Texan juries arrive at a guilty verdict more

petit jury
a jury of citizens selected randomly from voter registration lists or lists of licensed drivers that determines the guilt or innocence of a person during a criminal trial

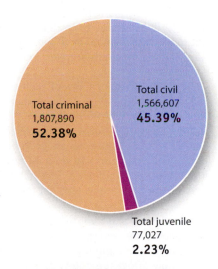

Total criminal
1,807,890
52.38%

Total civil
1,566,607
45.39%

Total juvenile
77,027
2.23%

Grand total: 3,451,524

FIGURE 25.3

Total Crimes in County and District Courts (2009)

SOURCE: The Texas Office of Court Administration Trial Court Judicial Data Management System, "County Level Courts Activity by Case Type, January 1, 2009 to December 31, 2009," and "District Courts Summary by Case Type from January 1, 2009 to December 31, 2009," http://dm.courts.state.tx.us/OCA/ReportSelection.aspx.

SHOULD VICTIMS' RIGHTS GROUPS BE ABLE TO INFLUENCE PAROLE BOARD DECISIONS?

The Issue: In July 2008, Austin's KVUE news announced that David Lopez was up for parole. Nearly thirty years earlier, 20-year-old Cydney Myers, a part-time college student, had been sexually assaulted and murdered. For nine years, the murder remained unsolved until in 1988 DNA evidence identified David Lopez as the killer. The case is famous for one reason: It kick-started the victims' rights movement in Texas. After Cydney's death, her mother, Nell Myers, found that there were very few resources to help her and her family deal with the justice system and the many issues they faced. In 1982, Myers founded People Against Violent Crime (PAVC), the group that is responsible for many of the achievements of the victims' rights movement. PAVC helped create the Texas Missing Person's Clearinghouse and a statewide ceremony honoring the victims of crime. PAVC also helped establish a Crime Victims Compensation Fund and fought to establish the Victim Services Section that is now part of the Texas Department of Criminal Justice. Finally, PAVC drafted the Crime Victim's Bill of Rights passed by the Texas legislature in 1989.

The Crime Victim's Bill of Rights gives victims and their families the right to be protected from threats that result from cooperating with the prosecution. It requires the state to pay for medical examinations and AIDS testing and counseling for victims of sexual assault. It guarantees the right to the prompt return of property not used as evidence, to a safe place to wait during trial, and to have the victim's safety taken into consideration when the judge sets bail.

The Crime Victim's Bill of Rights also gives victims and their families the right to be notified when parole proceedings are set. Nell Myers died in 2000, so when Lopez came up for parole in 2008, the parole board notified Whitney Myers, Cydney's sister. For the first time since her sister's death, Whitney Myers spoke out publicly, urging people to write letters to the parole board requesting that parole be denied. The parole board voted to deny Lopez parole. The next review was set for 2014.

Yes: Victims and their families are notified of parole procedures and should be allowed to testify at the parole hearing if they choose. The community is not notified, however. A convict's release may affect the safety and mental health not only of victims and their families but also of their friends and the community into which the convict will be released. Though the board is the final decision maker, the community should have a say about which criminals are released into their midst.

No: In deciding whether to grant parole, government officials should take into account the risk the convict presents to the community. The parole board should consider the convict's prison record, social history, and interactions with authority. The board should also review psychological assessments, the convict's prior criminal record, and any statements made by the judge at the time of sentencing. Public pressure should not be brought to bear on the board, however. Because the media often sensationalize a story to increase ratings or circulation, public opposition may be based on inaccurate or incomplete information spread by the media or by groups within the community, including victims' rights groups, which would almost always advocate denying parole. The board must make objective, responsible decisions.

Other approaches: In a democratic society, citizens have the right to voice their opinions. They also have a right to be informed about events that may affect their safety. However, the parole board is an experienced body with firsthand information. Therefore, although the board should listen to public concerns and explore issues that concerned citizens raise, public pressure should not determine the board's decision. The board members must have a measure of independence; regulations must be enacted so that members cannot be removed for making an unpopular decision.

What do you think?

① What role do you think the media have in the prosecution, conviction, and sentencing of people accused of violent crime? What role should they have?

② What rights and responsibilities does a community have toward violent offenders?

③ Should victims' rights groups exert public pressure against the release of a convict? Why or why not?

frequently when the defendant is a member of a minority. As shown in Figure 25.4, in 2008 Texas jails and prisons housed almost 10,000 more African Americans than Anglos. Yet, in that same year, almost three times the number of Anglos were arrested in Texas.[27]

The issue of racial disparity in the Texas judicial system attracted national attention because of a case that occurred in Tulia, a small farming town in the Texas panhandle with a population of about 5,000. On July 23, 1999, police officers and state troopers carried out an early-morning drug raid in the town. The raid was part of a federal and state war on drugs in rural areas. It was the fruit of an eighteen-month investigation on the part of undercover narcotics officer Tom Coleman, and it was a major operation: forty-six partially-dressed residents were dragged to the courthouse and charged with selling one to four grams of cocaine. The offense carried only a 20-year penalty, but many of those arrested were charged with more than one count or with selling cocaine in close proximity to a park or a school yard. So, of the thirty-eight who were convicted, twenty-two received long prison sentences—some as long as 60, 99, and 434 years. The case was widely acclaimed, and Coleman became the Department of Public Safety's Outstanding Lawman of the Year.

But some aspects of the case didn't sit right with a handful of Texans. For one, Tulia had a very small African American population, and yet all but a few of the forty-six arrested were African American, and they had been convicted by an almost all-white jury. Only five of those sentenced had previous convictions. Then, those who admitted selling to Coleman insisted they dealt only in marijuana and crack, narcotics that are more prevalent among low-income groups. Dealing in these drugs carries a lighter sentence in Texas. Finally, no drugs, paraphernalia, or stashes of money were found during the raid. The convictions were based entirely on the testimony of Coleman.

Jeff Blackburn, an Amarillo attorney and ACLU member working pro bono proved that Tanya White had been in Oklahoma City on the day and time Coleman claimed to have bought cocaine from her. As a result, in 2000, the ACLU filed a lawsuit with the U.S. Department of Justice. The *New York Times* picked up the story, and the national media turned to Coleman's shady past. Former friends and associates described him as unreliable and as racist. Coleman had committed theft in Cochran County, where he had previously worked as a deputy sheriff, and he pinned the department with thousands of dollars of debt. Finally, in early 2003, the Texas Court of Appeals arranged for an evidentiary hearing. Judge Ron Chapman determined that apart from Coleman's notes on the buys, he had collected no physical evidence to corroborate his testimony: no fingerprints, no photos—nothing.

By August 2003, all thirty-eight prisoners were released. Coleman, meanwhile, was indicted for perjury on multiple counts.

The Effect of Punishment on Crime Rates

As Figure 25.5 shows, the crime rate decreased in the United States and Texas from 1990 through 2006. Texas ranks third among the fifteen most populous states in total crimes committed per 100,000 population.[28] Total violent crime has increased, but the increase is not as great as suggested by the news media or by campaign rhetoric. Crime has increased in Texas less than in the nation as a whole.

Many factors contribute to the crime rate. Most crimes are committed in larger cities. If we compare the fifty states, we find a strong correlation

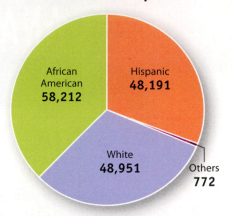

Texas Inmates by Race

African American **58,212**
Hispanic **48,191**
White **48,951**
Others **772**

Total incarcerated: 156,126

FIGURE 25.4

Texas Inmates by Race

SOURCE: Fiscal Year 2008 Statistical Report, Texas Department of Criminal Justice, www.tdcj.state.tx.us/publications/executive/FY08%20Stat%20Report.pdf.

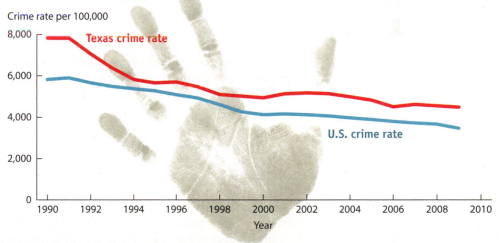

Crime Rates in Texas and the United States

Crime rate per 100,000

Texas crime rate

U.S. crime rate

Year

POLITICAL INQUIRY

FIGURE 25.5 ■ How does the Texas crime rate compare with the average rate in the United States? What factors might explain this difference?

SOURCE: www.disastercenter.com/crime/uscrime.htm.

ANALYZING THE SOURCES

WHO IS ARRESTED FOR CRIME?

It has been suggested that if society could lock up all men between 18 and 25 years of age, crime would decline tremendously. Race is also a factor in arrest rates. African Americans constitute about 12 percent of the U.S. population, yet, as shown in the accompanying table, they constitute almost 30 percent of persons arrested for various crimes.

Persons Arrested for Crime by Sex, Race, and Age

	PERCENTAGE OF ARRESTS, 2007
SEX	
Male	75.8
Female	24.2
RACE	
White	69.7
Black	28.2
Others	2.1
AGE	
Under 18	15.4
18–24	28.9
25–34	23.9
35–44	17.6
45–54	10.9
55 and over	3.3

SOURCES: The 2010 Statistical Abstract, Persons Arrested by Charge and Selected Characteristics: 2007, table 314, www.census.gov/prod/2009pubs/10statab/law.pdf; Arrests by Age, 2007, www.fbi.gov/ucr/cius2007/data/table_38.html.

Evaluating the Evidence

① How might these statistics—or your reaction to them—change, do you think, if the *types* of crimes for which people were arrested were specified?

② In light of the civil liberties guaranteed to all citizens, consider the suggestion that crime would decrease if young men could be "locked up." What other approaches might decrease crime levels while maintaining civil liberties?

③ What causes arrest rates to decrease once people reach the age of 35?

between the percentage of the population living in urban (metropolitan) areas and crime rates. This in part explains the crime rate in Texas, because about 80 percent of the population lives in metropolitan areas. There is also a strong relationship between age, sex, and crime. (See "Analyzing the Sources.") People below 25 years of age commit almost 45 percent of the crimes, and males commit 75 percent of all crimes. In Texas, the number of young men aged 18 to 24 has decreased in recent years. This has contributed to the reduced crime rate since 1989 in Texas.[29]

The attitude among most Texans is "if you do the crime, you should do the time." Juries in Texas give longer sentences than the average nationwide. However, the average time served in Texas is less than the national average, and the percentage of sentence served by violent offenders in Texas is also lower than the national average, because of the longer sentences imposed by juries. The length of time served has increased in recent years, because of an increase in available prison space.

Texas has one of the highest rates of incarceration in the country. (See "How Texas Compares: Incarceration Rates.") The argument advanced for more incarceration is that it will lead to a reduction in crime rates. Studies of Texas crime show that between 1989 and 1993, when the incarceration rate increased by 4 percent, there was a 1 percent decrease in the crime rate. Even if no other factors affecting crime rates were involved, this seems a high cost for such a small reduction in crime.

INCARCERATION RATES

Texas has one of the highest crime rates in the country, and Texas policy makers must find ways to combat this problem. Spending more on incarceration means less funding for juvenile justice programs and other crime preventive measures. How does Texas compare with other states in its incarceration rate? Should Texas reduce its level of incarceration and spend money on other programs?

SOURCES: Data from Texas Criminal Justice Policy Council, *Testing the Case for More Incarceration in Texas: The Record So Far* (Austin: State of Texas, 1995), 29; data for 1999, Texas Criminal Justice Policy Council Web page; data for 2001 and 2004, "Fiscal Size-up," table 56, www.lbb.state.tx.us; data for 2004, U.S. Department of Justice, Bureau of Judicial Studies, www.ojp.usdoj.gov/bjs/abstract/po4.htm; data for 2008 and 2009, "Prison Inmates at Midyear 2009—Statistical Tables NCJ," Bureau of Justice Statistics.

Death Penalty

Political values and attitudes influence not only the number of people sentenced but also the type of punishment they receive.

It has often been suggested that the death penalty can reduce crime. As discussed earlier in the book, the death penalty was outlawed in the United States in 1972 (*Furman v. Georgia*) because it was unfairly applied to many crimes and because of the lack of safeguards in place in many states. In 1976, the U.S. Supreme Court established guidelines under which a state could reinstate the death penalty (*Gregg v. Georgia*). To date, thirteen states do not have the death penalty: Alaska, Hawaii, Iowa, Maine, Massachusetts, Michigan, Minnesota, North Dakota, Rhode Island, Vermont, West Virginia, New Jersey, and Wisconsin.

Most executions (82%; 822 of 1,006) have been in southern states. The death penalty fits well within the dominant traditionalistic culture of the South. In Texas and many other southern states, juries can set the sentence for all crimes, and juries might be more inclined than judges to impose the death penalty.

Although Texas is still the leading state in the number of prisoners executed, the number of people sentenced to death has been in decline in recent years. Since the death penalty was reinstated in 1976, Texas has executed 452 of the 1,200 people executed nationwide. There is no shortage of people waiting to be executed. As of April 2010, 342 people sat on death row. However, Harris County, which was once known as the death penalty capital of the United States, has passed that title on to Los Angeles County in California, where in 2009 more people were sentenced to death than in the entire state of Texas.[30] In April 2010, a Harris County jury sentenced a defendant to death for the first time since 2007.

In 2001, the *Houston Chronicle* reported that nearly 70 percent of Texans supported the death penalty. Have Texans suddenly had a change of heart? It is more likely that there are other issues involved.

Money is often a factor in determining whether the prosecuting attorney will ask for a death sentence. Small rural counties often lack the money to prosecute a death sentence case. Even large urban counties often find that death sentence cases will strain their budgets. Until just a few years ago, the wealth of Harris County was seen as a reason it led the country in executions. Harris County could afford it. However, the economic crisis seems to have spurred prison reform across the nation as counties and states scramble to pinch pennies. During this time, the number of death sentences has also declined nationally. Harris County has implemented cost-saving "in-reach programs" that aim to reduce the number of repeat offenders by encouraging inmates to turn their lives around.

Another factor may simply be the negative attention that Harris County and Texas have received of late. The state had gained a reputation for showing little mercy or leniency regarding death penalty sentencing. The Texas Court of Criminal Appeals almost never reverses a death sentence, and the Texas Board of Pardons and Paroles, often the final recourse for those with failed appeals, is even less apt to make changes. Then, in 2007, one case in particular incited statewide and even national outrage.

On September 25, Michael Richard, convicted of two counts of murder, was scheduled to be executed. His lawyers were racing to complete the last-minute paperwork necessary for an appeal to the Texas Court of Criminal Appeals when they allegedly ran into computer problems. When the general counsel of the court called the presiding chief justice, Sharon Keller, to explain the predicament, she responded with four words, "We close at five." The appeal was never submitted, Michael Richard was executed, and a public uproar ensued.

Keller's words sparked immediate action within both the state judiciary and the legislature. Many called for her resignation or removal. A year and a half later, the Texas State Commission on Judicial Conduct charged Judge Sharon Keller with failing to follow execution-day protocol. In 2010, the judge presiding over her trial recommended that she neither lose her job nor receive further punishment.

In 2010, a federal district court judge in Harris County made, and later rescinded, a ruling that the manner in which the death penalty is administered is unconstitutional. Some in the media accused the judge of "judicial activism" and questioned whether a judge should be allowed to make a ruling that contradicted the values of those living within his jurisdiction.[31] Thus, it seems that although Texans may be moving away from death sentencing, they are still determined to keep their options open.

Tort Reform

In February 1992, 79-year-old Stella Liebeck ordered a cup of coffee at a McDonald's drive-through. She placed the Styrofoam cup between her knees to remove the plastic lid and add cream and sugar. The very hot coffee spilled, causing third-degree burns. In what became

> Jean Dember protests outside a Texas prison in February 2000 just before the execution of Betty Lou Beets, who was charged with murdering her fourth and fifth husbands. Beets became only the second woman to be executed in Texas since the 1860s.

known as the "McDonald's coffee case," a jury awarded Liebeck $2.7 million in **punitive damages**—damages meant as a punishment or a deterrent. The case brought national attention to frivolous civil lawsuits—personal injury, medical malpractice, and other lawsuits that end in excessive monetary awards to the plaintiff. Opponents of such suits argue that they are wasteful, clog the legal system, and extract a terrible financial and emotional price from both individuals and businesses. These people advocate **tort reform**—changes in the rules regarding compensation for damages—to limit the amount of damages that can be awarded and to define or restrict the circumstances under which a plaintiff can sue for damages.

Critics of tort reform argue that personal injury lawsuits are a means of holding large, powerful corporations accountable for practices that endanger worker safety and hurt consumers. They point to the role of asbestos lawsuits in establishing safe guidelines when it became clear that asbestos caused lung cancer. Other opponents of tort reform argue that it limits the power of the judiciary and its ability to act as a check on the other branches of government.

In the 2002 elections, tort reform became a major issue in Texas. The state was in the midst of an economic crisis, and Governor Perry and Republican candidates argued that frivolous civil lawsuits were preventing it from attracting new businesses, large industries, and potential employers. Because of the rise of these suits, they argued, Texas had gained a reputation as a "judicial hell hole." In fact, the number of personal injury and damage cases had risen in the 1990s. This was due in large part to the Supreme Court ruling in *Dow Chemical Co. v. Alfaro,* which determined that the legislature had abolished *forum non conveniens,* a doctrine that allows a court to refuse to hear a case if there is a more appropriate forum in which the matter may be settled.[32]

In addition, Governor Perry argued that Texas was in the midst of a medical crisis, with severe doctor shortages particularly in rural areas and in high-risk specializations, such as obstetrics and gynecology. Because of medical malpractice suits, doctors' insurance rates had skyrocketed. Only a few insurance companies still offered insurance to doctors in Texas. Governor Perry recounted personal testimonies of physicians closing their practices and moving to other states. The pro-tort reform lobby, which included HMOs, hospitals, doctors' associations, and nursing homes as well as insurance and pharmaceutical companies, had contributed a whopping $5.3 million to the 2002 campaign.[33]

In January 2003, Governor Perry officially designated medical malpractice reform as an emergency issue, directing legislators to address this problem within the first sixty days of the session. The legislature passed a bill to cap punitive damages for civil suits at $250,000. However, this was not the first time the legislature had tried to cap punitive damages. In 1977, the legislature had passed a similar law, but it had been struck down by the Texas Supreme Court on the grounds that the Texas Constitution did not give the legislature the power to limit the judicial process in this way. Therefore, the 2003 legislature passed another bill calling for a constitutional amendment providing the legislature with this authority. This amendment became known as Proposition 12. Citizens' rights groups such as Public Citizen staunchly opposed the proposition, but the amendment was approved by a narrow majority.

These laws and other lower-profile tort reforms have helped lower the number of injury and damage cases (see Figure 25.6). By 2005, fifteen new insurance companies had moved in, and insurance rates were becoming more affordable.[34] Between

punitive damages
damages awarded in a legal case as a punishment or a deterrent

tort reform
changing the legal rules regarding compensation for damages done by one party to another

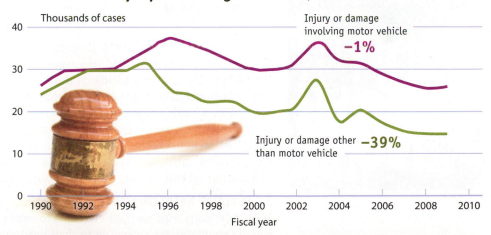

Injury or Damage Lawsuits, 1990–2009

Thousands of cases

Injury or damage involving motor vehicle **−1%**

Injury or damage other than motor vehicle **−39%**

Fiscal year

POLITICAL INQUIRY

FIGURE 25.6 ■ After a steady increase in injury and damage cases in the early 1990s, tort reform legislation has had an impact, decreasing the number of such lawsuits. **What impact, if any, will this have on Texas citizens who seek access to the courts? On product safety? On professional standards?**

SOURCE: Texas Courts Online, www.courts.state.tx.us/pubs/AR2007/trends/Caseload%20Trends%20by%20Case%20Type.pdf.

Issues in the Justice System   **751**

2003 and 2007, the number of new medical licenses granted climbed by 18 percent.[35] But critics argue that the number of patient complaints and disciplinary actions are up and that relief from the doctor shortage is coming mainly to urban areas. These critics lament the loss of the one big stick citizens had to keep big business from injuring those less powerful.

CONCLUSION

THINKING CRITICALLY ABOUT WHAT'S NEXT FOR TEXAS COURT SYSTEMS

In the twenty-first century, the court system in Texas faces many challenges. Methods of selecting judges will continue to be controversial, though some changes in these methods will probably occur. Texans may need to reconsider their approach to dealing with the high crime rates in the state. Although voters seem eager to approve bonds for the construction of more prisons, they have been reluctant to consider other approaches to crime control. However, budgetary constraints may force them to consider the long-term costs of having one of the highest prison populations and the highest execution rate in the United States—with the attendant costs of the appeals process—when weighed against the potential cost of alternative programs, such as expanded supervision and treatment programs, that might reduce crime more effectively.

The judicial system has been making progress in adopting methods to make the system more effective. In 1995, the state legislature established a Commission on Judicial Efficiency. One of the committee's four principal goals was to spearhead the adoption of information technologies. A good many of these efforts have been aimed at promoting a statewide court filing system that attorneys can use to file documents in civil cases. Dozens of counties are implementing these systems.[36] This and other measures should decrease the pressure on the county-level courts. As the population continues to grow rapidly, the Texas judicial system will have to find additional ways to accommodate its increasing caseload.

STUDY NOW

Summary

1. The Structure of State Courts
State court systems consist of trial, appellate, and supreme courts. Trial courts ascertain the facts of the case and decide on the defendant's guilt. Appellate courts review the trial court cases and determine whether proper procedures were followed. In addition, the Texas court system holds two types of trials: criminal and civil. Local courts of limited jurisdiction deal with matters such as small claims, magistrate functions, and civil actions of not more that $5,000. County trial courts deal with civil matters under $100,000, probate cases, some criminal misdemeanors, and appeals from lower courts. District courts deal with juvenile matters, felony crimes, and civil actions over $200 or $500.

2. Judicial Selection and Removal
Texas nominally uses partisan elections to select many judges, but in fact a good percentage of candidates are appointed to their positions before being elected. Most states have moved away from partisan elections, as a preference for some type of merit system is emerging. The Texas selection system has a number of disadvantages, including the tendency of voters to pick candidates with familiar names without any other knowledge of the candidate, and to vote a straight ticket and thus replace experienced judges with inexperienced judges, and the influence of campaign contributions on the partiality of judges. In Texas, supreme and district court judges can remove lower court judges, and the State Commission on Judicial Conduct can recommend the removal of judges.

3. Juries

All criminal defendants have the right to trial by jury. Texas has two types of juries. A grand jury serves as a screening mechanism to prevent arbitrary actions against citizens. Petit juries are trial juries that hear criminal and civil cases. Defendants may also waive their right to trial by jury.

4. Issues in the Justice System

Texas has recently implemented tort reform to decrease insurance rates for physicians and risks to businesses. Some argue these measures come at a cost to consumer and worker safety. High incarceration rates in Texas have achieved only a small reduction in crime rates. Although Texas still leads the nation in the number of individuals executed, the number of people sentenced to death has dropped significantly in recent years.

Key Terms

appointive-elective system 739

grand jury 744

information (administrative hearing) 744

magistrate functions 738

merit system (Missouri system) 739

minority representation in judgeships 742

nonpartisan election of judges 740

partisan election of judges 739

passive appearance 736

petit jury 745

punitive damages 751

strict procedural rules 736

strict rules of access 736

tort reform 751

trial *de novo* courts 738

For Review

1. What is the difference between criminal and civil cases?
2. What types of cases are heard by local, county, and district courts?
3. What types of cases are heard by the appellate and supreme courts?
4. How are judges selected and removed in Texas?
5. What is the function of grand juries and petit juries?
6. What is tort reform, and how was it implemented in Texas?

For Critical Thinking and Discussion

1. Give an example of a case you have heard of within your community or on the news. What type of case was it? Which court heard the case?
2. Which system of judicial selection do you think is best? Explain your reasoning.
3. When people vote for judges, they rarely know much about the candidates. How would you solve this problem within your community?
4. You are charged with a serious felony that you did not commit. Would you waive your right to review by a grand jury or not? Explain your answer.
5. What is your position on the death penalty in Texas? Prepare a brief speech that you could use when debating the issue.

PRACTICE QUIZ

MULTIPLE CHOICE: Choose the lettered item that answers the question correctly.

1. Texas has two types of minor or magistrate courts: municipal courts and _____ .
   a. courts of appeals
   b. principal courts
   c. justices of the peace (JPs)
   d. statutory probate courts

2. The amount of money an individual, PAC, law firm, or party organization can contribute to a judicial campaign
   a. decreases if the candidate is up for reelection.
   b. has no official or unofficial limit.
   c. is the same for local offices as it is for statewide offices.
   d. is proportional to the population of the district or county from which the judge is seeking election.

3. Which of the following phenomena tends to unseat experienced judges in the judicial system?
   a. straight ticket voting
   b. campaign contributions
   c. minority representation
   d. merit systems

4. A 1995 law that aimed to limit the influence of campaign contributions on judges has been ineffective because
   a. its limits are too large.
   b. its provisions are voluntary.
   c. its limits are too small.
   d. its limits are proportional based on population.

5. Which of the following groups has no authority to remove judges?
   a. Texas state Supreme Court
   b. probate judges
   c. district judges
   d. the State Commission on Judicial Conduct

6. Most judges in Texas are
   a. appointed only.
   b. appointed and then elected.
   c. elected only.
   d. appointed through a merit-selection plan.

7. How does the state locate individuals to serve on petit juries?
   a. randomly from voter registration lists or lists of licensed drivers
   b. randomly from a pool of interested applicants
   c. personally from the presiding judge's recommendations
   d. personally from the prosecution's recommendations

8. In 2008, the number of African Americans arrested was approximately _____ the number of Anglos arrested.
   a. three times
   b. twice
   c. the same as
   d. one-third

9. Supporters of tort reform argue that it will
   a. increase the accountability of large companies and improve consumer and worker safety.
   b. encourage new businesses and physicians to relocate to Texas.
   c. reduce trial costs to the state and local governments.
   d. eliminate corruption within the legal system.

10. Today, Texas is the leading state in
    a. both the number of death penalty sentences delivered annually and the total number of executions carried out.
    b. the number of death penalty sentences delivered annually, but not in the total number of executions carried out.
    c. the total number of executions carried out, but not in the number of death penalty sentences delivered annually.
    d. neither the number of death penalty sentences delivered annually nor the total number of executions carried out.

FILL IN THE BLANKS.

11. _____ damages are meant as a punishment or a deterrent, but opponents argue that they are wasteful and clog the legal system.

12. In Texas, _____ courts are local courts that hear cases in which juries often determine the outcome of the cases.

13. In Texas, _____ courts are higher-level courts that decide on points of law and not questions of guilt or innocence.

14. _____ are juries of citizens that determine whether a person will be charged with a crime.

15. _____ was once known as the death penalty capital of the nation.

RESOURCES FOR RESEARCH AND ACTION

Internet Resources

Death Penalty Information Center
www.deathpenaltyinfo.org   This site keeps track of death penalty information in all states.

Office of Court Administration
www.courts.state.tx.us   This is a good source of information on state courts in Texas. It keeps track of court data and serves as a watchdog agency for all state courts.

Texans for Public Justice
www.tpj.org   This advocacy group keeps track of many aspects of state government, including information on state courts and campaign contributions.

Internet Activism

The Texas Department of Public Safety provides crime records and statistics and general information about driving, handgun, and other laws. **www.txdps.state.tx.us/**.

Twitter
http://twitter.com/NCADP   Get updates from the National Coalition to Abolish the Death Penalty about issues related to Texas courts and national stories.

YouTube
www.youtube.com/watch?v=W8ZnR3ZpuQc   The Honorable Don Stevenson of Plano, Texas, takes viewers through a typical day at municipal court in this informative video.

Facebook
www.facebook.com/search/?flt=1&q=texas+court&o=65&s=40#!/ pages/Texas-Supreme-Court/136530906368210?ref=search
The Texas Supreme Court is centered in downtown Austin, and is composed of a Chief Justice and eight Associate Justices. It is the court of last resort for civil cases, including juvenile matters, acting alongside the Texas Court of Criminal Appeals, which handles criminal matters.

Recommended Readings

Abramson, Jeffrey. *We, the Jury*. New York: Basic Books, 1994.

Cheek, Kyle, and Anthony Champagne. "Money in Texas Supreme Court Elections," *Judicature* 84 (2000): 20–25.

Eisenstein, James, and Herbert Jacob. *Felony Justice*. Boston: Little Brown, 1977.

Herbert, Jacob. "Courts: The Least Visible Branch," in *Politics in the American States* (8th ed.), ed. Virginia Gray and Russell L. Hanson. Washington, DC: Congressional Quarterly Press, 2004.

Lawrence, Susan. *The Poor in Court*. Princeton, NJ: Princeton University Press, 1990.

Movie of Interest

At the Death House Door (2008)
This documentary investigates the case of Carlos DeLuna, who was executed in Texas in 1989 after prosecutors ignored evidence implicating another man for the crimes with which DeLuna had been charged.

Larry v. Lockney (2003)
This POV documentary charts the attempts by the ACLU and one small-town Texas farmer to oppose drug testing in public school.

The Life of David Gale (2003)
A fictional portrayal of an anti–death penalty activist and professor at the University of Texas who is wrongly sentenced to death for the rape and murder of his colleague. It stars Kevin Spacey and Kate Winslet.

Justice for Sale (1999)
This program was aired on *Frontline* by PBS and has received much attention. It explores the corrupting influence of campaign contributions on the judicial system in Texas.

The Thin Blue Line (1988)
A film by Errol Morris that successfully argues that a man was wrongly convicted for murder by a corrupt justice system in Dallas County, Texas. This film actually got the man released.

Public Policy in Texas

THEN

The Texas legislature approved and implemented a "pay as you go" budget that prevents the state from going into debt.

NOW

As the population of Texas grows, state and local governments scramble to fund education, social services, transportation, and public safety programs.

NEXT

Will Texans enact prison reforms to cut public safety costs?

Will the population growth precipitate a water crisis?

Will Texas turn increasingly to wind and other alternative power sources to meet its expanding energy needs?

In this chapter, we explore some of the major public policies in Texas state government and take a look at how Texas has implemented those policies.

FIRST, we cover *economic policies*, asking key questions such as where does the money come from and where does it go.

SECOND, we turn to *education policies* and consider who determines tuition rates, where college funding comes from, and how affirmative action is being pursued within the state.

THIRD, we examine *social policies* and how civil liberties, such as the right to privacy, fare in Texas.

FOURTH, we analyze Texas's *environmental policies* in view of the demands that arise from an increasing population and a booming economy.

public policy
any action or inaction by the government that has an impact on the lives of its citizens

As discussed in earlier chapters,

public policy can be any rule or regulation or the lack of rules and regulations that influence how government affects the lives of citizens. When the state legislature passes a law requiring that all students take two political science courses to graduate from a public university, that is a public policy. Had the legislature not passed such a rule, most students would not have registered for a course in state and local government.

By the same token, the lack of public policy can have an impact on citizens. The fact that the Texas legislature refused to appropriate more money to match federal dollars for the Children's Health Insurance Program (CHIP) is a public policy. The lack of funding for CHIP forces the uninsured to go to public hospital emergency rooms, increasing local property taxes. The landlord owner of the apartment where you live may have raised the rent to cover higher county taxes to support medical care for those uninsured children.

As a state much influenced by its past and the dominant traditionalistic political culture, Texas tends to pursue conservative public policy choices in comparison with other states. We will examine these policies within the spheres of economics, education, and social and environmental issues. These policies are an outcome of legislative initiatives, interest group activities, court decisions, executive branch decisions, and public opinion. They are the living product of the political system described in previous chapters.

Economic Policies

A budget can be thought of as a statement of policy in monetary terms, but where a state secures its revenue and how much it chooses to secure also reflect the state's values and political culture. Although a state may set priorities through laws that originate in any legislative committee, a state pursues its priorities by allocating funds to executive and legislative branch organizations that are then charged with executing those laws. An underfunded or unfunded law cannot be implemented. In this section, we analyze how the state's expenditures, sources of revenue, tax policies, and budgeting issues shape and produce its public policies.

Expenditures: Where Does the Money Go?

Today, much attention is focused on federal spending, and not all citizens realize that state governments also spend large sums of money to supply services to their citizens. In 2007, state and local governments, combined, spent $1.785 trillion. That amounted to $6,821 for each U.S. citizen. During the same year, the federal government spent $6,917 per citizen.[1] Some money spent by state and local governments comes from the federal government as grants, but state governments generate about 77 percent of their revenue from their own sources, and local governments generate about 67 percent of their revenue from their own sources.

What a state spends money for and how much it spends largely express its priorities. The budget becomes a statement of the dominant values in the state. The pattern of expenditures for Texas differs little from that of most states in terms of the items funded. In most states, three items consume most of the state budget—education, health and welfare, and transportation. In recent years, an increase in the prison population has greatly increased the amount spent for public safety, which includes prison operations. After those items, everything else pales in comparison. Figure 26.1 shows the major expenditure items in the state of Texas 2010–2011 biennium budget.

Whereas education eats up the lion's share of the state budget (about 42%), local school districts contribute about 60 percent of the funds for local schools. The state currently finances about 38 percent of the cost of elementary and secondary education. This is a decline in state contributions from a decade ago. The state's contribution has been steadily decreasing, and school districts have been forced to pick up a greater share of the cost of local education, which they are covering by assessing higher local property taxes.

Health and human services, about 33 percent of the state budget, is funded primarily with federal grants to the state. About 36 percent of the Texas budget comes from federal funds, most of which (about 52%) goes for health and human services (welfare and Medicare). Texas contributes less than most states to the cost of providing these services. The Texas Constitution prohibits spending more than an amount equal to 1 percent of the state budget on welfare.

A comparison of Texas with other large industrial states on the primary budget items will tell us more about what Texans value. Among the fifteen most populous states, Texas ranks near the bottom in expenditures for welfare and transportation. In education, Texas still ranks below the mean. Although Texas spends much money in total dollars, it spends less than the average comparable state in per capita dollars for most items. In recent years, most of the growth in state expenditures has been driven by population.

Revenue Sources: Where Does the Money Come From?

In addition to how a state spends its money, how a state funds its programs and how much funding it collects reveal a great deal about its public policy positions. To pay for the many services a state government provides, revenue must be raised from many sources. For state governments, the primary source of revenue is taxes paid by citizens and not service charges and fees. The most common single source of revenue for state governments is **consumer taxes,** such as sales and excise taxes on gasoline, tobacco, and liquor. Figure 26.2 shows the breakdown for Texas state tax revenue in 2010–2011, which totaled $77,726.7 billion for the

consumer taxes

taxes that citizens pay when they buy goods and services, such as sales taxes

Total Expenditures in Texas for 2010–2011

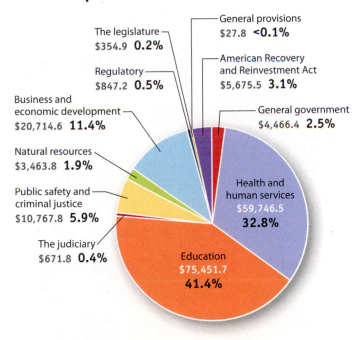

The legislature $354.9 **0.2%**

General provisions $27.8 **<0.1%**

Regulatory $847.2 **0.5%**

American Recovery and Reinvestment Act $5,675.5 **3.1%**

Business and economic development $20,714.6 **11.4%**

General government $4,466.4 **2.5%**

Natural resources $3,463.8 **1.9%**

Health and human services $59,746.5 **32.8%**

Public safety and criminal justice $10,767.8 **5.9%**

The judiciary $671.8 **0.4%**

Education $75,451.7 **41.4%**

Tax Revenue in Texas for 2010–2011

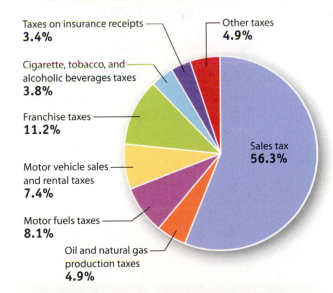

Taxes on insurance receipts **3.4%**

Other taxes **4.9%**

Cigarette, tobacco, and alcoholic beverages taxes **3.8%**

Franchise taxes **11.2%**

Sales tax **56.3%**

Motor vehicle sales and rental taxes **7.4%**

Motor fuels taxes **8.1%**

Oil and natural gas production taxes **4.9%**

POLITICAL INQUIRY

FIGURE 26.1 ■ The total expenditure was $182,880 million. What is most of this money spent on?

SOURCE: Legislative Budget Board.

POLITICAL INQUIRY

FIGURE 26.2 ■ The total tax revenue was $77,726.7 million. Where does most of this revenue come from?

SOURCE: *Texas Fact Book* 2010–2011.

two-year period. As you can see, most revenue comes from consumer taxes paid by individuals when they make purchases. Over 80 percent of all tax revenue comes from consumer taxes (sales, motor vehicle sales, motor fuels, alcoholic beverages, tobacco taxes).

Because of high sales taxes, most of the taxes in Texas are paid by consumers and not by businesses. There is only a limited tax on businesses, in the form of a corporate franchise tax. When compared with taxes on consumers, business taxes in Texas pale to insignificance at present. Texas has a form of corporate "income tax" that is called a **franchise fee.** Originally, it was assessed only on corporations doing business in the state. Some businesses changed to limited liability companies and other types of business structures to avoid the tax. The legislature was forced to eliminate many of these loopholes in 2007 and apply the franchise fee to most businesses in the state. In part, these loopholes were closed because of the school finance crisis. These reforms were implemented for the first time in 2008. The franchise fee is now the third largest source of tax revenue.

Texas is one of a handful of states without any form of personal income tax. Being in such a limited company of states without an income tax is not troublesome to most Texans. Politically there is great resistance to imposing such a tax. In 1992, the voters approved a constitutional amendment preventing the legislature from enacting an income tax without voter approval.

Service charges and fees are a source of **nontax revenue** for state governments. Governments often charge service charges and assess fees when a person can be excluded from receiving the service for nonpayment. When this exclusion is not possible, tax revenue is usually used to finance the service. Examples of these fees include tuition, driver's license fees, water bills, and fees for garbage collection. Figure 26.3 shows nontax revenue by source for the state of Texas in 2008–2009.

The trend in recent years has been to increase service charges and fees as a way to increase revenue and avoid raising taxes. All students attending state colleges and universities in Texas have experienced these increases as higher tuition and service charges. In total dollars in the state budget, the various service charges and fees provide 15 percent of total state revenue. The state lottery and interest income generates about 4 percent of total state revenue. (See Figure 26.4.) Federal aid made up about 35.5 percent of the Texas 2008–2009 biennium budget.

franchise fee
a type of business income tax levied in Texas

nontax revenue
governmental revenue derived from service charges, fees (tuition), the lottery, and other sources

Nontax Revenue in Texas for 2010–2011

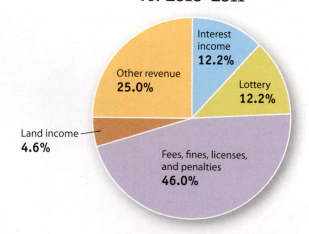

- Interest income **12.2%**
- Lottery **12.2%**
- Fees, fines, licenses, and penalties **46.0%**
- Land income **4.6%**
- Other revenue **25.0%**

POLITICAL INQUIRY

FIGURE 26.3 ■ The total nontax revenue was $29,600 million. Where does most of this revenue come from?

Revenue (All Sources) for Texas 2010–2011

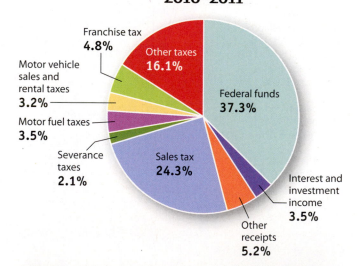

- Franchise tax **4.8%**
- Motor vehicle sales and rental taxes **3.2%**
- Motor fuel taxes **3.5%**
- Severance taxes **2.1%**
- Sales tax **24.3%**
- Other taxes **16.1%**
- Federal funds **37.3%**
- Interest and investment income **3.5%**
- Other receipts **5.2%**

POLITICAL INQUIRY

FIGURE 26.4 ■ Total revenue was $180,316.2 billion. Where does most of this revenue come from?

SOURCE: Legislative Budget Board, "Fiscal Size-up 2010–2011," figure 33.

Taxation: Who Is Targeted?

The question of who should pay the taxes raises many issues. The state shapes public policy by deciding whom to take money from, how to take it, and how much to take. "How Texas Compares: State Tax Capacity" examines the extent to which Texas exploits its **tax capacity**—the measure of its wealth in taxable resources—in relation to other states. In the following sections, we examine three additional categories of tax policy and show how Texas implements mostly conservative policies in line with its political culture.

BENEFIT-BASED TAXES AND ABILITY TO PAY Should those who benefit from public services pay taxes (**benefit-based taxes**), or should those who can most afford it pay the taxes? Some taxes are based more on the benefit a person receives, and others are based more on the **ability to pay.** For example, the excise tax on gasoline is an example of a tax based on benefit received rather than on ability to pay. A large portion of the gasoline tax is earmarked for highway construction. The more gasoline people buy, the more tax they pay and the more benefit they receive from using the streets and highways.

For most taxes, other than the gasoline tax, showing direct benefit is problematic. Benefit received is more applicable to service charges and fees than to taxes. Sometimes the service charge covers the actual cost of providing the service, such as a service charge for garbage collection. In other cases, the service charge might cover only part of the cost of providing the service. College students receive most of the benefit from attending classes, and they pay tuition and fees to attend. In state-supported universities and colleges, however, not all of the cost of a college education is covered by tuition and fees paid by students. Most of the cost is still paid by taxpayers.

Generally, when individual benefit can be measured, at least part of the cost of the service is paid as fees. People using a public golf course pay a green's fee, hunters pay for hunting licenses, and drivers pay a driver's license and tag fee. Often these funds go directly to the government unit providing the service. Taxpayers may pick up part of the cost through money paid in taxes. For example, green's fees paid by golfers often do not cover the total capital and operating costs of running a golf course. The difference is paid from revenue from other sources, typically from property tax revenues.

Other taxes, such as the federal income tax, are based more on ability to pay. The higher your net income, the higher your income tax bracket, and the higher the percentage of your net income you pay in federal income taxes. Most taxes, especially at the state level, are not based on ability to pay.

REGRESSIVE AND PROGRESSIVE TAXES Using the criterion of ability to pay, taxes can be ranked as regressive or progressive. A *regressive tax* takes a higher percentage of income from lower-income persons, and a *progressive tax* takes a higher percentage from higher-income people. Economists also talk about so-called proportional taxes, in which the tax paid is a fixed percentage of each person's income.

THEN NOW NEXT

The Budget for Education and Health and Human Services: The Money Trap

	THEN (1999)	NOW (2006–2010)
Amount spent on education	$12.5 billion	More than $33 billion
Amount spent on health and human services	$17 billion	Almost $33.5 billion
Total revenue	Just over $46 billion	Just over $84 billion

WHAT'S NEXT?

> How will Texas continue to fund increasing costs for education and health and human services?

> As expenses for public services grow, how will Texans pay for them during lean years when the state must also repay bond debt?

> Will Texans' attitude toward economic policy change?

SOURCES: Texas Comprehensive Annual Financial Report, Window on State Government, Texas Comptroller of Public Accounts, https://fmx.cpa.state.tx.us/fm/pubs/cafr/00/00CAFR185-197.pdf; Texas Net Expenditures by Function—Fiscal 2009, Window on State Government, www.window.state.tx.us/taxbud/expend.html; Revenue by Source for Fiscal Year 2009, Window on State Government, www.window.state.tx.us/taxbud/revenue.html.

tax capacity
the measure of wealth in taxable resources

benefit-based taxes
taxes for which there is a relationship between the amount paid in taxes and services received, such as gasoline taxes

ability to pay
taxes that are based not on the benefit received but on the wealth, or ability to pay, of an individual

STATE TAX CAPACITY

The amount of tax money available for any given state depends on the wealth of the citizens of that state. Some states, like some individuals, have a higher income capacity than others. The measure of a state's "wealth" is called the state tax capacity. How does Texas's tax capacity compare with that of other states?

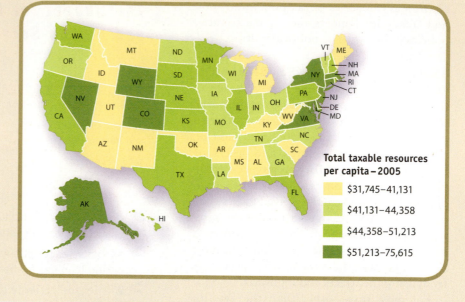

Total taxable resources per capita – 2005

- $31,745–41,131
- $41,131–44,358
- $44,358–51,213
- $51,213–75,615

SOURCE: The National Center for Higher Education Management Systems, "State Tax Capacity—Total Taxable Resources Per Capita," www .higheredinfo.org/dbrowser/index.php?submeasure=132&year=2005 &level=nation&mode=map&state=0.

Texas has one of the most regressive tax structures of all the states. The Institute for Taxation and Economic Policy, a Washington, D.C., advocacy group, issued a report in 2007 that ranked the fifty states based on how progressive or regressive their tax systems are. Texas made the "Terrible Ten" list, the list of states with the most regressive tax systems in the country.[2] Although all state tax structures are regressive, the tax structure in Texas is more regressive than average. States such as Texas that have no personal income tax have the most regressive tax systems. These states also have the lowest taxes on the rich.[3]

The degree to which taxes are regressive or progressive depends upon many factors. It is affected not only by the mix of taxes used in a state (income, sales, excise, property) but also by taxation rates and what is subject to tax. What is subject to taxation is called the *tax base*. For example, some states tax only unearned income (stock dividends and interest) and not earned income (wages and salaries). Others do the opposite. Some states have a flat rate (proportional) for state income tax rather than a progressive tax rate.

With the sales tax, the tax base is an important factor. If food and medicine are subject to a sales tax, the tax is more regressive. Only seventeen states exempt food items, forty-four exempt prescription drugs, and eleven exempt nonprescription drugs. If services used predominantly by the wealthy, such as legal and accounting fees, are subject to a sales tax, the tax is more progressive.

tax shifting
passing taxes on to other parties

tax incidence
the person actually paying the tax

TAX SHIFTING Another tax issue is the question of who actually pays the taxes: **tax shifting.** Some taxes can be shifted from the apparent payer of the tax to others, who become the true payers, or the **tax incidence.** For example, a person who purchases something in a store obtains a receipt from the store showing she paid so much in sales tax. It appears that she has paid a tax; she has a receipt that says so. Because of high competition

from other stores, however, the storeowner might lower the prices of goods and thus pay part of the tax in lower profits.

Students who rent apartments near their campus never receive a property tax bill. The landlord pays the tax each year; however, the landlord will try to pass along the property tax as part of the rent. Market conditions will determine when 100 percent of the tax gets passed along to the renter and when the landlord has to lower the rent and absorb part of the tax in lower profits.

Except for personal income tax, all taxes can be shifted to others. Market conditions will decide when taxes are shifted. People sometimes argue against business tax increases, advancing the argument that such increases will "simply result in higher prices to the customer." If taxes on businesses could always be shifted forward to customers as higher prices, no business would object to tax increases. Except for the inconvenience of collecting the tax and forwarding it to the government, there would be no cost involved. Obviously, taxes cannot always be shifted to the customer as higher prices, and businesses resist tax increases.

Budgeting and Crises

Because the legislature meets in regular sessions every other year (biennially), the Texas legislature approves budgets for two-year periods, called biennium budgets. In recent years, the Texas budget has been characterized by budget crises and an inability to pursue new policies.

THE BUDGET "FIX"   The legislature has a limited amount of discretion in spending money. Much of the revenues are earmarked for specific items, called fixed revenues, or **budget fixes.** Revenues are fixed in three ways: by constitutional or statutory provisions, by funding formulas, and by federal government rules. Although the legislature could change the statutory and funding formula rules, these are often politically fixed by past actions and, except in extraordinary circumstances, are not changed. Interest groups have a strong attachment to these appropriations and will fight to maintain them. Examples of fixes are the proceeds from the state lottery, which go to education, and the motor fuel tax, which goes primarily to state and local road programs.

The earmarking of revenues obviously limits the ability of the legislature to change budget priorities or to react to emergencies. If one fund is short, movement of money from another fund may not be possible. Last year's budget becomes the best predictor of next year's budget. Changes in the budget occur incrementally over a long period of time.

budget fix
a provision of the budget, mandated by state laws and constitutional amendments, that sets aside money to be spent on specific items

discretionary funding
those funds in the state budget that are not earmarked for specific purposes

income-elastic taxes
taxes that rise and fall quickly relative to changes in economic conditions; the Texas tax system is very income-elastic

Most funds in Texas are fixed, earmarked, or restricted. Only 19.5 percent of the moneys in the general fund are nonrestricted and available for change. That does not give the legislature much leeway in making changes in the budget. Similar patterns are found in most state budgets. Except for the Permanent University Fund, which applies only to the University of Texas and Texas A&M, university funding is part of the **discretionary funding.** That is why student tuition has increased in recent years. In per capita expenditures, the state has remained at about the same level over the past decade.

DEALING WITH BUDGET CRISES Over the past twenty years, Texas has experienced a number of fiscal shortfalls, and the legislature has been forced to meet in special sessions to correct those problems. Many of the fixes have been short-term, but there is a need for a long-term solution.

During the 1980s, there were ten special sessions of the legislature to attempt to correct revenue shortfalls. These shortfalls were caused primarily by a decline in the state economy attributable to a drop in oil prices from a high of $40 per barrel to a low of less than $10. The fiscal crisis was worsened by the state's tax structure. Texas depends heavily on **income-elastic taxes** (85 to 90 percent), which rise or fall very quickly relative to changes in economic conditions. When the economy is growing or contracting, tax revenue grows or contracts proportionately with the growth or contraction in the economy. For example, as retail sales grow, the sales tax grows. Texas is also very dependent on sales and excise taxes, which are also highly income-elastic. The same is true for the tax on oil and gas extracted in Texas. As the price of oil increases on world markets, the economy of the state booms and tax revenue increases. When an oil bust occurs, the opposite happens, and Texas finds itself extremely short of revenue. People quit buying goods and services subject to the sales and excise tax, and revenue falls accordingly.

The bar graph in "Analyzing the Sources" compares the tax dependency of the fifteen most populous states. As you can see, Texas is far more dependent on sales taxes than most other large states. Only Florida and Washington are about as dependent as Texas on consumer taxes. Washington, like Texas, lacks both a personal and a corporate income tax, and Florida lacks a personal income tax. Many states faced severe problems balancing their budgets in the wake of the global economic crisis that came to a climax in the fall of 2008.

In the 2003 session of the legislature, Texas faced at least a $10 billion revenue shortfall because of a downturn in the economy, and it will face another fiscal crisis so long as it remains dependent on consumer taxes. What recourses are available to the state? During past crises, the problem of revenue shortfall was often solved by raising sales and gasoline taxes and by increasing fees. Can those taxes be tapped again? Texas currently has one of the highest sales tax rates. The state tax is 6.25 percent and local tax is 2 percent, for a total of 8.25 percent. Raising the rate might not be possible. Only four states (Washington, Nevada, Rhode Island, and Mississippi) have higher state (excluding local) sales taxes.

Education Policies

The state regulates many education issues, but many are handled locally by special districts. We explore local issues in Chapter 27. Here, we look at state education policies pertaining to higher education, such as tuition, funding, and access.

College Tuition and Funding

For many years, the costs of college tuition and fees in Texas were very low and affordable to most people. Nonresidents of Texas often found it cheaper to come to Texas and pay a small out-of-state fee than to attend college in their own states. In the 1970s, the legislature began gradually to increase tuition and tie the amount students paid to semester hours taken. For most of the 1970s, the cost was four dollars per semester hour, or about twelve dollars per course, with a few fees for labs attached to some courses.

ANALYZING THE SOURCES

HOW STATES AND THE NATIONAL GOVERNMENT RAISE REVENUES

The bar graph compares the sources of tax revenue for the fifteen most populous states as well as the federal government. Note that Texas, Washington, and Florida rely most heavily on the total sales tax, whereas other populous states, such as California and New York, derive a large part of their revenue from an individual income tax, although both states also levy sales taxes.

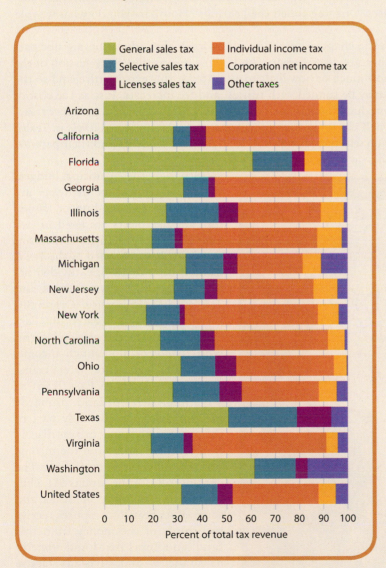

Legend:
- General sales tax
- Selective sales tax
- Licenses sales tax
- Individual income tax
- Corporation net income tax
- Other taxes

States (top to bottom): Arizona, California, Florida, Georgia, Illinois, Massachusetts, Michigan, New Jersey, New York, North Carolina, Ohio, Pennsylvania, Texas, Virginia, Washington, United States

x-axis: 0 10 20 30 40 50 60 70 80 90 100
Percent of total tax revenue

SOURCE: Legislative Budget Board, "Fiscal Size-up 2010–2011," 50, figure 59.

Evaluating the Evidence

① Based on what you've learned about state revenue, which states would you expect to experience the most severe budget crises? Explain your answer.

② Which states have the most regressive tax policies?

③ What conclusions can you draw about states that derive a large share of their revenues from individual income tax? From sales taxes? What kind of political culture do these states tend to have (see Chapter 19)?

Universities approached the legislature for more money during most of the 1980s and 1990s. For most of that time, the legislature refused to allow universities to set their own tuition rates but did allow the universities to charge additional fees for services provided to students. That included such charges as computer access fees, recreational fees, and transportation fees.

Texas A&M and the University of Texas at Austin approached the legislature about allowing the two "flagship" universities to charge a higher rate of tuition. They claimed flagship status as the lead universities in the state. Their request met considerable opposition in the legislature, especially from members who were graduates of "non-flagship" universities. Both schools continued to press this issue with the legislature, and in the 2003 session, the newly installed Republican majority and Republican Speaker Craddick agreed to allow what was called **deregulated tuition** for all state universities—a policy allowing them to set their own tuition. The legislature faced a $10 billion shortfall in revenues, and this seemed an easy solution to part of the problem. In 2002, the average cost for fifteen student credit hours for tuition and fees was $1,685. By 2007–2008, tuition had increased to an average of $6,000 per year.[4]

After the legislature changed the tuition policy, constituents began to complain about the increases. In the next session, the legislature held hearings and asked university officials to justify the increases. One wag called the hearings "How dare you do what we told you to do" hearings.

As indicated earlier in the chapter, operating funds for higher education are not part of the budget fix but, rather, are discretionary funds. This means that every session of the legislature must decide how much or how little to allocate for this expenditure, and so the cost of higher education may be funded with tuition and fee increases. Just as the cost of elementary and secondary education has been increasingly funded by local property taxes, which now equal almost half the total taxes collected at the state and local levels in Texas, the cost of higher education will increasingly fall to individual students and their parents, unless there is a drastic change in tuition policy.

deregulated tuition
a policy allowing universities to set their own tuition

> Students demonstrate in support of affirmative action, which remains a controversial issue in higher education.

Although the operating budgets for higher education in Texas are part of the regular budget, funds for capital projects are fixed in two funds. The Permanent University Fund (PUF), established by the Texas Constitution of 1876, is divided between the University of Texas and Texas A&M University. Originally, these lands were located in East Texas and were rather good farmland that generated much income. The state legislature later transferred these lands in East Texas to 2.1 million acres of land, primarily in West Texas. In the early part of the twentieth century, oil was discovered on these lands, and the income became substantial over time. The current value of the fund is $11.4 billion.[5] The University of Texas and some of its branch campuses receive two-thirds of the money from this fund, and Texas A&M and some of its branches and divisions receive one-third of the fund. Most of the money is committed to capital items and not operating budgets.[6]

Needless to say, many other colleges and universities in the state were upset that this policy did not give them any portion of these funds. The constitution specifically states that the money could be spent only at the University of Texas and its branch at College Station. The division of the money into two-thirds for the University of Texas and one-third for Texas A&M was an earlier agreement between the two schools.[7]

Because of pressure from other universities for a share in the PUF, the Texas legislature in 1984 proposed a policy change with an amendment to the state constitution, which the voters approved, that created the Higher Education Assistance Fund (HEAF). Beginning in 1985, the legislature set aside annual appropriations of $100 million for this fund. This was later increased to $175 million. Today, this fund provides about $275 million each year for colleges and universities not included within the PUF.[8]

Affirmative Action

From the 1950s to the 1970s, access to state colleges and universities in Texas was what could be called open enrollment, in which all students who were high school graduates and Texas residents would be automatically admitted without consideration of their high school standing or standardized test scores. Almost anyone could enroll in the university of his or her choice. In the 1980s, many schools, but especially Texas A&M and the University of Texas, began to impose higher standards for acceptance, primarily based on SAT scores and high school class standing.

This action to increase enrollment standards to some degree conflicted with the need to increase minority enrollment in the state's colleges and universities. Latinos and African Americans make up a majority of the state's population, but only about 20 percent were enrolled in colleges and fewer still at the top two state universities. This discrepancy was also true of law and other professional schools, where minority students were underrepresented.

Many colleges and universities began an affirmative action program to attempt to increase opportunities for members of minority groups to enroll in colleges and universities. These programs resulted in a lawsuit concerning the admission of minority students to the University of Texas law school. In 1996, the federal courts ended affirmative action practices at the University of Texas law school in the ***Hopwood* decision.**[9]

The attorney general of Texas, Daniel Morales, a beneficiary of affirmative action programs while a student in Texas higher education institutions, expanded the reach of the *Hopwood* case in Texas, effectively eliminating affirmative action admission policies in all colleges and universities in Texas. Thus, under the Morales interpretation, *Hopwood* was extended to prevent the consideration of race in areas beyond admissions.

In June 2003, *Hopwood* was overturned in a case originating in Michigan. The U.S. Supreme Court, in *Grutter v. Bollinger,* 539 U.S. 306 (2003), ruled that the U.S. Constitution does not prohibit the use of race as a factor in an admissions decision or policy. (For more on court decisions and affirmative action, see Chapter 5.)

Before the *Grutter v. Bollinger* decision, the Texas legislature, in an attempt to provide both equal opportunity and minority representation in higher education, changed the standards. It prevented admissions decisions and financial awards from being based primarily on any standardized test score such as the SAT, ACT, or GRE. Instead, the legislature allowed any student who graduated in the upper 10 percent of his or her high school class to gain automatic admission to any state college or university without consideration of other factors such as SAT scores. This ruling had the greatest impact on the University of Texas, where currently 81 percent of the freshman class has been admitted under the 10 percent rule. To a lesser degree, this is also the case at Texas A&M University.[10]

The 10 percent rule was supposed to increase minority enrollment by allowing students from inner-city minority high schools to attend the top schools in the state. There is some evidence that the 10 percent rule has increased minority enrollment, especially at the University of Texas and to a lesser degree at Texas A&M. It has created a problem for some high-performing students in the better high schools in the state, however, where students with SAT scores of 1,500 and higher often do not make the top 10 percent. There are also a few students with very low SAT scores from small rural schools who have been accepted under

Hopwood decision
a controversial 1996 case in which a federal court reversed affirmative action at the University of Texas law school

SHOULD THE TEXAS LEGISLATURE REFORM THE TOP 10 PERCENT LAW?

The Issue: In 1996, the Texas legislature passed the Top 10 Percent Law, which ensures that those who graduate in the top 10 percent of their high school class will be admitted to a Texas university or college. The hope was that the plan would increase diversity and minority representation at prestigious universities such as the University of Texas at Austin or Texas A&M University following the *Hopwood* decision. The plan has been praised by some, but not by all, and some maintain that it has created a problem for some high-performing students in the better high schools in the state. In some high schools, students with SAT scores above 1,500 do not automatically make the top 10 percent category. In contrast, a few students from small rural schools will get accepted to elite universities under the 10 percent rule despite having very low SAT scores. In 2007, the legislature initiated a bill to reform the plan. Under the revised plan, half of a university's freshman class would be admitted using the 10 percent plan. The rest would be admitted on the basis of other criteria. The bill passed in both the state House and the state Senate and proceeded to a conference committee. At the last minute, however, Texas representatives in the House from rural and minority districts blocked the bill. In 2009, the state legislature passed a less ambitious revision of the Top 10 Percent Law, allowing the University of Texas at Austin to admit 25 percent of its freshman class on the basis of other criteria. The other thirty-seven public universities, however, must continue to implement the 10 percent rule.

Yes: The Top 10 Percent Law discriminates against students of all races who attend the more competitive high schools. Students in the second or third highest decile of their graduating class in one high school may be just as capable as students from the top decile of another high school. University admissions should be based largely on ability, rather than on race or economic disadvantage. Moreover, the plan actually works against minorities who attend racially integrated high schools. These individuals, who may be present in a small percentage in their schools, may be represented in an even smaller percentage within the top 10 percent of their high school classes.

No: A recent study by Kim M. Lloyd, Kevin T. Leicht, and Teresa A. Sullivan found that the Top 10 Percent Law does increase minority representation at universities. Although some argue that minority representation isn't up to pre-*Hopwood* standards, raising awareness of the plan will encourage students who might not otherwise attend college to consider applying. Diversity is a key element of university education and is critical in a flagship university such as the University of Texas or Texas A&M. Students with good grades and SAT scores of 1,500 and above will find a place in a university; the Top 10 Percent Law provides opportunities for a broader range of students.

Other approaches: Apart from revising admissions procedures, there are many steps the state can take to improve minority representation and diversity on campus. Universities and colleges can target minorities and engage in more aggressive recruitment. The state can offer more financial aid and scholarships to low-income, rural, and minority students. In addition, efforts should be made to improve public schools in rural and minority districts.

What do you think?

① How has the Top 10 Percent Law affected you and your classmates?

② In what ways, if any, do you think the Top 10 Percent Law should be changed? What would be the effect of the changes you suggest?

③ What other measures would you take to improve diversity on campus?

the 10 percent rule. Some people think the 10 percent rule needs to be changed—the subject of this chapter's "Thinking Critically About Democracy."

Social Policies

Each session, the Texas legislature introduces bills relating to social issues. Compared with those of other states, the laws that are passed engender conservative social and economic policy. (See "How Texas Compares: Policy Liberalism.") This conservative approach to public policy becomes very clear when looking at the state's approach to right to privacy issues.

POLICY LIBERALISM

This index of policy liberalism examines state indicators of policy positions in three areas: gun control, abortion, and tax progressivity. From these policy areas the index of policy liberalism was constructed for each state. In the first column, each state is ranked with 1 as most liberal and 50 as most conservative (Texas is number 41). Each policy area is then ranked in the same way (1 = most liberal, 50 = most conservative), with a number for each state. Notice that some states rank high on some indicators of policy liberalism and near the bottom on others. Are there patterns among western states, southern states, or eastern states? How does Texas rank in each of these categories? Is the rank what you would expect?

State Rank on Policy Liberalism Index, 2005

STATE	POLICY LIBERALISM	GUN LAW INDEX	ABORTION INDEX	TAXES PROGRESSIVELY
California	1	2	1	10
Hawaii	2	4	12	34
New York	3	7	9	19
Vermont	4	27	6	3
New Jersey	5	6	16	21
Connecticut	6	9	3	24
Oregon	7	18	7	6
Massachusetts	8	1	17	18
Maine	9	35	5	5
Rhode Island	10	8	28	27
Maryland	11	3	4	12
Montana	12	50	11	2
Illinois	13	5	20	39
Minnesota	14	17	20	8
New Mexico	15	31	14	26
Delaware	16	21	22	1
Alaska	17	26	10	28
Washington	18	23	2	50
West Virginia	19	29	15	13
Pennsylvania	20	14	47	40
Wisconsin	21	15	32	14
Missouri	22	16	41	20
New Hampshire	23	41	13	43
Iowa	24	10	19	22
Michigan	25	11	43	37
Ohio	26	25	38	11
Kentucky	27	48	49	16
Colorado	28	33	25	33
Nebraska	29	13	36	7
Nevada	30	29	8	47
Kansas	31	32	31	25
South Carolina	32	19	37	4
Indiana	33	24	34	36
Tennessee	34	40	23	48
Arizona	35	29	18	38
Louisiana	36	37.5	50	41
North Carolina	37	20	24	15
Virginia	38	22	40	17
Utah	39	45	42	31
Florida	40	12	27	49
Texas	41	35	33	44
Idaho	42	37.5	35	9
Arkansas	43	44	43	23
Alabama	44	49	38	42
Oklahoma	45	39	30	29
Georgia	46	46	28	30
Mississippi	47	42	43	32
North Dakota	48	43	48	35
South Dakota	49	35	46	45
Wyoming	50	47	25	46

Note: The policy liberalism index also includes right-to-work laws that were not included in this table because the law is a binary variable.
SOURCE: Virginia Gray, "The Socioeconomic and Political Context of States," in *Politics in the American States: A Comparative Analysis* (9th ed.), ed. Virginia Gray and Russell Hanson (Washington, DC: Congressional Quarterly Press, 2008). Constructed by the author from data from the Brady Campaign to Prevent Gun Violence (for the gun law index), NAM Pro-Choice America (abortion index), Urban Institute (TAW index), and Institute on Taxation and Economic Policy (tax progressively).

Where infringement of privacy upholds conservative values, Texas laws have supported the right to privacy. Where the same type of infringement violates conservative values, Texas laws have opposed it.

Sex and Abortion: Upholding Texas's Conservative Tradition

Privacy and abortion were discussed in Chapter 4. As noted there, after the U.S. Supreme Court decided in the landmark *Roe v. Wade* case that the Texas law banning abortions was unconstitutional, *Planned Parenthood v. Casey* allowed states to impose regulations on women seeking an abortion, so long as those laws do not constitute an "undue burden." Many states have tried in a variety of ways to limit and restrict abortions. Texas is no exception. In the 2007 session of the legislature, twenty-five bills were introduced to restrict or define abortions and limit abortion rights. Each session of the legislature finds about this same number of bills filed that could have an impact on women's right to abortion. Often these bills restrict the right of a woman to have an abortion unless she obtains the consent of her parents or the father of the child grants permission. Most bills that have passed primarily affect younger women and require parental consent.

The legislature has also altered the rules in the state budget to make it easier for pro-life groups to receive funds for abortion counseling, and it has reduced the availability of funds for organizations such as Planned Parenthood that support a woman's right to choose.

Many legislators who file these bills do so out of strong religious convictions that abortions are wrong. They have a lot of vocal company supporting these actions. At the Planned Parenthood clinic in Bryan/College Station, the local Coalition for Life group keeps a constant vigil. They have a camera set up to photograph the license plates of everyone who visits the clinic. Parents of students who go to the clinic sometimes get a letter informing them that their daughter has visited the "abortion" clinic.

Some bills involving sex and teen behavior have been known to make the national news. One such bill in the 2005 session, introduced by former Representative Al Edwards of Houston, became known as the "Booty Bill." This bill would have prevented cheerleaders at high school events, such as football games, from doing dances and body movements that are sexually suggestive. Testifying before the committee when the bill was given a hearing,

> Youth from a San Marcos Catholic church march to an anti-abortion rally in Austin to hear Governor Rick Perry speak on the issue.

Edwards was unable to provide the words to describe what constituted such suggestive behavior. He knew what it looked like when he saw it but could not put it into words.

The Texas State Board of Education, however, has succeeded in introducing abstinence-only sex education curriculum in Texas high schools. In 2004, the SBE approved only textbooks that adopted this approach. By 2009, one study reported that 94 percent of Texas school districts provided only abstinence-only sex education and 2.3 percent skipped sex education altogether.[11] In 2005, Texas had the fourth highest teenage pregnancy rate and the highest live birth rate in the nation. Perhaps not surprisingly, Texas has one of the most restrictive birth control policies for minors. In almost one-third of the state's family planning clinics and in all school-based clinics, minors must obtain parental consent to obtain a prescription. Even teens who have already had a child of their own must obtain permission. The vast majority of teenagers who gave birth were unwed mothers: 81 percent of teens who give birth to their first child and 72 percent of teens who give birth to subsequent children. The percent of unwed teens that have given birth, however, falls below the national average, suggesting that more teens marry prior to giving birth.[12]

On other privacy issues, however, the Texas legislature has come down firmly on the side of the "get your laws off my body" argument—in cases where such an argument upholds conservative values. At the beginning of the 2007 session of the legislature, the governor, on very slim authority, issued an executive order requiring all schoolgirls to be vaccinated against the human papillomavirus to prevent cervical cancer later in life. Several members of the legislature expressed concern that if young women were to get the vaccine, it would encourage teen sex because they would not have to worry about getting cancer. In part, this logic assumed that teen behavior is rational when it comes to sex. Other legislators doubted this. Conservative groups also argued that requiring the vaccine was a violation of privacy and that Governor Perry had overstepped his authority. Several members of the House and Senate introduced legislation, which passed, preventing the vaccinations from taking place.

In March 2008, the Centers for Disease Control and Prevention (CDC) released a study that found one in four young women was infected with the virus. According to the *Houston Chronicle*, "Texas Gov. Rick Perry was right. Members of the Texas Legislature who last year shot down his plan to require schoolgirls be vaccinated against the human papillomavirus were shortsighted. This groundbreaking study shows how pressing is the need for sound public policy on teen sexual health—policy based on data and demonstrated best practices rather than emotion."[13]

Gay Rights and Gender Equality

One of the first rights won by gays and lesbians in the United States was the overturning of sodomy laws that ban this form of private consensual sex between adults of the same sex or the opposite sex. At one time, all states had antisodomy laws. However, by 2003 the number had decreased to thirteen states. Texas was one of the thirteen. In 2003, these laws were invalidated by the Supreme Court.[14]

The Texas legislature proposed an amendment to ban same-sex marriage, which was approved in the 2005 session. In November 2005, the voters overwhelmingly approved this amendment. Texas joined eighteen other states that had added amendments banning gay marriage to their constitutions.[15] Many of these bans follow the same language as the Defense of Marriage Act passed in 1996 by Congress that said states do not have to honor same-sex marriages performed in other states. This act goes against the Full Faith and Credit provision of the federal Constitution that requires states to recognize the acts and judicial proceedings of other states. There is no doubt that this amendment, which was primarily symbolic, has the support of most Texans, including many minority voters in the state.

Texas also lags slightly behind the other states in issues of gender equality. Regarding women's and men's salaries, for example, the median salary of a college-educated woman falls at 76 percent of the median salary of a college-educated man in the United States. In

Texas, the earnings gap is higher, with women's median salary at 71 percent.[16] Although most other southern states fare no better with this indicator, other southern states that have well-developed high-tech industries like Texas, such as North Carolina and Georgia, rank well above Texas.

Environmental Policies

Texas not only ranks number 1 in greenhouse gas emissions but also produces more carbon dioxide than California and Pennsylvania, the next two biggest polluters. If Texas declared itself an independent nation, it would rank seventh in the world among the top greenhouse gas polluters. Some point their finger at Texans' attachment to big gas-guzzling cars and air-conditioners, and others blame population growth and a booming economy that increases energy demands. Whatever the reason, the state's reliance on coal-burning power plants has loaded lakes and rivers with enough mercury to generate fish consumption warnings for hundreds of acres across the state, and about one in five U.S. women of childbearing age has mercury levels that are high enough to injure her unborn child.[17]

The nature of Texas politics and political culture does not support efforts to reduce pollution. In a state where the petrochemical and oil industries have been a mainstay of the economy, pollution has often been viewed as a sign of prosperity. In the past, if someone objected to the smell of oil production, the comeback was often, "Smells like money to me."

When George Bush was running for president in 2000, Texas already ranked as the top polluter among the states. Karen Hughes, a spokesperson for then governor Bush, was asked about the high pollution ranking of the state, and she said, "Governor Bush has done more than any governor in the history of Texas to hold the polluters' feet to the fire and force them to voluntarily comply." The news media reported that statement. No one in the news media asked the obvious question—"How many polluters have complied?" The press simply reported it. To a large degree, state leaders often deal with the problems by denying that they exist and thus foreclosing any need for a change in policy. Former congressman Tom DeLay called global warming data "political science," meaning that the data are driven by politics and not science.

In 2006, Environmental Defense Fund (EDF), an organization that works with governments, businesses, and communities to implement practical solutions to environmental problems, issued a report predicting the effects of global warming on Texas. As weather conditions change, the plant and animal life that inhabit the different regions of Texas will shift. Mosquito-born diseases will therefore migrate from the tropics northward. Malaria will spread. By 2006, Texas had already experienced its first cases of dengue fever. Over 600 miles of low-lying coastal lands will be inundated by rising sea levels. Some crops, such as cotton, will fair well, but others, such as corn, will fair badly. In general, however, longer droughts and surface-water evaporation will tax the water supply.[18]

Even if none of those predictions materialize, Texas still faces severe water shortages. Population growth, especially within urban areas, will mean a skyrocketing demand. Figure 26.5 shows projected demand, based solely on population estimates drawn from data from the U.S. census. Municipalities are already preparing for this eventuality. San Antonio and El Paso are leaders in this effort. San Antonio runs water conservation consumer education programs, provides rebates for water-efficient toilets

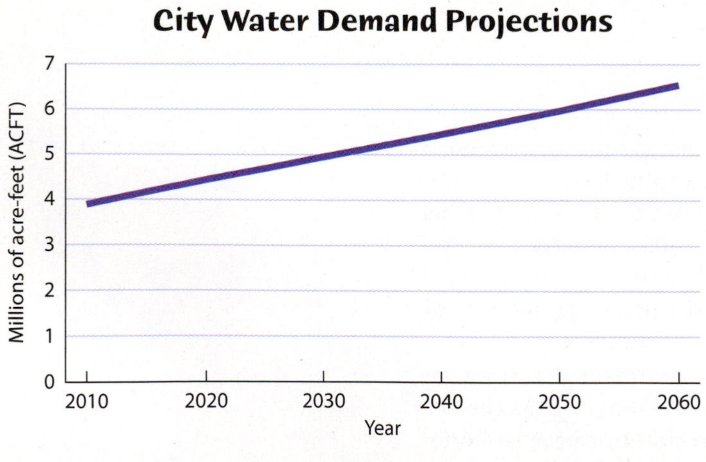

City Water Demand Projections

FIGURE 26.5

City Water Demand Projections in Acre-Feet (ACFT)

SOURCE: City Water Demand Projections: 2010–2060, The Texas Water Development Board, www.twdb.state.tx.us/wrpi/data/proj/popwaterdemand/2011Projections/Demand/5CityDemands.pdf.

and washing machines, and hired a four-person team to repair leaks quickly. The city's $5.5 million water conservation program reported a $4–7 savings on every $1 spent.[19]

Some entrepreneurs in Texas have been buying up rural lands in close proximity to urban areas to acquire water rights. Texas oilman T. Boone Pickens purchased land overlying the Ogallala aquifer, the largest underground water reservoir in North America. Pickens hopes to pump as much as 200,000 acre-feet of groundwater into municipalities such as Dallas. Environmental groups, however, have argued that pumps are already pulling water out of the acquifer ten times faster than it can be replaced.[20]

The water crisis, however, is not the only challenge presented by the rising number of Texans. As both industries and the population expand, Texas faces a steep rise in energy demands. To accommodate this growing need, Texas energy companies began applying for permits to build more coal-burning power plants. In 2005, Governor Perry issued an executive order to speed up the construction of seventeen of these new plants. Environmentalists and local government officials, who feared the new plants would put them out of compliance with federal law, joined together to fight this initiative and were successful in part. Energy companies agreed to cut the number of plants down and applied to build new nuclear power plants. The power companies agreed, as well, to pursue alternative energy schemes, and wind energy in particular. Today, Texas leads all fifty states in wind power generation. In 2009, Texas generated 9,400 megawatts of electricity, as compared with its closest competitor, Iowa, which produced 3,600. [21]

Despite the state's embrace of wind power, Texas shows little sign of changing its high-polluting ways. By contrast, California is a leader in pollution legislation. Its standards for auto emissions have forced the auto industry to reduce emissions nationwide. California is also leading efforts to reduce other emissions through the Global Warming Solutions Act. This act will require a reduction of carbon emissions from all sources by 25 percent by 2020.[22] Meanwhile, many Texas public officials deny that global warming is a problem. Texas's environmental policy is an example of how public policy can be created not by legislation but by the lack of it.

CONCLUSION

THINKING CRITICALLY ABOUT WHAT'S NEXT FOR TEXAS PUBLIC POLICY

The state of Texas spends a great deal of money, but measured in total dollars, it still ranks toward the bottom on per capita expenditures. School funding, discussed further in Chapter 27, will continue to be an issue. Prison funding will also become a major problem in the future if the state persists in its policy of increasing the number of state prisoners. The need for more health and human services will keep growing as the population increases. These expenditures cannot be funded through bonds, and yet they will have to be cut to repay bond debt in lean years.

State revenue is at or near capacity from most sources, and there is little room to raise existing state taxes. Tax revenue is highly dependent on income, and the current downturn in the economy can erase the surplus that existed in earlier sessions of the legislature. Perhaps this situation will force the state to evaluate the current tax system and its impact on the many segments of the state's economy. Politically, the prospects for change in the state tax structure are dim. The traditionalistic-individualistic political culture of the state does not support radical change. Without a major crisis, the status quo will probably prevail, and the current tax and spending structure in the state will continue.

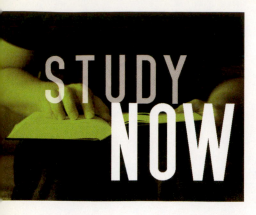
STUDY NOW

Summary

1. Economic Policies

A state pursues its priorities by deciding how much money to spend on a variety of governmental programs. Because of its budget fix, the budgetary process in the state of Texas restricts its ability to create and implement innovative policies. Change must occur slowly. In addition, how a state taxes individuals and businesses is a political policy. Most state tax systems are regressive, with lower-income individuals and families paying a greater percentage of their income to the state. Texas has one of the ten most regressive state tax systems in the nation.

2. Education Policies

As Texas universities have sought to become leading institutes of research and learning in the country, they have demanded the right to increase tuition. In 2003, tuition was deregulated. The *Hopwood* decision and the broadening of admissions policies have led the nation in the attempt to diversify campuses without using affirmative action.

3. Social Policies

Texas is conservative in other areas of public policy besides the economy and education. Where privacy rights support conservative family values, Texans favor privacy. Where privacy rights undermine those values, Texans tend to oppose them.

4. Environmental Policies

Texas has not considered innovative policies that states such as California have enacted, even though Texas faces rising energy demands and health issues caused by pollution. This is an example of how public policy is determined not by legislation but by the lack of it.

Key Terms

ability to pay 761	discretionary funding 764	public policy 758
benefit-based taxes 761	franchise fee 760	tax capacity 761
budget fix 763	*Hopwood* decision 767	tax incidence 762
consumer taxes 759	income-elastic taxes 764	tax shifting 762
deregulated tuition 766	nontax revenue 760	

For Review

1. What is public policy, and how is it created and implemented?

2. How is the budget a vehicle of public policy? To what extent do the legislature and the executive branch have the ability to shape policy through the budget?

3. How is the taxation system an expression of public policy? How do Texas's taxation policies compare with those in other states?

4. What was the impact of the *Hopwood* decision?

5. How do Texans feel about the right to privacy? Give examples.

6. Why has Texas failed to implement innovative environmental policies?

For Critical Thinking and Discussion

1. Design your ideal taxation system. What values would you promote, and how would you try to achieve them? What would be the disadvantages of the system you designed?

2. Texas faces budget crises because of its dependence on income-elastic taxes. What measures could you take to reduce this dependence, and what effect would these measures have on economic growth?

3. Do you support or oppose the *Hopwood* decision? Explain your answer.

4. Imagine the following scenario. The bird flu virus spreads to the United States, where researchers develop a vaccine. The Texas governor issues an executive order requiring that all schoolchildren be given vaccines. Will the majority of Texans support or oppose this measure? Justify your prediction.

5. Because of a population increase and economic growth, Texas is facing an energy crisis. Describe your solution to this problem.

MULTIPLE CHOICE: Choose the lettered item that answers the question correctly.

1. What is the result of Texas's policy of earmarking revenues?
   a. Texas has no stable source of revenue and many budget crises.
   b. The Texas legislature has a limited ability to set budget priorities.
   c. Texas tends to enact conservative taxation policies.
   d. Texas relies heavily on business taxes such as franchise fees.

2. Texas's taxation system is characterized by the lack of a
   a. sales tax.
   b. property tax.
   c. business tax.
   d. personal income tax.

3. An example of a source for nontax revenue would be
   a. playing the lottery.
   b. buying cigarettes.
   c. renting a car.
   d. purchasing fuel for your car.

4. All taxes can be shifted to others except
   a. sales tax.
   b. personal income tax.
   c. property tax.
   d. There are no exceptions.

5. The *Hopwood* decision is significant because it
   a. established the tax on corporations.
   b. provided tuition refunds for dissatisfied university students.
   c. reversed affirmative action in Texas universities.
   d. led to a quota system in higher education.

6. Funds for capital projects within higher education are fixed within which two funds?
   a. Deregulated Tuition Fund and Flagship University Fund
   b. Deregulated Tuition Fund and Permanent University Fund
   c. Permanent University Fund and Higher Education Assistance Fund
   d. Flagship University Fund and Higher Education Assistance Fund

7. Which ruling overturned the *Hopwood* decision?
   a. *Grutter v. Bollinger*
   b. *Roe v. Wade*
   c. *Planned Parenthood v. Casey*
   d. *Hopwood* still stands from the 1996 ruling.

8. Texas has passed a constitutional amendment banning
   a. same-sex marriage.
   b. abortion.
   c. cheerleading routines that are sexually suggestive.
   d. publicly mandated vaccinations.

9. When did Texas overturn its antisodomy law?
   a. in the 1970s, when the first states began to overturn these laws
   b. in the 1980s, when many states were overturning these laws
   c. in 2003, as one of the last thirteen states to overturn these laws
   d. never, because the law was finally invalidated by a Supreme Court ruling

10. Most bills regarding abortion that have passed
    a. deal with ethical matters instead of legal matters.
    b. are tied in to bills regarding gay rights.
    c. have been overturned because of efforts by local religious organizations.
    d. primarily affect younger women and require parental consent.

FILL IN THE BLANKS.

11. Some taxes are based more on the benefit a person receives, and others are based more on _____ —the wealth of the individual.

12. _____ are taxes that take a higher percentage of income from low-income persons.

13. Texas ranks number 1 in greenhouse gas emissions and produces more _____ than the next two biggest polluters combined.

14. _____ is the passing of taxes, such as sales tax, on to other parties.

15. A _____ is a provision of the budget, mandated by state laws and constitutional amendments, that sets aside money to be spent on specific items.

Answers: 1. b; 2. d; 3. a; 4. b; 5. c; 6. c; 7. a; 8. a; 9. c; 10. d; 11. ability to pay; 12. Regressive taxes; 13. carbon dioxide; 14. Tax shifting; 15. budget fix.

RESOURCES FOR RESEARCH AND ACTION

Internet Resources

Center for Public Policy Priorities
www.cppp.org/about/about_us.php   The CPPP is a research organization dedicated to improving the conditions of low-income and moderate-income families and individuals within Texas. Its research focuses on economic and social issues.

Texas Comptroller of Public Accounts
www.window.state.tx.us   This site provides information on sales, franchise, and property taxes, as well as other information on the state's finances and economy.

Texas Higher Education Coordinating Board
www.thecb.state.tx.us   At the Web site of the board established to help Texas meet its higher education goals, you'll find information on its Closing the Gaps program, college readiness, and financial aid.

Texas Public Policy Foundation
www.texaspolicy.com   The TPPF is a research institute that provides research and data on state issues. Its staff also makes recommendations to state policy makers based on the foundation's research.

Internet Activism

The Open Data section of the official Web site of the Texas government provides access to public information and databases to promote government transparency and civic participation. **www.texas .gov/en/Connect/Pages/open-data.aspx**

Twitter
twitter.com/ppnorthtexas   Get updates from Planned Parenthood of North Texas on relevant information and upcoming community events.

YouTube
www.youtube.com/watch?v=DfOiHMcrCbs   Watch this news story about why thieves stole cases of cigarettes just before a cigarette tax increase took effect.

Facebook
www.facebook.com/group.php?gid=2353465751&ref=search#!/ group.php?gid=2353465751&v=info&ref=search   NO Affirmative Action at A&M is a group open to anyone within the Texas A&M network who are against the implementation of affirmative action policies by businesses and universities.

Recommended Readings

Aronson, J. Richard, and John L. Hilley. *Financing State and Local Governments.* Washington, DC: Brookings Institution, 1986.

Mikesell, John L. *Fiscal Administration: Analysis and Applications for the Public Sector.* Pacific Grove, CA: Brooks/Cole, 1991.

Movies of Interest

2007 Global Conference:
The Eyes of Texas Are Upon the Future of TXU (2008)
This documentary examines the Texas Pacific Group (TPG) buyout of Texas utility company TXU, which led to a compromise over plans to build new coal plants. Interviews with Dallas Mayor Laura Miller, TPG founder David Bonderman, and others focus on environmental policies and the relationship between energy companies and environmental groups.

Overruled! (2008)
In 1998, the Houston police arrested John Lawrence and Tyron Garner in Lawrence's home for violating the Texas antisodomy law. This documentary captures the story of the court battle that followed in *Lawrence v. Texas,* which eventually led the U.S. Supreme Court to invalidate all sodomy laws. The documentary can be seen online at www.lambdalegal.org/campaigns/overruled/index.html.

Are the Kids Alright? (2004)
This documentary examines the state of mental health care for children in Texas. Capturing the experiences of children at home, in the courtroom, and at mental health institutions, this film offers a unique look at one important aspect of Texas public policy.

CHAPTER

27

Local Governments in Texas

THEN

Most cities used the mayor-council form of government.

NOW

Texas home-rule cities overwhelmingly adopt the council-manager form of government, increasing efficiency and professionalism.

NEXT

Will county governments change their structure to increase efficiency and allow them to provide better services?

How will the gap in capabilities between small general-law towns and home-rule cities shape Texas politics?

How will small Texas cities and counties deal with the growing problem of unfunded mandates?

In this chapter, we examine the forms of local governments, their authority, and the challenges that they face.

FIRST, we distinguish between *state and local authority* and identify local governments as "creatures of the state."

SECOND, we explore the different types of *municipal governments*, municipal elections, and the challenges municipalities face.

THIRD, we consider the structure of *county governments* and analyze policies that might help these governments overcome the disadvantage of their weak authority.

FOURTH, we review *special district governments* and the purposes for which they are created.

FIFTH, we take a look at *school districts* and the attempts to deal with school financing and improve the quality of education.

decentralized nation
a country, such as the United States, that possesses many units of local government controlled by citizens at the local level

Although the news media often

focus on state and national governments, in many respects local governments have a greater impact on the daily lives of citizens. Many services that local governments provide are taken for granted or expected by citizens, who notice local government only when it fails to properly perform its functions—when the water mains fail, the garbage is not collected, the pothole is not filled, stray animals are not impounded. When things work, local government goes unnoticed.

Citizens depend on local governments for many life-supporting services, such as water, sewers, and police and fire protection. Local governments also help maintain the environment and lifestyles of citizens by protecting neighborhoods through zoning and the regulation of land development. Finally, local governments assume the important, perhaps critical, function of educating children.

Though some citizens live in rural areas without many services, most people do not find that lifestyle appealing. Eighty percent of Texans live in urban areas and are very dependent on local governments. Even the 20 percent of citizens who live in rural areas expect services from county governments and special districts. Without the services provided by local governments, modern urban society would not be possible. Thus, the more we understand about how these local governments work and affect our lives, the more prepared we will be when local issues arise.

Citizens expect local governments not only to provide services but also to be very decentralized. In that respect, the United States is the most **decentralized nation** in the world. Nationwide there are nearly 90,000 units of local government; almost 5,000 of these are in Texas. Decentralization allows for local control. Many citizens become involved in their local governments, which has the effect of reducing conflict and increasing support for government at all levels. Average citizens feel they can have an impact on their local governments and influence outcomes. Attending a meeting of the school board, city council, or county government and participating in the deliberations is easy, and many citizens take part. In contrast, participation at the national and state levels is difficult, and few citizens have an opportunity to become involved.

Thus, local governments, decentralized and locally controlled, are central to the American system of government. Few citizens in other countries have the opportunity to become involved in their local government to the extent Americans do.

State and Local Authority

When citizens become involved in local governments, they do so under the power and authority given them by state governments. All local governments are creatures of the state, and whatever power or authority they possess is derived from state constitutions and statutes. Local governments are not mentioned in the U.S. Constitution. They are created under state constitutions to serve the interests of the state.

The amount of local authority granted and the degree to which governments can act independently of state government vary greatly from state to state and within states by type of government. One way to understand this variety is to distinguish between general-purpose and limited-purpose governments. **General-purpose governments** are those units given broad discretionary authority by the state government. They have the authority to perform many functions and can control their own finances, personnel, and government structure. **Limited-purpose governments** have very limited authority or control over their finances, and they are governed by a set structure. Personnel decisions are controlled by state law.[1]

An example of a limited-purpose government in Texas is a school district. It performs only one function (education), has limited revenue sources (property taxes and state funds), and is governed by a seven-member school board, with many personnel decisions (such as teacher certification) controlled by a state agency. Texas counties are also examples of limited-purpose governments. State laws limit their authority and revenue, they all operate under the same form of government, and state law often dictates personnel decisions.

Texas cities, on the other hand, are excellent examples of general-purpose governments. Under home rule (discussed next), Texas cities have the authority to pass any ordinance not prohibited by state law and have many sources of revenue. The structure of government varies greatly from city to city, and the state exerts limited control over personnel decisions.[2]

Thus, although all units of local government are creatures of the state, some units are granted more discretionary authority and operate relatively free of state control and supervision. Texas cities have very broad authority. Other units of local government in Texas are limited-purpose governments. This chapter examines cities, counties, special districts, and school districts in Texas and the differences among these units of government.

general-purpose government
a government given broad discretionary authority by the state government

limited-purpose government
a government that has very limited authority or control over its finances and is governed by a set structure

Municipal Governments

City governments are technically municipal corporations. The term *municipality* derives from the Roman *municipium,* which means "a free city capable of governing its local affairs, even though subordinate to the sovereignty of Rome."[3] In Texas, the state government grants charters to cities. A city charter is a document much like a state constitution, in that it provides the basic structure and organization of city government and the broad outlines of powers and authorities.

General-Law and Home-Rule Cities

general-law city
a city whose charter is created by state statutes

Texas cities are chartered as either general-law cities or home-rule cities. A **general-law city** can choose from seven charters specified in state statutes.[4] These options allow considerable choice as to form of government. There are 938 general-law cities in Texas.[5]

home-rule city
a city whose charter is created by the actions of local citizens

Since the passage of a constitutional amendment in 1912, any city in Texas with a population of at least 5,000 may be chartered as a **home-rule city.**[6] Most cities of this size adopt home-rule charters. Home rule means that the local citizens may adopt any form of government they want and pass any ordinance not prohibited by state law. For example, state law is silent on the number of members on city councils, but the state constitution limits the term of office to no more than four years.

implicit or explicit prohibition on city ordinance power
limitation on the power of cities, preventing them from passing ordinances that are explicitly prohibited by state law and from passing ordinances that by implication may violate state law

A prohibition in state law might be an **implicit or explicit prohibition on city ordinance power.** For example, there is no explicit prohibition against cities passing an ordinance prohibiting open alcohol containers in vehicles. Several Texas cities passed such ordinances in the 1980s before there was a state law against open containers. However, state courts ruled that the regulation of alcohol was a state function, and by implication (implicitly) Texas cities could not pass no-open-container ordinances.

The home-rule provisions of the Texas Constitution allow great latitude in governing local affairs. Once approved, home-rule charters may be amended only with the approval of the city voters. Usually the city council or a charter commission proposes changes. However, many home-rule charters in Texas allow voters to initiate charter changes.

Incorporation

incorporation
the process of creating a city government

The process of creating a city is known as **incorporation** because, as mentioned earlier, technically cities are municipal corporations. Creating a city normally involves the following steps: Local citizens must petition the state and ask to be incorporated as a city; an election is held, and voters must approve the creation of the city; the state then issues a charter.

In Texas, the requirements are as follows:

- There must be a population of at least 201 citizens living within a two-square-mile area. (This is a measure of density.)
- Petitions requesting that an election be called must be signed by 10 percent of the registered voters and 50 percent of the landowners in the area to be incorporated.
- If the petition is valid, the county judge calls an election.
- If voters approve, the city is created and a general-law charter is adopted. A second election is held to elect officials.[7]

extra territorial jurisdiction (ETJ)
city powers that extend beyond the city limits to an adjacent area

Although these procedures are not difficult, there are limitations about where cities can be created. Under Texas law, all cities have what is called **extra territorial jurisdiction (ETJ),** or power over an area that extends beyond the city limits of an existing city.[8] General-law cities have a half mile of ETJ. The distance increases as population increases, for up to as much as five miles for cities above 250,000 in population.[9] A city may not be incorporated within the ETJ of an existing city unless that city approves. This provision is intended to prevent the growth of smaller cities on the fringe of larger cities and to allow existing cities room to grow.

In addition, cities may annex land within their ETJ. Cities annex land by taking adjoining land that is unincorporated (not a part of another city). Texas cities have broad annexation powers. The city council, by majority vote, can unilaterally annex land, and the residents living in the area being annexed have no voice or vote in the process. This provision in state law, coupled with the ETJ provisions, provides Texas cities with room to expand. In every session of the Texas legislature, many bills are introduced to restrict the ability of Texas cities to annex land. Some restrictions are placed on home-rule cities; however, they still have broad annexation authority when compared with many other states.

THE CREATION OF IMPACT, TEXAS The city of Abilene surrounds the small city of Impact, Texas, which was incorporated in February 1960. The primary purpose of this incorporation was to allow for the sale of liquor. Under Texas law, the citizens of a city may vote to allow the sale of alcohol—so-called wet-dry elections. Abilene is noted for being a center of Christian fundamentalism and is the home of three religious colleges. Some citizens of Abilene were scandalized at the prospect of liquor sales in this dry corner of the state and attempted to block the incorporation. After the courthouse battles, the incorporation was allowed, and liquor sales took place for many years. Impact was the only place for miles around where liquor could be purchased.

The city of Abilene, using its annexation powers, surrounded the city of Impact, eliminating any chance for it to grow. In 1963, the Texas legislature passed the law creating the ETJ for all Texas cities and limiting the incorporation of cities within the ETJ of an existing city. The incorporation of Impact was a factor in the passage of this act.

In the 1980s, Abilene allowed for the sale of liquor within the city limits. The liquor store in Impact is now closed.

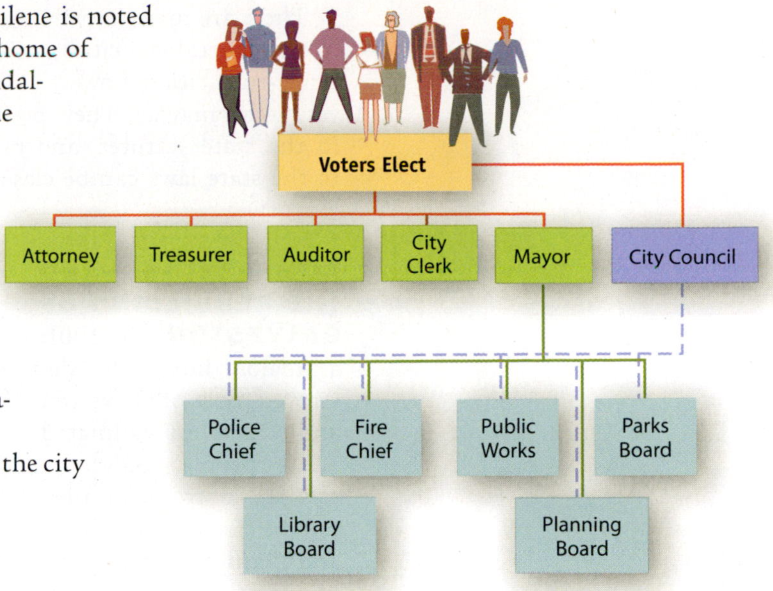

FIGURE 27.1

Mayor-Council Form of City Government, with a Weak Mayor

Forms of Municipal Governments

Cities use two basic forms of government in the United States and Texas: mayor-council and council-manager. A third form, commission, was tried once in Galveston but is not used by any Texas city and is used by only a few cities nationwide.

MAYOR-COUNCIL GOVERNMENT   The traditional form of city government that developed in the nineteenth century is mayor-council. There are two variations of mayor-council government—weak executive and strong executive. Under the weak executive, or weak mayor, form of government, the formal powers of the mayor are limited in much the same way that the Texas governor's formal powers are limited. First, the mayor shares power with other elected officials and with the city council, as shown in Figure 27.1. The weak mayor's executive/administrative authority is limited. Second, the mayor has limited control over budget formation and execution. Third, the number of terms the mayor can serve is limited. Last, the mayor has little or no veto authority.[10]

Under a strong executive, or strong mayor, form of government, the mayor can appoint and remove the major heads of departments, has control over budget formation and execution, is not limited by short terms or term limits, and can veto actions of the city council. (See Figure 27.2.)

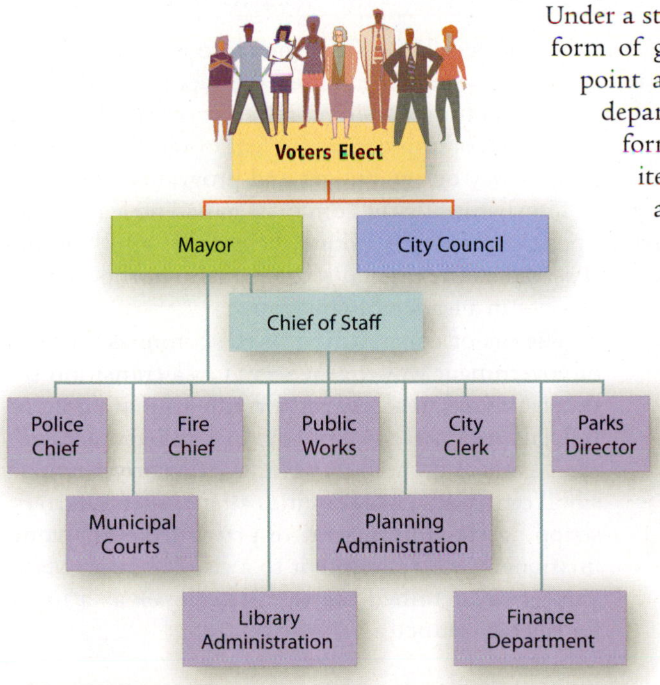

Only 39 of the 290 home-rule cities in Texas use the mayor-council form of government. Houston and Pasadena are the two largest cities using the form.[11] Of the two, only Houston has a strong mayor form. The Houston mayor can appoint and remove department heads and is responsible for budget formation and execution; however, the office has no veto authority, has a short term (two years), and is limited to three terms.

FIGURE 27.2

Mayor-Council Form of City Government, with a Strong Mayor

There are many more mayor-council forms in the general-law cities in Texas than in the home-rule cities; however, all have formally very weak mayors. Their powers are provided in the state statutes, and no form provided in the state laws can be classified as a strong executive.

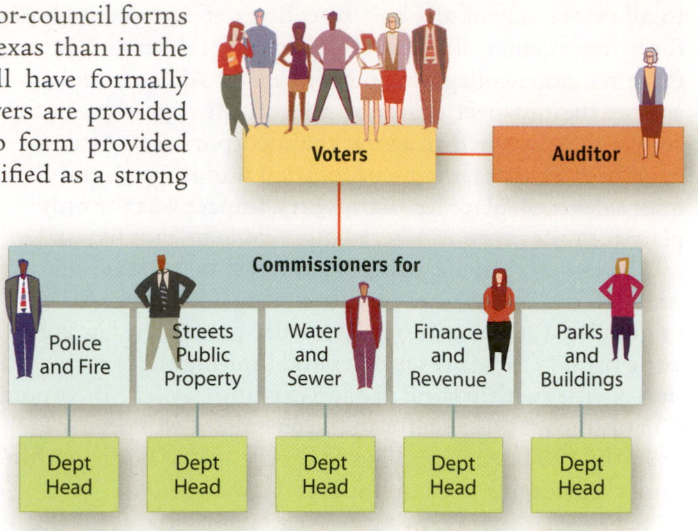

COMMISSIONS AND THE REBUILDING OF GALVESTON

In 1901, a major hurricane destroyed most of Galveston and killed an estimated 5,000 people. Galveston was the only major port on the Texas Gulf Coast and a kingpin in the cotton economy of the state. It was in the interests of all Texans to rebuild the city and port. A delegation of Galveston citizens approached the Texas legislature for funds to help in the rebuilding. Joseph D. Sayers, the governor then, proposed establishment of a local government of five commissioners to oversee the rebuilding of the city. The new commission in Galveston worked in an expeditious manner and quickly rebuilt the port city. This efficiency attracted nationwide attention. Many other cities adopted this new form of government, illustrated in Figure 27.3, assuming that the form had caused the efficiency.

It was a very simple form when compared with the older weak mayor system, and it seemed to allow for quick action. However, it also created many problems. The first weakness was that voters did not always elect competent administrators. For example, a failed banker might run for finance commissioner and stress his banking experience.[12] With no way of knowing that his banking experience had been a failure, voters might elect him on apparent qualifications, and the bank where he worked might want to see him depart and not challenge his qualifications.

Second, the system combined executive and legislative functions into a single body of government. Though efficient, this system eliminated the separation of powers and its checks and balances. Commissioners were reluctant to scrutinize the budget and the actions of other commissioners for fear of retaliation. Logrolling set in: You look the other way on my budget and programs, and I will look the other way on yours. Third, initially the commission had no leader. The commissioners rotated the position of mayor among themselves. This "mayor" presided over meetings and served as the official representative of the city but was not in a leadership position.

The major contribution of the commission form of government was that it served as a transition between the old weak mayor form, with many elected officials and a large city council, and the council-manager form, with no elected executives and a small city council. Many cities altered their charters, stripping the administrative power from the commissioners and assigning it to a city manager. Many Texas cities retained the term *commission* as a name for the city council.

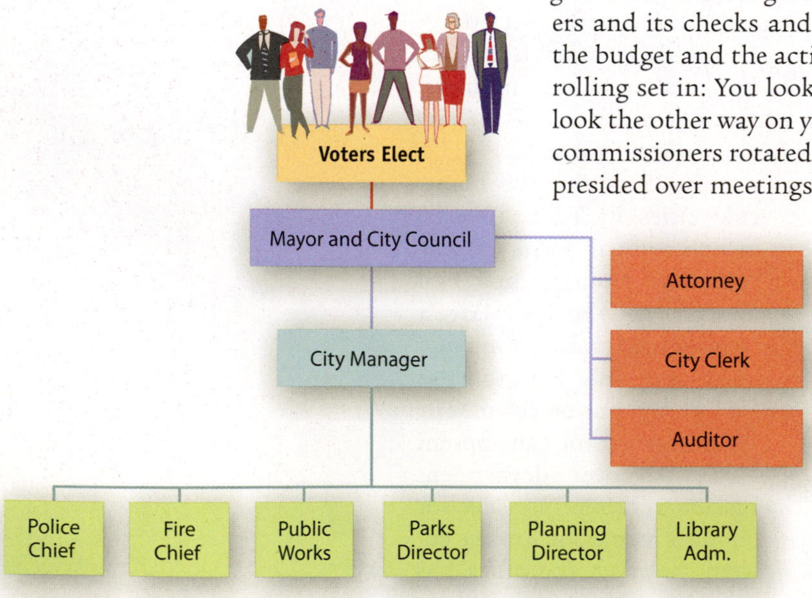

COUNCIL-MANAGER GOVERNMENT

The most popular form of government among Texas cities is the council-manager form, shown in Figure 27.4.

FIGURE 27.3

Commission Form of City Government

FIGURE 27.4

Council-Manager Form of City Government

Except Houston, all major cities in Texas use this form. Under the **council-manager** system, the voters elect a small city council (usually seven members), including a mayor. The council hires a city manager, who has administrative control over city government. The city manager appoints and removes the major heads of departments of government and is responsible for budget preparation and execution.

Administrative authority rests with the city manager, and the council is the policy-making body. The mayor and the city council are responsible for establishing the mission, policy, and direction of city government. Their roles in administration and management are greatly reduced. Figure 27.5 shows the roles of the council and the mayor on the four dimensions of city government: mission, policy, administration, and management. The council and the manager share in each of these areas, with the council dominating in mission and policy and the manager dominating in administration and management.

ROLES OF MAYORS The role of the mayor in city governments is often misunderstood because of the variations in strong mayor, weak mayor, and council-manager governments. This difference often escapes the average citizen.

In the strong mayor-council form, the mayor is the chief executive officer of the city, in charge of the city government. If the mayor possesses a veto authority, she or he can use the threat of a veto to extract some things from the council, just as the governor does with the legislature. There is a separation of powers between the mayor (the executive branch) and the city council (the legislative branch).

In a weak mayor form, the mayor is not the chief executive officer. The mayor may be the first among equals and the most visible member of city government but does not control administrative matters, although the mayor may have some administrative authority. The mayor's control over budgetary matters is limited and generally requires approval of the council even for minor matters such as paying bills. The mayor usually serves as a member of the council and generally lacks veto authority.

In council-manager government, the mayor is not the chief executive officer. The mayor does not control the city administration or the budget. Those powers rest with the city manager. The mayor is a member of the city council, and there is no separation of powers. The mayor serves as a leader of the council, presides over council meetings, usually helps set the council agenda, and serves as the official representative of the city. Some mayors in council-manager cities have been very successful leaders. They rule not from the formal powers granted in the charter but from personal abilities or informal leadership traits.

Henry Cisneros of San Antonio was one of the best examples of a successful mayor leader in a council-manager city. Cisneros led "by sheer personal magnetism and intellect, facilitating local successes through joint action of the total city council and professional staff."[13] Thus, mayors in council-manager cities are leaders, although the leadership style is quite different. They are not a driving force, as they can be in mayor-council governments, but they can serve as a guiding force.[14] No matter what the form of city government, the

council-manager form of government

a form of government in which voters elect a mayor and a city council; the mayor and the city council appoint a professional administrator to manage the city

Roles in the Council-Manager Form of Government

Dimensions of governmental process

Illustrative tasks for council	Council's sphere	Illustrative tasks for administrators
Determine "purpose," scope of services, tax level, constitutional issues.	Mission	Advise (what city "can" do may influence what it "should" do), analyze conditions and trends.
Pass ordinances, approve new projects and programs, ratify budget.	Policy	Make recommendations on all decisions, formulate budget, determine service distribution formulas.
Make implementing decisions, e.g., site selection, handle complaints, oversee administration.	Administration	Establish practices and procedures and make decisions for implementing policy.
Suggest management changes to manager, review organizational performance in manager's appraisal.	Management	Control the human, material, and informational resources of organization to support policy and administrative functions.

Manager's sphere

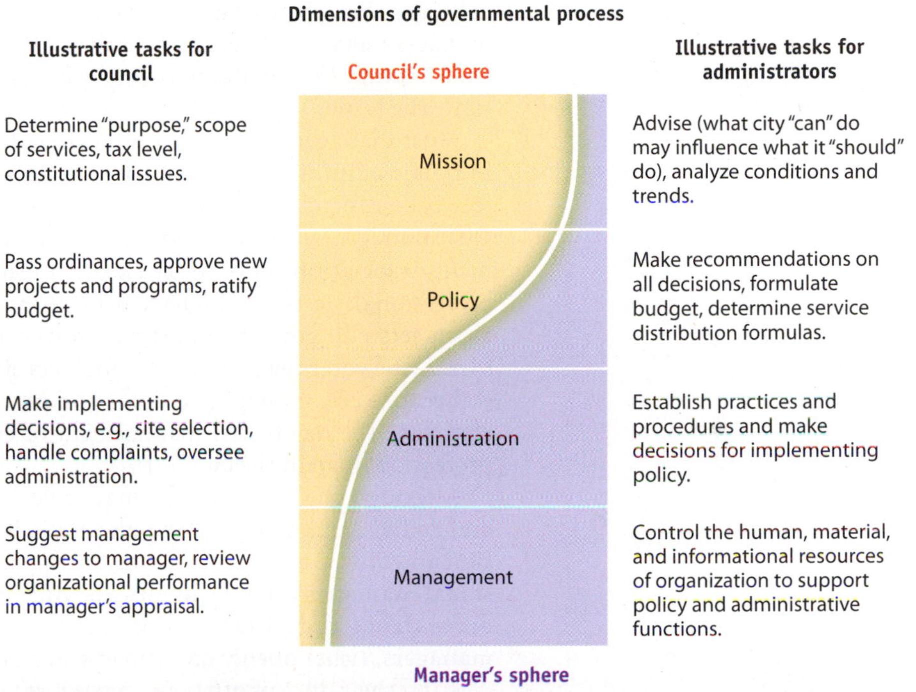

POLITICAL INQUIRY

FIGURE 27.5 ■ The curved line suggests the division between the council's and the manager's spheres of activity (the council's tasks to the left of the line, the manager's to the right). This division roughly approximates a "proper" degree of separation and sharing; shifts to the left or right would indicate improper incursions. What might cause the line to shift one way or the other?

SOURCE: James Svara, "Dichotomy and Duality: Reconceptualizing the Relationship Between Policy and Administration in Council-Manager Cities," *Public Administration Review* 450, no. 1 (1985): 228. Reprinted with permission from Public Administration Review. Copyright Blackwell Publishing, Ltd.

successful mayor must have political support within the community, the support and confidence of community leaders, popular support among the citizens, charisma, and the energy and stamina to lead, mold a coalition, and gain acceptance of his or her programs.

city manager
official hired by the city council to manage the city and serve as chief administrative officer

ROLES OF CITY MANAGERS   Because so many cities in Texas use the council-manager form of government, some understanding of the role of the **city manager** is essential. Texas has always been a leader in the use of this form of government. In 1913, Amarillo became the first city in the state to adopt the form. O. M. Carr, the first city manager in Amarillo, strongly influenced the formation of the International City Managers (Management) Association.[15]

Under the council-manager form of government, the voters elect a city council and a mayor. Generally, these are the only elected officials in city government. The council in turn appoints the city manager and may remove the manager for any reason at any time; managers serve at the pleasure of the city council. In smaller general-law cities in Texas, the position may be called a city administrator rather than manager, but the duties are essentially the same.

Most managers are trained professionals. Today, many managers have a master's degree in public administration and have served as an assistant city manager for several years before becoming city manager. All but a few city managers are members of the International City Management Association (ICMA) and, in Texas, members of the Texas City Management Association (TCMA). These organizations have a code of ethics and help to promote professionalism in the management of local governments. This expertise and professionalism sets city governments apart from county governments in Texas. In county governments, the voters elect most officeholders, and professionalism is often absent.

Because city managers appoint and can remove all major department heads and are in charge of the day-to-day management of city government, they can instill a high level of professionalism in the city staff.

Although the manager's primary role is to administer city government, managers can and do have an impact on the policies made by the city council. Managers provide information and advice to the council on the impact of policy changes in city government. Professional managers attempt to provide information that is impartial so that the council can make the final decision. Councils sometimes delegate this policy-making process to city managers, either openly or indirectly by failure to act. When that happens, councils are neglecting their duty of office and are not serving the citizens who elected them.

Over the last ninety years, the council-manager form of government has functioned well in Texas. Texas cities have a national reputation for being well managed and maintaining a high degree of professionalism in their operations.

Municipal Elections and Voter Turnout

single-member district
a system in which the city is divided into election districts and only the voters living in that district elect the council member from that district

The traditional method, used for most of the nineteenth century, to elect city council members was the **single-member district,** or ward system. The city is divided into election districts of approximately equal populations, and the voters in those districts elect a council member. There are a few cases of multimember districts, but none in Texas.

In the beginning of the twentieth century, many cities, led by early commission adoptions, moved away from the single-member-district system and began to elect council members at large by all voters in the city. There are several variations on the **at-large election system,** summarized in Figure 27.6. (For a thorough discussion of electoral systems in American cities, see Joseph Zimmerman in this chapter's "Recommended Readings.")

at-large election system
system in which all voters in the city elect the mayor and city council members

Some cities use a combination of at-large and single-member-district (SMD) systems. Houston is a prime example. Voters elect nine council members from single-member districts, and five council members and the mayor are elected at large by all voters in the city.[16]

cumulative voting
a system in which voters can concentrate (accumulate) all their votes on one candidate rather than casting one vote for each office up for election

Two other systems are used to elect council members. Under **cumulative voting,** each voter has votes equal to the number of city council seats open in the election. If five seats are open, each voter has five votes and may cast all five votes for one candidate (accumulating their votes), one vote each for five candidates, or any combination or variation. Several cities have adopted this system as an alternative to SMDs. Since 1991, forty school districts and fourteen cities in Texas have adopted cumulative voting. The Amarillo Independent School District is the largest government body using the system in Texas (160,000 people).

Preferential voting, also called instant runoff voting, is another system, which works by allowing voters to rank the candidates for city council. All candidates' names are listed on the ballot, and the voter indicates the order of his or her preferences (first, second, third, and so on). Using a complicated ballot-counting system, the most-preferred candidates are elected. Although no city in Texas currently uses this system, San Francisco and fifteen other cities use preferential voting nationwide. Advocates believe that both cumulative voting and preferential voting increase minority representation, but there is little evidence to support that claim.

Since the Voting Rights Act was amended in 1975 and applied to Texas, many cities have changed from an at-large system to single-member districts. Before 1975, almost no Texas cities used the SMD system. Most major cities have been forced to change to SMD for at least some of their city council seats.

In cities that have changed from at-large to SMD systems, the number of minority candidates elected to the city council has increased substantially. There is some evidence that SMD council members approach their role differently than at-large council members do. A study of council members in Houston, Dallas, San Antonio, and Fort Worth found that council members from SMDs showed greater concern for neighborhood issues, engaged in vote trading, increased their contacts with constituents in their districts regarding service requests, and became more involved in administrative affairs of the city.[17]

Although SMD council members might view their job as representing their districts first and the city as a whole second, there is no evidence that the distribution of services changes dramatically. District representation may be primarily symbolic. Symbolism is not insignificant, though, because support for local governments can be increased as minority groups feel they are represented on city councils and feel comfortable contacting their council member with problems.

At-large by place

This is the most common such system used in Texas. In this system, candidates file for at-large ballot positions, which are usually given a number designation—Place 1, Place 2, and so on. Voters cast one vote for each at-large ballot position, and the candidate with a majority is elected to that place on the city council.

At-large by place with residence wards required

In this system, candidates file for a specific place as in an at-large by place system; however, these candidates must live in a section, area, or ward of the city to file for a specific place. Mayors can live anywhere in the city. All voters in the city elect them at large.

At-large no place

This is the least common system used in Texas. In this system, all candidates seeking election to the council have their names placed on the ballot. If there are ten candidates seeking election and five open seats, each voter is instructed to cast one vote each for five candidates. The top five vote getters are elected. With this method it is not uncommon for a candidate to win with only a plurality (less than a majority) of the vote.

FIGURE 27.6

At-Large Voting Systems

preferential voting
a system that allows voters to rank candidates for the city council

ELECTION OF MAYORS The voters of the entire city generally elect mayors at large. During most of the nineteenth century, this was the prevailing system. With the coming of the commission form of government, and later the council-manager form, mayors were often selected by the members of the council, from among the members of the council. In recent years, the trend nationwide and in Texas has been toward at-large election of mayors in council-manager cities. In Texas, most mayors are elected at large. The election of mayors by the voters of the city gives the mayor some independence from the council and therefore the opportunity to function as the leader of the council.

NONPARTISAN ELECTIONS Nationwide, about 70 percent of city council members are elected in **nonpartisan elections.**[18] In Texas, all city elections are technically nonpartisan. Officially, in a nonpartisan election no party labels appear on the ballot, so voters cannot determine party affiliation by looking at the ballot. This differs from the general election ballot used in November.

Nonpartisan elections were a feature of the reform movement in the early part of the twentieth century and were aimed at undercutting the power of partisan big-city political machines. Reformers said there is no Democratic or Republican way to pave streets or provide police and fire protection, so partisanship should not be a factor in city decisions.

Texas cities adopted the nonpartisan system largely because the state was a one-party Democratic state for over a hundred years, and partisanship, even in state elections, was

nonpartisan elections
ballot form in which voters are unable to determine the party of candidates by looking at the ballot

not a factor as long as you ran as a Democrat. It was only natural that city elections used nonpartisan ballots. The Texas Election Code allows for partisan city elections in home-rule cities. To date, no city has officially used partisan elections.[19]

The use of a nonpartisan ballot does not eliminate partisanship from local politics. Partisanship simply takes new forms, and new labels are applied. For decades in several Texas cities, "nonpartisan organizations" successfully ran slates of candidates and dominated city politics. Most noted among these organizations were the Citizens Charter Association in Dallas, the Good Government League in San Antonio, and the Business and Professional Association in Wichita Falls and Abilene.[20] The influence of these groups has declined, but slate making is not unknown today in Texas city politics. Partisanship has been a factor in city elections recently in San Antonio, Houston, and Dallas, especially in mayoral races.

VOTER TURNOUT IN CITY ELECTIONS   Nationwide, voter turnout in city elections is quite low—often lower than in state elections. Turnout rates as low as 4 percent are not uncommon in Texas cities, and seldom do they exceed 25 percent. Off-year elections, a lack of contested races, and low levels of voter interest all contribute to low turnout in city elections.

State law provides two dates during the year when Texas cities may hold city council elections. Known as **off-year elections,** these elections are never held at the same time as state or national elections. The lack of contested races is so common in Texas that in 1996 a new state law went into effect that allows cities and school boards to dispense with elections if all seats are uncontested. The city or the school board declares the uncontested candidates elected. A standard joke is often told about a person sitting on a bench by city hall with a sign reading, "Will run for mayor for food."

The third factor in low turnout is a lack of publicity and interest in city elections. The news media might cover races in the major cities, especially in years when the mayor's office is up for election, but coverage of suburban city elections in a major metropolitan area is given scant attention by the press. Also, the average citizen does not think local elections are important. The races for president, governor, and other state offices are viewed as more important. These races are also given more attention by the news media.

Participation is largely class-based: The higher socioeconomic groups vote at higher rates. Thus, lower overall voter turnout tends to benefit the high-income, nonminority areas of a city. These groups often dominate city elections and city politics. The use of single-member district systems might overcome the class bias in voting and increase the number of minority members on the council, but there is little evidence that this produces great changes in policy. Also, SMD elections often lead to council members being elected with very small numbers of votes. For example, in a city with a population of 25,000 and six council seats elected from districts, it is quite common to have someone elected with a few hundred votes.

Low voter turnout can also heavily affect towns with a large percentage of students in the population. Students generally do not participate in local city elections, even though city governments have a big impact on the student population. For example, in Denton, the home of the University of North Texas, most students live off campus, and the city provides electrical, water, sewer, and other services for which fees are charged. These services affect off-campus students just as they do nonstudents. One consequence of students' not voting or participating in city government is that others make decisions that can have profound effects on the cost and the availability of housing.

One could argue that the fact that most citizens pay scant attention to elections may mean that people who live in cities are satisfied with the levels and kinds of services they are receiving. The main Texas cities have a reputation of being well run by professionals. This is in stark contrast to county government in the state, in which professionalism is often quite lacking. Patronage and politics more accurately describe what happens in county government.

Challenges to Cities: Revenues and Mandates

Local governments in Texas collect taxes from two primary sources—property tax and local sales tax. Almost all units of local government collect property tax. For school districts, the property tax is the largest source of revenue, exceeding state contributions. For so-called

off-year elections
local elections held at a different time of year from state and national elections

rich school districts, all of the cost of running local schools may come from the property tax, and it is a significant source of revenue for cities and counties. In addition, most cities, many counties, and all local transit authorities collect a local sales tax. In Texas, the local sales tax is fixed by state law at no more than 2 percent of the value of sales. Thus, in most urban areas in Texas, there is a 6.25 percent state sales tax, plus a 2.0 percent local tax, for a total of 8.25 percent sales tax.

There is effectively no state-level property tax in Texas. All but a small portion of property taxes goes to local governments. In recent years, property taxes have increased dramatically. In 2005, the most recent year for which data are available, a total of 3,748 local governments in Texas assessed a property tax. The total property tax levy was $30.9 billion, an increase of about 27 percent since 2000. Figure 27.7 shows this change. Texas local governments, especially school districts, have become more dependent upon the property tax. Texas ranks tenth in property tax revenue per $1,000 of personal income among the fifty states. As you can see in "How Texas Compares: Property Taxes," among the top twelve states, Texas has the second highest property tax per $1,000 of personal income. Only New Jersey is higher.

As taxes have climbed, local government must abide by an increasing number of mandates—laws passed by federal and state governments that apply to local governments. For example, the Texas Commission on Jail Standards inspects county jails to make sure the facilities and the personnel meet state laws. This state agency may require facilities to increase personnel or make other changes. On a federal level, the Clean Air Act forces city governments to comply with air quality standards. Yet municipalities cannot always control air quality in their jurisdiction. Although they can reduce pollution created by cars, buses, and other vehicles in their area, winds might blow air pollution from a power plant in the vicinity. Such considerations forced Dallas mayor Laura Miller to organize municipalities throughout the state to stop the building of over a dozen new coal-burning power plants in Texas. The efforts of municipalities and environmental groups eventually succeeded in reducing the number of new plants built.

The problem, however, goes beyond the mandates themselves. The mandates dictated by the federal government as well as state governments are often **unfunded or underfunded mandates.** This means that they do not give local governments the money they need to

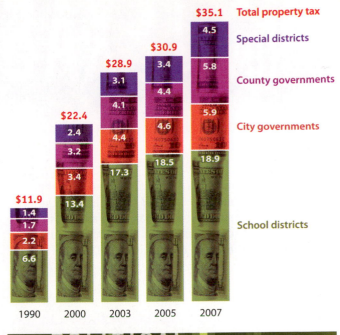

POLITICAL INQUIRY

FIGURE 27.7 ■ PROPERTY TAX COLLECTIONS BY TYPE OF LOCAL GOVERNMENTS IN TEXAS (BILLIONS OF DOLLARS) Which type of local governments have levied the highest hikes in property taxes? How can you explain this?

SOURCE: Legislative Budget Board, "Fiscal Size-up" in 1990, 2000, 2003, 2005, 2010.

unfunded or underfunded mandates

laws enacted by federal or state governments that impose responsibilities and financial burdens on city and county governments

> Municipalities organize to stop the construction of coal-burning power plants, such as this one, to reduce air pollution and comply with federally mandated air quality standards.

PROPERTY TAXES

How does the property tax in Texas compare with that in the other most populous states? Take a look at the states that have higher property tax rates and those that have lower property tax rates. What might cause some to have higher rates than others?

Rank among 50 states

State	Rank	Property tax revenues per $1,000 of personal income (in dollars)
North Carolina	39	$22.90
California	37	$24.48
Georgia	26	$28.04
Pennsylvania	22	$29.50
Ohio	21	$31.84
Florida	18	$32.96
Massachusetts	16	$34.17
Texas	13	$36.74
Illinois	12	$37.18
Michigan	11	$39.10
New York	6	$40.45
New Jersey	4	$47.97

Property tax revenues per $1,000 of personal income (in dollars)

SOURCE: Legislative Budget Board, "Fiscal Size-up 2009–2010," fig 60.

abide by these laws, and hence local governments must come up with the funds themselves. In 1995, the U.S. Congress passed the Unfunded Mandates Reform Act. The act specified that Congress committees obtain an estimate of the costs imposed on lower governments by their legislation. If the amount exceeds $50 million per year, the information would have to be discussed by legislators before the bill could be passed into law. The act has not been effective in preventing the federal government from increasing the financial burden placed on state and local governments by federal laws. A similar law was passed by the Texas state legislature with similar results.

In addition, when city governments fail to comply with state and federal mandates such as the Clean Air Act or No Child Left Behind, they may face penalties or loss of funds. With property taxes already high, with a traditionalistic-individualistic political culture opposed to high taxes, and with taxation limitations imposed on local governments by the state legislature, local governments face challenges finding the revenue necessary to meet federal and state mandates.

County Governments

The oldest type of local government in the United States is **county government,** an adaptation of the British county unit of government that was transported to this country. County governments exist in all states except Connecticut, which abolished them in 1963, and Rhode Island (which never needed them). Louisiana calls them "parishes," from the French influence, and Alaska calls them "boroughs." The number of counties varies greatly among the states. Alaska, Delaware, and Hawaii each have 3 county governments, and Texas has 254.[21]

County governments were originally intended to be a subdivision, or arm, of state government to perform state functions at the local level. For example, counties in Texas still serve as voter registrar, a state function; voters register to vote with the local county government. Other services of counties include recording vital statistics, operating state courts and jails, administering elections, and maintaining roads and bridges. In issuing marriage licenses, birth certificates, and automobile registrations, and in operating state courts, county governments are acting as an arm of state government. Texas counties can also assist in the creation of rural fire protection districts.

Besides performing state functions, county governments provide local services—in some states they provide many local services. In Texas, however, counties provide very limited local services. All Texas counties provide road construction and repair and police protection through the sheriff's department. Some urban county governments operate hospitals or health units, libraries, and parks.

The distinguishing feature of county government is population. Of the 3,043 counties in the United States, most are rural with small populations. About 700 counties have populations of less than 10,000, and fewer than 200 have populations of over 250,000. In Texas, 56 percent of the population live in the ten largest urban counties (see Table 27.1). Texas also has the distinction of having the smallest county in the United States. Loving County had a population of 70 in 2000, an increase from 18 in 1980 because of the oil boom.[22]

county government
the oldest type of local government, adapted from the British, whose numbers vary greatly among states; it is the primary administrative arm of a state government, providing services such as voter registration, operation of courts and jails, and maintenance of roads and bridges

TABLE 27.1

The Ten Largest Counties in Texas in 1990 and 2000

County and Major City	POPULATION	
	1990	2000
Harris (Houston)	2,925,965	3,400,578
Dallas (Dallas)	2,049,666	2,218,899
Bexar (San Antonio)	1,232,098	1,392,931
Tarrant (Fort Worth)	1,208,986	1,446,219
El Paso (El Paso)	614,927	679,622
Travis (Austin)	599,357	812,280
Hidalgo (McAllen)	398,648	569,463
Fort Bend (Richmond)	255,412	354,452
Denton (Denton)	212,792	432,976
Collin (Plano)	234,172	491,675
Total	**9,732,023**	**11,799,095**
Total state population	17,655,650	20,892,627
Percentage of population in the ten largest counties	55%	56%

SOURCE: Texas State Data Center, University of Texas at San Antonio, www.txsdc .utsa.edu.

The Structure of County Government

All Texas county governments have the same basic structure, regardless of the county's size. This structure, illustrated in Figure 27.8, mirrors the fragmented structure of state government. It can most accurately be described as weak or plural executive. Voters elect the heads of major departments. These provisions appeared in the constitution of 1876. The writers of this document distrusted appointive authority and trusted the electorate to choose administrators.[23]

The governing body of the county is the **county commissioner's court,** which is not really a court but a legislative body composed of the constitutional county judge and four county commissioners. The county judge is elected at large, and each commissioner is elected from a single-member district called a *commissioner precinct.* Like most other state officeholders, these officials are elected for four-year terms in partisan elections. Their duties include passing local ordinances, approving budgets and new programs, and overseeing county government.

The **constitutional county judge** presides as the chair of the commissioner's court, participates as a full member in deliberations, and has a vote on all matters. The constitution

county commissioner's court
legislative body made up of five elected officials that governs Texas counties

constitutional county judge
chief administrative officer of the county commissioner's court; may also have judicial duties in rural counties

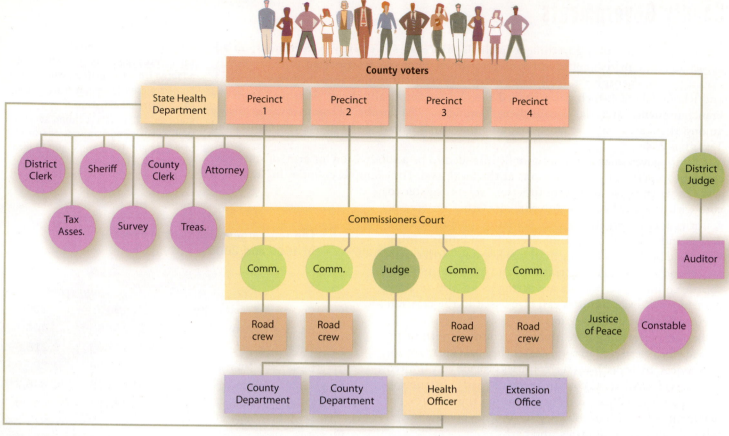

FIGURE 27.8

Structure of County Government in Texas

SOURCE: John A. Gilmartin and Joe M. Rothe, *County Government in Texas*, Issue 2, V. G. Young Institute of County Government, Texas Agricultural Extension Service, Texas A&M University.

assigns judicial duties to this office, but the occupant does not have to be a licensed attorney; the constitution states that she or he must be "well informed in the law." In seventy-two urban counties, where the state legislature has created county courts of law, the constitutional county judge performs very limited judicial functions. The judicial functions of county commissioner's courts are transferred to the county courts of law, and the constitutional county judge acts as the primary administrative officer of the county.

Like other legislative districts, commissioner precincts eventually became malapportioned. In 1968, the U.S. Supreme Court ruled that the one-person-one-vote rule applied to these election districts. The commissioner's court in Midland County claimed it was a court and not a legislative body, and therefore the one-person-one-vote rule did not apply. In *Avery v. Midland County,* the U.S. Supreme Court disagreed and ruled that it was a legislative body and not a court, and that election districts had to be equally apportioned.

The circled titles in Figure 27.8 indicate elected officials. Seven constitutionally prescribed officers are elected by the voters: sheriff, district attorney, county attorney, tax assessor collector, district clerk, county clerk, and county treasurer. These officials act as heads of departments of government. Some counties also have other minor elected officials, such as county surveyor and inspector of hides and wools.

The **county sheriff** is elected countywide for a four-year term and serves as the law enforcement officer for the county. Sheriffs can appoint deputy sheriffs. In rural counties, the sheriff may be the primary law enforcement officer. In urban counties, city police departments carry out most of these duties, and the sheriff's primary duty may be to operate the county jail. In the smaller counties (fewer than 1,800 residents), state law allows the sheriff

county sheriff

the elected head law enforcement officer for a county who in smaller counties may act as the tax assessor collector

to act as the tax assessor collector.[24] Some have suggested that combining sheriff and tax collector is a frightening leftover from Anglo-Saxon law, inspiring visions of Sherwood Forest, the Sheriff of Nottingham, and Robin Hood.

The voters also elect **constables,** who serve as law enforcement officers. Their primary function is to serve as court officers for the justice of the peace courts, delivering subpoenas and other court orders. Constables may also provide police protection in the precinct they serve.

The **county and district attorneys** are the chief prosecuting attorneys for criminal cases in the county. Not all counties have county attorneys. In those that have one, this office usually prosecutes the less serious criminal offenses before county courts, and the district attorney prosecutes major crimes before the district courts.

The **tax assessor collector** is responsible for collecting revenue for the state and the county. Before 1978, this office also assessed the value of all property in the county for property tax collection purposes. In 1978, these functions were transferred to a county-wide assessment district. There are 180 of these tax assessment districts in the state, and they are governed by a board elected by the governing bodies of all governments in the jurisdiction—counties, cities, school districts, and special districts. Though the tax assessor collector still has the title *assessor,* few occupants serve in that capacity today. Most still collect county property taxes, sell state vehicle licenses and permits, and serve as voter registrars. The voter registration function is a carryover from the days of the poll tax.[25]

The **county clerk** is the chief record keeper for the county and keeps track of all property records and issues marriage licenses, birth certificates, and other county records. Although normally the function of voter registration rests with the tax assessor collector, in some counties this function has been transferred to the county clerk, who in all counties is responsible for conducting elections. The **district clerk** is primarily a court official who maintains court records for county and district courts. The clerk schedules cases in these courts and maintains records. The **county treasurer** is responsible for receiving, maintaining, and disbursing county funds.

The **district judge** or judges in the county appoint the county auditor. The county auditor's responsibility is to oversee the collection and disbursement of county funds. The auditor reports to the district judge or judges. Not all counties have auditors. Counties with populations under 10,000 are not required to have auditors. In larger counties (populations above 250,000), the auditor acts as a budget officer unless the commissioner's court appoints its own budget officer.[26]

constables
elected county law enforcement and court officers

county and district attorneys
elected chief prosecuting attorneys for criminal cases

tax assessor collector
elected officer responsible for collecting revenue for the state and the county

county clerk
elected chief record keeper for the county

district clerk
elected official who maintains county and district court records

county treasurer
elected official who manages county funds

district judge
elected official who appoints the county auditor

> Inmates pass the time inside a general population cellblock at the Harris County Jail. County jails are facing an overcrowding crisis. Many blame judges who are determined to "get tough on crime." One study found that the number of people incarcerated before conviction has increased substantially in the past decade, which suggests that judges are setting bail too high. Others argue that the jails are being populated by nonviolent drug offenders who should be in treatment programs rather than prison.

Challenges to Counties: Weak Authority and Limited Financial Resources

The major issues county governments face are inherent weaknesses in the plural executive form of government and lack of power to confront many problems in urban areas.

The plural executive structure of county government in Texas is a product of the nineteenth century and the general distrust of centralized executive authority. As with the plural executive structure in state government, it lacks centralized authority, and the elected officials can, and often do, act quite independently of one another. Although the county commissioner's court does exercise some control over these department heads, it is primarily limited to budgetary matters. After a budget is approved, elected officials can make many independent decisions.

Elected officials also hire their own staff. After each election, personnel at the county courthouse can change dramatically. For example, new sheriffs hire their own deputy sheriffs. The patronage ("spoils") system in some courthouses results in a less professional staff.

Elections are imperfect instruments for determining the qualifications of candidates, and voters do not always select the most competent person to administer departments. Appointment of department heads is more likely to result in the selection of competent persons. A lack of professionalism and competence is a frequently noted problem with county officials in some counties.

County government was designed to meet the needs of and provide services to a rural population, and in rural areas of the state it still functions adequately. In large urban counties, however, this form of government has many weaknesses. The first of these weaknesses is the inability to provide urban-type services. Dense urban populations demand and need services that are unnecessary in rural areas. Usually, county governments are powerless under state law to provide even the most basic services common to city governments, such as water and sewer services. Citizens living on the fringes of cities are forced to provide these services themselves or to form other governments, such as a water district, to provide these services. In recent years, garbage (solid waste) collection and disposal have become a problem in the urban fringe areas. Many citizens must contract with private collectors for this service. Some counties help residents by providing collection centers, often operated by private contractors. In the area of fire protection, counties often help rural residents to establish volunteer fire departments. However, counties are not permitted to operate fire departments. Each rural fire department goes its own way, and there is often a lack of coordination between departments. Training and equipment are generally below the standards of full-time city fire departments. Counties sometimes contract with city governments in the county to provide fire protection for the county, although this practice has declined in recent years.

County governments also lack general ordinance authority. City governments in Texas may pass any ordinance not prohibited by state law, but county governments must seek legislative approval to pass specific ordinances. For example, county governments may not pass ordinances on land use (zoning) or building codes that regulate construction standards. A citizen buying a home in a rural area is largely dependent upon the integrity of the builder.

Finally, a problem for county governments related to their lack of power is the inequity of financial resources and expenditures. A few counties have a sales tax, but most rely almost exclusively on the property tax. Most of this tax is paid by citizens living inside cities and not in the unincorporated, rural areas of the county. Thus, most (89%) of the cost of county government is paid for by city residents paying county taxes. Although county residents pay little of the cost to operate county governments, they receive many services from county governments (such as road construction and repair, police protection) that are not provided to city residents by the county. City residents receive these services from their city and pay city taxes. City residents are paying twice for services they receive only once. This financial inequity goes unnoticed by most citizens.

Suggested Reforms of County Government

Since the 1930s, there have been suggestions to reform county government in Texas. The rhetoric often called for county government to be "brought into the twentieth century." In Texas, apparently all such reforms skipped the twentieth century and have to wait for the twenty-first century. While other states have modernized county governments, Texas has steadfastly refused all efforts at change. One suggestion that has been a frequent agenda item over the past seventy years is to allow for county home rule, which would allow the voters in each county to adopt a local option charter.[27] Voters could then approve any form of government not prohibited by state law; no county would be forced to change its form of government. This might result in the adoption of a strong executive form of government similar to the strong mayor or council-manager forms popular with Texas cities. Even though this suggestion seems quite reasonable, it has been strongly opposed by the many elected county officials in Texas who see this reform as a threat to their jobs.

The Texas Association of Counties (TAC) is an umbrella organization that represents elected county officials—sheriffs, tax collectors, treasurers, judges, commissioners, and so on. This politically powerful group has many supporters throughout the state and has opposed granting county governments home rule. One group within the TAC, the Conference of Urban Counties (CUC), has shown mild support for home rule. The CUC represents thirty metropolitan county governments in Texas where home rule would have the greatest impact. The CUC is not pushing home-rule issues and is more concerned with representing the unique interests of urban counties.

County officials have traditionally resisted changes in their powers to deal with urban problems. They have a provincial attitude toward providing service, and their view of county government does not extend much beyond that of a nineteenth-century official. This means that urban problems that are outside cities are often neglected. Even simple things such as the safety of home construction and septic systems are neglected. This lack of attention can have an effect on citizens' life and health.

County officials often will not even consider providing services that might enhance community amenities. For example, the city council in College Station once proposed that the city libraries be combined and made into a county library operated by Brazos County. A county commissioner was quoted as saying, "The last thing in the world we need is a bigger library. I was down at the Bryan Library once and they already got more books than anyone can read and every year they ask the county for more money to buy more books." The city council cooled on the idea of a county-run library with this provincial attitude among county officials.

At one time, county government was given the responsibility for inspecting septic systems in rural areas. One county never passed an ordinance or put in place an inspection system. When asked by a citizen why they did not have an ordinance and inspections, their reply was, "We just expect you to do it right." The state has since given this authority to the state health department, and septic installers must be licensed.

County government is often more concerned with problems of rural residents than with those living in cities. When the Brazos animal shelter confiscated a number of horses that it felt were malnourished and being mistreated, the county commissioner's court, at the request of rural residents, prevented the animal shelter from doing this in the future. They turned this function over to the sheriff, who is oriented toward policing in rural areas.

Improving the professionalism of county staff might prove difficult because each elected county official can hire his or her own people. Some county officials in some counties place great emphasis on professionalism. Other officials reward faithful campaign workers with appointments. In rural counties, these jobs are often well paid and much sought after by supporters.

> Firefighters search for victims after a building collapses. Some fire departments are part of a larger municipal organization while others are special districts.

Special District Governments

Another form of local government that provides services to local residents is known as special district government. Special districts have been referred to as *shadow governments* because they operate out of the view of most citizens. These governments are created for many reasons and perform many functions. Some districts are single function (such as fire) and others are multipurpose (such as water, sewer, street repair). Some special districts (such as metropolitan transit districts) cover several counties, and others (such as the municipal utility districts) are very small, covering only a few acres.

The primary reason special districts are created is to provide services when no other unit of government exists to provide that service. Sometimes the need extends beyond the geographical boundaries of existing units of government. Mass transportation is an example: Dallas/Fort Worth, Houston, San Antonio, Austin, El Paso, and other metropolitan areas have created transit districts that serve several counties. Sometimes the service involves natural boundaries that extend over county lines. Soil and water conservation and flood control are examples of this. In still other cases, the need for a service may be confined to a single county, but no government unit exists to provide the service. An excellent example of this is municipal utility districts (MUDs), which are multifunction districts generally created outside cities to provide water, sewage treatment, and other services. In Texas, these MUDs are created because county governments cannot provide these services. Finally, some districts are created for political reasons, when no existing unit of government wants to solve the service problem because of potential political conflicts. The creation of another unit of government to deal with a hot political issue is preferable. The Gulf Coast Waste Disposal Authority, created to clean up water pollution in the Houston area, is an example of this.

Special districts are often an efficient and expedient way to solve a problem, but they can also generate problems. One problem citizens face is keeping track of the many special districts that provide services to them. For example, a MUD, a soil and water conservation district, a flood control district, a fire protection district, a metropolitan transit authority, a hospital district, and a waste disposal district can govern a citizen living in the Houston suburbs. Most citizens have trouble distinguishing among a school district, a county, and a city. Dealing with seven or more units of government is even more complicated.

The governing boards of special districts in Texas are selected in two ways. Multicounty special districts (such as DART in Dallas and METRO in Houston) are governed by boards appointed by the governmental units (cities, counties) covered by the district. Single-county special districts (such as MUDs and flood control districts) usually have a board of directors elected by the voters.

Many special districts have taxation authority and can raise local property taxes. The remoteness of these districts from the electorate, their number, and their potential impact on the lives of citizens raise questions of democratic control.[28] The average citizen cannot be expected to know about, understand, and keep track of the decisions made by these remote governments. The alternatives are to consolidate governments, expand cities through the annexation of land, or expand the power of county governments. None of these alternatives is generally acceptable. Citizens demand and expect local governments to be decentralized. This is true even if they have only limited ability to watch and control the actions of local government and the government is ineffective. Big government is something most Texans want to avoid.

SHOULD AN ALTERNATIVE TO EVOLUTION BE TAUGHT IN PUBLIC SCHOOLS?

The Issue: In 2005, President George W. Bush announced his belief that intelligent design (ID) should be taught as another point of view along with the theory of evolution in biology classes. Governor Rick Perry indicated that he agreed with the president. In the summer of 2007, the Texas Board of Education met to discuss the issue. Several members of the board were creationists, and polls have shown that as many as two-thirds of Texans support teaching ID. Yet the board overwhelmingly rejected the idea. For now, only the theory of evolution will be taught in science classes.

The theory of intelligent design (ID) proposes that the existence of life on earth and the origin of the universe can best be explained not by undirected processes such as Darwin's theory of natural selection but, rather, by an intelligent cause. Proponents of ID claim that their theories are based on the principles of modern science. The movement challenges explanations of the origins of life that are based on the theory of natural selection.

Yes: Intelligent design is a scientific theory with a following in many communities in the United States and so should be taught in science classes when topics such as the origins of life on earth and the human species are discussed. There are biological phenomena that cannot be explained by the action of undirected forces, and students should be aware of deficiencies in currently accepted theories. Moreover, teachers should be allowed intellectual freedom to introduce ID as an alternative to more widely accepted scientific theories, and students should be allowed to examine the evidence for both theories and decide for themselves which one has more credibility. By suppressing the teaching of ID, the Texas Board of Education is suppressing academic freedom.

No: The U.S. Constitution guarantees the separation of church and state. As a result, it would be unconstitutional for public schools to force religious teachings into the minds of its students. intelligent design is pseudoscience, nothing more than creationism in new clothing. Religion is a belief system, not a field of scientific exploration. Intelligent design does not enjoy support within the scientific community and hence should not be taught in a science classroom. Parents who would like their children to learn about ID can teach it in their homes or through religious organizations.

Today, the study of science and technology is critical to our country's economic and military success. These subjects are challenging, and national test scores in math and science are falling. To take time away from the study of biology, chemistry, or physics for ID would throw obstacles in the path of our nation's future achievements.

Other approaches: Since ID is not accepted as a legitimate field of scientific exploration, it should not be studied in science class. It is, however, part of a social movement in the United States, and therefore it could be discussed as part of the social studies curriculum. In this way, teachers would not be presenting it as a legitimate field of scientific inquiry but, rather, as a social and philosophical movement.

What do you think?

1. Do you think ID has credibility? How do you think it differs from—or belongs within—modern scientific theory?

2. In your opinion, should ID be taught as an alternative to modern scientific explanations of the origins of life? Explain your answer.

3. Why do you think the Texas Board of Education decided not to allow the teaching of ID?

School Districts

A type of special district government that citizens generally watch and control very closely is the school district. One controversy that has gained a great deal of attention, for example, is the issue of whether to teach alternatives to the theory of evolution in the public schools; "Thinking Critically About Democracy" considers several approaches to this debate. Because school districts play such an important role in the lives of all citizens, we distinguish them from other special districts for discussion.

Texas experienced a slight decline in number of school districts in the 1990s and the first decade of the twenty-first century: from 1,100 in 1992 to 1,062 in 2007.[29] This decline is the result of consolidation, which has been driven by several factors. First, there have been demands for improved curriculum, especially in science and math, and many small rural school districts were unable to provide the desired range and diversity of curriculum. Second, there has been increased state financial aid to school districts that consolidate. Third, road conditions have continued to improve. For example, Texas developed the farm-to-market road system in the 1950s. This system, coupled with improved all-weather county roads, made it possible to bus students to urban schools, a trend that continues.

In the rural areas of Texas, there are still many school districts with a small student body that could consolidate with neighboring districts. Sometimes resistance to consolidation is driven by considerations for the school football program and the realization that closing the school will lead to the death of the town. Often the school is the only glue that holds a community together. Football and community pride are powerful forces, even if the football team has only six players.

The future will see few additional consolidations. The demand today is not for consolidation but for decentralization with the "open-enrollment charter school." In 1995, the legislature authorized the creation of "up to 20 charters for open-enrollment charter schools. These schools can be operated in school districts or non-school district facilities, by public or private higher education institutions, non-profit organizations or governmental entities."[30] Additional charter schools were authorized in the 1997 and 1999 sessions of the legislature. In 1998–1999, there were 89 charter schools operating in the state, and by 2010–2011, the number had increased to about 500. The exact implication of these charter schools is not known. Some preliminary reports and data are available from the Texas Education Agency, but whether these schools will produce substantial improvements in student achievement is unclear.[31] Thirty-two other states have some version of home-rule or charter schools. What is clear from the passage of these laws is that many citizens want to decentralize control over local schools. Further consolidation seems unlikely.

independent school districts
school districts that are not attached to any other unit of government and operate schools in Texas

All but one of the 1,089 school districts in Texas are called **independent school districts,** meaning that they are independent of any other unit of government. In seventeen states, 1,400 school systems are attached to, or dependent upon, another unit of government, most commonly a city or a county.[32] Most are located in the East and the Midwest, with few in the West and the South. In Texas, the Stafford School District in the Houston suburbs is the only school district attached to a city government. Reformers advocated making the school district independent of city government. Such independence was supposed to isolate the schools from evil political influences of city government.

A seven-member elected school board governs most independent school districts in Texas. School board elections are often held in April or May, at the same time as city elections. Some school boards are elected from single-member districts; most are at large, and all are chosen in nonpartisan ballot elections.

Challenges to School Districts: Financing, Quality, and Curriculum

Although the creation of independent school districts may have reduced the influence of city politics, school district elections are still quite political. Over the past several decades, many issues have dominated school politics, and we examine those of finance, quality, and certain areas of curriculum.

SCHOOL FINANCE   The first and perhaps most difficult issue for school districts to resolve is school finance. The state of Texas pays for part of the cost of education. Over the past twenty years, the state's share of the cost of education has declined, and local school districts have been forced to pick up a larger part of the cost. Today, the state pays about 38 percent of the cost of education, and local districts provide the remainder.[33] Because the only source of local financial support is the property tax, some school districts have been better able than others to absorb the higher local share. Some school districts have a high per-pupil property tax base (so-called rich districts), and others have a low per-pupil property tax base (so-called poor districts). Though the state does show preference to poor districts by providing increased funding, this support is still inadequate, and great disparities exist in the amount of money available to school districts on a per-pupil basis.

These inequities became a statewide issue in 1968 when parents in the Edgewood School District in San Antonio filed a lawsuit challenging the financing of schools in Texas (*Rodri-*

guez v. San Antonio Independent School District). The U.S. Supreme Court found the system of school financing to be unfair but said that it was a state problem and that its resolution rested with the state. Because of this case, the state did increase aid to poor school districts. However, severe inequities continued. In 1984, another lawsuit brought education finance to the forefront in Texas (Edgewood v. Kirby). This case was filed in state district court, and because of the efforts of the Mexican American Legal Defense and Education Fund and the Equity Center in Austin, the Texas Supreme Court in 1989 ruled the system of school finance in the state unconstitutional.

In an attempt to correct these inequities, the state legislature in 1991 consolidated property taxes within 188 units called *county education districts*. These districts collected property taxes to be used for school operations and distributed them to the school districts in their jurisdiction on a per-student basis. This system became known as the **"Robin Hood plan."** It was challenged in court by some rich districts, and the courts ruled that the plan violated the Texas Constitution. The state legislature proposed a constitutional amendment to make the system legal. In May 1993, the voters rejected this amendment by a large margin (63 percent against).[34]

The rejection of this issue had political implications in the 1994 governor's race. According to the *Dallas Morning News,* the Republican National Committee spent $400,000 to help defeat this amendment and to promote negative views about the governor, Ann Richards. The ads tied Richards to the amendment.[35] Richards was defeated by George W. Bush in 1994, although she may have lost even without the ads.

Following the defeat of this amendment, the legislature passed a new law that revised the Robin Hood plan by giving several options to rich districts. Under this plan, a school district's property tax wealth is capped at $305,000 per pupil. At that point, a district has several choices. It may send its excess wealth to the state, which will send the money to poor districts. It can also combine its wealth with a specific district. Most have sent the money to the state. After a district reaches the $305,000 per-pupil cap, it receives very little state money, although it still receives some federal funds. Ninety percent of the school districts in Texas are poor districts. Only 10 percent must give money to the state.

The 2003 session of the legislature again faced the problem of school finances. A new issue that has grown out of the present system is that school district taxes are capped by state law at no more than $1.50 per $100 of valuation for operations. Many districts reached the $1.50 limit and still did not have enough money to operate. In 2004, Governor Perry, intent on solving this crisis, called a special session of the legislature and proposed funding schools through gambling revenues. Public attention immediately focused on the pro-gambling lobby, which had contributed substantial sums to the campaigns of the governor and other top legislators. Many Republicans opposed gambling on moral grounds, and the 2004 legislative session failed to find a solution. The crisis was exacerbated when the so-called rich districts filed a lawsuit to throw out the Robin Hood plan in *Neeley v. West-Orange-Cove*

The Challenge of Funding Education

THEN (1990)	NOW (2010)
About 3.7 million children attended school in Texas.	The school-age population has increased by about 25 percent.*
School districts collected $6.6 billion in property tax revenue.	Property taxes collected by school districts have more than tripled since 1990.
Property taxes collected by school districts were high but still within state-mandated limits.	Property taxes collected by school districts have reached the cap imposed by state laws. Additional funds to pay for schools must come from other sources.

WHAT'S NEXT?

> How will Texas support its public schools without exceeding the mandatory cap on school district property taxes?

> Will larger, wealthier cities be able to fund their schools better than smaller, poorer ones?

> Will other revenue sources, such as the franchise fee, provide a much needed new source of funding for the public schools?

*"Texas Fact Sheet," National Council of La Raza, www.nclr.org/files/32314_file_TX_final.pdf.

"Robin Hood plan"

a nickname for the provision in the education statutes that consolidated property taxes so that they are distributed among rich and poor districts; revised later to require rich districts with a property tax base per pupil in excess of $305,000 to share their wealth with other school districts

Consolidated Independent School District. In September 2004, the district court ruled the current system unconstitutional on a number of grounds, including that school property taxes were so high that they constituted a virtual state income tax, which is forbidden by state law. Yet the 2005 legislative session was again unable to come to an agreement. In November 2005, the Texas Supreme Court upheld the district court's decision regarding the taxation and ordered the legislature to redo school finance before September 2006.

Under pressure from a decision by the Texas Supreme Court to close the schools in the fall of 2006, the legislature met in a special session to consider the changes in school finance. The legislature eventually produced a plan that provides some modest reduction of property tax for homeowners, additional property tax for businesses, a tax increase of a dollar per pack on cigarettes, and an increase in the franchise tax paid by businesses. This act solved the school finance issue temporarily. It cut the revenue taken from wealthier districts by almost half.[36] Some estimates, however, say that the state will face funding shortfalls of several million dollars over the next few years. In the meantime, wealthier districts are once again unhappy about the flow of funds out of their jurisdictions.

QUALITY OF EDUCATION   A second issue for school districts is the quality of education given to students. In the early 1980s, Governor Mark White, a Democrat, raised the profile of this issue. Working with Lt. Governor Hobby and House Speaker Gib Lewis, White appointed a select committee on public education. Texas billionaire Ross Perot was appointed chair of this committee. The recommendations of this committee led to the passage of House Bill 72, which contained two very controversial provisions. Although it provided funding for a teacher pay raise, it also required the state's teachers to pass a test to prove their competency. There was great resistance to this test by the teachers, although it was apparently a rather simple test designed to weed out the completely unqualified. Some referred to the test as a literacy test. Despite the easiness of the test, many teachers resented taking it and took it as a personal affront. Many blame this test and the teachers' reactions to it for Mark White's loss to Republican Bill Clements in the 1986 governor's race.

The second controversial provision in House Bill 72 was the no-pass, no-play provision. This new rule prohibited students from participating in extracurricular activities if they were not passing all their courses. In a state where Friday night football is an institution and in many small towns the premier social event, preventing students from participating because they failed a course was viewed as not only un-Texan but also perhaps a little "communistic." Students were also prohibited from participating in band, tennis, soccer, swimming, and cheerleading, but no one really much cared beyond football (although some communities cared about baseball). The no-pass, no-play rule also contributed to Mark White's defeat in 1986. The effects of no-pass, no-play and teacher literacy tests were probably more symbolic than real.

The first school accountability program was set up under Democratic Governor Ann Richards. When Republican George W. Bush was elected governor in 1994, many feared he would abolish this program. Instead, he championed school accountability. During his term, the first statewide achievement testing, Texas Assessment of Academic Skills (TAAS), for grades three through twelve was established. The tests were used to rank schools and hold them accountable for student progress. If schools scored high on these tests, they would receive financial rewards. If they scored too low, they could be subject to public hearings and risked being taken over by the state government. A study of test scores on the National Assessment of Educational Progress (NAEP) found that the quality of education improved measurably following the implementation of this new testing system. Detractors, however, argued that the study failed to look at important statistics that showed that the new system penalized low-income and minority students. In 2003, TAAS was replaced by Texas Assessment of Knowledge and Skills (TAKS), a new assessment system. (Another way of determining progress is to examine completion rates, as considered in "Analyzing the Sources.")

SEX EDUCATION, INTELLIGENT DESIGN, AND BILINGUAL EDUCATION
In school board elections in Texas and much of the nation, three curriculum issues have caused much controversy: sex education, intelligent design (ID), and bilingual education. Sex education (see Chapter 26) and ID are issues driven by members of the Christian Right, or Social Conservatives, who have a comfortable majority on the state board of education

ANALYZING THE SOURCES

MEASURING PROGRESS IN EDUCATION

Test scores are just one of many indicators that measure the performance of public education in Texas. In addition to NAEP and TAKS scores, the Texas Education Agency tracks measures such as enrollment trends, school and class size, and completion, graduation, and drop-out rates. The table below provides completion rates for students from seventh to twelfth grade. Completion rate consists of the percentage of students who graduated, received General Educational (GED) certificates, or continued high school.

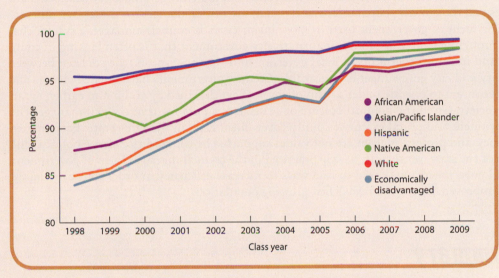

SOURCE: Secondary School Completion and Dropouts in Texas Public Schools, 2008–2009, Texas Education Agency, p. 50, table 14, www.tea.state.tx.us/index4.aspx?id=4080#reports.

Evaluating the Evidence

① How have completion rates changed over time? What does this say about the performance of public schools? What factors might explain this trend?

② Which socioeconomic groups have the highest completion rates? Which groups have the lowest completion rates?

③ Which socioeconomic groups have experienced the greatest improvement in completion rates? What does this say about the Texas public school system?

and are attempting to elect local school board members. Their aim is to limit sex education to abstinence-based programs and to require the teaching of ID as an alternative to evolution or along with evolution (see "Thinking Critically About Democracy"). The extent to which these groups have managed to control school boards is unknown, and the issues surrounding this are not likely to be resolved anytime soon. Members of the Christian Right have had an impact on choosing the state school board, which is elected by districts in the state. The legislature has reduced some authority of this board in the past ten years, and more restrictions are possible in future sessions, especially in the area of textbook content.

Bilingual education is a controversy dating to the early twentieth century, when Germans and Czechs in Texas wanted to teach their native languages in the schools. Following World War I, anti-German sentiment in the state killed those efforts, and in the 1920s the legislature prohibited the teaching of languages (other than English). There is an old story in the lore of Texas politics that claims when Governor Ma Ferguson signed the bill prohibiting the teaching of children in any language other than English, she reportedly said, "If English was good enough for Jesus Christ, it's good enough for the school children of Texas."

Currently, the bilingual issue revolves around teaching in Spanish and English to Latino children in the elementary schools. Many Anglo Texans object to using tax money for bilingual education. Some take the inconsistent position that everyone should speak English, but no tax money should be spent to ensure that they can. Governors Bush and Perry both helped soften the resistance to these education programs and reached out to Latino voters in the state.

CONCLUSION

THINKING CRITICALLY ABOUT WHAT'S NEXT FOR TEXAS LOCAL GOVERNMENT

Although local governments do not generate the same degree of interest that national and state governments do, they have an extremely important impact on the daily lives of citizens. Without the services provided by local governments, modern urban life would not be possible.

In Texas, city governments are the principal providers of local services. Many federal and state mandates are implemented at the local level. The increasing number of unfunded mandates and the growing population and economy are new challenges for these governments.

The form of government used in most major cities is council-manager, a system that has brought a degree of professionalism to city government that is often lacking in counties and in some other units of local government. In many respects, the contrast between county and city government is remarkable. County governments have resisted change and seem content to operate under a form of government designed by and for an earlier, agrarian society. Given the political culture of Texas, it is a paradox that council-manager city government and plural executive county government exist in the same state. Economy, efficiency, and professionalism are not values supported by the traditionalistic political culture of the state, yet they are widely practiced in the council-manager form of government. Local governments will need to find ways to increase efficiency in order to provide more, and improved, services to Texas's fast-growing population.

STUDY NOW

Summary

1. State and Local Authority
The authority of local governments is derived solely from state constitutions and statutes.

2. Municipal Governments
In Texas, cities are chartered as either general-law cities or home-rule cities. Most cities that are large enough to be eligible elect to become home-rule cities. There are two basic forms of city government: mayor-council and council-manager. Council-manager governments govern most major cities, a system that has brought a degree of professionalism to city government that is often lacking in county and some other units of local government. All cities face the challenge of finding the resources to finance state and federal unfunded or underfunded mandates.

3. County Governments
County governments have resisted change and seem content to operate under a plural executive, a form of government designed by and for an agrarian society. With this weak authority, county governments frequently cannot pass ordinances and raise the funds necessary to provide services to county residents.

4. Special District Governments
Some districts are created to perform a single function (for example, fire protection) or multiple functions (for example, water, sewer, street repair). Special districts are primarily created to provide services when no other unit of government exists to provide that service, and they often operate out of the view of most citizens. Some special districts serve several counties, and others are very small, covering only a few acres.

5. School Districts

School districts are one type of special district government. They face many problems; the most pressing is school finance. School funding has been chiefly derived from local property taxes, but these taxes have increased so dramatically that they have reached a cap set by the state. Finding new sources of state revenue has been and is expected to continue to be a challenge. Two additional, ongoing controversies for school districts are how to ensure they provide a high-quality education to all students and what the curriculum should be.

Key Terms

at-large election system 786

city manager 786

constables 793

constitutional county judge 791

council-manager form of government 785

county clerk 793

county commissioner's court 791

county and district attorneys 793

county government 791

county sheriff 792

county treasurer 793

cumulative voting 786

decentralized nation 780

district clerk 793

district judge 793

extra territorial jurisdiction (ETJ) 782

general-law city 782

general-purpose government 781

home-rule city 782

implicit or explicit prohibition on city ordinance power 782

incorporation 782

independent school districts 798

limited-purpose government 781

nonpartisan elections 787

off-year elections 788

preferential voting 787

"Robin Hood plan" 799

single-member district 786

tax assessor collector 793

unfunded or underfunded mandates 789

For Review

1. Why are local governments "creatures of the state"?
2. What is the difference between general-law and home-rule cities?
3. Describe the structure of a mayor-council government and a council-manager government.
4. What type of government do counties have, and what problems does this cause?
5. What are special district governments? Give some examples.
6. What problems do school districts in Texas face?

For Critical Thinking and Discussion

1. What are the advantages of the council-manager government over a mayor-council government?
2. The city of Houston uses a combination of at-large and single-member-district (SMD) systems to elect its city council. What would be the outcome if Houston abandoned the SMD and relied solely on at-large districts?
3. Give an example of a state or federal mandate that affects municipal governments. Explain who you think should fund the mandate.
4. What aspects of local government are strongly influenced by the traditionalistic-individualistic political culture?
5. Propose a solution to the school finance crisis. Ask another student to critique your proposal and find a way to improve it.

MULTIPLE CHOICE: Choose the lettered item that answers the question correctly.

1. Municipalities with populations under 5,000 are all
   a. general-law cities.
   b. home-rule cities.
   c. weak mayor-council governments.
   d. council-manager governments.

2. What is the main advantage of home-rule charters?
   a. They provide greater latitude in governing local affairs.
   b. They can be amended only with the approval of the voters.
   c. They allow the city to provide better services to its residents.
   d. They allow the city council to override certain state statutes.

3. Which of the following is not one of the powers or responsibilities of a city manager?
   a. appoints all major department heads
   b. has veto power over the city council on items dealing with administrative functions
   c. is in charge of the day-to-day management of city government
   d. provides information and advice to city council

4. Extra territorial jurisdiction is
   a. the process of creating a city.
   b. a form of special district that provides services to those in urban counties.
   c. an extension of city authority to areas adjacent to city limits.
   d. the legislative powers of a district judge.

5. The voting system that is most common in city council elections in Texas is called
   a. single-member districts.
   b. at-large by place.
   c. cumulative voting.
   d. preferential voting.

6. In Texas, property taxes
   a. are not primary source of taxes for local government.
   b. do not affect the revenue of school districts.
   c. have increased dramatically in recent years.
   d. all go to the state government.

7. An example of an underfunded or unfunded mandate is
   a. the incorporation of Impact, Texas.
   b. the Texas Board of Education.
   c. a multicounty special district such as DART.
   d. the Clean Air Act.

8. Which of the following does not operate at the county level?
   a. justice of the peace
   b. constables
   c. tax assessor collector
   d. police chief

9. Which of the following is a service Texas county governments typically provide?
   a. water supply service
   b. sewage disposal
   c. planning and zoning
   d. marriage licenses and birth certificates

10. What was the result of *Neely v. West-Orange-Cove Consolidated Independent School District*?
    a. The district court ruled the current school funding system unconstitutional.
    b. The legislature agreed to cut the revenue taken from wealthier school districts by 75 percent.
    c. The state legislature consolidated property taxes into county education districts.
    d. Long-term financial issues affecting school districts were resolved.

FILL IN THE BLANKS.

11. There are more _____ forms of government in the general-law cities in Texas than in the home-rule cities.

12. The governing body of the county is the _____, which is a legislative body composed of the constitutional county judge and four county commissioners.

13. The _____ is a nickname for the provision in the education statutes that requires so-called rich school districts to share their wealth with other school districts.

14. The _____ is the chief administrative officer of county government in Texas.

RESOURCES FOR RESEARCH AND ACTION

Internet Resources

Comptroller of Public Accounts
www.window.state.tx.us   This site is a good source on state expenditures and economic regions.

Legislative Budget Board
www.lbb.state.tx.us   This site gives information on Texas past and present and is a useful source of data on the state budget. The site includes a link to the *Texas Fact Book,* which contains a wealth of information about the state and is updated regularly.

The Texas Handbook
www.tsha.utexas.edu/handbook/online   Published online by the Texas Historical Society, this site has a lot of information on the history of the state and its people.

Texas Newspapers
www.usnpl.com/txnews.php   For information about Texas newspapers, use the links provided at this site.

Texas Online
www.texasonline.com   This "Official Portal of Texas" provides links to state agencies and popular online services.

Internet Activism

The Texas Municipal League provides legal and legislative assistance to cities throughout the state. You can learn more about policy issues on the local level or comb through job offerings posted by your own local governments. **www.tml.org**

Twitter
http://twitter.com/houstonchron   Get top headlines from the *Houston Chronicle* about relevant local and state issues.

YouTube
www.youtube.com/watch?v=ZuTF9DkQ5Rw   Watch the superintendent of the Harrold Independent School District in North Texas speak with a CBS reporter about a policy that allows teachers to carry guns at school.

Facebook
www.facebook.com/tom.leppert   Dallas Mayor Tom Leppert wants to be your Facebook friend. Message him with any questions or concerns about issues you may have that are local to Dallas, Texas.

Recommended Readings

Blodgett, Terrell. *Texas Home-rule Charters.* Austin: Texas Municipal League, 1994.

Frank, Nancy. *Charter Schools: Experiments in Reform, an Update.* Austin: Texas Legislative Budget Board, Public Education Team, 1995.

Halter, Gary M., and Gerald L. Dauthery. "The County Commissioners Court in Texas," in *Governing Texas: Documents and Readings* (3rd ed.), ed. Fred Gantt Jr. et al. New York: Thomas Y. Crowell, 1974.

Johnson, David R., John A. Booth, and Richard J. Harris. *The Politics of San Antonio: Community Progress and Power.* Lincoln: University of Nebraska Press, 1983.

Lyndon B. Johnson School of Public Affairs. *Local Government Election Systems,* Policy Research Report No. 62. Austin: University of Texas Press, 1984.

Martin, David L. *Running City Hall: Municipal Administration in the United States.* Tuscaloosa: University of Alabama Press, 1990.

Pernod, Virginia. *Special District, Special Purposes: Fringe Governments and Urban Problems in the Houston Area.* College Station: Texas A&M University Press, 1984.

Rice, Bradley Robert. *Progressive Cities: The Commission Government Movement in America, 1901–1920.* Austin: University of Texas Press, 1977.

Smith, Richard A. "How Business Failed Dallas," in *Governing Texas: Documents and Readings* (2nd ed.), ed. Fred Gantt Jr. et al. New York: Thomas Y. Crowell, 1970.

Stillman, Richard. *The Rise of the City Manager: A Public Professional in Local Government.* Albuquerque: University of New Mexico Press, 1974.

Svara, James A. *Official Leadership in the City: Patterns of Conflict and Cooperation.* New York: Oxford University Press, 1990.

Zimmerman, Joseph. *The Federal City: Community Control in Large Cities.* New York: St. Martin's Press, 1972.

Movies of Interest

Judgment Day: Intelligent Design on Trial (2007)
An award-winning documentary, produced by NOVA and Vulcan Productions, on the 2005 court case in which a federal judge ruled that a Pennsylvania school district could not require its teachers to present intelligent design as an alternative theory to the theory of evolution.

The Education of Shelby Knox (2005)
A critically acclaimed documentary that follows the experiences of a socially conservative teenage girl in Lubbock, Texas, as she joins a campaign for sex education in the public schools.

Lone Star (1996)
An American mystery film, written and directed by John Sayles and set in a small town in Texas. It deals with a sheriff's investigation into the murder of one of his predecessors.

THE DECLARATION OF INDEPENDENCE

In Congress, July 4, 1776

THE UNANIMOUS DECLARATION OF THE THIRTEEN UNITED STATES OF AMERICA

When in the Course of human Events, it becomes necessary for one People to dissolve the Political Bands which have connected them with another, and to assume, among the Powers of the Earth, the separate and equal Station to which the Laws of Nature and of Nature's God entitle them, a decent Respect to the Opinions of Mankind requires that they should declare the Causes which impel them to the Separation.

We hold these Truths to be self-evident, that all Men are created equal, that they are endowed, by their Creator, with certain unalienable Rights, that among these are Life, Liberty, and the Pursuit of Happiness.—That to secure these Rights, Governments are instituted among Men, deriving their just Powers from the Consent of the Governed, that whenever any Form of Government becomes destructive of these Ends, it is the Right of the People to alter or to abolish it, and to institute new Government, laying its Foundation on such Principles, and organizing its Powers in such Form, as to them shall seem most likely to effect their Safety and Happiness. Prudence, indeed, will dictate, that Governments long established, should not be changed for light and transient Causes; and accordingly all Experience hath shewn, that Mankind are more disposed to suffer, while Evils are sufferable, than to right themselves by abolishing the Forms to which they are accustomed. But when a long Train of Abuses and Usurpations, pursuing invariably the same Object, evinces a Design to reduce them under absolute Despotism, it is their Right, it is their Duty, to throw off such Government, and to provide new Guards for their future Security. Such has been the patient Sufferance of these Colonies; and such is now the Necessity which constrains them to alter their former Systems of Government. The History of the present King of Great-Britain is a History of repeated Injuries and Usurpations, all having in direct Object the Establishment of an absolute Tyranny over these States. To prove this, let Facts be submitted to a candid World.

He has refused his Assent to Laws, the most wholesome and necessary for the public Good.

He has forbidden his Governors to pass Laws of immediate and pressing Importance, unless suspended in their Operation till his Assent should be obtained; and when so suspended, he has utterly neglected to attend to them.

He has refused to pass other Laws for the Accommodation of large Districts of People, unless those People would relinquish the Right of Representation in the Legislature, a Right inestimable to them, and formidable to Tyranny only.

He has called together Legislative Bodies at Places unusual, uncomfortable, and distant from the Depository of their public Records, for the sole Purpose of fatiguing them into Compliance with his Measures.

He has dissolved Representative Houses repeatedly, for opposing with manly Firmness his Invasions on the Rights of the People.

He has refused for a long Time, after such Dissolutions, to cause others to be elected; whereby the Legislative Powers, incapable of Annihilation, have returned to the People at large for their exercise; the State remaining, in the mean Time, exposed to all the Dangers of Invasion from without, and Convulsions within.

He has endeavoured to prevent the Population of these States; for that Purpose obstructing the Laws for Naturalization of Foreigners; refusing to pass others to encourage their Migrations hither, and raising the Conditions of new Appropriations of Lands.

He has obstructed the Administration of Justice, by refusing his Assent to Laws for establishing Judiciary Powers.

He has made Judges dependent on his Will alone, for the Tenure of their Offices, and the Amount and Payment of their Salaries.

He has erected a Multitude of new Offices, and sent hither Swarms of Officers to harrass our People, and eat out their Substance.

He has kept among us, in Times of Peace, Standing Armies, without the Consent of our Legislatures.

He has affected to render the Military independent of and superior to the Civil Power.

He has combined with others to subject us to a Jurisdiction foreign to our Constitution, and unacknowledged by our Laws; giving his Assent to their Acts of pretended Legislation:

For quartering large Bodies of Armed Troops among us:

For protecting them, by a mock Trial, from Punishment for any Murders which they should commit on the Inhabitants of these States:

For cutting off our Trade with all Parts of the World:

For imposing Taxes on us without our Consent:

For depriving us, in many Cases, of the Benefits of Trial by Jury:

For transporting us beyond Seas to be tried for pretended Offences:

For abolishing the free System of English Laws in a neighbouring Province, establishing therein an arbitrary Government, and enlarging its Boundaries, so as to render it at once an Example and fit Instrument for introducing the same absolute Rule into these Colonies:

For taking away our Charters, abolishing our most valuable Laws, and altering fundamentally the Forms of our Governments:

For suspending our own Legislatures, and declaring themselves invested with Power to legislate for us in all Cases whatsoever.

He has abdicated Government here, by declaring us out of his Protection, and waging War against us.

He has plundered our Seas, ravaged our Coasts, burnt our Towns, and destroyed the Lives of our People.

He is, at this Time, transporting large Armies of foreign Mercenaries to complete the Works of Death, Desolation, and Tyranny, already begun with Circumstances of Cruelty and Perfidy, scarcely paralleled in the most barbarous Ages, and totally unworthy the Head of a civilized Nation.

He has constrained our fellow Citizens taken Captive on the high Seas to bear Arms against their Country, to become the Executioners of their Friends and Brethren, or to fall themselves by their Hands.

He has excited domestic Insurrections amongst us, and has endeavoured to bring on the Inhabitants of our Frontiers, the merciless Indian Savages, whose known Rule of Warfare, is an undistinguished Destruction, of all Ages, Sexes and Conditions.

In every Stage of these Oppressions we have Petitioned for Redress in the most humble Terms: Our repeated Petitions have been answered only by repeated Injury. A Prince, whose Character is thus marked by every Act which may define a Tyrant, is unfit to be the Ruler of a free People.

Nor have we been wanting in Attentions to our British Brethren. We have warned them, from Time to Time of Attempts by their Legislature to extend an unwarrantable Jurisdiction over us. We have reminded them of the Circumstances of our Emigration and Settlement here. We have appealed to their native Justice and Magnanimity, and we have conjured them by the Ties of our common Kindred to disavow these Usurpations, which would inevitably interrupt our Connections and Correspondence. They too have been deaf to the Voice of Justice and of Consanguinity. We must, therefore, acquiesce in the Necessity, which denounces our Separation, and hold them, as we hold the Rest of Mankind, Enemies in War, in Peace Friends.

We, therefore, the Representatives of the UNITED STATES OF AMERICA, in General Congress Assembled, appealing to the Supreme Judge of the World for the Rectitude of our Intentions, do, in the Name, and by Authority of the good People of these Colonies, solemnly Publish and Declare, That these United Colonies are, and of Right ought to be, Free and Independent States; that they are absolved from all Allegiance to the British Crown, and that all political Connection between them and the State of Great-Britain, is and ought to be totally dissolved; and that as Free and Independent States, they have full Power to levy War, conclude Peace, contract Alliances, establish Commerce, and to do all other Acts and Things which Independent States may of Right do. And for the Support of this Declaration, with a firm Reliance on the Protection of Divine Providence, we mutually pledge to each other our Lives, our Fortunes, and our sacred Honour.

John Hancock.

NEW-HAMPSHIRE
Josiah Bartlett
William Whipple
Matthew Thornton

MASSACHUSETTS BAY
Samuel Adams
John Adams
Robert Treat Paine
Elbridge Gerry

RHODE ISLAND
Stephen Hopkins
William Ellery

CONNECTICUT
Roger Sherman
Samuel Huntington
William Williams
Oliver Wolcott

NEW YORK
William Floyd
Philip Livingston
Francis Lewis
Lewis Morris

NEW JERSEY
Richard Stockton
John Witherspoon
Francis Hopkinson
John Hart
Abraham Clark

PENNSYLVANIA
Robert Morris
Benjamin Rush
Benjamin Franklin
John Morton
George Clymer
James Smith
George Taylor
James Wilson
George Ross

DELAWARE
Caesar Rodney
George Read
Thomas McKean

MARYLAND
Samuel Chase
William Paca
Thomas Stone
Charles Carroll

VIRGINIA
George Wythe
Richard Henry Lee
Thomas Jefferson
Benjamin Harrison
Thomas Nelson, Jr.
Francis Lightfoot Lee
Carter Braxton

NORTH CAROLINA
William Hooper
Joseph Hewes
John Penn

SOUTH CAROLINA
Edward Rutledge
Thomas Heyward, Jr.
Thomas Lynch, Jr.
Arthur Middleton

GEORGIA
Button Gwinnett
Lyman Hall
George Walton

November 22, 1787
JAMES MADISON

TO THE PEOPLE OF THE STATE OF NEW YORK:

Among the numerous advantages promised by a well constructed Union, none deserves to be more accurately developed than its tendency to break and control the violence of faction. The friend of popular governments never finds himself so much alarmed for their character and fate, as when he contemplates their propensity to this dangerous vice. He will not fail, therefore, to set a due value on any plan which, without violating the principles to which he is attached, provides a proper cure for it. The instability, injustice, and confusion introduced into the public councils, have, in truth, been the mortal diseases under which popular governments have everywhere perished; as they continue to be the favorite and fruitful topics from which the adversaries to liberty derive their most specious declamations. The valuable improvements made by the American constitutions on the popular models, both ancient and modern, cannot certainly be too much admired; but it would be an unwarrantable partiality, to contend that they have as effectually obviated the danger on this side, as was wished and expected. Complaints are everywhere heard from our most considerate and virtuous citizens, equally the friends of public and private faith, and of public and personal liberty, that our governments are too unstable, that the public good is disregarded in the conflicts of rival parties, and that measures are too often decided, not according to the rules of justice and the rights of the minor party, but by the superior force of an interested and overbearing majority. However anxiously we may wish that these complaints had no foundation, the evidence, of known facts will not permit us to deny that they are in some degree true. It will be found, indeed, on a candid review of our situation, that some of the distresses under which we labor have been erroneously charged on the operation of our governments; but it will be found, at the same time, that other causes will not alone account for many of our heaviest misfortunes; and, particularly, for that prevailing and increasing distrust of public engagements, and alarm for private rights, which are echoed from one end of the continent to the other. These must be chiefly, if not wholly, effects of the unsteadiness and injustice with which a factious spirit has tainted our public administrations.

By a faction, I understand a number of citizens, whether amounting to a majority or a minority of the whole, who are united and actuated by some common impulse of passion, or of interest, adversed to the rights of other citizens, or to the permanent and aggregate interests of the community.

There are two methods of curing the mischiefs of faction: the one, by removing its causes; the other, by controlling its effects.

There are again two methods of removing the causes of faction: the one, by destroying the liberty which is essential to its existence; the other, by giving to every citizen the same opinions, the same passions, and the same interests.

It could never be more truly said than of the first remedy, that it was worse than the disease. Liberty is to faction what air is to fire, an aliment without which it instantly expires. But it could not be less folly to abolish liberty, which is essential to political life, because it nourishes faction, than it would be to wish the annihilation of air, which is essential to animal life, because it imparts to fire its destructive agency.

The second expedient is as impracticable as the first would be unwise. As long as the reason of man continues fallible, and he is at liberty to exercise it, different opinions will be formed. As long as the connection subsists between his reason and his self-love, his opinions and his passions will have a reciprocal influence on each other; and the former will be objects to which the latter will attach themselves. The diversity in the faculties of men, from which the rights of property originate, is not less an insuperable obstacle to a uniformity of interests. The protection of these faculties is the first object of government. From the protection of different and unequal faculties of acquiring property, the possession of different degrees and kinds of property immediately results; and from the influence of these on the sentiments and views of the respective proprietors, ensues a division of the society into different interests and parties.

The latent causes of faction are thus sown in the nature of man; and we see them everywhere brought into different degrees of activity, according to the different circumstances of civil society. A zeal for different opinions concerning religion, concerning government, and many other points, as well of speculation as of practice; an attachment to different leaders ambitiously contending for pre-eminence and power; or to persons of other descriptions whose fortunes have been interesting to the human passions, have, in turn, divided mankind into parties, inflamed them with mutual animosity, and rendered them much more disposed to vex and oppress each other than to co-operate for their common good. So strong is this propensity of mankind to fall into mutual animosities, that where no substantial occasion presents itself, the most frivolous and fanciful distinctions have been sufficient to kindle their unfriendly passions and excite their most violent conflicts. But the most common and durable source of factions has been the various and unequal distribution of property. Those who hold and those who are without property have ever formed distinct interests in society. Those who are creditors, and those who are debtors, fall under a like discrimination. A landed interest, a manufacturing interest, a mercantile interest, a moneyed interest, with many lesser interests, grow up of necessity in civilized nations, and divide them into different classes, actuated by different sentiments and views. The regulation of these various and interfering interests forms the principal task of modern legislation, and involves the spirit of party and faction in the necessary and ordinary operations of the government.

No man is allowed to be a judge in his own cause, because his interest would certainly bias his judgment, and, not improbably, corrupt his integrity. With equal, nay with greater reason, a body of men are unfit to be both judges and parties at the same time; yet what are many of the most important acts of legislation, but so many judicial determinations, not indeed concerning the rights of single persons, but concerning the rights of large bodies of citizens? And what are the different classes of legislators but advocates and parties to the causes which they determine? Is a law proposed concerning private debts? It is a question to which the creditors are parties on one side and the debtors on the other. Justice ought to hold the balance between them. Yet the parties are, and must be, themselves the judges; and the most numerous party, or, in other words, the most powerful faction must be expected to prevail. Shall domestic manufactures be encouraged, and in what degree, by restrictions on foreign manufactures? are questions which would be differently decided by the landed and the manufacturing classes, and probably by neither with a sole regard to justice and the public good. The apportionment of taxes on the various descriptions of property is an act which seems to require the most exact impartiality; yet there is, perhaps, no legislative act in which greater opportunity and temptation are given to a predominant party to trample on the rules of justice. Every shilling with which they overburden the inferior number, is a shilling saved to their own pockets.

It is in vain to say that enlightened statesmen will be able to adjust these clashing interests, and render them all subservient to the public good. Enlightened statesmen will not always be at the helm. Nor, in many cases, can such an adjustment be made at all without taking into view indirect and remote considerations, which will rarely prevail over the immediate interest which one party may find in disregarding the rights of another or the good of the whole.

The inference to which we are brought is, that the causes of faction cannot be removed, and that relief is only to be sought in the means of controlling its *effects*.

If a faction consists of less than a majority, relief is supplied by the republican principle, which enables the majority to defeat its sinister views by regular vote. It may clog the administration, it may convulse the society; but it will be unable to execute and mask its violence under the forms of the Constitution. When a majority is included in a faction, the form of popular government, on the other hand, enables it to sacrifice to its ruling passion or interest both the public good and the rights of other citizens. To secure the public good and private rights against the danger of such a faction, and at the same time to preserve the spirit and the form of popular government, is then the great object to which our inquiries are directed. Let me add that it is the great desideratum by which this form of government can be rescued from the opprobrium under which it has so long labored, and be recommended to the esteem and adoption of mankind.

By what means is this object attainable? Evidently by one of two only. Either the existence of the same passion or interest in a major-

ity at the same time must be prevented, or the majority, having such coexistent passion or interest, must be rendered, by their number and local situation, unable to concert and carry into effect schemes of oppression. If the impulse and the opportunity be suffered to coincide, we well know that neither moral nor religious motives can be relied on as an adequate control. They are not found to be such on the injustice and violence of individuals, and lose their efficacy in proportion to the number combined together, that is, in proportion as their efficacy becomes needful.

From this view of the subject it may be concluded that a pure democracy, by which I mean a society consisting of a small number of citizens, who assemble and administer the government in person, can admit of no cure for the mischiefs of faction. A common passion or interest will, in almost every case, be felt by a majority of the whole; a communication and concert result from the form of government itself; and there is nothing to check the inducements to sacrifice the weaker party or an obnoxious individual. Hence it is that such democracies have ever been spectacles of turbulence and contention; have ever been found incompatible with personal security or the rights of property; and have in general been as short in their lives as they have been violent in their deaths. Theoretic politicians, who have patronized this species of government, have erroneously supposed that by reducing mankind to a perfect equality in their political rights, they would, at the same time, be perfectly equalized and assimilated in their possessions, their opinions, and their passions.

A republic, by which I mean a government in which the scheme of representation takes place, opens a different prospect, and promises the cure for which we are seeking. Let us examine the points in which it varies from pure democracy, and we shall comprehend both the nature of the cure and the efficacy which it must derive from the Union.

The two great points of difference between a democracy and a republic are: first, the delegation of the government, in the latter, to a small number of citizens elected by the rest; secondly, the greater number of citizens, and greater sphere of country, over which the latter may be extended.

The effect of the first difference is, on the one hand, to refine and enlarge the public views, by passing them through the medium of a chosen body of citizens, whose wisdom may best discern the true interest of their country, and whose patriotism and love of justice will be least likely to sacrifice it to temporary or partial considerations. Under such a regulation, it may well happen that the public voice, pronounced by the representatives of the people, will be more consonant to the public good than if pronounced by the people themselves, convened for the purpose. On the other hand, the effect may be inverted. Men of factious tempers, of local prejudices, or of sinister designs, may, by intrigue, by corruption, or by other means, first obtain the suffrages, and then betray the interests, of the people. The question resulting is, whether small or extensive republics are more favorable to the election of proper guardians of the public weal; and it is clearly decided in favor of the latter by two obvious considerations:

In the first place, it is to be remarked that, however small the republic may be, the representatives must be raised to a certain number, in order to guard against the cabals of a few; and that, however large it may be, they must be limited to a certain number, in order to guard against the confusion of a multitude. Hence, the number of representatives in the two cases not being in proportion to that of the two constituents, and being proportionally greater in the small republic, it follows that, if the proportion of fit characters be not less in the large than in the small republic, the former will present a greater option, and consequently a greater probability of a fit choice.

In the next place, as each representative will be chosen by a greater number of citizens in the large than in the small republic, it will be more difficult for unworthy candidates to practice with success the vicious arts by which elections are too often carried; and the suffrages of the people being more free, will be more likely to centre in men who possess the most attractive merit and the most diffusive and established characters.

It must be confessed that in this, as in most other cases, there is a mean, on both sides of which inconveniences will be found to lie. By enlarging too much the number of electors, you render the representatives too little acquainted with all their local circumstances and lesser interests; as by reducing it too much, you render him unduly attached to these, and too little fit to comprehend and pursue great and national objects. The federal Constitution forms a happy combination in this respect; the great and aggregate interests being referred to the national, the local and particular to the State legislatures.

The other point of difference is, the greater number of citizens and extent of territory which may be brought within the compass of republican than of democratic government; and it is this circumstance principally which renders factious combinations less to be dreaded in the former than in the latter. The smaller the society, the fewer probably will be the distinct parties and interests composing it; the fewer the distinct parties and interests, the more frequently will a majority be found of the same party; and the smaller the number of individuals composing a majority, and the smaller the compass within which they are placed, the more easily will they concert and execute their plans of oppression. Extend the sphere, and you take in a greater variety of parties and interests; you make it less probable that a majority of the whole will have a common motive to invade the rights of other citizens; or if such a common motive exists, it will be more difficult for all who feel it to discover their own strength, and to act in unison with each other. Besides other impediments, it may be remarked that, where there is a consciousness of unjust or dis-

honorable purposes, communication is always checked by distrust in proportion to the number whose concurrence is necessary.

Hence, it clearly appears, that the same advantage which a republic has over a democracy, in controlling the effects of faction, is enjoyed by a large over a small republic,—is enjoyed by the Union over the States composing it. Does the advantage consist in the substitution of representatives whose enlightened views and virtuous sentiments render them superior to local prejudices and schemes of injustice? It will not be denied that the representation of the Union will be most likely to possess these requisite endowments. Does it consist in the greater security afforded by a greater variety of parties, against the event of any one party being able to outnumber and oppress the rest? In an equal degree does the increased variety of parties comprised within the Union, increase this security? Does it, in fine, consist in the greater obstacles opposed to the concert and accomplishment of the secret wishes of an unjust and interested majority? Here, again, the extent of the Union gives it the most palpable advantage.

The influence of factious leaders may kindle a flame within their particular States, but will be unable to spread a general conflagration through the other States. A religious sect may degenerate into a political faction in a part of the Confederacy; but the variety of sects dispersed over the entire face of it must secure the national councils against any danger from that source. A rage for paper money, for an abolition of debts, for an equal division of property, or for any other improper or wicked project, will be less apt to pervade the whole body of the Union than a particular member of it; in the same proportion as such a malady is more likely to taint a particular county or district, than an entire State.

In the extent and proper structure of the Union, therefore, we behold a republican remedy for the diseases most incident to republican government. And according to the degree of pleasure and pride we feel in being republicans, ought to be our zeal in cherishing the spirit and supporting the character of Federalists.

Publius

February 6, 1788
JAMES MADISON

TO THE PEOPLE OF THE STATE OF NEW YORK:

To what expedient, then, shall we finally resort, for maintaining in practice the necessary partition of power among the several departments, as laid down in the Constitution? The only answer that can be given is, that as all these exterior provisions are found to be inadequate, the defect must be supplied, by so contriving the interior structure of the government as that its several constituent parts may, by their mutual relations, be the means of keeping each other in their proper places. Without presuming to undertake a full development of this important idea, I will hazard a few general observations, which may perhaps place it in a clearer light, and enable us to form a more correct judgment of the principles and structure of the government planned by the convention.

In order to lay a due foundation for that separate and distinct exercise of the different powers of government, which to a certain extent is admitted on all hands to be essential to the preservation of liberty, it is evident that each department should have a will of its own; and consequently should be so constituted that the members of each should have as little agency as possible in the appointment of the members of the others. Were this principle rigorously adhered to, it would require that all the appointments for the supreme executive, legislative, and judiciary magistracies should be drawn from the same fountain of authority, the people, through channels having no communication whatever with one another. Perhaps such a plan of constructing the several departments would be less difficult in practice than it may in contemplation appear. Some difficulties, however, and some additional expense would attend the execution of it. Some deviations, therefore, from the principle must be admitted. In the constitution of the judiciary department in particular, it might be inexpedient to insist rigorously on the principle: first, because peculiar qualifications being essential in the members, the primary consideration ought to be to select that mode of choice which best secures these qualifications; secondly, because the permanent tenure by which the appointments are held in that department, must soon destroy all sense of dependence on the authority conferring them.

It is equally evident, that the members of each department should be as little dependent as possible on those of the others, for the emoluments annexed to their offices. Were the executive magistrate, or the judges, not independent of the legislature in this particular, their independence in every other would be merely nominal.

But the great security against a gradual concentration of the several powers in the same department, consists in giving to those who administer each department the necessary constitutional means and personal motives to resist encroachments of the others. The provision for defense must in this, as in all other cases, be made commensurate to the danger of attack. Ambition must be made to counteract ambition. The interest of the man must be connected with the constitutional rights of the place. It may be a reflection on human nature, that such devices should be necessary to control the abuses of government. But what is government itself, but the greatest of all reflections on human nature? If men were angels, no government would be necessary. If angels were to govern men, neither external nor internal controls on government would be necessary. In framing a government which is to be administered by men over men, the great difficulty lies in this: you must first enable the government to control the governed; and in the next place oblige it to control itself. A dependence on the people is, no doubt, the primary control on the government; but experience has taught mankind the necessity of auxiliary precautions.

This policy of supplying, by opposite and rival interests, the defect of better motives, might be traced through the whole system of human affairs, private as well as public. We see it particularly displayed in all the subordinate distributions of power, where the constant aim is to divide and arrange the several offices in such a manner as that each may be a check on the other—that the private interest of every individual may be a sentinel over the public rights. These inventions of prudence cannot be less requisite in the distribution of the supreme powers of the State.

But it is not possible to give to each department an equal power of self-defense. In republican government, the legislative authority necessarily predominates. The remedy for this inconveniency is to divide the legislature into different branches; and to render them, by different modes of election and different principles of action, as little connected with each other as the nature of their common functions and their common dependence on the society will admit. It may even be necessary to guard against dangerous encroachments by still further precautions. As the weight of the legislative authority requires that it should be thus divided, the weakness of the executive may require, on the other hand, that it should be fortified. An absolute negative on the legislature appears, at first view, to be the natural defense with which the executive magistrate should be armed. But perhaps it would be neither altogether safe nor alone sufficient. On ordinary occasions it might not be exerted with the requisite firmness, and on extraordinary occasions it might be perfidiously abused. May not this defect of an absolute negative be supplied by some qualified connection between this weaker department and the weaker branch of the stronger department, by which the latter may be led to support the constitutional rights of the former, without being too much detached from the rights of its own department?

If the principles on which these observations are founded be just, as I persuade myself they are, and they be applied as a criterion to the several State constitutions, and to the federal Constitution it will be found that if the latter does not perfectly correspond with them, the former are infinitely less able to bear such a test.

There are, moreover, two considerations particularly applicable to the federal system of America, which place that system in a very interesting point of view.

First. In a single republic, all the power surrendered by the people is submitted to the administration of a single government; and the usurpations are guarded against by a division of the government into distinct and separate departments. In the compound republic of America, the power surrendered by the people is first divided between two distinct governments, and then the portion allotted to each subdivided among distinct and separate departments. Hence a double security arises to the rights of the people. The different governments will control each other, at the same time that each will be controlled by itself.

Second. It is of great importance in a republic not only to guard the society against the oppression of its rulers, but to guard one part of the society against the injustice of the other part. Different interests necessarily exist in different classes of citizens. If a majority be united by a common interest, the rights of the minority will be insecure. There are but two methods of providing against this evil: the one by creating a will in the community independent of the majority—that is, of the society itself; the other, by comprehending in the society so many separate descriptions of citizens as will render an unjust combination of a majority of the whole very improbable, if not impracticable. The first method prevails in all governments possessing an hereditary or self-appointed authority. This, at best, is but a precarious security; because a power independent of the society may as well espouse the unjust views of the major, as the rightful interests of the minor party, and may possibly be turned against both parties. The second method will be exemplified in the federal republic of the United States. Whilst all authority in it will be derived from and dependent on the society, the society itself will be broken into so many parts, interests, and classes of citizens, that the rights of individuals, or of the minority, will be in little danger from interested combinations of the majority. In a free government the security for civil rights must be the same as that for religious rights. It consists in the one case in the multiplicity of interests, and in the other in the multiplicity of sects. The degree of security in both cases will depend on the number of interests and sects; and this may be presumed to depend on the extent of country and number of people comprehended under the same government. This view of the subject must particularly recommend a proper federal system to all the sincere and considerate friends of republican government, since it shows that in exact proportion as the territory of the Union may be formed into more circumscribed Confederacies, or States oppressive combinations of a majority will be facilitated: the best security, under the republican forms, for the rights of every class of citizens, will be diminished: and consequently the stability and independence of some member of the government, the only other security, must be proportionately increased. Justice is the end of government. It is the end of civil society. It ever has been and ever will be pursued until it be obtained, or until liberty be lost in the pursuit. In a society under the forms of which the stronger faction can readily unite and oppress the weaker, anarchy may as truly be said to reign as in a state of nature, where the weaker individual is not secured against the violence of the stronger; and as, in the latter state, even the stronger individuals are prompted, by the uncertainty of their condition, to submit to a government which may protect the weak as well as themselves; so, in the former state, will the more powerful factions or parties be gradually induced, by a like motive, to wish for a government which will protect all parties, the weaker as well as the more powerful. It can be little doubted that if the State of Rhode Island was separated from the Confederacy and left to itself, the insecurity of rights under the popular form of government within such narrow limits would be displayed by such reiterated oppressions of factious majorities that some power altogether independent of the people would soon be called for by the voice of the very factions whose misrule had proved the necessity of it. In the extended republic of the United States, and among the great variety of interests, parties, and sects which it embraces, a coalition of a majority of the whole society could seldom take place on any other principles than those of justice and the general good; whilst there being thus less danger to a minor from the will of a major party, there must be less pretext, also, to provide for the security of the former, by introducing into the government a will not dependent on the latter, or, in other words, a will independent of the society itself. It is no less certain than it is important, notwithstanding the contrary opinions which have been entertained, that the larger the society, provided it lie within a practical sphere, the more duly capable it will be of self-government. And happily for the *republican cause,* the practicable sphere may be carried to a very great extent, by a judicious modification and mixture of the *federal principle.*

Publius

THE DECLARATION OF SENTIMENTS

Seneca Falls Conference, 1848

When, in the course of human events, it becomes necessary for one portion of the family of man to assume among the people of the earth a position different from that which they have hitherto occupied, but one to which the laws of nature and of nature's God entitle them, a decent respect to the opinions of mankind requires that they should declare the causes that impel them to such a course.

We hold these truths to be self-evident: that all men and women are created equal; that they are endowed by their Creator with certain inalienable rights; that among these are life, liberty, and the pursuit of happiness; that to secure these rights governments are instituted, deriving their just powers from the consent of the governed. Whenever any form of government becomes destructive of these ends, it is the right of those who suffer from it to refuse allegiance to it, and to insist upon the institution of a new government, laying its foundation on such principles, and organizing its powers in such form, as to them shall seem most likely to effect their safety and happiness. Prudence, indeed, will dictate that governments long established should not be changed for light and transient causes; and accordingly all experience hath shown that mankind are more disposed to suffer, while evils are sufferable, than to right themselves by abolishing the forms to which they are accustomed. But when a long train of abuses and usurpations, pursuing invariably the same object, evinces a design to reduce them under absolute despotism, it is their duty to throw off such government, and to provide new guards for their future security. Such has been the patient sufferance of the women under this government, and such is now the necessity which constrains them to demand the equal station to which they are entitled.

The history of mankind is a history of repeated injuries and usurpations on the part of man toward woman, having in direct object the establishment of an absolute tyranny over her. To prove this, let facts be submitted to a candid world.

He has never permitted her to exercise her inalienable right to the elective franchise.

He has compelled her to submit to laws, in the formation of which she had no voice.

He has withheld from her rights which are given to the most ignorant and degraded men—both natives and foreigners.

Having deprived her of this first right of a citizen, the elective franchise, thereby leaving her without representation in the halls of legislation, he has oppressed her on all sides.

He has made her, if married, in the eye of the law, civilly dead.

He has taken from her all right in property, even to the wages she earns.

He has made her, morally, an irresponsible being, as she can commit many crimes with impunity, provided they be done in the presence of her husband. In the covenant of marriage, she is compelled to promise obedience to her husband, he becoming, to all intents and purposes, her master—the law giving him power to deprive her of her liberty, and to administer chastisement.

He has so framed the laws of divorce, as to what shall be the proper causes, and in case of separation, to whom the guardianship of the children shall be given, as to be wholly regardless of the happiness of women—the law, in all cases, going upon a false supposition of the supremacy of man, and giving all power into his hands.

After depriving her of all rights as a married woman, if single, and the owner of property, he has taxed her to support a government which recognizes her only when her property can be made profitable to it.

He has monopolized nearly all the profitable employments, and from those she is permitted to follow, she receives but a scanty remuneration. He closes against her all the avenues to wealth and distinction which he considers most honorable to himself. As a teacher of theology, medicine, or law, she is not known.

He has denied her the facilities for obtaining a thorough education, all colleges being closed against her.

He allows her in church, as well as state, but a subordinate position, claiming apostolic authority for her exclusion from the ministry, and, with some exceptions, from any public participation in the affairs of the church.

He has created a false public sentiment by giving to the world a different code of morals for men and women, by which moral delinquencies which exclude women from society, are not only tolerated, but deemed of little account in man.

He has usurped the prerogative of Jehovah himself, claiming it as his right to assign for her a sphere of action, when that belongs to her conscience and to her God.

He has endeavored, in every way that he could, to destroy her confidence in her own powers, to lessen her self-respect, and to make her willing to lead a dependent and abject life.

Now, in view of this entire disfranchisement of one-half the people of this country, their social and religious degradation—in view of the unjust laws above mentioned, and because women do feel themselves aggrieved, oppressed, and fraudulently deprived of their most sacred rights, we insist that they have immediate admission to all the rights and privileges which belong to them as citizens of the United States.

In entering upon the great work before us, we anticipate no small amount of misconception, misrepresentation, and ridicule; but we shall use every instrumentality within our power to effect our object. We shall employ agents, circulate tracts, petition the State and national Legislatures, and endeavor to enlist the pulpit and the press in our behalf. We hope this Convention will be followed by a series of Conventions, embracing every part of the country.

Firmly relying upon the final triumph of the Right and the True, we do this day affix our signatures to this declaration.

Harriet Cady Eaton
Elizabeth M'Clintock
Mary M'Clintock
Margaret Pryor
Eunice Newton Foote
Margaret Schooley
Catherine F. Stebbins
Mary Ann Frink
Lydia Mount
Delia Matthews
Catharine C. Paine
Mary H. Hallowell
Sarah Hallowell
Catharine Shaw
Deborah Scott
Mary Gilbert
Sophrone Taylor
Cynthia Davis
Hannah Plant
Lucy Jones
Sarah Whitney
Elizabeth Conklin
Lucretia Coffin Mott
Mary Ann M'Clintock
Susan Quinn
Mary S. Mirror
Phebe King
Julia Ann Drake
Charlotte Woodard
Martha Underhill
Dorothy Matthews
Eunice Baker

Sarah R. Woods
Lydia Gild
Sarah Hoffman
Elizabeth Leslie
Martha Ridley
Rachel D. Bonnel
Betsey Tewksbury
Rhoda Palmer
Margaret Jenkins
Cynthia Fuller
Mary Martin
P. A. Culvert
Susan R. Doty
Rebecca Race
Martha Coffin Wright
Jane C. Hunt
Sarah A. Mosher
Mary E. Vail
Lucy Spaulding
Lavinia Latham
Sarah Smith
Eliza Martin
Maria E. Wilbur
Elizabeth D. Smith
Caroline Barker
Ann Porter
Experience Gibbs
Antoinette E. Segur
Hannah J. Latham
Sarah Sisson
Malvina Seymour
Phebe Mosher

Joel Bunker
Isaac Van Tassel
Thomas Dell
E. W. Capron
Stephen Shear
Henry Hatley
Amy Post
Frederick Douglass
Richard P. Hunt
Samuel D. Tillman
Justin Williams
Elisha Foote
Henry W. Seymour
David Salding
William G. Barker
Elias J. Doty
John Jones
William S. Dell
William Burroughs
Azaliah Schooley
Robert Smalldridge
Jacob Matthews
Charles L. Hoskins
Thomas M'Clintock
Saron Phillips
Jacob Chamberlain
Johnathan Metcalf
Nathan J. Milliken
S. E. Woodworth
Edward F. Underhill
George W. Pryor

GLOSSARY

A

ability to pay Taxes that are based not on the benefit received but on the wealth, or ability to pay, of an individual.

absentee voting The casting of a ballot in advance by mail in situations where illness, travel, or other circumstances prevent voters from voting in their precinct.

acting governor The position held by the lieutenant governor, who performs the functions of the office of governor when a governor leaves a state.

administrative adjudication The process by which agencies resolve disputes over the implementation of their administrative rules.

administrative discretion The authority delegated to bureaucrats to use their expertise and judgment when determining how to implement public policy.

administrative law The name given to agencies' rulemaking and resolution of conflicts regarding their rules.

administrative rule making The process by which an independent commission or agency fills in the details of a vague law by formulating, proposing, and approving rules, regulations, and standards that will be enforced to implement the policy.

advice and consent The Senate's authority to approve or reject the president's top appointments.

affirmative action In the employment arena, intentional efforts to recruit, hire, train, and promote underutilized categories of workers (women and minority men); in higher education, intentional efforts to diversify the student body.

agency review Part of the committee or subcommittee process of considering a bill, wherein committee members ask executive agencies that would administer the law for written comments on the measure.

agenda setting The determination by Congress of which public issues the government should consider for legislation.

agents of socialization The individuals, organizations, and institutions that facilitate the acquisition of political views.

agricultural associations Interest groups that represent different types of farmers and businesses that provide farming supplies.

al-Qaeda A radical international Islamic fundamentalist terror organization.

American dream The belief that in the United States hard work and persistence will reap a financially secure, happy and healthy life, with upward social mobility.

amicus curiae **brief ("friend of the court" brief)** A document submitted by parties interested in a certain case or issue in an attempt to provide the Court with information that may be used to decide the case.

annual voter registration A system that requires citizens to reregister every year.

Anti-Federalists Individuals who opposed ratification of the Constitution because they were deeply suspicious of the powers it gave to the national government and of the impact these powers would have on states' authority and individual freedoms.

appellate jurisdiction The authority of a court to review the decision reached by another court in a case.

appointive power The ability of a governor to appoint and remove important state administrators.

appointive-elective system The Texas system in which many judges are initially appointed to a seat on the court and later must stand for election.

appropriation law A law that gives bureaucracies and other government entities the legal authority to spend money.

approval ratings The percentage of survey respondents who say that they "approve" or "strongly approve" of the way the president is doing his job.

articles of impeachment Charges against the president during an impeachment.

at-large election system System in which all voters in the city elect the mayor and city council members.

attentive public The segment of voters who pay careful attention to political issues.

attorney general In Texas, chief counsel to the governor and state agencies; has limited criminal jurisdiction.

Australian ballot A secret ballot prepared by the government, distributed to all eligible voters, and, when balloting is completed, counted by government officials in an unbiased fashion, without corruption or regard to individual preferences.

authoritarianism A system of government in which the government holds strong powers but is checked by some forces.

authorization law A law that provides the plan of action to address a given societal concern and identifies the executive branch unit that will put the plan into effect.

B

bad tendency test A standard established in the 1925 case *Gitlow v. New York,* whereby any speech that has the tendency to incite crime or disturb the public peace can be silenced.

balance of power system A system of international alliances that, in theory, would balance the power of one group of nations against the power of another group and thus discourage war.

balanced budget A budget in which the government's expenditures are equal to or less than its revenues.

balanced ticket The selection of a running mate who brings diversity of ideology, geographic region, age, gender, race, or ethnicity to the slate.

ballot form The form used by voters to cast their ballot; in Texas, each county, with approval of the secretary of state, determines the form of the ballot.

ballot wording Description of a proposed amendment as it appears on the ballot, which can be noninstructive and misleading to voters.

bandwidth The amount of data that can travel through a network in a given time period.

benefit-based taxes Taxes for which there is a relationship between the amount paid in taxes and services received, such as gasoline taxes.

bicameral A legislative body composed of two chambers.

biennial session Meeting of the legislature every two years.

bill A proposed piece of legislation.

Bill of Rights The first ten amendments to the Constitution, which were ratified in 1791, constituting an enumeration of the individual liberties with which the government is forbidden to interfere.

"birthright" characteristics Social and economic characteristics of legislators that match certain demographic characteristics of many people in their district.

Black Codes Laws passed immediately after the Civil War by the confederate states that limited the rights of "freemen" (former slaves).

blanket primary A type of primary that allows voters to vote in either party's primary, and voters can choose to vote in *both* parties' primaries for different offices.

block grant The intergovernmental transfer of money that has fewer conditions of aid than a categorical grant and is used for broadly defined policy areas; it is distributed based on complicated formulas.

blogosphere A community, or social network, of bloggers.

brief A document detailing the legal argument for the desired outcome in a court case.

brinkmanship The Cold War–era practice of fooling the enemy by going to the edge (the brink), even if the party using the brinkmanship strategy had no intention of following it through.

Brown v. Board of Education of Topeka This 1954 Supreme Court decision ruled that segregated schools violated the equal protection clause of the Fourteenth Amendment.

budget authority The authority provided by law for agencies to obligate government spending.

budget deficit More money spent than collected through revenues.

budget fix A provision of the budget, mandated by state laws and constitutional amendments, that sets aside money to be spent on specific items.

budget reconciliation The annual process of rewriting authorization legislation to comply with the expenditure ceiling and revenue floor of the concurrent budget resolution for the upcoming fiscal year.

budget surplus Money left over after all expenses are paid.

budgetary powers The ability of a governor to formulate a budget, present it to the legislature, and execute or control it.

bureaucracy Any organization with a hierarchical structure, although most commonly used to designate a government agency or the collection of all national executive branch organizations.

bureaucrats People employed in a government executive branch unit to implement public policy; a public administrator; a public servant.

Bush Doctrine The argument, articulated by President George W. Bush, that unilateral action directly targeted at an enemy is both justifiable and feasible.

business regulation Government rules, regulations, and standards, directed at protecting competition in the marketplace.

C

cabinet The group of experts chosen by the president to serve as advisers on running the country.

calendars Procedures in the Texas House of Representatives used to consider different kinds of bills. Major bills and minor bills are considered under different procedures.

Calendars Committee Standing committee of the Texas House of Representatives that decides which bills will be considered for floor debate and to which committee they will be assigned.

campaign consultant A paid professional who specializes in the overall management of political campaigns or an aspect of campaigns.

campaign manager A professional whose duties comprise a variety of strategic and managerial tasks, from fund-raising to staffing a campaign.

campaign strategy The blueprint for the campaign, including a budget and fundraising plan, an advertising strategy, a staffing plan.

candidate committees Organizations that candidates form to support their individual election.

candidate-centered campaign A campaign in which the individual seeking election, rather than an entire party slate, is the focus.

capitalism An economic system in which the means of producing wealth are privately owned and operated to produce profits.

capture The situation in which a state agency or board falls under the heavy influence of its constituency interest groups.

casework Personal work by a member of Congress on behalf of a constituent or group of constituents, typically aimed at getting the government to do something the constituent wants done.

cash transfer The direct provision of cash (in forms including checks, debit cards, and tax breaks) to eligible individuals or to providers of goods or services to eligible individuals.

categorical formula grant The intergovernmental transfer of money for a specified program area for which the amount of money a government is eligible to receive is based on a legislated formula.

categorical project grant The intergovernmental transfer of money for a specified program area for which recipients compete by proposing specific projects they want to implement.

caucus A meeting of all members of the political party in one chamber in which they elect leaders, approve committee assignments, and elect committee chairpersons.

centralized federalism The relationship between the national and state governments whereby the national government imposes its policy preferences on state governments.

ceremonial duties A governor's duties to attend many functions and represent the state.

chad A ready-made perforation on a punch card ballot.

changing political climate Changing national politics and immigration are changing the politics of the state of Texas from Democratic to Republican domination.

checks and balances The mechanisms by which each branch of government can monitor and limit the functions of the other branches.

chief justice The leading justice on the Supreme Court, who provides both organizational and intellectual leadership.

chief legislator A role of governors in which they spend time and energy presenting an active agenda of legislation to the legislature and working to pass that agenda.

chief of staff Among the most important staff members of the White House Office (WHO); serves as both an adviser to the president and the manager of the WHO.

circuit courts Also known as *courts of appeals;* the middle level in the federal court structure.

circuit riding The practice of traveling around the circuits by early Supreme Court justices and district court judges to hear appeals cases.

citizens Those members of the polity who, through birth or naturalization, enjoy the rights, privileges, and responsibilities attached to membership in a given nation.

city manager Official hired by the city council to manage the city and serve as chief administrative officer.

civic engagement Individual and collective actions designed to identify and address issues of public concern.

civil law case A conflict between private individuals in which the plaintiff alleges that some action or inaction by the defendant has resulted in harm to him or her.

civil disobedience Active, but nonviolent, refusal to comply with laws or governmental policies that are morally objectionable.

civil liberties Constitutionally established guarantees that protect citizens, opinions, and property against arbitrary government interference.

civil rights The rights and privileges guaranteed to all citizens under the equal protection and due process clauses of the Fifth and Fourteenth amendments; the idea that individuals are protected from discrimination based on characteristics such as race, national origin, religion, and sex.

civil servants Bureaucrats hired through a merit-based personnel system who have job protection.

clash of civilizations thesis Samuel Huntington's idea that bitter cultural conflict will continue and escalate between modern Western democracies and fundamentalist Islamic states.

clear and present danger test A standard established in the 1919 Supreme Court case *Schenck v. U.S.,* whereby the government may silence speech or expression when there is a clear and present danger that this speech will bring about some harm that the government has the power to prevent.

clear and probable danger test A standard established in the 1951 case *Dennis v. U.S.* whereby the government could suppress speech to avoid grave danger, even if the probability of the dangerous result was relatively remote; replaced by the imminent lawless action (incitement) test in 1969.

climate control The practice of using public outreach to build favorable public opinion of an organization.

closed primary A type of primary in which voting in a party's primary is limited to members of that party.

closed rider Provision attached to appropriations bills of the Texas legislature that is not made public until the conference committee meets.

cloture A procedural move in which a supermajority of sixty senators agrees to end a filibuster.

coattail effect The phenomenon by which candidates running for a lower-level office such as city council benefit in an election from the popularity of a top-of-ticket nominee.

code law Laws created by legislators to regulate the behavior of individuals and organizations.

Cold War The political, ideological, and military conflict that lasted from 1945 until 1990 between communist nations led by the Soviet Union and Western democracies led by the United States.

collective bargaining Negotiations on wages, hours, and other working conditions between employers and employees.

collective defense The concept that allied nations agree to defend one another in the face of an invasion.

collective goods Outcomes shared by the general public; also called *public goods.*

collective security The idea that peace could be achieved if nations agreed to collectively oppose any nation that attacked another country.

collegial court A court made up of a group of judges who must evaluate a case together and decide on the outcome; significant compromise and negotiation take place as members try to build a majority coalition.

commercial speech Advertising statements that describe products.

committee assignments Decisions by the speaker of the Texas House of Representatives on which members of the House sit on each committee; some committees, such as appropriations, are more powerful than others.

common law Law made by judges who decide cases and articulate legal principles in their opinions; based upon the British system.

comptroller of public accounts Chief tax collector, revenue forecaster, and investor of state funds in Texas; the comptroller does not perform financial audits.

concurrent budget resolution A document approved by the House and Senate at the beginning of their budget process that establishes binding expenditure ceilings and a binding revenue floor as well as proposed expenditure levels for major policies.

concurrent powers The basic governing functions of all sovereign governments; in the United States they are held by the national, state, and local governments and include the authority to tax, to make policy, to implement policy, and the power of eminent domain.

concurring opinion A judicial opinion agreeing with how the majority decides the case but disagreeing with at least some of the legal interpretations or conclusions reached by the majority.

confederal system A structure of government in which several independent sovereign governments agree to cooperate on specified governmental matters while retaining sovereignty over all other governmental matters within their jurisdictions.

confederation A national government composed of a league of independent states and in which the central government has less power than the member states.

conference committee A bicameral, bipartisan committee composed of legislators whose job is to reconcile two versions of a bill.

conflict of interest In the case of public servants, the situation when they can personally benefit from a decision they make or an action they take in the process of doing their jobs.

conflicted federalism The current status of national-state relations that has elements of dual and cooperative federalism, with an overall centralizing tendency at the same time that elements of policy are devolved.

Connecticut Compromise (Great Compromise) At the constitutional convention, the compromise between the Virginia Plan and the New Jersey Plan that created a bicameral legislature with one chamber's representation based on population and the other having two members for each state.

consent of the governed The idea that, in a democracy, the government's power derives from the consent of the people.

conservatism An ideology that emphasizes preserving tradition and relying on community and family as mechanisms of continuity in society.

constables Elected county law enforcement and court officers.

constitution A document that describes three basic components of an organization: its mission, foundational structures, and essential processes.

constitutional convention An assembly of citizens who may propose changes to state constitutions for voter approval.

constitutional county judge Chief administrative officer of the county commissioner's court in Texas; may also have judicial duties in rural counties.

constitutional law The body of law that comes out of the courts in cases involving the interpretation of the Constitution.

constitutionalism Government that is structured by law, and in which the power of government is limited.

consumer price index (CPI) The most common measure of inflation, it measures the average change in prices over time of a "market basket" of goods and services.

consumer taxes Taxes that citizens pay when they buy goods and services, such as sales taxes.

containment The Cold War–era policy of preventing the spread of communism, mainly by providing military and economic aid as well as political advice to countries vulnerable to a communist takeover.

continuing resolution An agreement of the House and Senate that authorizes agencies not covered by approved appropriation laws to continue to spend money within their previous budget year's levels.

contracting-out Also called *outsourcing* or *privatizing;* a process by which the government contracts with a private for-profit or nonprofit organization to provide public services or resources needed by the government.

contributory program (social insurance program) A benefit provided only to those who paid the specific tax created to fund the benefit.

convergence The merging of various forms of media, including newspapers, television stations, radio networks, and blogs, under one corporate roof and one set of business editorial leaders.

cooperative federalism The relationship between the national and state governments whereby the two levels of government work together to address domestic matters reserved to the states, driven by the policy priorities of the states.

council-manager form of government A form of government in which voters elect a mayor and a city council; the mayor and the city council appoint a professional administrator to manage the city.

country desk The official operation of the U.S. government in each country that has diplomatic ties to the United States.

county chair Party official elected in each county to organize and support the party.

county clerk Elected chief record keeper for the county.

county commissioner's court Legislative body made up of five elected officials that governs Texas counties.

county and district attorneys Elected chief prosecuting attorneys for criminal cases.

county executive committee Committee made up of the county chair and all precinct chairs in the county; serves as the official organization for the party in each Texas county.

county government The oldest type of local government, adapted from the British, whose numbers vary greatly among states; it is the primary administrative arm of a state government, providing services such as voter registration, operation of courts and jails, and maintenance of roads and bridges.

county sheriff The elected head law enforcement officer for a county who in smaller counties may act as the tax assessor collector.

county treasurer Elected official who manages county funds.

courts of appeals The intermediate appellate courts in the federal system that review previous decisions made by courts in the federal or state judicial system.

creationism A theory of the creation of the earth and humankind that is based on a literal interpretation of the biblical story of Genesis.

criminal due process rights Safeguards for those accused of crime; these rights constrain government conduct in investigating crimes, trying cases, and punishing offenders.

criminal law case A case brought by the government or a prosecutor against a defendant, alleging that he or she has engaged in conduct resulting in injury to another person, and that this injury is so significant that it harms not only the individual but also the larger society.

cross pressuring The presence of two conditions or traits that pull a voter toward different political parties.

crossover voting A voting pattern in which voters from one party vote in the primaries of another party.

cumulative voting A system in which voters can concentrate (accumulate) all their votes on one candidate rather than casting one vote for each office up for election.

D

de facto segregation Segregation caused by the fact that people tend to live in neighborhoods with others of their own race, religion, or ethnic group.

de jure segregation Segregation mandated by law.

dealignment The situation in which fewer voters support the two major political parties, instead identifying themselves as independent, or splitting their ticket between candidates from more than one party.

decentralized nation A country, such as the United States, that possesses many units of local government controlled by citizens at the local level.

defendant A person who is defending himself or herself against a plaintiff's accusation.

defense conversion President Jimmy Carter's attempt to convert the nation's vast military apparatus to peacetime functions.

deficit spending Government expenditures costing more than is raised in taxes, leading to borrowing and debt.

democracy Government in which supreme power of governance lies in the hands of its citizens.

denials of power A way to limit the power of government by explicitly listing the powers that governments may not use.

department One of fifteen executive branch units responsible for a broadly defined policy area and whose top administrator (secretary) is appointed by the president, is confirmed by the Senate, and serves at the discretion of the president.

depression A long-term and severe recession.

deregulated tuition A policy allowing universities in Texas to set their own tuition.

deregulation The reduction or elimination of regulatory restrictions on firms and industries.

détente The easing of tensions between the United States and its communist rivals.

deterrence The idea that nations would be less likely to engage in nuclear war if adversaries each had first-strike capability.

devolution The process whereby the national government returns policy responsibilities to state and/or local governments.

digital divide The inequality of access to computers and Internet connections.

diplomacy The conduct of international relations, particularly involving the negotiation of treaties and other agreements between nations.

direct provision A policy tool whereby the government that creates a policy hires public servants to provide the service.

direct subsidy A cash transfer from general revenues to particular persons or private companies engaged in activities that the national government believes support the public good.

director of national intelligence (DNI) The person responsible for coordinating and overseeing all the intelligence agencies within the executive branch.

discharge petition A special tactic used to extract a bill from a committee in order to have it considered by the entire House.

discretionary funding Those funds in the state budget that are not earmarked for specific purposes.

discretionary spending Payment on programs for which Congress and the president must approve budget authority each year in appropriation legislation.

discuss list Compiled by the chief justice, the list of cases on review that he thinks may be appropriate for the Court to hear.

dissenting opinion A judicial opinion disagreeing both with the majority's disposition of a case and with their legal interpretations and conclusions.

district clerk Elected official who maintains county and district court records.

district judge Elected official who appoints the county auditor.

diversity of citizenship The circumstance in which the parties in a legal case are from different states or the case involves a U.S. citizen and a foreign government.

divided government The situation that exists when Congress is controlled by one party and the presidency by the other.

divine right of kings The assertion that monarchies, as a manifestation of God's will, could rule absolutely without regard to the will or well-being of their subjects.

domino theory The principle that if one nation fell to communism, other nations in its geographic vicinity also would succumb.

double jeopardy To be tried again for the same crime that one has been cleared of in court; barred by the Fifth Amendment.

dual court system A two-part judicial system such as that of the United States, which has both federal and state courts.

dual federalism The relationship between the national and state governments, dominant between 1789 and 1932, whereby the two levels of government functioned independently of each other to address their distinct constitutional responsibilities.

dual sovereignty The existence of two governments, each with sovereignty over different matters at the same time; neither level is sovereign over the other.

due process The legal safeguards that prevent the government from arbitrarily depriving citizens of life, liberty, or property; guaranteed by the Fifth and Fourteenth amendments.

E

earmark A designation within a spending bill that provides for a specific expenditure.

earmarked taxes Taxes dedicated to a specific expenditure.

e-campaigning The practice of mobilizing voters using the Internet.

economic boom Rapid economic growth.

economic diversity An economy based on many types of economic activity rather than one or a few activities.

economic incentives Motivation to join an interest group because the group works for policies that will provide members with material benefits.

economic regions Divisions of the state of Texas based on dominant economic activity.

economic regulation Government constraints on business practices aimed at ensuring competition in the marketplace and a healthy economy.

economy The system of transactions by which goods and services are distributed in the marketplace.

efficacy Citizens' belief that they have the ability to achieve something desirable and that the government listens to people like them.

electioneering Working to influence the election of candidates who support the organization's issues.

Electoral College A group of people elected by voters in each state to elect the president and the vice president.

elite theory A theory that holds that a group of wealthy, educated individuals wields most political power.

emergency powers Broad powers exercised by the president during times of national crisis.

eminent domain The authority of government to compel a property owner to sell private property to a government to further the public good.

entitlement program A government benefit guaranteed to all who meet the eligibility requirements.

enumerated powers The powers of the national government that are listed in the Constitution.

environmental racism The term for the higher incidence of environmental threats and subsequent health problems in lower-income communities, which frequently are also communities dominated by people of color.

equal protection clause The Fourteenth Amendment clause stating that no state shall "deny to any person within its jurisdiction the equal protection of the laws."

equity of representation Situation in which each member of a legislature represents about the same number of people.

establishment clause The First Amendment clause that bars the government from passing any law "respecting an establishment of religion"; often interpreted as a separation of church and state but increasingly questioned.

exclusionary rule The criminal procedural rule stating that evidence obtained illegally cannot be used in a trial.

executive agreement An international agreement between the United States and other nations, not subject to Senate approval and only in effect during the administration of the president who negotiates the agreement.

executive budget The budget document and budget message that explains the president's fiscal plan.

Executive Office of the President (EOP) The offices, counsels, and boards that help the president to carry out his day-to-day responsibilities.

executive order The power of the president to issue orders that carry the force of law.

executive privilege The right of the chief executive and members of the administration to withhold information from Congress or the courts, or the right to refuse to appear before legislative or judicial bodies.

exit polls Polls conducted at polling places on Election Day to determine the winner of an election before the polls close.

expressed powers Presidential powers enumerated in the Constitution.

extra territorial jurisdiction (ETJ) City powers that extend beyond the city limits to an adjacent area.

extradition The return of a person accused of a crime to the state in which the crime was committed upon the request of that state's governor.

extraordinary rendition Apprehending an individual believed to be a terrorist and transferring the person to another nation.

extraordinary session Legislative session called by the state legislature, rather than the governor; not used in Texas.

F

fairness doctrine The requirement that stations provide equal time to all parties regarding important public issues and equal access to airtime to all candidates for public office.

federal question A question of law based on interpretation of the U.S. Constitution, federal laws, or treaties.

federal system A governmental structure with two levels of government and in which each level has sovereignty over different governmental functions and policy matters.

The Federalist Papers A series of essays, written by James Madison, Alexander Hamilton, and John Jay, that argued for the ratification of the Constitution.

Federalists Individuals who supported the new Constitution as presented by the Constitutional Convention in 1787.

feminization of poverty The phenomenon of increasing numbers of unmarried, divorced, and separated women with children living in poverty.

fighting words Speech that is likely to bring about public disorder or chaos; the Supreme Court has held that this speech may be banned in public places to ensure the preservation of public order.

filibuster A procedural move by a member of the Senate to attempt to halt passage of a bill, during which the senator can speak for an unlimited time on the Senate floor.

fireside chats President Franklin Roosevelt's radio addresses to the country.

fiscal policy Government spending and taxing and their effect on the economy.

fiscal year (FY) The twelve months during which the government implements its annual budget, beginning on October 1 and ending on September 30 of the following year.

527 A tax-exempt group that raises money for political activities, much like those allowed under the soft money loophole.

focus group Opinion research technique in which a panel of "average citizens" is asked to react to issues or words.

food insecurity The situation in which people have a limited or an uncertain ability to obtain, in socially acceptable ways, enough nutritious food to live a healthy and active life.

foreign service officers The diplomatic and consular staff at U.S. embassies abroad.

fragmented government structure A government structure in which power is dispersed to many state agencies with no central control.

framing The process by which the media set a context that helps consumers understand important events and matters of shared interest.

franchise fee A type of business income tax levied in Texas.

free exercise clause The First Amendment clause prohibiting the government from enacting laws prohibiting an individual's practice of his or her religion; often in contention with the establishment clause.

free rider problem The phenomenon of someone deriving benefit from others' actions.

free trade policy The elimination of tariffs and nontariff trade barriers so that international trade is expanded.

freedom of assembly The right to form or join any type of organization, political party, or club without penalty.

full faith and credit clause The constitutional clause that requires states to comply with and uphold the public acts, records, and judicial decisions of other states.

fund-raising consultant A professional who works with candidates in identifying likely contributors to the campaign and arranging events and meetings with donors.

G

gender gap The measurable difference in the way women and men vote for candidates and in the way they view political issues.

general election An election that determines which candidates win the offices being sought.

general-law city A city whose charter is created by state statutes.

general-purpose government A government given broad discretionary authority by the state government.

generational effect The impact of an important external event in shaping the views of a generation.

gerrymandering The drawing of legislative district boundaries to benefit an incumbent, a political party, or another group.

global economy The worldwide economy created by the integration and interdependence of national economies.

global warming The rising temperature of the earth as a result of pollution that traps solar heat, keeping the air warmer than it would otherwise be.

globalism The interconnectedness between nations in contemporary times.

GOTV Get out the vote.

government The institution that creates and implements policy and laws that guide the conduct of the nation and its citizens.

government corporation An executive branch unit that sells a service and is expected to be financially self-sufficient.

grand jury A jury of citizens that determines whether a person will be charged with a crime.

grandfather clause A clause exempting individuals from voting conditions such as poll taxes or literacy tests if they or their ancestor had voted before 1870, thus sparing most white voters in the South.

grant-in-aid (intergovernmental transfer) The transfer of money from one government to another government (or from a government to a nonprofit organization, for-profit organization, or individual) that does not need to be paid back.

grants of power A way to limit the power of government by explicitly listing the powers that governments may use.

grassroots organizing Tasks that involve direct contact with voters or potential voters.

Great Depression Between 1929 and 1939, a time of devastating economic collapse and personal misery for people around the world.

greenhouse effect The heating of the earth's atmosphere as a result of humans' burning of fossil fuels and the resultant buildup of carbon dioxide and other gases.

gross domestic product (GDP) The total value of all goods and services produced by labor and properties within a country's borders.

H

habeas corpus An ancient right that protects an individual in custody from being held without the right to be heard in a court of law.

hard money Regulated campaign contributions that can specifically advocate the election of a candidate.

hate crime A crime committed against a person, property, or society, where the offender is motivated, in part or in whole, by his or her bias against the victim because of the victim's race, religion, disability, sexual orientation, or ethnicity.

hearings Sessions held by committees or subcommittees to gather information and views from experts.

heightened scrutiny test (intermediate scrutiny test) The guidelines used most frequently by the courts to determine the legality of sex-based discrimination; on the basis of this test, sex-based discrimination is legal if the government can prove that it is substantially related to the achievement of an important public interest.

Holocaust The genocide perpetrated by Adolf Hitler and the Nazis of six million Jews, along with political dissidents, Catholics, homosexuals, and gypsies.

home-rule city A city whose charter is created by the actions of local citizens.

honeymoon period A time early in a new president's administration characterized by optimistic approval by the public.

hopper A wooden box that sits on a desk at the front of the House of Representatives, into which House members place bills they want to introduce.

Hopwood **decision** A controversial 1996 case in which a federal court reversed affirmative action at the University of Texas law school.

horizontal federalism The state-to-state relationships created by the U.S. Constitution.

House majority leader The leader of the majority party, who helps the Speaker develop and implement strategy and work with other members of the House of Representatives.

House minority leader The leader of the minority party, whose job mirrors that of the majority leader but without the power that comes from holding a majority in the House of Representatives.

household income The total pretax earnings of all residents over the age of 15 living in a home.

housing insecurity The situation in which people have limited or uncertain ability to obtain, in socially acceptable ways, affordable, safe, and decent-quality permanent housing.

Human Development Index (HDI) A UN-created measure to determine how well a country's economy is providing for a long and healthy life, knowledge, and a decent standard of living.

I

imminent lawless action test (incitement test) A standard established in the 1969 *Brandenburg v. Ohio* case whereby speech is restricted only if it goes beyond mere advocacy, or words, to create a high likelihood of imminent disorder or lawlessness.

impeach Formally charging a government official with not fulfilling constitutional duties or with committing a high crime or misdemeanor.

impeachment The power of the House of Representatives to formally accuse the president (and other high-ranking officials, including the vice president and federal judges) of crimes.

implicit or explicit prohibition on city ordinance power Limitation on the power of cities, preventing them from passing ordinances that are explicitly prohibited by state law and from passing ordinances that by implication may violate state law.

implied powers The powers of the national government that are not enumerated in the Constitution but that Congress claims are necessary and proper for the national government to fulfill its enumerated powers in accordance with the necessary and proper clause of the Constitution.

impressment The forcible removal of merchant sailors from U.S. ships on the spurious grounds that the sailors were deserters from the British Navy.

income inequality The gap in the proportion of national income held by the richest compared to that held by the poorest.

income-elastic taxes Taxes that rise and fall quickly relative to changes in economic conditions; the Texas tax system is very income-elastic.

incorporation The process of creating a city government.

incumbency The situation of already holding the office that is up for reelection.

independent Often used as a synonym for unaffiliated voter.

independent administrative agency An executive branch unit created by Congress and the president that is responsible for a narrowly defined function and whose governing board is intended to be protected from partisan politics.

independent candidate A person who has collected a required number of signatures on a petition to have her or his name appear on the ballot without a political party designation.

independent expenditures Outlays by PACs and others, typically for advertising for or against a candidate, but uncoordinated with a candidate's campaign.

independent regulatory commission An executive branch unit responsible for developing standards of behavior within specific industries and businesses, monitoring compliance with these standards, and imposing sanctions on violators.

independent school districts School districts that are not attached to any other unit of government and operate schools in Texas.

indexed benefit A government benefit with an automatic cost of living increase based on the rate of inflation.

indirect democracy Sometimes called a *representative democracy,* a system in which citizens elect representatives who decide policies on behalf of their constituents.

individualistic subculture A political subculture that expects government to handle functions demanded of it by the people and to intervene in individuals' lives as little as necessary.

inflation The decreased value of money as evidenced by increased prices.

informal rules Set of norms or values that govern legislative behavior.

information (administrative hearing) A hearing before a judge who decides whether a person must stand trial; used in place of a grand jury.

information equilibrium The dissemination of information outside traditional channels of control.

infotainment News shows that combine entertainment and news, a hybrid of the words *information* and *entertainment.*

inherent characteristics Individual attributes such as race, national origin, religion, and sex.

inherent powers Presidential powers that are implied in the Constitution.

initiative A process that allows citizens to propose changes to the state constitution through the use of petitions signed by registered voters; Texas does not have these procedures at the state level.

in-kind assistance A benefit program in which the recipient shops for a service provider who will accept payment from the government for the service or item purchased.

inspectors general Political appointees who work within a government agency to ensure the integrity of public service by investigating allegations of misconduct by bureaucrats.

instant runoff election A special runoff election in which the computerized voting machine simulates the elimination of last-place vote-getters.

instructed delegate model A model of representation in which legislators, as representatives of their constituents, should vote in keeping with the constituents' views, even if those views contradict the legislators' personal views.

intelligent design The theory that the apparent design in the universe and in living things is the product of an intelligent cause rather than of an undirected process such as natural selection: its primary proponents believe that the designer is God and seek to redefine science to accept supernatural explanations.

interest groups Organizations that seek to achieve some of their goals by influencing government decision making.

intergovernmental coordinator A role of governors in which they coordinate activities with other state and federal officials.

intergovernmental lobbying Efforts by groups representing state and local governments to influence national domestic policy.

intergovernmental relations (IGR) The collaborative efforts of two or more levels of government working to serve the public.

interim committees Temporary committees of the Texas legislature that study issues between regular sessions and make recommendations on legislation.

intermestics The influence of domestic interests on foreign policy.

International Monetary Fund (IMF) The institution charged with regulating monetary relationships among nations, including establishment of exchange rates for major world currencies; established in 1944 by the Bretton Woods Agreement.

interstate compacts Agreements between states that Congress has the authority to review and reject.

interventionism A foreign policy characterized by a nation's willingness to participate and intervene in international situations, including another country's affairs.

iron triangle The interaction of mutual interests among members of Congress, executive agencies, and organized interests during policy making.

isolationism A foreign policy characterized by a nation's unwillingness to participate in international affairs.

issue network The web of connections among those concerned about a policy and those who create and administer the policy.

J

Jacksonian statehouse government A system in which most of the major department heads in state government are chosen by the voters at the ballot box.

Jim Crow laws Laws requiring the strict separation of racial groups, with whites and "nonwhites" required to attend separate schools, work in different jobs, and use segregated public accommodations, such as transportation and restaurants.

joint committee A bicameral committee composed of members of both chambers of Congress.

joint referral The practice, abolished in the 104th Congress, by which a bill could be referred to two different committees for consideration.

judicial activism An approach to judicial decision making whereby judges apply their authority to bring about specific social goals.

judicial powers of governors The ability of a governor to issue pardons, executive clemency, and parole for citizens convicted of a crime.

judicial restraint An approach to judicial decision making whereby judges defer to the democratically elected legislative and executive branches of government.

judicial review Court authority to determine that an action taken by any government official or governing body violates the Constitution.

judiciary The branch of government comprising the state and federal courts and the judges who preside over them.

jurisdiction The power of a court to hear a case and to resolve it, given to a court by either a constitution or a statute.

justice (of a court) Any of the nine judges who sit on the Supreme Court.

K

Keynesian economics The theory that recommends that during a recession the national government should increase its spending and decrease taxes, and during a boom, it should cut spending and increase taxes.

L

laissez-faire The hands-off stance of a government in regard to the marketplace.

land commissioner Elected official responsible for administration and oversight of state-owned lands and coastal lands extending 10.3 miles into the Gulf of Mexico.

land-based economy An economic system in which most wealth is derived from the use of the land.

lead committee The primary committee considering a bill.

League of Nations A representative body founded in the aftermath of World War I to establish the collective security of nations.

Legislative Audit Committee Legislative agency that performs audits on all Texas agencies.

Legislative Budget Board (LBB) Texas state agency that is controlled by the leadership in the state legislature and writes the state budget.

legislative powers of governors The formal powers, especially the veto authority and power to call special sessions, of the governor to force the legislature to enact his or her legislation.

Legislative Redistricting Board (LRB) State board composed of elected officials that can draw new legislative districts for the Texas House and Senate if the legislature fails to act.

legitimacy A quality conferred on government by citizens who believe that its exercise of power is right and proper.

Lemon **test** A three-part test established by the Supreme Court in the 1971 case *Lemon v. Kurtzman* to determine whether government aid to parochial schools is constitutional; the test is also applied to other cases involving the establishment clause.

letter to the editor A letter in which a reader responds to a story in a newspaper, knowing that the letter might be published in that paper.

libel False written statements about others that harm their reputation.

liberalism Ideology that advocates change in social, political, and economic realms to better protect the well-being of individuals and to produce equality in society.

libertarianism An ideology whose advocates believe that government should take a "hands off" approach in most matters.

liberty The most essential quality of American democracy; it is both the freedom from governmental interference in citizens' lives and the freedom to pursue happiness.

lieutenant governor Presiding officer of the Texas Senate, elected by the state voters.

limited war A combatant country's self-imposed limitation on the tactics and strategy it uses, particularly its avoidance of the use of nuclear weapons.

limited-purpose government A government that has very limited authority or control over its finances and is governed by a set structure.

line-item veto The power of the president or a governor to strike out specific line items on an appropriations bill while allowing the rest of the bill to become law; the presidential line-item veto was declared unconstitutional by the Supreme Court in 1997.

literacy test A test to determine eligibility to vote; designed so that few African Americans would pass.

litigation The process by which cases are brought and decided in the American legal system.

living wage A wage high enough to keep workers and their families out of poverty and to allow them to enjoy a basic living standard.

lobby To communicate directly with policy makers on an interest group's behalf.

Local and Consent Calendars Committee In the Texas House, the committee handling minor and noncontroversial bills that normally apply to only one county.

logrolling The practice of members of Congress agreeing to vote for a bill in exchange for their colleague's vote on another bill.

loyal opposition A role that the party out of power plays, highlighting its objections to policies and priorities of the government in power.

M

magistrate functions Preliminary hearings for persons charged with a serious criminal offense.

major party Any organization receiving 20 percent or more of the total votes cast for governor in the last election in Texas.

majority rule The idea that in a democracy, only policies with 50 percent plus one vote are enacted, and only candidates that win 50 percent plus one vote are elected.

majority whip A go-between with the majority leadership and party members in the House of Representatives.

majority-minority district A legislative district composed of a majority of a given minority community—say, African Americans—the intent of which is to make it likely that a member of that minority will be elected to Congress.

majority-minority state A state in which minority groups make up a majority of the population of the state; a change from Anglos being the majority in Texas.

mandates Clauses in legislation that direct state and local governments to comply with national legislation and national standards.

mandatory spending Payment for debt and government programs for which the legislation that creates the program also obligates the government to spend the money necessary to meet the program's commitments as long as the program is in existence.

manifest destiny The idea that it was the United States' destiny to spread throughout the North American continent; used to rationalize the expansion of U.S. territory.

Marbury v. Madison The 1803 Supreme Court case that established the power of judicial review, which allows the Court to strike down

laws passed by the other branches that it views to be in conflict with the Constitution.

margin of error Also called *sampling error;* a statistical calculation of the difference in results between a poll of the sample and a poll of the entire population.

market failure A condition in which competition for profits in the marketplace causes harms to society, such as environmental degradation, unsafe working conditions, and low pay.

marketplace of ideas A concept at the core of the freedoms of expression and press, based on the belief that true and free political discourse depends upon a free and unrestrained discussion of ideas.

markup The process by which the members of legislative committees "mark up" a bill with suggested language for changes and amendments.

Marshall Plan The U.S. government program that provided funds necessary for Western European countries to rebuild after World War II.

McCulloch v. Maryland The 1819 case that established that the necessary and proper clause justifies broad understandings of enumerated powers.

means-tested benefit A benefit for which eligibility is based on having an income below a specified amount, typically based on a percentage of the poverty guideline.

media consultant A professional who brings the campaign message to voters by creating handouts and all forms of media ads.

media segmentation The breaking down of the media according to the specific audiences they target.

median household income The middle of all household incomes—50 percent of households have incomes less than the median and 50 percent have incomes greater than the median.

merit A system of hiring and promotion based on an individual's competence.

merit system (Missouri system) A system of selecting judges in which the governor appoints judges from a list submitted by a screening committee, and after appointment, a judge serves for a set term and is then subjected to a retention election in which the voters decide whether the judge stays in office

merit-based civil service A personnel system in which bureaucrats are hired on the basis of the principles of competence, equal opportunity (open competition), and political neutrality; once hired, these public servants have job protection.

micro-lending Loaning poor entrepreneurs small amounts of money that enable them to buy what they need to create a business.

military powers of governors The governor's authority to use the National Guard in times of natural disaster or civil unrest.

minor party A party that receives 5 to 19 percent of the vote in any statewide election; candidates from minor parties are not required to file petitions to get on the ballot.

minority representation Requirement that in drawing legislative districts, the legislature should create districts that give members of minority groups an opportunity to be elected.

minority representation in judgeships Election of judges from single-member districts in major urban counties to allow minority judges to be elected.

minority whip The go-between with the minority leadership, whose job mirrors that of the majority whip but without the power that comes from holding a majority in the U.S. House of Representatives.

Miranda **rights** A criminal procedural rule, established in the 1966 case *Miranda v. Arizona,* requiring police to inform criminal suspects, on their arrest, of their legal rights, such as the right to remain silent and the right to counsel; these warnings must be read to suspects before interrogation.

modified one-party state A state in which one party regularly wins elections.

monarchy A government in which a member of a royal family, usually a king or queen, has absolute authority over a territory and its government.

monetarism The theory that says the government's proper economic role is to control the rate of inflation by controlling the amount of money in circulation.

monetary policy The body of government policies, controlled by the Federal Reserve System, aimed at influencing the supply of money in the marketplace to maintain price stability.

Monroe Doctrine President James Monroe's 1823 declaration that the Americas should not be considered subjects for future colonization by any European power.

moralistic subculture A political subculture that expects the government to act as a positive force to achieve a common good for all citizens.

muckraking Criticism and exposés of corruption in government and industry by journalists at the turn of the twentieth century.

multilateral Many-sided; having the support of numerous nations.

multimember district District having more than one member elected to the legislature.

mutual assured destruction (MAD) The doctrine that if one nation attacked another with nuclear weapons, the other would be capable of retaliating and would retaliate with such force as to assure mutual annihilation.

N

narrowcasting The practice of aiming media content at specific segments of the public.

national debt The total amount of money the government owes to others due to borrowing.

National Security Council (NSC) Consisting of top foreign policy advisers and relevant cabinet officials, this is an arm of the Executive Office of the President that the president consults on matters of foreign policy and national security.

natural law The assertion that standards that govern human behavior are derived from the nature of humans themselves and can be universally applied.

natural rights (unalienable rights) The rights possessed by all humans as a gift from nature, or God, including the rights to life, liberty, and the pursuit of happiness.

naturalization Becoming a citizen by means other than birth, as in the case of immigrants.

necessary and proper clause (elastic clause) A clause in Article I, section 8, of the Constitution that gives Congress the power to do whatever it deems necessary and constitutional to meet its enumerated obligations; the basis for the implied powers.

neoconservatism An ideology that advocates military over diplomatic solutions in foreign policy and is less concerned with restraining government activity in domestic politics than traditional conservatives.

Net neutrality The idea that Internet traffic—e-mail, Web site content, videos, and phone calls—should flow without interference or discrimination by those who own or run the Internet pipeline.

netroots The Internet-centered political efforts on behalf of candidates and causes.

New Deal Franklin Roosevelt's broad social welfare program in which the government would bear the responsibility of providing a "safety net" to protect the weakest members of society.

New Deal coalition The group composed of southern Democrats, northern city dwellers, immigrants, the poor, Catholics, labor union members, blue-collar workers, African Americans, and women that elected FDR to the presidency four times.

New Jersey Plan The proposal presented by states with smaller populations at the Constitutional Convention in response to James Madison's Virginia Plan.

new judicial federalism The practice whereby state judges base decisions regarding civil rights and liberties on their state's constitution, rather than the U.S. Constitution, when their state's constitution guarantees more than minimum rights.

new media Cable television, the Internet, blogs, and satellite technology.

Nixon Doctrine Policy emphasizing the responsibility of U.S. allies to provide for their own national defense and security, aimed at improving relations with the communist nations, including the Soviet Union and China.

noncontributory program A benefit provided to a targeted population, paid for by a proportion of the money collected from all taxpayers.

nonpartisan election of judges Election of judges in which party identification does not appear on the ballot.

nonpartisan elections Ballot form in which voters are unable to determine the party of candidates by looking at the ballot.

nontariff trade barrier Marketplace and social regulations as well as subsidies aimed at creating a competitive advantage in trade.

nontax revenue Governmental revenue derived from service charges, fees (tuition), the lottery, and other sources.

normal trade relations (NTR) status The international trade principle holding that the least restrictive trade conditions (best tariff rates) offered to any one national trading partner will be offered to every other nation in a trading network (also known as *most favored nations*).

North American Free Trade Agreement (NAFTA) An act passed by Congress in 1993 that established closer trade relations and economic cooperation between the United States, Canada, and Mexico.

North Atlantic Treaty Organization (NATO) An international mutual defense alliance formed in 1949 that created a structure for regional security for its fifteen member nations.

O

obscenity Indecent or offensive speech or expression.

Office of Management and Budget (OMB) The office that creates the president's annual budget.

office-block ballot A type of ballot that arranges all of the candidates for a particular office under the name of that office.

off-year elections Local elections held at a different time of year from state and national elections.

oligarchy A government in which an elite few hold power.

ombudsperson A role in which an elected or appointed leader acts as an advocate for citizens by listening to and investigating complaints against a government agency.

open primary A type of primary in which both parties' ballots are available in the voting booth, and the voters simply select one on which to register their preferences.

oral arguments The stage when appeals court judges or Supreme Court justices meet with the petitioner and the respondent to ask questions about the legal interpretations or information contained in their briefs.

ordinary scrutiny test The guidelines the courts used between 1873 and 1976 to determine the legality of sex-based discrimination; on the basis of this test, sex-based discrimination is legal if it is a reasonable means by which the government can achieve a legitimate public interest.

original jurisdiction The power of a court to hear a case first, before other courts have decided it.

outsourcing The situation in which the government signs contracts with private-sector employers to do work previously provided by government workers.

oversight The process by which the legislative branch "checks" the executive branch to ensure that the laws Congress has passed are being administered in keeping with legislators' intent.

P

parliamentarian Expert in legislative procedures.

partial preemption The authority of the national government to establish minimum regulatory standards that provide state and local governments the flexibility either to enforce the national standards or to establish their own more stringent standards, which they must enforce.

partial veto A veto that allows the legislature to recall a bill to answer a governor's objections to it; Texas does not have a formal partial veto process.

partisan election of judges Method used to select all judges (except municipal court judges) in Texas by using a ballot showing party identification.

party chief A role of governors that calls for them to aid their fellow party members in their reelection efforts, raise money for the party, and create a favorable party image.

party competition The principle that states with two active and competitive parties have higher rates of voter turnout than states, such as Texas, with weak or noncompetitive parties.

party dealignment The change from identifying with either major political party to identifying as independents.

party identifiers Individuals who identify themselves as a member of one party or the other.

party ideology Basic belief system that guides a political party.

party in government The partisan identifications of elected leaders in local, county, state, and federal government.

party in the electorate Individuals who identify with or tend to support a party.

party organization The formal party apparatus, including committees, party leaders, conventions, and workers.

party platform Statement of the primary beliefs and goals of a political party.

party realignment The change from a state dominated by one political party to the two-party system operating today in Texas.

party system The categorization of the number and competitiveness of political parties in a polity.

party-column ballot A ballot that organizes the candidates by political party.

passive appearance The procedure followed by courts in not initiating cases but waiting for cases to be brought to them.

patronage The system in which a party leader rewarded political supporters with jobs or government contracts in exchange for their support of the party.

peak business organizations Interest groups that represent statewide business organizations, such as a state's Chamber of Commerce.

penny press Newspapers that sold for a penny in the 1830s.

permanent party organization The series of elected officers in a political party who keep the party organization alive between elections.

permanent registration system A system that allows citizens to remain on the voter registration list if they continue to vote at prescribed intervals.

petit jury A jury of citizens selected randomly from voter registration lists or lists of licensed drivers that determines the guilt or innocence of a person during a criminal trial.

petitioner Also called *appellant*; the party seeking to have a lower court's decision reviewed by the Supreme Court under the Court's discretionary jurisdiction.

plaintiff The party bringing the case to court.

platform The formal statement of a party's principles and policy objectives.

Plessy v. Fergusson The 1896 Supreme Court ruling creating the separate but equal doctrine.

plum book A publication that lists the top jobs in the bureaucracy to which the president will appoint people via the patronage system.

plural executive structure System in which voters elect many statewide officeholders to serve as heads of departments.

pluralist theory A theory that holds that policy making is a competition among diverse interest groups that ensure the representation of individual interests.

pocket veto A special presidential veto of a bill passed at the conclusion of a legislative session, whereby the president waits ten days without signing the bill, and the bill dies.

police powers The states' reserved powers to protect the health, safety, lives, and properties of residents in a state.

political action committee (PAC) A group that raises and spends money in order to influence the outcome of an election.

political culture The people's collective beliefs and attitudes about government and political processes.

political engagement Citizen actions that are intended to solve public problems through political means.

political ideology An integrated system of ideas or beliefs about political values in general and the role of government in particular.

political machines Big-city organizations that exerted control over many aspects of life and lavishly rewarded supporters.

political party An organization that recruits, nominates, and elects party members to office in order to control the government.

political socialization The process by which we develop our political values and opinions.

politics The process of deciding who gets benefits in society and who is excluded from benefiting.

politics-administration dichotomy The concept that elected government officials, who are accountable to the voters, create and approve public policy, and then competent, politically neutral bureaucrats implement the public policy.

poll tax A fee for voting; levied to prevent poor African Americans in the South from voting.

pool memo Description written by Court clerks of the facts of a case filed with the Court, the pertinent legal arguments, and a recommendation as to whether the case should be taken.

popular sovereignty The theory that government is created by the people and depends on the people for the authority to rule.

population In a poll, the group of people whose opinions are of interest and/or about whom information is desired.

populism A philosophy supporting the rights and empowerment of the masses as opposed to elites.

pork barrel Legislators' appropriations of funds for special projects located within their congressional districts.

poverty The condition of lacking the income sufficient to purchase the necessities for an adequate living standard.

poverty guidelines A simplified version of the poverty thresholds developed each year by the Department of Health and Human Services; used to set financial eligibility criteria for benefits.

poverty rate The proportion of the population living below the poverty line as established by the national government.

poverty thresholds A set of income measures adjusted for family size that the Census Bureau establishes each year to define poverty for data collection purposes.

precedent Legal authority established by earlier cases.

precinct chair Party official elected in each voting precinct in Texas who organizes and supports the party.

preemption The constitutionally based principle that allows a national law to supersede state or local laws.

preferential voting A system that allows voters to rank candidates for the city council.

president pro tempore Also called *president pro tem*; theoretically, the chair of the Senate in the vice president's absence; in reality, an honorary title, with the senator of the majority party having the longest record of continuous service being elected to the position.

presidential preference primary Election held every four years by political parties to determine the preferences of delegates for presidential candidates.

press secretary The president's spokesperson to the media.

preventive war The strategy of waging war on countries that are regarded as threatening in order to avoid future conflicts.

primal scream format Loud, angry argument characteristic of many television and radio talk shows.

primary election An election in which voters choose the party's candidates who will run in the later general election.

priming Bringing certain policies on issues to the public agenda through media coverage.

prior restraint A form of censorship by the government whereby it blocks the publication of news stories viewed as libelous or harmful.

privileges and immunities The Constitution's requirement that a state extend to other states' citizens the privileges and immunities it provides for its citizens.

professional associations Organizations of people in professions such as teaching, medicine, law, architecture, cosmetology, and many others that generally require a license, have an element of state control, and lack the right to collective bargaining.

progressive tax A tax that takes a larger percentage of the income of wealthier taxpayers and a smaller percentage of the income of lower-income taxpayers.

property Anything that can be owned.

proportional representation system An electoral structure in which political parties win the number of parliamentary seats equal to the percentage of the vote the party receives.

proportional (flat) tax A tax that takes the same percentage of each taxpayer's income.

proposition A proposed measure placed on the ballot in an initiative election.

prospective voting A method of evaluating candidates in which voters focus on candidates' positions on issues important to them and vote for the candidates who best represent their views.

prosumers Individuals who simultaneously consume information and news and produce information in forms like videos, blogs, and Web sites.

protectionist trade policy The establishment of trade barriers to protect domestic goods from foreign competition.

public agenda The public issues that most demand the attention of government officials.

public diplomat An individual outside government who promotes his or her country's interests and thus contributes to shaping international perceptions of the nation.

public goods Services governments provide that are available to everyone, like clean air, clean water, airport security, and highways.

public opinion The public's expressed views about an issue at a specific point in time.

public opinion poll A survey of a given population's opinion on an issue or a candidate at a particular point in time.

public policy Any action or inaction by the government that has an impact on the lives of its citizens.

punitive damages Damages awarded in a legal case as a punishment or a deterrent.

pure capitalist economy Private individuals and companies own the modes of producing goods and services, and the government does not enact laws aimed at influencing the marketplace transactions that distribute these goods and services.

purposive incentives Motivation to join an interest group based on the belief in the group's cause from an ideological or a moral standpoint.

push polls A special type of poll that both provides information to campaigns about candidate strengths and weaknesses and attempts to skew public opinion about a candidate.

Q

quota sample A method by which pollsters structure a sample so that it is representative of the characteristics of the target population.

R

racially gerrymandered majority-minority districts Legislative districts that are drawn to the advantage of a minority group.

rally 'round the flag effect The peaks in presidential approval ratings during short-term military action.

random sampling A scientific method of selection for a poll in which each member of the population has an equal chance at being included in the sample.

rational abstention thesis A theory that some individuals decide the costs of voting are not worth the effort when compared to the benefits.

rational choice theory The idea that from an economic perspective it is not rational for people to participate in collective action when they can secure the collective good without participating.

real income Earned income adjusted for inflation.

realignment A shift in party allegiances or electoral support.

reapportionment Reallocation of seats in the House of Representatives to each state based on changes in the state's population since the last census.

recall of the governor The removal of the governor (or an elected official) by a petition signed by the required number of registered voters, followed by an election in which a majority votes to remove the person from office.

recession An economic downturn during which unemployment is high and the production of goods and services is low.

Reconstruction era The time after the Civil War between 1866 and 1877 when the institutions and infrastructure of the South were rebuilt.

redistricting The redrawing of congressional district boundaries within each state, based on the reapportionment from the census.

regime change The replacement of a country's government with another government by facilitating the deposing of its leader or leading political party.

regional security alliance An alliance typically between a superpower and nations that are ideologically similar in a particular region.

regressive tax A tax that takes a greater percentage of the income of lower-income earners than of higher-income earners.

regulated capitalist economy (mixed economy) An economy in which the government enacts policies to influence the health of the economy.

regulatory law (administrative law) A law made by executive and regulatory agencies, often pursuant to a delegation of lawmaking power from Congress.

regulatory policies Policies that mandate individual and group (corporate) behaviors that foster the general welfare.

report A legislative committee's explanation to the full chamber of a bill and its intent.

reserved powers The matters referred to in the Tenth Amendment over which states retain sovereignty.

respondent Also called *appellee;* the party opposing the hearing of a case on the Supreme Court's discretionary docket.

responsible party model Political scientists' view that a function of a party is to offer a clear choice to voters by establishing priorities or policy stances different from those of rival parties.

retrospective voting A method of evaluating candidates in which voters evaluate incumbent candidates and decide whether to support them based on their past performance.

rider Provision attached to a bill that may not be of the same subject matter as the main bill.

right to privacy The right of an individual to be left alone and to make decisions freely, without the interference of others.

"Robin Hood plan" In Texas, a nickname for the provision in the education statutes that consolidated property taxes so that they are distributed among rich and poor districts; revised later to require rich districts with a property tax base per pupil in excess of $305,000 to share their wealth with other school districts.

Roosevelt Corollary The idea advanced by President Theodore Roosevelt, stating that the United States had the right to act as an "international police power" in the Western Hemisphere in order to ensure stability in the region.

Rule of Four The Supreme Court practice by which the Court will agree to hear a case that comes to it under its discretionary jurisdiction if four or more justices vote to hear it.

Rules Committee One of the most important committees in the U.S. House of Representatives, which decides the length of debate and the scope of amendments that will be allowed on a bill.

runoff election A follow-up election that is held when no candidate receives the majority of votes cast in the original election.

runoff primary Election required if no person receives a majority in the primary election; primarily used in southern and border states.

S

safe election districts Noncompetitive districts that can be won only by the party with 55 percent or more of the votes in the district.

safety net A collection of public policies ensuring that the basic physiological needs of citizens are met.

salient Having resonance, in relation to a voting issue, reflecting intense interest.

SALT I The treaty signed in 1972 by the United States and the Soviet Union limiting the two countries' antiballistic missiles and freezing the number of offensive missiles that each nation could have at the number they already possessed, plus the number they had under construction.

SALT II The treaty signed in 1979 by the United States and the Soviet Union that set an overall limit on strategic nuclear launchers, limited the number of missiles that could carry multiple independently targeted reentry vehicles (MIRVs) with nuclear warheads, and limited each nation to the development of only one new type of intercontinental ballistic missile (ICBM).

sampling error Also called *margin of error;* a statistical calculation of the difference in results between a poll of a randomly drawn sample and a poll of the entire population.

sanctions Penalties that halt economic relations.

secretary of state (SOS) Chief election official and keeper of state records in Texas—appointed by the governor.

select committee A congressional committee created to consider a specific policy issue or address a specific concern.

selective incorporation The process by which, over time, the Supreme Court applied those freedoms that served some fundamental principle of liberty or justice to the states, thus rejecting total incorporation.

semiclosed primary A primary that allows voters to register or change their party registration on Election Day; registration as a member of a party is required on Election Day.

semiopen primary A nominating election in which registered voters can choose which primary to vote in on Election Day.

Senate majority leader The most powerful position in the U.S. Senate; the majority leader manages the legislative process and schedules debate on legislation.

Senate minority leader The leader of the minority party in the U.S. Senate, who works with the majority leader in negotiating legislation.

senatorial courtesy A custom that allows senators from the president's political party to veto the president's choice of federal district court judge in the senator's state.

senior executive service (SES) A unique personnel system for top managerial, supervisory, and policy positions offering less job security but higher pay than the merit-based civil service system.

seniority system The system in which the member with the longest continuous tenure on a standing committee is given preference when the committee chooses its chair

separate but equal doctrine Established by the Supreme Court in *Plessy v. Ferguson,* it said that separate but equal facilities for whites and nonwhites do not violate the Fourteenth Amendment's equal protection clause.

separation of powers The Constitution's delegation of authority for the primary governing functions among three branches of government so that no one group of government officials controls all the governing functions.

settlement patterns The many origins of first settlers to the state.

shadow bureaucrats People hired and paid by private for-profit and nonprofit organizations that implement public policy through a government contract.

Shivercrats Democrats who followed Texas Governor Allan Shivers's example and voted for Republican candidate Dwight Eisenhower in 1952 and 1956.

signing statement A written message that the president issues upon signing a bill into law.

sine die Adjourned; the legislature must adjourn at end of regular session and cannot continue to meet.

single-issue groups Groups that focus on one issue.

single-member district District having one member elected to the legislature; a system in which the city is divided into election districts and only the voters living in that district elect the council member from that district.

slander False verbal statements about others that harm their reputation.

social capital The ways in which our lives are improved in many ways by social connections.

social contract An agreement between the people and their leaders in which the people agree to give up some liberties so that their other liberties are protected.

social contract theory The idea that individuals possess free will, and every individual is equally endowed with the God-given right of self-determination and the ability to consent to be governed.

social movement The organized action of a broad segment of society to demand and effect improvement in the treatment of a specific group.

social regulation The government rules and regulations aimed at protecting workers, consumers, and the environment from market failure.

socialism An ideology that advocates economic equality, theoretically achieved by having the government or workers own the means of production (businesses and industry).

soft money loophole The Supreme Court's interpretation of campaign finance law that enabled political parties to raise unlimited funds for party-building activities such as voter registration drives and get-out-the-vote (GOTV) efforts.

soft news Events or topics that are not serious or broadly important.

solidary incentives The motivation to join an interest group based on the companionship and the satisfaction derived from socializing with others that it offers.

sound bites Short audio or video clips taken from a larger speech.

sound-bite commercial A brief, usually thirty-second, TV political advertisement that conveys a simple and memorable message about the candidate or the opponent.

Southeast Asia Treaty Organization (SEATO) A regional security agreement whose goal was to prevent communist encroachment in the countries of Southeast Asia.

sovereignty Having ultimate authority to govern, with no legal superior.

Speaker of the House The leader of the U.S. House of Representatives, chosen by the majority party; also member of the Texas House, elected by the other House members, who serves as presiding officer and generally controls the passage of legislation.

special session Session of the legislature called by the governor of Texas to consider legislation proposed by the governor only.

spoils system The practice of rewarding political supporters with jobs.

stagflation An economic condition in which the high unemployment of a recession occurs along with large increases in prices of consumer goods (high inflation) typical of an economic boom.

standing committee A permanent committee in Congress, with a defined legislative jurisdiction.

standing to sue The ability to bring lawsuits in court.

stare decisis From the Latin "let the decision stand," the principle that binds judges to rely upon the holdings of past judges in deciding cases.

state boards and commissions Administrative units for many Texas state agencies that carry out most of the work of state government; members are appointed by the governor for fixed terms.

state executive committee A committee that is made up of one man and one woman elected from each state senatorial district and functions as the governing body of the party.

state and local interest groups (SLIGs) Interest groups that represent state government employees, such as the Texas Association of Police Chiefs, and local governments, such as the Texas Association of County Officials.

statute A law enacted by Congress and the state legislatures to deal with particular issues or problems, sometimes more detailed and comprehensive than the common law.

statutory powers Powers explicitly granted to presidents by congressional action.

steering The practice by which realtors steered African American families to certain neighborhoods and white families to others.

straight ticket voting Casting all votes for candidates of one party.

strategic arms limitation talks (SALT talks) Discussions between the United States and the Soviet Union in the 1970s that focused on cooling down the nuclear arms race between the two superpowers.

strategic arms reduction talks (START talks) Talks between the United States and the Soviet Union in which reductions in missiles and nuclear warheads, not merely a limitation on increases, were negotiated.

strategic defense initiative (SDI, or "Star Wars") A ballistic missile defense system advocated by President Ronald Reagan.

stratified sampling A process of random sampling in which the national population is divided into fourths and representative counties and metropolitan statistical areas are selected as representative of the national population.

straw poll A poll conducted in an unscientific manner, used to predict election outcomes.

strict procedural rules The tight rules of courts regarding how cases must proceed and what evidence can be presented in court.

strict rules of access The limited access to courts because of special rules that determine whether the court will or can hear the case.

strict scrutiny test Guidelines the courts use to determine the legality of all but sex-based discrimination; on the basis of this test, discrimination is legal if it is a necessary means by which the government can achieve a compelling public interest.

subcommittee A subordinate committee in Congress that typically handles specific areas of a standing committee's jurisdiction.

subsidy A tax break or another kind of financial support that encourages business expansion or decreases the cost of doing business so that businesses can be more competitive.

Sunset Advisory Commission Agency responsible for making recommendations to the Texas legislature for change in the structure and organization of most state agencies.

sunset clause A clause in legislation that sets an expiration date for the authorized program/policy unless Congress reauthorizes it.

sunshine laws Legislation that opens up government functions and documents to the public.

Super Tuesday The Tuesday in early March on which the most primary elections are held, many of them in southern states; provided the basis for Super-Duper Tuesday in 2008.

superpowers Leader nations with dominating influence in international affairs.

supply-side economics The theory that advocates cutting taxes and deregulating business to stimulate the economy.

supremacy clause The paragraph in Article VI that makes the Constitution, and the treaties and laws created in compliance with it, the supreme law of the land.

supreme law of the land The U.S. Constitution's description of its own authority, meaning that all laws made by governments within the United States must be in compliance with the Constitution.

suspect classifications Distinctions based on race, religion, national origin, and sex, which are assumed to be illegitimate.

symbolic representation The attempt to ensure that the Supreme Court is representative of major demographic groups, such as women, African Americans, Jews, and Catholics.

symbolic speech Nonverbal "speech" in the form of an action such as picketing, flag burning, or wearing an armband to signify a protest.

T

take care clause The constitutional basis for inherent powers, which states that the president "shall take Care that the Laws be faithfully executed."

talk radio A format featuring conversations and interviews about topics of interest, along with call-ins from listeners.

tariff A special tax on imported goods.

tax assessor collector Elected officer responsible for collecting revenue for the state and the county.

tax base The overall *wealth* (income and assets of citizens and corporations) that the government can tax in order to raise revenue.

tax capacity The measure of wealth in taxable resources.

tax expenditures (Also, *tax breaks* or *loopholes*), government financial supports that allow individuals and corporations to pay reduced taxes, to encourage behaviors that foster the public good.

tax incidence The person actually paying the tax.

tax shifting Passing taxes on to other parties.

telegenic The quality of looking good on TV.

temporary party organization The series of conventions, or caucuses, that occur every two years at the precinct, county, and state levels.

tenure of office The legal ability of governors to succeed themselves in office and the length of term.

term limits Limit on the number of times a person can be elected to the same office.

Texas Ethics Commission State agency responsible for enforcing requirements to report information on money collected and activities by interest groups and candidates for public office.

Texas Railroad Commission (RRC) State agency, with a three-member elected board, that regulates some aspects of transportation and the oil and gas industry of the state.

third party A party organized in opposition or as an alternative to the existing parties in a two-party system.

Three-Fifths Compromise The negotiated agreement by the delegates to the Constitutional Convention to count each slave as three-fifths a free man for the purpose of representation and taxes.

ticket splitting The situation in which voters vote for candidates from more than one party.

time, place, and manner restrictions Regulations regarding when, where, or how expression may occur; must be content neutral.

tort A wrongful act involving a personal injury or harm to one's property or reputation.

tort reform Changing the legal rules regarding compensation for damages done by one party to another.

total incorporation The theory that the Fourteenth Amendment's due process clause requires the states to uphold all freedoms in the Bill of Rights; rejected by the Supreme Court in favor of selective incorporation.

totalitarianism A system of government in which the government essentially controls every aspect of people's lives.

tracking polls Polls that measure changes in public opinion over the course of days, weeks, or months by repeatedly asking respondents the same questions and measuring changes in their responses.

trade associations Interest groups that represent specific business interests, such as oil producers and highway contractors.

trade deficit The gap between the value of a nation's exports and the value of its imports.

trade policy A collection of tax laws and regulations that supports the country's international commerce.

traditionalistic subculture A political subculture that expects government to maintain the existing political order for the benefit of a small elite.

trial court The court in which a case is first heard and which determines the facts of a case.

trial de novo courts Courts that do not keep a written record of their proceedings; cases on appeal begin as new cases in the appellate courts.

Truman Doctrine Articulated by President Harry Truman, a foreign policy commitment by the United States to assist countries' efforts to resist communism in the Cold War era.

trustee model A model of representation in which a member of the House or Senate should articulate and vote for the position that best represents the views of constituents.

turnout rate The proportion of eligible voters who actually voted.

turnover The number of new members of the legislature each session

two-party competitive state A state in which parties switch control of the statewide elected offices and control of the state legislature.

U

umbrella organizations Interest groups that represent collective groups of industries or corporations.

unanimous consent An agreement by every senator to the terms of debate on a given piece of legislation.

unfunded or underfunded mandates Laws enacted by federal or state governments that impose responsibilities and financial burdens on city and county governments.

unicameral A legislative body with a single chamber.

unilateralism One-sided action, usually in foreign policy.

unitary system A governmental structure in which one central government has sovereignty, although it may create regional governments to which it delegates responsibilities.

United Nations (UN) Established in 1945, an international body whose founders hoped would develop the capacity to prevent future wars by achieving collective security and peace.

U.S. Code A compilation of all the laws passed by the U.S. Congress.

U.S. Supreme Court High court with a limited original jurisdiction whose decisions may not be appealed; it serves as the court of last resort in the U.S. judiciary.

V

vblog A video Weblog.

V-chip Required by the Telecommunications Act of 1996, a computer chip in television sets that lets parents block programming they consider unsuitable for children.

veto An executive power held by the president, who can reject a bill and return it to Congress with reasons for the rejection.

Virginia Plan James Madison's proposal at the Constitutional Convention for a new governmental structure, which favored states with larger populations.

voter fatigue The condition in which voters grow tired of all candidates by the time Election Day arrives, and may thus be less likely to vote.

voting-age population All citizens who meet the formal requirements to register to vote; in Texas, you must be 18 years of age and a resident of the state for thirty days before the election.

W

War Powers Act This law limits presidential use of military forces to sixty days, with an automatic extension of thirty additional days if the president requests such an extension.

Warsaw Pact A regional security structure formed in 1955 by the Soviet Union and its seven satellite states in Eastern Europe in response to the creation of the North Atlantic Treaty Organization (NATO).

Watergate During the Nixon administration, a scandal involving burglaries and the subsequent cover-up by high-level administration officials.

weapons of mass destruction (WMDs) Nuclear, chemical, and biological weapons.

whistleblower A civil servant who discloses mismanagement, fraud, waste, corruption, and/or threats to public health and safety to the government.

White House counsel The president's lawyer.

White House Office (WHO) The office that develops policies and protects the president's legal and political interests.

white primary A primary election in which a party's nominees for general election were chosen but in which only white people were allowed to vote.

winner-take-all An electoral system in which the candidate who receives the most votes wins that office, even if that total is not a majority.

Works Progress Administration (WPA) A New Deal program that would employ 8.5 million people at a cost of more than $11 million between 1935 and 1943.

World Bank The international financial institution created by the Bretton Woods Agreement of 1944 and charged with lending money to nations in need.

World Trade Organization (WTO) The organization created in 1995 to negotiate, implement, and enforce international trade agreements.

writ of *certiorari* Latin for "a request to make certain"; this is an order to a lower court to produce a certified record of a case so that the appellate court can determine whether any errors occurred during trial that warrant review of the case.

write-in candidate A person whose name does not appear on the ballot; voters must write in the name, and the person must have filed formal notice before the election that she or he is a write-in candidate.

Y

Yellow Dog Democrats People in Texas who voted straight ticket for Democrats—they would vote for a yellow dog if it ran as a Democrat.

yellow journalism An irresponsible, sensationalist approach to news reporting, so named after the yellow ink used in the "Yellow Kid" cartoons in the *New York World*.

Yellow Pup Republicans Younger voters in Texas who tend to vote straight ticket for Republican candidates.

REFERENCES

CHAPTER 1

1. Rogers Smith, *Civic Ideals: Conflicting Visions of Citizenship in U.S. History* (New Haven, CT: Yale University Press, 1997).
2. Robert A. Dahl, *Who Governs? Democracy and Power in an American City* (New Haven, CT: Yale University Press, 1961).
3. E. E. Schattschneider, *The Semi-Sovereign People* (New York: Holt, Rinehart, and Winston, 1960).
4. E. J. Dionne Jr., *Why Americans Hate Politics: The Death of the Democratic Process,* 2nd ed. (New York: Touchstone, 1992).
5. Gallup Poll, "Trust in Government," www.gallup.com/poll/5392/Trust-Government.aspx.
6. Institute of Politics at Harvard University, "Attitudes Towards Politics and Public Service: A National Survey of College Undergraduates," April 11–20, 2000, www.iop.harvard.edu/pdfs/survey/2000.pdf.
7. Ibid.
8. Ibid.
9. Ibid.
10. Barbara Roswell, "From Service-Learning to Service Politics: A Conversation with Rick Battistoni," http://reflectionsjournal.org/Articles/V3.N1.Battistoni.Rick.Roswell.Barbara.pdf.
11. Michael Delli Carpini, Director Pew Charitable Trusts, www.apa.org/ed/slce/civicengagement.html.
12. S. E. Finer, *The History of Government,* 3 vols. (London: Oxford University Press, 1997).
13. Martin A. Reddish, *The Constitution as Political Structure* (London: Oxford University Press, 1995).
14. Theodore Sky, *To Provide for the General Welfare: A History of the Federal Spending Power* (Newark, DE: University of Delaware Press, 2003).
15. David Epstein, *The Political Theory of the Federalist* (Chicago: University of Chicago Press, 1984).
16. Thomas Hobbes, *Leviathan* (1651; New York: Oxford University Press, 1996), chap. 14.
17. *New York Times,* "America Enduring," September 11, 2002, http://query.nytimes.com/gst/fullpage.html?res=9A00E0DE1431F932A2575AC0A9649C8B63&scp=1&sq=america+enduring&st=nyt.

CHAPTER 2

1. www.u-s-history.com/pages/h1211.html.
2. www.yale.edu/lawweb/avalon/amerrev/parliament/stamp_act_1765.htm.
3. www.historyplace.com/unitedstates/revolution/rev-prel.htm.
4. J. Alan Rogers, "Colonial Opposition to the Quartering of Troops During the French and Indian War," *Military Affairs* (1970): 7.
5. www.manhattanrarebooks-history.com/declaratory_act.htm.
6. http://ahp.gatech.edu/townshend_act_1767.html.
7. Russell Bourne, *Cradle of Violence: How Boston's Waterfront Mobs Ignited the American Revolution* (Hoboken, NJ: Wiley, 2006).
8. www.u-s-history.com/pages/h675.html.
9. C. Brian Kelly, *Best Little Stories from the American Revolution* (Nashville, TN: Cumberland House, 1999).
10. www.bostonteapartyship.com/.
11. www.ushistory.org/declaration/related/intolerable.htm.
12. www.usconstitution.net/intol.html#Rights.
13. www.usconstitution.net/assocart.html.
14. For further discussion of the impact of *Common Sense* on colonial attitudes and beliefs, see Edmund S. Morgan, *The Birth of the Republic: 1763–89* (Chicago: University of Chicago Press, 1992), 71–76.
15. www.geocities.com/presfacts/8/lee.html.
16. You can find these constitutions at http://avalon.law.yale.edu/subject_menus/18th.asp.
17. Jack N. Rakove, "A Tradition Born of Strife," in *American Politics: Classic and Contemporary Readings,* 6th ed., ed. Allan J. Cigler and Burdett A. Loomis (Boston: Houghton Mifflin, 2005), 4–5.
18. www.fordham.edu/halsall/mod/iroquois.html.
19. For an excellent discussion of how the Articles benefited the states, see Keith L. Dougherty, *Collective Action Under the Articles of Confederation* (New York: Cambridge University Press, 2001), 76–82.
20. http://avalon.law.yale.edu/18th_century/annapoli.asp.
21. Charles Beard, *An Economic Interpretation of the Constitution of the United States* (New York: Macmillan, 1913).
22. www.usconstitution.net/consttop_ccon.html.
23. www.africanaonline.com/slavery_timeline.htm.
24. Alexander Hamilton, "Federalist No. 9," *The Federalist Papers* (Cutchogue, NY: Buccaneer Books, 1992), 37.
25. James Madison, "Federalist No. 51," *The Federalist Papers* (Cutchogue, NY: Buccaneer Books, 1992), 261–65.
26. James Madison, "Federalist No. 10," *The Federalist Papers* (Cutchogue, NY: Buccaneer Books, 1992), 42–49.
27. Alexander Hamilton, "Federalist No. 84," *The Federalist Papers* (Cutchogue, NY: Buccaneer Books, 1992), 436–37.
28. Thomas Jefferson, Letter to James Madison on the Bill of Rights debate, March 15, 1789. Courtesy of Eigen's Political & Historical Quotations.
29. Larry M. Lane and Judith J. Lane, "The Columbian Patriot: Mercy Otis Warren and the Constitution," in *Women, Politics, and the Constitution,* ed. Naomi B. Lunn (New York: Harrington Park Press, 1990), 17–31.

18. Oscar Handlin and Mary Handlin, *The Dimensions of Liberty* (Cambridge, MA: Harvard University Press, 1961).
19. Richard Labunski, *James Madison and the Struggle for the Bill of Rights* (London: Oxford University Press, 2006).
20. Jack N. Rakove, *Original Meanings: Politics and Ideas in the Making of the Constitution* (New York: Knopf, 1996).
21. Ira Katznelson and Martin Shefter, eds., *Shaped by War and Trade: International Influences on American Political Development* (Princeton, NJ: Princeton University Press, 2002).
22. *Wing Hing v. City of Eureka* (Calif), 1886.
23. Clyde W. Barrow, *Critical Theories of the State: Marxist, Neo-Marxist, Post-Marxist* (Madison: University of Wisconsin Press, 1993).
24. Seymour Martin Lipset and Gary Marks, *It Didn't Happen Here: Why Socialism Failed in the United States* (New York: W. W. Norton, 2001).
25. Giovanni Sartori and Peter Mair, *Parties and Party Systems: A Framework for Analysis* (Oxford, England: European Consortium for Political Research.

30. John P. Roche, "The Founding Fathers: A Reform Caucus in Action," *American Political Science Review,* LV (1961).

31. Alexander Hamilton, "Federalist No. 78," *The Federalist Papers* (Cutchogue, NY: Buccaneer Books, 1992), 395–96.

32. Courtesy of Eigen's Political and Historical Quotations, www.politicalquotes.org/Quotedisplay.aspx?DocID=22447.

33. *Plessy v. Ferguson,* 163 U.S. 537 (1896).

34. *Brown v. Board of Education,* 347 U.S. 483 (1954).

35. Thomas Marshall, "Representing Public Opinion: American Courts and the Appeals Process," *Politics and Policy* 31, no. 4 (December 2003): 726–39.

CHAPTER 3

1. http://edocket.access.gpo.gov/2009/pdf/E9-27427.pdf.

2. U.S. Census, "Federal Grants-in-Aid to State and Local Governments," www.census.gov/compendia/statab/tables90s414.pdf.

3. *Marbury v. Madison,* 5 U.S. 137 (1803).

4. Joe R. Feagin and Clairece Booher Feagin, *Racial and Ethnic Relations,* 7th ed. (Upper Saddle River, NJ: Prentice Hall, 2003), 131.

5. Dennis L. Dresang and James J. Gosling, *Politics and Policy in American States and Communities,* 4th ed. (New York: Pearson Longman, 2004), 88.

6. *McCulloch v. Maryland,* 17 U.S. 316 (1819).

7. *Gibbons v. Ogden,* 22 U.S. 1 (1824).

8. *United States v. Lopez,* 514 U.S. 549 (1995).

9. www.oyez.org/cases/1990-1999/1994/1994_93_1260/.

10. *Helvering v. Davis,* 301 U.S. 619 (1937).

11. CNN, *CNN Reports: Katrina – State of Emergency* (Kansas City, KS: Andrews McMeel Publishing, 2005), 10.

12. Ibid., 11.

13. Ibid., 16.

14. Ibid., 176.

15. Ibid., 46.

16. *Pruneyard Shopping Center & Fred Sahadi v. Michael Robins et al.,* 447 U.S. 74, 100 S. Ct. 2035.

17. David B. Walker, *The Rebirth of Federalism,* 2nd ed. (New York: Chatham House, 2000).

18. *National League of Cities v. Usery,* 426 U.S. 833 (1976).

19. *Garcia v. San Antonio Transportation Authority,* 469 U.S. 528 (1985).

20. *United States v. Oakland Cannabis Buyers' Cooperative,* 532 U.S. 483 (2001).

21. www.drugpolicy.org/marijuana/medical/challenges/cases/conant/.

22. *Raich v. Gonzales,* 545 U.S. 1 (2005).

23. *Bush v. Gore,* 531 U.S. 98 (2000).

24. See, for example, David B. Walker, *The Rebirth of Federalism.*

25. Josh Goodman, "Where Have All the Dollars Gone?" *Governing* (October 2009): 45–48.

26. *Massachusetts v. Mellon,* 262 U.S. 447 (1923).

27. *South Dakota v. Dole,* 483 U.S. 208 (1987).

28. www2.potsdam.edu/hansondj/LegalDrinkingAge.html.

29. www.nih.gov/about/researchresultsforthepublic/AlcoholRelatedTrafficDeaths.pdf.

30. Goodman, "Where Have All the Dollars Gone?" 45–48.

CHAPTER 4

1. Stephen L. Carter, *The Dissent of the Governed: Law, Religion, and Loyalty* (Cambridge, MA: Harvard University Press, 1998).

2. For an accessible and lively account of the central role of liberty in the American Revolution, see Thomas Fleming, *Liberty! The American Revolution* (New York: Viking, 1997).

3. For a history of civil liberties in wartime, see Geoffrey R. Stone, *Perilous Times: Free Speech in Wartime from the Sedition Act of 1798 to the War on Terrorism* (New York: W. W. Norton, 2004).

4. *Barron v. Baltimore,* 32 U.S. 243 (1833).

5. See *Hurtado v. California,* 110 U.S. 516 (1884) and *Turning v. New Jersey,* 211 U.S. 78 (1908) for a discussion of the standard the Court uses to determine whether a particular liberty should be incorporated into the Fourteenth Amendment.

6. *Gitlow v. New York,* 268 U.S. 652 (1925).

7. *Near v. Minnesota,* 283 U.S. 697 (1931).

8. *Palko v. Connecticut,* 302 U.S. 319 (1937).

9. Presidential Proclamation of September 24, 1862, by President Abraham Lincoln, suspending the writ of habeas corpus.

10. For two detailed accounts of the acts, see John C. Miller, *Crisis in Freedom: The Alien and Sedition Acts* (Boston: Little, Brown, 1951), and James Morton Smith, *Freedom's Fetters: The Alien and Sedition Laws and American Civil Liberties* (Ithaca, NY: Cornell University Press, 1956).

11. Ron Fournier, "Bush Orders Terrorist Trials by Military Tribunals," Associated Press, November 13, 2001. Executive order available at www.whitehouse.gov/news/releases/releases/2001/11/20011113-27.html.

12. Associated Press, "Obama Administration Considering DC Trial for Guantanamo Detainee Riduan Isamuddin, aka Hambali," January 15, 2010, www.nydailynews.com/news/national/2010/01/15/2010-01-15_administration_considering_dc_for_gitmo_detainee.html.

13. Charlie Savage, "Detainees Will Still Be Held, but Not Tried, Official Says," January 22, 2010, www.nytimes.com/2010/01/22/us/22gitmo.html?hpw.

14. *Schenck v. United States,* 249 U.S. 47 (1919).

15. *Gitlow v. New York.*

16. *Dennis v. U.S.,* 341 U.S. 494 (1951).

17. *Brandenburg v. Ohio,* 395 U.S. 444 (1969).

18. *U.S. v. O'Brien,* 391 U.S. 367 (1968).

19. *Tinker et al. v. Des Moines Independent Community School District et al.,* 393 U.S. 503 (1969).

20. For a discussion of *Tinker* and similar cases, see Jamin B. Baskin, *We the Students: Supreme Court Cases for and About Students* (Washington, DC: CQ Press, 2000).

21. *Texas v. Johnson,* 491 U.S. 397 (1989).

22. *U.S. v. Eichman,* 496 U.S. 310 (1990).

23. *Citizens United v. Federal Election Commission,* 558 U.S. _____ (2010).

24. *Miller v. California,* 413 U.S. 15 (1973).

25. *Chaplinsky v. New Hampshire,* 315 U.S. 568 (1942).

26. *Reno v. ACLU,* 521 U.S. 844 (1997); *U.S. v. Playboy Entertainment Group,* 529 U.S. 803 (2000).

27. *Ashcroft v. Free Speech Coalition,* 535 U.S. 234 (2002).

28. James Risen and Eric Lightblau, "Bush Lets U.S. Spy on Callers Without Courts," *New York Times,* December 16, 2005.

29. Marc Ambinder, "Shut Up: It's Still a Secret," *The Atlantic,* April 7, 2009; www.theatlantic.com/politics/archive/2009/04/shut-up-its-still-a-secret/7304/.

30. David Kravets, "Obama Sides with Bush in Spy Case," January 22, 2009, www.wired.com/threatlivelevel/2009/01/obama-sides-wit/; Wayne Madsen, "Warrantless Electronic Surveillance Continues at Bush Levels under Obama," December 16, 2009, http://onlinejournal.com/artman/publish/article_5383.shtml.

31. *New York Times v. U.S.,* 403 U.S. 713 (1971).

32. www.gallup.com/poll/1690/Religion.aspx.

33. The phrase "wall of separation" first appeared in Thomas Jefferson's 1802 letter to the Danbury Baptist Association. This letter is available at the Library of Congress Web site: www.loc.gov/loc/lcib/9806/danpre.html.

34. For a discussion of the doctrine of accommodationism, see Kenneth D. Wald, *Religion and Politics in the United States,* 3rd ed. (Washington, DC: CQ Press, 1997). For a discussion of neutrality, see Robert Booth Fowler, Allen D. Hertzke, and Laura R. Olson, *Religion and Politics in America: Faith, Culture, & Strategic Choices,* 2nd ed. (Boulder, CO: Westview Press, 1999).

35. *Everson v. Board of Education,* 330 U.S. 1 (1947).

36. *Lemon v. Kurtzman,* 403 U.S. 602 (1971).

37. *Zelman v. Simmons-Harris,* 539 U.S. 639 (2002).

38. *Engel v. Vitale,* 370 U.S. 421 (1962).

39. See, for example, the U.S. District Court ruling in *Tammy Kitzmiller et al. v. Dover Area School District et al.,* 400 F. Supp. 2d 707 (M.D. Pa. 2005).

40. *Prince v. Massachusetts,* 321 U.S. 158 (1944).

41. *Employment Division, Department of Human Resources of the State of Oregon et al. v. Smith,* 494 U.S. 872 (1990).

42. *Griswold v. Connecticut,* 381 U.S. 479 (1965).

43. *Roberts v. U.S. Jaycees,* 468 U.S. 609 (1984).

44. *Roe v. Wade,* 410 U.S. 113 (1973).

45. *Planned Parenthood v. Casey,* 505 U.S. 833 (1992).

46. *Cruzan v. Director, Missouri Department of Health,* 497 U.S. 261 (1990).

47. Ibid.
48. *Bowers v. Hardwick,* 478 U.S. 186 (1986).
49. *Lawrence v. Texas,* 539 U.S. 558 (2003).
50. This is a point of agreement among the Court's opinion, the concurring opinion, and the dissenting opinion issued in *Lawrence v. Texas,* 539 U.S. 558 (2003).
51. *Weeks v. U.S.,* 232 U.S. 383 (1914).
52. *Mapp v. Ohio,* 367 U.S. 643 (1961).
53. See Chief Justice Warren E. Burger's dissent in *Coolidge v. New Hampshire,* 403 U.S. 443.
54. *Segura v. U.S.,* 468 U.S. 796 (1984).
55. *U.S. v. Leon,* 468 U.S. 897 (1984).
56. *California v. Greenwood,* 486 U.S. 35 (1988).
57. *Miranda v. Arizona,* 384 U.S. 436 (1966).
58. *Gideon v. Wainwright,* 312 U.S. 335 (1963).
59. *Furman v. Georgia,* 408 U.S. 238 (1972).
60. The de facto moratorium on the death penalty ended in 1976 in a series of cases starting with *Gregg v. Georgia,* 428 U.S. 153 (1976).
61. *Baze v. Rees,* 553 U.S. (2008).
62. *Wilkerson v. Utah,* 99 U.S. 130 (1878).
63. For a strong argument against gun control, see John R. Lott Jr., *More Guns, Less Crime: Understanding Crime and Gun Control Laws* (Chicago: University of Chicago Press, 1998).
64. For a detailed look at different historical interpretations of the Second Amendment, see Carl T. Bogus, ed., *The Second Amendment in Law and History: Historians and Constitutional Scholars on the Right to Bear Arms* (New York: New Press, 2000).
65. For an articulation of this argument, see Carl T. Bogus, "What Does the Second Amendment Restrict? A Collective Rights Analysis," *Constitutional Commentary* 18, no. 3 (Winter 2001): 485–516.
66. *McDonald v. City of Chicago,* 561 U.S. _____ (2010).
67. *District of Columbia v. Heller,* 554 U.S. (2008).
68. www.millionmommarch.com.
69. http://2asisters.org.
70. For a recent report, see ACLU, "History Repeated: The Dangers of Domestic Spying by Federal Law Enforcement," May 29, 2007, www.aclu.org/images/asset_upload_file893_29902.pdf.
71. Larry Siems, "Why We're Challenging the FAA," July 22, 2009, www.aclu.org/blog/national-security/why-were-challenging-FAA.
72. ACLU, "No Real Threat: The Pentagon's Secret Database on Peaceful Protest," January 17, 2007, available at www.aclu.org/safefree/spyfiles/27988pub20070117.html.
73. Jo Mannies, "Ashcroft Defends Bush on Spying," St. Louis *Post-Dispatch,* February 10, 2008.
74. The full title of the law (H.R. 3162) is the Uniting and Strengthening America by Providing Appropriate Tools Required to Intercept and Obstruct Terrorism (USA PATRIOT) Act of 2001.
75. Protect America Act of 2007 (Pub.L. 110-55, S. 1927) signed into law by George W. Bush on August 5, 2007.
76. Offices of Inspectors General of the Department of Defense, Department of Justice, the Central Intelligence Agency, the National Security Agency, and the Office of the Director of National Intelligence, "Unclassified Report on the President's Surveillance Progam," Report No. 2009-0013-AS, July 10, 2009.
77. For an articulation of this argument, see Charles Krauthammer, "The Truth About Torture," *The Weekly Standard,* December 5, 2005.
78. For an articulation of this viewpoint, see Andrew Sullivan, "The Abolition of Torture," *New Republic,* December 19, 2005.
79. The full text of the Detainee Treatment Act of 2005 (H.R. 2863, Title X) is available at http://thomas.loc.gov/cgi-bin/query/R?r109:FLD001:S10909.
80. The full text of a statement delivered by Condoleezza Rice, the former U.S. secretary of state, at Andrews Air Force base in Maryland is available at www.timesonline.co.uk/tol/news/world/us_and_americas/article745995.ece.
81. European Parliament report, January 22, 2006, "Alleged Secret Detentions and Unlawful Inter-State Transfers Involving Council of Europe Member States."
82. United States Department of Justice, "Special Task Force on Interrogations and Transfer Policies Issues Its Recommendations to the President," August 24, 2009, www.justice.gov/opa/pr/2009/August/09-ag-835.html.
83. David A. Harris, "'Flying While Arab,' Immigration Issues, and Lessons from the Racial Profiling Controversy," testimony before the U.S. Commission on Civil Rights (October 12, 2001).
84. Eric Love, "Obama Administration Official Ignores Non-Muslim Terrorists," Alternet, June 8, 2010, http://blogs.alternet.org/speakeasy/2010/06/08/obama-administration-only-muslims-can-be-terrorists/; Spencer Hsu, "Nawar Shora Takes Battle for Arab and Muslim Rights Inside the TSA," Washingtonpost.com, March 19, 2010, www.washingtonpost.com/wp-dyn/content/article/2010/03/18/AR2010031805190.html.

CHAPTER 5

1. Rolan J. Pennock, "Rights, Natural Rights, and Human Rights—A General View," in *Human Rights,* ed. J. R. Pennock and J. W. Chapman (New York: New York University Press, 1981).
2. *Loving v. Virginia,* 388 U.S. 1 (1967).
3. Donald E. Lively, *The Constitution and Race* (New York: Praeger, 1992).
4. John Hope Franklin, *From Slavery to Freedom,* 7th ed. (New York: McGraw-Hill, 1994).
5. *Dred Scott v. Sandford,* 60 U.S. 393 (1857).
6. *Plessy v. Ferguson,* 163 U.S. 537 (1896).
7. George T. Blakey, *Hard Times and New Deal in Kentucky, 1929–1939* (Lexington: University of Kentucky Press, 1986).
8. Richard Kluger, *Simple Justice: The History of* Brown v. Board of Education *and Black America's Struggle for Equality* (New York: Knopf, 1976).
9. Raymond Wolters, *The Burden of Brown: Thirty Years of School Desegregation* (Knoxville: University of Tennessee Press, 1984).
10. Jo Ann Robinson, *The Montgomery Bus Boycott and the Women Who Started It* (Knoxville: University of Tennessee Press, 1987).
11. Taylor Branch, *Parting the Waters: America During the King Years, 1954–1963* (New York: Simon & Schuster, 1988).
12. *Browder v. Gale,* 142 F. Supp. 707 (1956).
13. John Lewis, *Walking with the Wind: A Memoir of the Movement* (New York: Simon & Schuster, 1998).
14. David J. Garrow, *Protest at Selma: Martin Luther King, Jr., and the Voting Rights Act of 1965* (New Haven, CT: Yale University Press, 1978).
15. Taylor Branch, *Pillar of Fire: America in the King Years 1963–65* (New York: Simon & Schuster, 1998).
16. Stokely Carmichael, "What We Want," *New York Review of Books,* September 22, 1966: 5–7.
17. Stokely Carmichael and Mike Thelwell, "Toward Black Liberation," *Massachusetts Review* 7 (1966): 639–51.
18. Steven Lawson, *Black Ballots: Voting Rights in the South, 1944–1969* (New York: Columbia University Press, 1976).
19. www.census.gov/prod/2001pubs/statab/sec08.pdf.
20. *Bradwell v. Illinois,* 83 U.S. 130 (1873).
21. *Minor v. Happersett,* 88 U.S. 162 (1875).
22. www.now.org/history/purpos66.html.
23. *Reed v. Reed,* 404 U.S. 71 (1971).
24. *Craig v. Boren,* 429 U.S. 190 (1976).
25. *U.S. v. Virginia,* 518 U.S. 515 (1996).
26. Joe R. Feagin and Clairece Booher Feagin, *Racial and Ethnic Relations* (Upper Saddle River, NJ: Prentice Hall, 2003), 135.
27. www.nigc.gov/ReadingRoom/PressReleases/PressReleasesMain/PR113062009/tabid/918/Default.aspx.
28. Feagin and Feagin, *Racial and Ethnic Relations,* 135.
29. www.naacpldf.org/content/pdf/austin2/Navajo_Nation_Brief_14.pdf.
30. http://pewhispanic.org/files/factsheets/hispanics2007/Table-3.pdf.
31. Based on author's calculations using data from the William C. Velasquez Institute, www.wcvi.org/latino_voter_research/latino_voter_statistics.html.
32. www.lulac.org/about/history.html.
33. Ibid.
34. *Mendez v. Westminister,* 64 F. Supp. 544 (1946).
35. Feagin and Feagin, *Racial and Ethnic Relations,* 218.
36. *Corpus Christi Independent School District v. Cisneros,* 404 U.S. 1211 (1971).

37. Texas State Historical Association, "The Handbook of Texas Online," www .tshaonline.org/handbook/online/articles/ CC/jrc2.html.
38. www.naleo.org/directory. html.
39. http://minorityhealth.hhs.gov/templates/ content.aspx?ID=3005.
40. Feagin and Feagin, *Racial and Ethnic Relations,* 278 and 310.
41. Ibid., 315.
42. http://www.aasc.ucla.edu/archives/ pa_07_08.asp.
43. www.access-board.gov/about/laws/ ada-amendments.htm.
44. *Bowers v. Hardwick,* 478 U.S. 186 (1986).
45. *Lawrence v. Texas,* 539 U.S. 558 (2003).
46. Jon W. Davidson, "Celebrating Recent LGBT Legislative Advances," www .lambdalegal.org/our-work/publications/ facts-backgrounds/recent-lgbt-advances .html.
47. *Romer v. Evans,* 517 U.S. 620 (1996).
48. www.lambdalegal.org/publications/ articles/nationwide-status-same-sex -relationships.html#9.
49. www.adl.org/99hatecrime/state_hate _crime_laws.pdf.
50. *Regents of the University of California v. Bakke,* 438 U.S. 265 (1978).
51. Ward Connerly, "College Admissions, Let's Not Break the Law," 2007, www.acri.org/ chairman.html.
52. www.acri.org/.
53. *Grutter v. Bollinger,* 539 U.S. 306 (2003).
54. *Parents Involved in Community Schools v. Seattle School District No. 1 et al.,* 551 U.S. _____ (2007) and *Meredith v. Jefferson County Board of Education,* 551 U.S. _____ (2007).

CHAPTER 6

1. Steven Pinker, *How the Mind Works* (W. W. Norton, 1997), viii.
2. Aaron Nelson, "Update: Kids Tell Adults to 'Go Vote,'" *The Brownsville Herald,* November 7, 2006.
3. V. O. Key Jr., *Public Opinion and American Democracy* (New York: Knopf, 1961), 8.
4. Mark Hugo Lopez, Peter Levine, Deborah Both, Abby Kiesa, Emily Kirby, and Karlo Marcelo, *The 2006 Civic and Political Health of the Nation: A Detailed Look at How Youth Participate in Politics and Communities* (College Park, MD: Circle: The Center for Information and Research on Civic Learning and Engagement, 2006), 4.
5. Ibid.
6. Sidney Verba, Kay Lehman Schlozman, and Henry E. Brady, *Voice and Equality: Civic Voluntarism in American Politics* (Cambridge, MA: Harvard University Press, 1995), 439.
7. David L. Leal, Matt A. Barreto, Jongho Lee, and Rodolfo O. de la Garza, "The Latino Vote in the 2004 Election," *PS: Political Science and Politics* (2005): 46.
8. Lopez et al., *The 2006 Civic and Political Health of the Nation,* 20–21.

9. Karlo Barrios Marcelo, Mark Hugo Lopez, and Emily Hoban Kirby, *Civic Engagement Among Young Men and Women* (College Park, MD: Circle: The Center for Information and Research on Civic Learning and Engagement, 2007), 12.
10. David W. Moore, "Death Penalty Gets Less Support from Britons, Canadians Than Americans," Gallup News Service, February 20, 2006.
11. Elizabeth Noelle-Neumann, *The Spiral of Silence: Public Opinion—Our Social Skin,* 2nd ed. (Chicago: University of Chicago Press, 1993).
12. Susan Herbst, *Numbered Voices: How Opinion Polling Has Shaped American Politics* (Chicago: University of Chicago Press, 1993).
13. Robert S. Erikson, Gerald C. Wright, and John P. McIver, *Statehouse Democracy: Public Opinion and Policy in the American States* (New York: Cambridge University Press, 1994).
14. Walter Lippmann, *Public Opinion* (1929; repr. London: Free Press, 1997), 114.
15. "George Gallup, 1901–1984: Founder, The Gallup Organization," http://gallup.com/ content/?ci=21364.
16. Herbert Asher, *Polling and the Public: What Every Citizen Should Know* (Washington, DC: CQ Press, 2001).
17. Ibid., 2.
18. Joseph Carroll, "Many Americans Use Multiple Labels to Describe Their Ideology," December 6, 2006, www.gallup.com/poll/ 25771/Many-Americans-Use-Multiple -Labels-Describe-Their-Ideology.aspx.
19. Randolph Grossman and Douglas Weiland, "The Use of Telephone Directories as a Sample Frame: Patterns of Bias Revisited," *Journal of Advertising* 7 (1978): 31–36.
20. Stephen J. Blumberg and Julian V. Luke, "Coverage Bias in Traditional Telephone Surveys of Low-Income and Young Adults," *Public Opinion Quarterly* 71 (2007): 734–49.
21. Clyde Tucker, J. Michael Brick, and Brian Meekins, "Household Telephone Service and Usage Patterns in the United States in 2004: Implications for Telephone Samples," *Public Opinion Quarterly* 71 (2007): 3–22.
22. "Wireless Solution: Early Release Estimates from the National Health Interview Survey, July–December 2008," National Health Center for Health Statistics, Centers for Disease Control and Prevention, May 2009.
23. Blumberg and Luke, "Coverage Bias in Traditional Telephone Surveys of Low-Income and Young Adults," 734–49.
24. Ibid.
25. George Terhanian and John Bremer, "Confronting the Selection-Bias and Learning Effects Problems Associated with Internet Research," Harris Interactive white paper, August 16, 2000.
26. G. Terhanian, R. Smith, J. Bremer, and R. K. Thomas, "Exploiting Analytical Advances: Minimizing the Biases Associated with Internet-Based Surveys of Non-Random Samples," *ARF/ESOMAR: Worldwide Online Measurement* 248 (2001): 247–72.

27. Irving Crespi, *Pre-Election Polling: Sources of Accuracy & Error* (New York: Russell Sage Foundation, 1988).
28. Benjamin I. Page and Robert Y. Shapiro, *The Rational Public: Fifty Years of Trends in Americans' Policy Preferences* (Chicago: University of Chicago Press, 1992).
29. Frank Newport, *Polling Matters: Why Leaders Must Listen to the Wisdom of the People* (New York: Warner Books, 2004).
30. James A. Stimson, *Tides of Consent: How Public Opinion Shapes American Politics* (Cambridge: Cambridge University Press, 2004).
31. Frank Newport, "U.S. Satisfaction at 15%, Lowest Since 1992," April 14, 2008, www .gallup.com/poll/106498/US-Satisfaction -15-Lowest-Since-1992.aspx.
32. Frank Newport and Joseph Carroll, "Iraq Versus Vietnam: A Comparison of Public Opinion," August 24, 2005, www.galluppoll .com/content/default.aspx?ci=18097&pg=2.
33. Jeffrey M. Jones and Joseph Carroll, "National Satisfaction Level Dips to 25%, One of Lowest Since 1979," May 16, 2007, www. galluppoll.com/content/?ci=27601&pg=1.
34. David W. Moore, "Top Ten Gallup Presidential Approval Ratings," Gallup press release, September 24, 2001.

CHAPTER 7

1. Frank R. Baumgartner and Beth L. Leech, *Basic Interests: The Importance of Groups in Politics and in Political Science* (Princeton, NJ: Princeton University Press, 1998).
2. Peggy Daniels and Carol Schwartz, *Encyclopedia of Associations 1996* (Detroit: Gale Research, 1995).
3. Alexis De Tocqueville, *Democracy in America: The Complete and Unabridged Volumes I and II* (1835–1840; New York: Bantam, 2000), 51.
4. Everett Carll Ladd, *The Ladd Report* (New York: Free Press, 1999).
5. Publius (James Madison), *Federalist #10,* 1787, www.ourdocuments.gov/doc.php?doc =10.
6. Robert D. Putnam, *Bowling Alone: The Collapse and Revival of American Community* (New York: Touchstone, 2000).
7. Claude S. Fischer, "Bowling Alone: What's the Score?" *Social Networks* 27 (May): 155–67.
8. E. E. Schattschneider, *The Semi-Sovereign People* (New York: Holt, Rinehart, and Winston, 1960), 132.
9. Earl Latham, *The Group Basis of Politics* (Ithaca, NY: Cornell University Press, 1952).
10. David B. Truman, *The Governmental Process* (New York: Knopf, 1951).
11. Hugh Davis Graham, *The Civil Rights Era: Origins and Development of National Policy, 1960–1972* (London: Oxford University Press, 1990).
12. Sidney Verba, Kay Schlozman, and Nancy Burns, *The Private Roots of Public Action: Gender, Equality, and Political Participation*

(Cambridge, MA: Harvard University Press, 2001).

13. Quoted in Mark P. Petracca, *The Politics of Interests* (Boulder, CO: Westview, 1992), 347.

14. www.ama-assn.org/ama/pub/health -system-reform/repeal-medicare-sgr-video .shtml.

15. Julie Greene, *Pure and Simple Politics: The American Federation of Labor and Political Activism, 1881–1917* (New York: Cambridge University Press, 1998).

16. Elizabeth Sanders, *Roots of Reform: Farmers, Workers, and the American State, 1877–1917* (Chicago: University of Chicago Press, 1998).

17. Sharon E. Jarvis, Lisa Montoya, and Emily Mulvoy, "The Civic Participation of Working Youth and College Students: Working Paper 36" (Austin, TX: The Annette Strauss Institute for Civic Participation, and CIRCLE, the Center for Information and Research on Civic Learning and Engagement, 2005).

18. James Q. Wilson, *Political Organizations* (New York: Basic Books, 1973).

19. Dennis Hastert, *Speaker: Lessons from Forty Years in Coaching and Politics* (Washington, DC: Regnery Publishing, 2004), 256.

20. Jeffrey Berry, *The Interest Group Society*, 3rd ed. (New York: Longman, 1997).

21. Martin J. Smith, *Pressures, Power and Policy: Policy Networks and State Autonomy in Britain and the United States* (Pittsburgh, PA: University of Pittsburgh, 1994).

22. Herbert Alexander, *Money in Politics* (Washington, DC: Public Affairs Press, 1972).

23. Frank Sorauf, *Money in American Elections* (New York: Little, Brown, 1988).

24. Frank Sorauf, *Inside Campaign Finance: Myths and Realities* (New Haven, CT: Yale University Press, 1992).

25. Gary C. Jacobson, *Money in Congressional Elections* (New Haven, CT: Yale University Press, 1980).

26. Allan J. Cigler and Burdett A. Loomis, *Interest Group Politics* (Washington, DC: CQ Press, 1991).

27. Lucy G. Barber, *Marching on Washington: The Forging of an American Political Tradition* (Los Angeles: University of California Press, 2002).

28. www.cc.org/mission.cfm.

29. *Citizens United v. Federal Election Commission,* 558 U.S. _____ (2010).

30. American Music Conference Newsletter, "Sesame Street's Elmo Visits Congress on Behalf of Music Education," www .amc-music.com/AMCNews/newsletter Sp02/elmo_dc.html.

31. Louise Overacker, *Money in Elections* (New York: Macmillan, 1932), 378.

CHAPTER 8

1. E. E. Schattschneider, *Party Government* (New York: Farrar & Rinehart, 1942), 1.

2. L. Sandy Maisel and Kara Z. Buckley, *Parties and Elections in America,* 4th ed. (Lanham, MD: Rowman & Littlefield, 2004).

3. Jo Freeman, *A Room at a Time: How Women Entered Party Politics* (New York: Rowman & Littlefield, 2000).

4. Ibid.

5. Melanie Gustafson, Kristie Miller, and Elisabeth Israels Perry, *We Have Come to Stay: American Women and Political Parties, 1880–1960* (Albuquerque: University of New Mexico Press, 1999).

6. V. O. Key, *Politics, Parties, and Pressure Groups* (New York: Thomas Y. Crowell, 1964).

7. Seymour Martin Lipset and Stein Rokkan, *Party Systems and Voter Alignments* (New York: Free Press, 1967).

8. The Pew Research Center for the People and the Press, "Beyond Red vs. Blue: Republicans Divided About Role of Government—Democrats by Social and Personal Values" (Washington, DC: The Pew Research Center for the People and the Press, 2005).

9. Geoffrey Layman, *The Great Divide: Religious and Cultural Conflict in American Party Politics* (New York: Columbia University Press, 2002).

10. Walter Dean Burnham, *Critical Elections and the Mainsprings of American Politics* (New York: W. W. Norton, 1997).

11. John Aldrich, *Why Parties? The Origin and Transformation of Party Politics in America* (Chicago: University of Chicago Press, 1995).

12. *Buckley v. Valeo,* 424 U.S. 1 (1976).

13. Regina Dougherty, "Divided Government Defines the Era," in *America at the Polls: 1996,* ed. Regina Dougherty, Everett C. Ladd, David Wilber, and Lynn Zayachkiwsky (Storrs, CT: Roper Center for Public Opinion Research, 1997).

14. Richard Hofstadter, "A Constitution Against Parties: Madisonian Pluralism and the Anti-Party Tradition," *Government and Opposition* 4, no. 3 (1969), 345–66.

15. Jefferson and Washington quoted in Richard Hofstadter, *The Idea of a Party System: The Rise of Legitimate Opposition in the United States, 1780–1840* (Berkeley: University of California Press, 1969), 2, 123.

16. Hofstadter, *The Idea of a Party System.*

17. James L. Sundquist, *Dynamics of the Party System: Alignment and Realignment of Political Parties in the United States* (Washington, DC: Brookings, 1983).

18. Everett C. Ladd, *American Political Parties* (New York: W. W. Norton, 1970).

19. David R. Mayhew, *Electoral Realignments: A Critique of an American Genre* (New Haven, CT: Yale University Press, 2002).

20. William Nisbet Chambers, *Political Parties in a New Nation: The American Experience, 1776–1809* (New York: Oxford University Press, 1963).

21. Lance Banning, *The Jeffersonian Persuasion: Evolution of a Party Ideology* (Ithaca, NY: Cornell University Press, 1978).

22. Richard L. McCormick, *The Party Period and Public Policy: American Politics from the Age of Jackson to the Progressive Era* (New York: Oxford University Press, 1986).

23. Jules Witcover, *Party of the People: A History of the Democrats* (New York: Random House, 2003).

24. Lee Benson, *The Concept of Jacksonian Democracy* (Princeton, NJ: Princeton University Press, 1961).

25. Aileen Kraditor, *The Ideas of the Woman Suffrage Movement, 1890–1920* (New York: W. W. Norton, 1981).

26. Eric Foner, *Free Soil, Free Labor, Free Men: The Ideology of the Republican Party Before the Civil War* (New York: Oxford University Press, 1995).

27. William E. Gienapp, *The Origins of the Republican Party, 1852–1856* (New York: Oxford University Press, 1987).

28. Witcover, *Party of the People.*

29. McCormick, *The Party Period and Public Policy.*

30. Joel H. Silbey, *The Partisan Imperative: The Dynamics of American Politics Before the Civil War* (New York: Oxford University Press, 1985).

31. Lewis L. Gould, *Grand Old Party: A History of the Republicans* (New York: Random House, 2003).

32. Paul Kleppner, *The Third Electoral System, 1853–1892: Parties, Voters, and Political Cultures* (Chapel Hill: University of North Carolina Press, 1979).

33. Quoted in A. James Reichley, "Party Politics in a Federal Polity," in *Challenges to Party Government,* ed. John Kenneth White and Jerome M. Mileur (Carbondale: Southern Illinois University, 1992), 48.

34. Kristi Anderson, *After Suffrage* (Chicago: University of Chicago Press, 1996), 30.

35. John Petrocik, *Party Coalitions: Realignment and the Decline of the New Deal Party System* (Chicago: University of Chicago Press, 1981).

36. David G. Lawrence, *The Collapse of the Democratic Majority: Realignment, Dealignment, and Electoral Change from Franklin Roosevelt to Bill Clinton* (New York: Westview, 1997).

37. Edward G. Carmines, John P. McIver, and James A. Stimson, "Unrealized Partisanship: A Theory of Dealignment," *Journal of Politics* 49 (1987): 376–400.

38. www.galluppoll.com/content/default.aspx? ci=24655&pg=2.

39. David Karol, Hans Noel, John Zaller, and Marty Cohen, "Polls or Pols? The Real Driving Force Behind Presidential Nominations," www.brookings.edu/articles/ 2003/summer_politics_cohen.aspx.

40. Arend Lijphardt, *Electoral Systems and Party Systems: A Study of Twenty-Seven Democracies, 1945–1990* (New York: Oxford University Press, 1994).

41. Lipset and Rokkan, *Party Systems and Voter Alignments.*

42. Maurice Duverger, *Political Parties* (New York: Wiley, 1951).

43. Gary Orren, "The Changing Styles of American Party Politics," in *The Future of*

American Political Parties: The Challenge of Governance, ed. Joel L. Fleishman (Englewood Cliffs, NJ: Prentice Hall, 1982), 31.

44. This basis for this argument can be found in Larry J. Sabato and Bruce Larson, *The Party's Just Begun: Shaping Political Parties for America's Future,* 2nd ed. (New York: Longman, 2001).

45. Steven J. Rosenstone, Roy L. Behr, and Edward H. Lazarus, *Third Parties in America,* 2nd ed. (Princeton, NJ: Princeton University Press, 1996).

46. Stefan Halper and Jonathon Clarke, *America Alone: The Neo-Conservatives and the Global Order* (London: Cambridge University Press, 2004).

CHAPTER 9

1. V. O. Key, *The Responsible Electorate* (Cambridge, MA: Harvard University Press, 1966).

2. Samuel C. Patterson and Gregory A. Caldeira, "Getting Out the Vote: Participation in Gubernatorial Elections," *American Political Science Review* 77 (1983): 675–89.

3. Barbara Norrander, *Super Tuesday: Regional Politics and Presidential Primaries* (Lexington: University of Kentucky Press, 1992).

4. Thomas E. Cronin, *Direct Democracy: The Politics of Initiative, Referendum, and Recall* (Cambridge, MA: Harvard University Press, 1999).

5. David Broder, *Democracy Derailed: Initiative Campaigns and the Power of Money* (New York: Harvest Books, 2001).

6. *Perry v. Schwarzenegger,* 704 F. Supp. 2d 921 (N.D. Cal. 2010).

7. John F. Bibby, *Politics, Parties, and Elections in America* (Belmont, CA: Wadsworth, 2000), 253.

8. Pat Buchanan on NBC's *Today Show,* "The American Presidency Project," November 9, 2000, www.presidency.ucsb.edu/showflorida 2000.php?fileid=buchanan11-09.

9. Ibid.

10. Mark Trahant, "Vote by Mail? OK, So I Was Wrong . . . ," *Seattle Post-Intelligencer,* September 25, 2005, http://seattlepi.nwsource .com/opinion/242020_trahant25.html.

11. Pippa Norris, ed., *Politics and the Press: The News Media and Their Influences* (Boulder, CO: Lynne Rienner Publishers, 1997).

12. Ben Smith, "The Next Bob Shrum?" *Politico,* February 6, 2007, www.politico.com/ news/stories/0207/2667.html.

13. See, for example, Matthew Dowd, "Campaign Organization and Strategy," in *Electing the President 2004: An Insider's View,* ed. Kathleen Hall Jamieson (Philadelphia: University of Pennsylvania Press, 2006).

14. Vivé Griffith, "The Influence of Media in Presidential Politics," Think Democracy Project, University of Texas at Austin, www .utexas.edu/features/archive/2004/election _media.html.

15. Jose Antonio Vargas, "Obama Raised Half a Billion Online," January 20, 2008, http:// voices.washingtonpost.com/44/2008/11/20/ obama_raised_half_a_billion_on.html.

16. www.articles.latimes.com/2007/mar/11/ nation/na-actblue11

17. Gary Jacobson, *Money and Congressional Elections* (New Haven, CT: Yale University Press, 1980).

18. David Adamany, "Money, Politics and Democracy," *American Political Science Review* 71 (1977): 289–304.

19. *Buckley v. Valeo,* 424 U.S. (1976).

20. See Anthony Corrado, Thomas E. Mann, Dan Ortiz, Trevor Potter, and Frank Sorauf, *Campaign Finance Reform: A Sourcebook* (Washington, DC: Brookings Institute, 1997).

21. *Federal Election Commission v. National Conservative PAC,* 470 U.S. 480 (1985).

22. *McConnell v. Federal Election Commission,* 540 U.S. 93 (2003).

23. *Federal Election Commission v. Wisconsin Right to Life, Inc.,* 551 U.S. (2007).

24. Norman H. Nie, Sidney Verba, and John R. Petrocik, *The Changing American Voter* (Cambridge, MA: Harvard University Press, 1976).

25. Angus Campbell, Philip Converse, Warren Miller, and Donald Stokes, *The American Voter* (New York: Wiley, 1960).

26. Jan Leighley and Jonathan Nagler, "Who Votes Now? And Does It Matter?" (paper presented at the annual meeting of the Midwest Political Science Association Chicago, 2007).

27. Norman H. Nie, Jane Junn, and Kenneth Stehlik-Barry, *Education and Democratic Citizenship in America* (Chicago: University of Chicago Press, 1996).

28. Jan E. Leighley and Jonathan Nagler, "Socioeconomic Class Bias in Turnout, 1964–1988: The Voters Remain the Same," *American Political Science Review* 86 (1992): 725–36.

29. The Annenberg National Election Study (ANES), "Voter Turnout 1948–2004," www .electionstudies.org/nesguide/2ndtable/ t6a_2_2.htm.

30. Kim Nguyen and James Garand, "The Effects of Income Inequality on Political Attitudes and Behavior" (paper presented at the annual meeting of the Midwest Political Science Association, Chicago, 2007).

31. Richard A. Brody, "The Puzzle of Political Participation in America," in *The New American Political System,* ed. Anthony King (Washington, DC: American Enterprise Institute for Public Policy Research, 1978), 287–324.

32. www.census.gov/Press-Release/www/ releases/archives/voting/013995.html.

33. Pippa Norris, "Retrospective Voting in the 1984 Presidential Election: Peace, Prosperity, and Patriotism," *Political Studies* 35 (1987): 289–300.

34. Daniel M. Shea, *Campaign Craft: The Strategies, Tactics, and Art of Political Campaign Management* (Westport, CT: Praeger, 1996).

35. Nie, Verba, and Petrocik, *The Changing American Voter.*

36. Samuel Kernell, "Presidential Popularity and Negative Voting," *American Political Science Review* 71 (1977): 44–66.

37. Shanto Iyengar and Jennifer A. McGrady, *Media Politics: A Citizen's Guide* (New York: W. W. Norton, 2006).

38. Warren E. Miller, "Disinterest, Disaffection, and Participation," *Political Behavior* 2 (1980): 7–32.

39. E. E. Schattschneider, *The Semi-Sovereign People* (New York: Holt, Rinehart, and Winston, 1960).

40. Pew Research Center for People and the Press, "Beyond Red Versus Blue: Profiles of the Typology Groups," 2005, http://people -press.org/reports/display.php3?PageID=949.

41. Barbara Norrander and Bernard N. Grofman, "A Rational Choice Model of Citizen Participation in High and Low Commitment Electoral Activities," *Public Choice* 57 (1988): 187–92.

42. Sidney Verba and Norman H. Nie, *Participation in America: Political Democracy and Social Equality* (New York: Harper & Row, 1972).

43. Arend Lijphart, "Compulsory Voting Is the Best Way to Keep Democracy Strong," *The Chronicle of Higher Education,* October 18, 1996: B3–4.

44. Ruy A. Teixeira, "Just How Much Difference Does Turnout Really Make?" *The American Enterprise,* July/August, 1992: 52–59.

CHAPTER 10

1. www.guardian.co.uk/media/pda/2010/feb/ 16/george-polk-awards.

2. Pippa Norris, *Women, Media and Politics* (New York: Oxford, 1997).

3. David Weinberger, www.hillwatch.com/ PPRC/Quotes/Internet_and_Politics.aspx.

4. On April 7, 2005, General Motors pulled its advertising from the *Los Angeles Times* after columnist Dan McNeil, who covers the automotive trade for the newspaper, published several columns critical of GM, including one that chastised the company for not pursuing hybrid technology but, rather, pushing gas-guzzling SUVs and another that called for the "impeachment" of two of the company's top executives.

5. New editions of all of these works are available: Tarbell (New York: Norton, 1969); Steffens (New York: Sangamore Press, 1957); and Sinclair (Cambridge, MA: B. Bentley, 1971).

6. Mark Wheeler, *Politics and the Mass Media* (Oxford: Blackwell, 1997), 228.

7. Robert Smith, "Running for Office via the Web," *NPR: Morning Edition,* January 23, 2007.

8. Howard Rheingold, "Using Participatory Media and Public Voice to Encourage Civic Engagement," in *Civic Life Online: Learning How Digital Media Can Engage Youth,* ed. Lance W. Bennett, The John D. and Catherine T. MacArthur Foundation Series on

Digital Media and Learning (Cambridge, MA: MIT Press, 2008).

9. Norman H. Nie, Irena Stepanikova, Heili Pals, Lu Zheng, and Xiaobin He, *Ten Years after the Birth of the Internet: How Do Americans Use the Internet in Their Daily Lives?* www.stanford.edu/group/siqss/research/time_study_files/ProjectReport2005.pdf.

10. See Howard Kurtz, *Spin Cycle–How the White House and the Media Manipulate the News* (New York: Simon & Schuster, 1998).

11. Christine Gibbs Springer, "Mastering Strategic Conversations," *PA Times,* September 2006.

12. Jodi Wilgoren, "Shadowed by Threats, Judge Finds New Horror," *New York Times,* March 2, 2005, 1. See also Martin and Susan J. Tolchin, *A World Ignited: How Apostles of Ethnic, Religious and Racial Hatred Torch the Globe* (Lanham, MD: Rowman & Littlefield, 2006).

13. www.internetworldstats.com/stats.htm.

14. Cass Sunstein, *Republic.Com* (Princeton, NJ: Princeton University Press, 2002).

15. Republican National Convention Speech, July 14, 1964, *Eisenhower's Post-Presidential Speeches,* www.eisenhower.archives.gov/speeches/Post-Presidential_speeches.pdf.

16. C. Richard Hofstetter, *Bias in the News: Network Television Coverage of the 1972 Election Campaign* (Columbus, OH: Ohio State University Press, 1976); Michael J. Robinson and Margaret A. Sheehan, *Over the Wire and on TV: CBS and UPI in Campaign '80* (New York: Russell Sage Foundation, 1983).

17. William P. Eveland Jr. and Dhavan V. Shah, "The Impact of Individual and Interpersonal Factors on Perceived News Media Bias," *Political Psychology* 24, no. 1 (2003): 101–17.

18. Michael Parenti, *Inventing Reality: The Politics of the Mass Media* (New York: St. Martin's Press, 1986).

19. Tim Berners-Leer, "Neutrality of the Net," http://dig.csail.mit.edu/breadcrumbs/node/132.

CHAPTER 11

1. See, for example, David E. Price, *The Congressional Experience: A View from the Hill* (Boulder, CO: Westview, 1992).

2. Richard F. Fenno Jr., *Home Style: House Members in Their Districts* (New York: Longman, 2002).

3. www.electiondataservices.com/images/File/NR_Appor08wTables.pdf.

4. *Davis v. Bandemer,* 478 U.S. 109 (1986).

5. Samuel Kernell, ed., *James Madison: The Theory and Practice of Republican Government* (Stanford, CA: Stanford University Press, 2003).

6. Richard F. Fenno Jr., *Congressional Travels* (New York: Pearson Longman, 2007).

7. Sue Thomas, *How Women Legislate* (New York: Oxford University Press, 1994).

8. Edmund Burke, *Speeches at His Arrival at Bristol,* November, 3, 1774, http://books.google.com/books?id=eNILAAAAYAAJ&pg=PA81&dq=Edmund+Burke,.+1774.+Speeches+at+His+Arrival+at+Bristol.+3+November,+3,+1774.&source=gbs_toc_r&cad=0_0.

9. Ibid.

10. Diana Evans, *Greasing the Wheels: Using Pork Barrel Projects to Build Majority Coalitions in Congress* (New York: Cambridge University Press, 2004).

11. Bret Schulte, "A Bridge (Way) Too Far," *U.S. News and World Report,* August 8, 2005, www.usnews.com/usnews/news/articles/050808/8highway.htm.

12. Citizens Against Government Waste, *2010 Congressional Pig Book Summary,* p. 63, www.cagw.org/assets/pig-book-files/2010/2010-pig-book-summary.pdf.

13. See, for example, Bruce Cain, John Ferejohn, and Morris Fiorina, *The Personal Vote: Constituency Service and Electoral Independence* (Cambridge, MA: Harvard University Press, 1987).

14. Walter F. Mondale, testimony in hearing before the Joint Committee on the Organization of Congress, July 1, 1993, www.rules.house.gov/Archives/jcoc2av.htm.

15. Walter J. Oleszek, *Congressional Procedures and the Policy Process,* 7th ed. (Washington, DC: CQ Press, 2007).

16. See Janet M. Martin, *Lessons from the Hill: The Legislative Journey of an Education Program* (New York: St. Martin's, 1994).

17. Gary Cox and Matthew D. McCubbins, *Setting the Agenda* (Cambridge: Cambridge University Press, 2004).

18. Woodrow Wilson, *Constitutional Government in the United States* (New York: Columbia University Press, 1911), 87.

19. David Butler and Bruce Cain, *Congressional Redistricting: Comparative and Theoretical Perspectives* (New York: Macmillan, 1992).

20. Christopher J. Deering and Steven S. Smith, *Committees in Congress,* 3rd ed. (Washington, DC: Congressional Quarterly, 1997).

21. Garrison Nelson, *Committees in the U.S. Congress, 1947–1992,* 2 vols. (Washington, DC: CQ Press, 1993).

22. Steven S. Smith, Jason M. Roberts, and Ryan J. VanderWielen, *The American Congress,* 5th ed. (New York: Cambridge University Press, 2007).

23. Lawrence C. Dodd and Bruce I. Oppenheimer, *Congress Reconsidered,* 8th ed. (Washington, DC: CQ Press, 2004).

24. Sarah H. Binder, *Minority Rights, Majority Rule: Partisanship and the Development of Congress* (New York: Cambridge University Press, 1997).

25. David W. Brady and Mathew D. McCubbins, *Party, Process, and Political Change in Congress: New Perspectives on the History of Congress* (Stanford, CA: Stanford University Press, 2002).

26. Joseph Martin Hernon, *Profiles in Character: Hubris and Heroism in the U.S. Senate, 1789–1990* (Armonk, NY: M. E. Sharpe, 1997).

27. Gary W. Cox, *Legislative Leviathan: Party Government in the House* (Berkeley: University of California Press, 1993).

28. Ronald M. Peters Jr., *The American Speakership: The Office in Historical Perspective,* 2nd ed. (Baltimore: Johns Hopkins University Press, 1997).

29. Susan Webb Hammond, *Congressional Caucuses in National Policy Making* (Baltimore: Johns Hopkins University Press, 2001).

30. Charles Babington and Jonathan Weisman, "Reid, Pelosi Expected to Keep Tight Rein in Both Chambers," *Washington Post,* November 10, 2006: A12.

31. Barbara Sinclair, *Majority Leadership in the US House and the Transformation of the US Senate* (Baltimore: Johns Hopkins University Press, 1990).

32. Barry C. Burden, *Personal Roots of Representation* (Princeton, NJ: Princeton University Press, 2007).

33. Sean Theriault, "Party Polarization in Congress" (paper presented at the annual meeting of the American Political Science Association, Marriott Wardman Park, Omni Shoreham, Washington Hilton, Washington, DC, September 1, 2005), www.allacademic.com/meta/p40938_index.html.

34. Michael J. Malbin, *Unelected Representatives: Congressional Staff and the Future of Representative Government* (New York: Basic Books, 1980).

35. Burdett A. Loomis, *The Contemporary Congress,* 3rd ed. (Boston: Bedford/St. Martin's, 2000).

36. John R. Wright, *Interest Groups and Congress* (New York: Allyn and Bacon, 1996).

37. R. Douglas Arnold, *The Logic of Congressional Action* (New Haven, CT: Yale University Press, 1990).

38. For a discussion of the potential goals of demographic representation, see for example, David T. Canon, "Representing Racial and Ethnic Minorities," in *The Legislative Branch,* eds. Paul J. Quirk and Sarah A. Binder (New York: Oxford University Press, 2005).

CHAPTER 12

1. George C. Edwards III, John H. Kessel, and Bert A. Rockman, eds., *Researching the Presidency: Vital Questions, New Approaches* (Pittsburgh, PA: University of Pittsburgh Press, 1993).

2. Theodore J. Lowi, *The Personal President* (Ithaca, NY: Cornell University Press, 1985).

3. Jean Reith Schroedel, *Congress, the President, and Policymaking: A Historical Analysis* (Armonk, NY: M. E. Sharpe, 1994).

4. William W. Lammers, *The Presidency and Domestic Policy: Comparing Leadership Styles, FDR to Clinton* (Washington, DC: CQ Press, 2000).

5. Andrew Rudalevige, *Managing the President's Program: Presidential Leadership and*

Legislative Policy Formulation (Princeton, NJ: Princeton University Press, 2002).

6. Richard A. Watson, *Presidential Vetoes and Public Policy* (Lawrence: University of Kansas Press, 1993).

7. Robert J. Spitzer, *The Presidential Veto: Touchstone of the American Presidency* (Albany: SUNY Press, 1988).

8. Sidney M. Milkis and Mchael Nelson, *The American Presidency: Origins and Development, 1776–1998,* 4th ed. (Washington, DC: CQ Press, 2003).

9. www.abanet.org/media/releases/news072406.html.

10. http://online.wsj.com/article/SB125116264837455591.html.

11. George C. Edwards III and Steven J. Wayne, *Studying the Presidency* (Knoxville: University of Tennessee Press, 1983).

12. Louis Fisher, *Presidential War Power* (Lawrence: University of Kansas Press, 1995).

13. David S. Broder, "Obama in Command," *Washington Post,* May 21, 2009, www.washingtonpost.com/wp-dyn/content/article/2009/05/20/AR2009052003029.html.

14. Jon Meacham, "A Highly Logical Approach," *Newsweek,* May 16, 2009, www.newsweek.com/id/197891.

15. Cornell G. Hooton, *Executive Governance: Presidential Administrations and Policy Change in the Federal Bureaucracy* (Armonk, NY: M. E. Sharpe, 1997).

16. O. C. Fisher, *Cactus Jack: A Biography of John Nance Garner* (Waco, TX: Texian Press), chap. 11.

17. Bill Clinton, *My Life (*New York: Knopf, 2004), 414.

18. Stephen Skowronek, *The Politics Presidents Make: Leadership from John Adams to George Bush* (Cambridge, MA: Belknap Press, 1997).

19. MaryAnne Borrelli, *The President's Cabinet: Gender, Power, and Representation* (Boulder, CO: Lynne Rienner, 2002).

20. Joel D. Aberbach and Mark A. Peterson, eds., *The Executive Branch* (New York: Oxford University Press, 2005).

21. William E. Leuchtenburg, *In the Shadow of FDR: From Harry Truman to Ronald Reagan* (Ithaca, NY: Cornell University Press, 1989).

22. Kenneth R. Mayer, *With the Stroke of a Pen: Executive Orders and Presidential Power* (Princeton, NJ: Princeton University Press, 2002).

23. www.trumanlibrary.org/9981.htm.

24. *U.S. v. Curtiss-Wright Export Corp.,* 229 U.S. 304 (1936).

25. Mark J. Rozell, *Executive Privilege: Presidential Power, Secrecy, and Accountability,* 2nd ed. rev. (Lawrence: University of Kansas Press, 2002).

26. *U.S. v. Richard M. Nixon,* 418 U.S. 683 (1974).

27. Richard Neustadt, *The Power to Persuade* (New York: Wiley, 1960).

28. *Outlook,* February 27, 1909.

29. Richard E. Neustadt, *Presidential Power and the Modern President* (New York: The Free Press, 1990).

30. George C. Edwards III with Alec M. Gallup, *Presidential Approval: A Sourcebook [Eisenhower to Reagan]* (Baltimore: Johns Hopkins University Press, 1990).

31. Jeffrey K. Tulis, *The Rhetorical Presidency* (Princeton, NJ: Princeton University Press, 1988).

32. Harry A. Bailey Jr. and Jay M. Shafritz, *The American Presidency: Historical and Contemporary Perspectives* (Pacific Grove, CA: Brooks/Cole, 1988).

33. Marc Landy and Sidney M. Milkis, *Presidential Greatness* (Lawrence: University of Kansas Press, 2000).

34. Harold J. Laski, *The American Presidency* (New York: Harper & Row, 1940).

35. William M. Goldsmith, *The Growth of Presidential Power: A Documented History,* 3 vols. (New York: Chelsea House, 1974).

36. *New York Times Co. v. U.S.,* 403 U.S. 713 (1971).

37. Statement of Sen. Howard Baker (R-TN) during the Senate Committee investigation.

38. John Dean, the Nixon presidential transcripts, March 21, 1973.

39. http://nixon.archives.gov/find/tapes/excerpts/watergate.html.

40. David Frost, *I Gave Them a Sword* (New York: William Morrow, 1978).

41. http://blog.washingtonpost.com/the-trail/2007/08/29/a_party_in_disarray.html/.

42. Barbara Gamarekian, "Washington Talk: The Presidency; First Ladies Step Further Out of Shadows," *New York Times,* March 10, 1988, B5.

43. Barbara Bush, commencement address at Wellesley College, June 1, 1990.

44. Charles C. Thach Jr., *The Creation of the Presidency, 1775–1789: A Study in Constitutional History* (Baltimore: Johns Hopkins University Press, 1969).

CHAPTER 13

1. www.whitehouse.gov/omb/budget/Historicals.

2. For a review of the literature on public service motivation, see David J. Houston, "'Walking the Walk' of Public Service Motivation: Public Employees and Charitable Gifts of Time, Blood, and Money," *Journal of Public Administration Research and Theory* 16, no. 1 (2005): 67–86.

3. David J. Houston and Lauren K. Harding, "Trust in the Public Service: A Cross-National Examination" (presented at the 66th Annual National Conference of the Midwest Political Science Association, Chicago, April 3–6, 2008).

4. Charles T. Goodsell, *The Case for Bureaucracy: A Public Administration Polemic,* 4th ed. (Washington, DC: CQ Press, 2004): 104–106.

5. Norman J. Baldwin, "Public Versus Private Employees: Debunking Stereotypes," *Review of Public Personnel Administration* 12 (Winter 1991): 1–27.

6. Goodsell, *The Case for Bureaucracy,* 106.

7. Stuart Greenfield, "Public Sector Employment: The Current Situation" (Washington, DC: The Center for State & Local Government Excellence), www.slge.org/vertical/Sites/%7BA260E1DF-5Aee-459D-84C4-876EFE1E4032%7D/uploads/%7BB4579F88-660D-49DD-8D52-F6928BD43C46%7D.pdf.

8. John T. Woolley and Gerhard Peters, "The American Presidency Project," www.presidency.ucsb.edu/ws/?pid=30436 (Santa Barbara: University of California, hosted, Gerhard Peters, database).

9. www.bls.gov/news.release/union.

10. www.opm.gov/ses/features.asp.

11. www.usaspending.gov.

12. www.msnbc.msn.com/id/23919234.

13. Jeffrey L. Pressman and Aaron Wildavsky, *Implementation: How Great Expectations in Washington Are Dashed in Oakland: Or, Why It's Amazing That Federal Programs Work at All* (Berkeley: University of California Press, 1973).

14. Office of Management and Budget, *FY 2008 Report to Congress on Implementation of the E-Government Act of 2002,* March 1, 2009:3.

15. www.pogo.org/p/x/2007impact.html#contract.

16. Shaila Dewan, "FEMA Ordered to Restore Evacuees' Housing Aid," *New York Times,* November 30, 2006.

17. William T. Gormley Jr. and Steven J. Balla, *Bureaucracy and Democracy: Accountability and Performance* (Washington DC: CQ Press, 2004), 67.

18. Matt Kelley, "Probes at NASA Plummet Under Its Current IG," *USA Today,* January 11, 2008.

19. Charles T. Goodsell, *The Case for Bureaucracy,* 139.

20. Gormley and Balla, *Bureaucracy and Democracy,* 164–78.

21. Goodsell, The Case for Bureaucracy, 54.

22. Ibid., 30.

23. www.house.gov/etheridge/Press-FEMAcontracts.htm.

24. Richard Stillman, *The American Bureaucracy: The Core of Modern Government* (Chicago: Nelson Hall Publishers, 1996), 308.

25. http://media.washingtonpost.com/wp-serv/politics/documents/gov_experience_final_111609.pdf.

CHAPTER 14

1. "More Than Half of Americans Approve of the Job the Court Is Doing, Which Is Lower Than Approval Has Been at Some Recent Points but Still Much Higher Than Public Approval of President George W. Bush and Congress." Joseph Carroll, "1/3 of Americans Say U.S. Supreme Court Is

'Too Conservative,'" Gallup News Service, October 2, 2007.

2. Christopher N. May, *Constitutional Law— National Power and Federalism: Examples and Explanations* (New York: Aspen, 2004).

3. Morton J. Horowitz, *The Transformation of American Law, 1780–1860* (Cambridge, MA: Harvard University Press, 1977).

4. Charles D. Shipan, *Designing Judicial Review* (Ann Arbor: University of Michigan Press, 1997).

5. Joel B. Grossman, "Paths to the Bench: Selecting Supreme Court Justices in a 'Juristocratic' World," in *The Judicial Branch,* ed. Kermit L. Hall and Kevin T. McGuire (Oxford: Oxford University Press, 2005), 143.

6. Robert G. McCloskey, *The American Supreme Court,* 4th ed. (Chicago: University of Chicago Press, 2005).

7. Erwin Chemerinsky, *Constitutional Law: Principles and Policies* (New York: Aspen, 2006).

8. www.citmedialaw.org/threats/ simorangkir-v-love#description.

9. Robert A. Carp, Ronald Stidham, and Kenneth L. Manning, *Judicial Process in America* (Washington, DC: CQ Press, 2007).

10. Robert A. Carp and Ronald Stidham, *The Federal Courts,* 4th ed. (Washington, DC: CQ Press, 2001).

11. www.whitehouse.gov/news/releases/2008/ 05/20080517-2.html.

12. The exception is those cases whose original jurisdiction is the U.S. Supreme Court, which is not typically considered a trial court.

13. www.uscourts.gov/faq.html.

14. 50 U.S.C. §§1801–1811, 1821–29, 1841–46, and 1861–62.

15. Lawrence Baum, "The Future of the Judicial Branch," in *The Judicial Branch,* ed. Kermit L. Hall and Kevin T. McGuire (Oxford: Oxford University Press, 2005), 523.

16. See, for example, Hugh Hewitt, "Why the Right Was Wrong," *New York Times,* October 28, 2005, www.nytimes.com/2005/10/28/ opinion/28hewitt.html?ex=1288152000& en=53aee2bcf6872884&ei=5090&partner= rssuserland&emc=rss.

17. www.nytimes.com/interactive/2010/04/09/ us/politics/20100409-stevens-candidates .html.

18. Henry J. Abraham, *Justices and Presidents: A Political History of Appointments to the Supreme Court* (New York: Oxford University Press, 1974).

19. H. W. Perry Jr., *Deciding to Decide: Agenda Setting in the United States Supreme Court* (Cambridge, MA: Harvard University Press, 1994).

20. Bob Woodward, *The Brethren: Inside the Supreme Court* (New York: Simon & Schuster, 2005).

21. Henry J. Abraham, *The Judicial Process* (New York: Oxford University Press, 1998).

22. *Gratz v. Bollinger,* 539 U.S. 244 (2003) and *Grutter v. Bollinger,* 539 U.S. 306 (2003).

23. Benjamin N. Cardozo, *The Nature of the Judicial Process* (Mineola, NY: Dover, 2005).

24. Stephen Breyer, *Active Liberty: Interpreting Our Democratic Constitution* (New York: Vintage Books, 2006).

25. Gregory A. Caldeira and John R. Wright, "*Amicus Curiae* Before the Supreme Court: Who Participates, When, and How Much? *Journal of Politics* 52 (1990): 803.

26. William H. Rehnquist, *The Supreme Court* (New York: Vintage, 2002).

27. Bernard Schwartz, *Decision: How the Supreme Court Decides Cases* (New York: Oxford University Press, 1996).

28. Jeffrey A. Segal and Harold J. Spaeth, *The Supreme Court and the Attitudinal Model* (New York: Cambridge University Press, 2003).

29. Jeffrey Toobin, *The Nine: Inside the Secret World of the Supreme Court* (New York: Doubleday, 2007).

30. Lawrence Baum, *The Supreme Court* (Washington, DC: CQ Press, 2006).

31. Paul J. Wahlbeck, James F. Spriggs II, and Forrest Maltzman, "The Politics of Dissents and Concurrences on the U.S. Supreme Court," *American Politics Quarterly* 27 (1999): 488–514.

32. *New York Times,* "The Roberts Court Returns," www.nytimes.com/2007/09/30/ opinion/30sun1.html; Charles Lane, "Narrow Victories Move Court to the Right," *Washington Post,* June 29, 2007, p. A04; Linda Greenhouse, "Roberts Court Is a Conservative's Dream," *International Herald Tribune,* www.iht.com/articles/2007/07/01/news/ scotus.php.

33. www.gallup.com/poll/4732/Supreme-/ Court.aspx.

34. *Parents Involved in Community Schools v. Seattle School District No. 1,* 551 U.S. _____ (2007).

35. *Gonzales v. Carhart,* 550 U.S. (2007).

36. *Safford Unified School District v. Redding,* 557 U.S. _____ (2009).

37. *Horne v. Flores,* 57 U.S. _____ (2009).

38. *Melendez-Diaz v. Massachusetts,* 57 U.S. _____ (2009).

39. Lee Epstein and Jack Knight, *The Choices Justices Make* (Washington, DC: CQ Press, 1998).

40. Lee Cokorinos, *The Assault on Diversity: An Organized Challenge to Racial and Gender Justice* (Lanham, MD: Rowman & Littlefield, 2003), 9.

41. *Miranda v. Arizona,* 384 U.S. 436.

42. *Gideon v. Wainwright,* 372 U.S. 335 (1963).

43. *Griswold v. Connecticut,* 381 U.S. 479 (1965).

44. Antonin Scalia, *A Matter of Interpretation: Federal Courts and the Law* (Princeton, NJ: Princeton University Press, 1998).

45. Thomas M. Keck, *The Most Activist Supreme Court in History: The Road to Modern Judicial Conservatism* (Chicago: University of Chicago Press, 2004).

46. *Oregon v. Mitchell,* 400 U.S. 112 (1970).

47. Andrew Jay Koshner, *Solving the Puzzle of Interest Group Litigation* (Westport, CT: Greenwood, 1998).

48. John E. Nowak and Ronald D. Rotunda, *Constitutional Law (Hornbook Series)* (St. Paul, MN: West, 2004).

CHAPTER 15

1. Trudy Rubin, "Global Economy Waits for Next 'Conductor,'" *Philadelphia Inquirer,* January 27, 2008.

2. Bureau of Economic Analysis, "Measuring the Economy: A Primer on GDP and the National Income and Product Accounts," September 2007, www.bea.gov/national/ pdf/nipa_primer.pdf.

3. http://hdr.undp.org/en/statistics/.

4. www.census.gov/hhes/www/poverty/data/ threshld/thresh08.html.

5. www.whitehouse.gov/omb/budget/ Historicals/.

6. www.brillig.com/debt_clock.

7. Sherman Antitrust Act (1890); Clayton Antitrust Act (1914).

8. www.u-s-history.com/pages/h1603.html.

9. Ralph Nader, *Unsafe at Any Speed: The Designed-in Dangers of American Automobiles* (New York: Grossman Publishing, 1965), ix.

10. Alexei Barrionuevo, "Globalization in Every Loaf," *New York Times,* June 16, 2007.

11. L. Josh Bivens and John Irons, "A Feeble Recovery: The Fundamental Economic Weaknesses of the 2001–2007 Expansion," Economic Policy Institute Briefing Paper #214, May 1, 2008, www.epi.org/ publications/entry/4139.

12. Jared Bernstein, "Real Wages Decline in 2007," Economic Policy Issue Brief #240, 2008, www.epi.org/content.cfm/ib240.

13. Jared Bernstein, Elise Gould, and Lawrence Mishel; "Income Picture: Poverty, Income and Health Insurance Trends in 2006," August 28, 2007, www.epi.org/content .cfm/webfeatures_econindicators _income20070828.

14. Ibid.

15. Peter Grier, "Rich-poor gap gaining attention," *Christian Science Monitor,* June 14, 2005, viewed at www.csmonitor.com/ 2005/0614/p01s03-usec.htm.

16. Graham Bowley, "That 70's Look: Stagflation," *New York Times,* February 21, 2008.

17. Edmund L. Andrews, "Top Officials See Bleaker Outlook for the Economy," *New York Times,* February 15, 2008.

18. David Leonhardt, "Judging Stimulus by Job Data Reveals Success," *New York Times,* February 17, 2010.

19. Quoted in David Kamp: "Rethinking the American Dream," *Vanity Fair,* April 2009.

20. David Leonhardt, "Has the Jump in Wages Met Its End?" *New York Times,* September 12, 2007.

21. Bob Herbert, "Here Come the Millennials," *New York Times,* May 13, 2008.

CHAPTER 16

1. Visit the federal government's Web site (www.whitehouse.gov/omb/expectmore/index.html) for a more complete list of domestic programs.
2. http://earthday.wilderness.org/history/.
3. *Massachusetts v. EPA*, (2007) 549 U.S., 497.
4. David Hosansky, *The Environment: A to Z* (Washington, DC: CQ Press, 2001), 80–81.
5. Ibid., 243.
6. http://tonto.eia.doe.gov/energyexplained/index.cfm?page=about_home.
7. http://tonto.eia.doe.gov/energy_in_brief/foreign_oil_dependence.cfm.
8. Bill Vlasic, "Early Target for Fuel Economy Is Expected," *New York Times,* April 22, 2008.
9. Mary Cooper, "Energy Policy," in *Economic Issues: Selections from the CQ Researcher* (Washington, DC: CQ Press), 146–49.
10. Ibid., 139.
11. Josef Herbert, "Climate Bill May Spur Energy Revolution: President Claims Measure Will Strengthen Economy," Associated Press, June 28, 2009.
12. http://opencrs.com/document/RS22915.
13. Stephen Labaton, "Congress Passes Increase in the Minimum Wage," *New York Times,* May 25, 2007.
14. www.labotlawcenter.com/t-State-Minimum-Wage-Rates.aspx.
15. Center on Budget and Policy Priorities, "Policy Basics: The Earned Income Tax Credit," December 4, 2009, www.cbpp.org/cms/index.cfm?fa+view&id+2505#.
16. LaDonna Pavetti and Dottie Rosenbaum, "Creating a Safety Net That Works When the Economy Doesn't: The Role of the Food Stamp and TANF Programs" (Washington, DC: The Center on Budget and Policy Priorities, February 25, 2010), www.cbpp.org/cms/index.cfm?fa+view&id=3096.
17. www.census.gov/hhes/www/cpstables/032009/pov/new01_100.htm.
18. Joint Center for Housing Studies of Harvard University, *The State of the Nation's Housing 2005* (Boston: Harvard University, 2005), 24.
19. www.nationalhomeless.org/publications/facts.html.
20. www.hud.gov/offices/pih/programs/hcv/about/fact_sheet.cfm.
21. www.census.gov/hhes/www/hlthins08/hlth08asc.html.
22. Kendra Hovey and Harold A. Hovey, *CQ's State Fact Finder 2007* (Washington, DC: CQ Press, 2007), 143.
23. www.cms.hhs.gov/medicaideligibility/02?areyoueligible_asp.
24. www.whitehouse.gov/the-press-office/remarks-president-barack-obama-address-joint-session-congress.
25. Sheryl Gay Stolberg and Robert Peat, "Obama Signs Health Care Overhaul Bill, With a Flourish," www.nytimes.com/2010/03/24/health/policy/24health.html.
26. www.whitehouse.gov/news/releases/2006/02/print/20060223.html.
27. Deborah Macmillan, "Overview: Federal Immigration Policy and Proposed Reforms," www.lwv.org/AM/Template.cfm?Section=LWVUSImmigrationStudy&TEMPLATE=/CM/ContentDisplay.cfm&CONTENTID=7426.
28. Ibid.
29. Patricia Hatch, "What Motivates Immigration to America," www.lwv.org/AM/Template.cfm?Section=LWVUSImmigrationStudy&CONTENTID=8179&TEMPLATE=/CM/ContentDisplay.cfm.

CHAPTER 17

1. Congressional Research Service Report to Congress, "U.S. Foreign Aid to East and Southeast Asia: Selected Recipients," August 22, 2007, www.fas.org/sgp/crs/row/RL31362.pdf, p. 31.
2. Ibid., p. 36.
3. "About Those Billions," *Newsweek,* www.newsweek.com/id/218932.
4. "Dodd Assesses Efforts by U.S. to Increase Economic, Diplomatic, Political Pressure on Iran," March 21, 2007, http://dodd.senate.gov/index.php?q=node/3793.
5. Saul K. Padover, ed., *Wilson's Ideals* (Washington, DC: American Council on Public Affairs, 1942), 108.
6. www.unicef.org/sowc97/.
7. Secretary of State Colin L. Powell, remarks to the United Nations Security Council, February 5, 2003, www.state.gov/secretary/former/powell/remarks/2003/17300.htm.
8. www.npr.org/templates/story/story.php?storyId=4859238.
9. See, for example, James Risen, *State of War: The Secret History of the CIA and the Bush Administration* (New York: Free Press, 2006).
10. "Congress Abdicates War Powers," *The New American* (November 4, 2002): 5.
11. www.ourdocuments.gov/doc.php?flash=true&doc=90.
12. Roger H. Davidson, "Invitation to Struggle: An Overview of Legislative-Executive Relations," *Annals of the American Academy of Political and Social Science* 499 (1988): 1, 9–21.
13. Article 5 of the North Atlantic Treaty, Washington D.C., April 4, 1949, www.nato.int/docu/basictxt/treaty.htm.
14. President Harry S. Truman's address before a joint session of Congress on March 12, 1947.
15. George F. Kennan, writing under the pseudonym "X," "Sources of Soviet Conduct," *Foreign Affairs* (July 1947): 25.
16. Graham T. Allison and Philip Zelikow, *Essence of Decision: Explaining the Cuban Missile Crisis,* 2nd ed. (New York: Longman, 1999).
17. www.nps.gov/archive/eise/quotes2.htm.
18. Samuel P. Huntington, "The Clash of Civilizations?" *Foreign Affairs* 72, no. 3 (Summer 1993): 22–49.

CHAPTER 18

1. Theodore Roosevelt, "Charter of Democracy," speech to the 1912 Ohio constitutional convention.
2. www.iandrinstitute.org/IRI%20Initiative%20Use%20(2006-11).pdf.
3. www.iandrinstitute.org/IRI%20Initiative%20Use%20%281904-2008%29.pdf.
4. www.ncsl.org/default.aspx?tabid=18908; www.iandrinstitute.org/BW%202009-2%20Results%20%28v1%29.pdf.
5. M. Dane Waters, "The Initiative Industry: Its Impact on the Future of the Initiative Process," www.iandrinstitute.org/New%20IRI%20Website%20Info/I&R%20Research%20and%20History/I&R%20Studies/Waters%20-%20The%20Initiative%20Industry-Its%20Impact%20on%20the%20Future%20.pdf.
6. Alan Greenblatt, "Total Recall," in *State and Local Government 2004–2005,* ed. Thad L. Beyle (Washington, DC: CQ Press, 2004), 30.
7. http://igs.berkeley.edu/library/htRecall2003.html.
8. http://vote2003.sos.ca.gov/recall/1-1-proponents-grounds.html.
9. Thad Beyle, "The California Recall and Replacement Elections of 2003," in *State and Local Government 2004–2005* (Washington, DC: CQ Press), 34.
10. M. Dane Waters, "I Couldn't Recall," in *State and Local Government 2004–2005* (Washington, DC: CQ Press), 34.
11. www.ballotpedia.org/wiki/index.php/Jennifer_Granholm_recall,_Michigan,_2010.
12. "A Case of Faulty Recall," *Governing* (December 2009): 12.
13. Joel Lieske, "The Changing Regional Subcultures of the United States: A New Cultural Measure for Understanding Political Behavior" (paper presented at 2004 Annual Meeting of the Midwest Political Science Association, Chicago, April 15–18, 2004), p. 2.
14. Daniel Elazar, *American Federalist,* 3rd ed. (New York: Harper & Row, 1984).
15. Lieske, "The Changing Regional Subcultures of the United States, 5.
16. Ibid., 6.
17. Kendra A. Hovey and Harold A. Hovey, *CQ's State Fact Finder 2007* (Washington, DC: CQ Press, 2007), 33.
18. http://quickfacts.census.gov/qfd/states/06000.html.
19. http://quickfacts.census.gov/qfd/states/54000.html.
20. U.S. Census Burau, *Statistical Abstract of the United States: 2010* (Washington, DC: U.S. Government Printing Office, 2010), Table 449.
21. Hovey and Hovey, *CQ's State Fact Finder 2007,* 210; Kevin Smith, Alan Greenblatt, and John Buntin, *Governing States and Localities* (Washington, DC: CQ Press, 2005), 421.

22. Hovey and Hovey, *CQ's State Fact Finder 2007*, 231.

23. http://measuringup.highereducation.org/compare/state_addcomparison.cfm.

24. Hovey and Hovey, *CQ's State Fact Finder 2007*, 218, 225, 226.

25. "Financing America's Public Schools," www.nga.org/cda/files/PUBLICSCHOOLS.pdf.

26. U.S. Census Bureau, *Statistical Abstract of the United States: 2006*, 125th ed. (Washington, DC: U.S. Government Printing Office, 2005), Table 439.

27. Hovey and Hovey, *CQ's State Fact Finder 2007*, 143.

28. Josh Goodman, "Where Have all the Dollars Gone?" *Governing* (October 2009): 45–48.

29. Josh Goodman, "Uneven Stimulus," *Governing* (April 2009): 17.

30. Rob Gurwitt, "Broke and Broken," *Governing* (January 2010): 19–23.

31. Liz Sidoti, "Govs Expect Worst to Come: Joblessness, Bare budgets, to Continue," *The Scranton Sunday Times,* February 21, 2010, B3.

32. Ibid.

33. Thad Beyle, ed., *State and Local Government 2004–2005* (Washington, DC, CQ Press, 2004), 110.

34. www.nga.org/portal/site/nga/menuitem.42b929b1a5b9e4eac3363d10501010a0/?vgnextoid=d54c8aaa2ebbff00VgnVCM1000001a01010aRCRD&vgnextfmt=curgov.

35. www.afdc.energy.gov/afdc/laws/state.

36. Tom Arrandale, "A Bolder Boulder," *Governing* (February 2007): 56.

37. For more information on women in elected and appointed government positions, see the Web site of the Center for Women in Politics: www.cawp.rutgers.edu.

38. Statistics on race and ethnicity in state legislatures are available at www.ncsl.org/default.aspx?tabid=14767. Statistics on race and ethnicity in state populations are available at http://quickfacts.census.gov/qfd/index.html.

39. www.cawp.rutgers.edu/fast_facts/levels_of_office/Statewide-Current.php.

40. U.S. Census Bureau, *2007 Census of Government,* "Local Government and Public School Systems by Type and State," www.census.gov/govs/cog/GovOrgTab03ss.html.

41. Mayraj Fahim, "U.S. Voters Are Not Convinced That Big Is Better in Local Government," June 2005, www.citymayors.com/government/mergers_locgov.html.

42. U.S. Census Bureau, *2007 Census of Government,* "Local Government and Public School Systems by Type and State," www.census.gov/govs/cog/GovOrgTab03ss.html.

CHAPTER 19

1. From John Steinbeck, *Travels with Charley: In Search of America* (1962), in *The Columbia World of Quotations* (New York: Columbia University Press, 1996), n. 55679.

2. Terry G. Jordan, *German Seed in Texas Soil: Immigrant Farmers in Nineteenth Century Texas* (Austin: University of Texas Press, 1966).

3. Robert A. Calvert and Arnold DeLeon, *The History of Texas* (Arlington Heights, IL: Harland Davidson, 1990), 99–100.

4. Raul Gonzales was appointed by Governor Mark White to the Texas Supreme Court in 1984. He has subsequently been elected and reelected to the court.

5. Daniel J. Elazar, *American Federalism: A View from the States* (New York: HarperCollins, 1984).

6. Ibid., 90.

7. Ibid.

8. Ibid., 86.

9. Platforms of Beauford Jester, 1946 and 1948; Allan Shivers, 1950, 1952, and 1954; Price Daniel, 1956, 1958, and 1960. See James R. Soukup, Clifton McCleskey, and Harry Holloway, *Party and Factional Division in Texas* (Austin: University of Texas Press, 1964).

10. Roy Morris, *Sheridan: The Life and Wars of General Phil Sheridan* (New York: Crown, 1992).

11. T. R. Fehrenbach, *Lone Star: A History of Texas and the Texans* (New York: Collier, 1980), 276–77.

12. D'Ann Petersen, "Texas Transitions to Service Economy," *Southwest Economy,* Issue 3, May/June 2007; Federal Reserve Bank of Dallas, www.dallasfed.org/research/swe/2007/swe0703b.cfm.

13. California: Exports, Jobs, and Foreign Investment March 2010, Export.gov, www.trade.gov/td/industry/otea/state_reports/california.html.

14. "Texas: Crossroads to the World," Texas Ahead, 2010, Issue 3, www.texasahead.org/economic_developer/downloads/1313-3TexasAhead_Global.pdf.

15. Vivek Wadhwa, Ben Rissing, Aneesh Chopra, Ramakrishnan Balasubramanian, and Alyse Freilich, "U.S.-Based Global Intellectual Property Creation," Kauffman Foundation, www.kauffman.org/pdf/WIPO_103107.pdf.

16. Laila Assanie and Pia Orrenius, "Texas Economy Shakes Off Rough Ride in 2009," Federal Reserve Bank of Dallas, First Quarter 2010, www.dallasfed.org/research/swe/2010/swe1001b.cfm.

17. Julia Preston, "Texas Hospitals Reflect Debate on Immigration," *New York Times,* July 18, 2006, www.nytimes.com/2006/07/18/us/18immig.html?partner=rssnyt&emc=rss.

CHAPTER 20

1. T. R. Fehrenbach, *Lone Star,* 146–47 (see chap. 19, n. 11).

2. Ibid., 206.

3. Ibid., 222–23.

4. Ibid., 411–14.

5. Ibid., 434–35.

6. Ibid., 436.

7. Ibid.

8. Donald S. Lutz, "Toward a Theory of Constitutional Amendment," *American Political Science Review* 88 (June 1994): 355–70.

9. Texas Constitution, Art. I, Sec. 3a.

10. *The Book of the States 2003,* vol. 35 (Lexington, KY: Council of State Governments, 2003), 10, table 1.1.

11. Lutz, "Toward a Theory of Constitutional Amendment."

12. Texas Constitution, Art. XVII, Sec. 2.

13. Lutz, "Toward a Theory of Constitutional Amendment," 359.

14. Ibid., 360.

15. Ibid.

16. These figures are as of the general election in November 2005.

17. Number of amendments and dates of elections from Secretary of State, "Vote on Proposed Amendments to Texas Constitution, 1875–November 1993" (Austin: State of Texas, 1993), 12–29, data 1995–2003, www.sos.state.tx.us.

18. Constitutional amendments ballot general election, November 7, 1978, tax relief amendment, H.J.R. 1.

19. Dave Montgomery, "Texas' Gay Marriage Ban May Have Banned All Marriages," *Fort Worth Star-Telegram,* November 18, 2009, www.mcclatchydc.com/2009/11/18/79112/texas-gay-marriage-ban-may-have.html.

20. *The Book of the States 2005,* vol. 37, 10, table 1.1.

CHAPTER 21

1. Calvert and DeLeon, *The History of Texas,* 212 (see chap. 19, n. 3).

2. Ibid., 387.

3. *U.S. v. Texas,* 384 U.S. 155 (1966).

4. *Texas Almanac and State Industrial Guide, 1970–1971* (Dallas: A. H. Belo, 1969), 529.

5. *Texas Almanac and State Industrial Guide, 1974–1975* (Dallas: A. H. Belo, 1973), 529 (see chap. 20, n. 10).

6. *The Book of the States,* vol. 30, 23, table 5.6 (see chap. 20, n. 10).

7. *Nixon v. Herndon et al.,* 273 U.S. 536 (1927); *Nixon v. Condon et al.,* 286 U.S. 73 (1932).

8. *Grovey v. Townsend,* 295 U.S. 45 (1935).

9. *Smith v. Allwright,* 321 U.S. 649 (1944). Also, in *U.S. v. Classic,* 313 U.S. 299 (1941), the U.S. Supreme Court ruled that a primary in a one-party state (Louisiana) was an election within the meaning of the U.S. Constitution.

10. George McKenna, *The Drama of Democracy: American Government and Politics,* 2nd ed. (Guilford, CT: Dushkin, 1994), 129.

11. Wilbourn E. Benton, *Texas Politics: Constraints and Opportunities,* 5th ed. (Chicago: Nelson-Hall, 1984), 65.

12. C. Richard Hoffstedder, "Inter-Party Competition and Electoral Turnout: The Case of Indiana," *American Journal of Political Science* 17 (May 1973): 351–66.

13. Norman R. Luttbeg, "Differential Voting Turnout Decline in the American States," *Social Science Quarterly* 65 (March 1984): 60–73.

14. Ibid.

15. "Texas State Union," Unions.org, www.unions.org/home/umap43-.htm.

16. Robert Lineberry, *Equity and Urban Policy: The Distribution of Urban Services* (Newbury Park, CA: Sage, 1977).

17. David Knowles, "Texas Yanks Thomas Jefferson from Teaching Standard," AOL News, March 12, 2010, www.aolnews.com/nation/article/texas-removes-thomas-jefferson-from-teaching-standard/19397481.

18. Keith E. Hamm and Charles W. Wiggins, "The Transformation from Personnel to Information Lobbying," in *Interest Group Politics in the Southern States,* ed. Ronald J. Hrebenar and Clive S. Thomas (Tuscaloosa: University of Alabama Press, 1992), 152.

19. Ibid., 157.

20. Ibid.

21. Clive S. Thomas and Ronald J. Hrebenar, "Interest Groups in State Politics," in *Politics in the American States: A Comparative Analysis* (5th ed.), ed. Virginia Gray, Herbert Jacob, and Robert Albritton (Glenview, IL: Scott Foresman, 1990), 154.

22. The Texas Research League recently changed its name to the Texas Taxpayers and Research Association. It is headquartered in Austin.

23. Thomas R. Dye, *Politics in States and Communities,* 7th ed. (Englewood Cliffs, NJ: Prentice Hall, 1991), 112–13.

24. David F. Prindel, *Petroleum Politics and the Texas Railroad Commission* (Austin: University of Texas Press, 1981).

CHAPTER 22

1. Data for Figure 21.1, for 1952–1985, from James A. Dyer, Arnold Vedlitz, and David B. Hill, "New Voters, Switchers, and Political Party Realignment in Texas," *Western Political Quarterly* 41 (March 1988): 156; for 1994, from "The Texas Poll," 1994, Harte-Hanks Communications; for 1996, 1998, 2002, and 2005, from Texas Poll data, Scripps Howard, University of Texas at Austin.

2. V. O. Key Jr., *Southern Politics in State and Nation* (New York: Knopf, 1949), 7.

3. Calvert and DeLeon, *History of Texas,* 201–207 (see chap. 19, n. 3).

4. James R. Soukup, Clifton McCleskey, and Harry Holloway, *Party and Factional Division in Texas* (Austin: University of Texas Press, 1964), 8.

5. Ibid., 11.

6. Douglas O. Weeks, *Texas Presidential Politics in 1952* (Austin: University of Texas, Institute of Public Affairs, 1953), 3–4.

7. The budget actually increased during this period.

8. David A. Stockman, *The Triumph of Politics: How the Reagan Revolution Failed* (New York: Harper & Row, 1986).

9. Dyer, Vedlitz, and Hill, "New Voters, Switchers, and Political Party Realignment in Texas," 164.

10. John Williams, "Yellow Dogs Lose Bite in East Texas, *Houston Chronicle* (November 18, 2002): 17A, 24A.

11. Allan Turner, "Snapping Back: GOP Nipping on Heels of Yellow Dog Democrats," *Houston Chronicle* (March 5, 1995): 1D.

12. Ibid.

13. James A. Dyer, Jan E. Leighley, and Arnold Vedlitz, "Party Identification and Public Opinion: Establishing a Competitive Two Party System," in *Texas Reader,* ed. Tony Champagne and Ted Harpham (New York: Norton, 1997), 113–28.

14. Walter D. Burnham, *The Current Crisis in American Politics* (Oxford: Oxford University Press, 1982).

15. Texas Secretary of State, www.sos.state.tx.us.

16. James A. Anderson, Richard W. Murray, and Edward L. Farley, *Texas Politics: An Introduction,* 6th ed. (New York: HarperCollins, 1992), 34.

17. The Raza Unida party did not receive enough votes to qualify as a minor party but challenged this in court. The federal court sustained the challenge, and they were allowed to operate as a minor party.

18. The Libertarian Party of Texas, www.tx.lp.org.

19. Wayne Slater and Gromer Jeffers Jr., "Many Obama Voters Ignored Other Texas Primary Races," *Dallas Morning News,* March 9, 2008, www.dallasnews.com/sharedcontent/dws/dn/latestnews/stories/030908dnpoldemvoters.3a5249f.html.

20. Associated Press, "Clinton Campaign Wants Texas to Postpone Party Conventions," *Dallas Morning News,* March 16, 2008, www.dallasnews.com/sharedcontent/dws/dn/latestnews/stories/031708dnpoltxconventions.c4169f.html.

21. Interview with Neeley Lewis, Democratic Party chair for Brazos County, Texas, May 30, 1996.

22. Benton, *Texas Politics,* 80–81 (see chap. 21, n. 11).

23. Ann O. Bowman and Richard C. Kearney, *State and Local Government* (Boston: Houghton Mifflin, 1990), 158–59. Also see Charles S. Bullock III and Loch K. Johnson, *Runoff Elections in the United States* (Chapel Hill: University of North Carolina Press, 1992).

24. Jaime Powell, "High Duval Turnout Attracts State's Notice," *Caller-Times,* March 16, 2006, www.caller.com/ccct/local_news/

article/0,1641,CCCT_811_4546107,00.html.

25. Norman D. Brown, *Hood, Bonnet and Little Brown Jug: Texas Politics, 1921–1928* (College Station: Texas A&M University Press, 1984).

26. Bowman and Kearney, *State and Local Government,* 166. The "feel good" and "sainthood" classifications were adopted from this source.

27. Texans for Public Justice, "Tony Sanchez's War Chest: Who Gives to a $600 Million Man?" www.tpj.org/docs/2002/10/reports/sanchez/page3.html.

28. Texans for Public Justice, "Governor Perry's War Chest: Who Said Yes to Governor No?" www.tpj.org/docs/2002/10/reports/perry/page3.html.

29. Lobby Watch, "Texas Loan Stars Incurred $48 Million in Political Debts," www.tpj.org/lobby_Watch/latetrain.html.

CHAPTER 23

1. Samuel C. Patterson, "Legislators and Legislatures in the American States," in *Politics in the American States* (6th ed.), ed. Virginia Gray and Herbert Jacob (Washington, DC: CQ Press, 1996), 164.

2. Texas Constitution, Art. III, Sec. 26.

3. Leroy Hardy, Alan Heslop, and Stuart Anderson, *Reapportionment Politics* (Beverly Hills, CA: Sage, 1981), 18.

4. Gordon E. Baker, *The Reapportionment Revolution: Representation, Political Power and the Supreme Court* (New York: Random House, 1966).

5. Texas Constitution, Art. III, Sec. 28.

6. *Bush, Governor of Texas et al. v. Vera et al.,* No. 94-805. Case decided on June 13, 1996.

7. *Hunt v. Cromartie,* No. 562, U.S. 541 (2001).

8. Dye, *Politics in States and Communities,* 157 (see chap. 21, n. 23).

9. Harvey Tucker and Gary Halter, *Texas Legislative Almanac 2001* (College Station: Texas A&M University Press, 2001).

10. Gary C. Jacobson, *The Politics of Congressional Elections,* 3rd ed. (New York: HarperCollins, 1992).

11. Kevin A. Hill, "Does the Creation of Majority Black Districts Aid Republicans? An Analysis of the 1992 Congressional Election in Eight Southern States," *Journal of Politics* 57 (May 1995): 348–401.

12. Samuel C. Patterson, "Legislative Politics in the States," in *Politics in the American States,* 6th ed., 179–86.

13. Lawrence W. Miller, "Legislative Turnover and Political Careers: A Study of Texas Legislators, 1969–75," PhD dissertation, Texas Tech University, 1977, 43–45.

14. *The Book of the States 1994–1995,* 29, table A (see chap. 20, n. 10). Also see the National Conference of State Legislatures, www.ncsl.org.

15. *Presiding Officers of the Texas Legislature, 1846–2002* (Austin: Texas Legislative Council, 2002).

16. Interview with William P. Hobby, 1993, Texas A&M University, College Station.
17. *The Book of the States 1998–1999,* 48, table 2.13.
18. J. William Davis, *There Shall Also Be a Lieutenant Governor* (Austin: University of Texas, Institute of Public Affairs, 1967).
19. Harvey Tucker, "Legislative Calendars and Workload Management in Texas," *Journal of Politics* 51 (August 1989): 632.
20. Ibid., 633.
21. Ibid., 643.
22. Harvey J. Tucker, "Legislative Workload Congestion in Texas," *Journal of Politics* 49 (1987): 557.
23. Ibid., 569.
24. E. Lee Bernick and Charles W. Wiggins, "Legislative Norms in Eleven States," *Legislative Studies Quarterly* 7 (May 1983): 194–95.
25. Ibid.
26. National Conference of State Legislatures, *State Legislature* 20 (November 1994): 5.
27. Keith E. Hamm and Gary F. Moncrief, "Legislative Politics in the States," in *Politics in the American States* (7th ed.), ed. Virginia Gray, Russell L. Hanson, and Herbert Jacob (Washington, DC: Congressional Quarterly Press, 1999), 145, table 5.1.
28. Rich Jones, "State Legislatures," in *The Book of the States 1994–1995,* 99.
29. *The Book of the States 1998–1999,* 64–67, table 7.2.
30. Dye, *Politics in States and Communities,* 192.

CHAPTER 24

1. Thad L. Beyle, "Governors: The Middlemen and Women in Our Political System," in *Politics in the American States,* 6th ed., 197 (see chap. 23, n. 1).
2. Ibid.
3. *The Book of the States 2005,* 218, table 4.3 (see chap. 20, n. 10).
4. *The Book of the States 1994–1995,* 66.
5. Ibid.
6. Bowman and Kearney, *State and Local Government,* 206 (see chap. 22, n. 23).
7. Wilbourn E. Benton, *Texas: Its Government and Politics,* 2nd ed. (Englewood Cliffs, NJ: Prentice Hall, 1966), 222–24.
8. Victor E. Harlow, *Harlow's History of Oklahoma,* 5th ed. (Norman, OK: Author, 1967), 294–315.
9. Daniel R. Grant and Lloyd B. Omdahl, *State and Local Government in America* (Madison, WI: Brown & Benchmark, 1987), 260.
10. S. M. Morehouse, *State Politics, Parties and Policy* (New York: Holt, Rinehart & Winston, 1981), 206.
11. Beyle, "Governors," 230.
12. Ibid., 231.
13. Gromer Jeffers Jr., "Hutchison Proposes Term Limit for Governor, Other Changes," *Dallas Morning News,* January 19, 2010, www.dallasnews.com/sharedcontent/dws/news/localnews/stories/DN-hutchison_20pol.ART.State.Edition1.4ba632f.html;

Jason Embry and Corrie MacLaggan, "Newspapers' Poll: Perry Has Comfortable Lead as Voting Starts," *The Statesman,* February 13, 2010, www.statesman.com/news/texas-politics/newspapers-poll-perry-has-comfortable-lead-as-voting-237070.html.
14. Beyle, "Governors," 221.
15. Until 1996, the voters also elected a state treasurer. In 1996, the voters approved a constitutional amendment abolishing that office. These functions have been transferred to other state agencies.
16. *Guide to Texas State Agencies* (Austin: University of Texas, Lyndon B. Johnson School of Public Affairs, 1994).
17. Ibid.
18. Beyle, "Governors," 231.
19. *The Book of the States 1998–1999,* 22, table 2.4.
20. Beyle, "Governors," 234–35.
21. *The Book of the States 1998–1999,* 20, table 2.3.
22. Anderson, Murray, and Farley, *Texas Politics,* 122 (see chap. 22, n. 16).
23. Deborah K. Wheeler, "Two Men, Two Governors, Two Pardons: A Study of Pardon Policy of Governor Miriam Ferguson." Unpublished copyrighted paper, presented at State Historical Society Meeting, March 1998, Austin.
24. Bill Hobby, "Speaking of Pardons, Texas Has Had Its Share," *Houston Chronicle* (February 18, 2001): 4C.
25. *The Book of the States 1996–1997,* 33–34.
26. Legislative Budget Board, "Fiscal Size-up 2002–2003," 242.
27. Texas Sunset Advisory Commission, Guide to the Texas Sunset Process (Austin, 1997), 1.
28. Ibid.

CHAPTER 25

1. Herbert Jacob, "Courts: The Least Visible Branch," in *Politics in the American States,* 6th ed., 254 (see chap. 23, n. 1).
2. Ibid.
3. Dye, *Politics in States and Communities,* 8th ed., 227.
4. Ibid.
5. Jacob, "Courts," 253.
6. Ibid., 256–58.
7. Office of Court Administration, Texas Judicial Council, Texas Judicial System Annual Report (Austin: Author, 1994), 31–33.
8. *The Book of the States 1998–1999,* 131–32, table 4.2 (see chap. 20, n. 10).
9. Delaware, Maine, Massachusetts, New Hampshire, New Jersey, New York, and Vermont have some judges who are appointed by the governor and can be removed only for cause. Connecticut, Rhode Island, South Carolina, and Virginia have legislative elections. In the other three legislatures using elections, judges serve for life with good behavior. See Jacob, "Courts," 268, table 7.2. Also see *The Book of the States 1994–1995,* 190–93, table 4.4. There are some slight variations between the Jacob table and the table in *The Book of the States.*

This is probably due to interpretations by the writers. Owing to minor variations among states, classification differences are possible.
10. Richard H. Kraemer and Charldean Newell, *Essentials of Texas Politics* (St. Paul, MN: West, 1980), 281.
11. Anderson, Murray, and Farley, *Texas Politics,* 246–47 (see chap. 22, n. 16).
12. "A Closer Look at Harris County's Vote," *Houston Chronicle* (November 14, 2002): 32A.
13. Anthony Champagne, "Campaign Contributions in Texas Supreme Court Races," *Crime, Law and Social Change* 17 (1992): 91–106.
14. Gibson and Robison, *Government and Politics in the Lone Star State,* 6th ed. (New York: Prentice Hall, 2008), 281.
15. Herbert Jacob, "The Effect of Institutional Differences in the Recruitment Process: The Case of State Judges," *Journal of Public Law* 33, no. 113 (1964): 104–19.
16. Bradley Canon, "The Impact of Formal Selection Processes on Characteristics of Judges—Reconsidered," *Law and Society Review* 13 (May 1972): 570–93.
17. Richard Watson and Rondal G. Downing, *The Politics of the Bench and Bar: Judicial Selection Under the Missouri Nonpartisan Court Plan* (New York: John Wiley, 1969).
18. Dye, *Politics in States and Communities,* 8th ed., 236.
19. William K. Hall and Larry T. Aspin, "What Twenty Years of Judicial Retention and Elections Have Told Us," *Judicature* 70 (1987): 340–47.
20. Craig F. Emmert and Henry R. Glick, "The Selection of Supreme Court Judges," *American Politics Quarterly* 19 (October 1988): 444–65.
21. *The Book of the States 1998–1999,* 138–48, table 4.5.
22. Commission on Judicial Conduct, Annual Report (Austin: Author, 1994).
23. Office of Court Administration, Texas Judicial Council, Texas Judicial System Annual Report (1994), 173, 179.
24. Interview with District Court Judge John Delaney, Brazos County courthouse, November 1995.
25. Texas Code of Criminal Procedure, arts. 19.01–20.22.
26. "Murder Case Testing Grand Jury Selection," *Houston Chronicle* (March 2, 2002): 1A, 16A.
27. There were 880,759 Anglos as opposed to 301,981 African Americans according to the Texas Crime Report for 2008, Texas Department of Public Safety, www.txdps.state.tx.us/administration/crime_records/pages/crimestatistics.htm#2006.
28. Texas Criminal Justice Policy Council, Biennial Report to the Governor and the 78th Texas Legislature, January 2001.
29. Texas Criminal Justice Policy Council, *Testing the Case for More Incarceration in Texas: The Record So Far* (Austin: State of Texas, 1995), 43.

30. "Death in Decline '09: Los Angeles Holds California Back as Nation Shifts to Permanent Imprisonment," ACLU of Northern California, http://aclunc.org/docs/criminal_justice/death_penalty/death_in_decline_09.pdf.

31. See, for example, Sami Hartsfield, "Harris County District Judge Kevin Fine: Ruled Death Penalty Unconstitutional—Is It? Take the Poll!" *Houston Legal Issues Examiner,* March 7, 2010, www.examiner.com/x-12971-Houston-Legal-Issues-Examiner~y2010m3d7-Harris-County-District-Judge-Kevin-Fine-Ruled-death-penalty-unconstitutional-is-it-Take-the-poll, and Brian Rogers, "Judge Declares Death Penalty Unconstitutional," *Houston Chronicle,* March 5, 2010, www.chron.com/disp/story.mpl/metropolitan/6897252.html.

32. Annual Statistical Reports 2007, OCA & Texas Judicial Council, Texas Courts Online, www.courts.state.tx.us/pubs/AR2007/toc.htm.

33. "Prop. 12 Proponents Gave $5.3 Million to Perry, Dewhurst and Lawmakers in 2002," Texans for Public Justice, August 29, 2003, www.tpj.org/press_releases/prop12_interests.html.

34. American Tort Reform Association, www.atra.org/wrap/files.cgi/7964_howworks.html.

35. Ralph Blumenthal, "More Doctors in Texas After Malpractice Caps," *New York Times,* October 5, 2007, www.nytimes.com/2007/10/05/us/05doctors.html?pagewanted=1&ref=health.

36. JCIT Newsletter, "Reports of the Texas Judicial Council," www.courts.state.tx.us/jcit/reports/ReportsHome.asp.

CHAPTER 26

1. *Statistical Abstract of the United States,* 2003, table 421.

2. Institute on Taxation and Economic Policy, "Texas Taxes Hit Poor & Middle Class Far Harder Than the Wealthy," January 7, 2003, www.itepnet.org/wp2000/tx%20pr.pdf.

3. Ibid.

4. Texas Coordinating Board, www.thecb.state.tx.us/.

5. Permanent University Fund, "Overview," 2007, www.utimco.org/funds/allfunds/2007annual/puf_overview.asp.

6. Some at TAMU have suggested this is the source of the hook'm horns and the gigum Aggies hand gestures.

7. Texas Constitution, Art. VII, Sec. 18.

8. Texas Coordinating Board, www.thecb.state.tx.

9. *Hopwood v. Texas,* 78 F.3d 932 (5th Cir. 1996), cert. denied, *Texas v. Hopwood,* No. 95-1773 (July 1, 1996).

10. *Houston Chronicle,* "81% of U.T.'s Admissions Offers Go to Top 10% Graduates" (March 20, 2008): 1.

11. "Just Say Don't Know: Sexuality Education in Texas Public Schools," The Texas Freedom Network, www.tfn.org/site/DocServer/SexEdRort09_web.pdf?docID=981.

12. "U.S. Teenage Pregnancies, Births and Abortions: National and State Trends and Trends by Race and Ethnicity," Guttmacher Institute, January 2010, www.guttmacher.org/pubs/USTPtrends.pdf; "State Profiles—Texas," the National Campaign to Prevent Teen and Unplanned Pregnancy, www.thenationalcampaign.org/state-data/state-profile.aspx?state=texas; Robert T. Garrett, "Texas has Restrictive Birth Control Policy for Minors," *Dallas Morning News,* www.dallasnews.com/sharedcontent/dws/dn/latestnews/stories/090709dntexteenbirths.3eaae55.html.

13. *Houston Chronicle,* "One in Four Girls: Shocking Study on Sexually Transmitted Infections Must be a Wake-Up Call for Teen Health" (March 15, 2008): B8.

14. CNN, "Supreme Court Strikes Down Texas Sodomy Law," November 18, 2003, www.cnn.com/2003/LAW/06/26/scotus.sodomy/.

15. Robert T. Garrett and Wayne Slater, "Gay Marriage Foes Tackle Divorce Next," *Dallas Morning News,* November 10, 2005, www.dallasnews.com/sharedcontent/dws/news/texassouthwest/stories/111005dntexprop2.7a85398.html.

16. American Association of University Women, "Public Perceptions of the Pay Gap, 2005, www.aauw.org/research/statedata/upload/table_data.pdf.

17. Environmental Science and Technology Online, "One in Five U.S. Women Has High Mercury Levels," March 8, 2006, http://pubs.acs.org/subscribe/journals/esthag-w/2006/mar/science/pp_mercury.html.

18. Ramon Alvarez, Mary Sanger, Colin Rowan, and Lisa Moore, "Fair Warning: Global Warming and the Lone Star State," Environment Defense Fund, May 2006, www.edf.org/documents/5254_Fair Warning.pdf.

19. Texas Municipal Water Conservation, Issue Paper 1, 2009, Texas Water Matters, www.texaswatermatters.org/pdfs/issue_no1_conservation.pdf, and Forrest Wilder, "Water Conservation in Texas: Good, Bad And Ugly," *The Texas Observer,* March 10, 2010, www.texasobserver.org/forrestforthetrees/water-conservation-in-texas-good-bad-and-ugly.

20. Michael Milstein, "Beyond Wind Plan, Pickens Eyes Pipelines in Drought-Ridden U.S.," *Popular Mechanics,* October 1, 2009, www.popularmechanics.com/science/environment/4275059.

21. Clifford Bryan, "Texas is Undisputed Wind Power Leader—It's Not All About Oil Anymore," *Energy Policy Examiner,* April 17, 2010, www.examiner.com/x-43343-Energy-Policy-Examiner~y2010m4d17-Texas-is-undisputed-wind-power-leader-its-not-all-about-oil-anymore.

22. Virginia Gray, "The Socioeconomic and Political Context of States," in *Politics in the American States,* 9th ed.

CHAPTER 27

1. Federal Advisory Commission on Intergovernmental Relations, *State and Local Roles in the Federal System: A–88* (Washington, DC: U.S. Government Printing Office, 1982), 59.

2. Ibid.

3. Terrell Blodgett, *Texas Home-rule Charters* (Austin: Texas Municipal League, 1994).

4. There are three types (A, B, and C) of cities provided for in Texas state law. However, there are seven variations on the number of council members and their methods of election. See *Vernon's Texas Statutes and Codes Annotated,* vol. 1, 5.001–5.003.

5. Texas Municipal League, *Handbook for Mayors and Councilmembers in General-law Cities* (Austin: Texas Municipal League, 1994).

6. *Vernon's Texas Statutes and Codes Annotated,* "Local Government," vol. 1, 9.001–9.008.

7. Ibid., 7.005.

8. David L. Martin, *Running City Hall: Municipal Administration in the United States* (Tuscaloosa: University of Alabama Press, 1990), 21–22.

9. *Vernon's Texas Statutes and Codes Annotated,* "Local Government," vol. 1, 42.021.

10. James A. Svara, *Official Leadership in the City: Patterns of Conflict and Cooperation* (New York: Oxford University Press, 1990), chaps. 2 and 3.

11. Blodgett, *Texas Home-rule Charters,* 30–31.

12. Bradley Robert Rice, *Progressive Cities: The Commission Government Movement in America, 1901–1920* (Austin: University of Texas Press, 1977), 85.

13. Blodgett, *Texas Home-rule Charters,* 39.

14. Svara, *Official Leadership in the City.*

15. Richard Stillman, *The Rise of the City Manager: A Public Professional in Local Government* (Albuquerque: University of New Mexico Press, 1974), 15.

16. Blodgett, *Texas Home-rule Charters,* 46–47.

17. Svara, *Official Leadership in the City,* 136. Also see Lyndon B. Johnson School of Public Affairs, *Local Government Election Systems,* Policy Research Report No. 62 (Austin: University of Texas Press, 1984), 46–55, 145–46.

18. International City Management Association, *Municipal Year Book* (Washington, DC: Author, 1988), 17.

19. *Vernon's Texas Statutes and Codes Annotated,* "Elections," 41.003.

20. For a discussion of San Antonio, see David R. Johnson, John A. Booth, and Richard J. Harris, *The Politics of San Antonio: Community Progress and Power* (Lincoln: University of Nebraska Press, 1983). Also see Richard A. Smith, "How Business Failed Dallas," in *Governing Texas: Documents and Readings* (2nd ed.), ed. Fred Gantt Jr. et al. (New York: Thomas Y. Crowell, 1970), 122–29.

21. U.S. Department of Commerce, Bureau of the Census, *1997 Census of Governments: Government Organization,* vol. 1, no. 1 (Washington, DC: U.S. Government Printing Office, 1997), 18, table 13.

22. U.S. Census of Population 2000, www .census.gov.

23. Gary M. Halter and Gerald L. Dauthery, "The County Commissioners Court in Texas," in *Governing Texas* (3rd ed.), ed. Fred Gantt Jr. et al. (New York: Thomas Y. Crowell, 1974), 340–50.

24. Robert E. Norwood and Sabrina Strawn, *Texas County Government: Let the People Choose,* 2nd ed. (Austin: Texas Research League, 1984).

25. Ibid., 24. Also see John A. Gilmartin and Joe M. Rothe, *County Government in Texas: A Summary of the Major Offices and Officials,* Issue 2 (College Station: Texas Agricultural Extension Service).

26. Norwood and Strawn, *Texas County Government,* 27.

27. For an extensive explanation of the county home-rule efforts in Texas, see Wilbourn E. Benton, *Texas: Its Government and Politics,* 2nd ed. (Englewood Cliffs, NJ: Prentice Hall, 1966), 317–81.

28. For a discussion of the benefits and problems of special districts, see Virginia Pernod, *Special District, Special Purposes: Fringe Governments and Urban Problems in the Houston Area* (College Station: Texas A&M University Press, 1984).

29. *2002 Census of Governments,* 2:17, table 3.

30. Texas Legislative Budget Board home page, www.lbb.state.tx.us.

31. Nancy Frank, *Charter Schools: Experiments in Reform, an Update* (Austin: Texas Legislative Budget Board, Public Education Team, 1995).

32. *2002 Census of Governments,* 2:17, table 15.

33. Texas Legislative Budget Board home page, www.lbb.state.tx.us.

34. Secretary of State, State of Texas, *Votes on Proposed Amendments to the Texas Constitution, 1875–November 1993* (Austin: Author, 1994), 73.

35. *Dallas Morning News* (January 12, 1994): 1A.

36. Terrence Stutz, "Wimberley School District Challenging Texas' 'Robin Hood' Finance Law," *Dallas Morning News,* January 28, 2008, www.dallasnews.com/shared content/dws/news/texassouthwest/stories/012808dntexwimberley.2c73fcc.html.

CREDITS

Chapter 1 Opener: AP Photo/John Raoux; p. 7: © Mark Boulton/Alamy; p. 11: © Nancy G Spirit Wolf Photography/ Alamy; p. 13: © Enoch Seeman/The Bridgeman Art Library/ Getty Images; p. 15: AP Photo/Leslie Close; p. 16: © David Handschuh-Pool/Getty Images; p. 23 (left): © Hans F. Meier/ iStock; p. 23 (middle): © S. Greg Panosian/iStock; p. 23 (right): © S. Greg Panosian/iStock; p. 25 (left): © Charles Gatewood/The Image Works; p. 25 (right): © Tannin Maury/ epa/Corbis. **Chapter 2** Opener: © Ed Kashi/Corbis; p. 38: © Haley/SIPA/Newscom; p. 39: AP Photo; p. 41: AP Photo/ Kevin Rivoli; p. 46: © Mario Tama/Getty Images; p. 50: © Thaier Al-Sudani/Reuters/Corbis; p. 51 (left): © American School/The Bridgeman Art Library/Getty Images; p. 51 (middle): © FPG/Taxi/Getty Images; p. 51 (right): © Stock Montage/Hulton Archive/Getty Images; p. 52: The Granger Collection, New York; p. 56 (left): © Ron Sachs/CNP/Corbis; p. 56 (right): © Illustration by Art Lien/Pool/Reuters/Corbis. **Chapter 3** Opener: © Justin Sullivan/Getty Images; p. 85: © Photodisc/Getty Images; p. 86: AP Photo/Pablo Martinez Monsivais; p. 89: © iStockphoto.com/Pxlar8; p. 91: © Kent Steffens/iStock; p. 92: AP Photo/Matt York; p. 94: © Kevin Lamarque/Reuters/Corbis; p. 95: © David McNew/Getty Images; p. 98 (left): © Corbis; p. 98 (right): © Ethan Miller/ Getty Images; p. 99: © Rod Rolle/Getty Images; p. 100: © Rhona Wise/AFP/Getty Images; p. 102: © Richard Levine. **Chapter 4** Opener: AP Photo/M. Spencer Green; p. 115: © Valerie Berta/Journal-Courier/The Image Works; p. 116: © Marilyn Humphries/The Image Works; p. 121: © Tom Williams/Roll Call/Getty Images; p. 122: © Todd A. Gipstein/Corbis; p. 125: © Daniel Acker/Bloomberg via Getty Images; p. 126: © Digital Vision/Getty Images; p. 129: AP Photo/Evan Vucci; p. 130 (left): © Robert W. Ginn/Alamy; p. 130 (right): © Chip Somodevilla/Getty Images; p. 137 (left): © Jim West/Alamy; p. 137 (right): © Tim Boyle/Getty Images. **Chapter 5** Opener: © P-59 Photos/Alamy; p. 150 (left): The Everett Collection; p. 150 (middle): © New York Times Co./Hulton Archive/Getty Images; p. 150 (right): The Everett Collection; p. 157: © Carl Iwasaki/Time & Life Pictures/Getty Images; p. 158: © Bettmann/Corbis; p. 159: AP Photo; p. 160: © Newseum; p. 164 (top): AP Photo; p. 164 (bottom): Photo courtesy of the National Museum of American History; p. 165 (left): © Bettmann/Corbis; p. 165 (right): © Shawn Thew/EPA/Corbis; p. 167: AP Photo/Evan Vucci; p. 169: © Arthur Schatz/Getty Images; p. 171: AP Photo/David Duprey; p. 172: © John A. Rizzo/Getty Images; p. 173: © Brendan Smialowski/Getty Images; p. 174: © Bob Daemmrich/The Image Works. **Chapter 6** Opener: © Reuters/Corbis; p. 185: © Frances M. Roberts; p. 188: © Comstock Images/Getty Images; p. 192 (top left): AP Photo/David J. Phillip; p. 192 (top right): © AFP Photo/Paul J. Richards/Newscom; p. 192 (bottom): AP Photo/Lawrence Jackson; p. 193: AP Photo/Eugene Tanner; p. 198: AP Photo/ Byron Rollins; p. 202: © W. Eugene Smith//Time Life Pictures/Getty Images; p. 204: © Comstock/Corbis; p. 205: © Lara Seregni/iStock; p. 206 (top): © Eric Isselée/iStock; p. 206 (bottom): © Christine Balderas/iStock. **Chapter 7** Opener: © Karen Bleier/AFP/Getty Images; p. 215: © Duffy-Marie Arnoult/WireImage/Getty Images; p. 220: © The McGraw-Hill Companies, Inc./Jill Braaten, photographer; p. 221: © Mark Ralston/AFP/Getty Images; p. 223: AP Photo/Shizuo Kambayashi; p. 227: © Royalty-Free/ Corbis; p. 228: © John E Marriott/All Canada Photos/Getty Images; p. 229: AP Photo/Manuel Balce Ceneta; p. 232: AP Photo/Giles Communications, Ron Thomas. **Chapter 8** Opener: AP Photo/Gerald Herbert; p. 245: © Stan Honda/ AFP/Getty Images; p. 247: © Nicholas Piccillo/iStock; p. 251: © Chip Somodevilla/Getty Images News/Getty Images; p. 256 (left): © Bettmann/Corbis; p. 256 (right): © Richard Levine/Alamy; p. 258: Press Association via AP Images; p. 261: © Rick Gershon/Getty Images; p. 265: © Photodisc/ Getty Images; p. 267: Courtesy of Twitter. **Chapter 9** Opener: AP Photo/Matt York; p. 275: © Sally Ryan/The New York Times/Redux; p. 276: Julian Wasser/Time & Life Pictures/ Getty Images; p. 279: AP Photo/Ross D. Franklin; p. 280 (left): © Manic Photos/Alamy; p. 280 (right): © Manic Photos/Alamy; p. 281: © Comstock/PunchStock; p. 283: © Paul McMahon; p. 285: © Brooks Kraft/Corbis; p. 287: © Bettmann/Corbis; p. 291: © Goran Milic/iStock; p. 293: AP Photo/The News&Observer, Shawn Rocco; p. 295 (top): © ericsphotography/iStock; p. 295 (bottom): © Ryan McVay/ Getty Images; p. 300: © Raveendran/AFP/Getty Images; p. 301: © Bob Daemmrich/The Image Works. **Chapter 10** Opener: © Ed Hille/Philadelphia Inquirer/MCT/Newscom; p. 309: © HO/Reuters/Corbis; p. 311: Michael Becker/FOX/ PictureGroup via AP Images; p. 312: © Tamara Abdul Hadi/ The New York Times/Redux; p. 313: © Bettmann/Corbis; p. 314: © iStockphoto.com/Milos Luzanin; p. 315: © Doram/ iStock; p. 316 (left): © Bettmann/Corbis; p. 317 (top): AP Photo/Photo courtesy of Rush Limbaugh; p. 317 (bottom): © Yevgen Timashov/iStock; p. 321: © Andres Peiro Palme/ iStock; p. 322 (bottom): © Ramin Talaie/Corbis; p. 324: © Zuma/Nescom; p. 326: © Ryan McVay/Getty Images; p. 327: © Chris Hondros/Newsmakers/Getty Images; p. 328: © Adrian Wilson/Beateworks/Corbis; p. 331: © Thinkstock/ PunchStock. **Chapter 11** Opener: AP Photo/Eric Risberg; p. 338: © Tom Williams/Roll Call/Getty Images; p. 339: © P-59 Photos/Alamy; p. 340: © Bettmann/Corbis; p. 341: © Shawn Thew/Pool via Bloomberg/Getty Images; p. 345: © Jim Watson/AFP/Getty Images; p. 346: © Corbis; p. 350: © Craig Aurness/Corbis. **Chapter 12** Opener: © Official White House photo by Pete Souza; p. 372: AP Photo/Thomas Kienzle; p. 373: © P-59 Photos/Alamy; p. 374 (top): © Win McNamee/Getty Images; p. 374 (bottom): © Mandel Ngan/ AFP/Newscom; p. 376 (bottom): © Shawn Thew/epa/Corbis; p. 378: AP Photo/The Scranton Times-Tribune, Butch Comegys; p. 380 (Vilsack): Department of Agriculture; p. 380 (Locke): Department of Commerce; p. 380 (Gates): Department of Defense; p. 380 (Duncan): Department of Education; p. 380 (Salazar): Department of the Interior; p. 380 (Holder): Department of Justice; p. 380 (Solis): Department of Labor; p. 380 (Clinton): Department of State; p. 380 (Chu): Department of Energy; p. 380 (Sebelius): Department of Health and Human Services; p. 380 (Napolitano): Department of Homeland Security; p. 380 (Donovan): Department of Housing and Urban Development; p. 380 (LaHood): Department of Transportation; p. 380 (Geithner): Department of Treasury; p. 380 (Shinseki): Department of Veterans Affairs; p. 382: © George Skadding// Time Life Pictures/Getty Images; p. 383: © Stan Honda/AFP/ Getty Images; p. 386: © Greg Mathieson/Mai/Mai/Time Life Pictures/Getty Images; p. 390: © Bettmann/Corbis; p. 393: © Michael Newman/PhotoEdit.**Chapter 13** Opener: U.S. Coast Guard via Getty Images; p. 409: © Jim Young/Reuters/ Corbis; p. 413: © kativ/iStock; p. 417: © Michael Reynolds/ epa/Corbis; p. 421: © Scott J. Ferrell/Congressional Quarterly/Getty Images; p. 422: AP Photo/Ben Lowy/VII Network; p. 425 (left): AP Photo/Morry Gash; p. 425 (right): AP Photo/Jim Mone. **Chapter 14** Opener: © Pete Souza/ White House via Getty Images; p. 433: © North Wind Picture Archives/Alamy; p. 435: © Cathy Kapulka/UPI Photo; p. 436: © WidStock/Alamy; p. 438: © Brand X Pictures/PunchStock; p. 442: AP Photo/J. Scott Applewhite; p. 443: © PAUL J. RICHARDS/AFP/Getty Images; p. 446: © Brooks Kraft/ Corbis; p. 451 (top): © Gary Fabiano/Pool/Corbis; p. 451 (bottom): © Bettmann/Corbis; p. 454: Photo via Newscom; p. 456: © David J Sams/Stone/Getty Images. **Chapter 15** Opener: AP Photo/Eric Risberg; p. 467: © Corbis; p. 468 (left): © Bettmann/Corbis; p. 468 (right): © John Nordell/The Image Works; p. 469: © Emmanuel Dunand/AFP/Getty Images; p. 474: © Grigory Bibikov/iStock; p. 476: © Jonathan Ernst/Reuters/Corbis; p. 480: © Reuters/Corbis; p. 482: AP Photo/Nick Ut; p. 483: © Michael Siluk/The Image Works. **Chapter 16** Opener: © Mike Theiler/epa/Corbis; p. 496: © Larry Downing/Reuters/Corbis; p. 497: © Becky Olstad/ The Christian Science Monitor via Getty Images; p. 498 (left): © Topham/The Image Works; p. 498 (right): © Robert Brenner/PhotoEdit; p. 499: © Tom Williams/Roll Call/Getty Images; p. 500: © Ted Dayton Photography/Beateworks/ Corbis; p. 501: © Charles O. Cecil/The Image Works; p. 503: © Kate Davison/AFP Photo/Newscom; p. 512: © Shawn Thew/epa/Corbis; p. 514: © Monika Graff/The Image Works; p. 517: © Guadalupe Williams/AFP/Getty Images. **Chapter 17** Opener: © John Moore/Getty Images; p. 525: © Paula Bronstein/Getty Images; p. 528 (top): © Mandel Ngana/AFP/ Getty Images; p. 531 (left): © Swim Ink 2, LLC/Corbis; p. 531 (right): AP Photo/Nick Ut; p. 532: AP Photo; p. 533: AP Photo/ Kyodo News; p. 534: © SuperStock, Inc.; p. 535: © Diego Lezama Orezzoli/Corbis; p. 541: © Public Record Office/ HIP/The Image Works; p. 542: © Joe Raedle/Getty Images; p. 546: © Paula Bronstein/Getty Images; p. 548: AP Photo/ Hasan Sarbakhshin; p. 550: © Paul Miles/Axiom Photographic Agency/Getty Images; p. 550: © F./iStock. **Chapter 18** Opener: © Tim Boyle/Bloomberg via Getty Images; p. 559: Courtesy of Tuition Relief Now; p. 562 (left): © Justin Sullivan/Getty Images; p. 562 (right): © Jeff Kowalsky/Bloomberg via Getty Images; p. 563: © Shawn Thew/AFP/Getty Images; p. 566: © Najlah Feanny/Corbis; p. 576 (top left): © James Randklev/Corbis; p. 576 (top right): © Digital Vision/PunchStock; p. 576 (bottom left): © imageshop/PunchStock; p. 576 (bottom right): © Richard Ross/Photographer's Choice/Getty Images; p. 569 (top): © Arthur S. Aubry/Getty Images; p. 569 (bottom): © Doug Menuez/Photodisc/Getty Images; p. 574: AP Photo/Luis Cruz Hernandez; p. 578 (left): © Francis Miller//Time Life Pictures/Getty Images; p. 578 (right): AP Photo/John Stanmeyer/VII; p. 579: © Stefan Klein/iStock. **Chapter 19** Opener: © Eleanor Bentall/Corbis; p. 590: © Daughters of the Republic of Texas Library at the Alamo; Fig 19.1 (top, left): © Clint Spencer/iStock; Fig 19.1 (top, right) : © James Pauls/ iStock; Fig 19.1 648 (bottom, left): © Samuel Kessler/iStock; Fig 19.1 648 (bottom, right): Library of Congress; p. 592: Photo #C09258, Austin History Center, Austin Public Library; p. 594: AP Photo/Harry Cabluck; p. 959: © Bob Daemmrich/Daemmrich Photography; p. 598: Courtesy of Gary Halter; Fig 19.3 (top, left): © Hal Bergman/iStockphoto; Fig 19.3 (top, right): © Andrew Dean/iStock; Fig 19.3 (bottom, left): © Eric Foltz/iStock; Fig 19.3 (bottom, right): © Greg Cooksey/iStock; p. 600: © Glenn Chapman/AFP/ Getty Images. **Chapter 20** Opener: AP Photo/Donna McWilliam; p. 610: Reading of the Texas Declaration of Independence by Charles and Fanny Normann, Collection of the Joe Fultz estate, Navasota, Texas. Courtesy of the Star of the Republic Museum; p. 611: © Bettmann/Corbis; p. 613: © Texas State Library and Archives Commission; p. 614: © Brandon Seidel/Alamy; p. 615: AP Photo/Harry Cabluck; p. 620: © Index Stock/Alamy; p. 621: © John Anderson/ Austin Chronicle. **Chapter 21** Opener: AP Photo/The Daily Texan, Tamir Kalifa; p. 631 (top): © Bob Daemmrich/ Daemmrich Photography; p. 634: © Michael Silver Editorial/ Alamy; p. 635 (top): © Marjorie Kamys Cotera/Daemmrich Photography; p. 635 (bottom): © Bob Daemmrich/The Image Works; p. 637: © Bob Daemmrich/Daemmrich Photography. **Chapter 22** Opener: © Bob Daemmrich/The Image Works; p. 650: © SAMS/SIPA/Newscom; p. 653: AP Photo/Harry Cabluck; p. 659: © Louis DeLuca/Dallas Morning News; p. 664: AP Photo/L.M. Otero; p. 665: AP Photo/Waco Tribune Herald, Duane A. Laverty; p. 666: © Bob Daemmrich/The Image Works; p. 667: AP Photo/Eric Gay. **Chapter 23** Opener: © Bob Daemmrich/The Image Works; p. 680: AP Photo/ Harry Cabluck; p. 681: © Bob Daemmrich/The Image Works; p. 690: AP Photo/Harry Cabluck; p. 695: © Jon Arnold Images Ltd/Alamy; p. 696: AP Photo/Thomas Terry. **Chapter 24** Opener: © Chip Somodevilla/Getty Images; p. 711: © The McGraw-Hill Companies, Inc./Ken Karp photographer; p. 714: © Dave Einsel/Getty; p. 716: © Bob Daemmrich/ Daemmrich Photography; p. 725: © Bob Daemmrich/The Image Works. **Chapter 25** Opener: © Rodger Mallison/MCT/ Landov; p. 738: AP Photo/L.M. Otero; p. 741: © Larry Downing/Reuters/Corbis; p. 743: AP Photo/Harry Cabluck; p. 750: © Paul S. Howell/Getty; p. 75: © Stefan Klein/iStock. **Chapter 26** Opener: AP Photo/Harry Cabluck; p. 763: © Bob Daemmrich/The Image Works; p. 766: © Jim West/Alamy; p. 770: © Tom Reel/ZUMA/Newscom. **Chapter 27** Opener: © A.J.Sisco/UPI/Landov; p. 781: AP Photo/L.M. Otero; p. 789: © Ken Kramer/Sierra Club; p. 793: © Billy Smith/The Houston Chronicle; p. 794: © Peter Casolino/Alamy; p. 796 (top): © Joe Mitchell/Getty Images; p. 796 (bottom): © Edd Westmacott/Alamy.

Note: Page references followed by *f* or *t* refer to figures or photographs (*f*) or to tables (*t*).

A

AARP (American Association of Retired Persons), 222, 224, 328, 512
Abbott, Greg, 633, 721, 723, 741*f*
Abilene, Texas, 782–783
ability to pay, taxes and, 761
ABMs (antiballistic missiles), 543
abolitionists, 150–152
abortion
    arguments for and against legality of, 189, 189*f*
    interest groups on, 130*f*, 231, 232–233
    partial birth, 450
    right to privacy and, 130, 130*f*
    state laws on, 770–771, 770*f*
    Supreme Court on, 130, 130*f*, 189, 231–232, 357, 450, 453
Abraham, Spencer, 504
absentee voting, 281–282
abstinence-only sex education, 771, 801
Abu Ghraib prisoner abuse, 532, 532*f*
accommodationism, 126–127, 543
accountability, of schools, 800, 801*f*
accountability, of the federal bureaucracy, 419–423, 420*f*, 421*f*
ACLU (American Civil Liberties Union), 138, 747
ACORN, 421
ACRI (American Civil Rights Institute), 175
acting governor, 711
ACU (American Conservative Union), 234
ADA (Americans for Democratic Action), 234
ADA (Americans with Disabilities Act), 172, 172*f*
Adams, Abigail, 162
Adams, Franklin, 299
Adams, Gerry, 258
Adams, James Truslow, 486
Adams, John, 252–253
Adams, John Quincy, 253
Adams, Samuel, 37, 38
ADA Watch, 172
Adelsverein Society, 592
administrative adjudication, 418–419
administrative discretion, 418
administrative hearings, 744
administrative law, 438
Administrative Procedure Act (APA) of 1946, 419–420, 421
administrative rule making, 418
adolescents. *See* young people
adoptions, 171*f*, 174
advice and consent, 48
AFBF (American Farm Bureau Federation), 227
AFDC (Aid to Families with Dependent Children), 508
affirmative action, 174–177, 176*f*, 766*f*, 767–768
AFGE (American Federation of Government Employees), 409
Afghanistan. *See also* Afghanistan, U.S. war in
    challenges for the government of, 10, 10*f*
    Soviet invasion of, 543
Afghanistan, U.S. war in
    under Bush, 545–546

enemy combatants from, 529 (*See also* Guantánamo Bay detainees)
federal contracts in, 421
interim government and, 545
media coverage of, 532
under Obama, 377, 547
Pakistan-U.S. relations and, 525
Taliban regime and, 525, 526, 545
women's education and, 546*f*
AFL-CIO (American Federation of Labor-Congress of Industrial Organizations), 220, 226
African Americans. *See also* segregation; slavery
    affirmative action and, 174–176
    Black Codes, 153
    in cabinet positions, 379
    civil rights movement, 156–159, 157*f*, 158*f*, 159*f*, 160*f*
    in Congress, 359–360, 360*f*
    criminal justice system and, 747, 747*f*, 748*f*
    in elected office, 153
    Freemen's Bureau, 611*f*
    as governors, 578, 710
    Grange and, 651
    homeless children, 511
    Jim Crow laws, 150*f*, 153–155
    mean personal income of, 465, 465*t*
    in the military, 385, 437
    in New Deal coalition, 255, 256*f*
    newspapers for, 314
    party affiliation of, 190–191, 190*f*, 254, 255, 261, 655, 655*t*
    population of, 19, 20*f*, 21*f*
    poverty rates among, 510
    race riots, 711–712
    during Reconstruction, 153, 359, 393
    Republican Party and, 254
    settlement of Texas by, 591
    in state legislatures, 575–576
    steering of, by realtors, 161
    as Supreme Court justices, 444, 738*f*
    terminology, 19
    in Texas citizen groups, 636
    in Texas judiciary, 595
    in Texas legislature, 595, 684–685, 684*f*
    in Texas population, 594, 594*f*, 595
    Texas school completion rates by, 801*f*
    voter turnout by, 295, 295*f*, 595, 632
    voting rights of, 153, 154–155, 161–162, 161*f*
    white primaries, 630–631
age
    aging of population, 18–19, 19*f*, 20*f*
    discrimination based on, 150
    generational effect, 194
    party identification and, 9, 9*f*
    voter turnout by, 6–7, 7*f*, 8, 294–295, 295*f*
age-cohort effect, 194
agencies. *See* bureaucracy; Texas bureaucracy
agency review, 349
agenda setting, 187, 309–310, 345, 417, 532
agents of socialization, 186–195. *See also* political socialization
Agha-Soltan, Neda, 119, 308–309, 309*f*
agricultural associations, 634, 651
Agricultural Workers Organizing Committee (AWOC), 169
agriculture
    agricultural interest groups, 225, 226–227, 634, 651

farmworkers, 169, 169*f*, 507
pesticide contamination from, 498–499
subsidies to, 225, 227, 227*t*, 483
in Texas, 651, 724
water pollution from, 498–499, 500
Ahmadinejad, Mahmoud, 119, 324, 547
Aidid, Mohamed Farrah, 544
Aid to Dependent Children, 507, 508
Aid to Families with Dependent Children (AFDC), 508
AIG (American International Group), 468
AIM (American Indian Movement), 168
AIPAC (American Israel Public Affairs Committee), 230
air pollution, 499–500
Albright, Madeleine, 379
alcohol
    amendments on Prohibition of, 54*t*
    creation of Impact, Texas and, 782–783
    gender-based legal drinking age, 166
    national legal drinking age, 102–103
    state and local responsibilities, 569–570, 569*f*
    Texas laws on, 636, 718
Alien and Sedition Acts (1798), 112, 118
Alien Enemies Act (1789), 118
Alito, Justice Samuel, 357, 441, 444, 446*f*, 450
al-Qaeda, 526, 545
al-Zaid, Salama, 312, 312*f*
AMA (American Medical Association), 219–220
Amarillo, Texas, 786
amendment process, 49, 49*f*, 53–54, 71, 613
amendments, summary of, 52–53, 54*t*. *See also specific amendments*
American Anti-Slavery Society, 141
American Association of Retired Persons (AARP), 222, 224, 328, 512
American Bar Association, 219, 371
American Civil Liberties Union (ACLU), 138, 747
American Civil Rights Institute (ACRI), 175
American Clean Energy and Security Act (2009), 502
American Conservative Union (ACU), 234
American Dream, 464–465, 486
American Farm Bureau Federation (AFBF), 227
American Federalism (Elazar), 596
American Federation of Government Employees (AFGE), 409
American Federation of Labor-Congress of Industrial Organizations (AFL-CIO), 220, 226
American Idol, 311, 311*f*
American Indian Defense Association, 167
American Indian Movement (AIM), 168
American International Group (AIG), 468
American Israel Public Affairs Committee (AIPAC), 230
American Medical Association (AMA), 219–220
American Postal Workers Union, 409
American Recovery and Reinvestment Act (ARRA) of 2009. *See also* Great Recession
    as economic stimulus, 468, 468*f*
    as employment stimulus, 485–486
    grants to state and local governments in, 86*f*, 101–102, 572
    TANF Emergency Contingency Fund in, 510
Americans for Democratic Action (ADA), 234
American Society of Newspaper Editors, 420
Americans with Disabilities Act (ADA), 172, 172*f*
American Women's Suffrage Association (AWSA), 163

discrimination prohibited in hiring of, 406–407, 408*f*

distribution of, 87*f*, 402–404, 403*f*

former, as lobbyists, 231

merit-based selection of, 406–407

political appointees, 405, 414

restrictions on political actions of, 287, 407

salary ranges and education requirements for, 406*t*

in the senior executive service, 409–410

shadow, 403, 410–411

state and local, 410–411, 568

in Texas, 635

trends in number of, 412, 413*f*

unionization of, 409

Bureau of Consumer Financial Protection, 480

Bureau of Labor Statistics, 469, 470

Burke, Edmund, 342

Burning of the Frigate Philadelphia... (Moran), 534*f*

Burns, James McGregor, 52

Bush, Barbara, 394

Bush, George H. W.

in arms reduction talks, 544

foreign policy of, 544

increases in taxes by, 469

"thousand points of light" sound bite of, 666

veto of campaign finance bill, 289

war with Iraq over Kuwait, 526, 546

Bush, George W., Governor. *See also* Bush, George W., President

appeal to Mexican American voters by, 655

on bilingual education, 802

on Bush School at Texas A&M, 694

dove-hunting mistake by, 666

Latino appointments of, 715

platform of, 598

policy continuation under, 650

on polluters, 772

prior experience of, 709

Republican Party and, 653, 653*f*

on school accountability programs, 800

sound bites of, 667

Bush, George W., President. *See also* Afghanistan, U.S. war in; Iraq War; war on terror

"axis of evil" speech of, 548

Bush Doctrine, 545

on carbon dioxide regulation, 500

Christian interest group support of, 229

on discrimination lawsuit time limits, 372

divided government under, 252

domestic surveillance under, 124, 138, 139, 440

economic bailout plan of, 373

in election of 2000 (*See* election of 2000)

energy policy under, 504

executive orders of, 438

on global warming, 418–419

Guantánamo Bay detainees of, 56*f*, 116*f*, 140, 385–386, 529

Homeland Security Department creation, 379, 514

Hurricane Katrina response by, 93–94, 94*f*, 204, 205*f*, 424, 515

immigration reform efforts of, 516

on intelligent design taught in public schools, 797

on Iran, 548

loss of popular vote by, 369

Medicare prescription drug program of, 512, 514

on military tribunals, 118–119

neoconservatives and, 26, 545

Pakistan and, 525

politically motivated firing of U.S. attorneys, 386

presidential power under, 392

public opinion on, 387–388, 388*f*

public trust in, 205*f*, 206

regulatory policy of, 479–480

selling of Iraq War to the public, 546

signing statements by, 370–371, 373

Supreme Court justices selected by, 441, 444

tax cuts of, 468, 469, 484

use of inherent powers, 385

vetoes of, 370

voting rights extension, 161

Bush, Laura, 394

Bush Doctrine, 545

Bush School at Texas A&M University, 694

Bush v. Gore, 100, 100*f*, 280

business. *See* corporations

Business and Professional Association, 788

Business and Professional Women, 165*f*

business interest groups, 226

business regulation, 479–481, 480*f*, 482

Business Roundtable, 224, 226

butterfly ballot, 280–281

Byrd, James, Jr., 175

Byrd, Robert, 354

C

cabinet, 379, 381*t*

CAFÉ (Corporate Average Fuel Economy) standards, 504

CAIR (Council on American-Islamic Relations), 230

calendars, legislative, 694

Calendars Committee, 694

California

energy policy of, 773

higher education in, 569

on medical use of marijuana, 98–99

multilingual population in, 566

opposing interests in, 346, 346*f*

pollution standards in, 773

Proposition 8 (marriage), 278–279

Proposition 13 (property tax), 559

recall election in, 561

redistricting in, 683

California Marriage Protection Act, 278–279

Cameron, David, 375

campaign consultants, 284, 668

campaign fund-raising. *See also* Bipartisan Campaign Finance Reform Act; political action committees

Citizens United decision and, 123, 217, 224, 231, 288, 291

consultants in, 284

527 groups, 289–290

incumbency advantages in, 339

independent expenditures in, 288

interest groups and, 217–219, 233–236, 233*f*, 234*f*, 661, 661*t*

Internet and, 267, 286–287

for judges, 740–742, 741*f*

largest donors, 236*t*

regulation of, 287–291, 290*t*, 291*f*

soft money in, 249, 288–289

in Texas, 638–639, 661, 661*t*, 668–669, 668*f*

campaign managers, 283

campaigns. *See also* campaign fund-raising

candidate-centered politics, 261

candidate eligibility requirements, 283–284, 283*f*

congressional, 100, 338–340, 338*f*, 339*f*, 340*f*

corporations and labor unions in, 123, 217, 224, 231, 288, 291

costs of, 338

decision making by voters, 296–298, 297*f*, 298*f*

endorsements in, 233–234, 374*f*

grassroots organizing, 639

influences on voter choice, 297–298, 298*f*

interest groups in, 217, 233–234, 233*f*, 234*f*

Internet in, 266–267, 286–287, 319

media in, 285–286, 285*f*

national conventions, 249, 276, 292

negative, 297–299, 298*f*

presidential, 292–293, 292*f*

primaries (*See* primary elections)

professionalization of, 284–285

reasons for running for office, 282

technology use in, 5, 286–287

in Texas, 638–639

timeline of, 292*f*

campaign strategy, 284

cancer research funding, 621–622

candidate-centered campaigns, 261

candidate committees, 256–257

capital budgets, 567

capitalism

"creative," 485

definition of, 17

laissez-faire, 466–467

in political culture, 17

pure *vs.* regulated, 466–467

Capital News Group, 323

capital projects, 567

capital punishment. *See* death penalty

Capitol building, 348, 348*f*

capture, 641

carbon dioxide emission standards, 418–419

carbon emissions, 772–773

Carmichael, Stokely, 159

Carr, O. M., 786

Carson, Rachel, 499

Carter, Jimmy

in arms limitation talks, 543

civil service reform by, 408

on energy conservation, 504

foreign policy advisors of, 528

hostages held by Iran and, 548

on interest groups, 218

presidential power and, 392

response to OPEC embargo, 503–504

women's support of, 192

Carter, Stephen L., 112

casework, 339, 343–344

Cash, Bubbles, 658

cash transfers, 496–497, 511

Castro, Fidel, 533

categorical formula grants, 100–101

categorical project grants, 101

Catholic Church, 636

caucuses

congressional, 352

nominating, 276

presidential, 665

CBO (Congressional Budget Office), 476

CBPP (Center on Budget and Policy Priorities), 508

cell phones

in the Iranian election protests, 119, 308–309, 309*f*, 324, 550–551

public opinion polls and, 200, 201

censorship, 124–125

census, 101, 340

Census Bureau, 471

Center on Budget and Policy Priorities (CBPP), 508

Central Corridor, of Texas, 600

Central Intelligence Agency (CIA), 140, 514, 528

centralized federalism, 96–97

ceremonial duties, 708

cervical cancer vaccination of girls, 713–714, 771

chads, 279–280, 280*f*

Chamber of Commerce, 226

changing political climate, in Texas, 594

Chaplinsky v. New Hampshire, 123

Chapman, Ron, 747

charters, local, 84, 562, 563–564

charter schools, 798

Chavez, Cesar, 169, 169*f*

Chavez, Hugo, 504

checks and balances, 43–44, 45*f*, 56, 453–456

cheerleaders, banning suggestive behavior of, 770–771

chemical and biological weapons, 526, 547, 548

Cheney, Dick

energy policy of, 504

tie-breaking vote on spending bill, 353–354

as vice president, 378

Chertoff, Michael, 93

Chicano Movement, 169–170, 169*f*. *See also* Latinos/Latinas

chief executive, president as, 377

chief justice, 441

chief legislator, 708

chief of staff, 381

chief of state, president as, 377

child labor laws, 481

child pornography, 123

children

adoptions, 171*f*, 174

food insecurity among, 511

health care for, 511

health insurance for, 512, 758

homeless, 511

political socialization of, 185, 186–188, 311, 311*f*

in poverty, 508–510, 509*t*

trafficking of, 154

of unauthorized immigrants, 516

Children's Health Insurance Program (CHIP), 758

Houston, Texas
  mayor-council government in, 783, 783*f*
  school district in, 798
Hrebenar, Ronald J., 640
Huckabee, Mike, 711
Huerta, Dolores, 169, 169*f*
Hughes, Justice Charles Evans, 53
Hughes, Karen, 772
Human Development Index (HDI), 472, 473
Human Rights Campaign (HRC), 173, 224
Hume, John, 258
Humphrey, Hubert, 276
Huntington, Samuel P., 545, 547
Hussein, Saddam, 526, 546, 548. *See also* Iraq War
Hutchison, Kay Bailey, 652, 712, 720
hybrid agencies, 416

I

I-135W bridge, Minneapolis, 425*f*
ICBMs (intercontinental ballistic missiles), 543
ICC (Interstate Commerce Commission), 415, 480
ICMA (International City Management Association), 786
ID (intelligent design), 127–128, 797, 800–801
ideologically oriented parties, 262–263
ideology. *See* political ideology
IGR (intergovernmental relations), 84–86, 97, 104–105, 582
"I Have a Dream" (King), 158, 159*f*
Ikelle, Larissa, 192*f*
illegal aliens. *See* unauthorized immigrants
IMF (International Monetary Fund), 479, 539
immigration and immigrants
  American dream and, 464–465
  economic policy and, 467
  employment discrimination and, 170
  geographic regions for, 194
  global sources of, 515, 515*f*
  immigration eligibility, 515–516
  legal categories of immigrants, 515–516
  Mexico-U.S. border fence, 516–517, 517*f*
  policy reforms, 516–517
  political machines and, 254
  population growth through, 18, 18*f*
  in Texas, 592, 593–594
  unauthorized immigrants, 170, 516–517, 517*f*, 602–603, 602*f*
Immigration and Nationality Acts, 170, 515
Immigration and Naturalization Service (INS), 344
Immigration Reform and Control Act (1986), 170
imminent lawless action test, 121
Impact, Texas, creation of, 782–783
impeachment
  of Andrew Johnson, 392
  articles of, 392
  of Clinton, 355
  of federal judges, 454
  of governors, 711–712
  Nixon and, 391, 393
"imperial presidency," 389, 391, 392
implicit or explicit prohibitions on city ordinance power, 782
implied powers, 89, 92
import taxes, 474
impressment, 534
Inaba, Yoshimi, 345*f*
inalienable rights, 14, 39
incarceration rates, 748, 749*f*
incitement test, 121
inclusive model of federalism, 97
income. *See also* poverty; socioeconomic class
  earned *vs.* unearned, 508
  poverty thresholds, 472, 510
  race and sex and, 465, 465*t*
  real median household, 472
income-elastic taxes, 764
income inequality
  between 2000 and 2007, 484
  industrialization and, 467
  by race and ethnicity, 465, 465*t*
income security programs
  Earned Income Tax Credit program, 508
  government definitions of poverty, 510–511, 510*t*

housing and food insecurity and, 511
minimum wage laws, 98, 507–508
Social Security (*See* Social Security)
Temporary Assistance to Needy Families, 24, 497, 508–510, 509*t*
unemployment compensation, 507
income taxes
  corporate, 100, 474, 474*f*, 760
  national personal, 474, 474*f*
  Sixteenth Amendment and, 100
  state personal, 570*f*, 571
incorporation, of cities, 782–783
incumbency, advantages of, 233, 233*f*, 296–297, 338–339, 338*f*
indentured servants, 36
independent administrative agencies, 414–415
independent candidates, in Texas, 657
independent expenditures, 288
Independent Party, 263
independent regulatory commissions, 415
independent school districts, 798
independent voters
  definition of, 247
  demographics of, 9, 9*f*, 190–192, 191*f*, 191*t*
indexed benefits, 506
India, elections in, 300, 300*f*
Indian Citizenship Act (1924), 167
Indian Civil Rights Act (1968), 168
Indian Gaming Regulatory Act (1988), 168
Indian Removal Act (1830), 167
Indian Rights Association, 167
Indians. *See* Native Americans
Indian Self-Determination and Education Assistance Act (1975), 168
indirect democracy, 14–15
individualistic political culture, 17–18, 565
individualistic subculture, 596*f*, 597–598, 613
Individuals with Disabilities Education Act, 86
INF (Intermediate-Range Nuclear Forces Treaty), 544
inflation, 469, 470, 472, 479
inflation calculator website, 469
informal rules, in the Texas legislature, 695–696
information (administrative hearing), 744
infotainment, 309
inherent characteristics, 148–150, 150*f*
inherent powers, 384–385
initiatives, 278, 559–560, 560*f*, 618
injury lawsuits, 751, 751*f*
in-kind assistance, 496
inner ring, 453–454
Inouye, Daniel, 354
INS (Immigration and Naturalization Service), 344
Inspector General Act (1978), 423
inspectors general, 423
instant messaging, in campaigns, 286
instant runoff elections, 278, 787
Institute for Taxation and Economic Policy, 762
instructed delegate model of representation, 342–343
intelligence agencies, 528
intelligent design (ID), 127–128, 797, 800–801
intercontinental ballistic missiles (ICBMs), 543
interest groups, 214–237. *See also* lobbying; political action committees
  "capture" by, 641
  citizens' groups, 635–637, 635*f*
  civic participation and, 215
  Congress and, 357–358
  constitutional amendments and, 621
  definition of, 214
  downside of, 218–219
  economic, 225–227, 634–635
  electioneering by, 217, 233–234, 233*f*, 234*f*
  expert testimony and information from, 232, 232*f*
  financial resources of, 224
  foreign, 230
  fragmented government structure and, 640–641
  functions of, 217–218
  initiatives and referenda and, 560
  in iron triangles, 231, 231*f*, 417, 531, 641, 641*f*
  issue networks, 231, 417
  judiciary and, 455
  leadership in, 225
  litigation by, 231–232

membership patterns in, 219–220
membership resources of, 222, 224
motivations for joining, 220–222, 221*f*
opposition groups, 225
overall impact of, by state, 640, 640*f*
pluralist theory *vs.* elite theory, 215–217
political action committee influence, 224, 235–236
public and ideological, 227–230
public outreach by, 232–233
state and local, 637
Supreme Court justice selection and, 446
tactics and regulation of, 637–639, 637*f*, 638*f*
in Texas, 634–641, 637*f*, 638*f*
trends in group participation, 215, 216
value of, 214–219
interest rates, Fed and, 374, 478–479
Interfaith Alliance, 636
intergovernmental coordinator, governor as, 709, 712
intergovernmental lobbying, 102
intergovernmental relations (IGR), 84–86, 97, 104–105, 582
intergovernmental transfers. *See* grants-in-aid
interim committees, Texas, 691
Intermediate-Range Nuclear Forces Treaty (INF), 544
intermediate scrutiny test, 150
intermestics, 533
International City Management Association (ICMA), 786
International Covenant on Civil and Political Rights, 452
International Decade for Action on Water, 501
International Labor Organization, 484
International Monetary Fund (IMF), 479, 539
International Trade Commission, 482
Internet. *See also* social networking sites
  blogs, 286–287, 311, 320, 322, 323*f*
  in campaigns, 266–267, 286–287, 319
  digital divide, 319
  evolution of, 319–320
  as forum for political discussions, 274, 311
  fraud cases, 441
  freedom of speech on, 125, 324–325
  hate groups and, 324–325
  information and community on, 320
  misinformation on, 320
  mobilizing voters using, 321–322
  negative impact of, 323–324
  as news source, 187, 320–321, 321*f*
  opinion polls on, 201
  podcasts on, 320
  political dissent and, 119
  political influence of, 322, 323*f*
  political socialization through, 187
  pornography on, 123
  presidential use of, 389, 389*f*
  regulation of, 326–328
  sales tax on purchases from, 570
  sharing personal information on, 132
  sunshine laws and, 420–421, 420*f*
  talk radio on, 317
  Texas campaign fund-raising and, 667
  YouTube, 267, 308, 320, 322
interracial marriage, 149, 154
Inter-Religious Sponsoring Organization, 636
Interstate Commerce Commission (ICC), 415, 480
interstate compacts, 94–95
interventionism, 535
intimate association, 129, 131
Iowa caucuses, 665
Iran
  Bush on, 548
  economic sanctions on, 525, 548
  election protests in, 119, 308–309, 309*f*, 324, 324*f*, 550–551
  history of U.S. relations with, 548
  Iranian Revolution, 548
  Iran-Iraq War, 548
  nuclear weapons and, 548
  Obama on, 547
  support for U.S. after 9/11 attacks, 548, 548*f*
  U.S. hostages held by, 548
Iran-Iraq War, 548
Iran-Libya Sanctions Act (1996), 548

media (continued)
    campaign consultants on, 284–285
    campaign transformation by, 317–319, 318f
    competitive elections and, 296
    convergence in, 314, 323
    declining newspaper readership, 314, 314f
    definition of, 308
    foreign policy role of, 531–532, 531f
    as forum for political conversations, 311
    framing by, 309–310
    incumbency advantages with, 339
    as information providers, 309
    new media, 314–315
    penny papers, 313
    personality vs. policy in, 285–286, 285f
    political party decline from role of, 260–261
    political socialization by, 187, 311, 311f
    presidential use of, 316, 316f
    press in history, 313–314, 313f
    public confidence in, 310f
    regulation of, 326–327
    segmented, 318
    in Texas campaigns, 666–667
    yellow journalism, 313–314, 313f
media consultants, 284–285, 668
median household income, 472
media segmentation, 318
Medicaid
    beneficiaries of, 511–512
    as cash transfer, 497
    expansion of, 513
    federal grants to states for, 572, 572t
    formation of, 511
    as mandatory spending, 475
    state funding for, 569
medical malpractice reform, 751–752
medical treatment, right to terminate, 130–131
Medicare
    as mandatory spending, 475
    prescription drug plan, 512, 514
    provisions of, 512
    taxes collected for, 474, 474f
Medicare Prescription Drug, Improvement, and
    Modernization Act (2003), 512, 514
men, mean personal income of, 465, 465t. See also
    gender differences
Menendez, Robert, 266
mercury contamination, 772
merit-based civil service, 406
merit system, in judicial selection, 580, 739, 739f, 743
Merit System Protection Board (MSPB), 409
Metroplex region of Texas, 600
Mexican American Democrats (MAD), 635
Mexican American Legal Defense and Education
    Fund (MALDEF), 170, 636, 799
Mexican Americans. See also Latinos/Latinas
    Bush and, 655
    Chicano Movement, 169–170, 169f
    population of, 19
    in Texas, 593, 594
Mexico-U.S. border fence, 516–517, 517f
Mid-Continent Oil and Gas Association, 634
Miers, Harriet, 386, 442, 444, 741f
military
    budget for, 9
    commander in chief, 376–377, 377f, 533, 577
    Defense Department and, 527
    desegregation of, 385, 437
    Don't Ask, Don't Tell policy, 345
    in foreign policy, 526–527
    Geneva Conventions and, 529
    Guantánamo Bay detainees (See Guantánamo Bay
        detainees)
    impressment by British, 534
    Joint Chiefs of Staff, 527
    military courts, 118–119
    Quartering Act (1765), 37, 38
    rendition, 140
    torture of detainees by, 139–140, 529, 532, 532f
military-industrial complex, 530–531
military powers of governors, 718
military tribunals, 118–119
militias, 137
Millennial Generation, 5–6, 8, 192f, 486. See also
    young people

Miller, Laura, 789
Miller, Ola Babcock, 196, 198
Miller v. California, 123
Million Moms, 137, 137f
minimum legal drinking age, 102–103
minimum wage laws
    conflicted federalism and, 98
    current wage in, 507–508
    Fair Labor Standards Act creation of, 481, 507
    interest groups and, 225, 226
    as living wage, 507–508
Minneapolis I-135W bridge, 425f
Minor, Virginia, 163
minorities. See also demographics; race and ethnicity;
        specific minority groups
    in cabinet positions, 379, 381t
    in Congress, 358–360, 358t, 359f, 360f
    criminal justice system and, 745, 747, 747f, 748f,
        749f
    in federal bureaucracy, 408f
    Latinos as, 170
    majority-minority districts, 340
    mean personal income of, 465, 465t
    newsroom employment of, 315, 315t
    in the population, 19, 20f, 21f, 22, 22f
    poverty rates among, 510
    in presidential cabinets, 379
    redistricting and representation of, 678–679
    school completion by, 801f
    on the Supreme Court, 444–446
    in Texas, 594
minority representation, 678
minority representation in judgeships, 742
minority whip, 353
minor parties, 658. See also third parties
Minor v. Happersett, 163
Miranda rights, 134, 453
Miranda v. Arizona, 134
MIRVs (multiple independently targeted reentry
        vehicles), 543, 544
miscegenation laws, 154
Mississippi, African American state legislators in,
        575–576
Missouri Compromise, 151, 152
Missouri system, 739, 743
Mitchell, George, 258
Mitchell Principles, 258
mixed economy, 466, 467
modified one-party states, 648, 649f
monarchies, 12, 13, 14
Mondale, Walter F., 344
monetarism, 469–470
monetary policy, 478–479, 484
Monroe, James, 253, 535
Monroe Doctrine, 535
Montesquieu, Baron de, 43–44
Montgomery bus boycott, 157, 158, 158f
Morales, Daniel, 594, 767
Morales, Victor, 594, 660
moralistic political culture, 565, 575
moralistic subculture, 596–597, 596f
Moral Majority, 229, 665
Moran, Edward, 534f
Moran v. Burbine, 134t
mortgage crisis. See Great Recession
Mossadegh, Mohammed, 548
most favored nation status, 525, 539
Mothers Against Drunk Driving (MADD), 218
Motion Picture Association of America (MPAA), 226
"Motor Voter" Act, 299
Mott, Lucretia, 162
Mousavi, Mir-Hossein, 119, 324
MoveOn.org, 286, 290
MPAA (Motion Picture Association of America), 226
MSPB (Merit System Protection Board), 409
Mubasher FM, 312, 312f
muckraking, 314
MUDs (municipal utility districts), 796
multilateral agreements, 537
multilingual services, 566
multimember districts, 676
multiple independently targeted reentry vehicles
        (MIRVs), 543, 544
municipal courts, Texas, 737–738, 737f

municipal governments, 581
    elections and voter turnout, 786–788, 787f
    forms of, 783–786, 783f, 784f, 785f
    general-law and home-rule cities, 782
    as general-purpose government, 781
    incorporation and annexation, 782–783
    revenues and mandates, 788–790, 789f, 790f
municipal utility districts (MUDs), 796
Munn, Olivia, 221f
murder rates, 136f
Murray, Richard, 655, 740
Muslim Americans, 140, 141, 175, 230
mutual assured destruction (MAD), 543
Myers, Cydney, 746
Myers, Whitney, 746
MySpace, 132, 267

N

NAACP. See National Association for the
    Advancement of Colored People
Nader, Ralph
    on consumer protection, 228, 481
    third-party campaign of, 25, 260, 262, 263
NAEP (National Assessment of Educational
    Progress), 800
NAFTA (North American Free Trade Agreement),
    484, 525, 600, 601
Nagin, Ray, 93
Nakanishi, Don T., 171
NALEO (National Association of Latino Elected and
    Appointed Officials), 170
name recognition, 339, 739–740
Napoleonic Wars, 534
Napolitano, Janet, 379
NARAL Pro-Choice America, 221, 232–233
narrowcasting, 318
Nast, Thomas, 254f
National Aeronautics and Space Administration
    (NASA), 415
National American Women's Suffrage Association
    (NAWSA), 163
National Assessment of Educational Progress
    (NAEP), 800
National Association for the Advancement of
    Colored People (NAACP)
    Brown v. Board of Education of Topeka and, 156–157
    formation of, 156
    Montgomery bus boycott and, 157, 158, 158f
    motivations for joining, 221, 221f
    school desegregation and, 156–157, 455
National Association of Latino Elected and
    Appointed Officials (NALEO), 170
National Association of Police Organizations, 222
National Association of Realtors, 226
national bank, 92
National Beer Wholesalers Association, 226
National Biological Warfare Defense Analysis
    Center, 515
national chair, of the party, 249
National Coalition for the Homeless, 511
National Coalition of Disability Rights, 172
National Conference of State Legislatures, 700
national conventions, 249, 276, 292
National Council of Asian Pacific Americans
    (NCAPA), 171
national debt, 469, 475, 477–478
National Education Association (NEA), 220
National Farm Worker Association (NFWA), 169
National Firearms Association, 635f
National Gay and Lesbian Task Force, 173
national government. See federal system
National Guard, 577, 718
National Indian Education Association (NIEA), 168
National Indian Gaming Commission, 168
National Labor Relations Act (1935), 480–481
National League of Cities, 98
National League of Cities v. Usery, 98
National Organization for Women (NOW), 166
national primary elections, 277
National Restaurant Association, 225
National Rifle Association (NRA), 221
National Right to Life Committee (NRLC), 221, 224
National School Lunch Program, 511

national conventions, 249, 276, 292
national parties, 248–249
new party system, 256–257
in Northern Ireland, 258
organization of, 248–250, 248f, 249f
party-column ballots and, 280, 654
platform of, 244, 597–598
political machines, 254–255
power-sharing in, 258
presidential leadership of, 249, 374
primary process, 249, 260, 275–279, 292, 292f
realignments in, 252–256, 649, 650f, 651–657, 653f, 654f
red and blue designation and, 265f
responsible party model, 246
technology use by, 266–267
third parties, 253–254, 257, 259–265, 262f, 263f, 657–658, 658f
ticket splitting between, 256–257
two-party domination, 157–160, 257–260
in U.S. history, 252–257, 256f
voter turnout and, 296
winner-take-all electoral system, 259
political socialization
by churches, 188, 188f, 190
civic participation and, 184–186
definition of, 185
by families, 186–187, 220, 259
as function of government, 11, 11f
gender and, 192–194, 193f, 193t
generational effects on, 194
geographic region and, 194–195, 195t
by media, 187, 311, 311f
by peers and group norms, 190
by political and community leaders, 190
by political machines, 254–255
process of, 185
public opinion as, 195
race and ethnicity and, 190–192, 191f, 192f
by schools, 185–186, 187–188
technology use in, 187
to the two-party system, 259
political speech, 122
Politico, 323
politics, 4–8
politics-administration dichotomy, 416
politiqueras, 632, 633
polls. See public opinion polls
poll taxes, 155, 612, 629–630
Pompa, Delia, 615f
pool memo, 447
popular referendum, 559–560, 560f
popular sovereignty, 14, 41, 50, 613
population. See also demographics
aging of, 18–19, 19f
geographic distribution of, 18, 20f
growth of, 18, 18f, 411–412, 593, 593f
immigration and, 18, 18f
impact of trends on government, 21–22
race and ethnicity of, 20f, 21f, 22f
in Texas, 593–595, 593f, 594f, 595f, 773
in Texas counties, 791, 791t
voting-age, 628
population, in public opinion polls, 198
populism, 253, 389–390
Populist movement, 629–630
pork barrel, 343, 343t
pornography on the Internet, 123
Postal Service, 409, 415
poverty. See also income inequality
Earned Income Tax Credit and, 508
feminization of, 508–509
guidelines for, 510–511, 510t
housing insecurity and, 511
rate of, 472, 484
regional differences in, 565–566
TANF monthly benefits and, 508, 509f
thresholds for, 472, 510
working poor, 508
poverty guidelines, 510–511, 510t
poverty rate, 472
poverty thresholds, 472, 510
Powell, Colin, 379, 526
Powell, Justice Lewis, 175
power, in political parties, 248

power-sharing, 258
prayer in public schools, 127, 437
precedents, 436
precinct chair, in Texas, 659, 659f
precinct party committees, 249
preemption, 104, 410
preferential treatment standard, 126, 127
preferential voting, 787
Pregnancy Discrimination Act (1976), 454, 454f
premiers, 375
presidency/presidents, 368–395. See also executive branch
appointive powers of, 405
approval ratings of, 387–388, 388f
Article II on, 48, 67–69
bully pulpit of, 387
bureaucracy accountability to, 422
cabinet of, 379
campaigns of, 292–293, 292f
checks on judiciary by, 48
as chief executive, 377
as chief of state, 377
as commander in chief, 376–377, 377f, 533
as diplomat, 375–376
economic role of, 373–374, 374f
election of, 46, 253, 275–276, 292–293, 292f, 368–369
eligibility requirements for, 283–284
emergency powers of, 386
evaluation criteria for, 393
executive budget, 373–374, 476
Executive Office of the President, 377, 379, 381–382
executive orders of, 385–386, 437–438
executive privilege, 386
expressed and inherent powers of, 384–385
foreign policy role of, 374–377, 376f, 527–528, 533
governors elected to, 573
incapacitation of, 383
international opinion on, 549f
legislative role of, 351, 358, 370–372, 373
media use by, 387, 388–389, 389f
order of succession, 382–383, 382f, 383t
pardons by, 454
as party leader, 374
public opinion after Pentagon Papers, 391
scope of power in early, 389–390
signing statements by, 370–371, 373
statutory powers of, 384, 385–386
veto power of, 351, 370, 371f
War Powers Act and, 530
Watergate scandal and cynicism over, 382, 391, 392
women as future presidents, 394–395, 395f
presidential campaigns, 292–293, 292f
presidential preference primary, 664
presidential primaries, 275–278
presidential succession, 382–383, 382f, 383t
Presidential Succession Law (1947), 382, 383t
president of city council, 251
president pro tempore, 354, 691
press. See media; newspapers
Pressman, Jeffrey L., 419
press secretary, 381
preventive war, 546
primary elections
in 2008, 278, 298f, 379, 394
administration of, 665
African-American exclusion from, 155
blanket primaries, 662
crossover voting in, 662–663
Louisiana system of, 662
national conventions, 249, 276, 292
national primaries, 277
nomination process from, 275–278
open vs. closed, 276
political party decline from, 260
precinct conventions and, 663
presidential, 275–278
runoff, 664–665
schedule of, 276–278
semiclosed vs. semiopen, 662
state conventions in, 663–664, 663f
systems, by state, 663, 663f
in Texas, 638, 662–665, 663f, 664f
timeline of, 292f
white primaries, 630–631

prime ministers, 375
priming, 310
prior restraint, 124–125, 390
prisons, 793f
privacy. See right to privacy
privatizing, 403–404, 410–411, 424–425, 425f
privileges and immunities clause, 94–95
Product (RED) Campaign, 485
productivity, 470, 472
product safety, 415, 481–482
professional associations, 634–635
professional interest groups, 219, 227
professional legislatures, 640
Progressive Party, 254–255, 262, 265, 559
progressives, 199
progressive taxes, 474, 761–762
Project on Government Oversight (POGO), 421, 423
propaganda, 639
property
in political culture, 17
taxes on, 86, 559, 570f, 571
voting rights and, 631
property rights
of African Americans, 153, 161
environmental protection vs., 501
of Latinos/Latinas, 169
of women, 163
property taxes, 86, 559, 570f, 571, 788–790, 789f, 790f
proportional representation system, 259
proportional taxes, 474
Proposition 8 (California), 278–279
Proposition 13 (California), 559
propositions, 278–279, 559
prospective voting, 296
prosumers, 320
Protect America Act (2007), 139
protectionist trade policy, 483
Protestant Reformation, democracy and, 13, 13f
protests. See dissent and protest
Pruneyard Shopping Center and Fred Sahadi v. Michael Robins et al., 95
PRWORA (Personal Responsibility and Work Opportunity Reconciliation Act) of 1996, 509–510, 574
public agenda, 310
Public Citizen, 228, 751
public diplomats, 532–533, 533f
public employees. See bureaucrats
public goods, 11, 228
public health, 467, 481, 569–570
public housing, 511
public opinion. See also public opinion polls
on Americans by foreign countries, 197, 197f, 549f
approval ratings of the president, 387–388, 388f
on Bush's "axis of evil" speech, 548
on the death penalty, 750
definition of, 195
on a female president, 394, 395f
foreign policy role of, 204, 204f, 532
gender gap in, 192–194, 193f
generational effect in, 194
on the government, 203–206, 204f, 205f, 206f
on governors, 719
on the Iraq War, 194
judicial decisions and, 455–456, 456f
measurement of, 195–202
on the most important problem, 203, 203f
origin of polls on, 196–198
on partisan media bias, 326, 326f
on political ideology, 199, 199f
on political parties, 250f
on public employees, 403
on third parties, 262f
in wartime, 531f
Public Opinion (Lippmann), 196
public opinion polls
cell phones and, 200, 201
definition of, 196
online, 201
origins of, 196–198
population in, 198–199
sampling error in, 200–201
sampling in, 199–200
types of, 201–202
wording of questions in, 199